Computer and Information Security Handbook

The Morgan Kaufmann Series in Computer Security

Computer and Information Security Handbook
John Vacca

Disappearing Cryptography: Information Hiding: Steganography & Watermarking, Third Edition
Peter Wayner

Network Security: Know It All
James Joshi, et al.

Digital Watermarking and Steganography, Second Edition
Ingemar Cox, Matthew Miller, Jeffrey Bloom, Jessica Fridrich, and Ton Kalker

Information Assurance: Dependability and Security in Networked Systems
Yi Qian, David Tipper, Prashant Krishnamurthy, and James Joshi

Network Recovery: Protection and Restoration of Optical, SONET-SDH, IP, and MPLS
Jean-Philippe Vasseur, Mario Pickavet, and Piet Demeester

*For further information on these books and for a list of forthcoming titles,
please visit our Web site at http://www.elsevierdirect.com*

Computer and Information Security Handbook

Edited by
John R. Vacca

AMSTERDAM • BOSTON • HEIDELBERG • LONDON • NEW YORK
OXFORD • PARIS • SAN DIEGO • SAN FRANCISCO
SINGAPORE • SYDNEY • TOKYO
Morgan Kaufmann Publishers is an imprint of Elsevier

ELSEVIER

MORGAN KAUFMANN
PUBLISHERS

Morgan Kaufmann Publishers is an imprint of Elsevier.
30 Corporate Drive, Suite 400, Burlington, MA 01803, USA

This book is printed on acid-free paper.

Library of Congress Cataloging-in-Publication Data
Application submitted

British Library Cataloguing-in-Publication Data
A catalogue record for this book is available from the British Library.

ISBN: 978-0-12-374354-1

For information on all Morgan Kaufmann publications,
visit our Web site at www.mkp.com or www.elsevierdirect.com

Printed in the United States of America
09 10 11 12 13   5 4 3 2 1

Working together to grow
libraries in developing countries

www.elsevier.com | www.bookaid.org | www.sabre.org

ELSEVIER   BOOK AID
            International   Sabre Foundation

This book is dedicated to my wife, Bee.

Contents

Part III
Encryption Technology

Part VI
Physical Security

The Computer and Information Security Handbook is an essential reference guide for professionals in all realms of computer security. Researchers in academia, industry, and government as well as students of security will find the *Handbook* helpful in expediting security research efforts. The *Handbook* should become a part of every corporate, government, and university library around the world.

Dozens of experts from virtually every industry have contributed to this book. The contributors are the leading experts in computer security, privacy protection and management, and information assurance. They are individuals who will help others in their communities to address the immediate as well as long-term challenges faced in their respective computer security realms.

These important contributions make the *Handbook* stand out among all other security reference guides. I know and have worked with many of the contributors and can testify to their experience, accomplishments, and dedication to their fields of work.

John Vacca, the lead security consultant and managing editor of the *Handbook*, has worked diligently to see that this book is as comprehensive as possible. His knowledge, experience, and dedication have combined to create a book of more than 1400 pages covering every important aspect of computer security and the assurance of the confidentiality, integrity, and availability of information.

The depth of knowledge brought to the project by all the contributors assures that this comprehensive handbook will serve as a professional reference and provide a complete and concise view of computer security and privacy. The *Handbook* provides in-depth coverage of computer security theory, technology, and practice as it relates to established technologies as well as recent advancements in technology. Above all, the *Handbook* explores practical solutions to a wide range of security issues.

Another important characteristic of the *Handbook* is that it is a vendor-edited volume with chapters written by leading experts in industry and academia who do not support any specific vendor's products or services. Although there are many excellent computer security product and service companies, these companies often focus on promoting their offerings as one-and-only, best-on-the-market solutions. Such bias can lead to narrow decision making and product selection and thus was excluded from the *Handbook*.

Michael Erbschloe
Michael Erbschloe teaches information security courses
at Webster University in St. Louis, Missouri.

This comprehensive handbook serves as a professional reference to provide today's most complete and concise view of computer security and privacy available in one volume. It offers in-depth coverage of computer security theory, technology, and practice as they relate to established technologies as well as recent advancements. It explores practical solutions to a wide range of security issues. Individual chapters are authored by leading experts in the field and address the immediate and long-term challenges in the authors' respective areas of expertise.

The primary audience for this handbook consists of researchers and practitioners in industry and academia as well as security technologists and engineers working with or interested in computer security. This comprehensive reference will also be of value to students in upper-division undergraduate and graduate-level courses in computer security.

ORGANIZATION OF THIS BOOK

The book is organized into eight parts composed of 43 contributed chapters by leading experts in their fields, as well as 10 appendices, including an extensive glossary of computer security terms and acronyms.

Part 1: Overview of System and Network Security: A Comprehensive Introduction

Part 1 discusses how to build a secure organization; generating cryptography; how to prevent system intrusions; UNIX and Linux security; Internet and intranet security; LAN security; wireless network security; cellular network security, and RFID security. For instance:

Chapter 1, "Building a Secure Organization," sets the stage for the rest of the book by presenting insight into where to start building a secure organization.

Chapter 2, "A Cryptography Primer," provides an overview of cryptography. It shows how communications may be encrypted and transmitted.

Chapter 3, "Preventing System Intrusions," discusses how to prevent system intrusions and where an unauthorized penetration of a computer in your enterprise or an address in your assigned domain can occur.

Chapter 4, "Guarding Against Network Intrusions," shows how to guard against network intrusions by understanding the variety of attacks, from exploits to malware and social engineering.

Chapter 5, "UNIX and Linux Security," discusses how to scan for vulnerabilities; reduce denial-of-service (DoS) attacks; deploy firewalls to control network traffic; and build network firewalls.

Chapter 6, "Eliminating the Security Weakness of Linux and UNIX Operating Systems," presents an introduction to securing UNIX in general and Linux in particular, providing some historical context and describing some fundamental aspects of the secure operating system architecture.

Chapter 7, "Internet Security," shows you how cryptography can be used to address some of the security issues besetting communications protocols.

Chapter 8, "The Botnet Problem," describes the botnet threat and the countermeasures available to network security professionals.

Chapter 9, "Intranet Security," covers internal security strategies and tactics; external security strategies and tactics; network access security; and Kerberos.

Chapter 10, "Local Area Network Security," discusses network design and security deployment as well as ongoing management and auditing.

Chapter 11, "Wireless Network Security," presents an overview of wireless network security technology; how to design wireless network security and plan for wireless network security; how to install, deploy, and maintain wireless network security; information warfare countermeasures: the wireless network security solution; and wireless network security solutions and future directions.

Chapter 12, "Cellular Network Security," addresses the security of the cellular network; educates readers on the current state of security of the network and its vulnerabilities; outlines the cellular network specific attack taxonomy, also called *three-dimensional attack taxonomy*; discusses the vulnerability assessment tools for cellular networks; and provides insights into why the network is so vulnerable and why securing it can prevent communication outages during emergencies.

Chapter 13, "RFID Security," describes the RFID tags and RFID reader and back-end database in detail.

Part 2: Managing Information Security

Part 2 discusses how to protect mission-critical systems; deploy security management systems, IT security, ID management, intrusion detection and prevention systems, computer forensics, network forensics, firewalls, and penetration testing; and conduct vulnerability assessments. For instance:

Chapter 14, "Information Security Essentials for IT Managers: Protecting Mission-Critical Systems," discusses how security goes beyond technical controls and encompasses people, technology, policy, and operations in a way that few other business objectives do.

Chapter 15, "Security Management Systems," examines documentation requirements and maintaining an effective security system as well as conducting assessments.

Chapter 16, "Information Technology Security Management," discusses the processes that are supported with enabling organizational structure and technology to protect an organization's information technology operations and IT assets against internal and external threats, intentional or otherwise.

Chapter 17, "Identity Management," presents the evolution of identity management requirements. It also surveys how the most advanced identity management technologies fulfill present-day requirements. It discusses how mobility can be achieved in the field of identity management in an ambient intelligent/ubiquitous computing world.

Chapter 18, "Intrusion Prevention and Detection Systems," discusses the nature of computer system intrusions, the people who commit these attacks, and the various technologies that can be utilized to detect and prevent them.

Chapter 19, "Computer Forensics," is intended to provide an in-depth familiarization with computer forensics as a career, a job, and a science. It will help you avoid mistakes and find your way through the many aspects of this diverse and rewarding field.

Chapter 20, "Network Forensics," helps you determine the path from a victimized network or system through any intermediate systems and communication pathways, back to the point of attack origination or the person who should be held accountable.

Chapter 21, "Firewalls," provides an overview of firewalls: policies, designs, features, and configurations. Of course, technology is always changing, and network firewalls are no exception. However, the intent of this chapter is to describe aspects of network firewalls that tend to endure over time.

Chapter 22, "Penetration Testing," describes how testing differs from an actual "hacker attack" as well as some of the ways penetration tests are conducted, how they're controlled, and what organizations might look for when choosing a company to conduct a penetration test for them.

Chapter 23, "What Is Vulnerability Assessment?" covers the fundamentals: defining vulnerability, exploit, threat, and risk; analyzing vulnerabilities and exploits; and configuring scanners. It also shows you how to generate reports, assess risks in a changing environment, and manage vulnerabilities.

Part 3: Encryption Technology

Part 3 discusses how to implement data encryption, satellite encryption, public key infrastructure, and instant-messaging security. For instance:

Chapter 24, "Data Encryption," is about the role played by cryptographic technology in data security.

Chapter 25, "Satellite Encryption," proposes a method that enhances and complements satellite encryption's role in securing the information society. It also covers satellite encryption policy instruments; implementing satellite encryption; misuse of satellite encryption technology; and results and future directions.

Chapter 26, "Public Key Infrastructure," explains the cryptographic background that forms the foundation of PKI systems; the mechanics of the X.509 PKI system (as elaborated by the Internet Engineering Task Force); the practical issues surrounding the implementation of PKI systems; a number of alternative PKI standards; and alternative cryptographic strategies for solving the problem of secure public key distribution.

Chapter 27, "Instant-Messaging Security," helps you develop an IM security plan, keep it current, and make sure it makes a difference.

Part 4: Privacy and Access Management

Part 4 discusses Internet privacy, personal privacy policies, virtual private networks, identity theft, and VoIP security. For instance:

Chapter 28, "Net Privacy," addresses the privacy issues in the digital society from various points of view, investigating the different aspects related to the notion of privacy and the debate that the intricate essence of privacy has stimulated; the most common privacy threats and the possible economic aspects that may influence the way privacy is (and especially is not currently) managed in most firms; the efforts in the computer science community to face privacy threats, especially in the context of mobile and database systems; and the network-based technologies available to date to provide anonymity when communicating over a private network.

Chapter 29, "Personal Privacy Policies," begins with the derivation of policy content based on privacy legislation, followed by a description of how a personal privacy policy may be constructed semiautomatically. It then shows how to additionally specify policies so that negative unexpected outcomes can be avoided. Finally, it describes the author's Privacy Management Model, which explains how to use personal privacy policies to protect privacy, including what is meant by a "match" of consumer and service provider policies and how nonmatches can be resolved through negotiation.

Chapter 30, "Virtual Private Networks," covers VPN scenarios, VPN comparisons, and information assurance requirements. It also covers building VPN tunnels; applying cryptographic protection; implementing IP security; and deploying virtual private networks.

Chapter 31, "Identity Theft," describes the importance of understanding the human factor of ID theft security and details the findings from a study on deceit.

Chapter 32, "VoIP Security," deals with the attacks targeted toward a specific host and issues related to social engineering.

Part 5: Storage Security

Part 5 covers storage area network (SAN) security and risk management. For instance:

Chapter 33, "SAN Security," describes the following components: protection rings; security and protection; restricting access to storage; access control lists (ACLs) and policies; port blocks and port prohibits; and zoning and isolating resources.

Chapter 34, "Storage Area Networking Security Devices," covers all the issues and security concerns related to SAN security.

Chapter 35, "Risk Management," discusses physical security threats, environmental threats, and incident response.

Part 6: Physical Security

Part 6 discusses physical security essentials, biometrics, homeland security, and information warfare. For instance:

Chapter 36, "Physical Security Essentials," is concerned with physical security and some overlapping areas of premises security. It also looks at physical security threats and then considers physical security prevention measures.

Chapter 37, "Biometrics," discusses the different types of biometrics technology and verification systems and how the following work: biometrics eye analysis technology; biometrics facial recognition technology; facial thermal imaging; biometrics finger-scanning analysis technology; biometrics geometry analysis technology; biometrics verification technology; and privacy-enhanced, biometrics-based verification/authentication as well as biometrics solutions and future directions.

Chapter 38, "Homeland Security," describes some principle provisions of U.S. homeland security-related laws and Presidential directives. It gives the organizational changes that were initiated to support homeland security in the United States. The chapter highlights the 9/11 Commission that Congress charted to provide a full account of the circumstances surrounding the 2001 terrorist attacks and to develop recommendations for corrective measures that could be taken to prevent future acts of terrorism. It also details the Intelligence Reform and Terrorism Prevention Act of 2004 and the Implementation of the 9/11 Commission Recommendations Act of 2007.

Chapter 39, "Information Warfare," defines information warfare (IW) and discusses its most common tactics, weapons, and tools as well as comparing IW terrorism with conventional warfare and addressing the issues of liability and the available legal remedies under international law.

Part 7: Advanced Security

Part 7 discusses security through diversity, online reputation, content filtering, and data loss protection. For instance:

Chapter 40, "Security Through Diversity," covers some of the industry trends in adopting diversity in hardware, software, and application deployments. This chapter also covers the risks of uniformity, conformity, and the ubiquitous impact of adopting standard organizational principals without the consideration of security.

Chapter 41, "Reputation Management," discusses the general understanding of the human notion of reputation. It explains how this concept of reputation fits into computer security. The chapter presents the state of the art of attack-resistant reputation computation. It also gives an overview of the current market of online reputation services. The chapter concludes by underlining the need to standardize online reputation for increased adoption and robustness.

Chapter 42, "Content Filtering," examines the many benefits and justifications of Web-based content filtering such as legal liability risk reduction, productivity gains, and bandwidth usage. It also explores the downside and unintended consequences and risks that improperly deployed or misconfigured systems create. The chapter also looks into methods to subvert and bypass these systems and the reasons behind them.

Chapter 43, "Data Loss Protection," introduces the reader to a baseline understanding of how to investigate and evaluate DLP applications in the market today.

John R. Vacca
Editor-in-Chief
jvacca@frognet.net
www.johnvacca.com

There are many people whose efforts on this book have contributed to its successful completion. I owe each a debt of gratitude and want to take this opportunity to offer my sincere thanks.

A very special thanks to my senior acquisitions editor, Rick Adams, without whose continued interest and support this book would not have been possible. Assistant editor Heather Scherer provided staunch support and encouragement when it was most needed. Thanks to my production editor, A. B. McGee_and copyeditor, Darlene Bordwell, whose fine editorial work has been invaluable. Thanks also to my marketing manager, Marissa Hederson, whose efforts on this book have been greatly appreciated. Finally, thanks to all the other people at Computer Networking and Computer and Information Systems Security, Morgan Kaufmann Publishers/Elsevier Science & Technology Books, whose many talents and skills are essential to a finished book.

Thanks to my wife, Bee Vacca, for her love, her help, and her understanding of my long work hours. Also, a very, very special thanks to Michael Erbschloe for writing the Foreword. Finally, I wish to thank all the following authors who contributed chapters that were necessary for the completion of this book: John Mallery, Scott R. Ellis, Michael West, Tom Chen, Patrick Walsh, Gerald Beuchelt, Mario Santana, Jesse Walker, Xinyuan Wang, Daniel Ramsbrock, Bill Mansoor, Dr. Pramod Pandya, Chunming Rong, Prof. Erdal Cayirci, Prof. Gansen Zhao, Liang Yan, Peng Liu, Thomas F La Porta, Kameswari Kotapati, Albert Caballero, Joe Wright, Jim Harmening, Rahul Bhaskar, Prof. Bhushan Kapoor, Dr. Jean-Marc Seigneur, Christopher W. Day, Yong Guan, Dr. Errin W. Fulp, Sanjay Bavisi, Almantas Kakareka, Daniel S. Soper, Terence Spies, Samuel JJ Curry, Marco Cremonini, Chiara Braghin, Claudio Agostino Ardagna, Dr. George Yee, Markus Jacobsson, Alex Tsow, Sid Stamm, Chris Soghoian, Harsh Kupwade Patil, Dan Wing, Jeffrey S. Bardin, Robert Rounsavall, Sokratis K. Katsikas, William Stallings, Luther Martin, Jan Eloff, Anna Granova, Kevin Noble, Peter Nicoletti, and Ken Perkins.

John Vacca is an information technology consultant and bestselling author based in Pomeroy, Ohio. Since 1982 John has authored 60 books. Some of his most recent works include *Biometric Technologies and Verification Systems* (Elsevier, 2007); *Practical Internet Security* (Springer, 2006); *Optical Networking Best Practices* *Handbook* (Wiley-Interscience, 2006); *Guide to Wireless Network Security* (Springer, 2006); *Computer Forensics: Computer Crime Scene Investigation, 2nd Edition* (Charles River Media, 2005); *Firewalls: Jumpstart for Network and Systems Administrators* (Elsevier, 2004); *Public Key Infrastructure: Building Trusted Applications and Web Services* (Auerbach, 2004); *Identity Theft* (Prentice Hall/PTR, 2002); *The World's 20 Greatest Unsolved Problems* (Pearson Education, 2004); and more than 600 articles in the areas of advanced storage, computer security, and aerospace technology. John was also a configuration management specialist, computer specialist, and the computer security official (CSO) for NASA's space station program (Freedom) and the International Space Station Program from 1988 until his early retirement from NASA in 1995.

Claudio Agostino Ardagna (Chapter 28), Dept. of Information Technology, University of Milan, Crema, Italy

Jeffrey S. Bardin (Chapter 33), Independent Security Consultant, Barre, Massachusetts 01005

Jay Bavisi (Chapter 22), President, EC-Council, Albuquerque, New Mexico 87109

Gerald Beuchelt (Chapter 5), Independent Security Consultant, Burlington, Massachusetts 01803

Rahul Bhaskar (Chapter 38), Department of Information Systems and Decision Sciences, California State University, Fullerton, California 92834

Rahul Bhaskar (Chapter 16), Department of Information Systems and Decision Sciences, California State University, Fullerton, California 92834

Chiara Braghin (Chapter 28), Dept. of Information Technology, University of Milan, Crema, Italy

Albert Caballero CISSP, GSEC (Chapter 14), Security Operations Center Manager, Terremark Worldwide, Inc., Bay Harbor Islands, Florida 33154

Professor Erdal Cayirci (Chapters 11, 13), University of Stavanger, N-4036 Stavanger, Norway

Tom Chen (Chapter 4), Swansea University, Singleton Park, SA2 8PP, Wales, United Kingdom

Marco Cremonini (Chapter 28), Dept. of Information Technology, University of Milan, Crema, Italy

Sam Curry (Chapter 27), VP Product Management, RSA, the Security Division of EMC, Bedford, Massachusetts 01730

Christopher Day, CISSP, NSA:IEM (Chapter 18), Senior Vice President, Secure Information Systems, Terremark Worldwide, Inc., Miami, Florida 33131

Scott R. Ellis, EnCE (Chapters 2, 19), RGL – Forensic Accountants & Consultants, Forensics and Litigation Technology, Chicago, Illinois 60602

Jan H. P. Eloff (Chapter 39), Extraordinary Professor, Information & Computer Security Architectures Research Group, Department of Computer Science, University of Pretoria, and Research Director SAP Meraka UTD/SAP Research CEC, Hillcrest, Pretoria, South Africa, 0002

Michael Erbschloe (Foreword), Teaches Information Security courses at Webster University, St. Louis, Missouri 63119

Errin W. Fulp (Chapter 21), Department of Computer Science, Wake Forest University, Winston-Salem, North Carolina 27109

Anna Granova (Chapter 39), Advocate of the High Court of South Africa, Member of the Pretoria Society of Advocates, University of Pretoria, Computer Science Department, Hillcrest, Pretoria, South Africa, 0002

Yong Guan (Chapter 20), Litton Assistant Professor, Department of Electrical and Computer Engineering, Iowa State University, Ames, Iowa 50011

James T. Harmening (Chapters 15, 30), Computer Bits, Inc., Chicago, Illinois 60602

Markus Jakobsson (Chapter 31), Principal Scientist, CSL, Palo Alto Research Center, Palo Alto, California 94304

Almantas Kakareka (Chapter 23), Terremark World Wide Inc., Security Operations Center, Miami, Florida 33132

Bhushan Kapoor (Chapters 16, 24, 38), Department of Information Systems and Decision Sciences, California State University, Fullerton, California 92834

Sokratis K. Katsikas (Chapter 35), Department of Technology Education & Digital Systems, University of Piraeus, Piraeus 18532, Greece

Larry Korba (Chapter 29), Ottawa, Ontario, Canada K1G 5N7.

Kameswari Kotapati (Chapter 12), Department of Computer Science and Engineering, The Pennsylvania State University, University Park, Pennsylvania 16802

Thomas F. LaPorta (Chapter 12), Department of Computer Science and Engineering, The Pennsylvania State University, University Park, Pennsylvania 16802

Peng Liu (Chapter 12), College of Information Sciences and Technology, The Pennsylvania State University, University Park, Pennsylvania 16802

Tewfiq El Maliki (Chapter 17), Telecommunications labs, University of Applied Sciences of Geneva, Geneva, Switzerland

John R. Mallery (Chapter 1), BKD, LLP, Kansas City, Missouri 64105-1936

Bill Mansoor (Chapter 9), Information Systems Audit and Control Association (ISACA), Rancho Santa Margarita, California 92688-8741

Luther Martin (Chapter 37), Voltage Security, Palo Alto, California 94304

John McDonald (Chapter 33), EMC Corporation, Hopkinton, Massachusetts 01748

John McGowan (Chapter 33), EMC Corporation, Hopkinton, Massachusetts 01748

Peter F. Nicoletti (Chapter 42), Secure Information Systems, Terremark Worldwide, Miami, Florida

Kevin Noble, CISSP GSEC (Chapter 40), Director, Secure Information Services, Terremark Worldwide Inc., Miami, Florida 33132

Pramod Pandya (Chapters 10, 24), Department of Information Systems and Decision Sciences, California State University, Fullerton, California 92834

Harsh Kupwade Patil (Chapter 32), Department of Electrical Engineering, Southern Methodist University, Dallas, Texas 75205

Ken Perkins (Chapter 43), CIPP (Certified Information Privacy Professional), Sr. Systems Engineer, Blazent Incorporated, Denver, Colorado 80206

Daniel Ramsbrock (Chapter 8), Department of Computer Science, George Mason University, Fairfax, Virginia 22030

Chunming Rong (Chapters 11, 13), Professor, Ph.D., Chair of Computer Science Section, Faculty of Science and Technology, University of Stavanger, N-4036 Stavanger, Norway

Robert Rounsavall (Chapter 34), GCIA, GCWN, Director, SIS – SOC, Terremark Worldwide, Inc., Miami, Florida 33131

Mario Santana (Chapter 6), Terremark, Dallas, Texas 75226

Jean-Marc Seigneur (Chapters 17, 41), Department of Social and Economic Sciences, University of Geneva, Switzerland

Daniel S. Soper (Chapter 25), Information and Decision Sciences Department, Mihaylo College of Business and Economics, California State University, Fullerton, California 92834-6848

Terence Spies (Chapter 26), Voltage Security, Inc., Palo Alto, California 94304

William Stallings (Chapter 36), Independent consultant, Brewster Massachusetts 02631

Alex Tsow (Chapter 31), The MITRE Corporation, Mclean, Virginia 22102

Jesse Walker (Chapter 7), Intel Corporation, Hillboro, Oregon 97124

Patrick J. Walsh (Chapter 4), eSoft Inc., Broomfield, Colorado 80021

Xinyuan Wang (Chapter 8), Department of Computer Science, George Mason University, Fairfax, Virginia 22030

Michael A. West (Chapter 3), Independent Technical Writer, Martinez, California 94553

Dan Wing (Chapter 32), Security Technology Group, Cisco Systems, San Jose, California 95123

Joe Wright (Chapters 15, 30), Computer Bits, Inc., Chicago, Illinois 60602

George O.M. Yee (Chapter 29), Information Security Group, Institute for Information Technology, National Research Council Canada, Ottawa, Canada K1A 0R6

## Part I

Overview of System and Network Security: A Comprehensive Introduction

## Chapter 1

Building a Secure Organization

John Mallery
BKD, LLP

It seems logical that any business, whether a commercial enterprise or a not-for-profit business, would understand that building a secure organization is important to long-term success. When a business implements and maintains a strong security posture, it can take advantage of numerous benefits. An organization that can demonstrate an infrastructure protected by robust security mechanisms can potentially see a reduction in insurance premiums being paid. A secure organization can use its security program as a marketing tool, demonstrating to clients that it values their business so much that it takes a very aggressive stance on protecting their information. But most important, a secure organization will not have to spend time and money identifying security breaches and responding to the results of those breaches.

As of September 2008, according to the National Conference of State Legislatures, 44 states, the District of Columbia, and Puerto Rico had enacted legislation requiring notification of security breaches involving personal information.[1] Security breaches can cost an organization significantly through a tarnished reputation, lost business, and legal fees. And numerous regulations, such as the Health Insurance Portability and Accountability Act (HIPAA), the Gramm-Leach-Bliley Act (GLBA), and the Sarbanes-Oxley Act, require businesses to maintain the security of information. Despite the benefits of maintaining a secure organization and the potentially devastating consequences of not doing so, many organizations have poor security mechanisms, implementations, policies, and culture.

1. OBSTACLES TO SECURITY

In attempting to build a secure organization, we should take a close look at the obstacles that make it challenging to build a totally secure organization.

Security Is Inconvenient

Security, by its very nature, is inconvenient, and the more robust the security mechanisms, the more inconvenient the process becomes. Employees in an organization have a job to do; they want to get to work right away. Most security mechanisms, from passwords to multifactor authentication, are seen as roadblocks to productivity. One of the current trends in security is to add whole disk encryption to laptop computers. Although this is a highly recommended security process, it adds a second login step before a computer user can actually start working. Even if the step adds only one minute to the login process, over the course of a year this adds up to four hours of lost productivity. Some would argue that this lost productivity is balanced by the added level of security. But across a large organization, this lost productivity could prove significant.

To gain a full appreciation of the frustration caused by security measures, we have only to watch the Transportation Security Administration (TSA) security lines at any airport. Simply watch the frustration build as a particular item is run through the scanner for a third time while a passenger is running late to board his flight. Security implementations are based on a sliding scale; one end of the scale is total security and total inconvenience, the other is total insecurity and complete ease of use. When we implement any security mechanism, it should be placed on the scale where the level of security and ease of use match the acceptable level of risk for the organization.

Computers Are Powerful and Complex

Home computers have become storehouses of personal materials. Our computers now contain wedding videos, scanned family photos, music libraries, movie collections, and financial and medical records. Because computers contain such familiar objects, we have forgotten

---

1 www.ncsl.org/programs/lis/cip/priv/breachlaws.htm (October 2, 2008).

that computers are very powerful and complex devices. It wasn't that long ago that computers as powerful as our desktop and laptop computers would have filled one or more very large rooms. In addition, today's computers present a "user-friendly" face to the world. Most people are unfamiliar with the way computers truly function and what goes on "behind the scenes." Things such as the Windows Registry, ports, and services are completely unknown to most users and poorly understood by many computer industry professionals. For example, many individuals still believe that a Windows login password protects data on a computer. On the contrary—someone can simply take the hard drive out of the computer, install it as a slave drive in another computer, or place it in a USB drive enclosure, and all the data will be readily accessible.

Computer Users Are Unsophisticated

Many computer users believe that because they are skilled at generating spreadsheets, word processing documents, and presentations, they "know everything about computers." These "power users" have moved beyond application basics, but many still do not understand even basic security concepts. Many users will indiscriminately install software and visit questionable Web sites despite the fact that these actions could violate company policies. The "bad guys"— people who want to steal information from or wreak havoc on computers systems—have also identified that the average user is a weak link in the security chain. As companies began investing more money in perimeter defenses, attackers look to the path of least resistance. They send malware as attachments to email, asking recipients to open the attachment. Despite being told not to open attachments from unknown senders or simply not to open attachments at all, employees consistently violate this policy, wreaking havoc on their networks. The "I Love You Virus" spread very rapidly in this manner. More recently, phishing scams have been very effective in convincing individuals to provide their personal online banking and credit-card information. Why would an attacker struggle to break through an organization's defenses when end users are more than willing to provide the keys to bank accounts? Addressing the threat caused by untrained and unwary end users is a significant part of any security program.

Computers Created Without a Thought to Security

During the development of personal computers (PCs), no thought was put into security. Early PCs were very simple affairs that had limited computing power and no keyboards and were programmed by flipping a series of switches. They were developed almost as curiosities. Even as they became more advanced and complex, all effort was focused on developing greater sophistication and capabilities; no one thought they would have security issues. We only have to look at some of the early computers, such as the Berkeley Enterprises Geniac, the Heathkit EC-1, or the MITS Altair 8800, to understand why security was not an issue back then.[2] The development of computers was focused on what they could do, not how they could be attacked.

As computers began to be interconnected, the driving force was providing the ability to share information, certainly not to protect it. Initially the Internet was designed for military applications, but eventually it migrated to colleges and universities, the principal tenet of which is the sharing of knowledge.

Current Trend Is to Share, Not Protect

Even now, despite the stories of compromised data, people still want to share their data with everyone. And Web-based applications are making this easier to do than simply attaching a file to an email. Social networking sites such as SixApart provide the ability to share material: "Send messages, files, links, and events to your friends. Create a network of friends and share stuff. It's free and easy . . ."[3] In addition, many online data storage sites such as DropSend[4] and FilesAnywhere[5] provide the ability to share files. Although currently in the beta state of development, Swivel[6] provides the ability to upload data sets for analysis and comparison. These sites can allow proprietary data to leave an organization by bypassing security mechanisms.

Data Accessible from Anywhere

As though employees' desire to share data is not enough of a threat to proprietary information, many business professionals want access to data from anywhere they work, on a variety of devices. To be productive, employees now request access to data and contact information on their laptops, desktops, home computers, and mobile devices. Therefore, IT departments must now provide

---

2 "Pop quiz: What was the first personal computer?" www.blinkenlights. com/pc.shtml (October 26, 2008).
3 http://www.sixapart.com (March 24, 2009).
4 www.dropsend.com (October 26, 2008).
5 www.filesanywhere.com (October 26, 2008).
6 www.swivel.com (October 26, 2008).

the ability to sync data with numerous devices. And if the IT department can't or won't provide this capability, employees now have the power to take matters into their own hands.

Previously mentioned online storage sites can be accessed from both the home and office or anywhere there is an Internet connection. Though it might be possible to block access to some of these sites, it is not possible to block access to them all. And some can appear rather innocuous. For many, Google's free email service Gmail is a great tool that provides a very robust service for free. What few people realize is that Gmail provides more than 7 GB of storage that can also be used to store files, not just email. The Gspace plug-in[7] for the Firefox browser provides an FTP-like interface within Firefox that gives users the ability to transfer files from a computer to their Gmail accounts. This ability to easily transfer data outside the control of a company makes securing an organization's data that much more difficult.

Security Isn't About Hardware and Software

Many businesses believe that if they purchase enough equipment, they can create a secure infrastructure. Firewalls, intrusion detection systems, antivirus programs, and two-factor authentication products are just some of the tools available to assist in protecting a network and its data. It is important to keep in mind that no product or combination of products will create a secure organization by itself. Security is a process; there is no tool that you can "set and forget." All security products are only as secure as the people who configure and maintain them. The purchasing and implementation of security products should be only a percentage of the security budget. The employees tasked with maintaining the security devices should be provided with enough time, training, and equipment to properly support the products. Unfortunately, in many organizations security activities take a back seat to support activities. Highly skilled security professionals are often tasked with help-desk projects such as resetting forgotten passwords, fixing jammed printers, and setting up new employee workstations.

The Bad Guys Are Very Sophisticated

At one time the computer hacker was portrayed as a lone teenager with poor social skills who would break into systems, often for nothing more than bragging rights. As ecommerce has evolved, however, so has the profile of the hacker.

Now that there are vast collections of credit-card numbers and intellectual property that can be harvested, organized hacker groups have been formed to operate as businesses. A document released in 2008 spells it out clearly: "Cybercrime companies that work much like real-world companies are starting to appear and are steadily growing, thanks to the profits they turn. Forget individual hackers or groups of hackers with common goals. Hierarchical cybercrime organizations where each cybercriminal has his or her own role and reward system is what you and your company should be worried about."[8]

Now that organizations are being attacked by highly motivated and skilled groups of hackers, creating a secure infrastructure is mandatory.

Management Sees Security as a Drain on the Bottom Line

For most organizations, the cost of creating a strong security posture is seen as a necessary evil, similar to purchasing insurance. Organizations don't want to spend the money on it, but the risks of not making the purchase outweigh the costs. Because of this attitude, it is extremely challenging to create a secure organization. The attitude is enforced because requests for security tools are often supported by documents providing the average cost of a security incident instead of showing more concrete benefits of a strong security posture. The problem is exacerbated by the fact that IT professionals speak a different language than management. IT professionals are generally focused on technology, period. Management is focused on revenue. Concepts such as profitability, asset depreciation, return on investment, realization, and total cost of ownership are the mainstays of management. These are alien concepts to most IT professionals.

Realistically speaking, though it would be helpful if management would take steps to learn some fundamentals of information technology, IT professionals should take the initiative and learn some fundamental business concepts. Learning these concepts is beneficial to the organization because the technical infrastructure can be implemented in a cost-effective manner, and they are beneficial from a career development perspective for IT professionals.

---

7 www.getgspace.com (October 27, 2008).

8 "Report: Cybercrime groups starting to operate like the Mafia," published July 16, 2008, http://arstechnica.com/news.ars/post/20080716-report-cybercrime-groups-starting-to-operate-like-the-mafia.html (October 27, 2008).

A Google search on "business skills for IT professionals" will identify numerous educational programs that might prove helpful. For those who do not have the time or the inclination to attend a class, some very useful materials can be found online. One such document provided by the Government Chief Information Office of New South Wales is *A Guide for Government Agencies Calculating Return on Security Investment*.[9] Though extremely technical, another often cited document is *Cost-Benefit Analysis for Network Intrusion Detection Systems,* by Huaqiang Wei, Deb Frinke, Olivia Carter, and Chris Ritter.[10]

Regardless of the approach that is taken, it is important to remember that any tangible cost savings or revenue generation should be utilized when requesting new security products, tools, or policies. Security professionals often overlook the value of keeping Web portals open for employees. A database that is used by a sales staff to enter contracts or purchases or check inventory will help generate more revenue if it has no downtime. A database that is not accessible or has been hacked is useless for generating revenue.

Strong security can be used to gain a competitive advantage in the marketplace. Having secured systems that are accessible 24 hours a day, seven days a week means that an organization can reach and communicate with its clients and prospective clients more efficiently. An organization that becomes recognized as a good custodian of client records and information can incorporate its security record as part of its branding. This is no different than a car company being recognized for its safety record. In discussions of cars and safety, for example, Volvo is always the first manufacturer mentioned.[11]

What must be avoided is the "sky is falling" mentality. There are indeed numerous threats to a network, but we need to be realistic in allocating resources to protect against these threats. As of this writing, the National Vulnerability Database sponsored by the National Institute of Standards and Technology (NIST) lists 33,428 common vulnerabilities and exposures and publishes 18 new vulnerabilities per day.[12] In addition, the media is filled with stories of stolen laptops, credit-card numbers, and identities. The volume of threats to a network can be mind numbing. It is important to approach management with "probable threats" as opposed to

"describable threats." Probable threats are those that are most likely to have an impact on your business and the ones most likely to get the attention of management.

Perhaps the best approach is to recognize that management, including the board of directors, is required to exhibit a duty of care in protecting their assets that is comparable to other organizations in their industry. When a security breach or incident occurs, being able to demonstrate the high level of security within the organization can significantly reduce exposure to lawsuits, fines, and bad press.

The goal of any discussion with management is to convince them that in the highly technical and interconnected world we live in, having a secure network and infrastructure is a "nonnegotiable requirement of doing business."[13] An excellent resource for both IT professionals and executives that can provide insight into these issues is CERT's technical report, *Governing for Enterprise Security*.[14]

2. TEN STEPS TO BUILDING A SECURE ORGANIZATION

Having identified some of the challenges to building a secure organization, let's now look at 10 ways to successfully build a secure organization. The following steps will put a business in a robust security posture.

A. Evaluate the Risks and Threats

In attempting to build a secure organization, where should you start? One commonly held belief is that you should initially identify your assets and allocate security resources based on the value of each asset. Though this approach might prove effective, it can lead to some significant vulnerabilities. An infrastructure asset might not hold a high value, for example, but it should be protected with the same effort as a high-value asset. If not, it could be an entry point into your network and provide access to valuable data.

Another approach is to begin by evaluating the threats posed to your organization and your data.

Threats Based on the Infrastructure Model

The first place to start is to identify risks based on an organization's infrastructure model. What infrastructure is in place that is necessary to support the operational

9 www.gcio.nsw.gov.au/library/guidelines/resolveuid/87c81d4c6af bc1ae163024bd38aac9bd (October 29, 2008).

10 www.csds.uidaho.edu/deb/costbenefit.pdf (October 29, 2008).

11 "Why leaders should care about security" podcast, October 17, 2006, Julia Allen and William Pollak, www.cert.org/podcast/show/20061017allena.html (November 2, 2008).

12 http://nvd.nist.gov/home.cfm (October 29, 2008).

13 "Why leaders should care about security" podcast, October 17, 2006, Julia Allen and William Pollak, www.cert.org/podcast/show/20061017allena.html (November 2, 2008).

14 www.cert.org/archive/pdf/05tn023.pdf.

needs of the business? A small business that operates out of one office has reduced risks as opposed to an organization that operates out of numerous facilities, includes a mobile workforce utilizing a variety of handheld devices, and offers products or services through a Web-based interface. An organization that has a large number of telecommuters must take steps to protect its proprietary information that could potentially reside on personally owned computers outside company control. An organization that has widely dispersed and disparate systems will have more risk potential than a centrally located one that utilizes uniform systems.

Threats Based on the Business Itself

Are there any specific threats for your particular business? Have high-level executives been accused of inappropriate activities whereby stockholders or employees would have incentive to attack the business? Are there any individuals who have a vendetta against the company for real or imagined slights or accidents? Does the community have a history of antagonism against the organization? A risk management or security team should be asking these questions on a regular basis to evaluate the risks in real time. This part of the security process is often overlooked due to the focus on daily workload.

Threats Based on Industry

Businesses belonging to particular industries are targeted more frequently and with more dedication than those in other industries. Financial institutions and online retailers are targeted because "that's where the money is." Pharmaceutical manufacturers could be targeted to steal intellectual property, but they also could be targeted by special interest groups, such as those that do not believe in testing drugs on live animals.

Identifying some of these threats requires active involvement in industry-specific trade groups in which businesses share information regarding recent attacks or threats they have identified.

Global Threats

Businesses are often so narrowly focused on their local sphere of influence that they forget that by having a network connected to the Internet, they are now connected to the rest of the world. If a piece of malware identified on the other side of the globe targets the identical software used in your organization, you can be sure that you will eventually be impacted by this malware. Additionally, if extremist groups in other countries are targeting your specific industry, you will also be targeted.

Once threats and risks are identified, you can take one of four steps:

- *Ignore the risk.* This is never an acceptable response. This is simply burying your head in the sand and hoping the problem will go away—the business equivalent of not wearing a helmet when riding a motorcycle.
- *Accept the risk.* When the cost to remove the risk is greater than the risk itself, an organization will often decide to simply accept the risk. This is a viable option as long as the organization has spent the time required to evaluate the risk.
- *Transfer the risk.* Organizations with limited staff or other resources could decide to transfer the risk. One method of transferring the risk is to purchase specialized insurance targeted at a specific risk.
- *Mitigate the risk.* Most organizations mitigate risk by applying the appropriate resources to minimize the risks posed to their network.

For organizations that would like to identify and quantify the risks to their network and information assets, CERT provides a free suite of tools to assist with the project. Operationally Critical Threat, Asset, and Vulnerability Evaluation (OCTAVE) provides risk-based assessment for security assessments and planning.[15] There are three versions of OCTAVE: the original OCTAVE, designed for large organizations (more than 300 employees); OCTAVE-S (100 people or fewer); and OCTAVE-Allegro, which is a streamlined version of the tools and is focused specifically on information assets.

Another risk assessment tool that might prove helpful is the Risk Management Framework developed by Educause/Internet 2.[16] Targeted at institutions of higher learning, the approach could be applied to other industries.

Tracking specific threats to specific operating systems, products, and applications can be time consuming. Visiting the National Vulnerability Database and manually searching for specific issues would not necessarily be an effective use of time. Fortunately, the Center for Education and Research in Information Assurance and Security (CERIAS) at Purdue University has a tool called Cassandra that can be configured to notify you of specific threats to your particular products and applications.[17]

---

15 OCTAVE, www.cert.org/octave/ (November 2, 2008).
16 Risk Management Framework, https://wiki.internet2.edu/confluence/display/secguide/Risk+Management+Framework.
17 Cassandra, https://cassandra.cerias.purdue.edu/main/index.html.

B. Beware of Common Misconceptions

In addressing the security needs of an organization, it is common for professionals to succumb to some very common misconceptions. Perhaps the most common misconception is that the business is obscure, unsophisticated, or boring—simply not a target for malicious activity. Businesses must understand that any network that is connected to the Internet is a potential target, regardless of the type of business.

Attackers will attempt to gain access to a network and its systems for several reasons. The first is to look around to see what they can find. Regardless of the type of business, personnel information will more than likely be stored on one of the systems. This includes Social Security numbers and other personal information. This type of information is a target—always.

Another possibility is that the attacker will modify the information he or she finds or simply reconfigure the systems to behave abnormally. This type of attacker is not interested in financial gain; he is simply the technology version of teenagers who soap windows, egg cars, and cover property with toilet paper. He attacks because he finds it entertaining to do so. Additionally, these attackers could use the systems to store stolen "property" such as child pornography or credit-card numbers. If a system is not secure, attackers can store these types of materials on your system and gain access to them at their leisure.

The final possibility is that an attacker will use the hacked systems to mount attacks on other unprotected networks and systems. Computers can be used to mount denial-of-service (DoS) attacks, relay spam, or spread malicious software. To put it simply, no computer or network is immune from attack.

Another common misconception is that an organization is immune from problems caused by employees, essentially saying, "We trust all our employees, so we don't have to focus our energies on protecting our assets from them." Though this is common for small businesses in which the owners know everyone, it also occurs in larger organizations where companies believe that they only hire "professionals." It is important to remember that no matter how well job candidates present themselves, a business can never know everything about an employee's past. For this reason it is important for businesses to conduct preemployment background checks of all employees. Furthermore, it is important to conduct these background checks properly and completely.

Many employers trust this task to an online solution that promises to conduct a complete background check on an individual for a minimal fee. Many of these sites play on individuals' lack of understanding of how some of these online databases are generated. These sites might not have access to the records of all jurisdictions, since many jurisdictions either do not make their records available online or do not provide them to these databases. In addition, many of the records are entered by minimum wage data-entry clerks whose accuracy is not always 100 percent.

Background checks should be conducted by organizations that have the resources at their disposal to get court records directly from the courthouses where the records are generated and stored. Some firms have a team of "runners" who visit the courthouses daily to pull records; others have a network of contacts who can visit the courts for them. Look for organizations that are active members of the National Association of Professional Background Screeners.[18] Members of this organization are committed to providing accurate and professional results. And perhaps more important, they can provide counseling regarding the proper approach to take as well as interpreting the results of a background check.

If your organization does not conduct background checks, there are several firms that might be of assistance: Accurate Background, Inc., of Lake Forest, California[19]; Credential Check, Inc., of Troy, Michigan[20]; and Validity Screening Solutions in Overland Park, Kansas.[21] The Web sites of these companies all provide informational resources to guide you in the process. (*Note:* For businesses outside the United States or for U.S. businesses with locations overseas, the process might be more difficult because privacy laws could prevent conducting a complete background check. The firms we've mentioned should be able to provide guidance regarding international privacy laws.)

Another misconception is that a preemployment background check is all that is needed. Some erroneously believe that once a person is employed, he or she is "safe" and can no longer pose a threat. However, people's lives and fortunes can change during the course of employment. Financial pressures can cause otherwise law-abiding citizens to take risks they never would have thought possible. Drug and alcohol dependency can alter people's behavior as well. For these and other reasons it is a good idea to do an additional background check when an employee is promoted to a position of higher responsibility and trust. If this new position involves

18 National Association of Professional Background Screeners, www.napbs.com.
19 www.accuratebackground.com.
20 www.credentialcheck.com.
21 www.validityscreening.com.

handling financial responsibilities, the background check should also include a credit check.

Though these steps might sound intrusive, which is sometimes a reason cited not to conduct these types of checks, they can also be very beneficial to the employee as well as the employer. If a problem is identified during the check, the employer can often offer assistance to help the employee get through a tough time. Financial counseling and substance abuse counseling can often turn a potentially problematic employee into a very loyal and dedicated one.

Yet another common misconception involves information technology (IT) professionals. Many businesses pay their IT staff fairly high salaries because they understand that having a properly functioning technical infrastructure is important for the continued success of the company. Since the staff is adept at setting up and maintaining systems and networks, there is a general assumption that they know everything there is to know about computers. It is important to recognize that although an individual might be very knowledgeable and technologically sophisticated, no one knows *everything* about computers. Because management does not understand technology, they are not in a very good position to judge a person's depth of knowledge and experience in the field. Decisions are often based on the certifications a person has achieved during his or her career. Though certifications can be used to determine a person's level of competency, too much weight is given to them. Many certifications require nothing more than some time and dedication to study and pass a certification test. Some training companies also offer boot camps that guarantee a person will pass the certification test. It is possible for people to become certified without having any real-world experience with the operating systems, applications, or hardware addressed by the certification. When judging a person's competency, look at his or her experience level and background first, and if the person has achieved certifications in addition to having significant real-world experience, the certification is probably a reflection of the employee's true capabilities.

The IT staff does a great deal to perpetuate the image that they know everything about computers. One of the reasons people get involved with the IT field in the first place is because they have an opportunity to try new things and overcome new challenges. This is why when an IT professional is asked if she knows how to do something, she will always respond "Yes." But in reality the real answer should be, "No, but I'll figure it out." Though they frequently can figure things out, when it comes to security we must keep in mind that it is a specialized area,

and implementing a strong security posture requires significant training and experience.

C. Provide Security Training for IT Staff—Now and Forever

Just as implementing a robust, secure environment is a dynamic process, creating a highly skilled staff of security professionals is also a dynamic process. It is important to keep in mind that even though an organization's technical infrastructure might not change that frequently, new vulnerabilities are being discovered and new attacks are being launched on a regular basis. In addition, very few organizations have a stagnant infrastructure; employees are constantly requesting new software, and more technologies are added in an effort to improve efficiencies. Each new addition likely adds additional security vulnerabilities.

It is important for the IT staff to be prepared to identify and respond to new threats and vulnerabilities. It is recommended that those interested in gaining a deep security understanding start with a vendor-neutral program. A vendor-neutral program is one that focuses on concepts rather than specific products. The SANS (SysAdmin, Audit, Network, Security) Institute offers two introductory programs: Intro to Information Security (Security 301),[22] a five-day class designed for people just starting out in the security field, and the SANS Security Essentials Bootcamp (Security 401),[23] a six-day class designed for people with some security experience. Each class is also available as a self-study program, and each can be used to prepare for a specific certification.

Another option is start with a program that follows the CompTia Security + certification requirements, such as the Global Knowledge Essentials of Information Security.[24] Some colleges offer similar programs.

Once a person has a good fundamental background in security, he should then undergo vendor-specific training to apply the concepts learned to specific applications and security devices.

A great resource for keeping up with current trends in security is to become actively involved in a security-related trade organization. The key concept here is *actively involved*. Many professionals join organizations so that they can add an item to the "professional affiliations" section of their résumé. Becoming actively

---

22 SANS Intro to Computer Security, www.sans.org.
23 SANS Security Essentials Bootcamp, www.sans.org.
24 www.globalknowledge.com/training/course.asp?pageid=9&course id=10242&catid=191&country=United+States.

involved means attending meetings on a regular basis and serving on a committee or in a position on the executive board. Though this seems like a daunting time commitment, the benefit is that the professional develops a network of resources that can be available to provide insight, serve as a sounding board, or provide assistance when a problem arises. Participating in these associations is a very cost-effective way to get up to speed with current security trends and issues. Here are some organizations[25] that can prove helpful:

- ASIS International, the largest security-related organization in the world, focuses primarily on physical security but has more recently started addressing computer security as well.
- ISACA, formerly the Information Systems Audit and Control Association.
- High Technology Crime Investigation Association (HTCIA).
- Information Systems Security Association (ISSA).
- InfraGard, a joint public and private organization sponsored by the Federal Bureau of Investigation (FBI).

In addition to monthly meetings, many local chapters of these organizations sponsor regional conferences that are usually very reasonably priced and attract nationally recognized experts.

Arguably one of the best ways to determine whether an employee has a strong grasp of information security concepts is if she can achieve the Certified Information Systems Security Professional (CISSP) certification. Candidates for this certification are tested on their understanding of the following 10 knowledge domains:

- Access control
- Application security
- Business continuity and disaster recovery planning
- Cryptography
- Information security and risk management
- Legal, regulations, compliance, and investigations
- Operations security
- Physical (environmental) security
- Security architecture and design
- Telecommunications and network security

What makes this certification so valuable is that the candidate must have a minimum of five years of professional experience in the information security field or four years of experience and a college degree. To maintain

certification, a certified individual is required to attend 120 hours of continuing professional education during the three-year certification cycle. This ensures that those holding the CISSP credential are staying up to date with current trends in security. The CISSP certification is maintained by (ISC)² [26].

D. Think "Outside the Box"

For most businesses, the threat to their intellectual assets and technical infrastructure comes from the "bad guys" sitting outside their organizations, trying to break in. These organizations establish strong perimeter defenses, essentially "boxing in" their assets. However, internal employees have access to proprietary information to do their jobs, and they often disseminate this information to areas where it is no longer under the control of the employer. This dissemination of data is generally not performed with any malicious intent, simply for employees to have access to data so that they can perform their job responsibilities more efficiently. This also becomes a problem when an employee leaves (or when a person still-employed loses something like a laptop with proprietary information stored on it) and the organization and takes no steps to collect or control their proprietary information in the possession of their now ex-employee.

One of the most overlooked threats to intellectual property is the innocuous and now ubiquitous USB Flash drive. These devices, the size of a tube of lipstick, are the modern-day floppy disk in terms of portable data storage. They are a very convenient way to transfer data between computers. But the difference between these devices and a floppy disk is that USB Flash drives can store a very large amount of data. A 16 GB USB Flash drive has the same storage capacity as more than 10,000 floppy disks! As of this writing, a 16 GB USB Flash drive can be purchased for as little as $30. Businesses should keep in mind that as time goes by, the capacity of these devices will increase and the price will decrease, making them very attractive to employees.

These devices are not the only threat to data. Because other devices can be connected to the computer through the USB port, digital cameras, MP3 players, and external hard drives can now be used to remove data from a computer and the network to which it is connected. Most people would recognize that external hard drives pose a threat, but they would not recognize other devices as a threat. Cameras and music players are designed to store images and music, but to a computer they are simply

---

FIGURE 1.1 Identifying connected USB devices in the USBStor Registry key.

additional mass storage devices. It is difficult for people to understand that an iPod can carry word processing documents, databases, and spreadsheets as well as music. Fortunately, Microsoft Windows tracks the devices that are connected to a system in a Registry key, HKEY_Local_Machine\System\ControlSet00x\Enum\USBStor. It might prove interesting to look in this key on your own computer to see what types of devices have been connected. Figure 1.1 shows a wide array of devices that have been connected to a system that includes USB Flash drives, a digital camera, and several external hard drives.

Windows Vista has an additional key that tracks connected devices: HKEY_Local_Machine\Software\Microsoft\Windows Portable Devices\Devices.[27] (*Note:* Analyzing the Registry is a great way to investigate the activities of computer users. For many, however, the Registry is tough to navigate and interpret. If you are interested in understanding more about the Registry, you might want to download and play with Harlan Carvey's RegRipper.[28])

Another threat to information that carries data outside the walls of the organization is the plethora of handheld devices currently in use. Many of these devices have the ability to send and receive email as well as create, store, and transmit word processing, spreadsheet, and PDF files. Though most employers will not purchase these devices for their employees, they are more than happy to allow their employees to sync their personally owned

devices with their corporate computers. Client contact information, business plans, and other materials can easily be copied from a system. Some businesses feel that they have this threat under control because they provide their employees with corporate-owned devices and they can collect these devices when employees leave their employment. The only problem with this attitude is that employees can easily copy data from the devices to their home computers before the devices are returned.

Because of the threat of portable data storage devices and handheld devices, it is important for an organization to establish policies outlining the acceptable use of these devices as well as implementing an enterprise-grade solution to control how, when, or if data can be copied to them. Filling all USB ports with epoxy is a cheap solution, but it is not really effective. Fortunately there are several products that can protect against this type of data leak. DeviceWall from Centennial Software[29] and Mobile Security Enterprise Edition from Bluefire Security Technologies[30] are two popular ones.

Another way that data leaves control of an organization is through the use of online data storage sites. These sites provide the ability to transfer data from a computer to an Internet-accessible location. Many of these sites provide 5 GB or more of free storage. Though it is certainly possible to blacklist these sites, there are so many, and more are being developed on a regular basis, that it is difficult if not impossible to block access to all of them. One such popular storage location is the storage space provided with a Gmail account. Gmail provides a large amount of storage space with its free accounts (7260 MB as of this writing, and growing). To access this storage space, users must use the Firefox browser with the Gspace plugin installed.[31] Once logged in, users can transfer files simply by highlighting the file and clicking an arrow. Figure 1.2 shows the Gspace interface.

Another tool that will allow users to access the storage space in their Gmail account is the Gmail Drive shell extension.[32] This shell extension places a drive icon in Windows Explorer, allowing users to copy files to the online storage location as though it were a normal mapped drive. Figure 1.3 shows the Gmail Drive icon in Windows Explorer.

Apple has a similar capability for those users with a MobileMe account. This drive is called iDisk and

27 http://windowsir.blogspot.com/2008/06/portable-devices-on-vista.html (November 8, 2008).
28 RegRipper, www.regripper.net.

29 DeviceWall, www.devicewall.com.
30 Bluefire Security Technologies, 1010 Hull St., Ste. 210, Baltimore, Md. 21230.
31 Gspace, www.getgspace.com.
32 Gmail Drive, www.viksoe.dk/code/gmail.htm.

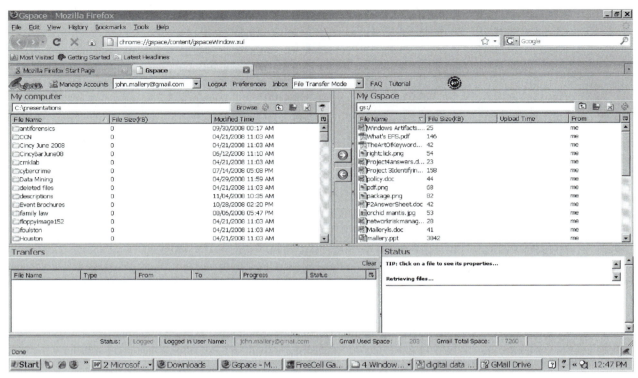

FIGURE 1.2 Accessing Gspace using the Firefox browser.

FIGURE 1.3 Gmail Drive in Windows Explorer.

appears in the Finder. People who utilize iDisk can access the files from anywhere using a Web browser, but they can also upload files using the browser. Once uploaded, the files are available right on the user's desktop, and they can be accessed like any other file. Figures 1.4 and 1.5 show iDisk features.

In addition, numerous sites provide online storage. A partial list is included here:

- ElephantDrive: www.elephantdrive.com
- Mozy: www.mozy.com
- Box: www.box.net
- Carbonite: www.carbonite.com
- Windows Live SkyDrive: www.skydrive.live.com
- FilesAnywhere: www.filesanywhere.com
- Savefile: www.savefile.com
- Spare Backup: www.sparebackup.com
- Digitalbucket.net: www.digitalbucket.net
- Memeo: www.memeo.com
- Biscu.com: www.biscu.com

Note: Though individuals might find these sites convenient and easy to use for file storage and backup purposes, businesses should think twice about storing data on them. The longevity of these sites is not guaranteed. For example, Xdrive, a popular online storage service created in 1999 and purchased by AOL in 2005 (allegedly for US$30 million), shut down on January 12, 2009.

E. Train Employees: Develop a Culture of Security

One of the greatest security assets is a business's own employees, but only if they have been properly trained to comply with security policies and to identify potential security problems.

Many employees don't understand the significance of various security policies and implementations. As mentioned previously, they consider these policies nothing

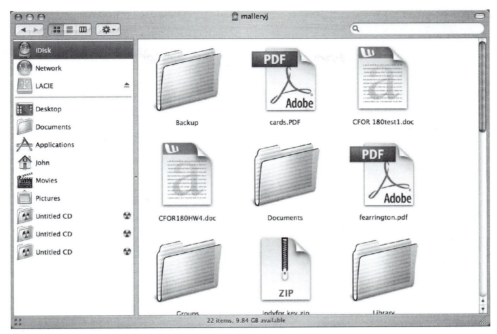

FIGURE 1.4 Accessing files in iDisk.

FIGURE 1.5 iDisk Upload window in Firefox.

more than an inconvenience. Gaining the support and allegiance of employees takes time, but it is time well spent. Begin by carefully explaining the reasons behind any security implementation. One of the reasons could be ensuring employee productivity, but focus primarily on the security issues. File sharing using LimeWire and eMule might keep employees away from work, but they can also open up holes in a firewall. Downloading and installing unapproved software can install malicious software that can infect user systems, causing their computers to function slowly or not at all.

Perhaps the most direct way to gain employee support is to let employees know that the money needed to respond to attacks and fix problems initiated by users is money that is then not available for raises and promotions. Letting employees know that they now have some

"skin in the game" is one way to get them involved in security efforts. If a budget is set aside for responding to security problems and employees help stay well within the budget, the difference between the money spent and the actual budget could be divided among employees as a bonus. Not only would employees be more likely to speak up if they notice network or system slowdowns, they would probably be more likely to confront strangers wandering through the facility.

Another mechanism that can be used to gain security allies is to provide advice regarding the proper security mechanisms for securing home computers. Though some might not see this as directly benefiting the company, keep in mind that many employees have corporate data on their home computers. This advice can come from periodic, live presentations (offer refreshments and attendance will be higher) or from a periodic newsletter that is either mailed or emailed to employees' personal addresses.

The goal of these activities is to encourage employees to approach management or the security team voluntarily. When this begins to happen on a regular basis, you will have expanded the capabilities of your security team and created a much more secure organization.

The security expert Roberta Bragg used to tell a story of one of her clients who took this concept to a high level. The client provided the company mail clerk with a WiFi hotspot detector and promised him a free steak dinner for every unauthorized wireless access point he could

FIGURE 1.6 Windows Server 2008 Security Guide Table of Contents.

find on the premises. The mail clerk was very happy to have the opportunity to earn three free steak dinners.

F. Identify and Utilize Built-In Security Features of the Operating System and Applications

Many organizations and systems administrators state that they cannot create a secure organization because they have limited resources and simply do not have the funds to purchase robust security tools. This is a ridiculous approach to security because all operating systems and many applications include security mechanisms that require no organizational resources other than time to identify and configure these tools. For Microsoft Windows operating systems, a terrific resource is the online Microsoft TechNet Library.[33] Under the Solutions Accelerators link you can find security guides for all recent Microsoft Windows operating systems. Figure 1.6 shows the table of contents for Windows 2008 Server.

TechNet is a great resource and can provide insight into managing numerous security issues, from Microsoft Office 2007 to security risk management. These documents can assist in implementing the built-in security features of Microsoft Windows products. Assistance is needed

in identifying many of these capabilities because they are often hidden from view and turned off by default.

One of the biggest concerns in an organization today is data leaks, which are ways that confidential information can leave an organization despite robust perimeter security. As mentioned previously, USB Flash drives are one cause of data leaks; another is the recovery of data found in the unallocated clusters of a computer's hard drive. Unallocated clusters, or *free space*, as it is commonly called, is the area of a hard drive where the operating system and applications dump their artifacts or residual data. Though this data is not viewable through a user interface, the data can easily be identified (and sometimes recovered) using a hex editor such as WinHex.[34] Figure 1.7 shows the contents of a deleted file stored on a floppy disk being displayed by WinHex.

Should a computer be stolen or donated, it is very possible that someone could access the data located in unallocated clusters. For this reason, many people struggle to find an appropriate "disk-scrubbing" utility. Many such commercial utilities exist, but there is one built into Microsoft Windows operating systems. The command-line program cipher.exe is designed to display or alter the encryption of directories (files) stored on NTFS partitions. Few people even know about this command; even fewer are familiar with the */w* switch. Here is a description of the switch from the program's Help file:

> *Removes data from available unused disk space on the entire volume. If this option is chosen, all other options are ignored. The directory specified can be anywhere in a local volume. If it is a mount point or points to a directory in another volume, the data on that volume will be removed.*

To use Cipher, click **Start | Run** and type **cmd**. When the cmd.exe window opens, type **cipher /w:*folder***, where *folder* is any folder in the volume that you want to clean, and then press **Enter**. Figure 1.8 shows Cipher wiping a folder.

For more on secure file deletion issues, see the author's white paper in the SANS reading room, "Secure file deletion: Fact or fiction?"[35]

Another source of data leaks is the personal and editing information that can be associated with Microsoft Office files. In Microsoft Word 2003 you can configure the application to remove personal information on save and to warn you when you are about to print, share, or send a document containing tracked changes or comments.

To access this feature, within Word click **Tools | Options** and then click the **Security** tab. Toward the

---

33 Microsoft TechNet Library, http://technet.microsoft.com/en-us/library/default.aspx.

34 WinHex, www.x-ways.net/winhex/index-m.html.
35 "Secure file deletion: Fact or fiction?" www.sans.org/reading_room/whitepapers/incident/631.php (November 8, 2008).

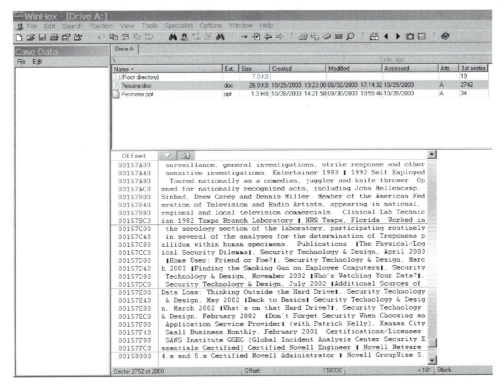

FIGURE 1.7 WinHex displaying the contents of a deleted Word document.

```
C:\>cipher /W:secretstuff
To remove as much data as possible, please close all other applications while
running CIPHER /W.
Writing 0x00
...........................................................................
Writing 0xFF
...........................................................................
Writing Random Numbers
...........................................................................
```

FIGURE 1.8 Cipher wiping a folder called Secretstuff.

bottom of the security window you will notice the two options described previously. Simply select the options you want to use. Figure 1.9 shows these options.

Microsoft Office 2007 made this tool more robust and more accessible. A separate tool called Document Inspector can be accessed by clicking the **Microsoft Office** button, pointing to **Prepare Document**, then clicking **Inspect Document**. Then select the items you want to remove.

Implementing a strong security posture often begins by making the login process more robust. This includes increasing the complexity of the login password. All passwords can be cracked, given enough time and resources, but the more difficult you make cracking a password, the greater the possibility the asset the password protects will stay protected.

All operating systems have some mechanism to increase the complexity of passwords. In Microsoft Windows XP Professional, this can be accomplished by

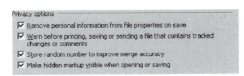

FIGURE 1.9 Security options for Microsoft Word 2003.

clicking **Start | Control Panel | Administrative Tools | Local Security Policy**. Under **Security Settings**, expand **Account Policies** and then highlight **Password Policy**. In the right-hand panel you can enable password complexity. Once this is enabled, passwords must contain at least three of the four following password groups[36]:

● English uppercase characters (A through Z)
● English lowercase characters (a through z)

---

[36] "Users receive a password complexity requirements message that does not specify character group requirements for a password," http://support.microsoft.com/kb/821425 (November 8, 2008).

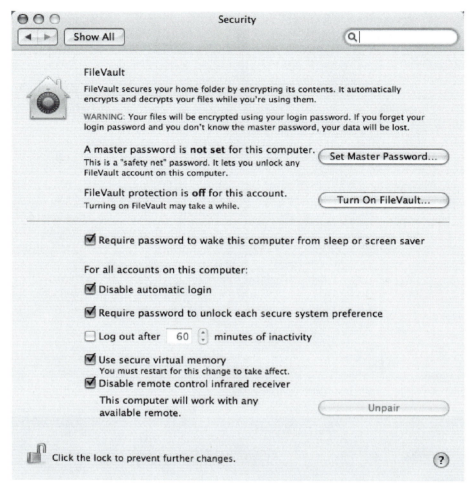

FIGURE 1.10 Security options for Mac OS X.

- Numerals (0 through 9)
- Nonalphabetic characters (such as !, $, #, %)

It is important to recognize that all operating systems have embedded tools to assist with security. They often require a little research to find, but the time spent in identifying them is less than the money spent on purchasing additional security products or recovering from a security breach.

Though not yet used by many corporations, Mac OS X has some very robust security features, including File Vault, which creates an encrypted home folder and the ability to encrypt virtual memory. Figure 1.10 shows the security options for Mac OS X.

G. Monitor Systems

Even with the most robust security tools in place, it is important to monitor your systems. All security products are manmade and can fail or be compromised. As

with any other aspect of technology, one should never rely on simply one product or tool. Enabling logging on your systems is one way to put your organization in a position to identify problem areas. The problem is, what should be logged? There are some security standards that can help with this determination. One of these standards is the Payment Card Industry Data Security Standard (PCI DSS).[37] Requirement 10 of the PCI DSS states that organizations must "Track and monitor access to network resources and cardholder data." If you simply substitute *confidential information* for the phrase *cardholder data,* this requirement is an excellent approach to a log management program. Requirement 10 is reproduced here:

Logging mechanisms and the ability to track user activities are critical. The presence of logs in all environments allows thorough tracking and analysis if something does go wrong. Determining the cause of a compromise is very difficult without system activity logs:

---

37 PCI DSS, www.pcisecuritystandards.org/.

1. Establish a process for linking all access to system components (especially access done with administrative privileges such as root) to each individual user.
2. Implement automated audit trails for all system components to reconstruct the following events:

- All individual user accesses to cardholder data
- All actions taken by any individual with root or administrative privileges
- Access to all audit trails
- Invalid logical access attempts
- Use of identification and authentication mechanisms
- Initialization of the audit logs
- Creation and deletion of system-level objects

3. Record at least the following audit trail entries for all system components for each event:

- User identification
- Type of event
- Date and time
- Success or failure indication
- Origination of event
- Identity or name of affected data, system component, or resource

4. Synchronize all critical system clocks and times.

5. Secure audit trails so they cannot be altered:

- Limit viewing of audit trails to those with a job-related need.
- Protect audit trail files from unauthorized modifications.
- Promptly back up audit trail files to a centralized log server or media that is difficult to alter.
- Copy logs for wireless networks onto a log server on the internal LAN.
- Use file integrity monitoring and change detection software on logs to ensure that existing log data cannot be changed without generating alerts (although new data being added should not cause an alert).

6. Review logs for all system components at least daily. Log reviews must include those servers that perform security functions like intrusion detection system (IDS) and authentication, authorization, and accounting protocol (AAA) servers (for example, RADIUS).

Note: Log harvesting, parsing, and alerting tools may be used to achieve compliance.

7. Retain audit trail history for at least one year, with a minimum of three months online availability.

Requirement 6 looks a little overwhelming, since few organizations have the time to manually review log files.

Fortunately, there are tools that will collect and parse log files from a variety of sources. All these tools have the ability to notify individuals of a particular event. One simple tool is the Kiwi Syslog Daemon[38] for Microsoft Windows. Figure 1.11 shows the configuration screen for setting up email alerts in Kiwi.

Additional log parsing tools include Microsoft's Log Parser[39] and, for Unix, Swatch.[40] Commercial tools include Cisco Security Monitoring, Analysis, and Response System (MARS)[41] and GFI EventsManager.[42]

An even more detailed approach to monitoring your systems is to install a packet-capturing tool on your network so you can analyze and capture traffic in real time. One tool that can be very helpful is Wireshark, which is "an award-winning network protocol analyzer developed by an international team of networking experts."[43] Wireshark is based on the original packet capture tool, Ethereal. Analyzing network traffic is not a trivial task and requires some training, but it is the perhaps the most accurate way to determine what is happening on your network. Figure 1.12 shows Wireshark monitoring the traffic on a wireless interface.

H. Hire a Third Party to Audit Security

Regardless of how talented your staff is, there is always the possibility that they overlooked something or inadvertently misconfigured a device or setting. For this reason it is very important to bring in an extra set of "eyes, ears, and hands" to review your organization's security posture.

Though some IT professionals will become paranoid having a third party review their work, intelligent staff members will recognize that a security review by outsiders can be a great learning opportunity. The advantage of having a third party review your systems is that the outsiders have experience reviewing a wide range of systems, applications, and devices in a variety of industries. They will know what works well and what might work but cause problems in the future. They are also more likely to be up to speed on new vulnerabilities and the latest product updates. Why? Because this is all they do.

38 Kiwi Syslog Daemon, www.kiwisyslog.com.
39 Log Parser 2.2, www.microsoft.com/downloads/details.aspx?Family ID=890cd06b-abf8-4c25-91b2-f8d975cf8c07&displaylang=en.
40 Swatch, http://sourceforge.net/projects/swatch/.
41 Cisco MARS, www.cisco.com/en/US/products/ps6241/.
42 GFI EventsManager, www.gfi.com/eventsmanager/.
43 Wireshark, www.wireshark.org.

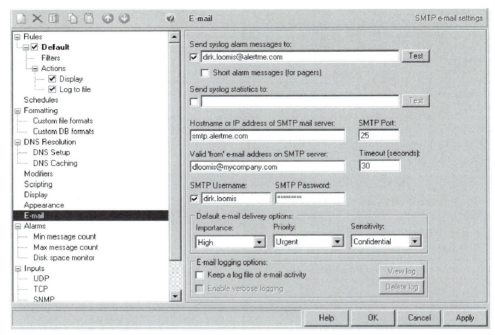

FIGURE 1.11 Kiwi Syslog Daemon Email Alert Configuration screen.

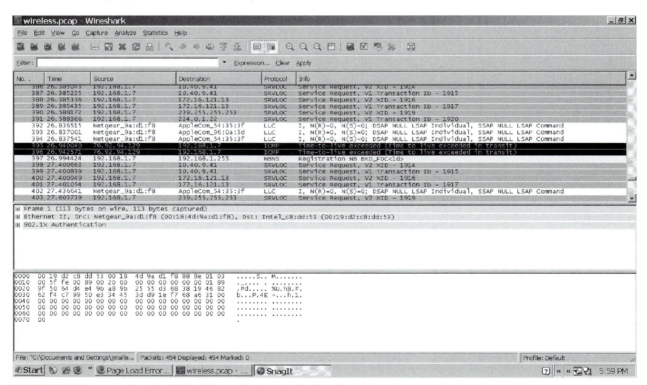

FIGURE 1.12 The protocol analyzer Wireshark monitoring a wireless interface.

They are not encumbered by administrative duties, internal politics, and help desk requests. They will be more objective than in-house staff, and they will be in a position to make recommendations after their analysis.

The third-party analysis should involve a two-pronged approach: They should identify how the network appears to attackers and how secure the system is, should attackers make it past the perimeter defenses. You don't want to have "Tootsie Pop security"—a hard crunchy shell with a soft center. The external review, often called a *penetration test,* can be accomplished in several ways; the first is a *no knowledge* approach, whereby the consultants are

7. Open an Internet browser, and type **http://192.168.0.1**.

If a "Configuration Assistant" appears immediately, then do not follow the rest of these instructions. Follow the Configuration Assistant instructions, instead. Once you are finished, test your Internet connection by browing online, for example to **http://kbserver.netgear.com**.

8. Type **admin** for User Name, and **password** for Password. (Older routers use 1234 as the password.)
9. Click **OK**. This logs you into the router.

FIGURE 1.13 Default username and password for Netgear router.

provided with absolutely no information regarding the network and systems prior to their analysis. Though this is a very realistic approach, it can be time consuming and very expensive. Using this approach, consultants must use publicly available information to start enumerating systems for testing. This is a realistic approach, but a *partial knowledge* analysis is more efficient and less expensive. If provided with a network topology diagram and a list of registered IP addresses, the third-party reviewers can complete the review faster and the results can be addressed in a much more timely fashion. Once the penetration test is complete, a review of the internal network can be initiated. The audit of the internal network will identify open shares, unpatched systems, open ports, weak passwords, rogue systems, and many other issues.

I. Don't Forget the Basics

Many organizations spend a great deal of time and money addressing perimeter defenses and overlook some fundamental security mechanisms, as described here.

Change Default Account Passwords

Nearly all network devices come preconfigured with a password/username combination. This combination is included with the setup materials and is documented in numerous locations. Very often these devices are the gateways to the Internet or other internal networks. If these default passwords are not changed upon configuration, it becomes a trivial matter for an attacker to get into these systems. Hackers can find password lists on the Internet,[44] and vendors include default passwords in their online manuals. For example, Figure 1.13 shows the default username and password for a Netgear router.

Use Robust Passwords

With the increased processing power of our computers and password-cracking software such as the Passware

products[45] and AccessData's Password Recovery Toolkit,[46] cracking passwords is fairly simple and straightforward. For this reason it is extremely important to create robust passwords. Complex passwords are hard for users to remember, though, so it is a challenge to create passwords that can be remembered without writing them down. One solution is to use the first letter of each word in a phrase, such as "**I** like **t**o **e**at **i**mported **c**heese **f**rom **H**olland." This becomes *IlteicfH*, which is an eight-character password using upper- and lowercase letters. This can be made even more complex by substituting an exclamation point for the letter *I* and substituting the number 3 for the letter *e*, so that the password becomes *!lt3icfH*. This is a fairly robust password that can be remembered easily.

Close Unnecessary Ports

Ports on a computer are logical access points for communication over a network. Knowing what ports are open on your computers will allow you to understand the types of access points that exist. The well-known port numbers are 0 through 1023. Some easily recognized ports and what they are used for are listed here:

- Port 21: FTP
- Port 23: Telnet
- Port 25: SMTP
- Port 53: DNS
- Port 80: HTTP
- Port 110: POP
- Port 119: NNTP

Since open ports that are not needed can be an entrance into your systems, and open ports that are open unexpectedly could be a sign of malicious software, identifying open ports is an important security process. There are several tools that will allow you to identify open ports. The built-in command-line tool *netstat*

44 www.phenoelit-us.org/dpl/dpl.html.

45 Passware, www.lostpassword.com.
46 Password Recovery Toolkit, www.accessdata.com/decryptionTool.html.

```
FPort v2.0 - TCP/IP Process to Port Mapper
Copyright 2000 by Foundstone, Inc.
http://www.foundstone.com

Pid     Process         Port  Proto Path
1284               ->   135   TCP
4       System     ->   139   TCP
4       System     ->   427   TCP
4       System     ->   445   TCP
2192               ->   1025  TCP
3632    ACIntUsr   ->   1027  TCP   C:\Program Files\Altiris\AClient\ACIntUsr.EXE
2736    firefox    ->   1080  TCP   C:\Program Files\Mozilla Firefox\firefox.exe
2736    firefox    ->   1081  TCP   C:\Program Files\Mozilla Firefox\firefox.exe
2736    firefox    ->   1082  TCP   C:\Program Files\Mozilla Firefox\firefox.exe
2736    firefox    ->   1083  TCP   C:\Program Files\Mozilla Firefox\firefox.exe
752     ZenRem32   ->   1761  TCP   C:\Program Files\Novell\ZENworks\RemoteManagement\RMAgent\ZenRem32.exe
1692               ->   2869  TCP
3252    dpmw32     ->   3017  TCP   C:\WINDOWS\system32\dpmw32.exe
416     InoRpc     ->   42510 TCP   C:\Program Files\CA\eTrust Antivirus\InoRpc.exe
272     AeXNSAgent ->   52028 TCP   C:\Program Files\Altiris\Altiris Agent\AeXNSAgent.exe

4       System     ->   123   UDP
2736    firefox    ->   123   UDP   C:\Program Files\Mozilla Firefox\firefox.exe
272     AeXNSAgent ->   137   UDP   C:\Program Files\Altiris\Altiris Agent\AeXNSAgent.exe
5177412            ->   138   UDP
1284               ->   401   UDP
4       System     ->   402   UDP
6029362            ->   427   UDP
3632    ACIntUsr   ->   445   UDP   C:\Program Files\Altiris\AClient\ACIntUsr.EXE
752     ZenRem32   ->   500   UDP   C:\Program Files\Novell\ZENworks\RemoteManagement\RMAgent\ZenRem32.exe
3866696            ->   1040  UDP
1692               ->   1058  UDP
2736    firefox    ->   1314  UDP   C:\Program Files\Mozilla Firefox\firefox.exe
416     InoRpc     ->   1761  UDP   C:\Program Files\CA\eTrust Antivirus\InoRpc.exe
2736    firefox    ->   1815  UDP   C:\Program Files\Mozilla Firefox\firefox.exe
4587552            ->   1900  UDP
3252    dpmw32     ->   1900  UDP   C:\WINDOWS\system32\dpmw32.exe
4       System     ->   1924  UDP
2192               ->   3024  UDP
2736    firefox    ->   4500  UDP   C:\Program Files\Mozilla Firefox\firefox.exe
6029420            ->   42508 UDP
3801155            ->   52029 UDP
```

FIGURE 1.14 Sample output from Fport.

will allow you to identify open ports and process IDs by using the following switches:

-a Displays all connections and listening ports
-n Displays addresses and port numbers in numerical form
-o Displays the owning process ID associated with each connection

(*Note:* In Unix, netstat is also available but utilizes the following switches: *-atvp.*)

Other tools that can prove helpful are ActivePorts,[47] a graphical user interface (GUI) tool that allows you to export the results in delimited format, and Fport,[48] a popular command-line tool. Sample results are shown in Figure 1.14.

J. Patch, Patch, Patch

Nearly all operating systems have a mechanism for automatically checking for updates. This notification system should be turned on. Though there is some debate as to whether updates should be installed automatically, systems administrators should at least be notified of updates. They might not want to have them installed automatically, since patches and updates have been known to cause more problems than they solve. However, administrators should not wait too long before installing updates, because this can unnecessarily expose systems to attack.

A simple tool that can help keep track of system updates is the Microsoft Baseline Security Analyzer,[49] which also will examine other fundamental security configurations.

Use Administrator Accounts for Administrative Tasks

A common security vulnerability is created when systems administrators conduct administrative or personal tasks while logged into their computers with administrator rights. Tasks such as checking email, surfing the Internet, and testing questionable software can expose the computer to malicious software. This means that the malicious software can run with administrator privileges, which can create serious problems. Administrators should log into their systems using a standard user account to prevent malicious software from gaining control of their computers.

Restrict Physical Access

With a focus on technology, it is often easy to overlook nontechnical security mechanisms. If an intruder can gain physical access to a server or other infrastructure asset, the intruder will own the organization. Critical systems should be kept in secure areas. A secure area is one that provides the ability to control access to only those who need access to the systems as part of their job

---

47 ActivePorts, www.softpile.com.
48 Fport, www.foundstone.com/us/resources/proddesc/fport.htm.

49 Microsoft Baseline Security Analyzer, http://technet.microsoft.com/en-us/security/cc184923.aspx.

responsibilities. A room that is kept locked using a key that is only provided to the systems administrator, with the only duplicate stored in a safe in the office manager's office, is a good start. The room should not have any windows that can open. In addition, the room should have no labels or signs identifying it as a server room or network operations center. The equipment should not be stored in a closet where other employees, custodians, or contractors can gain access. The validity of your security mechanisms should be reviewed during a third-party vulnerability assessment.

Don't Forget Paper!

With the advent of advanced technology, people have forgotten how information was stolen in the past—on paper. Managing paper documents is fairly straightforward. Locking file cabinets should be used—and locked consistently. Extra copies of proprietary documents, document drafts, and expired internal communications are some of the materials that should be shredded. A policy should be created to tell employees what they should and should not do with printed documents. The following example of the theft of trade secrets underscores the importance of protecting paper documents:

> A company surveillance camera caught Coca-Cola employee Joya Williams at her desk looking through files and "stuffing documents into bags," Nahmias and FBI officials said. Then in June, an undercover FBI agent met at the Atlanta airport with another of the defendants, handing him $30,000 in a yellow Girl Scout Cookie box in exchange for an Armani bag containing confidential Coca-Cola documents and a sample of a product the company was developing, officials said.[50]

The steps to achieving security mentioned in this chapter are only the beginning. They should provide some insight into where to start building a secure organization.

---

50 3 accused in theft of Coke secrets," *Washington Post*, July 26, 2006, www.washingtonpost.com/wp-dyn/content/article/2006/07/05/AR2006070501717.html (November 8, 2008).

## Chapter 2

A Cryptography Primer

Scott R. Ellis
RGL Forensics

Man is a warrior creature, a species that ritually engages in a type of warfare where the combat can range from the subtlety of inflicting economic damage, or achieving economic superiority and advantage, to moving someone's chair a few inches from sitting distance or putting rocks in their shoes, to the heinousness of the outright killing of our opponents. As such, it is in our nature to want to prevent others who would do us harm from intercepting private communications (which could be about them!). Perhaps nothing so perfectly illustrates this fact as the art of cryptography. It is, in its purpose, an art form entirely devoted to the methods whereby we can prevent information from falling into the hands of those who would use it against us—our enemies.

Since the beginning of sentient language, cryptography has been a part of communication. It is as old as language itself. In fact, one could make the argument that the desire and ability to encrypt communication, to alter a missive in such a way so that only the intended recipient may understand it, is an innate ability hardwired into the human genome. Aside from the necessity to communicate, it could very well be what led to the development of language itself. Over time, languages and dialects evolve, as we can see with Spanish, French, Portuguese, and Italian—all "Latin" languages. People who speak French have a great deal of trouble understanding people who speak Spanish, and vice versa. The profundity of Latin cognates in these languages is undisputed, but generally speaking, the two languages are so far removed that they are not dialects, they are separate languages. But why is this? Certain abilities, such as walking, are hardwired into our nervous systems. Other abilities, such as language, are not.

So why isn't language hardwired into our nervous system, as it is with bees, who are born knowing how to tell another bee how far away a flower is, as well as the quantity of pollen and whether there is danger present? Why don't we humans all speak the exact same language? Perhaps we do, to a degree, but we choose not to do so. The reason is undoubtedly because humans, unlike bees, understand that knowledge is power, and knowledge is communicated via spoken and written words. Plus we weren't born with giant stingers with which to simply sting people we don't like. With the development of evolving languages innate in our genetic wiring, the inception of cryptography was inevitable.

In essence, computer-based cryptography is the art of creating a form of communication that embraces the following precepts:

- Can be readily understood by the intended recipients
- Cannot be understood by unintended recipients
- Can be adapted and changed easily with relatively small modifications, such as a changed passphrase or word

Any artificially created lexicon, such as the Pig Latin of children, pictograph codes, gang-speak, or corporate lingo—and even the names of music albums, such as *Four Flicks*—are all manners of cryptography where real text, sometimes not so ciphered, is hidden in what appears to be plain text. They are attempts at hidden communications.

1. WHAT IS CRYPTOGRAPHY? WHAT IS ENCRYPTION?

Ask any ancient Egyptian and he'll undoubtedly define *cryptography* as the practice of burying their dead so that they cannot be found again. They were very good at it; thousands of years later, new crypts are still being discovered. The Greek root *krypt* literally means "a hidden place," and as such it is an appropriate base for any term involving cryptology. According to the Online Etymology Dictionary, *crypto-* as a prefix, meaning "concealed, secret," has been used since 1760, and from the Greek *graphikos*, "of or for writing, belonging to drawing, picturesque."[1] Together, *crypto + graphy* would then mean "hiding place for ideas, sounds, pictures, or words." *Graph*, technically from its Greek root, is "the art of writing." *Encryption*, in contrast, merely means the act of carrying out some aspect of cryptography. *Cryptology*, with its *-ology* ending, is the study of cryptography. Encryption is subsumed by cryptography.

How Is Cryptography Done?

For most information technology occupations, knowledge of cryptography is a very small part of a broader skill set, and is generally limited to relevant application. The argument could be made that this is why the Internet is so extraordinarily plagued with security breaches. The majority of IT administrators, software programmers, and hardware developers are barely cognizant of the power of true cryptography. Overburdened with battling the plague that they inherited, they can't afford to devote the time or resources needed to implement a truly secure strategy. And the reason, as we shall come to see, is because as good at cryptographers can be—well, just as it is said that everyone has an evil twin somewhere in the world, for every cryptographer there is a de cryptographer working just as diligently to decipher a new encryption algorithm.

Traditionally, cryptography has consisted of any means possible whereby communications may be encrypted and transmitted. This could be as simple as using a language with which the opposition is not familiar. Who hasn't been somewhere where everyone around you was speaking a language you didn't understand? There are thousands of languages in the world, nobody can know them all. As was shown in World War II, when Allied Forces used Navajo as a means of communicating freely, some languages are so obscure that an entire nation may not contain one person who speaks it! All true cryptography is composed of three parts: a cipher, an original message, and the resultant encryption. The *cipher* is the method of encryption used. Original messages are referred to as *plain text* or as *clear text*. A message that is transmitted without encryption is said to be sent "in the clear." The resultant message is called *ciphertext* or *cryptogram*. This section begins with a simple review of cryptography procedures and carries them through; each section building on the next to illustrate the principles of cryptography.

---

1 www.etymonline.com.

2. FAMOUS CRYPTOGRAPHIC DEVICES

The past few hundred years of technical development and advances have brought greater and greater means to decrypt, encode, and transmit information. With the advent of the most modern warfare techniques and the increase in communication and ease of reception, the need for encryption has never been greater.

World War II publicized and popularized cryptography in modern culture. The Allied Forces' ability to capture, decrypt, and intercept Axis communications is said to have hastened WWII's end by several years. Here we take a quick look at some famous cryptographic devices from that era.

The Lorenz Cipher

The Lorenz cipher machine was an industrial-strength ciphering machine used in teleprinter circuits by the Germans during WWII. Not to be confused with its smaller cousin, the Enigma machine, the Lorenz cipher could possibly be best compared to a virtual private network tunnel for a telegraph line—only it wasn't sending Morse code, it was using a code not unlike a sort of American Standard Code for Information Interchange (ASCII) format. A granddaddy of sorts, called Baudot code, was used to send alphanumeric communications across telegraph lines. Each character was represented by a series of 5 bits.

It is often confused with the famous Enigma, but unlike the Enigma (which was a portable field unit), the Lorenz cipher could receive typed messages, encrypt them, send them to another distant Lorenz cipher, which would then decrypt the signal. It used a pseudorandom cipher XOR'd with plaintext. The machine would be inserted inline as an attachment to a Lorenz teleprinter. Figure 2.1 is a rendered drawing from a photograph of a Lorenz cipher machine.

Enigma

The Enigma machine was a field unit used in WWII by German field agents to encrypt and decrypt messages and communications. Similar to the Feistel function of the 1970s, the Enigma machine was one of the first mechanized methods of encrypting text using an iterative cipher. It employed a series of rotors that, with some electricity, a light bulb, and a reflector, allowed the operator to either encrypt or decrypt a message. The original position of the rotors, set with each encryption and

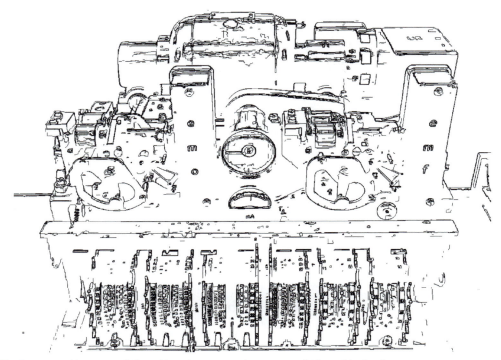

FIGURE 2.1 The Lorenz machine was set inline with a teletype to produce encrypted telegraphic signals.

based on a prearranged pattern that in turn was based on the calendar, allowed the machine to be used, even if it was compromised.

When the Enigma was in use, with each subsequent key press, the rotors would change in alignment from their set positions in such a way that a different letter was produced each time. The operator, with a message in hand, would enter each character into the machine by pressing a typewriter-like key. The rotors would align, and a letter would then illuminate, telling the operator what the letter *really* was. Likewise, when enciphering, the operator would press the key and the illuminated letter would be the cipher text. The continually changing internal flow of electricity that caused the rotors to change was not random, but it did create a polyalphabetic cipher that could be different each time it was used.

3. CIPHERS

Cryptography is built on one overarching premise: the need for a cipher that can reliably, and portably, be used to encrypt text so that, through any means of cryptanalysis—differential, deductive, algebraic, or the like—the ciphertext cannot be undone with any available technology. Throughout the centuries, there have been many attempts to create simple ciphers that can achieve this goal. With

the exception of the One Time Pad, which is not particularly portable, success has been limited.

Let's look at a few of these methods now.

The Substitution Cipher

In this method, each letter of the message is replaced with a single character. See Table 2.1 for an example of a substitution cipher. Because some letters appear more often and certain words appear more often than others, some ciphers are extremely easy to decrypt, and some can be deciphered at a glance by more practiced cryptologists.

By simply understanding probability and with some applied statistics, certain metadata about a language can be derived and used to decrypt any simple, one-for-one substitution cipher. Decryption methods often rely on understanding the context of the *ciphertext*. What was encrypted—business communication? Spreadsheets? Technical data? Coordinates? For example, using a hex editor and an access database to conduct some statistics, we can use the information in Table 2.2 to gain highly specialized knowledge about the data in Chapter 19, "Computer Forensics," by Scott R. Ellis, in this book. A long chapter at nearly 25,000 words, it provides a sufficiently large statistical pool to draw some meaningful analyses.

TABLE 2.1 A simple substitution cipher. Letters are numbered by their order in the alphabet, to provide a numeric reference key. To encrypt a message, the letters are replaced, or substituted, by the numbers. This is a particularly easy cipher to reverse.

A	B	C	D	E	F	G	H	I	J	K	L	M	N	O	P	Q	R	S	T	U	V	W	X	Y	Z
1	2	3	4	5	6	7	8	9	10	11	12	13	14	15	16	17	18	19	20	21	22	23	24	25	26
O	C	Q	W	B	X	Y	E	I	L	Z	A	D	R	J	S	P	F	G	K	H	N	T	U	M	V
15	3	17	23	2	24	25	5	9	12	26	1	4	18	10	19	16	6	7	11	8	14	20	21	13	22

TABLE 2.2 Statistical data of interest in encryption. An analysis of a selection of a manuscript (in this case, the preedited version of Chapter 19 of this book) can provide insight into the reasons that good ciphers need to be developed.

Character Analysis	Count
Number of distinct alphanumeric combinations	1958
Distinct characters	68
Number of four-letter words	984
Number of five-letter words	1375

Table 2.3 gives additional data about the occurrence of specific words in Chapter 19. Note that because it is a technical text, words such as *computer, files, email,* and *drive* emerge as leaders. Analysis of these leaders can reveal individual and paired alpha frequencies. Being armed with knowledge about the type of communication can be very beneficial in decrypting it.

Further information about types of data being encrypted include word counts by length of the word. Table 2.4 contains such a list for Chapter 19. This information can be used to begin to piece together useful and meaningful short sentences, which can provide cues to longer and more complex structures. It is exactly this sort of activity that good cryptography attempts to defeat.

Were it encrypted using a simple substitution cipher, a good start to deciphering Chapter 19 could be made using the information we've gathered. As a learning exercise, game, or logic puzzle, substitution ciphers are quite useful. Some substitution ciphers that are more elaborate can be just as difficult to crack. Ultimately, though, the weakness behind a substitution cipher is the fact that the ciphertext remains a one-to-one, directly corresponding substitution; ultimately anyone with a pen and paper and a large enough sample of the ciphertext can defeat it. Using a computer, deciphering a simple substitution cipher becomes child's play.

The Shift Cipher

Also known as the Caesar cipher, the shift cipher is one that anyone can readily understand and remember for decoding. It is a form of the substitution cipher. By shifting the alphabet a few positions in either direction, a simple sentence can become unreadable to casual inspection. Example 2.1 is an example of such a shift.

Interestingly, for cryptogram word games, the spaces are always included. Often puzzles use numbers instead of letters for the substitution. Removing the spaces in this particular example can make the ciphertext somewhat more secure. The possibility for multiple solutions becomes an issue; any number of words might fit the pattern.

Today many software tools are available to quickly and easily decode most cryptograms (at least, those that are not written in a dead language). You can have some fun with these tools; for example, the name Scott Ellis, when decrypted, turns into Still Books. The name of a friend of the author's decrypts to "His Sinless." It is apparent, then, that smaller-sample simple substitution ciphers can have more than one solution.

Much has been written and much has been said about frequency analysis; it is considered the "end-all and be-all" with respect to cipher decryption. This is not to be confused with cipher breaking, which is a modern attack against the actual cryptographic algorithms themselves. However, to think of simply plugging in some numbers generated from a Google search is a bit naïve. The frequency chart in Table 2.5 is commonplace on the Web.

It is beyond the scope of this chapter to delve into the accuracy of the table, but suffice it to say that our own analysis of Chapter 19's 118,000 characters, a technical text, yielded a much different result; see Table 2.6. Perhaps it is the significantly larger sample and the fact

TABLE 2.3 Five-letter word recurrences in Chapter 19: A glimpse of the leading five-letter words found in the preedited manuscript. Once unique letter groupings have been identified, substitution, often by trial and error, can result in a meaningful reconstruction that allows the entire cipher to be revealed.

Words Field	Number of Recurrences
files	125
drive	75
there	67
email	46
these	43
other	42
about	41
where	36
would	33
every	31
court	30
their	30
first	28
Using	28
which	24
could	22
table	22
After	21
image	21
Don't	19
tools	19
being	18
entry	18

TABLE 2.4 Leaders by word length in the preedited manuscript for Chapter 19. The context of the clear text can make the cipher less secure. There are, after all, only a finite number of words. Fewer of them are long.

Words Field	Number of Dupes	Word Length
XOriginalArrivalTime:	2	21
interpretations	2	15
XOriginatingIP:	2	15
electronically	4	14
investigations	5	14
interpretation	6	14
reconstructing	3	14
irreproducible	2	14
professionally	2	14
inexperienced	2	13
Demonstrative	2	13
XAnalysisOut:	8	13
Steganography	7	13
Understanding	8	13
certification	2	13
circumstances	8	13
unrecoverable	4	13
investigation	15	13
automatically	2	13
admissibility	2	13
XProcessedBy:	2	13
administrator	4	13
determination	3	13
investigative	3	13
practitioners	2	13
preponderance	2	13
intentionally	2	13
consideration	2	13
Interestingly	2	13

that it is a technical text that makes the results different after the top two. Additionally, where computers are concerned, an actual frequency analysis would take into consideration all ASCII characters, as shown in Table 2.6.

Frequency analysis is not difficult; once all the letters of a text are pulled into a database program, it is fairly straightforward to do a count of all the duplicate values. The snippet of code in Example 2.2 demonstrates one way whereby text can be transformed into a single column and imported into a database.

The cryptograms that use formatting (every word becomes the same length) are considerably more difficult for basic online decryption programs to crack. They

must take into consideration spacing and word lengths when considering whether or not a string matches a word. It stands to reason, then, that the formulation of the cipher, where a substitution that is based partially on frequency similarities and with a whole lot of obfuscation so that when messages are decrypted they have ambiguous or multiple meanings, would be desirable

Example 2.1   A sample cryptogram. Try this out:

Gv Vw, Dtwvg?
Hint: Caesar said it, and it is Latin.[2]

TABLE 2.5 "In a random sampling of 1000 letters," this pattern emerges.

Letter	Frequency
E	130
T	93
N	78
R	77
I	74
O	74
A	73
S	63
D	44
H	35
L	35
C	30
F	28
P	27
U	27
M	25
Y	19
G	16
W	16
V	13
B	9
X	5
K	3
Q	3
J	2
Z	1
Total	**1000**

TABLE 2.6 Using MS Access to perform some frequency analysis of Chapter 19 in this book. Characters with fewer repetitions than *z* were excluded from the return. Character frequency analysis of different types of communications yield slightly different results.

Chapter 19 Letters	Frequency
e	14,467
t	10,945
a	9239
i	8385
o	7962
s	7681
n	7342
r	6872
h	4882
l	4646
d	4104
c	4066
u	2941
m	2929
f	2759
p	2402
y	2155
g	1902
w	1881
b	1622
v	1391
.	1334
,	1110
k	698
0	490
x	490
q	166
7	160
*	149
5	147
)	147
(	146
j	145
3	142

---

2 *Et tu, Brute?*

TABLE 2.6 (Continued)

Chapter 19 Letters	Frequency
6	140
Æ	134
ò	134
ô	129
ö	129
4	119
z	116
Total	**116,798**

Example 2.2

```
 1:  Sub Letters2column ()
 2:    Dim bytText () As Byte
 3:    Dim bytNew() As Byte
 4:    Dim lngCount As Long
 5:    With ActiveDocument.Content
 6:    bytText = .Text
 7:    ReDim bytNew(((UBound(bytText()) + 1) * 2) - 5))
 8:    For lngCount = 0 To (UBound(bytText()) - 2) Step 2
 9:    bytNew((lngCount * 2)) = bytText(lngCount)
10:    bytNew(((lngCount * 2) + 2)) = 13
11:    Next lngCount
12:    .Text = bytNew()
13:    End With
14:  End Sub
```

for simple ciphers. However, this would only be true for very short and very obscure messages that could be code words to decrypt other messages or could simply be sent to misdirect the opponent. The amount of ciphertext needed to successfully break a cipher is called *unicity distance*. Ciphers with small unicity distances are weaker than those with large ones.

Ultimately, substitution ciphers are vulnerable to either word-pattern analysis, letter-frequency analysis, or some combination of both. Where numerical information is encrypted, tools such as Benford's Law can be used to elicit patterns of numbers that *should* be occurring. Forensic techniques incorporate such tools to uncover accounting fraud. So, though this particular cipher is a child's game, it is useful in that it is an underlying principle of cryptography and should be well understood

before continuing. The primary purpose of discussing it here is as an introduction to ciphers.

Further topics of interest and places to find information involving substitution ciphers are the chi-square statistic, Edgar Allan Poe, Sherlock Holmes, Benford's Law, Google, and Wikipedia.

The Polyalphabetic Cipher

The previous section clearly demonstrated that though the substitution cipher is fun and easy, it is also vulnerable and weak. It is especially susceptible to frequency analysis. Given a large enough sample, a cipher can easily be broken by mapping the frequency of the letters in the ciphertext to the frequency of letters in the language or dialect of the ciphertext (if it is known). To make ciphers more difficult to crack, Blaise de Vigenère from the 16th-century court of Henry III of France proposed a polyalphabetic substitution. In this cipher, instead of a one-to-one relationship, there is a one-to-many. A single letter can have multiple substitutes. The Vigenère solution was the first known cipher to use a keyword.

It works like this: First, a *tableau* is developed, as in Table 2.7. This tableau is a series of shift ciphers. In fact, since there can be only 26 additive shift ciphers, it is all of them.

In Table 2.7, a table in combination with a keyword is used to create the cipher. For example, if we choose the keyword *rockerrooks*, overlay it over the plaintext, and cross-index it to Table 2.7, we can produce the ciphertext. In this example, the top row is used to look up the plaintext, and the leftmost column is used to reference the keyword.

For example, we lay the word *rockerrooks* over the sentence, "Ask not what your country can do for you." Line 1 is the keyword, line 2 is the plain text, and line 3 is the ciphertext.

```
Keyword:    ROC  KER  ROOK  SROC  KERROOK  SRO  CK  ERR  OOK
Plaintext:  ASK  NOT  WHAT  YOUR  COUNTRY  CAN  DO  FOR  YOU
Ciphertext: RGM  XSK  NVOD  QFIT  MSLEHFI  URB  FY  JFI  MCE
```

The similarity of this tableau to a mathematical table like the one in Table 2.8 becomes apparent. Just think letters instead of numbers and it becomes clear how this works. The top row is used to "look up" a letter from the plaintext, the leftmost column is used to locate the overlaying keyword letter, and where the column and the row intersect is the ciphertext.

This similarity is, in fact, the weakness of the cipher. Through some creative "factoring," the length of the keyword can be determined. Since the tableau is, in practice, a series of shift ciphers, the length of the keyword

TABLE 2.7 Vigenère's tableau arranges all of the shift ciphers in a single table. It then implements a keyword to create a more complex cipher than the simple substitution or shift ciphers. The number of *spurious keys*, that is, bogus decryptions that result from attempting to decrypt a polyalphabetic encryption, is greater than those created during the decryption of a single shift cipher.

Letter	A	B	C	D	E	F	G	H	I	J	K	L	M	N	O	P	Q	R	S	T	U	V	W	X	Y	Z
A	A	B	C	D	E	F	G	H	I	J	K	L	M	N	O	P	Q	R	S	T	U	V	W	X	Y	Z
B	B	C	D	E	F	G	H	I	J	K	L	M	N	O	P	Q	R	S	T	U	V	W	X	Y	Z	A
C	C	D	E	F	G	H	I	J	K	L	M	N	O	P	Q	R	S	T	U	V	W	X	Y	Z	A	B
D	D	E	F	G	H	I	J	K	L	M	N	O	P	Q	R	S	T	U	V	W	X	Y	Z	A	B	C
E	E	F	G	H	I	J	K	L	M	N	O	P	Q	R	S	T	U	V	W	X	Y	Z	A	B	C	D
F	F	G	H	I	J	K	L	M	N	O	P	Q	R	S	T	U	V	W	X	Y	Z	A	B	C	D	E
G	G	H	I	J	K	L	M	N	O	P	Q	R	S	T	U	V	W	X	Y	Z	A	B	C	D	E	F
H	H	I	J	K	L	M	N	O	P	Q	R	S	T	U	V	W	X	Y	Z	A	B	C	D	E	F	G
I	I	J	K	L	M	N	O	P	Q	R	S	T	U	V	W	X	Y	Z	A	B	C	D	E	F	G	H
J	J	K	L	M	N	O	P	Q	R	S	T	U	V	W	X	Y	Z	A	B	C	D	E	F	G	H	I
K	K	L	M	N	O	P	Q	R	S	T	U	V	W	X	Y	Z	A	B	C	D	E	F	G	H	I	J
L	L	M	N	O	P	Q	R	S	T	U	V	W	X	Y	Z	A	B	C	D	E	F	G	H	I	J	K
M	M	N	O	P	Q	R	S	T	U	V	W	X	Y	Z	A	B	C	D	E	F	G	H	I	J	K	L
N	N	O	P	Q	R	S	T	U	V	W	X	Y	Z	A	B	C	D	E	F	G	H	I	J	K	L	M
O	O	P	Q	R	S	T	U	V	W	X	Y	Z	A	B	C	D	E	F	G	H	I	J	K	L	M	N
P	P	Q	R	S	T	U	V	W	X	Y	Z	A	B	C	D	E	F	G	H	I	J	K	L	M	N	O
Q	Q	R	S	T	U	V	W	X	Y	Z	A	B	C	D	E	F	G	H	I	J	K	L	M	N	O	P
R	R	S	T	U	V	W	X	Y	Z	A	B	C	D	E	F	G	H	I	J	K	L	M	N	O	P	Q
S	S	T	U	V	W	X	Y	Z	A	B	C	D	E	F	G	H	I	J	K	L	M	N	O	P	Q	R
T	T	U	V	W	X	Y	Z	A	B	C	D	E	F	G	H	I	J	K	L	M	N	O	P	Q	R	S
U	U	V	W	X	Y	Z	A	B	C	D	E	F	G	H	I	J	K	L	M	N	O	P	Q	R	S	T
V	V	W	X	Y	Z	A	B	C	D	E	F	G	H	I	J	K	L	M	N	O	P	Q	R	S	T	U
W	W	X	Y	Z	A	B	C	D	E	F	G	H	I	J	K	L	M	N	O	P	Q	R	S	T	U	V
X	X	Y	Z	A	B	C	D	E	F	G	H	I	J	K	L	M	N	O	P	Q	R	S	T	U	V	W
Y	Y	Z	A	B	C	D	E	F	G	H	I	J	K	L	M	N	O	P	Q	R	S	T	U	V	W	X
Z	Z	A	B	C	D	E	F	G	H	I	J	K	L	M	N	O	P	Q	R	S	T	U	V	W	X	Y

determines how many ciphers are used. The keyword *rockerrook*, with only six distinct letters, uses only six ciphers. Regardless, for nearly 300 years many people believed the cipher to be unbreakable.

The Kasiski/Kerckhoff Method

Now let's look at Kerckhoff's principle—"only secrecy of the key provides security" (not to be confused with Kirchhoff's law, a totally different man and rule). In the 19th century, Auguste Kerckhoff said that essentially, a system should still be secure, even when everyone knows everything about the system (except the password). Basically, his feeling was that if more than one person knows something, it's no longer a secret. Throughout modern cryptography, the inner workings of cryptographic techniques have been well known and published. Creating a portable, secure, unbreakable code is easy if nobody knows how it works. The problem lies in the fact that we people just can't keep a secret!

TABLE 2.8 The multiplication table is the inspiration for the Vigenère tableau

Multiplier 1	2	3	4	5	6	7	8	9	10
1	1	2	3	4	5	6	7	8	9	10
2	2	4	6	8	10	12	14	16	18	20
3	3	6	9	12	15	18	21	24	27	30
4	4	8	12	16	20	24	28	32	36	40
5	5	10	15	20	25	30	35	40	45	50
6	6	12	18	24	30	36	42	48	54	60
7	7	14	21	28	35	42	49	56	63	70
8	8	16	24	32	40	48	56	64	72	80
9	9	18	27	36	45	54	63	72	81	90
10	10	20	30	40	50	60	70	80	90	100

Example 2.3   A repetitious, weak keyword combines with plaintext to produce an easily deciphered ciphertext.

Keyword	to to toto to to toto o to
Plaintext	It is what it is, isn't it?
Ciphertext	BH BG PVTH BH BG BGG H BH

In 1863 Kasiski, a Prussian major, proposed a method to crack the Vigenère cipher. His method, in short, required that the cryptographer deduce the length of the keyword used and then dissect the cryptogram into a corresponding number of ciphers. Each cipher would then be solved independently. The method required that a suitable number of bigrams be located. A *bigram* is a portion of the ciphertext, two characters long, that repeats itself in a discernible pattern. In Example 2.3, a repetition has been deliberately made simple with a short keyword (*toto*) and engineered by crafting a harmonic between the keyword and the plaintext.

This might seem an oversimplification, but it effectively demonstrates the weakness of the polyalphabetic cipher. Similarly, the polyalphanumeric ciphers, such as the Gronsfeld cipher, are even weaker since they use 26 letters and 10 digits. This one also happens to decrypt to "On of when on of," but a larger sample with such a weak keyword would easily be cracked by even the least intelligent of Web-based cryptogram solvers. The harmonic is created by the overlaying keyword with the underlying text; when the bigrams "line up" and

repeat themselves, the highest frequency will be the length of the password. The distance between the two occurrences will be the length of the password. In Example 2.3, we see BH and BG repeating, and then we see BG repeating at a very tight interval of 2, which tells us the password might be two characters long and based on two shift ciphers that, when decrypted side by side, will be a real word. Not all bigrams will be indicators of this, so some care must be taken. As can be seen, BH repeats with an interval of 8, but the password is not eight digits long (but it is a factor of 8!). By locating the distance of all the repeating bigrams and factoring them, we can deduce the length of the keyword.

4. MODERN CRYPTOGRAPHY

Some of cryptography's greatest stars emerged in WWII. For the first time during modern warfare, vast resources were devoted to enciphering and deciphering communications. Both sides made groundbreaking advances in cryptography. Understanding the need for massive calculations (for the time—more is probably happening in the RAM of this author's PC over a period of five minutes than happened in all of WWII), both sides developed new machinery—predecessors to the modern solid-state computers—that could be coordinated to perform the calculations and procedures needed to crack enemy ciphers.

The Vernam Cipher (Stream Cipher)

Gilbert Sandford Vernam (1890–1960) was said to have invented the stream cipher in 1917. Vernam worked for

Example 2.4   Using the random cipher, a modulus shift instead of an XOR, and plaintext to produce ciphertext.

Plaintext 1

t h i s w i l l b e s o e a s y t o b r e a k i t w i l l b e f u n n y
20 8 9 19 23 9 12 12 2 5 19 15 5 1 19 25 20 15 2 18 5 1 11 9 20 23 9 12 12 2 5 6 21 14 14 25

Cipher One

q e r t y u i o p a s d f g h j k l z x c v b n m q a z w s x e r f v t
17 5 18 20 25 21 9 15 16 1 19 4 6 7 8 10 11 12 26 24 3 22 2 14 13 17 1 26 23 19 24 5 18 6 22 20

CipherText 1

11 13 1 13 22 4 21 1 18 6 12 19 11 8 1 9 5 1 2 16 8 23 13 23 7 14 10 12 9 21 3 11 13 20 10 19
k m a m v d u a r f l s k h a i e a b p h w m w g n j l w u c k m t j s

Plaintext 2

T h i s w i l l n o t b e e a s y t o b r e a k o r b e t o o f u n n y
20 8 9 19 23 9 12 12 14 15 20 2 5 5 1 19 25 20 15 2 18 5 1 11 15 18 2 5 20 15 15 6 21 14 14 25

Ciphertext 2, also using Cipher One.

11 13 1 13 22 4 21 1 4 16 13 6 11 12 9 3 10 6 15 0 21 1 3 25 2 9 3 5 17 8 13 11 13 20 10 19
k m a m v d u a e p m f k l i f j f o z u a c y b i c e q h m k m t j s

---

Bell Labs, and his patent described a cipher in which a prepared key, on a paper tape, combined with plaintext to produce a transmitted ciphertext message. The same tape would then be used to decrypt the ciphertext. In effect, the Vernam and "one-time pad" ciphers are very similar. The primary difference is that the "one-time pad" cipher implements an XOR for the first time and dictates that a truly random stream cipher be used for the encryption. The stream cipher had no such requirement and used a different method of relay logic to combine a pseudo-random stream of bits with the plaintext bits. More about the XOR process is discussed in the section on XOR ciphering. In practice today, the Vernam cipher is any stream cipher in which pseudo-random or random text is combined with plaintext to produce cipher text that is the same length as the cipher. RC4 is a modern example of a Vernam cipher.

The One-Time Pad

The "one-time pad" cipher, attributed to Joseph Mauborgne,[3] is perhaps one of the most secure forms of cryptography. It is very difficult to break if used properly, and if the key stream is perfectly random, the ciphertext gives away absolutely no details about the plaintext, which renders it unbreakable. And, just as the name suggests, it uses a single random key that is the same length as the entire message, and it uses the key only once. The word *pad* is derived from the fact that the key would be distributed in pads of paper, with each sheet torn off and destroyed as it was used.

There are several weaknesses to this cipher. We begin to see that the more secure the encryption, the more it will rely on other means of key transmission. The more a key has to be moved around, the more likely it is that someone who shouldn't have it will have it. The following weaknesses are apparent in this "bulletproof" style of cryptography:

- Key length has to equal plaintext length.
- It is susceptible to key interception; the key must be transmitted to the recipient, and the key is as long as the message!
- It's cumbersome, since it doubles the traffic on the line.
- The cipher must be perfectly random.
- One-time use is absolutely essential. As soon as two separate messages are available, the messages can be decrypted. Example 2.4 demonstrates this.

Since most people don't use binary, the author takes the liberty in Example 2.4 of using decimal numbers

---

3 Wikipedia, Gilbert Vernam entry.

> **TABLE 2.9** A simple key is created so that random characters and regular characters may be combined with a modulus function. Without the original cipher, this key is meaningless intelligence. It is used here in a similar capacity as an XOR, which is also a function that everyone knows how to do.
>
> Key
>
> | a | b | c | d | e | f | g | h | i | j | k | l | m | n | o | p | q | r | s | t | u | v | w | x | y | z |
> |---|---|---|---|---|---|---|---|---|---|---|---|---|---|---|---|---|---|---|---|---|---|---|---|---|---|
> | 1 | 2 | 3 | 4 | 5 | 6 | 7 | 8 | 9 | 10 | 11 | 12 | 13 | 14 | 15 | 16 | 17 | 18 | 19 | 20 | 21 | 22 | 23 | 24 | 25 | 26 |

Example 2.5

The two ciphertexts, side by side, show a high level of harmonics. This indicates that two different ciphertexts actually have the same cipher. Where letters are different, since XOR is a known process and our encryption technique is also publicly known, it's a simple matter to say that r = 18, e = 5 (see Table 2.9) and thusly construct an algorithm that can tease apart the cipher and ciphertext to produce plaintext.

```
k m a m v d u a r f l s k h a i e a b p h w m w g n j l w u c k m t j s (ciphertext 1)
k m a m v d u a e p m f k l i f j f o z u a c y b i c e q h m k m t j s (ciphertext 2)
```

modulus 26 to represent the XOR that would take place in a bitstream encryption (see the section on the XOR cipher) that uses the method of the one-time pad.

A numeric value is assigned to each letter, per Table 2.9. By assigning a numeric value to each letter, adding the plaintext value to the ciphertext value, modulus 26, yields a pseudo-XOR, or a wraparound Caesar shift that has a different shift for each letter in the entire message.

As this example demonstrates, by using the same cipher twice, a dimension is introduced that allows for the introduction of frequency analysis. By placing the two streams side by side, we can identify letters that are the same. In a large enough sample, where the cipher text is sufficiently randomized, frequency analysis of the aligned values will begin to crack the cipher wide open because we know that they are streaming in a logical order—the order in which they were written. One of the chief advantages of 21st-century cryptography is that the "eggs" are scrambled and descrambled during decryption based on the key, which you don't, in fact, want people to know. If the same cipher is used repeatedly, multiple inferences can be made and eventually the entire key can be deconstructed. Because plaintext 1 and plaintext 2 are so similar, this sample yields the following harmonics (in bold and boxed) as shown in Example 2.5.

Cracking Ciphers

One method of teasing out the frequency patterns is through the application of some sort of mathematical formula to test a hypothesis against reality. The chi-square test is perhaps one of the most commonly used; it allows someone to use what is called *inferential statistics* to draw certain inferences about the data by testing it against known statistical distributions.

Using the chi-square test against an encrypted text would allow certain inference to be made, but only where the contents, or the type of contents (random or of an expected distribution), of the text were known. For example, someone may use a program that encrypts files. By creating the null hypothesis that the text is completely random, and by reversing the encryption steps, a block cipher may emerge as the null hypothesis is disproved through the chi-square test. This would be done by reversing the encryption method and XORing against the bytes with a block created from the known text. At the point where the non-encrypted text matches the positioning of the encrypted text, chi-square would reveal that the output is not random and the block cipher would be revealed.

Chi-squared = ... (observed-expected)2/(expected)

Observed would be the actual zero/one ratio produced by XORing the data streams together, and expected

Some Statistical Tests for Cryptographic Applications By Adrian Fleissig

In many applications, it is often important to determine if a sequence is random. For example, a random sequence provides little or no information in cryptographic analysis. When estimating economic and financial models, it is important for the residuals from the estimated model to be random. Various statistical tests can be used to evaluate if a sequence is actually a random sequence or not. For a truly random sequence, it is assumed that each element is generated independently of any prior and/or future elements. A statistical test is used to compute the probability that the observed sequence is random compared to a truly random sequence. The procedures have test statistics that are used to evaluate the null hypothesis which typically assumes that the observed sequence is random. The alternative hypothesis is that the sequence is non random. Thus failing to accept the null hypothesis, at some critical level selected by the researcher, suggests that the sequence may be non random.

There are many statistical tests to evaluate for randomness in a sequence such as Frequency Tests, Runs Tests, Discrete Fourier Transforms, Serial Tests and many others. The tests statistics often have chi-square or standard normal distributions which are used to evaluate the hypothesis. While no test is overall superior to the other tests, a Frequency or Runs Test is a good starting point to examine for non-randomness in a sequence. As an example, a Frequency or Runs Test typically evaluates if the number of zeros and ones in a sequence are about the same, as would be the case if the sequence was truly random.

It is important to examine the results carefully. For example, the researcher may incorrectly fail to accept the null hypothesis that the sequence is random and thereby makes a Type I Error. Incorrectly accepting the null of randomness when the sequence is actually non random results in committing a Type II Error. The reliability of the results depends on having a sufficiently large number of elements in a sequence. In addition, it is important to perform alternative tests to evaluate if a sequence is random.[4]

would be the randomness of zeroes and ones (50/50) expected in a body of pseudorandom text.

Independent of having a portion of the text, a large body of encrypted text could be reverse encrypted using a block size of all zeroes; in this manner it may be possible to tease out a block cipher by searching for non random block sized strings. Modern encryption techniques generate many, many block cipher permutations that are layered against previous iterations (n-1) of permutated blocks. The feasibility of running such decryption techniques would require both a heavy-duty programmer, statistician, an incredible amount of processing power, and in-depth knowledge of the encryption algorithm used. An unpublished algorithm would render such testing worthless.

Notably, the methods and procedures used in breaking encryption algorithms are used throughout society in many applications where a null hypothesis needs to be tested. Forensic consultants use pattern matching and similar decryption techniques to combat fraud on a daily basis. Adrian Fleissig, a seasoned economist, makes use of many statistical tests to examine corporate data (see side bar, "Some Statistical Tests for Cryptographic Applications").

The XOR Cipher and Logical Operands

In practice, the XOR cipher is not so much a cipher as it is a mechanism whereby ciphertext is produced. *Random*

binary stream cipher would be a better term. The terms *XOR, logical disjunction,* and *inclusive disjunction* may be used interchangeably. Most people are familiar with the logical functions of speech, which are words such as *and, or, nor,* and *not*. A girl can tell her brother, "Mother is either upstairs or at the neighbor's," which means she could be in either state, but you have no way of knowing which one it is. The mother could be in either place, and you can't infer from the statement the greater likelihood of either. The outcome is undecided.

Alternately, if a salesman offers a customer either a blue car or a red car, the customer knows that he can have red or he can have blue. Both statements are true. Blue cars and red cars exist simultaneously in the world. A person can own both a blue car and a red car. But Mother will never be in more than one place at a time. Purportedly, there is widespread belief that no author has produced an example of an English *or* sentence that appears to be false because both of its inputs are true.[5] Quantum physics takes considerable exception to this statement (which explains quantum physicists) at the

---

4 Adrian Fleissig is the Senior Economist of Counsel for RGL Forensics, 2006–present. He is also a Full Professor, California State University Fullerton (CSUF) since 2003 with a joint Ph.D. in Economics and Statistics, North Carolina State University, 1993.

5 Barrett and Stenner, The myth of the exclusive "Or," *Mind,* 80 (317), 116–121, 1971.

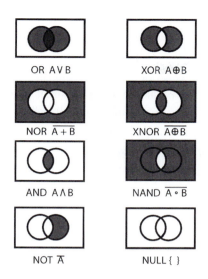

RELATI⊕NSHIPS

FIGURE 2.2 In each Venn diagram, the possible outcome of two inputs is decided.

Example 2.6   Line 1 and line 2 are combined with an XOR operand to produce line 3.

Line 1, plaintext :   1 0 0 1 1 1 0 1 0 1 1 0 1 1 1 1
Line 2, random cipher "": 1 0 0 0 1 1 0 1 0 1 0 0 1 0 0 1
Line 3, XOR ciphertext: 0 0 0 1 0 0 0 0 0 0 1 0 0 1 0 0

---

quantum mechanical level. In the Schrodinger cat experiment, the sentence "The cat is alive or dead" or the statement "The photon is a particle and a wave until you look at it, then it is a particle or a wave, depending on how you observed it" both create a quandary for logical operations, and there are no Venn diagrams or words that are dependant on time or quantum properties of the physical universe. Regardless of this exception, when speaking of things in the world in a more rigorously descriptive fashion (in the macroscopically nonphenomenological sense), greater accuracy is needed.

To create a greater sense of accuracy in discussions of logic, the operands as listed in Figure 2.2 were created. When attempting to understand this chart, the best thing to do is to assign a word to the A and B values and think of each Venn diagram as a universe of documents, perhaps in a document database or just on a computer being searched. If A stands for the word *tree* and B for *frog*, then each letter simply takes on a very significant and distinct meaning.

In computing, it is traditional that a value of 0 is false and a value of 1 is true. An XOR operation, then,

is the determination of whether two possibilities can be combined to produce a value of true or false, based on whether both operations are true, both are false, or one of the values is true.

1 XOR 1 = 0
0 XOR 0 = 0
1 XOR 0 = 1
0 XOR 1 = 1

In an XOR operation, if the two inputs are different, the resultant is TRUE, or 1. If the two inputs are the same, the resultant value is FALSE, or 0.

In Example 2.6, the first string represents the plaintext and the second line represents the cipher. The third line represents the ciphertext. If, and only exactly if, just one of the items has a value of TRUE, the results of the XOR operation will be true.

Without the cipher, and if the cipher is truly random, decoding the string becomes impossible. However, as in the one-time pad, if the same cipher is used, then (1) the cryptography becomes vulnerable to a known text attack, and (2) it becomes vulnerable to statistical analysis. Example 2.7 demonstrates this by showing exactly where the statistical aberration can be culled in the stream. If we know they both used the same cipher, can anyone solve for Plaintext A and Plaintext B?

Block Ciphers

Block ciphers work very similarly to the polyalphabetic cipher with the exception that a block cipher pairs together two algorithms for the creation of ciphertext and its decryption. It is also somewhat similar in that, where the polyalphabetic cipher used a repeating key, the block cipher uses a permutating, yet repeating, cipher block. Each algorithm uses two inputs: a key and a "block" of bits, each of a set size. Each output block is the same size as the input block, the block being transformed by the key. The key, which is algorithm based, is able to select the permutation of its bijective mapping from 2^n, where n is equal to the number of bits in the *input* block. Often, when 128-bit encryption is discussed, it is referring to the size of the *input* block. Typical encryption methods involve use of XOR chaining or some similar operation; see Figure 2.3.

Block ciphers have been very widely used since 1976 in many encryption standards. As such, cracking these ciphers became, for a long time, the top priority of cipher crackers everywhere. Block ciphers provide the backbone algorithmic technology behind most modern-era ciphers.

Example 2.7

To reconstruct the cipher if the plaintext is known, PlaintextA can be XOR'd to ciphertextB to produce cipherA! Clearly, in a situation where plaintext may be captured, using the same cipher key twice could completely expose the message. By using statistical analysis, the unique possibilities for PlaintextA and PlaintextB will emerge; *unique possibilities* means that for ciphertext = x, where the cipher is truly random, this should be at about 50% of the sample. Additions of ciphertext $n + 1$ will increase the possibilities for unique combinations because, after all, these binary streams must be converted to text and the set of binary stream possibilities that will combine into ASCII characters is relatively small. Using basic programming skills, you can develop algorithms that will quickly and easily sort through this data to produce a deciphered result. An intelligent person with some time on her hands could sort it out on paper or in an Excel spreadsheet. When the choice is "The red house down the street from the green house is where we will meet" or a bunch of garbage, it begins to become apparent how to decode the cipher.

CipherA and PlaintextA are XOR'd to produce ciphertextA:
PlaintextA: 0 0 0 0 0 0 0 0 1 1 1 1 1 1 1 1
cipherA: 1 1 1 1 1 1 1 1 0 0 0 0 0 0 0 0
ciphertextA: 1 1 1 1 1 1 1 1 1 1 1 1 1 1 1 1
PlaintextB and cipherA are XOR'd to produce ciphertextB:
ciphertextB: 0 0 0 0 0 0 0 0 1 1 1 1 1 1 1 1
cipherA: 1 1 1 1 1 1 1 1 0 0 0 0 0 0 0 0
PlaintextB: 1 1 1 1 1 1 1 1 0 0 0 0 0 0 0 0
| < ----- Column 1 --------- > | | < -------Column 2 ------|

Note: Compare ciphertextA to ciphertextB!

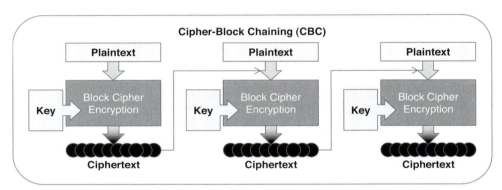

FIGURE 2.3 XOR chaining, or cipher-block chaining (CBC), is a method whereby the next block of plaintext to be encrypted is XOR'd with the previous block of ciphertext before being encrypted.

5. THE COMPUTER AGE

To many people, January 1, 1970, is considered the dawn of the computer age. That's when Palo Alto Research Center (PARC) in California introduced modern computing; the graphical user interface (no more command line and punch cards), networking on an Ethernet, and object-oriented programming have all been attributed to PARC. The 1970s also featured the Unix clock, Alan Shepherd on the moon, the U.S. Bicentennial, the civil rights movement, women's liberation, Robert Heinlein's sci-fi classic, *Stranger in a Strange Land*, and, most important to this chapter, modern cryptography. The late 1960s and early 1970s changed the face of the modern world at breakneck speed. Modern warfare reached tentative heights with radio-guided missiles, and warfare needed a new hero. And then there was the Data Encryption Standard, or DES; in a sense DES was the turning point for cryptography in that, for the first time, it fully leveraged the power of modern computing in its algorithms. The sky appeared to be the limit, but, unfortunately for those who wanted to keep their information secure, decryption techniques were not far behind.

Data Encryption Standard

In the mid-1970s the U.S. government issued a public specification, through its National Bureau of Standards (NBS), called the Data Encryption Standard or, most commonly, DES. This could perhaps be considered

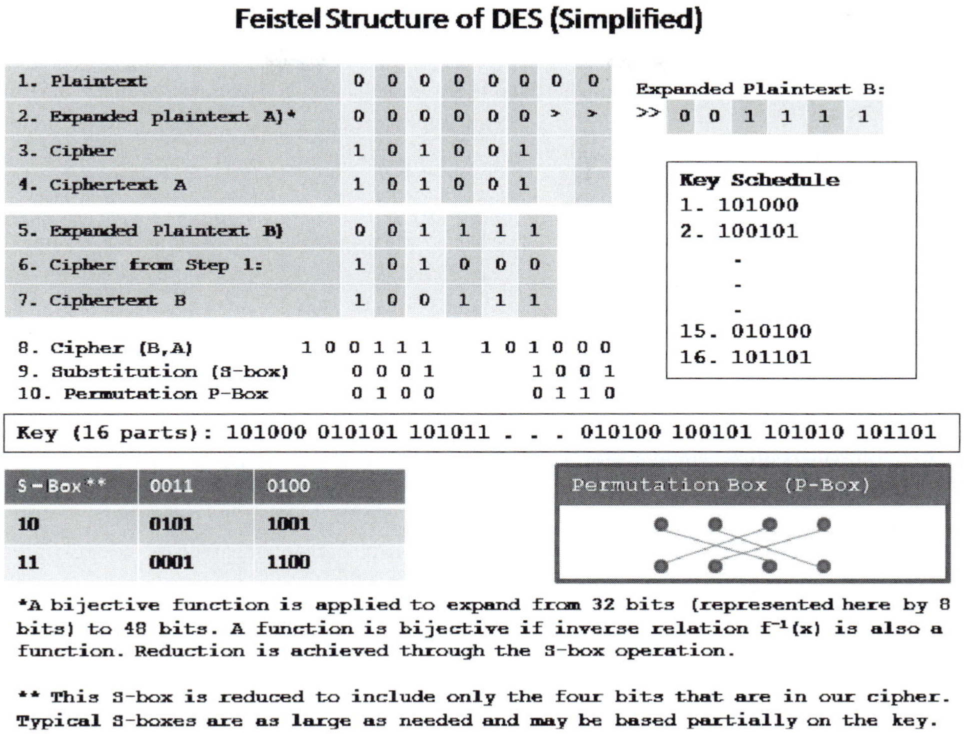

Feistel Structure of DES (Simplified)

									Expanded Plaintext B:
1. Plaintext	0	0	0	0	0	0	0	0	
2. Expanded plaintext A)*	0	0	0	0	0	0	>	>	>> 0 0 1 1 1 1
3. Cipher		1	0	1	0	0	1		
4. Ciphertext A		1	0	1	0	0	1		
5. Expanded Plaintext B)		0	0	1	1	1	1		
6. Cipher from Step 1:		1	0	1	0	0	0		
7. Ciphertext B		1	0	0	1	1	1		

```
Key Schedule
1. 101000
2. 100101
   .
   .
   .
15. 010100
16. 101101
```

```
8. Cipher (B,A)        1 0 0 1 1 1    1 0 1 0 0 0
9. Substitution (S-box)    0 0 0 1        1 0 0 1
10. Permutation P-Box      0 1 0 0        0 1 1 0
```

```
Key (16 parts): 101000 010101 101011 . . . 010100 100101 101010 101101
```

S-Box**	0011	0100
10	0101	1001
11	0001	1100

Permutation Box (P-Box)

*A bijective function is applied to expand from 32 bits (represented here by 8 bits) to 48 bits. A function is bijective if inverse relation $f^{-1}(x)$ is also a function. Reduction is achieved through the S-box operation.

** This S-box is reduced to include only the four bits that are in our cipher. Typical S-boxes are as large as needed and may be based partially on the key.

FIGURE 2.4 The Feistel function with a smaller key size.

the dawn of modern cryptography because it was very likely the first block cipher, or at least its first widespread implementation. But the 1970s were a relatively untrusting time. "Big Brother" loomed right around the corner (as per George Orwell's *1984*), and the majority of people didn't understand or necessarily trust DES. Issued under the NBS, now called the National Institute of Standards and Technology (NIST), hand in hand with the National Security Agency (NSA), DES led to tremendous interest in the reliability of the standard among academia's ivory towers. A shortened key length and the implementation of substitution boxes, or "S-boxes," in the algorithm led many to think that the NSA had deliberately weakened the algorithms and left a security "back door" of sorts.

The use of S-boxes in the standard was not generally understood until the design was published in 1994 by Don Coppersmith. The S-boxes, it turned out, had been deliberately designed to prevent a sort of cryptanalysis attack called *differential cryptanalysis*, as was discovered by IBM researchers in the early 1970s; the NSA had asked IBM to keep quiet about it. In 1990 the method was "rediscovered" independently and, when used against DES, the usefulness of the S-boxes became readily apparent.

Theory of Operation

DES used a 64-bit block cipher combined with a mode of operation based on cipher-block chaining (CBC) called the *Feistel function*. This consisted of an initial expansion permutation followed by 16 rounds of XOR key mixing via subkeys and a key schedule, substitution (S-boxes), and permutation.[6] In this strategy, a block is increased from 32 bits to 48 bits (expansion permutation). Then the 48-bit block is divided in half. The first half is XORs, with parts of the key according to a key schedule. These are called subkeys. Figure 2.4 shows this concept in a simplified format.

The resulting cipher is then XOR'd with the half of the cipher that was not used in step 1. The two halves switch sides. Substitution boxes reduce the 48 bits down to 32 bits via a nonlinear function and then a permutation, according to a permutation table, takes place. Then the entire process is repeated again, 16 times, except in the last step the two halves are not flipped. Finally, this diffusive strategy produced via substitution, permutation, and key schedules creates an effective ciphertext. Because a fixed-length cipher, a block cipher, is used,

---

6 A. Sorkin, LUCIFER: A cryptographic algorithm, *Cryptologia*, 8(1), 22–35, 1984.

the permutations and the S-box introduce enough confusion that the cipher cannot be deduced through brute-force methods without extensive computing power.

With the increase in size of hard drives and computer memory, the need for disk space and bandwidth still demand that a block cipher algorithm be portable. DES, Triple DES, and the Advanced Encryption Standard (AES) all provide or have provided solutions that are secure and practical.

Implementation

Despite the controversy at the time, DES was implemented. It became the encryption standard of choice until the late 1990s, when it was broken when Deep Crack and distributed.net broke a DES key in 22 hours and 15 minutes. Later that year a new form of DES called Triple DES, which encrypted the plaintext in three iterations, was published. It remained in effect until 2002, when it was superseded by AES.

Rivest, Shamir, and Adleman (RSA)

The release of DES also included the creation and release of Ron Rivest, Adi Shamir, and Leonard Adleman's encryption algorithm (RSA). Rivest, Shamir, and Adleman, based at the Massachusetts Institute of Technology (MIT), publicly described the algorithm in 1977. RSA is the first encryption standard to introduce (to public knowledge) the new concept of digital signing. In 1997 it was revealed through declassification of papers that Clifford Cocks, a British mathematician working for the U.K. Government Communications Headquarters (GCHQ), had, in 1973, written a paper describing this process. Assigned a status of top secret, the work had previously never seen the light of day. Because it was submitted in 1973, the method had been considered unattainable, since computing power at the time could not handle its methods.

Advanced Encryption Standard (AES or Rijndael)

AES represents one of the latest chapters in the history of cryptography. It is currently one of the most popular of encryption standards and, for people involved in any security work, its occurrence on the desktop is frequent.

It also enjoys the free marketing and acceptance that it received when it was awarded the title of official cryptography standard in 2001.[7] This designation went into effect in May of the following year.

Similarly to DES, AES encrypts plaintext in a series of rounds, involves the use of a key and block sizes, and leverages substitution and permutation boxes. It differs from DES in the following respects:

- It supports 128-bit block sizes.
- The key schedule is based on the S-box.
- It expands the key, not the plaintext.
- It is not based on a Feistel cipher.
- It is extremely complex.

The AES algorithms are to symmetric ciphers what a bowl of spaghetti is to the shortest distance between two points. Through a series of networked XOR operations, key substitutions, temporary variable transformations, increments, iterations, expansions, value swapping, S-boxing, and the like, a very strong encryption is created that, with modern computing, is impossible to break. It is conceivable that, with so complex a series of operations, a computer file and block could be combined in such a way as to produce all zeroes. Theoretically, the AES cipher could be broken by solving massive quadratic equations that take into consideration every possible vector and solve 8000 quadratic equations with 1600 binary unknowns. This sort of an attack is called an *algebraic attack* and, where traditional methods such as differential or differential cryptanalysis fail, it is suggested that the strength in AES lies in the current inability to solve supermultivariate quadratic equations with any sort of efficiency.

Reports that AES is not as strong as it should be are likely, at this time, to be overstated and inaccurate, because anyone can present a paper that is dense and difficult to understand and claims to achieve the incredible.[8] It is unlikely that, any time in the near or maybe not-so-near future (this author hedges his bets), AES will be broken using multivariate quadratic polynomials in thousands of dimensions. Mathematica is very likely one of the most powerful tools that can solve quadratic equations, and it is still many years away from being able to perform this feat.

---

7 U.S. FIPS PUB 197 (FIPS 197), November 26, 2001.
8 Bruce Schneier, *Crypto-Gram Newsletter*, September 15, 2002.

## Chapter 3

Preventing System Intrusions

Michael West

Independent senior technical writer

The moment you establish an active Web presence, you put a target on your company's back. And like the hapless insect that lands in the spider's web, your company's size determines the size of the disturbance you create on the Web—and how quickly you're noticed by the bad guys. How attractive you are as prey is usually directly proportionate to what you have to offer a predator. If yours is an ecommerce site whose business thrives on credit card or other financial information or a company with valuable secrets to steal, your "juiciness" quotient goes up; you have more of value there to steal. And if your business is new and your Web presence is recent, the assumption could be made that perhaps you're not yet a seasoned veteran in the nuances of cyber warfare and, thus, are more vulnerable to an intrusion.

Unfortunately for you, many of those who seek to penetrate your network defenses are educated, motivated, and quite brilliant at developing faster and more efficient methods of quietly sneaking around your perimeter, checking for the smallest of openings. Most IT professionals know that an enterprise's firewall is ceaselessly being probed for weaknesses and vulnerabilities by crackers from every corner of the globe. Anyone who follows news about software understands that seemingly every few months, word comes out about a new, exploitable opening in an operating system or application. It's widely understood that no one—not the most savvy network administrator or the programmer who wrote the software—can possibly find and close all the holes in today's increasingly complex software.

Bugs exist in applications, operating systems, server processes (daemons), and clients. System configurations can also be exploited, such as not changing the default administrator's password or accepting default system settings, or unintentionally leaving a hole open by configuring the machine to run in a nonsecure mode. Even Transmission Control Protocol/Internet Protocol (TCP/IP), the foundation on which all Internet traffic operates, can be exploited, since the protocol was designed before the threat of hacking was really widespread. Therefore it contains design flaws that can allow, for example, a cracker to easily alter IP data.

Once the word gets out that a new and exploitable opening exists in an application (and word *will* get out), crackers around the world start scanning sites on the Internet searching for any and all sites that have that particular opening.

Making your job even harder is the fact that many openings into your network can be caused by your employees. Casual surfing of porn sites can expose the network to all kinds of nasty bugs and malicious code, merely by an employee visiting the site. The problem is that, to users, it might not seem like such a big deal. They either don't realize or don't care that they're leaving the network wide open to intrusion.

1. SO, WHAT IS AN INTRUSION?

A network intrusion is an unauthorized penetration of a computer in your enterprise or an address in your assigned domain. An intrusion can be passive (in which penetration is gained stealthily and without detection) or active (in which changes to network resources are effected). Intrusions can come from outside your network structure or inside (an employee, customer, or business partner). Some intrusions are simply meant to let you know the intruder was there, defacing your Web site with various kinds of messages or crude images. Others are more malicious, seeking to extract critical information on either a one-time basis or as an ongoing parasitic relationship that will continue to siphon off data until it's discovered. Some intruders will seek to implant carefully crafted code designed to crack passwords, record keystrokes, or mimic your site while directing unaware users to their site. Others will embed themselves into the network and quietly siphon off data on a continuing basis or to modify public-facing Web pages with various kinds of messages.

An attacker can get into your system physically (by having physical access to a restricted machine and its hard drive and/or BIOS), externally (by attacking your Web servers or finding a way to bypass your firewall), or internally (your own users, customers, or partners).

2. SOBERING NUMBERS

So how often do these intrusions occur? The estimates are staggering: Depending on which reporting agency you listen to, anywhere from 79 million to over 160 million compromises of electronic data occurred worldwide between 2007 and 2008. U.S. government statistics show an estimated 37,000 known and reported incidents against federal systems alone in 2007, and the number is expected to rise as the tools employed by crackers become increasingly sophisticated.

In one case, credit- and debit-card information for over 45 million users was stolen from a large merchant in 2005, and data for an additional 130,000 were lifted in 2006. Merchants reported that the loss would cost them an estimated $5 million.

Spam continues to be one of the biggest problems faced by businesses today and has been steadily increasing every year. An Internet threat report published by Secure Computing Corporation in October 2008 states, "The acquisition of innocent machines via email and Web-based infections continued in Q3 with over 5000 new zombies created every hour."[1] And in the election year of 2008, election-related spam messages were estimated to exceed 100 million messages per day.

According to research done by Secure Computing, malware use is also on a steady rise, "with nearly 60% of all malware-infected URLs" coming from the United States and China. And Web-related attacks will become more widespread, with political and financially motivated attacks topping the list. With the availability of Web attack toolkits increasing, Secure Computing's research estimates that "about half of all Web-borne attacks will likely be hosted on compromised legitimate Web sites."

Alarmingly, there is also a rise in teenage involvement in cracking. Chris Boyd, director of malware research at FaceTime Security, was quoted in an October 29, 2008, posting on the BBC's Web site that he's "seeing kids of 11 and 12 sharing credit-card details and asking for hacks."[2] Some of the teens have resorted to posting videos of their work on YouTube, not realizing they've thus made it incredibly easy to track them down. But the fact that they exist and are sharing information via well-known venues is worrisome enough, the fumbling teen crackers of today are tomorrow's network security nightmares in the making.

Whatever the goal of the intrusion—fun, greed, bragging rights, or theft of data—the end result is the same: a weakness in your network security has been detected and exploited. And unless you discover that weakness—the intrusion entry point—it will continue to be an open door into your environment.

So, just who's out there looking to break into your network?

3. KNOW YOUR ENEMY: HACKERS VERSUS CRACKERS

An entire community of people—experts in programming and computer networking and those who thrive on solving complex problems—have been around since the earliest days of computing. The term *hacker* originated from the members of this culture, and they are quick to point out that it was hackers who built and make the Internet run, and hackers who created the Unix operating system. Hackers see themselves as members of a community who build things and make them work. And the term *cracker* is, to those in their culture, a badge of honor.

Ask a traditional hacker about people who sneak into computer systems to steal data or cause havoc, and he'll most likely correct you by telling you those people aren't true hackers. (In the cracker community, the term for these types is *cracker*, and the two labels aren't synonymous.) So, to not offend traditional hackers, I'll use the term *crackers* and focus on them and their efforts.

From the lone-wolf cracker seeking peer recognition to the disgruntled former employee out for revenge or the deep pockets and seemingly unlimited resources of a hostile government bent on taking down wealthy capitalists, crackers are out there in force, looking to find the chink in your system's defensive armor.

A cracker's specialty—or in some cases, his mission in life—is seeking out and exploiting vulnerabilities of an individual computer or network for their own purposes. Crackers' intentions are normally malicious and/

---

1 "Internet Threats Report and Predictions for 2009," October 27, 2008, Secure Computing Corporation.

2 http://news.bbc.co.uk, October 29, 2008.

or criminal in nature. They have, at their disposal, a vast library of information designed to help them hone their tactics, skills, and knowledge, and they can tap into the almost unlimited experience of other crackers through a community of like-minded individuals sharing information across underground networks.

They usually begin this life learning the most basic of skills: software programming. The ability to write code that can make a computer do what they want is seductive in and of itself. As they learn more and more about programming, they also expand their knowledge of operating systems and, as a natural course of progression, operating systems' weaknesses. They also quickly learn that, to expand the scope and type of their illicit handiwork, they need to learn HTML—the code that allows them to create phony Web pages that lure unsuspecting users into revealing important financial or personal data.

There are vast underground organizations to which these new crackers can turn for information. They hold meetings, write papers, and develop tools that they pass along to each other. Each new acquaintance they meet fortifies their skill set and gives them the training to branch out to more and more sophisticated techniques. Once they gain a certain level of proficiency, they begin their trade in earnest.

They start off simply by researching potential target firms on the Internet (an invaluable source for all kinds of corporate network related information). Once a target has been identified, they might quietly tiptoe around, probing for old forgotten back doors and operating system vulnerabilities. They can start off simply and innocuously by running basic DNS queries that can provide IP addresses (or ranges of IP addresses) as starting points for launching an attack. They might sit back and listen to inbound and/or outbound traffic, record IP addresses, and test for weaknesses by pinging various devices or users.

They can surreptitiously implant password cracking or recording applications, keystroke recorders, or other malware designed to keep their unauthorized connection alive—and profitable.

The cracker wants to act like a cyber-ninja, sneaking up to and penetrating your network without leaving any trace of the incursion. Some more seasoned crackers can put multiple layers of machines, many hijacked, between them and your network to hide their activity. Like standing in a room full of mirrors, the attack appears to be coming from so many locations you can't pick out the real from the ghost. And before you realize what they've done, they've up and disappeared like smoke in the wind.

4. MOTIVES

Though the goal is the same—to penetrate your network defenses—crackers' motives are often different. In some cases, a network intrusion could be done from the inside by a disgruntled employee looking to hurt the organization or steal company secrets for profit.

There are large groups of crackers working diligently to steal credit-card information that they then turn around and make available for sale. They want a quick grab and dash—take what they want and leave. Their cousins are the network parasites—those who quietly breach your network, then sit there siphoning off data.

A new and very disturbing trend is the discovery that certain governments have been funding digital attacks on network resources of both federal and corporate systems. Various agencies from the U.S. Department of Defense to the governments of New Zealand, France, and Germany have reported attacks originating from unidentified Chinese hacking groups. It should be noted that the Chinese government denies any involvement, and there is no evidence that it is or was involved. Furthermore, in October 2008, the South Korean Prime Minister is reported to have issued a warning to his cabinet that "about 130,000 items of government information had been hacked [by North Korean computer crackers] over the past four years."[3]

5. TOOLS OF THE TRADE

Crackers today are armed with an increasingly sophisticated and well-stocked tool kit for doing what they do. Like the professional thief with his custom-made lock picks, crackers today can obtain a frightening array of tools to covertly test your network for weak spots. Their tools range from simple password-stealing malware and keystroke recorders (loggers) to methods of implanting sophisticated parasitic software strings that copy data streams coming in from customers who want to perform an ecommerce transaction with your company. Some of the more widely used tools include these:

- *Wireless sniffers.* Not only can these devices locate wireless signals within a certain range, they can siphon off the data being transmitted over the signals. With the rise in popularity and use of remote wireless devices, this practice is increasingly responsible for the loss of critical data and represents a significant headache for IT departments.

---

3 Quoted from http://news.theage.com.au, October 15, 2008.

- *Packet sniffers.* Once implanted in a network data stream, these passively analyze data packets moving into and out of a network interface, and utilities capture data packets passing through a network interface.
- *Port scanners.* A good analogy for these utilities is a thief casing a neighborhood, looking for an open or unlocked door. These utilities send out successive, sequential connection requests to a target system's ports to see which one responds or is open to the request. Some port scanners allow the cracker to slow the rate of port scanning—sending connection requests over a longer period of time—so the intrusion attempt is less likely to be noticed. These devices' usual targets are old, forgotten "back doors," or ports inadvertently left unguarded after network modifications.
- *Port knocking.* Sometimes network administrators create a secret back-door method of getting through firewall-protected ports—a secret knock that enables them to quickly access the network. Port-knocking tools find these unprotected entries and implant a Trojan horse that listens to network traffic for evidence of that secret knock.
- *Keystroke loggers.* These are spyware utilities planted on vulnerable systems that record a user's keystrokes. Obviously, when someone can sit back and record every keystroke a user makes, it doesn't take long to obtain things like usernames, passwords, and ID numbers.
- *Remote administration tools.* Programs embedded on an unsuspecting user's system that allow the cracker to take control of that system.
- *Network scanners.* Explore networks to see the number and kind of host systems on a network, the services available, the host's operating system, and the type of packet filtering or firewalls being used.
- *Password crackers.* These sniff networks for data streams associated with passwords, then employ a brute-force method of peeling away any encryption layers protecting those passwords.

6. BOTS

A new and particularly virulent threat that has emerged over the past few years is one in which a virus is surreptitiously implanted in large numbers of unprotected computers (usually those found in homes), hijacking them (without the owners' knowledge) and turning them into slaves to do the cracker's bidding. These compromised computers, known as *bots*, are linked in vast and usually untraceable networks called *botnets*. Botnets are designed to operate in such a way that instructions come from a central PC and are rapidly shared among other botted computers in the network. Newer botnets are now using a "peer-to-peer" method that, because they lack a central identifiable point of control, makes it difficult if not impossible for law enforcement agencies to pinpoint. And because they often cross international boundaries into countries without the means (or will) to investigate and shut them down, they can grow with alarming speed. They can be so lucrative that they've now become the cracker's tool of choice.

Botnets exist, in large part, because of the number of users who fail to observe basic principles of computer security—installed and/or up-to-date antivirus software, regular scans for suspicious code, and so on—and thereby become unwitting accomplices. Once taken over and "botted," their machines are turned into channels through which large volumes of unwanted spam or malicious code can be quickly distributed. Current estimates are that, of the 800 million computers on the Internet, up to 40% are bots controlled by cyber thieves who are using them to spread new viruses, send out unwanted spam email, overwhelm Web sites in denial-of-service (DoS) attacks, or siphon off sensitive user data from banking or shopping Web sites that look and act like legitimate sites with which customers have previously done business.

It's such a pervasive problem that, according to a report published by security firm Damballa,[4] botnet attacks rose from an estimated 300,000 per day in August 2006 to over 7 million per day one year later, and over 90% of what was sent out was spam email. Even worse for ecommerce sites is a growing trend in which a site's operators are threatened with DoS attacks unless they pay protection money to the cyber extortionist. Those who refuse to negotiate with these terrorists quickly see their sites succumb to relentless rounds of cyber "carpet bombing."

Bot controllers, also called *herders*, can also make money by leasing their networks to others who need a large and untraceable means of sending out massive amounts of advertisements but don't have the financial or technical resources to create their own networks. Making matters worse is the fact that botnet technology is available on the Internet for less than $100, which makes it relatively easy to get started in what can be a very lucrative business.

---

4 Quoted from *USA Today*, March 17, 2008.

7. SYMPTOMS OF INTRUSIONS

As stated earlier, your company's mere presence on the Web places a target on your back. It's only a matter of time before you experience your first attack. It could be something as innocent looking as several failed login attempts or as obvious as an attacker having defaced your Web site or crippled your network. It's important that you go into this knowing you're vulnerable.

Crackers are going to first look for known weaknesses in the operating system (OS) or any applications you are using. Next, they would start probing, looking for holes, open ports, or forgotten back doors—faults in your security posture that can quickly or easily be exploited.

Arguably one of the most common symptoms of an intrusion—either attempted or successful—is repeated signs that someone is trying to take advantage of your organization's own security systems, and the tools you use to keep watch for suspicious network activity may actually be used against you quite effectively. Tools such as network security and file integrity scanners, which can be invaluable at helping you conduct ongoing assessments of your network's vulnerability, are also available and can be used by crackers looking for a way in.

Large numbers of unsuccessful login attempts are also a good indicator that your system has been targeted. The best penetration-testing tools can be configured with attempt thresholds that, when exceeded, will trigger an alert. They can passively distinguish between legitimate and suspicious activity of a repetitive nature, monitor the time intervals between activities (alerting when the number exceeds the threshold you set), and build a database of signatures seen multiple times over a given period.

The "human element" (your users) is a constant factor in your network operations. Users will frequently enter a mistyped response but usually correct the error on the next try. However, a sequence of mistyped commands or incorrect login responses (with attempts to recover or reuse them) can be a signs of brute-force intrusion attempts.

Packet inconsistencies—direction (inbound or outbound), originating address or location, and session characteristics (ingoing sessions vs. outgoing sessions)—can also be good indicators of an attack. If a packet has an unusual source or has been addressed to an abnormal port—say, an inconsistent service request—it could be a sign of random system scanning. Packets coming from the outside that have local network addresses that request services on the inside can be a sign that IP spoofing is being attempted.

Sometimes odd or unexpected system behavior is itself a sign. Though this is sometimes difficult to track, you should be aware of activity such as changes to system clocks, servers going down or server processes inexplicably stopping (with system restart attempts), system resource issues (such as unusually high CPU activity or overflows in file systems), audit logs behaving in strange ways (decreasing in size without administrator intervention), or unexpected user access to resources. If you note unusual activity at regular times on given days, heavy system use (possible DoS attack) or CPU use (brute-force password-cracking attempts) should always be investigated.

8. WHAT CAN YOU DO?

It goes without saying that the most secure network—the one that has the least chance of being compromised—is one that has no direct connection to the outside world. But that's hardly a practical solution, since the whole reason you have a Web presence is to do business. And in the game of Internet commerce, your biggest concern isn't the sheep coming in but the wolves dressed like sheep coming in with them. So, how do you strike an acceptable balance between keeping your network intrusion free and keeping it accessible at the same time?

As your company's network administrator, you walk a fine line between network security and user needs. You have to have a good defensive posture that still allows for access. Users and customers can be both the lifeblood of your business and its greatest potential source of infection. Furthermore, if your business thrives on allowing users access, you have no choice but to let them in. It seems like a monumentally difficult task at best.

Like a castle, imposing but stationary, every defensive measure you put up will eventually be compromised by the legions of very motivated thieves looking to get in. It's a game of move/countermove: You adjust, they adapt. So you have to start with defenses that can quickly and effectively adapt and change as the outside threats adapt.

First and foremost, you need to make sure that your perimeter defenses are as strong as they can be, and that means keeping up with the rapidly evolving threats around you. The days of relying solely on a firewall that simply does firewall functions are gone; today's crackers have figured out how to bypass the firewall by exploiting weaknesses in applications themselves. Simply being reactive to hits and intrusions isn't a very good option, either; that's like standing there waiting for someone to hit you before deciding what to do rather than seeing the oncoming punch and moving out of its way or blocking it. You need to be flexible in your approach to the newest technologies, constantly auditing your defenses to ensure that your network's defensive armor can meet the latest threat. You have to have a very dynamic and effective policy of constantly monitoring for suspicious activities that, when discovered, can be quickly dealt with so that someone doesn't slip something past without your noticing it. Once that happens, it's too late.

Next, and this is also a crucial ingredient for network administrators: You have to educate your users. No matter how good a job you've done at tightening up your network security processes and systems, you still have to deal with the weakest link in your armor—your users. It doesn't do any good to have bulletproof processes in place if they're so difficult to manage that users work around them to avoid the difficulty, or if they're so loosely configured that a casually surfing user who visits an infected site will pass that infection along to your network. The degree of difficulty in securing your network increases dramatically as the number of users goes up.

User education becomes particularly important where mobile computing is concerned. Losing a device, using it in a place (or manner) in which prying eyes can see passwords or data, awareness of hacking tools specifically designed to sniff wireless signals for data, and logging on to unsecured networks are all potential problem areas with which users need to be familiar.

Know Today's Network Needs

The traditional approach to network security engineering has been to try to erect preventative measures—firewalls—to protect the infrastructure from intrusion. The firewall acts like a filter, catching anything that seems suspicious and keeping everything behind it as sterile as possible. However, though firewalls are good, they typically don't do much in the way of identifying compromised applications that use network resources. And with the speed of evolution seen in the area of penetration tools, an approach designed simply to prevent attacks will be less and less effective.

Today's computing environment is no longer confined to the office, as it used to be. Though there are still fixed systems inside the firewall, ever more sophisticated remote and mobile devices are making their way into the workforce. This influx of mobile computing has expanded the traditional boundaries of the network to farther and farther reaches and requires a different way of thinking about network security requirements.

Your network's endpoint or perimeter is mutating—expanding beyond its historical boundaries. Until recently, that endpoint was the user, either a desktop system or laptop, and it was relatively easy to secure those devices. To use a metaphor: The difference between endpoints of early network design and those of today is like the difference between the battles of World War II and the current war on terror. In the battles of WWII there were very clearly defined "front lines"—one side controlled by the Allied powers, the other by the Axis. Today, however, the war on terror has no such front lines and is fought in multiple areas with different techniques and strategies that are customized for each combat theater.

With today's explosion of remote users and mobile computing, your network's endpoint is no longer as clearly defined as it once was, and it is evolving at a very rapid pace. For this reason, your network's physical perimeter can no longer be seen as your best "last line of defense," even though having a robust perimeter security system is still a critical part of your overall security policy.

Any policy you develop should be organized in such a way as to take advantage of the strength of your unified threat management (UTM) system. Firewalls, antivirus, and intrusion detection systems (IDSs), for example, work by trying to block all currently known threats—the "blacklist" approach. But the threats evolve more quickly than the UTM systems can, so it almost always ends up being an "after the fact" game of catch-up. Perhaps a better, and more easily managed, policy is to specifically state which devices are allowed access and which applications are allowed to run in your network's applications. This "whitelist" approach helps reduce the amount of time and energy needed to keep up with the rapidly evolving pace of threat sophistication, because you're specifying what gets in versus what you have to keep out.

Any UTM system you employ should provide the means of doing two things: specify which applications and devices are allowed and offer a policy-based approach to managing those applications and devices. It should allow you to secure your critical resources against unauthorized data extraction (or data leakage), offer protection from the most persistent threats (viruses, malware, and spyware), and evolve with the ever-changing spectrum of devices and applications designed to penetrate your outer defenses.

So, what's the best strategy for integrating these new remote endpoints? First, you have to realize that these new remote, mobile technologies are becoming increasingly ubiquitous and aren't going away anytime soon. In fact, they most likely represent the future of computing. As these devices gain in sophistication and function, they are unchaining end users from their desks and, for some businesses, are indispensible tools. iPhones, Blackberries, Palm Treos, and other smart phones and devices now have the capability to interface with corporate email systems, access networks, run enterprise-level applications, and do full-featured remote computing. As such, they also now carry an increased risk for network administrators due to loss or theft (especially if the device is unprotected by a robust authentication method) and unauthorized interception of their wireless signals from which data can be siphoned off.

To cope with the inherent risks, you engage an effective security policy for dealing with these devices: under what conditions can they be used, how many of your users need to employ them, what levels and types of access will they have, and how will they be authenticated?

Solutions are available for adding strong authentication to users seeking access via wireless LANs. Tokens, either of the hardware or software variety, are used to identify the user to an authentication server for verification of their credentials. For example, PremierAccess by Aladdin Knowledge Systems can handle incoming access requests from a wireless access point and, if the user is authenticated, pass them into the network.

Key among the steps you take to secure your network while allowing mobile computing is to fully educate the users of such technology. They need to understand, in no uncertain terms, the risks to your network (and ultimately to the company in general) represented by their mobile devices and that their mindfulness of both the

device's physical and electronic security is an absolute necessity.

Network Security Best Practices

So, how do you either "clean and tighten up" your existing network or design a new one that can stand up to the inevitable onslaught of attacks? Let's look at some basics. Consider the diagram shown in Figure 3.1.

The illustration in Figure 3.1 shows what could be a typical network layout. Users outside the DMZ approach the network via a secure (HTTPS) Web or VPN connection. They are authenticated by the perimeter firewall and handed off to either a Web server or a VPN gateway. If allowed to pass, they can then access resources inside the network.

If you're the administrator of an organization that has only, say, a couple dozen users with whom to contend, your task (and the illustration layout) will be relatively easy to manage. But if you have to manage several hundred (or several thousand) users, the complexity of your task increases by an order of magnitude. That makes a good security policy an absolute necessity.

9. SECURITY POLICIES

Like the tedious prep work before painting a room, organizations need a good, detailed, and well-written security policy. Not something that should be rushed through

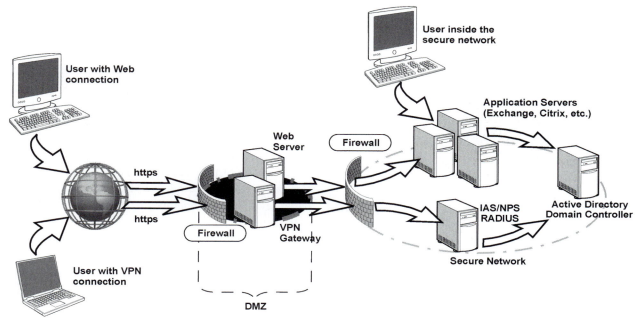

FIGURE 3.1 Network diagram.

"just to get it done," your security policy should be well thought out; in other words, the "devil is in the details." Your security policy is designed to get everyone involved with your network "thinking along the same lines."

The policy is almost always a work in progress. It must evolve with technology, especially those technologies aimed at surreptitiously getting into your system. The threats will continue to evolve, as will the systems designed to hold them at bay.

A good security policy isn't always a single document; rather, it is a conglomeration of policies that address specific areas, such as computer and network use, forms of authentication, email policies, remote/mobile technology use, and Web surfing policies. It should be written in such a way that, while comprehensive, it can be easily understood by those it affects. Along those lines, your policy doesn't have to be overly complex. If you hand new employees something that resembles *War and Peace* in size and tell them they're responsible for knowing its content, you can expect to have continued problems maintaining good network security awareness. Keep it simple.

First, you need to draft some policies that define your network and its basic architecture. A good place to start is by asking the following questions:

- What kinds of resources need to be protected (user financial or medical data, credit-card information, etc.)?
- How many users will be accessing the network on the inside (employees, contractors, etc.)?
- Will there need to be access only at certain times or on a 24/7 basis (and across multiple time zones and/ or internationally)?
- What kind of budget do I have?
- Will remote users be accessing the network, and if so, how many?
- Will there be remote sites in geographically distant locations (requiring a failsafe mechanism, such as replication, to keep data synched across the network)?

Next, you should spell out responsibilities for security requirements, communicate your expectations to your users (one of the weakest links in any security policy), and lay out the role(s) for your network administrator. It should list policies for activities such as Web surfing, downloading, local and remote access, and types of authentication. You should address issues such as adding users, assigning privileges, dealing with lost tokens or compromised passwords, and under what circumstances you will remove users from the access database.

You should establish a security team (sometimes referred to as a "tiger team") whose responsibility it will be to create security policies that are practical, workable, and sustainable. They should come up with the best plan for implementing these policies in a way that addresses both network resource protection and user friendliness. They should develop plans for responding to threats as well as schedules for updating equipment and software. And there should be a very clear policy for handling changes to overall network security—the types of connections through your firewall that will and will not be allowed. This is especially important because you don't want an unauthorized user gaining access, reaching into your network, and simply taking files or data.

10. RISK ANALYSIS

You should have some kind of risk analysis done to determine, as near as possible, the risks you face with the kind of operations you conduct (ecommerce, classified/ proprietary information handling, partner access, or the like). Depending on the determined risk, you might need to rethink your original network design. Though a simple extranet/intranet setup with mid-level firewall protection might be okay for a small business that doesn't have much to steal, that obviously won't work for a company that deals with user financial data or proprietary/ classified information. In that case, what might be needed is a tiered system in which you have a "corporate side" (on which things such as email, intranet access, and regular Internet access are handled) and a separate, secure network not connected to the Internet or corporate side. These networks can only be accessed by a user on a physical machine, and data can only be moved to them by "sneaker-net" physical media (scanned for viruses before opening). These networks can be used for data systems such as test or lab machines (on which, for example, new software builds are done and must be more tightly controlled, to prevent inadvertent corruption of the corporate side), or networks on which the storage or processing of proprietary, business-critical, or classified information are handled. In Department of Defense parlance, these are sometimes referred to as *red nets* or *black nets*.

Vulnerability Testing

Your security policy should include regular vulnerability testing. Some very good vulnerability testing tools, such as WebInspect, Acunetix, GFI LANguard, Nessus,

HFNetChk, and Tripwire, allow you to conduct your own security testing. Furthermore, there are third-party companies with the most advanced suite of testing tools available that can be contracted to scan your network for open and/or accessible ports, weaknesses in firewalls, and Web site vulnerability.

Audits

You should also factor in regular, detailed audits of all activities, with emphasis on those that seem to be near or outside established norms. For example, audits that reveal high rates of data exchanges after normal business hours, when that kind of traffic would not normally be expected, is something that should be investigated. Perhaps, after checking, you'll find that it's nothing more than an employee downloading music or video files. But the point is that your audit system saw the increase in traffic and determined it to be a simple Internet use policy violation rather than someone siphoning off more critical data.

There should be clearly established rules for dealing with security, use, and/or policy violations as well as attempted or actual intrusions. Trying to figure out what to do after the intrusion is too late. And if an intrusion does occur, there should be a clear-cut system for determining the extent of damage; isolation of the exploited application, port, or machine; and a rapid response to closing the hole against further incursions.

Recovery

Your plan should also address the issue of recovery after an attack has occurred. You need to address issues such as how the network will be reconfigured to close off the exploited opening. This might take some time, since the entry point might not be immediately discernable. There has to be an estimate of damage—what was taken or compromised, was malicious code implanted somewhere, and, if so, how to most efficiently extract it and clean the affected system. In the case of a virus in a company's email system, the ability to send and receive email could be halted for days while infected systems are rebuilt. And there will have to be discussions about how to reconstruct the network if the attack decimated files and systems.

This will most likely involve more than simply reinstalling machines from archived backups. Because the compromise will most likely affect normal business operations, the need to expedite the recovery will hamper efforts to fully analyze just what happened.

This is the main reason for preemptively writing a disaster recovery plan and making sure that all departments are represented in its drafting. However, like the network security policy itself, the disaster recovery plan will also be a work in progress that should be reviewed regularly to ensure that it meets the current needs. Things such as new threat notifications, software patches and updates, vulnerability assessments, new application rollouts, and employee turnover all have to be addressed.

11. TOOLS OF YOUR TRADE

Though the tools available to people seeking unauthorized entry into your domain are impressive, you also have a wide variety of tools to help keep them out. Before implementing a network security strategy, however, you must be acutely aware of the specific needs of those who will be using your resources.

Simple antispyware and antispam tools aren't enough. In today's rapidly changing software environment, strong security requires penetration shielding, threat signature recognition, autonomous reaction to identified threats, and the ability to upgrade your tools as the need arises.

The following discussion talks about some of the more common tools you should consider adding to your arsenal.

Firewalls

Your first line of defense should be a good firewall, or better yet, a system that effectively incorporates several security features in one. Secure Firewall (formerly Sidewinder) from Secure Computing is one of the strongest and most secure firewall products available, and as of this writing it has never been successfully hacked. It is trusted and used by government and defense agencies. Secure Firewall combines the five most necessary security systems—firewall, antivirus/spyware/spam, virtual private network (VPN), application filtering, and intrusion prevention/detection systems—into a single appliance.

Intrusion Prevention Systems

A good *intrusion prevention system* (IPS) is a vast improvement over a basic firewall in that it can, among other things, be configured with policies that allow it to make autonomous decisions as to how to deal with application-level threats as well as simple IP address or port-level attacks.

IPS products respond directly to incoming threats in a variety of ways, from automatically dropping (extracting) suspicious packets (while still allowing legitimate ones to pass) to, in some cases, placing an intruder into a "quarantine" file. IPS, like an application layer firewall, can be considered another form of access control in that it can make pass/fail decisions on application content.

For an IPS to be effective, it must also be very good at discriminating between a real threat signature and one that looks like but isn't one (false positive). Once a signature interpreted to be an intrusion is detected, the system must quickly notify the administrator so that the appropriate evasive action can be taken. The following are types of IPS:

- *Network-based.* Network-based IPSs create a series of choke points in the enterprise that detect suspected intrusion attempt activity. Placed inline at their needed locations, they invisibly monitor network traffic for known attack signatures that they then block.
- *Host-based.* These systems don't reside on the network per se but rather on servers and individual machines. They quietly monitor activities and requests from applications, weeding out actions deemed prohibited in nature. These systems are often very good at identifying post-decryption entry attempts.
- *Content-based.* These IPSs scan network packets, looking for signatures of content that is unknown or unrecognized or that has been explicitly labeled threatening in nature.
- *Rate-based.* These IPSs look for activity that falls outside the range of normal levels, such as activity that seems to be related to password cracking and brute-force penetration attempts, for example.

When searching for a good IPS, look for one that provides, at minimum:

- Robust protection for your applications, host systems, and individual network elements against exploitation of vulnerability-based threats as "single-bullet attacks," Trojan horses, worms, botnets, and surreptitious creation of "back doors" in your network
- Protection against threats that exploit vulnerabilities in specific applications such as Web services, mail, DNS, SQL, and any Voice over IP (VoIP) services
- Detection and elimination of spyware, phishing, and anonymizers (tools that hide a source computer's identifying information so that Internet activity can be undertaken surreptitiously)
- Protection against brute-force and DoS attacks, application scanning, and flooding

- A regular method of updating threat lists and signatures

Application Firewalls

Application firewalls (AFs) are sometimes confused with IPSs in that they can perform IPS-like functions. But an AF is specifically designed to limit or deny an application's level of access to a system's OS—in other words, closing any openings into a computer's OS to deny the execution of harmful code within an OS's structure. AFs work by looking at applications themselves, monitoring the kind of data flow from an application for suspicious or administrator-blocked content from specific Web sites, application-specific viruses, and any attempt to exploit an identified weakness in an application's architecture. Though AF systems can conduct intrusion prevention duties, they typically employ proxies to handle firewall access control and focus on traditional firewall-type functions. Application firewalls can detect the signatures of recognized threats and block them before they can infect the network.

Windows' version of an application firewall, called Data Execution Prevention (DEP), prevents the execution of any code that uses system services in such a way that could be deemed harmful to data or Virtual Memory (VM). It does this by considering RAM data as nonexecutable—in essence, refusing to run new code coming from the data-only area of RAM, since any harmful or malicious code seeking to damage existing data would have to run from this area.

The Macintosh Operating System (MacOS) Version 10.5.x also includes a built-in application firewall as a standard feature. The user can configure it to employ two-layer protection in which installing network-aware applications will result in an OS-generated warning that prompts for user authorization of network access. If authorized, MacOS will digitally sign the application in such a way that subsequent application activity will not prompt for further authorization. Updates invalidate the original certificate, and the user will have to revalidate before the application can run again.

The Linux OS has, for example, an application firewall called AppArmor that allows the admin to create and link to every application a security policy that restricts its access capabilities.

Access Control Systems

Access control systems (ACSs) rely on administrator-defined rules that allow or restrict user access to protected network resources. These access rules can, for example, require strong user authentication such as tokens or biometric devices to prove the identity of users requesting access. They can also restrict access to various network services based on time of day or group need.

Some ACS products allow for the creation of an *access control list* (ACL), which is a set of rules that define security policy. These ACLs contain one or more *access control entries* (ACEs), which are the actual rule definitions themselves. These rules can restrict access by specific user, time of day, IP address, function (department, management level, etc.), or specific system from which a logon or access attempt is being made.

A good example of an ACS is SafeWord by Aladdin Knowledge Systems. SafeWord is considered a two-factor authentication system in that it uses what the user knows (such as a personal identification number, or PIN) and what the user has (such as a one-time passcode, or OTP, token) to strongly authenticate users requesting network access. SafeWord allows administrators to design customized access rules and restrictions to network resources, applications, and information.

In this scheme, the tokens are a key component. The token's internal cryptographic key algorithm is made "known" to an authentication server when the token's file is imported into a central database.

When the token is assigned to a user, its serial number is linked to that user in the user's record. On making an access request, the authentication server prompts the user to enter a username and the OTP generated by the token. If a PIN was also assigned to that user, she must either prepend or append that PIN to the token-generated passcode. As long as the authentication server receives what it expects, the user is granted whatever access privileges she was assigned.

Unified Threat Management

The latest trend to emerge in the network intrusion prevention arena is referred to as *unified threat management*, or UTM. UTM systems are multilayered and incorporate several security technologies into a single platform, often in the form of a plug-in appliance. UTM products can provide such diverse capabilities as antivirus, VPN, firewall services, and antispam as well as intrusion prevention.

The biggest advantages of a UTM system are its ease of operation and configuration and the fact that its security features can be quickly updated to meet rapidly evolving threats.

Sidewinder by Secure Computing is a UTM system that was designed to be flexible, easily and quickly adaptable, and easy to manage. It incorporates firewall, VPN, trusted source, IPS, antispam and antivirus, URL filtering, SSL decryption, and auditing/reporting.

Other UTM systems include Symantec's Enterprise Firewall and Gateway Security Enterprise Firewall Appliance, Fortinet, LokTek's AIRlok Firewall Appliance, and SonicWall's NSA 240 UTM Appliance, to name a few.

12. CONTROLLING USER ACCESS

Traditionally users—also known as employees—have been the weakest link in a company's defensive armor. Though necessary to the organization, they can be a nightmare waiting to happen to your network. How do you let them work within the network while controlling their access to resources? You have to make sure your system of user authentication knows who your users are.

Authentication, Authorization, and Accounting

Authentication is simply proving that a user's identity claim is valid and authentic. Authentication requires some form of "proof of identity." In network technologies, physical proof (such as a driver's license or other photo ID) cannot be employed, so you have to get something else from a user. That typically means having the user respond to a challenge to provide genuine credentials at the time he requests access.

For our purposes, credentials can be something the user knows, something the user has, or something they are. Once they provide authentication, there also has to be authorization, or permission to enter. Finally, you want to have some record of users' entry into your network—username, time of entry, and resources. That is the accounting side of the process.

What the User Knows

Users know a great many details about their own lives— birthdays, anniversaries, first cars, their spouse's name— and many will try to use these nuggets of information as a simple form of authentication. What they don't realize is just how insecure those pieces of information are.

In network technologies, these pieces of information are often used as fixed passwords and PINs because they're easy to remember. Unless some strict guidelines are established on what form a password or PIN can take (for example, a minimum number of characters or a mixture of letters and numbers), a password will offer little to no real security.

Unfortunately, to hold down costs, some organizations allow users to set their own passwords and PINs as credentials, then rely on a simple challenge-response mechanism in which these weak credentials are provided to gain access. Adding to the loss of security is the fact that not only are the fixed passwords far too easy to guess, but because the user already has too much to remember, she writes them down somewhere near the computer she uses (often in some "cryptic" scheme to make it more difficult to guess). To increase the effectiveness of any security system, that system needs to require a much stronger form of authentication.

What the User Has

The most secure means of identifying users is by a combination of (1) hardware device in their possession that is "known" to an authentication server in your network, coupled with (2) what they know. A whole host of devices available today—tokens, smart cards, biometric devices—are designed to more positively identify a user. Since it's my opinion that a good token is the most secure of these options, I focus on them here.

Tokens

A *token* is a device that employs an encrypted key for which the encryption algorithm—the method of generating an encrypted password—is known to a network's authentication server. There are both software and hardware tokens. The software tokens can be installed on a user's desktop system, in their cellular phone, or on their smart phone. The hardware tokens come in a variety of form factors, some with a single button that both turns the token on and displays its internally generated passcode; others with a more elaborate numerical keypad for PIN input. If lost or stolen, tokens can easily be removed from the system, quickly rendering them completely ineffective. And the passcodes they generate are of the "one-time-passcode," or OTP, variety, meaning that a generated passcode expires once it's been used and cannot be used again for a subsequent logon attempt.

Tokens are either programmed onsite with token programming software or offsite at the time they are ordered from their vendor. During programming, functions such as a token's cryptographic key, password length, whether a PIN is required, and whether it generates passwords

based on internal clock timing or user PIN input are written into the token's memory. When programming is complete, a file containing this information and the token's serial number are imported into the authentication server so that the token's characteristics are known.

A token is assigned to a user by linking its serial number to the user's record, stored in the system database. When a user logs onto the network and needs access to, say, her email, she is presented with some challenge that she must answer using her assigned token.

Tokens operate in one of three ways: time synchronous, event synchronous, or challenge-response (also known as asynchronous).

Time Synchronous

In time synchronous operation, the token's internal clock is synched with the network's clock. Each time the token's button is pressed, it generates a passcode in hash form, based on its internal timekeeping. As long as the token's clock is synched with the network clock, the passcodes are accepted. In some cases (for example, when the token hasn't been used for some time or its battery dies), the token gets out of synch with the system and needs to be resynched before it can be used again.

Event Synchronous

In event synchronous operations, the server maintains an ordered passcode sequence and determines which passcode is valid based on the current location in that sequence.

Challenge-Response

In challenge-response, a challenge, prompting for username, is issued to the user by the authentication server at the time of access request. Once the user's name is entered, the authentication server checks to see what form of authentication is assigned to that user and issues a challenge back to the user. The user inputs the challenge into the token, then enters the token's generated response to the challenge. As long as the authentication server receives what it expected, authentication is successful and access is granted.

The User Is Authenticated, But Is She Authorized?

Authorization is independent of authentication. A user can be permitted entry into the network but not be authorized to access a resource. You don't want an employee having access to HR information or a corporate partner getting access to confidential or proprietary information.

Authorization requires a set of rules that dictate the resources to which a user will have access. These permissions are established in your security policy.

Accounting

Say that our user has been granted access to the requested resource. But you want (or in some cases are required to have) the ability to call up and view activity logs to see who got into what resource. This information is mandated for organizations that deal with user financial or medical information or DoD classified information or that go through annual inspections to maintain certification for international operations.

Accounting refers to the recording, logging, and archiving of all server activity, especially activity related to access attempts and whether they were successful. This information should be written into audit logs that are stored and available any time you want or need to view them. The audit logs should contain, at minimum, the following information:

- The user's identity
- The date and time of the request
- Whether the request passed authentication and was granted

Any network security system you put into place should store, or archive, these logs for a specified period of time and allow you to determine for how long these archives will be maintained before they start to age out of the system.

Keeping Current

One of the best ways to stay ahead is to not fall behind in the first place. New systems with increasing sophistication are being developed all the time. They can incorporate a more intelligent and autonomous process in the way the system handles a detected threat, a faster and more easily accomplished method for updating threat files, and configuration flexibility that allows for very precise customization of access rules, authentication requirements, user role assignment, and how tightly it can protect specific applications.

Register for newsletters, attend seminars and network security shows, read white papers, and, if needed, contract the services of network security specialists. The point is, you shouldn't go cheap on network security. The price you pay to keep ahead will be far less than the price you pay to recover from a security breach or attack.

13. CONCLUSION

Preventing network intrusions is no easy task. Like cops on the street—usually outnumbered and underequipped compared to the bad guys—you face an enemy with determination, skill, training, and a frightening array of increasingly sophisticated tools for hacking their way through your best defenses. And no matter how good your defenses are today, it's only a matter of time before a tool is developed that can penetrate them. If you know that ahead of time, you'll be much more inclined to keep a watchful eye for what "they" have and what you can use to defeat them.

Your best weapon is a logical, thoughtful, and nimble approach to network security. You have to be nimble—to evolve and grow with changes in technology, never being content to keep things as they are because "Hey, they're working just fine." Today's "just fine" will be tomorrow's "What the hell happened?"

Stay informed. There is no shortage of information available to you in the form of white papers, seminars, contract security specialists, and online resources, all dealing with various aspects of network security.

Have a good, solid, comprehensive, yet easy-to-understand network security policy in place. The very process of developing one will get all involved parties thinking about how to best secure your network while addressing user needs. When it comes to your users, you simply can't overeducate them where network security awareness is concerned. The more they know, the better equipped they'll be to act as allies against, rather than accomplices of, the hoards of crackers looking to steal, damage, hobble, or completely cripple your network.

Do your research and invest in good, multipurpose network security systems. Select systems that are easy to install and implement, are adaptable and quickly configurable, can be customized to suit your needs of today as well as tomorrow, and are supported by companies that keep pace with current trends in cracker technology.

Chapter 4

Guarding Against Network Intrusions

Tom Chen
Swansea University

Patrick J. Walsh
eSoft Inc.

Virtually all computers today are connected to the Internet through dialup, broadband, Ethernet, or wireless technologies. The reason for this Internet ubiquity is simple: Applications depending on the network, such as email, Web, remote login, instant messaging, and VoIP, have become essential to the computing experience. Unfortunately, the Internet exposes computer users to risks from a wide variety of possible attacks. Users have much to lose—their privacy, valuable data, control of their computers, and possibly theft of their identities. The network enables attacks to be carried out remotely, with relative anonymity and low risk of traceability.

The nature of network intrusions has evolved over the years. A few years ago, a major concern was fast worms such as Code Red, Nimda, Slammer, and Sobig. More recently, concerns shifted to spyware, Trojan horses, and botnets. Although these other threats still continue to be major problems, the Web has become the primary vector for stealthy attacks today.[1]

1. TRADITIONAL RECONNAISSANCE AND ATTACKS

Traditionally, attack methods follow sequential steps analogous to physical attacks, as shown in Figure 4.1: reconnaissance, compromise, and cover-up.[2] Here we are only addressing attacks directed at a specific target host. Some other types of attacks, such as worms, are not directed at specific targets. Instead, they attempt to hit as many targets as quickly as possible without caring who or what the targets are.

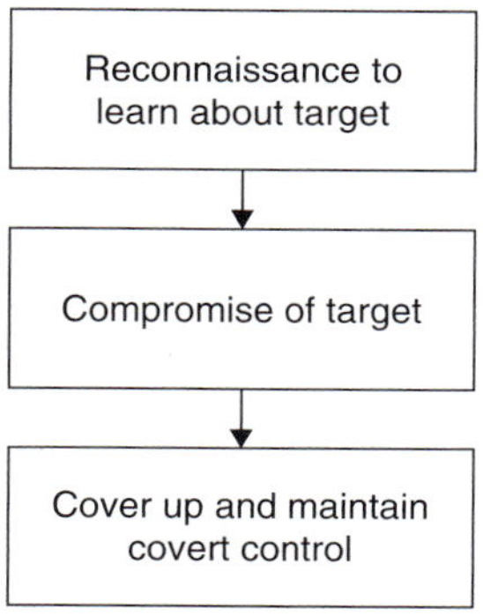

FIGURE 4.1 Steps in directed attacks.

In the first step of a directed attack, the attacker performs reconnaissance to learn as much as possible about the chosen target before carrying out an actual attack. A thorough reconnaissance can lead to a more effective attack because the target's weaknesses can be discovered. One might expect the reconnaissance phase to possibly tip off the target about an impending attack, but scans and probes are going on constantly in the "background noise" of network traffic, so systems administrators might ignore attack probes as too troublesome to investigate.

Through pings and traceroutes, an attacker can discover IP addresses and map the network around the target. Pings are ICMP echo request and echo reply messages that verify a host's IP address and availability. Traceroute is a network mapping utility that takes advantage of the time to live (TTL) field in IP packets. It sends out packets with TTL = 1, then TTL = 2, and so on. When the packets expire, the routers along the packets' path report that the packets have been discarded, returning ICMP "time exceeded" messages and thereby

1 Dean Turner, et al., Symantec Global Internet Security Threat Report: Trends for July–December 2007, available at www.symantec.com (date of access: July, 1, 2008).

2 Ed Skoudis, *Counter Hack Reloaded: A Step-by-Step Guide to Computer Attacks and Effective Defenses, 2nd ed.*, Prentice Hall, 2006.

Computer and Information Security Handbook

allowing the traceroute utility to learn the IP addresses of routers at a distance of one hop, two hops, and so on.

Port scans can reveal open ports. Normally, a host might be expected to have certain well-known ports open, such as TCP port 80 (HTTP), TCP port 21 (FTP), TCP port 23 (Telnet), or TCP port 25 (SMTP). A host might also happen to have open ports in the higher range. For example, port 12345 is the default port used by the Netbus remote access Trojan horse, or port 31337 is the default port used by the Back Orifice remote access Trojan horse. Discovery of ports indicating previous malware infections could obviously help an attacker considerably.

In addition to discovering open ports, the popular NMAP scanner (www.insecure.org/nmap) can discover the operating system running on a target. NMAP uses a large set of heuristic rules to identify an operating system based on a target's responses to carefully crafted TCP/IP probes. The basic idea is that different operating systems will make different responses to probes to open TCP/UDP ports and malformed TCP/IP packets. Knowledge of a target's operating system can help an attacker identify vulnerabilities and find effective exploits.

Vulnerability scanning tests a target for the presence of vulnerabilities. Vulnerability scanners such as SATAN, SARA, SAINT, and Nessus typically contain a database of known vulnerabilities that is used to craft probes to a chosen target. The popular Nessus tool (www.nessus.org) has an extensible plug-in architecture to add checks for backdoors, misconfiguration errors, default accounts and passwords, and other types of vulnerabilities.

In the second step of a directed attack, the attacker attempts to compromise the target through one or more methods. Password attacks are common because passwords might be based on common words or names and are guessable by a dictionary attack, although computer systems today have better password policies that forbid easily guessable passwords. If an attacker can obtain the password file from the target, numerous password-cracking tools are available to carry out a brute-force password attack. In addition, computers and networking equipment often ship with default accounts and passwords intended to help systems administrators set up the equipment. These default accounts and passwords are easy to find on the Web (for example, www.phenoelit-us.org/dpl/dpl.html). Occasionally users might neglect to change or delete the default accounts, offering intruders an easy way to access the target.

Another common attack method is an exploit attack code written to take advantage of a specific vulnerability.[3]

Many types of software, including operating systems and applications, have vulnerabilities. In the second half of 2007, Symantec observed an average of 11.7 vulnerabilities per day.[4] Vulnerabilities are published by several organizations such as CERT and MITRE as well as vendors such as Microsoft through security bulletins. MITRE maintains a database of publicly known vulnerabilities identified by common vulnerabilities and exposures (CVE) numbers. The severity of vulnerabilities is reflected in the industry-standard common vulnerability scoring system (CVSS). In the second half of 2007, Symantec observed that 3% of vulnerabilities were highly severe, 61% were medium-severe, and 36% were low-severe.[5] Furthermore, 73% of vulnerabilities were easily exploitable. For 2007, Microsoft reported that 32% of known vulnerabilities in Microsoft products had publicly available exploit code.[6] Microsoft released 69 security bulletins covering 100 unique vulnerabilities.

Historically, buffer overflows have been the most common type of vulnerability.[7] They have been popular because buffer overflow exploits can often be carried out remotely and lead to complete compromise of a target. The problem arises when a program has allocated a fixed amount of memory space (such as in the stack) for storing data but receives more data than expected. If the vulnerability exists, the extra data will overwrite adjacent parts of memory, which could mess up other variables or pointers. If the extra data is random, the computer might crash or act unpredictably. However, if an attacker crafts the extra data carefully, the buffer overflow could overwrite adjacent memory with a consequence that benefits the attacker. For instance, an attacker might overwrite the return pointer in a stack, causing the program control to jump to malicious code inserted by the attacker.

An effective buffer overflow exploit requires technical knowledge of the computer architecture and operating system, but once the exploit code is written, it can be reused again. Buffer overflows can be prevented by the programmer or compiler performing bounds checking or during runtime. Although C/C++ has received a good deal of blame as a programming language for not having built-in checking that data written to arrays stays within

3 S. McClure, J. Scambray, G. Kutz, *Hacking Exposed, third ed.,* McGraw-Hill, 2001.

4 Dean Turner, et al., Symantec Global Internet Security Threat Report: Trends for July–December 2007, available at www.symantec.com (date of access: July, 1, 2008).

5 Dean Turner, et al., Symantec Global Internet Security Threat Report: Trends for July–December 2007, available at www.symantec.com (date of access: July, 1, 2008).

6 B. Arsenault and V. Gullutto, Microsoft Security Intelligence Report: July–December 2007, available at www.microsoft.com (date of access: July 1, 2008).

7 J. Foster, V. Osipov, and N. Bhalla, *Buffer Overflow Attacks: Detect, Exploit, Prevent,* Syngress, 2005.

bounds, buffer overflow vulnerabilities appear in a wide variety of other programs, too.

Structured Query Language injection is a type of vulnerability relevant to Web servers with a database backend.[8] SQL is an internationally standardized interactive and programming language for querying data and managing databases. Many commercial database products support SQL, sometimes with proprietary extensions. Web applications often take user input (usually from a Web form) and pass the input into an SQL statement. An SQL injection vulnerability can arise if user input is not properly filtered for string literal escape characters, which can allow an attacker to craft input that is interpreted as embedded SQL statements and thereby manipulate the application running on the database.

Servers have been attacked and compromised by toolkits designed to automate customized attacks. For example, the MPack toolkit emerged in early 2007 and is sold commercially in Russia, along with technical support and regular software updates. It is loaded into a malicious or compromised Web site. When a visitor goes to the site, a malicious code is launched through an iframe (inline frame) within the HTML code. It can launch various exploits, expandable through modules, for vulnerabilities in Web browsers and client software.

Metasploit (www.metasploit.com) is a popular Perl-based tool for developing and using exploits with an easy-to-use Web or command-line interface. Different exploits can be written and loaded into Metasploit and then directed at a chosen target. Exploits can be bundled with a payload (the code to run on a compromised target) selected from a collection of payloads. The tool also contains utilities to experiment with new vulnerabilities and help automate the development of new exploits.

Although exploits are commonplace, not all attacks require an exploit. *Social engineering* refers to types of attacks that take advantage of human nature to compromise a target, typically through deceit. A common social engineering attack is *phishing*, used in identity theft.[9] Phishing starts with a lure, usually a spam message that appears to be from a legitimate bank or ecommerce business. The message attempts to provoke the reader into visiting a fraudulent Web site pretending to be a legitimate business. These fraudulent sites are often set up by automated phishing toolkits that spoof legitimate sites of various brands, including the graphics of those brands. The fraudulent site might even have links to the legitimate Web site, to appear more valid. Victims are thus tricked into submitting valuable personal information such as account numbers, passwords, and Social Security numbers.

Other common examples of social engineering are spam messages that entice the reader into opening an email attachment. Most people know by now that attachments could be dangerous, perhaps containing a virus or spyware, even if they appear to be innocent at first glance. But if the message is sufficiently convincing, such as appearing to originate from an acquaintance, even wary users might be tricked into opening an attachment. Social engineering attacks can be simple but effective because they target people and bypass technological defenses.

The third step of traditional directed attacks involves cover-up of evidence of the compromise and establishment of covert control. After a successful attack, intruders want to maintain remote control and evade detection. Remote control can be maintained if the attacker has managed to install any of a number types of malicious software: a backdoor such as Netcat; a remote access Trojan such as BO2K or SubSeven; or a bot, usually listening for remote instructions on an Internet relay chat (IRC) channel, such as phatbot.

Intruders obviously prefer to evade detection after a successful compromise, because detection will lead the victim to take remedial actions to harden or disinfect the target. Intruders might change the system logs on the target, which will likely contain evidence of their attack. In Windows, the main event logs are secevent.evt, sysevent.evt, and appevent.evt. A systems administrator looking for evidence of intrusions would look in these files with the built-in Windows Event Viewer or a third-party log viewer. An intelligent intruder would not delete the logs but would selectively delete information in the logs to hide signs of malicious actions.

A *rootkit* is a stealthy type of malicious software (*malware*) designed to hide the existence of certain processes or programs from normal methods of detection.[10] Rootkits essentially alter the target's operating system, perhaps by changing drivers or dynamic link libraries (DLLs) and possibly at the kernel level. An example is the kernel-mode FU rootkit that manipulates kernel memory in Windows 2000, XP, and 2003. It consists of a device driver, msdirectx.sys, that might be mistaken for Microsoft's DirectX tool. The rootkit can hide certain events and processes and change the privileges of running processes.

8 D. Litchfield, *SQL Server Security*, McGraw-Hill Osborne, 2003.
9 Markus Jakobsson and Steven Meyers, eds., *Phishing and Countermeasures: Understanding the Increasing Problem of Electronic Identity Theft*, Wiley-Interscience, 2006.
10 Greg Hoglund and Jamie Butler, *Rootkits: Subverting the Windows Kernel*, Addison-Wesley Professional, 2005.

If an intruder has installed malware for covert control, he will want to conceal the communications between himself and the compromised target from discovery by network-based *intrusion detection systems* (IDSs). Intrusion detection systems are designed to listen to network traffic and look for signs of suspicious activities. Several concealment methods are used in practice. *Tunneling* is a commonly used method to place packets of one protocol into the payload of another packet. The "exterior" packet serves a vehicle to carry and deliver the "interior" packet intact. Though the protocol of the exterior packet is easily understood by an IDS, the interior protocol can be any number of possibilities and hence difficult to interpret.

Encryption is another obvious concealment method. Encryption relies on the secrecy of an encryption key shared between the intruder and the compromised target. The encryption key is used to mathematically scramble the communications into a form that is unreadable without the key to decrypt it. Encryption ensures secrecy in practical terms but does not guarantee perfect security. Encryption keys can be guessed, but the time to guess the correct key increases exponentially with the key length. Long keys combined with an algorithm for periodically changing keys can ensure that encrypted communications will be difficult to break within a reasonable time.

Fragmentation of IP packets is another means to conceal the contents of messages from IDSs, which often do not bother to reassemble fragments. IP packets may normally be fragmented into smaller packets anywhere along a route and reassembled at the destination. An IDS can become confused with a flood of fragments, bogus fragments, or deliberately overlapping fragments.

2. MALICIOUS SOFTWARE

Malicious software, or malware, continues to be an enormous problem for Internet users because of its variety and prevalence and the level of danger it presents.[11,12,13] It is important to realize that malware can take many forms. A large class of malware is *infectious*, which includes viruses and worms. Viruses and worms are self-replicating, meaning that they spread from host to host by making copies of themselves. Viruses are pieces of code attached to a normal file or program. When the program is run, the virus code is executed and copies itself

to (or infects) another file or program. It is often said that viruses need a human action to spread, whereas worms are standalone automated programs. Worms look for vulnerable targets across the network and transfer a copy of themselves if a target is successfully compromised.

Historically, several worms have become well known and stimulated concerns over the possibility of a fast epidemic infecting Internet-connected hosts before defenses could stop it. The 1988 Robert Morris Jr. worm infected thousands of Unix hosts, at the time a significant portion of the Arpanet (the predecessor to the Internet). The 1999 Melissa worm infected Microsoft Word documents and emailed itself to addresses found in a victim's Outlook address book. Melissa demonstrated that email could be a very effective vector for malware distribution, and many subsequent worms have continued to use email, such as the 2000 Love Letter worm. In the 2001–04 interval, several fast worms appeared, notably Code Red, Nimda, Klez, SQL Slammer/Sapphire, Blaster, Sobig, and MyDoom.

An important feature of viruses and worms is their capability to carry a *payload*—malicious code that is executed on a compromised host. The payload can be virtually anything. For instance, SQL Slammer/Sapphire had no payload, whereas Code Red carried an agent to perform a denial-of-service (DoS) attack on certain fixed addresses. The Chernobyl or CIH virus had one of the most destructive payloads, attempting to overwrite critical system files and the system BIOS that is needed for a computer to boot up. Worms are sometimes used to deliver other malware, such as bots, in their payload. They are popular delivery vehicles because of their ability to spread by themselves and carry anything in their payload.

Members of a second large class of malware are characterized by attempts to conceal themselves. This class includes Trojan horses and rootkits. Worms are not particularly stealthy (unless they are designed to be), because they are typically indiscriminate in their attacks. They probe potential targets in the hope of compromising many targets quickly. Indeed, fast-spreading worms are relatively easy to detect because of the network congestion caused by their probes.

Stealth is an important feature for malware because the critical problem for antivirus software is obviously detection of malware. Trojan horses are a type of malware that appears to perform a useful function but hides a malicious function. Thus, the presence of the Trojan horse might not be concealed, but functionality is not fully revealed. For example, a video codec could offer to play certain types of video but also covertly steal the user's data in the background. In the second half of

11 David Harley and David Slade, *Viruses Revealed*, McGraw-Hill, 2001.
12 Ed Skoudis, *Malware: Fighting Malicious Code*, Prentice Hall PTR, 2004.
13 Peter Szor, *The Art of Computer Virus Research and Defense*, Addison-Wesley, 2005.

2007, Microsoft reported a dramatic increase of 300% in the number of Trojan downloaders and droppers, small programs to facilitate downloading more malware later.[4]

Rootkits are essentially modifications to the operating system to hide the presence of files or processes from normal means of detection. Rootkits are often installed as drivers or kernel modules. A highly publicized example was the extended copy protection (XCP) software included in some Sony BMG audio CDs in 2005, to prevent music copying. The software was installed automatically on Windows PCs when a CD was played. Made by a company called First 4 Internet, XCP unfortunately contained a hidden rootkit component that patched the operating system to prevent it from displaying any processes, Registry entries, or files with names beginning with sys. Although the intention of XCP was not malicious, there was concern that the rootkit could be used by malware writers to conceal malware.

A third important class of malware is designed for remote control. This class includes remote access Trojans (RATs) and bots. Instead of *remote access Trojan*, RAT is sometimes interpreted as *remote administration tool* because it can be used for legitimate purposes by systems administrators. Either way, RAT refers to a type of software usually consisting of server and client parts designed to enable covert communications with a remote controller. The client part is installed on a victim host and mainly listens for instructions from the server part, located at the controller. Notorious examples include Back Orifice, Netbus, and Sub7.

Bots are remote-control programs installed covertly on innocent hosts.[14] Bots are typically programmed to listen to IRC channels for instructions from a "bot herder." All bots under control of the same bot herder form a botnet. Botnets have been known to be rented out for purposes of sending spam or launching a distributed DoS (DDoS) attack.[15] The power of a botnet is proportional to its size, but exact sizes have been difficult to discover.

One of the most publicized bots is the Storm worm, which has various aliases. Storm was launched in January 2007 as spam with a Trojan horse attachment. As a botnet, Storm has shown unusual resilience by working in a distributed peer-to-peer manner without centralized control. Each compromised host connects to a small subset of the entire botnet. Each infected host shares lists of other infected hosts, but no single host has a full list of the entire botnet. The size of the Storm botnet has been estimated at more than 1 million compromised hosts, but an exact size has been impossible to determine because of the many bot variants and active measures to avoid detection. Its creators have been persistent in continually updating its lures with current events and evolving tactics to spread and avoid detection.

Another major class of malware is designed for data theft. This class includes keyloggers and spyware. A keylogger can be a Trojan horse or other form of malware. It is designed to record a user's keystrokes and perhaps report them to a remote attacker. Keyloggers are planted by criminals on unsuspecting hosts to steal passwords and other valuable personal information. It has also been rumored that the Federal Bureau of Investigation (FBI) has used a keylogger called Magic Lantern.

As the name implies, *spyware* is stealthy software designed to monitor and report user activities for the purposes of learning personal information without the user's knowledge or consent. Surveys have found that spyware is widely prevalent on consumer PCs, usually without knowledge of the owners. Adware is viewed by some as a mildly objectionable form of spyware that spies on Web browsing behavior to target online advertisements to a user's apparent interests. More objectionable forms of spyware are more invasive of privacy and raise other objections related to stealthy installation, interference with normal Web browsing, and difficulty of removal.

Spyware can be installed in a number of stealthy ways: disguised as a Trojan horse, bundled with a legitimate software program, delivered in the payload of a worm or virus, or downloaded through deception. For instance, a deceptive Web site might pop up a window appearing to be a standard Windows dialog box, but clicking any button will cause spyware to be downloaded. Another issue is that spyware might or might not display an end-user license agreement (EULA) before installation. If an EULA is displayed, the mention of spyware is typically unnoticeable or difficult to find.

More pernicious forms of spyware can change computer settings, reset homepages, and redirect the browser to unwanted sites. For example, the notorious CoolWebSearch changed homepages to Coolwebsearch.com, rewrote search engine results, and altered host files, and some variants added links to pornographic and gambling sites to the browser's bookmarks.

Lures and "Pull" Attacks

Traditional network attacks can be viewed as an "active" approach in which the attacker takes the initiative of a

---

14 Craig Schiller, et al., *Botnets: the Killer Web App*, Syngress Publishing, 2007.

15 David Dittrich, "Distributed denial of service (DDoS) attacks/tools," available at http://staff.washington.edu/dittrich/misc/ddos/ (date of access: July 1, 2008).

series of actions directed at a target. Attackers face the risk of revealing their malicious intentions through these actions. For instance, port scanning, password guessing, or exploit attempts can be readily detected by an IDS as suspicious activities. Sending malware through email can only be seen as an attack attempt.

Security researchers have observed a trend away from direct attacks toward more stealthy attacks that wait for victims to visit malicious Web sites, as shown in Figure 4.2.[16] The Web has become the primary vector for infecting computers, in large part because email has become better secured. Sophos discovers a new malicious Webpage every 14 seconds, on average.[17]

Web-based attacks have significant advantages for attackers. First, they are stealthier and not as "noisy" as active attacks, making it easier to continue undetected for a longer time. Second, Web servers have the intelligence to be stealthy. For instance, Web servers have been found that serve up an attack only once per IP address, and otherwise serve up legitimate content. The malicious server remembers the IP addresses of visitors. Thus, a visitor will be attacked only once, which makes the attack harder to detect. Third, a Web server can serve up different attacks, depending on the visitor's operating system and browser.

As mentioned earlier, a common type of attack carried out through the Web is phishing. A phishing site is typically disguised as a legitimate financial organization or ecommerce business. During the month of December 2007, the Anti-Phishing Working Group found 25,328 new unique phishing sites hijacking 144 brands (www. antiphishing.org).

Another type of Web-based attack is a malicious site that attempts to download malware through a visitor's

browser, called a *drive-by download*. A Web page usually loads a malicious script by means of an iframe (inline frame). It has been reported that most drive-by downloads are hosted on legitimate sites that have been compromised. For example, in June 2007 more than 10,000 legitimate Italian Web sites were discovered to be compromised with malicious code loaded through iframes. Many other legitimate sites are regularly compromised.

Drive-by downloading through a legitimate site holds certain appeal for attackers. First, most users would be reluctant to visit suspicious and potentially malicious sites but will not hesitate to visit legitimate sites in the belief that they are always safe. Even wary Web surfers may be caught off-guard. Second, the vast majority of Web servers run Apache (approximately 50%) or Microsoft IIS (approximately 40%), both of which have vulnerabilities that can be exploited by attackers. Moreover, servers with database applications could be vulnerable to SQL injection attacks. Third, if a legitimate site is compromised with an iframe, the malicious code might go unnoticed by the site owner for some time.

Pull-based attacks pose one challenge to attackers: They must attract visitors to the malicious site somehow while avoiding detection by security researchers. One obvious option is to send out lures in spam. Lures have been disguised as email from the Internal Revenue Service, a security update from Microsoft, or a greeting card. The email attempts to entice the reader to visit a link. On one hand, lures are easier to get through spam filters because they only contain links and not attachments. It is easier for spam filters to detect malware attachments than to determine whether links in email are malicious. On the other hand, spam filters are easily capable of extracting and following links from spam. The greater challenge is to determine whether the linked site is malicious.

3. DEFENSE IN DEPTH

Most security experts would agree with the view that perfect network security is impossible to achieve and that any single defense can always be overcome by an attacker with sufficient resources and motivation. The basic idea behind the *defense-in-depth strategy* is to hinder the attacker as much as possible with multiple layers of defense, even though each layer might be surmountable. More valuable assets are protected behind more layers of defense. The combination of multiple layers increases the cost for the attacker to be successful, and the cost is proportional to the value of the protected

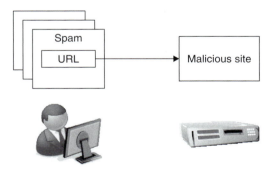

FIGURE 4.2 Stealthy attacks lure victims to malicious servers.

---

16 Joel Scambray, Mike Shema, and Caleb Sima, *Hacking Exposed Web Applications*, 2nd ed., McGraw-Hill, 2006.
17 Sophos, "Security Threat Report 2008," available at http://research. sophos.com/sophosthreatreport08 (date of access: July 1, 2008).

assets. Moreover, a combination of multiple layers will be more effective against unpredictable attacks than will a single defense optimized for a particular type of attack.

The cost for the attacker could be in terms of additional time, effort, or equipment. For instance, by delaying an attacker, an organization would increase the chances of detecting and reacting to an attack in progress. The increased costs to an attacker could deter some attempts if the costs are believed to outweigh the possible gain from a successful attack.

Defense in depth is sometimes said to involve people, technology, and operations. Trained security people should be responsible for securing facilities and information assurance. However, every computer user in an organization should be made aware of security policies and practices. Every Internet user at home should be aware of safe practices (such as avoiding opening email attachments or clicking suspicious links) and the benefits of appropriate protection (antivirus software, firewalls).

A variety of technological measures can be used for layers of protection. These should include firewalls, IDSs, routers with ACLs, antivirus software, access control, spam filters, and so on. These topics are discussed in more depth later.

The term *operations* refers to all preventive and reactive activities required to maintain security. Preventive activities include vulnerability assessments, software patching, system hardening (closing unnecessary ports), and access controls. Reactive activities should detect malicious activities and react by blocking attacks, isolating valuable resources, or tracing the intruder.

Protection of valuable assets can be a more complicated decision than simply considering the value of the assets. Organizations often perform a risk assessment to determine the value of assets, possible threats, likelihood of threats, and possible impact of threats. Valuable assets facing unlikely threats or threats with low impact might not need much protection. Clearly, assets of high value facing likely threats or high-impact threats merit the strongest defenses. Organizations usually have their own risk management process for identifying risks and deciding how to allocate a security budget to protect valuable assets under risk.

4. PREVENTIVE MEASURES

Most computer users are aware that Internet use poses security risks. It would be reasonable to take precautions to minimize exposure to attacks. Fortunately, several options are available to computer users to fortify their systems to reduce risks.

Access Control

In computer security, *access control* refers to mechanisms to allow users to perform functions up to their authorized level and restrict users from performing unauthorized functions.[18] Access control includes:

- Authentication of users
- Authorization of their privileges
- Auditing to monitor and record user actions

All computer users will be familiar with some type of access control.

Authentication is the process of verifying a user's identity. Authentication is typically based on one or more of these factors:

- Something the user knows, such as a password or PIN
- Something the user has, such as a smart card or token
- Something personal about the user, such as a fingerprint, retinal pattern, or other biometric identifier

Use of a single factor, even if multiple pieces of evidence are offered, is considered weak authentication. A combination of two factors, such as a password and a fingerprint, called *two-factor* (or *multifactor*) *authentication,* is considered strong authentication.

Authorization is the process of determining what an authenticated user can do. Most operating systems have an established set of permissions related to read, write, or execute access. For example, an ordinary user might have permission to read a certain file but not write to it, whereas a root or superuser will have full privileges to do anything.

Auditing is necessary to ensure that users are accountable. Computer systems record actions in the system in audit trails and logs. For security purposes, they are invaluable forensic tools to recreate and analyze incidents. For instance, a user attempting numerous failed logins might be seen as an intruder.

Vulnerability Testing and Patching

As mentioned earlier, vulnerabilities are weaknesses in software that might be used to compromise a computer. Vulnerable software includes all types of operating systems and application programs. New vulnerabilities are being discovered constantly in different ways. New vulnerabilities discovered by security researchers are usually

---

18 B. Carroll, *Cisco Access Control Security: AAA Administration Services*, Cisco Press, 2004.

reported confidentially to the vendor, which is given time to study the vulnerability and develop a path. Of all vulnerabilities disclosed in 2007, 50% could be corrected through vendor patches.[19] When ready, the vendor will publish the vulnerability, hopefully along with a patch.

It has been argued that publication of vulnerabilities will help attackers. Though this might be true, publication also fosters awareness within the entire community. Systems administrators will be able to evaluate their systems and take appropriate precautions. One might expect systems administrators to know the configuration of computers on their network, but in large organizations, it would be difficult to keep track of possible configuration changes made by users. Vulnerability testing offers a simple way to learn about the configuration of computers on a network.

Vulnerability testing is an exercise to probe systems for known vulnerabilities. It requires a database of known vulnerabilities, a packet generator, and test routines to generate a sequence of packets to test for a particular vulnerability. If a vulnerability is found and a software patch is available, that host should be patched.

Penetration testing is a closely related idea but takes it further. Penetration testing simulates the actions of a hypothetical attacker to attempt to compromise hosts. The goal is, again, to learn about weaknesses in the network so that they can be remedied.

Closing Ports

Transport layer protocols, namely Transmission Control Protocol (TCP) and User Datagram Protocol (UDP), identify applications communicating with each other by means of port numbers. Port numbers 1 to 1023 are well known and assigned by the Internet Assigned Numbers Authority (IANA) to standardized services running with root privileges. For example, Web servers listen on TCP port 80 for client requests. Port numbers 1024 to 49151 are used by various applications with ordinary user privileges. Port numbers above 49151 are used dynamically by applications.

It is good practice to close ports that are unnecessary, because attackers can use open ports, particularly those in the higher range. For instance, the Sub7 Trojan horse is known to use port 27374 by default, and Netbus uses port 12345. Closing ports does not by itself guarantee the safety of a host, however. Some hosts need to keep TCP port 80 open for HyperText Transfer Protocol (HTTP), but attacks can still be carried out through that port.

Firewalls

When most people think of network security, firewalls are one of the first things to come to mind. Firewalls are a means of perimeter security protecting an internal network from external threats. A firewall selectively allows or blocks incoming and outgoing traffic. Firewalls can be standalone network devices located at the entry to a private network or personal firewall programs running on PCs. An organization's firewall protects the internal community; a personal firewall can be customized to an individual's needs.

Firewalls can provide separation and isolation among various network zones, namely the public Internet, private intranets, and a demilitarized zone (DMZ), as shown in Figure 4.3. The semiprotected DMZ typically includes public services provided by a private organization. Public servers need some protection from the public Internet so they usually sit behind a firewall. This firewall cannot be completely restrictive because the public servers must be externally accessible. Another firewall typically sits between the DMZ and private internal network because the internal network needs additional protection.

There are various types of firewalls: packet-filtering firewalls, stateful firewalls, and proxy firewalls. In any case, the effectiveness of a firewall depends on the configuration of its rules. Properly written rules require detailed knowledge of network protocols. Unfortunately, some firewalls are improperly configured through neglect or lack of training.

Packet-filtering firewalls analyze packets in both directions and either permit or deny passage based on a set of rules. Rules typically examine port numbers, protocols, IP addresses, and other attributes of packet headers.

19 IBM Internet Security Systems, *X-Force 2007 Trend Statistics*, January 2008 (date of access: July 1, 2008).

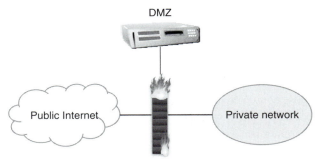

FIGURE 4.3 A firewall isolating various network zones.

There is no attempt to relate multiple packets with a flow or stream. The firewall is stateless, retaining no memory of one packet to the next.

Stateful firewalls overcome the limitation of packet-filtering firewalls by recognizing packets belonging to the same flow or connection and keeping track of the connection state. They work at the network layer and recognize the legitimacy of sessions.

Proxy firewalls are also called application-level firewalls because they process up to the application layer. They recognize certain applications and can detect whether an undesirable protocol is using a nonstandard port or an application layer protocol is being abused. They protect an internal network by serving as primary gateways to proxy connections from the internal network to the public Internet. They could have some impact on network performance due to the nature of the analysis.

Firewalls are essential elements of an overall defensive strategy but have the drawback that they only protect the perimeter. They are useless if an intruder has a way to bypass the perimeter. They are also useless against insider threats originating within a private network.

Antivirus and Antispyware Tools

The proliferation of malware prompts the need for antivirus software.[20] Antivirus software is developed to detect the presence of malware, identify its nature, remove the malware (disinfect the host), and protect a host from future infections. Detection should ideally minimize false positives (false alarms) and false negatives (missed malware) at the same time. Antivirus software faces a number of difficult challenges:

- Malware tactics are sophisticated and constantly evolving.
- Even the operating system on infected hosts cannot be trusted.
- Malware can exist entirely in memory without affecting files.
- Malware can attack antivirus processes.
- The processing load for antivirus software cannot degrade computer performance such that users become annoyed and turn the antivirus software off.

One of the simplest tasks performed by antivirus software is file scanning. This process compares the bytes in files with known signatures that are byte patterns indicative of a known malware. It represents the general approach of signature-based detection. When new malware is captured, it is analyzed for unique characteristics that can be described in a signature. The new signature is distributed as updates to antivirus programs. Antivirus looks for the signature during file scanning, and if a match is found, the signature identifies the malware specifically. There are major drawbacks to this method, however: New signatures require time to develop and test; users must keep their signature files up to date; and new malware without a known signature may escape detection.

Behavior-based detection is a complementary approach. Instead of addressing what malware is, behavior-based detection looks at what malware tries to do. In other words, anything attempting a risky action will come under suspicion. This approach overcomes the limitations of signature-based detection and could find new malware without a signature, just from its behavior. However, the approach can be difficult in practice. First, we must define what is suspicious behavior, or conversely, what is normal behavior. This definition often relies on heuristic rules developed by security experts, because normal behavior is difficult to define precisely. Second, it might be possible to *discern* suspicious behavior, but it is much more difficult to *determine* malicious behavior, because malicious intention must be inferred. When behavior-based detection flags suspicious behavior, more follow-up investigation is usually needed to better understand the threat risk.

The ability of malware to change or disguise appearances can defeat file scanning. However, regardless of its form, malware must ultimately perform its mission. Thus, an opportunity will always arise to detect malware from its behavior if it is given a chance to execute. Antivirus software will monitor system events, such as hard-disk access, to look for actions that might pose a threat to the host. Events are monitored by intercepting calls to operating system functions.

Although monitoring system events is a step beyond file scanning, malicious programs are running in the host execution environment and could pose a risk to the host. The idea of emulation is to execute suspected code within an isolated environment, presenting the appearance of the computer resources to the code, and to look for actions symptomatic of malware.

Virtualization takes emulation a step further and executes suspected code within a real operating system. A number of virtual operating systems can run above the host operating system. Malware can corrupt a virtual operating system, but for safety reasons a virtual operating system has limited access to the host operating system. A "sandbox" isolates the virtual environment from

---

20 Peter Szor, *The Art of Computer Virus Research and Defense*, Addison-Wesley, 2005.

tampering with the host environment, unless a specific action is requested and permitted. In contrast, emulation does not offer an operating system to suspected code; the code is allowed to execute step by step, but in a controlled and restricted way, just to discover what it will attempt to do.

Antispyware software can be viewed as a specialized class of antivirus software. Somewhat unlike traditional viruses, spyware can be particularly pernicious in making a vast number of changes throughout the hard drive and system files. Infected systems tend to have a large number of installed spyware programs, possibly including certain cookies (pieces of text planted by Web sites in the browser as a means of keeping them in memory).

Spam Filtering

Every Internet user is familiar with spam email. There is no consensus on an exact definition of spam, but most people would agree that spam is unsolicited, sent in bulk, and commercial in nature. There is also consensus that the vast majority of email is spam. Spam continues to be a problem because a small fraction of recipients do respond to these messages. Even though the fraction is small, the revenue generated is enough to make spam profitable because it costs little to send spam in bulk. In particular, a large botnet can generate an enormous amount of spam quickly.

Users of popular Webmail services such as Yahoo! and Hotmail are attractive targets for spam because their addresses might be easy to guess. In addition, spammers harvest email addresses from various sources: Web sites, newsgroups, online directories, data-stealing viruses, and so on. Spammers might also purchase lists of addresses from companies who are willing to sell customer information.

Spam is more than an inconvenience for users and a waste of network resources. Spam is a popular vehicle to distribute malware and lures to malicious Web sites. It is the first step in phishing attacks.

Spam filters work at an enterprise level and a personal level. At the enterprise level, mail gateways can protect an entire organization by scanning incoming messages for malware and blocking messages from suspicious or fake senders. A concern at the enterprise level is the rate of false positives, which are legitimate messages mistaken for spam. Users may become upset if their legitimate mail is blocked. Fortunately, spam filters are typically customizable, and the rate of false positives can be made very low. Additional spam filtering at the personal level can customize filtering even further, to account for individual preferences.

Various spam-filtering techniques are embodied in many commercial and free spam filters, such as DSPAM and SpamAssassin, to name two. Bayesian filtering is one of the more popular techniques.[21] First, an incoming message is parsed into tokens, which are single words or word combinations from the message's header and body. Second, probabilities are assigned to tokens through a training process. The filter looks at a set of known spam messages compared to a set of known legitimate messages and calculates token probabilities based on Bayes' theorem (from probability theory). Intuitively, a word such as *Viagra* would appear more often in spam, and therefore the appearance of a Viagra token would increase the probability of that message being classified as spam.

The probability calculated for a message is compared to a chosen threshold; if the probability is higher, the message is classified as spam. The threshold is chosen to balance the rates of false positives and false negatives (missed spam) in some desired way. An attractive feature of Bayesian filtering is that its probabilities will adapt to new spam tactics, given continual feedback, that is, correction of false positives and false negatives by the user.

It is easy to see why spammers have attacked Bayesian filters by attempting to influence the probabilities of tokens. For example, spammers have tried filling messages with large amounts of legitimate text (e.g., drawn from classic literature) or random innocuous words. The presence of legitimate tokens tends to decrease a message's score because they are evidence counted toward the legitimacy of the message.

Spammers are continually trying new ways to get through spam filters. At the same time, security companies respond by adapting their technologies.

Honeypots

The basic idea of a *honeypot* is to learn about attacker techniques by attracting attacks to a seemingly vulnerable host.[22] It is essentially a forensics tool rather than a line of defense. A honeypot could be used to gain valuable information about attack methods used elsewhere or imminent attacks before they happen. Honeypots are used routinely in research and production environments.

A honeypot has more special requirements than a regular PC. First, a honeypot should not be used for legitimate services or traffic. Consequently, every activity

---

21 J. Zdziarski, *Ending Spam: Bayesian Content Filtering and the Art of Statistical Language Classification*, No Starch Press, 2005.
22 The Honeynet Project, *Know Your Enemy: Learning About Security Threats*, 2nd ed., Addison-Wesley, 2004.

seen by the honeypot will be illegitimate. Even though honeypots typically record little data compared to IDS, for instance, their data has little "noise," whereas the bulk of IDS data is typically uninteresting from a security point of view.

Second, a honeypot should have comprehensive and reliable capabilities for monitoring and logging all activities. The forensic value of a honeypot depends on the detailed information it can capture about attacks.

Third, a honeypot should be isolated from the real network. Since honeypots are intended to attract attacks, there is a real risk that the honeypot could be compromised and used as a launching pad to attack more hosts in the network.

Honeypots are often classified according to their level of interaction, ranging from low to high. Low-interaction honeypots, such as Honeyd, offer the appearance of simple services. An attacker could try to compromise the honeypot but would not have much to gain. The limited interactions pose a risk that an attacker could discover that the host is a honeypot. At the other end of the range, high-interaction honeypots behave more like real systems. They have more capabilities to interact with an attacker and log activities, but they offer more to gain if they are compromised.

Honeypots are related to the concepts of black holes or network telescopes, which are monitored blocks of unused IP addresses. Since the addresses are unused, any traffic seen at those addresses is naturally suspicious (although not necessarily malicious).

Traditional honeypots suffer a drawback in that they are passive and wait to see malicious activity. The idea of honeypots has been extended to active clients that search for malicious servers and interact with them. The active version of a honeypot has been called a *honeymonkey* or *client honeypot*.

Network Access Control

A vulnerable host might place not only itself but an entire community at risk. For one thing, a vulnerable host might attract attacks. If compromised, the host could be used to launch attacks on other hosts. The compromised host might give information to the attacker, or there might be trust relationships between hosts that could help the attacker. In any case, it is not desirable to have a weakly protected host on your network.

The general idea of *network access control* (NAC) is to restrict a host from accessing a network unless the host can provide evidence of a strong security posture. The NAC process involves the host, the network (usually

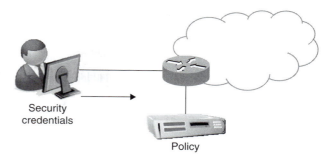

FIGURE 4.4 Network access control.

routers or switches, and servers), and a security policy, as shown in Figure 4.4.

The details of the NAC process vary with various implementations, which unfortunately currently lack standards for interoperability. A host's security posture includes its IP address, operating system, antivirus software, personal firewall, and host intrusion detection system. In some implementations, a software agent runs on the host, collects information about the host's security posture, and reports it to the network as part of a request for admission to the network. The network refers to a policy server to compare the host's security posture to the security policy, to make an admission decision.

The admission decision could be anything from rejection to partial admission or full admission. Rejection might be prompted by out-of-date antivirus software, an operating system needing patches, or firewall misconfiguration. Rejection might lead to quarantine (routing to an isolated network) or forced remediation.

5. INTRUSION MONITORING AND DETECTION

Preventive measures are necessary and help reduce the risk of attacks, but it is practically impossible to prevent all attacks. Intrusion detection is also necessary to detect and diagnose malicious activities, analogous to a burglar alarm. Intrusion detection is essentially a combination of monitoring, analysis, and response.[23] Typically an IDS supports a console for human interface and display. Monitoring and analysis are usually viewed as passive techniques because they do not interfere with ongoing activities. The typical IDS response is an alert to systems administrators, who might choose to pursue further investigation or not. In other words, traditional IDSs do

---

23 Richard Bejtlich, *The Tao of Network Security Monitoring: Beyond Intrusion Detection*, Addison-Wesley, 2005.

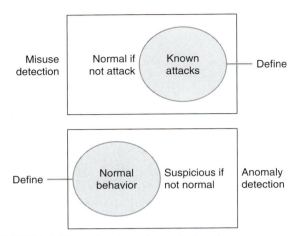

FIGURE 4.5 Misuse detection and anomaly detection.

not offer much response beyond alerts, under the presumption that security incidents need human expertise and judgment for follow-up.

Detection accuracy is the critical problem for intrusion detection. Intrusion detection should ideally minimize false positives (normal incidents mistaken for suspicious ones) and false negatives (malicious incidents escaping detection). Naturally, false negatives are contrary to the essential purpose of intrusion detection. False positives are also harmful because they are troublesome for systems administrators who must waste time investigating false alarms. Intrusion detection should also seek to more than identify security incidents. In addition to relating the facts of an incident, intrusion detection should ascertain the nature of the incident, the perpetrator, the seriousness (malicious vs. suspicious), scope, and potential consequences (such as stepping from one target to more targets).

IDS approaches can be categorized in at least two ways. One way is to differentiate host-based and network-based IDS, depending on where sensing is done. A host-based IDS monitors an individual host, whereas a network-based IDS works on network packets. Another way to view IDS is by their approach to analysis. Traditionally, the two analysis approaches are misuse (signature-based) detection and anomaly (behavior-based) detection. As shown in Figure 4.5, these two views are complementary and are often used in combination.

In practice, intrusion detection faces several difficult challenges: signature-based detection can recognize only incidents matching a known signature; behavior-based detection relies on an understanding of normal behavior, but "normal" can vary widely. Attackers are intelligent and evasive; attackers might try to confuse IDS with fragmented, encrypted, tunneled, or junk packets; an IDS might

not react to an incident in real time or quickly enough to stop an attack; and incidents can occur anywhere at any time, which necessitates continual and extensive monitoring, with correlation of multiple distributed sensors.

Host-Based Monitoring

Host-based IDS runs on a host and monitors system activities for signs of suspicious behavior. Examples could be changes to the system Registry, repeated failed login attempts, or installation of a backdoor. Host-based IDSs usually monitor system objects, processes, and regions of memory. For each system object, the IDS will usually keep track of attributes such as permissions, size, modification dates, and hashed contents, to recognize changes.

A concern for a host-based IDS is possible tampering by an attacker. If an attacker gains control of a system, the IDS cannot be trusted. Hence, special protection of the IDS against tampering should be architected into a host.

A host-based IDS is not a complete solution by itself. Though monitoring the host is logical, it has three significant drawbacks: visibility is limited to a single host; the IDS process consumes resources, possibly impacting performance on the host; and attacks will not be seen until they have already reached the host. Host-based and network-based IDS are often used together to combine strengths.

Traffic Monitoring

Network-based IDSs typically monitor network packets for signs of reconnaissance, exploits, DoS attacks, and malware. They have strengths to complement host-based IDSs: network-based IDSs can see traffic for a population of hosts; they can recognize patterns shared by multiple hosts; and they have the potential to see attacks before they reach the hosts.

IDSs are placed in various locations for different views, as shown in Figure 4.6. An IDS outside a firewall is useful for learning about malicious activities on the Internet. An IDS in the DMZ will see attacks originating from the Internet that are able to get through the outer firewall to public servers. Lastly, an IDS in the private network is necessary to detect any attacks that are able to successfully penetrate perimeter security.

Signature-Based Detection

Signature-based intrusion detection depends on patterns that uniquely identify an attack. If an incident matches

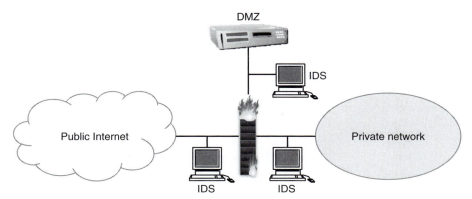

FIGURE 4.6 IDSs monitoring various network zones.

a known signature, the signature identifies the specific attack. The central issue is how to define signatures or model attacks. If signatures are too specific, a change in an attack tactic could result in a false negative (missed alarm). An attack signature should be broad enough to cover an entire class of attacks. On the other hand, if signatures are too general, it can result in false positives.

Signature-based approaches have three inherent drawbacks: new attacks can be missed if a matching signature is not known; signatures require time to develop for new attacks; and new signatures must be distributed continually.

Snort is a popular example of a signature-based IDS (www.snort.org). Snort signatures are rules that define fields that match packets of information about the represented attack. Snort is packaged with more than 1800 rules covering a broad range of attacks, and new rules are constantly being written.

Behavior Anomalies

A behavior-based IDS is appealing for its potential to recognize new attacks without a known signature. It presumes that attacks will be different from normal behavior. Hence the critical issue is how to define normal behavior, and anything outside of normal (anomalous) is classified as suspicious. A common approach is to define normal behavior in statistical terms, which allows for deviations within a range.

Behavior-based approaches have considerable challenges. First, normal behavior is based on past behavior. Thus, data about past behavior must be available for training the IDS. Second, behavior can and does change over time, so any IDS approach must be adaptive. Third, anomalies are just unusual events, not necessarily malicious ones. A behavior-based IDS might point out incidents to investigate further, but it is not good at discerning the exact nature of attacks.

Intrusion Prevention Systems

IDSs are passive techniques. They typically notify the systems administrator to investigate further and take the appropriate action. The response might be slow if the systems administrator is busy or the incident is time consuming to investigate.

A variation called an *intrusion prevention system* (IPS) seeks to combine the traditional monitoring and analysis functions of an IDS with more active automated responses, such as automatically reconfiguring firewalls to block an attack. An IPS aims for a faster response than humans can achieve, but its accuracy depends on the same techniques as the traditional IDS. The response should not harm legitimate traffic, so accuracy is critical.

6. REACTIVE MEASURES

When an attack is detected and analyzed, systems administrators must exercise an appropriate response to the attack. One of the principles in security is that the response should be proportional to the threat. Obviously, the response will depend on the circumstances, but various options are available. Generally, it is possible to block, slow, modify, or redirect any malicious traffic. It is not possible to delineate every possible response. Here we describe only two responses: quarantine and traceback.

Quarantine

Dynamic quarantine in computer security is analogous to quarantine for infectious diseases. It is an appropriate response, particularly in the context of malware, to prevent an infected host from contaminating other hosts. Infectious malware requires connectivity between an infected host and a new target, so it is logical to disrupt

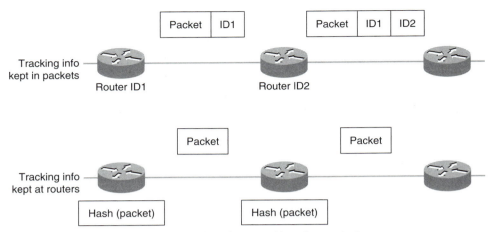

FIGURE 4.7 Tracking information stored at routers or carried in packets to enable packet traceback.

the connectivity between hosts or networks as a means to impede the malware from spreading further.

Within the network, traffic can be blocked by firewalls or routers with access control lists (ACLs). ACLs are similar to firewall rules, allowing routers to selectively drop packets.

Traceback

One of the critical aspects of an attack is the identity or location of the perpetrator. Unfortunately, discovery of an attacker in IP networks is almost impossible because:

- The source address in IP packets can be easily spoofed (forged).
- Routers are stateless by design and do not keep records of forwarded packets.
- Attackers can use a series of intermediary hosts (called *stepping stones* or *zombies*) to carry out their attacks.

Intermediaries are usually innocent computers taken over by an exploit or malware and put under control of the attacker. In practice, it might be possible to trace an attack back to the closest intermediary, but it might be too much to expect to trace an attack all the way back to the real attacker.

To trace a packet's route, some tracking information must be either stored at routers when the packet is forwarded or carried in the packet, as shown in Figure 4.7. An example of the first approach is to store a hash of a packet for some amount of time. If an attack occurs, the target host will query routers for a hash of the attack packet. If a router has the hash, it is evidence that the

packet had been forwarded by that router. To reduce memory consumption, the hash is stored instead of storing the entire packet. The storage is temporary instead of permanent so that routers will not run out of memory.

An example of the second approach is to stamp packets with a unique router identifier, such as an IP address. Thus the packet carries a record of its route. The main advantage here is that routers can remain stateless. The problem is that there is no space in the IP packet header for this scheme.

7. CONCLUSIONS

To guard against network intrusions, we must understand the variety of attacks, from exploits to malware to social engineering. Direct attacks are prevalent, but a class of *pull attacks* has emerged, relying on lures to bring victims to a malicious Web site. Pull attacks are much more difficult to uncover and in a way defend against. Just about anyone can become victimized.

Much can be done to fortify hosts and reduce their risk exposure, but some attacks are unavoidable. Defense in depth is a most practical defense strategy, combining layers of defenses. Although each defensive layer is imperfect, the cost becomes harder to surmount for intruders.

One of the essential defenses is *intrusion detection*. Host-based and network-based intrusion detection systems have their respective strengths and weaknesses. Research continues to be needed to improve intrusion detection, particularly behavior-based techniques. As more attacks are invented, signature-based techniques will have more difficulty keeping up.

## Chapter 5

Unix and Linux Security

Gerald Beuchelt

Sun Microsystems

When Unix was first booted on a PDP-8 computer at Bell Labs, it already had a basic notion of user isolation, separation of kernel and user memory space, and process security. It was originally conceived as a multiuser system, and as such, security could not be added on as an afterthought. In this respect, Unix was different from a whole class of computing machinery that had been targeted at single-user environments.

1. UNIX AND SECURITY

The examples in this chapter refer to the Solaris operating system and Debian-based Linux distributions, a commercial and a community developed operating system.

Solaris is freely available in open source and binary distributions. It derives directly from AT&T System V R4.2 and is one of the few operating systems that can legally be called Unix. It is distributed by Sun Microsystems, but there are independent distributions built on top of the open source version of Solaris.

The Aims of System Security

Linux is mostly a GNU software-based operating system with a kernel originally written by Linus Torvalds. Debian is a distribution originally developed by Ian Murdock of Purdue University. Debian's express goal is to use only open and free software, as defined by its guidelines.

Authentication

When a user is granted access to resources on a computing system, it is of vital importance to verify that he was granted permission for access. This process—establishing the identity of the user—is commonly referred to as *authentication* (sometimes abbreviated *AuthN*).

Authorization

As we mentioned, Unix was originally devised as a multiuser system. To protect user data from other users and nonusers, the operating system has to put up safeguards against unauthorized access. Determining the eligibility of an authenticated (or anonymous) user to access a resource is usually called *authorization* (*AuthZ*).

Availability

Guarding a system (including all its subsystems, such as the network) against security breaches is vital to keep the system available for its intended use. *Availability* of a system must be properly defined: Any system is physically available, even if it is turned off—however, a shutdown system would not be too useful. In the same way, a system that has only the core operating system running but not the services that are supposed to run on the system is considered not available.

Integrity

Similar to availability, a system that is compromised cannot be considered available for regular service. Ensuring that the Unix system is running in the intended way is most crucial, especially since the system might otherwise be used by a third party for malicious uses, such as a relay or member in a botnet.

Achieving Unix Security

Prior to anything else, it is vitally important to emphasize the need to keep Unix systems up to date. No operating system or other program can be considered safe without being patched up; this point cannot be stressed enough. Having a system with the latest security patches is the first and most often the best line of defense against intruders.

The term POSIX stands (loosely) for "Portable Operating System Interface for uniX". From the IEEE 1003.1 Standard, 2004 Edition:

"This standard defines a standard operating system interface and environment, including a command interpreter (or "shell"), and common utility programs to support applications portability at the source code level. This standard is the single common revision to IEEE Std 1003.1-1996, IEEE Std 1003.2-1992, and the Base Specifications of The Open Group Single UNIX Specification, Version 2." Partial or full POSIX compliance is often required for government contracts.

FIGURE 5.1 Various Unix and POSIX standards.

All Unix systems have a patching mechanism; this is a way to get the system up to date. Depending on the vendor and the mechanism used, it is possible to "back out" the patches. For example, on Solaris it is usually possible to remove a patch through the patchrm(1m) command. On Debian-based systems this is not quite as easy, since in a patch the software package to be updated is replaced by a new version. Undoing this is only possible by installing the earlier package.

Detecting Intrusions with Audits and Logs

By default, most Unix systems log kernel messages and important system events from core services. The most common logging tool is the syslog facility, which is controlled from the /etc/syslog.conf file.

2. BASIC UNIX SECURITY

Unix security has a long tradition, and though many concepts of the earliest Unix systems still apply, there have been a large number of changes that fundamentally altered the way the operating system implements these security principles.

One of the reasons that it's complicated to talk about Unix security is that there are a lot of variants of Unix and Unix-like operating systems on the market. In fact, if you only look at some of the core Portable Operating System Interface (POSIX) standards that have been set forth to guarantee a minimal consistency across different Unix flavors (see Figure 5.1), almost every operating system on the market qualifies as Unix (or, more precisely, POSIX compliant). Examples include not only the traditional Unix operating systems such as Solaris, HP-UX, or AIX but also Windows NT-based operating systems (such as Windows XP, either through the native POSIX subsystem or the Services for Windows extensions) or even z/OS.

Traditional Unix Systems

Most traditional Unix systems do share some internal features, though: Their authentication and authorization approaches are similar, their delineation between kernel space and user space goes along the same lines, and their security-related kernel structures are roughly comparable. In the last few years, however, there have been major advancements in extending the original security model by adding role-based access control (RBAC) models to some operating systems.

Kernel Space versus User Land

Unix systems typically execute instructions in one of two general contexts: the kernel or the user space. Code executed in a kernel context has (at least in traditional systems) full access to the entire hardware and software capabilities of the computing environment. Though there are some systems that extend security safeguards into the kernel, in most cases, not only can a rogue kernel execution thread cause massive data corruption, it can effectively bring down the entire operating system.

Obviously, a normal user of an operating system should not wield so much power. To prevent this, user execution threads in Unix systems are not executed in the context of the kernel but in a less privileged context, the user space—sometimes also facetiously called "user land." The Unix kernel defines a structure called *process* (see Figure 5.2) that associates metadata about the user as well as, potentially, other environmental factors with the execution thread and its data. Access to computing resources such as memory, I/O subsystems, and so on is safeguarded by the kernel; if a user process wants to allocate a segment of memory or access a device, it has to make a system call, passing some of its metadata as parameters to the kernel. The kernel then performs an authorization decision and either grants the request or returns an error. It is then the process's responsibility to properly react to either the results of the access or the error.

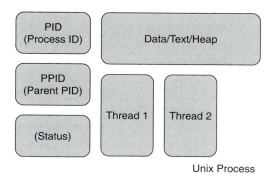

FIGURE 5.2 Kernel structure of a typical Unix process.

If this model of user space process security is so effective, why not implement it for all operating system functions, including the majority of kernel operations? The answer to this question is that to a large extent the overhead of evaluating authorization metadata is very compute expensive. If most or all operations (that are, in the classical kernel space, often hardware-related device access operations) are run in user space or a comparable way, the performance of the OS would severely suffer. There is a class of operating system with a microkernel that implements this approach; the kernel implements only the most rudimentary functions (processes, scheduling, basic security), and all other operations, including device access and other operations that are typically carried out by the kernel, run in separate user processes. The advantage is a higher level of security and better safeguards against rogue device drivers. Furthermore, new device drivers or other operating system functionality can be added or removed without having to reboot the kernel. The performance penalties are so severe, however, that no major commercial operating system implements a microkernel architecture.

User Space Security

In traditional Unix systems, security starts with access control to resources. Since users interact with the systems through processes, it is important to know that every user space process structure has two important security fields: the user identifier, or UID, and the group identifier, or GID. These identifiers are typically positive integers, which are unique for each user.[1] Every process that is started by (or on behalf of) a user inherits the UID

and GID values for that user account. These values are usually immutable for the live time of the process.

Access to system resources must go through the kernel by calling the appropriate function that is accessible to user processes. For example, a process that wants to reserve some system memory for data access will use the malloc() system call and pass the requested size and an (uninitialized) pointer as parameters. The kernel then evaluates this request, determines whether enough virtual memory (physical memory plus swap space) is available, reserves a section of memory, and sets the pointer to the address where the block starts.

Users who have the UID zero have special privileges: They are considered *superusers*, able to override many of the security guards that the kernel sets up. The default Unix superuser is named *root*.

Standard File and Device Access Semantics

File access is a very fundamental task, and it is important that only authorized users get read or write access to a given file. If any user was able to access any file, there would be no privacy at all, and security could not be maintained, since the operating system would not be able to protects its own permanent records, such as configuration information or user credentials.

The metadata describing who may access or modify files and directories is commonly referred to as an *access control list* (ACL). Note that there is more than just one type of ACL; the standard Unix ACLs are very well known, but different Unix variants or POSIX-like operating systems might implement different ACLs and only define a mapping to the simple POSIX 1003 semantics. A good example is the Windows NTFS ACL or the NFS v4 ACLs.

Read, Write, Execute

From its earliest days, Unix implemented a simple but effective way to set access rights for users. Normal files can be accessed in three fundamental ways: read, write, and execute. The first two ways are obvious; the execution requires a little more explanation. A file on disk may only be executed as either a binary program or a script if the user has the right to execute this file. If the execute permission is not set, the system call exec() will fail. In addition to a user's permissions, there must be a notion of ownership of files and sometimes other resources. In fact, each file on a traditional Unix file system is associated with a user and a group. The user and group are not identified by their name but by UID and GID instead.

---

[1] If two usernames are associated with the same UID, the operating system will treat them as the same user. Their authentication credentials (username and password) are different, but their authorization with respect to system resources is the same.

```
Making a directory readable for everyone:

# chmod o+r /tmp/mydir
# ls -ld /tmp/mydir

drwxr-xr-x   2 root      root           117 Aug  9 12:12 /tmp/mydir


Setting the SetID bit on an executable, thus enabling it to be run with super-user privileges:



# chmod u+s specialprivs
# ls -ld specialprivs

-rwsr-xr-x   2 root      root           117 Aug  9 12:12 specialprivs
```

FIGURE 5.3 Examples of chmod for files and directories.

In addition to setting permissions for the user owning the file, two other sets of permissions are set for files: for the group and for all others. Similar to being owned by a user, a file is also associated with one group. All members of this group[2] can access the file with the permissions set for the group. In the same way, the other set of permissions applies to all users of the system.

Special Permissions

In addition to the standard permissions, there are a few special permissions, discussed here.

Set-ID Bit

This permission only applies to executable files, and it can only be set for the user or the group. If this bit is set, the process for this program is not set to the UID or GID of the invoking user but instead the UID or GID of the file. For example, a program owned by the superuser can have the Set-ID bit set and execution allowed for all users. This way a normal user can execute a specific program with elevated privileges.

Sticky Bit

When the sticky bit is set on an executable file, its data (specifically the text segment) is kept in memory, even after the process exits. This is intended to speed execution of commonly used programs. A major drawback of setting the sticky bit is that when the executable file changes (for example, through a patch), the permission must be unset and the program started once more. When

this process exits, the executable is unloaded from memory and the file can be changed.

Mandatory Locking

Mandatory file and record locking refers to a file's ability to have its reading or writing permissions locked while a program is accessing that file.

In addition, there might be additional, implementation-specific permissions. These depend on the capabilities of the core operating facilities, including the kernel, but also on the type of file system. For example, most Unix operating systems can mount FAT-based file systems, which do not support any permissions or user and group ownership. Since the internal semantics require some values for ownership and permissions, these are typically set for the entire file system.

Permissions on Directories

The semantics of permissions on directories (see Figure 5.3) are different from those on files.

Read and Write

Mapping these permissions to directories is fairly straightforward: The read permission allows listing files in the directory, and the write permission allows us to create files. For some applications it can be useful to allow writing but not reading.

Execute

If this permission is set, a process can set its working directory to this directory. Note that with the basic permissions, there is no limitation on traversing directories, so a process might change its working directory to a child of a directory, even if it cannot do so for the directory itself.

---

2 It should be noted that users belong to one primary group, identified by the GID set in the password database. However, group membership is actually determined separately through the /etc/group file. As such, user can be (and often is) a member of more than one group.

SetID

Semantics may differ here. For example, on Solaris this changes the behavior for default ownership of newly created files from the System V to the BSD semantics.

Other File Systems

As mentioned, the set of available permissions and authorization policies depends on the underlying operating system capabilities, including the file system. For example, the UFS file system in Solaris since version 2.5 allows additional ACLs on a per-user basis. Furthermore, NFS version 4 defines additional ACLs for file access; it is obvious that the NFS server must have an underlying files system that is capable of recording this additional metadata.

4. PROTECTING USER ACCOUNTS AND STRENGTHENING AUTHENTICATION

For any interactive session, Unix systems require the user to log into the system. To do so, the user must present a valid credential that identifies him (he must authenticate to the system).

Establishing Secure Account Use

The type of credentials a Unix system uses depends on the capabilities of the OS software itself and on the configuration set forth by the systems administrator. The most traditional user credential is a username and a text password, but there are many other ways to authenticate to the operating system, including Kerberos, SSH, or security certificates.

The Unix Login Process

Depending on the desired authentication mechanism (see Figure 5.4), the user will have to use different access protocols or processes. For example, console or directly attached terminal sessions usually supports only password credentials or smart card logins, whereas a secure shell connection supports only RSA- or DSA-based cryptographic tokens over the SSH protocol.

The login process is a system daemon that is responsible for coordinating authentication and process setup for interactive users. To do this, the login process does the following:

1. Draw or display the login screen.
2. Collect the credential.

Overview of Unix authentication methods

- Simple: a username and a password are used to login to the operating system. The login process must receive both in cleartext. For the password, the Unix crypt hash is calculated and compared to the value in the password or shadow file.

- Kerberos: The user is supposed to have a ticket-granting ticket from the Kerberos Key Distribution Server (KDC). Using the ticket-granting ticket, he obtains a service ticket for an interactive login to the Unix host. This service ticket (encrypted, time limited) is then presented to the login process, and the Unix host validates it with the KDC.

- PKI based Smartcard: the private key on the smart card is used to authenticate with the system.

FIGURE 5.4 Various authentication mechanisms for Unix systems.

3. Present the user credential to any of the configured user databases (typically these can be files, NIS, Kerberos servers, or LDAP directories) for authentication.
4. Create a process with the user's default command-line shell, with the home directory as working directory.
5. Execute systemwide, user, and shell-specific startup scripts.

The commonly available X11 windowing system does not use the text-oriented login process but instead provides its own facility to perform roughly the same kind of login sequence.

Access to interactive sessions using the SSH protocol follows a similar general pattern, but the authentication is significantly different from the traditional login process.

Controlling Account Access

Simple files were the first method available to store user account data. Over the course of years many other user databases have been implemented. We examine these here.

The Local Files

Originally, Unix only supported a simple password file for storing account information. The username and the information required for the login process (UID, GID, shell, home directory, and GECOS information) are stored in this file, which is typically at /etc/passwd. This

```
# /etc/nsswitch.conf

#
# Example configuration of GNU Name Service Switch functionality.
#
passwd:          files nis

group:           files nis
shadow:          files nis

hosts:           files nis dns
networks:        files

protocols:       db files
services:        db files
ethers:          db files
rpc:             db files
netgroup:        nis
```

FIGURE 5.5 Sample nsswitch.conf for a Debian system.

approach is highly insecure, since this file needs to be readable by all for a number of different services, thus exposing the password hashes to potential hackers. In fact, a simple dictionary or even brute-force attack can reveal simple or even more complex passwords.

To protect against an attack like this, most Unix variants use a separate file for storing the password hashes (/etc/shadow) that is only readable and writable by the system.

Network Information System

The Network Information System (NIS) was introduced to simplify the administration of small groups of computers. Originally, Sun Microsystems called this service Yellow Pages, but the courts decided that this name constituted a trademark infringement on the British Telecom Yellow Pages. However, most commands that are used to administer the NIS still start with the yp prefix (such as ypbind, ypcat, etc.).

Systems within the NIS are said to belong to a NIS domain. Although there is absolutely no correlation between the NIS domain and the DNS domain of the system, it is quite common to use DNS-style domain names for naming NIS domains. For example, a system with DNS name system1.sales.example.com might be a member of the NIS domain nis.sales.Example.COM. Note that NIS domains—other than DNS domains—are case sensitive.

The NIS uses a simple master/slave server system: The master NIS server holds all authoritative data and uses an ONC-RPC-based protocol to communicate with the slave servers and clients. Slave servers cannot be easily upgraded to a master server, so careful planning of the infrastructure is highly recommended.

Client systems are bound to one NIS server (master or slave) during runtime. The addresses for the NIS master and the slaves must be provided when joining a system to the NIS domain. Clients (and servers) can always be members of only one NIS domain. To use the NIS user database (and other NIS resources, such as automount maps, netgroups, and host tables) after the system is bound, use the name service configuration file (/etc/nsswitch.conf), as shown in Figure 5.5.

Using PAMs to Modify AuthN

These user databases can easily be configured for use on a given system through the /etc/nsswitch.conf file. However, in more complex situations, the administrator might want to fine-tune the types of acceptable authentication methods, such as Kerberos, or even configure multifactor authentication. On many Unix systems, this is typically achieved through the pluggable authentication mechanism (PAM), as shown in Figure 5.6. Traditionally, the PAM is configured through the /etc/pam.conf file, but more modern implementations use a directory structure, similar to the System V init scripts. For these systems the administrator needs to modify the configuration files in the /etc/pam.d/ directory.

Noninteractive Access

The security configuration of noninteractive services can vary quite significantly. Especially popular network services, such as LDAP, HTTP, or NFS, can use a wide variety of authentication and authorization mechanisms that do not even need to be provided by the operating system. For example, an Apache Web server or a MySQL database server might use its own user database, without relying on any operating system services.

```
# /etc/pam.d/common-password - password-related modules common to all services
#

# This file is included from other service-specific PAM config files,
# and should contain a list of modules that define the services to be
# used to change user passwords.  The default is pam_unix.

# Explanation of pam_unix options:
#
# The "nullok" option allows users to change an empty password, else
# empty passwords are treated as locked accounts.
#

# The "md5" option enables MD5 passwords.  Without this option, the
# default is Unix crypt.
#

# The "obscure" option replaces the old `OBSCURE_CHECKS_ENAB' option in
# login.defs.
#

# You can also use the "min" option to enforce the length of the new
# password.
#
# See the pam_unix manpage for other options.

password    requisite   pam_unix.so nullok obscure md5

# Alternate strength checking for password. Note that this
# requires the libpam-cracklib package to be installed.
# You will need to comment out the password line above and
# uncomment the next two in order to use this.
# (Replaces the `OBSCURE_CHECKS_ENAB', `CRACKLIB_DICTPATH')
#

password required   pam_cracklib.so retry=3 minlen=6 difok=3

password required   pam_unix.so use_authtok nullok md5
```

FIGURE 5.6 Setting the password strength on a Debian-based system through the PAM system.

Other Network Authentication Mechanisms

In 1983, BSD introduced the rlogin service. Unix administrators have been using RSH, RCP, and other tools from this package for a long time; they are very easy to use and configure and provide simple access across a small network of computers. The login was facilitated through a very simple trust model: Any user could create a .rhosts file in her home directory and specify foreign hosts and users from which to accept logins without proper credential checking. Over the rlogin protocol (TCP 513), the username of the rlogin client would be transmitted to the host system, and in lieu of an authentication, the rshd daemon would simply verify the preconfigured values. To prevent access from untrusted hosts, the administrator could use the /etc/hosts.equiv file to allow or deny individual hosts or groups of hosts (the latter through the use of NIS netgroups).

Risks of Trusted Hosts and Networks

Since no authentication ever takes place, this trust mechanism should not be used. Not only does this system rely entirely on the correct functioning of the hostname resolution system, but in addition, there is no way to determine whether a host was actually replaced.[3] Also, though rlogin-based trust systems might work for very small deployments, they become extremely hard to set up and operate with large numbers of machines.

Replacing Telnet, rlogin, and FTP Servers and Clients with SSH

The most sensible alternative to the traditional interactive session protocols such as Telnet is the secure shell (SSH) system. It is very popular on Unix systems, and

---

3 This could actually be addressed through host authentication, but it is not a feature of the rlogin protocol.

pretty much all versions ship with a version of SSH. Where SSH is not available, the open source package OpenSSH can easily be used instead[4].

SSH combines the ease-of-use features of the rlogin tools with a strong cryptographic authentication system. On one hand, it is fairly easy for users to enable access from other systems; on the other hand, the secure shell protocol uses strong cryptography to:

- Authenticate the connection, that is, establish the authenticity of the user
- Protect the privacy of the connection through encryption
- Guarantee the integrity of the channel through signatures

This is done using either the RSA or DSA security algorithm, which are both available for the SSH v2[5] protocol. The cipher (see Figure 5.7) used for encryption can be explicitly selected.

The user must first create a public/private key pair through the ssh-keygen(1) tool. The output of the key generator is placed in the .ssh subdirectory of the user's home directory. This output consists of a private key file called id_dsa or id_rsa. This file must be owned by the user and can only be readable by the user. In addition, a file containing the public key is created, named in the same way, with the extension .pub appended. The public key file is then placed into the .ssh subdirectory of the user's home directory on the target system.

Once the public and private keys are in place and the SSH daemon is enabled on the host system, all clients that implement the SSH protocol can create connections. There are four common applications using SSH:

- Interactive session is the replacement for Telnet and rlogin. Using the ssh(1) command line, the sshd daemon creates a new shell and transfers control to the user.
- In a remotely executed script/command, ssh(1) allows a single command with arguments to pass. This way, a single remote command (such as a backup script) can be executed on the remote system as long as this command is in the default path for the user.
- An SSH-enabled file transfer program can be used to replace the standard FTP or FTP over SSL protocol.
- Finally, the SSH protocol is able to tunnel arbitrary protocols. This means that any client can use the privacy and integrity protection offered by SSH. In particular, the X-Window system protocol can tunnel

---

4 See [IEEE04]. www.opengroup.org/onlinepubs/009695399/
5 See [IETF4252]. http://tools.ietf.org/html/rfc4252

```
$ ssh host -luser1 -c aes192-cbc
```
FIGURE 5.7 Create an interactive session on Solaris to host for user1 using the AES cipher with 192 bits.

through an existing SSH connection by using the -X command-line switch.

5. REDUCING EXPOSURE TO THREATS BY LIMITING SUPERUSER PRIVILEGES

The superuser has almost unlimited power on a Unix system, which can be a significant problem.

Controlling Root Access

There are a number of ways to limit access for the root user.

Configuring Secure Terminals

Most Unix systems allow us to restrict root logins to special terminals, typically the system console. This approach is quite effective, especially if the console or the allowed terminals are under strict physical access control. The obvious downside of this approach is that remote access to the system can be very limited: using this approach, access through any TCP/IP-based connection cannot be configured, thus requiring a direct connection, such as a directly attached terminal or a modem.

Configuration is quite different for the various Unix systems. Figure 5.8 shows the comparison between Solaris and Debian.

Gaining Root Privileges with su

The su(1) utility allows changing the identity of an interactive session. This is an effective mediation of the issues that come with restricting root access to secure terminals: Though only normal users can get access to the machine through the network (ideally by limiting the access protocols to those that protect the privacy of the communication, such as SSH), they can change their interactive session to a superuser session.

Using Groups Instead of Root

If users should be limited to executing certain commands with superuser privileges, it is possible and common to create special groups of users. For these groups, we can set the execution bit on programs (while disabling execution for all others) and the SetID bit for the owner, in this case the superuser. Therefore, only users of such a special group can execute the given utility with superuser privileges.

On Solaris simply edit the file /etc/default/login:

```
# Copyright 2004 Sun Microsystems, Inc.  All rights reserved.
# Use is subject to license terms.

# If CONSOLE is set, root can only login on that device.
# Comment this line out to allow remote login by root.
#

CONSOLE=/dev/console

# PASSREQ determines if login requires a password.
#

PASSREQ=YES

# SUPATH sets the initial shell PATH variable for root
#

SUPATH=/usr/sbin:/usr/bin


# SYSLOG determines whether the syslog(3) LOG_AUTH facility should be used
# to log all root logins at level LOG_NOTICE and multiple failed login
# attempts at LOG_CRIT.
#

SYSLOG=YES

# The SYSLOG_FAILED_LOGINS variable is used to determine how many failed
# login attempts will be allowed by the system before a failed login
# message is logged, using the syslog(3) LOG_NOTICE facility.  For
example,
# if the variable is set to 0, login will log -all- failed login attempts.
#

SYSLOG_FAILED_LOGINS=5


On Debian:

# The PAM configuration file for the Shadow `login' service
#


# Disallows root logins except on tty's listed in /etc/securetty
# (Replaces the `CONSOLE' setting from login.defs)

auth       requisite  pam_securetty.so
# Disallows other than root logins when /etc/nologin exists
# (Replaces the `NOLOGINS_FILE' option from login.defs)

auth       requisite  pam_nologin.so

# Standard Un*x authentication.

@include common-auth

# This allows certain extra groups to be granted to a user
# based on things like time of day, tty, service, and user.
# Please edit /etc/security/group.conf to fit your needs
# (Replaces the `CONSOLE_GROUPS' option in login.defs)
```

FIGURE 5.8 Restricting root access.

```
auth       optional   pam_group.so

# Uncomment and edit /etc/security/time.conf if you need to set
# time restrainst on logins.
# (Replaces the `PORTTIME_CHECKS_ENAB' option from login.defs
# as well as /etc/porttime)

account    requisite  pam_time.so



# Uncomment and edit /etc/security/access.conf if you need to
# set access limits.
# (Replaces /etc/login.access file)

account  required       pam_access.so

# Sets up user limits according to /etc/security/limits.conf
# (Replaces the use of /etc/limits in old login)

session    required    pam_limits.so

# Prints the last login info upon succesful login
# (Replaces the `LASTLOG_ENAB' option from login.defs)

session    optional    pam_lastlog.so

# Standard Un*x account and session

@include common-account
@include common-session
@include common-password
```

FIGURE 5.8 (Continued).

Using the sudo(1) Mechanism

By far more flexible and easier to manage than the approach for enabling privileged execution based on groups is the sudo(1) mechanism. Originally an open source program, sudo(1) is available for most Unix distributions. The detailed configuration is quite complex, and the manual page is quite informative.

6. SAFEGUARDING VITAL DATA BY SECURING LOCAL AND NETWORK FILE SYSTEMS

For production systems, there is a very effective way of preventing the modification of system-critical resources by unauthorized users or malicious software. Critical portions of the file systems (such as the locations of binary files, system libraries, and some configuration files) do not necessarily change very often.

Directory Structure and Partitioning for Security

In fact, any systemwide binary code should probably only be modified by the systems administrators. In these cases, it is very effective to properly partition the file system.

Employing Read-Only Partitions

The reason to properly partition the file system (see Figure 5.9) is so that only frequently changing files (such as user data, log files, and the like) are hosted on readable file systems. All other storage can then be mounted on read-only partitions.

The following scheme is a good start for partitioning with read-only partitions:

- Binaries and Libraries: /bin, /lib, /sbin, /usr - read-only
- Logs and frequently changing system data: /var, /usr/var - writable
- User home directories: /home, /export/home - writable
- Additional software packages: /opt, /usr/local - read-only
- System configuration: /etc, /usr/local/etc - writable
- Everything else: Root (/) - read-only

Obviously, this can only be a start and should be evaluated for each system and application. Updating operating system files, including those on the root file system, should be performed in single-user mode with all partitions mounted writable.

FIGURE 5.9 Secure partitioning.

```
$ find /  \( -perm -04000 -o -perm -02000\) -type f -xdev -print
```
FIGURE 5.10 Finding files with SUID and SGID set.

Ownership and Access Permissions

To prevent inadvertent or malicious access to critical data, it is vitally important to verify the correct ownership and permission set for all critical files in the file system. The Unix find(1) command is an effective way to locate files with certain characteristics. In the following, a number of sample command-line options for this utility are given to locate files.

Locate SetID Files

Since executables with the SetID bit set are often used to allow the execution of a program with superuser

```
$ find / -nouser
```
FIGURE 5.11 Finding files without users.

privileges, it is vitally important to monitor these files on a regular basis.

Another critical permission set is that of world-writable files; there should be no system-critical files in this list, and users should be aware of any files in their home directories that are world-writable (see Figure 5.10).

Finally, files and directories that are not owned by current users can be found by the code shown in Figure 5.11.

For groups, just use -nogroup instead.

## Chapter 6

Eliminating the Security Weakness of Linux and UNIX Operating Systems

Mario Santana

Terremark

Linux and other Unix-like operating systems are prevalent on the Internet for a number of reasons. As an operating system designed to be flexible and robust, Unix lends itself to providing a wide array of host- and network-based services. Unix also has a rich culture from its long history as a fundamental part of computing research in industry and academia. Unix and related operating systems play a key role as platforms for delivering the key services that make the Internet possible.

For these reasons, it is important that information security practitioners understand fundamental Unix concepts in support of practical knowledge of how Unix systems might be securely operated. This chapter is an introduction to Unix in general and to Linux in particular, presenting some historical context and describing some fundamental aspects of the operating system architecture. Considerations for hardening Unix deployments will be contemplated from network-centric, host-based, and systems management perspectives. Finally, proactive considerations are presented to identify security weaknesses to correct them and to deal effectively with security breaches when they do occur.

1. INTRODUCTION TO LINUX AND UNIX

A simple Google search for "define:unix" yields many definitions, including this one from Microsoft: "A powerful multitasking operating system developed in 1969 for use in a minicomputer environment; still a widely used network operating system."[1]

What Is Unix?

Unix is many things. Officially, it is a brand and an operating system specification. In common usage the word

Unix is often used to refer to one or more of many operating systems that derive from or are similar to the operating system designed and implemented about 40 years ago at AT&T Bell Laboratories. Throughout this chapter, we'll use the term *Unix* to include official Unix-branded operating systems as well as Unix-like operating systems such as BSD, Linux, and even Macintosh OS X.

History

Years after AT&T's original implementation, there followed decades of aggressive market wars among many operating system vendors, each claiming that its operating system was Unix. The ever-increasing incompatibilities between these different versions of Unix were seen as a major deterrent to the marketing and sales of Unix. As personal computers grew more powerful and flexible, running inexpensive operating systems like Microsoft Windows and IBM OS/2, they threatened Unix as the server platform of choice. In response to these and other marketplace pressures, most major Unix vendors eventually backed efforts to standardize the Unix operating system.

Unix Is a Brand

Since the early 1990s, the Unix brand has been owned by The Open Group. This organization manages a set of specifications with which vendors must comply to use the Unix brand in referring to their operating system products. In this way, The Open Group provides a guarantee to the marketplace that any system labeled as Unix conforms to a strict set of standards.

Unix Is a Specification

The Open Group's standard is called the Single Unix Specification. It is created in collaboration with the Institute of Electrical and Electronics Engineers (IEEE), the International Standards Organization (ISO), and others.

---

1 Microsoft, n.d., "Glossary of Networking Terms for Visio IT Professionals", retrieved September 22, 2008, from Microsoft TechNet: http://technet.microsoft.com/en-us/library/cc751329.aspx#XSLT section142121120120.

The specification is developed, refined, and updated in an open, transparent process.

The Single Unix Specification comprises several components, covering core system interfaces such as system calls as well as commands, utilities, and a development environment based on the C programming language. Together, these describe a "functional superset of consensus-based specifications and historical practice."[2]

Lineage

The phrase *historical practice* in the description of the Single Unix Specification refers to the many operating systems historically referring to themselves as Unix. These include everything from AT&T's original releases to the versions released by the University of California at Berkeley and major commercial offerings by the likes of IBM, Sun, Digital Equipment Corporation (DEC), Hewlett-Packard (HP), the Santa Cruz Operation (SCO), Novell, and even Microsoft. But any list of Unix operating systems would be incomplete if it didn't mention Linux (see Figure 6.1).

What Is Linux?

Linux is a bit of an oddball in the Unix operating system lineup. That's because, unlike the Unix versions released by the major vendors, Linux did not reuse any existing source code. Instead, Linux was developed from scratch by a Finnish university student named Linus Torvalds.

Most Popular Unix-Like OS

Linux was written from the start to function very similarly to existing Unix products. And because Torvalds worked on Linux as a hobby, with no intention of making money, it was distributed for free. These factors and others contributed to making Linux the most popular Unix operating system today.

Linux Is a Kernel

Strictly speaking, Torvalds' pet project has provided only one part of a fully functional Unix operating system: the kernel. The other parts of the operating system, including the commands, utilities, development environment, desktop environment, and other aspects of a full Unix

operating system, are provided by other parties, including GNU, XOrg, and others.

Linux Is a Community

Perhaps the most fundamentally different thing about Linux is the process by which it is developed and improved. As the hobby project that it was, Linux was released by Torvalds on the Internet in the hopes that someone out there might find it interesting. A few programmers saw Torvalds' hobby kernel and began working on it for fun, adding features and fleshing out functionality in a sort of unofficial partnership with Torvald. At this point, everyone was just having fun, tinkering with interesting concepts. As more and more people joined the unofficial club, Torvalds' pet project ballooned into a worldwide phenomenon.

Today, Linux is developed and maintained by hundreds of thousands of contributors all over the world. In 1996, Eric S. Raymond[3] famously described the distributed development methodology used by Linux as a bazaar—a wild, uproarious collection of people, each developing whatever feature they most wanted in an operating system, or improving whatever shortcoming most impacted them; yet somehow, this quick-moving community resulted in a development process that was stable as a whole, and that produced an amazing amount of progress in a very short time.

This is radically different from the way in which Unix systems have typically been developed. If the Linux community is like a bazaar, then other Unix systems can be described as a cathedral—carefully preplanned and painstakingly assembled over a long period of time, according to specifications handed down by master architects from previous generations. Recently, however, some of the traditional Unix vendors have started moving toward a more decentralized, bazaar-like development model similar in many ways to the Linux methodology.

Linux Is Distributions

The Open Source movement in general is very important to the success of Linux. Thanks to GNU, XOrg, and other open-source contributors, there was an almost complete Unix already available when the Linux kernel was released. Linux only filled in the final missing component

---

2 The Open Group, n.d., "The Single Unix Specification", retrieved September 22, 2008, from What Is Unix: www.unix.org/what_is_unix/single_unix_specification.html.

3 E. S. Raymond, September 11, 2000, "The Cathedral and the Bazaar", retrieved September 22, 2008, from Eric S. Raymond's homepage: www.catb.org/esr/writings/cathedral-bazaar/cathedral-bazaar/index.html.

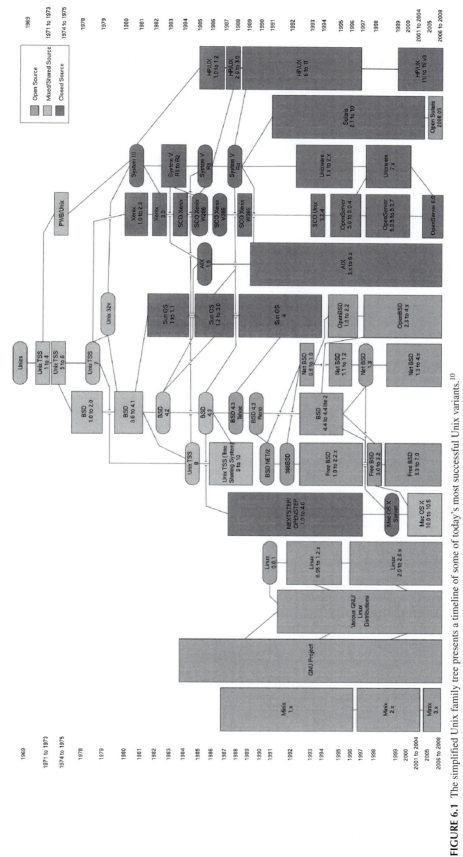

FIGURE 6.1 The simplified Unix family tree presents a timeline of some of today's most successful Unix variants.[10]

10 M. Hutton, July 9, 2008, "Image: Unix History", retrieved October 6, 2008, from Wikipedia: http://en.wikipedia.org/wiki/Image:Unix_history-simple.svg.

of a no-cost, open source Unix. Because the majority of the other parts of the operating system came from the GNU project, Linux is also known as GNU/Linux.

To actually install and run Linux, it is necessary to collect all the other operating system components. Because of the interdependency of the operating system components—each component must be compatible with the others—it is important to gather the right versions of all these components. In the early days of Linux, this was quite a challenge!

Soon, however, someone gathered up a self-consistent set of components and made them all available from a central download location. The first such efforts include H. J. Lu's "boot/root" floppies and MCC Interim Linux. These folks did not necessarily develop any of these components; they only redistributed them in a more convenient package. Other people did the same, releasing new bundles called *distributions* whenever a major upgrade was available.

Some distributions touted the latest in hardware support; others specialized in mathematics or graphics or another type of computing; still others built a distribution that would provide the simplest or most attractive user experience. Over time, distributions have become more robust, offering important features such as package management, which allows a user to safely upgrade parts of the system without reinstalling everything else.

Linux Standard Base

Today there are dozens of Linux distributions. Different flavors of distributions have evolved over the years. A primary distinguishing feature is the package management system. Some distributions are primarily volunteer community efforts; others are commercial offerings. See Figure 6.2 for a timeline of Linux development.[4]

The explosion in the number of different Linux distributions created a situation reminiscent of the Unix wars of previous decades. To address this issue, the Linux Standard Base was created to specify certain key standards of behavior for conforming Linux distributions. Most major distributions comply with the Linux Standard Base specifications.

System Architecture

The architecture of Unix operating systems is relatively simple. The kernel interfaces with hardware and provides

core functionality for the system. File systems provide permanent storage and access to many other kinds of functionality. Processes embody programs as their instructions are being executed. Permissions describe the actions that users may take on files and other resources.

Kernel

The operating system kernel manages many of the fundamental details that an operating system needs to deal with, including memory, disk storage, and low-level networking. In general, the kernel is the part of the operating system that talks directly to hardware; it presents an abstracted interface to the rest of the operating system components.

Because the kernel understands all the different sorts of hardware that the operating system deals with, the rest of the operating system is freed from needing to understand all those underlying details. The abstracted interface presented by the kernel allows other parts of the operating system to read and write files or communicate on the network without knowing or caring what kinds of disks or network adapter are installed.

File System

A fundamental aspect of Unix is its file system. Unix pioneered the hierarchical model of directories that contain files and/or other directories to allow the organization of data into a tree structure. Multiple file systems could be accessed by connecting them to empty directories in the root file system. In essence, this is very much like grafting one hierarchy onto an unused branch of another. There is no limit to the number of file systems that can be mounted in this way.

The file system hierarchy is also used to provide more than just access to and organization of local files. Network data shares can also be mounted, just like file systems on local disks. And special files such as device files, first in/first out (FIFO) or pipe files, and others give direct access to hardware or other system features.

Users and Groups

Unix was designed to be a time-sharing system, and as such has been multiuser since its inception. Users are identified in Unix by their usernames, but internally each is represented as a unique identifying integer called a *user ID*, or *UID*. Each user can also belong to one or more groups. Like users, groups are identified by their names, but they are represented internally as a unique integer called a *group ID*, or *GID*. Each file or

---

4 A. Lundqvist, May 12, 2008, "Image:Gldt", retrieved October 6, 2008, from Wikipedia: http://en.wikipedia.org/wiki/Image:Gldt.svg.

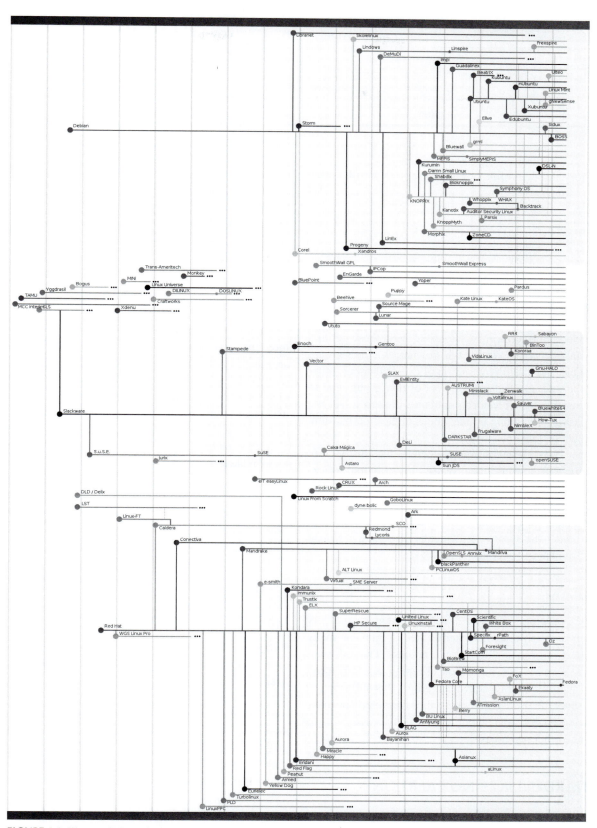

FIGURE 6.2 History of Linux distributions.

TABLE 6.1 Unix permissions and chmod

chmod usage	Read	Write	Execute	Special
User	u + r or 0004	u + w or 0002	u + x or 0001	u + s or 4000
Group	u + r or 0040	u + w or 0020	u + x or 0010	u + s or 2000
Other	u + r or 0400	u + w or 0200	u + x or 0100	u + s or 1000

directory in a Unix file system is associated with a user and a group.

Permissions

Unix has traditionally had a simple permissions architecture, based on the user and group associated with files in the file system. This scheme makes it possible to specify read, write, and/or execute permissions, along with a special permission setting whose effect is context-dependent. Furthermore, it's possible to set these permissions independently for the file's owner; the file's group, in which case the permission applies to all users, other than the owner, who are members of that group; and to all other users. The chmod command is used to set the permissions by adding up the values of each permission, as shown in Table 6.1.

The Unix permission architecture has historically been the target of criticism for its simplicity and inflexibility. It is not possible, for example, to specify a different permission setting for more than one user or more than one group. These limitations have been addressed in more recent file system implementations using extended file attributes and access control lists.

Processes

When a program is executed, it is represented in a Unix system as a process. The kernel keeps track of many pieces of information about each process. This information is required for basic housekeeping and advanced tasks such as tracing and debugging. This information represents the user, group, and other data used for making security decisions about a process's access rights to files and other resources.

2. HARDENING LINUX AND UNIX

With a basic understanding of the fundamental concepts of the Unix architecture, let's take a look at the practical work

of securing a Unix deployment. First we'll review considerations for securing Unix machines from network-borne attacks. Then we'll look at security from a host-based perspective. Finally, we'll talk about systems management and how different ways of administering a Unix system can impact security.

Network Hardening

Defending from network-borne attacks is arguably the most important aspect of Unix security. Unix machines are used heavily to provide network-based services, running Web sites, DNS, firewalls, and many more. To provide these services, Unix systems must be connected to hostile networks, such as the Internet, where legitimate users can easily access and make use of these services.

Unfortunately, providing easy access to legitimate users makes the system easily accessible to bad actors who would subvert access controls and other security measures to steal sensitive information, change reference data, or simply make services unavailable to legitimate users. Attackers can probe systems for security weaknesses, identify and exploit vulnerabilities, and generally wreak digital havoc with relative impunity from anywhere around the globe.

Minimizing Attack Surface

Every way in which an attacker can interact with the system poses a security risk. Any system that makes available a large number of network services, especially complex services such as the custom Web applications of today, suffers a higher likelihood that inadequate permissions or a software bug or some other error will present attackers with an opportunity to compromise security. In contrast, even a very insecure service cannot be compromised if it is not running.

A pillar of any security architecture is the concept of minimizing the attack surface. By reducing the number of enabled network services and by reducing the available functionality of those services that are enabled, a system presents a smaller set of functions that can be subverted by an attacker. Other ways to reduce attackable surface area are to deny network access from unknown hosts when possible and to limit the privileges of running services, to limit the extent of the damage they might be subverted to cause.

Eliminate Unnecessary Services

The first step in reducing attack surface is to disable unnecessary services provided by a server. In Unix, services are enabled in one of several ways. The "Internet daemon," or *inetd*, is a historically popular mechanism for managing network services. Like many Unix programs, inetd is configured by editing a text file. In the case of inetd, this text file is /etc/inetd.conf; unnecessary services should be commented out of this file. Today a more modular replacement for inetd, called *xinetd*, is gaining popularity. The configuration for xinetd is not contained in any single file but in many files located in the /etc/xinetd.d/ directory. Each file in this directory configures a single service, and a service may be disabled by removing the file or by making the appropriate changes to the file.

Many Unix services are not managed by inetd or xinetd, however. Network services are often started by the system's initialization scripts during the boot sequence. Derivatives of the BSD Unix family historically used a simple initialization script located in /etc/rc. To control the services that are started during the boot sequence, it is necessary to edit this script.

Recent Unices (the plural of Unix), even BSD derivatives, use something similar to the initialization scheme of the System V family. In this scheme, a "run level" is chosen at boot time. The default run level is defined in /etc/inittab; typically, it is 3 or 5. The initialization scripts for each run level are located in /etc/rcX.d, where X represents the run-level number. The services that are started during the boot process are controlled by adding or removing scripts in the appropriate run-level directory. Some Unices provide tools to help manage these scripts, such as the chkconfig command in Red Hat Linux and derivatives. There are also other methods of managing services in Unix, such as the Service Management Facility of Solaris 10.

No matter how a network service is started or managed, however, it must necessarily listen for network connections to make itself available to users. This fact makes it possible to positively identify all running network services by looking for processes that are listening for network connections. Almost all versions of Unix provide a command that makes this a trivial task. The netstat command can be used to list various kinds of information about the network environment of a Unix host. Running this command with the appropriate flags (usually –lut) will produce a listing of all open network ports, including those that are listening for incoming connections (see Figure 6.3).

Every such listening port should correspond to a necessary service that is well understood and securely configured.

Host-based

Obviously, it is impossible to disable all the services provided by a server. However, it is possible to limit the hosts that have access to a given service. Often it is possible to identify a well-defined list of hosts or subnets that should be granted access to a network service. There are several ways in which this restriction can be configured.

A classical way of configuring these limitations is through the *tcpwrappers* interface. The tcpwrappers functionality is to limit the network hosts that are allowed to access services provided by the server. These controls are configured in two text files, /etc/hosts.allow and /etc/hosts.deny. This interface was originally designed to be used by inetd and xinetd on behalf of the services they manage. Today most service-providing software directly supports this functionality.

Another, more robust method of controlling network access is through firewall configurations. Most modern Unices include some form of firewall capability: IPFilter, used by many commercial Unices; IPFW, used by most of the BSD variants, and IPTables, used by Linux. In all cases, the best way to arrive at a secure configuration is to create a default rule to deny all traffic, and to then create the fewest, most specific exceptions possible.

Modern firewall implementations are able to analyze every aspect of the network traffic they filter as well as aggregate traffic into logical connections and track the state of those connections. The ability to accept or deny connections based on more than just the originating network address and to end a conversation when certain conditions are met makes modern firewalls a much more powerful control for limiting attack surface than tcpwrappers.

chroot and Other Jails

Eventually some network hosts must be allowed to access a service if it is to be useful at all. In fact, it is often necessary to allow anyone on the Internet to access

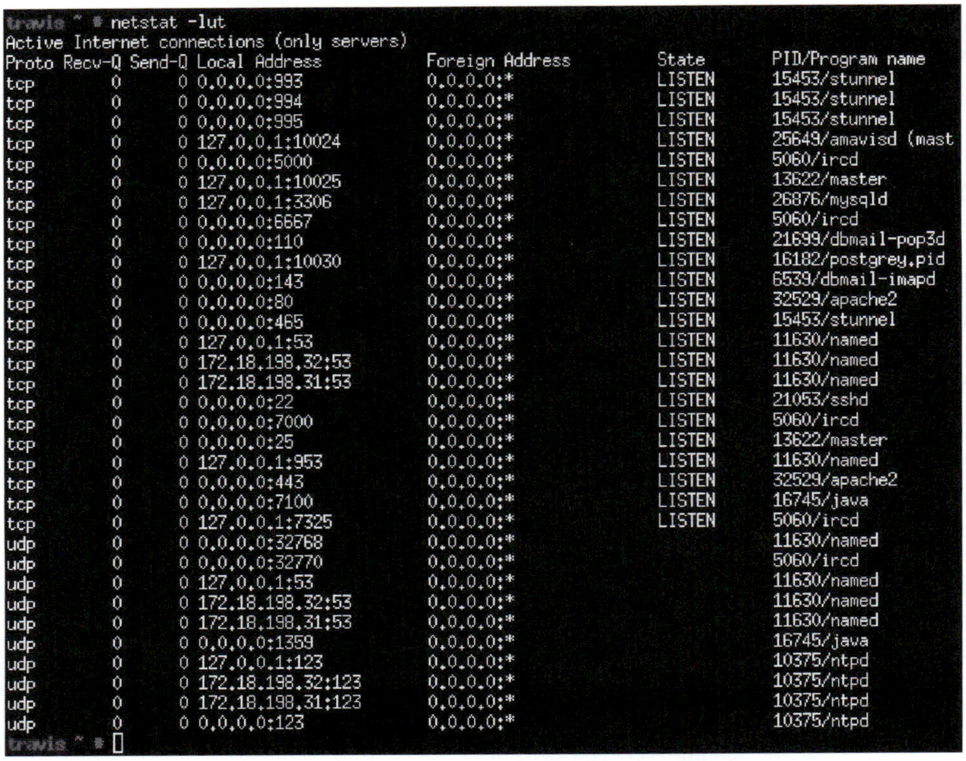

```
travis ~ # netstat -lut
Active Internet connections (only servers)
Proto Recv-Q Send-Q Local Address        Foreign Address      State    PID/Program name
tcp       0      0 0.0.0.0:993          0.0.0.0:*            LISTEN   15453/stunnel
tcp       0      0 0.0.0.0:994          0.0.0.0:*            LISTEN   15453/stunnel
tcp       0      0 0.0.0.0:995          0.0.0.0:*            LISTEN   15453/stunnel
tcp       0      0 127.0.0.1:10024      0.0.0.0:*            LISTEN   25649/amavisd (mast
tcp       0      0 0.0.0.0:5000         0.0.0.0:*            LISTEN   5060/ircd
tcp       0      0 127.0.0.1:10025      0.0.0.0:*            LISTEN   13622/master
tcp       0      0 127.0.0.1:3306       0.0.0.0:*            LISTEN   26876/mysqld
tcp       0      0 0.0.0.0:6667         0.0.0.0:*            LISTEN   5060/ircd
tcp       0      0 0.0.0.0:110          0.0.0.0:*            LISTEN   21699/dbmail-pop3d
tcp       0      0 127.0.0.1:10030      0.0.0.0:*            LISTEN   16182/postgrey.pid
tcp       0      0 0.0.0.0:143          0.0.0.0:*            LISTEN   6539/dbmail-imapd
tcp       0      0 0.0.0.0:80           0.0.0.0:*            LISTEN   32529/apache2
tcp       0      0 0.0.0.0:465          0.0.0.0:*            LISTEN   15453/stunnel
tcp       0      0 127.0.0.1:53         0.0.0.0:*            LISTEN   11630/named
tcp       0      0 172.18.198.32:53     0.0.0.0:*            LISTEN   11630/named
tcp       0      0 172.18.198.31:53     0.0.0.0:*            LISTEN   11630/named
tcp       0      0 0.0.0.0:22           0.0.0.0:*            LISTEN   21053/sshd
tcp       0      0 0.0.0.0:7000         0.0.0.0:*            LISTEN   5060/ircd
tcp       0      0 0.0.0.0:25           0.0.0.0:*            LISTEN   13622/master
tcp       0      0 127.0.0.1:953        0.0.0.0:*            LISTEN   11630/named
tcp       0      0 0.0.0.0:443          0.0.0.0:*            LISTEN   32529/apache2
tcp       0      0 0.0.0.0:7100         0.0.0.0:*            LISTEN   16745/java
tcp       0      0 127.0.0.1:7325       0.0.0.0:*            LISTEN   5060/ircd
udp       0      0 0.0.0.0:32768        0.0.0.0:*                     11630/named
udp       0      0 0.0.0.0:32770        0.0.0.0:*                     5060/ircd
udp       0      0 127.0.0.1:53         0.0.0.0:*                     11630/named
udp       0      0 172.18.198.32:53     0.0.0.0:*                     11630/named
udp       0      0 172.18.198.31:53     0.0.0.0:*                     11630/named
udp       0      0 0.0.0.0:1359         0.0.0.0:*                     16745/java
udp       0      0 127.0.0.1:123        0.0.0.0:*                     10375/ntpd
udp       0      0 172.18.198.32:123    0.0.0.0:*                     10375/ntpd
udp       0      0 172.18.198.31:123    0.0.0.0:*                     10375/ntpd
udp       0      0 0.0.0.0:123          0.0.0.0:*                     10375/ntpd
travis ~ #
```

FIGURE 6.3 Output of netstat –lut.

a service, such as a public Web site. Once a malicious user can access a service, there is a risk that the service will be subverted into executing unauthorized instructions on behalf of the attacker. The potential for damage is limited only by the permissions that the service process has to access resources and to make changes on the system. For this reason, an important security measure is to limit the power of a service to the bare minimum necessary to allow it to perform its duties.

A primary method of achieving this goal is to associate the service process with a user who has limited permissions. In many cases, it's possible to configure a user with very few permissions on the system and to associate that user with a service process. In these cases, the service can only perform a limited amount of damage, even if it is subverted by attackers.

Unfortunately, this is not always very effective or even possible. A service must often access sensitive server resources to perform its work. Configuring a set of permissions to allow access to only the sensitive information required for a service to operate can be complex or impossible.

In answer to this challenge, Unix has long supported the chroot and ulimit interfaces as ways to limit the access that a powerful process has on a system. The chroot interface limits a process's access on the file system.

Regardless of actual permissions, a process run under a chroot jail can only access a certain part of the file system. Common practice is to run sensitive or powerful services in a chroot jail and make a copy of only those file system resources that the service needs in order to operate. This allows a service to run with a high level of system access, yet be unable to damage the contents of the file system outside the portion it is allocated.[5]

The ulimit interface is somewhat different in that it can configure limits on the amount of system resources a process or user may consume. A limited amount of disk space, memory, CPU utilization, and other resources can be set for a service process. This can curtail the possibility of a denial-of-service attack because the service cannot exhaust all system resources, even if it has been subverted by an attacker.[6]

Access Control

Reducing the attack surface area of a system limits the ways in which an attacker can interact and therefore subvert a server. Access control can be seen as another way

5 W. Richard Stevens, (1992), *Advanced Programming in the UNIX Environment*, Addison-Wesley, Reading.
6 W. Richard Stevens, (1992), *Advanced Programming in the UNIX Environment*, Addison-Wesley, Reading.

FIGURE 6.4 Physical tokens used for two-factor authentication.

to reduce the attack surface area. By requiring all users to prove their identity before making any use of a service, access control reduces the number of ways in which an anonymous attacker can interact with the system.

In general, access control involves three phases. The first phase is identification, where a user asserts his identity. The second phase is authentication, where the user proves his identity. The third phase is authorization, where the server allows or disallows particular actions based on permissions assigned to the authenticated user.

Strong Authentication

It is critical, therefore, that a secure mechanism is used to prove the user's identity. If this mechanism were to be subverted, an attacker would be able to impersonate a user to access resources or issue commands with whatever authorization level has been granted to that user. For decades, the primary form of authentication has been through the use of passwords. However, passwords suffer from several weaknesses as a form of authentication, presenting attackers with opportunities to impersonate legitimate users for illegitimate ends. Bruce Schneier has argued for years that "passwords have outlived their usefulness as a serious security device."[7]

More secure authentication mechanisms include two-factor authentication and PKI certificates.

Two-Factor Authentication Two-factor authentication involves the presentation of two of the following types of information by users to prove their identity: something they know, something they have, or something they are. The first factor, something they know, is typified by a password or a PIN—some shared secret that only the legitimate user should know. The second factor, something they have, is usually fulfilled by a unique physical token (see Figure 6.4). RSA makes a popular line of such tokens, but cell phones, matrix cards, and other alternatives are becoming more common. The third factor, something they are, usually refers to biometrics.

Unix supports various ways to implement two-factor authentication into the system. Pluggable Authentication Modules, or PAMs, allow a program to use arbitrary authentication mechanisms without needing to manage any of the details. PAMs are used by Solaris, Linux, and other Unices. BSD authentication serves a similar purpose and is used by several major BSD derivatives.

With PAM or BSD authentication, it is possible to configure any combination of authentication mechanisms, including simple passwords, biometrics, RSA tokens, Kerberos, and more. It's also possible to configure a different combination for different services. This kind of flexibility allows a Unix security administrator to implement a very strong authentication requirement as a prerequisite for access to sensitive services.

PKI Strong authentication can also be implemented using a Private Key Infrastructure, or PKI. Secure Socket Layer, or SSL, is a simplified PKI designed for secure communications, familiar from its use in securing traffic on the Web. Using a similar foundation of technologies, it's possible to issue and manage certificates to authenticate users rather than Web sites. Additional technologies, such as a trusted platform module or a smart card, simplify the use of these certificates in support of two-factor authentication.

Dedicated Service Accounts

After strong authentication, limiting the complexity of the authorization phase is the most important part of access control. User accounts should not be authorized to perform sensitive tasks. Services should be associated with

---

7 B. Schneier, December 14, 2006, *Real-World Passwords*, retrieved October 9, 2008, from Schneier on Security: www.schneier.com/blog/archives/2006/12/realworld_passw.html.

dedicated user accounts, which should then be authorized to perform only those tasks required for providing that service.

Additional Controls

In addition to minimizing the attack surface area and implementing strong access controls, there are several important aspects of securing a Unix network server.

Encrypted Communications

One of the ways an attacker can steal sensitive information is to eavesdrop on network traffic. Information is vulnerable as it flows across the network, unless it is encrypted. Sensitive information, including passwords and intellectual property, are routinely transmitted over the network. Even information that is seemingly useless to an attacker can contain important clues to help a bad actor compromise security.

File Transfer Protocol (FTP), World Wide Web (WWW), and many other services that transmit information over the network support the Secure Sockets Layer standard, or SSL, for encrypted communications. For server software that doesn't support SSL natively, wrappers like *stunnel* provide transparent SSL functionality.

No discussion of Unix network encryption can be complete without mention of Secure Shell, or SSH. SSH is a replacement for Telnet and RSH, providing remote command-line access to Unix systems as well as other functionality. SSH encrypts all network communications using SSL, mitigating many of the risks of Telnet and RSH.

Log Analysis

In addition to encrypting network communications, it is important to keep a detailed activity log to provide an audit trail in case of anomalous behavior. At a minimum, the logs should capture system activity such as logon and logoff events as well as service program activity, such as FTP, WWW, or Structured Query Language (SQL) logs.

Since the 1980s, the *syslog* service has historically been used to manage log entries in Unix. Over the years, the original implementation has been replaced by more feature-rich implementations, such as *syslog-ng* and *rsyslog*. These systems can be configured to send log messages to local files as well as remote destinations, based on independently defined verbosity levels and message sources.

The syslog system can independently route messages based on the facility, or message source, and the level, or message importance. The facility can identify the message as pertaining to the kernel, the email system, user activity, an authentication event, or any of various other services. The level denotes the criticality of the message and can typically be one of *emergency, alert, critical, error, warning, notice, informational,* and *debug.* Under Linux, the *klog* process is responsible for handling log messages generated by the kernel; typically, klog is configured to route these messages through syslog, just like any other process.

Some services, such as the Apache Web server, have limited or no support for syslog. These services typically include the ability to log activity to a file independently. In these cases, simple scripts can redirect the contents of these files to syslog for further distribution and/or processing.

Relevant logs should be copied to a remote, secure server to ensure that they cannot be tampered with. Additionally, file hashes should be used to identify any attempt to tamper with the logs. In this way, the audit trail provided by the log files can be depended on as a source of uncompromised information about the security status of the system.

IDS/IPS

Intrusion detection systems (IDSs) and intrusion prevention systems (IPSs) have become commonplace security items on today's networks. Unix has a rich heritage of such software, including Snort, Prelude, and OSSEC. Correctly deployed, an IDS can provide an early warning of probes and other precursors to attack.

Host Hardening

Unfortunately, not all attacks originate from the network. Malicious users often gain access to a system through legitimate means, bypassing network-based defenses. There are various steps that can be taken to harden a Unix system from a host-based attack such as this.

Permissions

The most obvious step is to limit the permissions of user accounts on the Unix host. Recall that every file and directory in a Unix file system is associated with a single user and a single group. User accounts should each have permissions that allow full control of their respective home directories. Together with permissions to read and execute system programs, this allows most of the typical functionality required of a Unix user account. Additional permissions that might be required include mail spool files and directories as well as crontab files for scheduling tasks.

Administrative Accounts

Setting permissions for administrative users is a more complicated question. These accounts must access very powerful system-level commands and resources in the routine discharge of their administrative functions. For this reason, it's difficult to limit the tasks these users may perform. It's possible, however, to create specialized administrative user accounts, then authorize these accounts to access a well-defined subset of administrative resources. Printer management, Web site administration, email management, database administration, storage management, backup administration, software upgrades, and other specific administrative functions common to Unix systems lend themselves to this approach.

Groups

Often it is convenient to apply permissions to a set of users rather than a single user or all users. The Unix group mechanism allows for a single user to belong to one or more groups and for file system permissions and other access controls to be applied to a group.

File System Attributes and ACLs

It can become unfeasibly complex to implement and manage anything more than a simple permissions scheme using the classical Unix file system permission capabilities. To overcome this issue, modern Unix file systems support access control lists, or ACLs. Most Unix file systems support ACLs using extended attributes that could be used to store arbitrary information about any given file or directory. By recognizing authorization information in these extended attributes, the file system implements a comprehensive mechanism to specify arbitrarily complex permissions for any file system resource.

ACLs contain a list of *access control entries*, or ACEs, which specify the permissions that a user or group has on the file system resource in question. On most Unices, the chacl command is used to view and set the ACEs of a given file or directory. The ACL support in modern Unix file systems provides a fine-grained mechanism for managing complex permissions requirements. ACLs do not make the setting of minimum permissions a trivial matter, but complex scenarios can now be addressed effectively.

Intrusion Detection

Even after hardening a Unix system with restrictive user permissions and ACLs, it's important to maintain logs of system activity. As with activity logs of network services,

host-centric activity logs track security-relevant events that could show symptoms of compromise or evidence of attacks in the reconnaissance or planning stages.

Audit Trails

Again, as with network activity logs, Unix has leaned heavily on syslog to collect, organize, distribute, and store log messages about system activity. Configuring syslog for system messages is the same as for network service messages. The kernel's messages, including those messages generated on behalf of the kernel by klogd under Linux, are especially relevant from a host-centric point of view.

An additional source of audit trail data about system activity is the history logs kept by a login shell such as *bash*. These logs record every command the user issued at the command line. The bash shell and others can be configured to keep these logs in a secure location and to attach time stamps to each log entry. This information is invaluable in identifying malicious activity, both as it is happening as well as after the fact.

File Changes

Besides tracking activity logs, monitoring file changes can be a valuable indicator of suspicious system activity. Attackers often modify system files to elevate privileges, capture passwords or other credentials, establish backdoors to ensure future access to the system, and support other illegitimate uses. Identifying these changes early can often foil an attack in progress before the attacker is able to cause significant damage or loss.

Programs such as Tripwire and Aide have been around for decades; their function is to monitor the file system for unauthorized changes and raise an alert when one is found. Historically, they functioned by scanning the file system and generating a unique *hash*, or fingerprint, of each file. On future runs, the tool would recalculate the hashes and identify changed files by the difference in the hash. Limitations of this approach include the need to regularly scan the entire file system, which can be a slow operation, as well as the need to secure the database of file hashes from tampering.

Today many Unix systems support file change monitoring: Linux has dnotify and inotify; Mac OS X has FSEvents, and other Unices have File Alteration Monitor. All these present an alternative method of identifying file changes and reviewing them for security implications.

Specialized Hardening

Many Unices have specialized hardening features that make it more difficult to exploit software vulnerabilities or to do so without leaving traces on the system and/or to show that the system is so hardened. Linux has been a popular platform for research in this area; even the National Security Agency (NSA) has released code to implement its strict security requirements under Linux. Here we outline two of the most popular Linux hardening packages. Other such packages exist for Linux and other Unices, some of which use innovative techniques such as virtualization to isolate sensitive data, but they are not covered here.

GRSec/PAX

The grsecurity package provides several major security enhancements for Linux. Perhaps the primary benefit is the flexible policies that define fine-grained permissions it can control. This role-based access control capability is especially powerful when coupled with grsecurity's ability to monitor system activity over a period of time and generate a minimum set of privileges for all users. Additionally, through the PAX subsystem, grsecurity manipulates program memory to make it very difficult to exploit many kinds of security vulnerabilities. Other benefits include a very robust auditing capability and other features that strengthen existing security features, such as chroot jails.

SELinux

Security Enhanced Linux, or SELinux, is a package developed by the NSA. It adds Mandatory Access Control, or MAC, and related concepts to Linux. MAC involves assigning security attributes as well as system resources such as files and memory to users. When a user attempts to read, write, execute, or perform any other action on a system resource, the security attributes of the user and the resource are both used to determine whether the action is allowed, according to the security policies configured for the system.

Systems Management Security

After hardening a Unix host from network-borne attacks and hardening it from attacks performed by an authorized user of the machine, we will take a look at a few systems management issues. These topics arguably fall outside the purview of security as such; however, by taking certain considerations into account, systems management can both improve and simplify the work of securing a Unix system.

Account Management

User accounts can be thought of as keys to the "castle" of a system. As users require access to the system, they must be issued keys, or accounts, so they can use it. When a user no longer requires access to the system, her key should be taken away or at least disabled.

This sounds simple in theory, but account management in practice is anything but trivial. In all but the smallest environments, it is infeasible to manage user accounts without a centralized account directory where necessary changes can be made and propagated to every server on the network. Through PAM, BSD authentication, and other mechanisms, modern Unices support LDAP, SQL databases, Windows NT and Active Directory, Kerberos, and myriad other centralized account directory technologies.

Patching

Outdated software is perhaps the number-one cause of easily preventable security incidents. Choosing a modern Unix with a robust upgrade mechanism and history of timely updates, at least for security fixes, makes it easier to keep software up to date and secure from well-known exploits.

Backups

When all else fails—especially when attackers have successfully modified or deleted data in ways that are difficult or impossible to positively identify—good backups will save the day. When backups are robust, reliable, and accessible, they put a ceiling on the amount of damage an attacker can do. Unfortunately, good backups don't help if the greatest damage comes from disclosure of sensitive information; in fact, backups could exacerbate the problem if they are not taken and stored in a secure way.

3. PROACTIVE DEFENSE FOR LINUX AND UNIX

As security professionals, we devote ourselves to defending systems from attack. However, it is important to understand the common tools, mindsets, and motivations that drive attackers. This knowledge can prove invaluable in mounting an effective defense against attack. It's also important to prepare for the possibility of a successful attack and to consider organizational issues so that you can develop a secure environment.

Vulnerability Assessment

A vulnerability assessment looks for security weaknesses in a system. Assessments have become an established best practice, incorporated into many standards and regulations. They can be network-centric or host-based.

Network-Based Assessment

Network-centric vulnerability assessment looks for security weaknesses a system presents to the network. Unix has a rich heritage of tools for performing network vulnerability assessments. Most of these tools are available on most Unix flavors.

nmap is a free, open source tool for identifying hosts on a network and the services running on those hosts. It's a powerful tool for mapping out the true services being provided on a network. It's also easy to get started with nmap.

Nessus is another free network security tool, though its source code isn't available. It's designed to check for and optionally verify the existence of known security vulnerabilities. It works by looking at various pieces of information about a host on the network, such as detailed version information about the operating system and any software providing services on the network. This information is compared to a database that lists vulnerabilities known to exist in certain software configurations. In many cases, Nessus is also capable of confirming a match in the vulnerability database by attempting an exploit; however, this is likely to crash the service or even the entire system.

Many other tools are available for performing network vulnerability assessments. Insecure.Org, the folks behind the nmap tool, also maintain a great list of security tools.[8]

Host-Based Assessment

Several tools can examine the security settings of a system from a host-based perspective. These tools are designed to be run on the system that's being checked; no network connections are necessarily initiated. They check things such as file permissions and other insecure configuration settings on Unix systems.

One such tool, *lynis*, is available for various Linux distributions as well as some BSD variants. Another tool is the Linux Security Auditing Tool, or *lsat*. Ironically, lsat supports more versions of Unix than lynis does, including Solaris and AIX.

No discussion of host-based Unix security would be complete without mentioning *Bastille* (see Figure 6.5). Though lynis and lsat are pure auditing tools that report on the status of various security-sensitive host configuration settings, Bastille was designed to help remediate these issues. Recent versions have a reporting-only mode that makes Bastille work like a pure auditing tool.

Incident Response Preparation

Regardless of how hardened a Unix system is, there is always a possibility that an attacker—whether it's a worm, a virus, or a sophisticated custom attack—will successfully compromise the security of the system. For this reason, it is important to think about how to respond to a wide variety of security incidents.

Predefined Roles and Contact List

A fundamental part of incident response preparation is to identify the roles that various personnel will play in the response scenario. The manual, hands-on gestalt of Unix systems administration has historically forced Unix systems administrators to be familiar with all aspects of the Unix systems they manage. These should clearly be on the incident response team. Database, application, backup, and other administrators should be on the team as well, at least as secondary personnel that can be called on as necessary.

Simple Message for End Users

Incident response is a complicated process that must deal with conflicting requirements to bring the systems back online while ensuring that any damage caused by the attack—as well as whatever security flaws were exploited to gain initial access—is corrected. Often, end users without incident response training are the first to handle a system after a security incident has been identified. It is important that these users have clear, simple instructions in this case, to avoid causing additional damage or loss of evidence. In most situations, it is appropriate to simply unplug a Unix system from the network as soon as a compromise of its security is confirmed. It should not be used, logged onto, logged off from, turned off, disconnected from electrical power, or otherwise tampered with in any way. This simple action has the best chance, in most cases, to preserve the status of the incident for further investigation while minimizing the damage that could ensue.

Blue Team/Red Team Exercises

Any incident response plan, no matter how well designed, must be practiced to be effective. Regularly exercising these plans and reviewing the results are important parts of incident response preparation. A common way of organizing such exercises is to assign

---

8 Insecure.Org, 2008, "Top 100 Network Security Tools", retrieved October 9, 2008, from http://sectools.org.

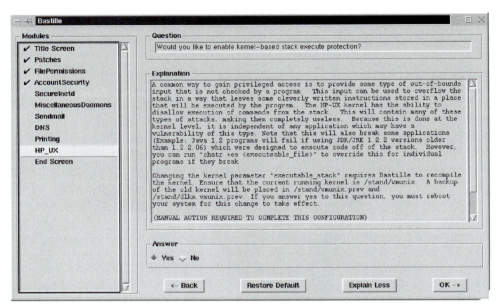

FIGURE 6.5 Bastille screenshot.

some personnel (the Red Team) to simulate a successful attack, while other personnel (the Blue Team) are assigned to respond to that attack according to the established incident response plan. These exercises, referred to as Red Team/Blue Team exercises, are invaluable for testing incident response plans. They are also useful in discovering security weaknesses and in fostering a sense of *esprit des corps* among the personnel involved.

Organizational Considerations

Various organizational and personnel management issues can also impact the security of Unix systems. Unix is a complex operating system. Many different duties must be performed in the day-to-day administration of Unix systems. Security suffers when a single individual is responsible for many of these duties; however, that is commonly the skill set of Unix system administration personnel.

Separation of Duties

One way to counter the insecurity of this situation is to force different individuals to perform different duties.

Often, simply identifying independent functions, such as backups and log monitoring, and assigning appropriate permissions to independent individuals is enough. Log management, application management, user management, system monitoring, and backup operations are just some of the roles that can be separated.

Forced Vacations

Especially when duties are appropriately separated, unannounced forced vacations are a powerful way to bring fresh perspectives to security tasks. It's also an effective deterrent to internal fraud or mismanagement of security responsibilities. A more robust set of requirements for organizational security comes from the Information Security Management Maturity Model, including its concepts of transparency, partitioning, separation, rotation, and supervision of responsibilities.[9]

---

9 ISECOM 2008, "Security Operations Maturity Architecture", retrieved October 9, 2008, from ISECOM: www.isecom.org/soma.

## Chapter 7

Internet Security

Jesse Walker
Intel Corporation

The Internet, and all its accompanying complications, has become integral to our lives. The security problems besetting the Internet are legendary and have been daily annoyances to many users. Given the Net's broad impact on our lives and the widespread security issues associated withit, it is worthwhile understanding what can be done to improve the immunity of our communications from attack.

The Internet can serve as a laboratory for studying network security issues; indeed, we can use it to study nearly every kind of security issue. We will pursue only a modest set of questions related to this theme. The goal of this chapter is to understand how cryptography can be used to address some of the security issues besetting communications protocols. To do so, it will be helpful to first understand the Internet architecture. After that we will survey the types of attacks that are possible against communications. With this background we will be in a position to understand how cryptography can be used to preserve the confidentiality and integrity of messages.

Our goal is modest. It is only to describe the network architecture and its cryptographic-based security mechanisms sufficiently to understand some of the major issues confronting security systems designers and to appreciate some of the major design decisions they have to make to address these issues.

1. INTERNET PROTOCOL ARCHITECTURE

The Internet was designed to create standardized communication between computers. Computers communicate by exchanging messages. The Internet supports message exchange through a mechanism called *protocols*. Protocols are very detailed and stereotyped rules explaining exactly how to exchange a particular set of messages. Each protocol is defined as a set of finite state automata and a set of message formats. Each protocol specification defines one automaton for sending a message and another for receiving a message. The automata specify the message timing; they play the role of grammar, indicating whether any particular message is meaningful or is interpreted by the receiver as gibberish. The protocol formats restrict the information that the protocol can express.

Security has little utility as an abstract, disembodied concept. What the word *security* should mean depends very much on the context in which it is applied. The architecture, design, and implementation of a system each determine the kind of vulnerabilities and opportunities for exploits that exist and which features are easy or hard to attack or defend.

It is fairly easy to understand why this is true. An attack on a system is an attempt to make the system act outside its specification. An attack is different from "normal" bugs that afflict computers and that occur through random interactions between the system's environment and undetected flaws in the system architecture, design, or implementation. An attack, on the other hand, is an explicit and systematic attempt by a party to search for flaws that make the computer act in a way its designers did not intend.

Computing systems consist of a large number of blocks or modules assembled together, each of which provides an intended set of functions. The system architecture hooks the modules together through *interfaces*, through which the various modules exchange information to activate the functions provided by each module in a coordinated way. An attacker exploits the architecture to compromise the computing system by interjecting inputs into these interfaces that do not conform to the specification for inputs of a specific module. If the targeted module has not been carefully crafted, unexpected inputs can cause it to behave in unintended ways. This implies that the security of a system is determined by its decomposition into modules, which an adversary exploits by injecting messages into the interfaces the architecture exposes. Accordingly, no satisfying discussion of any system is feasible without an understanding of the system architecture. Our first goal, therefore, is to review the architecture of the Internet communication protocols in an effort to gain a deeper understanding of its vulnerabilities.

Communications Architecture Basics

Since communication is an extremely complex activity, it should come as no surprise that the system components providing communication decompose into modules. One standard way to describe each communication module is as a black box with a well-defined service interface. A minimal communications service interface requires four primitives:

- A *send* primitive, which an application using the communications module uses to send a message via the module to a peer application executing on another networked device. The *send* primitive specifies a message payload and a destination. The communication module responding to the *send* transmits the message to the specified destination, reporting its requester as the message source.
- A *confirm* primitive, to report that the module has sent a message to the designated destination in response to a *send* request or to report when the message transmission failed, along with any failure details that might be known. It is possible to combine the *send* and *confirm* primitives, but network architectures rarely take this approach. The *send* primitive is normally defined to allow the application to pass a message to the communications module for transmission by transferring control of a buffer containing the message. The *confirm* primitive then releases the buffer back to the calling application when the message has indeed been sent. This scheme effects "a conservation of buffers" and enables the communications module and the application using it to operate in parallel, thus enhancing the overall communication performance.
- A *listen* primitive, which the receiving application uses to provide the communications module with buffers into which it should put messages arriving from the network. Each buffer the application posts must be large enough to receive a message of the maximum expected size.
- A *receive* primitive, to deliver a received message from another party to the receiving application. This

releases a posted buffer back to the application and usually generates a signal to notify the application of message arrival. The released buffer contains the received message and the (alleged) message source.

Sometimes the *listen* primitive is replaced with a *release* primitive. In this model the receive buffer is owned by the receiving communications module instead of the application, and the application must recycle buffers containing received messages back to the communication module upon completion. In this case the buffer size selected by the receiving module determines the maximum message size. In a moment we will explain how network protocols work around this restriction.

It is customary to include a fifth service interface primitive for communications modules:

- A *status* primitive, to report diagnostic and performance information about the underlying communications. This might report statistics, the state of active associations with other network devices, and the like.

Communications is effected by providing a communications module black box on systems, connected by a signaling medium. The medium connecting the two devices constitutes the network communications path. The media can consist of a direct link between the devices or, more commonly, several intermediate relay systems between the two communicating endpoints. Each relay system is itself a communicating device with its own communications module, which receives and then forward messages from the initiating system to the destination system.

Under this architecture, a message is transferred from an application on one networked system to an application on a second networked system as follows:

First the application sourcing the message invokes the *send* primitive exported by its communications module. This causes the communications module to (attempt) to transmit the message to a destination provided by the application in the *send* primitive.

The communications module encodes the message onto the network's physical medium representing a link to another system. If the communications module implements a *best-effort* message service, it generates the *confirm* primitive as soon as the message has been encoded onto the medium. If the communication module implements a *reliable* message service, the communication delays generation of the *confirm* until it receives an acknowledgment from the message destination. If it has not received an acknowledgment from the receiver after some period of time, it generates a *confirm* indicating that the message delivery failed.

The encoded message traverses the network medium and is placed into a buffer by the receiving communications module of another system attached to the medium. This communications module examines the destination. The module then examines the destination specified by the message. If the module's local system is not the destination, the module reencodes the message onto the medium representing another link; otherwise the module uses the *deliver* primitive to pass the message to the receiving application.

Getting More Specific

This stereotyped description of networked communications is overly simplified. Communications are actually torturously more difficult in real network modules. To tame this complexity, communications modules are themselves partitioned further into layers, each providing a different networking function. The Internet decomposes communications into five layers of communications modules:

- The PHY layer
- The MAC layer
- The network layer
- The transport layer
- The sockets layer

These layers are also augmented by a handful of cross-layer coordination modules. The Internet depends on the following cross-layer modules:

- ARP
- DHCP
- DNS
- ICMP
- Routing

An application using networking is also part of the overall system design, and the way it uses the network has to be taken into consideration to understand system security.

We next briefly describe each of these in turn.

The PHY Layer

The PHY (pronounced *fie*) layer is technically not part of the Internet architecture per se, but Ethernet jacks and cables, modems, Wi-Fi adapters, and the like represent the most visible aspect of networking, and no security treatment of the Internet can ignore the PHY layer entirely.

The PHY layer module is medium dependent, with a different design for each type of medium: Ethernet, phone lines, Wi-Fi, cellular phone, OC-48, and the like

are based on different PHY layer designs. It is the job of the PHY layer to translate between digital bits as represented on a computing device and the analog signals crossing the specific physical medium used by the PHY. This translation is a physics exercise.

To send a message, the PHY layer module encodes each bit of each message from the sending device as a media-specific signal, representing the bit value 1 or 0. Once encoded, the signal propagates along the medium from the sender to the receiver. The PHY layer module at the receiver decodes the medium-specific signal back into a bit.

It is possible for the encoding step at the transmitting PHY layer module to fail, for a signal to be lost or corrupted while it crosses the medium, and for the decoding step to fail at the receiving PHY layer module. It is the responsibility of higher layers to detect and recover from these potential failures.

The MAC Layer

Like the PHY layer, the MAC (pronounced *mack*) layer is not properly a part of the Internet architecture, but no satisfactory security discussion is possible without considering it. The MAC module is the "application" that uses and controls a particular PHY layer module. A MAC layer is always designed in tandem with a specific PHY (or vice versa), so a PHY-MAC pair together is often referred to as the *data link* layer.

MAC is an acronym for *media access control*. As its name suggests, the MAC layer module determines when to send and receive *frames*, which are messages encoded in a media-specific format. The job of the MAC is to pass frames over a link between the MAC layer modules on different systems.

Although not entirely accurate, it is useful to think of a MAC module as creating *links*, each of which is a communication channel between different MAC modules. It is further useful to distinguish physical links and virtual links. A *physical link* is a direct point-to-point channel between the MAC layers in two endpoint devices. A *virtual link* can be thought of as a shared medium to which more than two devices can connect at the same time. There are no physical endpoints per se; the medium acts as though it is multiplexing links between each pair of attached devices. Some media such as Ethernet are implemented as physical point-to-point links but act more like virtual links in that more than a single destination is reachable via the link. This is accomplished by MAC layer switching, which is also called *bridging*. Timing requirements for coordination among communicating MAC layer modules make it difficult to build worldwide networks based on MAC layer switching, however.

A MAC frame consists of a header and a data payload. The frame header typically specifies information such as the source and destination for the link endpoints. Devices attached to the medium via their MAC + PHY modules are identified by *MAC addresses*. Each MAC module has its own MAC address assigned by its manufacturer and is supposed to be a globally unique identifier. The destination MAC address in a frame allows a particular MAC module to identify frames intended for it, and the destination address allows it to identify the purported frame source. The frame header also usually includes a preamble, which is a set of special PHY timing signals used to synchronize the interpretation of the PHY layer data signals representing the frame bits.

The payload portion of a frame is the data to be transferred across the network. The maximum payload size is always fixed by the medium type. It is becoming customary for most MACs to support a maximum payload size of 1500 bytes = 12,000 bits, but this is not universal. The maximum fixed size allows the MAC to make efficient use of the underlying physical medium. Since messages can be of an arbitrary length exceeding this fixed size, a higher-layer function is needed to partition messages into segments of the appropriate length.

As we have seen, it is possible for bit errors to creep into communications as signals representing bits traverse the PHY medium. MAC layers differ a great deal in how they respond to errors. Some PHY layers, such as the Ethernet PHY, experience exceedingly low error rates, and for this reason, the MAC layers for these PHYs make no attempt to more than detect errors and discard the mangled frames. Indeed, with these MACs it is cheaper for the Internet to resend message segments at a higher layer than at the MAC layer. These are called *best-effort MACs*. Others, such as the Wi-Fi MAC, experience high error rates due to the shared nature of the channel and natural interference among radio sources, and experience has shown that these MACs can deliver better performance by retransmitting damaged or lost frames. It is customary for most MAC layers to append a checksum computed over the entire frame, called a *frame check sequence* (FCS). The FCS allows the receiver to detect bit errors accumulated due to random noise and other physical phenomena during transmission and due to decoding errors. Most MACs discard frames with FCS errors. Some MAC layers also perform error correction on the received bits to remove random bit errors rather than relying on retransmissions.

The Network Layer

The purpose of the network layer module is to represent messages in a media-independent manner and forward them between various MAC layer modules representing different links. The media-independent message format is called an *Internet Protocol*, or *IP, datagram*. The network layer implements the IP layer and is the lowest layer of the Internet architecture per se.

As well as providing media independence, the network layer provides a vital forwarding function that works even for a worldwide network like the Internet. It is impractical to form a link directly between each communicating system on the planet; indeed, the cabling costs alone are prohibitive—no one wants billions, or even dozens, of cables connecting their computer to other computers—and too many MAC + PHY interfaces can quickly exhaust the power budget for a single computing system. Hence, each machine is attached by a small number of links to other devices, and some of the machines with multiple links comprise a *switching fabric*. The computing systems constituting the switching fabric are called *routers*.

The forwarding function supported by the network layer module is the key component of a router and works as follows: When a MAC module receives a frame, it passes the frame payload to the network layer module. The payload consists of an *IP datagram*, which is the media-independent representation of the message. The receiving network layer module examines the datagram to see whether to deliver it locally or to pass it on toward the datagram's ultimate destination. To accomplish the latter, the network layer module consults a *forwarding table* to identify some neighbor router closer to the ultimate destination than itself. The forwarding table also identifies the MAC module to use to communicate with the selected neighbor and passes the datagram to that MAC layer module. The MAC module in turn retransmits the datagram as a frame encoded for its medium across its link to the neighbor. This process happens recursively until the datagram is delivered to its ultimate destination.

The network layer forwarding function is based on *IP addresses*, a concept that is critical to understanding the Internet architecture. An IP address is a media-independent name for one of the MAC layer modules within a computing system. Each IP address is structured to represent the "location" of the MAC module within the entire Internet. This notion of location is relative to the graph comprising routers and their interconnecting links, called the *network topology*, not to actual geography. Since this name represents a location, the forwarding table within each IP module can use the IP address of the ultimate destination as a sort of signpost pointing at the MAC module with the greatest likelihood of leading to the ultimate destination of a particular datagram.

An IP address is different from the corresponding MAC address already described. A MAC address is a permanent, globally unique identifier, whereas an IP address can be dynamic due to device mobility; an IP address cannot be assigned by the equipment manufacturer, since a computing device can change locations frequently. Hence, IP addresses are administered and blocks allocated to different organizations with an Internet presence. It is common, for instance, for an Internet service provider (ISP) to acquire a large block of IP addresses for use by its customers.

An IP datagram has a structure similar to that of a frame: It consists of an IP header, which is "extra" overhead used to control the way a datagram passes through the Internet, and a data payload, which contains the message being transferred. The IP header indicates the ultimate source and destinations, represented as IP addresses.

The IP header format limits the size of an IP datagram payload to 64K ($2^{16} = 65,536$) bytes. It is common to limit datagram sizes to the underlying media size, although datagrams larger than this do occur. This means that normally each MAC layer frame can carry a single IP datagram as its data payload. IP version 4, still the dominant version deployed on the Internet today, allows fragmentation of larger datagrams, to split large datagrams into chunks small enough to fit the limited frame size of the underlying MAC layer medium. IPv4 reassembles any fragmented datagrams at the ultimate destination.

Network layer forwarding of IP datagrams is best effort, not reliable. Network layer modules along the path taken by any message can lose and reorder datagrams. It is common for the network layer in a router to recover from congestion—that is, when the router is overwhelmed by more receive frames than it can process—by discarding late-arriving frames until the router has caught up with its forwarding workload. The network layer can reorder datagrams when the Internet topology changes, because a new path between source and destination might be shorter or longer than an old path, so datagrams in flight before the change can arrive after frames sent after the change. The Internet architecture delegates recovery from these problems to high-layer modules.

The Transport Layer

The transport layer is implemented by TCP and similar protocols. Not all transport protocols provide the same level of service as TCP, but a description of TCP will suffice to help us understand the issues addressed by the transport layer. The transport layer provides a multitude of functions.

First, the transport layer creates and manages instances of two-way channels between communication endpoints. These channels are called *connections*. Each connection represents a virtual endpoint between a pair of communication endpoints. A connection is named by a pair of IP addresses and *port numbers*. Two devices can support simultaneous connections using different port numbers for each connection. It is common to differentiate applications on the same host through the use of port numbers.

A second function of the transport layer is to support delivery of messages of arbitrary length. The 64K byte limit of the underlying IP module is too small to carry really large messages, and the transport layer module at the message source chops messages into pieces called *segments* that are more easily digestible by lower-layer communications modules. The segment size is negotiated between the two transport endpoints during connection setup. The segment size is chosen by discovering the smallest maximum frame size supported by any MAC + PHY link on the path through the Internet used by the connection setup messages. Once this is known, the transmitter typically partitions a large message into segments no larger than this size, plus room for an IP header. The transport layer module passes each segment to the network layer module, where it becomes the payload for a single IP datagram. The destination network layer module extracts the payload from the IP datagram and passes it to the transport layer module, which interprets the information as a message segment. The destination transport reassembles this into the original message once all the necessary segments arrive.

Of course, as noted, MAC frames and IP datagrams can be lost in transit, so some segments can be lost. It is the responsibility of the transport layer module to detect this loss and retransmit the missing segments. This is accomplished by a sophisticated acknowledgment algorithm defined by the transport layer. The destination sends a special acknowledgment message, often piggybacked with a data segment being sent in the opposite direction, for each segment that arrives. Acknowledgments can be lost as well, and if the message source does not receive the acknowledgment within a time window, the source retransmits the unacknowledged segment. This process is repeated some number of times, and if the failure continues, the network layer tears down the connection because it cannot fulfill its reliability commitment.

One reason for message loss is congestion at routers, something blind retransmission of unacknowledged segments will only exacerbate. The network layer is also responsible for implementing congestion control algorithms as part of its transmit function. TCP, for instance, lowers its transmit rate whenever it fails to receive an acknowledgment message in time, and it slowly increases its rate of transmission until another acknowledgment is lost. This allows TCP to adapt to congestion in the network, helping to minimize frame loss.

It can happen that segments arrive at the destination out of order, since some IP datagrams for the same connection could traverse the Internet through different paths due to dynamic changes in the underlying network topology. The transport layer is responsible for delivering the segments in the order sent, so the receiver caches any segments that arrive out of order prior to delivery. The TCP reordering algorithm is closed tied to the acknowledgment and congestion control scheme so that the receiver never has to buffer too many out-of-order received segments and the sender not too many sent but unacknowledged segments.

Segment data arriving at the receiver can be corrupted due to undetected bit errors on the data link and copy errors within routers and the sending and receiving computing systems. Accordingly, all transport layers use a checksum algorithm called a *cyclic redundancy check* (CRC) to detect such errors. The receiving transport layer module typically discards segments with errors detected by the CRC algorithm, and recovery occurs through retransmission by the receiver when it fails to receive an acknowledgment from the receiver for a particular segment.

The Sockets Layer

The top layer of the Internet, the sockets layer, does not *per se* appear in the architecture at all. The sockets layer provides a set of sockets, each of which represents a logical communications endpoint. An application can use the sockets layer to create, manage, and destroy connection instances using a socket as well as send and receive messages over the connection. The sockets layer has been designed to hide much of the complexity of utilizing the transport layer. The sockets layer has been highly optimized over the years to deliver as much performance as possible, but it does impose a performance penalty. Applications with very demanding performance requirements tend to utilize the transport layer directly instead of through the sockets layer module, but this comes with a very high cost in terms of software maintenance.

In most implementations of these communications modules, each message is copied twice, at the sender and the receiver. Most operating systems are organized into user space, which is used to run applications, and kernel space, where the operating system itself runs. The sockets layer occupies the boundary between user space and kernel space. The sockets layer's *send* function copies a message from memory controlled by the sending application into a buffer controlled by the kernel for transmission. This copy prevents the application from changing a message it has posted to send, but it also permits the application and kernel to continue their activities in parallel, thus better utilizing the device's computing resources. The sockets layer invokes the transport layer, which partitions the message buffer into segments and passes the address of each segment to the network layer. The network layer adds its headers to form datagrams from the segments and invokes the right MAC layer module to transmit each datagram to its next hop. A second copy occurs at the boundary between the network layer and the MAC layer, since the data link must be able to asynchronously match transmit requests from the network layer to available transmit slots on the medium provided by its PHY. This process is reversed at the receiver, with a copy of datagrams across the MAC-network layer boundary and of messages between the socket layer and application.

Address Resolution Protocol

The network layer uses Address Resolution Protocol, or ARP, to translate IP addresses into MAC addresses, which it needs to give to the MAC layer in order to deliver frames to the appropriate destination.

The ARP module asks the question, "Who is using IP address X?" The requesting ARP module uses a request/response protocol, with the MAC layer broadcasting the ARP module's requests to all the other devices on the same physical medium segment. A receiving ARP module generates a response only if its network layer has assigned the IP address to one of its MAC modules. Responses are addressed to the requester's MAC address. The requesting ARP module inserts the response received in an address translation table used by the network layer to identify the next hop for all datagrams it forwards.

Dynamic Host Configuration Protocol

Remember that unlike MAC addresses, IP addresses cannot be assigned in the factory, because they are dynamic and must reflect a device's current location within the Internet's topology. A MAC module uses Dynamic Host Configuration Protocol, or DHCP, to acquire an IP address for itself, to reflect the device's current location with respect to the Internet topology.

DHCP makes the request: "Please configure my MAC module with an IP address." When one of a device's MAC layer modules connects to a new medium, it invokes DHCP to make this request. The associated DHCP module generates such a request that conveys the MAC address of the MAC module, which the MAC layer module broadcasts to the other devices attached to the same physical medium segment. A DHCP server responds with a unicast DHCP response binding an IP address to the MAC address. When it receives the response, the requesting DHCP module passes the assigned IP address to the network layer to configure in its address translation table.

In addition to binding an IP address to the MAC module used by DHCP, the response also contains a number of network configuration parameters, including the address of one or more routers, to enable reaching arbitrary destinations, the maximum datagram size supported, and the addresses of other servers, such as DNS servers, that translate human-readable names into IP addresses.

Domain Naming Service

IP and MAC addresses are efficient means for identifying different network interfaces, but human beings are incapable of using these as reliably as computing devices can. Instead, human beings rely on names to identify the computing devices with which they want to communication. These names are centrally managed and called *domain names*. The Domain Naming Service, or DNS, is a mechanism for translating human-readable names into IP addresses.

The translation from human-readable names to IP addresses happens within the socket layer module. An application opens a socket with the name of the intended destination. As the first step of opening a connection to that destination, the socket sends a request to a DNS server, asking the server to translate the name into an IP address. When the server responds, the socket can open the connection to the right destination, using the IP address provided.

It is becoming common for devices to register their IP addresses under their names with DNS once DHCP has completed. This permits other devices to locate the registering device so that they can send messages to it.

Internet Control Message Protocol

Internet Control Message Protocol, or ICMP, is an important diagnostic tool for troubleshooting the Internet. Though ICMP provides many specialized message services, three are particularly important:

- *Ping.* Ping is a request/response protocol designed to determine reachability of another IP address. The requester sends a ping request message to a designated IP address. If it's delivered, the destination IP address sends a ping response message to the IP address that sourced the request. The responding ICMP module copies the contents of the ping request into the ping response so that the requester can match responses to requests. The requester uses pings to measure the roundtrip time to a destination.
- *Traceroute.* Traceroute is another request/response protocol. An ICMP module generates a traceroute request to discover the path it is using to traverse the Internet to a destination IP address. The requesting ICMP module transmits a destination. Each router that handles the traceroute request adds a description of its own IP address that received the message and then forwards the updated traceroute request. The destination sends all this information back to the message source in a traceroute response message.
- *Destination unreachable.* When a router receives a datagram for which it has no next hop, it generates a "destination unreachable" message and sends it back to the datagram source. When the message is delivered, the ICMP module marks the forwarding table of the message source so that its network layer will reject further attempts to send messages to the destination IP address. An analogous process happens at the ultimate destination when a message is delivered to a network layer, but the application targeted to receive the message is no longer on line. The purpose of "destination unreachable" messages is to suppress messages that will never be successfully delivered, to reduce network congestion.

Routing

The last cross-layer module we'll discuss is *routing*. Routing is a middleware application to maintain the forwarding tables used by the network layer. Each router advertises itself by periodically broadcasting "hello" messages through each of its MAC interfaces. This allows routers to discover the presence or loss of all neighboring routers, letting them construct the one-hop topology of the part of the Internet directly visible through their directly attached media. The routing application in a router then uses a sophisticated gossiping mechanism to exchange this mechanism with their neighbors. Since some of a router's neighbors are not its own direct neighbors, this allows each router to learn the two-hop topology of the Internet. This process repeats recursively until each router knows the entire topology of the Internet. The cost of using each link is part of the information gossiped. A routing module receiving this information uses all of it to compute a lowest-cost route to each destination. Once this is accomplished, the routing module reconfigures the forwarding table maintained by its network layer module. The routine module updates the forwarding table whenever the Internet topology changes, so each network layer can make optimal forwarding decisions in most situations and at the very worst at least reach any other device that is also connected to the Internet.

There are many different routing protocols, each of which are based on different gossiping mechanisms. The most widely deployed routing protocol between different administrative domains within the Internet is the Border Gateway Protocol (BGP). The most widely deployed routing protocols within wired networks controlled by a single administrative domain are OSPF and RIP. AODV, OLSR, and TBRPF are commonly used in Wi-Fi meshes. Different routing protocols are used in different environments because each one addresses different scaling and administrative issues.

Applications

Applications are the ultimate reason for networking, and the Internet architecture has been shaped by applications' needs. All communicating applications define their own language in which to express what they need to say. Applications generally use the sockets layer to establish communication channels, which they then use for their own purposes.

It is worth emphasizing that since the network modules have been designed to be a generic communications vehicle, that is, designed to meet the needs of all (or at least most) applications, it is rarely meaningful for the network to attempt to make statements on behalf of the applications. There is widespread confusion on this point around authentication and key management, which are the source of many exploitable security flaws.

2. AN INTERNET THREAT MODEL

Now that we have reviewed the architecture of the Internet protocol suite, it is possible to constructively consider security issues it raises. Before doing so, let's first set the scope of the discussion.

There are two general approaches to attacking a networked computer. The first is to compromise one of the communicating parties so that it responds to queries with lies or otherwise communicates in a manner not foreseen by the system designers of the receiver. For example, it has become common to receive email with virus-infected attachments, whereby opening the attachment infects the receiver with the virus. These messages typically are sent by a machine that has already been compromised, so the sender is no longer acting as intended by the manufacturer of the computing system. Problems of this type are called *Byzantine failures*, named after the Byzantine Generals problem.

The Byzantine Generals problem imagines several armies surrounding Byzantium. The generals commanding these armies can communicate only by exchanging messages transported by couriers between them. Of course the couriers can be captured and the messages replaced by forgeries, but this is not really the issue, since it is possible to devise message schemes that detect lost messages or forgeries. All the armies combined are sufficient to overwhelm the defenses of Byzantium, but if even one army fails to participate in a coordinated attack, the armies of Byzantium have sufficient strength to repulse the attack. Each general must make a decision as to whether to participate in an attack on Byzantium at dawn or withdraw to fight another day. The question is how to determine the veracity of the messages received on which the decision to attack will be made—that is, whether it is possible to detect that one or more generals have become traitors so will say their armies will join the attack when in fact they plan to hold back so that their allies will be slaughtered by the Byzantines.

Practical solutions addressing Byzantine failures fall largely within the purview of platform rather than network architecture. For example, since viruses infect a platform by buffer overrun attacks, platform mechanisms to render buffer overrun attacks futile are needed. Secure logging, to make an accurate record of messages exchanged, is a second deterrent to these sorts of attacks; the way to accomplish secure logging is usually a question of platform design. Most self-propagating viruses and worms utilize the Internet to propagate, but they do not utilize any feature of the Internet architecture per se for their success. The success of these attacks instead depends on the architecture, design, implementation, and policies of the receiving system. Although these sorts of problems are important, we will rarely focus on security issues stemming from Byzantine failures.

What will instead be the focus of the discussion are attacks on the messages exchanged between computers themselves. As we will see, even with this more limited scope, there are plenty of opportunities for things to go wrong.

The Dolev-Yao Adversary Model

Security analyses of systems traditionally begin with a model of the attacker, and we follow this tradition. Dolev and Yao formulated the standard attack model against messages exchanged over a network. The *Dolev-Yao model* makes the following assumptions about an attacker:

- *Eavesdrop.* An adversary can listen to any message exchanged through the network.
- *Forge.* An adversary can create and inject entirely new messages into the datastream or change messages in flight; these messages are called *forgeries.*
- *Replay.* A special type of forgery, called a *replay*, is distinguished. To replay a message, the adversary resends legitimate messages that were sent earlier.
- *Delay and rush.* An adversary can delay the delivery of some messages or accelerate the delivery of others.
- *Reorder.* An adversary can alter the order in which messages are delivered.
- *Delete.* An adversary can destroy in-transit messages, either selectively or all the messages in a datastream.

This model assumes a very powerful adversary, and many people who do not design network security solutions sometime assert that the model grants adversaries an unrealistic amount of power to disrupt network communications. However, experience demonstrates that it is a reasonably realistic set of assumptions in practice; examples of each threat abound, as we will see. One of the reasons for this is that the environment in which the network operates is exposed; unlike memory or microprocessors or other devices comprising a computer, there is almost no assurance that the network medium will be deployed in a "safe" way. That is, it is comparatively easy for an attacker to anonymously access the physical network fabric, or at least the medium monitored to identify attacks against the medium and the networked traffic it carries. And since a network is intended as a generic communications vehicle, it becomes necessary to adopt a threat model that addresses the needs of all possible applications.

Layer Threats

With the Dolev-Yao model in hand, we can examine each of the architectural components of the Internet protocol suite for vulnerabilities. We next look at threats each component of the Internet architecture exposes through the prism of this model. The first Dolev-Yao assumption about adversaries is that they can eavesdrop on any communications.

Eavesdropping

An attacker can eavesdrop on a communications medium by connecting a receiver to the medium. Ultimately such a connection has to be implemented at the PHY layer because an adversary has to access some physical media somewhere to be able to listen to anything at all. This connection to the PHY medium might be legitimate, such as when an authorized device is compromised, or illegitimate, such as an illegal wiretap; it can be intentional, as when an eavesdropper installs a rogue device, or unintentional, such as a laptop with wireless capabilities that will by default attempt to connect to any Wi-Fi network within range.

With a PHY layer connection, the eavesdropper can receive the analog signals on the medium and decode them into bits. Because of the limited scope of the PHY layer function—there are no messages, only analog signals representing bits—the damage an adversary can do with only PHY layer functionality is rather limited. In particular, to make sense of the bits, an adversary has to impose the higher-layer frame and datagram formats onto the received bits. That is, any eavesdropping attack has to take into account at least the MAC layer to learn anything meaningful about the communications. Real eavesdroppers are more sophisticated than this: They know how to interpret the bits as a medium-specific encoding with regards to the frames that are used by the MAC layer. They also know how to extract the media-independent representation of datagrams conveyed within the MAC frames, as well as how to extract the transport layer segments from the datagrams, which can be reassembled into application messages.

The defenses erected against any threat give some insight into the perceived danger of the threat. People are generally concerned about eavesdropping, and it is easy to illicitly attach listening devices to most PHY media, but detection and removal of wiretaps has not evolved into a comparatively large industry. An apparent explanation of why this is so is that it is easier and more cost effective for an attacker to compromise a legitimate device on the network and configure it to eavesdrop than it is to install an illegitimate device. The evidence for this view is that the antivirus/antibot industry is gigantic by comparison.

There is another reason that an antiwiretapping industry has never developed for the Internet. Almost every MAC module supports a special mode of operation called *promiscuous mode*. A MAC module in promiscuous mode receives every frame appearing on the medium, not just the frames addressed to itself. This allows one MAC module to snoop on frames that are intended for other parties. Promiscuous mode was intended as a troubleshooting mechanism to aid network administrators in diagnosing the source of problems. However, it is also a mechanism that can be easily abused by anyone motivated to enable promiscuous mode.

Forgeries

A second Dolev-Yao assumption is that the adversary can forge messages. Eavesdropping is usually fairly innocuous compared to forgeries, because eavesdropping merely leaks information, whereas forgeries cause an unsuspecting receiver to take actions based on false information. Hence, the prevention or detection of forgeries is one of the central goals of network security mechanisms. Different kinds of forgeries are possible for each architectural component of the Internet. We will consider only a few for each layer of the Internet protocol suite, to give a taste for their variety and ingenuity.

Unlike the eavesdropping threat, where knowledge of higher layers is essential to any successful compromise, an attacker with only a PHY layer transmitter (and no higher-layer mechanisms) can disrupt communications by *jamming* the medium—that is, outputting noise onto the medium in an effort to disrupt communications. A jammer creates signals that do not necessarily correspond to any bit patterns. The goal of a pure PHY layer jammer is denial of service (DoS)—that is, to fill the medium so that no communications can take place.

Sometimes it is feasible to create a jamming device that is sensitive to the MAC layer formats above it, to selectively jam only some frames. Selective jamming requires a means to interpret bits received from the medium as a higher-layer frame or datagram, and the targeted frames to jam are recognized by some criterion, such as being sent from or to a particular address. So that it can enable its own transmitter before the frame has been entirely received by its intended destination, the jammer's receiver must recognize the targeted frames before they are fully transmitted. When this is done correctly, the jammer's transmitter interferes with the legitimate signals, thereby introducing bit errors in the legitimate receiver's decoder. This results in the legitimate receiver's MAC layer detecting the bit errors while trying to verify the frame check sequence, causing it to discard the frame. Selective jamming is harder to implement than continuous jamming, PHY layer jamming, but it is also much harder to detect, because the jammer's signal source transmits only when legitimate devices transmit as well, and only the targeted frames are disrupted. Successful selective jamming usually causes administrators to look for the source of the communications failure on one of the communicating devices instead of in the network for a jammer.

There is also a higher-layer analog to jamming, called *message flooding*. Denial-of-service (DoS) is also the goal of message flooding. The technique used by message flooding is to create and send messages at a rate high enough to exhaust some resource. It is popular today, for instance, for hackers to compromise thousands of unprotected machines, which they use to generate simultaneous messages to a targeted site. Examples of this kind of attack are to completely fill the physical medium connecting the targeted site to the Internet with network layer datagrams—this is usually hard or impossible—or to generate transport layer connection requests at a rate faster than the targeted site can respond. Other variants—request operations that lead to disk I/O or require expensive cryptographic operations—are also common. Message flooding attacks have the property that they are legitimate messages from authorized parties but simply timed so that collectively their processing exceeds the maximum capacity of the targeted system.

Let's turn away from resource-clogging forgeries and examine forgeries designed to cause a receiver to take an unintended action. It is possible to construct this type of forgery at any higher layer: forged frames, datagrams, network segments, or application messages.

To better understand how forgeries work, we need to more closely examine Internet "identities"—MAC addresses, IP addresses, transport port numbers, and DNS names—as well as the modules that use or support their use. The threats are a bit different at each layer.

Recall that each MAC layer module is manufactured with its own "hardware" address, which is supposed to be a globally unique identifier for the MAC layer module instance. The hardware address is configured in the factory into nonvolatile memory. At boot time the MAC address is transferred from nonvolatile memory into operational RAM maintained by the MAC module.

A transmitting MAC layer module inserts the MAC address from RAM into each frame it sends, thereby advertising an "identity." The transmitter also inserts the MAC address of the intended receiver on each frame, and the receiving MAC layer matches the MAC address in its own RAM against the destination field in each frame sent over the medium. The receiver ignores the frame if the MAC addresses don't match and receives the frame otherwise.

In spite of this system, it is useful—even necessary sometimes—for a MAC module to change its MAC address. For example, sometimes a manufacturer recycles MAC addresses so that two different modules receive the same MAC address in the factory. If both devices are deployed on the same network, neither works correctly until one of the two changes its address. Because of this problem, all manufacturers provide a way for the MAC module to alter the address in RAM. This can always be specified by software via the MAC module's device driver, by replacing the address retrieved from hardware at boot time.

Since it can be changed, attacks will find it. A common attack in Wi-Fi networks, for instance, is for the adversary to put the MAC module of the attacking device into promiscuous mode, to receive frames from other nearby systems. It is usually easy to identify another client device from the received frames and extract its MAC address. The attacker then reprograms its own MAC module to transmit frames using the address of its victim. A goal of this attack is usually to "hijack" the session of a customer paying for Wi-Fi service; that is, the attacker wants free Internet access for which someone else has already paid. Another goal of such an attack is often to avoid attribution of the actions being taken by the attacker; any punishment for antisocial or criminal behavior will likely be attributed to the victim instead of the attacker because all the frames that were part of the behavior came from the victim's address.

A similar attack is common at the network layer. The adversary will snoop on the IP addresses appearing in the datagrams encoded in the frames and use these instead of their own IP addresses to source IP datagrams. This is a more powerful attack than that of utilizing only a MAC address, because IP addresses are global; an IP address is an Internet-wide locator, whereas a MAC address is only an identifier on the medium to which the device is physically connected.

Manipulation of MAC and IP addresses leads directly to a veritable menagerie of forgery attacks and enables still others. A very selective list of examples must suffice to illustrate the ingenuity of attackers:

- TCP uses sequence numbers as part of its reliability scheme. TCP is supposed to choose the first sequence number for a connection randomly. If an attacker can predict the first sequence number for a TCP connection, an attacker who spoofs the IP address of one of the parties to the connection can hijack the session by interjecting its own datagrams into the flow that use the correct sequence numbers. This desynchronizes the retry scheme for the device being spoofed, which then drops out from the conversation. This attack seems to have become relatively less common than other attacks over the past few years, since most TCP implementations have begun to utilize better random number generators to seed their sequence numbers.

- An attacker can generate an ARP response to any ARP request, thus claiming to use any requested IP address. This is a common method to hijack another machine's IP address; it is a very effective technique when the attacker has a fast machine and the victim machine responds more slowly.

- An attacker can generate DHCP response messages replying to DHCP requests. This technique is often used as part of a larger forgery, such as the evil twin attack, whereby an adversary masquerades as an access point for a Wi-Fi public hot spot. The receipt of DHCP response messages convinces the victim it is connecting to an access point operated by the legitimate hotspot.

- A variant is to generate a DHCP request with the hardware MAC address of another device. This method is useful when the attacker wants to ascribe action it takes over the Internet to another device.

- An attacker can impersonate the DNS server, responding to requests to resolve human-readable names into IP addresses. The IP address in the response messages point the victim to a site controlled by the attacker. This is becoming a common attack used by criminals attempting to commit financial fraud, such as stealing credit card numbers.

Replay

Replay is a special forgery attack. It occurs when an attacker records frames or datagrams and then retransmits them unchanged at a later time.

This might seem like an odd thing to do, but replay attacks are an especially useful way to attack stateful messaging protocols, such as a routing protocol. Since the goal of a routing protocol is to allow every router to know the current topology of the network, a replayed routing message can cause the routers receiving it to utilize out-of-date information.

An attacker might also respond to an ARP request sent to a sabotaged node or a mobile device that has migrated to another part of the Internet, by sending a replayed ARP response. This replay indicates the node is still present, thus masking the true network topology.

Replay is also often a valuable tool for attacking a message encryption scheme. By retransmitting a message, an attacker can sometimes learn valuable information from a message decrypted and then retransmitted without encryption on another link.

A primary use of replay, however, is to attack session startup protocols. Protocol startup procedures establish session state, which is used to operate the link or connection, and determine when some classes of failures occur. Since this state is not yet established when the session begins, startup messages replayed from prior instances of the protocol will fool the receiver into allocating a new session. This is a common DoS technique.

Delay and Rushing

Delay is a natural consequence of implementations of the Internet architecture. Datagrams from a single connection typically transit a path across the Internet in bursts. This happens because applications at the sender, when sending large messages, tend to send messages larger than a single datagram. The transport layer partitions these messages into segments to fit the maximum segment size along the path to the destination. The MAC tends to output all the frames together as a single blast after it has accessed the medium. Therefore, routers with many links can receive multiple datagram bursts at the same time. When this happens, a router has to temporarily buffer the burst, since it can output only one frame conveying a datagram per link at a time. Simultaneous arrival of bursts of datagrams is one source of congestion in routers. This condition usually manifests itself at the application by slow communications time over the Internet. Delay can also be introduced by routers intentionally, such as via traffic shaping.

There are several ways in which attackers can induce delays. We illustrate this idea by describing two different attacks. It is not uncommon for an attacker to take over a router, and when this happens, the attacker can introduce artificial delay, even when the router is uncongested. As a second example, attackers with bot armies can bombard a particular router with "filler" messages, the only purpose of which is to congest the targeted router.

Rushing is the opposite problem: a technique to make it appear that messages can be delivered sooner than can be reasonably expected. Attackers often employ rushing attacks by first hijacking routers that service parts of the Internet that are fairly far apart in terms of network topology. The attackers cause the compromised routers to form a *virtual link* between them. A virtual link emulates a MAC layer protocol but running over a transport layer connection between the two routers instead of a PHY layer. The virtual link, also called a *wormhole*, allows the routers to claim they are connected directly by a link and so are only one hop apart. The two compromised routers can therefore advertise the wormhole as a "low-cost" path between their respective regions of the Internet. The two regions then naturally exchange traffic through the compromised routers and the wormhole.

An adversary usually launches a rushing attack as a prelude to other attacks. By attracting traffic to the wormhole endpoints, the compromised routers can eavesdrop and modify the datagrams flowing through them. Compromised routers at the end of a wormhole are also an ideal vehicle for selective deletion of messages.

Reorder

A second natural event in the Internet is datagram *reordering*. The two most common reordering mechanisms are forwarding table updates and traffic-shaping algorithms. Reordering due to forwarding takes place at the network layer; traffic shaping can be applied at the MAC layer or higher.

The Internet reconfigures itself automatically as routers set up new links with neighboring routers and tear down links between routers. These changes cause the routing application on each affected router to send an update to its neighbors, describing the topology change. These changes are gossiped across the network until every router is aware of what happened. Each router receiving such an update modifies its forwarding table to reflect the new Internet topology.

Since the forwarding table updates take place asynchronously from datagram exchanges, a router can select a different forwarding path for each datagram between even the same two devices. This means that two datagrams sent in order at the message source can arrive in a different order at the destination, since a router can update its forwarding table between the selection of a next hop for different datagrams.

The second reordering mechanism is traffic shaping, which gets imposed on the message flow to make better use of the communication resources. One example is quality of service. Some traffic classes, such as voice or streaming video, might be given higher priority by routers than best-effort traffic, which constitutes file transfers. Higher-priority means the router will send datagrams carrying voice or video first while buffering the traffic longer. Endpoint systems also apply traffic-shaping algorithms in an attempt to make real-time applications work better, without gravely affecting the performance of applications that can wait for their data. Any layer of the protocol stack can apply traffic shaping to the messages it generates or receives.

An attacker can emulate reordering any messages it intercepts, but since every device in the Internet must recover from message reordering anyway, reordering attacks are generally useful only in very specific contexts. We will not discuss them further.

Message Deletion

Like reordering, *message deletion* can happen through normal operation of the Internet modules. A MAC layer will drop any frame it receives with an invalid frame check sequence. A network layer module will discard any datagram it receives with an IP header error. A transport layer will drop any data segment received with a data checksum error. A router will drop perfectly good datagrams after receiving too many simultaneous bursts of traffic that lead to congestion and exhaustion of its buffers. For these reasons, TCP was designed to retransmit data segments in an effort to overcome errors.

The last class of attack possible with a Dolev-Yao adversary is message deletion. Two message deletion attacks occur frequently enough to be named: *black-hole attacks* and *gray-hole attacks*.

Black-hole attacks occur when a router deletes all messages it is supposed to forward. From time to time a router is misconfigured to offer a zero-cost routes to every destination in the Internet. This causes all traffic to be sent to this router. Since no device can sustain such a load, the router fails. The neighboring routers cannot detect the failure rapidly enough to configure alternate routes, and they fail as well. This continues until a significant portion of the routers in the Internet fail, resulting in a black hole: Messages flow into the collapsed portion of the Internet and never flow out. A black-hole attack intentionally misconfigures a router. Black-hole attacks also occur frequently in small-scale sensor, mesh, and peer-to-peer file networks.

A gray-hole attack is a selective deletion attack. Targeted jamming is one type of selective message deletion attack. More generally, an adversary can discard any message it intercepts in the Internet, thereby preventing its ultimate delivery. An adversary intercepting and selectively deleting messages can be difficult to detect and diagnose, so is a powerful attack. It is normally accomplished via compromised routers.

A subtler, indirect form of message deletion is also possible through the introduction of *forwarding loops*. Each IP datagram header has a *time-to-live* (TTL) field, limiting the number of hops that a datagram can make. This field is set to 255 by the initiator and decremented by each router the datagram passes through. If a router decrements the TTL field to zero, it discards the datagram.

The reason for the TTL field is that the routing protocols that update the forwarding tables can temporarily cause forwarding loops because updates are applied asynchronously as the routing updates are gossiped through the Internet. For instance, if router A gets updated prior to router B, A might believe that the best path to some destination C is via B, whereas B believes the best route to C is via A as the next hop. Messages for C will ping-pong between A and B until one or both are updated with new topology information.

An attacker who compromises a router or forges its routing traffic can intentionally introduce forwarding routes. This causes messages addressed to the destinations affected by the forgery to circulate until the TTL field gets decremented to zero. These attacks are also difficult to detect, because all the routers are behaving according to their specifications, but messages are being mysteriously lost.

3. DEFENDING AGAINST ATTACKS ON THE INTERNET

Now that we have a model for thinking about the threats against communication and we understand how the Internet works, we can examine how its communications can be protected. Here we will explain how cryptography is used to protect messages exchanged between various devices on the Internet and illustrate the techniques with examples.

As might be expected, the techniques vary according to scenario. Methods that are effective for an active session do not work for session establishment. Methods that are required for session establishment are too expensive for an established session. It is interesting that similar methods are used at each layer of the Internet architecture for protecting a session and for session establishment and that each layer defines its own security protocols. Many find the similarity of security solutions at different layers curious and wonder why security is not centralized in a single layer. We will explain why the same mechanisms solve different problems at different layers of the architecture, to give better insight into what each is for.

Layer Session Defenses

A *session* is a series of one or more related messages. The easiest and most straightforward defenses protect the exchange of messages that are organized into sessions, so we will start with session-oriented defenses.

Cryptography, when used properly, can provide reliable defenses against eavesdropping. It can also be used to detect forgery and replay attacks, and the methods used also have some relevance to detecting reordering and message deletion attacks. We will discuss how this is accomplished and illustrate the techniques with TLS, IPsec, and 802.11i.

Defending against Eavesdropping

The primary method used to defend against eavesdropping is encryption. Encryption was invented with the goal of making it infeasible for any computationally limited adversary to be able to learn anything useful about a message that cannot already be deduced by some other means, such as its length. Encryption schemes that appear to meet this goal have been invented and are in widespread use on the Internet. Here we will describe how they are used.

There are two forms of encryption: symmetric encryption, in which the same key is used to both encrypt and decrypt, and asymmetric encryption, in which encryption and decryption use distinct but related keys. The properties of each are different. Asymmetric encryption tends to be used only for applications related to session initiation and assertions about policy (although this is not universally true). The reason for this is that a single asymmetric key operation is generally too expensive to be applied to a message stream of arbitrary length. We therefore focus on symmetric encryption and how it is used by network security protocols.

A symmetric encryption scheme consists of three operations: *key generate*, *encrypt*, and *decrypt*. The key generate operation creates a *key,* which is a secret. The key generate procedure is usually application specific; we describe some examples of key generate operations in our discussion of session startup. Once generated, the key is used by the encrypt operation to transform *plaintext* messages—that is, messages that can be read by anyone—into *ciphertext*, which is messages that cannot be read by any computationally limited party who does not possess the key. The key is also used by the decrypt primitive to translate ciphertext messages back into plaintext messages.

There are two kinds of symmetric encryption algorithms. The first is type is called a *block cipher* and the second a *stream cipher*. Block and stream ciphers make different assumptions about the environment in which they operate, making each more effective than the other at different protocol layers.

A block cipher divides a message into chunks of a fixed size called *blocks* and encrypts each block separately. Block ciphers have the random access property, meaning that a block cipher can efficiently encrypt or decrypt any block utilizing an *initialization vector* in conjunction with the key. This property makes block ciphers a good choice for encrypting the content of MAC layer frames and network layer datagrams, for two reasons. First, the chunking behavior of a block cipher corresponds nicely to the packetization process used to form datagrams from segments and frames from datagrams. Second, and perhaps more important, the Internet architecture models the lower layers as "best-effort" services, meaning that it assumes that datagrams and frames are sent and then forgotten. If a transmitted datagram is lost due to congestion or bit error (or attack), it is up to the transport layer or application to recover. The random access property makes it easy to restart a block cipher anywhere it's needed in the datastream. Popular examples of block ciphers include AES, DES, and 3DES, used by Internet security protocols.

Block ciphers are used by the MAC and network layers to encrypt as follows: First, a block cipher mode of operation is selected. A block cipher itself encrypts and decrypts only single blocks. A mode of operation is a set of rules extending the encryption scheme from a single block to messages of arbitrary length. The most popular modes of operation used in the Internet are counter mode and cipher-block chaining (CBC) mode. Both require an initialization vector, which is a counter value for counter mode and a randomly generated bit vector for cipher-block chaining mode. To encrypt a message, the mode of operation first partitions the message into a sequence of blocks whose sizes equal that of the cipher's block size, padding if needed to bring the message length up to a multiple of the block size. The mode of operation then encrypts each block under the key while combining initialization vectors with the block in a mode-specific fashion.

For example, counter mode uses a counter as its initialization vector, which it increments, encrypts, and then exclusive-ORs the result with the block:

$$\text{counter} \rightarrow \text{counter} + 1; \text{E} \leftarrow \text{Encrypt}_{\text{Key}}(\text{counter});$$
$$\text{CipherTextBlock} \leftarrow \text{E} \oplus \text{PlainTextBlock}$$

where $\oplus$ denotes exclusive OR. The algorithm output the new (unencrypted) counter value, which is used to encrypt the next block, and CipherTextBlock.

The process of assembling a message from a message encrypted under a mode of operation is very simple: Prepend the original initialization vector to the sequence of ciphertext blocks, which together replace the plaintext payload for the message. The right way to think of this is that the initialization vector becomes a new message header layer. Also prepended is a *key identifier*, which indicates to the receiver which key it should utilize to decrypt the payload. This is important because in many cases it is useful to employ multiple connections between the same pair of endpoints, and so the receiver can have multiple decryption keys to choose from for each message received from a particular source.

A receiver reverses this process: First it extracts the initialization vector from the data payload, then it uses this and the ciphertext blocks to recover the original plaintext message by reversing the steps in the mode of operation.

This paradigm is widely used in MAC and network layer security protocols, including 802.11i, 802.16e, 802.1ae, and IPsec, each of which utilizes AES in modes related to counter and cipher-block chaining modes.

A stream cipher treats the data as a continuous stream and can be thought of as encrypting and decrypting data one bit at a time. Stream ciphers are usually designed so that each encrypted bit depends on all previously encrypted ones, so decryption becomes possible only if all the bits arrive in order; most true stream ciphers lack the random access property. This means that in principle stream ciphers only work in network protocols when they're used on top of a reliable data delivery service such as TCP, and so they only work correctly below the transport layer when used in conjunction with reliable data links. Stream ciphers are attractive from an implementation perspective because they can often achieve much higher throughputs than block ciphers. RC4 is an example of a popular stream cipher.

Stream ciphers typically do not use a mode of operation or an initialization vector at all, or at least not in the same sense as a block cipher. Instead, they are built as pseudo-random number generators, the output of which is based on a key. The random number generator is used to create a sequence of bits that appear random, called a *key stream*, and the result is exclusive OR'd with the plaintext data to create ciphertext. Since XOR is an idempotent operation, decryption with a stream cipher is just the same operation: Generate the same key stream and exclusive OR it with the ciphertext to recover the plaintext. Since stream ciphers do not utilize initialization vectors, Internet protocols employing stream ciphers do not need the extra overhead of a header to convey the initialization vector needed by the decryptor in the block cipher case. Instead, these protocols rely on the sender and receiver being able to keep their respective key stream generators synchronized for each bit transferred. This implies that stream ciphers can only be used over a reliable medium such as TCP—that is, a transport that guarantees delivery of all bits in the proper order and without duplication.

Transport layer security (TLS) is an example of an Internet security protocol that uses the stream cipher RC4. TLS runs on top of TCP.

Assuming that a symmetric encryption scheme is well designed, its efficacy against eavesdropping depends on four factors. Failing to consider *any* of these can cause the encryption scheme to fail catastrophically.

Independence of Keys

This is perhaps the most important consideration for the use of encryption. All symmetric encryption schemes assume that the encryption key for each and every session is generated independently of the encryption keys used for every other session. Let's parse this thought:

- *Independent* means selected or generated by a process that is indistinguishable by *any* polynomial time statistical test from the uniform distribution applied to the key space. One common failure is to utilize a key generation algorithm that is not random, such as using the MAC address or IP address of a device or time of session creation as the basis for a key. Schemes that use such public values instead of randomness for keys are easily broken using brute-force search techniques such as dictionary attacks. A second common failure is to pick an initial key randomly but create successive keys by some simple transformation, such as incrementing the initial key, exclusive OR'ing the MAC address of the device with the key, and so on. Encryption using key generation schemes of this sort are easily broken using differential cryptanalysis and related key attacks.

- *Each and every* mean each and every. For a block cipher, reusing the same key twice with the same initialization vector can allow an adversary to recover the plaintext data from the ciphertext *without* using the key. Similarly, each key always causes the pseudo-random number generator at the heart of a stream cipher to generate the same key stream, and reuse of the same key stream again will leak the plaintext data from the ciphertext without using the key.
- Methods effective for the coordinated generation of random keys at the beginning of each session constitute a complicated topic. We address it in our discussion of session startup later in the chapter.

Limited Output

Perhaps the second most important consideration is to limit the amount of information encrypted under a single key. The modern definition of security for an encryption scheme revolves around the idea of indistinguishability of the scheme's output from random. This goes back to a notion of ideal security proposed by Shannon. This has a dramatic effect on how long an encryption key may be safely used before an adversary has sufficient information to begin to learn something about the encrypted data.

Every encryption scheme is ultimately a deterministic algorithm, and no deterministic algorithm can generate an infinite amount of output that is indistinguishable from random. This means that encryption keys must be replaced on a regular basis. The amount of data that can be safely encrypted under a single key depends very much on the encryption scheme. As usual, the limitations for block ciphers and stream ciphers are a bit different.

Let the block size for a block cipher be some integer $n > 0$. Then, for any key K, for every string S_1 there is another string S_2 so that:

$$\text{Encrypt}_K(S_2) = S_1 \text{ and } \text{Decrypt}_K(S_1) = S_2$$

This says that a block cipher's encrypt and decrypt operations are *permutations* of the set of all bit strings whose length equals the block size. In particular, this property says that every pair of distinct n bit strings results in distinct n bit ciphertexts for any block cipher. However, by an elementary theorem from probability called the birthday paradox, random selection of n bit strings should result in a 50% probability that some string is chosen at least twice after about $2^{n/2}$ selections. This has an important consequence for block ciphers. It says that an algorithm as simple as naïve guessing can

distinguish the output of the block cipher from random after about $2^{n/2}$ blocks have been encrypted. This means that an encryption key should never be used to encrypt even close to $2^{n/2}$ blocks before a new, independent key is generated.

To make this specific, DES and 3DES have a block size of 64 bits; AES has a 128-bit block size. Therefore a DES or 3DES key should be used much less than to encrypt $2^{64/2} = 2^{32}$ blocks, whereas an AES key should never be used to encrypt as many as 2^{64} blocks; doing so begins to leak information about the encrypted data without use of the encryption key. As an example, 802.11i has been crafted to limit each key to encrypting 2^{48} before forcing generation of a new key.

This kind of arithmetic does not work for a stream cipher, since its block size is 1 bit. Instead, the length of time a key can be safely used is governed by the periodicity of the pseudorandom number generator at the heart of the stream cipher. RC4, for instance, becomes distinguishable from random after generating about 2^{31} bytes. Note that $31 \approx 32 = \sqrt{256}$, and 256 bytes is the size of the RC4 internal state. This illustrates the rule of thumb that there is a birthday paradox relation between the maximum number of encrypted bits of a stream cipher key and its internal state.

Key Size

The one "fact" about encryption that everyone knows is that larger keys result in stronger encryption. This is indeed true, provided that the generate keys operation is designed according to the independence condition. One common mistake is to properly generate a short key—say, 32 bits long—that is then concatenated to get a key of the length needed by the selected encryption scheme—say, 128 bits. Another similar error is to generate a short key and manufacture the remainder of the key with known public data, such as an IP address. These methods result in a key that is only as strong as the short key that was generated randomly.

Mode of Operation

The final parameter is the mode of operation—that is, the rules for using a block cipher to encrypt messages whose length is different than the block cipher width. The most common problem is failure to respect the document terms and conditions defined for using the mode of operation.

As an illustration of what can go wrong—even by people who know what they are doing—cipher-block chaining mode requires that the initialization vector be chosen randomly. The earliest version of the IPsec standard used cipher-block chaining mode exclusively for encryption. This standard recommended choosing initialization vectors as the final block of any prior message sent. The reasoning behind this recommendation was that, because an encrypted block cannot be distinguished from random if the number of blocks encrypted is limited, a block of a previously encrypted message ought to suffice. However, the advice given by the standard was erroneous because the initialization vector selection algorithm failed to have one property that a real random selection property has: The initialization vector is not unpredictable. A better way to meet the randomness requirement is to increment a counter, prepend it to the message to encrypt, and then encrypt the counter value, which becomes the initialization vector. This preserves the unpredictability property at a cost of encrypting one extra block.

A second common mistake is to design protocols using a mode of operation that was not designed to encrypt multiple blocks. For example, failing to use a mode of operation at all—using the naked encrypt and decrypt operations, with no initialization vector—is itself a mode of operation called *electronic code book* mode. Electronic code book mode was designed to encrypt messages that never span more than a single block—for example, encrypting keys to distribute for other operations. Using electronic code book mode on a message longer than a single block leaks a bit per block, however, because this mode allows an attacker to disguise when two plaintext blocks are the same or different. A classical example of this problem is to encrypt a photograph using electronic code book mode. The main outline of the photograph shows through plainly. This is not a failure of the encryption scheme; it is rather using encryption in a way that was never intended.

Now that we understand how encryption works and how it is used in Internet protocols, we should ask why is it needed at different layers. What does encryption at each layer of the Internet architecture accomplish? The best way to answer this question is to watch what it does.

Encryption applied at the MAC layer encrypts a single link. Data is encrypted prior to being put on a link and is decrypted again at the other end of a link. This leaves the IP datagrams conveyed by the MAC layer frames exposed inside each router as they wend their way across the Internet. Encryption at the MAC layer is a good way to transparently prevent data from leaking, since many devices never use encryption. For example, many organizations are distributed geographically and use direct point-to-point links to connect sites; encrypting the links connecting sites prevents an outsider from learning the organization's confidential information merely by eavesdropping. Legal wiretaps also depend on this arrangement because they monitor data inside routers. The case of legal wiretaps also illustrates the problem with link layer encryption only: If an unauthorized party assumes control of a router, they are free to read all the datagrams that traverse the router.

IPsec operates essentially at the network layer. Applying encryption via IPsec prevents exposure of the datagrams' payload end to end, so the data is still protected within routers. Since the payload of a datagram includes both the transport layer header as well as its data segments, applying encryption at the IPsec layer hides the applications being used as well as the data. This provides a big boost in confidentiality but also leads to more inefficient use of the Internet, since traffic-shaping algorithms in routers critically depend on having complete access to the transport headers. Using encryption at the IPsec layer also means the endpoints do not have to know whether each link a datagram traverses through the Internet applies encryption; using encryption at this layer simplifies the security analysis over encryption applied at the MAC layer alone. Finally, like MAC layer encryption, IPsec is a convenient tool for introducing encryption transparently to protect legacy applications, which by and large ignored confidentiality issues.

The transport layer encryption function can be illustrated by TLS. Like IPsec, TLS operates end to end, but TLS encrypts only the application data carried in the transport data segments, leaving the transport header exposed. Thus, with TLS, routers can still perform their traffic-shaping function, and we still have the simplified security analysis that comes with end-to-end encryption. The first downside of this method is that the exposure of the transport headers gives the attacker greater knowledge about what might be encrypted in the payload. The second downside is that it is somewhat more awkward to introduce encryption transparently at the transport layer; encryption at the transport layer requires cooperation by the application to perform properly.

This analysis says that it is reasonable to employ encryption at any one of the network protocol layers, because each solves a slightly different problem.

Before leaving the topic of encryption, it is worthwhile to emphasize what encryption does and does not do. Encryption, when properly used, is a *read access control*. If used properly, no one who lacks access to the encryption key can read the encrypted data. Encryption, however, is *not* a *write access control*; that is, it does not maintain the integrity of the encrypted data. Counter mode and stream ciphers are subject to bit-flipping attacks, for instance. An attacker launches a bit-flipping attack by capturing a frame or datagram, changing one or more bits from 0 to 1 (or vice versa) and retransmitting the altered frame. The resulting frame decrypts to some result—the altered message decrypts to something—and if bits are flipped judiciously, the result can be intelligible. As a second example, cipher-block chaining mode is susceptible to cut-and-paste attacks, whereby the attack cuts the final few blocks from one message in a stream and uses them to overwrite the final blocks of a later stream. At most one block decrypts to gibberish; if the attacker chooses the paste point judiciously, for example, so that it falls where the application ought to have random data anyway, this can be a powerful attack. The upshot is that even encrypted data needs an integrity mechanism to be effective, which leads us to the subject of defenses against forgeries.

Defending against Forgeries and Replays

Forgery and replay detection are usually treated together because replays are a special kind of forgery. We follow this tradition in our own discussion. Forgery detection, not eavesdropping protection, is the central concern for designs to secure network protocol. This is because every accepted forgery of an encrypted frame or datagram is a question for which the answer can tell the adversary about the encryption key or plaintext data. Just as in school, an attacker can learn about the encrypted stream or encryption key faster by asking questions rather than sitting back and passively listening.

Since eavesdropping is a passive attack, whereas creating forgeries is active, turning from the subject of eavesdropping to that of forgeries changes the security goals subtly. Encryption has a security goal of prevention—to prevent the adversary from learning anything useful about the data that cannot be derived in other ways. The comparable security goal for forgeries is to prevent the adversary from creating forgeries, which is infeasible. This is because any device with a transmitter appropriate for the medium can send forgeries by creating frames and datagrams using addresses employed by other parties. What is feasible is a form of asking forgiveness instead of permission: Prevent the adversary from creating *undetected* forgeries.

The cryptographic tool underlying forgery detection is called a *message authentication code*. Like an encryption scheme, a message authentication code consists of three operations: a *key generation* operation, a *tagging* operation, and a *verification* operation. Also like encryption, the key generation operation, which generates a symmetric key shared between the sender and receiver, is usually application specific. The tagging and verification operations, however, are much different from encrypt and decrypt.

The tagging operation takes the symmetric key, called an *authentication key*, and a message as input parameters and outputs a *tag*, which is a cryptographic checksum depending on the key and message as its output.

The verification operation takes three input parameters: the symmetric key, the message, and its tag. The verification algorithm recomputes the tag from the key and message and compares the result against the tag input into the algorithm. If the two fail to match, the verify algorithm outputs a signal that the message is a forgery. If the input and locally computed tag match, the verify algorithm declares that the message is authenticated.

The conclusion drawn by the verify algorithm of a message authentication code is not entirely logically correct. Indeed, if the tag is n bits in length, an attacker could generate a random n bit string as its tag and it would have one chance in 2^n of being valid. A message authentication scheme is considered good if there are no polynomial time algorithms that are significantly better than random guessing at producing correct tags.

Message authentication codes are incorporated into network protocols in a manner similar to encryption. First, a sequence number is prepended to the data that is being forgery protected; the sequence number, we will see, is used to detect replays. Next, a message authentication code tagging operation is applied to the sequence number and message body to produce a tag. The tag is appended to the message, and a key identifier for the authentication key is prepended to the message. The message can then be sent. The receiver determines whether the message was a forgery by first finding the authentication key identified by the key identifier, then by checking the correctness of the tag using the message authentication code's verify operation. If these checks succeed, the receiver finally uses the sequence number to verify that the message is not a replay.

How does replay detection work? When the authentication key is established, the sender initializes to zero the counter that is used in the authenticated message. The receiver meanwhile establishes a replay window, which is a list of all recently received sequence numbers. The replay window is initially empty. To send a replay protected frame, the sender increments his counter by one and prepends this at the front of the data to be authenticated prior to tagging. The receiver extracts the counter value from the received message and compares this to the replay window. If the counter falls before the replay window, which means it is too old to be considered valid, the receiver flags the message as a replay. The receiver does the same thing if the counter is already represented in the replay window data structure. If the counter is greater than the bottom of the replay window and is a counter value that has not yet been received, the frame or datagram is considered "fresh" instead of a replay.

The process is simplest to illustrate for the MAC layer. Over a single MAC link it is ordinarily impossible for frames to be reordered, because a single device can access the medium at a time and, because of the speed of electrons or photons comprising the signals representing bits, at least some of the bits at the start of a frame are received prior to the final bits being transmitted (satellite links are an exception). If frames cannot be reordered by a correctly operating MAC layer, the replay window data structure records the counter for the last received frame, and the replay detection algorithm merely has to decide whether the replay counter value in a received frame is larger than that recorded in its replay window. If the counter is less than or equal to the replay window value, the frame is a forgery; otherwise it is considered genuine. 802.11i, 802.16, and 802.1ae all employ this approach to replay detection. This same approach can be used by a message authentication scheme operating above the transport layer, by protocols such as TLS and SSH (Secure Shell), since the transport eliminates duplicates and delivers bits in the order sent. The replay window is more complicated at the network layer, however, because some reordering is natural, given that the network reorders datagrams. Hence, for the network layer the replay window is usually sized to account for the maximum reordering expected in the "normal" Internet. IPsec uses this more complex replay window.

The reason that this works is the following: Every message is given a unique, incrementing sequence number in the form of its counter value. The transmitter computes the message authentication code tag over the sequence number and the message data. Since it is infeasible for a computationally bounded adversary to create a valid tag for the data with probability significantly greater than $1/2^n$, a tag validated by the receiver implies that the message, including its sequence number, was created by the transmitter. The worst thing that could have happened, therefore, is that the adversary has delayed the message. However, if the sequence number falls within the replay window, the message could not have been delayed longer than reordering due to the normal operation of forwarding and traffic shaping within the Internet.

A replay detection scheme limits an adversary's opportunities to delete and to reorder messages. If a message does not arrive at its destination, its sequence number is never set in the receive window, so it can be declared a lost message. It is easy to track the percentage of lost messages, and if this exceeds some threshold, then communications become unreliable, but more important, the cause of the unreliability can be investigated. Similarly, messages received outside the replay window can also be tracked, and if the percentage becomes too high, messages are arriving out of order more frequently than might be expected from normal operation of the Internet, pointing to a configuration problem, an equipment failure, or an attack. Again, the cause of the anomaly can be investigated. Mechanisms like these are often the way that attacks are discovered in the first place. The important lesson is that attacks and even faulty equipment or misconfigurations are often difficult to detect without collecting reliability statistics, and the forgery detection mechanisms can provide some of the best reliability statistics available.

Just like encryption, the correctness of this analysis depends critically on the design enforcing some fundamental assumptions, regardless of the quality of the message authentication code on which it might be based. If any of the following assumptions are violated, the forgery detection scheme can fail catastrophically to accomplish its mission.

Independence of Authentication Keys

This is absolutely paramount for forgery detection. If the message authentication keys are not independent, an attacker can easily create forged message authentication tags based on authentication keys learned in other ways. This assumption is so important that it is useful to examine in greater detail.

The first point is that a message authentication key utterly fails to accomplish its mission if it is shared among even three parties; only two parties must know any particular authentication key. This is very easy to illustrate. Suppose A, B, and C were to share a message authentication key, and suppose A creates a forgery-protected message it sends to C. What can C conclude when it receives this message? C cannot conclude that the message actually originated from A, even though its addressing indicates it did, because B could have produced the same message and used A's address. C cannot even conclude that B did not change some of the message in transit. Therefore, the algorithm loses all its efficacy for detecting forgeries if message authentication keys are known by more than two parties. They must be known by at least two parties or the receiver cannot verify that the message and its bits originated with the sender.

This is much different than encryption. An encryption/decryption key can be distributed to every member of a group, and as long as the key is not leaked from the group to a third party, the encryption scheme remains an effective read access control against parties that are not members of the group. Message authentication utterly fails if the key is shared beyond two parties. This is due to the active nature of forgery attacks and the fact that forgery handling, being a detection rather than a prevention scheme, already affords the adversary more latitude than encryption toward fooling the good guys.

So message authentication keys must be shared between exactly two communicating devices for forgery detection schemes to be effective. As with encryption keys, a message authentication key must be generated randomly because brute-force searches and related key attacks can recover the key by observing messages transiting the medium.

No Reuse of Replay Counter Values with a Key

Reusing a counter with a message authentication key is analogous to reusing an initialization vector with an encryption key. Instead of leaking data, however, replay counter value reuse leads automatically to trivial forgeries based on replayed messages. The attacker's algorithm is trivial: Using a packet sniffer, record each of the messages protected by the same key and file them in a database. If the attacker ever receives a key identifier and sequence number pair already in the database, the transmitter has begun to reuse replay counter values with a key. The attacker can then replay any message with a higher sequence number and the same key identifier. The receiver will be fooled into accepting the replayed message.

An implication of this approach is that known forgery detection schemes cannot be based on static keys. We could to the contrary attempt to design such a scheme. One could try to checkpoint in nonvolatile memory the replay counter at the transmitter and the replay window at the receiver. This approach does not work, however, in the presence of a Dolev-Yao adversary. The adversary can capture a forgery-protected frame in flight and then delete all successive messages. At its convenience later, the adversary resends the captured message. The receiver, using its static message authentication key, will verify the tag and, based on its replay window retrieved from nonvolatile storage, verify that the message is indeed in sequence and so accept the message as valid. This experiment demonstrates that forgery detection is not entirely satisfactory, because sequence numbers do not take timeliness into account. Secure clock

synchronization, however, is a difficult problem with solutions that enjoy only partial success. The construction of better schemes that account for timing remains an open research problem.

Key Size

If message authentication keys must be randomly generated, they must also be of sufficient size to discourage brute-force attack. The key space has to be large enough to make exhaustive search for the message authentication key cost prohibitive. Key sizes for message authentication comparable with those for encryption are sufficient for this task.

Message Authentication Code Tag Size

We have seen many aspects that make message authentication codes somewhat more fragile encryption schemes. Message authentication code size is one in which forgery detection can on the contrary effectively utilize a smaller block size than an encryption scheme. Whereas an encryption scheme based on a 128-bit block size has to replace keys every 2^{48} or so blocks to avoid leaking data, an encryption scheme can maintain the same level of security with about a 48-bit message authentication code tag. The difference is that the block cipher-based encryption scheme leaks information about the encrypted data due to the birthday paradox, whereas an attacker has to create a valid forgery based on exhaustive search due to the active nature of a forgery attack. In general, to determine the size of a tag needed by a message authentication code, we have only to determine the maximum number of messages sent in the lifetime of the key. If this number of messages is bounded by 2^n, the tag need only be $n + 1$ bits long.

As with encryption, many find it confusing that forgery detection schemes are offered at nearly every layer of the Internet architecture. To understand this, it is again useful to ask the question about what message forgery detection accomplishes at each layer.

If a MAC module requires forgery detection for every frame received, physical access to the medium being used by the module's PHY layer affords an attacker no opportunity to create forgeries. This is a very strong property. It means that the only MAC layer messages attacking the receiver are either generated by other devices authorized to attach to the medium or else are forwarded by the network layer modules of authorized devices, because all frames received directly off the medium generated by unauthorized devices will be discarded by the forgery detection scheme. A MAC layer forgery detection scheme therefore essentially provides a write access control of the physical medium, closing it to unauthorized parties. Installing a forgery detection scheme at any other layer will not provide this kind of protection. Requiring forgery detection at the MAC layer is therefore desirable whenever feasible.

A different kind of assurance is provided by forgery detection at the network layer. IPsec is the protocol designed to accomplish this function. If a network layer module requires IPsec for every datagram received, this essentially cuts off attacks against the device hosting the module to other authorized machines in the entire Internet; datagrams generated by unauthorized devices will be dropped. With this forgery detection scheme it is still possible for an attacker on the same medium to generate frames attacking the device's MAC layer module, but attacks against higher layers become computationally infeasible. Installing a forgery detection scheme at any other layer will not provide this kind of protection. Requiring forgery detection at the network layer is therefore desirable whenever feasible as well.

Applying forgery detection at the transport layer offers different assurances entirely. Forgery detection at this level assures the receiving application that the arriving messages were generated by the peer application, not by some virus or Trojan-horse program that has linked itself between modules between protocol layers on the same or different machine. This kind of assurance cannot be provided by any other layer. Such a scheme at the network or MAC layers only defends against message injection by unauthorized devices on the Internet generally or directly attached to the medium, not against messages generated by unauthorized processes running on an authorized machine. Requiring forgery detection at the transport layer therefore is desirable whenever it is feasible.

The conclusion is that forgery detection schemes accomplish different desirable functions at each protocol layer. The security goals that are achievable are always architecturally dependent, and this sings through clearly with forgery detection schemes.

We began the discussion of forgery detection by noting that encryption by itself is subject to attack. One final issue is how to use encryption and forgery protection together to protect the same message. Three solutions could be formulated to this problem. One approach might be to add forgery detection to a message first—add the authentication key identifier, the replay sequence number, and the message authentication code tag—followed by encryption of the message data and forgery detection headers. TLS is an example Internet protocol that takes this approach. The second approach is to reverse the order of encryption and forgery detection: First encrypt, then compute the tag over the encrypted data and the encryption headers. IPsec is an example Internet protocol defined to use this approach. The last approach is to apply both simultaneously to the plaintext data. SSH is an Internet protocol constructed in this manner.

Session Startup Defenses

If encryption and forgery detection techniques are such powerful security mechanisms, why aren't they used universally for all network communications? The problem is that not everyone is your friend; everyone has enemies, and in every human endeavor there are those with criminal mindsets who want to prey on others. Most people do not go out of their way to articulate and maintain relationships with their enemies unless there is some compelling reason to do so, and technology is powerless to change this.

More than anything else, the keys used by encryption and forgery detection are relationship signifiers. Possession of keys is useful not only because they enable encryption and forgery detection but because their use assures the remote party that messages you receive will remain confidential and that messages the peer receives from you actually originated from you. They enable the accountable maintenance of a preexisting relationship. If you receive a message that is protected by a key that only you and I know, and you didn't generate the message yourself, it is reasonable for you to conclude that I sent the message to you and did so intentionally.

If keys are signifiers of preexisting relationships, much of our networked communications cannot be defended by cryptography, because we do not have preexisting relationships with everyone. We send and receive email to and from people we have never met. We buy products online from merchants we have never met. None of these relationships would be possible if we required all messages to be encrypted or authenticated. What is always required is an open, unauthenticated, risky channel to establish new relationships; cryptography can only assure us that communication from parties with whom we already have relationships is indeed occurring with the person with whom we think we are communicating.

A salient and central assumption for both encryption and forgery detection is that the keys these mechanisms use are fresh and independent across sessions. A session is an instance of exercising a relationship to effect communication. This means that secure communications require a state change, transitioning from a state in which two communicating parties are not engaged in an instance of communication to one in which they are. This state change is *session establishment*.

Session establishment is like a greeting between human beings. It is designed to synchronize two entities communicating over the Internet and establish and synchronize their keys, key identifiers, sequence numbers and replay windows, and, indeed, all the states to provide mutual assurance that the communication is genuine and confidential.

The techniques and data structures used to establish a secure session are different from those used to carry on a conversation. Our next goal is to look at some representative mechanisms in this area. The field is vast and it is impossible to do more than skim the surface briefly to give the reader a glimpse of the beauty and richness of the subject.

Secure session establishment techniques typically have three goals, as described in the following subsections.

Mutual Authentication

First, session establishment techniques seek to mutually authenticate the communicating parties to each other. *Mutually authenticate* means that both parties learn the "identity" of the other. It is not possible to know what is proper to discuss with another party without also knowing the identity of the other party. If only one party learns the identity of the other, it is always possible for an imposter to masquerade as the unknown party.

Key Secrecy

Second, session establishment techniques seek to establish a session key that can be maintained as a secret between the two parties and is known to no one else. The session key must be independent from all other keys for all other session instances and indeed from all other keys. This implies that no adversary with limited computational resources can distinguish the key from random. Generating such an independent session key is both harder and easier than it sounds; it is always possible to do so if a preexisting relationship already exists between the two communicating parties, and it is impossible to do so reliably if a preexisting relationship does not exist. Relationships begat other relationships, and nonrelationships are sterile with respect to the technology.

Session State Consistency

Finally, the parties need to establish a consistent view of the session state. This means that they both agree on the identities of both parties; they agree on the session

key instance; they agree on the encryption and forgery detection schemes used, along with any associated state such as sequence counters and replay windows; and they agree on which instance of communication this session represents. If they fail to agree on a single shared parameter, it is always possible for an imposter to convince one of the parties that it is engaged in a conversation that is different from its peer's conversation.

Mutual Authentication

There are an enormous number of ways to accomplish the mutual authentication function needed to initiate a new session. Here we examine two that are used in various protocols within the Internet.

A Symmetric Key Mutual Authentication Method

Our old friend the message authentication code can be used with a static, long-lived key to create a simple and robust mutual authentication scheme. Earlier we stressed that the properties of message authentication are incompatible with the use of a static key to provide forgery detection of session-oriented messages. The incompatibility is due to the use of sequence numbers for replay detection. We will replace sequence numbers with unpredictable quantities in order to resocialize static keys. The cost of this resocialization effort will be a requirement to exchange extra messages.

Suppose parties A and B want to mutually authenticate. We will assume that ID_A is B's name for A, whereas ID_B is A's name for B. We will also assume that A and B share a long-lived message authentication key K, and that K is known only to A and B. We will assume that A initiates the authentication. A and B can mutually authenticate using a three-message exchange, as follows: For message 1, A generates a random number R_A and sends a message containing its identity ID_A and random number to B:

$$\text{A} \rightarrow \text{B}: ID_A, R_A \qquad (1)$$

The notation $\text{A} \rightarrow \text{B}: m$ means that A sends message m to B. Here the message being passed is specified as ID_A, R_A, meaning it conveys A's identity ID_A and A's random number R_A. This message asserts B's name for A, to tell B which is the right long-lived key it should use in this instance of the authentication protocol. The random number R_A plays the role of the sequence number in the session-oriented case.

If B is willing to have a conversation with A at this time, it fetches the correct message authentication key

K, generates its own random number R_B, and computes a message authentication code tag T over the message ID_B, ID_A, R_A, R_B, that is, over the message consisting of both names and both random numbers. B appends the tag to the message, which it then sends to A in response to message 1:

$$B \rightarrow A:\ ID_B,\ ID_A,\ R_A,\ R_B,\ T \qquad (2)$$

B includes A's name in the message to tell A which key to use to authenticate the message. It includes A's random number R_A in the message to signal the protocol instance to which this message responds.

The magic begins when A validates the message authentication code tag T. Since independently generated random numbers are unpredictable, A knows that the second message could not have been produced before A sent the first, because it returns R_A to A. Since the authentication code tag T was computed over the two identities ID_B and ID_A and the two random numbers R_A and R_B using the key K known only to A and B, and since A did not create the second message itself, A knows that B must have created message 2. Hence, message 2 is a response from B to A's message 1 for this instance of the protocol. If the message were to contain some other random number than R_A, A would know the message is not a response to its message 1.

If A verifies message 2, it responds by computing a message authentication code tag T' computed over ID_A and B's random number RB, which it includes in message 3:

$$A \rightarrow B:\ ID_A,\ R_B,\ T' \qquad (3)$$

Reasoning as before, B knows A produced message 3 in response to its message 2, because message 3 could not have been produced prior to message 2 and only A could have produced the correct tag T'. Thus, after message 3 is delivered, A and B both have been assured of each other's identity, and they also agree on the session instance, which is identified by the pair of random numbers R_A and R_B.

A deeper analysis of the protocol reveals that message 2 must convey both identities and both random numbers protected from forgery by the tag T. This construction binds A's view of the session with B's. This binding prevents interleaving or man-in-the-middle attacks. As an example, without this binding, a third party, C, could masquerade as B to A and as A to B.

It is worth noting that message 1 is not protected from either forgery or replay. This lack of any protections is an intrinsic part of the problem statement. During the protocol, A and B must transition from a state where they are unsure about the other's identity and have no communication instance instantiating the long-term relationship signified by the encryption key K to a state where they fully agree on each other's identities and a common instance of communication expressing their long-lived relationship. A makes the transition upon verifying message 2, and there are no known ways to reassure it about B until this point of the protocol. B makes the state transition once it has completed verification of message 3. The point of the protocol is to transition from a mutually suspicious state to a mutually trusted state.

An Asymmetric Key Mutual Authentication Method

Authentication based on asymmetric keys is also possible. In addition to asymmetric encryption there is also an asymmetric key analog of a message authentication code called a *signature scheme*. Just like a message authentication code, a signature scheme consists of three operations: *key generate*, *sign*, and *verify*. The key generate operation outputs two parameters, a signing key S and a related verification key V. S's key holder is never supposed to reveal S to another party, whereas V is meant to be a public value. Under these assumptions the sign operation takes the signing key S and a message M as input parameters and output a signature s of M. The verify operation takes the verification key V, message M and signature s as inputs, and returns whether it verifies that s was created from S and M. If the signing key S is indeed known by only one party, the signature s must have been produced by that party. This is because it is infeasible for a computationally limited party to compute the signature s without S. Asymmetric signature schemes are often called *public/private key schemes* because S is maintained as a secret, never shared with another party, whereas the verification key is published to everyone.

Signature schemes were invented to facilitate authentication. To accomplish this goal, the verification key must be public, and it is usually published in a certificate, which we will denote as $cert(ID_A, V)$, where ID_A is the identity of the key holder of S, and V is the verification key corresponding to A. The certificate is issued by a well-known party called a *certificate authority*. The sole job of the certificate authority is to introduce one party to another. A certificate $cert(ID_A, V)$ issued by a certificate authority is an assertion that entity A has a public verification key V that is used to prove A's identity.

As with symmetric authentication, hundreds of different authentication protocols can be based on signature schemes. The following is one example among legion:

$$A \rightarrow B: \ cert(ID_A, V), R_A \qquad (4)$$

Here $cert(ID_A, V)$ is A's certificate, conveying its identity ID_A and verification key V; R_A is a random number generated by A. If B is willing to begin a new session with A, it responds with the message:

$$B \rightarrow A: \ cert(ID_B, V'), R_B, R_A, \text{sig}_B(ID_A, R_B, R_A) \qquad (5)$$

R_B is a random number generated by B, and $\text{sig}_B(ID_A, R_B, R_A)$ is B's signature over the message with fields ID_A, R_B, and R_A. Including IDA under B's signature is essential because it is B's way of asserting that A is the target of message 2. Including RB and RA in the information signed is also necessary to defeat man-in-the-middle attacks. A responds with a third message:

$$A \rightarrow B: \ cert(ID_A, V), R_b, \text{sig}_B(ID_B, R_B) \qquad (6)$$

A Caveat

Mutual authentication is necessary to establish identities. Identities are needed to decide on the access control policies to apply to a particular conversation, that is, to answer the question, Which information that the party knows is suitable for sharing in the context of this communications instance? Authentication—mutual or otherwise—has very limited utility if the communications channel is not protected against eavesdropping and forgeries.

One of the most common mistakes made by Wi-Fi hotspot operators, for instance, is to require authentication but disable eavesdropping and forgery protection for the subsequent Internet access via the hotspot. This is because anyone with a Wi-Fi radio transmitter can access the medium and hijack the session from a paying customer. Another way of saying this is that authentication is useful only when it's used in conjunction with a secure channel. This leads to the topic of session key establishment. The most common use of mutual authentication is to establish ephemeral session keys using the long-lived authentication keys. We will discuss session key establishment next.

Key Establishment

Since it is generally infeasible for authentication to be meaningful without a subsequent secure channel, and since we know how to establish a secure channel across the Internet if we have a key, the next goal is to add key establishment to mutual authentication protocols. In this model, a mutual authentication protocol establishes an ephemeral session key as a side effect of its successful operation; this session key can then be used to construct all the encryption and authentication keys needed to establish a secure channel. All the session states, such as sequence number, replay windows, and key identifiers, can be initialized in conjunction with the completion of the mutual authentication protocol.

It is usually feasible to add key establishment to an authentication protocol. Let's illustrate this with the symmetric key authentication protocol, based on a message authentication code, discussed previously. To extend the protocol to establish a key, we suppose instead that A and B share two long-lived keys K and K'. The first key K is a message authentication key as before. The second key K' is a derivation key, the only function of which is to construct other keys within the context of the authentication protocol. This is accomplished as follows: After verifying message 2 (from line 2 previously), A computes a session key SK as:

$$SK \leftarrow prf(K', R_A, R_B, ID_A, ID_B, length) \qquad (7)$$

Here prf is another cryptographic primitive called a *pseudo random function*. A pseudo random function is characterized by the properties that (a) its output is indistinguishable from random by any computationally limited adversary and (b) it is hard to invert, that is, given a fixed output O, it is infeasible for any computationally limited adversary to find an input I so that $O \leftarrow prf(I)$. The output SK of (7) is *length* bits long and can be split into two pieces to become encryption and message authentication keys. B generates the same SK when it receives message 3. An example of a pseudo-random function is any block cipher, such as AES, in cipher-block chaining MAC mode. Cipher-block chaining MAC mode is just like Cipher-block chaining mode, except all but the last block of encrypted data is discarded.

This construction meets the goal of creating an independent, ephemeral set of encryptions of message authentication keys for each session. The construction creates independent keys because any two outputs of a *prf* appear to be independently selected at random to any adversary that is computationally limited. A knows that all the outputs are statistically distinct, because A picks the parameter to the prf R_A randomly for each instance of the protocol; similarly for B. And using the communications instances identifiers RA, RB along with A and B's identities ID_A and ID_B are interpreted as a "contract" to use SK only for this session instance and only between A and B.

Public key versions of key establishment based on signatures and asymmetric encryption also exist, but we will close with one last public key variant based on a completely different asymmetric key principle called the *Diffie-Hellman algorithm*.

The Diffie-Hellman algorithm is based on the discrete logarithm problem in finite groups. A group G is a mathematical object that is closed under an associative multiplication and has inverses for each element in G. The prototypical example of a finite group is the integers under addition modulo a prime number p.

The idea is to begin with an element g of a finite group G that has a long period. This means to $g^1 = g$, $g^2 = g \times g$, $g^3 = g^2 \times g$, ... Since G is finite, this sequence must eventually repeat. It turns out that $g = g^{n+1}$ for some integer $n > 1$, and $g^n = e$ is the group's neutral element. The element e has the property that $h \times e = e \times h = h$ for every element h in G, and n is called the *period* of g. With such an element it is easy to compute powers of g, but it is hard to compute the logarithm of g^k. If g is chosen carefully, no polynomial time algorithm is known that can compute k from g^k. This property leads to a very elegant key agreement scheme:

$$A \rightarrow B: cert(ID_A, V), g^a$$
$$B \rightarrow A: g^b, cert(ID_B, V'), sig_B(g^a, g^b, ID_A)$$
$$A \rightarrow B: sig_A(g^b, g^a, ID_B)$$

The session key is then computed as $SK \leftarrow prf(K, g^a g^b, ID_A, ID_B)$, where $K \leftarrow prf(0, g^{ab})$. In this protocol, a is a random number chosen by A, b is a random number chosen by B, and 0 denotes the all zeros key. Note that A sends g^a unprotected across the channel to B.

The quantity g^{ab} is called the Diffie-Hellman key. Since B knows the random secret b, it can compute $g^{ab} = (g^a)^b$ from A's public value g^a, and similarly A can compute g^{ab} from B's public value g^b. This construction poses no risk, because the discrete logarithm problem is intractable, so it is computationally infeasible for an attacker to determine a from g^a. Similarly, B may send g^b across the channel in the clear, because a third party cannot extract b from g^b. B's signature on message 2 prevents forgeries and assures that the response is from B. Since no method is known to compute g^{ab} from g^a and g^b, only A and B will know the Diffie-Hellman key at the end of the protocol. The step $K \leftarrow prf(0, g^{ab})$ extracts

all the computational entropy from the Diffie-Hellman key. The construction $SK \leftarrow prf(K, g^a g^b, ID_A, ID_B)$ computes a session key, which can be split into encryption and message authentication keys as before.

The major drawback of Diffie-Hellman is that it is subject to man-in-the-middle attacks. The preceding protocol uses signatures to remove this threat. B's signature authenticates B to a and also binds g^a and g^b together, preventing man-in-the-middle attacks. Similarly, A's signature on message 3 assures B that the session is with A.

These examples illustrate that is practical to construct session keys that meet the requirements for cryptography, if a preexisting long-lived relationship already exists.

State Consistency

We have already observed that the protocol specified in (1) through (3) achieves state consistency when the protocol succeeds. Both parties agree on the identities and on the session instance. When a session key SK is derived, as in (7), both parties also agree on the key. Determining which parties know which pieces of information after each protocol message is the essential tool for a security analysis of this kind of protocol. The analysis of this protocol is typical for authentication and key establishment protocols.

4. CONCLUSION

This chapter examined how cryptography is used on the Internet to secure protocols. It reviewed the architecture of the Internet protocol suite, as even what security means is a function of the underlying system architecture. Next it reviewed the Dolev-Yao model, which describes the threats to which network communications are exposed. In particular, all levels of network protocols are completely exposed to eavesdropping and manipulation by an attacker, so using cryptography properly is a first-class requirement to derive any benefit from its use. We learned that effective security mechanisms to protect session-oriented and session establishment protocols are different, although they can share many cryptographic primitives. Cryptography can be very successful at protecting messages on the Internet, but doing so requires preexisting, long-lived relationships. How to build secure open communities is still an open problem; it is probably intractable because a solution would imply the elimination of conflict between human beings who do not know each other.

## Chapter 8

The Botnet Problem

Xinyuan Wang
George Mason University

Daniel Ramsbrock
George Mason University

A *botnet* is a collection of compromised Internet computers being controlled remotely by attackers for malicious and illegal purposes. The term comes from these programs being called *robots*, or *bots* for short, due to their automated behavior.

Bot software is highly evolved Internet malware, incorporating components of viruses, worms, spyware, and other malicious software. The person controlling a botnet is known as the *botmaster* or *bot-herder*, and he seeks to preserve his anonymity at all costs. Unlike previous malware such as viruses and worms, the motivation for operating a botnet is financial. Botnets are extremely profitable, earning their operators hundreds of dollars per day. Botmasters can either rent botnet processing time to others or make direct profits by sending spam, distributing spyware to aid in identity theft, and even extorting money from companies via the threat of a distributed denial-of-service (DDoS) attack.[1] It is no surprise that many network security researchers believe that botnets are one of the most pressing security threats on the Internet today.

> *Bots are at the center of the undernet economy. Almost every major crime problem on the Net can be traced to them.*
>
> —Jeremy Linden, formerly of Arbor Networks[2]

1. INTRODUCTION

You sit down at your computer in the morning, still squinting from sleep. Your computer seems a little slower than usual, but you don't think much of it. After checking the news, you try to sign into eBay to check on your auctions. Oddly enough, your password doesn't seem to work. You try a few more times, thinking maybe you changed it recently—but without success.

Figuring you'll look into it later, you sign into online banking to pay some of those bills that have been piling up. Luckily, your favorite password still works there—so it must be a temporary problem with eBay. Unfortunately, you are in for more bad news: The $0.00 balance on your checking and savings accounts isn't just a "temporary problem." Frantically clicking through the pages, you see that your accounts have been completely cleaned out with wire transfers to several foreign countries.

You check your email, hoping to find some explanation of what is happening. Instead of answers, you have dozens of messages from "network operations centers" around the world, informing you in no uncertain terms that your computer has been scanning, spamming, and sending out massive amounts of traffic over the past 12 hours or so. Shortly afterward, your Internet connection stops working altogether, and you receive a phone call from your service provider. They are very sorry, they explain, but due to something called "botnet activity" on your computer, they have temporarily disabled your account. Near panic now, you demand an explanation from the network technician on the other end. "What exactly is a botnet? How could it cause so much damage overnight?"

Though this scenario might sound far-fetched, it is entirely possible; similar things have happened to thousands of people over the last few years. Once a single bot program is installed on a victim computer, the possibilities are nearly endless. For example, the attacker can get your online passwords, drain your bank accounts, and use your computer as a remote-controlled "zombie" to scan for other victims, send out spam emails, and even launch DDoS attacks.

---

1 T. Holz, "A short visit to the bot zoo," *IEEE Security and Privacy*, 3(3), 2005, pp. 76–79.

2 S. Berinato, "Attack of the bots," *WIRED*, Issue 14.11, November 2006, www.wired.com/wired/archive/14.11/botnet.html.

This chapter describes the botnet threat and the countermeasures available to network security professionals. First, it provides an overview of botnets, including their origins, structure, and underlying motivation. Next, the chapter describes existing methods for defending computers and networks against botnets. Finally, it addresses the most important aspect of the botnet problem: how to identify and track the botmaster in order to eliminate the root cause of the botnet problem.

2. BOTNET OVERVIEW

Bots and botnets are the latest trend in the evolution of Internet malware. Their black-hat developers have built on the experience gathered from decades of viruses, worms, Trojan horses, and other malware to create highly sophisticated software that is difficult to detect and remove. Typical botnets have several hundred to several thousand members, though some botnets have been detected with over 1.5 million members.[3] As of January 2007, Google's Vinton Cerf estimated that up to 150 million computers (about 25% of all Internet hosts) could be infected with bot software.[4]

Origins of Botnets

Before botnets, the main motivation for Internet attacks was fame and notoriety. By design, these attacks were noisy and easily detected. High-profile examples are the Melissa email worm (1999), ILOVEYOU (2000), Code Red (2001), Slammer (2003), and Sasser (2004).[5,6] Though the impact of these viruses and worms was severe, the damage was relatively short-lived and consisted mainly of the cost of the outage plus man-hours required for cleanup. Once the infected files had been removed from the victim computers and the vulnerability patched, the attackers no longer had any control.

By contrast, botnets are built on the very premise of extending the attacker's control over his victims. To achieve long-term control, a bot must be stealthy during every part of its lifecycle, unlike its predecessors.[2] As a result, most bots have a relatively small network footprint and do not create much traffic during typical operation. Once a bot is in place, the only required traffic consists of incoming commands and outgoing responses, constituting the botnet's command and control (C&C) channel. Therefore, the scenario at the beginning of the chapter is not typical of all botnets. Such an obvious attack points to either a brazen or inexperienced botmaster, and there are plenty of them.

The concept of a remote-controlled computer bot originates from Internet Relay Chat (IRC), where benevolent bots were first introduced to help with repetitive administrative tasks such as channel and nickname management.[1,2] One of the first implementations of such an IRC bot was Eggdrop, originally developed in 1993 and still one of the most popular IRC bots.[6,7] Over time, attackers realized that IRC was in many ways a perfect medium for large-scale botnet C&C. It provides an instantaneous one-to-many communications channel and can support very large numbers of concurrent users.[8]

Botnet Topologies and Protocols

In addition to the traditional IRC-based botnets, several other protocols and topologies have emerged recently. The two main botnet topologies are centralized and peer-to-peer (P2P). Among centralized botnets, IRC is still the predominant protocol,[9,10,11] but this trend is decreasing and several recent bots have used HTTP for their C&C channels.[9,11] Among P2P botnets, many different protocols exist, but the general idea is to use a decentralized collection of peers and thus eliminate the single point of failure found in centralized botnets. P2P is becoming the most popular botnet topology because it has many advantages over centralized botnets.[12]

3 Joris Evers, "'Bot herders' may have controlled 1.5 million PCs," http://news.cnet.com/Bot-herders-may-have-controlled-1.5-million-PCs/2100-7350_3-5906896.html

4 A. Greenberg, "Spam crackdown 'a drop in the bucket,'" *Forbes*, June 14, 2007, www.forbes.com/security/2007/06/14/spam-arrest-fbi-tech-security-cx_ag_0614spam.html.

5 Wikipedia contributors, "Timeline of notable computer viruses and worms," http://en.wikipedia.org/w/index.php?title=Timeline_of_notable_computer_viruses_and_worms&oldid=207972502 (accessed May 3, 2008).

6 P. Barford and V. Yegneswaran, "An inside look at botnets," Special Workshop on Malware Detection, Advances in Information Security, Springer Verlag, 2006.

7 Wikipedia contributors, "Eggdrop," http://en.wikipedia.org/w/index.php?title=Eggdrop&oldid=207430332 (accessed May 3, 2008).

8 E. Cooke, F. Jahanian, and D. McPherson, "The zombie roundup: Understanding, detecting, and disturbing botnets," in Proc. 1st Workshop on Steps to Reducing Unwanted Traffic on the Internet (SRUTI), Cambridge, July 7, 2005, pp. 39–44.

9 N. Ianelli and A. Hackworth, "Botnets as a vehicle for online crime," in Proc. 18th Annual Forum of Incident Response and Security Teams (FIRST), Baltimore, June 25–30, 2006.

10 M. Rajab, J. Zarfoss, F. Monrose, and A. Terzis, "A multifaceted approach to understanding the botnet phenomenon," in Proc. of the 6th ACM SIGCOM Internet Measurement Conference, Rio de Janeiro, Brazil, October 2006.

11 Trend Micro, "Taxonomy of botnet threats," Trend Micro Enterprise Security Library, November 2006.

12 Symantec, "Symantec internet security threat report, trends for July–December 2007," Volume XIII, April 2008.

Centralized

Centralized botnets use a single entity (a host or a small collection of hosts) to manage all bot members. The advantage of a centralized topology is that it is fairly easy to implement and produces little overhead. A major disadvantage is that the entire botnet becomes useless if the central entity is removed, since bots will attempt to connect to nonexistent servers. To provide redundancy against this problem, many modern botnets rely on dynamic DNS services and/or fast-flux DNS techniques. In a fast-flux configuration, hundreds or thousands of compromised hosts are used as proxies to hide the identities of the true C&C servers. These hosts constantly alternate in a round-robin DNS configuration to resolve one hostname to many different IP addresses (none of which are the true IPs of C&C servers). Only the proxies know the true C&C servers, forwarding all traffic from the bots to these servers.[13]

As we've described, the IRC protocol is an ideal candidate for centralized botnet control, and it remains the most popular among in-the-wild botmasters,[9,10,11] although it appears that will not be true much longer. Popular examples of IRC bots are Agobot, Spybot, and Sdbot.[13] Variants of these three families make up most active botnets today. By its nature, IRC is centralized and allows nearly instant communication among large botnets. One of the major disadvantages is that IRC traffic is not very common on the Internet, especially in an enterprise setting. As a result, standard IRC traffic can be easily detected, filtered, or blocked. For this reason, some botmasters run their IRC servers on nonstandard ports. Some even use customized IRC implementations, replacing easily recognized commands such as JOIN and PRIVMSG with other text. Despite these countermeasures, IRC still tends to stick out from the regular Web and email traffic due to uncommon port numbers.

Recently, botmasters have started using HTTP to manage their centralized botnets. The advantage of using regular Web traffic for C&C is that it must be allowed to pass through virtually all firewalls, since HTTP comprises a majority of Internet traffic. Even closed firewalls that only provide Web access (via a proxy service, for example) will allow HTTP traffic to pass. It is possible to inspect the content and attempt to filter out malicious C&C traffic, but this is not feasible due to the large number of existing bots and variants. If botmasters use HTTPS (HTTP

encrypted using SSL/TLS), then even content inspection becomes useless and all traffic must be allowed to pass through the firewall. However, a disadvantage of HTTP is that it does not provide the instant communication and built-in, scale-up properties of IRC: Bots must manually poll the central server at specific intervals. With large botnets, these intervals must be large enough and distributed well to avoid overloading the server with simultaneous requests. Examples of HTTP bots are Bobax[14,11] and Rustock, with Rustock using a custom encryption scheme on top of HTTP to conceal its C&C traffic.[15]

Peer-to-Peer

As defenses against centralized botnets have become more effective, more and more botmasters are exploring ways to avoid the pitfalls of relying on a centralized architecture and therefore a single point of failure. Symantec reports a "steady decrease" in centralized IRC botnets and predicts that botmasters are now "accelerating their shift…to newer, stealthier control methods, using protocols such as…peer-to-peer."[12] In the P2P model, no centralized server exists, and all member nodes are equally responsible for passing on traffic. "If done properly, [P2P] makes it near impossible to shut down the botnet as a whole. It also provides anonymity to the [botmaster], because they can appear as just another node in the network," says security researcher Joe Stewart of Lurhq.[16] There are many protocols available for P2P networks, each differing in the way nodes first join the network and the role they later play in passing traffic along. Some popular protocols are BitTorrent, WASTE, and Kademlia.[13] Many of these protocols were first developed for benign uses, such as P2P file sharing.

One of the first malicious P2P bots was Sinit, released in September 2003. It uses random scanning to find peers, rather than relying on one of the established P2P bootstrap protocols.[13] As a result, Sinit often has trouble finding peers, which results in overall poor connectivity.[17] Due to the large amount of scanning traffic, this bot is easily detected by intrusion detection systems (IDSs).[18]

13 J. Grizzard, V. Sharma, C. Nunnery, B. Kang, and D. Dagon, "Peer-to-peer botnets: Overview and case study," in Proc. First Workshop on Hot Topics in Understanding Botnets (HotBots), Cambridge, April 2007.

14 J. Stewart, "Bobax Trojan analysis," SecureWorks, May 17, 2004, http://secureworks.com/research/threats/bobax.

15 K. Chiang and L. Lloyd, "A case study of the Rustock Rootkit and Spam Bot," in Proc. First Workshop on Hot Topics in Understanding Botnets (HotBots), Cambridge, April 10, 2007.

16 R. Lemos, "Bot software looks to improve peerage," SecurityFocus, May 2, 2006, www.securityfocus.com/news/11390/.

17 P. Wang, S. Sparks, and C. Zou, "An advanced hybrid peer-to-peer botnet," in Proc. First Workshop on Hot Topics in Understanding Botnets (HotBots), Cambridge, April 10, 2007.

18 J. Stewart, "Sinit P2P Trojan analysis," SecureWorks, December 8, 2004, www.secureworks.com/research/threats/sinit/.

Another advanced bot using the P2P approach is Nugache, released in April 2006.[13] It initially connects to a list of 22 predefined peers to join the P2P network, then downloads a list of active peer nodes from there. This implies that if the 22 "seed" hosts can be shut down, no new bots will be able to join the network, but existing nodes can still function.[19] Nugache encrypts all communications, making it harder for IDSs to detect and increasing the difficulty of manual analysis by researchers.[16] Nugache is seen as one of the first more sophisticated P2P bots, paving the way for future enhancements by botnet designers.

The most famous P2P bot so far is Peacomm, more commonly known as the Storm Worm. It started spreading in January 2007 and continues to have a strong presence.[20] To communicate with peers, it uses the Overnet protocol, based on the Kademlia P2P protocol. For bootstrapping, it uses a fixed list of peers (146 in one observed instance) distributed along with the bot. Once the bot has joined Overnet, the botmaster can easily update the binary and add components to extend its functionality. Often the bot is configured to automatically retrieve updates and additional components, such as an SMTP server for spamming, an email address harvesting tool, and a DoS module. Like Nugache, all of Peacomm's communications are encrypted, making it extremely hard to observe C&C traffic or inject commands appearing to come from the botmaster. Unlike centralized botnets relying on a dynamic DNS provider, Peacomm uses its own P2P network as a distributed DNS system that has no single point of failure. The fixed list of peers is a potential weakness, although it would be challenging to take all these nodes offline. Additionally, the attackers can always set up new nodes and include an updated peer list with the bot, resulting in an "arms race" to shut down malicious nodes.[13]

3. TYPICAL BOT LIFE CYCLE

Regardless of the topology being used, the typical life cycle of a bot is similar:

1. *Creation.* First, the botmaster develops his bot software, often reusing existing code and adding custom features. He might use a test network to perform dry runs before deploying the bot in the wild.

2. *Infection.* There are many possibilities for infecting victim computers, including the following four. Once a victim machine becomes infected with a bot, it is known as a *zombie.*
   - *Software vulnerabilities.* The attacker exploits a vulnerability in a running service to automatically gain access and install his software without any user interaction. This was the method used by most worms, including the infamous Code Red and Sasser worms.[5]
   - *Drive-by download.* The attacker hosts his file on a Web server and entices people to visit the site. When the user loads a certain page, the software is automatically installed without user interaction, usually by exploiting browser bugs, misconfigurations, or unsecured ActiveX controls.
   - *Trojan horse.* The attacker bundles his malicious software with seemingly benign and useful software, such as screen savers, antivirus scanners, or games. The user is fully aware of the installation process, but he does not know about the hidden bot functionality.
   - *Email attachment:* Although this method has become less popular lately due to rising user awareness, it is still around. The attacker sends an attachment that will automatically install the bot software when the user opens it, usually without any interaction. This was the primary infection vector of the ILOVEYOU email worm from 2000.[5] The recent Storm Worm successfully used enticing email messages with executable attachments to lure its victims.[20]

3. *Rallying.* After infection, the bot starts up for the first time and attempts to contact its C&C server(s) in a process known as *rallying.* In a centralized botnet, this could be an IRC or HTTP server, for example. In a P2P botnet, the bots perform the bootstrapping protocol required to locate other peers and join the network. Most bots are very fault-tolerant, having multiple lists of backup servers to attempt if the primary ones become unavailable. Some C&C servers are configured to immediately send some initial commands to the bot (without botmaster intervention). In an IRC botnet, this is typically done by including the commands in the C&C channel's topic.

4. *Waiting.* Having joined the C&C network, the bot waits for commands from the botmaster. During this time, very little (if any) traffic passes between the victim and the C&C servers. In an IRC botnet, this traffic would mainly consist of periodic keep-alive messages from the server.

19 R. Schoof and Ralph Koning, "Detecting peer-to-peer botnets," unpublished paper, University of Amsterdam, February 4, 2007, http://staff.science.uva.nl/~delaat/sne-2006-2007/p17/report.pdf.
20 Wikipedia contributors, "Storm worm," http://en.wikipedia.org/w/index.php?title=Storm_Worm&oldid=207916428 accessed May 4, 2008).

5. *Executing.* Once the bot receives a command from the botmaster, it executes it and returns any results to the botmaster via the C&C network. The supported commands are only limited by the botmaster's imagination and technical skills. Common commands are in line with the major uses of botnets: scanning for new victims, sending spam, sending DoS floods, setting up traffic redirection, and many more.

Following execution of a command, the bot returns to the waiting state to await further instructions. If the victim computer is rebooted or loses its connection to the C&C network, the bot resumes in the rallying state. Assuming it can reach its C&C network, it will then continue in the waiting state until further commands arrive.

Figure 8.1 shows the detailed infection sequence in a typical IRC-based botnet:

1. An existing botnet member computer launches a scan, then discovers and exploits a vulnerable host.
2. Following the exploit, the vulnerable host is made to download and install a copy of the bot software, constituting an infection.
3. When the bot starts up on the vulnerable host, it enters the rallying state: It performs a DNS lookup to determine the current IP of its C&C server.
4. The new bot joins the botnet's IRC channel on the C&C server for the first time, now in the waiting state.
5. The botmaster sends his commands to the C&C server on the botnet's IRC channel.
6. The C&C server forwards the commands to all bots, which now enter the executing state.

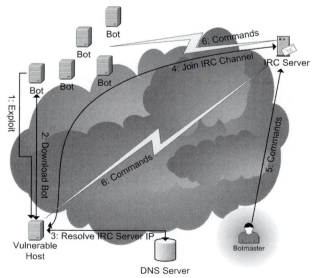

FIGURE 8.1 Infection sequence of a typical centralized IRC-based botnet.

4. THE BOTNET BUSINESS MODEL

Unlike the viruses and worms of the past, botnets are motivated by financial profit. Organized crime groups often use them as a source of income, either by hiring "freelance" botmasters or by having their own members create botnets. As a result, network security professionals are up against motivated, well-financed organizations that can often hire some of the best minds in computers and network security. This is especially true in countries such as Russia, Romania, and other Eastern European nations where there is an abundance of IT talent at the high school and university level but legitimate IT job prospects are very limited. In such an environment, criminal organizations easily recruit recent graduates by offering far better opportunities than the legitimate job market.[21,22,23,24] One infamous example of such a crime organization is the Russian Business Network (RBN), a Russian Internet service provider (ISP) that openly supports criminal activity.[21,25] They are responsible for the Storm Worm (Peacomm),[25] the March 2007 DDoS attacks on Estonia,[25] and a high-profile attack on the Bank of India in August 2007,[26] along with many other attacks.

It might not be immediately obvious how a collection of computers can be used to cause havoc and produce large profits. The main point is that botnets provide *anonymous* and *distributed* access to the Internet. The anonymity makes the attackers untraceable, and a botnet's distributed nature makes it extremely hard to shut down. As a result, botnets are perfect vehicles for criminal activities on the Internet. Some of the main profit-producing methods are explained here,[27] but criminals are always devising new and creative ways to profit from botnets:

- *Spam.* Spammers send millions of emails advertising phony or overpriced products, phishing for financial

21 D. Bizeul, "Russian business network study," unpublished paper, November 20, 2007, www.bizeul.org/files/RBN_study.pdf.

22 A. E. Cha, "Internet dreams turn to crime," *Washington Post*, May 18, 2003, www.washingtonpost.com/ac2/wp-dyn/A2619-2003May17.

23 B. I. Koerner, "From Russia with løpht," *Legal Affairs*, May–June 2002, http://legalaffairs.org/issues/May-June-2002/feature_koerner_may jun2002.msp.

24 M. Delio, "Inside Russia's hacking culture," *WIRED*, March 12, 2001, www.wired.com/culture/lifestyle/news/2001/03/42346.

25 Wikipedia contributors, "Russian business network," http://en.wikipedia.org/w/index.php?title=Russian_Business_Network&oldid=209665215 (accessed May 3, 2008).

26 L. Tung, "Infamous Russian ISP behind Bank of India hack" *ZDNet*, September 4, 2007, http://news.zdnet.co.uk/security/0,1000000189,39289057,00.htm?r=2.

27 P. Bächer, T. Holz, M. Kötter, and G. Wicherski, "Know your enemy: Tracking botnets," March 13, 2005, see www.honeynet.org/papers/bots/.

data and login information, or running advance-fee schemes such as the Nigerian 419 scam.[28] Even if only a small percentage of recipients respond to this spam, the payoff is considerable for the spammer. It is estimated that up to 90% of all spam originates from botnets.[2]

- *DDoS and extortion.* Having amassed a large number of bots, the attacker contacts an organization and threatens to launch a massive DDoS attack, shutting down its Web site for several hours or even days. Another variation on this method is to find vulnerabilities, use them steal financial or confidential data, and then demand money for the "safe return" of the data and to keep it from being circulated in the underground economy.[23] Often, companies would rather pay off the attacker to avoid costly downtime, lost sales, and the lasting damage to its reputation that would result from a DDoS attack or data breach.

- *Identity theft.* Once a bot has a foothold on a victim's machine, it usually has complete control. For example, the attacker can install keyloggers to record login and password information, search the hard drive for valuable data, or alter the DNS configuration to redirect victims to look-alike Web sites and collect personal information, known as *pharming.*[29] Using the harvested personal information, the attacker can make fraudulent credit card charges, clean out the victim's bank account, and apply for credit in the victim's name, among many other things.

- *Click fraud.* In this scenario, bots are used to repeatedly click Web advertising links, generating per-click revenue for the attacker.[2] This represents fraud because only the clicks of human users with a legitimate interest are valuable to advertisers. The bots will not buy the product or service as a result of clicking the advertisement.

These illegal activities are extremely profitable. For example, a 2006 study by the Germany Honeynet Project estimated that a botmaster can make about $430 per day just from per-install advertising software.[30] A 20-year-old California botmaster indicted in February 2006 earned $100,000 in advertising revenue from his

botnet operations.[31] However, both of these cases pale in comparison to the estimated $20 million worth of damage caused by an international ring of computer criminals known as the A-Team.[32]

Due to these very profitable uses of botnets, many botmasters make money simply by creating botnets and then renting out processing power and bandwidth to spammers, extortionists, and identity thieves. Despite a recent string of high-profile botnet arrests, these are merely a drop in the bucket.[4] Overall, botmasters still have a fairly low chance of getting caught due to a lack of effective traceback techniques. The relatively low risk combined with high yield makes the botnet business very appealing as a fundraising method for criminal enterprises, especially in countries with weak computer crime enforcement.

5. BOTNET DEFENSE

When botnets emerged, the response was similar to previous Internet malware: Antivirus vendors created signatures and removal techniques for each new instance of the bot. This approach initially worked well at the host level, but researchers soon started exploring more advanced methods for eliminating more than one bot at a time. After all, a botnet with tens of thousands of members would be very tedious to combat one bot at a time.

This section describes the current defenses against centralized botnets, moving from the host level to the network level, then to the C&C server, and finally to the botmaster himself.

Detecting and Removing Individual Bots

Removing individual bots does not usually have a noticeable impact on the overall botnet, but it is a crucial first step in botnet defense. The basic antivirus approach using signature-based detection is still effective with many bots, but some are starting to use polymorphism, which creates unique instances of the bot code and evades signature-based detection. For example, Agobot is known to have thousands of variants, and it includes built-in support for polymorphism to change its signature at will.[33]

28 Wikipedia contributors, "E-mail spam," http://en.wikipedia.org/w/index.php?title=E-mail_spam&oldid=209902571 (accessed May 3, 2008).

29 Wikipedia contributors, "Pharming," http://en.wikipedia.org/w/index.php?title=Pharming&oldid=196469141 (accessed May 3, 2008).

30 R. Naraine, "Money bots: Hackers cash in on hijacked PCs," *eWeek*, September 8, 2006, www.eweek.com/article2/0,1759,2013924,00.asp.

31 P. F. Roberts, "DOJ indicts hacker for hospital botnet attack," *eWeek*, February 10, 2006, www.eweek.com/article2/0,1759,1925456,00.asp.

32 T. Claburn, "New Zealander 'AKILL' pleads guilty to botnet charges," *Information Week*, April 3, 2008, www.informationweek.com/news/security/cybercrime/showArticle.jhtml?articleID=207001573.

33 Wikipedia contributors, "Agobot (computer worm)," http://en.wikipedia.org/w/index.php?title=Agobot_%28computer_worm%29&oldid=201957526 (accessed May 3, 2008).

To deal with these more sophisticated bots and all other polymorphic malware, detection must be done using behavioral analysis and heuristics. Researchers Stinson and Mitchell have developed a taint-based approach called BotSwat that marks all data originating from the network. If this data is used as input for a system call, there is a high probability that it is bot-related behavior, since user input typically comes from the keyboard or mouse on most end-user systems.[34]

Detecting C&C Traffic

To mitigate the botnet problem on a larger scale, researchers turned their attention to network-based detection of the botnet's C&C traffic. This method allows organizations or even ISPs to detect the presence of bots on their entire network, rather than having to check each machine individually.

One approach is to examine network traffic for certain known patterns that occur in botnet C&C traffic. This is, in effect, a network-deployed version of signature-based detection, where signatures have to be collected for each bot before detection is possible. Researchers Goebel and Holz implemented this method in their Rishi tool, which evaluates IRC nicknames for likely botnet membership based on a list of known botnet naming schemes. As with all signature-based approaches, it often leads to an "arms race" where the attackers frequently change their malware and the network security community tries to keep up by creating signatures for each new instance.[35]

Rather than relying on a limited set of signatures, it is also possible to use the IDS technique of anomaly detection to identify unencrypted IRC botnet traffic. This method was successfully implemented by researchers Binkley and Singh at Portland State University, and as a result they reported a significant increase in bot detection on the university network.[36]

Another IDS-based detection technique called BotHunter was proposed by Gu et al. in 2007. Their approach is based on IDS dialog correlation techniques: It deploys three separate network monitors at the network perimeter, each detecting a specific stage of bot infection. By correlating these events, BotHunter can reconstruct the traffic dialog between the infected machine and the outside Internet. From this dialog, the engine determines whether a bot infection has taken place with a high accuracy rate.[37]

Moving beyond the scope of a single network/organization, traffic from centralized botnets can be detected at the ISP level based only on transport layer flow statistics. This approach was developed by Karasaridis et al., and it solves many of the problems of packet-level inspection. It is passive, highly scalable, and only uses flow summary data (limiting privacy issues). Additionally, it can determine the size of a botnet without joining and can even detect botnets using encrypted C&C. The approach exploits the underlying principle of centralized botnets: Each bot has to contact the C&C server, producing detectable patterns in network traffic flows.[38]

Beyond the ISP level, a heuristic method for Internet-wide bot detection was proposed by Ramachandran et al. in 2006. In this scheme, query patterns of DNS black-hole lists (DNSBLs) are used to create a list of possible bot-infected IP addresses. It relies on the fact that botmasters need to periodically check whether their spam-sending bots have been added to a DNSBL and have therefore become useless. The query patterns of botmasters to a DNSBL are very different from those of legitimate mail servers, allowing detection.[39] One major limitation is that this approach focuses mainly on the sending of spam. It would most likely not detect bots engaged in other illegal activities, such as DDoS attacks or click fraud, since these do not require DNSBL lookups.

Detecting and Neutralizing the C&C Servers

Though detecting C&C traffic and eliminating all bots on a given local network is a step in the right direction, it still doesn't allow the takedown of an entire botnet at once. To achieve this goal in a centralized botnet, access

34 E. Stinson and J. Mitchell, "Characterizing bots' remote control behavior," in Proc. 4th International Conference on Detection of Intrusions & Malware and Vulnerability Assessment (DIMVA), Lucerne, Switzerland, July 12–13, 2007.

35 J. Goebel and T. Holz, "Rishi: Identify bot contaminated hosts by IRC nickname evaluation," in Proc. First Workshop on Hot Topics in Understanding Botnets (HotBots), Cambridge, April 10, 2007.

36 J. Binkley and S. Singh, "An algorithm for anomaly-based botnet detection," in Proc. 2nd Workshop on Steps to Reducing Unwanted Traffic on the Internet (SRUTI), San Jose, July 7, 2006, pp. 43–48.

37 G. Gu, P. Porras, V. Yegneswaran, M. Fong, and W. Lee, "BotHunter: Detecting malware infection through IDS-driven dialog correlation," in Proc. 16th USENIX Security Symposium, Boston, August 2007.

38 A. Karasaridis, B. Rexroad, and D. Hoeflin, "Wide-scale botnet detection and characterization," in Proc. First Workshop on Hot Topics in Understanding Botnets (HotBots), Cambridge, MA, April 10, 2007.

39 A. Ramachandran, N. Feamster, and D. Dagon, "Revealing botnet membership using DNSBL counter-intelligence," in Proc. 2nd Workshop on Steps to Reducing Unwanted Traffic on the Internet (SRUTI), San Jose, CA, July 7, 2006, pp. 49–54.

to the C&C servers must be removed. This approach assumes that the C&C servers consist of only a few hosts that are accessed directly. If hundreds or thousands of hosts are used in a fast-flux proxy configuration, it becomes extremely challenging to locate and neutralize the true C&C servers.

In work similar to BotHunter, researchers Gu et al. developed BotSniffer in 2008. This approach represents several improvements, notably that BotSniffer can handle encrypted traffic, since it no longer relies only on content inspection to correlate messages. A major advantage of this approach is that it requires no advance knowledge of the bot's signature or the identity of C&C servers. By analyzing network traces, BotSniffer detects the spatial-temporal correlation among C&C traffic belonging to the same botnet. It can therefore detect both the bot members and the C&C server(s) with a low false positive rate.[40]

Most of the approaches mentioned under "Detecting C&C Traffic" can also be used to detect the C&C servers, with the exception of the DNSBL approach.[39] However, their focus is mainly on detection and removal of individual bots. None of these approaches mentions targeting the C&C servers to eliminate an entire botnet.

One of the few projects that has explored the feasibility of C&C server takedown is the work of Freiling et al. in 2005.[41] Although their focus is on DDoS prevention, they describe the method that is generally used in the wild to remove C&C servers when they are detected. First, the bot binary is either reverse-engineered or run in a sandbox to observe its behavior, specifically the hostnames of the C&C servers. Using this information, the proper dynamic DNS providers can be notified to remove the DNS entries for the C&C servers, preventing any bots from contacting them and thus severing contact between the botmaster and his botnet. Dagon et al. used a similar approach in 2006 to obtain experiment data for modeling botnet propagation, redirecting the victim's connections from the true C&C server to their sinkhole host.[42] Even though effective, the manual analysis and contact with the DNS operator is a slow process. It can take up to several days until all C&C servers are located and neutralized. However, this process is essentially the best available approach for shutting down entire botnets in the wild. As we mentioned, this technique becomes much harder when fast-flux proxies are used to conceal the real C&C servers or a P2P topology is in place.

Attacking Encrypted C&C Channels

Though some of the approaches can detect encrypted C&C traffic, the presence of encryption makes botnet research and analysis much harder. The first step in dealing with these advanced botnets is to penetrate the encryption that protects the C&C channels.

A popular approach for adding encryption to an existing protocol is to run it on top of SSL/TLS; to secure HTTP traffic, ecommerce Web sites run HTTP over SSL/TLS, known as HTTPS. Many encryption schemes that support key exchange (including SSL/TLS) are susceptible to man-in-the-middle (MITM) attacks, whereby a third party can impersonate the other two parties to each other. Such an attack is possible only when no authentication takes place prior to the key exchange, but this is a surprisingly common occurrence due to poor configuration.

The premise of an MITM attack is that the client does not verify that it's talking to the real server, and vice versa. When the MITM receives a connection from the client, it immediately creates a separate connection to the server (under a different encryption key) and passes on the client's request. When the server responds, the MITM decrypts the response, logs and possibly alters the content, then passes it on to the client reencrypted with the proper key. Neither the client or the server notice that anything is wrong, because they are communicating with each other over an encrypted connection, as expected. The important difference is that unknown to either party, the traffic is being decrypted and reencrypted by the MITM in transit, allowing him to observe and alter the traffic.

In the context of bots, two main attacks on encrypted C&C channels are possible: (1) "gray-box" analysis, whereby the bot communicates with a local machine impersonating the C&C server, and (2) a full MITM attack, in which the bot communicates with the true C&C server. Figure 8.2 shows a possible setup for both attacks, using the DeleGate proxy[43] for the conversion to and from SSL/TLS.

40 G. Gu, J. Zhang, and W. Lee, "BotSniffer: Detecting botnet command and control channels in network traffic," in Proc. 15th Network and Distributed System Security Symposium (NDSS), San Diego, February 2008.

41 F. Freiling, T. Holz, and G. Wicherski, "Botnet tracking: Exploring a root-cause methodology to prevent denial-of-service attacks," in Proc. 10th European Symposium on Research in Computer Security (ESORICS), Milan, Italy, September 12–14, 2005.

42 D. Dagon, C. Zou, and W. Lee, "Modeling botnet propagation using time zones," in Proc. 13th Network and Distributed System Security Symposium (NDSS), February 2006.

43 "DeleGate multi-purpose application gateway," www.delegate.org/delegate/ (accessed May 4, 2008).

The first attack is valuable to determine the authentication information required to join the live botnet: the address of the C&C server, the IRC channel name (if applicable), plus any required passwords. However, it

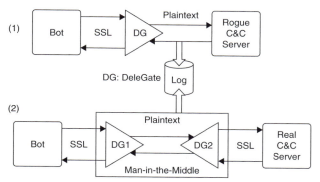

FIGURE 8.2 Setups for man-in-the-middle attacks on encrypted C&C channels.

does not allow the observer to see the interaction with the larger botnet, specifically the botmaster. The second attack reveals the full interaction with the botnet, including all botmaster commands, the botmaster password used to control the bots, and possibly the IP addresses of other bot members (depending on the configuration of the C&C server). Figures 8.3–8.5 show the screenshots of the full MITM attack on a copy of Agobot configured to connect to its C&C server via SSL/TLS. Specifically, Figure 8.3 shows the botmaster's IRC window, with his commands and the bot's responses. Figure 8.4 shows the encrypted SSL/TLS trace, and Figure 8.5 shows the decrypted plaintext that was observed at the DeleGate proxy. The botmaster password *botmasterPASS* is clearly visible, along with the required username, *botmaster*.

Armed with the botmaster username and password, the observer could literally take over the botnet. He

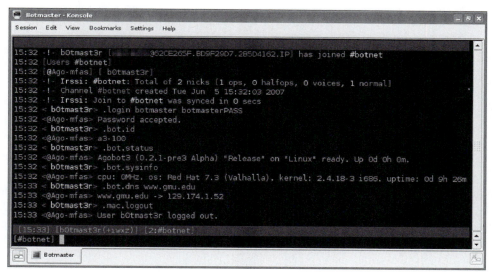

FIGURE 8.3 Screenshot showing the botmaster's IRC window.

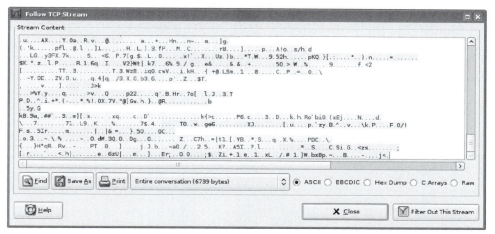

FIGURE 8.4 Screenshot showing the SSL/TLS-encrypted network traffic.

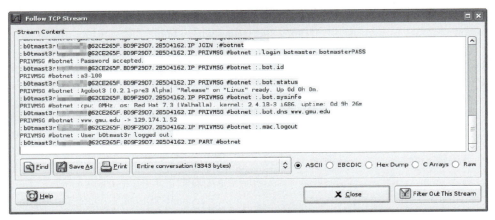

FIGURE 8.5 Screenshot showing decrypted plaintext from the DeleGate proxy.

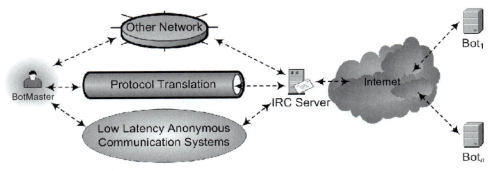

FIGURE 8.6 Botnet C&C traffic laundering.

could log in as the botmaster, then issue a command such as Agobot's .bot.remove, causing all bots to disconnect from the botnet and permanently remove themselves from the infected computers. Unfortunately, there are legal issues with this approach because it constitutes unauthorized access to all the botnet computers, despite the fact that it is in fact a benign command to remove the bot software.

Locating and Identifying the Botmaster

Shutting down an entire botnet at once is a significant achievement, especially when the botnet numbers in the tens of thousands of members. However, there is nothing stopping the botmaster from simply deploying new bots to infect the millions of vulnerable hosts on the Internet, creating a new botnet in a matter of hours. In fact, most of the machines belonging to the shut-down botnet are likely to become infected again because the vulnerabilities and any attacker-installed backdoors often remain active, despite the elimination of the C&C servers. Botnet-hunting expert Gadi Evron agrees: "When we disable a command-and-control server, the botnet is

immediately recreated on another host. We're not hurting them anymore," he said in a 2006 interview.[44]

The only permanent solution of the botnet problem is to go after the root cause: the botmasters. Unfortunately, most botmasters are very good at concealing their identities and locations, since their livelihood depends on it. Tracking the botmaster to her true physical location is a complex problem that is described in detail in the next section. So far, there is no published work that would allow automated botmaster traceback on the Internet, and it remains an open problem.

6. BOTMASTER TRACEBACK

The botnet field is full of challenging problems: obfuscated binaries, encrypted C&C channels, fast-flux proxies protecting central C&C servers, customized communication protocols, and many more (see Figure 8.6). Arguably the most challenging task is locating the botmaster. Most botmasters take precautions on multiple

---

44 R. Naraine, "Is the botnet battle already lost?" *eWeek*, October 16, 2006, www.eweek.com/article2/0,1895,2029720,00.asp.

levels to ensure that their connections cannot be traced to their true locations.

The reason for the botmaster's extreme caution is that a successful trace would have disastrous consequences. He could be arrested, his computer equipment could be seized and scrutinized in detail, and he could be sentenced to an extended prison term. Additionally, authorities would likely learn the identities of his associates, either from questioning him or by searching his computers. As a result, he would never again be able to operate in the Internet underground and could even face violent revenge from his former associates when he is released.

In the United States, authorities have recently started to actively pursue botmasters, resulting in several arrests and convictions. In November 2005, 20-year-old Jeanson James Ancheta of California was charged with botnet-related computer offenses.[45] He pleaded guilty in January 2006 and could face up to 25 years in prison.[46] In a similar case, 20-year-old Christopher Maxwell was indicted on federal computer charges. He is accused of using his botnet to attack computers at several universities and a Seattle hospital, where bot infections severely disrupted operations.[31]

In particular, the FBI's Operation Bot Roast has resulted in several high-profile arrests, both in the United States and abroad.[47] The biggest success was the arrest of 18-year-old New Zealand native Owen Thor Walker, who was a member of a large international computer crime ring known as the A-Team. This group is reported to have infected up to 1.3 million computers with bot software and caused about $20 million in economic damage. Despite this success, Walker was only a minor player, and the criminals in control of the A-Team are still at large.[32]

Unfortunately, botmaster arrests are not very common. The cases described here represent only several individuals; thousands of botmasters around the world are still operating with impunity. They use sophisticated techniques to hide their true identities and locations, and they often operate in countries with weak computer crime enforcement. The lack of international coordination, both on the Internet and in law enforcement, makes it hard to trace botmasters and even harder to hold them accountable to the law.[22]

Traceback Challenges

One defining characteristic of the botmaster is that he originates the botnet C&C traffic. Therefore, one way to find the botmaster is to track the botnet C&C traffic. To hide himself, the botmaster wants to disguise his link to the C&C traffic via various traffic-laundering techniques that make tracking C&C traffic more difficult. For example, a botmaster can route his C&C traffic through a number of intermediate hosts, various protocols, and low-latency anonymous networks to make it extremely difficult to trace. To further conceal his activities, a botmaster can also encrypt his traffic to and from the C&C servers. Finally, a botmaster only needs to be online briefly and send small amounts of traffic to interact with his botnet, reducing the chances of live traceback. Figure 8.6 illustrates some of the C&C traffic-laundering techniques a botmaster can use.

Stepping Stones

The intermediate hosts used for traffic laundering are known as *stepping stones*. The attacker sets them up in a chain, leading from the botmaster's true location to the C&C server. Stepping stones can be SSH servers, proxies (such as SOCKS), IRC bouncers (BNCs), virtual private network (VPN) servers, or any number of network redirection services. They usually run on compromised hosts, which are under the attacker's control and lack audit/logging mechanisms to trace traffic. As a result, manual traceback is tedious and time-consuming, requiring the cooperation of dozens of organizations whose networks might be involved in the trace.

The major challenge posed by stepping stones is that all routing information from the previous hop (IP headers, TCP headers, and the like) is stripped from the data before it is sent out on a new, separate connection. Only the content of the packet (the application layer data) is preserved, which renders many existing tracing schemes useless. An example of a technique that relies on routing header information is *probabilistic packet marking* (PPM). This approach was introduced by Savage et al. in 2000, embedding tracing information in an unused IP header field.[48] Two years later, Goodrich expanded this approach, introducing "randomize-and-link" for better scalability.[49] Another technique for IP-level traceback

45 P. F. Roberts, "California man charged with botnet offenses," *eWeek*, November 3, 2005, www.eweek.com/article2/0,1759,1881621,00.asp.
46 P. F. Roberts, "Botnet operator pleads guilty," *eWeek*, January 24, 2006, www.eweek.com/article2/0,1759,1914833,00.asp.
47 S. Nichols, "FBI 'bot roast' scores string of arrests" *vnunet. com*, December 3, 2007, www.vnunet.com/vnunet/news/2204829/bot-roast-scores-string-arrests.

48 S. Savage, D. Wetherall, A. Karlin, and T. Anderson, "Practical network support for IP traceback," in Proc. ACM SIGCOMM 2000, Sept. 2000, pp. 295–306.
49 M. T. Goodrich, "Efficient packet marking for large-scale IP traceback," in Proc. 9th ACM Conference on Computer and Communications Security (CCS 2002), October 2002, pp. 117–126.

is the log/hash-based scheme introduced by Snoeren et al.[50] and enhanced by Li et al.[51] These techniques were very useful in combating the fast-spreading worms of the early 2000s, which did not use stepping stones. However, these approaches do not work when stepping stones are present, since IP header information is lost.

Multiple Protocols

Another effective and efficient method to disguise the botmaster is to launder the botnet C&C traffic across other protocols. Such protocol laundering can be achieved by either *protocol tunneling* or *protocol translation*. For example, a sophisticated botmaster could route its command and control traffic through SSH (or even HTTP) tunnels to reach the command and control center. The botmaster could also use some intermediate host X as a stepping stone, use some real-time communication protocols other than IRC between the botmaster host and host X, and use IRC between the host X and the IRC server. In this case, host X performs the protocol translation at the application layer and serves as a conduit of the botnet C&C channel. One protocol that is particularly suitable for laundering the botnet command and control is instant messaging (IM), which supports real-time text-based communication between two or more people.

Low-Latency Anonymous Network

Besides laundering the botnet C&C across stepping stones and different protocols, a sophisticated botmaster could anonymize its C&C traffic by routing it through some low-latency anonymous communication systems. For example, Tor—the second generation of onion routing—uses an overlay network of onion routers to provide anonymous outgoing connections and anonymous hidden services. The botmaster could use Tor as a virtual tunnel to anonymize his TCP-based C&C traffic to the IRC server of the botnet. At the same time, the IRC server of the botnet could utilize Tor's hidden services to anonymize the IRC server of the botnet in such a way that its network location is unknown to the bots and yet it could communicate with all the bots.

Encryption

All or part of the stepping stone chain can be encrypted to protect it against content inspection, which could reveal information about the botnet and botmaster. This can be done using a number of methods, including SSH tunneling, SSL/TLS-enabled BNCs, and IPsec tunneling. Using encryption defeats all content-based tracing approaches, so the tracer must rely on other network flow characteristics, such as packet size or timing, to correlate flows to each other.

Low-Traffic Volume

Since the botmaster only has to connect briefly to issue commands and retrieve results from his botnet, a low volume of traffic flows from any given bot to the botmaster. During a typical session, only a few dozen packets from each bot can be sent to the botmaster. Tracing approaches that rely on analysis of packet size or timing will most likely be ineffective because they typically require a large amount of traffic (several hundred packets) to correlate flows with high statistical confidence. Examples of such tracing approaches[52,53,54] all use timing information to embed a traceable watermark. These approaches can handle stepping stones, encryption, and even low-latency anonymizing network, but they cannot be directly used for botmaster traceback due to the low traffic volume.

Traceback Beyond the Internet

Even if all three technical challenges can be solved and even if all Internet-connected organizations worldwide cooperate to monitor traffic, there are additional traceback challenges beyond the reach of the Internet (see Figure 8.7). Any IP-based traceback method assumes that the true source IP belongs to the computer the attacker is using and that this machine can be physically located. However, in many scenario this is not true—for example, (1) Internet-connected mobile phone networks, (2) open wireless (Wi-Fi) networks, and (3) public computers, such as those at libraries and Internet cafés.

50 A. Snoeren, C. Patridge, L. A. Sanchez, C. E. Jones, F. Tchakountio, S. T. Kent, and W. T. Strayer, "Hash-based IP traceback," in Proc. ACM SIGCOMM 2001, September 2001, pp. 3–14.

51 J. Li, M. Sung, J. Xu, and L. Li, "Large-scale IP traceback in high-speed internet: Practical techniques and theoretical foundation," in Proc. 2004 IEEE Symposium on Security and Privacy, IEEE, 2004.

52 X. Wang, S. Chen, and S. Jajodia, "Network flow watermarking attack on low-latency anonymous communication systems," in Proc. 2007 IEEE Symposium on Security and Privacy, May 2007.

53 X. Wang, S. Chen, and S. Jajodia, "Tracking anonymous, peer-to-peer VoIP calls on the internet," in Proc. 12th ACM Conference on Computer and Communications Security (CCS 2005), October 2005.

54 X. Wang and D. Reeves, "Robust correlation of encrypted attack traffic through stepping stones by manipulation of interpacket delays," in Proc. 10th ACM Conference on Computer and Communications Security (CCS 2003), October 2003, pp. 20–29.

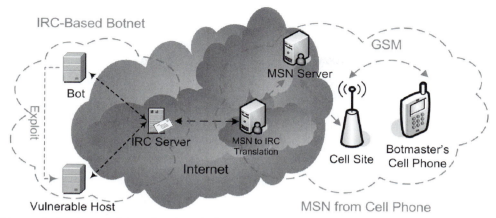

FIGURE 8.7 Using a cell phone to evade Internet-based traceback.

Most modern cell phones support text-messaging services such as Short Message Service (SMS), and many smart phones also have full-featured IM software. As a result, the botmaster can use a mobile device to control her botnet from any location with cell phone reception. To enable her cell phone to communicate with the C&C server, a botmaster needs to use a protocol translation service or a special IRC client for mobile phones. She can run the translation service on a compromised host, an additional stepping stone. For an IRC botnet, such a service would receive the incoming SMS or IM message, then repackage it as an IRC message and send it on to the C&C server (possibly via more stepping stones), as shown in Figure 8.7. To eliminate the need for protocol translation, the botmaster can run a native IRC client on a smart phone with Internet access. Examples of such clients are the Java-based WLIrc[55] and jmIrc[56] open source projects. In Figure 8.8, a Nokia smartphone is shown running MSN Messenger, controlling an Agobot zombie via MSN-IRC protocol translation. On the screen, a new bot has just been infected and has joined the IRC channel following the botmaster's .scan.dcom command.

When a botnet is being controlled from a mobile device, even a perfect IP traceback solution would only reach as far as the gateway host that bridges the Internet and the carrier's mobile network. From there, the tracer can ask the carrier to complete the trace and disclose the name and even the current location of the cell phone's owner. However, there are several problems with this approach. First, this part of the trace again requires lots

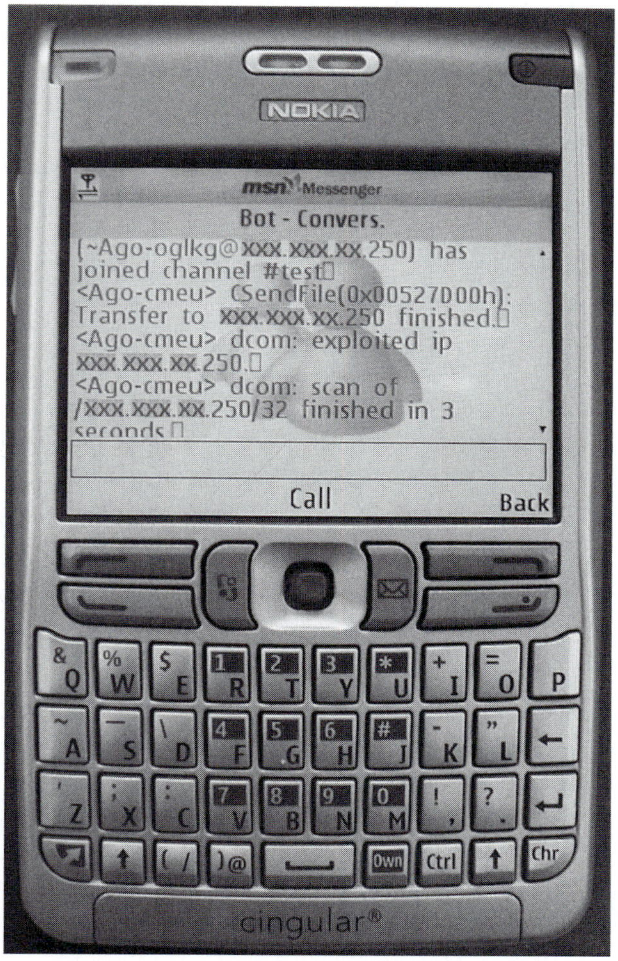

FIGURE 8.8 Using a Nokia smartphone to control an Agobot-based botnet. (Photo courtesy of Ruishan Zhang.)

of manual work and cooperation of yet another organization, introducing further delays and making a real-time trace unlikely. Second, the carrier won't be able to determine the name of the subscriber if he is using a prepaid

---

55 "WLIrc wireless IRC client for mobile phones," http://wirelessirc. sourceforge.net/ (accessed May 3, 2008).

56 "jmIrc: Java mobile IRC-client (J2ME)," http://jmirc.sourceforge. net/ (accessed May 3, 2008).

cell phone. Third, the tracer could obtain an approximate physical location based on cell site triangulation. Even if he can do this in real time, it might not be very useful if the botmaster is in a crowded public place. Short of detaining all people in the area and checking their cell phones, police won't be able to pinpoint the botmaster.

A similar situation arises when the botmaster uses an unsecured Wi-Fi connection. This could either be a public access point or a poorly configured one that is intended to be private. With a strong antenna, the botmaster can be located up to several thousand feet away. In a typical downtown area, such a radius can contain thousands of people and just as many computers. Again, short of searching everyone in the vicinity, the police will be unable to find the botmaster.

Finally, many places provide public Internet access without any logging of the users' identities. Prime examples are public libraries, Internet cafés, and even the business centers at most hotels. In this scenario, a real-time trace would actually find the botmaster, since he would be sitting at the machine in question. However, even if the police are late by only several minutes, there might no longer be any record of who last used the computer. Physical evidence such as fingerprints, hair, and skin cells would be of little use, since many people use these computers each day. Unless a camera system is in place and it captured a clear picture of the suspect on his way to/from the computer, the police again will have no leads.

This section illustrates a few common scenarios where even a perfect IP traceback solution would fail to locate the botmaster. Clearly, much work remains on developing automated, integrated traceback solutions that work across various types of networks and protocols.

7. SUMMARY

Botnets are one of the biggest threats to the Internet today, and they are linked to most forms of Internet crime. Most spam, DDoS attacks, spyware, click fraud, and other attacks originate from botnets and the shadowy organizations behind them. Running a botnet is immensely profitable, as several recent high-profile arrests have shown. Currently, many botnets still rely on a centralized IRC C&C structure, but more and more botmasters are using P2P protocols to provide resilience and avoid a single point of failure. A recent large-scale example of a P2P botnet is the Storm Worm, widely covered in the media.

A number of botnet countermeasures exist, but most are focused on bot detection and removal at the host and network level. Some approaches exist for Internet-wide detection and disruption of entire botnets, but we still lack effective techniques for combating the root of the problem: the botmasters who conceal their identities and locations behind chains of stepping-stone proxies.

The three biggest challenges in botmaster traceback are stepping stones, encryption, and the low traffic volume. Even if these problems can be solved with a technical solution, the trace must be able to continue beyond the reach of the Internet. Mobile phone networks, open wireless access points, and public computers all provide an additional layer of anonymity for the botmasters.

Short of a perfect solution, even a partial traceback technique could serve as a very effective deterrent for botmasters. With each botmaster that is located and arrested, many botnets will be eliminated at once. Additionally, other botmasters could decide that the risks outweigh the benefits when they see more and more of their colleagues getting caught. Currently, the economic equation is very simple: Botnets can generate large profits with relatively low risk of getting caught. A botmaster traceback solution, even if imperfect, would drastically change this equation and convince more botmasters that it simply is not worth the risk of spending the next 10–20 years in prison.

## Chapter 9

Intranet Security

Bill Mansoor

Information Systems Audit and Control Association (ISACA)

Intranet Security as News in the Media

- "State Department Contract Employees Fired, Another Disciplined for Looking at Passport File"[1]
- "Laptop stolen with a million customer data records"[2]
- "eBayed VPN kit hands over access to council network"[3]
- "(Employee) caught selling personal and medical information about . . . FBI agent to a confidential source . . . for $500."[4]
- "Data thieves gain access to TJX through unsecured wireless access point"[5]

Headline drama like these in the mainstream media are embarrassing nightmares to top brass in any large corporation. These events have a lasting impact on a company's bottom line because the company reputation and customer trust take a direct hit. Once events like these transpire, customers and current and potential investors never look at the company in the same trusting light again, regardless of remediation measures. The smart thing, then, is to avoid this kind of limelight. The onus of preventing such embarrassing security gaffes falls squarely on the shoulders of IT security chiefs (CISOs and security officers), who are sometimes hobbled by unclear mandates from government regulators and lack of sufficient budgeting to tackle the mandates.

However, federal governments across the world are not taking breaches of personal data lightly (see side bar, "TJX: Data Breach with 45 Million Data Records Stolen"). In view of a massive plague of publicized data thefts in the past decade, recent mandates such as the Health Insurance Portability and Accountability Act (HIPAA), Sarbanes-Oxley, and the Payment Card Industry-Data Security Standard (PCI-DSS) Act within the United States now have teeth. These go so far as to spell out stiff fines and personal jail sentences for CEOs who neglect data breach issues.

TJX: Data Breach with 45 Million Data Records Stolen

The largest-scale data breach in history occurred in early 2007 at TJX, the parent company for the TJ Maxx, Marshalls, and HomeGoods retail chains.

In the largest identity-theft case ever investigated by the U.S. Department of Justice, 11 people were convicted of wire fraud in the case. The primary suspect was found to perpetrate the intrusion by wardriving and taking advantage of an unsecured Wi-Fi access point to get in and set up a "sniffer" software instance to capture credit-card information from a database.[12]

Though the intrusion was earlier believed to have taken place from May 2006 to January 2007, TJX later found that it took place as early as July 2005. The data compromised included portions of the credit- and debit-card transactions for approximately 45 million customers.[6]

As seen in the TJX case, intranet data breaches can be a serious issue, impacting a company's goodwill in

---

1 Jake, Tapper, and Kirit, Radia, "State Department contract employees fired, another disciplined for looking at passport file," ABCnews.com, March 21, 2008, http://abcnews.go.com/Politics/story?id=4492773&page=1.

2 Laptop security blog, Absolute Software, http://blog.absolute.com/category/real-theft-reports/.

3 John Leyden, "eBayed VPN kit hands over access to council network", theregister.co.uk, September 29, 2008, www.theregister.co.uk/2008/09/29/second_hand_vpn_security_breach.

4 Bob, Coffield, "Second criminal conviction under HIPAA," Health Care Law Blog, March 14, 2006, http://healthcarebloglaw.blogspot.com/2006/03/second-criminal-conviction-under-hipaa.html

5 "TJX identity theft saga continues: 11 charged with pilfering millions of credit cards," Networkworld.com magazine, August 5, 2008, www.networkworld.com/community/node/30741?nwwpkg=breaches?ap1=rcb.

6 "The TJX Companies, Inc. updates information on computer systems intrusion," February 21, 2007, www.tjx.com/Intrusion_Release_email.pdf.

the open marketplace as well as spawning class-action lawsuits.[7]

Gone are the days when intranet security was a superficial exercise; security inside the firewall was all but nonexistent. There was a feeling of implicit trust in the internal user. After all, if you hired that person, trained him for years, how could you not trust him?

In the new millennium, the Internet has come of age, and so have its users. The last largely computer-agnostic generation has exited the user scene; their occupational shoes have been filled with the "X and Y" generations. Many of these young people have grown up with the Internet, often familiar with it since elementary school. It is not uncommon today to find young college students who started their programming interests in the fifth or sixth grade.

With such a level of computer-savvy in users, the game of intranet security has changed (see side bar, "Network Breach Readiness: Many Are Still Complacent"). Resourceful as ever, these new users have gotten used to the idea of being hyperconnected to the Internet using mobile technology such as personal digital assistants (PDAs) and smart phones and firewalled barriers. For a corporate intranet that uses older ideas of using access control as the cornerstone of data security, such mobile access to the Internet at work needs careful analysis and control. The idea of building a virtual moat around your well-constructed castle (investing in a firewall and hoping to call it an intranet) is gone. Hyperconnected "knowledge workers" with laptops, PDAs and USB keys that have whole operating systems built in have made sure of it.

Network Breach Readiness: Many Are Still Complacent

The level of readiness for breaches among IT shops across the country is still far from optimal. The Ponemon Institute, a security think tank, surveyed some industry personnel and came up with some startling revelations. Hopefully these will change in the future:

- Eighty-five percent of industry respondents reported that they had experienced a data breach.
- Of those responding, 43% had no incident response plan in place, and 82% did not consult legal counsel before responding to the incident.
- Following a breach, 46% of respondents still had not implemented encryption on portable devices (laptops, PDAs) with company data stored on them.[8]

---

7 "TJX class action lawsuit settlement site," The TJX Companies, Inc., and Fifth Third Bancorp, Case No. 07-10162, www.tjxsettlement.com/.
8 "Ponemon Institute announces result of survey assessing the business impact of a data security breach," May 15, 2007, www.ponemon.org/press/Ponemon_Survey_Results_Scott_and_Scott_FINAL1.pdf.

If we could reuse the familiar vehicle ad tagline of the 1980s, we would say that the new intranet is not "your father's intranet anymore." The intranet as just a simple place to share files and to list a few policies and procedures has ceased to be. The types of changes can be summed up in the following list of features, which shows that the intranet has become a combined portal as well as a public dashboard. Some of the features can include:

- A searchable corporate personnel directory of phone numbers by department. Often the list is searchable only if the exact name is known.
- Expanded activity guides and a corporate calendar with links for various company divisions.
- Several RSS feeds for news according to divisions such as IT, HR, Finance, Accounting, and Purchasing.
- Company blogs (weblogs) by top brass that talk about the current direction for the company in reaction to recent events, a sort of "mission statement of the month."
- Intranets frequently feature a search engine for searching company information, often helped by a search appliance from Google. Microsoft also has its own search software on offer that targets corporate intranets.
- One or several "wiki" repositories for company intellectual property, some of it of a mission-critical nature. Usually granular permissions are applied for access here. One example could be court documents for a legal firm with rigorous security access applied.
- A section describing company financials and other mission-critical indicators. This is often a separate Web page linked to the main intranet page.
- A "live" section with IT alerts regarding specific downtimes, outages, and other critical time-sensitive company notifications. Often embedded within the portal, this is displayed in a "ticker-tape" fashion or like an RSS-type dynamic display.

Of course, this list is not exhaustive; some intranets have other unique features not listed here. But in any case, intranets these days do a lot more than simply list corporate phone numbers.

Recently, knowledge management systems have presented another challenge to intranet security postures. Companies that count knowledge as a prime protected asset (virtually all companies these days) have started deploying "mashable" applications that combine social networking (such as Facebook and LinkedIn), texting, and microblogging (such as Twitter) features to encourage employees to "wikify" their knowledge and information within intranets.

One of the bigger vendors in this space, Socialtext, has introduced a mashable wiki app that operates like a corporate dashboard for intranets.[9,10]

Socialtext has individual widgets, one of which, "Socialtext signals," is a microblogging engine. In the corporate context, microblogging entails sending short SMS messages to apprise colleagues of recent developments in the daily routine. Examples could be short messages on progress on any major project milestone—for example, joining up major airplane assemblies or getting Food and Drug Administration (FDA) testing approval for a special experimental drug.

These emerging scenarios present special challenges to security personnel guarding the borders of an intranet. The border as it once existed has ceased to be. One cannot block stored knowledge from leaving the intranet when a majority of corporate mobile users are accessing intranet wikis from anywhere using inexpensive mini-notebooks that are given away with cellphone contracts.[11]

If we consider the impact of national and international privacy mandates on these situations, the situation is compounded further for C-level executives in multinational companies who have to come up with responses to privacy mandates in each country in which the company does business. The privacy mandates regarding private customer data have always been more stringent in Europe than in North America, which is a consideration for doing business in Europe.

It is hard enough to block entertainment-related Flash video traffic from time-wasting Internet abuse without blocking a video of last week's corporate meeting at headquarters. Only letting in traffic on an exception basis becomes untenable or impractical because of a high level of personnel involvement needed for every ongoing security change. Simply blocking YouTube.com or Vimeo.com is not sufficient. Video, which has myriad legitimate work uses nowadays, is hosted on all sorts of content-serving (caching and streaming) sites worldwide, which makes it well near impossible to block using Web filters. The evolution of the Internet Content Adaptation Protocol (ICAP), which standardizes Web site categories for content-filtering purposes, is under way. However, ICAP still does not solve the problem of the dissolving networking "periphery."[12]

Guarding movable and dynamic data—which may be moving in and out of the perimeter without notice, flouting every possible mandate—is a key feature of today's intranet. The dynamic nature of data has rendered the traditional confidentiality, integrity, and availability (CIA) architecture somewhat less relevant. The changing nature of data security necessitates some specialized security considerations:

- Intranet security policies and procedures (P&Ps) are the first step toward a legal regulatory framework. The P&Ps needed on any of the security controls listed below should be compliant with federal and state mandates (such as HIPAA, Sarbanes-Oxley, the European Directive 95/46/EC on the protection of personal data, and PCI-DSS, among others). These P&Ps have to be signed off by top management and placed on the intranet for review by employees. There should be sufficient teeth in all procedural sections to enforce the policy, explicitly spelling out sanctions and other consequences of noncompliance, leading up to discharge.

- To be factual, none of these government mandates spell out details on implementing any security controls. That is the vague nature of federal and international mandates. Interpretation of the security controls is better left after the fact to an entity such as the National Institute of Standards and Technology (NIST) in the United States or the Geneva-based International Organization for Standardization (ISO). These organizations have extensive research and publication guidance for any specific security initiative. Most of NIST's documents are offered as free downloads from its Web site.[13] ISO security standards such as 27002~27005 are also available for a nominal fee from the ISO site.

Policies and procedures, once finalized, need to be automated as much as possible (one example is mandatory password changes every three months). Automating policy compliance takes the error-prone human factor out of the equation (see side bar, "Access Control in the Era of Social Networking"). There are numerous software tools available to help accomplish security policy automation.

9 Mowery, James, "Socialtext melds media and collaboration", cmswire.com, October 8, 2008, www.cmswire.com/cms/enterprise-20/socialtext-melds-media-and-collaboration-003270.php.

10 Rob, Hof, "Socialtext 3.0: Will wikis finally find their place in business?" Businessweek.com magazine, September 30, 2008, www.businessweek.com/the_thread/techbeat/archives/2008/09/socialtext_30_i.html.

11 Hickey, Matt, "MSI's 3.5G Wind 120 coming in November, offer subsidized by Taiwanese Telecom," Crave.com, October 20, 2008, http://news.cnet.com/8301-17938_105-10070911-1.html?tag=mncol;title.

12 Network Appliance, Inc., RFC Standards white paper for Internet Content Adaptation Protocol (ICAP), July 30, 2001, www.content-networking.com/references.html.

13 National Institute of Standards and Technology, Computer Security Resource Center, http://csrc.nist.gov/.

Access Control in the Era of Social Networking

In an age in which younger users have grown up with social networking sites as part of their digital lives, corporate intranet sites are finding it increasingly difficult to block them from using these sites at work. Depending on the company, some are embracing social networking as part of their corporate culture; others, especially government entities, are actively blocking these sites. Detractors mention as concerns wasted bandwidth, lost productivity, and the possibility of infections with spyware and worms.

However, blocking these sites can be difficult because most social networking and video sites such as Vimeo and YouTube can use port 80 to vector Flash videos into an intranet—which is wide open for HTTP access. Flash videos have the potential to provide a convenient Trojan horse for malware to get into the intranet.

To block social networking sites, one needs to block either the Social Networking category or block the specific URLs (such as YouTube.com) for these sites in the Web-filtering proxy appliance. Flash videos are rarely downloaded from YouTube itself. More often a redirected caching site is used to send in the video. The caching sites also need to be blocked; this is categorized under Content Servers.

---

1. PLUGGING THE GAPS: NAC AND ACCESS CONTROL

The first priority of an information security officer in most organizations is to ensure that there is a relevant corporate policy on access controls. Simple on the surface, the subject of access control is often complicated by the variety of ways the intranet is connected to the external world.

Remote users coming in through traditional or SSL (browser-based) virtual private networks (VPNs), control over use of USB keys, printouts, and CD-ROMs all require that a comprehensive endpoint security solution be implemented.

The past couple of years have seen large-scale adoption of network access control (NAC) products in the midlevel and larger IT shops to manage endpoint security. Endpoint security ensures that whomever is plugging into or accessing any hardware anywhere within the intranet has to comply with the minimum baseline corporate security policy standards. This can include add-on access credentials but goes far beyond access. Often these solutions ensure that traveling corporate laptops are compliant with a minimum patching level, scans, and antivirus definition levels before being allowed to connect to the intranet.

The NAC appliances that enforce these policies often require that a NAC fat client is installed on every PC and laptop. This rule can be enforced during logon using a logon script. The client can also be a part of the standard OS image for deploying new PCs and laptops.

Microsoft has built a NAC-type framework into some versions of its client OSs (Vista and XP SP3) to ease compliance with its NAC server product called MS Network Policy Server, which closely works with its Windows 2008 Server product (see side bar, "The Cost of a Data Breach"). The company has been able to convince quite a few industry networking heavyweights (notably Cisco and Juniper) to adopt its NAP standard.[14]

The Cost of a Data Breach

- As of July 2007, the average breach cost per incident was $4.8 million.
- This works out to $182 per exposed record.
- It represents an increase of more than 30% from 2005.
- Thirty-five percent of these breaches involved the loss or theft of a laptop or other portable device.
- Seventy percent were due to a mistake or malicious intent by an organization's own staff.
- Since 2005 almost 150 million individuals' identifiable information has been compromised due to a data security breach.
- Nineteen percent of consumers notified of a data breach discontinued their relationship with the business, and a further 40% considered doing so.[15]

Essentially the technology has three parts: a policy-enforceable client, a decision point, and an enforcement point. The client could be an XP SP3 or Vista client (either a roaming user or guest user) trying to connect to the company intranet. The decision point in this case would be the Network Policy Server product, checking to see whether the client requesting access meets the minimum baseline to allow it to connect. If it does not, the decision point product would pass this data on to the enforcement point, a network access product such as a router or switch, which would then be able to cut off access.

The scenario would repeat itself at every connection attempt, allowing the network's health to be maintained

---

14 "Juniper and Microsoft hook up for NAC work," May 22, 2007, PHYSORG.com, www.physorg.com/news99063542.html.
15 Bocek, Kevin, "What does a data breach cost?" SCmagazine.com, July 2, 2007, www.scmagazineus.com/What-does-a-data-breach-cost/article/35131.

on an ongoing basis. Microsoft's NAP page has more details and animation to explain this process.[16]

Access control in general terms is a relationship triad among internal users, intranet resources, and the actions internal users can take on those resources. The idea is to give users only the least amount of access they require to perform their job. The tools used to ensure this in Windows shops utilize Active Directory for Windows logon scripting and Windows user profiles. Granular classification is needed for users, actions, and resources to form a logical and comprehensive access control policy that addresses who gets to connect to what, yet keeping the intranet safe from unauthorized access or data-security breaches. Quite a few off-the-shelf solutions geared toward this market often combine inventory control and access control under a "desktop life-cycle" planning umbrella.

Typically, security administrators start with a "Deny–All" policy as a baseline before slowly building in the access permissions. As users migrate from one department to another, are promoted, or leave the company, in large organizations this job can involve one person by herself. This person often has a very close working relationship with Purchasing, Helpdesk, and HR, getting coordination and information from these departments on users who have separated from the organization and computers that have been surplused, deleting and modifying user accounts and assignments of PCs and laptops.

Helpdesk software usually has an inventory control component that is readily available to Helpdesk personnel to update and/or pull up to access details on computer assignments and user status. Optimal use of form automation can ensure that these details occur (such as deleting a user on the day of separation) to avoid any possibility of an unwelcome data breach.

2. MEASURING RISK: AUDITS

Audits are another cornerstone of a comprehensive intranet security policy. To start an audit, an administrator should know and list what he is protecting as well as knowing the relevant threats and vulnerabilities to those resources.

Assets that need protection can be classified as either tangible or intangible. *Tangible assets* are, of course, removable media (USB keys), PCs, laptops, PDAs, Web servers, networking equipment, DVR security cameras, and employees' physical access cards. *Intangible assets* can include company intellectual property such as corporate email and wikis, user passwords, and, especially

for HIPAA and Sarbanes-Oxley mandates, personally identifiable health and financial information, which the company could be legally liable to protect.

Threats can include theft of USB keys, laptops, PDAs, and PCs from company premises, resulting in a data breach (for *tangible assets*) and weak passwords and unhardened operating systems in servers (for *intangible assets*).

Once a correlated listing of assets and associated threats and vulnerabilities has been made we have to measure the impact of a breach, which is known as *risk*. The common rule of thumb to measure risk is:

$$Risk = Value of asset \times Threat \times Vulnerability$$

It is obvious that an Internet-facing Web server faces greater risk and requires priority patching and virus scanning because the vulnerability and threat components are high in that case (these servers routinely get sniffed and scanned over the Internet by hackers looking to find holes in their armor). However, this formula can standardize the priority list so that the actual audit procedure (typically carried out weekly or monthly by a vulnerability-scanning device) is standardized by risk level. Vulnerability-scanning appliances usually scan server farms and networking appliances only because these are high-value targets within the network for hackers who are looking for either unhardened server configurations or network switches with default factory passwords left on by mistake. To illustrate the situation, look at Figure 9.1, which illustrates an SQL injection attack on a corporate database.[17]

The value of an asset is subjective and can be assessed only by the IT personnel in that organization (see sidebar, "Questions for a Nontechnical Audit of Intranet Security"). If the IT staff has an ITIL (Information Technology Infrastructure Library) process under way, the value of an asset will often already have been classified and can be used. Otherwise, a small spreadsheet can be created with classes of various tangible and intangible assets (as part of a hardware/software cataloguing exercise) and values assigned that way.

> **Questions for a Nontechnical Audit of Intranet Security**
>
> Is all access (especially to high-value assets) logged?
> In case of laptop theft, is encryption enabled so that the records will be useless to the thief?
> Are passwords verifiably strong enough to comply with the security policy? Are they changed frequently and held to strong encryption standards?

16 NAP Program program details, Microsoft.com, www.microsoft.com/windowsserver2008/en/us/nap-features.aspx.

17 "Web application security—check your site for web application vulnerabilities," www.acunetix.com/websitesecurity/webapp-security.htm.

Are all tangible assets (PCs, laptops, PDAs, Web servers, networking equipment) tagged with asset tags?

Is the process for surplusing obsolete IT assets secure (meaning, are disks wiped for personally identifiable data before surplusing happens)?

Is email and Web usage logged?

Are peer-to-peer (P2P) and instant messaging (IM) usage controlled?

Based on the answers you get (or don't), you can start the security audit procedure by finding answers to these questions.

3. GUARDIAN AT THE GATE: AUTHENTICATION AND ENCRYPTION

To most lay users, authentication in its most basic form is two-factor authentication—meaning a username and a password. Although adding further factors (such as additional autogenerated personal identification numbers [PINs] and/or biometrics) makes authentication stronger by magnitudes, one can do a lot with just the password within a two-factor situation. Password strength is determined by how hard the password is to crack using a password-cracker application that uses repetitive tries using common words (sometimes from a stored dictionary) to match the password. Some factors will prevent the password from being cracked easily and make it a stronger password:

- Password length (more than eight characters)
- Use of mixed case (both uppercase and lowercase)
- Use of alphanumeric characters (letters as well as numbers)
- Use of special characters (such as !, ?, %, and #)

The ACL in a Windows AD environment can be customized to demand up to all four factors in the

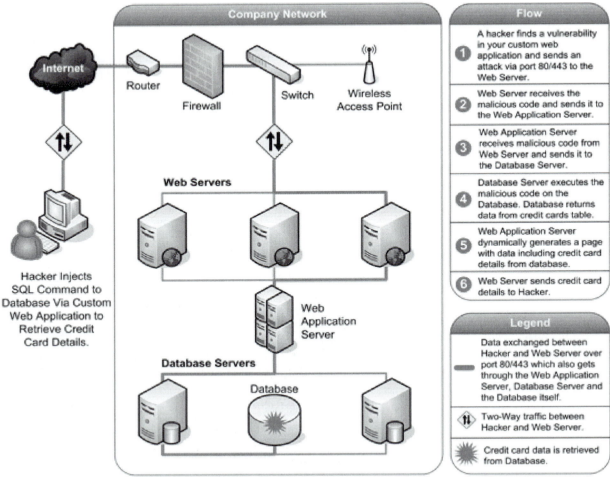

FIGURE 9.1 SQL injection attack. Source: © acunetix.com

setting or renewal of a password, which will render the password strong.

Prior to a few years ago, the complexity of a password (the last three items in the preceding list) was favored as a measure of strength in passwords. However, the latest preference as of this writing is to use uncommon passwords—joined-together sentences to form passphrases that are quite long but don't have much in the way of complexity. Password authentication ("what you know") as two-factor authentication is not as secure as adding a third factor to the equation (a dynamic token password). Common types of third-factor authentication include biometrics (fingerprint scan, palm scan, or retina scan—in other words, "what you are") and token-type authentication (software or hardware PIN–generating tokens—that is, "what you have").

Proximity or magnetic swipe cards and tokens have seen common use for physical premises-access authentication in high-security buildings (such as financial and R&D companies) but not for network or hardware access within IT.

When remote or teleworker employees connect to the intranet via VPN tunnels or Web-based SSL VPNs (the outward extension of the intranet once called an *extranet*), the connection needs to be encrypted with strong 3DES or AES type encryption to comply with patient data and financial data privacy mandates. The standard authentication setup is usually a username and a password, with an additional hardware token-generated random PIN entered into a third box. Until lately, RSA as a company was one of the bigger players in the hardware-token field; it incidentally also invented the RSA algorithm for public-key encryption.

As of this writing, hardware tokens cost under $30 per user in quantities of greater than a couple hundred pieces, compared to about a $100 only a decade ago. Most vendors offer free lifetime replacements for hardware tokens. Instead of a separate hardware token, some inexpensive software token generators can be installed within PC clients, smart phones, and BlackBerry devices. Tokens are probably the most cost-effective enhancement to security today.

4. WIRELESS NETWORK SECURITY

Employees using the convenience of wireless to log into the corporate network (usually via laptop) need to have their laptops configured with strong encryption to prevent data breaches. The first-generation encryption type known as Wireless Equivalent Privacy (WEP) was easily deciphered (cracked) using common hacking tools and is no longer widely used. The latest standard in wireless authentication is WPA or WPA2 (802.11i), which offer stronger encryption compared to WEP. Though wireless cards in laptops can offer all the previously noted choices, they should be configured with WPA or WPA2 if possible.

There are quite a few hobbyists roaming corporate areas looking for open wireless access points (transmitters) equipped with powerful Wi-Fi antennas and wardriving software, a common package being Netstumbler. Wardriving was originally meant to log the presence of open Wi-Fi access points on Web sites (see side bar, "Basic Ways to Prevent Wi-Fi Intrusions in Corporate Intranets"), but there is no guarantee that actual access and use (*piggybacking*, in hacker terms) won't occur, curiosity being human nature. If there is a profit motive, as in the TJX example, access to corporate networks will take place, although the risk of getting caught and resulting risk of criminal prosecution will be high. Furthermore, installing a RADIUS server is a must to check access authentication for roaming laptops.

Basic Ways to Prevent Wi-Fi Intrusions in Corporate Intranets

1. Reset and customize the default Service Set Identifier (SSID) or Extended Service Set Identifier (ESSID) for the access point device before installation.
2. Change the default admin password.
3. Install a RADIUS server, which checks for laptop user credentials from an Active Directory database (ACL) from the same network before giving access to the wireless laptop. See Figures 9.2 and 9.3 for illustrated explanations of the process.
4. Enable WPA or WPA2 encryption, not WEP, which is easily cracked.
5. Periodically try to wardrive around your campus and try to sniff (and disable) nonsecured network-connected rogue access points set up by naïve users.
6. Document the wireless network by using one of the leading wireless network management software packages made for that purpose.

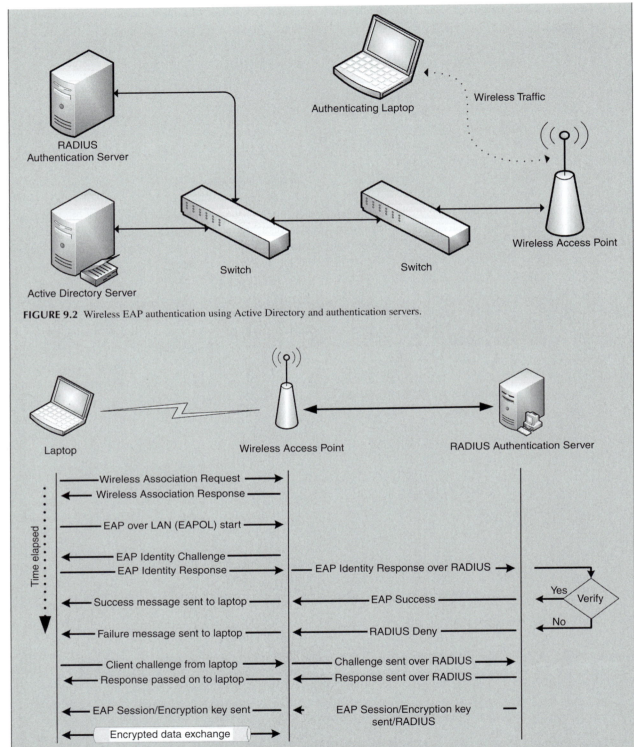

FIGURE 9.2 Wireless EAP authentication using Active Directory and authentication servers.

FIGURE 9.3 High-level wireless Extensible Authentication Protocol (EAP) workflow.

Note: Contrary to common belief, turning off SSID broadcast won't help unless you're talking about a home access point situation. Hackers have an extensive suite of tools with which to sniff SSIDs for lucrative corporate targets, which will be broadcast anyway when connecting in clear text (unlike the real traffic, which will be encrypted).

5. SHIELDING THE WIRE: NETWORK PROTECTION

Firewalls are, of course, the primary barrier to a network. Typically rule based, firewalls prevent unwarranted traffic from getting into the intranet from the Internet. These days firewalls also do some stateful inspections within packets to peer a little into the header contents of an incoming packet, to check validity—that is, to check whether a streaming video packet is really what it says it is, and not malware masquerading as streaming video.

Intrusion prevention systems (IPSs) are a newer type of inline network appliance that uses heuristic analysis (based on a weekly updated signature engine) to find patterns of malware identity and behavior and to block malware from entering the periphery of the intranet. The IPS and the intrusion detection system (IDS), however, operate differently.

IDSs are typically *not* sitting inline; they sniff traffic occurring anywhere in the network, cache extensively, and can correlate events to find malware. The downside of IDSs is that unless their filters are extensively modified, they generate copious amounts of false positives—so much so that "real" threats become impossible to sift out of all the noise.

IPSs, in contrast, work *inline* and inspect packets rapidly to match packet signatures. The packets pass through many hundreds of parallel filters, each containing matching rules for a different type of malware threat. Most vendors publish new sets of malware signatures for their appliances every week. However, signatures for common worms and injection exploits such as SQL-slammer, Code-red, and NIMDA are sometimes hardcoded into the application-specific integrated chip (ASIC) that controls the processing for the filters. Hardware-enhancing a filter helps avert massive-scale attacks more efficiently because it is performed in hardware, which is more rapid and efficient compared to software signature matching. Incredible numbers of malicious packets can be dropped from the wire using the former method.

The buffers in an enterprise-class IPS are smaller compared to those in IDSs and are quite fast—akin to a high-speed switch to preclude latency (often as low as 200 microseconds during the highest load). A top-of-the-line midsize IPS box's total processing threshold for all input and output segments can exceed 5 gigabits per second using parallel processing.[18]

However, to avoid overtaxing CPUs and for efficiency's sake, IPSs usually block only a very limited number of important threats out of the thousands of malware signatures listed. Tuning IPSs can be tricky—just enough blocking to silence the false positive noise but making sure all critical filters are activated to block important threats.

The most important factors in designing a critical data infrastructure are resiliency, robustness, and redundancy regarding the operation of inline appliances. Whether one is talking about firewalls or inline IPSs, redundancy is paramount (see side bar, "Types of Redundancy for Inline Security Appliances"). Intranet robustness is a primary concern where data has to available on a 24/7 basis.

Types of Redundancy for Inline Security Appliances

1. Security appliances usually have dual power supplies (often hot-swappable) and are designed to be connected to two separate UPS devices, thereby minimizing chances of a failure within the appliance itself. The hot-swap capability minimizes replacement time for power supplies.

2. We can configure most of these appliances to either shut down the connection or fall back to a level-two switch (in case of hardware failure). If reverting to a fallback state, most IPSs become basically a bump in the wire and, depending on the type of traffic, can be configured to fail open so that traffic remains uninterrupted. Also, inexpensive, small third-party switchboxes are available to enable this failsafe high-availability option for a single IPS box. The idea is to keep traffic flow active regardless of attacks.

3. IPS or firewall devices can be placed in dual-redundant failover mode, either in active-active (load-sharing) or active-passive (primary-secondary) mode. The devices commonly use a protocol called Virtual Router Redundancy Protocol (VRRP) where the secondary pings the primary every second to check live status and assumes leadership to start processing traffic in case pings are not returned from the primary. The switchover is instantaneous and transparent to most network users. Prior to the switchover, all data and connection settings are fully synchronized at identical states between both boxes to ensure failsafe switchover.

4. Inline IPS appliances are relatively immune to attacks because they have highly hardened Linus/Unix operating systems and are designed from the ground up to be robust and low-maintenance appliances (logs usually clear themselves by default).

---

18 IPS specification datasheet. "TippingPoint® intrusion prevention system (IPS) technical specifications," www.tippingpoint.com/pdf/resources/datasheets/400918-007_IPStechspecs.pdf.

Most security appliances come with syslog reporting (event and alert logs sent usually via port 514 UDP) and email notification (set to alert beyond a customizable threshold) as standard. The syslog reporting can be forwarded to a security events management (SEM) appliance, which consolidates syslogs into a central threat console for benefit of event correlation and forwards warning emails to administrators based on preset threshold criteria. Moreover, most firewalls and IPSs can be configured to forward their own notification email to administrators in case of an impending threat scenario.

For those special circumstances where a wireless-type LAN connection is the primary one (whether microwave beam, laser beam, or satellite-type connection), redundancy can be ensured by a secondary connection of equal or smaller capacity. For example, in certain northern Alaska towns where digging trenches into the hardened icy permafrost is expensive and rigging wire across the tundra is impractical due to the extreme cold, the primary network connections between towns are always via microwave link, often operating in dual redundant mode.

6. WEAKEST LINK IN SECURITY: USER TRAINING

Intranet security awareness is best communicated to users in two primary ways—during new employee orientation and by ongoing targeted training for users in various departments, with specific user audiences in mind.

A formal security training policy should be drafted and signed off by management, with well-defined scopes, roles, and responsibilities of various individuals, such as the CIO and the information security officer, and posted on the intranet. New recruits should be given a copy of all security policies to sign off on before they are granted user access. The training policy should also spell out the HR, Compliance, and PR departments' roles in the training program.

Training can be given using the PowerPoint Seminar method in large gatherings before monthly "all-hands" departmental meetings and also via an emailed Web link to a Flash video format presentation. The latter can also be configured to have an interactive quiz at the end, which should pique audience interest on the subject and help them remember relevant issues.

As far as topics to be included in the training, any applicable federal or industry mandate such as HIPAA, SOX, PCI-DSS, or ISO 27002 should be discussed extensively first, followed by discussions on tackling social engineering, spyware, viruses, and so on.

The topics of data theft and corporate data breaches are frequently in the news. This subject can be extensively discussed with emphasis on how to protect personally identifiable information in a corporate setting. Password policy and access control topics are always good things to discuss; users at a minimum need to be reminded to sign off their workstations before going on break.

7. DOCUMENTING THE NETWORK: CHANGE MANAGEMENT

Controlling the IT infrastructure configuration of a large organization is more about change control than other things. Often the change control guidance comes from documents such as the ITIL series of guidebooks.

After a baseline configuration is documented, change control—a deliberate and methodical process that ensures that any changes made to the baseline IT configuration of the organization (such as changes to network design, AD design, and so on)—is extensively documented and authorized only after prior approval. This is done to ensure that unannounced or unplanned changes are not allowed to hamper the day-to-day efficiency and business functions of the overall intranet infrastructure.

In most government entities, even very small changes are made to go through change management (CM); however, management can provide leeway to managers to approve a certain minimal level of ad hoc change that has no potential to disrupt operations. In most organizations where mandates are a day-to-day affair, no ad hoc change is allowed unless it goes through supervisory-level change management meetings.

The goal of change management is largely to comply with mandates—but for some organizations, waiting for a weekly meeting can slow things significantly. If justified, an emergency CM meeting can be called to approve a time-sensitive change.

Practically speaking, the change management process works like this; A formal change management document is filled out (usually a multitab online Excel spreadsheet) and forwarded to the change management ombudsman (maybe a project management person). See the side bar "Change Management Spreadsheet Details to Submit to a CM Meeting" for some CM form details.

The document must have supervisory approval from the requestor's supervisor before proceeding to the

> **Change Management Spreadsheet Details to Submit to a CM Meeting**
>
> - Name and organizational details of the change-requestor
> - Actual change details, such as the time and duration of the change
> - Any possible impacts (high, low, medium) to significant user groups or critical functions
> - The amount of advance notice needed for impacted users via email (typically two working days)
> - Evidence that the change has been tested in advance
> - Signature and approval of the supervisor and her supervisor (manager)
> - Whether and how rollback is possible
> - Post-change, a "post-mortem tab" has to confirm whether the change process was successful and any revealing comments or notes for the conclusion
> - One of the tabs can be an "attachment tab" containing embedded Visio diagrams or word documentation embedded within the Excel sheet to aid discussion

ombudsman. The ombudsman posts this change document on a section of the intranet for all other supervisors and managers within the CM committee to review in advance. Done this way, the change management committee, meeting in its weekly or biweekly change approval meetings, can voice reservations or ask clarification questions of the change-initiating person, who is usually present to explain the change. At the end of the deliberations the decision is then voted on to either approve, deny, modify, or delay the change (sometimes with preconditions).

If approved, the configuration change is then made (usually within the following week). The post-mortem section of the change can then be updated to note any issues that occurred during the change (such as a rollback after change reversal and the causes).

In recent years, some organizations have started to operate the change management collaborative process using social networking tools at work. This allows disparate flows of information, such as emails, departmental wikis, and file-share documents, to belong to a unified thread for future reference.

8. REHEARSE THE INEVITABLE: DISASTER RECOVERY

Possible disaster scenarios can range from the mundane to the biblical in proportion. In intranet or general IT terms, successfully recovering from a disaster can mean resuming critical IT support functions for mission-critical business functions. Whether such recovery is smooth and hassle-free depends on how prior disaster-recovery planning occurs and how this plan is tested to address all relevant shortcomings adequately.

The first task when planning for disaster recovery (DR) is to assess the business impact of a certain type of disaster on the functioning of an intranet using business impact analysis (BIA). BIA involves certain metrics; again, off-the shelf software tools are available to assist with this effort. The scenario could be a natural hurricane-induced power outage or a human-induced critical application crash. In any one of these scenarios, one needs to assess the type of impact in time, productivity, and financial terms.

BIAs can take into consideration the breadth of impact. For example, if the power outage is caused by a hurricane or an earthquake, support from generator vendors or the electricity utility could be hard to get because of the large demands for their services. BIAs also need to take into account historical and local weather priorities. Though there could be possibilities of hurricanes occurring in California or earthquakes occurring along the Gulf Coast of Florida, for most practical purposes the chances of those disasters occurring in those locales are pretty remote. Historical data can be helpful for prioritizing contingencies.

Once the business impacts are assessed to categorize critical systems, a disaster recovery (DR) plan can be organized and tested. The criteria for recovery have two types of metrics: a recovery point objective (RPO) and a recovery time objective (RTO).

In the DR plan, the RPO refers to how far back or "back to what point in time" that backup data has to be recovered. This timeframe generally dictates how often tape backups are taken, which can again depend on the criticality of the data. The most common scenario for medium-sized IT shops is daily incremental backups and a weekly full backup on tape. Tapes are sometimes changed automatically by the tape backup appliances.

One important thing to remember is to rotate tapes (that is, put them on a life-cycle plan by marking them for expiry) to make sure that tapes have complete data integrity during a restore. Most tape manufacturers have marking schemes for this task. Although tapes are still relatively expensive, the extra amount spent on always having fresh tapes ensures that there are no nasty surprises at the time of a crucial data recovery.

RTO refers to how long it takes to restore backed up or recovered data to its original state for resuming normal business processes. The critical factor here is cost. It will cost much more to restore data within an hour using an online backup process or to resume operations using a hotsite rather than a five-hour restore using stored tape backups. If business process resumption is critical, cost becomes less a factor.

DR also has to take into account resumption of communication channels. If network and telephone links aren't up, having a timely tape restore does little good to resume business functions. Extended campus network links are often dependent on leased lines from major vendors such as Verizon and AT&T, so having a trusted vendor relationship with agreed-on SLA standards is a requirement.

Depending on budgets, one can configure DR to happen almost instantly, if so desired, but that is a far more costly option. Most shops with "normal" data-flows are okay with business being resumed within the span of about three to fours hours or even a full working day after a major disaster. Balancing costs with business expectations is the primary factor in the DR game. Spending inordinately for a rare disaster that might never happen is a waste of resources. It is fiscally imprudent (not to mention futile) to try to prepare for every contingency possible.

Once the DR plan is more or less finalized, a DR committee can be set up under an experienced DR professional to orchestrate the routine training of users and managers to simulate disasters on a frequent basis. In most shops this means management meeting every two months to simulate a DR "war room" (command center) situation and employees going through a mandatory interactive six-month disaster recovery training, listing the DR personnel to contact.

Within the command center, roles are preassigned, and each member of the team carries out his or her role as though it were a real emergency or disaster. DR coordination is frequently modeled after the U.S. Federal Emergency Management Agency (FEMA) guidelines, an active entity that has training and certification tracks for DR management professionals.

There are scheduled simulated "generator shutdowns" in most shops on a biweekly or monthly basis to see how the systems actually function. The systems can include uninterruptible power supplies (UPSs), emergency lighting, email and cell phone notification methods, and alarm enunciators and sirens. Since electronics items in a server room are sensitive to moisture damage, gas-based Halon fire-extinguishing systems are used. These Halon systems also have a provision to test them (often twice a year) to determine their readiness. The vendor will be happy to be on retainer for these tests, which can be made part of the purchasing agreement as a service-level agreement (SLA). If equipment is tested on a regular basis, shortcomings and major hardware maintenance issues with major DR systems can be easily identified, documented, and redressed.

In a severe disaster situation, priorities need to be exercised on what to salvage first. Clearly, trying to recover employee records, payroll records, and critical business mission data such as customer databases will take precedence. Anything irreplaceable or not easily replaceable needs priority attention.

We can divide the levels of redundancies and backups to a few progressive segments. The level of backup sophistication would of course be dependent on (1) criticality and (2) time-to-recovery criteria of the data involved.

At the very basic level, we can opt not to back up any data or not even have procedures to recover data, which means that data recovery would be a failure. Understandably, this is not a common scenario.

More typical is contracting with an archival company of a local warehouse within a 20-mile periphery. Tapes are backed up onsite and stored offsite, with the archival company picking up the tapes from your facility on a daily basis. The time to recover is dependent on retrieving the tapes from archival storage, getting them onsite, and starting a restore. The advantages here are lower cost. However, the time needed to transport tapes and recover them might not be acceptable, depending on the type of data and the recovery scenario.

Often a "coldsite" or "hotsite" is added to the intranet backup scenario. A coldsite is a smaller and scaled-down copy of the existing intranet data center that has only the most essential pared-down equipment supplied and tested for recovery but not in a perpetually ready state (powered down as in "cold," with no live connection). These coldsites can house the basics, such as a Web server, domain name servers, and SQL databases, to get an informational site started up in very short order.

A hotsite is the same thing as a coldsite except that in this case the servers are always running and the Internet and intranet connections are "live" and ready to be switched over much more quickly than on a coldsite. These are just two examples of how the business resumption and recovery times can be shortened.

Recovery can be made very rapidly if the hotsite is linked to the regular data center using fast leased-line links (such as a DS3 connection). Backups synched in real time with identical RAID disks at the hotsite over redundant high-speed data links afford the shortest recovery time.

In larger intranet shops based in defense-contractor companies, there are sometimes requirements for even faster data recovery with far more rigid standards for data integrity. To-the-second real-time data synchronization in addition to hardware synchronization ensures that duplicate sites thousands of miles away can be up and running within a matter of seconds—even faster than a hotsite. Such extreme redundancy is typically needed for critical national databases (that is, air traffic control or customs databases that are accessed 24/7, for example).

At the highest level of recovery performance, most large database vendors offer "zero data loss" solutions, with a variety of cloned databases synchronized across the country that automatically failover and recover in an instantaneous fashion to preserve a consistent status— often free from human intervention. Oracle's version is called Data Guard; most mainframe vendors offer a similar product varying in tiers and features offered.

The philosophy here is simple: The more dollars you spend, the more readiness you can buy. However, the expense has to be justified by the level of criticality for the availability of the data.

9. CONTROLLING HAZARDS: PHYSICAL AND ENVIRONMENTAL PROTECTION

Physical access and environmental hazards are very relevant to security within the intranet. People are the primary weak link in security (as previously discussed), and controlling the activity and movement of authorized personnel and preventing access to unauthorized personnel fall within the purview of these security controls.

This important area of intranet security must first be formalized within a management-sanctioned and published P&P.

Physical access to data center facilities (as well as IT working facilities) is typically controlled using card readers. These were scanning types in the last two decades but are increasingly being converted to near-field or proximity-type access card systems. Some high-security facilities (such as bank data centers) use smartcards, which use encryption keys stored within the cards for matching keys.

Some important and common-sense topics should be discussed within the subject of physical access. First, disbursal of cards needs to be a deliberate and high-security affair requiring the signatures of at least two supervisory-level people who can be responsible for the authenticity and actual need for access credentials for a person to specific areas.

Access-card permissions need to be highly granular. An administrative person will probably never need to be in server room, so that person's access to the server room should be blocked. Areas should be categorized and catalogued by sensitivity and access permissions granted accordingly.

Physical data transmission access points to the intranet have to be monitored via digital video recording (DVR) and closed-circuit cameras if possible. Physical electronic eavesdropping can occur to unmonitored network access points in both wireline and wireless ways. There have been known instances of thieves intercepting LAN communication from unshielded Ethernet cable (usually hidden above the plenum or false ceiling for longer runs). All a data thief needs is to place a TAP box and a miniature (Wi-Fi) wireless transmitter at entry or exit points to the intranet to copy and transmit all communications. At the time of this writing, these transmitters are the size of a USB key. The miniaturization of electronics has made data theft possible for part-time thieves. Spy-store sites give determined data thieves plenty of workable options at relatively little cost.

Using a DVR solution to monitor and store access logs to sensitive areas and correlating them to the timestamps on the physical access logs can help forensic investigations in case of a physical data breach, malfeasance, or theft. It is important to remember that DVR records typically rotate and are erased every week. One person has to be in charge of the DVR so records are saved to optical disks weekly before they are erased. DVR tools need some tending to because their sophistication level often does not come up to par with other network tools.

Written or PC-based sign-in logs must be kept at the front reception desk, with timestamps. Visitor cards should have limited access to private and/or secured areas. Visitors must provide official identification, log times coming in and going out, and names of persons to be visited and the reason for their visit. If possible, visitors should be escorted to and from the specific person to be visited, to minimize the chances of subversion or sabotage.

Entries to courthouses and other special facilities have metal detectors but these may not be needed for every facility. The same goes for bollards and concrete entry barriers to prevent car bombings. In most government facilities where security is paramount, even physical entry points to parking garages have special personnel (usually deputed from the local sheriff's department) to check under cars for hidden explosive devices.

Contractor laptops must be registered and physically checked in by field support personnel, and if these laptops are going to be plugged into the local network, the laptops need to be virus-scanned by data-security personnel and checked for unauthorized utilities or suspicious software (such as hacking utilities, Napster, or other P2P threats).

Supply of emergency power to the data center and the servers has to be robust to protect the intranet from corruption due to power failures. Redundancy has to be exercised all the way from the utility connection to the servers themselves. This means there has to be more than one power connection to the data center (from more than one substation/transformer, if it is a larger data center). There has to be provision of alternate power supply (a ready generator to supply some, if not all, power requirements) in case of failure of utility power to the facility.

Power supplied to the servers has to come from more than one single UPS because most servers have two removable power inputs. Data center racks typically have two UPSs on the bottom supplying power to two separate power strips on both sides of the rack for this redundancy purpose (for seamless switchover). In case of a power failure, the UPSs instantly take over the supply of power and start beeping, alerting personnel to gracefully shut down servers. UPSs usually have reserve power for brief periods (less than 10 minutes) until the generator kicks in, relieving the UPS of the large burden of the server power loads. Generators come on trailers or are skid-mounted and are designed to run as long as there is fuel available in the tank, which can be about three to five days, depending on the model and capacity to generate (in thousands of kilowatts).

Increasingly, expensive polluting batteries have made UPSs in larger datacenters fall out of favor compared to flywheel power supplies, which is a cleaner, battery-less technology to supply interim power. Maintenance of this technology is half as costly as UPS and it offers the same functionality.[19]

There has to be provision for rechargeable emergency luminaires within the server room as well as all areas occupied by administrators, so entry and exit are not hampered during a power failure.

Provision for fire detection and firefighting must also be made. As mentioned previously, Halon gas fire-suppression systems are appropriate for server rooms because sprinklers will inevitably damage expensive servers if the servers are still turned on during sprinkler activation.

Sensors have to be placed close to the ground to detect moisture from plumbing disasters and resultant flooding. Master shutoff valve locations for water have to be marked and identified and personnel trained on performing shutoffs periodically. Complete environmental control packages with cameras geared toward detecting any type of temperature, moisture, and sound abnormality are offered by many vendors. These sensors are connected to monitoring workstations using Ethernet LAN cabling. Reporting can occur through emails if customizable thresholds are met or exceeded.

10. KNOW YOUR USERS: PERSONNEL SECURITY

Users working within intranet-related infrastructures have to be known and trusted. Often data contained within the intranet is highly sensitive, such as new product designs and financial or market-intelligence data gathered after much research and at great expense.

Assigning personnel to sensitive areas in IT entails attaching security categories and parameters to the positions, especially within IT. Attaching security parameters to a position is akin to attaching tags to a photograph or blog. Some parameters will be more important than others, but all describe the item to some extent. The categories and parameters listed on the personnel access form should correlate to access permissions to sensitive installations such as server rooms. Access permissions should be compliant to the organizational security policy in force at the time.

Personnel, especially those who will be handling sensitive customer data or individually identifiable health records, should be screened before hiring to ensure that they do not have felonies or misdemeanors on their records.

During transfers and terminations, all sensitive access tools should be reassessed and reassigned (or deassigned, in case of termination) for logical and physical access. Access tools can include such items as encryption tokens, company cell phones, laptops or PDAs, card keys, metal keys, entry passes, and any other company identification provided for employment. For people who are leaving the organization, an exit interview should be taken. System access should be terminated on the hour after former personnel have ceased to be employees of the company.

11. PROTECTING DATA FLOW: INFORMATION AND SYSTEM INTEGRITY

Information integrity protects information and data flows while they are in movement to and from the users'

---

19 Flywheel energy storage, Wikipedia.com, http://en.wikipedia.org/wiki/Flywheel_energy_storage.

desktops to the intranet. System integrity measures protect the systems that process the information (usually servers such as email or file servers). The processes to protect information can include antivirus tools, IPS and IDS tools, Web-filtering tools, and email encryption tools.

Antivirus tools are the most common security tools available to protect servers and users' desktops. Typically, enterprise-level antivirus software from larger vendors such as Symantec or McAfee will contain a console listing all machines on the network and will enable the administrators to see graphically (color or icon differentiation) which machines need virus remediation or updates. All machines will have a software client installed that does some scanning and reporting of the individual machines to the console. To save bandwidth, the management server that contains the console will be updated with the latest virus (and spyware) definition from the vendor. Then it is the management console's job to slowly update the software client in each computer with the latest definitions. Sometimes the client itself will need an update, and the console allows this to be done remotely.

IDS used to detect malware within the network from the traffic and communication malware used. There are certain patterns of behavior attached to each type of malware, and those signatures are what IDSs are used to match. IDSs are mostly defunct nowadays. The major problems with IDSs were that (1) IDSs used to produce too many false positives, which made sifting out actual threats a huge, frustrating exercise, and (2) IDSs had no teeth, that is, their functionality was limited to reporting and raising alarms. IDS devices could not stop malware from spreading because they could not block it.

Compared to IDSs, IPSs have seen much wider adoption across corporate intranets because IPS devices sit inline processing traffic at the periphery and they can block traffic or malware, depending on a much more sophisticated heuristic algorithm than IDS devices. Although IPS are all mostly signature based, there are already experimental IPS devices that can stop threats, not on signature, but based only on suspicious or anomalous behavior. This is good news because the numbers of "zero-day" threats are on the increase, and their signatures are mostly unknown to the security vendors at the time of infection.

Web-filtering tools have gotten more sophisticated as well. Ten years ago Web filters could only block traffic to specific sites if the URL matched. Nowadays most Web filter vendors have large research arms that try to categorize specific Web sites under certain categories.

Some vendors have realized the enormity of this task and have allowed the general public to contribute to this effort. The Web site www.trustedsource.org is an example; a person can go in and submit a single or multiple URLs for categorization. If they're examined and approved, the site category will then be added to the vendor's next signature update for their Web filter solution.

Web filters not only match URLs, they do a fair bit of packet-examining too these days—just to make sure that a JPEG frame is indeed a JPEG frame and not a worm in disguise. The categories of Web sites blocked by a typical midsized intranet vary, but some surefire blocked categories would be pornography, erotic sites, discrimination/hate, weapons/illegal activities, and dating/relationships.

Web filters are not just there to enforce the moral values of management. These categories—if not blocked at work—openly enable an employee to offend another employee (especially pornography or discriminatory sites) and are fertile grounds for a liability lawsuit against the employer.

Finally, email encryption has been in the news because of the various mandates such as Sarbanes-Oxley and HIPAA. Both mandates specifically mention email or communication encryption to encrypt personally identifiable financial or patient medical data while in transit. Lately the state of California (among other states) has adopted a resolution to discontinue fund disbursements to any California health organization that does not use email encryption as a matter of practice. This has caught quite a few California companies and local government entities unaware because email encryption software is relatively hard to implement. The toughest challenge yet is to train users to get used to the tool.

Email encryption works by entering a set of credentials to access the email rather than just getting email pushed to the user, as within the email client Outlook.

12. SECURITY ASSESSMENTS

A security assessment (usually done on a yearly basis for most midsized shops) not only uncovers various misconfigured items on the network and server-side sections of IT operations, it serves as a convenient blueprint for IT to activate necessary changes and get credibility for budgetary assistance from the accounting folks.

Typically most consultants take two to four weeks to conduct a security assessment (depending on the size of the intranet) and they primarily use open-source vulnerability scanners such as Nessus. GFI LANguard, Retina, and Core Impact are other examples of commercial vulnerability-testing tools. Sometimes testers also use other proprietary suites of tools (special open-source tools like the Metasploit Framework or Fragrouter) to conduct "payload-bearing attack exploits," thereby evading the firewall and the IPS to gain entry. In the case of intranet Web servers, cross-site scripting attacks can occur (see sidebar, "Types of Scans Conducted on Servers and Network Appliances During a Security Assessment").

Types of Scans Conducted on Servers and Network Appliances During a Security Assessment

- Firewalls and IPS devices configuration
- Regular and SSL VPN configuration
- Web server hardening (most critical; available as guides from vendors such as Microsoft)
- DMZ configuration
- Email vulnerabilities
- DNS server anomalies
- Database servers (hardening levels)
- Network design and access control vulnerabilities
- Internal PC health such as patching levels and incidence of spyware, malware, and so on

---

The results of these penetration tests are usually compiled as two separate items: (1) as a full-fledged technical report for IT and (2) as a high-level executive summary meant for and delivered to top management to discuss strategy with IT after the engagement.

13. RISK ASSESSMENTS

Risk is defined as the probability of loss. In IT terms we're talking about compromising data CIA (confidentiality, integrity, or availability). Risk management is a way to manage the probability of threats causing an impact. Measuring risks using a risk assessment exercise is the first step toward managing or mitigating a risk. Risk assessments can identify network threats, their probabilities, and their impacts. The reduction of risk can be achieved by reducing any of these three factors.

Regarding intranet risks and threats, we're talking about anything from threats such as unpatched PCs getting viruses and spyware (with hidden keylogging software) to network-borne denial-of-service attacks and even large, publicly embarrassing Web vandalism threats, such as someone being able to deface the main page of the company Web site. The last is a very high-impact threat but mostly perceived to be a remote probability—unless, of course, the company has experienced this before. The awareness among vendors as well as users regarding security is at an all-time high due to security being a high-profile news item.

Any security threat assessment needs to explore and list exploitable vulnerabilities and gaps. Many mid-sized IT shops run specific vulnerability assessment (VA) tools in-house on a monthly basis. eEye's Retina Network Security Scanner and Foundstone's scanning tools appliance are two examples of VA tools that can be found in use at larger IT shops. These tools are consolidated on ready-to-run appliances that are usually managed through remote browser-based consoles. Once the gaps are identified and quantified, steps can be taken to gradually mitigate these vulnerabilities, minimizing the impact of threats.

In intranet risk assessments, we identify primarily Web server and database threats residing within the intranet, but we should also be mindful about the periphery to guard against breaches through the firewall or IPS.

14. CONCLUSION

It is true that the level of Internet hyperconnectivity among generation X and Y users has mushroomed lately, and the network periphery that we used to take for granted as a security shield has been diminished, to a large extent, because of the explosive growth of social networking and the resulting connectivity boom. However, with the various new types of incoming application traffic (VoIP, SIP, and XML traffic) to their networks, security administrators need to stay on their toes and deal with these new protocols by implementing newer tools and technology. One recent example of new technology is the application-level firewall for connecting outside vendors to intranets (also known as an XML firewall, placed within a DMZ) that protects the intranet from malformed XML and SOAP message exploits coming from outside sourced applications.[20]

In conclusion, we can say that with the myriad security issues facing intranets today, most IT shops are still well equipped to defend themselves if they assess risks and, most important, train their employees regarding data security practices on an ongoing basis. The problems with threat mitigation remain largely a matter of meeting gaps in procedural controls rather than technical measures. Trained and security-aware employees are the biggest deterrent to data thefts and security breaches.

---

20 Latest standard (version 1.1) for SOAP message security standard from OASIS, a consortium for Web Services Security, www.oasis-open.org/committees/download.php/16790/wss-v1.1-spec-os-SOAPMessageSecurity.pdf.

## Chapter 10

Local Area Network Security

Dr. Pramod Pandya
California State University

Securing available resources on any corporate or academic data network is of paramount importance because most of these networks connect to the Internet for commercial or research activities. Therefore, the network is under attack from hackers on a continual basis, so network security technologies are ever evolving and playing catch-up with hackers. Around 20 years ago the number of potential users was small and the scope of any activity on the network was limited to local networks only. As the Internet expanded in its reach across national boundaries and as the number of users increased, potential risk to the network grew exponentially. Over the past 10 years ecommerce-related activities such as online shopping, banking, stock trading, and social networking have permeated extensively, creating a dilemma for both service providers and their potential clients, as to who is a trusted service provider and a trusted client on the network. Of course, this being a daunting task for security professionals, they have needed to design security policies appropriate for both the servers and their clients. The security policy must be a factor in clients' level of access to the resources. So, in whom do we place trust, and how much trust? Current network designs implement three levels of trust: most trusted, less trusted, and least trusted. Figure 10.1 reflects these levels of trust, as described here:

- The most trusted users belong to the *intranet*. These users have to authenticate to a centralize administrator to access the resources on the network.
- The less trusted users may originate from the intranet as well as the external users who are authenticated to access resources such as email and Web services.
- The least trusted users are the unauthenticated users; most of them are simply browsing the resources on the Internet with no malice intended. Of course, some are scanning the resources with the intent to break in and steal data.

These are the objectives of network security:

- *Confidentiality.* Only authorized users have access to the network.
- *Integrity.* Data cannot be modified by unauthorized users.
- *Access.* Security must be designed so that authorized users have uninterrupted access to data.

Finally, the responsibility for the design and implementation of network security is headed by the chief

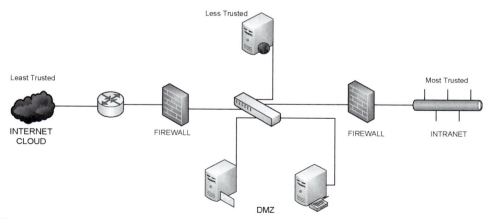

FIGURE 10.1 The DMZ.

information officer (CIO) of the enterprise network. The CIO has a pool of network administrators and legal advisers to help with this task. The network administrators define the placing of the network access controls, and the legal advisors underline the consequences and liabilities in the event of network security breaches. We have seen cases of customer records such as credit-card numbers, Social Security numbers, and personal information being stolen. The frequency of these reports have been on the increase in the past years, and consequently this has led to a discussion on the merits of encryption of stored data. One of the most quoted legal requirements on the part of any business, whether small or big, is the protection of consumer data under the Health Insurance Portability and Accountability Act (HIPAA), which restricts disclosure of health-related data and personal information.

1. IDENTIFY NETWORK THREATS

Network security threats can be in one of two categories: (1) disruptive type or (2) unauthorized access type.

Disruptive

Most LANs are designed as collapsed backbone networks using a layer-2 or layer-3 switch. If a switch or a router were to fail due to power failure, a segment or the entire network may cease to function until the power is restored. In some case, the network failure may be due to a virus attack on the secondary storage, thus leading to loss of data.

Unauthorized Access

This access type can be internal (employee) or external (intruder), a person who would attempt to break into resources such as database, file, and email or web servers that they have no permission to access. Banks, financial institutions, major corporations, and major retail businesses employ data networks to process customer transactions and store customer information and any other relevant data. Before the birth of the Internet Age, interinstitutional transactions were secured because the networks were not accessible to intruders or the general public. In the past 10 years, access to the Internet is almost universal; hence institutional data networks have become the target of frequent intruder attacks to steal customer records. One frequently reads in the news about data network security being compromised by hackers, leading to loss of credit card and debit card numbers, Social Security numbers, drivers' license numbers, and other sensitive information

such as purchasing profiles. Over the years, although network security has increased, the frequency of attacks on the networks has also increased because the tools to breach the network security have become freely available on the Internet. In 1988 the U.S. Department of Defense established the Computer Emergency Response Team (CERT), whose mission is to work with the Internet community to prevent and respond to computer and network security breaches. Since the Internet is widely used for commercial activities by all kinds of businesses, the federal government has enacted stiffer penalties for hackers.

2. ESTABLISH NETWORK ACCESS CONTROLS

In this section we outline steps necessary to secure networks through network controls. These network controls are either software or hardware based and are implemented in a hierarchical structure to reflect the network organization. This hierarchy is superimposed on the network from the network's perimeter to the access level per user of the network resources. The functions of the network control are to detect an unauthorized access, to prevent network security from being breached, and finally, to respond to a breach—thus the three categories of detect, prevent, and respond.

The role of prevention control is to stop unauthorized access to any resource available on the network. This could be implemented as simply as a password required to authenticate the user to access the resource on the network. For an authorized user this password can grant login to the network to access the services of a database, file, Web, print, or email server. The network administrator would need a password to access the switch or a router. The prevention control in this case is software based. An analog of hardware-based control would be, for example, if the resources such as server computers, switches, and routers are locked in a network access control room.

The role of the detection control is to monitor the activities on the network and identify an event or a set of events that could breach network security. Such an event may be a virus, spyware, or adware attack. The detection control software must, besides registering the attack, generate or trigger an alarm to notify of an unusual event so that a corrective action can be taken immediately, without compromising security.

The role of the response control is to take corrective action whenever network security is breached so that the same kind of breach is detected and any further damage is prevented.

TABLE 10.1 Mission-Critical Components of Any Enterprise Network

Threats / Resources	Fire, Flood, Earthquake	Power Failure	Spam	Virus	Spyware, Adware	Hijacking
Perimeter Router						
DNS Server						
WEB Server						
Email Server						
Core Switches						
Databases						

3. RISK ASSESSMENT

During the initial design phase of a network, the network architects assess the types of risks to the network as well as the costs of recovering from attacks for all the resources that have been compromised. These cost factors can be realized using well-established accounting procedures such as cost/benefit analysis, return on investment (ROI), and total cost of ownership (TCO). These risks could range from natural disaster to an attack by a hacker. Therefore, you need to develop levels of risks to various threats to the network. You need to design some sort of spreadsheet that lists risks versus threats as well as responses to those identified threats. Of course, the spreadsheet would also mark the placing of the network access controls to secure the network.

4. LISTING NETWORK RESOURCES

We need to identify the assets (resources) that are available on the corporate network. Of course, this list could be long, and it would make no sense to protect all the resources, except for those that are mission-critical to the business functions. Table 10.1 identifies mission-critical components of any enterprise network. You will observe that these mission-critical components need to be prioritized, since they do not all provide the same functions. Some resources provide controlled access to a network; other resources carry sensitive corporate data. Hence the threats posed to these resources do not carry the same degree of vulnerabilities to the network. Therefore, the network access control has to be articulated and applied to each of the components listed, in varying degrees. For example, threats to DNS server pose a different set of problems from threats to the database servers. In the next section we itemize the threats to these resources and specific network access controls.

5. THREATS

We need to identify the threats posed to the network from internal users as opposed to those from external users. The reason for such a distinction is that the internal users are easily traceable, compared to the external users. If a threat to the data network is successful, and it could lead to loss or theft of data or denial of access to the services offered by the network, it would lead to monetary loss for the corporation. Once we have identified these threats, we can rank them from most probable to least probable and design network security policy to reflect that ranking.

From Table 10.2, we observe that most frequent threats to the network are from viruses, and we have seen a rapid explosion in antivirus, antispamware, and spyware and adware software. Hijacking of resources such as domain name services, Web services, and perimeter routers would lead to what's most famously known as denial of service (DoS) or distributed denial of service (DDoS). Power failures can always be complemented by standby power supplies that could keep the essential resources from crashing. Natural disasters such as fire, floods, or earthquakes can be most difficult to plan for; therefore we see a tremendous growth in data protection and backup service provider businesses.

6. SECURITY POLICIES

The fundamental goals of security policy are to allow uninterrupted access to the network resources for authenticated

TABLE 10.2 The Most Frequent Threats to the Network Are from Viruses

Rank	Threat
1	Virus
2	Spam
3	Spyware, Adware
4	Hijacking
5	Power Failure
6	Fire, Flood, Earthquake

users and to deny access to unauthenticated users. Of course, this is always a balancing act between the users' demands on network resources and the evolutionary nature of information technology. The user community would prefer open access, whereas the network administrator insists on restricted and monitored access to the network.

The hacker is, in the final analysis, the arbitrator of the network security policy, since it is always the unauthorized user who discovers the potential flaw in the software. Hence, any network is as secure as the last attack that breached its security. It would be totally unrealistic to expect a secured network at all times, once it is built and secured. Therefore, network security design and its implementation represent the ultimate battle of the minds between the chief information security officer (CISO) and the devil, the hacker. We can summarize that the network security policy can be as simple as to allow access to resources, or it can be several hundred pages long, detailing the levels of access and punishment if a breach is discovered. Most corporate network users now have to sign onto the usage policy of the network and are reminded that security breaches are a punishable offence.

The critical functions of a good security policy are:

- Appoint a security administrator who is conversant with users' demands and on a continual basis is prepared to accommodate the user community's needs.
- Set up a hierarchical security policy to reflect the corporate structure.
- Define ethical Internet access capabilities.
- Evolve the remote access policy.
- Provide a set of incident-handling procedures.

7. THE INCIDENT-HANDLING PROCESS

The incident-handling process is the most important task of a security policy for the reason that you would not want to shut down the network in case of a network security breach. The purpose of the network is to share the resources; therefore an efficient procedure must be developed to respond to a breach. If news of the network security breach becomes public, the corporation's business practices could become compromised, thus resulting in compromise of its business operations. Therefore set procedures must be developed jointly with the business operations manager and the chief information officer. This calls for a modular design of the enterprise network so that its segments can be shut down in an orderly way, without causing panic.

Toward this end, we need a set of tools to monitor activities on the network—we need an intrusion detection and prevention system. These pieces of software will monitor network activities and log and report an activity that does not conform to usual or acceptable standards as defined by the software. Once an activity is detected and logged, response is activated. It is not merely sufficient to respond to an incident; the network administrator also has to activate tools to trace back to the source of this breach. This is critical so that the network administrator can update the security procedures to make sure that this particular incident does not take place.

8. SECURE DESIGN THROUGH NETWORK ACCESS CONTROLS

A network is as secure as its weakest link in the overall design. To secure it, we need to identify the entry and exit points into the network. Since most data networks have computational nodes to process data and storage nodes to store data, stored data may need to be encrypted so that if network security is breached, stolen data may still remain confidential unless the encryption is broken. As we hear of cases of stolen data from either hacked networks or stolen nodes, encrypting data while it's being stored appears to be necessary to secure data.

The entry point to any network is a perimeter router, which sits between the external firewall and the Internet; this model is applicable to most enterprise networks that engage in some sort of ecommerce activities. Hence our first network access control is to define security policy on the perimeter router by configuring the appropriate parameters on the router. The perimeter router will filter traffic based on the range of IP addresses.

Next in the line of defense is the external firewall that filters traffic based on the state of the network connection. Additionally, the firewall could also check the contents of the traffic packet against the nature of the Transmission Control Protocol (TCP) connection requested. Following the firewall we have the so-called demilitarized zone, or DMZ, where we would place the following servers: Web, DNS, and email. We could harden these servers so that potential threatening traffic can be identified and appropriate incident response generated.

The DMZ is placed between two firewalls, so our last line of defense is the next firewall that would inspect the traffic and possibly filter out the potential threat. The nodes that are placed on the intranet can be protected by commercially available antivirus software. Last but not least, we could install on the network an intrusion detection and prevention system that will generate real-time response to a threat.

Next we address each of the network control access points. The traditional network design includes an access layer, a distribution layer, and the core layer. In the case of a local area network (LAN) we will use the access and distribution layers; the core layer would simply be our perimeter router that we discussed earlier in this section. Thus the LAN will consist of a number of segments reflecting the organizational structure. The segments could sit behind their firewall to protect one another as well, in case of network breach; segments under attack can be isolated, thus preventing a cascade-style attack on the network.

9. IDS DEFINED

An intrusion detection system, or IDS, can be both software and hardware based. IDSs listen to all the activities taking place on both the computer (node on a network) and the network itself. One could think of an IDS as like traffic police, whose function is to monitor the data packet traffic and detect and identify those data packets that match predefined unusual pattern of activities. An IDS can also be programmed to teach itself from its past activities to refine the rules for unusual activities. This should not come as a surprise, since the hackers also get smarter over time.

As we stated, the IDS collects information from a variety of system and network resources, but in actuality it captures packets of data as defined by the TCP/IP protocol stack. In this sense IDS is both a sniffer and analyzer software. IDS in its sniffer role would either capture all the data packets or select ones as specified by the configuration script. This configuration script is a set of rules that tell the analyzer what to look for in a captured data packet, then make an educated guess per rules and generate an alert. Of course, this could lead to four possible outcomes with regard to intrusion detection: false positive, false negative, true positive, or true negative. We address this topic in more detail later in the chapter.

IDSs performs a variety of functions:

- Monitor and analyze user and system activities
- Verify the integrity of data files
- Audit system configuration files
- Recognize activity of patterns, reflecting known attacks
- Statistical analysis of any undefined activity pattern

An IDS is capable of distinguishing different types of network traffic, such as an HTTP request over port 80 from some other application such as SMTP being run over port 80. We see here that an IDS understands which TCP/IP applications run over which preassigned port numbers, and therefore falsifying port numbers would be trivially detectable. This is a very easy illustration, but there are more complex attacks that are not that easy to identify, and we shall cover them later in this chapter.

The objective of intrusion detection software packages is to make possible the complex and sometimes virtually impossible task of managing system security. With this in mind, it might be worthwhile to bring to our attention two industrial-grade IDS software packages: Snort (NIDS), which runs on both Linux and Windows, and GFI LANguard S.E.L.M., a host intrusion detection system (HIDS), which runs on Windows only. Commercial-grade IDS software is designed with user-friendly interfaces that make it easy to configure scripts, which lay down the rules for intrusion detection.

Next let's examine some critical functions of an IDS:

- Can impose a greater degree of flexibility to the security infrastructure of the network
- Monitors the functionality of routers, including firewalls, key servers, and critical switches
- Can help resolve audit trails, thus often exposing problems before they lead to loss of data
- Can trace user activity from the network point of entry to the point of exit
- Can report on file integrity checks
- Can detect whether a system has been reconfigured by an attack
- Can recognize a potential attack and generate an alert
- Can make possible security management of a network by nonexpert staff

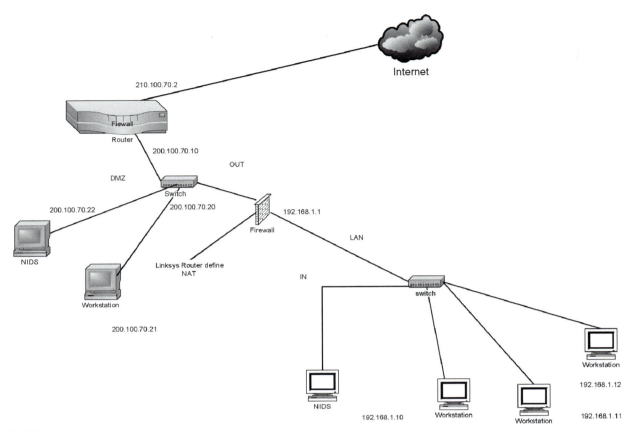

FIGURE 10.2 An example of a network-based intrusion detection system.

10. NIDS: SCOPE AND LIMITATIONS

Network-based IDS (NIDS) sensors scan network packets at the router or host level, auditing data packets and logging any suspicious packets to a log file. Figure 10.2 is an example of a NIDS. The data packets are captured by a sniffer program, which is a part of the IDS software package. The node on which the IDS software is enabled runs in promiscuous mode. In promiscuous mode, the NIDS node captures all the data packets on the network as defined by the configuration script. NIDSs have become a critical component of network security management as the number of nodes on the Internet has grown exponentially over last few years. Some of the common malicious attacks on networks are:

- IP address spoofing
- MAC address spoofing
- ARP cache poisoning
- DNS name corruption

11. A PRACTICAL ILLUSTRATION OF NIDS

In this section, we illustrate the use of Snort as an example of a NIDS. The signature files are kept in the directory

signatures under the directory .doc. Signature files are used to match defined signature against a pattern of bytes in the data packets, to identify a potential attack. Files marked as rules in the rules directory are used to trigger an alarm and write to the file alert.ids. Snort is installed on a node with IP address 192.168.1.22. The security auditing software Nmap is installed on a node with IP address 192.168.1.20. Nmap software is capable of generating ping sweeps, TCP SYN (half-open) scanning, TCP connect() scanning, and much more. Figure 10.2 has a node labeled *NIDS* (behind the Linksys router) on which Snort would be installed. One of the workstations would run Nmap software.

UDP Attacks

A UDP attack is generated from a node with IP address 192.168.1.20 to a node with IP address 192.168.1.22. Snort is used to detect a possible attack. Snort's detect engine uses one of the files in DOS under directory rules to generate the alert file alert.ids. We display a partial listing (see Listing 10.1) of the alert.ids file.

Listing 10.2 shows a partial listing of DOS rules file. The rules stated in the DOS rules file are used to generate the alert.ids file.

```
[**] [1:0:0] DOS Teardrop attack [**]
[Priority: 0]
01/26-11:37:10.667833 192.168.1.20:1631 -> 192.168.1.22:21
UDP TTL:128 TOS:0x0 ID:60940 IpLen:20 DgmLen:69
Len: 41
[**] [1:0:0] DOS Teardrop attack [**]
[Priority: 0]
01/26-11:37:10.668460 192.168.1.20:1631 -> 192.168.1.22:21
UDP TTL:128 TOS:0x0 ID:60940 IpLen:20 DgmLen:69
Len: 41
[**] [1:0:0] DOS Teardrop attack [**]
[Priority: 0]
01/26-11:37:11.667926 192.168.1.20:1631 -> 192.168.1.22:21
UDP TTL:128 TOS:0x0 ID:60941 IpLen:20 DgmLen:69
Len: 41
[**] [1:0:0] DOS Teardrop attack [**]
[Priority: 0]
01/26-11:37:11.669424 192.168.1.20:1631 -> 192.168.1.22:21
UDP TTL:128 TOS:0x0 ID:60941 IpLen:20 DgmLen:69
Len: 41
[**] [1:0:0] DOS Teardrop attack [**]
[Priority: 0]
01/26-11:37:12.669316 192.168.1.20:1631 -> 192.168.1.22:21
UDP TTL:128 TOS:0x0 ID:60942 IpLen:20 DgmLen:69
Len: 41
```

LISTING 10.1 An alert.ids file.

```
# (C) Copyright 2001, Martin Roesch, Brian Caswell, et al.  All rights reserved.
# $Id: dos.rules,v 1.30.2.1 2004/01/20 21:31:38 jh8 Exp $
#----------
# DOS RULES
#----------
alert ip $EXTERNAL_NET any -> $HOME_NET any (msg:"DOS Jolt attack";
fragbits: M; dsize:408; reference:cve,CAN-1999-0345;
classtype:attempted-dos; sid:268; rev:2;)
alert udp $EXTERNAL_NET any -> $HOME_NET any (msg:"DOS Teardrop attack";
id:242; fragbits:M; reference:cve,CAN-1999-0015;
reference:url,www.cert.org/advisories/CA-1997-28.html;
reference:bugtraq,124; classtype:attempted-dos; sid:270; rev:2;)
alert udp any 19 <> any 7 (msg:"DOS UDP echo+chargen bomb";
reference:cve,CAN-1999-0635; reference:cve,CVE-1999-0103;
classtype:attempted-dos; sid:271; rev:3;)
alert ip $EXTERNAL_NET any -> $HOME_NET any (msg:"DOS IGMP dos attack";
content:"|02 00|"; depth: 2; ip_proto: 2; fragbits: M+;
reference:cve,CVE-1999-0918; classtype:attempted-dos; sid:272; rev:2;)
alert ip $EXTERNAL_NET any -> $HOME_NET any (msg:"DOS IGMP dos attack";
content:"|00 00|"; depth:2; ip_proto:2; fragbits:M+; reference:cve,CVE-
1999-0918; classtype:attempted-dos; sid:273; rev:2;)
alert icmp $EXTERNAL_NET any -> $HOME_NET any (msg:"DOS ath";
content:"+++ath"; nocase; itype: 8; reference:cve,CAN-1999-1228;
reference:arachnids,264; classtype:attempted-dos; sid:274; rev:2;)
```

LISTING 10.2 The DOS rules file.

TCP SYN (Half-Open) Scanning

This technique is often referred to as *half-open* scanning because you don't open a full TCP connection. You send a SYN packet, as though you were going to open a real connection, and wait for a response. A SYN|ACK indicates that the port is listening. An RST is indicative of a nonlistener. If a SYN|ACK is received, you immediately send an RST to tear down the connection (actually, the kernel does this for you). The primary advantage of this scanning technique is that fewer sites will log it! SYN scanning is the -s option of Nmap.

A SYN attack is generated using Nmap software from a node with IP address 192.168.1.20 to a node with IP address 192.168.1.22. Snort is used to detect for a possible attack. Snort's detect engine uses scan and ICMP rules files under directory rules to generate the alert file alert.ids. A partial listing of alert.ids file is shown in Listing 10.3.

A partial listing of the scan rules appears in Listing 10.4.

Listing 10.5 contains a partial listing of the ICMP rules.

The following points must be noted about NIDS:

- One NIDS is installed per LAN (Ethernet) segment.
- Place NIDS on the auxiliary port on the switch and then link all the ports on the switch to that auxiliary port.
- When the network is saturated with traffic, the NIDS might drop packets and thus create a potential "hole."
- If the data packets are encrypted, the usefulness of an IDS is questionable.

Some Not-So-Robust Features of NIDS

Network security is a complex issue with myriad possibilities and difficulties. In networks, security is also a weakest link phenomenon, since it takes vulnerability on one node to allow a hacker to gain access to a network and thus create chaos on the network. Therefore IDS products are vulnerable.

An IDS cannot compensate for weak identification and authentication. Hence you must rely on other means of identification and authentication of users. This is best implemented by token-based or biometric schemes and one-time passwords.

An IDS cannot conduct investigations of attacks without human intervention. Therefore when an incident does occur, steps must be defined to handle the incident. The incident must be followed up to determine the responsible party, then the vulnerability that allowed the problem to occur should be diagnosed and corrected. You will observe that an IDS is not capable of identifying the attacker, only the IP address of the node that served as the hacker's point of entry.

```
[**] [1:469:1] ICMP PING NMAP [**]
[Classification: Attempted Information Leak] [Priority: 2]
01/24-19:28:24.774381 192.168.1.20 -> 192.168.1.22
ICMP TTL:44 TOS:0x0 ID:29746 IpLen:20 DgmLen:28
Type:8 Code:0 ID:35844  Seq:45940  ECHO
[Xref => http://www.whitehats.com/info/IDS162]
[**] [1:469:1] ICMP PING NMAP [**]
[Classification: Attempted Information Leak] [Priority: 2]
01/24-19:28:24.775879 192.168.1.20 -> 192.168.1.22
ICMP TTL:44 TOS:0x0 ID:29746 IpLen:20 DgmLen:28
Type:8 Code:0 ID:35844  Seq:45940  ECHO
[Xref => http://www.whitehats.com/info/IDS162]
[**] [1:620:6] SCAN Proxy Port 8080 attempt [**]
[Classification: Attempted Information Leak] [Priority: 2]
01/24-19:28:42.023770 192.168.1.20:51530 -> 192.168.1.22:8080
TCP TTL:50 TOS:0x0 ID:53819 IpLen:20 DgmLen:40
******S* Seq: 0x94D68C2 Ack: 0x0 Win: 0xC00 TcpLen: 20
[**] [1:620:6] SCAN Proxy Port 8080 attempt [**]
[Classification: Attempted Information Leak] [Priority: 2]
01/24-19:28:42.083817 192.168.1.20:51530 -> 192.168.1.22:8080
TCP TTL:50 TOS:0x0 ID:53819 IpLen:20 DgmLen:40
******S* Seq: 0x94D68C2 Ack: 0x0 Win: 0xC00 TcpLen: 20
[**] [1:615:5] SCAN SOCKS Proxy attempt [**]
[Classification: Attempted Information Leak] [Priority: 2]
01/24-19:28:43.414083 192.168.1.20:51530 -> 192.168.1.22:1080
TCP TTL:59 TOS:0x0 ID:62752 IpLen:20 DgmLen:40
******S* Seq: 0x94D68C2 Ack: 0x0 Win: 0x1000 TcpLen: 20
[Xref => http://help.undernet.org/proxyscan/]
```

LISTING 10.3 Alert.ids file.

An IDS cannot compensate for weaknesses in network protocols. IP and MAC address spoofing is a very common form of attack in which the source IP or MAC address does not correspond to the real source IP or MAC address of the hacker. Spoofed addresses can be mimicked to generate DDoS attacks.

An IDS cannot compensate for problems in the integrity of information the system provides. Many hacker tools target system logs, selectively erasing records corresponding to the time of the attack and thus covering the hacker's tracks. This calls for redundant information sources.

An IDS cannot analyze all the traffic on a busy network. A network-based IDS in promiscuous mode can capture all the data packets, and as the traffic level raises, NIDS can reach a saturation point and begin to lose data packets.

An IDS cannot always deal with problems involving packet-level attacks. The vulnerabilities lie in the difference between IDS interpretation of the outcome of a network transaction and the destination node for that network session's actual handling of the transaction. Therefore, a hacker can send a series of fragmented

```
# (C) Copyright 2001,2002, Martin Roesch, Brian Caswell, et al.
#    All rights reserved.
# $Id: scan.rules,v 1.21.2.1 2004/01/20 21:31:38 jh8 Exp $
#-----------
# SCAN RULES
#-----------
# These signatures are representitive of network scanners.  These include
# port scanning, ip mapping, and various application scanners.
#
# NOTE: This does NOT include web scanners such as whisker.  Those are
# in web*
#
alert tcp $EXTERNAL_NET 10101 -> $HOME_NET any (msg:"SCAN myscan";
stateless; ttl: >220; ack: 0; flags: S;reference:arachnids,439;
classtype:attempted-recon; sid:613; rev:2;)
alert tcp $EXTERNAL_NET any -> $HOME_NET 113 (msg:"SCAN ident version
request"; flow:to_server,established; content: "VERSIONI0AI"; depth:
16;reference:arachnids,303; classtype:attempted-recon; sid:616; rev:3;)
alert tcp $EXTERNAL_NET any -> $HOME_NET 80 (msg:"SCAN cybercop os
probe"; stateless; flags: SF12; dsize: 0; reference:arachnids,146;
classtype:attempted-recon; sid:619; rev:2;)
alert tcp $EXTERNAL_NET any -> $HOME_NET 3128 (msg:"SCAN Squid Proxy
attempt"; stateless; flags:S,12; classtype:attempted-recon; sid:618;
rev:5;)
alert tcp $EXTERNAL_NET any -> $HOME_NET 1080 (msg:"SCAN SOCKS Proxy
attempt"; stateless; flags:S,12;
reference:url,help.undernet.org/proxyscan/; classtype:attempted-recon;
sid:615; rev:5;)
alert tcp $EXTERNAL_NET any -> $HOME_NET 8080 (msg:"SCAN Proxy Port 8080
attempt"; stateless; flags:S,12; classtype:attempted-recon; sid:620;
rev:6;)
alert tcp $EXTERNAL_NET any -> $HOME_NET any (msg:"SCAN FIN"; stateless;
flags:F,12; reference:arachnids,27; classtype:attempted-recon; sid:621;
rev:3;)
alert tcp $EXTERNAL_NET any -> $HOME_NET any (msg:"SCAN ipEye SYN scan";
flags:S; stateless; seq:1958810375; reference:arachnids,236;
classtype:attempted-recon; sid:622; rev:3;)
alert tcp $EXTERNAL_NET any -> $HOME_NET any (msg:"SCAN NULL";
stateless; flags:0; seq:0; ack:0; reference:arachnids,4;
classtype:attempted-recon; sid:623; rev:2;)
```

LISTING 10.4 Scan rules.

```
# (C) Copyright 2001,2002, Martin Roesch, Brian Caswell, et al.
#    All rights reserved.
# $Id: icmp.rules,v 1.19 2003/10/20 15:03:09 chrisgreen Exp $
#-----------
# ICMP RULES
#-----------
#
# Description:
# These rules are potentially bad ICMP traffic.  They include most of the
# ICMP scanning tools and other "BAD" ICMP traffic (Such as redirect
host)
#
# Other ICMP rules are included in icmp-info.rules
alert icmp $EXTERNAL_NET any -> $HOME_NET any (msg:"ICMP ISS Pinger";
content:"|495353504e475251|";itype:8;depth:32; reference:arachnids,158;
classtype:attempted-recon; sid:465; rev:1;)
alert icmp $EXTERNAL_NET any -> $HOME_NET any (msg:"ICMP L3retriever
Ping"; content: "ABCDEFGHIJKLMNOPQRSTUVWABCDEFGHI"; itype: 8; icode: 0;
depth: 32; reference:arachnids,311; classtype:attempted-recon; sid:466;
rev:1;)
alert icmp $EXTERNAL_NET any -> $HOME_NET any (msg:"ICMP Nemesis v1.1
Echo"; dsize: 20; itype: 8; icmp_id: 0; icmp_seq: 0; content:
"|00000000000000000000000000000000000000000|"; reference:arachnids,449;
classtype:attempted-recon; sid:467; rev:1;)
alert icmp $EXTERNAL_NET any -> $HOME_NET any (msg:"ICMP PING NMAP";
dsize: 0; itype: 8; reference:arachnids,162; classtype:attempted-recon;
sid:469; rev:1;)
alert icmp $EXTERNAL_NET any -> $HOME_NET any (msg:"ICMP icmpenum
v1.1.1"; id: 666; dsize: 0; itype: 8; icmp_id: 666 ; icmp_seq: 0;
reference:arachnids,450; classtype:attempted-recon; sid:471; rev:1;)
alert icmp $EXTERNAL_NET any -> $HOME_NET any (msg:"ICMP redirect
host";itype:5;icode:1; reference:arachnids,135; reference:cve,CVE-1999-
0265; classtype:bad-unknown; sid:472; rev:1;)
alert icmp $EXTERNAL_NET any -> $HOME_NET any (msg:"ICMP redirect
net";itype:5;icode:0; reference:arachnids,199; reference:cve,CVE-1999-
0265; classtype:bad-unknown; sid:473; rev:1;)
alert icmp $EXTERNAL_NET any -> $HOME_NET any (msg:"ICMP superscan
echo"; content:"|0000000000000000|"; itype: 8; dsize:8;
classtype:attempted-recon; sid:474; rev:1;)
alert icmp $EXTERNAL_NET any -> $HOME_NET any (msg:"ICMP traceroute
ipopts"; ipopts: rr; itype: 0; reference:arachnids,238; classtype
```

LISTING 10.5 ICMP rules.

packets that elude detection and can also launch attacks on the destination node. Even worse, the hacker can lead to DoS on the IDS itself.

An IDS has problems dealing with fragmented data packets. Hackers would normally use fragmentation to confuse the IDS and thus launch an attack.

12. FIREWALLS

A firewall is either a single node or a set of nodes that enforce an access policy between two networks. Firewall technology evolved to protect the intranet from unauthorized users on the Internet. This was the case in the earlier years of corporate networks. Since then, the network administrators have realized that networks can also be attacked from trusted users as well as, for example, the employee of a company. The corporate network consists of hundreds of nodes per department and thus aggregates to over a thousand or more, and now there is a need to protect data in each department from other departments. Hence, a need for internal firewalls arose to protect data from unauthorized access, even if they are employees of the corporation.

This need has, over the years, led to design of segmented IP networks, such that internal firewalls would form barriers within barriers, to restrict a potential break-in to an IP segment rather than expose the entire corporate network to a hacker. For this reason, network security has grown into a multibillion-dollar business.

Almost every intranet, whether of one node or many nodes, is always connected to the Internet, and thus a potential number of hackers wait to attack it. Thus every intranet is an IP network, with TCP- and UDP-based applications running over it. The design of TCP and UDP protocols require that every client/server application interacts with other client/server applications through TCP and UDP port numbers. As we stated earlier, these TCP and UDP port numbers are well known and hence give rise to a necessary weakness in the network. TCP and UDP port numbers open up "holes" in the networks by their very design. Every Internet and intranet point of entry has to be guarded, and you must monitor the traffic (data packets) that enter and leave the network.

A firewall is a combination of hardware and software technology, namely a sort of sentry, waiting at the points of entry and exit to look out for an unauthorized data packet trying to gain access to the network. The network administrator, with the help of other IT staff, must first identify the resources and the sensitive data that need to be protected from the hackers. Once this task has been accomplished, the next task is to identify who would have access to these identified resources and the data. We should pointed out that most of the networks in any corporation are never designed and built from scratch but are added to an existing network as the demand for networking grows with the growth of the business. So, the design of the network security policy has multilayered facets as well.

Once the network security policy is defined and understood, we can identify the proper placement of the firewalls in relation to the resources on the network. Hence, the next step would be to actually place the firewalls in the network as nodes. The network security policy now defines access to the network, as implemented in the firewall. These access rights to the network resources are based on the characteristics of TCP/IP protocols and the TCP/UDP port numbers.

Firewall Security Policy

The firewall enables the network administrator to centralize access control to the campuswide network.

A firewall logs every packet that enters and leaves the network. The network security policy implemented in the firewall provides several types of protection, including the following:

- Block unwanted traffic
- Direct incoming traffic to more trustworthy internal nodes
- Hide vulnerable nodes that cannot easily be secured from external threats
- Log traffic to and from the network

A firewall is transparent to authorized users (both internal and external), whereas it is not transparent to unauthorized users. However, if the authorized user attempts to access a service that is not permitted to that user, a denial of that service will be echoed, and that attempt will be logged.

Firewalls can be configured in a number of architectures, providing various levels of security at different costs of installation and operations. Figure 10.2 is an example of a design termed a *screened Subnet*. In this design, the internal network is a private IP network, so the resources on that network are completely hidden from the users who are external to that network, such as users from the Internet. In an earlier chapter we talked about public versus private IP addresses. It is agreed to by the IP community that nodes with private IP addresses will not be accessible from outside that network. Any number of corporations may use the same private IP network address without creating packets with duplicated IP addresses. This feature of IP networks, namely private IP networks, adds to network security. In Figure 10.2, we used a Linksys router to support a private IP network (192.168.1.0) implementation. For the nodes on the 192.168.1.0 network to access the resources on the Internet, the Linksys router has to translate the private IP address of the data packet to a public IP address. In our scenario, the Linksys router would map the address of the node on the 192.168.1.0 network, to an address on the public network, 200.100.70.0. This feature is known as Network Address Translation (NAT), which is enabled on the Linksys router. You can see in Figure 10.2 that the Linksys router demarks the internal (IN) network from the external (OUT) network.

We illustrate an example of network address translation, as shown in Listing 10.6. The script configures a Cisco router that translates an internal private IP address to a public IP address. Of course, configuring a Linksys router is much simpler using a Web client. An explanation of the commands and their details follow the script.

```
ip nat pool net-sf 200.100.70.50 200.100.70.60 netmask 255.255.255.0
ip nat inside source list 1 pool net-sf
!
interface Ethernet0
 ip address 192.168.1.1 255.255.255.0
 ip nat inside
!
interface Ethernet1
 ip address 200.100.70.20 255.255.255.0
 ip nat outside
 access-list 1 deny 192.168.1.0 0.0.0.255
```

LISTING 10.6 Network Address Translation (NAT).

Configuration Script for sf Router

The access-list command creates an entry in a standard traffic filter list:

- Access-list "access-list-number" permit|deny source [source-mask]
- Access-list number: identifies the list to which the entry belongs; a number from 1 to 99
- Permit|deny: this entry allows or blocks traffic from the specified address
- Source: identifies source IP address
- Source-mask: identifies the bits in the address field that are matched; it has a 1 in position indicating "don't care" bits, and a 0 in any position that is to be strictly followed

The IP access-group command links an existing access list to an outbound interface. Only one access list per port, per protocol, and per direction is allowed.

- Access-list-number: indicates the number of the access list to be linked to this interface
- In|out: selects whether the access list is applied to the incoming or outgoing interface; out is the default

NAT is a feature that operates on a border router between an inside private addressing scheme and an outside public addressing scheme. The inside private address is 192.168.1.0 and the outside public address is chosen to be 200.100.70.0. Equivalently, we have an intranet on the inside and the Internet on the outside.

13. DYNAMIC NAT CONFIGURATION

First a NAT pool is configured from which outside addresses are allocated to the requesting inside hosts: IP NAT pool "pool name" "start outside IP address" "finish outside IP address." Next the access-list is defined to determine which inside networks are translated by the NAT router: access-list "unique access-list number" permit|deny "inside IP network address." Finally the NAT pool and the access list are correlated:

- IP NAT inside source list "unique access list number" pool "pool name"
- Enable the NAT on each interface of the NAT router
- IP NAT inside + + + + + + + + + + + + + + + IP NAT outside

You will note that only one interface may be configured as outside, yet multiple interfaces may be configured as inside, with regard to Static NAT configuration:

- IP NAT inside source static "inside IP address" "outside IP address"
- IP NAT inside source static 192.168.1.100 200.100.70.99

14. THE PERIMETER

In Figure 10.3, you will see yet another IP network labeled *demilitarized zone* (DMZ). You may ask, why yet another network? The rationale behind this design is as follows.

The users that belong to IN might want to access the resources on the Internet, such as read their email and send email to the users on the Internet. The corporation needs to advertise its products on the Internet.

The DMZ is the perimeter network, where resources have public IP addresses, so they are seen and heard on the Internet. The resources such as the Web (HTTP), email (SMTP), and domain name server (DNS) are placed in the DMZ, whereas the rest of the resources that belong to this corporation are completely hidden behind the Linksys router. The resources in the DMZ can be attacked by the hacker because they are open to users on the Internet. The relevant TCP and UDP port numbers on the servers in the DMZ have to be left open to the incoming and outgoing

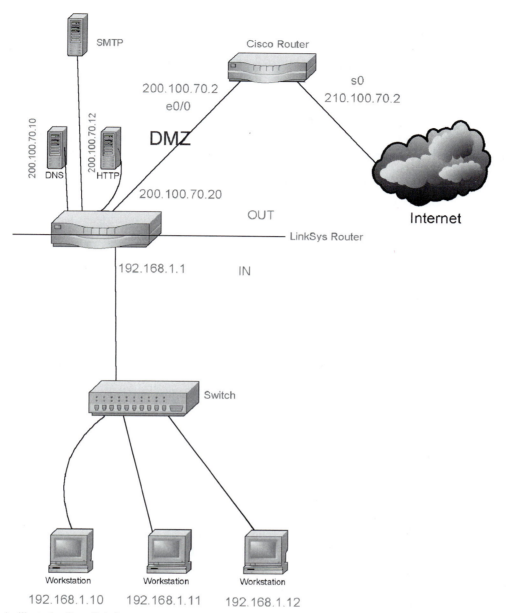

FIGURE 10.3 An illustrative firewall design.

traffic. Does this create a potential "hole" in the corporate network? The answer to this is both yes and no. Someone can compromise the resources in the DMZ without the entire network being exposed to a potential attack.

The first firewall is the Cisco router, and it is the first line of defense, were network security policy implemented. On the Cisco router it is known as the Access Control List (ACL). This firewall will allow external traffic to inbound TCP port 80 on the Web server, TCP port 25 on the email server, and TCP and UDP port 53 on the DNS server. The external traffic to the rest of the ports will be denied and logged.

The second line of defense is the Linksys router that will have well-known ports closed to external traffic. It too will monitor and log the traffic. It is acceptable to place email and the Web server behind the Linksys router on the private IP network address. Then you will have to open up the TCP ports 80 and 25 on the Linksys router so that the external traffic can be mapped to ports 80 and 25, respectively. This would slow down the traffic because the Linksys router (or any commercial-grade router) would have to constantly map the port numbers back and forth. Finally, the DNS server would always need to be placed in the DMZ with a public IP address, since it will be used to resolve domain names by both internal and external users. This decision has to be left to the corporate IT staff.

15. ACCESS LIST DETAILS

The Cisco router in Figure 10.3 can be configured with the following access list to define network security policy. Building an access list in the configuration script of the router does not activate the list unless it is applied to an interface. "ip access-group 101 in" applies the access-list 101 to the serial interface of the router. Some of the access-list commands are explained here. For more information on Cisco access-list commands, visit the Cisco Web site (www.cisco.com):

- ip access-group group no. {in|out}: default is out
- What is the group number?
- The group number is the number that appears in the access-list command line
- What is {in|out}?
- In implies that the packet enters the router's interface from the network
- Out implies that the packet leaves the router's interface to the network

All TCP packets are IP packets, but all IP packets are not TCP packets. Therefore, entries matching on IP packets are more generic than matching on TCP, UDP, or ICMP packets. Each entry in the access list is interpreted (see Listing 10.7) from top to bottom for each packet on the specified interface. Once a match is reached, the remaining access-list entries are ignored. Hence, the order of entries in an access list is very critical, and therefore more specific entries should appear earlier on.

This permits TCP from any host to any host if the ACK or RST bit is set, which indicates that it is part of an established connection. You will note that in a TCP Full Connect, the first packet from the source node does not have the ACK bit set. The keyword *established* is meant to prevent an untrusted user from initiating a connection while allowing packets that are part of already established TCP connections to go through:

- Access-list 101 permit udp any gt 1023 host 200.100.70.10 eq 53

```
interface serial0
ip address 210.100.70.2
ip access-group 101 in
!
access-list 101 permit tcp any any established
```

LISTING 10.7 Access-list configuration script.

- Permit UDP protocol from any host with port greater than 1023 to the DNS server at port 53
- Access-list 101 permit ip any host 200.100.70.12
- Permit IP from any host to 200.100.70.12

or

- Access-list 101 permit TCP any 200.100.70.12 eq 80
- Permit any host to engage with our HTTP server on port 80 only
- Access-list 101 permit icmp any echo-reply
- Permit ICMP from any host to any host if the packet is in response to a ping request
- Access-list 101 deny ip any any

The last access-list command is implicit (that is, not explicitly stated). The action of this last access-list is to deny all other packets.

16. TYPES OF FIREWALLS

Conceptually, there are three types of firewalls:

- *Packet filtering.* Permit packets to enter or leave the network through the interface on the router on the basis of protocol, IP address, and port numbers.
- *Application-layer firewall.* A proxy server that acts as an intermediate host between the source and the destination nodes.
- *Stateful-inspection layer.* Validates the packet on the basis of its content.

17. PACKET FILTERING: IP FILTERING ROUTERS

An IP packet-filtering router permits or denies the packet to either enter or leave the network through the interface (incoming and outgoing) on the basis of the protocol, IP address, and the port number. The protocol may be TCP, UDP, HTTP, SMTP, or FTP. The IP address under consideration would be both the source and the destination addresses of the nodes. The port numbers would correspond to the well-known port numbers. The packet-filtering firewall has to examine every packet and make a decision on the basis of defined ACL; additionally it will log the following guarded attacks on the network:

- A hacker will attempt to send IP spoofed packets using raw sockets (we will discuss more about usage of raw sockets in the next chapters)
- Log attempted network scanning for open TCP and UDP ports—NIDS will carry out this detective work in more detail

- SYN attacks using TCP connect(), and TCP half open
- Fragment attacks

18. APPLICATION-LAYER FIREWALLS: PROXY SERVERS

These are proxy servers that act as an intermediary host between the source and the destination nodes. Each of the sources would have to set up a session with the proxy server, then the proxy server would set up a session with the destination node. The packets would have to flow through the proxy server. There are examples of Web and FTP proxy servers on the Internet. The proxy servers would also have to be used by the internal users, that is, the traffic from the internal users will have to run through the proxy server to the outside network. Of course, this slows the flow of packets, but you must pay the price for added network security.

19. STATEFUL INSPECTION FIREWALLS

In here the firewall will examine the contents of the packets before permitting them to either enter or leave the network. The contents of the packets must conform with the protocol declared with the packet. For example, if the protocol declared is HTTP, the contents of the packet must be consistent with the HTTP packet definition.

20. NIDS COMPLEMENTS FIREWALLS

A firewall acts as a barrier, if so designed, among various IP network segments. Firewalls may be defined among IP intranet segments to protect resources. In any corporate network, there will always be more than one firewall because an intruder could be one of the authorized network users. Hence the following points should be noted:

- Not all threats originate outside the firewall.
- The most trusted users are also the potential intruders.
- Firewalls themselves may be subject to attack.

Since the firewall sits at the boundary of the IP network segments, it can only monitor the traffic entering and leaving the interface on the firewall that connects to the network. If the intruder is internal to the firewall, the firewall will not be able to detect the security breach. Once an intruder has managed to transit through the interface of the firewall, the intruder would go undetected,

which could possibly lead to stealing sensitive information, destroying information, leaving behind viruses, staging attacks on other networks, and most important, leaving spyware software to monitor the activities on the network for future attacks. Hence, a NIDS would play a critical role in monitoring activities on the network and continually looking for possible anomalous patterns of activities.

Firewall technology has been around for the past 20 years, so much has been documented about its weaknesses and strengths. Information about firewalls is freely available on the Internet. Hence a new breed of hackers have utilized *tunneling* as a means of bypassing firewall security policy. NIDS enhances security infrastructure by monitoring system activities for signs of attack and then, based on the system settings, responds to the attack as well as generates an alarm. Response to a potential attack is known as the *incident response* or *incident handling*, which combines investigation and diagnosis phases. Incident response has been an emerging technology in the past couple of years and is now an integral part of intrusion detection and prevention technology.

Finally, but not least, securing network systems is an ongoing process in which new threats arise all the time. Consequently, firewalls, NIDS, and intrusion prevention systems are continuously evolving technologies. In this chapter and subsequent chapters our focus has been and will be wired networks. However, as wireless data networks proliferate and seamlessly connect to the cellular voice networks, the risk of attacks on the wired networks is growing exponentially.

21. MONITOR AND ANALYZE SYSTEM ACTIVITIES

Figure 10.1 shows the placement of a NIDS, one in the DMZ and the other in the private network. This suggests at least two points on the network from which we capture data packets. The next question is the timing of the information collection, although this depends on the degree of threat perceived to the network.

If the level of perceived threat to the network is low, an immediate response to the attack is not very critical. In such a case, interval-oriented data capturing and analysis is most economical in terms of load placed on a NIDS and other resources on the network. Additionally, there might not be full-time network security personnel to respond to an alarm triggered by the NIDS.

If the level of perceived threat is imminent and the time and the data are mission-critical to the organization, real-time data gathering and analysis are of extreme importance. Of course, the real-time data gathering would impact the CPU cycles on the NIDS and would lead to a massive amount of data storage. With real-time data capturing and analysis, real-time response to an attack can be automated with notification. In such a case, network activities can be interrupted, the incident could be isolated, and system and network recovery could be set in motion.

Analysis Levels

Capturing and storing data packets are among the manageable functions of any IDS. How do we analyze the data packets that represent potential or imminent threats to the network?

We need to examine the data packets and look for evidence that could point to a threat. Let's examine the makeup of data packets. Of course, any packet is almost encapsulated by successive protocols from the Internet model, with the data as its kernel. Potential attacks could be generated by IP or MAC spoofing, fragmented IP packets leading to some sort of DoS, saturating the resource with flooding, and much more. We should remind readers that since humans are not going to examine the data packets, this process of examination is relegated to an algorithm. This algorithm must compare the packets with a known format of the packet (signature) that suggests an attack is in progress, or it could be that there is some sort of unusual activity on the network. How does one distinguish abnormal from normal sets of activities? There must be some baseline (statistical) that indicates normal, and deviation from it would be an indicator of abnormal. We explore these concepts in the following paragraphs.

We can identify two levels of analysis: signature and statistical.

22. SIGNATURE ANALYSIS

Signature analysis includes some sort of pattern matching of the contents of the data packets. There are patterns corresponding to known attacks. These known attacks are stored in a database, and a pattern is examined against the known pattern, which defines signature analysis. Most commercial NIDS products perform signature analysis against a database of known attacks, which is part of the NIDS software. Even though the databases of known attacks may be proprietary to the vendor, the client of this software should be able to increase the scope of the NIDS software by adding signatures to the database. Snort is open-source NIDS software, and the database of known attacks is maintained and updated by the user community. This database is an ASCII (human-readable) file.

23. STATISTICAL ANALYSIS

First we have to define what constitutes a normal traffic pattern on the network. Then we must identify deviations away from normal patterns as potential threats. These deviations must be arrived at by statistical analysis of the traffic patterns. A good example would be how many times records are written to a database over a given time interval, and deviations from normally accepted numbers would be an indication of an impending attack. Of course, a clever hacker could mislead the detector into accepting attack activity as normal by gradually varying behavior over time. This would be an example of a false negative.

24. SIGNATURE ALGORITHMS

Signature analysis is based on these algorithms:

- Pattern matching
- Stateful pattern matching
- Protocol decode-based analysis
- Heuristic-based analysis
- Anomaly-based analysis

Pattern Matching

Pattern matching is based on searching for a fixed sequence of bytes in a single packet. In most cases the pattern is matched against only if the suspect packet is associated with a particular service or, more precisely, destined to and from a particular port. This helps to reduce the number of packets that must get examined and thus speed up the process of detection. However, it tends to make it more difficult for systems to deal with protocols that do not live on well-defined ports.

The structure of a signature based on the simple pattern-matching approach might be as follows: First, the packet is IPv4 and TCP, the destination port is 3333, and the payload contains the fictitious string *psuw*, trigger an alarm. In this example, the pattern *psuw* is what we were searching for, and one of the IDS rules implies to trigger an alarm. One could do a variation on this example to set up more convoluted data packets. The advantage of this simple algorithm is:

- This method allows for direct correlation of an exploit with the pattern; it is highly specific.
- This method is applicable across all protocols.

- This method reliably alerts on the pattern matched.

The disadvantages of this pattern-matching approach are as follows:

- Any modification to the attack can lead to missed events (false negatives).
- This method can lead to high false-positive rates if the pattern is not as unique as the signature writer assumed.
- This method is usually limited to inspection of a single packet and, therefore, does not apply well to the stream-based nature of network traffic such as HTTP traffic. This scenario leads to easily implemented evasion techniques.

Stateful Pattern Matching

This method of signature development adds to the pattern-matching concept because a network stream comprises more than a single atomic packet. Matches should be made in context within the state of the stream. This means that systems that perform this type of signature analysis must consider arrival order of packets in a TCP stream and should handle matching patterns across packet boundaries. This is somewhat similar to a stateful firewall.

Now, instead of looking for the pattern in every packet, the system has to begin to maintain state information on the TCP stream being monitored. To understand the difference, consider the following scenario. Suppose that the attack you are looking for is launched from a client connecting to a server and you have the pattern-match method deployed on the IDS. If the attack is launched so that in any given single TCP packet bound for the target on port 3333 the string is present, this event triggers the alarm. If, however, the attacker causes the offending string to be sent such that the fictitious *gp* is in the first packet sent to the server and *o* is in the second, the alarm does not get triggered. If the stateful pattern-matching algorithm is deployed instead, the sensor has stored the *gp* portion of the string and is able to complete the match when the client forwards the fictitious *p*. The advantages of this technique are as follows:

- This method allows for direct correlation of an exploit with the pattern.
- This method is applicable across all protocols.
- This method makes evasion slightly more difficult.
- This method reliably alerts on the pattern specified.

The disadvantages of the stateful pattern matching-based analysis are as follows:

- Any modification to the attack can lead to missed events (false negatives).

- This method can lead to high false-positive rates if the pattern is not as unique as the signature writer assumed.

Protocol Decode-based Analysis

In many ways, intelligent extensions to stateful pattern matches are protocol decode-based signatures. This class of signature is implemented by decoding the various elements in the same manner as the client or server in the conversation would. When the elements of the protocol are identified, the IDS applies rules defined by the request for comments (RFCs) to look for violations. In some instances, these violations are found with pattern matches within a specific protocol field, and some require more advanced techniques that account for such variables as the length of a field or the number of arguments.

Consider the fictitious example of the *gwb* attack for illustration purposes. Suppose that the base protocol that the attack is being run over is the fictitious OBL protocol, and more specifically, assume that the attack requires that the illegal fictitious argument *gpp* must be passed in the OBL Type field. To further complicate the situation, assume that the Type field is preceded by a field of variable length called OBL Options. The valid list of fictitious options are *gppi, nppi, upsnfs,* and *cvjmep*. Using the simple or the stateful pattern-matching algorithm in this case leads to false positives because the option *gppi* contains the pattern that is being searched for. In addition, because the field lengths are variable, it would be impossible to limit such false positives by specifying search start and stop locations. The only way to be certain that *gpp* is being passed in as the OBL type argument is to fully decode the protocol.

If the protocol allows for behavior that the pattern-matching algorithms have difficulty dealing with, not doing full protocol decodes can also lead to false negatives. For example, if the OBL protocol allows every other byte to be a NULL if a value is set in the OBL header, the pattern matchers would fail to see fx00ox00ox00. The protocol decode-enabled analysis engine would strip the NULLS and fire the alarm as expected, assuming that *gpp* was in the Type field. Thus, with the preceding in mind, the advantages of the protocol decode-based analysis are as follows:

- This method can allow for direct correlation of an exploit.
- This method can be more broad and general to allow catching variations on a theme.
- This method minimizes the chance for false positives if the protocol is well defined and enforced.

- This method reliably alerts on the violation of the protocol rules as defined in the rules script.

  The disadvantages of this technique are as follows:

- This method can lead to high false-positive rates if the RFC is ambiguous and allows developers the discretion to interpret and implement as they see fit. These gray area protocol violations are very common.
- This method requires longer development times to properly implement the protocol parser.

Heuristic-Based Analysis

A good example of this type of signature is a signature that would be used to detect a port sweep. This signature looks for the presence of a threshold number of unique ports being touched on a particular machine. The signature may further restrict itself through the specification of the types of packets that it is interested in (that is, SYN packets). Additionally, there may be a requirement that all the probes must originate from a single source. Signatures of this type require some threshold manipulations to make them conform to the utilization patterns on the network they are monitoring. This type of signature may be used to look for very complex relationships as well as the simple statistical example given.

The advantages for heuristic-based signature analysis are that some types of suspicious and/or malicious activity cannot be detected through any other means. The disadvantages are that algorithms may require tuning or modification to better conform to network traffic and limit false positives.

Anomaly-Based Analysis

From what is seen normally, anomaly-based signatures are typically geared to look for network traffic that deviates. The biggest problem with this methodology is to first define what normal is. Some systems have hard-coded definitions of normal, and in this case they could be considered heuristic-based systems. Some systems are built to learn normal, but the challenge with these systems is in eliminating the possibility of improperly classifying abnormal behavior as normal. Also, if the traffic pattern being learned is assumed to be normal, the system must contend with how to differentiate between allowable deviations and those not allowed or representing attack-based traffic. The work in this area has been mostly limited to academia, although there are a few commercial products that claim to use anomaly-based detection methods. A subcategory of this type of detection is the profile-based

detection methods. These systems base their alerts on changes in the way that users or systems interact on the network. They incur many of the same limitations and problems that the overarching category has in inferring the intent of the change in behavior.

Statistical anomalies may also be identified on the network either through learning or teaching of the statistical norms for certain types of traffic, for example, systems that detect traffic floods, such as UDP, TCP, or ICMP floods. These algorithms compare the current rate of arrival of traffic with a historical reference; based on this, the algorithms will alert to statistically significant deviations from the historical mean. Often, a user can provide the statistical threshold for the alerts. The advantages for anomaly-based detection are as follows:

- If this method is implemented properly, it can detect unknown attacks.
- This method offers low overhead because new signatures do not have to be developed.

  The disadvantages are:

- In general, these systems are not able to give you intrusion data with any granularity. It looks like something terrible may have happened, but the systems cannot say definitively.
- This method is highly dependent on the environment in which the systems learn what normal is.

  The following are Freeware tools to monitor and analyze network activities:

- Network Scanner, Nmap, is available from www. insecure.org. Nmap is a free open-source utility to monitor open ports on a network. The MS-Windows version is a zip file by the name nmap-3.75-win32. zip. You also need to download a packet capture library, WinPcap, under Windows. It is available from http://winpcap.polito.it. In addition to these programs, you need a utility to unzip the zipped file, which you can download from various Internet sites.
- PortPeeker is a freeware utility for capturing network traffic for TCP, UDP, or ICMP protocols. With PortPeeker you can easily and quickly see what traffic is being sent to a given port. This utility is available from www.Linklogger.com.
- Port-scanning tools such as Fport 2.0 and SuperScan 4.0 are easy to use and freely available from www. Foundstone.com.
- Network sniffer Ethereal is available from www. ethereal.com. Ethereal is a packet sniffer and analyzer for a variety of protocols.

- EtherSnoop light is a free network sniffer designed for capturing and analyzing the packets going through the network. It captures the data passing through your network Ethernet card, analyzes the data, and represents it in a readable form. EtherSnoop light is a fully configurable network analyzer program for Win32 environments. It is available from www.arechisoft.com.
- A fairly advanced tool, Snort, an open-source NIDS, is available from www.snort.org.
- UDPFlood is a stress testing tool that could be identified as a DoS agent; it is available from www.Foundstone.com.
- An application that allows you to generate a SYN attack with a spoofed address so that the remote host's CPU cycle's get tied up is Attacker, and is available from www.komodia.com.

## Chapter 11

Wireless Network Security

Chunming Rong
University of Stavanger

Erdal Cayirci
University of Stavanger

With the rapid development of technology in wireless communication and microchips, wireless technology has been widely used in various application areas. The proliferation of wireless devices and wireless networks in the past decade shows the widespread use of wireless technology.

Wireless networks is a general term to refer to various types of networks that communicate without the need of wire lines. Wireless networks can be broadly categorized into two classes based on the structures of the networks: wireless ad hoc networks and cellular networks. The main difference between these two is whether a fixed infrastructure is present.

Three of the well-known cellular networks are the GSM network, the CDMA network, and the 802.11 wireless LAN. The GSM network and the CDMA network are the main network technologies that support modern mobile communication, with most of the mobile phones and mobile networks that are built based on these two wireless networking technologies and their variants. As cellular networks require fixed infrastructures to support the communication between mobile nodes, deployment of the fixed infrastructures is essential. Further, cellular networks require serious and careful topology design of the fixed infrastructures before deployment, because the network topologies of the fixed infrastructures are mostly static and will have a great impact on network performance and network coverage.

Wireless ad hoc networks do not require a fixed infrastructure; thus it is relatively easy to set up and deploy a wireless ad hoc network (see Figure 11.1). Without the fixed infrastructure, the topology of a wireless ad hoc network is dynamic and changes frequently. It is not realistic to assume a static or a specific topology for a wireless ad hoc network. On the other hand, wireless ad hoc networks

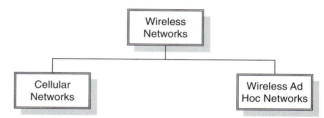

FIGURE 11.1 Classification of wireless networks.

need to be self-organizing; thus mobile nodes in a wireless ad hoc network can adapt to the change of topology and establish cooperation with other nodes at runtime.

Besides the conventional wireless ad hoc networks, there are two special types that should be mentioned: wireless sensor networks and wireless mesh networks. Wireless sensor networks are wireless ad hoc networks, most of the network nodes of which are sensors that monitor a target scene. The wireless sensors are mostly deprived devices in terms of computation power, power supply, bandwidth, and other computation resources. Wireless mesh networks are wireless networks with either a full mesh topology or a partial mesh topology in which some or all nodes are directly connected to all other nodes. The redundancy in connectivity of wireless networks provides great reliability and excellent flexibility in network packet delivery.

1. CELLULAR NETWORKS

Cellular networks require fixed infrastructures to work (see Figure 11.2). A cellular network comprises a fixed infrastructure and a number of mobile nodes. Mobile nodes connect to the fixed infrastructure through wireless links. They may move around from within the range of

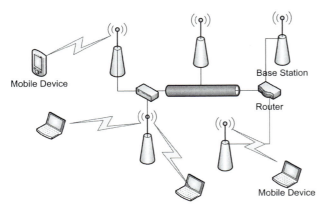

FIGURE 11.2 Cellular networking.

one base station to outside the range of the base station, and they can move into the ranges of other base stations. The fixed infrastructure is stationary, or mostly stationary, including base stations, links between base stations, and possibly other conventional network devices such as routers. The links between base stations can be either wired or wireless. The links should be more substantial than those links between base stations and mobile nodes in terms of reliability, transmission range, bandwidth, and so on.

The fixed infrastructure serves as the backbone of a cellular network, providing high speed and stable connection for the whole network, compared to the connectivity between a base station and a mobile node. In most cases, mobile nodes do not communicate with each other directly without going through a base station. A packet from a source mobile node to a destination mobile node is likely to be first transmitted to the base station to which the source mobile node is connected. The packet is then relayed within the fixed infrastructures until reaching the destination base station to which the destination mobile node is connected. The destination base station can then deliver the packet to the destination mobile node to complete the packet delivery.

Cellular Telephone Networks

Cellular telephone networks offer mobile communication for most of us. With a cellular telephone network, base stations are distributed over a region, with each base station covering a small area. Each part of the small area is called a *cell*. Cell phones within a cell connect to the base station of the cell for communication. When a cell phone moves from one cell to another, its connection will also be migrated from one base station to a new base station. The new base station is the base station of the cell into which the cell phone just moved.

Two of the technologies are the mainstream for cellular telephone networks: the global system for mobile communication (GSM) and code division multiple access (CDMA).

GSM is a wireless cellular network technology for mobile communication that has been widely deployed in most parts of the world. Each GSM mobile phone uses a pair of frequency channels, with one channel for sending data and another for receiving data. Time division multiplexing (TDM) is used to share frequency pairs by multiple mobiles.

CDMA is a technology developed by a company named Qualcomm and has been accepted as an international standard. CDMA assumes that multiple signals add linearly, instead of assuming that colliding frames are completely garbled and of no value. With coding theory and the new assumption, CDMA allows each mobile to transmit over the entire frequency spectrum at all times. The core algorithm of CDMA is how to extract data of interest from the mixed data.

802.11 Wireless LANs

Wireless LANs are specified by the IEEE 802.11 series standard [1], which describes various technologies and protocols for wireless LANs to achieve different targets, allowing the maximum bit rate from 2 Mbits per second to 248 Mbits per second.

Wireless LANs can work in either access point (AP) mode or ad hoc mode, as shown in Figure 11.3. When a wireless LAN is working in AP mode, all communication passes through a base station, called an *access point*. The access point then passes the communication data to the destination node, if it is connected to the access point, or forwards the communication data to a router for further routing and relaying. When working in ad hoc mode, wireless LANs work in the absence of base stations. Nodes directly communicate with other nodes within their transmission range, without depending on a base station.

One of the complications that 802.11 wireless LANs incur is medium access control in the data link layer. Medium access control in 802.11 wireless LANs can be either distributed or centralized control by a base station. The distributed medium access control relies on the Carrier Sense Multiple Access (CSMA) with Collision Avoidance (CSMA/CA) protocol. CSMA/CA allows network nodes to compete to transmit data when a channel is idle and uses the Ethernet binary exponential backoff algorithm to decide a waiting time before retransmission when a collision occurs. CSMA/CA can also operate based on MACAW (Multiple Access with Collision

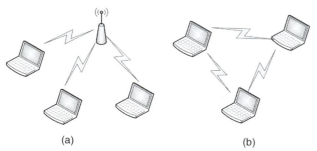

FIGURE 11.3 (a) A wireless network in AP mode; (b) a wireless network in ad hoc mode.

Avoidance for Wireless) using virtual channel sensing. Request packets and clear-to-send (CTS) packets are broadcast before data transmission by the sender and the receiver, respectively. All stations within the range of the sender or the receiver will keep silent in the course of data transmission to avoid interference on the transmission.

The centralized medium access control is implemented by having the base station broadcast a beacon frame periodically and poll nodes to check whether they have data to send. The base station serves as a central control over the allocation of the bandwidth. It allocates bandwidth according to the polling results. All nodes connected to the base station must behave in accordance with the allocation decision made by the base station. With the centralized medium access control, it is possible to provide quality-of-service guarantees because the base station can control on the allocation of bandwidth to a specific node to meet the quality requirements.

2. WIRELESS AD HOC NETWORKS

Wireless ad hoc networks are distributed networks that work without fixed infrastructures and in which each network node is willing to forward network packets for other network nodes. The main characteristics of wireless ad hoc networks are as follows:

- Wireless ad hoc networks are distributed networks that do not require fixed infrastructures to work. Network nodes in a wireless ad hoc network can be randomly deployed to form the wireless ad hoc network.
- Network nodes will forward network packets for other network nodes. Network nodes in a wireless ad hoc network directly communicate with other nodes within their ranges. When these networks communicate with network nodes outside their ranges, network packets will be forwarded by the nearby network nodes and other nodes that are on the path from the source nodes to the destination nodes.

- Wireless ad hoc networks are self-organizing. Without fixed infrastructures and central administration, wireless ad hoc networks must be capable of establishing cooperation between nodes on their own. Network nodes must also be able to adapt to changes in the network, such as the network topology.
- Wireless ad hoc networks have dynamic network topologies. Network nodes of a wireless ad hoc network connect to other network nodes through wireless links. The network nodes are mostly mobile. The topology of a wireless ad hoc network can change from time to time, since network nodes move around from within the range to the outside, and new network nodes may join the network, just as existing network nodes may leave the network.

Wireless Sensor Networks

A wireless sensor network is an ad hoc network mainly comprising sensor nodes, which are normally used to monitor and observe a phenomenon or a scene. The sensor nodes are physically deployed within or close to the phenomenon or the scene. The collected data will be sent back to a base station from time to time through routes dynamically discovered and formed by sensor nodes.

Sensors in wireless sensor networks are normally small network nodes with very limited computation power, limited communication capacity, and limited power supply. Thus a sensor may perform only simple computation and can communicate with sensors and other nodes within a short range. The life spans of sensors are also limited by the power supply.

Wireless sensor networks can be self-organizing, since sensors can be randomly deployed in some inaccessible areas. The randomly deployed sensors can cooperate with other sensors within their range to implement the task of monitoring or observing the target scene or the target phenomenon and to communicate with the base station that collects data from all sensor nodes. The cooperation might involve finding a route to transmit data to a specific destination, relaying data from one neighbor to another neighbor when the two neighbors are not within reach of each other, and so on.

Mesh Networks

One of the emerging technologies of wireless network is wireless mesh networks (WMNs). Nodes in a WMN include mesh routers and mesh clients. Each node in a WMN works as a router as well as a host. When it's a router, each node needs to perform routing and to forward packets for other nodes when necessary, such as when two nodes are not within direct reach of each other and when a route to a specific destination for packet delivery is required to be discovered.

Mesh routers may be equipped with multiple wireless interfaces, built on either the same or different wireless technologies, and are capable of bridging different networks. Mesh routers can also be classified as access mesh routers, backbone mesh routers, or gateway mesh routers. Access mesh routers provide mesh clients with access to mesh networks; backbone mesh routers form the backbone of a mesh network; and a gateway mesh router connects the backbone to an external network.

Each mesh client normally has only one network interface that provides network connectivity with other nodes. Mesh clients are not usually capable of bridging different networks, which is different from mesh routers.

Similar to other ad hoc networks, a wireless mesh network can be self-organizing. Thus nodes can establish and maintain connectivity with other nodes automatically, without human intervention. Wireless mesh networks can divided into backbone mesh networks and access mesh networks.

3. SECURITY PROTOCOLS

Wired Equivalent Privacy (WEP) was defined by the IEEE 802.11 standard [2]. WEP is designed to protect linkage-level data for wireless transmission by providing confidentiality, access control, and data integrity, to provide secure communication between a mobile device and an access point in a 802.11 wireless LAN.

WEP

Implemented based on shared key secrets and the RC4 stream cipher [3], WEP's encryption of a frame includes two operations (see Figure 11.4). It first produces a checksum of the data, and then it encrypts the plaintext and the checksum using RC4:

- *Checksumming.* Let c be an integrity checksum function. For a given message M, a checksum $c(M)$ is calculated and then concatenated to the end of M, obtaining a plaintext $P = <M, c(M)>$. Note that the checksum $c(M)$ does not depend on the shared key.
- *Encryption.* The shared key k is concatenated to the end of the initialization vector (IV) v, forming $<v,k>$. $<v,k>$ is then used as the input to the RC4 algorithm to generate a keystream $RC4(v,k)$. The plaintext P is exclusive-or'ed (XOR, denoted by $\oplus$) with the keystream to obtain the ciphertext: $C = P \oplus RC4(v,k)$.

Using the shared key k and the IV v, WEP can greatly simplify the complexity of key distribution because it

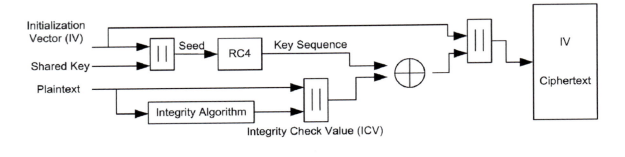

(a) WEP Encryption

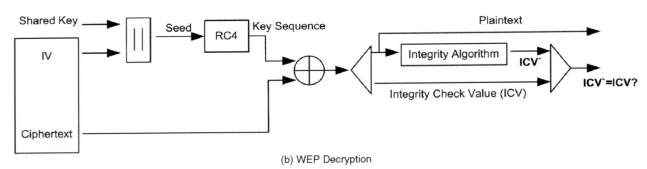

(b) WEP Decryption

FIGURE 11.4 WEP encryption and decryption.

needs only to distribute k and v but can achieve a relatively very long key sequence. IV changes from time to time, which will force the $RC4$ algorithm to produce a new key sequence, avoiding the situation where the same key sequence is used to encrypt a large amount of data, which potentially leads to several types of attacks [4, 5].

WEP combines the shared key k and the IV v as inputs to seed the $RC4$ function. 802.11B [6] specifies that the seed shall be 64 bits long, with 24 bits from the IV v and 40 bits from the shared key k. Bits 0 through 23 of the seed contain bits 0 through 23 of the IV v, and bits 24 through 63 of the seed contain bits 0 through 39 of the shared key k.

When a receiver receives the ciphertext C, it will XOR the ciphertext C with the corresponding keystream to produce the plaintext M' as follows:

$$M' = C \oplus RC4(k,v) = (P \oplus RC4(k,v)) \oplus RC4(k,v) = M$$

WPA and WPA2

Wi-Fi Protected Access (WPA) is specified by the IEEE 802.11i standard, which is aimed at providing stronger security compared to WEP and is expected to tackle most of the weakness found in WEP [7, 8, 9].

WPA

WPA has been designed to target both enterprise and consumers. Enterprise deployment of WPA is required to be used with IEEE 802.1x authentication, which is responsible for distributing different keys to each user. Personal deployment of WPA adopts a simpler mechanism, which allows all stations to use the same key. This mechanism is called the *Pre-Shared Key* (PSK) mode.

The WPA protocol works in a similar way to WEP. WPA mandates the use of the $RC4$ stream cipher with a 128–bit key and a 48–bit initialization vector (IV), compared with the 40–bit key and the 24–bit IV in WEP.

WPA also has a few other improvements over WEP, including the Temporal Key Integrity Protocol (TKIP) and the Message Integrity Code (MIC). With TKIP, WPA will dynamically change keys used by the system periodically. With the much larger IV and the dynamically changing key, the stream cipher $RC4$ is able to produce a much longer keystream. The longer keystream improved WPA's protection against the well-known key recovery attacks on WEP, since finding two packets encrypted using the same key sequences is literally impossible due to the extremely long keystream.

With MIC, WPA uses an algorithm named Michael to produce an authentication code for each message, which is termed the *message integrity code*. The message integrity code also contains a frame counter to provide protection over replay attacks.

WPA uses the Extensible Authentication Protocol (EAP) framework [10] to conduct authentication. When a user (supplicant) tries to connect to a network, an authenticator will send a request to the user asking the user to authenticate herself using a specific type of authentication mechanism. The user will respond with corresponding authentication information. The authenticator relies on an authentication server to make the decision regarding the user's authentication.

WPA2

WPA2 is not much different from WPA. Though TKIP is required in WPA, Advanced Encryption Standard (AES) is optional. This is aimed to provide backward compatibility for WPA over hardware designed for WEP, as TKIP can be implemented on the same hardware as those for WEP, but AES cannot be implemented on this hardware. TKIP and AES are both mandatory in WPA2 to provide a higher level of protection over wireless connections. AES is a block cipher, which can only be applied to a fixed length of data block. AES accepts key sizes of 128 bits, 196 bits, and 256 bits.

Besides the mandatory requirement of supporting AES, WPA2 also introduces supports for fast roaming of wireless clients migrating between wireless access points. First, WPA2 allows the caching of a Pair-wise Master Key (PMK), which is the key used for a session between an access point and a wireless client; thus a wireless client can reconnect a recently connected access point without having to reauthenticate. Second, WPA2 enables a wireless client to authenticate itself to a wireless access point that it is moving to while the wireless client maintains its connection to the existing access point. This reduces the time needed for roaming clients to move from one access point to another, and it is especially useful for timing-sensitive applications.

SPINS: Security Protocols for Sensor Networks

Sensor nodes in sensor networks are normally low-end devices with very limited resources, such as memory, computation power, battery, and network bandwidth.

Perrig et al. [11] proposed a family of security protocols named SPINS, which were specially designed for low-end devices with severely limited resources, such as sensor nodes in sensor networks. SPINS consists of two building blocks: Secure Network Encryption Protocol (SNEP) and the "micro" version of the Timed, Efficient, Streaming, Loss-tolerant Authentication Protocol (μTESLA). SNEP uses symmetry encryption to provide data confidentiality, two-party data authentication, and data freshness. μTESLA provides authentication over broadcast streams. SPINS assumes that each sensor node shares a master key with the base station. The master key serves as the base of trust and is used to derive all other keys.

SNEP

As illustrated in Figure 11.5, SNEP uses a block cipher to provide data confidentiality and message authentication code (MAC) to provide authentication. SNEP assumes a shared counter C between the sender and the receiver and two keys, the encryption key K_{encr} and the authentication key K_{mac}.

For an outgoing message D, SNEP processes it as follows:

- The message D is first encrypted using a block cipher in counter mode with the key K_{encr} and the counter C, forming the encrypted text $E = \{D\}_{<Kencr,C>}$.
- A message authentication code is produced for the encrypted text E with the key K_{mac} and the counter C, forming the MAC $M = MAC(K_{mac},C|E)$ where $MAC()$ is a one-way function and $C|E$ stands for the concatenation of C and E.
- SNEP increments the counter C.

To send the message D to the recipient, SNEP actually sends out E and M. In other words, SNEP encrypts D to E using the shared key K_{encr} between the sender and the receiver to prevent unauthorized disclosure of the data, and it uses the shared key K_{mac}, known only to the sender and the receiver, to provide message authentication. Thus data confidentiality and message authentication can both be implemented.

The message D is encrypted with the counter C, which will be different in each message. The same message D will be encrypted differently even it is sent multiple times. Thus semantic security is implemented in SNEP. The MAC is also produced using the counter C; thus it enables SNEP to prevent replying to old messages.

μTESLA

TESLA [12, 13, 14] was proposed to provide message authentication for multicast. TESLA does not use any asymmetry cryptography, which makes it lightweight in terms of computation and overhead of bandwidth.

μTESLA is a modified version of TESLA, aiming to provide message authentication for multicasting in sensor networks. The general idea of μTESLA is that the sender splits the sending time into intervals. Packets sent out in different intervals are authenticated with different keys. Keys to authenticate packets will be disclosed after a short delay, when the keys are no longer used to send out messages. Thus packets can be authenticated when the authentication keys have been disclosed. Packets will not be tampered with while they are in transit since the keys have not been disclosed yet. The disclosed authentication keys can be verified using previous known keys to prevent malicious nodes from forging authentication keys.

μTESLA has four phases: sender setup, sending authenticated packets, bootstrapping new receivers, and authenticating packets. In the sender setup phase, a sender generates a chain of keys, K_i ($0 \leq i \leq n$). The keychain is a one-way chain such that K_i can be derived from K_j if $i \leq j$, such as a keychain K_i ($i = 0,...,n$), $K_i = F(K_{i+1})$, where F is a one-way function. The sender also decides on the starting time T_0, the interval duration T_{int}, and the disclosure delay d (unit is interval), as shown in Figure 11.6.

To send out authenticated packets, the sender attaches a MAC with each packet, where the MAC is produced using a key from the keychain and the data in the network packet. μTESLA has specific requirements on the

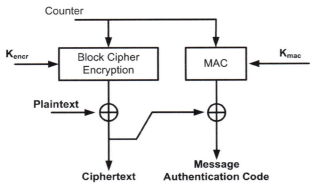

FIGURE 11.5 Sensor Network Encryption Protocol (SNEP).

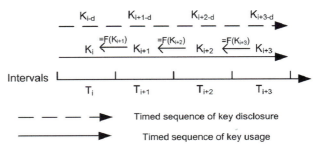

FIGURE 11.6 Sequences of intervals, key usages, and key disclosure.

use of keys for producing MACs. Keys are used in the same order as the key sequence of the keychain. Each of the keys is used in one interval only. For the interval $T_i = T_0 + i \times T_{int}$, the key K_i is used to produce the MACs for the messages sent out in the interval T_i. Keys are disclosed with a fixed delay d such that the key K_i used in interval T_i will be disclosed in the interval T_{i+d}. The sequence of key usage and the sequence of key disclosure are demonstrated in Figure 11.6.

To bootstrap a new receiver, the sender needs to synchronize the time with the receiver and needs to inform the new receiver of a key K_j that is used in a past interval T_j, the interval duration T_{int}, and the disclosure delay d. With a previous key K_j, the receiver will be able to verify any key K_p where $j \leq p$ using the one-way keychain's property. After this, the new receiver will be able to receive and verify data in the same way as other receivers that join the communication prior to the new receiver.

To receive and authenticate messages, a receiver will check all incoming messages if they have been delayed for more than d. Messages with a delay greater than d will be discarded, since they are suspect as fake messages constructed after the key has been disclosed. The receiver will buffer the remaining messages for at least d intervals until the corresponding keys are disclosed. When a key K_i is disclosed at the moment $T_i + d$, the receiver will verify K_i using K_{i-1} by checking if $K_{i-1} = F(K_i)$. Once the key K_i is verified, K_i will be used to authenticate those messages sent in the interval T_i.

4. SECURE ROUTING

Secure Efficient Ad hoc Distance (SEAD) [15] vector routing is designed based on Destination-Sequenced Distance Vector (DSDV) routing [16]. SEAD augments DSDV with authentication to provide security in the construction and exchange of routing information.

SEAD

Distance vector routing works as follows. Each router maintains a routing table. Each entry of the table contains a specific destination, a metric (the shortest distance to the destination), and the next hop on the shortest path from the current router to the destination. For a packet that needs to be sent to a certain destination, the router will look up the destination from the routing table to get the matching entry. Then the packet is sent to the next hop specified in the entry.

To allow routers to automatically discover new routes and maintain their routing tables, routers exchange routing information periodically. Each router advises its neighbors of its own routing information by broadcasting its routing table to all its neighbors. Each router will update its routing table according to the information it hears from its neighbors. If a new destination is found from the information advertised by a neighbor, a new entry is added to the routing table with the metric recalculated based on the advertised metric and the linking between the router and the neighbor. If an existing destination is found, the corresponding entry is updated only when a new path that is shorter than the original one has been found. In this case, the metric and the next hop for the specified destination are modified based on the advertised information.

Though distance vector routing is simple and effective, it suffers from possible routing loops, also known as the counting to infinity problem. DSDV [17] is one of the extensions to distance vector routing to tackle this issue. DSDV augments each routing update with a sequence number, which can be used to identify the sequence of routing updates, preventing routing updates being applied in an out-of-order manner. Newer routing updates are advised with sequence numbers greater than those of the previous routing updates. In each routing update, the sequence number will be incremented to the next even number. Only when a broken link has been detected will the router use the next odd sequence number as the sequence number for the new routing update that is to be advertised to all its neighbors. Each router maintains an even sequence number to identify the sequence of every routing update. Neighbors will only accept newer routing updates by discarding routing updates with sequence numbers less than the last sequence number heard from the router.

SEAD provides authentication on metrics' lower bounds and senders' identities by using the one-way hash chain. Let H be a hash function and x be a given value. A list of values is computed as follows:

$$h_0, h_1, h_2, \ldots, h_n$$

where $h_0 = x$ and $h_{i+1} = H(h_i)$ for $0 \leq i \leq n$. Given any value h_k that has been confirmed to be in the list, to authenticate if a given value d is on the list or not one can compute if d can be derived from h_k by applying H a certain number of times, or if h_k can be derived from d by applying H to d a certain number of times. If either d can be derived from h_k or h_k can be derived from d within a certain number of steps, it is said that d can be authenticated by h_k.

SEAD assumes an upper bound $m - 1$ on the diameter of the ad hoc network, which means that the metric of a routing entry will be less than m. Let h_0, h_1, h_2, ..., h_n be a hash chain where $n = m \times k$ and $k \in Z^+$.

For an update with the sequence number i and the metric value of j, the value $h_{(k-i)m+j}$ is used to authenticate the routing update entry.

By using $h_{(k-i)m+j}$ to authenticate the routing update entry, a node is actually disclosing the value $h_{(k-i)m+j}$ and subsequently all h_p where $p \geq (k - i)m + j$, but not any value h_q where $q \leq (k - i)m + j$.

Using a hash value corresponding to the sequence number and metric in a routing update entry allows the authentication of the update and prevents any node from advertising a route to some destination, forging a greater sequence number or a smaller metric.

To authenticate the update, a node can use any given earlier authentic hash value h_p from the same hash chain to authenticate the current update with sequence number i and metric j. The current update uses the hash value $h_{(k-i)m+j}$ and $(k - i)m + j \leq p$, thus h_p can be computed from $h_{(k-i)m+j}$ by applying H for $(k - i)m + j - p$ times.

The disclosure of $h_{(k-i)m+j}$ does not disclose any value h_q where $q \leq (k - i)m + j$. Let a fake update be advised with a sequence number p and metric q, where $p \geq i$ *and* $q \leq j$, or $q \leq j$. The fake update will need to use the hash value $h_{(k-p)m+q}$. If the sequence number p is greater than i or the metric q is less than j, $(k - p)m + q < (k - i)m + j$. This means that a hash value $h_{(k-p)m+q}$ that has not been disclosed is needed to authenticate the update. Since the value $h_{(k-p)m+q}$ has not been disclosed, the malicious node will not be able to have it to fake a routing update.

Ariadne

Ariadne [18] is a secure on-demand routing protocol for ad hoc networks. Ariadne is built on the Dynamic Source Routing protocol (DSR) [19].

Routing in Ariadne is divided into two stages: the route discovery stage and the route maintenance stage. In the route discovery stage, a source node in the ad hoc network tries to find a path to a specific destination node. The discovered path will be used by the source node as the path for all communication from the source node to the destination node until the discovered path becomes invalid. In the route maintenance stage, network nodes identify broken paths that have been found. A node sends a packet along a specified route to some destination. Each node on the route forwards the packet to the next node on the specified route and tries to confirm the delivery of the packet to the

next node. If a node fails to receive an acknowledgment from the next node, it will signal the source node using a ROUTE ERROR packet that a broken link has been found. The source node and other nodes on the path can then be advised of the broken link.

The key security features Ariadne adds onto the route discovery and route maintenance are node authentication and data verification for the routing relation packets. Node authentication is the process of verifying the identifiers of nodes that are involved in Ariadne's route discovery and route maintenance, to prevent forging routing packets. In route discovery, a node sends out a ROUTE REQUEST packet to perform a route discovery. When the ROUTE REQUEST packet reaches the destination node, the destination node verifies the originator identity before responding. Similarly, when the source node receives a ROUTE REPLY packet, which is a response to the ROUTE REQUEST packet, the source node will also authenticate the identity of the sender. The authentication of node identities can be of one of the three methods: TELSA, digital signatures, and Message Authentication Code (MAC).

Data verification is the process of verifying the integrity of the node list in route discovery for the prevention of adding and removing nodes from the node list in a ROUTE RQUEST. To build a full list of nodes for a route to a destination, each node will need to add itself into the node list in the ROUTE REQUEST when it forwards the ROUTE REQUEST to its neighbor. Data verification protects the node list by preventing unauthorized adding of nodes and unauthorized removal of nodes.

ARAN

Authenticated Routing for Ad hoc Networks (ARAN) [20] is a routing protocol for ad hoc networks with authentication enabled. It allows routing messages to be authenticated at each node between the source nodes and the destination nodes. The authentication that ARAN has implemented is based on cryptographic certificates.

ARAN requires a trusted certificate server, the public key of which is known to all valid nodes. Keys are assumed to have been established between the trusted certificate server and nodes. For each node to enter into a wireless ad hoc network, it needs to have a certificate issued by the trusted server. The certificate contains the IP address of the node, the public key of the node, a time stamp indicating the issue time of the certification, and the expiration time of the certificate. Because all nodes have the public key of the trusted server, a certificate can be verified by all nodes to check whether it is authentic.

With an authentic certificate and the corresponding private key, the node that owns the certificate can authenticate itself using its private key.

To discover a route from a source node to the destination node, the source node sends out a route discovery packet (RDP) to all its neighbors. The RDP is signed by the source node's private key and contains a nonce, a time stamp, and the source node's certificate. The time stamp and the nonce work to prevent replay attacks and flooding of the RDP.

The RDP is then rebroadcast in the network until it reaches the destination. The RDP is rebroadcast with the signature and the certificate of the rebroadcaster. On receiving an RDP, each node will first verify the source's signature and the previous node's signature on the RDP.

On receiving an RDP, the destination sends back a reply packet (REP) along the reverse path to the source after validating the RDP. The REP contains the nonce specified in the RDP and the signature from the destination node.

The REP is unicast along the reverse path. Each node on the path will put its own certificate and its own signature on the RDP before forwarding it to the next node. Each node will also verify the signatures on the RDP. An REP is discarded if one or more invalid signatures are found on the REP.

When the source receives the REP, it will first verify the signatures and then the nonce in the REP. A valid REP indicates that a route has been discovered. The node list on a valid REP suggests an operational path from the source node to the destination node that is found.

As an on-demand protocol, nodes keep track of route status. If there has been no traffic for a route's lifetime or a broken link has been detected, the route will be deactivated. Receiving data on an inactive route will force a node to signal an error state by using an error (ERR) message. The ERR message is signed by the node that produces it and will be forwarded to the source without modification. The ERR message contains a nonce and a time stamp to ensure that the ERR message is fresh.

SLSP

Secure Link State Routing Protocol (SLSP) [21] is a secure routing protocol for ad hoc network building based on link state protocols. SLSP assumes that each node has a public/private key pair and has the capability of signing and verifying digital signatures. Keys are bound with the Medium Access Code and the IP address, allowing neighbors within transmission range to uniquely verify nodes if public keys have been known prior to communication.

In SLSP, each node broadcasts its IP address and the MAC to its neighbor with its signature. Neighbors verify the signature and keep a record of the pairing IP address and the MAC. The Neighbor Lookup Protocol (NLP) of SLSP extracts and retains the MAC and IP address of each network frame received by a node. The extracted information is used to maintain the mapping of MACs and IP addresses.

Nodes using SLSP periodically send out link state updates (LSUs) to advise the state of their network links. LSU packets are limited to propagating within a zone of their origin node, which is specified by the maximum number of hops. To restrict the propagation of LSU packets, each LSU packet contains the *zone radius* and the *hops traversed* fields. Let the maximum hop be R; X, a random number; and H be a hash function. *Zone–radius* will be initialized to $H^R(X)$ and *hops_traversed* be initialized to $H(X)$. Each LSU packet also contains a *TTL* field initialized as $R - 1$. If $TTL < 0$ or $H(hops\text{–}traversed) = zone\text{–}radius$, a node will not rebroadcast the LSU packet. Otherwise, the node will replace the *hops–traversed* field with $H(hops\text{–}traversed)$ and decrease *TTL* by one. In this way, the hop count is authenticated. SLSP also uses signatures to protect LSU packets. Receiving nodes can verify the authenticity and the integrity of the received LSU packets, thus preventing forging or tampering with LSU packets.

5. KEY ESTABLISHMENT

Because wireless communication is open and the signals are accessible by anyone within the vicinity, it is important for wireless networks to establish trust to guard the access to the networks. Key establishment builds relations between nodes using keys; thus security services, such as authentication, confidentiality, and integrity can be achieved for the communication between these nodes with the help of the established keys.

The dynamically changing topology of wireless networks, the lack of fixed infrastructure of wireless ad hoc and sensor networks, and the limited computation and energy resources of sensor networks have all added complication to the key establishment process in wireless networks.

Bootstrapping

Bootstrapping is the process by which nodes in a wireless network are made aware of the presence of others in the network. On bootstrapping, a node gets its identifying credentials that can be used in the network the node is trying to join. Upon completion of the bootstrapping, the wireless network should be ready to accept the node as a valid node to join the network.

To enter a network, a node needs to present its identifying credential to show its eligibility to access the network. This process is called *preauthentication*. Once the credentials are accepted, network security associations are established with other nodes.

These network security associations will serve as further proof of authorization in the network. Security associations can be of various forms, including symmetric keys, public key pairs, hash key chains, and so on. The security associations can be used to authenticate nodes. Security associations may expire after a certain period of time and can be revoked if necessary. For example, if a node is suspected of being compromised, its security association will be revoked to prevent the node accessing the network. The actual way of revocation depends on the form of the security associations.

Bootstrapping in Wireless Ad Hoc Networks

Wireless ad hoc networks bring new challenges to the bootstrapping process by their lack of a centralized security infrastructure. It is necessary to build a security infrastructure in the bootstrapping phase. The trust infrastructure should be able to accept nodes with valid credentials to enter the network but stop those nodes without valid credentials from joining the network and establish security association between nodes within the network.

To build such a trust infrastructure, we can use any one of the following three supports: prior knowledge, trusted third parties, or self-organizing capability. Prior knowledge is information that has been set on valid nodes in advance, such as predistributed secrets or preset shared keys. This information can be used to distinguish legitimate nodes from malicious ones. Only nodes with prior knowledge will be accepted to enter the network. For example, the predistributed secrets can be used to authenticate legitimate nodes, so the network can simply reject those nodes without the predistributed secrets so that they can't enter the network.

Trusted third parties can also be used to support the establishment of the trust infrastructure. The trusted third party can be a Certificate Authority (CA), a base station of the wireless network, or any nodes that are designated to be trusted. If trusted third parties are used, all nodes must mutually agree to trust them and derive their trust on others from the trusted third parties. One of the issues with this method is that trusted third parties are required to be available for access by all nodes across the whole network, which is a very strong assumption for wireless networks as well as an impractical requirement.

It is desirable to have a self-organizing capability for building the trust infrastructure for wireless networks, taking into account the dynamically changing topology of wireless ad hoc networks. Implementing a self-organizing capability for building the trust infrastructure often requires an out-of-band authenticated communication channel or special hardware support, such as tamper-proof hardware tokens.

Bootstrapping in Wireless Sensor Networks

Bootstrapping nodes in wireless sensor networks is also challenging for the following reasons:

- *Node capture.* Sensor nodes are normally deployed in an area that is geographically close or inside the monitoring environment, which might not be a closed and confined area under guard. Thus sensor nodes are vulnerable to physical capture because it might be difficult to prevent physical access to the area.

- *Node replication.* Once a sensor node is compromised, it is possible for adversaries to replicate sensor nodes by using the secret acquired from the compromised node. In this case, adversaries can produce fake legitimate node that cannot be distinguished by the network.

- *Scalability.* A single-sensor network may comprise a large number of sensor nodes. The more nodes in a wireless sensor network, the more complicated it is for bootstrapping.

- *Resource limitation.* Sensor nodes normally have extremely limited computation power and memory as well as limited power supply and weak communication capability. This makes some of the deliberate algorithms and methods not applicable to wireless sensor networks. Only those algorithms that require a moderate amount of resources can be implemented in wireless sensor networks.

Bootstrapping a sensor node is achieved using an incremental communication output power level to discover neighbors nearby. The output power level is increased step by step from the minimum level to the maximum level, to send out a HELLO message. This will enable the sensor node to discover neighbors in the order of their distance from the sensor node, from the closest to the farthest away.

Key Management

Key management schemes can be classified according to the way keys are set up (see Figure 11.7). Either keys

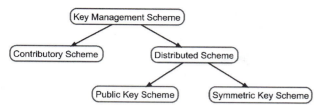

FIGURE 11.7 Key management schemes.

are managed based on the contribution from all participating nodes in the network or they are managed based on a central node in the network. Thus key management schemes can be divided into contributory key management schemes, in which all nodes work equally together to manage the keys, and distributed key management schemes, in which only one central node is responsible for key management [22].

Classification

The distributed key management scheme can be further divided into symmetric schemes and public key schemes. Symmetric key schemes are based on private key cryptography, whereby shared secrets are used to authenticate legitimate nodes and to provide secure communication between them. The underlying assumption is that the shared secrets are known only to legitimate nodes involved in the interaction. Thus proving the knowledge of the shared secrets is enough to authenticate legitimate nodes. Shared secrets are distributed via secure channels or out-of-band measures. Trust on a node is established if the node has knowledge of a shared secret.

Public key schemes are built on public key cryptography. Keys are constructed in pairs, with a private key and a public key in each pair. Private keys are kept secret by the owners. Public keys are distributed and used to authenticate nodes and to verify credentials. Keys are normally conveyed in certificates for distribution. Certificates are signed by trusted nodes for which the public keys have been known and validated. Trust on the certificates will be derived from the public keys that sign the certificates. Note that given g^i *(mod p)* and g^j *(mod p)*, it is hard to compute g^{i*j} *(mod p)* without the knowledge of i and j.

Contributory Schemes

Diffie-Hellman (D-H) [23] is a well-known algorithm for establishing shared secrets. The D-H algorithm's strength depends on the discrete log problem: It is hard to calculate s if given the value g^s (mod p), where p is a large prime number.

Diffie-Hellman Key Exchange

D-H was designed for establishing a shared secret between two parties, namely node A and node B. Each party agrees on a large prime number p and a generator g. A and B each choose a random value i and j, respectively. A and B are then exchanged with the public values g^i (mod p) and g^j (mod p). On the reception of g^j (mod p) from B, A is then able to calculate the value $g^{j \times i}$ (mod p). Similarly, B computes $g^{i \times j}$ (mod p). Thus a shared secret, $g^{i \times j}$ (mod p), has been set up between A and B.

ING

Ingemarsson, Tang, and Wong (ING) [24] extends the D-F key exchange to a group of n members, $d_1, ..., d_n$. All group members are organized in a ring, where each member has a left neighbor and a right neighbor. Node d_i has a right neighbor d_{i-1} and a left neighbor d_{i+1}. Note that for node d_i, its right neighbor is d_{i+1}; for node d_{i+1}, its left neighbor is d_i.

Same as the D-F algorithm, all members in an ING group assume a large prime number p and a generator g. Initially, node d_i will choose a random number r_i. At the first round of key exchange, node d_i will compute g^{r_i} (mod p) and send it to its left neighbor d_{i+1}. At the same time, node d_i also receives the public value $g^{r_{i-1}}$ (mod p) from its right neighbor d_{i-1}. From the second round on, let q be the value that node d_i received in the previous round, node d_i will compute a new public value q^{d_i} (mod p). After $n-1$ rounds, the node d_i would have received a public value, g^k (mod p) where $k = \Pi_{m=1}^{i-1} r_m \times \Pi_{s=i+1}^{n} r_s$, from its right neighbors. With the public value received at the $n-1$th round, the node d_i can raise it to the power of r_i to compute the value g^l (mod p) where $l = \Pi_{m=1}^{n} r_m$.

Hypercube and Octopus (H&O)

The Hypercube protocol [25] assumes that there are 2^d nodes joining to establish a shared secret and all nodes are organized as a d-dimensional vector space $GF(2)^d$ Let $b_1, ..., b_d$ be the basic of $GF(2)^d$ The hypercube protocol takes d rounds to complete:

- In the first round, every participant $v \in GF(2)^d$ chooses a random number r_v and conducts a D-H key exchange with another participant $v + b_1$, with the random values r_v and r_{v+b1}, respectively.

- In the ith round, every participant $v \in GF(2)^d$ performances a D-H key exchange with the participant $v + b_i$, where both v and $v + b_i$ use the value generated in the previous round as the random number for D-H key exchange.

This algorithm can be explained using a complete binary tree to make it more comprehensible. All the nodes are put in a complete binary tree as leaves, with leaves at the 0–level and the root at the d-level. D-H key exchanges are performed from the leaves up to the root. The key exchange takes d rounds:

- In the first round, each leaf chooses a random number k and performs a D-H key exchange with its sibling leaf, which has a random number j, and the resulting value $g^{k \times j} \pmod{p}$ is saved as the random value for the parent node of the above two leaves.

- In the ith round, each node at the $i − 1$ level performs a D-H key exchange with its sibling node using the random numbers m and n, respectively, that they received in the previous round. The resulting value $g^{m \times n} \pmod{p}$ is saved as the random value for the parent node of the above two nodes.

After d rounds, the root of the complete binary tree contains the established shared secret s.

The hypercube protocol assumes that there are 2^d network nodes. The octopus protocol removes the assumption and extends the hypercube protocol to work with an arbitrary number of nodes. Thus the octopus protocol can be used to establish a shared key for a node set containing an arbitrary number of nodes.

Distributed Schemes

A partially distributed threshold CA scheme [26] works with a normal PKI system where a CA exists. The private key of the CA is split and distributed over a set of n server nodes using a (k,n) secret-sharing scheme [27]. The (k,n) secret-sharing scheme allows any k or more server nodes within the n server nodes to work together to reveal the CA's private key. Any set of nodes with fewer than k nodes will not be able to reveal the CA's private key. With the threshold signature scheme [28], any k of the n nodes can cooperate to sign a certificate. Each of the k nodes produces a piece of the signature on the request of signing a given certificate. With all the k pieces of the signature, a valid signature, which is the same as the one produced using the CA's private key, can be produced by combining the k pieces of the signature.

Partially Distributed Threshold CA Scheme

In this way, the partial distributed threshold CA scheme can avoid the bottleneck of the centralized CA of conventional PKI infrastructures. As long as there are at least k of the n nodes available, the network can always issue and sign new certificates. Attacks to any single node will not bring the whole CA down. Only when an attack manages to paralyze $n − k$ or more nodes will the CA's signing service not be available.

To further improve the security of the private key that is distributed over the n nodes, proactive security [29] can be imposed. Proactive security forces the private key shares to be refreshed periodically. Each refreshment will invalidate the previous share held by a node. Attacks on multiple nodes must complete within a refresh period to succeed. To be specific, only when an attack can compromise k or more nodes within a refresh period can the attack succeed.

While conventional PKI systems depend on directories to publish public key certificates, it is suggested that certificates should be disseminated to communication peers when establishing a communication channel with the partial distributed threshold CA scheme. This is due to the fact that the availability of centralized directories cannot be guaranteed in wireless networks. Therefore it is not realistic to assume the availability of a centralized directory.

Self-Organized Key Management (PGP-A)

A self-organized key management scheme (PGP-A) [30] has its basis in the Pretty Good Privacy (PGP) [31] scheme. PGP is built based on the "web of trust" model, in which all nodes have equal roles in playing a CA. Each node generates its own public/private key pair and signs other nodes' public keys if it trusts the nodes. The signed certificates are kept by nodes in their own certificate repositories instead of being published by centralized directories in the X.509 PKI systems [32].

PGP-A treats trust as transitive, so trust can be derived from a trusted node's trust on another node, that is, if node A trusts node B, and node B trusts node C, then A should also trust C if A knows the fact that node B trusts node C.

To verify a key of a node u, a node j will merge its certificate repository with those of j's trusted nodes, and those of the nodes trusted by j's trusted nodes, and so forth. In this way, node j can build up a web of trust in which node j is at the center of the web and j's directly trusted nodes as node j's neighbors. Node l is linked with node k if node k trusts node l. Node j can search the web of trust built as above to find a path from j to u. If such as path exists, let it be a sequence of nodes S: $node_i$ where $i = 1, ..., n$, n be the length of the path, and $node_1 = j$ and $node_n = u$. This means that $node_i$ trust $node_{i+1}$ for all $i = 1, ..., n − 1$. Therefore u can be trusted by j. The path S represents a verifiable chain of certificates. PGP-A does not guarantee that a node u that should be trusted by node j will always be trusted by node j, since there are chances that the node j fails to find a path from node j to node u in the web of trust. This might be due to the reason that node j has not acquired enough certificates from its trusted nodes to cover the path from node j to node u.

Self-Healing Session Key Distribution

The preceding two key management schemes are public key management schemes. The one discussed here, a self-healing session key distribution [33], is a symmetric key management scheme. In such a scheme, keys can be distributed either by an online key distribution server or by key predistribution. A key predistribution scheme normally comprises the key predistribution phase, the shared-key discovery phase, and the path key establishment phase.

In the key predistribution phase, a key pool of a large number of keys is created. Every key can be identified by a unique key identifier. Each network node is given a set of keys from the key pool. The shared-key discovery phase begins when a node tries to communicate with the others. All nodes exchange their key identifiers to find out whether there are any keys shared with others. The shared keys can then be used to establish a secure channel for communication. If no shared key exists, a key path will need to be discovered. The key path is a sequence of nodes with which all adjacent nodes share a key. With the key path, a message can travel from the first node to the last node securely, by which a secure channel can be established between the first node and the last node.

The self-healing session key distribution (S-HEAL) [34] assumes the existence of a group manager and pre-shared secrets. Keys are distributed from the group manager to group members. Let h be a polynomial, where for a node i, node i knows about $h(i)$. Let K be the group key to be distributed, K is covered by h in the distribution: $f(x) = h(x) + K$. The polynomial $f(x)$ is the information that the group manager sends out to all its group members. For node j, node j will calculate $K = f(j) - h(j)$ to reveal the group key. Without the knowledge of $h(j)$, node j will not be able to recover K.

To enable revocation in S-HEAL, the polynomial $h(x)$ is replaced by a bivariate polynomial $s(x,y)$. The group key is covered by the bivariate polynomial $s(x,y)$ when it is distributed to group members, in the way that $f(N,x) = s(N,x) + K$. Node i must calculate $s(N,i)$ to recover K. The revocation enabled S-HEAL tries to stop revoked nodes to calculate $s(N,i)$, thus preventing them to recover K.

Let s of degree t; then $t + 1$ values are needed to compute $s(x,i)$. Assuming that $s(i,i)$ is predistributed to node i, node i will need another t values to recover $s(N,i)$, namely $s(r_1,x)$, ..., $s(r_t,x)$. These values will be disseminating to group members together with the key update. If the group manager wants to revoke node i, the group manager can set one of the values $s(r_1,x)$, ..., $s(r_t,x)$ to $s(i,x)$. In this case, node i obtains only t values instead of $t + 1$ values. Therefore, node i will not be able to compute $s(x,i)$, thus it will not be able to recover K. This scheme can only revoke maximum t nodes at the same time.

REFERENCES

[1] L. M. S. C. of the IEEE Computer Society. Wireless LAN medium access control (MAC) and physical layer (PHY) specifications, technical report, IEEE Standard 802.11, 1999 ed., 1999.

[2] L. M. S. C. of the IEEE Computer Society. Wireless LAN medium access control (MAC) and physical layer (PHY) specifications, technical report, IEEE Standard 802.11, 1999 ed., 1999.

[3] R.L. Rivest, The RC4 encryption algorithm, RSA Data Security, Inc., March 1992 technical report.

[4] E. Dawson, L. Nielsen, Automated cryptanalysis of XOR plaintext strings, *Cryptologia*, 20 (2), April 1996.

[5] S. Singh, *The code book: the evolution of secrecy from Mary, Queen of Scots, to quantum cryptography*, Doubleday, 1999.

[6] L. M. S. C. of the IEEE Computer Society. Wireless LAN medium access control (MAC) and physical layer (PHY) specifications, technical report, IEEE Standard 802.11, 1999 ed., 1999.

[7] W.A. Arbaugh, An inductive chosen plaintext attack against WEP/WEP2, IEEE Document 802.11-01/230, May 2001.

[8] J.R. Walker, Unsafe at any key size; an analysis of the WEP encapsulation, IEEE Document 802.11-00/362, October 2000.

[9] N. Borisov, I. Goldberg, D. Wagner, Intercepting Mobile Communications: The Insecurity of 802.11, MobiCom 2001.

[10] B. Aboba, L. Blunk, J. Vollbrecht, J. Carlson, E.H. Levkowetz, Extensible Authentication Protocol (EAP), request for comment, Network Working Group, 2004.

[11] A. Perrig, R. Szewczyk, V. Wen, D. Culler, J.D. Tygar, SPINS: Security protocols for sensor networks, MobiCom '01: Proceedings of the 7th annual international conference on Mobile computing and networking, 2001.

[12] A. Perrig, R. Canetti, D. Xiaodong Song, J.D. Tygar, Efficient and secure source authentication for multicast, NDSS 01: Network and Distributed System Security Symposium, 2001.

[13] A. Perrig, J.D. Tygar, D. Song, R. Canetti, Efficient authentication and signing of multicast streams over lossy channels, SP '00: Proceedings of the 2000 IEEE Symposium on Security and Privacy, 2000.

[14] A. Perrig, R. Canetti, J.D. Tygar, D. Song, RSA CryptoBytes, 5, 2002.

[15] Yih-Chun Hu, D.B. Johnson, A. Perrig, SEAD: Secure efficient distance vector routing for mobile wireless ad hoc networks, in: WMCSA '02: Proceedings of the Fourth IEEE Workshop on Mobile Computing Systems and Applications, IEEE Computer Society, Washington, DC, 2002, p. 3.

[16] C.E. Perkins, P. Bhagwat, Highly dynamic destination-sequenced distance-vector routing (DSDV) for mobile computers, SIGCOMM Comput. Commun. Rev. 24 (4), 1994, 234–244.

[17] C.E. Perkins, P. Bhagwat, Highly dynamic destination-sequenced distance-vector routing (DSDV) for mobile computers, SIGCOMM Comput. Commun. Rev. 24 (4) (1994) 234–244.

[18] Yih-Chun Hu, A. Perrig, D. Johnson, Ariadne: a secure on-demand routing protocol for ad hoc networks, *Wireless Networks Journal*, 11, (1), 2005.

[19] D.B. Johnson, D.A. Maltz, Dynamic source routing in ad hoc wireless networks, *Mobile Computing*, Kluwer Academic Publishers, 1996, pp. 153–181.

[20] K. Sanzgiri, B. Dahill, B.N. Levine, C. Shields, E.M. Belding-Royer, A secure routing protocol for ad hoc networks, 10th IEEE International Conference on Network Protocols (ICNP'02), 2002.

[21] P. Papadimitratos, Z.J. Haas, Secure link state routing for mobile ad hoc networks, *saint-w*, 00, 2003.

[22] E. Cayirci, C. Rong, *Security in wireless ad hoc, sensor, and mesh networks*, John Wiley & Sons, 2008.

[23] W. Diffie, M.E. Hellman, New directions in cryptography, *IEEE Transactions on Information Theory*, IT-22 (6), 644–654, 1976.

[24] I. Ingemarsson, D. Tang, C. Wong, A conference key distribution system, *IEEE Transactions on Information Theory*, 28, (5), 714–720, September 1982.

[25] K. Becker, U. Wille, Communication complexity of group key distribution, *ACM conference on computer and communications security*, 1998.

[26] L. Zhou, Z.J. Haas, Securing ad hoc networks, IEEE Network 13, 24–30, 1999.

[27] A. Shamir, How to share a secret, *Comm. ACM*, 22 (11), 1979.

[28] Y. Desmedt, Some recent research aspects of threshold cryptography, *ISW*, 158–173, 1997.

[29] R. Canetti, A. Gennaro, Herzberg, D. Naor, Proactive security: Long-term protection against break-ins, *CryptoBytes* 3 (1), Spring 1997.

[30] S. Capkun, L. Buttyán, J.-P. Hubaux, Self-organized public-key management for mobile ad hoc networks, *IEEE Trans. Mob. Comput.*, 2 (1), 52–64, 2003.

[31] P. Zimmermann, *The Official PGP User's Guide*, The MIT Press, 1995.

[32] ITU-T. Recommendation X.509, ISO/IEC 9594-8, *Information Technology: Open Systems Interconnection–The Directory: Public-key and Attribute Certificate Frameworks, 4th ed.*, 2000, ITU.

[33] J. Staddon, S.K. Miner, M.K. Franklin, D. Balfanz, M. Malkin, D. Dean, Self-healing key distribution with revocation, *IEEE Symposium on Security and Privacy*, 2002.

[34] J. Staddon, S.K. Miner, M.K. Franklin, D. Balfanz, M. Malkin, D. Dean, Self-healing key distribution with revocation, *IEEE Symposium on Security and Privacy*, 2002.

## Chapter 12

Cellular Network Security

Peng Liu
Pennsylvania State University

Thomas F. LaPorta
Pennsylvania State University

Kameswari Kotapati
Pennsylvania State University

In recent years, cellular networks have become open public networks to which end subscribers have direct access. This has greatly increased the threats to the cellular network. Though cellular networks have vastly advanced in their performance abilities, the security of these networks still remains highly outdated. As a result, they are one of the most insecure networks today—so much so that using simple off-the-shelf equipment, any adversary can cause major network outages affecting millions of subscribers.

In this chapter, we address the security of the cellular network. We educate readers on the current state of security of the network and its vulnerabilities. We also outline the cellular network specific attack taxonomy, also called the *three-dimensional attack taxonomy*. We discuss the vulnerability assessment tools for cellular networks. Finally, we provide insights as to why the network is so vulnerable and why securing it can prevent communication outages during emergencies.

1. INTRODUCTION

Cellular networks are high-speed, high-capacity voice and data communication networks with enhanced multimedia and seamless roaming capabilities for supporting cellular devices. With the increase in popularity of cellular devices, these networks are used for more than just entertainment and phone calls. They have become the primary means of communication for finance-sensitive business transactions, lifesaving emergencies, and life-/mission-critical services such as E-911. Today these networks have become the lifeline of communications.

A breakdown in the cellular network has many adverse effects, ranging from huge economic losses due to financial transaction disruptions; loss of life due to loss of phone calls made to emergency workers; and communication outages during emergencies such as the September 11, 2001, attacks. Therefore, it is a high priority for the cellular network to function accurately.

It must be noted that it is not difficult for unscrupulous elements to break into the cellular network and cause outages. The major reason for this is that cellular networks were not designed with security in mind. They evolved from the old-fashioned telephone networks that were built for performance. To this day, the cellular network has numerous well-known and unsecured vulnerabilities providing access to adversaries. Another feature of cellular networks is network relationships (also called *dependencies*) that cause certain types of errors to propagate to other network locations as a result of regular network activity. Such propagation can be very disruptive to the network, and in turn it can affect subscribers. Finally, Internet connectivity to the cellular network is another major contributor to the cellular network's vulnerability because it gives Internet users direct access to cellular network vulnerabilities from their homes.

To ensure that adversaries do not access the network and cause breakdowns, a high level of security must be maintained in the cellular network. However, though great efforts have been made to improve the cellular network in terms of support for new and innovative services, greater number of subscribers, higher speed, and larger bandwidth, very little has been done to update the security of the cellular network. Accordingly, these networks have become highly attractive targets to adversaries, not only because of their lack of security but also due to the ease with which these networks can be exploited to affect millions of subscribers.

In this chapter we analyze the security of cellular networks. Toward understanding the security issues in cellular networks, the rest of the chapter is organized as follows. We present a comprehensive overview of cellular networks with a goal of providing a fundamental understanding of their functioning. Next we present the current state of cellular network security through an in-depth discussion on cellular network vulnerabilities and possible attacks. In addition, we present the cellular network specific attack taxonomy. Finally, we present a review of current cellular network vulnerability assessment techniques and conclude with a discussion.

2. OVERVIEW OF CELLULAR NETWORKS

The current cellular network is an evolution of the early-generation cellular networks that were built for optimal performance. These early-generation cellular networks were proprietary and owned by reputable organizations. They were considered secure due to their proprietary ownership and their *closed nature*, that is, their control infrastructure was unconnected to any public network (such as the Internet) to which end subscribers had direct access. Security was a nonissue in the design of these networks.

Recently, connecting the Internet to the cellular network has not only imported the Internet vulnerabilities to the cellular network, it has also given end subscribers direct access to the control infrastructure of the cellular network, thereby opening the network. Also, with the increasing demand for these networks, a large number of new network operators have come into the picture. Thus, the current cellular environment is no longer a safe, closed network but rather an insecure, open network with many unknown network operators having nonproprietary access to it. Here we present a brief overview of the cellular network architecture.

Overall Cellular Network Architecture

Subscribers gain access to the cellular network via radio signals enabled by the radio access network, as shown in Figure 12.1. The radio access network is connected to the wireline portion of the network, also called the *core network*. Core network functions include servicing subscriber requests and routing traffic. The core network is also connected to the Public Switched Telephone Network (PSTN) and the Internet, as illustrated in Figure 12.1 [1].

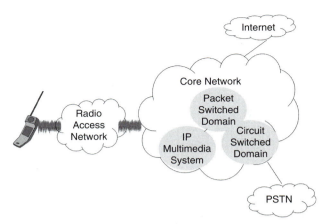

FIGURE 12.1 Cellular network architecture.

The PSTN is the circuit-switched public voice telephone network that is used to deliver voice telephone calls on the *fixed landline telephone network*. The PSTN uses Signaling System No. 7 (SS7), a set of telephony signaling protocols defined by the International Telecommunication Union (ITU) for performing telephony functions such as call delivery, call routing, and billing. The SS7 protocols provide a universal structure for telephony network signaling, messaging, interfacing, and network maintenance. PSTN connectivity to the core network enables mobile subscribers to call fixed network subscribers, and vice versa. In the past, PSTN networks were also closed networks because they were unconnected to other public networks.

The core network is also connected to the Internet. Internet connectivity allows the cellular network to provide innovative multimedia services such as weather reports, stock reports, sports information, chat, and electronic mail. Interworking with the Internet is possible using protocol gateways, federated databases, and multiprotocol mobility managers [2]. Interworking with the Internet has created a new generation of services called *cross-network services*. These are multivendor, multidomain services that use a combination of Internet-based data and data from the cellular network to provide a variety of services to the cellular subscriber. A sample cross-network service is the *Email Based Call Forwarding Service* (CFS), which uses Internet-based email data (in a mail server) to decide on the call-forward number (in a call-forward server) and delivers the call via the cellular network.

From a functional viewpoint, the core network may also be further divided into the circuit-switched (CS) domain, the packet-switched (PS) domain, and the IP Multimedia Subsystem (IMS). In the following, we further discuss the core network organization.

Core Network Organization

Cellular networks are organized as collections of inter-connected *network areas*, where each network area covers a fixed geographical region (as shown in Figure 12.2). Every subscriber is affiliated with two networks: the *home network* and the *visiting network*.

Every subscriber is permanently assigned to the home network, from which they can roam onto other visiting networks. The home network maintains the subscriber profile and current subscriber location. The visiting network is the network where the subscriber is currently roaming. It provides radio resources, mobility management, routing, and services for roaming subscribers. The visiting network provides service capabilities to the subscribers on behalf of the home environment [3].

The core network is facilitated by network servers (also called *service nodes*). Service nodes are composed of (1) a variety of *data sources* (such as cached read-only, updateable, and shared data sources) to store data such as subscriber profile and (2) *service logic* to perform functions such as computing data items, retrieving data items from data sources, and so on.

Service nodes can be of different types, with each type assigned specific functions. The major service node types in the circuit-switched domain include the Home Location Register (HLR), the Visitor Location Register (VLR), the Mobile Switching Center (MSC), and the Gateway Mobile Switching Center (GMSC) [4].

All subscribers are permanently assigned to a fixed HLR located in the home network. The HLR stores permanent subscriber profile data and relevant temporary data such as current subscriber location (pointer to VLR) of all subscribers assigned to it. Each network area is assigned a VLR. The VLR stores temporary data of subscribers currently roaming in its assigned area; this subscriber data is received from the HLR of the subscriber. Every VLR is always associated with an MSC. The MSC acts as an interface between the radio access network and the core network. It also handles circuit-switched services for subscribers currently roaming in its area. The GMSC is in charge of routing the call to the actual location of the mobile station. Specifically, the GMSC acts as interface between the fixed PSTN network and the cellular network. The radio access network comprises a transmitter, receiver, and speech transcoder called the base station (BS) [5].

Service nodes are geographically distributed and service the subscriber through collaborative functioning of various network components. Such collaborative functioning is possible due to the network relationships (called dependencies). A *dependency* means that

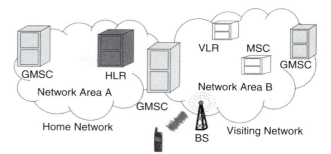

FIGURE 12.2 Core network organization.

a network component must rely on other network components to perform a function. For example, there is a *dependency* between service nodes to service subscribers. Such a dependency is made possible through signaling messages containing data items. Service nodes typically request other service nodes to perform specific operations by sending them signaling messages containing data items with predetermined values. On receiving signaling messages, service nodes realize the operations to perform based on values of data items received in signaling messages. Further, dependencies may exist between data items so that received data items may be used to derive other data items. Several application layer protocols are used for signaling messages. Examples of signaling message protocols include Mobile Application Part (MAP), ISDN User Part (ISUP), and Transaction Capabilities Application Part (TCAP) protocols.

Typically in the cellular network, to provide a specific service a preset group of signaling messages is exchanged between a preset group of service node types. The preset group of signaling messages indicates the operations to be performed at the various service nodes and is called a *signal flow*. In the following, we use the *call delivery service* [6] to illustrate a signal flow and show how the various geographically distributed service nodes function together.

Call Delivery Service

The *call delivery service* is a basic service in the circuit-switched domain. It is used to deliver incoming calls to any subscriber with a mobile device regardless of their location. The signal flow of the call delivery service is illustrated in Figure 12.3. The call delivery service signal flow comprises MAP messages SRI, SRI_ACK, PRN, and PRN_ACK; ISUP message IAM; and TCAP messages SIFIC, Page MS, and Page.

Figure 12.3 illustrates the exchange of signal messages between different network areas. It shows that when

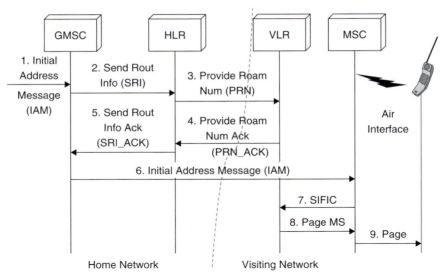

FIGURE 12.3 Signal flow in the call delivery service.

a subscriber makes a call using his mobile device, the call is sent in the form of a signaling message IAM to the nearest GMSC, which is in charge of routing calls and passing voice traffic between different networks. This signaling message IAM contains data items such as *called number* that denotes the mobile phone number of the subscriber receiving this call. The *called number* is used by the GMSC to locate the address of the HLR (home network) of the called party. The GMSC uses this address to send the signaling message SRI.

The SRI message is an intimation to the HLR of the arrival of an incoming call to a subscriber with *called number* as mobile phone number. It contains data items such as the *called number* and *alerting pattern*. The *alerting pattern* denotes the pattern (*packet-switched data, short message service,* or *circuit-switched call*) used to alert the subscriber receiving the call. The HLR uses the *called number* to retrieve from its database the current location (pointer to VLR) of the subscriber receiving the call. The HLR uses this subscriber location to send the VLR the message PRN. The PRN message is a request for call routing information (also called *roaming number*) from the VLR where the subscriber is currently roaming. The PRN message contains the *called number*, *alerting pattern*, and other *subscriber call profile* data items.

The VLR uses the *called number* to store the *alerting pattern* and *subscriber call profile* data items and assign the *roaming number* for routing the call. This *roaming number* data item is passed on to the HLR (in message PRN_ACK), which forwards it to the GMSC (in message SRI_ACK). The GMSC uses this *roaming number* to route the call (message IAM) to the MSC where the subscriber

is currently roaming. On receipt of the message IAM, the MSC assigns the *called number* resources for the call and also requests the *subscriber call profile* data items, and *alerting pattern* for the *called number* (using message SIFIC) from the VLR, and receives the same in the Page MS message. The MSC uses the *alerting pattern* in the incoming call profile to *derive* the *page type* data item. The *page type* data item denotes the manner in which to alert the mobile station. It is used to page the mobile subscriber (using message Page). Thus subscribers receive incoming calls irrespective of their locations in the network.

If data item values are inaccurate, the network can misoperate and subscribers will be affected. Hence, accurate functioning of the network is greatly dependent on the integrity of data item values. Thus signal flows allow the various service nodes to function together, ensuring that the network services its subscribers effectively.

3. THE STATE OF THE ART OF CELLULAR NETWORK SECURITY

This part of the chapter presents the current state of the art of cellular network security. Because the security of the cellular network is the security of each aspect of the network, that is, radio access network, core network, Internet connection, and PSTN connection, we detail the security of each in detail.

Security in the Radio Access Network

The radio access network uses radio signals to connect the subscriber's cellular device with the core wireline network. Hence it would seem that attacks on the radio access network could easily happen because anyone with a transmitter/receiver could capture these signals. This was very true in the case of early-generation cellular networks (first and second generations), where there were no guards against eavesdropping on conversations between the cellular device and BS; cloning of cellular devices to utilize the network resources without paying; and cloning BSs to entice users to camp at the cloned BS in an attack called a *false base station attack*, so that the target user provides secret information to the adversary.

In the current generation (third-generation) cellular network, all these attacks can be prevented because the network provides adequate security measures. Eavesdropping on signals between the cellular device and BS is not possible, because cipher keys are used to encrypt these signals. Likewise, replay attacks on radio signals are voided by the use of nonrepeated random values. Use of integrity keys on radio conversations voids the possibility of deletion and modification of conversations between cellular devices and BSs. By allowing the subscriber to authenticate the network, and vice versa, this generation voids the attacks due to cloned cellular devices and BSs. Finally, as the subscriber's identity is kept confidential by only using a temporary subscriber identifier on the radio network, it is also possible to maintain subscriber location privacy [7].

However, the current generation still cannot prevent a denial-of-service attack from occurring if a large number of registration requests are sent via the radio access network (BS) to the visiting network (MSC). Such a DoS attack is possible because the MSC cannot realize that the registration requests are fake until it attempts to authenticate each request and the request fails. To authenticate each registration request, the MSC must fetch the authentication challenge material from the corresponding HLR. Because the MSC is busy fetching the authentication challenge material, it is kept busy and the genuine registration requests are lost [8]. Overall there is a great improvement in the radio network security in the current third-generation cellular network.

Security in Core Network

Though the current generation network has seen many security improvements in the radio access network, the security of the core network is not as improved. Core network security is the security at the service nodes and security on links (or wireline signaling message) between service nodes.

With respect to wireline signaling message security, of the many wireline signaling message protocols, protection is only provided for the Mobile Application Part (MAP) protocol. The MAP protocol is the cleartext application layer protocol that typically runs on the security-free SS7 protocol or the IP protocol. MAP is an essential protocol and it is primarily used for message exchange involving subscriber location management, authentication, and call handling. The reason that protection is provided for only the MAP protocol is that it carries authentication material and other subscriber-specific confidential data; therefore, its security was considered top priority and was standardized [9–11]. Though protection for other signaling message protocols was also considered important, its was left as an improvement for the next-generation network [12].

Security for the MAP protocol is provided in the form of the newly proposed protocol called Mobile Application Part Security (MAPSec) when MAP runs on the SS7 protocol stack, or Internet Protocol Security (IPSec) when MAP runs on the IP protocol.

Both MAPSec and IPSec, protect MAP messages on the link between service nodes by negotiating security associations. Security associations comprise keys, algorithms, protection profiles, and key lifetimes used to protect the MAP message. Both MAPSec and IPSec protect MAP messages by providing source service node authentication and message encryption to prevent eavesdropping, MAP corruption, and fabrication attacks.

It must be noted that though MAPSec and IPSec are deployed to protect individual MAP messages on the link between service nodes, signaling messages typically occur as a group in a signal flow, and hence signaling messages must be protected not only on the link but also in the intermediate service nodes. Also, the deployment of MAPSec and IPSec is optional; hence if any service provider chooses to omit MAPSec/IPSec's deployment, the efforts of all other providers are wasted. Therefore, to completely protect MAP messages, MAPSec/IPSec must be used by every service provider.

With respect to wireline service nodes, while MAPSec/IPSec protects links between service nodes, there is no standardized method for protecting service nodes [13]. Remote and physical access to service nodes may be subject to operator's security policy and hence could be exploited (insider or outsider) if the network operator is lax with security. Accordingly, the network suffers from the possibility of node impersonation, corruption of data sources, and service logic attacks. For example, unauthorized access to the HLR could deactivate customers or activate customers not seen by the building system. Similarly, unauthorized access to the MSC could cause outages for a large number of users in a given network area.

Corrupt data sources or service logic in service nodes have the added disadvantage of propagating this corruption to other service nodes in the network [14–16] via signaling messages. This fact was recently confirmed by a security evaluation of cellular networks [17] that showed the damage potential of a compromised service node to be much greater than the damage potential of compromised signaling messages. Therefore, it is of utmost importance to standardize a scheme for protecting service nodes in the interest of not only preventing node impersonation attacks but also preventing the corruption from propagating to other service nodes.

In brief, the current generation core network is lacking in security for all types of signaling messages, for MAP signaling messages in service nodes, and a standardized method for protecting service nodes. To protect all types of signaling message protocols and ensure that messages are secured not only on the link between service nodes but also on the intermediate service nodes (that is, secured end to end), and prevent service logic corruption from propagating to other service nodes, the End-to-End Security (EndSec) protocol was proposed [18].

Because signaling message security essentially depends on security of data item values contained in these messages, EndSec focuses on securing data items. EndSec requires every data item to be signed by its source service nodes using public key encryption. By requiring signatures, if data items are corrupt by compromised intermediate service nodes en route, the compromised status of the service node is revealed to the service nodes receiving the corrupt data items. Revealing the compromised status of service nodes prevents corruption from propagating to other service nodes, because service nodes are unlikely to accept corrupt data items from compromised service nodes.

EndSec also prevents misrouting and node impersonation attacks by requiring every service node in a signal flow to embed the PATH taken by the signal flow in every EndSec message. Finally, EndSec introduces several control messages to handle and correct the detected corruption. Note that EndSec is not a standardized protocol.

Security Implications of Internet Connectivity

Internet connectivity introduces the biggest threat to the security of the cellular network. This is because cheap PC-based equipment with Internet connectivity can now access gateways connecting to the core network. Therefore, any attack possible in the Internet can now filter into the core cellular network via these gateways. For example, Internet connectivity was the reason for the slammer worm to filter into the E-911 service in Bellevue, Washington, making it completely unresponsive [19]. Other attacks that can filter into the core network from the Internet include spamming and phishing of short messages [20].

We expect low-bandwidth DoS attacks to be the most damaging attacks brought on by Internet connectivity [21–23]. These attacks demonstrate that by sending just 240 short messages per second, it is possible to saturate the cellular network and cause the MSC in charge of the region to be flooded and lose legitimate short messages per second. Likewise, it shows that it is possible to cause a specific user to lose short messages by flooding that user with a large number of messages, causing a buffer overflow. Such DoS attacks are possible because the short message delivery time in the cellular network is much greater than the short message submission time using Internet sites [24].

Also, short messages and voices services use the same radio channel, so contention for these limited resources may still occur and cause a loss of voice service. To avoid loss of voice services due to contention, separation of voice and data services on the radio network has been suggested [16]. However, such separation requires major standardization and overhaul of the network and is therefore unlikely be implemented very soon. Other minor techniques such as queue management and resource provisioning have been suggested [25].

Though such solutions could reduce the impact of short message flooding, they cannot eliminate other types of low-bandwidth, DoS attacks such as attacks on connection setup and teardown of data services. The root cause for such DoS attacks from the Internet to the core network was identified as the difference in the design principles of these networks. Though the Internet makes no assumptions on the content of traffic and simply passes it on to the next node, the cellular network identifies the traffic content and provides a highly tailored service involving multiple service nodes for each type of traffic [26].

Until this gap is bridged, such attacks will continue, but bridging the gap itself is a major process because either the design of the cellular network must be changed to match the Internet design, or vice versa, which is unlikely to happen soon. Hence a temporary fix would be to secure the gateways connecting the Internet and core network. As a last note, Internet connectivity filters attacks not only into the core network, but also into the PSTN network. Hence PSTN gateways must also be guarded.

Security Implications of PSTN Connectivity

PSTN connectivity to the cellular network allows calls between the fixed and cellular networks. Though the PSTN was a closed network, the security-free SS7 protocol stack on which it is based was of no consequence. However, by connecting the PSTN to the core network that is in turn connected to the Internet, the largest open public network, the SS7-based PSTN network has "no security left" [27].

Because SS7 protocols are plaintext and have no authentication features, it is possible to introduce fake messages, eavesdrop, cause DoS by traffic overload, and incorrectly route signaling messages. Such introduction of SS7 messages into the PSTN network is very easily done using cheap PC-based equipment. Attacks in which calls for 800 and 900 numbers were rerouted to 911 servers so that legitimate calls were lost are documented [28]. Such attacks are more so possible due to the IP interface of the PSTN service nodes and Web-based control of these networks.

Because PSTN networks are to be outdated soon, there is no interest in updating these networks. So, they will remain "security free" until their usage is stopped [29].

So far, we have addressed the security and attacks on each aspect of the cellular network. But an attack that is common to all the aspects of the cellular network is the *cascading attack*. Next we detail the cascading attack and present vulnerability assessment techniques to identify the same.

4. CELLULAR NETWORK ATTACK TAXONOMY

In this part of the chapter, we present the cellular network specific attack taxonomy. This attack taxonomy is called the *three-dimensional taxonomy* because attacks are classified based on the following three dimensions: (1) adversary's physical access to the network when the attack is launched; (2) type of attack launched; and (3) vulnerability exploited to launch the attack.

The three-dimensional attack taxonomy was motivated by the *cellular network specific abstract model*, which is an atomic model of cellular network service nodes. It enabled better study of interactions within the cellular network and aided in derivation of several insightful characteristics of attacks on the cellular network.

The abstract model not only led to the development of the three-dimensional attack taxonomy that has been instrumental in uncovering (1) *cascading attacks*, a type of attack in which the adversary targets a specific network location but attacks another location, which in turn propagates the attack to the target location, and (2) *cross-infrastructure cyber attack*, a new breed of attack

in which the cellular network may be attacked from the Internet [30]. In this part of the chapter we further detail the three-dimensional attack taxonomy and cellular network abstract model.

Abstract Model

The abstract model dissects functionality of the cellular network to the basic atomic level, allowing it to systematically isolate and identify vulnerabilities. Such identification of vulnerabilities allows attack classification based on vulnerabilities, and isolation of network functionality aids in extraction of interactions between network components, thereby revealing new vulnerabilities and attack characteristics.

Because service nodes in the cellular network comprise sophisticated *service logic* that performs numerous network functions, the abstract model logically divides the service logic into basic atomic units, called *agents* (represented by the elliptical shape in Figure 12.4). Each agent performs a single function. Service nodes also manage data, so the abstract model also logically divides data sources into data units specific to the agents they support. The abstract model also divides the data sources into *permanent* (represented by the rectangular shape in Figure 12.4) or *cached* (represented by the triangular shape in Figure 12.4) from other service nodes.

The abstract model developed for the CS domain is illustrated in Figure 12.4. It shows agents, permanent, and cached data sources for the CS service nodes. For example, the *subscriber locator agent* in the HLR is the agent that tracks the subscriber location information. It receives and responds to location requests during an incoming call and stores a subscriber's location every time they move. This location information is stored in the *location data source*. Readers interested in further details may refer to [31,32].

Abstract Model Findings

The abstract model had lead to many interesting findings. We outline them as follows:

Interactions

To study the network interactions, service nodes in signal flows (e.g. call delivery service) were replaced by their corresponding abstract model agents and data sources. Such an abstract-model–based signal flow based on the call delivery service is shown in Figure 12.5.

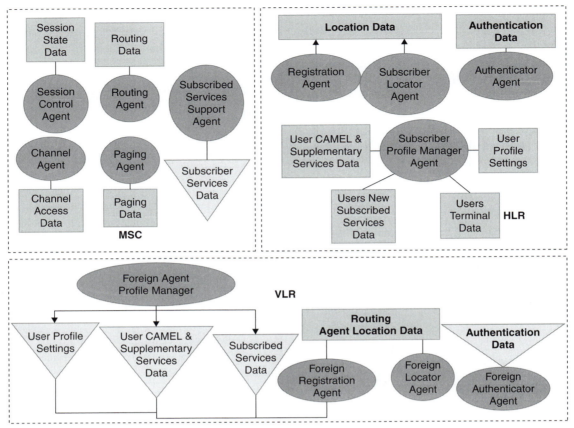

FIGURE 12.4 Abstract model of circuit-switched service nodes.

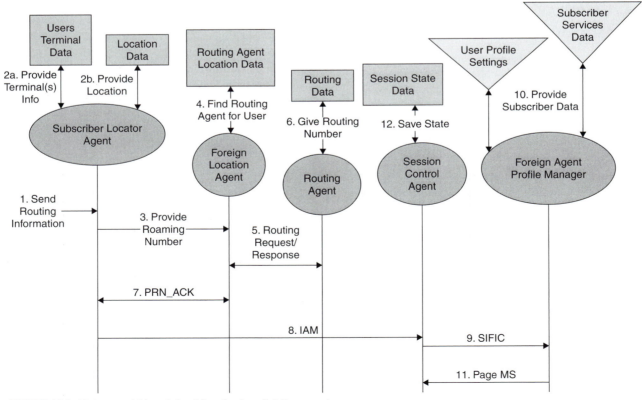

FIGURE 12.5 Abstract model-based signal flow for the call delivery service.

In studying the abstract model signal flow, it was observed that interactions happen (1) between agents typically using procedure calls containing data items; (2) between agents and data sources using queries containing data items; and (3) between agents belonging to different service nodes using signaling messages containing data items.

The common behavior in all these interactions is that they typically involve *data items* whose values are set or modified in agents or data source, or it involves data items passed between agents, data sources, or agents and data sources. Hence, the value of a data item not only can be corrupt in an agent or data source, it can also be easily passed on to other agents, resulting in propagation of corruption. This propagation of corruption is called the *cascading effect*, and attacks that exhibit this effect are called *cascading attacks*. In the following, we present a sample of the cascading attack.

Sample Cascading Attack

In this sample cascading attack, cascading due to corrupt data items and ultimately their service disruption are illustrated in Figure 12.6. Consider the call delivery service explained previously. Here the adversary may corrupt the *roaming number* data item (used to route the call) in the VLR. This corrupt *roaming number* is passed on in message PRN_ACK to the HLR, which in turn passes this information to the GMSC. The GMSC uses the incorrect *roaming number* to route the call to the incorrect MSC$_B$, instead of the correct MSC$_A$. This results in the caller

losing the call or receiving a wrong-number call. Thus corruption cascades and results in service disruption.

The type of corruption that can cascade is *system-acceptable incorrect value corruption*, a type of corruption in which corrupt values taken on system-acceptable values, albeit incorrect values. Such a corruption can cause the roaming number to be incorrect but a system-acceptable value.

Note that it is easy to cause such system-acceptable incorrect value corruption due to the availability of Web sites that refer to proprietary working manuals of service nodes such as the VLR [33,34]. Such command insertion attacks have become highly commonplace, the most infamous being the telephone tapping of the Greek government and top-ranking civil servants [35].

Cross-Infrastructure Cyber Cascading Attacks

When cascading attacks cross into the cellular networks from the Internet through *cross-network services*, they're called *cross-infrastructure cyber cascading attacks*. This attack is illustrated on the CFS in Figure 12.7.

As the CFS forwards calls based on the emails received, corruption is shown to propagate from the mail server to a call-forward (CF) server and finally to the MSC. In the attack, using any standard mail server vulnerabilities, the adversary may compromise the mail server and corrupt the email data source by deleting emails from people the victim is expecting to call. The CF server receives and caches incorrect email from the mail server.

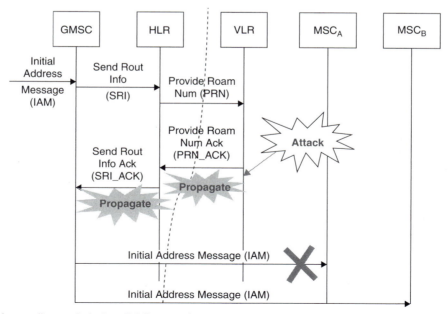

FIGURE 12.6 Sample cascading attacks in the call delivery service.

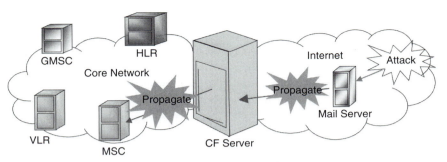

FIGURE 12.7 Cross-infrastructure cyber cascading attacks on call-forward service.

When calls arrive for the subscriber, the call-forwarding service is triggered, and the MSC queries the CF server on how to forward the call. The CF server checks its incorrect email cache, and because there are no emails from the caller, it responds to the MSC to forward the call to the victim's voicemail when in reality the call should have been forwarded to the cellular device. Thus the effect of the attack on the mail server propagates to the cellular network service node. This is a classic example of a cross-infrastructure cyber cascading attack, whereby the adversary gains access to the cross-network server, and attacks by modifying data in the data source of the cross-network server.

Note that it has become highly simplified to launch such attacks due to easy accessibility to the Internet and subscriber preference for Internet-based cross-network services.

Isolating Vulnerabilities

From the abstract model, the major network components that are vulnerable to adversaries are (1) data sources; (2) agents (more generally called service logic); and (3) signaling messages. By exploiting each of these vulnerabilities, data items that are crucial to the correct working of the network can be corrupted, leading to ultimate service disruption through cascading effects.

In addition, the effect of corrupt signaling messages is different from the effect of corrupt data sources. By corrupting data items in a data source of a service node, all the subscribers attached to this service node may be affected. However, by corrupting a signaling message, only the subscribers (such as the caller and called party in case of call delivery service) associated with the message are affected. Likewise, corrupting the agent in the service node can affect all subscribers using the agent in the service node. Hence, in the three-dimensional taxonomy, a vulnerability exploited is considered as an attack dimension, since the effect on each vulnerability is different.

Likewise, the adversary's physical access to the network also affects how the vulnerability is exploited and

how the attack cascades. For example, consider the case when a subscriber has access to the air interface. The adversary can only affect messages on the air interface. Similarly, if the adversary has access to a service node, the data sources and service logic may be corrupted. Hence, in the three-dimensional taxonomy, the physical access is considered a category as it affects how the vulnerability is exploited and its ultimate effect on the subscriber.

Finally, the way the adversary chooses to launch an attack ultimately affects the service in a different way. Consider a passive attack such as *interception*. Here the service is not affected, but it can have a later effect on the subscriber, such as identity theft or loss of privacy. An active attack such as *interruption* can cause complete service disruption. Hence, in the three-dimensional taxonomy, the attack means are considered a category due the ultimate effect on service.

In the next part of the chapter, we detail the cellular network specific three-dimensional taxonomy and the way the previously mentioned dimensions are incorporated.

Three-Dimensional Attack Taxonomy

The three dimensions in the taxonomy include Dimension I: Physical Access to the Network, Dimension II: Attack Categories, and Dimension III: Vulnerability Exploited. In the following, we outline each dimension.

Dimension I: Physical Access to the Network

In this dimension, attacks are classified based on the adversary's level of physical access to the cellular network. Dimension I may be further classified into *single infrastructure attacks* (Level I–III) and *cross-infrastructure cyber attacks* (Level IV–V):

Level I: Access to air interface with physical device. Here the adversary launches attacks via access to the radio access network using standard inexpensive "off-the-shelf" equipment [36]. Attacks include false base station attacks, eavesdropping, and man-in-the-middle attacks and correspond to attacks previously mentioned.

Level II: Access to links connecting core service nodes. Here the adversary has access to links connecting to core service nodes. Attacks include disrupting normal transmission of signaling messages and correspond to message corruption attacks previously mentioned.

Level III: Access core service nodes. In this case, the adversary could be an insider who managed to gain physical access to core service nodes. Attacks include editing the service logic or modifying data sources, such as subscriber data (profile, security and services) stored in the service node and corresponding to corrupt service logic, data source, and node impersonation attacks previously mentioned.

Level IV: Access to links connecting the Internet and the core network service nodes. This is a cross-infrastructure cyber attack. Here the adversary has access to links connecting the core network and Internet service nodes. Attacks include editing and deleting signaling messages between the two networks. This level of attack is easier to achieve than Level II.

Level V: Access to Internet servers or cross-network servers: This is a cross-infrastructure cyber attack. Here the adversary can cause damage by editing the service logic or modifying subscriber data (profile, security and services) stored in the cross-network servers. Such an attack was previously outlined earlier in the chapter. This level of attack is easier to achieve than Level III.

Dimension II: Attack Type

In this dimension, attacks are classified based on the type of attack. The attack categories are based on Stallings [37]:

Interception. The adversary intercepts signaling messages on a cable (Level II) but does not modify or delete them. This is a passive attack. This affects the privacy of the subscriber and the network operator. The adversary may use the data obtained from interception to analyze traffic and eliminate the competition provided by the network operator.

Fabrication or replay. In this case, the adversary inserts spurious messages, data, or service logic into the system, depending on the level of physical access. For example, in a Level II, the adversary inserts fake signaling messages, and in a Level III, the adversary inserts fake service logic or fake subscriber data into this system.

Modification of resources. Here the adversary modifies data, messages, or service logic. For example, in a Level II, the adversary modifies signaling messages on the link, and in a Level III, the adversary modifies service logic or data.

Denial of service. In this case, the adversary takes actions to overload the network results in legitimate subscribers not receiving service.

Interruption. Here the adversary causes an interruption by destroying data, messages, or service logic.

Dimension III: Vulnerability Exploited

In this dimension, attacks are classified based on the vulnerability exploited to cause the attack. Vulnerabilities exploited are explained as follows:

Data. The adversary attacks the data stored in the system. Damage is inflicted by modifying, inserting, and deleting the data stored in the system.

Messages. The adversary adds, modifies, deletes, or replays signaling messages.

Service logic. Here the adversary inflicts damage by attacking the service logic running in the various cellular core network service nodes.

Attack classification. In classifying attacks, we can group them according to *Case 1: Dimension I versus Dimension II*, and *Case 2: Dimension II versus Dimension III*. Note that the Dimension I versus Dimension III case can be transitively inferred from Case 1 and Case 2.

Table 12.1 shows a sample tabulation of Level 1 attacks grouped in Case 1. For example, with Level 1 access an adversary causes interception attacks by observing traffic and eavesdropping. Likewise, fabrication attacks due to Level I include sending spurious registration messages. Modification of resources due to Level 1 includes modifying conversations in the radio access network. DoS due to Level 1 occurs when a large number of fake registration messages are sent to keep the network busy so as to not provide service to legitimate subscribers. Finally, interruption attacks due to Level 1 occur when adversaries jam the radio access channel so that legitimate subscribers cannot access the network. For further details on attack categories, refer to [38].

5. CELLULAR NETWORK VULNERABILITY ANALYSIS

Regardless of how attacks are launched, if attack actions cause a system-acceptable incorrect value corruption, the corruption propagates, leading to many unexpected cascading effects. To detect remote cascading effects and identify the origin of cascading attacks, cellular network vulnerability assessment tools were developed.

These tools, the *Cellular Network Vulnerability Assessment Toolkit* (CAT) and the *advanced Cellular*

TABLE 12.1 Sample Case 1 Classification

	Interception	Fabrication/Insertion	Modification of Resources	Denial of Service	Interruption
Level I	• Observe time, rate, length, source, and destination of victim's locations. • With modified cellular devices, eavesdrop on victim.	• Using modified cellular devices, the adversary can send spurious registration messages to the target network. • Likewise, using modified base stations, the adversary can signal victims to camp at their locations.	• With a modified base station and cellular devices, the adversary modifies conversations between subscribers and their base stations.	• The adversary can cause DoS by sending a large number of fake registration messages.	• Jam victims' traffic channels so that victims cannot access the channels. • Broadcast at a higher intensity than allowed, thereby hogging the bandwidth.

Network Vulnerability Assessment Toolkit (aCAT) [39,40] allow users to input the data item that might be corrupted and output an attack graph. The CAT attack graph not only shows the network location and the network service where the corruption might originate, it also shows the various messages and service nodes through which the corruption propagates.

An attack graph is a diagrammatic representation of an attack on a real system. It shows various ways an adversary can break into a system or cause corruption and the various ways in which the corruption may propagate within the system. Attack graphs are typically produced manually by red teams and used by systems administrators for protection. CAT and aCAT attack graphs allow users to trace the effect of an attack through the network and determine its side effects, thereby making them the ultimate service disruption.

The cellular network is at the nascent stage of development with respect to security, so it is necessary to evaluate security protocols before deploying them. Hence, aCAT can be extended with security protocol evaluation capabilities into a tool [41] called *Cellular Network Vulnerability Assessment Toolkit for evaluation* (eCAT). eCAT allows users to quantify the benefits of security solutions by removing attack effects from attack graphs based on the defenses provided. One major advantage of this approach is that solutions may be evaluated before expensive development and deployment.

It must be noted that developing such tools—CAT, aCAT, and eCAT—presented many challenges: (1) cellular networks are extremely complex systems; they comprise several types of service nodes and control protocols, contain hundreds of data elements, and support

hundreds of services; hence developing such toolkits requires in-depth working knowledge of these systems; and (2) every deployment of the cellular network comprises a different physical configuration; toolkits must be immune to the diversity in physical configuration; and finally (3) attacks cascade in the network due to regular network activity as a result of dependencies; toolkits must be able to track the way that corruption cascades due to network dependencies.

The challenge of in-depth cellular network knowledge was overcome by incorporating the toolkits with cellular network specifications defined by the Third Generation Partnership Project (3GPP) and is available at no charge [42]. The 3GPP is a telecommunications standards body formed to produce, maintain, and develop globally applicable "technical specifications and technical reports" for a third-generation mobile system based on evolved GSM core networks and the radio access technologies that they support [43].

Usage of specifications allows handling of the diversity of physical configuration, as they detail the functional behavior and not the implementation structure of the cellular network. Specifications are written using simple flow-like diagrams called the Specification and Description Language (SDL) [44], and are referred to as *SDL specifications*. Equipment and service providers use these SDL specifications as the basis for their service implementations.

Corruption propagation is tracked by incorporating the toolkits with novel dependency and propagation models to trace the propagation of corruption. Finally, Boolean properties are superimposed on the propagation model to capture the impact of security solutions.

CAT is the first version of the toolkit developed for cellular network vulnerability assessment. CAT works by taking user input of *seeds* (data items directly corrupted by the adversary and the cascading effect of which leads to a goal) and *goals* (data parameters that are derived incorrectly due to the direct corruption of seeds by the adversary) and uses SDL specification to identify cascading attacks. However, SDL is limited in its expression of relationships and inexplicit in its assumptions and hence cannot capture all the dependencies; therefore CAT misses several cascading attacks.

To detect a complete set of cascading effects, CAT was enhanced with new features, to aCAT. The new features added to aCAT include (1) a network dependency model that explicitly specifies the exact dependencies in the network; (2) infection propagation rules that identify the reasons that cause corruption to cascade; and (3) a small amount of expert knowledge. The network dependency model and infection propagation rules may be applied to SDL specifications and help alleviate their limited expression capability. The expert knowledge helps capture the inexplicit assumptions made by SDL.

In applying these features, aCAT captures all those dependencies that were previously unknown to CAT, and thereby aCAT was able to detect a complete set of cascading effects. Through extensive testing of aCAT, several interesting attacks were found and the areas where SDL is lacking was identified.

To enable evaluation of new security protocols, aCAT was extended to eCAT. eCAT uses Boolean probabilities in attack graphs to detect whether a given security protocol can eliminate a certain cascading effect. Given a security protocol, eCAT can measure effective coverage, identify the types of required security mechanisms to protect the network, and identify the most vulnerable network areas. eCAT was also used to evaluate MAPSec, the new standardized cellular network security protocol. Results from MAPSec's evaluation gave insights into MAPSec's performance and the network's vulnerabilities. In the following, we detail each toolkit.

Cellular Network Vulnerability Assessment Toolkit (CAT)

In this part of the chapter, we present an overview of CAT and its many features. CAT is implemented using the Java programming language. It is made up of a number of subsystems (as shown in Figure 12.8). The *knowledge base* contains the cellular network knowledge obtained from SDL specifications. SDL specifications contain simple flowchart-like diagrams. The flowcharts

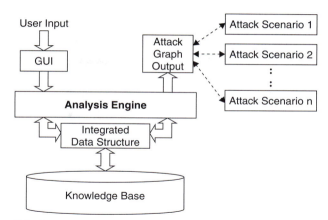

FIGURE 12.8 Architecture of CAT.

are converted into data in the *knowledge base*. The *integrated data structure* is similar to that of the knowledge base; it holds intermediate attack graph results.

The GUI subsystem takes user input in the form of seeds and goals. The analysis engine contains algorithms (forward and midpoint) incorporated with cascading effect detection rules. It explores the possibility of the user input *seed* leading to the cascading effect of the user input *goal*, using the knowledge base, and outputs the cascading attack in the form of attack graphs.

Using these attack graphs, realistic attack scenarios may be derived. Attack scenarios explain the effect of the attack on the subscriber in a realistic setting. Each attack graph may have multiple interpretations and give rise to multiple scenarios. Each scenario gives a different perspective on how the attack may affect the subscriber:

- *Cascading effect detection rules.* These rules were defined to extract cascading effects from the SDL specifications contained in the knowledge base. They are incorporated into the algorithms in the analysis engine. These rules define what constitutes propagation of corruption from a signaling message to a block, and vice versa, and propagation of corruption within a service node. For example, when a service node receives a signaling message with a corrupt data item and stores the data item, it constitutes propagation of corruption from a signaling message to a block. Note that these rules are high level.
- *Attack graph.* The CAT attack graph may be defined as a state transition showing the paths through a system, starting with the conditions of the attack, followed by attack action, and ending with its cascading effects.

In Figure 12.9, we present the CAT attack graph output, which was built using user input of *ISDN Bearer Capability* as a seed and *Bearer Service* as goal. The

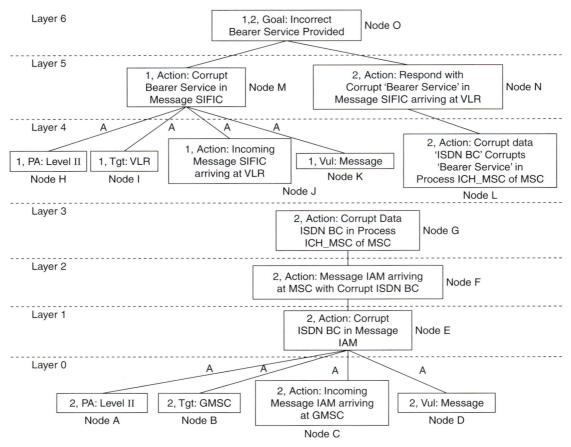

FIGURE 12.9 CAT attack graph output.

attack graph constitutes nodes and edges. Nodes represent states in the network with respect to the attack, and *edges* represent network state transitions. For description purposes, each node has been given a node label followed by an alphabet, and the attack graph has been divided into layers.

Nodes may be broadly classified as *conditions, actions,* and *goals,* with the conditions of the attack occurring at the lowest layer and the final cascading effect at the highest layer. In the following, we detail each node type:

- *Condition nodes.* Nodes at the lowest layer typically correspond to the conditions that must exist for the attack to occur. These condition nodes directly follow from the taxonomy. They are an adversary's physical access, target service node, and vulnerability exploited. For example, the adversary has access to links connecting to the GMSC service node, that is, Level II physical access; this is represented as Node A in the attack graph. Likewise, the adversary corrupts data item ISDN Bearer Capability in the IAM message arriving at the GMSC. Hence the target of

the attack is the GMSC and is represented by Node B. Similarly, the adversary exploits vulnerabilities in a message (IAM), and this is represented by Node D in the attack graph.

The CAT attack graphs show all the possible conditions for an attack to happen, that is, we see not only the corruption due to the seed ISDN Bearer Capability in signaling message IAM arriving at the GMSC but also other possibilities such as the corruption of goal Bearer Service in signaling message SIFIC, represented by Node M.

- *Action nodes.* Nodes at higher layers are actions that typically correspond to effects of the attack propagating through the network. Effects typically include propagation of corruption between service nodes, such as from MSC to VLR (Node N), propagation of corruption within service nodes such as ISDN Bearer Capability corrupting Bearer Service (Node L), and so on. Actions may further be classified as adversary actions, normal network operations, or normal subscriber activities. Adversary actions include insertion, corruption, or deletion of data, signaling messages, or service logic represented by Node E. Normal network operations include sending (Node N) and receiving signaling messages (Node E). Subscriber activity may include updating personal data or initiating service.

- *Goal nodes.* Goal nodes typically occur at the highest layer of the attack graph. They indicate corruption of the goal items due to the direct corruption of seeds by the adversary (Node A).

- *Edges.* In our graph, edges represent network transitions due to both normal network actions and adversary actions. Edges help show the global network view of adversary action. This is the uniqueness of our attack graph. Transitions due to adversary action are indicated by an edge marked by the letter A (edges connecting Layer 0 and Layer 1). By inclusion of normal network transitions in addition to the transitions caused by the adversary, our attack graph shows not only the adversary's activity but also the *global network view of the adversary's action.* This is a unique feature of the attack graph.

- *Trees.* In the graph, trees are distinguished by the tree numbers assigned to its nodes. For example, all the nodes marked with number 2 belong to Tree 2 of the graph. Some nodes in the graph belong to multiple trees. Tree numbers are used to distinguish between AND and OR nodes in the graph. Nodes at a particular layer with the same tree number(s) are AND nodes. For example, at Layer 4, Nodes H, I, J, and K are AND nodes; they all must occur for Node M at Layer 5 to occur. Multiple tree numbers on a node are called OR nodes. The OR node may be arrived at using alternate ways. For example, Node O at Layer 6 is an OR node, the network state indicated by Node O may be arrived at from Node M or Node N.

Each attack tree shows the attack effects due to corruption of a seed at a specific network location (such as signaling message or process in a block). For example, Tree 1 shows the attack due to the corruption of the seed Bearer Service at the VLR. Tree 2 shows the propagation of the seed ISDN Bearer Capability in the signaling message IAM. These trees show that the vulnerability of the cellular network is not limited to one place but can be realized due to the corruption of data in many network locations.

In constructing the attack graph, CAT assumes that an adversary has all the necessary conditions for launching the attack. The CAT attack graph format is well suited to cellular networks because data propagates through the network in various forms during the normal operation of a network; thus an attack that corrupts a data item manifests itself as the corruption of a different data item in a different part of the network after some network operations take place.

- Attack scenario derivation. The CAT attack graph is in cellular network semantics, and realistic attack scenarios may be derived to understand the implications of the attack graph. Here we detail the principles involved in the derivation of realistic attack scenarios:

  1. *End-user effect.* Goal node(s) are used to infer the end effect of the attack on the subscriber. According to the goal node in Figure 12.9, the SIFIC message to the VLR has incorrect goal item Bearer Service. The SIFIC message is used to inform the VLR the calling party's preferences such as voice channel requirements and request the VLR to set up the call based on the calling party and receiving party preferences.

     If the calling party's preferences (such as Bearer Service) are incorrect, the call setup by the VLR is incompatible with the calling party, and the communication is ineffective (garbled speech). From the goal node, it can be inferred that Alice, the receiver of the call, is unable to communicate effectively with Bob, the caller, because Alice can only hear garbled speech from Bob's side.

  2. *Origin of attack.* Nodes at Layer 0 indicate the origin of the attack, and hence the location of the attack may be inferred. The speech attack may originate at the signaling messages IAM, or the VLR service node.

  3. *Attack propagation and side effects.* Nodes at all other layers show the propagation of corruption across the various service nodes in the network. From other layers in Figure 12.9, it can be inferred that the seed is the ISDN Bearer Capability and the attack spreads from the MSC to the VLR.

- Attack Scenario: Using these guidelines, an attack scenario may be derived as follows. Trudy, the adversary, corrupts the ISDN Bearer Capability of Bob, the victim, at the IAM message arriving at the GMSC. The GMSC propagates this corruption to the MSC, which computes, and hence corrupts, the Bearer Service. The corrupt Bearer Service is passed on to the VLR, which sets up the call between Bob, the caller, and Alice, the receiver. Bob and Alice cannot communicate effectively because Alice is unable to understand Bob.

Though CAT has detected several cascading attacks, its output to a great extent depends on SDL's ability to capture data dependencies. SDL is limited in its expression capability in the sense that it does not always accurately capture the relationship between data items, and in many cases, SDL does even specify the relationship. Without these details CAT may miss some cascading effects due to loss of data relationships. CAT's output to a minor extent also depends on user input in the sense that to accurately capture all the cascading effect of a seed, the user's input must comprise all the seeds that can occur in the cascading effect; otherwise the exact cascading effect is not captured. To alleviate CAT's inadequacies, aCAT was developed.

Advanced Cellular Network Vulnerability Assessment Toolkit (aCAT)

In this part of the chapter, we present aCAT, an extension of CAT with enhanced features. These enhanced features include (1) incorporating expert knowledge to compensate for the lacking caused by SDL's inexplicit assumptions; expert knowledge added to the knowledge base with the SDL specifications; (2) defining a network dependency model that accurately captures the dependencies in the cellular network; the network dependency model is used to format the data in knowledge base,

thereby clarifying the nature of the network dependency; and (3) defining infection propagation rules that define fine-grained rules to detect cascading attacks; these infection propagation rules are incorporated into the analysis engine, which comprises the forward, reverse, and combinatory algorithms. aCAT is also improved in terms of its user input requirements. It requires as input either seeds or goals, whereas CAT required both seeds and goals.

In principle, cascading attacks are the result of propagation of corruption between network components (such as signaling messages, caches, local variables, and service logic) due to dependencies that exist between these network components. Hence, to uncover these attacks, the network dependency model and infection propagation (IP) rules were defined. In the following, we detail the network dependency model and infection propagation model using Figure 12.10.

- *Network dependency model.* The network dependency model accurately defines fine-grained dependencies between the various network components. Given that service nodes comprise agents and data sources (from the abstract model), the dependencies are defined as follows. In interagent dependency, agents communicate with each other using agent

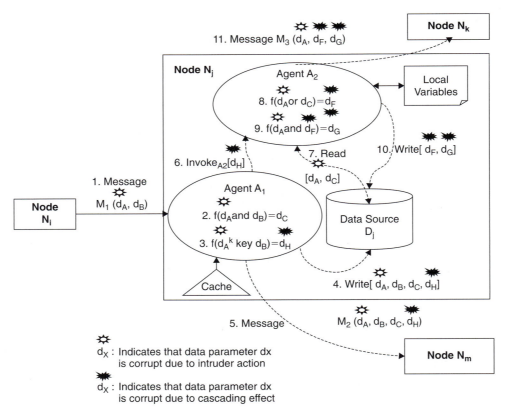

FIGURE 12.10 Network dependency model.

invocations (as shown by 6 in Figure 12.10) containing data items. Thus, agents are related to each other through data items. Likewise, in agent to data source dependency, agents communicate with data sources using Read and Write operations containing data items. Therefore, agents and data items are related to each other through data items. Within agents, derivative dependencies define relationships between data items. Here data items are used as input to derive data items using derivation operations such as AND, OR operations. Therefore, data items are related to each other through derivation operation. For further detail on the network dependency model, refer to [45].

- *Infection propagation (IP) rules.* These are fine-grained rules to detect cascading effects. They are incorporated into the algorithms in the analysis engine. An example of the IP rule is that an output data item in the AND dependency is corrupt only if both the input data items are corrupt (as shown by 9 in Figure 12.10). Likewise, an output data item in the OR dependency is corrupt if a single input data item is corrupt (as shown by 8 in Figure 12.10). Similarly, corruption propagates between agents when the data item used to invoke the agent is corrupt, and the same data item is used as an input in the derivative dependency whose output may be corrupt (as shown by 6, 8 in Figure 12.10). Accordingly, corruption propagates from an agent to a data source if the data item written to the data source is corrupt (as shown by 4 in Figure 12.10). Finally, corruption propagates between service nodes if a data item used in the signaling message between the service nodes is corrupt, and the corrupt data item is used to derive corrupt output items or the corrupt data item is stored in the data source (as shown by 1, 3 or 1, 4 in Figure 12.10) [46].

With such a fine-grained dependency model and infection propagation rules, aCAT was very successful in identifying cascading attacks in several of the key services offered by the cellular network, and it was found that aCAT can indeed identify a better set of cascading effects in comparison to CAT. aCAT has also detected several interesting and unforeseen cascading attacks that are subtle and difficult to identify by other means. These newly identified cascading attacks include the alerting attack, power-off/power-on attack, mixed identity attack, call redirection attack, and missed calls attack.

- *Alerting attack.* In the following we detail aCAT's output, a cascading attack called the *alerting attack,* shown in Figure 12.11. From goal nodes (Node A at Level 5, and Node C at Level 4) in the alerting attack, it can be inferred that the Page message has

incorrect data item *page type.* The Page message is used to inform subscribers of the arrival of incoming calls, and "page type" indicates the type of call. "Page type" must be compatible with the subscriber's mobile station or else the subscriber is not alerted. From the goal node it may be inferred that Alice, a subscriber of the system, is not alerted on the arrival of an incoming call and hence does not receive incoming calls. This attack is subtle to detect because network administrators find that the network processes the incoming call correctly and that the subscriber is alerted correctly. They might not find that this alerting pattern is incompatible with the mobile station itself.

Also, nodes at Level 0 indicate the origin of the attack as signaling messages SRI, PRN, the service nodes VLR, or the HLR. From the other levels it may be inferred that the seed is the *alerting pattern* that the adversary corrupts in the SRI message and the attack spreads from the HLR to the VLR and from the VLR to the MSC. For more details on these attacks, refer to [47].

Cellular Network Vulnerability Assessment Toolkit for evaluation (eCAT)

In this part of the chapter, we present eCAT an extension to aCAT. eCAT was developed to evaluate new security protocols before their deployment. Though the design goals and threat model of these security protocols are common knowledge, eCAT was designed to find (1) the effective protection coverage of these security protocols in terms of percentage of attacks prevented; (2) the other kinds of security schemes required to tackle the attacks that can evade the security protocol under observation; and (3) the most vulnerable network areas (also called *hotspots*) [48].

eCAT computes security protocol coverage using attack graphs generated by aCAT and Boolean probabilities in a process called *attack graph marking* and quantifies the coverage using *coverage measurement formulas* (CMF). Attack graph marking also identifies network hotspots and exposes if the security protocol being evaluated protects these hotspots. eCAT was also used to evaluate MAPSec, as it is a relatively new protocol, and evaluation results would aid network operators.

- *Boolean probabilities.* Boolean probabilities are used in attack graphs to distinguish between nodes eliminated (denoted by 0, or shaded node in attack graph) and nodes existing (denoted by 1, or unshaded node in attack graph) due to the security protocol under evaluation. By computing Boolean probabilities for

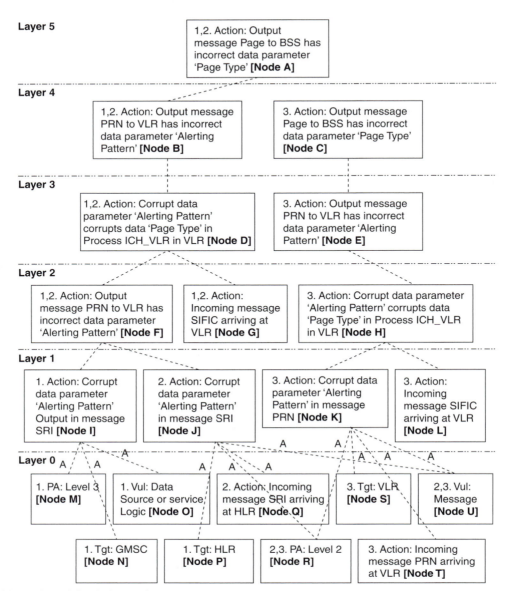

FIGURE 12.11 Attack graph for alerting attack.

each node in the attack graph, eCAT can extract the attack effects that may be eliminated by the security protocol under evaluation.

- *Attack graph marking.* To mark attack graphs, user input of Boolean probabilities must be provided for Layer 0 nodes. For example, if the security protocol under evaluation is MAPSec, then because MAPSec provides security on links between nodes, it eliminates Level 2 physical access. For example, consider the attack graph generated by eCAT shown in Figure 12.12. Here, Node 5 is set to 0, while all other nodes are set to 1.

eCAT uses the input from Layer 0 nodes to compute the Boolean probabilities for the rest of the nodes

starting from Layer 1 and moving upward. For example, the Boolean probability of the AND node (Node 18) is the product of all the nodes in the previous layer with the same tree number. Because Node 5 has the same tree number as Node 18, and Node 5's Boolean probability is 0, Node 18's Boolean probability is also 0. This process of marking attack graphs is continued until Boolean probability of all the nodes is computed till the topmost layer.

- *Hotspots.* Graph marking also marks the network hotspots in the attack graph. With respect to the attack graph, hotspots are the Layer 0 nodes with the highest tree number count. For example in Figure 12.12, Node 3 and Node 4 are the hotspots. A high

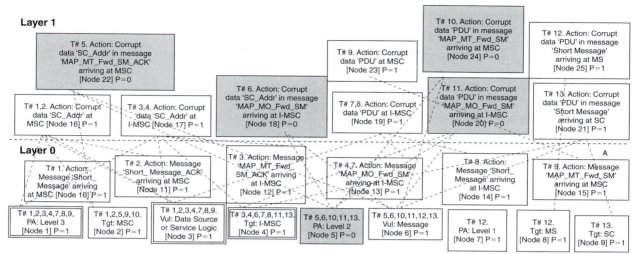

FIGURE 12.12 Fragment of a marked attack graph generated by eCAT.

tree number count indicates an increased attractiveness of the network location to adversaries. This is because by breaking into the network location indicated by the hotspot node, the adversary has a higher likelihood of success and can cause the greatest amount of damage.

Extensive testing of eCAT on several of the network services using MAPSec has revealed hotspots to be "Data Sources and Service Logic." This is because a corrupt data source or service logic may be used by many different services and hence cause many varied cascading effects, spawning a large number of attacks (indicated by multiple trees in attack graphs). Thus attacks that occur due to exploiting service logic and data source vulnerabilities constitute a major portion of the networkwide vulnerabilities and so a major problem. In other words, by exploiting service logic and data sources, the likelihood of attack success is very high. Therefore data source and service logic protection mechanisms must be deployed. It must be noted that MAPSec protects neither service logic nor data sources; rather, it protects MAP messages.

- *Coverage measurement formulas.* The CMF comprises the following set of three formulas to capture the coverage of security protocols: (1) *effective coverage*, to capture the average effective number of attacks eliminated by the security protocol; the higher the value of Effective Coverage the greater the protection the security protocol; (2) *deployment coverage*, to capture the coverage of protocol deployments; and (3) *attack coverage*, to capture the attack coverage provided by the security protocol; the higher this value, the greater is the security solution's

efficacy in eliminating a large number of attacks on the network.

Extensive use of CMF on several of the network services has revealed that MAPSec has an average networkwide attack coverage of 33%. This may be attributed to the fact that message corruption has a low spawning effect. Typically a single message corruption causes a single attack, since messages are typically used by a single service. Hence MAPSec is a solution to a small portion of the total network vulnerabilities.

Finally, in evaluating MAPSec using eCAT, it was observed that though MAPSec is 100% effective in preventing MAP message attacks, it cannot prevent a successfully launched attack from cascading. For MAPSec to be truly successful, every leg of the MAP message transport must be secured using MAPSec. However, the overhead for deploying MAPSec can be high, in terms of both processing load and monetary investment. Also, as MAP messages travel through third-party networks en route to their destinations, the risk level of attacks without MAPSec is very high. Hence, MAPSec is vital to protect MAP messages.

In conclusion, because MAPSec can protect against only 33% of attacks, it alone is insufficient to protect the network. A complete protection scheme for the network must include data source and service logic protection.

6. DISCUSSION

Next to the Internet, the cellular network is the most highly used communication network. It is also the most vulnerable, with inadequate security measures making it a most attractive target to adversaries that want to cause communication outages during emergencies. As the cellular network is moving in the direction of the Internet, becoming an amalgamation of several types of diverse networks, more attention must be paid to securing these networks. A push from government agencies requiring mandatory security standards for operating cellular networks would be just the momentum needed to securing these networks.

Of all the attacks discussed in this chapter, cascading attacks have the most potential to stealthily cause major network misoperation. At present there is no standardized scheme to protect from such attacks. EndSec is a good solution for protecting from cascading attacks, since it requires every data item to be signed by the source service node. Because service nodes are unlikely to corrupt data items and they are to be accounted for by their signatures, the possibility of cascading attacks is greatly reduced. EndSec has the added advantage of providing end-to-end security for all types of signaling messages. Hence, standardizing EndSec and mandating its deployment would be a good step toward securing the network.

Both Internet and PSTN connectivity are the open gateways that adversaries can use to gain access and attack the network. Because the PSTN's security is not going to be improved, at least its gateway to the core network must be adequately secured. Likewise, since neither the Internet's design nor security will be changed to suit the cellular network, at least its gateways to the core network must be adequately secured.

Finally, because the cellular network is an amalgamation of many diverse networks, it has too many vulnerable points. Hence, the future design of the network must be planned to reduce the number of vulnerable network points and reduce the number of service nodes that participate in servicing the subscriber, thereby reducing the number of points from which an adversary may attack.

REFERENCES

[1] 3GPP, architectural requirements, Technical Standard 3G TS 23.221 V6.3.0, 3G Partnership Project, May 2004.

[2] K. Murakami, O. Haase, J. Shin, T. F. LaPorta, Mobility management alternatives for migration to mobile internet session-based services, IEEE Journal on Selected Areas in Communications (J-SAC), special issue on Mobile Internet, 22 (June 2004) 834–848.

[3] 3GPP, 3G security, Security threats and requirements, Technical Standard 3G TS 21.133 V3.1.0, 3G Partnership Project, December 1999.

[4] 3GPP, network architecture, Technical Standard 3G TS 23.002 V3.3.0, 3G Partnership Project, May 2000.

[5] V. Eberspacher, *GSM Switching, Services and Protocols*, John Wiley & Sons, 1999.

[6] 3GPP, Basic call handling - technical realization, Technical Standard 3GPP TS 23.018 V3.4.0, 3G Partnership Project, April 1999.

[7] 3GPP, A guide to 3rd generation security, Technical Standard 3GPP TR 33.900 V1.2.0, 3G Partnership Project, January 2001.

[8] 3GPP, A guide to 3rd generation security, Technical Standard 3GPP TR 33.900 V1.2.0, 3G Partnership Project, January 2001.

[9] B. Chatras, C. Vernhes, Mobile application part design principles, in: Proceedings of XIII International Switching Symposium, vol. 1, June 1990, pp. 35–42.

[10] J.A. Audestad, The mobile application part (map) of GSM, technical report, Telektronikk 3.2004, Telektronikk, March 2004.

[11] 3GPP, Mobile Application part (MAP) specification, Technical Standard 3GPP TS 29.002 V3.4.0, 3G Partnership Project, April 1999.

[12] K. Boman, G. Horn, P. Howard, V. Niemi, Umts security, Electronics Communications Engineering Journal 14 (5) (October 2002) 191–204 Special issue security for mobility.

[13] 3GPP, A guide to 3rd generation security, Technical Standard 3GPP TR 33.900 V1.2.0, 3G Partnership Project, January 2001.

[14] K. Kotapati, P. Liu, T. F. LaPorta, Dependency relation-based vulnerability analysis of 3G networks: can it identify unforeseen cascading attacks? Special Issue of Springer Telecommunications Systems on Security, Privacy and Trust for Beyond 3G Networks, March 2007.

[15] K. Kotapati, P. Liu, T. F. LaPorta, Evaluating MAPSec by marking attack graphs, ACM/Kluwer Journal of Wireless Networks Journal (WINET) (March 2008).

[16] K. Kotapati, P. Liu, T. F. LaPorta, EndSec: An end-to-end message security protocol for cellular networks, IEEE Workshop on Security, Privacy and Authentication in Wireless Networks (SPAWN 2008) in IEEE International Symposium on a World of Wireless Mobile and Multimedia Networks (WOWMOM), June 2008.

[17] K. Kotapati, P. Liu, T. F. LaPorta, Evaluating MAPSec by marking attack graphs, ACM/Kluwer Journal of Wireless Networks Journal (WINET) (March 2008).

[18] K. Kotapati, P. Liu, T. F. LaPorta, Evaluating MAPSec by marking attack graphs, ACM/Kluwer Journal of Wireless Networks Journal (WINET) (March 2008).

[19] D. Moore, V. Paxson, S. Savage, C. Shannon, S. Staniford, N. Weaver, Inside the slammer worm, IEEE Security and Privacy 1 (4) (2003) 33–39.

[20] W. Enck, P. Traynor, P. McDaniel, T. F. LaPorta, Exploiting open functionality in sms-capable cellular networks, in: CCS '05: Proceedings of the 12th ACM Conference on Computer and Communications Security, ACM Press, 2005.

[21] W. Enck, P. Traynor, P. McDaniel, T. F. LaPorta, Exploiting open functionality in sms-capable cellular networks, in: CCS '05: Proceedings of the 12th ACM Conference on Computer and Communications Security, ACM Press, 2005.

[22] P. Traynor, W. Enck, P. McDaniel, T. F. LaPorta, Mitigating attacks on open functionality in sms-capable cellular networks, in: MobiCom '06: Proceedings of the 12th Annual International Conference on Mobile Computing and Networking, ACM Press, 2006, pp. 182–193.

[23] P. Traynor, P. McDaniel, T. F. LaPorta, On attack causality in internet-connected cellular networks, USENIX Security Symposium (SECURITY), August 2007.

[24] P. Traynor, W. Enck, P. McDaniel, T. F. LaPorta, Mitigating attacks on open functionality in SMS-capable cellular networks, in: MobiCom '06: Proceedings of the 12th Annual International Conference on Mobile Computing and Networking, ACM Press, 2006, pp. 182–193.

[25] P. Traynor, W. Enck, P. McDaniel, T. F. LaPorta, Mitigating attacks on open functionality in sms-capable cellular networks, in: MobiCom '06: Proceedings of the 12th Annual International Conference on Mobile Computing and Networking, ACM Press, 2006, pp. 182–193.

[26] P. Traynor, P. McDaniel, T. F LaPorta, On attack causality in internet-connected cellular networks, USENIX Security Symposium (SECURITY), August 2007.

[27] T. Moore, T. Kosloff, J. Keller, G. Manes, S. Shenoi. Signaling system 7 (SS7) network security, in: Proceedings of the IEEE 45th Midwest Symposium on Circuits and Systems, August 2002.

[28] G. Lorenz, T. Moore, G. Manes, J. Hale, S. Shenoi, Securing SS7 telecommunications networks, in: Proceedings of the 2001 IEEE Workshop on Information Assurance and Security, June 2001.

[29] T. Moore, T. Kosloff, J. Keller, G. Manes, S. Shenoi, Signaling system 7 (SS7) network security, in: Proceedings of the IEEE 45th Midwest Symposium on Circuits and Systems, August 2002.

[30] K. Kotapati, P. Liu, Y. Sun, T. F. LaPorta, A taxonomy of cyber attacks on 3G networks, in: Proceedings IEEE International Conference on Intelligence and Security Informatics, ISI, Lecture Notes in Computer Science, Springer-Verlag, May 2005, pp. 631–633.

[31] K. Kotapati, P. Liu, Y. Sun, T. F. LaPorta, a taxonomy of cyber attacks on 3G networks, in: Proceedings IEEE International Conference on Intelligence and Security Informatics, ISI, Lecture Notes in Computer Science, Springer-Verlag, May 2005, pp. 631–633.

[32] K. Kotapati, Assessing Security of Mobile Telecommunication Networks, Ph. D dissertation, Penn State University, August 2008.

[33] Switch, 5ESS Switch, www.alleged.com/telephone/5ESS/.

[34] Telcoman, Central Offices, www.thecentraloffice.com/.

[35] V. Prevelakis, D. Spinellis, The Athens affair, IEEE Spectrum (July 2007).

[36] H. Hannu, Signaling Compression (SigComp) Requirements & Assumptions, RFC 3322 (Informational), January 2003.

[37] W. Stallings, *Cryptography and Network Security: Principles and Practice*, Prentice Hall, 2000.

[38] K. Kotapati, Assessing Security of Mobile Telecommunication Networks, Ph. D dissertation, Penn State University, August 2008.

[39] K. Kotapati, P. Liu, T. F. LaPorta, CAT - a practical graph & SDL based toolkit for vulnerability assessment of 3G networks, in: Proceedings of the 21st IFIP TC-11 International Information Security Conference, Security and Privacy in Dynamic Enviro-nments, SEC 2006, May 2006.

[40] K. Kotapati, P. Liu, T. F. LaPorta, Dependency relation-based vulnerability analysis of 3G networks: can it identify unforeseen cascading attacks? Special Issue of Springer Telecommunications Systems on Security, Privacy and Trust for Beyond 3G Networks, March 2007.

[41] K. Kotapati, P. Liu, T. F. LaPorta, Evaluating MAPSec by mark-ing attack graphs, ACM/Kluwer Journal of Wireless Networks Journal (WINET) 12 (March 2008).

[42] 3GPP2 3GPP, Third Generation Partnership Project, www.3gpp.org/, 2006.

[43] Telcoman, Central Offices, www.thecentraloffice.com/.

[44] J. Ellsberger, D. Hogrefe, A. Sarma, SDL, *Formal Object-oriented Language for Communicating Systems*, Prentice Hall, 1997.

[45] K. Kotapati, P. Liu, T. F. LaPorta, Dependency relation-based vulnerability analysis of 3G networks: can it identify unforeseen cascading attacks? Special Issue of Springer Telecommunications Systems on Security, Privacy and Trust for Beyond 3G Networks, March 2007.

[46] K. Kotapati, P. Liu, T. F. LaPorta, Dependency relation-based vulnerability analysis of 3G networks: can it identify unforeseen cascading attacks? Special Issue of Springer Telecommunications Systems on Security, Privacy and Trust for Beyond 3G Networks, March 2007.

[47] K. Kotapati, P. Liu, T. F. LaPorta, Dependency relation-based vulnerability analysis of 3G networks: can it identify unforeseen cascading attacks? Special Issue of Springer Telecommunications Systems on Security, Privacy and Trust for Beyond 3G Networks, March 2007.

[48] K. Kotapati, P. Liu, T. F. LaPorta, Evaluating MAPSec by mark-ing attack graphs, ACM/Kluwer Journal of Wireless Networks Journal (WINET) 12 (March 2008).

## Chapter 13

RFID Security

Chunming Rong
University of Stavanger

Erdal Cayirci
University of Stavanger

Radiofrequency identification (RFID) systems use RFID tags to annotate and identify objects. When objects are processed, an RFID reader is used to read information from the tags attached to the objects. The information will then be used with the data stored in the back-end databases to support the handling of business transactions.

1. RFID INTRODUCTION

Generally, an RFID system consists of three basic components: RFID tags, RFID readers, and a back-end database.

- *RFID tags or RFID transponders.* These are the data carriers attached to objects. A typical RFID tag contains information about the attached object, such as an identifier (ID) of the object and other related properties of the object that may help to identify and describe it.
- *The RFID reader or the RFID transceiver.* These devices can read information from tags and may write information into tags if the tags are rewritable.
- *Back-end database.* This is the data repository responsible for the management of data related to the tags and business transactions, such as ID, object properties, reading locations, reading time, and so on.

RFID System Architecture

RFID systems' architecture is illustrated in Figure 13.1. Tags are attached to or embedded in objects to identify or annotate them. An RFID reader will send out signals to a tag for requesting information stored on the tag. The tag responsed to the request by sending back the appropriate information. With the data from the back-end database,

applications can then use the information from the tag to proceed with the business transaction related to the object.

Next we describe the RFID tags, RFID reader, and back-end database in detail.

Tags

In RFID systems, objects are identified or described by information on RFID tags attached to the objects. An RFID tag basically consists of a microchip that is used for data storage and computation and a coupling element for communicating with the RFID reader via radio frequency communication, such as an antenna. Some tags may also have an on-board battery to supply a limited amount of power.

RFID tags can respond to radio frequencies sent out by RFID readers. On receiving the radio signals from a RFID reader, an RFID tag will either send back the requested data stored on the tag or write the data into the tag, if the tag is rewritable. Because radio signals are used, RFID tags do not require line of sight to connect with the reader and precise positioning, as barcodes do. Tags may also generate a certain amount of electronic power from the radio signals they receive, to power the computation and transmission of data.

RFID tags can be classified based on four main criteria: power source, type of memory, computational power, and functionality.

A basic and important classification criterion of RFID tags is to classify tags based on power source. Tags can be categorized into three classes: active, semiactive, and passive RFID tags.

Active RFID tags have on-board power sources, such as batteries. Active RFID tags can proactively send radio signals to an RFID reader and possibly to other tags [1]

FIGURE 13.1 RFID system architecture.

as well. Compared with tags without on-board power, active tags have longer transmission range and are more reliable. Active tags can work in the absence of an RFID reader. On the other hand, the on-board power supply also increases the costs of active tags.

Semiactive RFID tags also have on-board power sources for powering their microchips, but they use RFID readers' energy field for actually transmitting their data [2] when responding to the incoming transmissions. Semiactive tags have the middle transmission range and cost.

Passive RFID tags do not have internal power sources and cannot initiate any communications. Passive RFID tags generate power from radio signals sent out by an RFID reader in the course of communication. Thus passive RFID tags can only work in the presence of an RFID reader. Passive tags have the shortest transmission range and the cheapest cost. The differences of active tags, semiactive tags and passive tags are shown in Table 13.1.

RFID tags may have read-only memory, write-once/read-many memory, or fully rewritable memory. RFID tags can be classified into three categories according to the type of memory that a tag uses: read-only tags, write-once/read-many tags, and fully rewritable tags. The information on read-only tags cannot be changed in the life-cycle of the tags. Write-once/read-many tags can be initialized with application-specific information. The information on fully rewritable tags can be rewritten many times by an RFID reader.

According to the computational power, RFID tags can be classified into three categories: basic tags, symmetric-key tags, and public-key tags. Basic tags do not have the ability to perform cryptography computation. Symmetric-key tags and public-key tags have the ability to perform symmetric-key and public–key cryptography computation, respectively.

RFID tags can also be classified according to their functionality. The MIT Auto-ID Center defined five classes of tags according to their functionality in 2003 [3]: Class 0, Class 1, Class 2, Class 3, and Class 4 tags. Every

TABLE 13.1 Tags classified by power source

Power Source	Active Tags	Semiactive Tags	Passive Tags
On-board power supply	Yes	Yes	No
Transmission range	Long	Medium	Short
Communication pattern	Proactive	Passive	Passive
Cost	Expensive	Medium	Cheap

class has different functions and different requirements for tag memory and power resource. Class 0 tags are passive and do not contain any memory. They only announce their presence and offer electronic article surveillance (EAS) functionality. Class 1 tags are typically passive. They have read-only or write-once/read-many memory and can only offer identification functionality. Class 2 tags are mostly semiactive and active. They have fully rewritable memory and can offer data-logging functionality. Class 3 tags are semiactive and active tags. They contain on-board environmental sensors that can record temperature, acceleration, motion, or radiation and require fully rewritable memory. Class 4 tags are active tags and have fully rewritable memory. They can establish ad hoc wireless networks with other tags because they are equipped with wireless networking components.

RFID Readers

An RFID reader (transceiver) is a device used to read information from and possibly also write information into RFID tags. An RFID reader is normally connected to a back-end database for sending information to that database for further processing.

An RFID reader consists of two key functional modules: a high-frequency (HF) interface and a control unit.

The HF interface can perform three functions: generating the transmission power to activate the tags, modulating the signals for sending requests to RFID tags, and receiving and demodulating signals received from tags. The control unit of an RFID reader has also three basic functions: controlling the communication between the RFID reader and RFID tags, encoding and decoding signals, and communicating with the back-end server for sending information to the back-end database or executing the commands from the back-end server. The control unit can perform more functions in the case of complex RFID systems, such as executing anticollision algorithms in the cause of communicating with multitags, encrypting requests sent by the RFID reader and decrypting responses received from tags, and performing the authentication between RFID readers and RFID tags [4].

RFID readers can provide high-speed tag scanning. Hundreds of objects can be dealt with by a single reader within a second; thus it is scalable enough for applications such as supply chain management, where a large number of objects need to be dealt with frequently. RFID readers need only to be placed at every entrance and exit. When products enter or leave the designated area by passing through an entrance or exit, the RFID readers can instantly identify the products and send the necessary information to the back-end database for further processing.

Back-End Database

The back-end database is in the back-end server that manages the information related to the tags in an RFID system. Every object's information can be stored as a record in the database, and the information on the tag attached to the object can serve as a pointer to the record.

The connection between an RFID reader and a back-end database can be assumed as secure, no matter via wireless link or TCP/IP, because constraints for readers are not very tight and security solutions such as SSL/TLS can be implemented for them [5].

RFID Standards

Currently, as different frequencies are used for RFID systems in various countries and many standards are adopted for different kinds of application, there is no agreement on a universal standard that's accepted by all parties. Several kinds of RFID standards [6] are being used today. These standards include contactless smart cards, item management tags, RFID systems for animal identification, and

EPC tags. These standards specify the physical layer and the link layer characteristics of RFID systems but do not cover the upper layers.

Contactless smart cards can be classified into three types according to the communication ranges. The ISO standards for them are ISO 10536, ISO 14443, and ISO 15693. ISO 10536 sets the standard for close-coupling smart cards, for which the communication range is about 0–1 cm. ISO 14443 sets the standard for proximity-coupling smart cards, which have a communication range of about 0–10 cm. ISO 15693 specifies vicinity-coupling smart cards, which have a communication range of about 0–1 m. The proximity-coupling and vicinity-coupling smart cards have already been implemented with some cryptography algorithms such as 128-bit AES, triple DES, and SHA-1 and challenge-response authentication mechanisms to improve system security [7].

Item management tag standards include ISO 15961, ISO 15962, ISO 15963, and ISO 18000 series [8]. ISO 15961 defines the host interrogator, tag functional commands, and other syntax features of item management. ISO 15962 defines the data syntax of item management, and ISO 15963 is "Unique Identification of RF tag and Registration Authority to manage the uniqueness." For the ISO 18000 standards series, part 1 describes the reference architecture and parameters definition; parts 2, 3, 4, 5, 6, and 7 define the parameters for air interface communications below 135 kHz, at 13.56 MHz, at 2.45 GHz, at 860 MHz, at 960 MHz, and at 433 MHz, respectively.

Standards for RFID systems for animal identification include ISO 11784, ISO 11785, and ISO 14223 [9]. ISO 11784 and ISO 11784 define the code structure and technical concepts for radiofrequency identification of animals. ISO 14223 includes three parts: air interface, code and command structure, and applications. These kinds of tags use low frequency for communication and have limited protection for animal tracking [10].

The EPC standard was created by the MIT Auto-ID, which is an association of more than 100 companies and university labs. The EPC system is currently operated by EPCglobal [11]. A typical EPC network has four parts [12]: the electronic product code, the identification system that includes RFID tags and RFID readers, the Savant middleware, and the object naming service (ONS). The first- and second-generation EPC tags cannot support strong cryptography to protect the security of the RFID systems due to the limitation of computational resources, but both of them can provide a kill command to protect the privacy of the consumer [13].

EPC tag encoding includes a Header field followed by one or more Value fields. The Header field defines the

TABLE 13.2 EPC basic format

Header	EPC Manager Number	Object Class	Serial Number

TABLE 13.3 RFID application purpose

Application Type	Identification Purpose
Asset management	Determine item presence
Tracking	Determine item location
Authenticity verification	Determine item source
Matching	Ensure affiliated items are not separated
Process control	Correlate item information for decision making
Access control	Person authentication
Automated payment	Conduct financial transaction

overall length and format of the Value fields. There are two kinds of EPC format: EPC 64-bit format and EPC 96-bit format. In the most recent version [14], the 64-bit format was removed from the standard. As shown in Table 13.2, both the formats include four fields: a header (8 bits), an EPC manager number (28 bits), an object class (24 bits), and a serial number (36 bits). The header and the EPC manager number are assigned by EPCglobal [15], and the object class and the serial number are assigned by EPC manager owner. The EPC header identifies the length, type, structure version, and generation of the EPC. The EPC manager number is the entity responsible for maintaining the subsequent partitions of the EPC. The object class identifies a class of objects. Serial number identifies the instance.

RFID Applications

Recently more and more companies and organizations have begun to use RFID tags rather than traditional barcode because RFID systems have many advantages over traditional barcode systems. First, the information stored in the RFID tags can be read by RFID readers without line of sight, whereas barcodes can only be scanned within the line of sight. Second, the distance between a tag and a reader is longer compared with the barcode system. For example, an RFID reader can read information from a tag at a distance as long as 300 feet, whereas the read range for a barcode is typically no more than 15 feet. Third, RFID readers can scan hundreds of tags in seconds. Fourth, since today most RFID tags are produced using silicon technology, more functions can be added to them, such as large memory for more information storage and calculation ability to support various kinds of encryption and decryption algorithms, so privacy can be better protected and the tags cannot be easily cloned by attackers. In addition, the information stored in the barcode cannot be changed after being imprinted on the barcode, whereas for the RFID tags with rewritable memory the information can be updated when needed.

With these characteristics and advantages, RFID has been widely adopted and deployed in various areas. Currently, RFID can be used in passports, transportation

payments, product tracking, lap scoring, animal identification, inventory systems, RFID mandates, promotion tracking, human implants, libraries, schools and universities, museums, and social retailing. These myriad applications of RFID can be classified into seven classes according to the purpose of identifying items [16]. These classes are asset management, tracking, authenticity verification, matching, process control, access control, and automated payment. Table 13.3 lists the identification purposes of various application types.

Asset management involves determining the presence of tagged items and helping manage item inventory. One possible application of asset management is electronic article surveillance (EAS). For example, every good in a supermarket is attached to an EAS tag, which will be deactivated if it is properly checked out. Then RFID readers at the supermarket exits can detect unpaid goods automatically when they pass through.

Tracking is used to identify the location of tagged items. If the readers are fixed, a single reader can cover only one area. To effectively track the items, a group of readers is needed, together with a central system to deal with the information from different readers.

Authenticity verification methods are used to verify the source of tagged items. For example, by adding a cryptography-based digital signature in the tag, the system can prevent tag replication to make sure that the good is labeled with the source information.

Matching is used to ensure that affiliated items are not separated. Samples for matching applications include mothers and their newborn babies to match each other in the hospital and for airline passengers to match their checked luggage and so prevent theft.

Access control is used for person authentication. Buildings may use contactless RFID card systems to identify authorized people. Only those authorized people with the correct RFID card can authenticate themselves to the reader to open a door and enter a building. Using a car key with RFID tags, a car owner can open his own car automatically, another example of RFID's application to access control.

Process control involves decision making by correlating tagged item information. For example, RFID readers in different parts of an assembly line can read the information on the products, which can be used to help production managers make suitable decisions.

Automated payment is used to conduct financial transactions. The applications include payment for toll expressways and at gas stations. These applications can improve the speed of payment to hasten the processing of these transactions.

2. RFID CHALLENGES

RFID systems have been widely deployed in some areas. Perhaps this happened before the expectations of RFID researchers and RFID services providers were satisfied. There are many limitations of the RFID technology that restrain the deployment of RFID applications, such as the lack of universal standardization of RFID in the industry and the concerns about security and privacy problems that may affect the privacy and security of individuals and organizations. The security and privacy issues pose a huge challenge for RFID applications. Here we briefly summarize some of the challenges facing RFID systems.

Counterfeiting

As described earlier in the chapter, RFID tags can be classified into three categories based on the equipped computation power: basic tags, symmetric-key tags, and public-key tags. Symmetric-key and public-key tags can implement cryptography protocols for authentication with private key, and public keys, respectively. Basic tags are not capable of performing cryptography computation. Although they lack the capability to perform cryptography computation, they are most widely used for applications such as supply chain management and travel systems. With the widespread application of fully writable or even reprogrammable basic tags, counterfeiters can easily forge basic tags in real-world applications, and these counterfeit tags can be used in multiple places at the same time, which can cause confusion.

The counterfeiting of tags can be categorized into two areas based on the technique used for tampering with tag data: modifying tag data and adding data to a blank tag. In real-world applications, we face counterfeit threats such as the following [7]:

- The attacker can modify valid tags to make them invalid or modify invalid tags to make them valid.
- The attacker can modify a high-priced object's tag as a low-priced object or modify a low-priced object's tag as a high-priced object.
- The attacker can modify an object's tag to be the same as the tags attached to other objects.
- The attacker can create an additional tag for personal reasons by reading the data from an authorized tag and adding this data to a blank tag in real-world applications, such as in a passport or a shipment of goods.

Sniffing

Another main issue of concern in deploying RFID systems is the sniffing problem. It occurs when third parties use a malicious and unauthorized RFID reader to read the information on RFID tags within their transmission range. Unfortunately, most RFID tags are indiscriminate in their responses to reading requests transmitted by RFID readers and do not have access control functions to provide any protection against an unauthorized reader. Once an RFID tag enters a sufficiently powered reader's field, it receives the reader's requests via radio frequency. As long as the request is well formed, the tag will reply to the request with the corresponding information on the tag. Then the holder of the unauthenticated reader may use this information for other purposes.

Tracking

With multiple RFID readers integrated into one system, the movements of objects can be tracked by fixed RFID readers [18]. For example, once a specific tag can be associated with a particular person or object, when the tag enters a reader's field the reader can obtain the specific identifier of the tag, and the presence of the tag within the range of a specific reader implies specific location information related to the attached person or object. With location information coming from multiple RFID readers, an attacker can follow movements of people or objects. Tracking can also be performed without decrypting the encrypted messages coming from RFID readers [19]. Generally, the more messages the attacker describes, the more location or privacy information can be obtained from the messages.

One way to track is to generate maps of RFID tags with mobile robots [20]. A sensor model is introduced to compute the likelihood of tag detections, given the relative pose of the tag with respect to the robot. In this model a highly accurate FastSLAM algorithm is used to learn the geometrical structure of the environment around the robots, which are equipped with a laser range scanner; then it uses the recursive Bayesian filtering scheme to estimate the posterior locations of the RFID tags, which can be used to localize robots and people in the environment with the geometrical structure of the environment learned by the FastSLAM algorithm.

There is another method to detect the motion of passive RFID tags that are within a detecting antenna's field. Response rate at the reader is used to study the impact of four cases of tag movements that can provide prompt and accurate detection and the influence of the environment. The idea of multiple tags/readers is introduced to improve performance. The movement-detection algorithms can be improved and integrated into the RFID monitoring system to localize the position of the tags. The method does not require any modification of communication protocols nor the addition of hardware.

In real-world applications, there exists the following tracking threat:

- The attacker can track the potential victim by monitoring the movement of the person and performing some illegal actions against the potential victim [21].

Denial of Service

Denial of service (DoS) takes place when RFID readers or back-end servers cannot provide excepted services. DoS attacks are easy to accomplish and difficult to guard against [22]. The following are nine DoS threats:

- *Killing tags to make them disabled to disrupt readers' normal operations.* EPCglobal had proposed that a tag have a "kill" command to destroy it and protect consumer privacy. If an attacker knows the password of a tag, it can "kill" the tag easily in real-world applications. Now Class-0, Class-1 Generation-1, and Class-1 Generation-2 tags are all equipped with the kill command.
- *Carry a blocker tag that can disrupt the communication between an RFID reader and RFID tags.* A blocker tag is a cheap, passive RFID device that can simulate many basic RFID tags at one time and render specific zones private or public. An RFID reader can only communicate with a single RFID tag

at any specific time. If more than one tag responds to a request coming from the reader at the same time, "collision" happens. In this case, the reader cannot receive the information sent by the tags, which makes the system unavailable to authorized uses.

- *Carry a special absorbent tag that can be tuned to the same radio frequencies used by legitimate tags.* The absorbent tag can absorb the energy or power generated by radiofrequency signals sent by the reader, and the resulting reduction in the reader's energy may make the reader unavailable to communicate with other tags.
- *Remove, physically destroy, or erase the information on tags attached to or embedded in objects.* The reader will not communicate with the dilapidated tags in a normal way.
- *Shield the RFID tags from scrutiny using a Faraday cage.* A Faraday cage is a container made of a metal enclosure that can prevent reading radio signals from the readers [23].
- *Carry a device that can actively broadcast more powerful return radio signals or noises than the signals responded to by the tags so as to block or disrupt the communication of any nearby RFID readers and make the system unavailable to authorized users.* The power of the broadcast is so high that it could cause severe blockage or disruption of all nearby RFID systems, even those in legitimate applications where privacy is not a concern [24].
- *Perform a traditional Internet DoS attack and prevent the back-end servers from gathering EPC numbers from the readers.* The servers do not receive enough information from the readers and cannot provide the additional services from the server.
- *Perform a traditional Internet DoS attack against the object-naming service (ONS).* This can deny the service.
- *Send URL queries to a database and make the database busy with these queries.* The database may then deny access to authorized users.

Other Issues

Besides the four basic types of attack—counterfeiting, sniffing, tracking, and denial of service—in real-world applications, there also exists some other threats of RFID systems.

Spoofing

Spoofing attacks take place when an attacker successfully poses as an authorized user of a system [25]. Spoofing attacks are different from counterfeiting and sniffing attacks, though they are all falsification types of attack. Counterfeiting takes place when an attacker forges the RFID tags that can be scanned by authorized readers. Sniffing takes place when an attacker forges authorized readers that can scan the authorized tags to obtain useful information. But the forging object of spoofing is an authorized user of a system. There exist the following spoofing threats in real-world applications [26]:

- *The attacker can pose as an authorized EPC global Information Service Object Naming Service (ONS) user.* If the attacker successfully poses as an authorized ONS user, he can send queries to the ONS to gather EPC numbers. Then, from the EPC numbers, the attacker may easily obtain the location, identification, or other privacy information.
- *The attacker can pose as an authorized database user in an RFID system.* The database stores the complete information from the objects, such as manufacturer, product name, read time, read location, and other privacy information. If the attacker successfully poses as an authorized database user and an authorized user of ONS, he can send queries to the ONS for obtaining the EPC number of one object, then get the complete information on the object by mapping the EPC number to the information stored in the database.
- *The attacker can also pose as an ONS server.* If the attacker's pose is successful, he can easily use the ONS server to gather EPC numbers, respond to invalid requests, deny normal service, and even change the data or write malicious data to the system.

Repudiation

Repudiation takes place when a user denies doing an action or no proof exists to prove that the action has been implemented [27]. There are two kinds of repudiation threats:

- The sender or the receiver denies performing the send and receive actions. A nonrepudiation protocol can be used to resolve this problem.
- The owner of the EPC number or the back-end server denies that it has the information from the objects to which the tags are attached.

Insert Attacks

Insert attacks take place when an attacker inserts some system commands to the RFID system where data is

normally expected [28]. In real-world applications, there exists the following attack:

- A system command rather than valid data is carried by a tag in its data storage memory.

Replay Attacks

Replay attacks take place when an attacker intercepts the communication signals between an RFID reader and an RFID tag and records the tag's response. Then the RFID tag's response can be reused if the attacker detects that the reader sends requests to the other tags for querying [29]. There exist the following two threats:

- The attacker can record the communications between proximity cards and a building access reader and play it back to access the building.
- The attacker can record the response that an RFID card in a car gives to an automated highway toll collection system, and the response can be used when the car of the attacker wants to pass the automated toll station.

Physical Attacks

Physical attacks are very strong attacks that physically obtain tags and have unauthorized physical operations on the tags. But it is fortunate that physical attacks cannot be implemented in public or on a widespread scale, except for Transient Electromagnetic Pulse Emanation Standard (TEMPEST) attacks. There exist the following physical attacks [30,31]:

- *Probe attacks.* The attacker can use a probe directly attached to the circuit to obtain or change the information on tags.
- *Material removal.* The attacker can use a knife or other tools to remove the tags attached to objects.
- *Energy attacks.* The attacks can be either of the contact or contactless variety. It is required that contactless energy attacks be close enough to the system.
- *Radiation imprinting.* The attacker can use an X-ray band or other radial bands to destroy the data unit of a tag.
- *Circuit disruption.* The attacker can use strong electromagnetic interference to disrupt tag circuits.
- *Clock glitch.* The attacker can lengthen or shorten the clock pulses to a clocked circuit and destroy normal operations.

Viruses

Viruses are old attacks that threaten the security of all information systems, including RFID systems. RFID viruses always target the back-end database in the server, perhaps destroying and revealing the data or information stored in the database. There exist the following virus threats:

- An RFID virus destroys and reveals the data or information stored in the database.
- An RFID virus disturbs or even stops the normal services provided by the server.
- An RFID virus threatens the security of the communications between RFID readers and RFID tags or between back-end database and RFID readers.

Social Issues

Due to the security challenges in RFID, many people do not trust RFID technologies and fear that they could allow attackers to purloin their privacy information.

Weis [32] presents two main arguments. These arguments make some people choose not to rely on RFID technology and regard RFID tags as the "mark of the beast." However, security issues cannot prevent the success of RFID technology.

The first argument is that RFID tags are regarded as the best replacement for current credit cards and all other ways of paying for goods and services. But RFID tags can also serve as identification. The replacement of current ways of paying by RFID tag requires that people accept RFID tags instead of credit cards, and they cannot sell or buy anything without RFID tags.

There is a second argument [33]: "Since RFID tags are also used as identification, they should be implanted to avoid losing the ID or switching it with someone. Current research has shown that the ideal location for the implant is indeed the forehead or the hand, since they are easy to access and unlike most other body parts they do not contain much fluid, which interferes with the reading of the chip."

Comparison of All Challenges

Previously in this chapter we introduced some of the challenges that RFID systems are facing. Every challenge or attack can have a different method or attack goal, and the consequences of the RFID system after an attack may also be different. In this part of the chapter, we briefly analyze the challenges according to attack methods, attack goals, and the consequences of RFID systems after attacks (see Table 13.4).

The first four challenges are the four basic challenges in RFID systems that correspond to the four basic use

cases. *Counterfeiting* happens when counterfeiters forge RFID tags by copying the information from a valid tag or adding some well-formed format information to a new tag in the RFID system. *Sniffing* happens when an unauthorized reader reads the information from a tag, and the information may be utilized by attackers. *Tracking* happens when an attacker who holds some readers unlawfully monitors the movements of objects attached by an RFID tag that can be read by those readers. *Denial of service* happens when the components of RFID systems deny the RFID service.

The last seven challenges or attacks can always happen in RFID systems (see Table 13.4). *Spoofing* happens when an attacker poses as an authorized user of an RFID system on which the attacker can perform invalid operations. *Repudiation* happens when a user or component of an RFID system denies the action it performed and there is no proof that the user did perform the action. *Insert attacks* happen when an attacker inserts some invalid system commands into the tags and some operations may be implemented by the invalid command. *Replay attacks* happen when an attacker intercepts the response of the tag and reuses the response for another communication. *Physical attacks* happen when an attacker does some physical operations on RFID tags and these attacks disrupt communications between the RFID readers and tags. A *virus* is the security challenge of all information systems; it can disrupt the operations of RFID systems or reveal the information in those systems. *Social issues* involve users' psychological attitudes that can influence the users' adoption of RFID technologies for real-world applications.

3. RFID PROTECTIONS

According to their computational power, RFID tags can be classified into three categories: basic tags, symmetric-key tags, and public-key tags. In the next part of the chapter, we introduce some protection approaches for these three kinds of RFID tags.

Basic RFID System

Prices have been one of the biggest factors to be considered when we're making decisions on RFID deployments. Basic tags are available for the cheapest price, compared with symmetric-key tags and public-key tags. Due to the limited computation resources built into a basic tag, basic tags are not capable of performing

TABLE 13.4 Comparison of all challenges or attacks in RFID systems

Challenge or Attack	Attack Method	Attack Goal	Direct Consequence
Counterfeiting	Forge tags	Tag	Invalid tags
Sniffing	Forge readers	Reader	Reveals information
Tracking	Monitor the movement of objects	Objects of an RFID system	Tracks the movement of object
Denial of service	RF jamming, kill normal command, physical destroy, and so on	Reader, back-end database or server	Denies normal services
Spoofing	Pose as an authorized user	User	Invalid operations by invalid user
Repudiation	Deny action or no proof that the action was implemented	Tag, reader, back-end database or server	Deniable actions
Insert attacks	Insert invalid command	Tag	Invalid operations by invalid commands
Replay attacks	Reuse the response of tags	Communication between RFID tags and readers	Invalid identification
Physical attacks	Physical operations on tag	Tag	Disrupts or destroys communication between RFID tags and readers
Virus	Insert invalid data	Back-end database or server	Destroys the data or service of system
Social issues	Social attitude	Psychology of potential user	Restricts the widespread application

cryptography computations. This imposes a huge challenge to implement protections on basic tags; cryptography has been one of the most important and effective methods to implement protection mechanisms. Recently several approaches have been proposed to tackle this issue.

Most of the approaches to security protection for basic tags focus on protecting consumer privacy. A usual method is by tag killing, proposed by EPCglobal. In this approach, when the reader wants to kill a tag, it sends a kill message to the tag to permanently deactivate it. Together with the kill message, a 32-bit tag-specific PIN code is also sent to the object tag, to avoid killing other tags. On receiving this kill message, a tag will deactivate itself, after which the tag will become inoperative. Generally, tags are killed when the tagged items are checked out in shops or supermarkets. This is very similar to removing the tags from the tagged items when they are purchased. It is an efficient method of protecting the privacy of consumers, since a killed tag can no longer send out information.

The disadvantage of this approach is that it will reduce the post-purchase benefits of RFID tags. In some cases, RFID tags need to be operative only temporarily. For example, RFID tags used in libraries and museums for tagging

books and other items need to work at all times and should not be killed or be removed from the tagged items. In these cases, instead of being killed or removed, tags can be made temporarily inactive. When a tag needs to be reawoken, an RFID reader can send a wake message to the tag with a 32-bit tag-specific PIN code, which is sent to avoid waking up other tags. This also results in the management of PIN codes for tags, which brings some inconvenience.

Another approach to protecting privacy is tag relabeling, which was first proposed by Sarma et al [34]. In this scheme, to protect consumers' privacy, identifiers of RFID tags are effaced when tagged items are checked out, but the information on the tags will be kept for later use. Inoue and Yasuuran [35] proposed that consumers can store the identifiers of the tags and give each tag a new identifier. When needed, people can reactivate the tags with the new identifiers. This approach allows users to manage tagged items throughout the items' life cycle. A third approach is to allocate each tag a new random number at each checkout; thus attackers cannot rely on the identifiers to collect information about customers [36]. This method does not solve the problem of tracking [37]. To prevent tracking, random numbers need to be refreshed frequently, which will increase the burden on consumers. Juels proposed a system called the *minimalist system* [38], in which every tag has a list of pseudonyms, and for every reader query, the tag will respond with a different pseudonym from the list and return to the beginning of the list when this list is exhausted. It is assumed that only authorized readers know all these tag pseudonyms. Unauthorized readers that do not know these pseudonyms cannot identify the tags correctly. To prevent unauthorized readers getting the pseudonyms list by frequent query, the tags will response to an RFID reader's request with a relatively low rate, which is called *pseudonym throttling*. Pseudonym throttling is useful, but it cannot provide a high level of privacy for consumers, because with the tag's small memory, the number of pseudonyms in the list is limited. To tackle this problem, the protocol allows an authorized RFID reader to refresh a tag's pseudonyms list.

Juels and Pappu [39] proposed to protect consumers' privacy by using tagged banknotes. The proposed scheme used public-key cryptography to protect the serial numbers of tagged banknotes. The serial number of a tagged banknote is encrypted using a public key to generate a ciphertext, which is saved in the memory of the tag. On receiving a request of the serial number, the tag will respond with this ciphertext. Only law enforcement agencies know the related private key and can decrypt this ciphertext to recover the banknote's serial number. To prevent tracking of banknotes, the ciphertext will be reencrypted periodically. To avoid the ciphertext of a banknote being reencrypted by an attacker, the tagged banknote can use an optical write–access key. A reader that wants to reencrypt this ciphertext needs to scan the write–access key first. In this system only one key pair, a public key and a private key, is used. But this is not enough for the general RFID system. Using multiple key pairs will impair the privacy of RFID systems, since if the reader wants to reencrypt the ciphertext, it needs to know the corresponding public key of this tag.

So, a universal reencryption algorithm has been introduced [40]. In this approach, an RFID reader can reencrypt the ciphertext without knowing the corresponding public key of a tag. The disadvantage of this approach is that attackers can substitute the ciphertext with a new ciphertext, so the integrity of the ciphertext cannot be protected. By signing the ciphertext with a digital signature, this problem can be solved [41], since only the authenticated reader can access the ciphertext.

Floerkemeier et al. [42] introduced another approach to protect consumer privacy by using a specially designed protocol. In their approach, they first designed the communication protocol between RFID tags and RFID readers. This protocol requires an RFID reader to provide information about the purpose and the collection type for the query. In addition, a privacy-enforcing device called a *watchdog tag* is used in the system. This watchdog tag is a kind of sophisticated RFID tag that is equipped with a battery, a small screen, and a long-range communication channel. A watchdog tag can be integrated into a PDA or a cell phone and can decode the messages from an RFID reader and display them on the screen for the user to read. With a watchdog tag, a user can know not only the information from the RFID readers in the vicinity of the tag but also the ID, the query purpose, and the collection type of the requests sent by the RFID readers. With this information, the user is able to identify the unwanted communications between tags and an RFID reader, making this method useful for users to avoid the reader ID spoofing attack.

Rieback, Crispo, and Tanebaum [43] proposed another privacy-enforcing device called RFID Guardian, which is also a battery-powered RFID tag that can be integrated into a PDA or a cell phone to protect user privacy. RFID Guardian is actually a user privacy protection platform in RFID systems. It can also work as an RFID reader to request information from RFID tags, or it can work like a tag to communicate with a reader. RFID Guardian has four different security properties: auditing, key management, access control, and authentication. It can audit RFID readers in its vicinity and record information about the RFID readers, such as commands, related parameters, and data, and provide these kinds of information to the user. Using this information, the user can sufficiently identify illegal scanning. In some cases, a user might not know or could forget the tags in his vicinity. With the help of RFID Guardian, the user can detect all the tags within radio range. Then the user can deactivate the tags according to his choice.

For RFID tags that use cryptography methods to provide security, one important issue is key management. RFID Guardian can perform two-way RFID communications and can generate random values. These features are very useful for key exchange and key refresh. Using the features of coordination of security primitives, context awareness, and tag-reader mediation, RFID Guardian can provide access control for RFID systems [44]. Also, using two-way RFID communication and standard challenge-response algorithms, RFID Guardian can provide off-tag authentication for RFID readers.

Another approach for privacy protecting is proposed by Juels, Rivest, and Szydlo [45]. In this approach, a cheap, passive RFID tag is used as the blocker tag. Since this blocker tag can simulate many RFID tags at the same time, it is very difficult for an RFID reader to identify the real tag carried by the user. The blocker tag can both simulate all the possible RFID tags and simulate only a select set of the tags, making it convenient for the user to manage the RFID tags. For example, the user can tell the blocker tag to block only the tags that belong to a certain company. Another advantage of this approach is that if the user wants to reuse these RFID tags, unlike the "killed" tags that need to be activated by the user, the user need only remove the blocker tag. Since the blocker tag can shield the serial numbers of the tags from being read by RFID readers, it can also be used by attackers to disrupt proper operation of an RFID system. A thief can also use the blocker tag to shield the tags attached to the commodities in shops and take them out without being detected.

RFID System Using Symmetric-Key Cryptography

Symmetric-key cryptography, also called *secret-key cryptography* or *single-key cryptography,* uses a single key to perform both encryption and decryption. Due to the limited amount of resources available on an RFID chip, most available symmetric-key cryptographs are too costly to be implemented on an RFID chip. For example, a typical implementation of Advanced Encryption Standard (AES) needs about 2000–3000 gates. This is not appropriate for low-cost RFID tags. It is only possible to implement AES in high-end RFID tags. A successful case of implementing a 128-bit AES on high-end RFID tags has been reported [46].

Using the Symmetric Key to Provide Authentication and Privacy

Symmetric-key cryptography can be applied to prevent tag cloning in RFID systems using a challenge and response protocol. For example, if a tag shares a secret key K with a reader and the tag wants to authenticate itself to the reader, it will first send its identity to the reader. The reader will then generate a nonce N and send it to the tag. The tag will use this nonce and the secret K to generate a hash code $H = h(K,N)$ and send this hash code to the reader. The reader can also generate a hash code $H' = h(K,N)$ and compare these two codes to verify this tag. Using this scheme, it is difficult for an attacker to clone the tags without knowing the secret keys.

Different kinds of symmetric-key cryptography protocol-based RFID tags have been used recently in daily life. For example, an RFID device that uses this symmetric-key challenge-response protocol, called a digital signature transponder, has been introduced by Texas Instruments. This transponder can be built into cars to prevent car theft and can be implemented into wireless payment devices used in filling stations.

One issue of RFID systems that use symmetric-key cryptography is key management. To authenticate itself to an RFID reader, each tag in the system should share a different secret key with the reader, and the reader needs to keep all the keys of these tags. When a tag wants to authenticate itself to an RFID reader, the reader needs to know the secret key shared between them. If the reader does not know the identification of the tag in advance, it cannot determine which key can be used to authenticate this tag. If the tag sends its identification to the reader before the authentication for the reader to search the secret key, the privacy of the tag cannot be protected, since other readers can also obtain the identification of this tag.

To tackle this problem, one simple method is *key searching*. The reader will search all the secret keys in its memory to find the right key for the tag before authentication. There are some protocols proposed for the key search for RFID tags. One general kind of key search scheme [47] has been proposed. In this approach, the tag first generates a random nonce N and hashes this N using its secret key K to generate the hash code. Then it sends both this hash code and N to the reader. Using this nonce N, the reader will generate the hash code with all the secret keys and compare them with the received hash code from the tag. If there is a match, it means it found the right key. In this scheme, since the nonce N is generated randomly every time, the privacy of the tag can be protected.

The problem with this approach is that if there are a large number of tags, the key searching will be very costly. To reduce the cost of the key searching, a modification of this scheme was proposed [48]; in [20], in this approach, a scheme called *tree of secret* is used. Every tag is assigned to a leaf in the tree, and every node in the tree has its secret key. This way the key search cost for each tag can be reduced, but it will add some overlap to the sets of keys for each tag.

Another approach to reduce the cost of key searching is for the RFID tags and RFID reader to keep synchronization with each other. In this kind of approach, every tag will maintain a counter for the reader query times. For each reader's query, the tag should respond with a different value. The reader will also maintain counters for all the tags' responses and maintain a table of all the possible response values. Then, if the reader and tags can keep synchronization, the reader can know the approximate

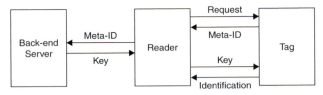

FIGURE 13.2 Tag unlock.

current counter number of the tags. When the reader receives a response from a tag, it can search the table and quickly identify this tag.

Other Symmetric-Key Cryptography-Based Approaches

In addition to the basic symmetric-key challenge-response protocol, some symmetric-key cryptography-based approaches have been proposed recently to protect the security and privacy of RFID systems.

One approach is called YA-TRAP: Yet Another Trivial RFID Authentication Protocol, proposed by Tsudik [49]. In this approach, a technique for the inexpensive untraceable identification of RFID tags is introduced. Here *untraceable* means it is computationally difficult to gather the information about the identity of RFID tags from the interaction with them. In YA-TRAP, for the purpose of authentication, only minimal communication between the reader and tags is needed, and the computational burden on the back-end server is very small.

The back-end server in the system is assumed to be secure and maintains all tag information. Each tag should be initialized with three values: K_i, T_0, and T_{max}. K_i is both the identifier and the cryptographic key for this tag. The size of K_i depends on the number of tags and the secure authentication requirement; in practice, 160 bits is enough. T_0 is the initial timestamp of this tag. The value of T_0 of each tag does not need to vary. This means that a group of tags can have the same T_0. T_{max} is the maximum value of T_0, and a group of tags can also have the same T_{max} value. In addition, each tag has a seeded pseudorandom number generator.

YA-TRAP works as follows: First, each tag should store a timestamp T_t in its memory. When an RFID reader wants to interrogate a RFID tag, it will send the current timestamp T_r to this tag. Receiving T_r, the tag will compare T_r with the timestamp value it stores and with T_{max}. If $T_r < T_t$ or $T_r > T_{max}$, this tag will respond to the reader with a random value generated by the seeded pseudo random number generator. Otherwise, the tag will replace T_t with T_r and calculate $H_r = HMACK_i(T_t)$, and then send H_r to the reader. Then the reader will send T_r and H_r to

the back-end server. The server will look up its database to find whether this tag is a valid tag. If it's not, the server will send a tag-error message to the reader. If this is a valid tag, the server will send the meta-ID of this tag or the valid message to the reader, according to different application requirements. Since the purpose of this protocol is to minimize the interaction between the reader and tags and minimize the computation burden of the back-end server, it has some vulnerability. One of them is that the adversary can launch a DoS attack to the tag. For example, the attack can send a timestamp $t < T_{max}$, but this t is wildly inaccurate with the current time. In this case, the tag will update its timestamp with the wrong time and the legal reader cannot get access to this tag.

In Ref. [33], another approach called *deterministic hash locks* [50] was proposed. In this scheme, the security of RFID systems is based on the one-way hash function. During initialization, every tag in the system will be given a meta-ID, which is the hash code of a random key. This meta-ID will be stored in the tag's memory. Both the meta-ID and the random key are also stored in the back-end server. After initialization, all the tags will enter the locked state. When they stay in the locked state, tags will respond only with the meta-ID when interrogated by an RFID reader. When a legitimate reader wants to unlock a tag, as shown in Figure 13.2, it will first send a request to the tag. After receiving the meta-ID from the tag, the reader will send this meta-ID to the back-end server. The back-end server will search in its database using this meta-ID to get the random key. Then it will send this key to the reader, and the reader will send it to the tag. Using this random key, the tag will hash this key and compare the hash code with its meta-ID. The tag will unlock itself and send its actual identification to the reader if these two values match. Then the tag will return to the locked state to prevent hijacking of illegal readers. Since the illegal reader cannot contact the back-end server to get the random key, it cannot get the actual identification of the tag.

One problem with deterministic hash locks is that when the tag is queried, it will respond with its meta-ID. Since the meta-ID of the tag is a static one and cannot change, the tag can be tracked easily. To solve this problem, Weis, Sarma, Rivest, and Engels proposed the Randomized Hash Locks protocol to prevent tracking of the tag. In this protocol, each tag is equipped with not only the one-way hash function but also a random number generator. When the tag is requested by a reader, it will use the random number generator to generate a random number and will hash this random number together with its identification. The tag will respond with this hash code and the random number to the reader. After receiving this response from the tag, the reader will get all identifications of the tags from the back-end server. Using these identifications, the reader will perform brute-force search by hashing the identification of each tag together with the random number and compare the hash code. If there is a match, the reader can know the identification of the tag. In this approach, the tag response to the reader is not dependent on the request of the reader, which means that the tag is vulnerable to replay attack. To avoid this, Juels and Weis proposed a protocol called Improved Randomized Hash-Locks [51].

RFID System Using Public-key Cryptography

Symmetric-key cryptography can provide security for RFID systems, but it is more suitable to be implemented in a closed environment. If the shared secret keys between them are leaked, it will impose a big problem for the security of RFID systems. Public-key cryptography is more suitable for open systems, since both RFID readers and tags can use their public keys to protect the security of RFID systems. In addition, using public-key cryptography can not only prevent leakage of any information to the eavesdropper attack during communication between reader and tags, it also can provide digital signatures for both the readers and tags for authentication. In the public-key cryptography system, an RFID reader does not need to keep all the secret keys for each tag and does not need to search the appropriate key for each tag as it does in a symmetric-key cryptography system. This will reduce the system burden for key management. Although public-key cryptography has some advantages over symmetric-key cryptography, it is commonly accepted that public-key cryptography is computationally more expensive than symmetric-key cryptography. Because of the limitations of memory and computational power of the ordinary RFID tags, it is difficult for the public-key cryptography to be implemented in RFID systems. In recent years, some research shows that some kinds of public key-based cryptographies such as elliptic curve cryptography and hyperelliptic curve cryptography are feasible to be implemented in high-end RFID tags [52].

Authentication with Public-Key Cryptography

Basically, there are two different kinds of RFID tag authentication methods using public-key cryptography: one is online authentication and the other is offline authentication [53].

For the authentication of RFID tags in an online situation, the reader is connected with a database server. The database server stores a large number of challenge-response pairs for each tag, making it difficult for the attacker to test all the challenge-response pairs during a limited time period. During the challenge-response pairs enrollment phase, the physical uncloneable function part of RFID systems will be challenged by a Certification Authority with a variety of challenges, and accordingly it will generate responses for these challenges. The physical uncloneable function is embodied in a physical object and can give responses to the given challenges [54]. Then these generated challenge-response pairs will be stored in the database server.

In the authentication phase, when a reader wants to authenticate a tag, first the reader will send a request to the tag for its identification. After getting the ID of the tag, the reader will search the database server to get a challenge-response pair for this ID and send the challenge to the tag. After receiving the challenge from the reader, the tag will challenge its physical uncloneable function to get a response for this challenge and then send this response to the reader. The reader will compare this received response with the response stored in the database server. If the difference between these two responses is less than a certain predetermined threshold, the tag can pass the authentication. Then the database server will remove this challenge-response pair for this ID.

One paper [55] details how the authentication of RFID tags works in an offline situation using public key cryptography. To provide offline authentication for the tags, a PUF-Certificate-Identify-based identification scheme is proposed. In this method, a standard identification scheme and a standard signature scheme are used. Then the security of RFID systems depends on the security of the PUF, the standard identification scheme, and the standard signature scheme. For the standard identification scheme, an elliptic curve discrete log based on Okamoto's Identification protocol [56] is used. This elliptic curve discrete log protocol is feasible to be implemented in the RFID tags.

Identity-Based Cryptography Used in the RFID Networks

An identity-based cryptographic scheme is a kind of public-key-based approach that was first proposed by Shamir [57] in 1984. To use identity-based cryptography in RFID systems, since both the RFID tags and the reader have their identities, it is convenient for them to use their own identities to generate their public keys.

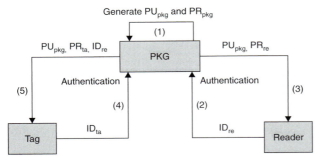

FIGURE 13.3 Key generation and distribution.

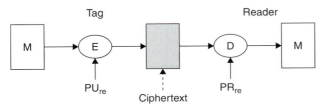

FIGURE 13.4 Message encryption.

An RFID system based on identity-based cryptography should be set up with the help of a PKG. When the reader and tags enter the system, each of them is allocated a unique identity stored in their memory. The process of key generation and distribution in the RFID system that uses identity-based cryptography is shown in Figure 13.3 and is outlined here:

1. PKG generates a "master" public key PU_{pkg} and a related "master" private key PR_{pkg} and saves them in its memory.
2. The RFID reader authenticates itself to the PKG with its identity ID_{re}.
3. If the reader can pass the authentication, PKG generates a unique private key PR_{re} for the reader and sends this private key together with PU_{pkg} to reader.
4. When an RFID tag enters the system, it authenticates itself to the PKG with its identity ID_{ta}.
5. If the tag can pass the authentication, PKG generates a unique private key PR_{ta} for the tag and sends PR_{ta} together with PU_{pkg} and the identity of the reader ID_{re} to the tag.

After this process, the reader can know its private key PR_{re} and can use PU_{pkg} and its identity to generate its public key. Every tag entered into the system can know its own private key and can generate a public key of its own and a public key of the reader.

If an RFID tag is required to transmit messages to the reader in security, since the tag can generate the reader's public key PU_{re}, it can use this key PU_{re} to encrypt the message and transmit this encrypted message to the

reader. As shown in Figure 13.4, after receiving the message from the tag, the reader can use its private key PR_{re} to decrypt the message. Since only the reader can know its private key PR_{re}, the security of the message can be protected.

Figure 13.5 illustrates the scheme for the reader to create its digital signature and verify it. First, the reader will use the message and the hash function to generate a hash code, and then it uses its private key PR_{re} to encrypt this hash code to generate the digital signature and attach it to the original message and send both the digital signature and message to the tag. After receiving them, the RFID tag can use the public key of the reader PU_{re} to decrypt the digital signature to recover the hash code. By comparing this hash code with the hash code generated from the message, the RFID tag can verify the digital signature.

Figure 13.6 illustrates the scheme for the RFID tag to create its digital signature and verify it. In RFID systems, the reader cannot know the identity of the tag before reading it from the tag. The reader cannot generate the public key of the tag, so the general protocol used in identity-based networks cannot be used here. In our approach, first, the tag will use its identity and its private key PR_{ta} to generate a digital signature. When the tag needs to authenticate itself to the reader, it will add this digital signature to its identity, encrypt it with the public key of the reader PU_{re}, and send to the reader; only the reader can decrypt this ciphertext and get the identity of the tag and the digital signature. Using the tag identity, the reader can generate the tag's public key PU_{ta}. Then the reader can use this public key to verify the digital signature.

As mentioned, the most important problem for the symmetric-key approach in RFID systems is the key management. The RFID tags need a great deal of memory to store all the secret keys related with each tag in the system for message decryption. Also, if the RFID reader receives a message from a tag, it cannot know which tag this message is from and therefore cannot know which key it can use to decrypt the message. The reader needs to search all the keys until it finds the right one. In RFID systems using identity-based cryptography, every tag can use the public key of the reader to generate the ciphertext that can be decrypted using the reader's private key, so the reader does not need to know the key of the tags; all it needs to keep is its own private key.

In some RFID applications such as epassports and visas, tag authentication is required. However, the symmetric-key approach cannot provide digital signatures for RFID tags to authenticate them to RFID readers. By using an identity-based scheme, the tags can generate digital signatures using their private keys and store them in the tags.

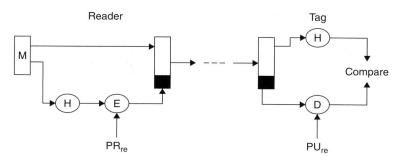

FIGURE 13.5 A digital signature from a reader.

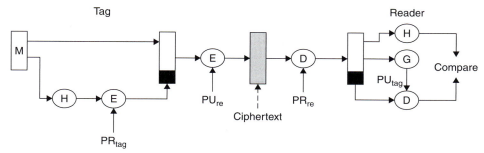

FIGURE 13.6 A digital signature from a tag.

When they need to authenticate themselves to RFID readers, they can transmit these digital signatures to the reader, and the reader can verify them using the tags' public keys.

In identity-based cryptography RFID systems, since the identity of the tags and reader can be used to generate public keys, the PKG does not need to keep the key directory, so it can reduce the resource requirements. Another advantage of using identity-based cryptography in RFID systems is that the reader does not need to know the public keys of the tags in advance. If the reader wants to verify the digital signature of an RFID tag, it can read the identity of the tag and use the public key generated from the identity to verify the digital signature.

An inherent weakness of identity-based cryptography is the key escrow problem. But in RFID systems that use identity-based cryptography, because all the devices can be within one company or organization, the PKG can be highly trusted and protected, and the chance of key escrow can be reduced.

Another problem of identity-based cryptography is revocation. For example, people always use their public information such as their names or home addresses to generate their public key. If their private keys are compromised by an attacker, since their public information cannot be changed easily, this will make it difficult to regenerate their new public keys. In contrast, in RFID systems the identity of the tag is used to generate the public key. If the private key of one tag has been compromised, the system can allocate a new identity to the tag and use this new identity to effortlessly create a new private key to the tag.

REFERENCES

[1] S.A. Weis, Security and Privacy in Radio-Frequency Identification Devices.

[2] M. Langheinrich, RFID and Privacy.

[3] Auto-ID Center, Draft Protocol Specification for a Class 0 Radio Frequency Identification Tag, February 2003.

[4] K. Finkenzeller, RFID Handbook: Fundamentals and Applications in Contactless Smart Cards and Identification.

[5] P. Peris-Lopez, J.C. Hernandez-Castro, J. Estevez-Tapiador, A. Ribagorda, RFID systems: A survey on security threats and proposed solutions, in: 11th IFIP International Conference on Personal Wireless Communications – PWC06, Volume 4217 of Lecture Notes in Computer Science, Springer-Verlag, September 2006, pp. 159–170.

[6] J. Wiley & Sons, RFID Handbook, second ed.

[7] T. Phillips, T. Karygiannis, R. Huhn, Security standards for the RFID market, IEEE Security & Privacy (November/December 2005) 85–89.

[8] RFID Handbook, second ed., J. Wiley & Sons.

[9] RFID Handbook, second ed., J. Wiley & Sons.

[10] T. Phillips, T. Karygiannis, R. Huhn, Security standards for the RFID market, IEEE Security & Privacy (November/December 2005) 85–89.

[11] EPCglobal, www.epcglobalinc.org/, June 2005.

[12] P. Peris-Lopez, J.C. Hernandez-Castro, J. Estevez-Tapiador, A. Ribagorda, RFID systems: a survey on security threats and proposed solutions, in: 11th IFIP International Conference on Personal Wireless Communications – PWC06, Volume 4217 of Lecture Notes in Computer Science, Springer-Verlag, September 2006, pp. 159–170.

[13] T. Phillips, T. Karygiannis, R. Huhn, Security standards for the RFID market, IEEE Security & Privacy (2005) 85–89.

[14] EPCglobal Tag Data Standards, Version 1.3.

[15] EPCglobal, www.epcglobalinc.org/, June 2005.

[16] Guidelines for Securing Radio Frequency Identification (RFID) Systems, Recommendations of the National Institute of Standards and Technology, NIST Special Publication 800–98.

[17] D.R. Thompson, N. Chaudhry, C.W. Thompson, RFID Security Threat Model.

[18] S. Weis, S. Sarma, R. Rivest, D. Engels, Security and privacy aspects of low-cost radio frequency identification systems, in: W. Stephan, D. Hutter, G. Muller, M. Ullmann (Eds.), International Conference on Security in Pervasive computing-SPC 2003, vol. 2802, Springer-Verlag, 2003, pp. 454–469.

[19] P. Peris-Lopez, J.C. Hernandez-Castro, J. Estevez-Tapiador, A. Ribagorda, RFID systems: a survey on security threats and proposed solutions, in: 11th IFIP International Conference on Personal Wireless Communications – PWC06, Volume 4217 of Lecture Notes in Computer Science, Springer-Verlag, September 2006, pp. 159–170.

[20] D. Haehnel, W. Burgard, D. Fox, K. Fishkin, M. Philipose, Mapping and localization with WID technology, International Conference on Robotics & Automation, 2004.

[21] D.R. Thompson, N. Chaudhry, C.W. Thompson, RFID Security Threat Model.

[22] D.R. Thompson, N. Chaudhry, C.W. Thompson, RFID Security Threat Model.

[23] A. Juels, R.L. Rivest, M. Syzdlo, The blocker tag: selective blocking of RFID tags for consumer privacy, in: V. Atluri (Ed.), 8th ACM Conference on Computer and Communications Security, 2003, pp. 103–111.

[24] A. Juels, R.L. Rivest, M. Syzdlo, The blocker tag: selective blocking of RFID tags for consumer privacy, in: V. Atluri (Ed.), 8th ACM Conference on Computer and Communications Security, 2003, pp. 103–111.

[25] D.R. Thompson, N. Chaudhry, C.W. Thompson, RFID Security Threat Model.

[26] D.R. Thompson, N. Chaudhry, C.W. Thompson, RFID Security Threat Model.

[27] D.R. Thompson, N. Chaudhry, C.W. Thompson, RFID Security Threat Model.

[28] F. Thornton, B. Haines, A.M. Das, H. Bhargava, A. Campbell, J. Kleinschmidt, RFID Security.

[29] C. Jechlitschek, A Survey Paper on Radio Frequency Identification (RFID) Trends.

[30] S.H. Weingart, Physical Security Devices for Computer Subsystems: A Survey of Attacks and Defenses.

[31] S.A. Weis, Security and Privacy in Radio-Frequency Identification Devices.

[32] C. Jechlitschek, A Survey Paper on Radio Frequency Identification (RFID) Trends.

[33] C. Jechlitschek, A Survey Paper on Radio Frequency Identification (RFID) Trends.

[34] S.E. Sarma, S.A. Weis, D.W. Engels, RFID systems security and privacy implications, Technical Report, MITAUTOID-WH-014, AutoID Center, MIT, 2002.

[35] S. Inoue, H. Yasuura, RFID privacy using user-controllable uniqueness, in: RFID Privacy Workshop, MIT, November 2003.

[36] N. Good, J. Han, E. Miles, D. Molnar, D. Mulligan, L. Quilter, J. Urban, D. Wagner, Radio frequency ID and privacy with information goods, in: Workshop on Privacy in the Electronic Society (WPES), 2004.

[37] N. Good, J. Han, E. Miles, D. Molnar, D. Mulligan, L. Quilter, J. Urban, D. Wagner, Radio frequency ID and privacy with information goods, in: Workshop on Privacy in the Electronic Society (WPES), 2004.

[38] A. Juels, Minimalist cryptography for low-cost RFID tags, in: C. Blundo, S. Cimato (Eds.), The Fourth International Conference on Security in Communication Networks – SCN 2004, Vol. 3352 of Lecture Notes in Computer Science, Springer-Verlag, 2004, pp. 149–164.

[39] A. Juels, R. Pappu, Squealing euros: privacy protection in RFID-enabled banknotes. in: R. Wright (Ed.), Financial Cryptography '03, vol. 2742, Springer-Verlag, 2003, pp. 103–121.

[40] P. Golle, M. Jakobsson, A. Juels, P. Syverson, Universal re-encryption for mixnets, in: T. Okamoto (Ed.), RSA Conference-Cryptographers' Track (CT-RSA), vol. 2964, 2004, pp. 163–178.

[41] G. Ateniese, J. Camenisch, B. de Madeiros, Untraceable RFID tags via insubvertible encryption, in: 12th ACM Conference on Computer and Communication Security, 2005.

[42] C. Floerkemeier, R. Schneider, M. Langheinrich, Scanning with a Purpose Supporting the Fair Information Principles in RFID Protocols, 2004.

[43] M.R. Rieback, B. Crispo, A. Tanenbaum, RFID Guardian: a battery-powered mobile device for RFID privacy management, in: C. Boyd, J.M. Gonz´alez Nieto (Eds.), Australasian Conference on Information Security and Privacy – ACISP 2005, Vol. 3574 of Lecture Notes in Computer Science, Springer-Verlag, 2005, pp. 184–194.

[44] M.R. Rieback, B. Crispo, A. Tanenbaum, RFID guardian: a battery-powered mobile device for RFID privacy management, in: C. Boyd, J.M. Gonz´alez Nieto (Eds.), Australasian Conference on Information Security and Privacy – ACISP 2005, vol. 3574 of Lecture Notes in Computer Science, Springer-Verlag, 2005, pp. 184–194.

[45] A. Juels, R.L. Rivest, M. Syzdlo, The blocker tag: selective blocking of RFID tags for consumer privacy, in: V. Atluri (Ed.), 8th ACM Conference on Computer and Communications Security, 2003, pp. 103–111.

[46] M. Feldhofer, S. Dominikus, J. Wolkerstorfer, Strong authentication for RFID systems using the AES algorithm, in: M. Joye, J.-J. Quisquater (Eds.), Workshop on Cryptographic Hardware and Embedded Systems CHES 04, Vol. 3156 of Lecture Notes in Computer Science, Springer-Verlag, 2004, pp. 357–370.

[47] S. Weis, S. Sarma, R. Rivest, D. Engels, Security and privacy aspects of low-cost radio frequency identification systems, in: W. Stephan, D. Hutter, G. Muller, M. Ullmann (Eds.), International Conference on Security in Pervasive computing-SPC 2003, vol. 2802, Springer-Verlag, 2003, pp. 454–469.

[48] D. Molnar, D. Wagner, Privacy and security in library RFID: issues, practices, and architectures, in: B. Pfitzmann, P. McDaniel (Eds.),

ACM Conference on Communications and Computer Security, ACM Press, 2004, pp. 210– 219.

[49] G. Tsudik, YA-TRAP: Yet another trivial RFID authentication protocol, in: Fourth Annual IEEE International Conference on Pervasive Computing and Communications Workshops (PERCOMW'06), 2006, pp. 640–643.

[50] S. Weis, S. Sarma, R. Rivest, D. Engels, Security and privacy aspects of low-cost radio frequency identification systems, in: W. Stephan, D. Hutter, G. Muller, M. Ullmann (Eds.), International Conference on Security in Pervasive computing-SPC 2003, vol. 2802, Springer-Verlag, 2003, pp. 454–469.

[51] A. Juels, S. Weis, Defining strong privacy for RFID, in: Pervasive Computing and Communications Workshops, 2007.

[52] P. Tuyls, L. Batina, RFID tags for anticounterfeiting, in: D. Pointcheval (Ed.), Topics in Cryptology-CT-RSA 2006, Springer-Verlag, 2006.

[53] L. Batina, J. Guajardo, T. Kerins, N. Mentens, P. Tuyls, I. Verbauwhede, Public-key cryptography for RFID-tags. in:

Printed handout of Workshop on RFID Security," RFIDSec06, 2006, pp. 61–76.

[54] P. Tuyls, L. Batina, RFID tags for anticounterfeiting, in: D. Pointcheval (Ed.), Topics in Cryptology-CT-RSA 2006, Springer-Verlag, 2006.

[55] P. Tuyls, L. Batina, RFID tags for anticounterfeiting, in: D. Pointcheval (Ed.), Topics in Cryptology-CT-RSA 2006, Springer-Verlag, 2006.

[56] T, Okamoto, (1992). Provably secure and practical identification schemes and corresponding signature schemes. In: E.F. Brickell (Ed.), Advances in Cryptology | CRYPTO'92, Vol. 740 of LNCS, Springer-Verlag, 1992, pp. 31–53.

[57] A. Shamir, Identity-based cryptosystems and signature scheme, Advances in Cryptology: Proceedings of CRYPTO 84, LNCS, 1984, pp. 47–53.

Part II

Managing Information Security

Information Security Essentials for IT Managers: Protecting Mission-Critical Systems

Albert Caballero

Terremark Worldwide, Inc.

Information security involves the protection of organizational assets from the disruption of business operations, modification of sensitive data, or disclosure of proprietary information. The protection of this data is usually described as maintaining the confidentiality, integrity, and availability (CIA) of the organization's assets, operations, and information.

1. INFORMATION SECURITY ESSENTIALS FOR IT MANAGERS, OVERVIEW

Information security management as a field is ever increasing in demand and responsibility because most organizations spend increasingly larger percentages of their IT budgets in attempting to manage risk and mitigate intrusions, not to mention the trend in many enterprises of moving all IT operations to an Internet-connected infrastructure, known as enterprise cloud computing.[1] For information security managers, it is crucial to maintain a clear perspective of all the areas of business that require protection. Through collaboration with all business units, security managers must work security into the processes of all aspects of the organization, from employee training to research and development. Security is not an IT problem, it is a business problem.

Information security means protecting information and information systems from unauthorized access, use, disclosure, disruption, modification, or destruction.[2]

Scope of Information Security Management

Information security is a business problem in the sense that the entire organization must frame and solve security problems based on its own strategic drivers, not solely on technical controls aimed to mitigate one type of attack. As identified throughout this chapter, security goes beyond technical controls and encompasses people, technology, policy, and operations in a way that few other business objectives do. The evolution of a risk-based paradigm, as opposed to a technical solution paradigm for security, has made it clear that a secure organization does not result from securing technical infrastructure alone. Furthermore, securing the organization's technical infrastructure cannot provide the appropriate protection for these assets, nor will it protect many other information assets that are in no way dependent on technology for their existence or protection. Thus, the organization would be lulled into a false sense of security if it relied on protecting its technical infrastructure alone.[3]

CISSP Ten Domains of Information Security

In the information security industry there have been several initiatives to attempt to define security management and how and when to apply it. The leader in certifying information security professionals is the Internet Security Consortium, with its CISSP (see sidebar, "CISSP Ten Domains: Common Body of Knowledge") certification.[4]

---

1 "Cloud computing, the enterprise cloud," Terremark Worldwide Inc. Website, http://www.theenterprisecloud.com/

2 "Definition of information security," Wikipedia, http://en.wikipedia.org/wiki/Information_security

3 Richard A. Caralli, William R. Wilson, "The challenges of security management," Survivable Enterprise Management Team, Networked Systems Survivability Program, Software Engineering Institute, http://www.cert.org/archive/pdf/ESMchallenges.pdf

4 "CISSP Ten domains" ISC2 Web site https://www.isc2.org/cissp/default.aspx

CISSP Ten Domains: Common Body of Knowledge:

- *Access control.* Methods used to enable administrators and managers to define what objects a subject can access through authentication and authorization, providing each subject a list of capabilities it can perform on each object. Important areas include access control security models, identification and authentication technologies, access control administration, and single sign-on technologies.

- *Telecommunications and network security.* Examination of internal, external, public, and private network communication systems, including devices, protocols, and remote access.

- *Information security and risk management.* Including physical, technical, and administrative controls surrounding organizational assets to determine the level of protection and budget warranted by highest to lowest risk. The goal is to reduce potential threats and money loss.

- *Application security.* Application security involves the controls placed within the application programs and operating systems to support the security policy of the organization and measure its effectiveness. Topics include threats, applications development, availability issues, security design and vulnerabilities, and application/data access control.

- *Cryptography.* The use of various methods and techniques such as symmetric and asymmetric encryption to achieve desired levels of confidentiality and integrity. Important areas include encryption protocols and applications and Public Key Infrastructures.

- *Security architecture and design.* This area covers the concepts, principles, and standards used to design and implement secure applications, operating systems, and all platforms based on international evaluation criteria such as Trusted Computer Security Evaluation Criteria (TCSEC) and Common Criteria.

- *Operations security.* Controls over personnel, hardware systems, and auditing and monitoring techniques such as maintenance of AV, training, auditing, and resource protection; preventive, detective, corrective, and recovery controls; and security and fault-tolerance technologies.

- *Business continuity and disaster recovery planning.* The main purpose of this area is to preserve business operations when faced with disruptions or disasters. Important aspects are to identify resource values, perform a business impact analysis, and produce business unit priorities, contingency plans, and crisis management.

- *Legal, regulatory, compliance, and investigations.* Computer crime, government laws and regulations, and geographic locations will determine the types of actions that constitute wrongdoing, what is suitable evidence, and what type of licensing and privacy laws your organization must abide by.

- *Physical (environmental) security.* Concerns itself with threats, risks, and countermeasures to protect facilities, hardware, data, media, and personnel. Main topics include restricted areas, authorization models, intrusion detection, fire detection, and security guards.

In defining required skills for information security managers, the ISC has arrived at an agreement on ten domains of information security that is known as the *Common Body of Knowledge* (CBK). Every security manager must understand and be well versed in all areas of the CBK.[5]

In addition to individual certification there must be guidelines to turn these skills into actionable items that can be measured and verified according to some international standard or framework. The most widely used standard for maintaining and improving information security is ISO/IEC 17799:2005. ISO 17799 (see Figure 14.1) establishes guidelines and principles for initiating, implementing, maintaining, and improving information security management in an organization.[6]

A new and popular framework to use in conjunction with the CISSP CBK and the ISO 17799 guidelines is ISMM. ISMM is a framework (see Figure 14.2) that describes a five-level evolutionary path of increasingly organized and systematically more mature security layers. It is proposed for the maturity assessment of information security management and the evaluation of the level of security awareness and practice at any organization, whether public or private. Furthermore, it helps us better understand where, and to what extent, the three main processes of security (prevention, detection, and recovery) are implemented and integrated.

ISMM helps us better understand the application of information security controls outlined in ISO 17799. Figure 14.3 shows a content matrix that defines the scope of applicability between various security controls mentioned in ISO 17799's ten domains and the corresponding scope of applicability on the ISMM Framework.[7]

---

5 Micki, Krause, Harold F. Tipton, *Information Security Management Handbook sixth edition* CRC Press LLC

6 "ISO 17799 security standards," ISO Web site, http://www.iso.org/iso/support/faqs/faqs_widely_used_standards/widely_used_standards_other/information_security.htm

7 Saad Saleh AlAboodi, *A New Approach for Assessing the Maturity of Information Security*, CISSP

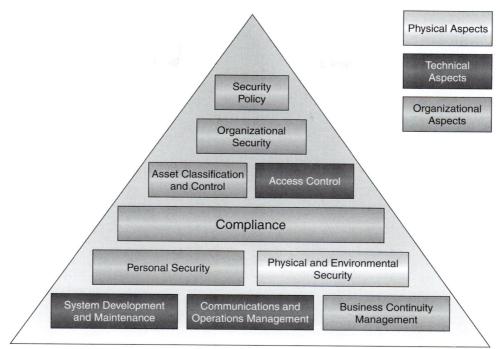

FIGURE 14.1 ISO 17799:2005 security model.[8]

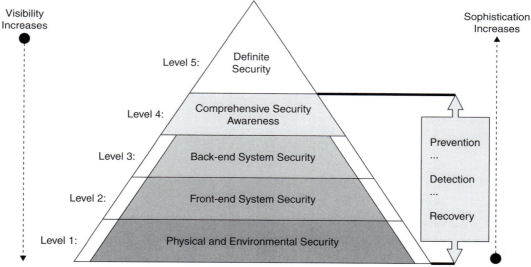

FIGURE 14.2 ISMM framework.[9]

What is a Threat?

Threats to information systems come in many flavors, some with malicious intent, others with supernatural powers or unexpected surprises. Threats can be deliberate acts of espionage, information extortion, or sabotage, as in many targeted attacks between foreign nations;

however, more often than not it happens that the biggest threats can be forces of nature (hurricane, flood) or acts of human error or failure. It is easy to become consumed in attempting to anticipate and mitigate every threat, but this is simply not possible. Threat agents are threats only when they are provided the opportunity to take advantage of a vulnerability, and ultimately there is no guarantee that the vulnerability will be exploited. Therefore, determining which threats are important can only be done in the context of your organization. The process by which a threat can actually cause damage to your information assets is as follows: A threat agent *gives rise to*

8 "ISO 17799 security standards," ISO Web site, http://www.iso.org/iso/support/faqs/faqs_widely_used_standards/widely_used_standards_other/information_security.htm

9 Saad Saleh AlAboodi, *A New Approach for Assessing the Maturity of Information Security*, CISSP

ISO 17799			ISMM (Scope of Applicability)				
Domain Number	Domain Name	Domain Subname	Layer 1	Layer 2	Layer 3	Layer 4	Layer 5
1	Security policy	N/A	✓	✓	✓	✓	
2	Organizational security	Information security infrastructure	✓	✓	✓		
		Security of third-party access	✓	✓	✓	✓	
		Outsourcing	✓	✓	✓	✓	
3	Asset classification and control	Accountability for assets	✓	✓	✓		
		Information classification	✓	✓	✓		
4	Personnel security	Security in job definition and resourcing	✓				
		User training	✓	✓	✓	✓	
		Responding to security incidents/malfunctions	✓	✓	✓	✓	
5	Physical and environmental security	Secure areas	✓				
		Equipment security	✓				
		General controls	✓				
6	Communications and operations management	Operational procedures and responsibilities		✓	✓		
		System planning and acceptance		✓	✓		
		Protection against malicious software		✓			
		Housekeeping		✓	✓		
		Network management			✓		
		Media handling and security	✓				
		Exchange of information and software		✓			
7	Access control	Business requirement for access control	✓	✓	✓		
		User access management		✓			
		User responsibilities		✓			
		Network access control			✓		
		Operating system access control			✓		
		Application access control		✓			
		Monitoring system access and use		✓	✓		
		Mobile computing and teleworking		✓	✓		
8	System development and maintenance	Security requirement of systems		✓	✓		
		Security in application systems		✓			
		Cryptographic controls			✓		
		Security of system files		✓	✓		
		Security in development and support processes		✓	✓		
9	Business continuity management	N/A				✓	✓
10	Compliance	Compliance with legal requirements				✓	
		Review of security policy and compliance				✓	
		System audit considerations				✓	

FIGURE 14.3 A content matrix for ISO 17799 and its scope of applicability.

a threat that *exploits* a vulnerability and can *lead to* a security risk that *can damage* your assets and *cause* an exposure. This can be *counter-measured by* a safeguard that *directly affects* the threat agent. Figure 14.4 shows the building blocks of the threat process.

Common Attacks

Threats are exploited with a variety of attacks, some technical, others not so much. Organizations that focus on the technical attacks and neglect items such as policies and procedures or employee training and awareness are setting information security up for failure. The mantra that the IT department or even the security department, by themselves, can secure an organization is as antiquated as black-and-white television. Most threats today are a mixed blend of automated information gathering, social engineering, and combined exploits, giving the perpetrator endless vectors through which to gain access. Examples of attacks vary from a highly technical remote exploit over the Internet, social-engineering an administrative assistant to reset his password, or simply walking right through an unprotected door in the back of your building. All scenarios have the potential to be equally devastating to the integrity of the organization. Some of the most common attacks are briefly described in the sidebar, "Common Attacks."[10]

---

10 Symantec Global Internet, Security Threat Report, Trends for July–December 07, Volume XII, Published April 2008 http://eval.symantec.com/mktginfo/enterprise/white_papers/b-whitepaper_internet_security_threat_report_xiii_04-2008.en-us.pdf

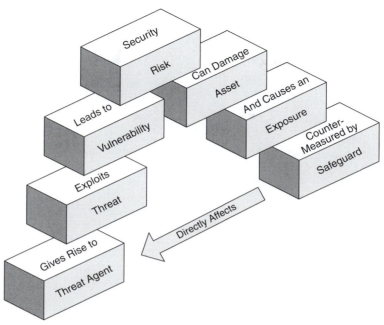

FIGURE 14.4 The threat process.

Common Attacks

- *Malicious code (malware).* Malware is a broad category; however, it is typically software designed to infiltrate or damage a computer system without the owner's informed consent. As shown in Figure 14.5, the most commonly identifiable types of malware are viruses, worms, backdoors, and Trojans. Particularly difficult to identify are root kits, which alter the kernel of the operating system.

- *Social engineering.* The art of manipulating people into performing actions or divulging confidential information. Similar to a confidence trick or simple fraud, the term typically applies to trickery to gain information or computer system access; in most cases, the attacker never comes face to face with the victim.

- *Industrial espionage.* Industrial espionage describes activities such as theft of trade secrets, bribery, blackmail, and

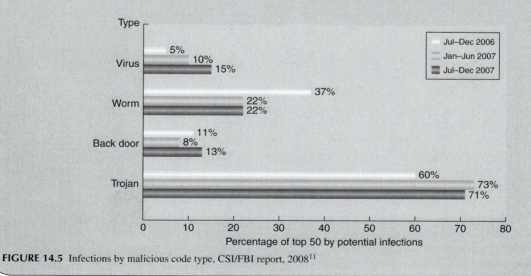

FIGURE 14.5 Infections by malicious code type, CSI/FBI report, 2008[11]

---

11 Robert Richardson, "2008 CSI Computer Crime & Security Survey," (The latest results from the longest-running project of its kind) http://i.cmpnet.com/v2.gocsi.com/pdf/CSIsurvey2008.pdf

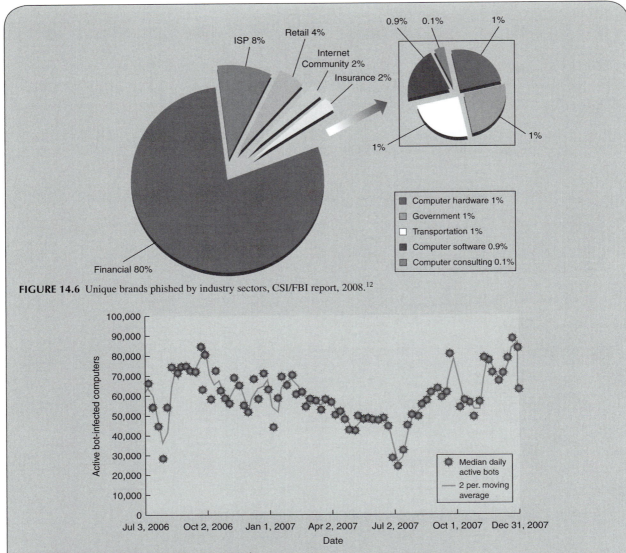

FIGURE 14.6 Unique brands phished by industry sectors, CSI/FBI report, 2008.[12]

FIGURE 14.7 Botnet activity, CSI/FBI report, 2008[13]

technological surveillance as well as spying on commercial organizations and sometimes governments.

- *Spam, phishing, and hoaxes.* Spamming and phishing (see Figure 14.6), although different, often go hand in hand. Spamming is the abuse of electronic messaging systems to indiscriminately send unsolicited bulk messages, many of which contain hoaxes or other undesirable contents such as links to phishing sites. Phishing is the criminally fraudulent process of attempting to acquire sensitive information such as usernames, passwords, and credit-card details by masquerading as a trustworthy entity in an electronic communication.
- *Denial-of-service (DoS) and distributed denial-of-service (DDoS).* These are attempts to make a computer resource unavailable to its intended users. Although the means to carry out, motives for, and targets of a DoS attack may vary, it generally consists of the concerted, malevolent efforts of a person or persons to prevent an Internet site or service from functioning efficiently or at all, temporarily or indefinitely.
- *Botnets.* The term *botnet* (see Figure 14.7) can be used to refer to any group of bots, or software robots, such as IRC bots, but this word is generally used to refer to a collection of compromised computers (called zombies) running software, usually installed via worms, Trojan horses, or backdoors, under a common command-and-control infrastructure. The majority of these computers are running Microsoft Windows operating systems, but other operating systems can be affected.

12 Robert Richardson, "2008 CSI Computer Crime & Security Survey," (The latest results from the longest-running project of its kind) http://i.cmpnet.com/v2.gocsi.com/pdf/CSIsurvey2008.pdf

13 Robert Richardson, "2008 CSI Computer Crime & Security Survey," (The latest results from the longest-running project of its kind) http://i.cmpnet.com/v2.gocsi.com/pdf/CSIsurvey2008.pdf

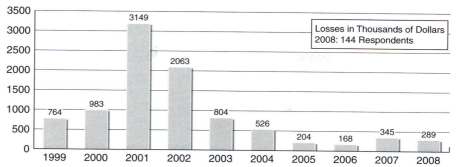

FIGURE 14.8 2008 CSI/FBI Security Survey results.[15]

Impact of Security Breaches

The impact of security breaches on most organizations can be devastating; however, it's not just dollars and cents that are at stake. Aside from the financial burden of having to deal with a security incident, especially if it leads to litigation, other factors could severely damage an organization's ability to operate, or damage the reputation of an organization beyond recovery. Some of the preliminary key findings from the 2008 CSI/FBI Security Report[14] (see Figure 14.8) include:

- Financial fraud cost organizations the most, with an average reported loss of close to $500,000.
- The second most expensive activity was dealing with bots within the network, reported to cost organizations an average of nearly $350,000.
- Virus incidents occurred most frequently, respondents said—at almost half (49%) of respondent organizations.

Some things to consider:

- How much would it cost your organization if your ecommerce Web server farm went down for 12 hours?
- What if your mainframe database that houses your reservation system was not accessible for an entire afternoon?
- What if your Web site was defaced and rerouted all your customers to a site infected with malicious Java scripts?
- Would any of these scenarios significantly impact your organization's bottom line?

2. PROTECTING MISSION-CRITICAL SYSTEMS

The IT core of any organization is its mission-critical systems. These are systems without which the mission of the organization, whether building aircraft carriers for the U.S. military or packaging Twinkies to deliver to food markets, could not operate. The major components to protecting these systems are detailed throughout this chapter; however, with special emphasis on the big picture an information security manager must keep in mind, there are some key components that are crucial for the success and continuity of any organization. These are information assurance, information risk management, defense in depth, and contingency planning.

Information Assurance

Information assurance is achieved when information and information systems are protected against attacks through the application of security services such as availability, integrity, authentication, confidentiality, and nonrepudiation. The application of these services should be based on the protect, detect, and react paradigm. This means that in addition to incorporating protection mechanisms, organizations need to expect attacks and include attack detection tools and procedures that allow them to react to and recover from these unexpected attacks.[16]

Information Risk Management

Risk is, in essence, the likelihood of something going wrong and damaging your organization or information

14 Robert Richardson, "2008 CSI Computer Crime & Security Survey," (The latest results from the longest-running project of its kind) http:// i.cmpnet.com/v2.gocsi.com/pdf/CSIsurvey2008.pdf

15 Robert Richardson, "2008 CSI Computer Crime & Security Survey," (The latest results from the longest-running project of its kind) http:// i.cmpnet.com/v2.gocsi.com/pdf/CSIsurvey2008.pdf

16 "Defense in Depth: A practical strategy for achieving Information Assurance in today's highly networked environments,"

assets. Due to the ramifications of such risk, an organization should try to reduce the risk to an acceptable level. This process is known as *information risk management*. Risk to an organization and its information assets, similar to threats, comes in many different forms. Some of the most common risks and/or threats are:

- *Physical damage.* Fire, water, vandalism, power loss and natural disasters.
- *Human interaction.* Accidental or intentional action or inaction that can disrupt productivity.
- *Equipment malfunctions.* Failure of systems and peripheral devices.
- *Internal or external attacks.* Hacking, cracking, and attacking.
- *Misuse of data.* Sharing trade secrets; fraud, espionage, and theft.
- *Loss of data.* Intentional or unintentional loss of information through destructive means.
- *Application error.* Computation errors, input errors, and buffer overflows.

The idea of risk management is that threats of any kind must be identified, classified, and evaluated to calculate their damage potential.[17] This is easier said than done.

Administrative, Technical, and Physical Controls

For example, administrative, technical, and physical controls, are as follows:

- Administrative controls consist of organizational policies and guidelines that help minimize the exposure of an organization. They provide a framework by which a business can manage and inform its people how they should conduct themselves while at the workplace and provide clear steps employees can take when they're confronted with a potentially risky situation. Some examples of administrative controls include the corporate security policy, password policy, hiring policies, and disciplinary policies that form the basis for the selection and implementation of logical and physical controls. Administrative controls are of paramount importance because technical and physical controls are manifestations of the administrative control policies that are in place.
- Technical controls use software and hardware resources to control access to information and computing systems, to help mitigate the potential for errors and blatant security policy violations. Examples of technical controls include passwords, network- and host-based firewalls, network intrusion detection systems, and access control lists and data encryption. Associated with technical controls is the *Principle of Least Privilege*, which requires that an individual, program, or system process is not granted any more access privileges than are necessary to perform the task.
- Physical controls monitor and protect the physical environment of the workplace and computing facilities. They also monitor and control access to and from such facilities. Separating the network and workplace into functional areas are also physical controls. An important physical control is also separation of duties, which ensures that an individual cannot complete a critical task by herself.

Risk Analysis

During risk analysis there are several units that can help measure risk. Before risk can be measured, though, the organization must identify the vulnerabilities and threats against its mission-critical systems in terms of business continuity. During risk analysis, an organization tries to evaluate the cost for each security control that helps mitigate the risk. If the control is cost effective relative to the exposure of the organization, then the control is put in place. The measure of risk can be determined as a product of threat, vulnerability, and asset values—in other words:

$$\text{Risk} = \text{Asset} \times \text{Threat} \times \text{Vulnerability}$$

There are two primary types of risk analysis: quantitative and qualitative. *Quantitative risk analysis* attempts to assign meaningful numbers to all elements of the risk analysis process. It is recommended for large, costly projects that require exact calculations. It is typically performed to examine the viability of a project's cost or time objectives. Quantitative risk analysis provides answers to three questions that cannot be addressed with deterministic risk and project management methodologies such as traditional cost estimating or project scheduling[18]:

- What's the probability of meeting the project objective, given all known risks?

---

17 Shon Harris, *All in One CISSP Certification Exam Guide 4th Edition*, McGraw Hill Companies

18 Lionel Galway, *Quantitative Risk Analysis for Project Management, A Critical Review*, WR-112-RC, February 2004, http://www.rand.org/pubs/working_papers/2004/RAND_WR112.pdf

- How much could the overrun or delay be, and therefore how much contingency do we need for the organization's desired level of certainty?
- Where in the project is the most risk, given the model of the project and the totality of all identified and quantified risks?

Qualitative risk analysis does not assign numerical values but instead opts for general categorization by severity levels. Where little or no numerical data is available for a risk assessment, the qualitative approach is the most appropriate. The qualitative approach does not require heavy mathematics; instead, it thrives more on the people participating and their backgrounds. Qualitative analysis enables classification of risk that is determined by people's wide experience and knowledge captured within the process. Ultimately it is not an exact science, so the process will count on expert opinions for its base assumptions. The assessment process uses a structured and documented approach and agreed likelihood and consequence evaluation tables. It is also quite common to calculate risk as a single loss expectancy (SLE) or annual loss expectancy (ALE) by project or business function.

Defense in Depth

The principle of *defense in depth* is that layered security mechanisms increase security of a system as a whole. If an attack causes one security mechanism to fail, other mechanisms may still provide the necessary security to protect the system.[19] This is a process that involves people, technology, and operations as key components to its success; however, those are only part of the picture. These organizational layers are difficult to translate into specific technological layers of defenses, and they leave out areas such as security monitoring and metrics. Figure 14.9 shows a mind map that organizes the major categories from both the organizational and technical aspects of defense in depth and takes into account people, policies, monitoring, and security metrics.

Contingency Planning

Contingency planning is necessary in several ways for an organization to be sure it can withstand some sort of security breach or disaster. Among the important steps

required to make sure an organization is protected and able to respond to a security breach or disaster are business impact analysis, incident response planning, disaster recovery planning, and business continuity planning. These contingency plans are interrelated in several ways and need to stay that way so that a response team can change from one to the other seamlessly if there is a need. Figure 14.10 shows the relationship between the four types of contingency plans with the major categories defined in each.

Business impact analysis must be performed in every organization to determine exactly which business process is deemed mission-critical and which processes would not seriously hamper business operations should they be unavailable for some time. An important part of a business impact analysis is the recovery strategy that is usually defined at the end of the process. If a thorough business impact analysis is performed, there should be a clear picture of the priority of each organization's highest-impact, therefore risky, business processes and assets as well as a clear strategy to recover from an interruption in one of these areas.[20]

An Incident Response (IR) Plan

It is a detailed set of processes and procedures that anticipate, detect, and mitigate the impact of an unexpected event that might compromise information resources and assets. Incident response plans are composed of six major phases:

1. *Preparation.* Planning and readying in the event of a security incident.
2. *Identification.* To identify a set of events that have some negative impact on the business and can be considered a security incident.
3. *Containment.* During this phase the security incident has been identified and action is required to mitigate its potential damage.
4. *Eradication.* After it's contained, the incident must be eradicated and studied to make sure it has been thoroughly removed from the system.
5. *Recovery.* Bringing the business and assets involved in the security incident back to normal operations.
6. *Lessons learned.* A thorough review of how the incident occurred and the actions taken to respond to it where the lessons learned get applied to future incidents

---

19 OWASP Definition of Defense in Depth http://www.owasp.org/index.php/Defense_in_depth

20 M. E. Whitman, H. J. Mattord, *Management of Information Security*, Course Technology, 2nd Edition, March 27, 2007.

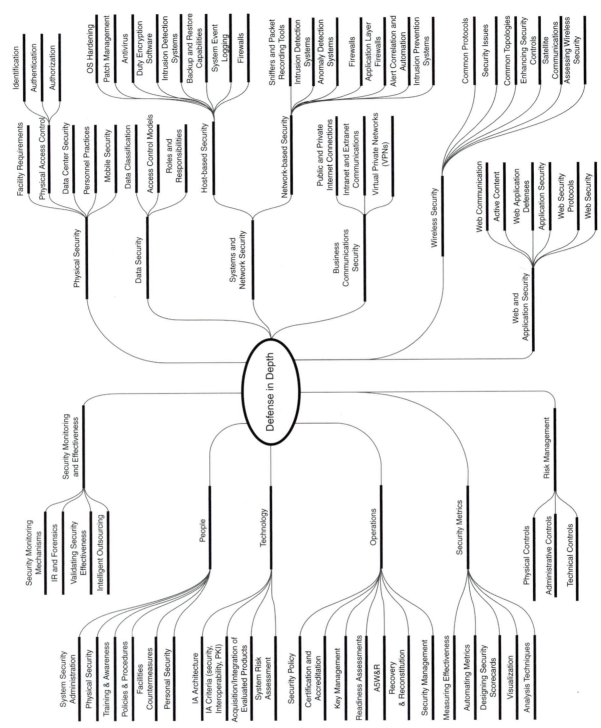

FIGURE 14.9 Defense-in-depth mind map.

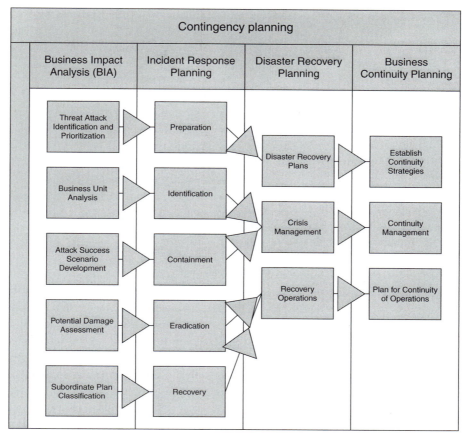

FIGURE 14.10 The relationship between the four types of contingency plans.

When a threat becomes a valid attack, it is classified as an information security incident if[21]:

- It is directed against information assets
- It has a realistic chance of success
- It threatens the confidentiality, integrity, or availability of information assets

Business Continuity Planning (BCP)

It ensures that critical business functions can continue during a disaster and is most properly managed by the CEO of the organization. The BCP is usually activated and executed concurrently with *disaster recovery planning* (DRP) when needed and reestablishes critical functions at alternate sites (DRP focuses on reestablishment at the primary site). BCP relies on identification of critical business functions and the resources to support them using several continuity strategies, such as exclusive-use options like

hot, warm, and cold sites or shared-use options like time-share, service bureaus, or mutual agreements.[22]

Disaster recovery planning is the preparation for and recovery from a disaster. Whether natural or manmade, it is an incident that has become a disaster because the organization is unable to contain or control its impact, or the level of damage or destruction from the incident is so severe that the organization is unable to recover quickly. The key role of DRP is defining how to reestablish operations at the site where the organization is usually located.[23] Key points in a properly designed DRP:

- Clear delegation of roles and responsibilities
- Execution of alert roster and notification of key personnel
- Clear establishment of priorities
- Documentation of the disaster
- Action steps to mitigate the impact

---

21 M. E. Whitman, H. J. Mattord, *Management of Information Security*, Course Technology, 2nd Edition, March 27, 2007.

22 M. E. Whitman, H. J. Mattord, *Management of Information Security*, Course Technology, 2nd Edition, March 27, 2007.

23 M. E. Whitman, H. J. Mattord, *Management of Information Security*, Course Technology, 2nd Edition, March 27, 2007.

- Alternative implementations for various systems components
- DRP must be tested regularly

3. INFORMATION SECURITY FROM THE GROUND UP

The core concepts of information security management and protecting mission-critical systems have been explained. Now, how do you actually apply these concepts to your organization from the ground up? You literally start at the ground (physical) level and work yourself up to the top (application) level. This model can be applied to many IT frameworks, ranging from networking models such as OSI or TCP/IP stacks to operating systems or other problems such as organizational information security and protecting mission-critical systems.

There are many areas of security, all of which are interrelated. You can have an extremely hardened system running your ecommerce Web site and database; however, if physical access to the system is obtained by the wrong person, a simple yanking of the right power plug can be game over. In other words, to think that any of the following components is not important to the overall security of your organization is to provide malicious attackers the only thing they need to be successful—that is, the path of least resistance. The next parts of this chapter each contain an overview of the technologies

(see Figure 14.11) and processes of which information security managers must be aware to successfully secure the assets of any organization:

- Physical security
- Data security
- Systems and network security
- Business communications security
- Wireless security
- Web and application security
- Security policies and procedures
- Security employee training and awareness

Physical Security

Physical security as defined earlier concerns itself with threats, risks, and countermeasures to protect facilities, hardware, data, media and personnel. Main topics include restricted areas, authorization models, intrusion detection, fire detection, and security guards. Therefore physical safeguards must be put in place to protect the organization from damaging consequences. The security rule defines physical safeguards as "physical measures, policies, and procedures to protect a covered entity's electronic information systems and related buildings and equipment, from natural and environmental hazards, and unauthorized intrusion."[24] A brief description of the baseline requirements to implement these safeguards at your facility follow.

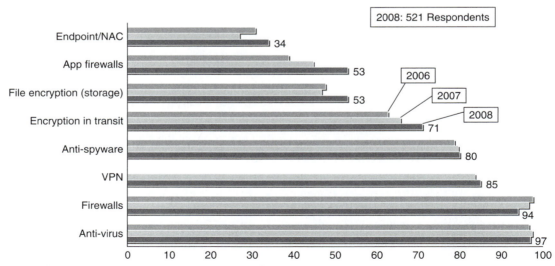

FIGURE 14.11 Security technologies used by organizations, CSI/FBI report, 2008.

---

24 45 C.F.R. § 164.310 Physical safeguards, http://law.justia.com/us/cfr/title45/45-1.0.1.3.70.3.33.5.html

Facility Requirements

Entering and accessing information systems to any degree within any organization must be controlled. What's more, it is necessary to understand what is allowed and what's not; if those parameters are clearly defied, the battle is half won. Not every building is a high-security facility, so it's understandable that some of the following items might not apply to your organization; however, there should be a good, clear reason as to why they don't. Sample questions to consider:[25]

- Are policies and procedures developed and implemented that address allowing authorized and limiting unauthorized physical access to electronic information systems and the facility or facilities in which they are housed?
- Do the policies and procedures identify individuals (workforce members, business associates, contractors, etc.) with authorized access by title and/ or job function?
- Do the policies and procedures specify the methods used to control physical access, such as door locks, electronic access control systems, security officers, or video monitoring?

The facility access controls standard has four implementation specifications[26]:

- *Contingency operations.* Establish (and implement as needed) procedures that allow facility access in support of restoration of lost data under the disaster recovery plan and emergency mode operations plan in the event of an emergency.
- *Facility security plan.* Implement policies and procedures to safeguard the facility and the equipment therein from unauthorized physical access, tampering, and theft.
- *Access control and validation procedures.* Implement procedures to control and validate a person's access to facilities based on her role or function, including visitor control and control of access to software programs for testing and revision.
- *Maintenance records.* Implement policies and procedures to document repairs and modifications to the physical components of a facility that are related to security (for example, hardware, walls, doors, and locks).

25 45 C.F.R. § 164.310 Physical safeguards, http://law.justia. com/us/cfr/title45/45-1.0.1.3.70.3.33.5.html
26 45 C.F.R. § 164.310 Physical safeguards, http://law.justia. com/us/cfr/title45/45-1.0.1.3.70.3.33.5.html

Administrative, Technical, and Physical Controls

Understanding what it takes to secure a facility is the first step in the process of identifying exactly what type of administrative, technical, and physical controls will be necessary for your particular organization. Translating the needs for security into tangible examples, here are some of the controls that can be put in place to enhance security:

- *Administrative controls.* These include human resources exercises for simulated emergencies such as fire drills or power outages as well as security awareness training and security policies.
- *Technical controls.* These include physical intrusion detection systems and access control equipment such as biometrics.
- *Physical controls.* These include video cameras, guarded gates, man traps, and car traps.

Data Security

Data security is at the core of what needs to be protected in terms of information security and mission-critical systems. Ultimately it is the data that the organization needs to protect in many cases, and usually data is exactly what perpetrators are after, whether trade secrets, customer information, or a database of Social Security numbers—the data is where it's at!

To be able to properly classify and restrict data, the first thing to understand is how data is accessed. Data is accessed by a *subject*, whether that is a person, process, or another application, and what is accessed to retrieve the data is called an *object*. Think of an object as a cookie jar with valuable information in it, and only select subjects have the permissions necessary to dip their hands into the cookie jar and retrieve the data or information that they are looking for. Both subjects and objects can be a number of things acting in a network, depending on what action they are taking at any given moment, as shown in Figure 14.12.

Data Classification

Various *data classification* models are available for different environments. Some security models focus on the confidentiality of the data (such as Bell-La Padula) and use different classifications. For example, the U.S. military uses a model that goes from most confidential (Top Secret) to least confidential (Unclassified) to classify the data on any given system. On the other hand, most

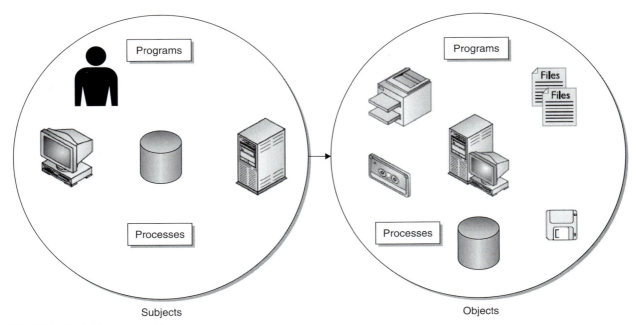

FIGURE 14.12 Subjects access objects.

corporate entities prefer a model whereby they classify data by business unit (HR, Marketing, R&D...) or use terms such as Company Confidential to define items that should not be shared with the public. Other security models focus on the integrity of the data (for example, Bipa); yet others are expressed by mapping security policies to data classification (for example, Clark-Wilson). In every case there are areas that require special attention and clarification.

Access Control Models

Three main *access control models* are in use today: RBAC, DAC, and MAC. In Role-Based Access Control (RBAC), the job function of the individual determines the group he is assigned to and determines the level of access he can attain on certain data and systems. The level of access is usually defined by IT personnel in accordance with policies and procedures. In Discretionary Access Control (DAC), the end user or creator of the data object is allowed to define who can and who cannot access the data; this has become less popular in recent history. Mandatory Access Control (MAC) is more of a militant style of applying permissions, where permissions are the same across the board to all members of a certain level or class within the organization.

The following are data security "need to knows":

- *Authentication versus authorization*. It's crucial to understand that simply because someone becomes

authenticated does not mean that they are authorized to view certain data. There needs to be a means by which a person, after gaining access through authentication, is limited in the actions they are authorized to perform on certain data (such as read-only permissions).

- *Protecting data with cryptography* is important for the security of both the organization and its customers. Usually the most important item that an organization needs to protect, aside from trade secrets, is its customers' personal data. If there is a security breach and the data that is stolen or compromised was previously encrypted, the organization can feel more secure in that the collateral damage to their reputation and customer base will be minimized.

- *Data leakage prevention and content management* is an up-and-coming area of data security that has proven extremely useful in preventing sensitive information from leaving an organization. With this relatively new technology, a security administrator can define the types of documents, and further define the content within those documents, that cannot leave the organization and quarantine them for inspection before they hit the public Internet.

- *Securing email systems* is one of the most important and overlooked areas of data security. With access to the mail server, an attacker can snoop through anyone's email, even the company CEO's! Password files, company confidential documents, and contacts for all address books are only some of the things that a compromised mail server can reveal about an organization, not to mention root/administrator access to a system in the internal network.

Systems and Network Security

Systems and network security[27] is at the core of information security. Though physical security is extremely important and a breach could render all your systems and network security safeguards useless, without hardened systems and networks, anyone from the comfort of her own living room can take over your network, access your confidential information, and disrupt your operations at will. Data classification and security are also quite important, if for nothing else to be sure that only those who need to access certain data can and those who do not need access cannot; however, that usually works well for people who play by the rules. In many cases when an attacker gains access to a system, the first order of business is escalation of privileges. This means that the attacker gets in as a regular user and attempts to find ways to gain administrator or root privileges.

The following are brief descriptions of each of the components that make for a complete security infrastructure for all host systems and network connected assets.

Host-Based Security

The host system is the core of where data sits and is accessed, so it is therefore also the main target of many intruders. Regardless of the operating system platform that is selected to run certain applications and databases, the principles of hardening systems are the same and apply to host systems as well as network devices, as we will see in the upcoming sections. Steps required to maintain host systems in as secure a state as possible are as follows:

1. *OS hardening.* Guidelines by which a base operating system goes through a series of checks to make sure no unnecessary exposures remain open and that security features are enabled where possible. There is a series of organizations that publish OS hardening Guides for various platforms of operating systems.
2. *Removing unnecessary services.* In any operating system there are usually services that are enabled

but have no real business need. It is necessary to go through all the services of your main corporate image, on both the server side and client side, to determine which services are required and which would create a potential vulnerability if left enabled.

3. *Patch management.* All vendors release updates for known vulnerabilities on some kind of schedule. Part of host-based security is making sure that all required vendor patches, at both the operating system and the application level, are applied as quickly as business operations allow on some kind of regular schedule. There should also be an emergency patch procedure in case there is an outbreak and updates need to be pushed out of sequence.

4. *Antivirus.* Possibly more important than patches are antivirus definitions, specifically on desktop and mobile systems. Corporate antivirus software should be installed and updated frequently on all systems in the organization.

5. *Intrusion detection systems (IDSs).* Although many seem to think IDSs are a network security function, there are many good host-based IDS applications, both commercial and open source, that can significantly increase security and act as an early warning system for possibly malicious traffic and/or files for which the AV does not have a definition.

6. *Firewalls.* Host-based firewalls are not as popular as they once were because many big vendors such as Symantec, McAfee, and Checkpoint have moved to a host-based client application that houses all security functions in one. There is also another trend in the industry to move toward application-specific host-based firewalls like those specifically designed to run on a Web or database server, for example.

7. *Data encryption software.* One item often overlooked is encryption of data while it is at rest. Many solutions have recently come onto the market that offer the ability to encrypt sensitive data such as credit card and Social Security numbers that sit on your file server or inside the database server. This is a huge protection in the case of information theft or data leakage.

8. *Backup and restore capabilities.* Without the ability to back up and restore both servers and clients in a timely fashion, an issue that could be resolved in short order can quickly turn into a disaster. Backup procedures should be in place and restored on a regular basis to verify their integrity.

9. *System event logging.* Event logs are significant when you're attempting to investigate the root cause

---

27 "GSEC, GIAC Security Essentials Outline," SANS Institute, https://www.sans.org/training/description.php?tid=672

of an issue or incident. In many cases, logging is not turned on by default and needs to be enabled after the core installation of the host operating system. The OS hardening guidelines for your organization should require that logging be enabled.

Network-Based Security

The network is the communication highway for everything that happens between all the host systems. All data at one point or another passes over the wire and is potentially vulnerable to snooping or spying by the wrong person. The controls implemented on the network are similar in nature to those that can be applied to host systems; however, network-based security can be more easily classified into two main categories: detection and prevention. We will discuss security monitoring tools in another section; for now the main functions of network-based security are to either detect a potential incident based on a set of events or prevent a known attack.

Most network-based security devices can perform detect or protect functions in one of two ways: signature-based or anomaly-based. Signature-based detection or prevention is similar to AV signatures that look for known traits of a particular attack or malware. Anomaly-based systems can make decisions based on what is expected to be "normal" on the network or per a certain set of standards (for example, RFC), usually after a period of being installed in what is called "learning" or "monitor" mode.

Intrusion Detection

Intrusion detection is the process of monitoring the events occurring in a computer system or network and analyzing them for signs of possible incidents that are violations or imminent threats of violation of computer security policies, acceptable-use policies, or standard security practices. Incidents have many causes, such as malware (e.g., worms, spyware), attackers gaining unauthorized access to systems from the Internet, and authorized system users who misuse their privileges or attempt to gain additional privileges for which they are not authorized.[28] The most common detection technologies and their security functions on the network are as follows:

- *Packet sniffing and recording tools.* These tools are used quite often by networking teams to troubleshoot

connectivity issues; however, they can be a security professional's best friend during investigations and root-cause analysis. When properly deployed and maintained, a packet capture device on the network allows security professionals to reconstruct data and reverse-engineer malware in a way that is simply not possible without a full packet capture of the communications.

- *Intrusion detection systems.* In these systems, appliances or servers monitor network traffic and run it through a rules engine to determine whether it is malicious according to its signature set. If the traffic is deemed malicious, an alert will fire and notify the monitoring system.

- *Anomaly detection systems.* Aside from the actual packet data traveling on the wire, there are also traffic trends that can be monitored on the switches and routers to determine whether unauthorized or anomalous activity is occurring. With Net-flow and S-flow data that can be sent to an appliance or server, aggregated traffic on the network can be analyzed and can alert a monitoring system if there is a problem. Anomaly detection systems are extremely useful when there is an attack for which the IDS does not have a signature or if there is some activity occurring that is suspicious.

Intrusion Prevention

Intrusion prevention is a system that allows for the active blocking of attacks while they are inline on the network, before they even get to the target host. There are many ways to prevent attacks or unwanted traffic from coming into your network, the most common of which is known as a firewall. Although a firewall is mentioned quite commonly and a lot of people know what a firewall is, there are several different types of controls that can be put in place in addition to a firewall that can seriously help protect the network. Here are the most common prevention technologies:

- *Firewalls.* The purpose of a firewall is to enforce an organization's security policy at the border of two networks. Typically most firewalls are deployed at the edge between the internal network and the Internet (if there is such a thing) and are configured to block (prevent) any traffic from going in or out that is not allowed by the corporate security policy. There are quite a few different levels of protection a firewall can provide, depending on the type of firewall that is deployed, such as these:

- *Packet filtering.* The most basic type of firewalls perform what is called *stateful packet filtering*, which

28 Karen Scarfone and Peter Mell, NIST Special Publication 800-94: "Guide to Intrusion Detection and Prevention Systems (IDPS)," Recommendations of the National Institute of Standards and Technology, http://csrc.nist.gov/publications/nistpubs/800-94/SP800-94.pdf

means that they can remember which side initiated the connection, and rules (called access control lists, or ACLs) can be created based not only on IPs and ports but also depending on the state of the connection (meaning whether the traffic is going into or out of the network).

- *Proxies.* The main difference between proxies and stateful packet-filtering firewalls is that proxies have the ability to terminate and reestablish connections between two end hosts, acting as a proxy for all communications and adding a layer of security and functionality to the regular firewalls.

- *Application layer firewalls.* The app firewalls have become increasingly popular; they are designed to protect certain types of applications (Web or database) and can be configured to perform a level of blocking that is much more intuitive and granular, based not only on network information but also application-specific variables so that administrators can be much more precise in what they are blocking. In addition, app firewalls can typically be loaded with server-side SSL certificates, allowing the appliance to decrypt encrypted traffic, a huge benefit to a typical proxy or stateful firewall.

- *Intrusion prevention systems.* An intrusion prevention system (IPS) is software that has all the capabilities of an intrusion detection system and can also attempt to stop possible incidents using a set of conditions based on signatures or anomalies.

Business Communications Security

Businesses today tend to communicate with many other business entities, not only over the Internet but also through private networks or guest access connections directly to the organization's network, whether wired or wireless. Business partners and contractors conducting business communications obviously tend to need a higher level of access than public users but not as extensive as permanent employees, so how does an organization handle this phenomenon? External parties working on internal projects are also classed as business partners. Some general rules for users to maintain security control of external entities are shown in Figure 14.13.

General Rules for Self-Protection

The general rules for self-protection are as follows:

- Access to a user's own IT system must be protected in such a way that system settings (e.g., in the BIOS) can only be changed subject to authentication.

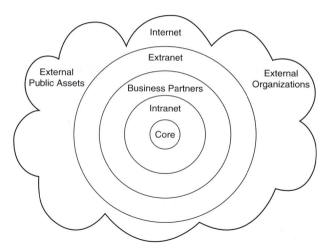

FIGURE 14.13 The business communications cloud.

- System start must always be protected by requiring appropriate authentication (e.g., requesting the boot password). Exceptions to this rule can apply if:
- Automatic update procedures require this, and the system start can only take place from the built-in hard disk.
- The system is equipped for use by a number of persons with their individual user profiles, and system start can only take place from the built-in hard disk.
- Unauthorized access to in-house resources including data areas (shares, folders, mailboxes, calendar, etc.) must be prevented in line with their need for protection. In addition, the necessary authorizations for approved data access must be defined.
- Users are not permitted to operate resources without first defining any authorizations (such as no global sharing). This rule must be observed particularly by those users who are system managers of their own resources.
- Users of an IT system must lock the access links they have opened (for example, by enabling a screensaver or removing the chip card from the card reader), even during short periods of absence from their workstations.
- When work is over, all open access links must be properly closed or protected against system/data access (such as if extensive compilation runs need to take place during the night).
- Deputizing rules for access to the user's own system or data resources must be made in agreement with the manager and the acting employee.

Handling Protection Resources

The handling of protection resources are as follows:

- Employees must ensure that their protection resources cannot be subject to snooping while data required for authentication is being entered (e.g., password entry during login).
- Employees must store all protection resources and records in such a way that they cannot be subjected to snooping or stolen.
- Personal protection resources must never be made available to third parties.
- In the case of chip cards, SecurID tokens, or other protection resources requiring a PIN, the associated PIN (PIN letter) must be stored separately.
- Loss, theft, or disclosure of protection resources is to be reported immediately.
- Protection resources subject to loss, theft, or snooping must be disabled immediately.

Rules for Mobile IT Systems

In addition to the general rules for users, the following rules may also apply for mobile IT systems:

- Extended self-protection.
- A mobile IT system must be safeguarded against theft (that is, secured with a cable lock, locked away in a cupboard).
- The data from a mobile IT system using corporate proprietary information must be safeguarded as appropriate (e.g., encryption). In this connection, CERT rules in particular are to be observed.
- The software provided by the organization for system access control may only be used on the organization's own mobile IT systems.

Operation on Open Networks

Rules for operation on open networks are as follows:

- The mobile IT system must be operated in open network environments using a personal firewall.
- The configuration of the personal firewall must be in accordance with the corporate policy or, in the case of other personal firewall systems, must be subject to restrictive settings.
- A mobile IT system must be operated in an unprotected open network only for the duration of a secure access link to the organization's own network. The connection establishment for the secure access link must be performed as soon as possible, at least within five minutes.

- Simultaneous operation on open networks (protected or unprotected) and the organization's own networks is forbidden at all times.
- Remote access to company internal resources must always be protected by means of strong authentication.
- For the protection of data being transferred via a remote access link, strong encryption must always be used.

Additional Business Communications Guidelines

Additional business communications guidelines should be defined for the following:

- External IT systems may not be connected directly to the intranet. Transmission of corporate proprietary data to external systems should be avoided wherever possible, and copies of confidential or strictly confidential data must never be created on external IT systems.
- Unauthorized access to public data areas (shares, folders, mailboxes, calendars, etc.) is to be prevented. The appropriate authentication checks and authorization requirements must be defined and the operation of resources without such requirements is not permitted (e.g., no global sharing).
- Remote data access operations must be effected using strong authentication and encryption, and managers must obtain permission from the owner of the resources to access.
- For secure remote maintenance by business partners, initialization of the remote maintenance must take place from an internal system, such as via an Internet connection protected by strong encryption. An employee must be present at the system concerned during the entire remote maintenance session to monitor the remote maintenance in accordance with the policy, and the date, nature, and extent of the remote maintenance must be logged at a minimum.

Wireless Security

Wireless networking enables devices with wireless capabilities to use information resources without being physically connected to a network. A wireless local area network (WLAN) is a group of wireless networking nodes within a limited geographic area that is capable of radio communications. WLANs are typically used by devices within a fairly limited range, such as

IEEE Standard or Amendment	Maximum Data Rate	Typical Range	Frequency Band	Comments
802.11	2 Mbps	50–100 meters	2.4 GHz	
802.11a	54 Mbps	50–100 meters	5 GHz	Not compatible with 802.11b
802.11b	11 Mbps	50–100 meters	2.4 GHz	Equipment based on 802.11b has been the dominant WLAN technology
802.11g	54 Mbps	50–100 meters	2.4 GHz	Backward compatible with 802.11b

FIGURE 14.14 IEEE Common Wireless Standards: NIST SP800-97.[30]

an office building or building campus, and are usually implemented as extensions to existing wired local area networks to provide enhanced user mobility. Since the beginning of wireless networking, many standards and technologies have been developed for WLANs. One of the most active standards organizations that address wireless networking is the Institute of Electrical and Electronics Engineers (IEEE), as outlined in Figure 14.14.[29] Like other wireless technologies, WLANs typically need to support several security objectives. This is intended to be accomplished through a combination of security features built into the wireless networking standard.

The most common security objectives for WLANs are as follows:

- *Access control.* Restrict the rights of devices or individuals to access a network or resources within a network.
- *Confidentiality.* Ensure that communication cannot be read by unauthorized parties.
- *Integrity.* Detect any intentional or unintentional changes to data that occur in transit.
- *Availability.* Ensure that devices and individuals can access a network and its resources whenever needed.

Access Control

Typically there are two means by which to validate the identities of wireless devices attempting to connect to a WLAN: open-system authentication and shared-key authentication. Neither of these alternatives is secure. The security provided by the default connection means is unacceptable; all it takes for a host to connect to your system is a Service Set Identifier (SSID) for the AP (which is a name that is broadcast in the clear) and, optionally, a MAC Address. The SSID was never intended to be used as an access control feature.

A MAC address is a unique 48-bit value that is permanently assigned to a particular wireless network interface. Many implementations of IEEE 802.11 allow administrators to specify a list of authorized MAC addresses; the AP will permit devices with those MAC addresses only to use the WLAN. This is known as *MAC address filtering.* However, since the MAC address is not encrypted, it is simple to intercept traffic and identify MAC addresses that are allowed past the MAC filter. Unfortunately, almost all WLAN adapters allow applications to set the MAC address, so it is relatively trivial to spoof a MAC address, meaning that attackers can easily gain unauthorized access. Additionally, the AP is not authenticated to the host by open-system authentication. Therefore, the host has to trust that it is communicating to the real AP and not an impostor AP that is using the same SSID. Therefore, open system authentication does not provide reasonable assurance of any identities and can easily be misused to gain unauthorized access to a WLAN or to trick users into connecting to a malicious WLAN.[31]

Confidentiality

The WEP protocol attempts some form of confidentiality by using the RC4 stream cipher algorithm to encrypt

---

29 Sheila Frankel, Bernard Eydt, Les Owens, Karen Scarfone, NIST Special Publication 800-97: "Establishing Wireless Robust Security Networks: A Guide to IEEE 802.11i," Recommendations of the National Institute of Standards and Technology, http://csrc.nist.gov/publications/nistpubs/800-97/SP800-97.pdf

30 Sheila Frankel, Bernard Eydt, Les Owens, Karen Scarfone, NIST Special Publication 800-97: "Establishing Wireless Robust Security Networks: A Guide to IEEE 802.11i," Recommendations of the National Institute of Standards and Technology, http://csrc.nist.gov/publications/nistpubs/800-97/SP800-97.pdf

31 Sheila Frankel, Bernard Eydt, Les Owens, Karen Scarfone, NIST Special Publication 800-97: "Establishing Wireless Robust Security Networks: A Guide to IEEE 802.11i," Recommendations of the National Institute of Standards and Technology, http://csrc.nist.gov/publications/nistpubs/800-97/SP800-97.pdf

wireless communications. The standard for WEP specifies support for a 40-bit WEP key only; however, many vendors offer nonstandard extensions to WEP that support key lengths of up to 128 or even 256 bits. WEP also uses a 24-bit value known as an *initialization vector* (IV) as a seed value for initializing the cryptographic keystream. Ideally, larger key sizes translate to stronger protection, but the cryptographic technique used by WEP has known flaws that are not mitigated by longer keys. WEP is not the secure alternative you're looking for.

A possible threat against confidentiality is network traffic analysis. Eavesdroppers might be able to gain information by monitoring and noting which parties communicate at particular times. Also, analyzing traffic patterns can aid in determining the content of communications; for example, short bursts of activity might be caused by terminal emulation or instant messaging, whereas steady streams of activity might be generated by videoconferencing. More sophisticated analysis might be able to determine the operating systems in use based on the length of certain frames. Other than encrypting communications, IEEE 802.11, like most other network protocols, does not offer any features that might thwart network traffic analysis, such as adding random lengths of padding to messages or sending additional messages with randomly generated data.[32]

Integrity

Data integrity checking for messages transmitted between hosts and APs exists and is designed to reject any messages that have been changed in transit, such as by a man-in-the-middle attack. WEP data integrity is based on a simple encrypted checksum—a 32-bit cyclic redundancy check (CRC-32) computed on each payload prior to transmission. The payload and checksum are encrypted using the RC4 keystream, and then transmitted. The receiver decrypts them, recomputes the checksum on the received payload, and compares it with the transmitted checksum. If the checksums are not the same, the transmitted data frame has been altered in transit, and the frame is discarded. Unfortunately, CRC-32 is subject to bit-flipping attacks, which means that an attacker knows which CRC-32 bits will change when message bits are altered. WEP attempts to counter this problem by encrypting the CRC-32 to produce an integrity check value (ICV). WEP's

creators believed that an enciphered CRC-32 would be less subject to tampering. However, they did not realize that a property of stream ciphers such as WEP's RC4 is that bit flipping survives the encryption process—the same bits flip whether or not encryption is used. Therefore, the WEP ICV offers no additional protection against bit flipping.[33]

Availability

Individuals who do not have physical access to the WLAN infrastructure can cause a denial of service for the WLAN. One threat is known as jamming, which involves a device that emits electromagnetic energy on the WLAN's frequencies. The energy makes the frequencies unusable by the WLAN, causing a denial of service. Jamming can be performed intentionally by an attacker or unintentionally by a non-WLAN device transmitting on the same frequency. Another threat against availability is flooding, which involves an attacker sending large numbers of messages to an AP at such a high rate that the AP cannot process them, or other STAs cannot access the channel, causing a partial or total denial of service. These threats are difficult to counter in any radio-based communications; thus, the IEEE 802.11 standard does not provide any defense against jamming or flooding. Also, as described in Section 3.2.1, attackers can establish rogue APs; if STAs mistakenly attach to a rogue AP instead of a legitimate one, this could make the legitimate WLAN effectively unavailable to users. Although 802.11i protects data frames, it does not offer protection to control or management frames. An attacker can exploit the fact that management frames are not authenticated to deauthenticate a client or to disassociate a client from the network.[34]

Enhancing Security Controls

The IEEE 802.11i amendment allows for enhanced security features beyond WEP and the simple IEEE 802.11 shared-key challenge-response authentication. The amendment introduces the concepts of Robust Security Networks

32 Sheila Frankel, Bernard Eydt, Les Owens, Karen Scarfone, NIST Special Publication 800-97: "Establishing Wireless Robust Security Networks: A Guide to IEEE 802.11i," Recommendations of the National Institute of Standards and Technology, http://csrc.nist.gov/publications/nistpubs/800-97/SP800-97.pdf

33 Sheila Frankel, Bernard Eydt, Les Owens Karen, Scarfone, NIST Special Publication 800-97: "Establishing Wireless Robust Security Networks: A Guide to IEEE 802.11i," Recommendations of the National Institute of Standards and Technology, http://csrc.nist.gov/publications/nistpubs/800-97/SP800-97.pdf

34 Sheila Frankel, Bernard Eydt, Les Owens Karen, Scarfone, NIST Special Publication 800-97: "Establishing Wireless Robust Security Networks: A Guide to IEEE 802.11i," Recommendations of the National Institute of Standards and Technology, http://csrc.nist.gov/publications/nistpubs/800-97/SP800-97.pdf

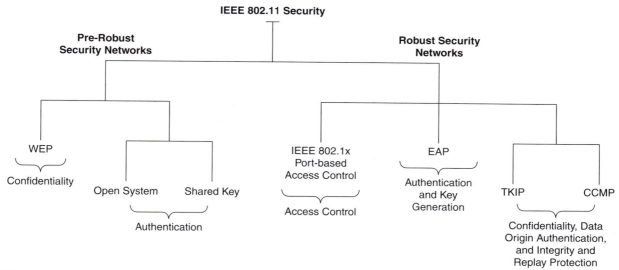

FIGURE 14.15 High-level taxonomy of the major pre-RSN and RSN security mechanisms.[35]

(RSNs) (see Figure 14.15) and Robust Security Network Associations (RSNAs). There are two RSN data confidentiality and integrity protocols defined in IEEE 802.11i—Temporal Key Integrity Protocol (TKIP) and Counter Mode with Cipher-Block Chaining Message Authentication Code Protocol (CCMP).

At a high level, RSN includes IEEE 802.1x port-based access control, key management techniques, and the TKIP and CCMP data confidentiality and integrity protocols. These protocols allow for the creation of several diverse types of security networks because of the numerous configuration options. RSN security is at the link level only, providing protection for traffic between a wireless host and its associated AP or between one wireless host and another. It does not provide end-to-end application-level security, such as between a host and an email or Web server, because communication between these entities requires more than just one link. For infrastructure mode, additional measures need to be taken to provide end-to-end security.

The IEEE 802.11i amendment defines an RSN as a wireless network that allows the creation of RSN Associations (RSNAs) only. An RSNA is a security relationship established by the IEEE 802.11i 4-Way Handshake. The 4-Way Handshake validates that the parties to the protocol instance possess a pairwise master key (PMK), synchronize the installation of temporal keys, and confirm the selection of cipher suites. The PMK is the cornerstone of a number of security features absent from WEP. Complete robust security is considered possible only when all devices in the network use RSNAs. In practice, some networks have a mix of RSNAs and non-RSNA connections. A network that allows the creation of both pre-RSN associations (pre-RSNA) and RSNAs is referred to as a Transition Security Network (TSN). A TSN is intended to be an interim means to provide connectivity while an organization migrates to networks based exclusively on RSNAs. RSNAs enable the following security features for IEEE 802.11 WLANs:

- Enhanced user authentication mechanisms
- Cryptographic key management
- Data confidentiality
- Data origin authentication and integrity
- Replay protection

An RSNA relies on IEEE 802.1x to provide an authentication framework. To achieve the robust security of RSNAs, the designers of the IEEE 802.11i amendment used numerous mature cryptographic algorithms and techniques. These algorithms can be categorized as being used for confidentiality, integrity (and data origin authentication), or key generation. All the algorithms specifically referenced in the IEEE 802.11 standard (see Figure 14.16) are symmetric algorithms, which use the same key for two different steps of the algorithm, such as encryption and decryption.

TKIP is a cipher suite for enhancing WEP on pre-RSN hardware without causing significant performance

---

35 Sheila Frankel, Bernard Eydt, Les Owens Karen, Scarfone, NIST Special Publication 800-97: "Establishing Wireless Robust Security Networks: A Guide to IEEE 802.11i," Recommendations of the National Institute of Standards and Technology, http://csrc.nist.gov/publications/nistpubs/800-97/SP800-97.pdf

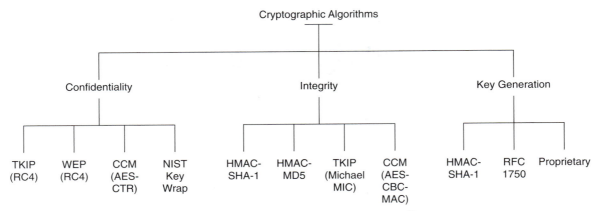

FIGURE 14.16 Taxonomy of the cryptographic algorithms included in the IEEE 802.11 standard.[36]

degradation. TKIP works within the processing constraints of first-generation hosts and APs and therefore enables increased security without requiring hardware replacement. TKIP provides the following fundamental security features for IEEE 802.11 WLANs:

- Confidentiality protection using the RC4 algorithm[38]
- Integrity protection against several types of attacks[39] using the Michael message digest algorithm (through generation of a message integrity code [MIC])[40]
- Replay prevention through a frame-sequencing technique
- Use of a new encryption key for each frame to prevent attacks, such as the Fluhrer-Mantin-Shamir (FMS) attack, which can compromise WEP-based WLANs[41]
- Implementation of countermeasures whenever the STA or AP encounters a frame with a MIC error, which is a strong indication of an active attack

Web and Application Security

Web and application security has come to center stage recently because Web sites and other public-facing applications have had so many vulnerabilities reported that it is often trivial to find some part of the application that is vulnerable to one of the many exploits out there. When an attacker compromises a system at the application level, often it is too trivial to take advantage of all

the capabilities said application has to offer, including querying the back-end database or accessing proprietary information. In the past it was not necessary to implement security during the development phase of an application, and since most security professionals are not programmers, that worked out just fine; however, due to factors such as rushing software releases and a certain level of complacency where end users expect buggy software and apply patches, the trend of inserting security earlier in the development process is catching steam.

Web Security

Web security is unique to every environment; any application and service that the organization wants to deliver to the customer will have its own way of performing transactions. Static Web sites with little content or searchable areas of course pose the least risk, but they also offer the least functionality. Who wants a Web site they can't sell anything from? Implementing something like a shopping cart or content delivery on your site opens up new, unexpected aspects of Web security. Among the things that need to be considered are whether it is worth developing the application in-house or buying one off the shelf and rely on someone else for the maintenance ad patching. With some of these thoughts in mind, here are some of the biggest threats associated with having a public-facing Web site:

- Vandalism
- Financial fraud
- Privileged access
- Theft of transaction information
- Theft of intellectual property
- Denial-of-service (DoS) attacks
- Input validation errors

36 Sheila Frankel, Bernard Eydt, Les Owens, Karen Scarfone, NIST Special Publication 800-97: "Establishing Wireless Robust Security Networks: A Guide to IEEE 802.11i," Recommendations of the National Institute of Standards and Technology, http://csrc.nist.gov/publications/nistpubs/800-97/SP800-97.pdf

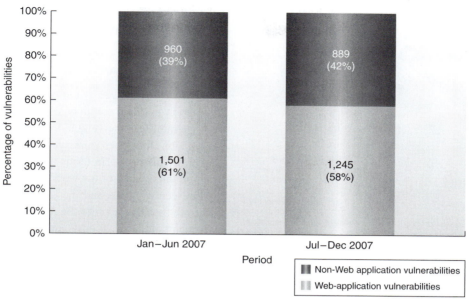

FIGURE 14.17 Symantec Web application vulnerabilities by share.

- Path or directory traversal
- Unicode encoding
- URL encoding
  Some Web application defenses that can be implemented have already been discussed; they include:

- Web application firewalls
- Intrusion prevention systems
- SYN proxies on the firewall

Application Security

An integrated approach to application security (see Figure 14.17) in the organization is required for successful deployment and secure maintenance of all applications. A corporate initiative to define, promote, assure, and measure the security of critical business applications would greatly enhance an organization's overall security. Some of the biggest obstacles, as mentioned in the previous section, are that security professionals are not typically developers, so this means that often application security is left to IT or R&D personnel, which can lead to gaping holes. Components of an application security program consist of[37]:

- *People.* Security architects, managers, technical leads, developers and testers.

- *Policy.* Integrate security steps into your SDLC and ADLC; have security baked in, not bolted on. Find security issues early so that they are easier and cheaper to fix. Measure compliance; are the processes working? Inventory and categorize your applications.
- *Standards.* Which controls are necessary, and when and why? Use standard methods to implement each control. Provide references on how to implement and define requirements.
- *Assessments.* Security architecture/design reviews, security code reviews, application vulnerability tests, risk acceptance review, external penetration test of production applications, white-box philosophy. Look inside the application, and use all the advantages you have such as past reviews, design documents, code, logs, interviews, and so on. Attackers have advantages over you; don't tie your hands.
- *Training.* Take awareness and training seriously. All developers should be performing their own input validation in their code and need to be made aware of the security risks involved in sending unsecure code into production.

Security Policies and Procedures

A quality information security program begins and ends with the correct information security policy (see Figure 14.18). Policies are the least expensive means of control and often the most difficult to implement.

37 "AppSec2005DC-Anthony Canike-Enterprise AppSec Program PowerPoint Presentation," OWASP, http://www.owasp.org/index.php/Image:AppSec2005DC-Anthony_Canike-Enterprise_AppSec_Program.ppt

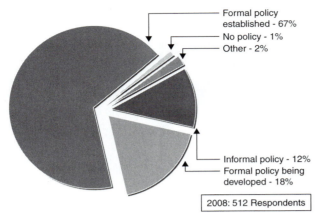

Formal policy established - 67%
No policy - 1%
Other - 2%
Informal policy - 12%
Formal policy being developed - 18%

2008: 512 Respondents

FIGURE 14.18 Information security policy within your organization, CSI/FBI report, 2008.

An information security policy is a plan that influences and determines the actions taken by employees who are presented with a policy decision regarding information systems. Other components related to a security policy are practices, procedures, and guidelines, which attempt to explain in more detail the actions that are to be taken by employees in any given situation. For policies to be effective, they must be properly disseminated, read, understood, and agreed to by all employees as well as backed by upper management. Without upper management support, a security policy is bound to fail. Most information security policies should contain at least:

- An overview of the corporate philosophy on security
- Information about roles and responsibilities for security shared by all members of the organization
- Statement of purpose
- Information technology elements needed to define certain controls or decisions
- The organization's security responsibilities defining the security organization structure
- References to IT standards and guidelines, such as Government Policies and Guidelines, FISMA, http://iase.disa.mil/policy-guidance/index.html#FISMA and NIST Special Publications (800 Series), and http://csrc.nist.gov/publications/PubsSPs.html.

Some basic rules must be followed when you're shaping a policy:

- Never conflict with the local or federal law.
- Your policy should be able to stand up in court.
- It must be properly supported and administered by management.
- It should contribute to the success of the organization.

- It should involve end users of information systems from the beginning.

Security Employee Training and Awareness

The Security Employee Training and Awareness (SETA) program is a critical component of the information security program. It is the vehicle for disseminating security information that the workforce, including managers, need to do their jobs. In terms of the total security solution, the importance of the workforce in achieving information security goals and the importance of training as a countermeasure cannot be overstated. Establishing and maintaining a robust and relevant information security awareness and training program as part of the overall information security program is the primary conduit for providing employees with the information and tools needed to protect an agency's vital information resources. These programs will ensure that personnel at all levels of the organization understand their information security responsibilities to properly use and protect the information and resources entrusted to them. Agencies that continually train their workforces in organizational security policy and role-based security responsibilities will have a higher rate of success in protecting information.[38]

As cited in audit reports, periodicals, and conference presentations, people are arguably the weakest element in the security formula that is used to secure systems and networks. The people factor, not technology, is a critical one that is often overlooked in the security equation. It is for this reason that the Federal Information Security Management Act (FISMA) and the Office of Personnel Management (OPM) have mandated that more and better attention must be devoted to awareness activities and role-based training, since they are the only security controls that can minimize the inherent risk that results from the people who use, manage, operate, and maintain information systems and networks. Robust and enterprisewide awareness and training programs are needed to address this growing concern.[39]

---

38 Pauline Bowen, Joan Hash and Mark Wilson, NIST Special Publication 800-100: Information Security Handbook: A Guide for Managers. Recommendations of the National Institute of Standards and Technology, http://csrc.nist.gov/publications/nistpubs/800-100/SP800-100-Mar07-2007.pdf

39 Pauline Bowen, Joan Hash and Mark Wilson, NIST Special Publication 800-100: Information Security Handbook: A Guide for Managers. Recommendations of the National Institute of Standards and Technology, http://csrc.nist.gov/publications/nistpubs/800-100/SP800-100-Mar07-2007.pdf

	Awareness	Training	Education
Attribute:	"What"	"How"	"Why"
Level:	Information	Knowledge	Insight
Objective:	Recognition	Skill	Understanding
Teaching Method:	<u>Media</u> Videos Newsletters Posters, etc.	<u>Practical Instruction</u> Lecture Case study workshop Hands-on practice	<u>Theoretical Instruction</u> Discussion Seminar Background reading
Test Measure:	True/False Multiple Choice (identify learning)	Problem Solving (apply learning)	Essay (interpret learning)
Impact Timeframe:	Short-term	Intermediate	Long-term

FIGURE 14.19 Matrix of security teaching methods and measures that can be implemented.

The Ten Commandments of SETA

The Ten Commandments of SETA consist of the following:

1. Information security is a people, rather than a technical, issue.
2. If you want them to understand, speak their language.
3. If they cannot see it, they will not learn it.
4. Make your point so that you can identify it and so can they.
5. Never lose your sense of humor.
6. Make your point, support it, and conclude it.
7. Always let the recipients know how the behavior that you request will affect them.
8. Ride the tame horses.
9. Formalize your training methodology.
10. Always be timely, even if it means slipping schedules to include urgent information.

Depending on the level of targeted groups within the organization, the goal is first awareness, then training, and eventually the education of all users as to what is acceptable security. Figure 14.19 shows a matrix of teaching methods and measures that can be implemented at each level.

Targeting the right people and providing the right information are crucial when you're developing a security awareness program. Therefore, some of the items that must be kept in mind are focusing on people, not so much on technologies; refraining from using technical jargon; and using every available venue, such as newsletters or memos, online demonstrations, and in-person classroom sessions. By not overloading users and helping them understand their roles in information security, you can establish a program that is effective, identifies target audiences, and defines program scope, goals, and objectives. Figure 14.20 presents a snapshot according to the 2008 CSI/FBI Report, showing where the SETA program stands in 460 different U.S. organizations.

4. SECURITY MONITORING AND EFFECTIVENESS

Security monitoring and effectiveness are the next evolutions to a constant presence of security-aware personnel who actively monitor and research events in real time. A substantial number of suspicious events occur within most enterprise networks and computer systems every day and go completely undetected. Only with an effective security monitoring strategy, an incident response plan, and security validation and metrics in place will an optimal level of security be attained. The idea is to automate and correlate as much as possible between both events and vulnerabilities and to build intelligence into security tools so that they alert you if a known bad set of events has occurred or a known vulnerability is actually being attacked.

To come full circle; You need to define a security monitoring and log management strategy, an integrated incident response plan, validation, and penetration exercises against security controls and security metrics to help measure whether there has been improvement in your organization's handling of these issues.

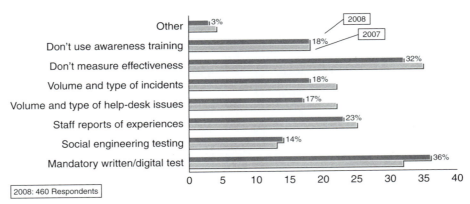

FIGURE 14.20 Awareness training metrics.

Security Monitoring Mechanisms

Security monitoring involves real-time or near-real-time monitoring of events and activities happening on all your organization's important systems at all times. To properly monitor an organization for technical events that can lead to an incident or an investigation, usually an organization uses a security information and event management (SIEM) and/or log management tool. These tools are used by security analysts and managers to filter through tons of event data and to identify and focus on only the most interesting events.

Understanding the regulatory and forensic impact of event and alert data in any given enterprise takes planning and a thorough understanding of the quantity of data the system will be required to handle. The better logs can be stored, understood, and correlated, the better the possibility of detecting an incident in time for mitigation. In this case, what you don't know *will* hurt you. Responding to incidents, identifying anomalous or unauthorized behavior, and securing intellectual property has never been more important. Without a solid log management strategy it becomes nearly impossible to have the necessary data to perform a forensic investigation, and without monitoring tools, identifying threats and responding to attacks against confidentiality, integrity, or availability become much more difficult. For a network to be compliant and an incident response or forensics investigation to be successful, it is critical that a mechanism be in place to do the following:

- Securely acquire and store raw log data for as long as possible from as many disparate devices as possible while providing search and restore capabilities of these logs for analysis.
- Monitor interesting events coming from all important devices, systems, and applications in as near real time as possible.
- Run regular vulnerability scans on your hosts and devices and correlate these vulnerabilities to

intrusion detection alerts or other interesting events, identifying high-priority attacks as they happen and minimizing false positives.

SIEM and log management solutions in general can assist in security information monitoring (see Figure 14.21) as well as regulatory compliance and incident response by:

- Aggregating and normalizing event data from unrelated network devices, security devices, and application servers into usable information.
- Analyze and correlate information from various sources such as vulnerability scanners, IDS/IPS, firewalls, servers, and so on, to identify attacks as soon as possible and help respond to intrusions more quickly.
- Conduct network forensic analysis on historical or real-time events through visualization and replay of events.
- Create customized reports for better visualization of your organizational security posture.

FIGURE 14.21 Security monitoring.

- Increase the value and performance of existing security devices by providing a consolidated event management and analysis platform.
- Improve the effectiveness and help focus IT risk management personnel on the events that are important.
- Meet regulatory compliance and forensics requirements by securely storing all event data on a network for long-term retention and enabling instant accessibility to archived data.

Incidence Response and Forensic Investigations

Network forensic investigation is the investigation and analysis of all the packets and events generated on any given network in hope of identifying the proverbial needle in a haystack. Tightly related is incident response, which entails acting in a timely manner to an identified anomaly or attack across the system. To be successful, both network investigations and incident response rely heavily on proper event and log management techniques. Before an incident can be responded to there is the challenge of determining whether an event is a routine system event or an actual incident. This requires that there be some framework for incident classification (the process of examining a possible incident and determining whether or not it requires a reaction). Initial reports from end users, intrusion detection systems, host- and network-based malware detection software, and systems administrators are all ways to track and detect incident candidates.[40]

As mentioned in earlier sections, the phases of an incident usually unfold in the following order: preparation, identification (detection), containment, eradication, recovery and lessons learned. The preparation phase requires detailed understanding of information systems and the threats they face; so to perform proper planning an organization must develop predefined responses that guide users through the steps needed to properly respond to an incident. Predefining incident responses enables rapid reaction without confusion or wasted time and effort, which can be crucial for the success of an incident response. Identification occurs once an actual incident has been confirmed and properly classified as an incident that requires action. At that point the IR team moves from identification to containment. In the containment phase, a number of action steps are taken by the IR team and others. These steps to respond to an incident must occur quickly and may occur concurrently, including notification of key personnel, the assignment of tasks, and documentation of the incident. Containment strategies focus on two tasks: first, stopping the incident from getting any worse, and second, recovering control of the system if it has been hijacked.

Once the incident has been contained and system control regained, eradication can begin, and the IR team must assess the full extent of damage to determine what must be done to restore the system. Immediate determination of the scope of the breach of confidentiality, integrity, and availability of information and information assets is called *incident damage assessment*. Those who document the damage must be trained to collect and preserve evidence in case the incident is part of a crime investigation or results in legal action.

At the moment that the extent of the damage has been determined, the recovery process begins to identify and resolve vulnerabilities that allowed the incident to occur in the first place. The IR team must address the issues found and determine whether they need to install and/or replace/upgrade the safeguards that failed to stop or limit the incident or were missing from system in the first place. Finally, a discussion of lessons learned should always be conducted to prevent future similar incidents from occurring and review what could have been done differently.[41]

Validating Security Effectiveness

The process of validating security effectiveness comprises making sure that the security controls that you have put in place are working as expected and that they are truly mitigating the risks they claim to be mitigating. There is no way to be sure that your network is not vulnerable to something if you haven't validated it yourself. Ensuring that the information security policy addresses your organizational needs and assessing compliance with your security policy across all systems, assets, applications, and people is the only way to have a concrete means of validation.

Here are some areas where actual validation should be performed—in other words, these are areas where assigned IT personnel should go with policy in hand, log in, and verify the settings and reports before the auditors do:

- Verifying operating system settings
- Reviewing security device configuration and management

---

40 M. E. Whitman, H. J. Mattord, *Management of Information Security*, Course Technology, 2nd Edition, March 27, 2007.

41 M. E. Whitman, H. J. Mattord, *Management of Information Security*, Course Technology, 2nd Edition, March 27, 2007.

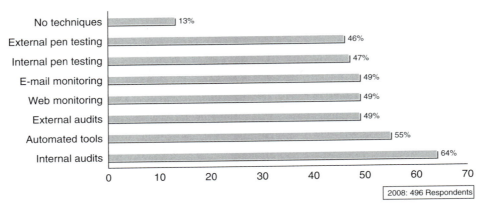

FIGURE 14.22 Security validation techniques, CSI/FBI survey, 2008.

- Establishing ongoing security tasks
- Maintaining physical security
- Auditing security logs
- Creating an approved product list
- Reviewing encryption strength
- Providing documentation and change control

Vulnerability Assessments and Penetration Tests

Validating security (see Figure 14.22) with internal as well as external vulnerability assessments and penetration tests is a good way to measure an increase or decrease in overall security, especially if similar assessments are conducted on a regular basis. There are several ways to test security of applications, hosts, and network devices. With a vulnerability assessment, usually limited scanning tools or just one scanning tool is used to determine vulnerabilities that exist in the target system. Then a report is created and the manager reviews a holistic picture of security. With authorized penetration tests it's a little different. In that case the data owner is allowing someone to use just about any means within reason (in other words, many different tools and techniques) to gain access to the system or information. A successful penetration test does not provide the remediation avenues that a vulnerability assessment does; rather, it is a good test of how difficult it would be for someone to truly gain access if he were trying.

REFERENCES

[1] R. Richardson, CSI Director, 2008 CSI Computer Crime & Security Survey, CSI Website, http://i.cmpnet.com/v2.gocsi.com/pdf/CSIsurvey2008.pdf.

[2] 45 C.F.R. § 164.310 Physical safeguards, Justia Website, http://law.justia.com/us/cfr/title45/45-1.0.1.3.70.3.33.5.html.

[3] S. Saleh AlAboodi, A New Approach for Assessing the Maturity of Information Security, CISSP, www.isaca.org/Template.cfm?Section=Home&CONTENTID=34805&TEMPLATE=/ContentManagement/ContentDisplay.cfm.

[4] A. Jaquith, Security Metrics: Replacing Fear, Uncertainty and Doubt, Addison-Wesley, 2007.

[5] AppSec2005DC-Anthony Canike-Enterprise AppSec Program PowerPoint Presentation, OWASP, www.owasp.org/index.php/Image:AppSec2005DC-Anthony_Canike-Enterprise_AppSec_Program.ppt.

[6] CISSP 10 Domains ISC2 Website, https://www.isc2.org/cissp/default.aspx.

[7] Cloud Computing: The Enterprise Cloud, Terremark Worldwide Inc. Web site, www.theenterprisecloud.com/.

[8] Defense in Depth: A Practical Strategy for Achieving Information Assurance in Today's Highly Networked Environments, National Security Agency, Information Assurance Solutions Group – STE 6737.

[9] Definition of Defense in Depth, OWASP Web site, www.owasp.org/index.php/Defense_in_depth.

[10] Definition of Information Security, Wikipedia, http://en.wikipedia.org/wiki/Information_security.

[11] GSEC, GIAC Security Essentials Outline, SANS Institute, https://www.sans.org/training/description.php?tid=672.

[12] ISO 17799 Security Standards, ISO Web site, www.iso.org/iso/support/faqs/faqs_widely_used_standards/widely_used_standards_other/information_security.htm.

[13] M.E. Whitman, H.J. Mattord., Management of Information Security.

[14] M. Krause, H.F. Tipton, Information Security Management Handbook, sixth ed., Auerbach Publications, CRC Press LLC.

[15] K. Scarfone, P. Mell, NIST Special Publication 800-94: Guide to Intrusion Detection and Prevention Systems (IDPS), Recommendations of the National Institute of Standards and Technology, http://csrc.nist.gov/publications/nistpubs/800-94/SP800-94.pdf.

[16] S. Frankel Bernard, E.L. Owens, K. Scarfone, NIST Special Publication 800-97: Establishing Wireless Robust Security Networks: A Guide to IEEE 802.11i, Recommendations of the National Institute of Standards and Technology, http://csrc.nist.gov/publications/nistpubs/800-97/SP800-97.pdf.

[17] P. Bowen, J. Hash, M. Wilson, NIST Special Publication 800-100: Information Security Handbook: A Guide for Managers, Recommendations of the National Institute of Standards and Technology, http://csrc.nist.gov/publications/nistpubs/800-100/SP800-100-Mar07-2007.pdf.

[18] R.A. Caralli, W.R. Wilson, and the Survivable Enterprise Management Team, The Challenges of Security Management, Networked Systems Survivability Program, Software Engineering Institute, www.cert.org/archive/pdf/ESMchallenges.pdf.

[19] S. Harris, All in One CISSP Certification Exam Guide, fourth ed., McGraw Hill.

[20] Symantec Global Internet Security Threat Report, Trends for July–December 2007, Vol. XII, published April 2008, Symantec Web site, http://eval.symantec.com/mktginfo/enterprise/white_papers/b-whitepaper_internet_security_threat_report_xiii_04-2008.en-us.pdf

[21] L. Galway, Quantitative Risk Analysis for Project Management, A Critical Review, WR-112-RC, February 2004, Rand.org Web site, www.rand.org/pubs/working_papers/2004/RAND_WR112.pdf.

## Chapter 15

Security Management Systems

Joe Wright
Computer Bits, Inc.

Jim Harmening
Computer Bits, Inc.

Today, when most companies and government agencies rely on computer networks to store and manage their organizations' data, it is essential that measures are put in place to secure those networks and keep them functioning optimally. Network administrators need to define their security management systems to cover all parts of their computer and network resources.

Security management systems are sets of policies put place by an organization to maintain the security of their computer and network resources. These policies are based on the types of resources that need to be secured, and they depend on the organization. Some groups of policies can be applied to entire industries; others are specific to an individual organization.

A security management system starts as a set of policies that dictate the way in which computer resources can be used. The policies are then implemented by the organization's technical departments and enforced. This can be easy for smaller organizations but can require a team for larger international organizations that have thousands of business processes. Either way, measures need to be put in place to prevent, respond to, and fix security issues that arise in an organization.

1. SECURITY MANAGEMENT SYSTEM STANDARDS

To give organizations a starting point to develop their own security management systems, the International Organization for Standardization (ISO) and the International Electrotechnical Commission (IEC) have developed a family of standards known as the Information Security Management System 27000 Family of Standards. This group of standards, starting with ISO/IEC 27001, gives organizations the ability to certify their security management systems.

The certification process takes place in several stages. The first stage is an audit of all documentation and policies that currently exist for a system. The documentation is usually based directly on the requirements of the standard, but it does not have to be. Organizations can come up with their own sets of standards, as long as all aspects of the standard are covered. The second stage actually tests the effectiveness of the existing policies. The third stage is a reassessment of the organization to make sure it still meets the requirements. This third stage keeps organizations up to date over time as standards for security management systems change. This certification process is based on a Plan-Do-Check-Act iterative process:

- *Plan* the security management system and create the policies that define it.
- *Do* implement the policies in your organization.
- *Check* to ensure the security management system's policies are protecting the resources they were meant to protect.
- *Act* to respond to incidents that breach the implemented policies.

Certifying your security management system helps ensure that you keep the controls and policies constantly up to date to meet certification requirements. Getting certified also demonstrates to your partners and customers that your security management systems will help keep your business running smoothly if network security events were to occur.

Though the ISO/IEC 27000 Family of Standards allows for businesses to optionally get certified, the Federal Information Security Management Act (FISMA) requires all government agencies to develop security management systems. The process of complying with FISMA is very similar to the process of implementing the ISO 27000 family of standards.

The first step of FISMA compliance is determining what constitutes the system you're trying to protect. Next, you need to perform risk assessment to determine what controls you'll need to put in place to protect your system's assets. The last step is actually implementing the planned controls. FISMA then requires mandatory yearly inspections to make sure an organization stays in compliance.

2. TRAINING REQUIREMENTS

Many security management system training courses for personnel are available over the Internet. These courses provide information for employees setting up security management systems and for those using the computer and network resources of the company that are referenced in the policies of the security management system.

Training should also include creating company security policies and creating user roles that are specific to the organization. Planning policies and roles ahead of time will help prevent confusion in the event of a problem, since everyone will know what systems they are responsible for.

3. PRINCIPLES OF INFORMATION SECURITY

The act of securing information has been around for as long as the idea of storing information. Over time, three main objectives of information security have been defined:

- *Confidentiality.* Information is only available to the people or systems that need access to it. This is done by encrypting information that only certain people are able to decrypt or denying access to those who don't need it. This might seem simple at first, but confidentiality must be applied to all aspects of a system. This means preventing access to all backup locations and even log files if those files can contain sensitive information.
- *Integrity.* Information can only be added or updated by those who need to update that data. Unauthorized changes to data cause it to lose its integrity, and access to the information must be cut off to everyone until the information's integrity is restored. Allowing access to compromised data will cause those unauthorized changes to propagate to other areas of the system.
- *Availability.* The information needs to be available in a timely manner when requested. Access to no data is just as bad as access to compromised data. No

process can be performed if the data on which the process is based is unavailable.

4. ROLES AND RESPONSIBILITIES OF PERSONNEL

All personnel who come into contact with information systems need to be aware of the risks from improper use of those systems. Network administrators need to know the effects of each change they make to their systems and how that affects the overall security of that system. They also need to be able to efficiently control access to those systems in cases of emergency, when quick action is needed.

Users of those systems need to understand what risks can be caused by their actions and how to comply with company policy.

Several roles should be defined within your organization:

- *Chief information officer/director of information technology.* This person is responsible for creating and maintaining the security policies for your organization.
- *Network engineer.* This person is responsible for the physical connection of your network and the connection of your network to the Internet. He or she is also responsible for the routers, firewalls, and switches that connect your organization.
- *Network administrator.* This person handles all other network devices within the organization, such as servers, workstations, printers, copiers, and wireless access devices. Server and workstation software is also the responsibility of the network administrator.
- *End users.* These people are allowed to operate the computer in accordance with company policies, to perform their daily tasks. They should not have administrator access to their PCs or, especially, servers.

There are also many other specific administrators some companies might require. These are Microsoft Exchange Administrators, Database Administrators, and Active Directory Administrators, to name a few. These administrators should have specific tasks to perform and a specific scope in which to perform them that is stated in the company policy.

5. SECURITY POLICIES

Each organization should develop a company policy detailing the preferred use of company data or a company application. An example of a policy is one that restricts transfer of data on any device that was not purchased by the company. This can help prevent unauthorized access to company data. Some companies also prefer not to allow any removable media to be used within the organization.

Security policies should also govern how the computer is to be used on a day-to-day basis. Very often, computer users are required to have Internet access to do research pertaining to their jobs. This isn't hard to restrict in a specialized setting such as a law firm where only a handful of sites contain pertinent information. In other cases it can be nearly impossible to restrict all Web sites except the ones that contain information that applies to your organization or your research. In those cases it is imperative that you have company policies that dictate what Web sites users are able to visit and for what purposes. When unrestricted Internet access is allowed, it is a good practice to use software that will track the Web sites a user visits, to make sure they are not breaking company policy.

6. SECURITY CONTROLS

There are three types of security controls that need to be implemented for a successful security policy to be put into action. They are physical controls, technical controls, and administrative controls.

Physical controls consist of things such as magnetic swipe cards, RFID, or biometric security to prevent access to stored information or network resources. Physical controls also consist of environmental controls such as HVAC units, power generators, and fire suppression systems.

Technical controls are used to limit access to network resources and devices that are used in the organization. They can be individual usernames and passwords used to access individual devices or access control lists that are part of a network operating system.

Administrative controls consist of policies created by an organization that determine how the organization will function. These controls guide employees by describing how their jobs are to be done and what resources they are supposed to use to do them.

7. NETWORK ACCESS

The first step in developing a security management system is documenting the network resources to which each group of users should have access to. Users should only have access to the resources that they need to complete their jobs efficiently. An example of when this will come in handy is when the president of the company wants access to every network resource and then his computer becomes infected with a virus that starts infecting all network files. Access Control Lists (ACLs) should be planned ahead of time and then implemented on the network to avoid complications with the network ACL hierarchy.

An ACL dictates which users have access to certain network resources. Network administrators usually have access to all files and folders on a server. Department administrators will have access to all files used by their departments. End users will have access to a subset of the department files that they need to perform their jobs. ACLs are developed by the head of IT for an organization and the network administrator and implemented by the network administrator.

Implementing ACLs prevents end users from being able to access sensitive company information and helps them perform their jobs better by not giving them access to information that can act as a distraction.

Access control can also apply to physical access as well as electronic access. Access to certain networking devices could cause an entire organization to stop functioning for a period of time, so access to those devices should be carefully controlled.

8. RISK ASSESSMENT

Before security threats can be blocked, all risks must first be identified and assessed. Risk assessment forms the foundation of a good security management system. Network administrators must document all aspects of their network setup. This documentation should provide information on the network firewall, servers, clients, and any other devices physically connected or wirelessly connected to the network. The most time should be spent documenting how the private computer network will be connected to the Internet for Web browsing and email. Some common security risks are:

- *USB storage devices.* Devices that can be used to copy proprietary company data off the internal network. Many organizations use software solutions to disable unused USB ports on a system; others physically block the connections.
- *Remote control software.* Services such as GoToMyPc or Log Me In do not require any special router or firewall configuration to enable remote access.
- *Email.* Filters should be put in place that prevent sensitive company information from simply being emailed outside the organization.

- *General Internet use.* There is always a possibility of downloading a malicious virus from the Internet unless all but trusted and necessary Web sites are restricted to internal users. This can be accomplished by a content-filtering firewall or Web proxy server.
- *Laptops.* Lost laptops pose a very large security risk, depending on the type on data stored on them. Policies need to be put in place to determine what types of information can be stored on these devices and what actions should be taken if a laptop is lost.
- *Peer-to-peer applications.* P2P applications that are used to download illegal music and software cause a risk because the files that are downloaded are not coming from known sources. People who download an illegal version of an application could be downloading a worm that can affect the entire network.

9. INCIDENT RESPONSE

Knowing what to do in case of a security incident is crucial to being able to track down what happened and how to make sure it never happens again. When a security incident is identified, it is imperative that steps are taken so that forensic evidence is not destroyed in the investigation process. Forensic evidence includes the content of all storage devices attached to the system at the time of the incident and even the contents stored in memory of a running computer.

Using an external hard drive enclosure to browse the content of the hard drive of a compromised system will destroy date and timestamps that a forensic technician can use to tie together various system events.

When a system breach or security issue has been detected, it is recommended to consult someone familiar with forensically sound investigation methods. If forensic methods are not used, it can lead to evidence not being admissible in court if the incident results in a court case.

There are specific steps to take with a computer system, depending on the type of incident that occurred. Unless a system is causing damage to itself by deleting files or folders that can be potential evidence, it is best to leave the system running for the forensic investigator. The forensic investigator will:

- Document what is on the screen by photographing it. She will also photograph the actual computer system and all cable connections.

- Capture the contents of the system's memory. This is done using a small utility installed from a removable drive that will create a forensic image of what is in the system's physical memory. This can be used to document Trojan activity. If memory is not imaged and the computer was used to commit a crime, the computer's user can claim that a malicious virus, which was only running in memory, was responsible.
- Turn off the computer. If the system is running a Windows workstation operating system such as Windows 2000 Workstation or Windows XP, the forensic technician will pull the plug on the system. If the system is running a server operating system such as Windows 2000 Server, Windows 2003 Server, or a Linux- or Unix-based operating system such as Red Hat, Fedora, or Ubuntu, the investigator will properly shut down the system.
- Create a forensic image of the system's hard drive. This is done using imaging software and usually a hardware write-blocker to connect the system's hard drive to the imaging computer. A hardware write-blocker is used to prevent the imaging computer from writing anything at all to the hard drive. Windows, by default, will create a recycle bin on a new volume that it is able to mount, which would cause the evidence to lose forensic value.

Investigators are then able to search through the system without making any changes to the original media.

10. SUMMARY

Organizations interested in implementing a comprehensive security management system should start by documenting all business processes that are critical to an organization and then analyzing the risks associated with them, then implement the controls that can protect those processes from external and internal threats. Internet threats are not usually the cause of someone with malicious intent but someone who accidentally downloads a Trojan or accidentally moves or deletes a directory or critical files. The final step is performing recursive checking of the policies your organization has put in place to adjust for new technologies that need to be protected or new ways that external threats can damage your network. The easiest way to implement security management systems is to use the Plan-Do-Act-Check (PDAC) process to step though the necessary procedures.

## Chapter 16

Information Technology Security Management

Rahul Bhasker
California State University

Bhushan Kapoor
California State University

Information technology security management can be defined as processes that supported enabling organizational structure and technology to protect an organization's IT operations and assets against internal and external threats, intentional or otherwise. The principle purpose of IT security management is to ensure confidentiality, integrity, and availability (CIA) of IT systems. Fundamentally, security management is a part of the risk management process and business continuity strategy in an organization.

1. INFORMATION SECURITY MANAGEMENT STANDARDS

A range of standards are specified by various industry bodies. Although specific to an industry, these standards can be used by any organization and adapted to its goals.

Here we discuss the main organizations that set standards related to information security management.

Federal Information Security Management Act

At the U.S. federal level, the National Institute of Standards and Technology (NIST) has specified guidelines for implementing the Federal Information Security Management Act (FISMA). This act aims to provide the following standards shown in Figure 16.1.

The "Federal Information Security Management Framework Recommended by NIST"[2] sidebar describes the risk management framework as specified in FISMA. The activities specified in this framework are paramount in implementing an IT security management plan.

• Standards for categorizing information and information systems by mission impact
• Standards for minimum security requirements for information and information systems
• Guidance for selecting appropriate security controls for information systems
• Guidance for assessing security controls in information systems and determining security control effectiveness
• Guidance for certifying and accrediting information systems

FIGURE 16.1 Specifications in the Federal Information Security Management Act.[1]

---

1 "Federal Information Security Management Act," National Institute of Standards and Technology, http://csrc.nist.gov/groups/SMA/fisma/index.html, 2008 (downloaded 10/20/2008).

2 "Federal Information Security Management Act," National Institute of Standards and Technology, http://csrc.nist.gov/groups/SMA/fisma/index.html, 2008 (downloaded 10/20/2008).

Although specified for the federal government, this framework can be used as a guideline by any organization.

> ### Federal Information Security Management Framework Recommended by NIST
>
> **Step 1: Categorize**
>
> In this step, information systems and internal information should be categorized based on impact.
>
> **Step 2: Select**
>
> Use the categorization in the first step to select an initial set of security controls for the information system and apply tailoring guidance as appropriate, to obtain a starting point for required controls.
>
> **Step 3: Supplement**
>
> Assess the risk and local conditions, including the security requirements, specific threat information, and cost/benefit analyses or special circumstances. Supplement the initial set of security controls with the supplement analyses.
>
> **Step 4: Document**
>
> The original set of security controls and the supplements should be documented.
>
> **Step 5: Implement**
>
> The security controls you identified and supplemented should be implemented in the organization's information systems.
>
> **Step 6: Assess**
>
> The security controls should be assessed to determine whether the controls are implemented correctly, are operating as intended, and are producing the desired outcome with respect to meeting the security requirements for the system.
>
> **Step 7: Authorize**
>
> Upon a determination of the risk to organizational operations, organizational assets, or individuals resulting from their operation, authorize the information systems.
>
> **Step 8: Monitor**
>
> Monitor and assess selected security controls in the information system on a continuous basis, including documenting changes to the system.

International Standards Organization

Another influential international body, the International Standards Organization and the International Electro

Technical Commission, published ISO/IEC 17799:2005.[3] These standards establish guidelines and general principles for initiating, implementing, maintaining, and improving information security management in an organization. The objectives outlined provide general guidance on the commonly accepted goals of information security management. The standards consist of best practices of control objectives and controls in the areas of information security management shown in Figure 16.2.

These objectives and controls are intended to be implemented to meet the requirements identified by a risk assessment.

Other Organizations Involved in Standards

Other organizations that are involved in information security management include The Internet Society[4] and the Information Security Forum.[5] These are professional societies with members in the thousands. The Internet Society is the organization home for the groups responsible for Internet infrastructure standards, including the Internet Engineering Task Force (IETF) and the Internet Architecture Board (IAB). The Information Security Forum is a global nonprofit organization of several hundred leading organizations in financial services, manufacturing, telecommunications, consumer goods, government, and other areas. It provides research into best practices and advice, summarized in its biannual Standard of Good Practice, which incorporates detailed specifications across many areas.

2. INFORMATION TECHNOLOGY SECURITY ASPECTS

The various aspects to IT security in an organization that must be considered include:

- Security policies and procedures
- Security organization structure

3 "Information technology | Security techniques | Code of practice for information security management, ISO/IEC 17799," The International Standards Organization and The International Electro Technical Commission, www.iso.org/iso/iso_catalogue/catalogue_tc/catalogue_detail.htm?csnumber=39612, 2005 (downloaded 10/20/2008).

4 "ISOC's Standards and Technology Activities," Internet Society, www.isoc.org/standards, 2008 (downloaded 10/20/2008).

5 "The Standard of Good Practice," Information Security Forum, https://www.securityforum.org/html/frameset.htm, 2008 (downloaded 10/20/2008).

Security Policy
Organization of Information Security
Asset Management
Human Resources Security
Physical and Environmental Security
Communication and Operations Management
Access Control
Information Systems Acquisition, Development and Maintenance
Information Security Incident Management
Business Continuity Management
Compliance

FIGURE 16.2 International Standards Organization best-practice areas.[6]

- IT security processes
  - Processes for a business continuity strategy
  - Processes for IT security governance planning
- Rules and regulations

Security Policies and Procedures

Security policies and procedures constitute the main part of any organization's security. These steps are essential for implementing IT security management: authorizing security roles and responsibilities to various security personnel; setting rules for expected behavior from users and security role players; setting rules for business continuity plans; and more. The security policy should be generally agreed to by most personnel in the organization and should have the support of the highest-level management. This helps in prioritization at the overall organization level.

The following list, illustrated in Figure 16.3, is a sample of some of the issues an organization is expected to address in its policies.[7] Note, however, that the universal list is virtually endless, and each organization's list will consist of issues based on several factors, including its size and the value and sensitivity of the information it owns or deals with. Some important issues included in most security policies are:

- *Access control standards.* These are standards on controlling the access to various systems. These include password change standards.

Access Control Standards
Accountability
Audit Trails
Backups
Disposal of Media
Disposal of Printed Matter
Information Ownership
Managers Responsibility
Equipment
Communication
Procedures and Processes at Work

FIGURE 16.3 Security aspects an organization is expected to address in its policies.

- *Accountability.* Every user should be responsible for her own accounts. This implies that any activity under a particular user ID should be the responsibility of the user whose ID it is.
- *Audit trails.* There should be an audit trail recorded of all the activities under a user ID. For example, all the login, log-out activities for 30 days should be recorded. Additionally, all unauthorized attempts to access, read, write, and delete data and execute programs should be logged.
- *Backups.* There should be a clearly defined backup policy. Any backups should be kept in a secure area. A clear policy on the frequency of the backups and their recovery should be communicated to the appropriate personnel.
- Disposal of media. A clear policy should be defined regarding the disposal of media. This includes a policy on which hardware and storage media, such as disk drives, diskettes, and CD-ROMs, are to be destroyed. The level and method of destruction of business-critical information that is no longer needed should be well defined and documented. Personnel should be trained regularly on the principles to follow.

---

6 "Information technology | Security techniques | Code of practice for information security management, ISO/IEC 17799," The International Standards Organization and The International Electro Technical Commission, www.iso.org/iso (downloaded 10/20/2008).

7 "Information technology | Security techniques | Code of practice for information security management, ISO/IEC 17799," The International Standards Organization and The International Electro Technical Commission, www.iso.org/iso (downloaded 10/20/2008).

- *Disposal of printed matter.* Guidelines as to the disposal of printed matter should be specified and implemented throughout the organization. In particular, business-critical materials should be disposed properly and securely.
- *Information ownership.* All the data and information available in the organization should have an assigned owner. The owner should be responsible for deciding on access rights to the information for various personnel.
- *Managers' responsibility.* Managers at all levels should ensure that their staff understands the security policy and adheres to it continuously. They should be held responsible for recording any deviations from the core policy.
- *Equipment.* An organization should have specific guidelines about modems, portable storage, and other devices. These devices should be kept in a secured physical environment.
- *Communication.* Well-defined policy guidelines are needed for communication using corporate information systems. These include communications via emails, instant messaging, and so on.
- *Work procedures and processes.* Employees of an organization should be trained to secure their workstations when not in use. The policy can impose a procedure of logging off before leaving a workstation. It can also include quarantining any device (such as a laptop) brought from outside the organization before plugging it into the network.

Security Organization Structure

Various security-related roles need to be maintained and well defined. These roles and their brief descriptions are described here.[8]

End User

End users have a responsibility to protect information assets on a daily basis through adherence to the security policies that have been set and communicated. End-user compliance with security policies is key to maintaining information security in an organization because this group represents the most consistent users of the organization's information.

Executive Management

Top management plays an important role in protecting the information assets in an organization. Executive management can support the goal of IT security by conveying the extent to which management supports security goals and priorities. Members of the management team should be aware of the risks that they are accepting for the organization through their decisions or failure to make decisions. There are various specific areas on which senior management should focus, but some that are specifically appropriate are user training, inculcating and encouraging a security culture, and identifying the correct policies for IT security governance.

Security Officer

The security officer "directs, coordinates, plans, and organizes information security activities throughout the organization."[9]

Data/Information Owners

Every organization should have clearly identified data and information owners. These executives or managers should review the classification and access security policies and procedures. They should also be responsible for periodic audit of the information and data and its continuous security. They may appoint a data custodian in case the work required to secure the information and data is extensive and needs more than one person to complete.

Information System Auditor

Information system auditors are responsible for ensuring that the information security policies and procedures have been adhered to. They are also responsible for establishing the baseline, architecture, management direction, and compliance on a continuous basis. They are an essential part of unbiased information about the state of information security in the organization.

Information Technology Personnel

IT personnel are responsible for building IT security controls into the design and implementations of the systems. They are also responsible for testing these controls periodically or whenever there is a change. They work

---

8 Tipton and Krause, "Information Security Governance," *Information Security Management Handbook*, Auerbach Publications, 2008.

9 Tipton and Krause, "Information Security Governance," *Information Security Management Handbook*, Auerbach Publications, 2008.

with the executives and other managers to ensure compliance in all the systems under their responsibility.

Systems Administrator

A systems administrator is responsible for configuring the hardware and the operating system to ensure that the information systems and their contents are available for business as and when needed. These adminstrators are placed ideally in an organization to ensure security of these assets. They play a key role because they own access to the most vulnerable information assets of an organization.

IT Security Processes

To achieve effective IT security requires processes related to security management. These processes include business continuity strategy, processes related to IT security governance planning, and IT security management implementation.

Processes for a Business Continuity Strategy

As is the case with any strategy, the business continuity strategy depends on a commitment from senior management. This can include some of the analysis that is obtained by business impact assessment/risk analysis focused on business value drivers. These business value drivers are determined by the main stakeholders from the organizations. Examples of these value drivers are customer service and intellectual property protection.[10]

The Disaster Recovery Institute International (DRII) associates eight tasks with the contingency planning process.[11] These are as follows:

- Business impact analysis, to analyze the impact of outage on critical business function operations.
- Risk assessment, to assess the risks to the current infrastructure and the incorporation of safeguards to reduce the likelihood and impact of disasters.
- Recovery strategy identification, to develop a variety of disaster scenarios and identify recovery strategies.

- Recovery strategy selection, to select the appropriate recovery strategies based on the perceived threats and the time needed to recover.
- Contingency plan development, to document the processes, equipment, and facilities required to restore the IT assets.
- User training, to develop training programs to enable all affected users to perform their tasks.
- Plan verification, for accuracy and adequacy.
- Plan maintenance, for continuous upkeep of the plan as needs change.

Processes for IT Security Governance Planning

IT security governance planning includes prioritization as its major function. This helps in utilizing the limited sources of the organization. Determining priorities among the potential conflicting interests is the main focus of these processes. This includes budget setting, resource allocation, and, most important, the political process needed to prioritize in an organization.

Rules and Regulations

An organization is influenced by rules and regulations that influence its business. In a business environment marked by globalization, organizations have to be aware of both national and international rules and regulations. From an information security management perspective, various rules and regulations must be considered. These are listed in Figure 16.4.

We give more details on some rules and regulations here:

- The Health Insurance Portability and Accountability Act (HIPAA) requires the adoption of national standards for electronic healthcare transactions and national identifiers for providers, health insurance plans, and employers. Healthcare providers have to protect the personal medical information of the customer to comply with this law. Similarly, the Gramm-Leach-Bliley Act of 1999 (GLBA), also known as the Financial Services Modernization Act of 1999, requires financial companies to protect the information about individuals that it collects during transactions.
- The Sarbanes-Oxley Act of 2002 (SOX). This law requires companies to protect and audit their financial data. The chief information officer and other senior executives are held responsible for reporting and auditing an organization's financial information to regulatory and other agencies.

---

10 C. R. Jackson, "Developing Realistic Continuity Planning Process Metrics," *Information Security Management Handbook*, Auerbach Publications, 2008.

11 "Contingency Planning Process," DRII – The Institute for Continuity Management, https://www.drii.org/professional_prac/profprac_appendix.html#BUSINESS_CONTINUITY_PLANNING_INFORMATION, 2008 (downloaded 10/24/2008).

| Health Insurance Portability and Accountability Act (HIPAA) |
| Gramm-Leach-Bliley Act |
| Sarbanes-Oxley Act of 2002 |
| Security Breach Notification Laws |
| Personal Information Protection and Electronic Document Act (PIPEDA) |
| Computer Fraud and Abuse Act |
| USA PATRIOT Act |

FIGURE 16.4 Rules and regulations related to information security management.

- State Security Breach Notification Laws (California and many others) require businesses, nonprofits, and state institutions to notify consumers when unencrypted "personal information" might have been compromised, lost, or stolen.
- The Personal Information Protection and Electronics Document Act (PIPEDA) supports and promotes electronic commerce by protecting personal information that is collected, used, or disclosed in certain circumstances, by providing for the use of electronic means to communicate or record information or transactions, and by amending the Canada Evidence Act, the Statutory Instruments Act, and the Statute Revision Act that is in fact the case.
- The Computer Fraud and Abuse Act, or CFAA (also known as Fraud and Related Activity in Connection with Computers), is a U.S. law passed in 1986 and intended to reduce computer crimes. It was amended in 1994, 1996, and 2001 by the U.S.A. PATRIOT Act.[12]

The following sidebar, "Computer Fraud and Abuse Act Criminal Offences," lists criminal offences covered under this law.[13]

Computer Fraud and Abuse Act Criminal Offences

(a) Whoever—

(1) having knowingly accessed a computer without authorization or exceeding authorized access, and by means of such conduct having obtained information that has been determined by the United States Government pursuant to an Executive order or statute to require protection against unauthorized disclosure for reasons of national defense or foreign relations, or any restricted data, as defined in paragraph y. of section 11 of the Atomic Energy Act of 1954, with reason to believe that such information so obtained could be used to the injury of the United States, or to the advantage of any foreign nation willfully communicates, delivers, transmits, or causes to be communicated, delivered, or transmitted, or attempts to communicate, deliver, transmit or cause to be communicated, delivered, or transmitted the same to any person not entitled to receive it, or willfully retains the same and fails to deliver it to the officer or employee of the United States entitled to receive it;

(2) intentionally accesses a computer without authorization or exceeds authorized access, and thereby obtains—

(A) information contained in a financial record of a financial institution, or of a card issuer as defined in section 1602 (n) of title 15, or contained in a file of a consumer reporting agency on a consumer, as such terms are defined in the Fair Credit Reporting Act (15 U.S.C. 1681 et seq.);

(B) information from any department or agency of the United States; or

(C) information from any protected computer if the conduct involved an interstate or foreign communication;

(3) intentionally, without authorization to access any non-public computer of a department or agency of the United States, accesses such a computer of that department or agency that is exclusively for the use of the Government of the United States or, in the case of a computer not exclusively for such use, is used by or for the Government of the United States and such conduct affects that use by or for the Government of the United States;

---

12 "Fraud and Related Activities in Relation to the Computers," U.S. Code Collection, Cornell University Law School, www4.law.cornell.edu/uscode/18/1030.html, 2008 (downloaded 10/24/2008).

13 "Fraud and Related Activities in Relation to the Computers," U.S. Code Collection, Cornell University Law School, www4.law.cornell.edu/uscode/18/1030.html, 2008 (downloaded 10/24/2008).

(4) knowingly and with intent to defraud, accesses a protected computer without authorization, or exceeds authorized access, and by means of such conduct furthers the intended fraud and obtains anything of value, unless the object of the fraud and the thing obtained consists only of the use of the computer and the value of such use is not more than $5,000 in any 1-year period;

(5)

(A)

(i) knowingly causes the transmission of a program, information, code, or command, and as a result of such conduct, intentionally causes damage without authorization, to a protected computer;

(ii) intentionally accesses a protected computer without authorization, and as a result of such conduct, recklessly causes damage; or

(iii) intentionally accesses a protected computer without authorization, and as a result of such conduct, causes damage; and

(B) by conduct described in clause (i), (ii), or (iii) of subparagraph (A), caused (or, in the case of an attempted offense, would, if completed, have caused)—

(i) loss to 1 or more persons during any 1-year period (and, for purposes of an investigation, prosecution, or other proceeding brought by the United States only, loss resulting from a related course of conduct affecting 1 or more other protected computers) aggregating at least $5,000 in value;

(ii) the modification or impairment, or potential modification or impairment, of the medical examination, diagnosis, treatment, or care of 1 or more individuals;

(iii) physical injury to any person;

(iv) a threat to public health or safety; or

(v) damage affecting a computer system used by or for a government entity in furtherance of the administration of justice, national defense, or national security;

(6) knowingly and with intent to defraud traffics (as defined in section 1029) in any password or similar information through which a computer may be accessed without authorization, if—

(A) such trafficking affects interstate or foreign commerce; or

(B) such computer is used by or for the Government of the United States; [1]

(7) with intent to extort from any person any money or other thing of value, transmits in interstate or foreign commerce any communication containing any threat to cause damage to a protected computer;
shall be punished as provided in subsection (c) of this section.

(b) Whoever attempts to commit an offense under subsection (a) of this section shall be punished as provided in subsection (c) of this section.

(c) The punishment for an offense under subsection (a) or (b) of this section is—

(1)

(A) a fine under this title or imprisonment for not more than ten years, or both, in the case of an offense under subsection (a)(1) of this section which does not occur after a conviction for another offense under this section, or an attempt to commit an offense punishable under this subparagraph; and

(B) a fine under this title or imprisonment for not more than twenty years, or both, in the case of an offense under subsection (a)(1) of this section which occurs after a conviction for another offense under this section, or an attempt to commit an offense punishable under this subparagraph;

(2)

(A) except as provided in subparagraph (B), a fine under this title or imprisonment for not more than one year, or both, in the case of an offense under subsection (a)(2), (a)(3), (a)(5)(A)(iii), or (a)(6) of this section which does not occur after a conviction for another offense under this section, or an attempt to commit an offense punishable under this subparagraph;

(B) a fine under this title or imprisonment for not more than 5 years, or both, in the case of an offense under subsection (a)(2), or an attempt to commit an offense punishable under this subparagraph, if—

(i) the offense was committed for purposes of commercial advantage or private financial gain;

(ii) the offense was committed in furtherance of any criminal or tortious act in violation of the Constitution or laws of the United States or of any State; or

(iii) the value of the information obtained exceeds $5,000; and

(C) a fine under this title or imprisonment for not more than ten years, or both, in the case of an offense under subsection (a)(2), (a)(3) or (a)(6) of this section which occurs after a conviction for another offense under this section, or an attempt to commit an offense punishable under this subparagraph;

(3)

(A) a fine under this title or imprisonment for not more than five years, or both, in the case of an offense under subsection (a)(4) or (a)(7) of this section which does not occur after a conviction for another offense under this section, or an attempt to commit an offense punishable under this subparagraph; and

(B) a fine under this title or imprisonment for not more than ten years, or both, in the case of an offense under subsection (a)(4), (a)(5)(A)(iii), or (a)(7) of this section which occurs after a conviction for another offense under this section, or an attempt to commit an offense punishable under this subparagraph;

(4)

(A) except as provided in paragraph (5), a fine under this title, imprisonment for not more than 10 years, or both, in the case of an offense under subsection (a)(5)(A)(i), or an attempt to commit an offense punishable under that subsection;

(B) a fine under this title, imprisonment for not more than 5 years, or both, in the case of an offense under subsection (a)(5)(A)(ii), or an attempt to commit an offense punishable under that subsection;

(C) except as provided in paragraph (5), a fine under this title, imprisonment for not more than 20 years, or both, in the case of an offense under subsection (a)(5)(A)(i) or (a)(5)(A)(ii), or an attempt to commit an offense punishable under either subsection, that occurs after a conviction for another offense under this section; and

(5)

(A) if the offender knowingly or recklessly causes or attempts to cause serious bodily injury from conduct in violation of subsection (a)(5)(A)(i), a fine under this title or imprisonment for not more than 20 years, or both; and

(B) if the offender knowingly or recklessly causes or attempts to cause death from conduct in violation of subsection (a)(5)(A)(i), a fine under this title or imprisonment for any term of years or for life, or both.

(d)

(1) The United States Secret Service shall, in addition to any other agency having such authority, have the authority to investigate offenses under this section.

(2) The Federal Bureau of Investigation shall have primary authority to investigate offenses under subsection (a)(1) for any cases involving espionage, foreign counterintelligence, information protected against unauthorized disclosure for reasons of national defense or foreign relations, or Restricted Data (as that term is defined in section 11y of the Atomic Energy Act of 1954 (42 U.S.C. 2014 (y)), except for offenses affecting the duties of the United States Secret Service pursuant to section 3056 (a) of this title.

(3) Such authority shall be exercised in accordance with an agreement which shall be entered into by the Secretary of the Treasury and the Attorney General.

(e) As used in this section—

(1) the term "computer" means an electronic, magnetic, optical, electrochemical, or other high speed data processing device performing logical, arithmetic, or storage functions, and includes any data storage facility or communications facility directly related to or operating in conjunction with such device, but such term does not include an automated typewriter or typesetter, a portable hand held calculator, or other similar device;

(2) the term "protected computer" means a computer—

(A) exclusively for the use of a financial institution or the United States Government, or, in the case of a computer not exclusively for such use, used by or for a financial institution or the United States Government and the conduct constituting the offense affects that use by or for the financial institution or the Government; or

(B) which is used in interstate or foreign commerce or communication, including a computer located outside the United States that is used in a manner that affects interstate or foreign commerce or communication of the United States;

(3) the term "State" includes the District of Columbia, the Commonwealth of Puerto Rico, and any other commonwealth, possession or territory of the United States;

(4) the term "financial institution" means—

(A) an institution, with deposits insured by the Federal Deposit Insurance Corporation;

(B) the Federal Reserve or a member of the Federal Reserve including any Federal Reserve Bank;

(C) a credit union with accounts insured by the National Credit Union Administration;

(D) a member of the Federal home loan bank system and any home loan bank;

(E) any institution of the Farm Credit System under the Farm Credit Act of 1971;

(F) a broker-dealer registered with the Securities and Exchange Commission pursuant to section 15 of the Securities Exchange Act of 1934;

(G) the Securities Investor Protection Corporation;

(H) a branch or agency of a foreign bank (as such terms are defined in paragraphs (1) and (3) of section 1(b) of the International Banking Act of 1978); and

(I) an organization operating under section 25 or section 25(a) [2] of the Federal Reserve Act;

(5) the term "financial record" means information derived from any record held by a financial institution pertaining to a customer's relationship with the financial institution;

(6) the term "exceeds authorized access" means to access a computer with authorization and to use such access to obtain or alter information in the computer that the accesser is not entitled so to obtain or alter;

(7) the term "department of the United States" means the legislative or judicial branch of the Government or one of the executive departments enumerated in section 101 of title 5;

(8) the term "damage" means any impairment to the integrity or availability of data, a program, a system, or information;

(9) the term "government entity" includes the Government of the United States, any State or political subdivision of the United States, any foreign country, and any state,

province, municipality, or other political subdivision of a foreign country;

(10) the term "conviction" shall include a conviction under the law of any State for a crime punishable by imprisonment for more than 1 year, an element of which is unauthorized access, or exceeding authorized access, to a computer;

(11) the term "loss" means any reasonable cost to any victim, including the cost of responding to an offense, conducting a damage assessment, and restoring the data, program, system, or information to its condition prior to the offense, and any revenue lost, cost incurred, or other consequential damages incurred because of interruption of service; and

(12) the term "person" means any individual, firm, corporation, educational institution, financial institution, governmental entity, or legal or other entity.

(f) This section does not prohibit any lawfully authorized investigative, protective, or intelligence activity of a law enforcement agency of the United States, a State, or a political subdivision of a State, or of an intelligence agency of the United States.

(g) Any person who suffers damage or loss by reason of a violation of this section may maintain a civil action against the violator to obtain compensatory damages and injunctive relief or other equitable relief. A civil action for a violation of this section may be brought only if the conduct involves 1 of the factors set forth in clause (i), (ii), (iii), (iv), or (v) of subsection (a)(5)(B). Damages for a violation involving only conduct described in subsection (a)(5)(B)(i) are limited to economic damages. No action may be brought under this subsection unless such action is begun within 2 years of the date of the act complained of or the date of the discovery of the damage. No action may be brought under this subsection for the negligent design or manufacture of computer hardware, computer software, or firmware.

(h) The Attorney General and the Secretary of the Treasury shall report to the Congress annually, during the first 3 years following the date of the enactment of this subsection, concerning investigations and prosecutions under subsection (a)(5).

The U.S.A. PATRIOT Act of 2001 increased the scope and penalties of this act by[14]:

- Raising the maximum penalty for violations to ten years (from five) for a first offense and 20 years (from ten) for a second offense
- Ensuring that violators only need to intend to cause damage generally, not intend to cause damage or other specified harm over the $5000 statutory damage threshold
- Allowing aggregation of damages to different computers over a year to reach the $5000 threshold
- Enhancing punishment for violations involving any (not just $5000 in) damage to a government computer involved in criminal justice or the military
- Including damage to foreign computers involved in U.S. interstate commerce
- Including state law offenses as priors for sentencing;
- Expanding the definition of loss to expressly include time spent investigating
- Responding (this is why it is important for damage assessment and restoration)

These details are summarized in Figure 16.5.

| Maximum Penalty |
| Extent of Damage |
| Aggregation of Damage |
| Enhancement of Punishment |
| Damage to Foreign Computers |
| State Law Offenses |
| Expanding the Definition of Loss |
| Response |

FIGURE 16.5 U.S.A. PATRIOT Act increase in scope and penalties.

The PATRIOT Act of 2001 came under criticism for a number of reasons. There are fears that the Act is an invasion of privacy and infringement on freedom of speech. Critics also feel that the Act unfairly expands the powers of the executive branch and strips away many crucial checks and balances.

The original act has a sunset clause that would have caused many of the law's provisions to expire in 2005. The Act was reauthorized in early 2006 with some new safeguards and with expiration dates for its two most controversial powers, which authorize roving wiretaps and secret searches of records.

3. CONCLUSION

Information technology security management consists of processes to enable organizational structure and

---

14 "Computer Fraud and Abuse Act," Wikipedia, http://en.wikipedia.org/wiki/Computer_Fraud_and_Abuse_Act, 2008 (downloaded 10/24/2008).

technology to protect an organization's IT operations and assets against internal and external threats, intentional or otherwise. These processes are developed to ensure confidentiality, integrity, and availability of IT systems. There are various aspects to the IT security in an organization that need to be considered. These include security policies and procedures, security organization structure, IT security processes, and rules and regulations.

Security policies and procedures are essential for implementing IT security management: authorizing security roles and responsibilities to various security personnel; setting rules for expected behavior from users and security role players; setting rules for business continuity plans; and more. The security policy should be generally agreed to by most personnel in the organization and have support from the highest-level management. This helps in prioritization at the overall organization level. The IT security processes are essentially part of an organization's risk management processes and business continuity strategies. In a business environment marked by globalization, organizations have to be aware of both national and international rules and regulations. Their information security and privacy policies must conform to these rules and regulations.

## Chapter 17

Identity Management

Dr. Jean-Marc Seigneur
University of Geneva

Dr. Tewfiq El Maliki
University of Applied Sciences of Geneva

Digital identity lays the groundwork necessary to guarantee that the Internet infrastructure is strong enough to meet basic expectations for security and privacy. "Anywhere, anytime" mobile computing is becoming real; in this ambient intelligent world, the choice of identity management mechanisms will have a large impact on social, cultural, business, and political aspects of our lives. Privacy is a human need, and all of society would suffer from its demise; people have hectic lives and cannot spend all their time administering their digital identities. The choice of identity mechanisms will change the social, cultural, business, and political environment. Furthermore, identity management is also a promising topic for modern society.

Recent technological advances in user identity management have highlighted the paradigm of federated identity management and user-centric identity management as improved alternatives. The first empowers the management of identity; the second allows users to actively manage their identity information and profiles. It also allows providers to easily deal with privacy aspects regarding user expectations. This problem has been tackled with some trends and emerging solutions, as described in this chapter. First, we provide an overview of identity management from Identity 1.0 to 2.0, with emphasis on user-centric approaches. We survey how the requirements for user-centric identity management and their associated technologies have evolved, with emphasis on federated approaches and user-centricity. Second, we focus on related standards XRI and LID, issued from the Yadis project, as well as platforms, mainly ID-WSF, OpenID, CardSpace, Sxip, and Higgins. Finally, we treat identity management in the field of mobility and focus on the future of mobile identity management.

1. INTRODUCTION

Anytime, anywhere mobile computing is becoming easier, more attractive, and even cost-effective: Mobile devices carried by roaming users offer more and more computing power and functionalities, including sensing and providing location awareness.[1] Many computing devices are also deployed in the environments where the users evolve—for example, intelligent home appliances or RFID-enabled fabrics. In this ambient intelligent world, the choices of identity mechanisms will have a large impact on social, cultural, business and political aspects. Moreover, the Internet will generate more complicated privacy problems.[2]

Identity has become a burden in the online world. When it is stolen, it engenders a massive fraud, principally in online services, which generates a lack of confidence in doing business with providers and frustration for users.

Therefore, the whole of society would suffer from the demise of privacy, which is a real human need. Because people have hectic lives and cannot spend their time administering their digital identities, we need consistent identity management platforms and technologies enabling usability and scalability, among other things.[3] In this chapter, we survey how the requirements have evolved for mobile user-centric identity management and its associated technologies.

2. EVOLUTION OF IDENTITY MANAGEMENT REQUIREMENTS

First, we define what we mean by a digital identity. Later, we summarize all the various requirements and detail the most important ones: namely, privacy, usability, and mobility.

---

1 G. Roussos and U. Patel, "Mobile identity management: An enacted view," Birkbeck College, University of London, 2003.
2 A. Westin, *Privacy and Freedom*, Athenaeum, 1967.
3 J. Madelin et al., BT report, "Comprehensive identity management balancing cost, risk and convenience in identity management," 2007.

Digital Identity Definition

A digital identity is a representation of an entity in a specific context.[4] For a long time, a digital identity was considered the equivalent of a user's real-life identity that indicates some of our attributes:

- Who we are: Name, citizenship, birthday
- What we like: Our favorite reading, food, clothes
- What our reputation is: Whether we are honest, without any problems

A digital identity was seen as an extended identity card or passport containing almost the same information.

However, recent work[5] has argued that the link between the real-world identity and a digital identity is not always mandatory. For example, on eBay, what matters is to know whether the seller's digital reputation has been remarkable and that the seller can prove that she controls that digital identity. It is less important to know that her real-world national identity is the Bermuda Islands, where suing anybody is rather unlikely to succeed. It should be underlined that in a major identity management initiative,[6] a digital identity is defined as "the distinguishing character or personality of an individual. An identity consists of traits, attributes, and preferences upon which one may receive personalized services. Such services could exist online, on mobile devices at work, or in many other places"—that is, without mentioning a mandatory link to the real-world identity behind the digital identity.

The combination of virtual world with ubiquitous connectivity has changed the physical constraints to an entirely new set of requirements as associated security issues such as phishing, spam, and identity theft have emerged. They are aggravated by the mobility of the user and the temporary anonymity of cyberrelationships. We are going toward a new, truly virtual world, always with the implication of humanity. Therefore, we are facing the problem of determining the identity of our interlocutors and the accuracy of their claims. Simply using strong authentication will not resolve all these security issues.

Digital identity management is a key issue that will ensure not only service and functionality expectations but also security and privacy.

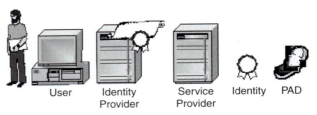

FIGURE 17.1 Identity management main components.

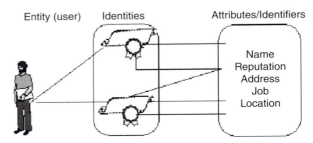

FIGURE 17.2 Relationship among identities, identifiers, and entity.

Identity Management Overview

A model of identity[7] can been as follows:

- A user who wants to access to a service
- Identity Provider (IdP), the issuer of user identity
- Service Provider (SP), the relay party imposing an identity check
- Identity (Id), a set of user attributes
- Personal Authentication Device (PAD), which holds various identifiers and credentials and could be used for mobility

Figure 17.1 lists the main components of identity management.

The relationship between entities, identities and identifiers are shown in Figure 17.2 which illustrates that an entity, such as a user, may have multiple identities, and each identity may consist of multiple attributes that can be unique or non-unique identifiers.

Identity management refers to "the process of representing, using, maintaining, deprovisioning and authenticating entities as digital identities in computer networks."[8]

Authentication is the process of verifying claims about holding specific identities. A failure at this stage will threaten the validity of the entire system. The technology is constantly finding stronger authentication using claims based on:

- Something you know (password, PIN)
- Something you have (one-time-password)

4 T. Miyata et al., "A survey on identity management protocols and standards," IEICE TRANS. INF & SYST, 2006.

5 J.-M. Seigneur, "Trust, security and privacy in global computing," Ph. D. thesis, Trinity College Dublin, 2005.

6 Introduction to the Liberty Alliance Identity Architecture, Rev. 1.0, March 2003.

7 A.B. Spantzel et al., "User centricity: A taxonomy and open issues," IBM Zurich Research Laboratory, 2006.

8 Phillip J. Windley : "Unmasking identity management architecture: digital identity" O'Reilly, August 2005.

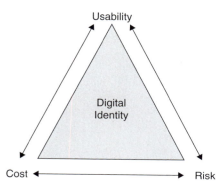

FIGURE 17.3 Digital identity environment to be managed.

- Something you are (your voice, face, fingerprint [biometrics])
- Your position
- Some combination of the four

The BT report[9] has highlighted some interesting points to meet the challenges of identity theft and fraud:

- Developing risk calculation and assessment methods
- Monitoring user behavior to calculate risk
- Building trust and value with the user or consumer
- Engaging the cooperation of the user or consumer with transparency and without complexity or shifting the liability to the consumer
- Taking a staged approach to authentication deployment and process challenges using more advanced technologies

Digital identity should manage three connected vertexes: usability, cost, and risk, as illustrated in Figure 17.3.

The user should be aware of the risk she is facing if her device's or software's security is compromised. Usability is the second aspect that should be guaranteed to the user unless he will find the system difficult to use, which could be the source of a security problem. Indeed, many users, when flooded with passwords to remember, write them down and hide them in a "secret" place under their keyboard. Furthermore, the difficulty of deploying and managing a large number of identities discourages the use of an identity management system. The cost of a system should be well studied and balanced related to risk and usability. Many systems such as one-time password tokens are not widely used because they are too costly for widespread deployment in large institutions. Traditionally, identity management was seen as being service provider-centric because it was designed to fulfill the requirements of service providers, such as cost effectiveness and scalability.

Users were neglected in many aspects because they were forced to memorize difficult or too many passwords.

Identity management systems are elaborated to deal with the following core facets[10]:

- *Reducing identity theft.* The problem of identity theft is becoming a major one, mainly in the online environment. Providers need more efficient systems to tackle this issue.
- *Management.* The number of digital identities per person will increase, so users need convenient support to manage these identities and the corresponding authentication.
- *Reachability.* The management of reachability allows a user to handle their contacts to prevent misuse of their email address (spam) or unsolicited phone calls.
- *Authenticity.* Ensuring authenticity with authentication, integrity, and nonrepudiation mechanisms can prevent identity theft.
- *Anonymity and pseudonymity.* Providing anonymity prevents tracking or identifying the users of a service.
- *Organization personal data management.* A quick method to create, modify, or delete work accounts is needed, especially in big organizations.

Without improved usability of identity management[11]—for example, weak passwords used on many Web sites—the number of successful attacks will remain high. To facilitate interacting with unknown entities, simple recognition rather than authentication of a real-world identity has been proposed, which usually involves manual enrollment steps in the real world.[12] Usability is indeed enhanced if no manual task is needed. There might be a weaker level of security, but that level might be sufficient for some actions, such as logging to a mobile game platform. Single Sign-On (SSO) is the name given to the requirements of eliminating multiple-password issues and dangerous passwords. When we use multiple user IDs and passwords just to use email systems and file servers at work, we feel the inconvenience that comes from having multiple identities. The second problem is the scattering of identity data, which causes problems for the integration of IT systems. SSO simplifies the end-user experience and enhances security via identity-based access technology.

---

9 J. Madelin et al., BT report, "Comprehensive identity management Balancing cost, risk and convenience in identity management," 2007.

10 Independent Center for Privacy Protection (ICPP) and Studio Notarile Genghini (SNG), "Identity management systems (IMS): Identification and comparison study," 2003.

11 Independent Center for Privacy Protection (ICPP) and Studio Notarile Genghini (SNG), "Identity management systems (IMS): Identification and comparison study," 2003.

12 J.-M. Seigneur, "Trust, security and privacy in global computing," Ph. D. thesis, Trinity College Dublin, 2005.

Microsoft's first large identity management system was the Passport Network. It was a very large and widespread Microsoft Internet service, an identity provider for the MSN and Microsoft properties and for the Internet. However, with Passport, Microsoft was suspected by many of intending to have absolute control over the identity information of Internet users and thus exploiting them for its own interests. Passport failed to become "the" Internet identity management tool.

Since then, Microsoft has clearly come to understand that an identity management solution cannot succeed unless some basic rules are respected.[13] That's why Microsoft's Identity Architect, Kim Cameron, has stated the seven laws of identity. His motivation was purely practical in determining the prerequisites of creating a successful identity management system. He formulated these essential principles to maintain privacy and security;

- User control and consent over the handling of their data
- Minimal disclosure of data, and for a specified purpose
- Information should only be disclosed to people who have a justifiable need for it
- The system must provide identifiers for both bilateral relationships between parties and for incoming unsolicited communications
- It must support diverse operators and technologies
- It must be perceived as highly reliable and predictable
- There must be a consistent user experience across multiple identity systems and using multiple technologies.

Most systems do not fulfill several of these tests; they are particularly deficient in fine-tuning the access control over identity to minimize disclosure of data.

Cameron's principles are very clear but they are not explicit enough to compare identity management systems. That's why we will explicitly define the identity requirements.

Privacy Requirement

Privacy is a central issue due to the fact that the official authorities of almost all countries have strict legal policies related to identity. It is often treated in the case of identity management because the management deals with personal information and data. Therefore, it is important to give a definition. Alan F. Westin defines privacy as "the claim of individuals, groups and institutions to determine for themselves, when, how and to what extent information about them is communicated to others."[14] However, we will use Cooley's broader definition of privacy[15]: "the right to be let alone," because it also emphasizes the problems related to disturbing the user's attention, for example, with email spam.

User-Centricity

The evolution of identity management systems is toward the simplification of the user experience and reinforcing authentication. It is well known that poor usability implies a weakness in authentication. Mainly federated management has responded to some of these requirements by facilitating the use and the managing of identifiers and credentials in the boundary of a federated domain. Nevertheless, it is improbable that only one federated domain will subsist. Moreover, different levels of sensitivity and risks of various services will need different kinds of credentials. It is obvious that we should give support and atomization of identity management on the user's side.

A new paradigm must be introduced to solve the problems of usability, scalability, and universal SSO. A user-oriented paradigm, called *user-centric identity management*, has emerged. The expression *user-controlled management*[16] was the first used to explain the user-centric management model. Recent federated identity management systems keep strong end-user controls over how identity information is disseminated among members of the federation. This new paradigm gives the user full control over his identity by notifying him of the information collected and by guaranteeing his consent for any type of manipulation of collected information. User control and consent is also defined as the first law in Cameron's Laws of Identity.[17] A user-centric identity management system supports the user's control and considers user-centric architecture and usability aspects.

There is no uniform definition, but one is "User-centric identity management is understood to mean digital identity infrastructure where an individual end-user has substantially independent control over the dissemination and use of their identifier(s) and personally identifiable information (PII)."[18] See Figure 17.4.

---

13 K. Cameron, "Laws of identity," May, 2005.

14 A. Westin, *Privacy and Freedom*, Athenaeum, 1967.
15 T. M. Cooley, "A treatise on the law of torts," Callaghan, Chicago, 1888.
16 Independent Center for Privacy Protection (ICPP) and Studio Notarile Genghini (SNG), "Identity management systems (IMS): identification and comparison study," 2003.
17 K. Cameron, "Laws of identity," May, 2005.
18 David Recordon VeriSign Inc, Drummond Reed, "OpenID 2.0: A platform for user-centric identity management," 2006.

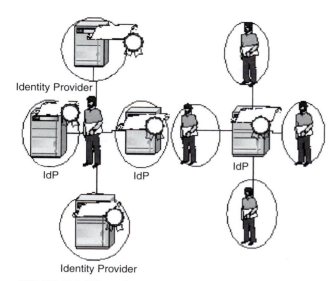

Identity Provider

IdP **IdP** **IdP**

Identity Provider

FIGURE 17.4 IdP-centric and user-centric models.

We can also give this definition of user centricity: "In user-centric identity management, the user has full control over her identity and consistent user experience during all transactions when accessing her services."

In other words, the user is allowed to keep at least some or total control over his personal data.

One of the principles of a user-centric identity is the idea that the user of a Web service should have full control over his identity information. A lot of technology discussion and solutions have focused on service provider's and rarely on user's perspectives. The user-centric identity paradigm is a real evolution because it moves IT architecture forward for users, with the following advantages:

- Empowering users to have total control over their privacy
- Usability, as users are using the same identity for each identity transaction
- Consistent user experience, thanks to uniformity of the identity interface
- Limiting identity attacks, such as phishing
- Limiting reachability/disturbances, such as spam
- Reviewing policies on both sides, both identity providers and service providers (Web sites), when necessary
- Huge scalability advantages, since the identity provider does not need any prior knowledge about the service provider
- Assuring secure conditions when exchanging data
- Decoupling digital identity from applications
- Pluralism of operators and technologies

The user-centric approach allows users to gain access anonymously because they retain full control over their identities. Of course, full anonymity[19] and unlinkability may lead to increased misuse by anonymous users. Then, pseudonymity is an alternative that is more suitable to the ecommerce environment. In this regard, anonymity must be guaranteed at the application and network levels. Some frameworks have been proposed to ensure user-centric anonymity using the concepts of one-task authorization keys and binding signatures.[20]

Usability Requirement

Security is compromised with the proliferation of user passwords and even by their weakness. Indeed, some users note their passwords on scratchpads because their memorization poses a problem. The recent FFIEC guidelines on authentication in online banking reports state that "Account fraud and identity theft are frequently the result of single-factor (e.g., ID/password) authentication exploitation."[21] From then on, security must be user oriented because the user is the effective person concerned with it, and many recent attacks take advantage of users' lack of awareness of attacks (such as spoofing, pharming, and phishing).[22] Without strong control and improved usability[23] of identity management, some attacks will always be possible. To facilitate interacting with unknown entities, simple recognition rather than authentication of a real-world identity, which usually involves manual enrollment steps in the real world, has been proposed.[24] Usability is indeed enhanced if no manual task is needed. A weaker level of security might be reached, but that level might be sufficient for some actions, such as logging to a mobile game platform.

As we've seen, SSO is the name given to the requirements of eliminating multiple password issues and dangerous passwords. When we use multiple user IDs and passwords to use the email systems and file servers at

19 R. Au, H. Vasanta, K. Kwang, R. Choo, M. Looi, "A user-centric anonymous authorisation framework in ecommerce, environment information security research centre," Queensland University of Technology, Brisbane, Australia.

20 R. Au, H. Vasanta, K. Kwang, R. Choo, M. Looi, "A user-centric anonymous authorisation framework in ecommerce, environment information security research centre," Queensland University of Technology, Brisbane, Australia.

21 Federal Financial Institutions Examination Council, authentication in an internet banking environment, October 2005, www.ffiec.gov/press/pr101205.htm.

22 A. Erzberg and A. Gbara, TrustBar: protecting (even Naïve) web users from spoofing and phishing attacks, www.cs.biu.ac.il/~erzbea/papaers/ecommerce/spoofing.htm, 2004.

23 Introduction to usability, www.usabilityfirst.com/intro/index.tx1, 2005.

24 J.-M. Seigneur, "Trust, security and privacy in global computing," Ph. D. thesis, Trinity College Dublin, 2005.

work, we feel the pain that comes from having multiple identities. The second problem is the scattering of identity data, which causes problems for the integration of IT systems. Moreover, it simplifies the end-user experience and enhances security via identity-based access technology.

Therefore, we offer these features:

- Flexible authentication
- Directory independence
- Session and password management
- Seamlessness

3. THE REQUIREMENTS FULFILLED BY CURRENT IDENTITY MANAGEMENT TECHNOLOGIES

This part of the chapter provides an overview of identity management solutions from Identity 1.0 to Identity 2.0 and how they address the requirements introduced earlier. We focus on related standards XRI and LID, issued from the Yadis project, and platforms, mainly ID-WSF, OpenID, Higgins, CardSpace, and Sxip. Then we discuss identity management in the field of mobility.

Evolution of Identity Management

This part of the chapter provides an overview of almost all identity management 1.0 (see Figure 17.5). We begin by describing the silo model, then different kinds of centralized model and federated identity management.

Identity Management 1.0

In the real world I use my identity card to prove who I am. How about in the online world?

FIGURE 17.5 Identity 1.0 principle.

The first digital identity appeared when a user was associated with the pair (username, password) or any other shared secret. This method is used for authentication when connecting to an account or a directory. It proves your identity if you follow the guidelines strictly; otherwise there is no proof.

In fact, it is a single authority using opaque trust decisions without any credentials (cryptographic proofs), choice, or portability.

In the context of Web access, the user must enroll for every unrelated service, generally with different user interfaces, and follow diverse policies and protocols. Thus, the user has an inconsistent experience and deals with different identity copies. In addition, some problems related to privacy have also emerged. Indeed, our privacy was potentially invaded by Web sites. It is clear that sites have a privacy policy, but there is no user control over her own identity. What are the conditions for using these data? How can we improve our privacy? And to what granularity do we allow Web sites to use our data?

The same problem is revealed when we have access to resources. The more resources, the more management we have to perform. It is an asymmetric trust. And the policy decision may be opaque.

It allows access with an opaque trust decision and a single centralized authority without a credentials choice. It is a silo model[25] because it is neither portable nor scalable. This is Identity 1.0.

Identity management appeared with these problems in the 1980s. The first identity management system was the Rec. X.500, developed by the ITU[26] and covering directory services such as Directory Access Protocol (DAP). The ISO was also associated with development of the standard. Like a lot of ITU standards, this one was very heavy and complex. A light version appeared in the 1990s for DAP. It was LDAP, which was standardized by the IETF and became widespread and adopted by Netscape. Microsoft has invented an equivalent Active Directory, and for users it introduced Passport. It is also the ITU that standardized X.509 for identities related to certificates and it is the format currently recognized. It is a small file, generated by an authority of certification. If there is a loss or a usurpation of the certificate, it can always be revoked by the authority of certification.

This is for single users; what about business corporations that have automated their procedures and have a proliferation of applications with deprovisioning but still

25 A. Jøsang and S. Pope, "User-centric identity management," AusCERT Conference 2005.

26 International telecommunication union (ITU), Geneva, www.itu. org.

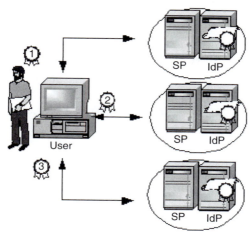

FIGURE 17.6 Identity silo model.

in a domain-centric model? What about resources shared between domains?

Silo Model

The main identity management system deployed currently on the Internet is called the *silo model*, shown in Figure 17.6. Indeed, the identity provider and service provider are mixed up and they share the same space. The identity management environment is put in place and operated by a single entity for a fixed user community.

Users of different services must have different accounts and therefore reenter the same information about their identity which increases the difficulty of management. Moreover, the users are overloaded with identities and passwords to memorize, which produce a significant barrier to usage.

A real problem is the "forgetability" of passwords due to the infrequent use of some of these data. This can obviously lead to a higher cost of service provisions.

This is for single users. What about enterprises that have automated their procedures and have a proliferation of applications with deprovisioning but are still in a domain-centric model? What about resources shared between domains?

The silo model is not interoperable and is deficient in many aspects. That's why the federated identity management model is now emerging, and it is very appreciated by enterprises. A federated identity management system consists of software components and protocols that handle in a decentralized manner the identity of individuals throughout their identity life-cycle.[27]

Solution by Aggregation

Aggregating identity information and finding the relationship between identity records is important to aggregating identity. There are some alternatives:

- The first approach consolidates authentication and attributes in only one site and is called a *centralized management solution,* such as Microsoft Passport. This solution avoids the redundancies and inconsistencies in the silo model and gives the user a seamless experience.[28] The evolution[29,30] was as follows:
  - Building a single central identity data store, which is feasible only for small organizations
  - Creating a metadirectory that synchronizes data from other identities, data stored elsewhere
  - Creating a virtual directory that provides a single integrated view of the identity data stored
  - An SSO identity model that allows users to be authenticated by one service provider
- The second approach decentralizes the responsibility of IdP to multiple such IdPs, which can be selected by end users. This is a federate system whereby some attributes of identity are stored in distributed IdPs. A federated directories model, by linking identity data stored together, has emerged. Protocols are defined in several standards such as Shibboleth,[31] Web services federation language 2003.

Centralized versus Federation Identity Management

Microsoft Passport is a centralized system entirely controlled by Microsoft and closely tied to other Microsoft products. Individuals and companies have proven reluctant adopters of a system so tightly controlled by one dominant company.

Centrally managed repositories in centralized identity infrastructures can't solve the problem of cross-organizational authentication and authorization. This approach has several drawbacks because the IdP not only becomes a single point of failure, it may also not be trusted. That's why Microsoft Passport was not successful. In contrast, the federation identity will leave the identity resources in their various distributed locations but produce

27 A. Jøsang et al., "Usability and privacy in identity management architectures," (AISW2007), Ballarat, Australia, 2007.

28 A.B. Spantzel et al., "User centricity: A taxonomy and open issues," IBM Zurich Research Laboratory, 2006.

29 A. Jøsang and S. Pope, "User-centric identity management," ausCERT conference 2005.

30 A. Jøsang et al., "Usability and privacy in identity management architectures," (AISW2007), Ballarat, Australia, 2007.

31 Internet2, Shibboleth project, http://shibboleth.Internet2.edu.

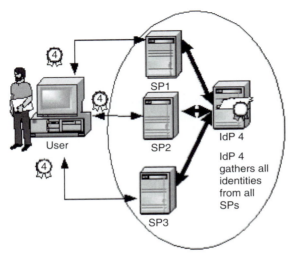

FIGURE 17.7 Simple centralized identity management.

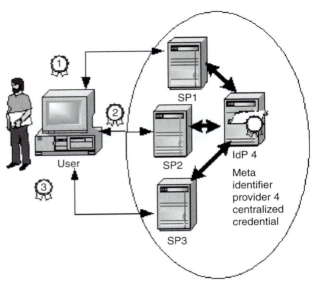

FIGURE 17.8 Metadirectory model.

a federation that links them to solve identity duplication, provision, and management.

A Simple Centralized Model

A relatively simple centralized identity management model is to build a platform that centralizes identities. A separate entity acts as an exclusive user credentials provider for all service providers. This approach merges both authentication and attributes in only one site. This architecture, which could be called the common user identity management model, is illustrated in Figure 17.7. All identities for each SP are gathered to a unique identity management site (IdP). SPs have to provide each identity to the IdP.

In this environment, users can have access to all service providers using the same set of identifiers and credentials. A centralized certificate (CA) could be implemented with a Public Key Infrastructure (PKI) or Simple Public Key Infrastructure (SKPI).[32] This architecture is very efficient in a close domain where users could be identified by a controlled email address. Although such architecture seems to be scalable, the concentration of privacy-related information has a great deal of difficulty in terms of social acceptance.[33]

Metadirectories

SPs can share certain identity-related data on a meta level. This can be implemented by consolidating all service providers' specific identities to a meta-identifier linked to credentials.

There are collections of directory information from various directory sources. We aggregated them to

provide a single view of data. Therefore, we can show these advantages:

- A single point of reference provides an abstraction boundary between application and actual implementation. A single point of administration avoids multiple directories, too.
- Redundant directory information can be eliminated, reducing administration tasks.

This approach can be seen from the user's point of view as password synchronization across multiple service providers. Thus, the password is automatically changed with all the others.

This architecture can be used in large enterprises where all services are linked to a metadirectory, as shown in Figure 17.8. In this case, the ease of use is clear because the administration is done by a single authority.

Virtual Directories

Virtual directories (VDs) are directories that are not located in the same physical structure as the Web home directory but look as though they are to Web clients. The actual directories may be at a completely different location in the physical directory structure—for example, on another hard disk or on a remote computer. They are similar in concept to metadirectories in that they provide a single directory view from multiple independent directories. They differ in the means used to accomplish this goal. Metadirectories (MD) software agents replicate and synchronize data from various directories in what might be batch processes. In contrast, Various Directories (VDs) provide a single view of multiple directories using real-time queries based on mapping from fields in the

---

32 C. Esslison et al., RFC 2693- SPKI Certification Theory. IETF, Sep. 1999, www.ietf.org/rfc/rfc2693.txt.
33 T. Miyata et al., "A survey on identity management protocols and standards," IEICE TRANS. INF & SYST, 2006.

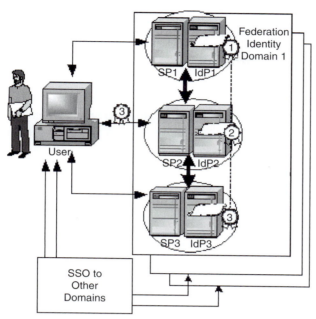

FIGURE 17.9 Single sign-on model.

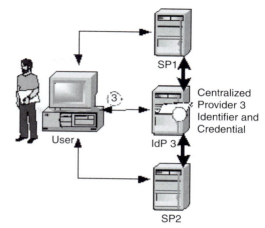

FIGURE 17.10 Federated identity management model.

virtual scheme to fields in the physical schemes of the real directories.

Single Sign-On (SSO)

Single sign-on, or SSO (see Figure 17.9), is a solution proposed to eliminate multiple password issues and dangerous passwords. Moreover, it simplifies the end-user experience and enhances security via identity-based access technology.

Therefore, it offers these features:

- Flexible authentication
- Seamlessness
- Directory independence
- Session and password management

Federated Identity Management

We have seen different approaches to manage user identity; they are not clearly interoperable and are deficient in unifying standard-based frameworks. On one hand, maintenance of privacy and identity control are fundamental when offering identity to users; on the other hand, the same users ask for more easy and rapid access. The balance of the two sides leads to federated network identity. That's why these environments are now emerging. A federated identity management system (see Figure 17.10) consists of software components and protocols that handle the identity of individuals throughout their identity life cycle.

This architecture gives the user the illusion that there is a single identifier authority. Even though the user has many identifiers, he doesn't need to know all of them.

Only one identifier is enough to have access to all services in the federated domain.

Each SP is responsible for the namespace of his users, and all SPs are federated by linking the identity domains. Thus, the federated identity model is based on a set of SPs, called a *circle of trust* by the Liberty Alliance. This set of SPs follows an agreement on mutual security and authentication to allow SSO. Indeed, the federated identity management combines SSO and authorization tools using a number of mutual SPs' technologies and standards. This practice makes the recognition and entitlement of user identities by other SPs easy. Figure 17.10 shows the set of federated domains and the possibility for other SPs to have access to the same user with different identifiers.

The essential difference between federated identity systems and centralized identity management is that there is no single entity that operates the identity management system. Federated systems support multiple identity providers and a distributed and partitioned store for identity information. Therefore, a federated identity network allows a simplified sign-on to users by giving rapid access to resources, but it doesn't require the user's personal information to be stored centrally. With this identity network approach, users authenticate themselves once and can control how their personal information and preferences are used by the service providers.

Federated identity standards, like those produced by the Liberty Alliance, provide SSO over all offered services and enable users to manage the sharing of their personal information through identity and service providers as well as the use of personalized services to give them access to convergent services. The interoperability between disparate security systems is assumed by an encapsulation layer through a trust domain, which links a set of trusted service providers.

However, there are some disadvantages with federated identity management. The first is the user's lack of privacy, because his personnel attributes and information can be mapped using correlation between identifiers. Anonymity could be violated. The second is the scalability of users because they have access to the network from different domains by authentication to their relative IdPs. Therefore, the problem of passwords will continue across multiple federated domains.

A major challenge is to integrate all these components into a distributed network and to deal with these drawbacks. This challenge cannot be taken up without new paradigms and supported standards.

The evolution of identity management systems is toward simplification of user experience and reinforcing authentication. It is very known that poor usability implies the weakness of authentication. A new paradigm should be introduced to solve those problems while still being compatible at least with federated identity management.

That is why user-centric identity management has emerged.[34,35] This paradigm is embraced by multiple industry products and initiatives such as Microsoft CardSpace,[36] Sxip,[37] and Higgins Trust Framework.[38] This is Identity 2.0.

Identity 2.0

The user of Internet services is overcome with identities. She is seldom able to transfer her identity from one site to another. The reputation that she gains in one network is useful to transfer to other networks. Nevertheless, she cannot profit from her constructed reputation, and she must rebuild her identity and reputation time and again. The actual systems don't allow users to decide about the sharing of their attributes related to their identity with other users. This causes a lack of privacy control. Some solutions propose an advanced social system that would model the social interaction after the real world.

The solutions must be easy to use and enable users to share credentials among many services and must be transparent from the end-user perspective.

The principle of modern identity is to separate the acquisition process from the presentation process. It is the same for the identification process and the authorization process. Moreover, it provides scalability and privacy. Doing so, we can have more control over our identities.

The scale, security, and usability advantages of user-centric identity make it the underpinning for Identity 2.0. The main objective of the Identity 2.0 protocol is to provide users with full control over their virtual identities. An important aspect of Identity 2.0 is protection against increasing Web attacks such as phishing as well as the inadvertent disclosure of confidential information while enabling convenient management.

Identity 2.0 would allow users to use one identity respecting transparency and flexibility. It is focused around the user and not around directory or identity providers. It requires identified transactions between users and relaying party using credentials, thus providing more traceable transactions. To maximize the privacy of users, some credentials could be given to the users in advance. Doing so, the IdP could not easily know when the user is utilizing the credentials.

The Identity 2.0 (see Figure 17.11) completely endorses the paradigms of user-centric identity management, enabling users' full control over their identities. Service providers will therefore be required to change their approaches by including requests for and authentication of users' identity. Identity 2.0 systems are interested in using the concept of a user's identity as credentials for the user, based on attributes such as user name and address to less traditional things such as their desires, customer service history, and other attributes that are usually not so associated with a user identity.

Identity 2.0 initiatives

When a Web site collects data from users, it cannot confirm whether or not the collected data is pertinent and

34 A.B. Spantzel et al., "User centricity: A taxonomy and open issues," IBM Zurich Research Laboratory, 2006.

35 A. Jøsang and S. Pope, "User-centric identity management," AusCERT Conference 2005.

36 Microsoft, A technical ref. for InfoCard in Windows, http://msdn.microsoft.com/winfx/reference/infocard/ 2005.

37 G. Roussos and U. Patel, "Mobile identity management: An enacted view," Birkbeck College, University of London, 2003.

38 Higgins Trust Framework project, www.eclipse.org/higgins/, 2006.

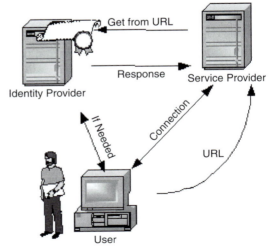

FIGURE 17.11 URL-based Id 2.0.

reliable, since users often enter nonsense information into online forms. This is due to the lack of Web sites to control and verify users' data. Furthermore, due to the legal limitation on requested data, a Web site cannot provide true customized services, even though users require them. On the other side, users have no direct control over what the Web site will do with their data. In addition, users enter the same data many times when accessing Web sites for the first time. Doing so, they have a huge difficulty in managing their large numbers of identities.

To mitigate these problems, various models of identity management have been considered. One such model, Identity 2.0, proposes an Internet-scalable and user-centric identity architecture that mimics real-world interactions.

Many research labs have collaborated to develop the Identity 2.0 Internet-based Identity Management services. They are based on the concept of user-centric identity management, supporting enhanced identity verification and privacy and user consent and control over any access to personal information for Internet-based transactions.

There are various Identity 2.0 initiatives:

- LID
- XRI
- SAML
- Shibboleth
- ID-WSF
- OpenID
- Microsoft's CardSpace (formerly InfoCard)
- SXIP
- Higgins

LID

Like LDAP, Light-Weight Identity (LID) is based on the principle of simplicity, since many existing identity schemes are too complicated to be largely adoptable. It simplifies more complex protocols; but instead of being less capable due to fewer features, it has had success that more complex predecessors lacked. This was because their simplification reduced the required complexity to the point where many people could easily support them, and that was one of the goals of LID.

LID is a set of protocols capable of representing and using digital identities on the Internet in a simple manner, without relying on any central authority. LID is the original URL-based identity protocol, part of the OpenID movement.

LID supports digital identities for humans, human organizations, and nonhumans (such as software agents,

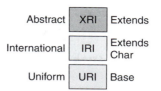

FIGURE 17.12 XRI layers.

and Web sites). It implements Yadis[39], a metadata discovery service, and is pluggable on all levels.

XRI/XDI

The XRI EXtensible Resource Identifier (see Figure 17.12) and XDI[40] represent the fractional solution without the integration of Web services. They are open standards and royalty-free. XRI is about Addressing, whereas XDI is a Data Sharing protocol that uses XRI. Both XRI and XDI are being developed under the support of OASIS. I-name and I-number registry services for privacy-protected digital addressing use XRI. It can be used as an identifier for persons, machines and agents.

XRI offers a human-friendly form of persistent identifier. That's why it is a convenient identifier for SSO systems. It supports both persistent and reassignable identifiers in the same syntax and establishes global context symbols. Moreover, it enables identification of the same logical resource across multiple contexts and multiple versions of the same logical resource.

XDI is a Secure Distributed Data Sharing Protocol. It is also an architecture and specification for privacy-controlled data exchange in which all data is identified using XRIs. The XDI platform includes explicit specification for caching with both push and pull synchronization. XDI universal schema can represent any complex data and have the ability to do cross-context addressing and linking.

SAML

The Security Assertion Markup Language (SAML) is an OASIS specification[41] that provides a set of rules for the structure of identity assertions, protocols to move assertions, bindings of protocols for typical message transport mechanisms, and profiles. Indeed, SAML (see Figure 17.13) is a set of XML and SOAP-based services and formats for the exchange of authentication and authorization information between security systems.

The initial versions of SAML v1.0 and v1.1 define protocols for SSO, delegated administration, and policy management. The most recent version is SAML 2.0. It is

39 Yadis, "Yadis specification 1.0," released March 2006, http://yadis.org.
40 OASIS Working Draft Version 04, "An Introduction to XRIs," March 14, 2005.
41 OASIS, "Conformance requirements for the OASIS Security Assertion Markup Language (SAML)," Vol. 20, 2005.

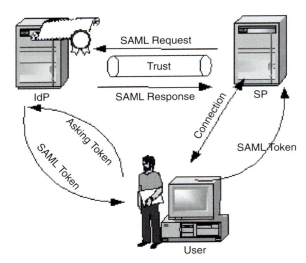

FIGURE 17.13 SAML token exchange.

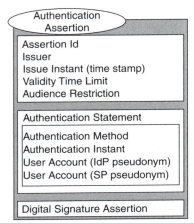

FIGURE 17.14 SAML assertion.

now the most common language to the majority of platforms that need to change the unified secure assertion. It is very useful and simple because it is based on XML.

An assertion is a datum produced by a SAML authority referring to authentication, attribute information, or authorizations applying to the user with respect to a specified resource.

This protocol (see Figure 17.14) enables interoperability between security systems (browser SSO, Web services security, and so on). Other aspects of federated identity management as permission-based attribute sharing are also supported.

SAML is sometimes criticized for its complexity of the specifications and the relative constraint of its security rules. Recently, the SAML community has shown significant interest in extending SAML to reach less stringent requirements for low-sensitivity use cases. The advantages of SAML are robustness of its security and privacy model and the guarantee of its interoperability

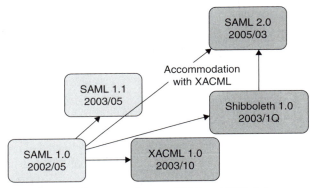

FIGURE 17.15 Convergence between SAML and Shibboleth.

between multiple-vendor implementations through the Liberty Alliance's Conformance Program.

Shibboleth

Shibboleth[42] is a project for which the goal is to allow universities to share Web resources subject to control access. Thereafter, it allows interoperation between institutions using it. It develops architectures, policy structure, practical technologies, and an open-source implementation. It is building components for both the identity providers and the reliant parties. The key concept includes "federated" management identity, the meaning of which is almost the same as the Liberty term's.[43] Access control is fundamentally based on user attributes, validated by SAML assertions. In Figure 17.15, we can see the evolution of SAML, Shibboleth, and XACML.[44]

ID-WSF

In 2001, a business alliance was formed to serve as an open standards organization for federated identity management; it was named the Liberty Alliance.[45] Its goals are to guarantee interoperability, support privacy, and promote adoption of its specifications, guidelines, and best practices. The key objectives of the Liberty Alliance (see Figure 17.16) are to:

- Enable users to protect their privacy and identity
- Enable SPs to manage their clients
- Provide an open, federated SSO
- Provide a network identity infrastructure that supports all current emerging network access devices

---

42 Internet2, Shibboleth project, http://shibboleth.Internet2.edu.
43 Liberty Developer Tutorial, www.projectliberty.org/resources/ LAP_ DIDW_Oct-15_2003_jp.pdf.
44 SACML, www.oasis-open.org/committees/tc_home.php?wg_ abbrev=xacml.
45 Liberty Alliance, "Liberty ID-FF architecture overview," Liberty Alliance Project, 2005.

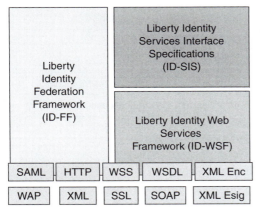

FIGURE 17.16 High-level overview of the Liberty Alliance architecture.

The Liberty Alliance's work in the first phase is to enable federated network identity management[46]. It offers, among other things, SSO and linking accounts in the set of SPs in the boundary of the circle of trust. The work of this phase is referred to as the *Identity Federation Framework* (ID-FF).

In the second phase, the specifications offer enhancing identity federation and interoperable identity-based Web services. This body is referred to as the *Identity Web Services Framework* (ID-WSF). This framework involves support of the new open standard such as WS-Security developed in OASIS. ID-WSF is a platform for the discovery and invocation of identity services—Web services associated with a given identity. In the typical ID-WSF use case, after a user authenticates to an IdP, this fact is asserted to an SP through SAML-based SSO. Embedded within the assertion is information that the SP can optionally use to discover and invoke potentially numerous and distributed identity services for that user. Some scenarios present an unacceptable privacy risk because they suggest the possibility of a user's identity being exchanged without that user's consent or even knowledge. ID-WSF has a number of policy mechanisms to guard against this risk, but ultimately, it is worth noting that many identity transactions (such as automated bill payments) already occur without the user's active real-time consent—and users appreciate this efficiency and convenience.

To build additional interoperable identity services such as registration services, contacts, calendar, geolocation services, and alert services, it's envisaged to use ID-WSF. This specification is referred to as the *Identity Services Interface Specification* (ID-SIS).

The Liberty Alliance specifications define the protocol messages, profiles, and processing rules for identity federation and management. They rely heavily on other standards such as SAML and WS-Security, which is another OASIS specification that defines mechanisms implemented in SOAP headers.

These mechanisms are designed to enhance SOAP messaging by providing a quality of protection through message integrity, message confidentiality, and single message authentication. Additionally, Liberty has contributed portions of its specification back into the technical committee working on SAML. Other identity management enabling standards include:

- Service Provisioning Markup Language (SPML)
- XML Access Control Markup Language (XACML)
- XML Key Management Specification (XKMS)
- XML Signature
- XML Encryption

The WS-* (the Web Services protocol specifications) are a set of specifications currently under development by Microsoft and IBM. It is part of a larger effort to define a security framework for Web services; the results of proposals are often referred to as WS-*. It includes such specifications as WS-Policy, WS-Security Conversation, WS-Trust, and WS-Federation. This last one has functionality for enabling pseudonyms and attribute-based interactions. Therefore, WS-Trust has the ability to ensure security tokens as a means of brokering identity and trust across domain boundaries.[47]

The Liberty Alliance is developing and delivering a specification that enables federate network identity management. Figure 17.16 shows an overview of the Liberty Alliance architecture as described in the introduction to the Liberty Alliance identity architecture.

OpenID 2.0

Brad Fitzpatrick is at the origin of the development of OpenID 1.0. The intent of the OpenID framework is to specify layers that are independent and small enough to be acceptable and adopted by the market.[48] OpenID is basically providing simple attribute sharing for low-value transactions. It does not depend on any preconfigured trust model. Version 1.0 has a deal with an HTTP-based URL authentication protocol. OpenID authentication 2.0 is becoming an open platform that supports both URL and XRI user identifiers. In addition, it would like to be modular, lightweight, and user oriented. Indeed, OpenID auth. 2.0 allows users to choose, control and manage

46 Liberty Alliance, "Liberty developer tutorial," http://www.project-liberty.orgwww.projectliberty.org.

47 T. Miyata et al., "A survey on identity management protocols and standards," IEICE TRANS. INF & SYST, 2006.

48 David Recordon VeriSign Inc, Drummond Reed, "OpenID 2.0: A platform for user-centric identity management," 2006.

their identity addresses. Moreover, the user chooses his identity provider and has a large interoperability of his identity and can dynamically use new services that stand out, such as attribute verification and reputation, without any loss of features. No software is required on the user's side because the user interacts directly with the identity provider's site. This approach jeopardizes the user identity because it could be hacked or stolen. Also, the user has no ability to examine tokens before they are sent.

At the beginning of identity management, each technology came with its own futures, without any interest in others. Later, the OpenID 1.0 community realized the importance of integrating other technologies as OASIS Extensible Resource Description Sequence (XRDS), which is useful for its simplicity and extensibility.

OpenID Stack

The first layer is for supporting users' identification. Using URL or XRI forms, we can identify a user. URLs use IP or DNS resolution and are unique and ubiquitously supported. They can be a personal digital address as used by bloggers, even though these are not yet widely used.

XRI is being developed under the support of OASIS and is about addressing.

I-names are a generic term for XRI authority names that provide abstract identifiers for the entity to which they are assigned. They can be used as the entry point to access data under the control of that authority. Like a domain name, the physical location of the information is transparent to the requester.

OpenID 2.0 provides a private digital address to allow a user to be identified only in specific conditions. This guarantees the user privacy in a public domain.

Discovery

Yadis is used for identity service discovery for URLs and XRI resolution protocol for XRIs. They both use the OASIS format XRDS. The protocol is simple and describes any type of service.

Authentication

This service lets a user prove his URL or I-name using credentials (cryptographic proof). This protocol is explained in Figure 17.17. The OpenID doesn't need a centralized authority for enrollment and it is therefore a federated identity management. With OpenID 2.0 the IdP offers the user the option of selecting a digital address to send to the SP. To ensure anonymity, IdP can randomly generate a digital address used specially for this SP.

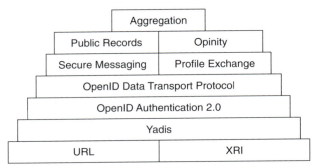

FIGURE 17.17 OpenID protocol stack.

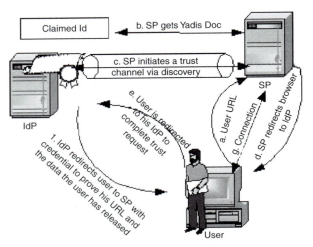

FIGURE 17.18 OpenID 1.1 protocol flow.

Data Transport

This layer ensures data exchange between the IdP and SP. It supports push and pull methods and it is independent from authentication procedures. Therefore, the synchronization of data and secure messaging and other services will be enabled. The data formats are those defined by SAML, SDI (XRI Data interchange), or any other data formats. This approach will enable evolution of the OpenID platform.

The four layers construct the foundation of the OpenID ensuring user centricity (see Figure 17.18). There are three points to guarantee this paradigm:

- User chooses his digital identity
- User chooses IdP
- User chooses SP

OpenID is decentralized and well founded and at the same time simple and easy to use and to deploy. It provides an open development process and SSO for the Web and ease of integration into scripted Web platforms (such as Drupal and WordPress). Thus it has a great future. You can learn about OpenID at www.openidenabled.com or join the OpenID community www.openid.net.

CardSpace

Rather than invent another technology for creating and representing digital identities, Microsoft has adopted the federated user-centric identity meta-system. This is a serious solution that provides a consistent way to work with multiple digital identities. Using standard protocols that anyone can implement on any platform, the identity meta-system allows the acquisition and use of any kind of security tokens to convey identity.

CardSpace is Microsoft's code name for this new technology that tackles the problem of managing and disclosing identity information. CardSpace implements the core of the identity meta-system, using open standard protocols to negotiate, request, and broker identity information between trusted IdPs and SPs. CardSpace is a technology that helps developers integrate a consistent identity infrastructure into applications, Web sites, and Web services.

By providing a way for users to select identities and more, Windows CardSpace[49] plays an important part in the identity meta-system. It provides the consistent user experience required by the identity meta-system. It is specifically hardened against tampering and spoofing, to protect the end user's digital identities and maintain end-user control. Windows CardSpace enables users to provide their digital identities in a familiar, secure, and easy way.

In the terminology of Microsoft, the relying party is in the model service provider (SP).

To prove an identity over a network, the user gives credentials, which are some proofs about her identity. For example, in the simplest digital identity the username is the identity whereas the password is said to be the authentication credential. In the terminology of Microsoft and others, these are called *security tokens* and contain one or more claims. Each claim contains information about the user, such as username or home address. In addition, the security token proves that the claims are correctly emitted by the real user and are belonging to him. This could be done cryptographically using various forms such as X.509 certificates and Kerberos tickets, but unfortunately these are not practical to convey some kinds of claims. The standard SAML as seen before is indicated for this purpose because it can be used to define security tokens. Indeed, SAML tokens could enclose any desired information and thus become as largely useful in the network to show and control digital identity.

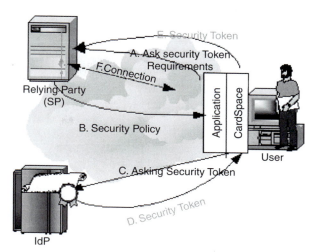

FIGURE 17.19 Interactions among the users, identity providers, and relying party.

CardSpace runs on Windows Vista, XP, Server 2003, and Server 2008, based on .NET3, and uses Web service protocols:

- WS-Trust
- WS-Policy
- WS-SecurityPolicy
- WS-MetaDataExchange

CardSpace runs in a virtual desktop on the PC, thereby locking out other processes and reducing the possibility of spyware intercepting information.

Figure 17.19 shows that the architecture exactly fits the principle of Identity 2.0. The user accesses one of any of his relying parties (SPs) using an application that supports CardSpace.

When the choice is made, the application asks for the requirement of a security token of this specific SP that will answer with SP policy. It really contains information about the claims and the accepted token formats.

Once this is done, the application passes these requirements to CardSpace, which asks for the security token from an appropriate identity provider.

Once this security token has been received, CardSpace transmits via application to the relying party. The relying party can then use this token to authenticate the user.

Note that each identity is emitted by an identity provider and is stored on the user side. It contains the emitter, the kind of security token the user can issue and the details about the identity claims. All difficulties are hidden from the user; he has only to choose one CardSpace when the process of authentication is launched. Indeed, once the required information is returned and passed to CardSpace, the system displays the card selection matching the requirements on screen. In this regard, the user

49 Microsoft, "A technical ref. for InfoCard in Windows," http://msdn.microsoft.com/winfx/reference/infocard/, 2005.

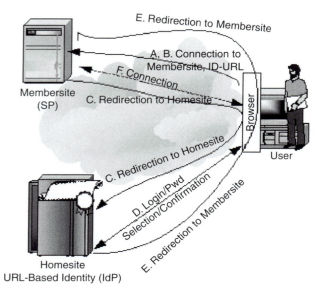

FIGURE 17.20 SXIP entity interactions.

has a consistent experience, since all applications based on CardSpace will have the same interface, and the user does not have to worry about the protocol used to express his identity's security token. The PIN is entered by the user and the choice of his card is done in a private Windows desktop to prevent locally running processes.

SXIP 2.0

In 2004, SXIP 1.0 grew from efforts to build a balanced online identity solution that met the requirements of the entire online community. Indeed, SXIP 2.0 is the new generation of the SXIP 1.0 protocol, a platform that gives users control over their online identities and enables online communities to have richer relationships with their members. SXIP 2.0 defines entities' terminology as:

- Home site: URL-based identity given by IdP
- Membersite: SP that uses SXIP 2.0
- User: Equivalent to the user in our model

The Simple eXtensible Identity Protocol (SXIP)[50] was designed to address the principles defined by the Identity 2.0 model (see Figure 17.20), which proposes an Internet-scalable and user-centric identity architecture that mimics real-world interactions.

If an SP has integrated an SXIP to its Web site, which is easily done using SDKs, it is a Membersite. When a subscriber of SXIP would like to access this Membersite:

1. He types his URL address and clicks **Sxip in**.
2. He types his URL identity issued by IdP (called the Homesite).
3. The browser is redirected to the Homesite.

---

50 J. Merrels, "SXIP identity. DIX: Digital Identity Exchange protocol." Internet draft, March 2006.

4. He enters his username and password and is informed that the Membersite has requested data, selects the related data, verifies it and can select to automatically release data for other visits to this Membersite, and confirms.
5. The browser is redirected to the Membersite.
6. The user gains access to the content of the site.

SXIP 2.0 is a platform based on a fully decentralized architecture providing an open and simple set of processes for exchanging identity information. SXIP 2.0 has significantly reduced the problems resulting from moving identity data from one site to another. It is a URL-based protocol that allows a seamless user experience and fits exactly the user-centric paradigm. In that sense, the user has full control of her identity and has an active role in the exchange of her identity data. Therefore, she can use portable authentication to connect to many Web sites. Doing so, the user has more choice and convenience when exchanging her identity data; this method also indirectly enables Web sites to offer enhanced services to their subscribers.

SXIP 2.0 provides the following features:

- *Decentralized architecture.* SXIP 2.0 is completely decentralized and is a federated identity management system. The online identity is URL-based and the user identity is separated from the authority that issues the identifiers for this identity. In this regard, we can easily move the location of the identity data without losing the associated identifier.

- *Dynamic discovery.* A simple and dynamic discovery mechanism ensures that users are always informed online about the Homesite that is exporting their identity data.

- *Simple implementation.* SXIP 2.0 is open source using various high-level development languages such as Perl, Python, PHP, and Java. Therefore, the integration of SXIP 2.0 into a Web site is effortless. It does not require PKI, because it uses a URL-based protocol.

- *Support for existing technologies.* SXIP 2.0 uses simple Web browsers, the primary client and means of data exchange, providing users with choices in the release of their identity data.

- *Interoperability.* SXIP 2.0 can coexist with other URL-based protocols.

- *Richer data on an Internet scale.* SXIP 2.0 messages consist of lists of simple name value pairs. It can exchange simple text, claims using SAML, and third-party claims in one exchange and present them in many separate exchanges. In addition, the identity provider is not bothersome every time an identity is requested.

Finally, using SXIP 2.0, Web sites can also be authoritative about users regarding data, such as third-party claims. Those are keys to build an online reputation, further enriching the online exchange of identity data.

Higgins

Higgins[51] is a project supported principally by IBM and it is a part of IBM's Eclipse open-source foundation. It will also offer libraries for Java, C, and C++ as well as plug-ins for popular browsers. It is really an open-source trust framework, the goals of which are to support existing and new applications that give users more convenience, privacy, and control over their identity information. The objective is to develop an extensible, platform-independent, identity protocol-independent software framework that provides a foundation for user-centric identity management. Indeed, it enables applications to integrate identity, profiles, and relationships across heterogeneous systems.

The main goals of Higgins as an identity management system are interoperability, security, and privacy in a decoupled architecture. This system is a true user-centric one based on federated identity management. The user has the ability to use a pseudonym or simply reply anonymously.

We use the term *context* to cover a range of underlying implementations. A context can be thought of as a distributed container-like object that contains digital identities of multiple people or processes.

The platform intends to address four challenges:

- The need to manage multiple contexts
- The need for interoperability
- The need to respond to regulatory, public, or customer pressure to implement solutions based on trusted infrastructure that offers security and privacy
- The lack of common interfaces to identity/networking systems

Higgins matches exactly the user-centric paradigms because it offers a consistent user experience based on card icons for management and release of identity data. Therefore there is less vulnerability to phishing and other attacks. Moreover, user privacy is enabled by sharing only what is needed. Thus, the user has full control over his personal data. The Identity Attribute Service enables aggregation and federation of identity systems and even silos.

For enterprises, Higgins integrates all data related to identity, profile, reputation, and relationship information across and among complex systems.

Higgins is a trust framework that enables users and enterprises to adopt, share across multiple systems, and integrate to new or existing applications digital identity, profiles, and cross-relationship information. In fact, it facilitates as well the integration of different identity management systems in the management of identity, profile, reputation and relationship data across repositories. Using context providers, directories and communications technologies (such as Microsoft/IBM WS-*, LDAP, email, etc.) can be plugged into the Higgins framework. Higgins has become an Eclipse plug-in and is a project of the Eclipse Foundation. Any application developed with Higgins will enable users to share identities with other users, under strict control.

Higgins is beneficial for developers, users, and enterprise. It relieves developers of knowing all the details of multiple identity systems, thanks to one API that supports many protocols and technologies: CardSpace, OpenID, XRI, LDAP, and so on. An application written to the Higgins API can integrate identity, profile, and relationship information across these heterogeneous systems. The goal of the framework is to be useful in the development of applications accessed through browsers, rich clients, and Web services. Thus, the Higgins Project is supported by IBM and Novell and attempts to thwart CardSpace, Microsoft's project.

The Higgins framework intends to define, in terms of service descriptions, messages and port types consistent with an SOA model and to develop a Java binding and implementation as an initial reference.

Applications can use Higgins to create a unified, virtual view of identity, profile, and relationship information. A key focus of Higgins is providing a foundation for a new "user-centric identity" and personal information management applications.

Finally, Higgins provides virtual integration, a user-centric federated management model and trust brokering that are applied to identity, profile, and relationship information. Furthermore, Higgins provides common interfaces to identity and, thanks to data context, it includes an enhanced automation process. Those features are also offered across multiple contexts, disparate systems, and implementations. In this regard, Higgins is a fully interoperable framework.

The Higgins service acts together with a set of so-called context providers that can represent a department, association, informal network, and so on. A context is the Higgins environment and digital identities, the policies and protocols that govern their interactions. Context providers adjust existing legacy systems to the framework or implement new ones; context providers may also contain the identities of a machine or a human. A context encloses a group of digital identities and their related claims and

---

51 U. Jendricke et al., Mobile Identity Management, UBICOMP 2002.

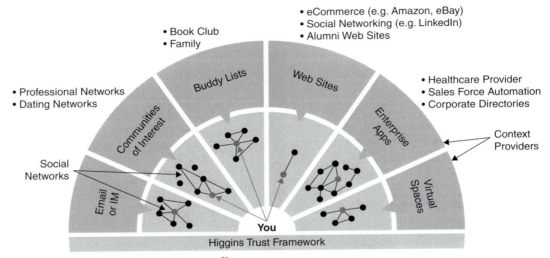

FIGURE 17.21 The Higgins Trust Framework and context.[52]

links. A context maintains a set of claims about properties and values (name, address, etc.). It is like a security token for CardSpace. The set of profile properties, the set of roles, and the access rights for each role are defined by and controlled by the context provider.

Context providers act as adapters to existing systems. Adapter providers can connect, for example, to LDAP servers, identity management systems like CardSpace, or mailing list and social networking systems. A Higgins context provider (see Figure 17.21) has the ability to implement the context interface and thus empower the applications layered on top of Higgins.

The 10 requirements in the first column of Table 17.1 are those discussed earlier in the chapter. In the table, white means that the requirement is not covered, and gray that it's fully fulfilled.

At the moment, service providers have to choose between many authentications and identity management systems and users are left to face the inconvenience of carrying a variety of digital identities. The main initiatives have different priorities and some unique advantages while overlapping in many areas. The most pressing requirements for users are interoperability, usability, and centricity. Thanks to Higgins, the majority of identity requirements are guaranteed. Therefore, using Higgins the user is free to visit all Web sites without worrying about the identity management system used by the provider.

4. IDENTITY 2.0 FOR MOBILE USERS

Now let's talk about mobility, its evolution and its future.

The number of devices such as mobile phones, smart cards, and RFIDs[53] is increasing daily and becoming huge. Mobile phones have attracted particular interest because of their large penetration and pervasiveness that exceeds that of personal computers. Furthermore, the emergence of both IP-TV and wireless technology has facilitated the proliferation of intelligent devices, mobile phones, RFIDs, and other forms of information technology that are developing at a rapid speed. These devices include a fixed identifier that can be linked to a user's identity. This identifier provides a mobile identity that takes into account information about the location and the mobile user's personal data.[54]

Mobile Web 2.0

Mobile Web 2.0 as a content-based service is an up-to-date offering of services within the mobile network. As the number of people with access to mobile devices exceeds those using a desktop computer, *mobile Web* will be a key factor for the next-generation network. At the moment, mobile Web suffers from lack of interoperability and usability due to the small screen size and lower computational capability. Fortunately, these limitations are only temporary, and within five years they will be easily overcome. The next-generation public networks will converge toward the mobile network, which will bring mobility to the forefront. Thus, mobile identity management will play a central role in addressing issues such as usability, privacy, and security, which are Wkey challenges for researchers in

52 Higgins Trust Framework project, www.eclipse.org/higgins/ ,2006.

53 S. Garfinkel and B. Rosenberg, *RFID, Applications, Security and Privacy*, Addison-Wesley, 2006.

54 S. A. Weis et al., "Security and privacy aspects of low-cost radio frequency identification systems," *Proc. Of First International Conference on Security in Pervasive Computing*, March 2003

TABLE 17.1 Evaluating identity 2.0 technologies

Requirement	XRI/XDI	ID/WSF	Shibboleth	CardSpace	OpenID	SXIP	Higgins
Empowering total control of users over their privacy	■	■	■	■	■	■	■
Usability; users are using the same identity for each identity transaction	■	■		■	■	■	■
Giving a consistent user experience due to uniformity of identity interface		■		■	■	■	■
Limiting identity attacks such as phishing		■		■	■	■	■
Limiting reachability/disturbances such as spam		■		■	■	■	■
Reviewing policies on both sides when necessary, identity providers and service providers		■		■			■
Huge scalability advantages because the identity provider does not have to get any prior knowledge about the service provider				■	■	■	■
Assuring secure conditions when exchanging data	■	■	■	■	■	■	■
Decoupling digital identity from applications	■	■		■	■	■	■
Pluralism of operators and technologies	■	■	■	■		■	■

the mobile network. Since the initial launch of mobile Web services, customers have increasingly turned to their wireless phones to connect with family and friends and to obtain the latest news and information or even to produce content with their mobiles and then publish it. Mobile Web 2.0[55] is the enforcement of evolution and will enhance the user experience by providing connections in an easier and more efficient way. For this reason, it will be welcomed by the key actors as a well-established core service identity management tool for the next-generation mobile network. This mobile identity management will be used not only to identify, acquire, access, and pay for services but also to offer context-aware services as well as location-based services.

Mobility

The mobile identity may not be stored in one location but could be distributed among many locations, authorities, and devices.

Indeed, identity is mobile in many respects[56]:

- There is device mobility, where a person is using the same identity while using different devices

- There is location mobility, where a person is using the same devices while changing location.
- There is context mobility, where a person is receiving services based on different societal roles: as a parent, as a professional, and so on.

The three kinds of mobility are not isolated; they interact often and became concurrently modified, creating much more complex situations than that implied from single mode. Mobile identity management addresses three main challenges: usability via context awareness, trust based on the perception of secure operation, and privacy protection.[57]

Evolution of Mobile Identity

Mobile identity management is in its infancy. GSM networks, for example, provide management of Subscriber Identity Module (SIM) identities as a kind of mobile identity management, but they do not meet all the requirements for complete mobile identity management.

---

55 A. Jaokar and T. Fish, *Mobile Web 2.0, A book,* 2007.

56 G. Roussos and U. Patel, "Mobile identity management: An enacted view," Birkbeck College, University of London, 2003.

57 G. Roussos and U. Patel, "Mobile identity management: An enacted view," Birkbeck College, University of London, 2003.

Unlike static identity, already implemented in the Web 2.0 identity, dynamic aspects, such as the user's position or the temporal context, gain increasing importance for new kinds of mobile applications.[58]

Mobile identity (MId) infrastructure solutions have evolved over time and can be classified into three solutions. The first is just an extension of wired identity management to the mobile Internet. This is a widespread solution that is limited to the users of mobile devices running the same operating system as wired solutions. This limitation is expected to evolve over time, mainly with the large deployment of Web services. Some specifications, such as Liberty Alliance specifications, have been developed for identity management, including mobility. However, several limitations are observed when the MId system is derived from a fixed context. These limitations are principally due to the assumptions during their design and they do not match well with extra requirements of mobility.[59]

Many improvements such as interoperability, privacy, and security are to come, and also older centralized PKI must be replaced by modern trust management systems, or at least a decentralized PKI.

The second solution is capable of providing an alternative to the prevalent Internet-derived MId infrastructure consisting of either connected (cellular phones) or unconnected (smart cards) mobile devices. The third consists of using implantable radiofrequency identifier (RFID) devices. This approach is expected to increase rapidly, even if the market penetration is smaller than that of cellular phones.

In addition, the sensitivity risk of data related to different applications and services is seldom at the same level, and the number of identifiers used by a person is constantly increasing. Thus, there is a real need of different kinds of credentials associated with different kinds of applications. Indeed, a tool on the user side that's capable of managing user credentials and identities is inevitable. With the increasing capacity of CPU power and the spreading number of mobile phones with SIM cards, a mobile phone can be considered a personal authentication device (PDA). Cell phones can securely hold user credentials, passwords, and even identities. Therefore we introduce a new, efficient identity management device on the user side that's able to on one hand facilite memorization and on the other hand, strengthen security by limiting the number of passwords and their weaknesses. All wired identity management can be deployed using PADs. In addition, many different

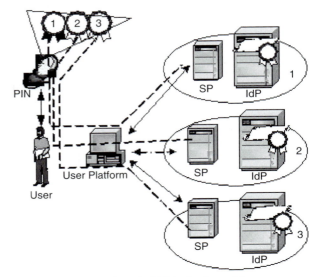

FIGURE 17.22 Integration of a PAD in the silo model.

authentication architectures, such as dual-channel authentication, become possible and easy to implement.

PADs as a Solution to Strong Authentication

A PAD[60] is a tamper-resistant hardware device that could include smart cards and sensors or not. This term was used early in the context of security by Wong et al.[61] The approach is the same; the only thing changed so far is that the performance of the mobile device has radically changed. This is the opportunity to emphasize the user centricity, since the PAD can strengthen the user experience and facilitate the automation and system support of identity management on the user side. Figure 17.22 illustrates the combination of the PAD and silo model. The user stores his identity in the PAD; whenever he would like to connect to a service provider:

1. He authenticates himself with a PIN code to use the PAD.
2. He chooses the password to be used for his connection to the specific service provider.
3. He launches and logs in to the specific service provider by entering his username and password.

The PAD is a good device to tackle the weakness and inconvenience of password authentication. It provides a user-friendly and user-centric application and even introduces stronger authentication. The fundamental

58 M. Hoffmann, "User-centric identity management in open mobile environments," Fraunhofer-Institute for Secure Telecooperation (SIT). 59 G. Roussos and U. Patel, "Mobile Identity Management: An enacted view," Birkbeck College, University of London, 2003.

60 A. Jøsang et al., "Trust requirements in identity management," AISW 2005. 61 Wong et al. "Polonius: an identity authentication system," *Proceedings of the 1985 IEEE Symposium on Security and Privacy.*

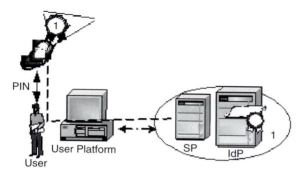

FIGURE 17.23 Single-channel authentication.

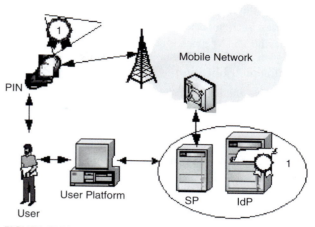

FIGURE 17.24 Dual-channel authentication.

advantage of PADs compared with common PCs using common operating systems such as Windows or Linux is that PADs have a robust isolation of processes. Therefore, compromising one application does not compromise all the applications. This advantage is becoming less important for mobile phones; as manufacturers introduce flexibility, many vulnerabilities are also introduced. We have seen many viruses for mobile phones and even nowadays we have viruses for RFID. This vulnerability can compromise authentication and even biometrics authentication. That's why we should be very vigilant in implementing security in PAD devices. An ideal device is the USB stick running a standalone OS and integrating a biometric reader and mobile network access. You can find some of these with fingerprint readers for a reasonable price.

Two main categories can group many authentication architectures that could be implemented in a PAD. They are single- and dual-channel authentications. Thereby, the cost, risk, and inconvenience can be tackled at the same time.

Figure 17.23 illustrates the principle of single-channel authentication, which is the first application of the PAD. Figure 17.24 illustrates the second principle of dual-channel authentication, which is more secure.

Types of Strong Authentication Through Mobile PADs

The mobile network, mainly GSM, can help overcome many security vulnerabilities, such as phishing or man-in-the-middle (MITM) attacks. It attracts all businesses that would like to deploy dual-channel authentication but worry about cost and usability. The near-ubiquity of the mobile network has made feasible the utilization of this approach, which is even being adopted by some banks.

SMS-Based One-Time Password (OTP)

The main advantages of mobile networks are the facility and usability to send and receive SMSs. Moreover, they could be used to set up and easily download Java

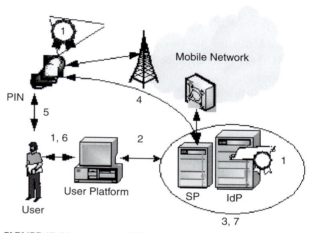

FIGURE 17.25 A scenario of SMS double-channel authentication.

programs to a mobile device. In addition, mobile devices are using smart cards that can securely calculate and store claims.

The cost is minimized by adopting a mobile device using SMS to receive OTP instead of special hardware that can generate OTP.

The scenario implemented by some banks is illustrated in Figure 17.25 and described as follows. First, the user switches on her mobile phone and enters her PIN code. Then:

1. The user logs in to her online account by entering her username and password (U/P).
2. The Web site receives the U/P.
3. The server verifies the U/P.
4. The server sends an SMS message with OTP.
5. The user reads the message.
6. The user enters the OTP into her online account.
7. The server verifies the OTP and gives access.

The problem with this approach is the fact that the cost is assumed by the service provider. In addition, some drawbacks are very common, mainly in some developing countries, such as lack of coverage and SMS latency. Of course, the MITM attack is not overcome by this approach.

Soft-Token Application

In this case, the PAD is used as a token emitter. The application is previously downloaded. SMS could be sent to the user to set up the application that will play the role of soft token.

The scenario is identical to the SMS, only the user generates her OTP using the soft token instead of waiting for an SMS message. The cost is less than the SMS-based OTP. This approach is a single-channel authentication that is not dependent on mobile network coverage nor latency. Furthermore, the MITM attack is not tackled.

Full-Option Mobile Solution

We have seen in the two previously scenarios that the MITM attack is not addressed. There exists a counterattack to this security issue consisting of using the second channel to completely control all the transactions over the online connection. Of course, the security of this approach is based on the assumption that it is difficult for an attacker to steal a user's personal mobile phone or attack the mobile network. Anyway, we have developed an application to crypt the SMS message, which minimizes the risk of attacks. The scenario is illustrated in Figure 17.26 and is as follows:

1. The user logs in to his online account using a token.
2. The server receives the token.
3. The server verifies the token.
4. Access is given to the service.
5. The user requests a transaction.
6. An SMS message is sent with the requested transaction and a confirmation code.
7. The user verifies the transaction.

8. He enters the confirmation code.
9. The server verifies and executes the transaction.
10. The server sends a transaction confirmation.

The Future of Mobile User-Centric Identity Management in an Ambient Intelligence World

Ambient intelligence (AmI) manifests itself through a collection of everyday devices incorporating computing and networking capabilities that enable them to interact with each other, make intelligent decisions, and interact with users through user-friendly multimodal interfaces. AmI is driven by users' needs, and the design of its capabilities should be driven by users' requirements.

AmI technologies are expected to combine concepts of ubiquitous computing and intelligent systems, putting humans in the center of technological developments. Indeed, with the Internet extension to home and mobile networks, the multiplication of modes of connection will make the individual the central point. Therefore, user identity is a challenge in this environment and will guarantee infatuation with AmI. Moreover, AmI will be the future environment where we will be surrounded by mobile devices that will be increasingly used for mobile interactions with things, places, and people.

The low cost and the shrinking size of sensors as well as the ease of deployment will aid AmI research efforts for rapid prototyping. Evidently, a sensor combined with unique biometric identifiers is becoming more frequently utilized in accessing systems and supposedly provides proof of a person's identity and thus accountability for subsequent actions.

To explore these new AmI technologies, it is easiest to investigate a scenario related to ubiquitous computing in an AmI environment.

AmI Scenario

A person with a mobile device, GPS (or equivalent), and an ad hoc communication network connected to sensors visits an intelligent environment supermarket and would like to acquire some merchandise. Here we illustrate how this person can benefit from a mobile identity.

When she enters the supermarket, she is identified by means of her mobile device or implemented RFID tag, and a special menu is displayed to her. Her profile, related to her context identity, announces a discount on goods, if there is one.

The members of her social network could propose a connection to her, if they are present, and could even guide her to their location. Merchandise on display could

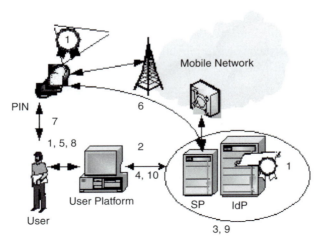

FIGURE 17.26 Secure transaction via SMS.

communicate with her device to show prices and details. Location-based services could be offered to quickly find her specific articles.

Her device could help her find diabetic foods or any restrictions associated with specific articles. A secure Web connection could be initiated to give more information about purchases and the user account. The supermarket could use an adaptive screen to show her information that is too extensive for her device screen.

Payment could be carried out using the payment identity stored in the user's device, and even a biometric identity to prevent identity theft. Identity information and profiling should be portable and seamless for interoperability. The identity must be managed to ensure user control. Power and performance management in this environment is a must. The concept of authentication between electronic devices is also highlighted.

To use identity management, the user needs an appropriate tool to facilitate managing disclosure of personal data. A usable and secure tool should be proposed to help even inexperienced users manage their general security needs when using the network.

We need mobile identity management, which is a concept that allows the user to keep her privacy, depending on the situation. By using identity management, the user's device acts in a similar way to the user. In different contexts, the user presents a different appearance. Devices controlled by identity management change their behavior, similar to the way a user would.

Requirements for Mobile User-Centric Identity Management in an AmI World

As the network evolution is toward mobility with the proliferation of ubiquitous and pervasive computing systems, the importance of identity management to build trust relationships in the context of electronic and mobile (e/m) government and business is evident.[62,63] All these systems require advanced, automated identity management processes to be cost effective and easy to use.

Several mobile devices such as mobile phones, smart cards, and RFID are used for mobility. Because mobile devices have fixed identifiers, they are essentially providing a mobile identity that can be likened to a user. Mobile identity takes into account location data of mobile users in addition to their personal data. A court decision in the United Kingdom established, as proof of location of the accused, the location trace of his mobile phone, which

implies a de facto recognition of the identity of a citizen as the identity of his mobile telephone.[64]

That is why mobile identity management (MIdm) is necessary to empower mobile users to manage their mobile identities, to enforce their security and privacy interests. Mobile identity management is a special kind of identity management. For this purpose, mobile users must be able to control the disclosure of their mobile identities, dependent on the respective service provider, and their location via mobile identity management systems.

Ambient intelligence emphasizes the principles of secure communication anywhere, anytime, with anything. The evolution of AmI will directly influence identity management with this requirement to ensure mutual interaction between users and things. *Being anywhere* will imply more and more mobility, interoperability, and profiling. *At any time* will imply that online as well as offline connection because the network does not have 100% coverage and will imply power as well as performance management to optimize battery use. *With anything* will imply sensor use, biometrics, and RFID interaction; and *securely* implies more and more integration of privacy, authentication, anonymity, and prevention of identity theft.

From multilateral security,[65,66] Jendricke[67] has derived privacy principles for MIdm; we have completed them below with a few other important principles.

Management systems:

1. Context-detection
   - Sensors
   - Biometrics
   - RFID
2. Anonymity
3. Security
   - Confidentiality
   - Integrity
   - Nonrepudiation
   - Availability
4. Privacy
   - Protection of location information
5. Trustworthiness
   - Segregation of power, separating knowledge, integrating independent parties
   - Using open source

---

62 MyGrocer Consortium, "MyGrocer white paper," 2002.

63 M. Wieser, "The computer for the twenty-first century," *Scientific American*, 1991.

64 G. Roussos and U. Patel, "Mobile identity management: An enacted view," Birkbeck College, University of London, 2003.

65 K. Rannenberg, "Multilateral security? A concept and examples for balanced security," *Proc. 9th ACM New Security Paradigms Workshop*, 2000.

66 K. Reichenbach et al. "Individual management of personal reachability in mobile communications," Proc. IFIP TC11 (September '97).

67 U. Jendricke et al., "Mobile identity management," UBICOMP 2002.

- Trusted seals of approval seal
6. Law enforcement/liability
   - Digital evidence
   - Digital signatures
   - Data retention
7. Usability
   - Comfortable and informative user interfaces
   - Training and education
   - Reduction of system complexity
   - Raising awareness
8. Affordability
   - Power of market: Produce Mobile Identity Management Systems (MIMS) that are competitive and are able to reach a remarkable penetration of market
   - Using open-source building blocks
   - Subsidies for development, use, operation, etc.
9. Power management: the energy provided by the batteries of mobile devices is limited and that energy must be used with care on energy-friendly applications and services
10. Online and offline identity proof
11. Small screen size and lower computational capability
12. Interoperability
    - Identity needs to be portable to be understood by any device

Research Directions

Future identity management solutions will play a more central role in the IT industry due to the pervasiveness and increased presence of identity information in all components of the IT stack. The Liberty Alliance specifications provide a standardized solution to the problem of lack of capability for mobile identity. The specified architecture will have an impact on the architecture of mobile services. However, many open issues remain to be considered.

There will be many issues raised concerning identity and mobility. All strong platforms combining identity management and mobility play a central role and will be key elements for the progress of the ambient intelligence network; they will also represent the main vehicle for the information society.

Here we list a few of the most important research questions in the field of mobile user-centric identity management:

- *Requirements*. How can we satisfy the requirements of mobile identity management in mobile systems and devices?
- *Mobility*. How can we manage identity when the device is offline? How can we manage biometric information? How can mobility and biometrics help in authentication?
- *Privacy*. What are the needed identity management controls to preserve individual privacy? How can we guarantee anonymity? How can we protect the user from location/activity tracking?
- *Forensic science*. What is the reliability of the identity management system, and how can evidence extracted from the system be used in court? What protections are in place for the identity holder or for the relaying party?
- *Costs of infrastructure*. How can we limit the cost of mobile identity management?
- *Interoperability*. How can we evolve toward higher levels of interoperability?
- *Efficiencies*. How can we efficiently integrate sensors, RFIDs, and biometrics into mobile identity management systems? How can we manage performance of mobile devices? How can we integrate usability into mobile identity usage?
- *Identity theft*. Does large-scale deployment of identity management systems make it easier or harder to perpetrate identity theft or identity fraud? How can we deal with theft of devices or identities?
- *Longevity of information*. Do mobile identity management systems provide adequate care in tracking changes in identity information over time?
- *Authenticity of identity*. What are the trust services that must be in place to generate confidence in the identity management service?

5. CONCLUSION

The Internet is increasingly used, but the fact that the Internet has not been developed with an adequate identity layer is a major security risk. Password fatigue and online fraud are a growing problem and are damaging user confidence.

Currently, major initiatives are under way to try to provide a more adequate identity layer for the Internet, but their convergence has not yet been achieved. Higgins and Liberty Alliance seem to be the most promising ones.

In any case, future identity management solutions will have to work in mobile computing settings, anywhere and anytime.

This chapter has underlined the necessity of mobility and the importance of identity in future ambient intelligent environments. Mobile identity management will have to support a wide range of information technologies and devices with critical requirements such as usability on the move, privacy, scalability, and energy-friendliness.

## Chapter 18

Intrusion Prevention and Detection Systems

Christopher Day
Terremark Worldwide, Inc.

With the increasing importance of information systems in today's complex and global economy, it has become mission and business critical to defend those information systems from attack and compromise by any number of adversaries. Intrusion prevention and detection systems are critical components in the defender's arsenal and take on a number of different forms. Formally, intrusion detection systems (IDSs) can be defined as "software or hardware systems that automate the process of monitoring the events occurring in a computer system or network, analyzing them for signs of security problems."[1] Intrusion prevention systems (IPSs) are systems that attempt to actually stop an active attack or security problem. Though there are many IDS and IPS products on the market today, often sold as self-contained, network-attached computer appliances, truly effective intrusion detection and prevention are achieved when viewed as a process coupled with layers of appropriate technologies and products. In this chapter, we will discuss the nature of computer system intrusions, those who commit these attacks, and the various technologies that can be utilized to detect and prevent them.

1. WHAT IS AN "INTRUSION," ANYWAY?

Information security concerns itself with the confidentiality, integrity, and availability of information systems and the information or data they contain and process. An intrusion, then, is any action taken by an adversary that has a negative impact on the confidentiality, integrity, or availability of that information.

Given such a broad definition of "intrusion," it is instructive to examine a number of commonly occurring classes of information system (IS) intrusions.

Physical Theft

Having physical access to a computer system allows an adversary to bypass most security protections put in place to prevent unauthorized access. By stealing a computer system, the adversary has all the physical access he could want, and unless the sensitive data on the system is encrypted, the data is very likely to be compromised. This issue is most prevalent with laptop loss and theft. Given the processing and storage capacity of even low-cost laptops today, a great deal of sensitive information can be put at risk if a laptop containing this data is stolen. In May 2006, for example, it was revealed that over 26 million military veterans' personal information, including names, Social Security numbers, addresses, and some disability data, was on a Veteran Affairs staffer's laptop that was stolen from his home.[2] The stolen data was of the type that is often used to commit identity theft, and due to the large number of impacted veterans, there was a great deal of concern about this theft and the lack of security around such a sensitive collection of data.

Abuse of Privileges (The Insider Threat)

An insider is an individual who, due to her role in the organization, has some level of authorized access to the IS environment and systems. The level of access can range from that of a regular user to a systems administrator with nearly unlimited privileges. When an insider

---

[1] "NIST special publication on intrusion detection systems," NIST, Washington, D.C., 2006.

[2] M. Bosworth, "VA loses data on 26 million veterans," Consumeraffairs. com, www.consumeraffairs.com/news04/2006/05/va_laptop.html, 2006.

abuses her privileges, the impact can be devastating. Even a relatively limited-privilege user is already starting with an advantage over an outsider due to that user's knowledge of the IS environment, critical business processes, and potential knowledge of security weaknesses or soft spots. An insider may use her access to steal sensitive data such as customer databases, trade secrets, national security secrets, or personally identifiable information (PII), as discussed in the sidebar, "A Definition of Personally Identifiable Information." Because she is a trusted user, and given that many IDSs are designed to monitor for attacks from outsiders, an insider's privileged abuse can go on for a long time unnoticed, thus compounding the damage. An appropriately privileged user may also use her access to make unauthorized modifications to systems, which can undermine the security of the environment. These changes can range from creating "backdoor" accounts to preserving access in the event of termination to installing so-called logic bombs, which are programs designed to cause damage to systems or data at some predetermined point in time, often as a form of retribution for some real or perceived slight.

A Definition of Personally Identifiable Information

Personally identifiable information (PII) is a set of information such as name, address, Social Security number, financial account number, credit-card number, and driver's license number. This class of information is considered particularly sensitive due to its value to identity thieves and others who commit financial crimes such as credit-card fraud. Most U.S. states have some form of data breach disclosure law that imposes a burden of notification on any organization that suffers unauthorized access, loss, or theft of unencrypted PII. It is worth noting that all the current laws provide a level of "safe harbor" for organizations that suffer a PII loss if the PII was encrypted. California's SB1386 was the first and arguably most well known of the disclosure laws.

2. UNAUTHORIZED ACCESS BY AN OUTSIDER

An outsider is considered anyone who does not have authorized access privileges to an information system or environment. To gain access, the outsider may try to gain possession of valid system credentials via social engineering or even by guessing username and password pairs in a brute-force attack. Alternatively, the outsider may attempt to exploit a vulnerability in the target system to gain access. Often the result of successfully exploiting a system vulnerability leads to some form of high-privileged access to the target, such as an Administrator or Administrator-equivalent account on a Microsoft Windows system or a root or root-equivalent account on a Unix- or Linux-based system. Once an outsider has this level of access on a system, he effectively "owns" that system and can steal data or use the system as a launching point to attack other systems.

3. MALWARE INFECTION

Malware (see sidebar, "Classifying Malware") can be generally defined as "a set of instructions that run on your computer and make your system do something that allows an attacker to make it do what he wants it to do."[3] Historically, malware in the form of viruses and worms was more a disruptive nuisance than a real threat, but it has been evolving as the weapon of choice for many attackers due to the increased sophistication, stealthiness, and scalability of intrusion-focused malware. Today we see malware being used by intruders to gain access to systems, search for valuable data such as PII and passwords, monitor real-time communications, provide remote access/control, and automatically attack other systems, just to name a few capabilities. Using malware as an attack method also provides the attacker with a "stand-off" capability that reduces the risk of identification, pursuit, and prosecution. By "stand-off" we mean the ability to launch the malware via a number of anonymous methods such as an insecure, open public wireless access point. Once the malware has gained access to the intended target or targets, the attacker can manage the malware via a distributed command and control system such as Internet Relay Chat (IRC). Not only does the command and control network help mask the location and identity of the attacker, it also provides a scalable way to manage many compromised systems at once, maximizing the results for the attacker. In some cases the number of controlled machines can be astronomical, such as with the Storm worm infection, which, depending on the estimate, ranged somewhere between 1 million and 10 million compromised systems.[4] These large collections of compromised systems are often referred to as *botnets*.

---

3 E. Skoudis, *Malware: Fighting Malicious Code*, Prentice Hall, 2003.
4 P. Gutman, "World's most powerful supercomputer goes online," *Full Disclosure*, http://seclists.org/fulldisclosure/2007/Aug/0520.html, 2007.

Classifying Malware

Malware takes many forms but can be roughly classified by function and replication method:

- *Virus*. Self-replicating code that attaches itself to another program. It typically relies on human interaction to start the host program and activate the virus. A virus usually has a limited function set and its creator has no further interaction with it once released. Examples are Melissa, Michelangelo, and Sobig.
- *Worm*. Self-replicating code that propagates over a network, usually without human interaction. Most worms take advantage of a known vulnerability in systems and compromise those that aren't properly patched. Worm creators have begun experimenting with updateable code and payloads, such as seen with the Storm worm.[5] Examples are Code Red, SQL Slammer, and Blaster.
- *Backdoor*. A program that bypasses standard security controls to provide an attacker access, often in a stealthy way. Backdoors rarely have self-replicating capability and are installed either manually by an attacker after compromising a system to facilitate future access or by other self-propagating malware as payload. Examples are Back Orifice, Tini, and netcat (netcat has legitimate uses as well).
- *Trojan horse*. A program that masquerades as a legitimate, useful program while performing malicious functions in the background. Trojans are often used to steal data or monitor user actions and can provide a backdoor function as well. Examples of two well-known programs that have had Trojan versions circulated on the Internet are tcpdump and Kazaa.

- *User-level root kit*. Trojan/backdoor code that modifies operating system software so that the attacker can maintain privileged access on a machine but remain hidden. For example, the root kit will remove malicious processes from user-requested process lists. This form of root kit is called *user-level* because it manipulates operating system components utilized by users. This form of root kit can often be uncovered by the use of trusted tools and software since the core of the operating system is still unaffected. Examples of user-level root kits are the Linux Rootkit (LRK) family and FakeGINA.
- *Kernel-level root kit*. Trojan/backdoor code that modifies the core or kernel of the operating system to provide the intruder the highest level of access and stealth. A kernel-level root kit inserts itself into the core of the operating system, the kernel, and intercepts system calls and thus can remain hidden even from trusted tools brought onto the system from the outside by an investigator. Effectively nothing the compromised system tells a user can be trusted, and detecting and removing kernel-level root kits is very difficult and often requires advanced technologies and techniques. Examples are Adore and Hacker Defender.
- *Blended malware*. More recent forms of malware combine features and capabilities discussed here into one program. For example, one might see a Trojan horse that, once activated by the user, inserts a backdoor utilizing user-level root-kit capabilities to stay hidden and provide a remote handler with access. Examples of blended malware are Lion and Bugbear.

4. THE ROLE OF THE "0-DAY"

The Holy Grail for vulnerability researchers and exploit writers is to discover a previously unknown and exploitable vulnerability, often referred to as a *0-day exploit* (pronounced *zero day* or *oh day*). Given that the vulnerability has not been discovered by others, all systems running the vulnerable code will be unpatched and possible targets for attack and compromise. The danger of a given 0-day is a function of how widespread the vulnerable software is and what level of access it gives the attacker. For example, a reliable 0-day for something as widespread as the ubiquitous Apache Web server that somehow yields root- or Administrator-level access to the attacker is far more dangerous and valuable than an exploit that works against an obscure point-of-sale system used by only a few hundred users (unless the attacker's target is that very set of users).

In addition to potentially having a large, vulnerable target set to exploit, the owner of a 0-day has the advantage that most intrusion detection and prevention systems will not trigger on the exploit for the very fact that it has never been seen before and the various IDS/IPS technologies will not have signature patterns for the exploit yet. We will discuss this issue in more detail later.

It is this combination of many unpatched targets and the ability to potentially evade many forms of intrusion detection and prevention systems that make 0-days such a powerful weapon in the hands of attackers. Many legitimate security and vulnerability researchers explore software systems to uncover 0-days and report them to the appropriate software vendor in the hopes of preventing malicious individuals from finding and using them first. Those who intend to use 0-days for illicit purposes guard the knowledge of a 0-day very carefully lest it become widely and publically known and effective countermeasures, including vendor software patches, can be deployed.

---

5 P. Gutman, "World's most powerful supercomputer goes online," *Full Disclosure*, http://seclists.org/fulldisclosure/2007/Aug/0520.html, 2007.

One of the more disturbing issues regarding 0-days is their lifetimes. The lifetime of a 0-day is the amount of time between the discovery of the vulnerability and public disclosure through vendor or researcher announcement, mailing lists, and so on. By the very nature of 0-day discovery and disclosure it is difficult to get reliable statistics on lifetimes, but one vulnerability research organization claims their studies indicate an average 0-day lifetime of 348 days.[6] Hence, if malicious attackers have a high-value 0-day in hand, they may have almost a year to put it to most effective use. If used in a stealthy manner so as not to tip off system defenders, vendors, and researchers, this sort of 0-day can yield many high-value compromised systems for the attackers. Though there has been no official substantiation, there has been a great deal of speculation that the Titan Rain series of attacks against sensitive U.S. government networks between 2003 and 2005 utilized a set of 0-days against Microsoft software.[7,8]

5. THE ROGUE'S GALLERY: ATTACKERS AND MOTIVES

Now that we have examined some of the more common forms computer system intrusions take, it is worthwhile to discuss the people who are behind these attacks and attempt to understand their motivations. The appropriate selection of intrusion detection and prevention technologies is dependent on the threat being defended against, the class of adversary, and the value of the asset being protected.

Though it is always risky to generalize, those who attack computer systems for illicit purposes can be placed into a number of broad categories. At minimum this gives us a "capability spectrum" of attackers to begin to understand motivations and, therefore, threats:

- *Script kiddy.* The pejorative term *script kiddy* is used to describe those who have little or no skill at writing or understanding how vulnerabilities are discovered and exploits are written, but download and utilize others' exploits, available on the Internet, to attack vulnerable systems. Typically, script kiddies are not a threat to a well-managed, patched environment since they are usually relegated to using publicly known and available exploits for which patches and detection signatures already exist.

- *Joy rider.* This type of attacker is often represented by people with potentially significant skills in discovering vulnerabilities and writing exploits but who rarely have any real malicious intent when they access systems they are not authorized to access. In a sense they are "exploring" for the pleasure of it. However, though their intentions are not directly malicious, their actions can represent a major source of distraction and cost to system administrators, who must respond to the intrusion anyway, especially if the compromised system contained sensitive data such as PII where a public disclosure may be required.

- *Mercenary.* Since the late 1990s there has been a growing market for those who possess the skills to compromise computer systems and are willing to sell them from organizations willing to purchase these skills.[9] Organized crime is a large consumer of these services. Computer crime has seen a significant increase in both frequency and severity over the last decade, primarily driven by direct, illicit financial gain and identity theft.[10] In fact, so successful have these groups become that a full-blown market has emerged, including support organizations offering technical support for rented botnets and online trading environments for the exchange of stolen credit card data and PII. Stolen data has a tangible financial value, as shown in Table 18.1, which indicates the dollar-value ranges for various types of PII.

- *Nation-state backed.* Nations performing espionage against other nations do not ignore the potential for intelligence gathering via information technology systems. Sometimes this espionage takes the form of malware injection and system compromises such as the previously mentioned Titan Rain attack; other times it can take the form of electronic data interception of unencrypted email and other messaging protocols. A number of nations have developed or are developing an information warfare capability designed to impair or incapacitate an enemy's Internet-connected systems, command-and-control systems, and other information

---

6 J. Aitel, "The IPO of the 0-day," www.immunityinc.com/downloads/0day_IPO.pdf, 2007.

7 M. H. Sachs, "Cyber-threat analytics," www.cyber-ta.org/downloads/files/Sachs_Cyber-TA_ThreatOps.ppt, 2006.

8 J. Leyden, "Chinese crackers attack US.gov," *The Register*, www.theregister.co.uk/2006/10/09/chinese_crackers_attack_us/, 2006.

9 P. Williams, "Organized crime and cyber-crime: Implications for business," www.cert.org/archive/pdf/cybercrime-business.pdf, 2002.

10 C. Wilson, "Botnets, cybercrime, and cyberterrorism: Vulnerabilities and policy issues for Congress," http://fas.org/sgp/crs/terror/RL32114.pdf, 2008.

TABLE 18.1 PII Values

Goods and Services	Percentage	Range of Prices
Financial Accounts	22%	$10–$1,000
Credit Card Information	13%	$.40–$20
Identity Information	9%	$1–$15
eBay Accounts	7%	$1–$8
Scams	7%	$2.5–$50/week for hosting, $25 for design
Mailers	6%	$1–$10
Email Addresses	5%	$.83–$10/MB
Email Passwords	5%	$4–$30
Drop (request or offer)	5%	10%–50% of drop amount
Proxies	5%	$1.50–$30

(Compiled from Miami Electronic Crimes Task Force and Symantec Global Internet Security Threat Report (2008))

technology capability.[11] These sorts of capabilities were demonstrated in 2007 against Estonia, allegedly by Russian sympathizers utilizing a sustained series of denial-of-service attacks designed to make certain Web sites unreachable as well as to interfere with online activities such as email and mission-critical systems such as telephone exchanges.[12]

6. A BRIEF INTRODUCTION TO TCP/IP

Throughout the history of computing, there have been numerous networking protocols, the structured rules computers use to communicate with each other, but none have been as successful and become as ubiquitous as the Transmission Control Protocol/Internet Protocol (TCP/IP) suite of protocols. TCP/IP is the protocol suite used on the Internet, and the vast majority of enterprise and government networks have now implemented TCP/IP on their networks. Due to this ubiquity almost all attacks against computer systems today are designed to be launched over a TCPI/IP network, and thus the majority of intrusion detection and prevention systems are designed to operate with and monitor TCP/IP-based networks. Therefore, to better understand the nature of these technologies it is important to have a working knowledge of TCP/IP. Though a complete description of TCP/IP is beyond the scope of this chapter, there are numerous excellent references and tutorials for those interested in learning more.[13,14]

Three features that have made TCP/IP so popular and widespread are[15]:

- *Open protocol standards that are freely available.* This and independence from any particular operating system or computing hardware means that TCP/IP can be deployed on nearly any computing device imaginable.
- *Hardware, transmission media, and device independence.* TCP/IP can operate over numerous physical devices and network types such as Ethernet, Token Ring, optical, radio, and satellite.
- *A consistent and globally scalable addressing scheme.* This ensures that any two uniquely addressed network nodes can communicate with each other (notwithstanding any traffic restrictions implemented for security or policy reasons), even if those nodes are on different sides of the planet.

11 M. Graham, "Welcome to cyberwar country, USA," *WIRED*, www.wired.com/politics/security/news/2008/02/cyber_command, 2008.

12 M. Landler and J. Markoff, "Digital fears emerge after data siege in Estonia," *New York Times*, www.nytimes.com/2007/05/29/technology/29estonia.html, 2007.

13 R. Stevens, *TCP/IP Illustrated, Volume 1: The Protocols,* Addison-Wesley Professional, 1994.

14 D. E. Comer, *Internetworking with TCP/IP Vol. 1: Principles, Protocols, and Architecture*, 4th ed., Prentice Hall, 2000.

15 C. Hunt, *TCP/IP Network Administration*, 3rd ed., O'Reilly Media, Inc., 2002.

7. THE TCP/IP DATA ARCHITECTURE AND DATA ENCAPSULATION

The best way to describe and visualize the TCP/IP protocol suite is to think of it as a layered stack of functions, as in Figure 18.1.

Each layer is responsible for a set of services and capabilities provided to the layers above and below it. This layered model allows developers and engineers to modularize the functionality in a given layer and minimize the impacts of changes on other layers. Each layer performs a series of functions on data as it is prepared for network transport or received from the network. The way those functions are performed internal to a given layer is hidden from the other layers, and as long as the agreed rules and standards are adhered to with regard to how data is passed from layer to layer, the inner workings of a given layer are isolated from any other layer.

The Application Layer is concerned with applications and processes, including those with which users interact, such as browsers, email, instant messaging, and other network-aware programs. There can also be numerous applications in the Application Layer running on a computer system that interact with the network, but users have little interaction with such as routing protocols.

The Transport Layer is responsible for handling data flow between applications on different hosts on the network. There are two Transport protocols in the TCP/IP suite: the Transport Control Protocol (TCP) and the User Datagram Protocol (UDP). TCP is a connection- or session-oriented protocol that provides a number of services to the application, such as reliable delivery via Positive Acknowledgment with Retransmission (PAR), packet sequencing to account for out-of-sequence receipt of packets, receive buffer management, and error detection. In contrast, UDP is a low-overhead, connectionless protocol that provides no delivery acknowledgment or other session services. Any necessary application reliability must be built into the application, whereas with TCP, the application need not worry about the details of packet delivery. Each protocol serves a specific purpose and allows maximum flexibility to application developers and engineers. There may be numerous network services running on a computer system, each built on either TCP or UDP (or, in some cases, both), so both protocols utilize the concept of *ports* to identify a specific network service and direct data appropriately. For example, a computer may be running a Web server, and standard Web services are offered on TCP port 80. That same computer could also be running an email system utilizing the Simple Mail Transport Protocol (SMTP),

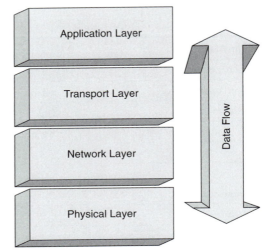

FIGURE 18.1 TCP/IP data architecture stack.

which is by standard offered on TCP port 25. Finally, this server may also be running a Domain Name Service (DNS) server on both TCP and UDP port 53. As can be seen, the concept of ports allows multiple TCP and UDP services to be run on the same computer system without interfering with each other.

The Network Layer is primarily responsible for packet addressing and routing through the network. The Internet Protocol (IP) manages this process within the TCP/IP protocol suite. One very important construct found in IP is the concept of an IP address. Each system running on a TCP/IP network must have at least one unique address for other computer systems to direct traffic to it. An IP address is represented by a 32-bit number, which is usually represented as four integers ranging from 0 to 255 separated by decimals, such as 192.168.1.254. This representation is often referred to as a *dotted quad*. The IP address actually contains two pieces of information: the network address and the node address. To know where the network address ends and the node address begins, a *subnet mask* is used to indicate the number of bits in the IP address assigned to the network address and is usually designated as a slash and a number, such as /24. If the example address of 192.168.1.254 has a subnet mask of /24, we know that the network address is 24 bits, or 192.168.1, and the node address is 254. If we were presented with a subnet mask of /16, we would know that the network address is 192.168 while the node address is 1.254. Subnet masking allows network designers to construct subnets of various sizes, ranging from two nodes (a subnet mask of /30) to literally millions of nodes (a subnet of /8) or anything in between. The topic of subnetting and its impact

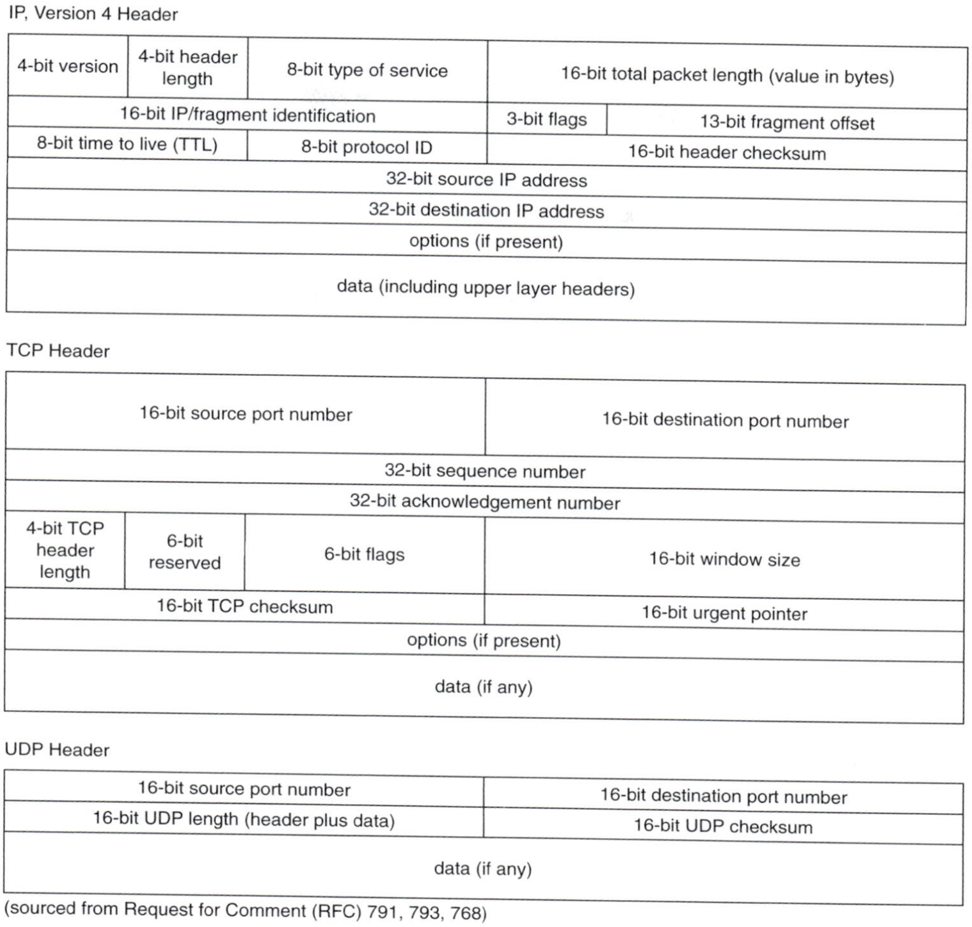

IP, Version 4 Header

4-bit version	4-bit header length	8-bit type of service	16-bit total packet length (value in bytes)	
16-bit IP/fragment identification			3-bit flags	13-bit fragment offset
8-bit time to live (TTL)		8-bit protocol ID	16-bit header checksum	
32-bit source IP address				
32-bit destination IP address				
options (if present)				
data (including upper layer headers)				

TCP Header

16-bit source port number			16-bit destination port number	
32-bit sequence number				
32-bit acknowledgement number				
4-bit TCP header length	6-bit reserved	6-bit flags	16-bit window size	
16-bit TCP checksum			16-bit urgent pointer	
options (if present)				
data (if any)				

UDP Header

16-bit source port number	16-bit destination port number
16-bit UDP length (header plus data)	16-bit UDP checksum
data (if any)	

(sourced from Request for Comment (RFC) 791, 793, 768)

FIGURE 18.2 IP, TCP, and UDP headers.

on addressing and routing is a complex one, and the interested reader is referred to[16] for more detail.

The Physical Layer is responsible for interaction with the physical network medium. Depending on the specifics of the medium, this can include functions such as collision avoidance, the transmission and reception of packets or datagrams, basic error checking, and so on. The Physical Layer handles all the details of interfacing with the network medium and isolates the upper layers from the physical details.

Another important concept in TCP/IP is that of data encapsulation. Data is passed up and down the stack as it travels from a network-aware program or application in the Application Layer, is packaged for transport across the network by the Transport and Network Layer, and eventually is placed on the transmission medium (copper or fiber-optic cable, radio, satellite, and so on) by

the Physical Layer. As data is handed down the stack, each layer adds its own header (a structured collection of fields of data) to the data passed to it by the above layer. Figure 18.2 illustrates three important headers: the IP header, the TCP header, and the UDP header. Note that the various headers are where layer-specific constructs such as IP address and TCP or UDP port numbers are placed, so the appropriate layer can access this information and act on it accordingly.

The receiving layer is not concerned with the content of the data passed to it, only that the data is given to it in a way compliant with the protocol rules. The Physical Layer places the completed packet (the full collection of headers and application data) onto the transmission medium for handling by the physical network. When a packet is received, the reverse process occurs. As the packet travels up the stack, each layer removes its respective header, inspects the header content for instructions on which upper layer in the protocol stack to hand the remaining data to, and passes the data to the

---

16 R. Stevens, *TCP/IP Illustrated, Volume 1: The Protocols,* Addison-Wesley Professional, 1994.

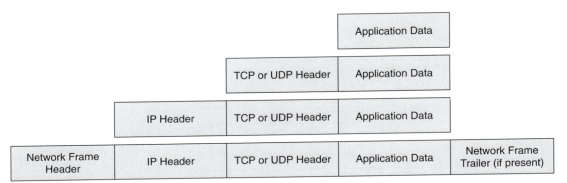

FIGURE 18.3 TCP/IP encapsulation.

appropriate layer. This process is repeated until all TCP/IP headers have been removed and the appropriate application is handed the data. The encapsulation process is illustrated in Figure 18.3.

To best illustrate these concepts, let's explore a somewhat simplified example. Figure 18.4 illustrates the various steps in this example. Assume that a user, Alice, want to send an email to her colleague Bob at CoolCompany.com.

1. Alice launches her email program and types in Bob's email address, *bob@coolcompany.com*, as well as her message to Bob. Alice's email program constructs a properly formatted SMTP-compliant message, resolves Cool Company's email server address utilizing a DNS query, and passes the message to the TCP component of the Transport Layer for processing.

2. The TCP process adds a TCP header in front of the SMTP message fields including such pertinent information as the source TCP port (randomly chosen as a port number greater than 1024, in this case 1354), the destination port (port 25 for SMTP email), and other TCP-specific information such as sequence numbers and receive buffer sizes.

3. This new data package (SMTP message plus TCP header) is then handed to the Network Layer and an IP header is added with such important information as the source IP address of Alice's computer, the destination IP address of Cool Company's email server, and other IP-specific information such as packet lengths, error-detection checksums, and so on.

4. This complete IP packet is then handed to the Physical Layer for transmission onto the physical network medium, which will add network layer headers as appropriate. Numerous packets may be needed to fully transmit the entire email message depending on the various network media and protocols that must be traversed by the packets as they leave Alice's network and travel the Internet to Cool

Company's email server. The details will be handled by the intermediate systems and any required updates or changes to the packet headers will be made by those systems.

5. When Cool Company's email server receives the packets from its local network medium via the Physical Layer, it removes the network frame and hands the remaining data to the Network Layer.

6. The Network Layer strips off the IP header and hands the remaining data to the TCP component of the Transport Layer.

7. The TCP process removes and examines the TCP header to, among other tasks, examine the destination port (again, 25 for email) and finally hand the SMTP message to the SMTP server process.

8. The SMTP application performs further application specific processing as well delivery to Bob's email application by starting the encapsulation process all over again to transit the internal network between Bob's PC and the server.

It is important to understand that network-based computer system attacks can occur at every layer of the TCP/IP stack and thus an effective intrusion detection and prevention program must be able to inspect at each layer and act accordingly. Intruders may manipulate any number of fields within a TCP/IP packet to attempt to bypass security processes or systems including the application-specific data, all in an attempt to gain access and control of the target system.

8. SURVEY OF INTRUSION DETECTION AND PREVENTION TECHNOLOGIES

Now that we have discussed the threats to information systems and those who pose them as well as examined the underlying protocol suite in use on the Internet and enterprise networks today, we are prepared to explore the various technologies available to detect and prevent

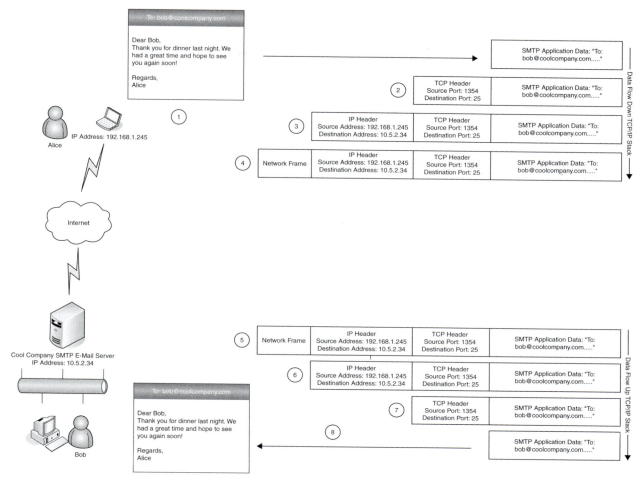

FIGURE 18.4 Application and network interaction example.

intrusions. It is important to note that though technologies such as firewalls, a robust patching program, and disk and file encryption (see sidebar, "A Definition of Encryption") can be part of a powerful intrusion prevention program, these are considered static preventative defenses and will not be discussed here. In this part of the chapter, we discuss various dynamic systems and technologies that can assist in the detection and prevention of attacks on information systems.

9. ANTI-MALWARE SOFTWARE

We have discussed malware and its various forms previously. Anti-malware software (see Figure 18.5), in the past typically referred to as *antivirus software*, is designed to analyze files and programs for known signatures, or patterns, in the data that make up the file or program and that indicate malicious code is present. This signature scanning is often accomplished in a multitiered

---

A Definition of Encryption

Encryption is the process of protecting the content or meaning of a message or other kinds of data.[17] Modern encryption algorithms are based on complex mathematical functions that scramble the original, cleartext message or data in such a way that makes it difficult or impossible for an adversary to read or access the data without the proper key to reverse the scrambling. The encryption key is typically a large number of values, that when fed into the encryption algorithm, scrambles and unscrambles the data being protected and without which it is extremely difficult or impossible to decrypt encrypted data. The science of encryption is called *cryptography* and is a broad and technical subject.

---

17 B. Schneier, *Applied Cryptography,* Wiley, 1996.

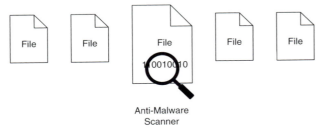

FIGURE 18.5 Anti-malware file scanning.

approach where the entire hard drive of the computer is scanned sequentially during idle periods and any file accessed is scanned immediately to help prevent dormant code in a file that has not been scanned from becoming active. When an infected file or malicious program is found, it is prevented from running and either quarantined (moved to a location for further inspection by a systems administrator) or simply deleted from the system. There are also appliance-based solutions that can be placed on the network to examine certain classes of traffic such as email before they are delivered to the end systems.

In any case, the primary weakness of the signature-based scanning method is that if the software does not have a signature for a particular piece of malware, the malware will be effectively invisible to the software and will be able to run without interference. A signature might not exist because a particular instance of the anti-malware software may not have an up-to-date signature database or the malware may be new or modified so as to avoid detection. To overcome this increasingly common issue, more sophisticated anti-malware software will monitor for known-malicious behavioral patterns instead of, or in addition to, signature-based scanning. Behavioral pattern monitoring can take many forms such as observing the system calls all programs make and identifying patterns of calls that are anomalous or known to be malicious. Another common method is to create a whitelist of allowed known-normal activity and prevent all other activity, or at least prompt the user when a non-whitelisted activity is attempted. Though these methods overcome some of the limitations of the signature-based model and can help detect previously never seen malware, they come with the price of higher false-positive rates and/or additional administrative burdens.

While anti-malware software can be evaded by new or modified malware, it still serves a useful purpose as a component in a defense-in-depth strategy. A well maintained anti-malware infrastructure will detect and prevent known forms, thus freeing up resources to focus on other threats, but it can also be used to help speed and simplify containment and eradication of a malware

infection once an identifying signature can be developed and deployed.

10. NETWORK-BASED INTRUSION DETECTION SYSTEMS

For many years, network-based intrusion detection systems (NIDS) have been the workhorse of information security technology and in many ways have become synonymous with intrusion detection.[18] NIDS function in one of three modes: signature detection, anomaly detection, and hybrid.

A signature-based NIDS operates by passively examining all the network traffic flowing past its sensor interface or interfaces and examines the TCP/IP packets for signatures of known attacks, as illustrated in Figure 18.6.

TCP/IP packet headers are also often inspected to search for nonsensical header field values sometimes used by attackers in an attempt to circumvent filters and monitors. In much the same way that signature-based anti-malware software can be defeated by never-before-seen malware or malware sufficiently modified to no longer possess the signature used for detection, signature-based NIDS will be blind to any attack for which it does not have a signature. Though this can be a very serious limitation, signature-based NIDS are still useful due to most systems' ability for the operator to add custom signatures to sensors. This allows security and network engineers to rapidly deploy monitoring and alarming capability on their networks in the event they discover an incident or are suspicious about certain activity. Signature-based NIDS are also useful to monitor for known attacks and ensure that none of those are successful at breaching systems, freeing up resources to investigate or monitor other, more serious threats.

NIDS designed to detect anomalies in network traffic build statistical or baseline models for the traffic they monitor and raise an alarm on any traffic that deviates significantly from those models. There are numerous methods for detecting network traffic anomalies, but one of the most common involves checking traffic for compliance with various protocol standards such as TCP/IP for the underlying traffic and application layer protocols such as HTTP for Web traffic, SMTP for email, and so on. Many attacks against applications or the underlying network attempt to cause system malfunctions by violating the protocol standard in ways unanticipated by the system developers and which the targeted protocol-handling

---

18 S. Northcutt, *Network Intrusion Detection*, 3rd ed., Sams, 2002.

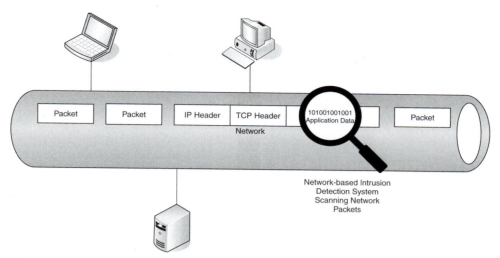

FIGURE 18.6 NIDS device-scanning packets flowing past a sensor interface.

layer does not deal with properly. Unfortunately, there are entire classes of attacks that do not violate any protocol standard and thus will not be detected by this model of anomaly detection. Another commonly used model is to build a model for user behavior and to generate an alarm when a user deviates from the "normal" patterns. For example, if Alice never logs into the network after 9:00 p.m. and suddenly a logon attempt is seen from Alice's account at 3:00 a.m., this would constitute a significant deviation from normal usage patterns and generate an alarm. Some of the main drawbacks of anomaly detection systems are defining the models of what is normal and what is malicious, defining what is a significant enough deviation from the norm to warrant an alarm, and defining a sufficiently comprehensive model or models to cover the immense range of behavioral and traffic patterns that are likely to be seen on any given network. Due to this complexity and the relative immaturity of adaptable, learning anomaly detection technology, there are very few production-quality systems available today. However, due to not relying on static signatures and the potential of a successful implementation of an anomaly detection, NIDS for detecting 0-day attacks and new or custom malware is so tantalizing that much research continues in this space.

A hybrid system takes the best qualities of both signature-based and anomaly detection NIDS and integrates them into a single system to attempt to overcome the weaknesses of both models. Many commercial NIDS now implement a hybrid model by utilizing signature matching due to its speed and flexibility while incorporating some level of anomaly detection to, at minimum, flag suspicious traffic for closer examination by those responsible for monitoring the NIDS alerts.

Aside from the primary criticism of signature-based NIDS their depending on static signatures, common additional criticisms of NIDS are they tend to produce a lot of false alerts either due to imprecise signature construction or poor tuning of the sensor to better match the environment, poor event correlation resulting in many alerts for a related incident, the inability to monitor encrypted network traffic, difficulty dealing with very high-speed networks such as those operating at 10 gigabits per second, and no ability to intervene during a detected attack. This last criticism is one of the driving reasons behind the development of intrusion prevention systems.

11. NETWORK-BASED INTRUSION PREVENTION SYSTEMS

NIDS are designed to passively monitor traffic and raise alarms when suspicious traffic is detected, whereas network-based intrusion prevention systems (NIPS) are designed to go one step further and actually try to prevent the attack from succeeding. This is typically achieved by inserting the NIPS device inline with the traffic it is monitoring. Each network packet is inspected and only passed if it does not trigger some sort of alert based on a signature match or anomaly threshold. Suspicious packets are discarded and an alert is generated.

The ability to intervene and stop known attacks, in contrast to the passive monitoring of NIDS, is the greatest benefit of NIPS. However, NIPS suffers from the same drawbacks and limitations as discussed for NIDS, such as heavy reliance on static signatures, inability to examine encrypted traffic, and difficulties with very high network speeds. In addition, false alarms are much more significant due to the fact that the NIPS may discard that traffic even though it is not really malicious. If the destination system is business or mission critical, this action could have significant negative impact on the functioning of the system. Thus, great care must be taken to tune the NIPS during a training period where there is no packet discard before allowing it to begin blocking any detected, malicious traffic.

12. HOST-BASED INTRUSION PREVENTION SYSTEMS

A complementary approach to network-based intrusion prevention is to place the detection and prevention system on the system requiring protection as an installed software package. Host-based intrusion prevention systems (HIPS), though often utilizing some of the same signature-based technology found in NIDS and NIPS, also take advantage of being installed on the protected system to protect by monitoring and analyzing what other processes on the system are doing at a very detailed level. This process monitoring is very similar to that which we discussed in the anti-malware software section and involves observing system calls, interprocess communication, network traffic, and other behavioral patterns for suspicious activity. Another benefit of HIPS is that encrypted network traffic can be analyzed after the decryption process has occurred on the protected system, thus providing an opportunity to detect an attack that would have been hidden from a NIPS or NIDS device monitoring network traffic.

Again, as with NIPS and NIDS, HIPS is only as effective as its signature database, anomaly detection model, or behavioral analysis routines. Also, the presence of HIPS on a protected system does incur processing and system resource utilization overhead and on a very busy system, this overhead may be unacceptable. However, given the unique advantages of HIPS, such as being able to inspect encrypted network traffic, it is often used as a complement to NIPS and NIDS in a targeted fashion and this combination can be very effective.

13. SECURITY INFORMATION MANAGEMENT SYSTEMS

Modern network environments generate a tremendous amount of security event and log data via firewalls, network routers and switches, NIDS/NIPS, servers, anti-malware systems, and so on. Envisioned as a solution to help manage and analyze all this information, security information management (SIM) systems have since evolved to provide data reduction, to reduce the sheer quantity of information that must analyzed, and event correlation capabilities that assist a security analyst to make sense of it all.[19] A SIM system not only acts as a centralized repository for such data, it helps organize it and provides an analyst the ability to do complex queries across this entire database. One of the primary benefits of a SIM system is that data from disparate systems is normalized into a uniform database structure, thus allowing an analyst to investigate suspicious activity or a known incident across different aspects and elements of the IT environment. Often an intrusion will leave various types of "footprints" in the logs of different systems involved in the incident; bringing these all together and providing the complete picture for the analyst or investigator is the job of the SIM.

Even with modern and powerful event correlation engines and data reduction routines, however, a SIM system is only as effective as the analyst examining the output. Fundamentally, SIM systems are a reactive technology, like NIDS, and because extracting useful and actionable information from them often requires a strong understanding of the various systems sending data to the SIM, the analysts' skill set and experience become very critical to the effectiveness of the SIM as an intrusion detection system.[20] SIM systems also play a significant role during incident response because often evidence of an intrusion can be found in the various logs stored on the SIM.

14. NETWORK SESSION ANALYSIS

Network session data represents a high-level summary of "conversations" occurring between computer systems.[21] No specifics about the content of the conversation such as packet payloads are maintained, but various elements about the conversation are kept and can be very useful in investigating an incident or as an indicator of suspicious activity. There are a number of ways to generate and process network session data ranging from vendor-specific implementations such as Cisco's NetFlow[22] to session data reconstruction from full traffic analysis using tools such as Argus.[23] However the session data is generated, there are a number of common elements constituting the session, such as source IP address, source

---

19 http://en.wikipedia.org/wiki/Security_Information_Management.

20 www.schneier.com/blog/archives/2004/10/security_inform.html.

21 R. Bejtlich, *The Tao of Network Security Monitoring: Beyond Intrusion Detection,* Addison-Wesley Professional, 2004.

22 Cisco NetFlow, wwww.cisco.com/web/go/netflow.

23 Argus, http://qosient.com/argus/.

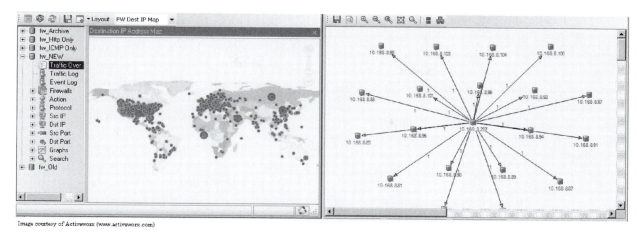

FIGURE 18.7 Network Session Analysis Visualization Interface.

port, destination IP address, destination port, time-stamp information, and an array of metrics about the session, such as bytes transferred and packet distribution.

Using the collected session information, an analyst can examine traffic patterns on a network to identify which systems are communicating with each other and identify suspicious sessions that warrant further investigation. For example, a server configured for internal use by users and having no legitimate reason to communicate with addresses on the Internet will cause an alarm to be generated if suddenly a session or sessions appear between the internal server and external addresses. At that point the analyst may suspect a malware infection or other system compromise and investigate further. Numerous other queries can be generated to identify sessions that are abnormal in some way or another such as excessive byte counts, excessive session lifetime, or unexpected ports being utilized. When run over a sufficient timeframe, a baseline for traffic sessions can be established and the analyst can query for sessions that don't fit the baseline. This sort of investigation is a form of anomaly detection based on high-level network data versus the more granular types discussed for NIDS and NIPS. Figure 18.7 illustrates a visualization of network session data. The pane on the left side indicates one node communicating with many others; the pane on the right is displaying the physical location of many IP addresses of other flows.

Another common use of network session analysis is to combine it with the use of a honeypot or honeynet (see sidebar, "Honeypots and Honeynets"). Any network activity, other than known-good maintenance traffic such as patch downloads, seen on these systems is, by definition, suspicious since there are no production business functions or users assigned to these systems. Their sole

purpose is to act as a lure for an intruder. By monitoring network sessions to and from these systems, an early warning can be raised without even necessarily needing to perform any complex analysis.

> **Honeypots and Honeynets**
>
> A honeypot is a computer system designed to act as a lure or trap for intruders. This is most often achieved by configuring the honeypot to look like a production system that possibly contains valuable or sensitive information and provides legitimate services, but in actuality neither the data or the services are real. A honeypot is carefully monitored and, since there is no legitimate reason for a user to be interacting with it, any activity seen targeting it is immediately considered suspicious. A honeynet is a collection of honeypots designed to mimic a more complex environment than one system can support.[24]

15. DIGITAL FORENSICS

Digital forensics is the "application of computer science and investigative procedures for a legal purpose involving the analysis of digital evidence."[25] Less formally, digital forensics is the use of specialized tools and techniques to investigate various forms of computer-oriented crime including fraud, illicit use such as child pornography, and many forms of computer intrusions.

Digital forensics as a field can be divided into two subfields: network forensics and host-based forensics. Network forensics focuses on the use of captured network traffic and session information to investigate computer

24 www.honeynet.org.
25 K. Zatyko, "Commentary: Defining digital forensics," *Forensics Magazine*, www.forensicmag.com/articles.asp?pid=130, 2007.

crime. Host-based forensics focuses on the collection and analysis of digital evidence from individual computer systems to investigate computer crime. Digital forensics is a vast topic, and a comprehensive discussion is beyond the scope of this chapter; interested readers are referred to[26] for more detail.

In the context of intrusion detection, digital forensic techniques can be utilized to analyze a suspected compromised system in a methodical manner. Forensic investigations are most commonly used when the nature of the intrusion is unclear, such as those perpetrated via a 0-day exploit, but wherein the root cause must be fully understood either to ensure that the exploited vulnerability is properly remediated or to support legal proceedings. Due to the increasing use of sophisticated attack tools and stealthy and customized malware designed to evade detection, forensic investigations are becoming increasingly common, and sometimes only a detailed and methodical investigation will uncover the nature of an intrusion. The specifics of the intrusion may also require a forensic investigation such as those involving the theft of Personally Identifiable Information (PII) in regions covered by one or more data breach disclosure laws.

16. SYSTEM INTEGRITY VALIDATION

The emergence of powerful and stealthy malware, kernel-level root kits, and so-called clean-state attack frameworks that leave no trace of an intrusion on a computer's hard drive have given rise to the need for technology that can analyze a running system and its memory and provide a series of metrics regarding the integrity of the system. System integrity validation (SIV) technology is still in its infancy and a very active area of research but primarily focuses on live system memory analysis and the notion of deriving trust from known-good system elements.[27] This is achieved by comparing the system's running state, including the processes, threads, data structures, and modules loaded into memory, to the static elements on disk from which the running state was supposedly loaded. Through a number of cross-validation processes, discrepancies between what is running in memory and what should be running can be identified. When properly implemented, SIV can be a powerful tool for detecting intrusions, even those utilizing advanced techniques.

17. PUTTING IT ALL TOGETHER

It should now be clear that intrusion detection and prevention are not single tools or products but a series of layered technologies coupled with the appropriate methodologies and skill sets. Each of the technologies surveyed in this chapter has its own specific strengths and weaknesses, and a truly effective intrusion detection and prevention program must be designed to play to those strengths and minimize the weaknesses. Combining NIDS and NIPS with network session analysis and a comprehensive SIM, for example, helps offset the inherent weakness of each technology as well as provide the information security team greater flexibility to bring the right tools to bear for an ever-shifting threat environment.

An essential element in a properly designed intrusion detection and prevention program is an assessment of the threats faced by the organization and a valuation of the assets to be protected. There must be an alignment of the value of the information assets to be protected and the costs of the systems put in place to defend them. The program for an environment processing military secrets and needing to defend against a hostile nation state must be far more exhaustive than that for a single server containing no data of any real value that must simply keep out assorted script kiddies.

For many organizations, however, their information systems are business and mission critical enough to warrant considerable thought and planning with regard to the appropriate choices of technologies, how they will be implemented, and how they will be monitored. Only through flexible, layered, and comprehensive intrusion detection and prevention programs can organizations hope to defend their environment against current and future threats to their information security.

---

26 K. Jones, *Real Digital Forensics: Computer Security and Incident Response*, Addison-Wesley Professional, 2005.

27 www.volatilesystems.com.

## Chapter 19

Computer Forensics

Scott R. Ellis
RGL

This guide is intended to provide in-depth information on computer forensics as a career, a job, and a science. It will help you *avoid mistakes* and find your way through the many aspects of this diverse and rewarding field.

1. WHAT IS COMPUTER FORENSICS?

Definition: Computer forensics is the acquisition, preservation, and analysis of electronically stored information (ESI) in such a way that ensures its admissibility for use as either evidence, exhibits, or demonstratives in a court of law.

Rather than discussing at great length what computer forensics is (the rest of the chapter will take care of that), let's, for the sake of clarity, define what computer forensics is *not*. It is not an arcane ability to tap into a vast, secret repository of information about every single thing that ever happened on, or to, a computer. Often, it involves handling hardware in unique circumstances and doing things with both hardware and software that are not, typically, things that the makers or manufacturers ever intended (see sidebar: "Angular Momentum").

Not every single thing a user ever did on a computer is 100% knowable beyond a shadow of a doubt or even beyond reasonable doubt. Some things are certainly *knowable* with varying degrees of certainty. and there is nothing that can happen on a computer through the use of a keyboard and a mouse that cannot be replicated with a software program or macro of some sort. It is fitting, then, that many of the arguments of computer forensics become philosophical, and that *degrees of certainty* exist and beg definition. Such as: How heavy is the burden of proof? Right away, lest arrogant thoughtlessness prevail, anyone undertaking a study of computer forensics must understand the core principles of what it means to be in a position of authority and to what varying degrees of certainty an examiner may attest to without finding he has overstepped his mandate (see sidebar, "Angular Momentum"). The sections "Testifying in Court" and "Beginning to End in Court" in this chapter, and the article "Computer Forensics and Ethics, Green Home Plate Gallery View," address these concerns as they relate to ethics and testimonial work.

Angular Momentum

Hard drive platters spin very fast. The 5¼-inch floppy disk of the 1980s has evolved into heavy, metallic platters that spin at ridiculous speeds. If your car wheels turned at 10,000 RPM, you would zip along at 1000 mph. Some hard drives spin at 15,000 RPM. That's really fast. But though HD platters will not disintegrate (as CD-ROMs have been known to do), anecdotal evidence suggests that in larger, heavier drives, the bearings can become so hot that they liquefy, effectively stopping the drive in its tracks. Basic knowledge of surface coating magnetic properties tells us that if the surface of a hard drive becomes overly hot, the basic magnetic properties, the "zeroes and ones" stored by the particulate magnetic domains, will become unstable.

The stability of these zeroes and ones maintains the consistency of the logical data stored by the medium. The high speeds of large, heavy hard drives generate heat and ultimately result in drive failure.

Forensic technicians are often required to handle hard drives, sometimes while they have power attached to them. For example, a computer may need to be moved while it still has power attached to it. Here is where a note about angular momentum becomes necessary: A spinning object translates pressure applied to its axis of rotation 90 degrees from the direction of the force applied to it. Most hard drives are designed to park the heads at even the slightest amount of detected g-shock. They claim to be able to

---

withstand thousands of "g's," but this simply means that if the hard drive was parked on a neutron star it would still be able to park its heads. This is a relatively meaningless, static attribute. Most people should understand that if you drop your computer, you may damage the internal mechanics of a hard drive and, if the platters are spinning, the drive may be scored. Older drives, those that are more than three years old, are especially susceptible to damage. Precautions should be taken to keep older drives vibration free and cool.

With very slight, gentle pressures, a spinning hard drive can be handled much as you would handle a gyro and with little potential for damage. It can be handled in a way that won't cause the heads to park.

Note: Older drives are the exception, and any slight motion at all can cause them to stop functioning.

Most hard drives have piezoelectric shock detectors that will cause the heads to park the instant a certain g-shock value is reached. Piezoelectrics work under the principle that when a force is exerted along a particular axis, certain types of crystals will emit an electrical charge. Just like their pocket-lighter counterparts, they don't always work and eventually become either desensitized or oversensitized; if the internal mechanism of the hard drive is out of tolerance, the shock detector may either work or it won't park the heads correctly and the heads will shred the surface of the platters. Or, if it does work, it may thrash the surface anyway as the heads park and unpark during multiple, repeated shocks. A large, heavy drive (such as a 1TB drive) will behave exactly as would any heavy disk spinning about an axis—just like a gyro (see Figure 19.1). So, when a vector of force is applied to a drive and it is forced to turn in the same direction as the vector, instead of its natural 90 degree offset, the potential for damage to the drive increases dramatically.

Such is the case of a computer mounted in brackets inside a PC in transit. The internal, spinning platters of the drive try to shift in opposition to the direction the external drive turned; it is an internal tug of war. As the platters attempt to lean forward, the drive leans to the left instead. If there is any play in the bearings at all, the cushion of air that floats the drive heads can be disrupted and the surface

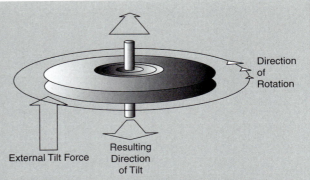

Direction of Rotation

External Tilt Force

Resulting Direction of Tilt

FIGURE 19.1 A spinning object distributes applied force differently than a stationary object. Handle operating hard drives with extreme care.

of the platters can scratch. If you must move a spinning drive (and sometimes you must), be very careful, go very slowly, and let the drive do all the work. If you must transport a running hard drive, ensure that the internal drive is rotating about the x axis, that it is horizontally mounted inside the computer, and that there is an external shock pad. Some PCs have vertically mounted drives.

Foam padding beneath the computer is essential. If you are in the business of transporting running computers that have been seized, a floating platform of some sort wouldn't be a bad idea. A lot of vibrations, bumps, and jars can shred less durably manufactured HDs. This author once shredded his own laptop hard drive by leaving it turned on, carrying it 15 city blocks, and then for an hour-long ride on the train. You can transport and move computers your entire life and not have an issue. But the one time you do, it could be an unacceptable and unrecoverable loss.

Never move an older computer. If the computer cannot be shut down, then the acquisition of the computer must be completed on site. Any time a computer is to be moved while it's running, everyone involved in the decision-making process should sign off on the procedure and be aware of the risk.

Lesson learned: Always make sure that a laptop put into standby mode has actually gone into standby mode before closing the lid. Windows can be tricky like that sometimes.

2. ANALYSIS OF DATA

Never underestimate the power of a maze. There are two types of mazes that maze experts generally agree on: unicursive and multicursive. In the unicursive maze, the maze has only one answer; you wind along a path and with a little patience you end up at the end. Multicursory mazes, according to the experts, are full of wrong turns and dead ends.

The fact of the matter is, however, when one sets foot into a multicursive maze, one need only recognize that it

is, in fact, two unicursory mazes put together, with the path through the maze being the seam. If you take the unicursory tack and simply *always stay to the right (or the left,* as long as you are consistent), you will traverse the entire maze and have no choice but to traverse and complete it successfully.

This is not a section about mazes, but they are analogous in that there are two approaches to computer forensics: one that churns through every last bit of data and one that takes shortcuts. This is called *analysis*. Quite often as a forensic analyst, the sheer amount of data that needs to be sifted will seem enormous and unrelenting. But there is a path that, if you know it, you can follow it through to success. Here are a few guidelines on how to go about conducting an investigation. For starters, we talk about a feature that is built into most forensic toolsets. It allows the examiner to "reveal all" in a fashion that can place hundreds of thousands of files at the fingertips for examination. It can also create a bad situation, legally and ethically.

Computer Forensics and Ethics, Green Home Plate Gallery View[1]

A simplified version of this article was published on the Chicago Bar Association blog in late 2007. This is the original version, unaltered.

EnCase is a commonly used forensic software program that allows a computer forensic technologist to conduct an investigation of a forensic hard disk copy. One of the functions of the software is something known as "green-home-plate-gallery-view." This function allows the forensic technologist to create, in *plain view*, a gallery of every single image on the computer.

In EnCase, the entire folder view structure of a computer is laid out just as in Windows Explorer with the exception that to the left of every folder entry are two boxes. One is shaped like a square, and the other like a little "home plate" that turns green when you click on it; hence the "green-home-plate." The technical name for the home plate box is "Set Included Folders." With a single click, every single file *entry* in that folder and its subfolders becomes visible in a table view. An additional option allows the examiner to switch from a table view of entries to a gallery view of *thumbnails*. Both operations together create the "green-home-plate-gallery-view" action.

With two clicks of the mouse, the licensed EnCase user can gather up every single image that exists on the computer and place it into a single, scrollable, thumbnail gallery. In a court-ordered investigation where the search may be for text-based documents such as correspondence, green-home-plate-gallery-view has the potential of being *misused* to visually search the computer for imaged/scanned documents. I emphasize *misused* because, ultimately, this action puts every single image on the computer in *plain view*. It is akin to policemen showing up for a domestic abuse response with an x-ray machine in tow and x-raying the contents of the whole house.

Because this action enables one to view every single image on a computer, including those that may not have anything to do with the forensic search at hand, it raises a question of ethics, and possibly even legality. Can a forensic examiner green-home-plate-gallery-view without reasonable cause?

In terms of a search where the search or motion specifically authorized searching for text-based "documents," green-home-plate-gallery-view is not the correct approach, nor is it the most efficient. The action exceeds the scope of the search and it may raise questions regarding the violation of rights and/or privacy. To some inexperienced examiners, it may seem to be the quickest and easiest route to locating all the documents on a computer. More experienced examiners may use it as a quick litmus test to "peek under the hood" to see if there are documents on the computer.

Many documents that are responsive to the search may be in the form of image scans or PDFs. Green-home-plate-gallery-view renders them visible and available, just for the scrolling. Therein lies the problem: If anything incriminating turns up, it also has the ring of truth in a court of law when the examiner suggests that he was innocently searching for financial documents when he inadvertently discovered, in *plain view*, offensive materials that were outside the scope of his original mandate. But just because something has the ring of truth does not mean that the bell's been rung.

For inexperienced investigators, green-home-plate-gallery-view (see Figure 19.2) may truly seem to be the only recourse and it may also be the one that has yielded the most convictions. However, because there is a more efficient method to capture and detect text, one that can protect privacy and follows the constraints of the search mandate, it should be used.

Current forensic technology allows us, through electronic file signature analysis, sizing, and typing of images, to capture and export every image from the subject file system. Next, through optical character recognition (OCR), the experienced professional can detect every image that has text and discard those that do not. In this manner, images are protected from being viewed, the subject's privacy is protected, and all images with text are located efficiently. The resultant set can then be hashed and reintroduced into EnCase as single files, hashed, and indexed so that the notable files can be bookmarked and a report generated.

Technically, this is a more difficult process because it requires extensive knowledge of imaging, electronic file signature analysis, automated OCR discovery techniques, and hash libraries. But to a trained technician, this is

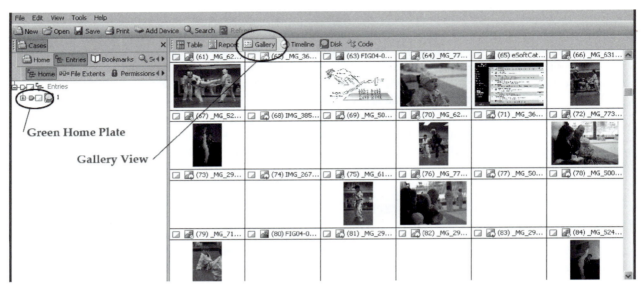

FIGURE 19.2 Green-home-plate-gallery-view.

actually faster than green-home-plate-gallery-view, which may yield thousands of images and may take hundreds of hours to accurately review.

In practice, the easiest way is seldom the most ethical way to solve a problem; neither is it always the most efficient method of getting a job done. Currently, there are many such similar scenarios that exist within the discipline of computer forensics. As the forensic technology industry grows and evolves, professional organizations may eventually emerge that will provide codes of ethics and some syncretism in regard to these issues. For now, however, it falls on attorneys to retain experienced computer forensic technologists who place importance on developing appropriate ethical protocols. Only when these protocols are in place can we successfully understand the breadth and scope of searches and prevent possible violations of privacy.

Database Reconstruction

A disk that hosts an active database is a very busy place. Again and again throughout this chapter, a single recurring theme will emerge: Data that has been overwritten cannot, by any conventionally known means, be recovered. If it could be, then Kroll Ontrack and every other giant in the forensics business would be shouting this service from the rooftops and charging a premium price for it. Experimentally, accurate statistics on the amount of data that will be overwritten by the seemingly random action of a write head may be available, but most likely it functions by rules that are different for every system based on the amount of usage, the size of the files, and the size of the unallocated clusters. Anecdotally, the

formula goes something like this; the rules change under any given circumstances, but this story goes a long way toward telling how much data will be available:

On a server purposed with storing surveillance video, there are three physical hard drives. Drive C serves as the operating system (OS) disk and program files disk; Drives E and F, 350 gigabytes (GB) each, serve as storage disks. When the remote DVR units synchronize each evening, every other file writes to every other disk of the two storage drives. Thirty-day-old files automatically get deleted by the synchronization tool.

After eight months of use, the entire unallocated clusters of each drive, 115 GB on one drive and 123 GB on the other, are completely filled with MPG data. An additional 45 GB of archived deleted files are available to be recovered from each drive.

In this case, the database data were MPG movie files. In many databases, the data, the records (as the database indexes and grows and shrinks and is compacted and optimized), will grow to populate the unallocated clusters. Database records found in the unallocated clusters are not an indicator of deleted records. Database records that exist in the unallocated clusters that don't exist in the live database *are* a sign of deleted records.

Lesson learned: Don't believe everything you see. Check it out and be sure. Get second, third, and fourth opinions when you're uncertain.

3. COMPUTER FORENSICS IN THE COURT SYSTEM

Computer forensics is one of the few computer-related fields in which the practitioner will be found in the courtroom on a given number of days of the year. With that in mind, the following sections are derived from the author's experiences in the courtroom, the lessons learned there, and the preparation leading up to giving testimony. To most lawyers and judges, computer forensics is a mysterious black art. It is as much a discipline of the art to demystify and explain results in plain English as it is to conduct an examination. It was with special consideration of the growing prevalence of the use of electronically stored information (ESI) in the courtroom, and the general unfamiliarity with how it must be handled as evidence, that spawned the idea for the sidebar "Preserving Digital Evidence in the Age of eDiscovery."

Preserving Digital Evidence in the Age of eDiscovery[2]

Society has awoken in these past few years to the realities of being immersed in the digital world. With that, the harsh realities of how we conduct ourselves in this age of binary processing are beginning to take form in terms of both new laws and new ways of doing business. In many actions, both civil and criminal, digital documents are the new "smoking gun." And with the new Federal laws that open the floodgates of accessibility to your digital media, the sanctions for mishandling such evidence become a fact of law and a major concern.

At some point, most of us (any of us) could become involved in litigation. Divorce, damage suits, patent infringement, intellectual property theft, and employee misconduct are just some examples of cases we see. When it comes to digital evidence, most people simply aren't sure of their responsibilities. They don't know how to handle the requests for and subsequent handling of the massive amounts of data that can be crucial to every case. Like the proverbial smoking gun, "digital evidence" must be handled properly.

Recently, a friend forwarded us an article about a case ruling in which a routine email exhibit was found inadmissible due to authenticity and hearsay issues. What we should take away from that ruling is that electronically stored information (ESI), just like any other evidence, must clear standard evidentiary hurdles. Whenever ESI is offered as evidence, the following evidence rules must be considered.

In most courts, there are four types of evidence. Computer files that are extracted from a subject machine and presented in court typically fall into one or more of these types:

- *Documentary evidence* is paper or digital evidence that contains human language. It must meet the authenticity requirements outlined below. It is also unique in that it may be disallowed if it contains hearsay. Emails fall into the category of documentary evidence.
- *Real evidence* must be competent (authenticated), relevant, and material. For example, a computer that was involved in a court matter would be considered real evidence provided that it hasn't been changed, altered, or accessed in a way that destroyed the evidence. The ability to use these items as evidence may be contingent on this fact, and that's is why preservation of a computer or digital media must be done.

- *Witness testimony.* With ESI, the technician should be able to verify how he retrieved the evidence and that the evidence is what it purports to be, and he should be able to speak to all aspects of computer use. The witness must both remember what he saw and be able to communicate it.
- *Demonstrative evidence* uses things like PowerPoint, photographs, or computer-aided design (CAD) drawings of crime scenes to demonstrate or reconstruct an event. For example, a flowchart that details how a person goes to a Web site, enters her credit-card number, and makes a purchase would be considered demonstrative.

For any of these items to be submitted in court, they each must, to varying degrees, pass the admissibility requirements of relevance, materiality, and competence. For evidence to be *relevant*, it must make the event it is trying to prove either more or less probable. A forensic analyst may discover a certain Web page on the subject hard drive that shows the subject visited a Web site where flowers are sold and that he made a purchase. In addition to perhaps a credit-card statement, this shows that it is more probable that the subject of an investigation visited the site on his computer at a certain time and location.

Materiality means that something not only proves the fact (it is relevant to the fact that it is trying to prove) but is also *material* to the issues in the case. The fact that the subject of the investigation purchased flowers on a Web site may not be material to the matter at hand.

Finally, *competency* is the area where the forensic side of things becomes most important. Assuming that the purchase of flowers from a Web site is material (perhaps it is a stalking case), how the evidence was obtained and what happened to it after that will be put under a microscope by both the judge and the party objecting to the evidence. The best evidence collection experts are trained professionals with extensive experience in their field. The best attorneys will understand this and will use experts when and where needed. Spoliation results from mishandled ESI, and spoiled data is generally inadmissible. It rests upon everyone involved in a case—IT directors, business owners, and attorneys—to get it right. Computer forensics experts cannot undo damage that has been done, but if involved in the *beginning*, they can prevent it from happening.

---

2 Scott R. Ellis, "Preserving digital evidence in the age of ediscovery," *Daily Southtown*, 2007.

4. UNDERSTANDING INTERNET HISTORY

Of the many aspects of user activity, the Internet history is usually of the greatest interest. In most investigations, people such as HR, employers, and law enforcement seek to understand the subject's use of the Internet. What Web sites did he visit? When did he visit them? Did he visit them more than once? The article "What Have You Been Clicking On" (see sidebar) seeks to demystify the concept of temporary Internet files (TIF).

What Have You Been Clicking On?

You've probably heard the rumor that whenever you click on something on a Web page, you leave a deeply rooted trail behind you for anyone (with the right technology) to see. In computer forensics, just like in archeology, these pieces that a user leaves behind are called *artifacts*. An artifact is a thing made by a human. It tells the story of a behavior that happened in the past.

On your computer, that story is told by metadata stored in databases as well as by files stored on your local machine. They reside in numerous places, but this article will address just three: Internet history, Web cache, and temporary Internet files (TIF). Because Internet Explorer (IE) was developed in a time when bandwidth was precious, storing data locally prevents a browser from having to retrieve the same data every time the same Web page is visited. Also, at the time, no established technology existed that, through a Web browser, could show data on a local machine without first putting the file on the local machine. A Web browser, essentially, was a piece of software that combined FTP and document-viewing technology into one application platform, complete with its own protocol, HTTP.

In IE, press **Ctrl + H** to view your history. This will show a list of links to all the sites that were viewed over a period of four weeks. The history database only stores the name and date the site was visited. It holds no information about files that may be cached locally. That's the job of the Web cache.

To go back further in history, an Internet history viewer is needed. A Google search for "history.dat viewer" will turn up a few free tools.

The Web cache database, index.dat, is located in the TIF folder; it tracks the date, the time the Web page downloaded, the original Web page filename, and its local name and location in the TIF. Information stays in the index.dat for a long time, much longer than four weeks. You will notice that if you set your computer date back a few weeks and then press **Ctrl + H**, you can always pull the last four weeks of data for as long as you have had your computer (and not cleared your cache). Using a third-party viewer to view the Web cache shows you with certainty the date and origination of a Web page. The Web cache is a detailed inventory of everything in the TIF. Some history viewers will show Web cache information, too.

The TIF is a set of local folders where IE stores Web pages your computer has downloaded. Typically, the size varies depending on user settings. But Web sites are usually small, so 500 MB can hold thousands of Web pages and images! Viewing these files may be necessary. Web mail, financial, and browsing interests are all stored in the TIF. However, malicious software activity, such as pop-ups, exploits, viruses, and Trojans, can cause many strange files to appear in the TIF. For this reason, files that are in the TIF should be compared to their entry in the Web cache. Time stamps on files in the TIF may or may not accurately show when a file was written to disk. System scans periodically alter Last Accessed and Date Modified time stamps! Because of hard-disk caching and delayed writing, the Date Created time stamp may not be the actual time the file arrived. Computer forensics uses special tools to analyze the TIF, but much is still left to individual interpretations.

Inspection of all the user's Internet artifacts, when intact, can reveal what a user was doing and whether or not a click trail exists. Looking just at time stamps or IE history isn't enough. Users can easily delete IE history, and time stamps aren't always accurate. Missing history can disrupt the trail. Missing Web cache entries or time stamp–altering system scans can destroy the trail. Any conclusions are best not preceded by a suspended leap through the air (you may land badly and trip and hurt yourself). Rather, check for viruses and bad patching, and get the artifacts straight. If there is a click trail, it will be revealed by the Web cache, the files in the TIF, and the history. Bear in mind that when pieces are missing, the reliability of the click trail erodes, and professional examination may be warranted.

---

5. TEMPORARY RESTRAINING ORDERS AND LABOR DISPUTES

A temporary restraining order (TRO) will often be issued in intellectual property or employment contract disputes.

The role of the forensic examiner in a TRO may be multifold, or it may be limited to a simple, one-time acquisition of a hard drive. Often when an employee leaves an organization under less than amicable terms, accusations will be fired in both directions and the resulting lawsuit will be a many-headed beast. Attorneys on both sides may file motions that result in forensic analysis of emails, user activity, and possible contract violations as well as extraction of information from financial and customer relationship management (CRM) databases.

Divorce

Typically the forensic work done in a divorce case will involve collecting information about one of the parties to be used to show that trust has been violated. Dating sites, pornography, financial sites, expatriate sites, and email should be collected and reviewed.

Patent Infringement

When one company begins selling a part that is patented by another company, a lawsuit will likely be filed in federal court. Subsequently, the offending company will be required to produce all the invoices relating to sales of that product. This is where a forensic examiner may be required. The infringed-on party may find through their own research that a company has purchased the part from the infringer and that the sale has not been reported. A thorough examination of the financial system will reveal all the sales. It is wise when doing this sort of work to contact the financial system vendor to get a data dictionary that defines all the fields and the purpose of the tables.

Invoice data is easy to collect. It will typically reside in just two tables: a header and a detail table. These tables will contain customer codes that will need to be joined to the customer table, so knowing some SQL will be a great help. Using the database server for the specific database technology of the software is the gold standard for this sort of work. Getting the collection to launch into VMware is the platinum standard, but sometimes an image won't want to boot. Software utilities such as Live View do a great job of preparing the image for deployment in a virtualized environment.

When to Acquire, When to Capture Acquisition

When a forensics practitioner needs to capture the data on a hard disk, he does so in a way that is forensically sound. This means that, through any actions on the part of the examiner, no data on the hard drive is altered and a complete and total copy of the surface of the hard drive

platters is captured. Here are some common terms used to describe this process:

- Collection
- Mirror
- Ghost
- Copy
- Acquisition

Any of these terms is sufficient to describe the process. The one that attorneys typically use is *mirror* because they seem to understand it best. A "forensic" acquisition simply means that the drive was write-protected by either a software or hardware write blocker while the acquisition was performed.

Acquisition of an entire hard drive is the standard approach in any case that will require a deep analysis of the behaviors and activities of the user. It is not always the standard procedure. However, most people will agree that a forensic procedure must be used whenever information is copied from a PC. Forensic, enterprise, and ediscovery cases all vary in their requirements for the amount of data that must be captured. In discovery, much of what is located on a computer may be deemed "inaccessible," which is really just fancy lawyer talk for "it costs too much to get it." Undeleting data from hundreds of computers in a single discovery action in a civil case would be a very rare thing to happen and would only take place if massive malfeasance was suspected. In these cases, forensic creation of logical evidence files allows the examiner to capture and copy relevant information without altering the data.

Creating Forensic Images Using Software and Hardware Write Blockers

Both software and hardware write blockers are available. Software write blockers are versatile and come in two flavors. One is a module that "plugs" into the forensic software and can generally be used to write block any port on the computer. The other method of software write blocking is to use a forensic boot disk. This will boot the computer from the hard drive. Developing checklists that can be repeatable procedures is an ideal way to ensure solid results in any investigation.

Software write blockers are limited by the port speed of the port they are blocking, plus some overhead for the write-blocking process. But then, all write blockers are limited in this manner.

Hardware write blockers are normally optimized for speed. Forensic copying tools such as Logicube and Tableau are two examples of hardware write blockers, though there are many companies now that make them. LogiCube will both hash and image a drive at a rate of about 3GB a minute. They are small and portable and can replace the need for bulky PCs on a job site. There are also appliances and large enterprise software packages that are designed to automate and alleviate the labor requirements of large discovery/disclosure acquisitions that may span thousands of computers.

Live Capture of Relevant Files

Before conducting any sort of a capture, all steps should be documented and reviewed with counsel before proceeding. Preferably, attorneys from both sides on a matter and the judge agree to the procedure before it is enacted. Whenever a new procedure or technique is introduced late on the job site, if there are auditors or observers present, the attorneys will argue, which can delay the work by several hours. Most forensic software can be loaded to a USB drive and launched on a live system with negligible forensic impact to the operating environment. Random Access Memory (RAM) captures are becoming more popular; currently this is the only way to capture an image of physical RAM. Certain companies are rumored to be creating physical RAM write blockers. Launching a forensic application on a running system will destroy a substantial amount of physical RAM as well as the paging file. If either RAM or the paging file is needed, the capture must be done with a write blocker.

Once the forensic tool is launched, either with a write blocker or on a live system, the local drive may be previewed. The examiner may only be interested in Word documents, for example. Signature analysis is a lengthy process in preview mode, as are most searches. A better method, if subterfuge is not expected: Filtering the table pane by extension produces a list of all the docs. "Exporting" them will damage the forensic information, so instead you need to create a logical evidence file (LEF). Using EnCase, a user can create a condition to view all the .DOC files and then dump the files into a logical evidence file in about 30 seconds. Once the logical evidence file is created, it can later be used to create a CD-ROM. There are special modules available that will allow an exact extraction of native files to CD to allow further processing for a review tool.

Redundant Array of Independent (or Inexpensive) Disks (RAID)

Acquiring an entire RAID set disk by disk and then reassembling them in EnCase is probably the easiest way of dealing with a RAID and may be the only way to capture a software RAID. Hardware RAIDs can be most efficiently captured using a boot disk. This allows the capture of a single volume that contains all the unique data in an array. It can be trickier to configure and as with everything, practice makes perfect. Be sure you understand how it works. The worst thing that can happen is that the wrong disk or an unreadable disk gets imaged and the job has to be redone at your expense.

File System Analyses

FAT12, FAT16, and FAT32 are all types of file systems. Special circumstances aside, most forensic examiners will find themselves regularly dealing with either FAT or NTFS file systems. FAT differs from NTFS primarily in the way that it stores information about how it stores information. Largely, from the average forensic examiner's standpoint, very little about the internal workings of these file systems is relevant. Most modern forensic software will do the work of reconstructing and extracting information from these systems, at the system level, for you. Nonetheless, an understanding of these systems is critical because, at any given time, an examiner *just might* need to know it. The following are some examples showing where you might need to know about the file system:

- Rebuilding RAID arrays
- Locating lost or moved partitions
- Discussions of more advanced information that can be gleaned from entries in the MFT or FAT

The difference between FAT12, 16, and 32 is in the size of each item in the File Allocation Table (FAT). Each has a correspondingly sized entry in the FAT. For example, FAT12 has a 12-bit entry in the FAT. Each 12-bit sequence represents a cluster. This places a limitation on the file system regarding the number of file extents available to a file. The FAT stores the following information:

- Fragmentation
- Used or unused clusters
- A list of entries that correspond to each cluster on the partition
- Marks a cluster as used, reserved, unused, or bad
- The cluster number of the next cluster in the chain

Sector information is stored in the directory. In the FAT file system, directories are actually files that contain as many 32-byte slots as there are entries in the folder. This is also where deleted entries from a folder can be

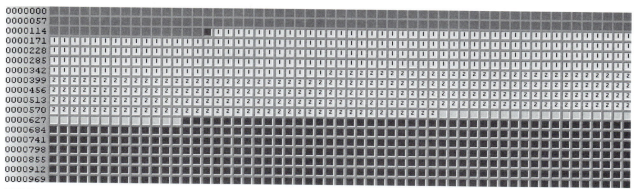

FIGURE 19.3 The sector view.

discovered. Figure 19.3 shows how the sector view is represented by a common forensic analysis tool.

NTFS

NTFS is a significant advancement in terms of data storage. It allows for long filenames, almost unlimited storage, and a more efficient method of accessing information. It also provides for much greater latency in deleted files, that is, deleted files stick around a lot longer in NTFS than they do in FAT. The following items are unique to NTFS. Instead of keeping the filenames in folder files, the entire file structure of NTFS is retained in a flat file database called the Master File Table (MFT):

- Improved support for metadata
- Advanced data structuring improves performance and reliability

- Improved disk space utilization with a maximum disk size of 7.8TB, or 2^{64} sectors; sector sizes can vary in NTFS and are most easily controlled using a third-party partitioning tool such as Partition Magic.
- Greater security

The Role of the Forensic Examiner in Investigations and File Recovery

The forensic examiner is at his best when he is searching for deleted files and attempting to reconstruct a pattern of user behavior. The sidebar "Oops! Did I Delete That?" first appeared in the Chicago *Daily Southtown* column "Bits You Can Use." In addition, this section also includes a discussion of data recovery and an insurance investigation article (see sidebar, "Don't Touch That Computer! Data Recovery Following Fire, Flood, or Storm").

Oops! Did I Delete That?

The file is gone. It's not in the recycle bin. You've done a complete search of your files for it, and now the panic sets in. It's vanished. You may have even asked people to look through their email because maybe you sent it to them (you didn't). Oops. Now what?

Hours, days, maybe even years of hard work seem to be lost. Wait! Don't touch that PC! Every action you take on your PC at this point may be destroying what is left of your file. It's not too late yet. You've possibly heard that things that are deleted are never really deleted, but you may also think that it will cost you thousands of dollars to recover deleted files once you've emptied the recycle bin. Suffice it to say, unless you are embroiled in complicated ediscovery or forensic legal proceedings where preservation is a requirement, recovering some deleted files for you may cost no more than a tune-up for your car.

Now the part where I told you: "Don't touch that PC!" I meant it. Seriously: Don't touch that PC. The second you realize you've lost a file, stop doing anything. Don't visit

any Web sites. Don't install software. Don't reformat your hard drive, do a Windows repair, or install undelete software. In fact, if it's not a server or running a shared database application, pull the plug from the back of the PC. Every time you "write" to your hard drive, you run the risk that you are destroying your lost file. In the case of one author we helped, ten years of a book were "deleted." With immediate professional help, her files were recovered.

Whether you accidentally pulled your USB drive from the slot without stopping it first (corrupting your MFT), intentionally deleted it, or have discovered an "OS not found" message when you booted your PC, you need your files back and you need them now. However, if you made the mistake of actually overwriting a file with a file that has the same name and thereby replaced it, "Abandon hope all ye who enter here." Your file is trashed, and all that may be left are some scraps of the old file, parts that didn't get overwritten but can be extracted from file slack. If your hard drive is physically damaged, you may also be looking at an expensive recovery.

Here's the quick version of how deleted files become "obliterated" and unrecoverable:

Step 1: The MFT that contains a reference to your file marks the deleted file space as available.

Step 2: The actual sectors where the deleted file resides *might* be either completely or partially overwritten.

Step 3: The MFT record for the deleted file is over-written and destroyed. Any ability to *easily* recover your deleted file at this point is lost.

Step 4: The sectors on the PC that contain your deleted file *are* overwritten and eventually only slight traces of your lost file remain. Sometimes the MFT record may be destroyed before the actual sectors are over-written. This happens a lot, and these files are recov-erable with a little extra work.

It's tremendously amazing how fast this process can occur. It's equally amazing how slowly this process can occur. Recently I retrieved hundreds of files from a system that had periodically been deleting files, and new files were written to the disk on a daily basis. Yet recovery software successfully recovered hundreds of complete files from nearly six months ago! A lot of free space on the disk contri-buted to this success. A disk that is in use and is nearly full will be proportionally less likely to contain old, deleted files.

The equipment and training investment to perform these operations is high, so expect that labor costs will be higher, but you can also expect some degree of success when attempting to recover files that have been acciden-tally deleted. Let me leave you with two dire warnings: Disks that have experienced surface damage (scored plat-ters) are unrecoverable with current technology. And never, ever, ever disrupt power to your PC when it's performing a defrag. The results are disastrous.

Don't Touch That Computer! Data Recovery Following Fire, Flood, or Storm

Fire, flood, earthquakes, landslides, and other catastrophes often result in damaged computer equipment—and loss of electronic data. For claims managers and adjusters, this data loss can manifest itself in an overwhelming number of insurance claims, costing insurers millions of dollars each year.

The improper handling of computers immediately fol-lowing a catastrophic event is possibly one of the leading causes of data loss—and once a drive has been improperly handled, the chances of data retrieval plummet. Adjusters often assume a complete loss when, in fact, there are methods that can save or salvage data on even the most damaged computers.

Methods to Save or Salvage Data

One of the first steps toward salvaging computer data is to focus on the preservation of the hard drive. Hard drives are highly precise instruments, and warping of drive compo-nents by even fractions of a millimeter will cause damage to occur in the very first moments of booting up. During these moments the drive head can shred the surface of the platters, rendering the data unrecoverable.

Hard drives are preserved in different ways, depending on the damaging event. If the drive is submerged in a flood, the drive should be removed and resubmerged in clean, dis-tilled water and shipped to an expert. It is important that this is done immediately. Hard drive platters that are allowed to corrode after being exposed to water, especially if the drive experienced seepage, will oxidize and data will be destroyed. A professional can completely disassemble the

drive to ensure that all of its parts are dry, determine what level of damage has already occurred, and then decide how to proceed with the recovery. Care must always be taken during removal from the site to prevent the drive from breaking open and being exposed to dust.

Fire or Smoke Damage

After a fire or a flood, the hard drive should not be moved and in no circumstances should it be powered up. A certi-fied computer forensic expert with experience in handling damaged drives should be immediately contacted. Typically, these experts will be able to dismantle the drive and move it without causing further damage. They are able to assess the external damage and arrive at a decision that will safely triage the drive for further recovery steps. Fire-damaged drives should never be moved or handled by laymen.

Shock Damage

Shock damage can occur when someone drops a compu-ter or it is damaged via an automobile accident; in more catastrophic scenarios, shock damage can result when serv-ers fall through floors during a fire or are even damaged by bulldozers that are removing debris. This type of crush-ing damage often results in bending of the platters and can be extensive. As in fire and flood circumstances, the drive should be isolated and power should not be applied.

A drive that has been damaged by shock presents a unique challenge: from the outside, the computer may look fine. This is typical of many claims involving laptop computers damaged during an automobile collision. If the computer consultant can verify that the drive was powered down at the time the accident occurred, most will be comfortable attempting to power up a drive that has been in a collision, to begin the data capture process. At the first sign of a change in the dynamics of the drive, a head clicking or a drive spinning down, power will be cut from the drive and the restoration will continue in a clean room where the drive will be opened up and protected from harmful dust.

The Importance of Off-Site Computer Backup

One of the best ways to maximize computer data recovery efforts is to have off-site computer backup. For adjusters arriving at the scene, this should be one of the first questions asked. An offsite backup can take many forms. Some involve the use of special data centers that synchronize data constantly. There are companies that provide this service. Other backups, for smaller companies, may be as mundane (but effective) as removing a tape backup of critical data from the site on a daily basis. With proper rotation and several tapes, a complete backup of data is always offsite. Prices for these services vary widely depending on how much data needs to be backed up and how often.

Case Studies

Scenario 1

John ran a home-based IT business. After his home burned down, John posted an insurance claim for a $500,000 loss for lost income, damaged computer equipment, and lost wages. He also charged the insurance company $60,000 for the three months he spent recovering data from the drives. Because he was only able to recover 25% of the data, he posted an additional claim for the cost of reconstructing the Web sites that he hosted from his home.

For the computer forensic consultant, this case raised several questions. As an IT professional, John should have known better than to touch the hard drive and attempt to recover any of the data himself. Also, when a claimant intentionally or unintentionally inflicts damage on his or her own property after an event, who is responsible? Through a thorough evaluation of the circumstances and intense questioning of the claimant, the claim was eventually reduced to a substantially smaller amount.

Scenario 2

Sammie's Flowers has 113 retail outlets and one central headquarters where they keep photography, custom software, catalog masters, and the like. There is no offsite backup. Everything is on CD-ROMs or on the hard drive of the company's server.

One night lightning struck the headquarters building and it burned down. An IT appraiser lacking the appropriate computer forensic skills evaluated the computer equipment after the fire. No attempts were made to recover data from the hard drives or to start the computers; because of their damaged physical condition, they were simply thrown into a dumpster.

One year later, the insured filed a claim for $37 million. Under the terms of the insured's policy, coverage for valuable papers and business personal property was most pertinent to the case. The policy limit for valuable papers is small and easily reached. The coverage limit for business personal property, on the other hand, *will* cover the $37 million claim—if the court decides that the computer data that was lost qualifies as "business valuable papers." Though this case is still pending, the cost of resolving this claim could be astronomic, and had a computer data recovery expert been consulted, the claim amount could have been reduced by millions.

Scenario 3

Alisa, a professional photographer, was in a car accident that damaged her laptop computer. She had been using the PC at a rest stop prior to the accident and later reported to the adjuster that when she booted it up after the accident she heard "a strange clicking and clacking sound." Unfortunately for Alisa, that was the sound of data being destroyed. She posted a $500,000 claim to her insurance company under her business policy—including the cost of 2000 lost images and the cost of equipment, site, model, and agency fees for a one-day photography shoot. Had the PC, which had a noticeable crack in it caused by the accident, been professionally handled, the chances are good the data could have been recovered and the claim would have been significantly reduced.

Computer equipment is always at risk of being damaged—whether by flood, fire, lightning, or other catastrophic means. However, damage does not always equal data loss. Indeed, companies and their adjusters can be quick to write off damaged storage media when, in fact, recovery may be possible. By taking the immediate measures of protecting the computers from touch and power and by calling in professional computer forensic experts to assess the damage, insurers can reap the benefits in reduced claim amounts.

Password Recovery

The following is a short list of the ways and types of passwords that can be recovered. Many useful tools that can be downloaded from the Internet for free will crack open system files that store passwords. Software programs, such as Peachtree (a financial database), Windows 98, certain FTP programs, and the like all store passwords in a way that allows their easy retrieval.

Recovering license keys for software is often an important step in reconstructing or virtualizing a disk image. Like passwords, without a valid license key the software won't work. There are a number of useful programs that can recover software license keys from the registry of a computer that can be found with a quick Google search. Understanding the mind of the user can also be helpful in locating things such as password storage tools or simply thinking to search a computer for the word *password*. Many, many Web sites will pass the password down to a client machine through the Password field in HTML documents. Some developers have wised up to this "feature" and they strip it out before it comes down, but most of them do it on the client side. This means that with the proper intercepting tool, the password can be captured midstream on its way down to the client, before it gets stripped out.

Password cracking can be achieved with a minimal amount of skill and a great deal of patience. Having some idea of what the password is before cracking it will be helpful. You can also purchase both online services as well as software tools that will strip the password right out of a file, removing it completely. Word documents are particularly vulnerable, and zip files are particularly invulnerable. However, there is a method (and a free download) that can figure out the password of a zip file if a sample of a file that is known to be in the zip can be provided.

File Carving

In most investigations, the very first place a file system examination begins is with live files. Live files are those files that still have MFT entries. Link file, trash bin, Outlook Temporary (OLK) folders, recent items, ISO lists, Internet history, TIF, and thumb databases all constitute a discernible, unique pattern of user activity. As such, they hold particular interest. By exploring these files an examiner can make determinations about file origins, the usage of files, the distribution of files, and of course the current location of the files. But sometimes the subject has been very clever and removed all traces of activity. Or the suspect item may be a server, used merely as a repository for the files. Or maybe someone just wants to recover a file that they deleted a long, long time ago (see sidebar, "Oops, Did I Delete That?").

When such need arises, the vast graveyard called the *unallocated clusters* could hold the last hope that the file can be recovered. By searching the unallocated clusters using a search tool designed for such things, and by using a known keyword in the file, one may locate the

portion within the unallocated clusters where a file used to reside. Typically, search hits will be stored under a tab or in a particular area of the forensic toolset, and they may be browsed, one by one, along with a small excerpt from the surrounding bits. By clicking on the search hit, another pane of the software window may show a more expanded view of the hit location. If it is a document, with text, then that is great and you may see other words that were also known to have been in the target file. Now, in TV shows like *CSI*, of course the document is always there, and by running some reverse 128-bit decryption sequencer to an inverted 12-bit decryption sequencer that reloops the hashing algorithm through a 256-bit decompiler by rethreading it into a multiplexing file marker, they can just right click and say "export this" and the file will print out, even if it's not even on the computer that is being examined and never was. (Yes, I made all that up.)

In the real world, more often than not we find that our examinations are spurred and motivated and wholly created by someone's abject paranoia. In these cases, no amount of digging will ever create the evidence that they want to see. That leaves only creative use of time stamps on documents to attempt to create an aroma of guilt about the subject piece. Sometimes we find that even after rooting through 300GB of unallocated clusters, leaving no stone unturned, the file *just isn't there*. But sometimes, all pessimism aside, we find little bits and pieces of interesting things all salted around throughout the unallocated clusters.

The first place to turn is the automated carvers. By familiarizing ourselves with the hexadecimal patterns of file signatures (and I've provided a nice table for you here), we may view the hex of the unallocated clusters in a hex editor or in the hex pane of the examination tool. Or possibly we already know the type of file. Let's say that we know the type of file because our client told us that they only use Word as their document editor. We scroll to the beginning of the section of text, which might look like this:

Figure sample file signature
From the text pane view of EnCase:
ĐÏ·à¡±á·············· > ···þÿ ·········
From the Hex view:
00 00 00 00 00 00 00 00 00 00 00 00 00 00 4F 6F 70 73
21 20 20 44 69 64
20 49 20 64 65 6C 65 74 65 20 74 68 61 74 3F 0D 42 79
20 53 63 6F 74 74 20
52 2E 20 45 6C 6C 69 73 0D 73 65 6C 6C 69 73 40 75 73
2E 72 67 6C 2E 63 6F
6D 0D 0D 54 68 65 20 66 69 6C 65 20 69 73 20 67 6F 6E
65 2E 20 20 49 74 92

73 20 6E 6F 74 20 69 6E 20 74 68 65 20 72 65 63 79 63
6C 65 20 62 69 6E 2E
20 59 6F 75 92 76 65 20 64 6F 6E 65 20 61 20 63 6F 6D
70 6C 65 74 65 20 73

Scrolling down in the text pane, we then find the following:

> ··············*Oops! Did I delete that? By Scott R. Ellis The file is gone. It's not in the recycle bin. You've.......*

By simply visually scanning the unallocated clusters, we can pick up where the file begins and, if the file signature isn't in the provided list of signatures or if for some reason the carving scripts in the forensic software are incorrectly pulling files, they may need to be manually set up. Truly, for Word files, that is all you need to know. You need to be able to determine the end and the beginning of a file. Some software will ignore data in the file before and after the beginning and end of file signatures. This is true for many, many file types; I can't tell you which ones because I haven't tried them all. There are some file types that need a valid end-of-file (EOF) marker, but most don't. However, if you *don't* capture the true EOF (sensible marker or no), the file may look like garbage or all the original formatting will be scrambled or it won't open. Some JPEG viewers (such as Adobe Photoshop) will throw an error if the EOF is not found. Others, such as Internet Explorer, won't even notice. Here's the trick—and it is a trick, and don't let anyone tell you differently; they might not teach this in your average university computer forensics class: Starting with the file signature, highlight as many of the unallocated clusters *after* the file signature that you think would possibly be big enough to hold the entire file size. Now double that, and export it as raw data. Give it a .DOC extension and open it in Word. *Voilá!* The file has been reconstructed. Word will know where the document ends and it will show you that document. If you happen to catch a few extra documents at the end, or a JPG or whatever, Word will ignore them and show only the first document.

Unless some sort of drastic "wiping action" has taken place, as in the use of a third-party utility to delete data, I have almost always found that a great deal of deleted data is *immediately* available in EnCase (forensic software) within 20–25 minutes after a hard disk image is mounted, simply by running "recover folders" and sitting back and waiting while it runs. This is especially true when the drive has not been used at all since the time the data was deleted. Preferably, counsel will have taken steps to ensure that this is the case when a computer is the prime subject of an investigation. Often this is not the case, however. Many attorneys, IT, and HR directors "poke around" for information all on their own.

It is conceivable that up to 80% of deleted data on a computer may be readily available, without the necessity of carving, for up to two or three years, as long as the computer hasn't seen extreme use (large amounts of files, or large amounts of copying and moving of very large files) that could conceivably overwrite the data.

Even so, searching unallocated clusters for file types typically does not require the creation of an index. Depending on the size of the drive, it may take four or five hours for the carving process to complete, and it may or may not be entirely successful, depending on the type of files that are being carved. For example, MPEG videos do not carve well at all, but there are ways around that. DOC and XLS files usually carve out quite nicely.

Indexing is something that is done strictly for the purpose of searching massive amounts of files for large numbers of keywords. We rarely use EnCase to search for keywords; we have found it better to use Relativity, our review environment, to allow the people who are interested in the keywords to do the keyword searching themselves as they perform their review. Relativity is built on an SQL platform on which indexing is a known and stable technology.

In other words (as in the bottom line), spending 15 to 25 minutes with a drive, an experienced examiner can provide a very succinct answer as to how long it would take to provide the files that they want. And, very likely, the answer could be, "Another 30 minutes and it will be yours." Including time to set up, extract, and copy to disk, if everything is in perfect order, two hours is the upper limit. This is based on the foundation that the deleted data they are looking for was deleted in the last couple of weeks of the use of the computer. If they need to go back more than a couple of months, an examiner may end up carving into the unallocated clusters to find "lost" files—these are files for which part of or all of the master file table entry has been obliterated and portions of the files themselves may be overwritten.

Carving is considered one of the consummate forensic skills. Regardless of the few shortcuts that exist, carving requires a deep, disk-level knowledge of how files are stored, and it requires a certain intuition that cannot be "book taught." Examiners gain this talent from years of looking at raw disk data. Regardless, even the most efficient and skilled of carvers will turn to their automated carving tools. Two things that the carving tools excel at is carving out images and print spool files (EMFs). What are they really bad at? The tools I use don't even begin to work properly to carve out email files. General regular program (GREP) searching doesn't provide for branching logic, so you can't locate a qualified email header, every single time, and capture the end of it. The best you can do is create your own script to carve out the emails. GREP does not allow for any sort of true logic that would be useful or even efficient at capturing something as complex as the many variations of email headers that exist, but it does allow for many alterations of a single search term to be formulated with a single expression. For example, the words *house, housing, houses,* and *housed* could all be searched for with a single statement such as "hous[(e)|(es)|(ing)|(ed)]". GREP can be useful, but it is not really a shortcut. Each option added to a GREP statement doubles the length of time the search will take to run. Searching for *house(s)* has the same run time as two separate keywords for *house* and *houses*. It also allows for efficient pattern matching. For example, if you wanted to find all the phone numbers on a computer for three particular area codes, you could formulate a GREP expression like this. Using a test file and running the search each time, an expression can be built that finds phone numbers in any of three area codes:

> (708)|(312)|(847) *Checks for the three area codes*
> [\(]?(708)|(312)|(847)[\-\)\.]? *Checks for parentheses and other formatting*
> [\(]?(708)|(312)|(847)[\-\)\.]?###[\-\.]?#### *Checks for the rest of the number*

This statement will find any 10-digit string that is formatted like a phone number, as well as any 10-digit string that contains one of the three area codes. This last option, to check for any 10-digit number string, if run against an entire OS, will likely return numerous results that aren't phone numbers. The question marks render the search for phone number formatting optional.

The following are the characters that are used to formulate a GREP expression. Typically, the best use of GREP is its ability to formulate pattern-matching searches. In GREP, the following symbols are used to formulate an expression:

- · The period is a wildcard and means a space must be occupied by any character.
- * The asterisk is a wildcard that means any character or no character. It will match multiple repetitions of the character as well.
- ? The character preceding the question mark must repeat 0 or 1 times. It provides instructions as to how to search for the character or grouping that precedes it.

- + This is like the question mark, only it *must* exist at least one or more times.
- # Matches a number.
- [·] Matches a list of characters. *[hH]i* matches *hi* and *Hi* (but not *hHi!*).
- ∧ This is a "not" and will exclude a part from a string.
- [-] A range of characters such as (a-z) will find any single letter, a through z.
- \ This will escape the standard GREP search symbols so that it may be included as part of the search. For example, a search string that has the (symbol in it (such as a phone number) needs to have the parentheses escaped so that the string can be included as part of the search.
- | This is an "or." See previous sample search for area codes.
- \x Searches for the indicated hex string.

By preceding a hex character with \x marks the next two characters as hexadecimal characters. Using this to locate a known hex string is more efficient than relying on it to be interpreted from Unicode or UTF.

Most forensic applications have stock scripts included that can carve for you. Many of the popular computer forensics applications can carve for you. They have scripted modules that will run, and all you have to do is select the signature you want and *voilá*, it carves it right out of the unallocated clusters for you. Sounds pretty slick, and it is slick—when it works. The problem is that some files, such as MPEG video, don't have a set signature at the beginning and end of each file. So how can we carve them? Running an MPEG carver will make a mess. It's a far better thing to do a "carve" by locating MPEG data, highlighting it, exporting it to a file, and giving it an MPEG extension.

Things to Know: How Time stamps Work

Let's take an example: Bob in accounting has been discovered to be pilfering from the cash box. A forensics examiner is called in to examine his computer system to see if he has been engaging in any activities that would be against company policy and to see if he has been accessing areas of the network that he shouldn't be. They want to know what he has been working on. A quick examination of his PC turns up a very large cache of pornography. A casual glance at the Entry Modified time stamp shows that the images were created nearly one year before Bob's employment, so automatically the investigator disregards the images and moves onto his search for evidence of copying and deleting sensitive files to his local machine. The investigator begins to look at the deleted files. His view is filtered, so he is not looking at anything but deleted files. He leaves the view in "gallery" view so that he can see telltale images that may give clues as to any Web sites used during the timeframe of the suspected breaches. To his surprise, the investigator begins seeing images from that porn cache. He notices now that when a deleted file is overwritten, in the gallery view of the software the image that overwrote the deleted file is displayed. He makes the logical conclusion that the Entry Modified time stamp is somehow wrong.

On a Windows XP machine, an archive file is extracted. Entry Modified time stamps are xx:xx:xx, even though the archive was extracted to the file system on yy:yy:yy. Normally when a file is created on a system, it takes on the system date as its Date Created time stamp. Such is not the case with zip files.

Entry Modified, in the world of computer forensics, is that illustrious time stamp that has cinched many a case. It is a hidden time stamp that users never see, and few of them actually know about it. As such, they cannot change it. A very little-known fact about the Entry Modified time stamp is that it is constrained. It can be no later than the Date Created time stamp. (This is not true in Vista.)

When a zip file is created, the Date Created and Date Modified time stamps become the same.

Experimental Evidence

Examining and understanding how time stamps behave on individual PCs and operating systems provide some of the greatest challenges facing forensic examiners. This is not due to any great difficulty, but rather because of the difficulty in clearly explaining it to others. This examiner once read a quote from a prosecutor in a local newspaper that said, "We will clearly show that he viewed the image on three separate occasions." In court the defense's expert disabused her of the notion she held that Last Written, Last Accessed, Entry Modified, and Date Created time stamps were convenient little recordings of user activity. Rather, they are references mostly used by the operating system for its own arcane purposes. Table 19.1 compares the three known Windows time stamps with the four time stamps in EnCase.

XP

A zip file was created using a file with a Date Created time stamp of 12/23/07 10:40:53AM (see ID 1 in Table 19.2). It was then extracted and the time stamps were examined.

Using Windows XP compressed folders, the file was then extracted to a separate file on a different system (ID 2 in Table 19.2). Date Created and Entry Modified time stamps, upon extraction, inherited the original Date Created time stamp of 12/23/07 10:40:53AM and Last Accessed of 04/28/08 01:56:07PM.

TABLE 19.1 Comparison of Three Known Windows Time stamps with the Four EnCase Time stamps

Windows	EnCase	Purpose
Date Created	Date Created	Typically this is the first time a file appeared on a system. It is not always accurate.
Date Modified	Last Written	Usually this is the time when a system last finished writing or changing information in a file.
Last Accessed	Last Accessed	This time stamp can be altered by any number of user and system actions. It should not be interpreted as the file having been opened and viewed.
N/A	Entry Modified	This is a system pointer that is inaccessible to users through the Explorer interface. It changes when the file changes size.

TABLE 19.2 Date Created Time stamp

ID	Name	Last Accessed	File Created	Entry Modified
1	*IMG_3521.CR2*	*04/28/08 01:56:07PM*	**12/23/07 10:40:53AM**	*03/15/08 09:11:15AM*
2	IMG_3521.CR2	04/28/08 01:56:07PM	**12/23/07 10:40:53AM**	04/28/08 01:57:12PM

TABLE 19.3 Altering the Entry Modified Time stamp

ID	Name	Last Accessed	File Created	Entry Modified
1	IMG_3521.CR2	04/28/08 01:56:07PM	12/23/07 10:40:53AM	03/15/08 09:11:15AM
2	IMG_3521.CR2	05/21/08 03:32:01PM	12/23/07 10:40:53AM	05/21/08 03:32:01PM

The system Entry Modified (not to be confused with Date Modified) became 04/28/08 01:57:12PM.

Various operating systems can perform various operations that will, *en masse*, alter the Entry Modified time stamp (see Table 19.3). For example, a tape restoration of a series of directories will create a time stamp adjustment in Entry Modified that corresponds to the date of the restoration. The original file is on another system somewhere and is inaccessible to the investigator (because he doesn't know about it).

In Table 19.3, Entry Modified becomes a part of a larger pattern of time stamps after an OS event. On a computer on which most of the time stamps have an Entry Modified time stamp that is sequential to a specific timeframe, it is now more difficult to determine when the file actually arrived on the system. As long as the date stamps are not inherited from the overwriting file by the overwritten file, examining the files that were overwritten by ID2 (Table 19.3), can reveal a No Later Than time. In other words, the file could not have appeared on the system prior to the file that it overwrote.

Vista

A zip file was created using a file with a Date Created time stamp of dd:mm:yyyy(a) and a date modified of dd:mm:yy(a). Using Windows Vista compressed folders, the file was then extracted to a separate file on the same system. Date Modified time stamps, on extraction, inherited the original time stamp of dd:mm:yyyy(a), but the Date Created time stamp reflected the true date. This is a significant change from XP. There are also tools available that will allow a user to mass-edit time stamps. Forensic examiners must always bear in mind that there are some very savvy users who research and understand antiforensics.

Email Headers and Time stamps, Email Receipts, and Bounced Messages

There is much confusion in the ediscovery industry and in computer forensics in general about how best to interpret email time stamps. Though it might not offer the perfect "every case" solution, this section reveals the intricacies of dealing with time stamps and how to interpret them correctly.

Regarding sources of email, SMTP has to relay email to its own domain. HELO/EHLO allows a user to connect to the SMTP port and send email.

As most of us are aware, in 2007 the U.S. Congress enacted the Energy Policy Act of 2005 (http://www.epa.gov/oust/fedlaws/publ_109-058.pdf, Section 110. Daylight Savings). This act was passed into law by President George W. Bush on August 8, 2005. Among other provisions, such as subsidies for wind energy, reducing air pollution, and providing tax breaks to homeowners for making energy-conserving changes to their homes, it amended the Uniform Time Act of 1966 by changing the start and end dates for Daylight Savings Time (DST) beginning in 2007. Previously, clocks would be set ahead by an hour on the first Sunday of April and set back on the last Sunday of October. The new law changed this as follows: Starting in 2007 clocks were set ahead one hour on the first Sunday of March and then set back on the first Sunday in November. Aside from the additional confusion now facing everyone when we review email and attempt to translate Greenwich Mean Time (GMT) to a sensible local time, probably the only true noteworthy aspect of this new law is the extra daylight time afforded to children trick-or-treating on Halloween. Many observers have questioned whether or not the act actually resulted in a net energy savings.

In a world of remote Web-based email servers, it has been observed that some email sent through a Web mail interface will bear the time stamp of the time zone wherein the server resides. Either your server is in the Central Time zone or the clock on the server is set to the wrong time/time zone. Servers that send email mark the header of the email with the GMT stamp numerical value (noted in bold in the example that follows) as opposed to the actual time zone stamp. For example, instead of saying 08:00 CST, the header will say 08:00 (-0600). The GMT differential is used so that every email client interprets that stamp based on the time zone and time setting of itself and is able to account for things like Daylight Savings Time offsets. This is a dynamic interpretation; if I change the time zone of my computer, it will change the way Outlook *shows* me the time of each email, but it doesn't actually physically change the email itself. For example, if an email server is located in Colorado, every email I send appears to have been sent from the Mountain Time zone. My email client interprets the Time Received of an email based on when my server received the mail, *not* when my email client downloads the email from my server.

If a server is in the Central Time zone and the client is in Mountain Time, the normal Web mail interface will not be cognizant of the client's time zone. Hence those are the times you'll see. I checked a Webmail account on a server in California that I use and it does the same thing. Here I've broken up the header to show step by step how it moved. Here is, first, the entire header in its original context, followed by a breakdown of how I interpret each transaction in the header:

****

Received: from p01c11m096.mxlogic.net (208.65.144.247) by mail.us.rgl.com
(192.168.0.12) with Microsoft SMTP Server id 8.0.751.0; Fri, 30 Nov 2007
21:03:15 -0700
Received: from unknown [65.54.246.112] (EHLO bay0-omc1-s40.bay0.hotmail.com)
by p01c11m096.mxlogic.net (mxl_mta-5.2.0-1) with ESMTP id 23cd0574.3307895728.120458.00-105.p01c11m096.
mxlogic.net (envelope-from
<timezone32@hotmail.com>); Fri, 30 Nov 2007 20:59:46 -0700 (MST)
Received: from BAY108-W37 ([65.54.162.137]) by bay0-omc1-s40.bay0.hotmail.com
with Microsoft SMTPSVC(6.0.3790.3959); Fri, 30 Nov 2007 19:59:46 -0800
Message-ID: <BAY108-W374BF59F8292A9D2C95F08BA720@phx.gbl>
Return-Path: timezone32@hotmail.com
Content-Type: multipart/alternative; boundary="=_reb-r538638D0-t4750DC32"
X-Originating-IP: [71.212.198.249]
From: Test Account <timezone3@hotmail.com>
To: Bill Nelson <attorney@attorney12345.com>, Scott Ellis <sellis@us.rgl.com>
Subject: FW: Norton Anti Virus
Date: Fri, 30 Nov 2007 21:59:46 -0600
Importance: Normal
In-Reply-To: <BAY108-W26EE80CDDA1C4C632124ABA720@phx.gbl>
References: <BAY108-W26EE80CDDA1C4C632124ABA720@phx.gbl>

MIME-Version: 1.0
X-OriginalArrivalTime: 01 Dec 2007 03:59:46.0488 (UTC) FILETIME=[9CAC5B80:01C833CE]
X-Processed-By: Rebuild v2.0-0
X-Spam: [F=0.0038471784; B=0.500(0); spf=0.500; CM=0.500; S=0.010(2007110801); MH=0.500(2007113048); R=0.276(1071030201529); SC=none; SS=0.500]
X-MAIL-FROM: <timezone3@hotmail.com>
X-SOURCE-IP: [65.54.246.112]
X-AnalysisOut:[v=1.0c=0a=Db0T9Pbbji75CibVOCAA:9 a=rYVTvsE0vOPdh0IEP8MA:]
X-AnalysisOut: [7 a=TaS_S6-EMopkTzdPlCr4MVJL5DQA:4 a=NCG-xuS670wA:10 a=T-0]
X-AnalysisOut:[QtiWyBeMA:10a=r9zUxlSq4yJzxRie7pAA:7 a=EWQMng83CrhB0XWP0h]
X-AnalysisOut: [vbCEdheDsA:4 a=EfJqPEOeqlMA:10 a=37WNUvjkh6kA:10]

****

Looks like a bunch of garbage, right? Here it is, step by step, transaction by transaction, in reverse chronological order:

1. My server in Colorado receives the email (GMT differential is in bold):

   Received: from p01c11m096.mxlogic.net (208.65.144.247) by mail.us.rgl.com
   (192.168.0.12) with Microsoft SMTP Server id 8.0.751.0; Fri, 30 Nov 2007 21:03:15 **-0700**

2. Prior to that, my mail-filtering service in Colorado receives the email:

   Received: from unknown [65.54.246.112] (EHLO bay0-omc1-s40.bay0.hotmail.com)
   by p01c11m096.mxlogic.net (mxl_mta-5.2.0-1) with ESMTP id 23cd0574.3307895728.120458.00-105.p01c11m096.
   mxlogic.net (envelope-from
   <timezone3@hotmail.com>); Fri, 30 Nov 2007 20:59:46 **-0700** *(MST)*

   – The email server receives the sender's email in this next section. On most networks, the mail server is rarely the same machine on which a user created the email. This next item in the header of the email shows that the email server is located in the Pacific Time zone. 65.54.246.112, the x-origin stamp, is the actual IP address of the computer that sent the email:

   Received: from BAY108-W37 ([65.54.162.137]) by bay0-omc1-s40.bay0.hotmail.com
   with Microsoft SMTPSVC(6.0.3790.3959); Fri, 30 Nov 2007 19:59:46 **-0800**

*Message-ID: <BAY108-W374BF59F8292A9D2C95F08B
A720@phx.gbl>*
Return-Path: timezone310@hotmail.com

— This content was produced on the server where the
Webmail application resides. Technically, the email
was created on the Web client application with only
one degree of separation between the originating IP
and the sender IP. By examining the order and type
of IP addresses logged in the header, a trail can be
created that shows the path of mail servers that the
email traversed before arriving at its destination.
This machine is the one that is likely in the Central
Time zone, since it can be verified by the -0600 in
the following. The X-originating IP address is the
IP address of the sender's external Internet connection IP address in her house and the X-Source
IP address is the IP address of the Webmail server
she logged into on this day. This IP address is
also subject to change because they have many
Webmail servers as well. In fact, comparisons to
older emails sent on different dates show that it is
different. Originating IP address is also subject to
change since a DSL or cable Internet is very likely
a dynamic account, but it (likely) won't change as
frequently as the X-source:

*Content-Type: multipart/alternative; boundary="=_reb-
r538638D0-t4750DC32"*
X-Originating-IP: [71.212.198.249]
From: Test Account <@hotmail.com>
*To: Bill Nelson <attorney@attorney12345.com>, Scott
Ellis <sellis@us.rgl.com>*
Subject: FW: Norton Anti Virus
Date: Fri, 30 Nov 2007 21:59:46 -0600
Importance: Normal
*In-Reply-To: <BAY108-W26EE80CDDA1C4C632124ABA
720@phx.gbl>*
*References: <BAY108-W26EE80CDDA1C4C632124ABA7
20@phx.gbl>*
MIME-Version: 1.0
*X-OriginalArrivalTime: 01 Dec 2007 03:59:46.0488
(UTC) FILETIME=[9CAC5B80:01C833CE]*
X-Processed-By: Rebuild v2.0-0
*X-Spam: [F=0.0038471784; B=0.500(0); spf=0.500;
CM=0.500; S=0.010(2007110801); MH=0.500(2007113
048); R=0.276(1071030201529); SC=none; SS=0.500]*
X-MAIL-FROM: <timezone310@hotmail.com>
X-SOURCE-IP: [65.54.246.112]
*X-AnalysisOut:[v=1.0c=0a=Db0T9Pbbji75CibVOCAA:9
a=rYVTvsE0vOPdh0IEP8MA:]*
*X-AnalysisOut:[7a=TaS_S6-EMopkTzdPlCr4MVJL5DQA:4
a=NCG-xuS670wA:10 a=T-0]*

*X-AnalysisOut: [QtiWyBeMA:10 a = r9zUxlSq4yJzxRie7p
AA:7 a = EWQMng83CrhB0XWP0h]*
*X-AnalysisOut: [vbCEdheDsA:4 a = EfJqPEOeqlMA:10
a = 37WNUvjkh6kA:10]*

From: *Test Account [mailto:timezone310@hotmail.com]*
Sent: *Friday, November 30, 2007 10:00 PM*
To: *Bill Nelson; Scott Ellis*
Subject: *FW: Norton Anti Virus*

Bill and Scott,

*By the way, it was 8:57 my time when I sent the last email,
however, my hotmail shows that it was 9:57 pm. Not sure if
their server is on Central time or not. Scott, can you help
with that question? Thanks.*

Anonymous

From: *timezone310@hotmail.com*
To: *attorney@attorney12345.com; sellis@us.rgl.com*
CC: *timezone310@hotmail.com*
Subject: Norton Anti Virus
Date: Fri, 30 Nov 2007 21:57:16 -0600

Bill and Scott,

*I am on the computer now and have a question for you.
Can you please call me?*

Anonymous

Steganography "Covered Writing"

Steganography tools provide a method that allows a
user to hide a file in plain sight. For example, there are a
number of stego software tools that allow the user to hide
one image inside another. Some of these do it by simply
appending the "hidden" file at the tail end of a JPEG file
and then add a pointer to the beginning of the file. The
most common way that steganography is discovered on
a machine is through the detection of the steganography
software on the machine. Then comes the arduous task
of locating 11 of the files that may possibly contain hidden data. Other, more manual stego techniques may be
as simple as hiding text behind other text. In Microsoft
Word, text boxes can be placed right over the top of other
text, formatted in such a way as to render the text undetectable to a casual observer. Forensic tools will allow
the analyst to locate this text, but on opening the file the
text won't be readily visible. Another method is to hide
images behind other images using the layers feature of
some photo enhancement tools, such as Photoshop.

StegAlyzerAS is a tool created by Backbone Security
to detect steganography on a system. It works by both
searching for known stego artifacts as well as by searching

for the program files associated with over 650 steganography toolsets. Steganography hash sets are also available within the NIST database of hash sets. Hash sets are databases of MD5 hashes of known unique files associated with a particular application.

5. FIRST PRINCIPLES

In science, *first principles* refer to going back to the most basic nature of a thing. For example, in physics, an experiment is *ab initio* (from first principles) if it only subsumes a parameterization of known irrefutable laws of physics. The experiment of calculation does not make assumptions through modeling or assumptive logic.

First principles, or *ab initio,* may or may not be something that a court will understand, depending on the court and the types of cases it tries. Ultimately the very best evidence is that which can be easily duplicated. In observation of a compromised system in its live state, even if the observation photographed or videoed may be admitted as evidence but the events viewed cannot be duplicated, the veracity of the events will easily be questioned by the opposition.

During an investigation of a defendant's PC, an examiner found that a piece of software on the computer behaved erratically. This behavior had occurred after the computer had been booted from a restored image of the PC. The behavior was photographed and introduced in court as evidence. The behavior was mentioned during a cross-examination and had not, originally, been intended as use for evidence; it was simply something that the examiner recalled seeing during his investigation, that the list of files a piece of software would display would change. The prosecution was outraged because this statement harmed his case to a great deal. The instability and erratic behavior of the software was one of the underpinnings of the defense. The examiner, in response to the prosecutor's accusations of ineptitude, replied that he had a series of photographs that demonstrated the behavior. The prosecutor requested the photos, but the examiner didn't have them in court. He brought them the next day, at which time, when the jury was not in the room, the prosecutor requested the photos, reviewed them, and promptly let the matter drop.

It would have been a far more powerful thing to have produced the photographs at the time of the statement; but it may have also led the prosecution to an *ab initio* effort—one that may have shown that the defense expert's findings were irreproducible. In an expert testimony, the more powerful and remarkable a piece of evidence, the more likely it is to be challenged by the opposition. It is an intricate game because such a challenge may ultimately destroy the opposition's case, since a corroborative result would only serve to increase the veracity and reliability of the expert's testimony. Whether you are defense, prosecution, or plaintiff, the strongest evidence is that which is irrefutable and relies on first principles. Aristotle defined it as those circumstances where "for the same (characteristic) simultaneously to belong and not belong to the same (object) in the same (way) is impossible." In less obfuscating, 21st-century terms, the following interpretation is applicable: One thing can't be two different things at the same time in the same circumstance; there is only one truth, and it is self-evidentiary and not open to interpretation. For example, when a computer hard drive is imaged, the opposition may also image the same hard drive. If proper procedures are followed, there is no possible way that different MD5 hashes could result. Black cannot be white.

The lesson learned? Never build your foundation on irreproducible evidence. To do so is tantamount to building the case on "circumstantial" evidence.

6. HACKING A WINDOWS XP PASSWORD

There are many, many methods to decrypt or "hack" a Windows password. This section lists some of them. One of the more interesting methods of cracking passwords through the use of forensic methods is hacking the Active Directory. It is not covered here, but suffice it to say that there is an awesome amount of information stored in the Active Directory file of a domain server. With the correct tools and settings in place, Bitlocker locked PCs can be accessed and passwords can be viewed in plaintext with just a few simple, readily available scripts.

Net User Password Hack

If you have access to a machine, this is an easy thing, and the instructions to do it can easily be found on YouTube. Type **net users** at the Windows command line. Pick a user. Type **net user** *username* *. (You have to type the asterisk or it won't work.) You will then, regardless of your privileges, be allowed to change any password, including the local machine administrator password.

Lanman Hashes and Rainbow Tables

- The following procedure can be used to "reverse-engineer" the password from where it is stored in Windows. Lan Manager (or Lanman, or LM) has been used by Windows, in versions prior to Windows Vista, to store passwords that are shorter than 15 characters. The vast majority of passwords are stored in this format. LM hashes are computed via a short series of actions. The following items contribute to the weakness of the hash:

- Password is converted to all uppercase.
- Passwords longer than seven characters are divided into two halves. By visual inspection of the hash, this allows us to determine whether the second half is padding. We can do this by viewing all the LM hashes on a system and observing whether the second halves of any of the hashes are the same. This will speed up the process of decrypting the hash.
- There is no salt. In cryptography, *salt* is random bits that are thrown in to prevent large lookup tables of values from being developed.

Windows will store passwords using the Lanman hash. Windows Vista has changed this. For all versions of Windows except Vista, about 70GB of what are called *rainbow tables* can be downloaded from the Internet. Using a tool such as the many that are found on Backtrack will capture the actual hashes that are stored for the password on the physical disk. Analysis of the hashes will show whether or not the hashes are in use as passwords. Rainbow tables, which can be downloaded from the Web in a single 70GB table, are simply lookup tables of every possible iteration of the hashes. By entering the hash value, the password can be easily and quickly reverse-engineered and access to files can be gained. A favorite method of hackers is to install command-line software on remote machines that will allow access to the Lanman hashes and will send them via FTP to the hacker. Once the hacker has admin rights, he owns the machine.

Password Reset Disk

Emergency Boot CD (EBCD) is a Linux-based tool that allows you to boot a computer that has an unknown password. Using this command-line tool, you can reset the administrator password very easily. It will not tell you the plaintext of the password, but it will clear it so that the machine can be accessed through something like VMware with a blank password.

Memory Analysis and the Trojan Defense

One method of retrieving passwords and encryption keys is through memory analysis—physical RAM. RAM can be acquired using a variety of relatively nonintrusive methods. HBGary.com offers a free tool that will capture RAM with very minimal impact. In addition to extracting encryption keys, RAM analysis can be used to either defeat or corroborate the Trojan defense. The Responder tool from HBGary (single-user license) provides in-depth analysis and reporting on the many malware activities that can be detected in a RAM environment. The Trojan defense is commonly used by innocent and guilty parties to explain unlawful actions that have occurred on their computers. The following items represent a brief overview of the types of things that can be accomplished through RAM analysis:

- A hidden driver is a 100% indicator of a bad guy. Hidden drivers can be located through analysis of the physical memory.
- Using tools such as FileMon, TCPView, and RegMon, you can usually readily identify malware infections. There is a small number of advanced malwares that are capable of doing things such as rolling up completely (poof, it's gone!) when they detect the presence of investigative tools or that are capable of escaping a virtualized host. All the same, when conducting a malware forensic analysis, be sure to isolate the system from the network.
- RAM analysis using a tool such as HBGary's Responder can allow reverse-engineering of the processes that are running and can uncover potential malware behavioral capabilities. As this science progresses, a much greater ability to easily and quickly detect malware can be expected.

User Artifact Analysis

There is nothing worse than facing off against an opposing expert who has not done his artifact analysis on a case. Due to an increasing workload in this field, experts are often taking shortcuts that, in the long run, really make more work for everyone. In life and on computers, the actions people take leave behind artifacts. The following is a short list of artifacts that are readily viewed using any method of analysis:

- Recent files
- OLK files
- Shortcuts
- Temporary Internet Files (TIF)
- My Documents
- Desktop
- Recycle Bin
- Email
- EXIF data

Users create all these artifacts, either knowingly or unknowingly, and aspects of them can be reviewed and understood to indicate that certain actions on the computer took place—for example, a folder in My Documents called "fast trains" that contains pictures of Europe's TGV and surrounding countryside, TIF sites that show the user booking travel to Europe, installed software for a Casio Exilim digital camera, EXIF data that shows the photos were taken with a Casio Exilim, and email confirmations and discussions about the planned trip all work together to show that the user of that account on that PC did very likely take a trip to Europe and did take the photos. Not that there is anything wrong with taking pictures of trains, but if the subject of the investigation is a suspected terrorist and he has ties with a group that was discovered to be planning an attack on a train, this evidence would be very valuable.

It is the sum of the parts that matters the most. A single image of a train found in the user's TIF would be virtually meaningless. Multiple pictures of trains in his TIF could also be meaningless; maybe he likes trains or maybe someone sent him a link that he clicked to take him to a Web site about trains. *It's likely he won't even remember having visited the site.* It is the forensic examiner's first priority to ensure that all the user artifacts are considered when making a determination about any behavior.

Recovering Lost and Deleted Files

Unless some sort of drastic "wiping action" has taken place, as in the use of a third-party utility to delete data or if the disk is part of a RAIDed set, I have almost always found that deleted data is *immediately* available in EnCase (forensic software I use) within 20 to 25 minutes after a hard disk image is mounted. This is especially true when the drive has not been used at all since the time the data was deleted.

Software Installation

Nearly every software installation will offer to drop one on your desktop, in your Start menu, and on your quick launch tool bar at the time of program installation. Whenever a user double-clicks on a file, a link file is created in the Recent folder located at the root of Documents and Settings. This is a hidden file.

Recent Files

In Windows XP (and similar locations exist in other versions), link files are stored in the Recent folder under Documents and Settings. Whenever a user double-clicks on a file, a link file is created. Clicking the Start button in Windows and navigating to the My Recent Documents link will show a list of the last 15 documents that a user has clicked on. What most users don't realize is that the C:\Documents and Settings\$user name$\Recent folder will potentially reveal *hundreds* of documents that have been viewed by the user. This list is indisputably a list of documents that the user has viewed. Interestingly, in Windows 2000, if the Preserve History feature of the Windows Media Player is turned off, no link files will be created. The only way to make any legitimate determination about the use of a file is to view the Last Accessed time, which has been shown in several cases to be inconsistent and unreliable in certain circumstances. Be very careful when using this time stamp as part of your defense or prosecution. It is a loaded weapon, ready to go off.

Start Menu

The Start menu is built on shortcuts. Every item in the Start file has a corresponding .LNK file. Examining Last Accessed or Date Created time stamps may shed light on when software was installed and last used.

Email

Extracting email is an invaluable tool for researching and finding out thoughts and motives of a suspect in any investigation. Email can be extracted from traditional client-based applications such as Outlook Express, Lotus Notes, Outlook, Eudora, and Netscape Mail as well as from common Webmail apps such as Gmail, Hotmail, Yahoo Mail, and Excite. Reviewing log files from server-based applications such as Outlook Webmail can show a user, for example, accessing and using his Webmail after employment termination. It is important that companies realize that they should terminate access to such accounts the day a user's employment is terminated.

Internet History

Forensic analysis of a user's Internet history can reveal much useful information. It can also show the exact code that may have downloaded on a client machine and resulted in an infection of the system with a virus. Forensic examiners should actively familiarize themselves with the most recent, known exploits.

Typed URLs is a registry key. It will store the last 10 addresses that a user has typed into a Web browser

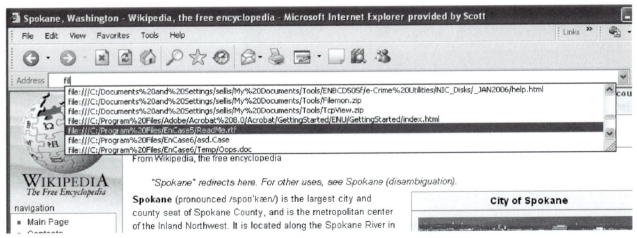

FIGURE 19.4 Spawning a list of URLs that were never typed (the Google one is deleted).

address field. I once had a fed try to say that everything that appeared in the drop-down window was a "typed" URL. This is not the case. The only definitive source of showing the actual typed URLs is the registry key. Just one look at the screen shown in Figure 19.4 should clearly demonstrate that the user never would have "typed" all these entries. Yet that is exactly what a Department of Homeland Security Agent sat on the witness stand and swore, under oath, was true. In Figure 19.4, simply typing in **fil** spawns a list of URLs that were never typed but rather are the result of either the user having opened a file or a program having opened one. The highlighted file entered the history shown as a result of installing the software, not as a result of the user "typing" the filename. Many items in the history wind their way into it through regular software use, with files being accessed as an indirect result of user activity.

7. NETWORK ANALYSIS

Many investigations require a very hands-off approach in which the only forensics that can be collected is network traffic. Every machine is assigned an IP address and a MAC address. It is like an IP address on layer 3, but the MAC address sits on Layer 2. It is quite like a phone number in that it is unique. Software that is used to examine network traffic is categorized as a *sniffer*. Tools such as Wireshark and Colasoft are two examples of sniffers. They can be used to view, analyze, and capture all the IP traffic that comes across a port.

Switches are not promiscuous, however. To view the traffic coming across a switch you can either put a hub in line with the traffic (between the target and the switch) and plug the sniffer into the hub with it, or ports can be spanned. Spanning, or mirroring, allows one port on a switch to copy and distribute network traffic in a way such that the sniffer can see everything. The argument could be made in court that the wrong port was accidentally spanned, but this argument quickly falls apart because all network packets contain both the machine and IP address of a machine. ARP poisoning is the practice of spoofing another user's IP address, however. This would be the smartest defense, but if a hub is used on a switched port, with the hub wired directly to the port, a greater degree of forensic certainty can be achieved. The only two computers that should be connected to the hub are the examiner and target machines.

Protocols

In the world of IP, the various languages of network traffic that are used to perform various tasks and operations are called *protocols*. Each protocol has its own special way of organizing and forming its packets. Unauthorized protocols viewed on a port are a good example of a type of action that might be expected from a rogue machine or employee. Network sniffing for email (SMTP and POP) traffic and capturing it can, depending on the sniffer used, allow the examiner to view live email traffic coming off the target machine. Viewing the Web (HTTP) protocol allows the examiner to capture images and text from Web sites that the target is navigating, in real time.

Analysis

Once the capture of traffic has been completed, analysis must take place. Colasoft offers a packet analyzer that can carve out and filter out the various types of traffic. A good deal of traffic can be eliminated as just "noise" on the line. Filters can be created that will capture the specific protocols, such as VoIP. Examination of the protocols for protocol obfuscation can (if it is not found) eliminate the possibility that a user has a malware infection, and it can identify a user that is using open ports on the firewall to transmit illicit traffic. They sneak legitimate traffic over open ports, masking their nefarious activities over legitimate ports, knowing that the ports are open. This can be done with whitespace inside of an existing protocol, with HTTP, VoIP, and many others. The thing to look for, which will usually be clearly shown, is something like:

> VOIP > SMTP

This basically means that VOIP is talking to a mail server. This is not normal.[3]

Another thing to look for is protocols coming off a box that isn't purposed for that task. It's all context: who should be doing what with whom. Why is the workstation suddenly popping a DNS server? A real-world example is when a van comes screaming into your neighborhood. Two guys jump out and break down the door of your house and grab your wife and kids and drag them out of the house. Then they come and get you. Seems a little fishy, right? But it is a perfectly normal thing to have happen if the two guys are firemen, the van was a fire truck, and your house is on fire.

8. COMPUTER FORENSICS APPLIED

This section details the various ways in which computer forensics is applied professionally. By no means does this cover the extent to which computer forensics is becoming one of the hottest computer careers. It focuses on the consulting side of things, with less attention to corporate or law enforcement applications. Generally speaking, the average forensic consultant handles a broader variety of cases than corporate or law enforcement disciplines, with a broader applicability.

Tracking, Inventory, Location of Files, Paperwork, Backups, and So On

These items are all useful areas of knowledge in providing consultative advisement to corporate, legal, and law-enforcement clients. During the process of discovery and warrant creation, knowledge of how users store and access data at a very deep level is critical to success.

---

3 M. J. Staggs, FireEye, Network Analysis talk at CEIC 2008.

Testimonial

Even if the work does not involve the court system directly—for example, a technician that provides forensic backups of computers and is certified—you may someday be called to provide discovery in a litigation matter. Subsequently, you may be required to testify.

Experience Needed

In computer forensics, the key to a successful technologist is experience. Nothing can substitute for experience, but a good system of learned knowledge that represents at least the last 10 years is welcome.

Job Description, Technologist

Practitioners must possess extreme abilities in adapting to new situations. The environment is always changing.

Job description:

Senior Forensic Examiner and eDiscovery Specialist
Prepared by Scott R. Ellis, 11/01/2007

- Forensics investigative work which includes imaging hard drives, extracting data and files for ediscovery production, development of custom scripts as required to extract or locate data. On occasion this includes performing detailed analyses of user activity, images, and language that may be of an undesirable, distasteful, and potentially criminal format. For this reason, a manager must be notified immediately upon the discovery of any such materials.
- Creation of detailed reports that lay out findings in a meaningful and understandable format. All reports will be reviewed and OK'd by manager before delivery to clients.
- Use of software tools such as FTK, EnCase, VMware, Recovery for Exchange, IDEA, LAW, and Relativity.
- Processing ediscovery and some paper discovery.
- Be responsive to opportunities for publication such as papers, articles, blog, or book chapter requests. All publications should be reviewed by manager and marketing before being submitted to requestor.
- Use technology such as servers, email, time reporting, and scheduling systems to perform job duties and archive work in client folders.

- Managing lab assets (installation of software, Windows updates, antivirus, maintaining backup strategy, hardware installation, tracking hardware and software inventory).
- Some marketing work
- Work week will be 40 hours per week, with occasional weekends as needed to meet customer deadlines.
- Deposition or testimony as needed.
- Occasional evenings and out of town to accommodate client schedules for forensic investigative work.
- Occasional evenings and out of town to attend seminars, CPE or technology classes as suggested by self or by manager, and marketing events.
- Other technology related duties as may be assigned by manager in the support of the company mission as it relates to technology or forensic technology matters

Job Description Management

A manager in computer forensics is usually a working manager. He is responsible for guiding and developing staff as well as communicating requirements to the executive level. His work duties will typically encompass everything mentioned in the previous description.

Commercial Uses

Archival, ghosting images, dd, recover lost partitions, etc. are all applications of computer forensics at a commercial level. Data recovery embraces a great many of the practices typically attributed to computer forensics. Archival and retrieval of information for any number of purposes, not just litigation, is required as is a forensic level of system knowledge.

Solid Background

To become a professional practitioner of computer forensics, there are three requirements to a successful career. Certainly there are people, such as many who attain certification through law-enforcement agencies, that have skipped or bypassed completely the professional experience or scientific training necessary to be a true computer forensic scientist. That is not to degrade the law-enforcement forensic examiner. His mission is traditionally quite different from that of a civilian, and these pros are frighteningly adept and proficient at accomplishing

their objective, which is to locate evidence of criminal conduct and prosecute in court. Their lack of education in the traditional sense should never lead one to a desultory conclusion. No amount of parchment will ever broaden a mind; the forensic examiner must have a broad mind that eschews constraints and boxed-in thinking.

The background needed for a successful career in computer forensics is much like that of any other except that, as a testifying expert, publication will give greater credence to a testimony than even the most advanced pedigree. The exception would be the computer forensic scientist who holds a Ph. D. and happened to write her doctoral thesis on just the thing that is being called into question on the case. Interestingly, at this time, this author has yet to meet anyone with a Ph. D. (or any university degree for that matter), in computer forensics. We can then narrow down the requirements to these three items. Coincidentally, these are also the items required to qualify as an expert witness in most courts:

- Education
- Programming and Experience
- Publications

The weight of each of these items can vary. To what degree depends on who is asking, but suffice it to say that a deficiency in any area may be overcome by strengths in the other two. The following sections provide a more in-depth view of each requirement.

Education/Certification

A strong foundation at the university level in mathematics and science provides the best mental training that can be obtained in computer forensics. Of course, anyone with an extremely strong understanding of computers can surpass and exceed any expectations in this area. Of special consideration are the following topics. The best forensic examiner has a strong foundation in these areas and can qualify not just as a forensic expert with limited ability to testify as to the functions and specific mechanical abilities of software, but as a computer expert who can testify to the many aspects of both hardware and software.

Understand how database technologies, including MS SQL, Oracle, Access, My SQL, and others, interact with applications and how thin and fat clients interact and transfer data. Where do they store temporary files? What happens during a maintenance procedure? How are indexes built, and is the database software disk aware?

Programming and Experience

Background in computer programming is an essential piece. The following software languages must be understood by any well-rounded forensic examiner:

- Java
- JavaScript
- ASP/.NET
- HTML
- XML
- Visual Basic
- SQL

Develop a familiarity with the purpose and operation of technologies that have not become mainstream but have a devoted cult following. At one time such things as virtualization, Linux, and even Windows lived on the bleeding edge, but from being very much on the "fringe" have steadily become more mainstream.

- If it runs on a computer and has an installed base of greater than 10,000 users, it is worth reviewing.
- Internet technologies should be well understood. JavaScript, Java, HTML, ASP, ASPRX, cold fusion, databases, etc. are all Internet technologies that may end up at the heart of a forensic examiner's investigation.
- Experience. Critical to either establishing oneself in a career as a corporate computer forensic examiner or as a consultant, experience working in the field provides the confidence and knowledge-base needed to successfully complete a forensic examination. From cradle to grave, from the initial interviews with the client to forensic collection, examination, reporting, and testifying, experience will guide every step. No suitable substitute exists. Most forensic examiners come into the career later in life after serving as a network or software consultant. Some arrive in this field after years in law enforcement where almost anyone who can turn on a computer winds up taking some computer forensic training.

Communications

- Computer forensics is entirely about the ability to look at a computer system and subsequently explain, in plain English, the analysis. A typical report may consist of the following sections:
  - Summary
  - Methodology
  - Narrative

  - Healthcare information data on system
  - User access to credit-card numbers
  - Date range of possible breach and order handlers
  - Distinct list of operators
  - Russell and Crist Handlers
  - All other users logged in during Crist/Russel Logins
- Login failures activity coinciding with account activity
- All Users
  - User access levels possible ingress/egress
  - Audit trail
  - Login failures
  - Conclusion
  - Contacts/examiners

Each section either represents actual tables, images, and calculated findings, or it represents judgments, impressions, and interpretations of those findings. Finally, the report should contain references to contacts involved in the investigation. A good report conveys the big picture, and translates findings into substantial knowledge without leaving any trailing questions asked and unanswered. Sometimes findings are arrived at through a complex procedure such as a series of SQL queries. Conclusions that depend on such findings should be as detailed as necessary so that opposing experts can reconstruct the findings without difficulty.

Almost any large company requires some measure of forensic certified staff. Furthermore, the forensic collection and ediscovery field continues to grow. Virtually every branch of law enforcement—FBI, CIA, Homeland Security, and state and local agencies—all use computer forensics to some degree. Accounting firms and law firms of almost any size greater than 20 need certified forensic and ediscovery specialists that can both support their forensic practice areas as well as grow business.

Publications

Publishing articles in well-known trade journals goes a long way toward establishing credibility. The following things are nearly always true:

- A long list of publications not only creates in a jury the perception that the expert possess special knowledge that warrants publication; it also shows the expert's ability to communicate. Articles published on the Internet typically do not count unless they are for well-known publications that have a printed publication as well as an online magazine.

- Publishing in and of itself creates a certain amount of risk. Anything that an expert writes or says or posts online may come back to haunt him in court. Be sure to remember to check, double check, and triple check anything that could be of questionable interpretation.
- When you write, you get smarter. Writing forces an author to conduct research and refreshes the memory on long unused skills.

Getting published in the first place is perhaps the most difficult task. Make contact with publishers and editors at trade shows. Ask around, and seek to make contact and establish relationships with published authors and bloggers. Most important, always seek to gain knowledge and deeper understanding of the work.

9. TESTIFYING AS AN EXPERT

Testifying in court is difficult work. As with any type of performance, the expert testifying must know her material, inside and out. She must be calm and collected and have confidence in her assertions. Often, degrees of uncertainty may exist within a testimony. It is the expert's duty to convey those "gray" areas with clarity and alacrity. She must be able to confidently speak of things in terms of degrees of certainty and clear probabilities, using language that is accessible and readily understood by the jury.

In terms of degrees of certainty, often we find ourselves discussing the "degree of difficulty" of performing an operation. This is usually when judges ask whether or not an operation has occurred through direct user interaction or through an automated, programmatic, or normal maintenance procedure. For example, it is well within the normal operation of complex database software to reindex or compact its tables and reorganize the way the data is arranged on the surface of the disk. It is not, however, within the normal operation of the database program to completely obliterate itself and all its program, help, and system files 13 times over a period of three weeks, all in the time leading up to requests for discovery from the opposition. Such information, when forensically available, will then be followed by the question of "Can we know *who* did it?" And that question, if the files exist on a server where security is relaxed, can be nearly impossible to answer.

Degrees of Certainty

Most computer forensic practitioners ply their trade in civil court. A typical case may involve monetary damages or loss. From a computer forensics point of view, evidence that you have extracted from a computer may be used by the attorneys to establish liability, that the plaintiff was damaged by the actions of the defendant. Your work may be the lynchpin of the entire case. You cannot be wrong. The burden to prove the amount of damages is less stringent once you've established that damage was inflicted, and since a single email may be the foundation for that proof, its provenance should prevail under even the most expert scrutiny. Whether or not the damage was inflicted may become a point of contention that the defense uses to pry and crack open your testimony.

The following sections may prove useful in your answers. The burden of proof will fall on the defense to show that the alleged damages are not accurate. There are three general categories of "truth" that can be used to clarify for a judge, jury, or attorney the weight of evidence. See the section on "Rules of Evidence" for more on things such as relevance and materiality.

Generally True

Generally speaking, something is generally true if under normal and general use the same thing always occurs. For example, if a user deletes a file, generally speaking it will go into the recycle bin. This is not true if:

- The user holds down a Shift key when deleting
- The recycle bin option "Do not move files to the recycle bin. Remove files immediately when deleted," is selected
- An item is deleted from a server share or from another computer that is accessing a local user share

Reasonable Degree of Certainty

If it smells like a fish and looks like a fish, generally speaking, it is a fish. However, without dissection and DNA analysis, there is the possibility that it is a fake, especially if someone is jumping up and down and screaming that it is a fake. Short of expensive testing, one may consider other factors. Where was the fish found? Who was in possession of the fish when it was found? We begin to rely on more than just looking at the fish to see if it is a fish.

Computer forensic evidence is much the same. For example, in an employment dispute, an employee may be accused of sending sensitive and proprietary documents to her personal Webmail account. The employer introduces forensic evidence that the files were sent from her work email account during her period of employment on days when she was in the office.

Pretty straightforward, right? Not really. Let's go back in time to two months before the employee was fired. Let's go back to the day after she got a very bad performance review and left for the day because she was so upset. Everyone knew what was going on, and they knew that her time is limited. Two weeks later she filed an EEOC complaint. The IT manager in this organization, a seemingly mild-mannered, helpful savant, was getting ready to start his own company as a silent partner in competition with his employer. He wanted information. His partners want information in exchange for a 20% stake. As an IT manager, he had administrative rights and could access the troubled employee's email account and began to send files to her Webmail account. As an IT administrator, he had system and network access that would easily allow him to crack her Webmail account and determine the password. All he had to do was spoof her login page and store it on a site where he could pick it up from somewhere else. If he was particularly interested in keeping his own home and work systems free of the files, he could wardrive her house, hack her home wireless (lucky him, it is unsecured), and then use terminal services to access her home computer, log into her Webmail account (while she is home), and view the files to ensure that they appear as "read." This scenario may seem farfetched but it is not; this is not hard to do.

For anyone with the IT manager's level of knowledge, lack of ethics, and opportunity, this is likely the *only* way that he would go about stealing information. There is no other way that leaves him so completely out of the possible running of suspects.

There is no magic wand in computer forensics. The data is either there or it isn't, despite what Hollywood says about the subject. If an IT director makes the brash decision to reinstall the OS on a system that has been compromised and later realizes he might want to use a forensic investigator to find out what files were viewed, stolen, or modified, he can't just dial up his local forensics tech and have him pop in over tea, wave his magic wand, and recover all the data that was overwritten. Here is the raw, unadulterated truth: If you have 30GB of unallocated clusters and you copy the DVD *Finding Nemo* onto the drive until the disk is full, nobody (and I really mean this), *nobody* will be able to extract a complete file from the unallocated clusters. Sure, they might find a couple of keyword hits in file slack and maybe, just maybe, if the stars align and Jupiter is in retrograde and Venus is rising, maybe they can pull a tiny little complete file out of the slack or out of the MFT. Small files, less than 128 bytes, are stored directly in the MFT

and won't ever make it out to allocated space. This can be observed by viewing the $MFT file.

When making the determination "reasonable degree of forensic certainty," *all* things must be considered. Every possible scenario that could occur must flash before the forensic practitioner's eyes until only the most reasonable answer exists, an answer that is supported by all the evidence, not just part of it. This is called *interpretation*, and it is a weigh of whether or not a preponderance of evidence actually exists. The forensic expert's job is not to decide whether a preponderance of evidence exists. His job is to fairly, and truthfully, present the facts and his interpretation of the individual facts. Questions an attorney might ask a computer forensics practitioner on the stand:

- Did the user delete the file?
- Could someone else have done it?
- Could an outside process have downloaded the file to the computer?
- Do you know for certain how this happened?
- Did you see Mr. Smith delete the files?
- How do you know he did?
- Isn't it true, Mr. Expert, that you are being paid to be here today?

These are not "Yes or no" questions. Here might be the answers:

- I'm reasonably certain he did.
- Due to the security of this machine, it's very unlikely that someone else did it.
- There is evidence to strongly indicate that the photos were loaded to the computer from a digital camera, not the Internet.
- I am certain, without doubt, that the camera in Exhibit 7a is the same camera that was used to take these photos and that these photos were loaded to the computer while username CSMITH was logged in.
- I have viewed forensic evidence that strongly suggests that someone with Mr. Smith's level of access and permissions to this system did, in fact, delete these files on 12/12/2009.
- I'm not sure I didn't just answer that.
- I am an employee of The Company. I am receiving my regular compensation and today is a normal workday for me.

Be careful, though. Reticence to answer in a yes-or-no fashion may be interpreted by the jury as uncertainty. If certainty exists, say so. But it is always better to be honest and admit uncertainty than to attempt to inflate one's own ego by expressing certainty where none

TABLE 19.4 Example of a Forensic View of Files Showing Some Alteration or Masking of Dates

Filename	Date Created	File Properties	Original Path
Kitty.jpg	5/12/2007	File, Archive	
summaryReport.doc	7/12/2007	File, Deleted, Overwritten	Kitty.jpg
Marketing_flyer.pdf	2/12/2008	File, Deleted, Overwritten	Kitty.jpg

exists. Never worry about the outcome of the case. You can't care about the outcome of the trial. Guilt or innocence cannot be a factor in your opinion. You must focus on simply answering the questions in front of you that demand to be answered.

Certainty without Doubt

Some things on a computer can happen only in one fashion. For example, if a deleted item is found in the recycle bin, there are steps that must be taken to ensure that "it is what it is":

- Was the user logged in at the time of deletion?
- Are there link files that support the use or viewing of the file?
- Was the user with access to the user account at work that day?
- What are the permissions on the folder?
- Is the deleted file in question a system file or a user-created file located in the user folders?
- Is the systems administrator beyond reproach or outside the family of suspects?

If all of these conditions are met, you may have arrived at certainty without doubt. Short of reliable witnesses paired with physical evidence, it is possible that there will always be other explanations, that uncertainty to some degree can exist. It is the burden of the defense and the plaintiff to understand and resolve these issues and determine if, for example, hacker activity is a plausible defense. I have added the stipulation of reliable witnesses because, in the hands of a morally corrupt forensic expert with access to the drive and a hex editor, a computer can be undetectably altered. Files can be copied onto a hard drive in a sterile manner that, to most trained forensic examiners, could appear to be original. Even advanced users are capable of framing the evidence in such a way as to render the appearance of best evidence, but a forensic examination may lift the veil of uncertainty and show that data has been altered, or

that something *isn't quite right*. For example, there are certain conditions that can be examined that can show with certainty that the time stamps on a file have been somehow manipulated or are simply incorrect, and it is likely that the average person seeking to plant evidence will not know these tricks (see Table 19.4). The dates on files that were overwritten may show that "old" files overwrote newer files. This is impossible.

As shown here, the file kitty.jpg overwrites files that appear to have been created on the system after it. Such an event may occur when items are copied from a CD-ROM or unzipped from a zip file.

10. BEGINNING TO END IN COURT

In most courts in the world, the accuser goes first and then the defense presents its case. This is for the very logical reason that if the defense goes first, nobody would know what they are talking about. The Boulder Bar has a Bar manual located at www.boulder-bar.org[4] that provides a more in-depth review of the trial process than can be presented here. Most states and federal rules are quite similar, but nothing here should be taken as legal advice; review the rules for yourself for the courts where you will be testifying. The knowledge isn't necessary, but the less that you seem to be a fish out of water, the better. This section *does not* replace true legal advice, it is strictly intended for the purpose of education. The manual located at the Boulder Bar Web site was created for a similar reason that is clearly explained on the site. The manual there was specifically developed without any "legalese," which makes it very easy to understand.

Defendants, Plaintiffs, and Prosecutors

When someone, an individual or an organization, decides it has a claim of money or damages against another individual or entity, they file a claim in court.

---

4 Boulder Bar, www.boulder-bar.org/bar_media/index.html.

The group filing the claim is the plaintiff, the other parties are the defendants. Experts may find themselves working for strictly defendants, strictly plaintiffs, or a little bit of both. In criminal court, charges are "brought" by an indictment, complaint, information, or a summons and complaint.

Pretrial Motions

Prior to the actual trial, there may be many, many pretrial motions and hearings. When a motion is filed, such as when the defense in a criminal case is trying to prevent certain evidence from being seen or heard by the jury, a hearing is called and the judge decides whether the motion has any merit. In civil court, it may be a hearing to decide whether the defense has been deleting, withholding, or committing other acts of discovery abuse. Computer forensic practitioners will find that they may be called to testify at any number of hearings prior to the trial, and then they may not be needed at the trial at all, or the defense and plaintiff may reach a settlement and there will be no trial at all.

Trial: Direct and Cross-Examination

Assuming that there is no settlement or plea agreement, a case will go to trial. The judge will first ask the prosecutor or plaintiff whether they want to make an opening statement. Then the defense will be asked. Witnesses will be called, and if it is the first time appearing in the particular trial as an expert, the witness will be qualified, as discussed in a moment. The party putting on the witness will conduct a direct examination and the other side will very likely cross-examine the witness afterward. Frequently the two sides will have reviewed the expert report and will ask many questions relating directly to it. "Tricks" may be pulled by either attorney at this point. Certain prosecutors have styles and techniques that are used in an attempt to either rattle the expert's cage or simply intimidate him into a state of nervousness so that he will appear uncertain and unprepared. These prosecutors are not interested in justice. They are interested in winning because their career rotates around their record of wins/losses.

Rebuttal

After a witness has testified and undergone direct examination and cross-examination, the other side may decide to bring in an expert to discuss or refute. The defendant may then respond to the prosecution's witness in *rebuttal*. In criminal court, when the state or the government (sometimes affectionately referred to by defense attorneys as "The G") brings a case against an individual or organization, the attorneys that prosecute the case are called the state's attorney, district attorney, assistant U.S. attorney (AUSA), or simply prosecutor.

Surrebuttal

This is the plaintiff (or prosecutor's!) response to rebuttal. Typically the topics of surrebuttal will be limited to those topics that are broached in rebuttal, but the rules for this are probably best left to attorneys to decipher; this author has occasionally been asked questions that should have been deemed outside the bounds of the rebuttal. This could most likely be attributed to a lack of technical knowledge on the part of the attorneys involved in the case.

Testifying: Rule 702. Testimony by Experts

Rule 702 is a federal rule of civil procedure that governs expert testimony. The judge is considered the "gatekeeper," and she alone makes the decision as to whether or not the following rule is satisfied:

> *If scientific, technical, or other specialized knowledge will assist the trier of fact to understand the evidence or to determine a fact in issue, a witness qualified as an expert by knowledge, skill, experience, training, or education, may testify thereto in the form of an opinion or otherwise, if (1) the testimony is based upon sufficient facts or data, (2) the testimony is the product of reliable principles and methods, and (3) the witness has applied the principles and methods reliably to the facts of the case (U.S. Courts, Federal Rules of Evidence, Rule 702).*

There are certain rules for qualifying as an expert. In court, when an expert is presented, both attorneys may question the expert on matters of background and expertise. This process is referred to as *qualification* and, if an "expert" does not meet the legal definition of expert, he may not be allowed to testify. This is a short bullet list of items that will be asked in qualifying as an expert witness:

- How long have you worked in the field?
- What certifications do you hold in this field?
- Where did you go to college?
- Did you graduate? What degrees do you have?
- What are your publications?

You may also be asked if you have testified in other proceedings. It is important to always be honest when on the stand. Perjury is a very serious crime and can result in jail time. All forensics experts should familiarize themselves with Federal Rules 701–706 as well as understand the purpose, intent, and results of a successful *Daubert* challenge, wherein an expert's opinion or the expert himself may be challenged and, if certain criteria are met, may have his testimony thrown out. It is accepted and understood that experts may have reasonably different conclusions given the same evidence.

When testifying, stay calm (easier said than done). If you've never done it, approaching the bench and taking the witness stand may seem like a lot of fun. In a case where a lot is on the line and it all depends on the expert's testimony, nerves will shake and cages will be rattled. The best advice is to stay calm. Drink a lot of water. Drinking copious amounts of water will, according to ex-Navy Seal Mike Lukas, dilute the affect of adrenalin in the bloodstream.

Testifying in a stately and austere court of law may seem like it is the domain of professors and other ivory tower enthusiasts. However, it is something that pretty much anyone can do that has a valuable skill to offer, regardless of educational background. Hollywood often paints a picture of the expert witness as a consummate professorial archetype bent on delivering "just the facts." It is true that expert witnesses demand top dollar in the consulting world. Much of this is for the reason that a great deal is at stake once the expert takes the stand. There is also a very high inconvenience factor. When on the stand for days at a time, one can't simply take phone calls, respond to emails, or perform other work for other clients. There is a certain amount of business interruption that the fees must make up for somehow.

Testifying is interesting. Distilling weeks of intense, technical investigation into a few statements that can be understood by everyone in the courtroom is no small task. It is a bit nerve wracking, and one can expect to have high blood pressure and overactive adrenalin glands for the day. Drinking lots of water will ease the nerves better than anything (nonpharmaceutical). It can have other side effects, however, but it is better to be calm and ask the judge for a short recess as needed than to have shaky hands and a trembling voice from nerves. Caffeine is a bad idea.

Correcting Mistakes: Putting Your Head in the Sand

The interplay of examiner and expert in the case of computer forensics can be difficult. Often the forensic examiner can lapse into speech and explanations that are so commonplace to her that she doesn't realize she is speaking fluent geek-speak. The ability to understand how she sounds to someone who doesn't understand technology must be cultivated. Practice by explaining to any six-year-old what it is you do.

Direct Testimony

Under direct questioning, your attorney will ask questions to which you will know the answer. A good expert will, in fact, have prepared a list of questions and reviewed the answers with the attorney and explained the context and justification for each question thoroughly. If it is a defense job, you will likely go first and testify as to what your investigation has revealed. Avoid using big words and do make some eye contact with the jury if you feel you need to explain something to them, but generally speaking, you should follow the attorney's lead. If she wants you to clarify something for the jury, you should do so, and at that time you should look at the jury. Generally, the rule of thumb is to look at the attorney who asked you the question. If the judge says, "Please explain to the jury . . ." then by all means, look at the jury.

Cross-Examination

The purpose of a cross-examination is to get the testifying expert to make a mistake or to discredit him. Sometimes (rarely) it is actually used to further understand and clarify things that were discussed in direct. In most cases, the attorney will do this by asking you questions about your experience or about the testimony the expert gave under direct. But there is another tactic that attorneys use. They ask a question that is completely unrelated to the topic you talked about. They know that the vast majority of time you spend is on the issues in your direct. For example, you may give a testimony about Last Accessed time stamps. Your entire testimony may be about Last Accessed time stamps. It may be the only issue in the case you are aware of. Then, on cross, the attorney asks a question about the behavior of the mail icon that appears on each line next to the subject line in an email. "Great," the expert thinks. "They recognize my expertise and are asking questions."

Stop. They are about to ask you an arcane question about a behavior in a piece of software in the hopes that you are overconfident and will answer from the hip and get the answer wrong. Because if you get this wrong, then everything else you said must be wrong, too. *Whenever* you are asked a question that does not relate to your previous testimony, pause. Pause for a long time. Give your attorney time to object. He might not know that he should object, but the fact is that you might get the answer wrong and even if there is no doubt in your mind that you know the answer, you should respond that you had not prepared to answer that question and would like to know more details. For example, what is the version of the software? What is the operating system? What service pack? If it is Office, what Office service pack? You need to make it clear that you need more information before you answer the question because, frankly, if the opposition goes down this road, they will try to turn *whatever* you say into the wrong answer.

As a forensic examiner, you may find yourself thinking that the reason they are asking these questions in such a friendly manner is because they forgot to ask their own expert and are trying to take advantage of your time because possibly this came up in a later conversation. This could very well be the case. Maybe the counselor is not trying to trip up the expert. Maybe the Brooklyn Bridge *can* be purchased for a dollar, too.

What is the best response to a question like this? If you give it a 10 count and your attorney hasn't objected, and the asking attorney has not abandoned the question, you may have to answer. There are many schools of thought on this. It is best to understand that a number of responses can facilitate an answer to difficult questions. One such response might be, "That is not really a forensics question" (if it's not), or "I'm not sure how that question relates back to the testimony I just gave."

Or, if it is a software question, you can say, "Different software behaves differently, and I don't think I can answer that question without more details. I don't typically memorize the behavior of every piece of software, and I'm afraid that if I answer from memory I may not be certain." At the end of the day, the expert should only speak to what he knows *with certainty*. There is very little room for error. Attorneys can back-pedal a certain amount to "fix" a mistake, but a serious mistake can follow you for a very long time and can hamper future testimony. For example, if you make statements about time stamps in one trial, and then in the next trial you make statements that interpret them differently, there is a good chance that the opposition will use this against you.

Fortunately, when computer forensic experts testify in a defense trial, the testimony can last a number of hours. Great care is usually taken by the judge to ensure that understanding of all the evidence is achieved. This can create a very long transcript that is difficult to read, understand, and recall with accuracy. For this reason, rarely will bits and pieces of testimony be used against a testifying expert in a future trial. This is not, of course, to say that it can't or won't happen.

It is important, in terms of both setting expectations and understanding legal strategy, for an expert witness to possess passable knowledge of the trial process. Strong familiarity with the trial process can benefit both the expert and the attorneys as well as the judge and the court reporter.

## Chapter 20

Network Forensics

Yong Guan
Iowa State University

Today's cyber criminal investigator faces a formidable challenge: tracing network-based cyber criminals. The possibility of becoming a victim of cyber crime is the number-one fear of billions of people. This concern is well founded. The findings in the annual *CSI/ FBI Computer Crime and Security Surveys* confirm that cyber crime is real and continues to be a significant threat. Traceback and attribution are performed during or after cyber violations and attacks, to identify where an attack originated, how it propagated, and what computer(s) and person(s) are responsible and should be held accountable. The goal of network forensics capabilities is to determine the path from a victimized network or system through any intermediate systems and communication pathways, back to the point of attack origination or the person who is accountable. In some cases, the computers launching an attack may themselves be compromised hosts or be controlled remotely. *Attribution* is the process of determining the identity of the source of a cyber attack. Types of attribution can include both digital identity (computer, user account, IP address, or enabling software) and physical identity (the actual person using the computer from which an attack originated).

Cyber crime has become a painful side effect of the innovations of computer and Internet technologies. With the growth of the Internet, cyber attacks and crimes are happening every day and everywhere. It is very important to build the capability to trace and attribute attacks to the real cyber criminals and terrorists, especially in this large-scale human-built networked environment.

In this chapter, we discuss the current network forensic techniques in cyber attack traceback. We focus on the current schemes in IP spoofing traceback and stepping-stone attack attribution. Furthermore, we introduce the traceback issues in Voice over IP, Botmaster, and online fraudsters.

1. SCIENTIFIC OVERVIEW

With the phenomenal growth of the Internet, more and more people enjoy and depend on the convenience of its provided services. The Internet has spread rapidly almost all over the world. Up to December 2006, the Internet had been distributed to over 233 countries and world regions and had more than 1.09 billion users.[1] Unfortunately, the wide use of computers and the Internet also opens doors to cyber attackers. There are different kinds of attacks that an end user of a computer or Internet can meet. For instance, there may be various viruses on a hard disk, several backdoors open in an operating system, or a lot of phishing emails in an emailbox. According to the annual *Computer Crime Report* of the Computer Security Institute (CSI) and the U.S. Federal Bureau of Investigation (FBI), released in 2006, cyber attacks cause massive money losses each year.

However, the FBI/CSI survey results also showed that a low percentage of cyber crime cases have been reported to law enforcement (in 1996, only 16%; in 2006, 25%), which means that in reality, the vast majority of cyber criminals are never caught or prosecuted. Readers may ask why this continues to happen. Several factors contribute to this fact:

- In many cases, businesses are often reluctant to report and publicly discuss cyber crimes related to them. The concern of negative publicity becomes the number-one reason because it may attract other cyber attackers, undermine the confidence of customers, suppliers, and investors, and invite the ridicule of competitors.
- Generally, it is much harder to detect cyber crimes than crimes in the physical world. There are

---

1 Internet World Stats, www.internetworldstats.com.

various antiforensics techniques that can help cyber criminals evade detection, such as information-hiding techniques (steganography, covert channels), anonymity proxies, stepping stones, and botnets. Even more challenging, cyber criminals are often insiders or employees of the organizations themselves.

- Attackers may walk across the boundaries of multiple organizations and even countries. To date, the lack of effective solutions has significantly hindered efforts to investigate and stop the rapidly growing cyber criminal activities. It is therefore crucial to develop a forensically sound and efficient solution to track and capture these criminals.

Here we discuss the basic principles and some specific forensic techniques in attributing real cyber criminals.

2. THE PRINCIPLES OF NETWORK FORENSICS

Network forensics can be generally defined as a science of discovering and retrieving evidential information in a networked environment about a crime in such a way as to make it admissible in court. Different from intrusion detection, all the techniques used for the purpose of network forensics should satisfy both legal and technical requirements. For example, it is important to guarantee whether the developed network forensic solutions are practical and fast enough to be used in high-speed networks with heterogeneous network architecture and devices. More important, they need to satisfy general forensics principles such as the rules of evidence and the criteria for admissibility of novel scientific evidence (such as the *Daubert* criteria).[2,3,4] The five rules are that evidence must be:

- *Admissible*. Must be able to be used in court or elsewhere.
- *Authentic*. Evidence relates to incident in relevant way.
- *Complete*. No tunnel vision, exculpatory evidence for alternative suspects.
- *Reliable*. No question about authenticity and veracity.
- *Believable*. Clear, easy to understand, and believable by a jury.

---

2 G. Palmer, "A road map for digital forensic research," Digital Forensic Research Workshop (DFRWS), Final Report, Aug. 2001.

3 C. M. Whitcomb, "An historical perspective of digital evidence: A forensic scientist's view," IJDE, 2002.

4 S. Mocas, "Building theoretical underpinnings for digital forensics research," Digital Investigation, Vol. 1, pp. 61–68, 2004.

The evidence and the investigative network forensics techniques should satisfy the criteria for admissibility of novel scientific evidence (*Daubert v. Merrell*):

- Whether the theory or technique has been reliably tested
- Whether the theory or technique has been subject to peer review and publication
- What is the known or potential rate of error of the method used?
- Whether the theory or method has been generally accepted by the scientific community

The investigation of a cyber crime often involves cases related to homeland security, corporate espionage, child pornography, traditional crime assisted by computer and network technology, employee monitoring, or medical records, where privacy plays an important role.

There are at least three distinct communities within digital forensics: law enforcement, military, and business and industry, each of which has its own objectives and priorities. For example, prosecution is the primary objective of the law enforcement agencies and their practitioners and is often done after the fact. Military operations' primary objective is to guarantee the continuity of services, which often have strict real-time requirements. Business and industry's primary objectives vary significantly, many of which want to guarantee the availability of services and put prosecution as a secondary objective.

Usually there are three types of people who use digital evidence from network forensic investigations: police investigators, public investigators, and private investigators. The following are some examples:

- Criminal prosecutors. Incriminating documents related to homicide, financial fraud, drug-related records.
- Insurance companies. Records of bill, cost, services to prove fraud in medical bills and accidents.
- Law enforcement officials. Require assistance in search warrant preparation and in handling seized computer equipment.
- Individuals. To support a possible claim of wrongful termination, sexual harassment, or age discrimination.

The primary activities of network forensics are investigative in nature. The investigative process encompasses the following:

- Identification
- Preservation
- Collection

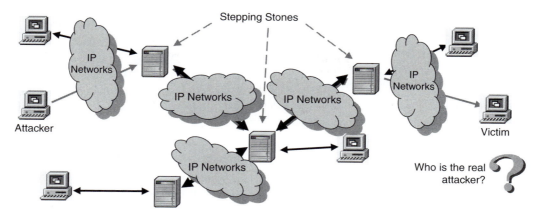

FIGURE 20.1 Stepping-stone attack attribution.

- Examination
- Analysis
- Presentation
- Decision

In the following discussion, we focus on several important network forensic areas.

3. ATTACK TRACEBACK AND ATTRIBUTION

When we face the cyber attacks, we can detect them and take countermeasures. For instance, an intrusion detection system (IDS) can help detect attacks; we can update operating systems to close potential backdoors; we can install antivirus software to defend against many known viruses. Although in many cases we can detect attacks and mitigate their damage, it is hard to find the real attackers/criminals. However, if we don't trace back to the attackers, they can always conceal themselves and launch new attacks. If we have the ability to find and punish the attackers, we believe this will help significantly reduce the attacks we face every day.

Why is traceback difficult in computer networks? One reason is that today's Internet is stateless. There is too much data in the Internet to record it all. For example, a typical router only forwards the passed packets and does not care where they are from; a typical mail transfer agent (MTA) simply relays emails to the next agent and never minds who is the sender. Another reason is that today's Internet is almost an unauthorized environment. Alice can make a VoIP call to Bob and pretend to be Carol; an attacker can send millions of emails using your email address and your mailbox will be bombed by millions of replies. Two kinds of attacks are widely used by attackers and also interesting to researchers all over the world. One is IP spoofing; the other is the stepping-stone attack. Each IP packet header contains the source IP address. Using IP spoofing, an attacker can change the source IP address in the header to that of a different machine and thus avoid traceback.

In a stepping-stone attack, the attack flow may travel through a chain of stepping stones (intermediate hosts) before it reaches the victim. Therefore, it is difficult for the victim to know where the attack came from except that she can see the attack traffic from the last hop of the stepping-stone chain. Figure 20.1 shows an example of IP stepping-stone attack.

Next we introduce the existing schemes to trace back IP spoofing attacks, then we discuss current work on stepping-stone attack attribution.

IP Traceback

Here we review major existing IP traceback schemes that have been designed to trace back to the origin of IP packets through the Internet. We roughly categorize them into four primary classes:

- Active probing[5,6]
- ICMP traceback[7,8,9]

5 H. Burch and B. Cheswick, "Tracing anonymous packets to their approximate source," in *Proceedings of USENIX LISA 2000*, Dec. 2000, pp. 319–327.

6 R. Stone, "Centertrack: An IP overlay network for tracking DoS floods," in *Proceedings of the 9th USENIX Security Symposium*, Aug. 2000, pp. 199–212.

7 S. M. Bellovin, "ICMP traceback messages," Internet draft, 2000.

8 A. Mankin, D. Massey, C.-L. Wu, S. F. Wu, and L. Zhang, "On design and evaluation of 'Intention-Driven' ICMP traceback," in *Proceedings of 10th IEEE International Conference on Computer Communications and Networks*, Oct. 2001.

9 S. F. Wu, L. Zhang, D. Massey, and A. Mankin, "Intention-driven ICMP trace-back," Internet draft, 2001.

- Packet marking[10,11,12,13,14]
- Log-based traceback[15,16,17,18]

Active Probing

Stone[19] proposed a traceback scheme called *CenterTrack*, which selectively reroutes the packets in question directly from edge routers to some special tracking routers. The tracking routers determine the ingress edge router by observing from which tunnel the packet arrives. This approach requires the cooperation of network administrators, and the management overhead is considerably large.

Burch and Cheswick[20] outlined a technique for tracing spoofed packets back to their actual source without relying on the cooperation of intervening ISPs. The victim actively changes the traffic in particular links and observes the influence on attack packets, and thus can determine where the attack comes from. This technique cannot work well on distributed attacks and requires that the attacks remain active during the time period of traceback.

ICMP Traceback (iTrace)

Bellovin[21] proposed a scheme named *iTrace* to trace back using ICMP messages for authenticated IP marking. In this scheme, each router samples (with low probability) the forwarding packets, copies the contents into a special ICMP traceback message, adds its own IP address as well as the IP of the previous and next-hop routers, and forwards the packet to either the source or destination address. By combining the information obtained from several of these ICMP messages from different routers, the victim can then reconstruct the path back to the origin of the attacker.

A drawback of this scheme is that it is much more likely that the victim will get ICMP messages from routers nearby than from routers farther away. This implies that most of the network resources spent on generating and utilizing iTrace messages will be wasted. An enhancement of iTrace, called *Intention-Driven iTrace*, has been proposed.[22,23] By introducing an extra "intention-bit," it is possible for the victim to increase the probability of receiving iTrace messages from remote routers.

Packet Marking

Savage et al.[24] proposed a *Probabilistic Packet Marking* (PPM) scheme. Since then several other PPM-based schemes have been developed.[25,26,27] The baseline idea of PPM is that routers probabilistically write partial path information into the packets during forwarding. If the attacks are made up of a sufficiently large number of packets, eventually the victim may get enough information by combining a modest number of marked packets to reconstruct the entire attack path. This allows victims to locate the approximate source of attack traffic without requiring outside assistance.

10 A. Belenky and N. Ansari, "IP traceback with deterministic packet marking," *IEEE Communications Letters*, Vol. 7, No. 4, pp. 162–164, April 2003.

11 D. Dean, M. Franklin, and A. Stubblefield, "An algebraic approach to IP traceback," *Information and System Security*, Vol. 5, No. 2, pp. 119–137, 2002.

12 K. Park and H. Lee, "On the effectiveness of probabilistic packet marking for IP traceback under denial of service attack," in *Proceedings of IEEE INFOCOM 2001*, Apr. 2001, pp. 338–347.

13 S. Savage, D. Wetherall, A. Karlin, and T. Anderson, "Network support for IP traceback," *IEEE/ACM Transactions on Networking*, Vol. 9, No. 3, pp. 226–237, June 2001.

14 D. Song and A. Perrig, "Advanced and authenticated marking schemes for IP traceback," in *Proceedings of IEEE INFOCOM 2001*, Apr. 2001.

15 J. Li, M. Sung, J. Xu, and L. Li, "Large-scale IP traceback in high-speed Internet: Practical techniques and theoretical foundation," in *Proceedings of 2004 IEEE Symposium on Security and Privacy*, May 2004.

16 S. Matsuda, T. Baba, A. Hayakawa, and T. Nakamura, "Design and implementation of unauthorized access tracing system," in *Proceedings of the 2002 Symposium on Applications and the Internet (SAINT 2002)*, Jan. 2002.

17 K. Shanmugasundaram, H. Brönnimann, and N. Memon, "Payload attribution via hierarchical Bloom filters," in *Proceedings of the 11th ACM Conference on Computer and Communications Security*, Oct. 2004.

18 A.C. Snoeren, C. Partridge, L. A. Sanchez, C. E. Jones, F. Tchakountio, B. Schwartz, S. T. Kent, and W. T. Strayer, "Single-packet IP traceback," *IEEE/ACM Transactions on Networking*, Vol. 10, No. 6, pp. 721–734, Dec. 2002.

19 R. Stone, "Centertrack: An IP overlay network for tracking DoS floods," in *Proceedings of the 9th USENIX Security Symposium*, Aug. 2000, pp. 199–212.

20 H. Burch and B. Cheswick, "Tracing anonymous packets to their approximate source," in *Proceedings of USENIX LISA 2000*, Dec. 2000, pp. 319–327.

21 S. M. Bellovin, "ICMP traceback messages," Internet draft, 2000.

22 A. Mankin, D. Massey, C.-L. Wu, S. F. Wu, and L. Zhang, "On design and evaluation of 'Intention-Driven' ICMP traceback," in *Proceedings of 10th IEEE International Conference on Computer Communications and Networks*, Oct. 2001.

23 S. F. Wu, L. Zhang, D. Massey, and A. Mankin, "Intention-driven ICMP trace back," Internet draft, 2001.

24 S. Savage, D. Wetherall, A. Karlin, and T. Anderson, "Network support for IP traceback," *IEEE/ACM Transactions on Networking*, Vol. 9, No. 3, pp. 226–237, June 2001.

25 D. Song and A. Perrig, "Advanced and authenticated marking schemes for IP traceback," in *Proceedings of IEEE INFOCOM 2001*, Apr. 2001.

26 K. Park and H. Lee, "On the effectiveness of probabilistic packet marking for IP traceback under denial of service attack," in *Proceedings of IEEE INFOCOM 2001*, Apr. 2001, pp. 338–347.

27 D. Dean, M. Franklin, and A. Stubblefield, "An algebraic approach to IP traceback," *Information and System Security*, Vol. 5, No. 2, pp. 119–137, 2002.

The *Deterministic Packet Marking* (DPM) scheme proposed by Belenky and Ansari[28] involves marking each individual packet when it enters the network. The packet is marked by the interface closest to the source of the packet on the edge ingress router. The mark remains unchanged as long as the packet traverses the network. However, there is no way to get the whole paths of the attacks.

Dean et al.[29] proposed an *Algebraic Packet Marking* (APM) scheme that reframes the traceback problem as a polynomial reconstruction problem and uses techniques from algebraic coding theory to provide robust methods of transmission and reconstruction. The advantage of this scheme is that it offers more flexibility in design and more powerful techniques that can be used to filter out attacker-generated noise and separate multiple paths. But it shares similarity with PPM in that it requires a sufficiently large number of attack packets.

Log-Based Traceback

The basic idea of log-based traceback is that each router stores the information (digests, signature, or even the packet itself) of network traffic through it. Once an attack is detected, the victim queries the upstream routers by checking whether they have logged the attack packet in question. If the attack packet's information is found in a given router's memory, that router is deemed to be part of the attack path. Obviously, the major challenge in log-based traceback schemes is the storage space requirement at the intermediate routers.

Matsuda et al.[30] proposed a hop-by-hop log-based IP traceback method. Its main features are a logging *packet feature* that is composed of a portion of the packet for identification purposes and an algorithm using a data-link identifier to identify the routing of a packet. However, for each received packet, about 60 bytes of data should be recorded. The resulting large memory space requirement prevents this method from being applied to high-speed networks with heavy traffic.

Although today's high-speed IP networks suggest that classical log-based traceback schemes would be too prohibitive because of the huge memory requirement, log-based traceback became attractive after Bloom filter-based (i.e., hash-based) traceback schemes were proposed. *Bloom filters* were presented by Burton H. Bloom[31] in 1970 and have been widely used in many areas such as database and networking.[32] A Bloom filter is a space-efficient data structure for representing a set of elements to respond to membership queries. It is a vector of bits that are all initialized to the value 0. Then each element is inserted into the Bloom filter by hashing it using several independent uniform hash functions and setting the corresponding bits in the vector to value 1. Given a query as to whether an element is present in the Bloom filter, we hash this element using the same hash functions and check whether all the corresponding bits are set to 1. If any one of them is 0, then undoubtedly this element is not stored in the filter. Otherwise, we would say that it is present in the filter, although there is a certain probability that the element is determined to be in the filter though it is actually not. Such false cases are called *false positives*.

The space-efficiency of Bloom filters is achieved at the cost of a small, acceptable false-positive rate. Bloom filters were introduced into the IP traceback area by Snoeren et al.[33] They built a system named the *Source Path Isolation Engine* (SPIE), which can trace the origin of a single IP packet delivered by the network in the recent past. They demonstrated that the system is effective, space-efficient, and implementable in current or next-generation routing hardware. Bloom filters are used in each SPIE-equipped router to record the digests of all packets received in the recent past. The digest of a packet is exactly several hash values of its nonmutable IP header fields and the prefix of the payload. Strayer et al.[34] extended this traceback architecture to IP-v6. However, the inherent false positives of Bloom filters caused by unavoidable collisions restrain the effectiveness of these

28 A. Belenky and N. Ansari, "IP traceback with deterministic packet marking," *IEEE Communications Letters*, Vol. 7, No. 4, pp. 162–164, April 2003.

29 D. Dean, M. Franklin, and A. Stubblefield, "An algebraic approach to IP traceback," *Information and System Security*, Vol. 5, No. 2, pp. 119–137, 2002.

30 S. Matsuda, T. Baba, A. Hayakawa, and T. Nakamura, "Design and implementation of unauthorized access tracing system," in *Proceedings of the 2002 Symposium on Applications and the Internet (SAINT 2002)*, Jan. 2002.

31 B. H. Bloom, "Space/time trade-offs in hash coding with allowable errors," *Communications of the ACM*, Vol. 13, No. 7, pp. 422–426, July 1970.

32 A. Broder and M. Mitzenmacher, "Network applications of Bloom filters: A survey," *Proceedings of the 40th Annual Allerton Conference on Communication, Control, and Computing*, Oct. 2002, pp. 636–646.

33 A.C. Snoeren, C. Partridge, L. A. Sanchez, C. E. Jones, F. Tchakountio, B. Schwartz, S. T. Kent, and W. T. Strayer, "Single-packet IP traceback," *IEEE/ACM Transactions on Networking*, Vol. 10, No. 6, pp. 721–734, Dec. 2002.

34 W.T. Strayer, C. E. Jones, F. Tchakountio, and R. R. Hain, "SPIE-IPv6: Single IPv6 packet traceback," in *Proceedings of the 29th IEEE Local Computer Networks Conference (LCN 2004)*, Nov. 2004.

systems. To reduce the impact of unavoidable collisions in Bloom filters, Zhang and Guan[35] propose a topology-aware single-packet IP traceback system, namely TOPO. The router's local topology information, that is, its immediate predecessor information, is utilized. The performance analysis shows that TOPO can reduce the number and scope of unnecessary queries and significantly decrease false attributions. When Bloom filters are used, it is difficult to decide their optimal control parameters *a priori*. They designed a *k*-adaptive mechanism that can dynamically adjust the parameters of Bloom filters to reduce the false-positive rate.

Shanmugasundaram et al.[36] proposed a *payload attribution system* (PAS) based on a *hierarchical Bloom filter* (HBF). HBF is a Bloom filter in which an element is inserted several times using different parts of the same element. Compared with SPIE, which is a packet-digesting scheme, PAS only uses the payload excerpt of a packet. It is useful when the packet header is unavailable.

Li et al.[37] proposed a Bloom filter-based IP traceback scheme that requires an order of magnitude smaller processing and storage cost than SPIE, thereby being able to scale to much higher link speed. The baseline idea of their approach is to sample and log a small percentage of packets, and 1 bit packet marking is used in their sampling scheme. Therefore, their traceback scheme combines packet marking and packet logging together. Their simulation results showed that the traceback scheme can achieve high accuracy and scale well to a large number of attackers. However, as the authors also pointed out, because of the low sampling rate, their scheme is no longer capable of tracing one attacker with only one packet.

Stepping-Stone Attack Attribution

Ever since the problem of detecting stepping stones was first proposed by Staniford-Chen and Heberlein,[38] several approaches have been proposed to detect encrypted stepping-stone attacks.

The ON/OFF based approach proposed by Zhang and Paxson[39] is the first timing-based method that can trace stepping stones, even if the traffic were to be encrypted. In their approach, they calculated the correlation of different flows by using each flow's OFF periods. A flow is considered to be in an OFF period when there is no data traffic on it for more than a time period threshold. Their approach comes from the observation that two flows are in the same connection chain if their OFF periods coincide.

Yoda and Etoh[40] presented a deviation-based approach for detecting stepping-stone connections. The deviation is defined as the difference between the average propagation delay and the minimum propagation delay of two connections. This scheme comes from the observation that the deviation for two unrelated connections is large enough to be distinguished from the deviation of connections in the same connection chain.

Wang et al.[41] proposed a correlation scheme using interpacket delay (IPD) characteristics to detect stepping stones. They defined their correlation metric over the IPDs in a sliding window of packets of the connections to be correlated. They showed that the IPD characteristics may be preserved across many stepping stones.

Wang and Reeves[42] presented an active watermark scheme that is designed to be robust against certain delay perturbations. The watermark is introduced into a connection by slightly adjusting the interpacket delays of selected packets in the flow. If the delay perturbation is not quite large, the watermark information will remain along the connection chain. This is the only active stepping-stone attribution approach.

Strayer et al.[43] presented a State-Space algorithm that is derived from their work on wireless topology discovery. When a new packet is received, each node is given

35 L. Zhang and Y. Guan, "TOPO: A topology-aware single packet attack traceback scheme," in *Proceedings of the 2nd IEEE Communications Society/CreateNet International Conference on Security and Privacy in Communication Networks (SecureComm 2006),* Aug. 2006.

36 S. Savage, D. Wetherall, A. Karlin, and T. Anderson, "Network support for IP traceback," *IEEE/ACM Transactions on Networking,* Vol. 9, No. 3, pp. 226–237, June 2001.

37 J. Li, M. Sung, J. Xu, and L. Li, "Large-scale IP traceback in high-speed Internet: Practical techniques and theoretical foundation," in *Proceedings of 2004 IEEE Symposium on Security and Privacy,* May 2004.

38 S. Staniford-Chen and L. T. Heberlein, "Holding intruders accountable on the Internet," in *Proceedings of the 1995 IEEE Symposium on Security and Privacy,* May 1995.

39 Y. Zhang and V. Paxson, "Detecting stepping stones," in *Proceedings of the 9th USENIX Security Symposium,* Aug. 2000, pp. 171¨C184.

40 K. Yoda and H. Etoh, "Finding a connection chain for tracing intruders," in *Proceedings of the 6th European Symposium on Research in Computer Security (ESORICS 2000),* Oct. 2000.

41 X. Wang, D. S. Reeves, and S. F. Wu, "Inter-packet delay based correlation for tracing encrypted connections through stepping stones," in *Proceedings of the 7th European Symposium on Research in Computer Security (ESORICS 2002),* Oct. 2002.

42 X. Wang and D. S. Reeves, "Robust correlation of encrypted attack traffic through stepping stones by manipulation of interpacket delays," in *Proceedings of the 10th ACM Conference on Computer and Communications Security (CCS 2003),* Oct. 2003.

43 W. T. Strayer, C. E. Jones, I. Castineyra, J. B. Levin, and R. R. Hain, "An integrated architecture for attack attribution," BBN Technologies, Tech. Rep. BBN REPORT-8384, Dec. 2003.

a weight that decreases as the elapsed time from the last packet from that node increases. Then the connections on the same connection chain will have higher weights than other connections.

However, none of these previous approaches can effectively detect stepping stones when delay and chaff perturbations exist simultaneously. Although no experimental data is available, Donoho et al.[44] indicated that there are theoretical limits on the ability of attackers to disguise their traffic using evasions for sufficiently long connections. They assumed that the intruder has a maximum delay tolerance, and they used wavelets and similar multiscale methods to separate the short-term behavior of the flows (delay or chaff) from the long-term behavior of the flows (the remaining correlation). However, this method requires the intrusion connections to remain for long periods, and the authors never experimented to show the effectiveness against chaff perturbation. These evasions consist of local jittering of packet arrival times and the addition of superfluous packets.

Blum et al.[45] proposed and analyzed algorithms for stepping-stone detection using ideas from computational learning theory and the analysis of random walks. They achieved provable (polynomial) upper bounds on the number of packets needed to confidently detect and identify stepping-stone flows with proven guarantees on the false positives and provided lower bounds on the amount of chaff that an attacker would have to send to evade detection. However, their upper bounds on the number of packets required is large, while the lower bounds on the amount of chaff needed for attackers to evade detection is very small. They did not discuss how to detect stepping stones without enough packets or with large amounts of chaff and did not show experimental results.

Zhang et al.[46] proposed and analyzed algorithms that represent that attackers cannot always evade detection only by adding limited delay and independent chaff perturbations. They provided the upper bounds on the number of packets needed to confidently detect stepping-stone

connections from nonstepping stone connections with any given probability of false attribution.

Although there have been many stepping-stone attack attribution schemes, there is a lack of comprehensive experimental evaluation of these schemes. Therefore, there are no objective, comparable evaluation results on the effectiveness and limitations of these schemes. Xin et al.[47] designed and built a scalable testbed environment that can evaluate all existing stepping-stone attack attribution schemes reproducibly, provide a stable platform for further research in this area, and be easily reconfigured, expanded, and operated with a user-friendly interface. This testbed environment has been established in a dedicated stepping-stone attack attribution research laboratory. An evaluation of proposed stepping-stone techniques is currently under way.

A group from Iowa State University proposed the first effective detection scheme to detect attack flows with both delay and chaff perturbations. A scheme named "datatick" is proposed that can handle significant packet merging/splitting and can attribute multiple application layer protocols (e.g., X-Windows over SSH, Windows Remote Desktop, VNC, and SSH). A scalable testbed environment is also established that can evaluate all existing stepping-stone attack attribution schemes reproducibly. A group of researchers from North Carolina State University and George Mason University utilizes timing-based watermarking to trace back stepping-stone attacks. They have proposed schemes to handle repacketization of the attack flow and a "centroid-based" watermarking scheme to detect attack flows with chaff. A group from Johns Hopkins University demonstrates the feasibility of a "post-mortem" technique for traceback through indirect attacks. A group from Telcordia Technologies proposed a scheme that reroutes the attack traffic from uncooperative networks to cooperative networks such that the attacks can be attributed. The BBN Technologies' group integrates single-packet traceback and stepping-stone correlation. A distributed traceback system called FlyTrap is developed for uncooperative and hostile networks. A group from Sparta integrates multiple complementary traceback approaches and tests them in a TOR anonymous system.

A research project entitled Tracing VoIP Calls through the Internet, led by Xinyuan Wang from George Mason University, aims to investigate how VoIP calls can be effectively traced. Wang et al. proposed to use the

44 D. L. Donoho, A. G. Flesia, U. Shankar, V. Paxson, J. Coit, and S. Staniford, "Multiscale stepping-stone detection: Detecting pairs of jittered interactive streams by exploiting maximum tolerable delay," in *Proceedings of the 5th International Symposium on Recent Advances in Intrusion Detection (RAID 2002),* Oct. 2002.

45 A. Blum, D. Song, and S. Venkataraman, "Detection of interactive stepping stones: Algorithms and confidence bounds," in *Proceedings of the 7th International Symposium on Recent Advances in Intrusion Detection* (RAID 2004), Sept. 2004.

46 L. Zhang, A. G. Persaud, A. Johnson, and Y. Guan, "Detection of Stepping Stone Attack under Delay and Chaff Perturbations," in *25th IEEE International Performance Computing and Communications Conference (IPCCC 2006),* Apr. 2006.

47 J. Xin, L. Zhang, B. Aswegan, J. Dickerson, J. Dickerson, T. Daniels, and Y. Guan, "A testbed for evaluation and analysis of stepping stone attack attribution techniques," in *Proceedings of TridentCom 2006,* Mar. 2006.

watermarking technology in stepping-stone attack attribution into VoIP attribution and showed that VoIP calls can still be attributed.[48]

Strayer et al. has been supported by the U.S. Army Research Office to research how to attribute attackers using botnets. Their approach for detecting botnets is to examine flow characteristics such as bandwidth, duration, and packet timing, looking for evidence of botnet command and control activity.[49]

4. CRITICAL NEEDS ANALYSIS

Although large-scale cyber terrorism seldom happens, some cyber attacks have already shown their power in damaging homeland security. For instance, on October 21, 2002, all 13 Domain Name System (DNS) root name servers sustained a DoS attack.[50] Some root name servers were unreachable from many parts of the global Internet due to congestion from the attack traffic. Even now, we do not know the real attacker and what his intention was.

Besides the Internet itself, many sensitive institutions, such as the U.S. power grid, nuclear power plants, and airports, may also be attacked by terrorists if they are connected to the Internet, although these sites have been carefully protected physically. If the terrorists want to launch large-scale attacks targeting these sensitive institutions through the Internet, they will probably have to try several times to be successful. If we only sit here and do not fight back, they will finally find our vulnerabilities and reach their evil purpose. However, if we can attribute them to the source of attacks, we can detect and arrest them before they succeed.

Although there have been a lot of traceback and attribution schemes on IP spoofing and stepping-stone attacks, we still have a lot of open issues in this area. The biggest issue is the deployment of these schemes. Many schemes (such as packet marking and log-based traceback) need the change of Internet protocol on each intermediate router. Many schemes need many network monitors placed all over the world. These are very difficult to implement in the current Internet without support

from government, manufacturers, and academics. It is necessary to consider traceback demands when designing and deploying next-generation networks.

5. RESEARCH DIRECTIONS

There are still some open problems in attack traceback and attribution.

VoIP Attribution

Like the Internet, the Voice over Internet Protocol (VoIP) also provides unauthorized services. Therefore, some security issues existing in the Internet may also appear in VoIP systems. For instance, a phone user may receive a call with a qualified caller ID from her credit-card company, so she answers the critical questions about Social Security number, data of birth, and so on. However, this call actually comes from an attacker who fakes the caller ID using a computer. Compared with a Public Switched Telephone Network (PSTN) phone or mobile phone, IP phones lack monitoring. Therefore, it is desirable to provide schemes that can attribute or trace back to the VoIP callers.

Tracking Botnets

A botnet is a network of compromised computers, or bots, commandeered by an adversarial botmaster. Botnets usually spread through viruses and communicate through the IRC channel. With an army of bots, bot controllers can launch many attacks, such as spam, phishing, key logging, and denial of service. Today more and more scientists are interested in how to detect, mitigate, and trace back botnet attacks.

Traceback in Anonymous Systems

Another issue is that there exist a lot of anonymous systems available all over the world, such as Tor.[51] Tor is a toolset for anonymizing Web browsing and publishing, instant messaging, IRC, SSH, and other applications that use TCP. It provides anonymity and privacy for legal users, and at the same time, it is a good platform via which to launch stepping-stone attacks. Communications over Tor are relayed through several distributed servers called *onion routers*. So far there are more than 800 onion routers all over the world. Since Tor may be seen as a special stepping-stone attack platform, it is interesting to consider how to trace back attacks over Tor.

48 X. Wang, S. Chen, and S. Jajodia "Tracking anonymous peer-to-peer VoIP calls on the Internet," In *Proceedings of the 12th ACM Conference on Computer Communications Security (CCS 2005),* November 2005.

49 W.T. Strayer, R. Walsh, C. Livadas, and D. Lapsley, "Detecting botnets with tight command and control," *Proceedings of the 31st IEEE Conference on Local Computer Networks (LCN),* November 15–16, 2006.

50 P. Vixie, G. Sneeringer, and M. Schleifer, "Events of Oct. 21, 2002", November 24, 2002, www.isc.org/ops/f-root/october21.txt.

51 Tor system, http://tor.eff.org.

Online Fraudster Detection and Attribution

One example is the auction frauds on eBay-like auction systems. In the past few years, Internet auctions have become a thriving and very important online business. Compared with traditional auctions, Internet auctions virtually allow everyone to sell and buy anything at anytime from anywhere, at low transaction fees. However, the increasing number of cases of fraud in Internet auctions has harmed this billion-dollar worldwide market. Due to the inherent limitation of information asymmetry in Internet auction systems, it is very hard, if not impossible, to discover all potential (i.e., committed and soon to be committed) frauds. Auction frauds are reported as ascending in recent years and have become serious problems. The Internet Crime Complaint Center (IC3) and Internet FraudWatch have both reported Internet auction frauds as the most prevalent type of Internet fraud.[52,53] Internet FraudWatch reported that auction fraud represented 34% (the highest percentage) of total Internet frauds in 2006, resulting in an average loss of $1331. Internet auction houses had tried to prevent frauds by using certain types of reputation systems, but it has been shown that fraudulent users are able to manipulate these reputation systems. It is important that we develop the capability to detect and attribute auction fraudsters.

Tracing Phishers

Another serious problem is the fraud and identity theft that result from phishing, pharming, and email spoofing of all types. Online users are lured to a faked web site and tricked to disclose sensitive credentials such as passwords, Social Security numbers, and credit-card numbers. The phishers collect these credentials in order to illegitimately gain access to the user's account and cause financial loss or other damages to the user. In the past, phishing attacks often involve various actors as a part of a secret criminal network and take approaches similar to those of money laundering and drug trafficking. Tracing phishers is a challenging forensic problem and the solutions thereof would greatly help law enforcement practitioners and financial fraud auditors in their investigation and deterrence efforts.

Tracing Illegal Content Distributor in P2P Systems

Peer-to-peer (P2P) file sharing has gained popularity and achieved a great success in the past 10 years. Though the well-known and popular P2P file sharing applications such as BitTorrent (BT), eDonkey, and Foxy may vary from region to region, the trend of using P2P networks can be seen almost everywhere. In North America, a recent report stated that around 41%–44% of all bandwidth was used up by P2P file transfer traffic. With the increasing amount of sensitive documents and files accidentally shared through P2P systems, it is important to develop forensic solutions for locating initial illegal content uploaders in P2P systems. However, one technique would not be applicable to all P2P systems due to their architectural and algorithmic differences among different P2P systems. There are many legal and technical challenges for tracing illegal content distributors in P2P systems.

---

52 Internet Crime Complaint Center, Internet crime report, 2006 ic3 annual report, 2006.

53 Internet National Fraud Information Center, 2006 top 10 Internet scam trends from NCL's fraud center, 2006.

## Chapter 21

Firewalls

Dr. Errin W. Fulp
Wake Forest University

Providing a secure computing environment continues to be an important and challenging goal of any computer administrator. The difficulty is in part due to the increasing interconnectivity of computers via networks, which includes the Internet. Such interconnectivity brings great economies of scale in terms of resources, services, and knowledge, but it has also introduced new security risks. For example, interconnectivity gives illegitimate users much easier access to vital data and resources from almost anywhere in the world.

In a secure environment it is important to maintain the privacy, integrity, and availability of data and resources. *Privacy* refers to limiting information access and disclosures to authorized users and preventing access by or disclosure to illegitimate users. In the United States, a range of state and federal laws—for example, FERPA, FSMA, and HIPAA—define the legal terms of privacy. *Integrity* is the trustworthiness of information. It includes the idea of *data integrity*, which means data has not been changed inappropriately. It can also include *source integrity*, which means the source of the data is who it claims to be. *Availability* is the accessibility of resources. Of course these security definitions can also form the basis of *reputation*, which is vital to businesses.

1. NETWORK FIREWALLS

Network firewalls are a vital component for maintaining a secure environment and are often the first line of defense against attack. Simply stated, a firewall is responsible for controlling access among devices, such as computers, networks, and servers. Therefore the most common deployment is between a secure and an insecure network (for example, between the computers you control and the Internet), as shown in Figure 21.1. This chapter refers to the secure network as the internal network; the insecure network is the external network.

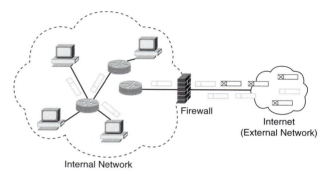

FIGURE 21.1 Example network consisting of an internal network (which is to be secured) and an external network (not trusted). The firewall controls access between these two networks, allowing and denying packets according to a security policy.

The purpose of the firewall and its location is to have network connections traverse the firewall, which can then stop any unauthorized packets. A simple firewall will filter packets based on IP addresses and ports. A useful analogy is filtering your postal mail based only on the information on the envelope. You typically accept any letter addressed to you and return any letter addressed to someone else. This act of filtering is essentially the same for firewalls.

However, in response to the richer services provided over modern networks (such as multimedia and encrypted connections), the role of the firewall has grown over time. Advanced firewalls may also perform Network Address Translation (NAT), which allows multiple computers to share a limited number of network addresses (explained later in this chapter). Firewalls may provide service differentiation, giving certain traffic priority to ensure that data is received in a timely fashion. Voice over IP (VoIP) is one type of application that needs differentiation to ensure proper operation. This idea is discussed several times in this chapter, since the use of multimedia services will only continue to increase. Assuming that email and VoIP packets arrive at the firewall at the same time, VoIP packets should be processed first because the application is more susceptible to delays.

Firewalls may also inspect the contents (the data) of packets. This can be done to filter other packets (learn new connections), block packets that contain offensive information, and/or block intrusion attempts. Using the mail analogy again, in this case you open letters and determine what to accept based on what is inside. For example, you unfortunately have to accept bills, but you can deny credit-card solicitations.

The remainder of this chapter provides an overview of firewall policies, designs, features, and configurations. Of course, technology is always changing, and network firewalls are no exception. However, the intent of this chapter is to describe aspects of network firewalls that tend to endure over time.

2. FIREWALL SECURITY POLICIES

When a packet arrives at a firewall, a security policy is applied to determine the appropriate action. Actions include accepting the packet, which means the packet is allowed to travel to the intended destination. A packet can be denied, which means the packet is not permitted to travel to the intended destination (it is dropped or possibly is bounced back). The firewall may also log information about the packet, which is important to maintain certain services.

It is easy to consider a firewall policy as an ordered list of rules, as shown in Table 21.1. Each firewall rule consists of a set of tuples and an action. Each tuple corresponds to a field in the packet header, and there are five such fields for an Internet packet: Protocol, Source Address, Source Port, Destination Address, and Destination Port.

The firewall rule tuples can be fully specified or contain wildcards (*) in standard prefix format. However, each tuple represents a finite set of values; therefore, the set of all possible packets is also finite. (A more concise mathematical model will be introduced later in the chapter.) It is possible to consider the packet header consisting of tuples, but each tuple must be fully specified.

As packets pass through a firewall, their header information is sequentially compared to the fields of a rule. If a packet's header information is a subset of a rule, it is said to be a match, and the associated action, to accept or reject, is performed. Otherwise, the packet is compared to the next sequential rule. This is considered a *first-match policy* since the action associated with the first rule that is matched is performed. Other matching strategies are discussed at the end of this section.

For example, assume that a packet has the following values in the header: The protocol is TCP, source IP is 210.1.1.1, source port is 3080, destination IP is 220.2.33.8, and destination port is 80. When the packet arrives it is compared to the first rule, which results in no match since the rule is for UDP packets. The firewall then compares the packet second rule, which results in no match since the source IP is different. The packet does not match the third rule, but it does match the fourth rule. The rule action is performed and so the packet is allowed to pass the firewall.

A default rule, or catch-all, is often placed at the end of a policy with action reject. The addition of a default rule makes a policy comprehensive, indicating that every packet will match at least one rule. In the event that a packet matches multiple rules, the action of the first matching rule is taken. Therefore the order of rules is very important.

If a default rule (a rule that matches all possible packets) is placed at the beginning of a first-match policy, no

TABLE 21.1 A Security Policy Consisting of Six Rules, Each of Which Has Five Parts (Tuples)

No.	Protocol	Source IP	Source Port	Destination IP	Destination Port	Action
1	UDP	190.1.1.*	*	*	80	deny
2	TCP	180.*	*	180.*	90	accept
3	UDP	210.1.*	*	*	90	accept
4	TCP	210.*	*	220.*	80	accept
5	UDP	190.*	*	*	80	accept
6	*	*	*	*	*	deny

other rule will match. This situation is an anomaly referred to as *shadowing*. We'll talk more about policy anomalies later in this chapter. Policies that employ this form of short-circuit evaluation are called *first-match policies* and account for the majority of firewall implementations.

Rule-Match Policies

Multiple rules of a single firewall policy may match a packet—for example, a packet could match rules 1, 5, and 6 of the policy in Table 21.1. Given multiple possible matches, the rule-match policy describes the rule the firewall will apply to the packet. The previous section described the most popular match policy, first match, which will apply the first rule that is a match.

Other match policies are possible, including best match and last match. For best-match policies, the packet is compared against every rule to determine which rule most closely matches every tuple of the packet. Note that the relative order of the rules in the policy does not impact determining the best-match result; therefore shadowing is not an issue. It is interesting to note that best match is the default criterion for IP routing, which is not surprising since firewalls and routers do perform similar tasks. If a packet matches multiple rules with a last-match criterion, the action of the last rule matched is performed. Note that rule order is important for a last-match policy.

3. A SIMPLE MATHEMATICAL MODEL FOR POLICIES, RULES, AND PACKETS

At this point it is perhaps useful to describe firewall policies, firewall rules, and network packets using set theory.[1] The previous section defined the parts and fields of rules and packets as *tuples*. A tuple can be modeled as a set. For example, assume the tuple for IP source addresses is 198.188.150.*. Then this tuple represents the set of 256 addresses that range from 198.188.150.0 to 198.180.150.255. Each tuple of a packet consists of a single value, which is expected, since a packet only has one source and one destination.

The tuples (which are sets) that form a rule collective define a set of packets that match. For example, consider the following rule:

Proto = TCP, SIP = 190.150.140.38, SP = 188,
DIP = 190.180.39.* DP = 80, action = accept

This rule defines a set of 256 unique TCP packet headers with source address 190.150.140.38 and source port 188 destined for any of the 256 computers with destination port 80 and destination IP address 190.180.39.0 through 190.180.39.255, perhaps a Web server farm. Therefore the rule describes a set of 256 packets that will be accepted. If the source port was defined as *, the rule would describe a set of 16,777,216 different packet headers.

$$2^{16} \times 2^8 = 65,536 \times 256 = 16,777,216$$

Using set theory also provides a simple definition of a match. A match occurs when every tuple of a packet is a proper subset of the corresponding rule. In this chapter a proper set can be thought of as one set completely contained within another. For example, every tuple in the following packet is a proper subset of the preceding rule; therefore it is considered a match.

Proto = TCP, SIP = 190.150.140.38, SP = 188,
DIP = 190.180.39.188 DP = 80

A set model can also be used to describe a firewall policy. The list of rules in a firewall policy collectively describes a set of packets. There are three distinct (nonoverlapping) sets of possible packets. The first set, $A(R)$, describes packets that will be accepted by the policy R. The second set, $D(R)$, defines the set of packets that will be dropped by the policy. The last set, $U(R)$, is the set of packets that do not match any rule in the policy. Since the sets do not overlap, the intersection of $A(R)$, $D(R)$, and $U(R)$ should be the empty set.

Using set theory we can also define the set P that describes all possible packet headers, of which there are approximately 7.7×10^{25} possible packet headers. A packet is a single element in this large set.

Using accept, drop, nonmatch, and possible packet sets, we can describe useful attributes of a firewall policy. A firewall policy R is considered comprehensive if any packet from P will match at least one rule. In other words, the union of $A(R)$ and $D(R)$ equals P (therefore $A(R)D(R) = P$), or $U(R)$ is the empty set (therefore $U(R) = \emptyset$). Of course, it is better if a policy is comprehensive, and generally the last rule (catch-all) makes this true.

Finally, these mathematical models also allow the comparison of policies, the most important reason for introducing a somewhat painful section. Assume two firewall policies R and S exist. We can say the two polices are equivalent if the accept, drop, and nonmatch sets are the same. This does not imply that the two policies have the same rules, just that given a packet, both policies will

---

1 Errin W. Fulp, "Optimization of network firewall policies using directed acyclic graphs," In *Proceedings of the IEEE Internet Management Conference*, 2005.

have the same action. This is an important property that will be mentioned again and again in this chapter.

4. FIRST-MATCH FIREWALL POLICY ANOMALIES

As described in the previous sections, for most firewalls the first rule that matches a packet is typically applied. Given this match policy, more specific rules (those that match few packets) typically appear near the beginning of the policy, whereas more general rules are located at the end. Using the set theory model, the number of elements in the rules sets increases as you move toward the last rule.

Unfortunately, it is easy to introduce anomalies when developing and managing a firewall policy. This is especially true as the policy grows in size (number of rules) and complexity. An anomaly is an unintended consequence of adding rules in a certain order.

A simple and very common anomaly is rule shadowing. Shadowing occurs when an earlier rule r_i matches every packet that another lower rule r_j matches, where i and j are rule numbers. Assume rules are numbered sequentially starting at the first rule and $i < j$. Using the mathematical model, shadowing occurs when every tuple in r_j is a proper subset of r_i.

For example, shadowing occurs between the following two rules:

Proto = TCP, SIP = 190.150.140.38, SP = 188,
DIP = 190.180.39.* DP = 80, action = accept
Proto = TCP, SIP = 190.150.140.38, SP = 188,
DIP = 190.180.39.180 DP = 80, action = drop

What is the problem? Nothing, if the two rules have the same action (there is a performance issue described in the next section). However, if the rules have different actions, there is a potential issue. In the preceding example the second rule is never matched; therefore the packet [Proto = TCP, SIP = 190.150.140.38, SP = 188, DIP = 190.180.39.180 DP = 80] will always be accepted. Was this the intent? If so, the second rule should be removed.

Another policy anomaly is half shadowing, where only a portion of the packets of a later rule matches an earlier rule (although not necessarily half of the packets in the set). For example, consider the following two rules:

Proto = TCP, SIP = 190.150.140.38, SP = 188,
DIP = 190.180.39.* DP = 80, action = accept
Proto = TCP, SIP = 190.150.140.38, SP = *,
DIP = 190.180.39.180 DP = 80, action = drop

In this example, the second rule is partially shadowed by the first rule. By itself, the second rule will drop any TCP packet arriving from the address 190.150.140.38 and destined for the Web server (because of destination port 80) 190.180.39.180. When the first rule is added, a packet from the address 190.150.140.38 and port 188 will be accepted. Was this the intent? Only the firewall administrator would know. Regardless, it is difficult to detect.

Other firewall policy anomalies are possible. Unfortunately, detecting these problems is not easy, since the anomaly may be introduced on purpose (then technically it is not an anomaly). This has created a new area of research, and some software packages are available to help find problems. However, only the administrator can ultimately determine whether the rule ordering is correct. Note that best-match policies do not have these issues, and this reason is often used to promote their use. However, best-match policies are typically considered difficult for the administrator to manage.

5. POLICY OPTIMIZATION

Given that a network firewall will inspect all packets transmitted between multiple networks, these devices need to determine the appropriate match with minimal delay. Often the number of firewall rules in a policy will impact the firewall performance. Given that every rule requires some processing time, more rules will require more time, on average. There are a few ways to improve firewall performance with regard to the security policy. Note that this section is more applicable to software-based than hardware-based firewalls.

Policy Reordering

Given a security policy, it may be possible to reorder the rules such that more popular rules appear earlier.[2] *More popular* refers to how often the rule is a match. For example, over time it is possible to determine how many times a rule is matched. Dividing this number by the total number of packets matched for the entire policy yields the probability that this rule is considered the first match.

If the match policy is first match, then placing more popular rules earlier in the policy will reduce the average number of rule comparisons. The average number of rule

---

2 Errin W. Fulp, "Optimization of network firewall policies using directed acyclical graphs," In *Proceedings of the IEEE Internet Management Conference*, 2005.

comparisons performed, $E[n]$, is given by the following equation:

$$E[n] = \sum_{i=1}^{n} i \times p_i$$

where n is the number of rules in the policy and p_i is the probability that rule i is the first match. Although reordering is advantageous, it must be done so that the policy's integrity is maintained.

Policy integrity refers to the policy intent, so the policy will accept and deny the same packets before and after the reorganization of rules. For example, rule six in Table 21.1 may be the most popular rule (the default deny), but placing it at the beginning of the policy does not maintain integrity. However, if rule two is more popular than rule one, it could be placed at the beginning of the policy and integrity will be maintained. Therefore the order between certain rules must be maintained.

This can be described mathematically using the models introduced in the earlier section. Assume a firewall policy R exists. After reordering the rules, let's call the firewall policy S. If $A(R) = A(S)$ and $D(R) = D(S)$, then the policies R and S are equivalent and integrity is maintained. As a result S can be used in place of R in the firewall, which should improve performance.

Although a simple concept, reordering rules to maintain integrity is provably difficult for large policies.[3,4] Fortunately, commercial software packages are now available to optimize rules to improve performance.

Combining Rules

Another method for improving firewall performance is removing unnecessary rules. This can be accomplished by first removing redundant rules (rules that are shadowed with the same action). For example, the second rule here is unnecessary:

Proto = TCP, SIP = 190.150.140.38, SP = 188,
DIP = 190.180.39.* DP = 80, action = drop
Proto = TCP, SIP = 190.150.140.38, SP = 188,
DIP = 190.180.39.180 DP = 80, action = drop

This is because the first rule matches any packet the second rule does, and the first rule has the same action

(different actions would be an anomaly, as described in the earlier sections).

Another example occurs when two nonshadowing rules can be combined into a single rule. Consider the following two rules:

Proto = TCP, SIP = 190.150.140.38, SP = 188,
DIP = 190.180.39.* DP = 80, action = accept
Proto = UDP, SIP = 190.150.140.38, SP = 188,
DIP = 190.180.39.* DP = 80, action = accept

These two rules can be combined into the following rule, which substitutes the wildcard for the protocol field:

Proto = *, SIP = 190.150.140.38, SP = 188,
DIP = 190.180.39.* DP = 80, action = accept

Combining rules to form a smaller policy is better in terms of performance as well as management in most cases, since fewer rules should be easier for the administrator to understand. Finding such combinations takes practice; fortunately, there are some software packages available to help.

Default Accept or Deny?

It may be worth a few lines to discuss whether a default accept policy provides better performance than a default deny. This debate occurs from time to time; generally speaking, the question is better answered with regard to management of the policy and security. Is it easier to define the appropriate policy in terms of what is denied or what should be accepted?

Assuming that the administrator defines one (accepted or denied), the default behavior becomes the other. A "define what is accepted and default deny" is the most common. It can be considered pessimistic, since it assumes that if you are not certain about a packet, then drop it.

6. FIREWALL TYPES

Firewalls can be categorized into three general classes: packet filters, stateful firewalls, and application layer firewalls.[5] Each type provides a certain type of security and is best described within the context of a network layer model—for example, the Open Systems Interconnection (OSI) or TCP/IP model, as shown in Figure 21.2.

3 Errin W. Fulp, "Optimization of network firewall policies using directed acyclical graphs," In *Proceedings of the IEEE Internet Management Conference*, 2005.
4 M. Yoon and Z. S. Zhang, "Reducing the size of rule set in a firewall," In *Proceedings of the IEEE International Conference on Communications*, 2007.

5 J.R. Vacca and S. R. Ellis, *Firewalls Jumpstart for Network and Systems Administrators*, Elsevier, 2005.

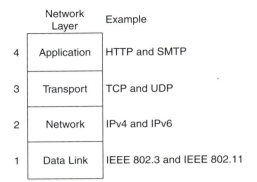

	Network Layer	Example
4	Application	HTTP and SMTP
3	Transport	TCP and UDP
2	Network	IPv4 and IPv6
1	Data Link	IEEE 802.3 and IEEE 802.11

FIGURE 21.2 Layered model for computer networks and example implementations for each layer.

Recall that the TCP/IP model consists of four basic layers: data link, networking (IP), transport (TCP and UDP), and application. Each layer is responsible for providing a certain service to the layer above it. The first layer (data link) is responsible for transmitting information across the local area network (LAN); examples include Ethernet and 802.11 networks. The network layer (routing, implemented IP) concerns routing information across interconnected LANs. The third layer (transport, implemented as TCP and UDP) concerns the end-to-end connection between communicating devices. The highest layer (application) is the application using the network.

Packet Filter

A packet filter is the most basic type of a firewall since it only filters at the network and transport layers (layers two and three). Therefore a packet filter's operations are similar to a network router's. The packet filter receives a packet, determines the appropriate action based on the policy, then performs the action on the packet. This will be based on the information from the network and transport layers. Therefore, a packet filter only considers the IP addresses (layer two information), the port numbers (layer one information), and the transport protocol type (layer three information). Furthermore, since all this information resides in the packet header, there is no need to inspect the packet data (payload). It is possible to filter based on the data link layer, but this chapter only considers the network layer and above. Another important note is that the packet filter has no memory (or state) regarding the packets that have arrived and departed.

Stateful Packet Firewalls

Stateful firewalls perform the same operations as packet filters but also maintain state about the packets that have arrived. Given this additional functionality, it is now possible to create firewall rules that allow network sessions (sender and receiver are allowed to communicate), which is critical given the client/server nature of most communications (that is, if you send packets, you probably expect something back). Also note the change in terminology from packet filter to firewall. Many people say that when state is added to a packet filter, it becomes a firewall. This is really a matter of opinion.

For example, assume a user located in the internal (protected) network wants to contact a Web server located in the Internet. The request would be sent from the user to the Web server, and the Web server would respond with the requested information. A packet filter would require two rules, one allowing departing packets (user to Web server) and another allowing arriving packets (Web server to user). There are several problems with this approach, since it is difficult to determine in advance what Web servers a user will connect to. Consider having to add a new rule for every Web server that is or would ever be contacted.

A stateful firewall allows connection tracking, which can allow the arriving packets associated with an accepted departing connection. Recall that a connection or session can be considered all the packets belonging to the conversation between computers, both sender to receiver, and vice versa. Using the Web server example, a single stateful rule can be created that accepts any Web requests from the secure network and the associated return packets. A simple way to add this capability is to have the firewall add to the policy a new rule allowing return packets. Of course, this new rule would be eliminated once the connection is finished. Knowing when a connection is finished is not an easy task, and ultimately timers are involved. Regardless, stateful rules were a significant advancement for network firewalls.

Application Layer Firewalls

Application layer firewalls can filter traffic at the network, transport, and application layer. Filtering at the application layer also introduces new services, such as proxies. Application proxies are simply intermediaries for network connections. Assume that a user in the internal network wants to connect to a server in the external network. The connection of the user would terminate at the firewall; the firewall would then create a connection to the Web server. It is important to note that this occurs seamlessly to the user and server.

As a result of the proxy the firewall can potentially inspect the contents of the packets, which is similar to an intrusion detection system (IDS). This is increasingly important since a growing number of applications, as well as illegitimate users, are using nonstandard port numbers to transmit data. Application layer firewalls are also necessary if an existing connection may require the establishment of another connection—for example, the Common Object Resource Broker Architecture (CORBA).

Increasingly, firewalls and other security devices are being merged into a single device that can simplify management. For example, an intrusion prevention system (IPS) is a combination firewall and IDS. An IPS can filter packets based on the header, but it can also scan the packet contents (payload) for viruses, spam, and certain types of attacks.

7. HOST AND NETWORK FIREWALLS

Firewalls can also be categorized based on where they are implemented or what they are intended to protect—host or network.[6] Host firewalls typically protect only one computer. Host firewalls reside on the computer they are intended to protect and are implemented in software (this is described in the next section).

In contrast, network firewalls are typically standalone devices. Located at the gateway(s) of a network (for example, the point at which a network is connected to the Internet), a network firewall is designed to protect all the computers in the internal network. As a result, a network firewall must be able to handle high bandwidth, as fast as the incoming connection, and process packets quickly. A network firewall gives administrators a single point at which to implement and manage security, but it is also a single point of failure.

There are many different network configurations that involve firewalls. Each provides different levels of security and management complexity. These configurations are described in detail in a later section.

8. SOFTWARE AND HARDWARE FIREWALL IMPLEMENTATIONS

As described in the previous sections, a firewall applies a policy to an arriving packet to determine the appropriate match. The policy is an ordered list of rules, and typically the first rule that matches the packet is performed. This operation can be performed primarily in either software or hardware. Performance is the principal reason to choose one implementation.

Software firewalls are application software that can execute on commercial hardware. Most operating systems provide a firewall to protect the host computer (often called a *host firewall*). For example, iptables is the firewall application provided as a part of the Linux operating system. Several major firewall companies offer a software version of their network firewall. It is possible to buy off-the-shelf hardware (for example, a server) and run the firewall software. The advantage of software firewalls is their ability to upgrade without replacing the hardware. In addition, it is easier to add new features—for example, iptables can easily perform stateful filtering, NATing, and quality-of-service (QoS) operations. It is as simple as updating and configuring the firewall software.

Hardware firewalls rely on hardware to perform packet filtering. The policy and matching operation is performed in dedicated hardware—for example, using a field-programmable gate array (FPGA). The major advantages of a hardware firewall are increased bandwidth and reduced latency. Note that bandwidth is the number of packets a firewall can process per unit of time, and latency is the amount of time require to process a packet. They are not the same thing, and IETF RFC 3511 provides a detailed description of the process of testing firewall performance.[7]

Hardware firewalls can operate at faster bandwidths, which translates to more packets per second (10 Gbps is easily achieved). In addition, hardware firewalls can operate faster since processing is performed in dedicated hardware. The firewall operates almost at wireline speeds; therefore, very little delay is added to accepted packets. This is important since more applications, such as multimedia, need QoS for their operation. The disadvantage is that upgrading the firewall may require replacement of hardware, which can be more expensive.

9. CHOOSING THE CORRECT FIREWALL

The previous sections have described several categories of firewalls. Firewalls can be packet filters or stateful firewalls and/or provide application layer processing; implemented at the host or network or implemented in software or hardware. Given the possible combinations, it can be difficult to choose the appropriate technology.

When determining the appropriate technology, it is important to first understand the current and future security needs of the computer system being protected. Given a large number of hosts, a network firewall is probably

---

6 J.R. Vacca and S. R. Ellis, *Firewalls Jumpstart for Network and Systems Administrators*, Elsevier, 2005.

7 B. Hickman, D. Newman, S. Tadjudin, and T. Martin, *Benchmarking Methodology for Firewall Performance*, IETF RFC 3511, 2003.

the easiest to manage. Requiring and relying on every computer in an internal network to operate a host firewall may not be realistic.

Furthermore, updating the policy in a multiple host-based firewall system would be difficult. However, a single network firewall may imply that a single policy is suitable for all computers in the internal network. This generally is not the case when there are servers and computers in the internal network. More expensive network firewalls will allow the implementation of multiple policies or objects (described in more detail in the next section). Of course, if speed is an issue, a hardware firewall may justify the generally higher cost.

If scanning for viruses and spam and/or discovering network attacks are also requirements, a more advanced firewall is needed. Sometimes called an intrusion prevention system (IPS), these advanced devices filter based on packet headers and inspect the data transmitted for certain signatures. In addition, these devices can monitor traffic (usage and connection patterns) for attacks. For example, a computer that attempts to connect to a range of ports on another computer is probably *port scanning*. This can be done to determine what network-oriented programs are running and in some cases even the operating system can be determined. It is a good idea to block this type of network reconnaissance, which an advanced firewall can do.

Although already introduced in this chapter, it is worth mentioning IETF RFC 3511 again. This document describes how firewalls should be tested to measure performance. This information helps the buyer understand the performance numbers cited by manufacturers. It is also important to ask whether the device was tested under RFC 3511 conditions.

10. FIREWALL PLACEMENT AND NETWORK TOPOLOGY

A simple firewall typically separates two networks: one trusted (internal—for example, the corporate network) and one untrusted (external—for example, the Internet). In this simple arrangement, one security policy is applied to secure all the devices connected to the internal network. This may be sufficient if all the computers perform the same duties, such as desktop computers; however, if the internal network consists of different types of computers (in terms of the services provided), a single policy or level of protection is not sufficient or is difficult to create and maintain.

For example, the security policy for a Web server will be different from the security policy for a desktop computer. This is primarily due to the type of external network access each type of computer needs. Web servers would probably accept almost any unsolicited HTTP (port 80) requests arriving from the Internet. However, desktop computers probably do not serve Web pages and should not be subject to such requests.

Therefore it is reasonable to expect that different classes of computers will need different security policies. Assume an internal network consists of one Web server and several desktop computers. It is possible to locate the Web server on the outside, on the firewall (on the side of the external network), but that would leave the Web server without any firewall protection. Furthermore, given that the Web server is on the outside, should the administrator trust it?

Of course, the Web server could be located in the internal network (see Figure 21.3) and a rule can be added to the policy to allow Web traffic to the Web server (often

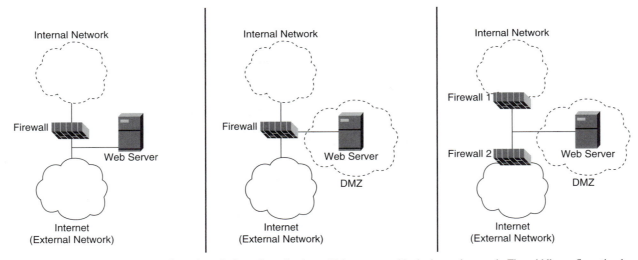

FIGURE 21.3 Example firewall configurations. Left configuration has a Web server outside the internal network. The middle configuration has the Web server in a demilitarized zone. The right configuration is another example of a demilitarized zone.

called *poking a hole*). However, if the Web server is compromised, the remaining computers in the internal network are vulnerable. Most attacks are multistage, which means the first target of attack is rarely the objective. Most attackers use one computer to compromise another until the objective is achieved. Therefore it is a good practice to separate machines and services, even in the internal network.

Demilitarized Zones

Another strategy often employed to provide different types of protection is a *demilitarized zone* (DMZ), as shown in Figure 21.3. Assume the firewall has three connections (sometimes called a *multihomed* device)—one for the external network (Internet), one for the Web server, and another for the internal network. For each connection to the firewall (referred to as an *interface*), a different firewall policy can be enforced, providing different forms of protection. The connection for the Web server is called the DMZ, and it prevents users from the external network getting direct access to the other computers in the internal network. Furthermore, if the Web server is compromised, the internal network still has some protection, since the intruder would have to cross the firewall again to access the internal network.

If the firewall only supports two interfaces (or just one policy), multiple firewalls can be used to achieve the same DMZ effect. The first firewall would be placed between the external network and the Web server. The second firewall would connect the Web server to the internal network. Given this design, the first firewall policy would be less restrictive than the second. Again, different levels of security are now possible.

Grouping machines together based on similar firewall security needs is increasingly common and is seen as a good practice. Large networks may have server farms or a group of servers that perform similar services. As such, each farm is connected to a firewall and given a unique security policy. For example, users from the internal network may have access to administrative servers, but Web servers may have no access to the administrative servers. Such groupings are also referred to as *enclaves*.

Perimeter Networks

A perimeter network is a subnetwork of computers located outside the internal network.[8] Given this definition, a DMZ can be considered a type of perimeter

network. The primary difference between a DMZ and a perimeter network is the way packets arriving and departing the subnetwork are managed.

In a perimeter network, the device that connects the external network to the perimeter network is a *router*, whereas a DMZ uses a firewall to connect to the Internet. For a DMZ, a firewall policy will be applied to all packets arriving from the external network (Internet). The firewall can also perform advanced services such as NATing and packet payload inspection. Therefore it is easy to see that a DMZ offers a higher level of protection to the computers that are part of the perimeter and internal networks.

Two-Router Configuration

Another interconnection of subnetworks is the two-router configuration.[9] This system consists of an external router, a bastion host, an internal router, and an internal network. The *bastion host* is a computer that serves as a filter and/or proxy for computers located in the internal network.

Before describing the specifics of the two-router configuration, let's define the duties of a bastion host. A bastion host is the first device any external computer will contact before accessing a computer in the internal network. Therefore the bastion host is fully exposed to the Internet and should be made as secure as possible. There are several types of bastion hosts, including victim machines that provide insecure but necessary services. For our discussion the bastion host will provide proxy services, shielding (to a limited degree) internal computers from external threats.

For the two-router configuration, the external network connects to the external router, which connects to the bastion host. The bastion host then connects to the internal router, which also connects to the internal network. The routers can provide limited filtering, whereas the bastion host provides a variety of proxy services—for example, HTTP, SSH, IRC, and FTP. This provides some level of security, since attackers are unaware of some internal network details. The bastion host can be viewed as a part of a very small perimeter network.

Compared to the DMZ, a two-router system provides less security. If the bastion host is compromised, the computers in the internal network are not immediately vulnerable, but it would only be a matter of time before they were. Therefore the two-router design should be limited

---

8 J.R. Vacca and S. R. Ellis, *Firewalls Jumpstart for Network and Systems Administrators*, Elsevier, 2005.

9 J.R. Vacca and S. R. Ellis, *Firewalls Jumpstart for Network and Systems Administrators*, Elsevier, 2005.

to separating internal subnetworks. If the internal router is a firewall, the design is considerably more secure.

Dual-Homed Host

A *dual-homed host* system consists of a single computer separating the external network from internal computers.[10] Therefore the dual-homed computer needs at least two network interface cards (NICs). One NIC connects to the external network; the other connects to the internal network—hence the term *dual-homed*. The internal connection is generally a switch that connects the other internal computers.

The dual-homed computer is the location where all traffic arriving and departing the internal network can be processed. The dual-homed computer can perform various tasks such as packet filtering, payload inspection, NAT, and proxy services. Given the simple design and low cost, this setup is popular for home networks. Unfortunately, the dual-homed approach introduces a single point of failure. If the computer fails, then the internal network is isolated from the external network. Therefore this approach is not appropriate for businesses that rely on the Internet.

Network Configuration Summary

This section described various network configurations that can be used to provide varying levels of security. There are certainly variations, but this part of the chapter attempted to describe the most prevalent:

- *Demilitarized zones (DMZs).* When correctly configured, DMZs provide a reasonable level of security. Servers that need to be available to the external network are placed outside the internal network but have a firewall between them and the external network.
- *Perimeter networks.* A perimeter network consists of a subnetwork of systems (again, those that need to be available to the external network) located outside the internal network. The perimeter subnetwork is separated from the external network by a router that can provide some basic packet filtering.
- *Two-router configuration.* The two-router configuration places a bastion host between the internal and external networks. One router is placed between the internal network and bastion host, and

the other router is placed between the bastion host and the external network. The bastion host provides proxy services, which affords some security (but not much).
- *Dual-homed configuration.* A dual-homed configuration has one computer that has at least two network connections—one connected to the external network and another to the internal network. All traffic must transmit through the dual-homed system; thus is can act as a firewall, NAT, and/or IDS. Unfortunately, this system has a single point of failure.

11. FIREWALL INSTALLATION AND CONFIGURATION

Before a firewall is actually deployed, it is important to determine the required services and realize the vulnerabilities that may exist in the computer system that is to be secured. Determining the services requires a detailed understanding of how the computers in the network are interconnected, both physically and from a service-oriented perspective. This is commonly referred to as *object discovery*.

For example, given a database server, which services should the server provide? Which computers should be allowed to connect? Restated, which ports should be open and to whom? Often object discovery is difficult since it is common that a server will be asked to do various tasks over time. Generally a multiservice server is cheaper (one server providing Web, email, and database), but it is rarely more secure. For example, if a multiservice server is compromised via one service, the other services are vulnerable to attack. In other words, the rules in the firewall policy are usually established by the list of available services and secure computers.

Scanning for vulnerabilities is also helpful when you're installing a firewall. Several open-source tools are available to detect system vulnerabilities, including netstat, which shows open services. Why not simply patch the vulnerability? Perhaps the patch is not available yet, or perhaps the application is deemed necessary but it is simply insecure (FTP is an example). Network mappers such as Nessus are also valuable in showing what information about the internal network is available from the outside. Knowing the internal network layout is invaluable in attacking a system, since must modern attacks are multistaged. This means that one type of system vulnerability is typically leveraged to gain access elsewhere within the network.

---

10 J.R. Vacca and S. R. Ellis, *Firewalls Jumpstart for Network and Systems Administrators*, Elsevier, 2005.

A simple and unfortunately common security risk is a Web server that is connected to another internal server for data. Assume that Network File System (NFS) is used to gain access to remote data. If the Web server is compromised, which will probably occur at some time, then all the data inside the data server may be at risk (depending on how permissions have been set) and access to the data could be the true objective of the attacker. Therefore, understanding the interconnection of internal machines can help identify possible multistage attacks.

Of course the process of determining services, access rights, and vulnerabilities is not a one-time occurrence. This process should repeat over time as new computers, operating systems, users, and so on are introduced. Furthermore, firewall changes can cause disruption to legitimate users; these cases require tracing routes, defining objects, and reading policies. Managing a firewall and its policy requires constant vigilance.

12. SUPPORTING OUTGOING SERVICES THROUGH FIREWALL CONFIGURATION

As described in the first section, a firewall and the policy govern access to and from an internal network (the network being administered). A firewall applies a policy to arriving packets, then determines the type of access. The policy can be represented as an ordered set of rules; again, assume that the first-match criterion is used. When a packet arrives, it is compared to the first rule to determine whether it is a match. If it is, then the associated action is performed; otherwise the next rule is tested. Actions include accepting, denying, and logging the packet.

For a simple packet filter, each rule in the policy will describe a certain range of packet headers that it will match. This range of packets is then defined by describing certain parts of the packet header in the rule. For the Internet (TCP/IP networks) there are five such parts that can be described: source IP, source port, destination IP, destination port, and protocol.

Recall that the source IP is the address of the computer that originated the packet. The source port is the number associated with the application that originated the packet. Given the IP address and port number, it is possible to determine the machine and application, within reason. The destination IP and port number describe the computer and the program that will receive the packet. Therefore, given these four pieces of information, it is possible to control the access to and from a certain computer and program. The fifth piece of information is the communication protocol, UDP or TCP.

At this point it is important to also consider the direction of traffic. When referring to a packet, did it come from the external network and is it destined for an internal computer, or vice versa? If the packet is considered inbound, the source and destination addresses are in one order; outbound would reverse the order. Unfortunately, many firewalls will consider any arriving packet as inbound, regardless of where it originated (external or internal network), so the administrator must consider the direction when designing the policy. For example, iptables considers packets as locally or nonlocally generated. Locally generated packets are created at the computer running the firewall; all others are nonlocal, regardless of the source network.

Many firewalls can go beyond the five tuples (TCP/IP packet header parts) described. It is not uncommon to have a rule check the Medium Access Control (MAC) address or hardware address. This can be applied to filter-spoofed addresses. Filtering on the Type of Service (ToS) field is also possible to treat packets differently—for better service, for example.

As previously described, maintaining the state of a connection is important for filtering traffic. For example, maintaining state allows the returning traffic to be accepted if the request was initiated from the internal network. Note that in these simple cases we are only considering two computers communicating—for example, an internal workstation connecting to an external Web server.

Forms of State

The state of a connection can be divided into three main categories: new, established, and related. The new state indicates that this is the first packet in a connection. The established state has observed traffic from both directions, so the minimum requirement is that the source computer sends a packet and receives a packet in reply. The new state will change to *established* once the reply packet is processed by the firewall.

The third type of state is *related*, which is somewhat complicated. A connection is considered related if it is associated with an established connection. Therefore an established connection may create a new connection, separate from the original, which is considered related. The common example of this process is the File Transfer Protocol (FTP), which is used to transmit data from a source computer to a destination computer. The process begins with one connection from source to destination on port 21, the command connection. If there is data to be transferred, a second connection is created on port 20 for the data. Hence the data connection is related to the initial control connection. To simplify the firewall policy, it is possible to add a single rule to permit related connections.

In the previous example, the two computers communicating remained the same, but new connections were created, which can be managed in a table. However, understanding related connections is problematic for many new services. One example is the Common Object Resource Broker Architecture (CORBA), which allows software components to be executed on different computers. This communication model may initiate new connections from different computers, similar to peer-to-peer networking. Therefore it is difficult to associate related connections.

Payload Inspection

Although firewalls originally only inspected the packet header, content filtering is increasingly commonplace. In this case the packet payload (also called *contents* or *data*) is examined for certain patterns (analogous to searching for certain words on a page). These patterns, or signatures, could be for inappropriate or illegal content, spam email messages, or intrusion attempts. For example, it is possible to search for certain URLs in the packet payload.

The patterned searched for is often called a *signature*. If the pattern is found, the packet can be simply dropped, or the administrator may want to log the connection. In terms of intrusion signatures, this includes known patterns that may cause a buffer overflow in a network service.

Content filtering can be used to provide differentiated services as well. For example if the firewall can detect that a connection is used for multimedia, it may be possible to provide more bandwidth or disconnect it, depending on the policy. Of course, content filtering assumes that the content is available (readable), which is not the case when encryption is used. For example, many worms encrypt their communications to prevent content filtering at the firewall.

Examining the packet payload normally requires significantly more processing time than normal header inspection. A signature may actually contain several patterns to match, specifying where they should occur relative to the packet beginning and the distance between patterns in the signature. This is only a short list of potential signature characteristics.

A signature can also span multiple packets—for example, a 20-byte signature could occur over two 10-byte IP fragments. Recall that IP may fragment packets based on the maximum transfer unit (MTU) of a link. Therefore the system may have to reassemble fragments before the scanning can begin. This necessary reassembly will further delay the transmission of data, which is problematic for certain types of applications (for example, multimedia). However, at this point, the discussion is more about intrusion detection systems (IDSs) than firewalls.

Over the years several techniques have been developed to decrease the amount of time required for payload inspection. Faster searching algorithms, dedicated hardware, and parallel searching techniques have all shown promise in this regard. However, payload inspection at high bandwidths with low latency often requires expensive equipment.

13. SECURE EXTERNAL SERVICES PROVISIONING

Often we need a server that will provide services that are widely available to the external network. A Web server is a simple example of providing a service (Web pages) to a potentially large set of users (both honest and dishonest). As a result the server will be subjected to malicious intrusion attempts during its deployment.

Therefore systems that provide external services are often deployed on the edge or perimeter of the internal network. Given the location, it is it important to maintain secure communications between it and other servers. For example, assume that the Web server needs to access a database server for content (PHP and MySQL); the connection between these machines must be secure to ensure proper operation.

A common solution to secure communications is the use of a virtual private network (VPN), which uses encryption to tunnel through an insecure network and provide secrecy. Advanced firewalls can create VPNs to different destinations, including mobile users. The first and most popular protocol for VPN is Internet Security Protocol (IPsec), which consists of standards from IPv6 ported to IPv4.

14. NETWORK FIREWALLS FOR VOICE AND VIDEO APPLICATIONS

The next generation of network applications is expected to better leverage different forms of media. This is evident with the increased use of Voice over IP (VoIP) instead of traditional line-line telephones. Teleconferencing is another application that is seeing a steady increase in use because it provides an easy method for collaborating with others.

Teleoperations is another example that is seeing recent growth. These applications allow operators to control equipment that is at another location over the network (for example, telemedicine). Of course these examples assume that the network can provide QoS guarantees, but that is a separate discussion.

Generally speaking, these applications require special handling by network firewalls. In addition, they normally use more than one connection. For example, the audio, video, and control information of a multimedia application often uses multiple network connections.

Multimedia applications also use multiple transport protocols. Control messages can be sent using TCP, which provides a reliable service between the sender and receiver. The media (voice and/or video) is typically sent using UDP. Often Realtime Transport Protocol (RTP) is used, but this protocol is built on UDP. UDP is unreliable but faster than TCP, which is more important for multimedia applications.

As a result, these connections must be carefully managed by the firewall to ensure the proper operation of the application. This includes maintaining state across multiple connections and ensuring that packets are filtered with minimal delay.

Packet Filtering H.323

There are a few multimedia standards for transmitting voice and video over the Internet. Session Initiation Protocol (SIP) and H.323 are two examples commonly found in the Internet. The section briefly describes H.323 to illustrate the support required by network firewalls.

H.323 is the International Telecommunications Union (ITU) standard for videoconferencing. It is a high-level standard that uses other lower-level standards for the actual setup, transmission, control, and tear-down of a videoconference. For example, G.711 is used for encoding and decoding speech, and H.245 is used to negotiate the connections.

During H.323's operation, one port will be used for call setup using the static port 1720 (easy for firewalls). Each datastream will require one dynamically allocated TCP port for control and one dynamically allocated UDP port for data. As previously described, audio and video are transmitted separately.

Therefore an H.323 session will generate at least eight dynamic connections, which makes packet processing at the firewall very difficult. How does a firewall know which ports to open for an H.323 session? This is referred as a *lack of symmetry* between the computer

located in the internal network and the computer located in the external network.

A stateful firewall can inspect the packet payloads and determine the dynamic connection port numbers. This information (negotiated port numbers) is placed in higher-level protocols, which are difficult to quickly parse and can be vendor specific.

In 2005 the ITU ratified the H.460.17/.18/.19 standards, which describe how to allow H.323 to traverse a firewall (or a NAT router/firewall, which essentially has the same problem). H.460.17 and H.460.18 deal with signaling, whereas H.460.19 concerns media. The H.460 standards require the deployment of stateful firewalls and updated H.323 equipment. This is a solution, but it remains a complex problem.

15. FIREWALLS AND IMPORTANT ADMINISTRATIVE SERVICE PROTOCOLS

There are a large number of administrative network protocols that are used to manage computer systems. These protocols are typically not complex to control at the firewall since dynamic connections are not used and little state information is necessary. The administrator should be aware of these services when designing the security policy, since many can be leveraged for attacks. This section reviews some of these important protocols.

Routing Protocols

Routing protocols are used to distribute routing information between routing devices. This information will change over time based on network conditions; therefore this information is critical to ensure that packets will get to their destinations. Of course, attackers can also use routing protocols for attacks. For example, maliciously setting routes such that a certain network is not reachable can be considered a denial-of-service (DoS) attack. Securing routers and routing protocols is a continuing area of research. The firewall can help prevent these attacks (typically by not forwarding such information).

In considering routing protocols, it is important to first determine which devices in the internal network will need to receive and submit routing information. More than likely only devices that are directly connected to the external network will need to receive and respond to external routing changes—for example, the gateway router(s) for the internal network. This is primarily due to the hierarchical nature of routing tables, which does not require an external host to know the routing specifics of a distant subnetwork. As a result, there is typically no need to forward routing information from the external network into the internal network, and vice versa.

Routing Information Protocol (RIP) is the oldest routing protocol for the Internet. The two versions of RIP differ primarily by the inclusion of security measures. RIPv1 is the original protocol, and RIPv2 is the same but supports classless addresses and includes some security. Devices that use RIP will periodically (approximately every 30 seconds) broadcast routing information to neighboring hosts. The information sent by a host describes the devices they are directly connected to and the cost. RIP is not very scalable so is primarily used for small networks. RIP uses UDP to broadcast messages; port 520 is used by servers, whereas clients use a port above 1023.

Another routing protocol is Open Short Path First (OSPF), which was developed after RIP. As such OSPF is considered an improvement because it converges faster and it incorporates authentication. Interestingly, OSPF is not built on the transport layer but instead talks directly to IP. It is considered protocol 89 by the IP layer. OSPF messages are broadcast using two special multicast IP addresses: 224.0.0.5 (all SPF/link state routers) and 224.0.0.6 (all designated routers). The use of multicast addresses and setting the packet Time to Live (TTL) to one (which is done by OSPF) typically means a firewall will not pass this routing information.

Internet Control Message Protocol

Internet Control Message Protocol (ICMP) is used to send control messages to network devices and hosts. Routers and other network devices monitor the operation of the network. When an error occurs, these devices can send a message using ICMP. Messages that can be sent include destination unreachable, time exceeded, and echo request.

Although ICMP was intended to help manage the network, unfortunately attackers can use it as well. Several attacks are based on ICMP messages since they were originally allowed through the firewall. For example, simply forging a "destination unreachable" ICMP message can cause problems.

The program ping is one program that uses ICMP to determine whether a system is connected to the Internet (it uses the ICMP messages Echo Request and Echo Reply). However, this program can also be used for a smurf attack, which causes a large number of unsolicited ping replies to be sent toward one computer. As a result most firewall administrators do not allow ping requests or replies across the firewall.

Another program that uses ICMP is traceroute, which determines the path (list of routers) between a source and destination. Finding the path is done by sending multiple packets, each with an increasing TTL number (starting at one). When a router encounters a packet that it cannot forward due to the TTL, an ICMP message is sent back to the source. This reveals the router on the path (assuming that the path remains the same during the process). Most administrators do not want to provide this information, since it can show addresses assigned to hosts, which is useful to attackers. As a result firewalls are often configured to only allow traceroute requests originating from the internal network or limiting replies to traceroute originating from known external computers.

ICMP is built on the IP layer, like TCP and UDP. A firewall can filter these messages based on the message code field, which is a number that corresponds to each type of error message. Although this section described the problems with allowing ICMP messages through the firewall, an administrator may not want to block all ICMP packets. For example, Maximum Transfer Unit (MTU) messages are important for the transmission of packets and probably should be allowed.

Network Time Protocol

Network Time Protocol (NTP) is a protocol that allows the synchronization of system clocks (from desktops to servers). Having synchronized clocks is not only convenient but required for many distributed applications. Therefore the firewall policy must allow the NTP service if the time comes from an external server.

NTP is a built-on UDP, where port 123 is used for NTP server communication and NTP clients use port 1023 (for example, a desktop). Unfortunately, like many legacy protocols, NTP suffers from security issues. It is possible to spoof NTP packets, causing clocks to set to various times (an issue for certain services that run periodically). There are several cases of NTP misuse and abuse where servers are the victim of DoS attacks.

As a result, if clock synchronization is needed, it may be better to provide an internal NTP server (master clock) that synchronizes the remaining clocks in the internal network. If synchronization is needed by an NTP server in the Internet, consider using a bastion host.

Central Log File Management

Almost every operating system maintains a system log where important information about a system's state is reported. This log is a valuable resource for managing system resources and investigating security issues.

Given that almost every system (especially a server) generates log messages, having this information at a central location is beneficial. The protocol syslog provides this functionality, whereby messages can be forwarded to a syslog server, where they are stored. An attacker will commonly attempt to flood the syslog server with fake messages in an effort to cover their steps or to cause the server disk to fill, causing syslog to stop.

Syslog runs on UDP, where syslog servers listen to UDP port 514 and clients (sending log messages) use a port above 1023. Note that a syslog server will not send a message back to the client, but the syslog log server can communicate, normally using port 514.

Generally allowing syslog communication between the external and internal network is not needed or advised. Syslog communications should be limited to internal computers and servers; otherwise a VPN should be used to prevent abuse from others and to keep the information in the messages private.

Dynamic Host Configuration Protocol

The Dynamic Host Configuration Protocol (DHCP) provides computers essential information when connecting to an IP network. This is necessary because a computer (for example, a mobile laptop) does not have an IP address to use.

The computer needing an IP address will first send a broadcast request for an IP address. A DHCP server will reply with the IP address, netmask, and gateway router information the computer should use. The address provided comes from a pool of available IP addresses, which is managed by the DHCP server. Therefore the DHCP provides a method of sharing IP addresses among a group of hosts that will change over time.

The actual exchange of information is more elaborate than described here, but this is enough information for our discussion. In general the DHCP server providing addresses will be located in the internal network. As a result, this information should not be transmitted across the firewall that separates the internal and external networks. Why would you want to provide IP addresses to computers in the external network?

16. INTERNAL IP SERVICES PROTECTION

Domain Name Service (DNS) provides the translation between the hostname and the IP address, which is

necessary to send packets in the Internet. Given the number of hostnames in the Internet, DNS is built on a hierarchical structure. The local DNS server cannot store all the possible hostnames and IP addresses, so this server will need to occasionally request a translation from another DNS server located in the external network. As a result it is important to configure the firewall to permit this type of lookup.

In many cases the service provider provides the address of a DNS server that can be used to translate external hostnames. There is no need to manage a local DNS server in this case. However, it is possible to manage a local DNS, which allows the internal network to use local hostnames (these can be published to the external network). Some advanced firewalls can provide DNS, which can help hide internal computer hostnames and IP addresses. As a result, external computers have a limited view of the internal network.

Another important service that can be provided by the firewall is Network Address Translation (NAT). NAT is a popular method for sharing a smaller set of IP addresses across a larger number of computers. Recall that every packet has a source IP, source port, destination IP, and destination port. Assume that a small network only has one external IP address but has multiple computers that need to access the Internet. Note the external address is a routable address, whereas the internal computers would use a private address (addresses have no meaning outside the internal network). NAT will allow the internal machines to share the single external IP address.[11]

When a packet arrives from a computer in the internal network, its source address is replaced with the external address, as shown in Figure 21.4. The packet is sent to the destination computer, which returns a packet. The return packet has the external address (which is routable), so it is forwarded to the firewall. The firewall can then replace the external destination address with the correct internal destination address. What if multiple internal machines send a packet to a server in the external network? The firewall will replace the source address with the external address, but how will the firewall differentiate the return packets? NAT will also change the source port number, so each connection can be separated.

The NAT process described in the preceding paragraph is *source NAT*[12], which works for packets initiated in the internal network. There is also *destination NAT*,

11 B. Hickman, D. Newman, S. Tadjudin, and T. Martin, *Benchmarking Methodology for Firewall Performance*, IETF RFC 3511, 2003.
12 K. Egevang and P. Francis, *The IP Network Address Translator (NAT)*, IETF RFC 1631, 1994.

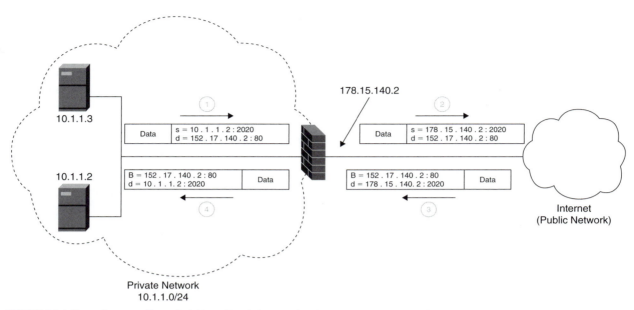

FIGURE 21.4 Example source Network Address Translation (NAT). The connection originates from a computer in the internal network and is sent to a computer in the external network. Note the address and port number exchange performed at the firewall.

which works in a similar fashion for packets initiated in the external network. In this case the firewall needs to know which machine to forward packets to in the internal network.

17. FIREWALL REMOTE ACCESS CONFIGURATION

As described in the first section, firewalls are deployed to help maintain the privacy of data and authenticate the source. Privacy can be provided using encryption, for which there are several possible algorithms to use. These algorithms can be categorized as either secret key or public key. Secret key techniques use the same key to encrypt and decrypt information. Examples include IDEA, RC4, Twofish, and AES. Though secret key algorithms are fast, they require the key to be distributed between the two parties in advance, which is not trivial.

Public key encryption uses two keys—one to encrypt (the public key) and another to decrypt (the private key). The public key can be freely available for others to use to encrypt messages for the owner of the private key, since only the private key can decrypt a message. Key management sounds easy, but secure key distribution is difficult. How do you know the public key obtained is the correct one? Perhaps it is a man-in-middle attack. The Public Key Infrastructure (PKI), one method of distributing public keys, depends on a system of trusted key servers.

Authentication is another important component of security; it attempts to confirm a person is who he or she claims to be. This can be done based on what the user has (ID card or security token) or by something a person knows (for example, a password). A very familiar method of authentication is requesting a username and password, which is common for VPNs.

Secrecy and authentication are also important when an entity manages multiple separate networks. In this case the administrator would like to interconnect the networks but must do so using an insecure network (for example, the Internet).

Tunneling from one firewall to another firewall can create a secure interconnection. This can be done using application proxies or VPN. Application firewalls implement a proxy for each application supported. A user first contacts the firewall and authenticates before connecting to the server. The firewall then connects to the destination firewall, which then connects to the destination server. Three connections are thus involved.

An alternative is to construct a VPN from one firewall to another. Now a secure connection exists between the two networks. However, note that the VPN could also be used as an easy connection for an attacker who has successfully broken into one of the networks.

It is also important to note that tunneling can be used to transport packets over a network with a different transport protocol—for example, carrying TCP/IP traffic over Frame Relay.

18. LOAD BALANCING AND FIREWALL ARRAYS

As network speeds continue to increase, firewalls must continue to process packets with minimal delay (latency). Unfortunately, firewalls that can operate at these extreme data rates are also typically very expensive and cannot easily be upgraded to meet future demands. Load-balancing firewalls can provide an answer to this important problem.[13]

Load balancing (or *parallelization*) provides a scalable firewall solution for high-bandwidth networks and/or low-latency applications. This approach consists of an array of firewalls that process arriving packets in parallel. A simple system would consist of two load balancers connected to an array of firewalls, where each firewall is identically configured (same firewall policy), as depicted in Figure 21.5. One balancer connects to the Internet, then to the array (arriving traffic); the other balancer connects to the internal network, then to the array (departing traffic). Of course, one load balancer can be used instead of two separate load balancers.

When a packet arrives, it is sent to a firewall that currently has the lightest load (fewest number of packets awaiting processing), hence the term *load balancing*. As a result, the amount of traffic each firewall must process is roughly $1/n$ of the total traffic, where n is the number of firewalls in the array.

As with any new firewall implementation, the integrity of the policy must be maintained. This means that given a policy, a traditional single firewall and a load-balancing firewall will accept the same packets and deny the same packets. For static rules, integrity is provided,

since the policy is duplicated at every firewall; therefore the set of accepted and denied packets at each firewall is also the same. As will be discussed in the next sections, maintaining integrity for stateful rules is not easy.

Load Balancing in Real Life

A simple supermarket analogy can help describe the system and the potential performance increase. Consider a market consisting of an array of n cashiers. As with the firewall system, each cashier in the market is identical and performs the same duties. When a customer wants to pay for her items, she is directed to the cashier with the shortest line. The load balancer is the entity that would direct the customer, but in reality such a person rarely exists. A customer must guess which line is actually the best to join, which as we all know is not simple to determine.

Obviously, as more cashiers are added, the market can check out more customers. This is akin to increasing the bandwidth of the firewall system. Another important advantage of a load-balancing system is robustness. Even if a cashier takes a break (or a firewall in the array fails), the system will still function properly, albeit more slowly.

How to Balance the Load

An important problem with load-balancing firewalls is how to quickly balance the lines (queues) of packets. We are all aware that customers require different amounts of time to check out of a market. This is dependent on the number of items (which is observable) and their ability to pay (not easily observable). Similarly, it is difficult to determine how much time a packet will require at a firewall (for software-based systems). It will depend on the number of rules, organization of the rules, and which rule the packet will match.

A more important problem with load balancing is how to maintain state. As described in the preceding sections, some firewall rules will maintain the state of a connection. For example, a firewall rule may allow traffic arriving from the Internet only if an internal computer requested it. If this is the case, a new temporary rule will be generated to handle traffic arriving from the Internet. In a parallel system, where should this rule reside? Which firewall? The objective is to ensure that the integrity of the policy is maintained in the load-balancing system.

To use the market analogy again (and this will be a stretch), assume that a mother leaves her credit card with one cashier, then sends her children into the market to buy certain items. When the children are ready to pay for

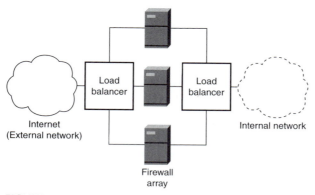

FIGURE 21.5 Load-balancing firewall array consisting of a three-firewall array and a load balancer.

13 Errin W. Fulp and Ryan J. Farley, "A function-parallel architecture for high-speed firewalls," In *Proceedings of the IEEE International Conference on Communications*, 2006.

their items they must go to the cashier that has the credit card. If the children don't know which cashier has the credit card the load balancer must not only balance lines but also check a list to make certain the children join the correct line.

Maintaining state increases the amount of time the load balancer will spend per packet, which increases the latency of the system. An alternative solution is it to replicate the stateful rules across every firewall (or the credit card across every cashier). This requires an interconnection and state-aware program per firewall. Maintaining network connections is also difficult for applications that dynamically create new connections. Examples include FTP (one connection for control, the other for data), multimedia, and CORBA. Again, a new rule must be added to handle the new traffic.

Advantages and Disadvantages of Load Balancing

Given these issues, firewall load balancing is still done. There are several advantages and disadvantages to this approach. Disadvantages of load balancing include:

- *Load balancing is not trivial.* The load balancer seeks to ensure that the lines of packets across the array of firewalls remains equal. However, this assumes that the balancer can predict how much time a packet will require.
- *Maintaining state is difficult.* All packets that belong to a session will need to traverse the same firewall, or state information must be shared across the firewalls. Either solution is difficult to manage.

There are several advantages to load balancing:

- *Scalable solution for higher throughput.* If higher throughput is needed, adding more firewalls is simple and cost effective.
- *Robustness.* If a firewall fails in the array, the integrity of the system remains. The only loss is throughput.
- *Easy policy management.* If the rules change, simply update the policy at each firewall.

The load balancer can be implemented in software or hardware. Hardware load balancers provide better performance, but they will also have a much higher price.

19. HIGHLY AVAILABLE FIREWALLS

As previously discussed, a network firewall is generally considered easier to manage than multiple host-based firewalls. The administrator only manages one firewall and one policy, but this design also introduces a single point of failure. If the network firewall fails in the system, the entire internal network is isolated from the Internet. As a result, there is a real need to provide a highly available, or robust, firewall system.

The load-balancing system described in the previous section provides a greater degree of robustness. If a firewall in the array fails, the system is still functional; however, the capacity of the system is reduced, which is considered acceptable under the circumstances. Unfortunately, the design still has a single point of failure—the load distributor. If the load distributor fails, the entire system fails.

A simple solution to this problem simply replicates the load distributor. The incoming connection is duplicated to both load distributors, and the distributors are then connected to the firewalls in the array. The distributors are interconnected via a lifeline to detect failure and possibly share information.

Load Balancer Operation

The two load balancers described in the previous section can operate in one of two modes: active-backup or active-active. In active-backup mode, one balancer operates as normal distributing packets to minimize delays and maintain state information. The second distributor is in backup mode and monitors the status of the active load balancer and duplicates any necessary state information. Upon load-balance failure, the backup device can quickly take over operation.

In contrast, active-active operation operates both load balancers in parallel. When a packet arrives at the system, it is processed by one of the load balancers, which forwards the packet to a firewall in the array. Of course, this seems as though there will be a load balancer for the load balancers, but this is not necessary. Under active-active mode, the load balancers use the lifeline to synchronize and determine which packets to process. Although the active-active mode can increase performance by using both load balancers simultaneously, it is more difficult to implement and complex to manage.

Interconnection of Load Balancers and Firewalls

In our simple example, the additional load balancer requires double the number of ports per firewall (one per load balancer). This design provides greater robustness but may also be cost prohibitive.

An alternative solution uses active-active mode and divides the array into two equal groups. One group is then connected to one load-balancer and the other group is connected to the other. For example, consider an array of six firewalls. Three firewalls would be connected to one load balancer and the other six firewalls connected to the second load balancer. Although this design only requires one port per firewall (on one side), if a load balancer fails, half the firewalls are nonoperational.

20. FIREWALL MANAGEMENT

Once a firewall has been deployed and policy created, it is important to determine whether it is providing the desired security. Auditing is the process of verifying the firewall and policy and consists of two steps. First, the administrator should determine whether the firewall is secure. If an attacker can exploit the firewall, the attacker has a significant advantage. Consider the information that can be gained just from knowing the firewall policy.

The firewall should be in a secure location and have the latest security patches (recall that many firewalls are implemented in software). Also ensure that the firewall only provides the necessary services, such as SSH, if remote access to the firewall is needed. Exploiting a firewall operating system or provided services is the most common method for breaking into a firewall. Therefore the services and access should be tightly controlled. User authentication with good passwords and secure connections should always be used.

Once the firewall has been secured, the administrator should review the policy and verify that it provides the security desired. Does it block the illegitimate traffic and permit legitimate traffic? This is not a trivial task, given the first-match criterion and the number of rules in the policy. It is easy to create firewall policies with anomalies, such as shadowing (a subsequent rule that is never matched because of an earlier rule). Some software packages are available to assist this process, but in general it is a difficult problem.

An administrator should periodically audit the firewall rules and test the policy to verify that the system performs as expected. In addition, the system should undergo penetration testing to verify correct implementation. This includes seeded and blind penetration testing. *Seeded testing* includes detailed information about the network and configuration, so target systems and services can be tested. *Blind testing* is done without any knowledge of the system, so it is more complete but also more time consuming.

Keeping backups of configurations and policies should be done in case of hardware failure or an intrusion. Logging at the firewall should also be performed, which can help measure performance. In addition, logs can show connections over time, which is useful for forensics and verifying whether the security policy is sufficient.

21. CONCLUSION

Network firewalls are a key component of providing a secure environment. These systems are responsible for controlling access between two networks, which is done by applying a security policy to arriving packets. The policy describes which packets should be accepted and which should be dropped. The firewall inspects the packet header and/or the payload (data portion).

There are several different types of firewalls, each briefly described in this chapter. Firewalls can be categorized based on what they inspect (packet filter, stateful, or application), their implementation (hardware or software), or their location (host or network). Combinations of the categories are possible, and each type has specific advantages and disadvantages.

Placement of the firewall with respect to servers and internal computers is key to the way these systems will be protected. Often servers that are externally available, such as Web servers, will be located away from other internal computers. This is often accomplished by placing these servers in a demilitarized zone (DMZ). A different security policy is applied to these computers so the access between computers in the DMZ and the internal network is limited.

Improving the performance of the firewall can be achieved by minimizing the rules in the policy (primarily for software firewalls). Moving more popular rules near the beginning of the policy can also reduce the number of rules comparisons that are required. However, the order of certain rules must be maintained (any rules that can match the same packet).

Parallel firewalls can provide greater performance improvements. These systems consist of a load balancer and an array of firewalls, where all the firewalls in the array are identical. When a packet arrives at the system, it is sent to one of the firewalls in the array. The load balancer maintains short packet queues, which can provide greater system bandwidth and possibly a lower latency.

Regardless of the firewall implementation, placement, or design, deployment requires constant vigilance. Developing the appropriate policy (set of rules) requires a detailed understanding of the network topology and the necessary services. If either of these items change (and they certainly will), that will require updating the policy. Finally, it is important to remember that a firewall is not a complete security solution but is a key part of a security solution.

## Chapter 22

Penetration Testing

Sanjay Bavisi
EC-Council

Last year I walked into a restaurant in Rochester, New York, with a business partner; I was wearing an EC-Council official polo shirt. The back of the shirt was embroidered with the words "Licensed Penetration Tester." On reading those words on my shirt, a group of young executives seated behind me started an intense dialogue among themselves.

They were obviously not amused at my "behavior," since that was a restaurant for decent people! On my way out, I walked up to them and asked if they were amazed at what that statement meant. They replied "Absolutely!" When I explained to them the meaning of a Licensed Penetration Tester, they gave a loud laugh and apologized to me. They admitted that they had thought I was a pervert.

Each time I am at an airport, I get some stares when I put on that shirt. So the question is, what is penetration testing?

In this chapter, we'll talk about penetration testing and what it is (and isn't!), how it differs from an actual "hacker attack," some of the ways penetration tests are conducted, how they're controlled, and what organizations might look for when they're choosing a company to conduct a penetration test for them.

Because this is a chapter and not an entire book, there are a lot of things that I just don't have the space to talk about. What you're about to read is, quite literally, just the tip of the iceberg when it comes to penetration testing. Keep that in mind when you think to yourself: "What about . . .?" The answer to your question (whatever it might be) is probably a part of our licensed penetration tester certification course!

1. WHAT IS PENETRATION TESTING?

Penetration testing is the exploitation of vulnerabilities present in an organization's network. It helps determine which vulnerabilities are exploitable and the degree of information exposure or network control that the organization could expect an attacker to achieve after successfully exploiting a vulnerability. No penetration test is or ever can be "just like a hacker would do it," due to necessary limitations placed on penetration tests conducted by "white hats." Hackers don't have to follow the same rules as the "good guys" and they could care less whether your systems crash during one of their "tests." We'll talk more about this later. Right now, before we can talk any more about penetration testing, we need to talk about various types of vulnerabilities and how they might be discovered.

Before we can exploit a vulnerability in a penetration test, we have to discover what vulnerabilities exist within (and outside of) the organization. A vulnerability is a potential weakness in an organization's security. I use the term "potential" because not all vulnerabilities are exploitable or worth exploiting. A flaw may exist and may even be documented, but perhaps no one has figured out (yet) how to exploit it. Some vulnerabilities, although exploitable, might not yield enough information in return for the time or resources necessary to exploit them. Why break into a bank and steal only a dollar? That doesn't make much sense, does it?

Vulnerabilities can be thought of in two broad categories: logical and physical. We normally think of logical vulnerabilities as those associated with the organization's computers, infrastructure devices, software, or applications. Physical vulnerabilities, on the other hand, are normally thought of as those having to do with either the actual physical security of the organization (such as a door that doesn't always lock properly), the sensitive information that "accidentally" ends up in the dumpster, or the vulnerability of the organization's employees to social engineering (a vendor asking to use a computer to send a "quick email" to the boss).

Logical vulnerabilities can be discovered using any number of manual or automated tools and even by browsing the Internet. For those of you who are familiar with Johnny Long's *Google Hacking* books: "*Passwords, for the love of God!!!* Google found *passwords!*" The discovery of logical vulnerabilities is usually called *security scanning, vulnerability scanning,* or just *scanning.* Unfortunately, there are a number of "security consultants" who run a scan, put a fancy report cover on the output of the tool, and pass off these scans as a penetration test.

Physical vulnerabilities can be discovered as part of a physical security inspection, a "midnight raid" on the organization's dumpsters, getting information from employees, or via unaccompanied access to a usually nonpublic area (I really need to use the bathroom!).

Vulnerabilities might also exist due to a lack of company policies or procedures or an employee's failure to follow the policy or procedure. Regardless of the cause of the vulnerability, it might have the potential to compromise the organization's security. So, of all the vulnerabilities that have been discovered, how do we know which ones pose the greatest danger to the organization's network? We test them! We test them to see which ones we can exploit and exactly what could happen if a "real" attacker exploited that vulnerability.

Because few organizations that I know of have enough money, time, or resources to eliminate every vulnerability discovered, they have to prioritize their efforts; this is one of the best reasons for an organization to conduct a penetration test. At the conclusion of the penetration test, they will know which vulnerabilities can be exploited and what can happen if they are exploited. They can then plan to correct the vulnerabilities based on the amount of critical information exposed or network control gained by exploiting the vulnerability. In other words, a penetration test helps organizations strike a balance between security and business functionality. Sounds like a perfect solution, right? If only it were so!

There are organizations that do not care about the "true risks" that their organizations face. Instead, they are more interested in being able to tell their shareholders or their regulating agencies that they've conducted a penetration test and "passed" it. If the penetration test is structured so that only certain systems are tested, or if the test is conducted during a known timeframe, the test results will be favorable to the organization, but the test isn't a true reflection of its network security posture. This kind of "boutique testing" can lead to a false sense of security for the organization, its employees, and its stakeholders.

2. HOW DOES PENETRATION TESTING DIFFER FROM AN ACTUAL "HACK?"

Earlier, I mentioned that penetration testing isn't and never can be "just like a hacker would do it." How come? Except in the case of "directed" sabotage or espionage, it's not personal between your organization and attackers. They don't care who you are, where you are, or what your organization does to earn its living. They just want to hack something. The easier it is to attack your network, the more likely it is that you'll be a target. Ask your network administrator to look at the network intrusion detection logs (or look at them yourself if you're a network admin). See how many times in a 24-hour period your organization's network gets scanned for potential vulnerabilities.

Once an attacker has decided that you're his or her (yes, there *are* female hackers—good ones, too!) next target, they may take weeks or months to perform the first step of an attack: reconnaissance. As a penetration tester or company providing penetration testing services, I doubt that you're going to get hired to spend six months doing reconnaissance and another couple of months conducting an attack. So, the first difference between a penetration test and a real attack is the length of time taken to conduct all the activities needed to produce a successful outcome. As "good guys," we don't have the luxury of time that the "bad guys" do. So we're handicapped to begin with.

In some (not all) cases, once attackers find a suitable vulnerability to attack, they will. They don't care that the vulnerability resides on a mission-critical system, if the vulnerability will crash the system, or that the system might become unusable in the middle of the busiest time of day. If that vulnerability doesn't "pan out," they find another and try again. They keep it up until they run out of vulnerabilities that they can exploit, or they're discovered, or they manage to successfully breach the network or crash the system. Penetration test teams normally don't have this luxury, either. Usually the test team has *X* amount of time to find a vulnerability and get in or the test is over and the network is declared "safe and secure." If the test team didn't have enough time to test all the vulnerabilities—oh, well. The test is still over, they still didn't get in, and so our network *must* be safe! Few seem to think about the fact that a "real" attacker may, just by blind luck, choose one of the unable-to-be-tested-because-of-time-limitations vulnerabilities and be able to waltz right into the network without being detected.

Some systems are declared "off limits" to testing because they're "too important to have crash" during a test. An organization may specify that testing can only occur during certain hours or on certain days because of a real or perceived impact on business operations. This is the second difference between a penetration test and a real attack: Hackers don't play by any rules. They attack what they want when they want and how they want. Just to be clear: I'm not advocating denial-of-service testing during the busiest time of an organization's day, or unrestricted testing at any time. I'm just trying to make a point that *no* system is too critical to test. From a hacker's perspective, there are no "off-limits" systems, just opportunities for attack. We'll talk more about differences between real attacks and penetration tests when we talk about the various types of testing in the next section.

3. TYPES OF PENETRATION TESTING

Some sources classify penetration testing into two types—internal and external—and then talk about the "variations" of these types of tests based on the amount of information the test team has been given about the organization prior to starting the test. Other sources use a reverse-classification system, typing the penetration test based on the amount of information available to the test team and then the location from which the test is conducted. I much prefer the latter method, since it removes any chance of misunderstanding about what testing is going to be conducted where. *Warning:* If you're planning to take the CISSP or some of the other network security certification examinations, stick with the "old skool" "classification by location, then type" definitions for penetration testing types and variations.

When a penetration test is conducted against Internet-facing hosts, it is known as *external testing*. When conducted against hosts inside the organization's internal network, it is known as *internal testing*. Obviously, a complete penetration test will encompass testing of both external and internal hosts. The "variations" of penetration tests are normally classified based on how much information the test team has been given about the organization. The three most commonly used terms for penetration types are *white-box, gray-box,* and *black-box testing.* Before we talk about these penetration testing variations, you need to understand that we can conduct any of them (white, gray, or black) either externally or internally. If we want a complete test, we need to test both externally *and* internally. Got it? Good! Now we can talk about what is involved with each type of testing.

We'll start with white-box testing. The "official" definition of white-box testing usually includes verbiage

about providing information so as to be able to assess the security of a specific target or assess security against a specific attack. There are several problems with this definition in real life. The first is that it sounds as though you would only conduct a white-box test if you were looking to verify the security of one specific host or looking to verify the security of your network against one specific attack. But it would be foolhardy to test for only one vulnerability. Since the "variations" we're talking about are supposed to be centered on the amount of information available to the test team, let's look at a white-box test from an information availability perspective.

Who in your organization knows the most about your network? Probably the network administrator. Any organization that has recently terminated employment of a network administrator or member of the IT Department under less than favorable circumstances has a big problem. There is the potential that the organization's network could be attacked by this former employee who has extreme knowledge about the network. In a white-box test, therefore, the test team should be given about the same amount of information that a network administrator would have. Probably the team won't be given passwords, but they'll be given network ranges, topologies, and so on.

Gray-box testing, by "official" definition, provides "some" knowledge to the test team, about the sort of thing a normal, unprivileged user might have: hostnames, maybe a few IP addresses, the fact that the organization allows senior management to "remote" into the network, and so on. Common, though not necessarily public, knowledge about the "inner workings" of the organization's network is the level of information provided to the test team. Some sources claim that this testing type (as well as the information disclosed in a white-box test) "puts the tester at an advantage" over an attacker because the test team possesses information that an attacker wouldn't have. But that's not necessarily the case. Any organization that has terminated a "normal user" has the potential for an attack based on that user's inside knowledge of the network.

Now let's talk about everyone's favorite: black-box penetration testing. Again, we'll start with the common definition, which usually says something like "provides the test team with little or no information except for possibly the company name." The test team is required to obtain all their attack information from public sources such as the Internet. There's usually some sentence somewhere in the description that says how a black-box test is always much better than any other type of test because it most closely mimics the way an attacker would conduct an attack. The definition might be right (and I might even be inclined to agree with it) if the organization has never terminated a network admin or any other employee with network access. I might also be more in agreement with this train of thought if the majority of attacks were conducted by unknown persons from the far reaches of the globe instead of former employees or currently employed "insiders"!

Depending on what article or book you happen to be reading at the time, you might also see references to application penetration testing, Web penetration testing, shrink-wrap penetration testing, wireless penetration testing, telephony penetration testing, Bluetooth penetration testing . . . and the list goes on. I've seen every possible device in a network listed as a separate penetration test. The bottom line is that if it's present in the network, an organization needs to discover what vulnerabilities exist on it and then test those vulnerabilities to discover what could happen if they're successfully exploited.

I guess since Morgan Kaufmann asked me to write this chapter, I can give you my opinion: I don't like black-box penetration testing. I don't want any network of mine tested "just like a hacker would do it." I want my network tested *better* than any hacker ever could, because I don't want to end up on the front page of *The New York Times* as the subject of a "latest breach" article. My client's data are much too important to take that chance.

The success of every penetration test rests on the experience of the test team. If some hacker has more experience than the test team I hire, I'm in trouble! So how do I even the odds? Instead of hiring a team to do a black box, in which they're going to spend hours searching for information and poking around, I give them the necessary information to test the network thoroughly, right up front. By doing so, their time is actually spent testing the network, not carrying out a high-tech scavenger hunt. Any good penetration test team is still going to do reconnaissance and tell me what information is available about my organization from public sources anyway. No, I'm not going to give up the administrative password to my network. But I am going to tell them what my IP ranges are, whether or not I have wireless, and whether I allow remote access into the network, among other things.

In addition to the types and variations of penetration testing, we also need to talk about announced and unannounced testing. Which of these two methods will be used depends on whether your intent is to test the network itself or the network's security staff. In an announced test, the penetration testing team works in "full cooperation" with the IT staff and the IT staff has "full knowledge" about the test, such as what will be tested and when. In an unannounced test, only specific members of the tested organization (usually the higher levels of management) are aware that the testing will take place. Even they may only know a "window" of time for testing, not the exact times or dates.

If you follow the published guidelines, an unannounced test is used when testing an organization's incident response capability is called for. Announced tests are used when the organization simply wants to test network devices. Is this really how it happens in the real world? Sometimes it isn't.

Most organizations that conduct annual testing do so at about the same time every year, especially if it's a government organization. So there's really no such thing as an "unannounced" test. Everyone knows that sometime between X and Y dates, they're going to be tested. In some organizations this means that during that timeframe there suddenly appears to be an increased awareness of network security. Machines get patched quicker. Logs are reviewed daily. Abnormal activities are reported immediately. After the testing window is over, however, it's back to the same old routine until the next testing window, next year.

What about announced testing, you ask? Think about it: If you're a network administrator and you know a test is coming, you're going to make sure that everything is as good as you can make it. Once again, there's that increased emphasis on security—until the testing window is over, that is.

Let's take a minute to recap what we've talked about so far. We've learned that a penetration test is used to exploit discovered vulnerabilities and to help determine what an attacker could do if they successfully exploited a vulnerability. We learned that not all vulnerabilities are actually a concern, because there might not be a way to exploit them or what we'd get by exploiting them wouldn't justify the time or effort we spent in doing so. We learned that there are different types and variations of penetration tests, that they can be announced or unannounced, and that none of them are actually "just like a hacker would do it." Probably the most important thing we've learned so far is that if we really and truly want to protect our network from a real-life attack, we have to offset the biggest advantage that a hacker has: time. We discovered that we can do this by giving the testing team sufficient information to thoroughly test the network instead of surfing the Internet on our dime.

What's next? Let's talk about how a penetration test might be conducted.

4. PHASES OF PENETRATION TESTING

There are three phases in a penetration test, and they mimic the phases that an attacker would use to conduct a real attack. These phases are the pre-attack phase, the attack phase, and the post-attack phase, as shown in Figure 22.1.

The activities that take place in each phase (as far as the penetration testing team is concerned) depend on how the rules of engagement have specified that the penetration test be conducted. To give you a more complete picture, we talk about these phases from the perspective of a hacker and from that of a penetration team conducting the test under "black-box" conditions.

The Pre-Attack Phase

The pre-attack phase (see Figure 22.2) consists of the penetration team's or hacker's attempts to investigate or explore the potential target. This reconnaissance effort is normally categorized into two types: active reconnaissance and passive reconnaissance.

Beginning with passive reconnaissance, which does not "touch" the network and is therefore undetectable by

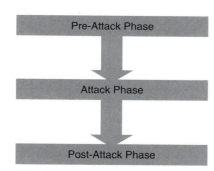

FIGURE 22.1 The three phases in a penetration test.

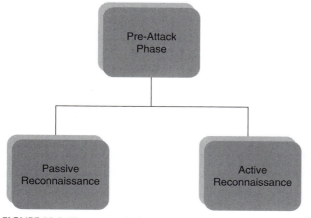

FIGURE 22.2 The pre-attack phase.

the target organization, the hacker or penetration tester will gather as much information as possible about the target company. Once all available sources for passive reconnaissance have been exhausted, the test team or attacker may move into active reconnaissance.

During active reconnaissance, the attacker may actually "touch" the network, thereby increasing the chance that they will be detected or alert the target that someone is "rattling the doorknobs." Some of the information gathered during reconnaissance can be used to produce a provisional map of the network infrastructure for planning a more coordinated attack strategy later. Ultimately it boils down to information gathering in all its many forms. Hackers will often spend more time on pre-attack or reconnaissance activities than on the actual attack itself.

The Attack Phase

This stage involves the actual compromise of the target. The hacker or test team may exploit a logical or physical vulnerability discovered during the pre-attack phase or use other methods such as a weak security policy to gain access to a system. The important point here is to understand that although there could be several possible vulnerabilities, the hacker needs only one to be successful to compromise the network.

By comparison, a penetration test team will be interested in finding and exploiting as many vulnerabilities as possible because neither the organization nor the test team will know which vulnerability a hacker will choose to exploit first (see Figure 22.3). Once inside, the attacker may attempt to escalate his or her privileges, install one or more applications to sustain their access, further exploit the compromised system, and/or attempt to extend their control to other systems within the network. When they've finished having their way with the system or network, they will attempt to eliminate all evidence of their presence in a process some call "covering their tracks."

The Post-Attack Phase

The post-attack phase is unique to the penetration test team. It revolves around returning any modified system(s) to the pretest state. With the exception of covering their tracks, a real attacker couldn't care less about returning a compromised system to its original state. The longer the system remains compromised, the longer they can legitimately claim credit for "pwning" (owning) the system.

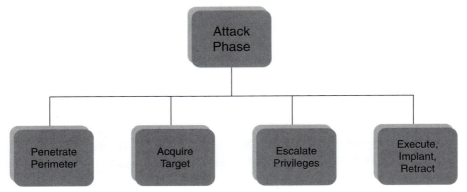

FIGURE 22.3 The attack phase.

Obviously, in a real penetration test, the following list would include reversal of each and every change made to the network to restore it to its pre-attack state. Some of the activities that the test team may have to accomplish are shown here:

- Removal of any files, tools, exploits, or other test-created objects uploaded to the system during testing
- Removal or reversal of any changes to the registry made during system testing
- Reversal of any access control list (ACL) changes to file(s) or folder(s) or other system or user object(s)
- Restoration of the system, network devices, and network infrastructure to the state the network was in prior to the beginning of the test

The key element for the penetration test team to be able to restore the network or system to its pre-attack state is documentation. The penetration testing team documents every step of every action taken during the test, for two reasons. The obvious one is so that they can reverse their steps to "cleanse" the system or network. The second reason is to ensure repeatability of the test. Why is repeatability an issue?

An important part of the penetration test team's job is not only to find and exploit vulnerabilities but also to recommend appropriate mitigation strategies for discovered vulnerabilities. This is especially true for those vulnerabilities that were successfully exploited. After the tested organization implements the recommended corrections, it should repeat the penetration test team's actions to ensure that the vulnerability has indeed been eliminated and that the applied mitigation has not had "unintended consequences" by creating a new vulnerability. The only way to do that is to recreate the original test that found the vulnerability in the first place, make sure it's gone, and then make sure there are no new vulnerabilities as a result of fixing the original problem.

As you might imagine, there are lots of possible ways for Murphy to stick his nose into the process we just talked about. How do penetration test teams and tested organizations try to keep Murphy at bay? Rules!

5. DEFINING WHAT'S EXPECTED

Someone once said: "You can't win the game if you don't know the rules!" That statement makes good sense for a penetration test team as well. Every penetration test must have a clearly defined set of rules by which the penetration test "game" is played. These rules are put into place to help protect both the tested organization and the penetration test team from errors of omission and commission (under normal circumstances). According to the National Institute of Standards and Technology (NIST), the "rule book" for penetration tests is often called the "Rules of Engagement." Rules of Engagement define things like which IP addresses or hosts are and are not allowed to be tested, which techniques are and are not allowed to be used, when testing is permitted or prohibited, points of contact for both the test team and the tested organization, IP addresses of machines from which testing is conducted, and measures to prevent escalation of an incident response to law enforcement, just to name a few.

There isn't a standard format for the Rules of Engagement, so it is not the only document that can be used to control a penetration test. Based on the complexity of the tested organization and the scope of the penetration test, the penetration test team may also use detailed test plan(s) for either or both logical and physical testing. In addition to these documents, both the client and the penetration test company conducting the operation will require some type of formal contact that spells out either explicitly, or incorporates by reference, such items as how discovered sensitive material will be handled, an indemnification statement, nondisclosure statement, fees, project schedule, reporting, and responsibilities. These are but a few of the many items that penetration testing control documents cover, but they should be sufficient for you to understand that all aspects of the penetration test need to be described somewhere in a document.

We now know what's expected during the penetration test. Armed with this information, how does the penetration test team plan to deliver the goods? It starts with a methodology.

6. THE NEED FOR A METHODOLOGY

When you leave for vacation and you've never been to your destination before, you're likely make a list of things you need or want to do before, during, or after the trip. You might also take a map along so you know how to get there and not get lost or sidetracked along the way. Penetration test teams also use a map of sorts. It's called their *methodology*.

A methodology is simply a way to ensure that a particular activity is conducted in a standard manner, with documented and repeatable results. It's a planning tool to help ensure that all mandatory aspects of an activity are performed.

Just as a map will show you various ways to get to your destination, a good penetration testing methodology does not restrict the test team to a single way of compromising the network. While on the road to your dream vacation, you might find your planned route closed or under construction and you might have to make a detour. You might want to do some sightseeing, or maybe visit long-lost relatives along the way.

Similarly, in a penetration test, your primary attack strategy might not work, forcing you to find a way around a particular network device, firewall, or intrusion prevention system. While exploiting one vulnerability, you may discover another one that leads you to a different host or a different subnet. A well-written methodology allows the test team the leeway necessary to explore these "targets of opportunity" while still ultimately guiding them to the stated goals of the test.

Most penetration test companies will have developed a standard methodology that covers all aspects of a penetration test. This baseline methodology document is the starting point for planning a particular test. Once the control documentation has been finalized, the penetration test team will know exactly what they can and cannot test. They will then modify that baseline methodology based on the scope statement in the Rules of Engagement for the penetration test that they are going to conduct.

Different clients are subject to different regulatory requirements such as HIPAA, Sarbanes-Oxley, Gramm-Leach-Bliley, or others, so the penetration test team's methodology must also be flexible enough to cover these and other government or private industry regulations.

In a minute, we'll talk about the sources of penetration testing methodologies, but for now, just understand that a methodology is not a "nice to have," it's a "must have." Without a methodology to be used as the basis to plan and execute a penetration test, there is no reliability. The team will be lost in the network, never knowing if they've fulfilled the requirements of the test or not until they're writing the report. By then, it's too late—for them and for the organization.

7. PENETRATION TESTING METHODOLOGIES

Back to our map example for a minute. Unless you're a cartographer, you're probably not going to make your own map to get to your dream vacation destination. You'll rely on a map that someone else has drawn, tested, and published. The same holds true for penetration testing methodologies. Before we talk about how a methodology, any methodology, is used in a penetration test, let's discuss penetration testing methodologies in general. There are probably as many different methodologies as there are companies conducting penetration tests, but all of them fit into one of two broad categories: open source or proprietary.

Open-source methodologies are just that: available for use by anyone. Probably the best-known open-source methodology, and de facto standard, is the Open Source Security Testing Methodology Manual (OSSTMM), the brainchild of Pete Herzog. You can get the latest copy of this document at www.isecom.org. Another valuable open-source methodology is the Open Web Application Security Project (OWASP), geared to securing Web applications, available at www.owasp.org.

Proprietary methodologies have been developed by particular entities offering network security services or certifications. The specific details of the processes that produce the output of the methodology are usually kept private. Companies wanting to use these proprietary methodologies must usually undergo specific training in their use and abide by quality standards set by the methodology proponent. Some examples of proprietary methodologies include IBM, ISS, Foundstone, and our own EC Council Licensed Penetrator Tester methodology.

8. METHODOLOGY IN ACTION

A comprehensive penetration test is a systematic analysis of all security controls in place at the tested organization. The penetration test team will look at not only the logical and physical vulnerabilities that are present but also at the tested organization's policies and procedures to assess whether or not the controls in place adequately protect the organization's information infrastructure.

Let's examine the use of a penetration testing methodology in more detail to demonstrate how it's used to conduct a penetration test. Of course, as the President of the EC-Council, I'm going to take the liberty of using our LPT methodology as the example.

EC-Council LPT Methodology

Figure 22.4 is a block representation of some of the major areas of the LPT methodology as taught in the EC-Council's Licensed Penetration Tester certification course. The first two rows of the diagram (except for the Wireless Network Penetration Testing block) represent a fairly normal sequence of events in the conduct of a penetration test. The test team will normally start by gathering information, then proceed with vulnerability discovery and analysis, followed by penetration testing from the network perimeter, and graduating to the internal network.

After that, beginning with wireless testing, what the test team actually does will depend on what applications or services are present in the network and what is allowed to be tested under the Rules of Engagement. I've chosen not to show every specific step in the process as part of the diagram. After all, if I told you everything, there wouldn't be any reason for you to get certified as a Licensed Penetration Tester, would there?

The methodology (and course) assumes that the penetration test team has been given authorization to conduct a complete test of the target network, including using denial-of-service tactics so that we can acquaint our LPT candidates with the breadth of testing they may be called on to perform. In real life, a test team may seldom actually perform DoS testing, but members of the penetration test team must still be proficient in conducting this type of test, to make recommendations in their reports as to the possible consequences of an attacker conducting a DoS attack on the company's network infrastructure. Here I give you a quick overview of each of the components.

Information Gathering

The main purpose of information gathering is to understand more about the target company. As we've already talked about, there are a number of ways to gather information

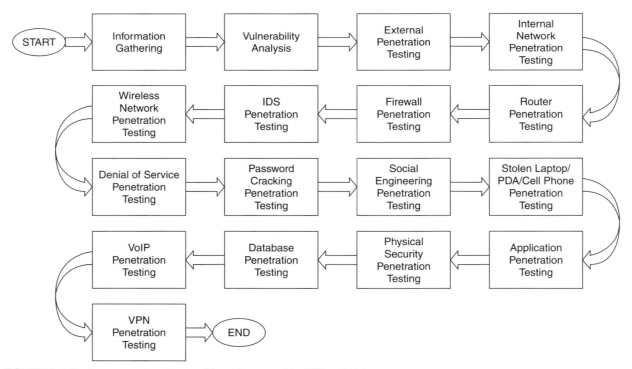

FIGURE 22.4 Block representation of some of the major areas of the LPT methodology.

about the company from public domain sources such as the Internet, newspapers, and third-party information sources.

Vulnerability Analysis

Before you can attack, you have to find the weak points. A vulnerability analysis is the process of identifying logical weaknesses in computers and networks as well as physical weaknesses and weaknesses in policies, procedures, and practices relating to the network and the organization.

External Penetration Testing

External testing is normally conducted before internal testing. It exploits discovered vulnerabilities that are accessible from the Internet to help determine the degree of information exposure or network control that could be achieved by the successful exploitation of a particular vulnerability from outside the network.

Internal Network Penetration Testing

Internal testing is normally conducted after external testing. It exploits discovered vulnerabilities that are accessible from inside the organization to help determine the degree of information exposure or network control that could be achieved by the successful exploitation of a particular vulnerability from inside the network.

Router Penetration Testing

Depending on where they are located in the network infrastructure, routers may forward data to points inside or outside the target organization's network. Take down a router; take down all hosts connected to that router. Because of their importance, routers that connect the target organization to the Internet may be tested twice: once from the Internet and again from inside the network.

Firewall Penetration Testing

Firewall(s) are another critical network infrastructure component that may be tested multiple times, depending on where they reside in the infrastructure. Firewalls that are exposed to the Internet are a primary line of defense for the tested organization and so will usually be tested from the Internet and from within the DMZ for both ingress and egress vulnerabilities and proper rule sets. Internal firewalls are often used to segregate portions of the internal network from each other. Those firewalls are also tested from both sides and for ingress and egress filtering to ensure that only applicable traffic can be passed.

IDS Penetration Testing

As networks have grown more complex and the methods to attack them have multiplied, more and more organizations have come to rely on intrusion detection (and prevention) systems (IDS/IPS) to give them warning or prevent an intrusion from occurring. The test team will be extremely interested in testing these devices for any vulnerabilities that will allow an attacker to circumvent setting of the IPS/IDS alarms.

Wireless Network Penetration Testing

If the target company uses wireless (and who doesn't these days), the test team will focus on the availability of "outside" wireless networks that can be accessed by employees of the target company (effectively circumventing the company's firewalls), the "reach" of the company's own wireless signal outside the physical confines of the company's buildings, and the type and strength of encryption employed by the wireless network.

Denial-of-Service Penetration Testing

If the test team is lucky enough to land a penetration test that includes DoS testing, they will focus on crashing the company's Web sites and flooding the sites or the internal network with enough traffic to bring normal business processes to a standstill or a crawl. They may also attempt to cause a DoS by locking out user accounts instead of trying to crack the passwords.

Password-Cracking Penetration Testing

Need we say more?

Social Engineering Penetration Testing

The test team may use both computer- and human-based techniques to try to obtain not only sensitive and/or nonpublic information directly from employees but also to gain unescorted access to areas of the company that are normally off-limits to the public. Once alone in an off-limits area, the social engineer may then try to obtain additional sensitive or nonpublic information about the company, its data, or its customers.

Stolen Laptop, PDA, and Cell Phone Penetration Testing

Some organizations take great pains to secure the equipment that is located within the physical confines of their buildings but fail to have adequate policies and procedures in place to maintain that security when mobile equipment leaves the premises. The test team attempts to temporarily "liberate" mobile equipment and then conducts testing to gain access to the data stored on those devices. They will most often attempt to target either or both members of the IT Department and the senior members of an organization in the hopes that their mobile devices will contain the most useful data.

Application Penetration Testing

The test team will perform meticulous testing of an application to check for code-related or "back-end" vulnerabilities that might allow access to the application itself, the underlying operating system, or the data that the application can access.

Physical Security Penetration Testing

The test team may attempt to gain access to the organizational facilities before, during, or after business hours using techniques meant to defeat physical access control systems or alarms. They may also conduct an overt "walk-thorough" accompanied by a member of the tested organization to provide the tested company with an "objective perspective" of the physical security controls in place. Either as a part of physical security testing or as a part of social engineering, the team may rifle through the organization's refuse to discover what discarded information could be used by an attacker to compromise the organization and to observe employee reaction to an unknown individual going through the trash.

Database Penetration Testing

The test team may attempt to directly access data contained in the database using account password-cracking techniques or indirectly access data by manipulating triggers and stored procedures that are executed by the database engine.

Voice-Over-IP Penetration Testing

The test team may attempt to gain access to the VoIP network for the purpose of recording conversations or to perform a DoS to the company's voice communications network. In some cases, if the organization has not followed the established "best practices" for VoIP, the team may attempt to use the VoIP network as a jumping-off point to conduct further compromise of the organization's network backbone.

VPN Penetration Testing

A number of companies allow at least some of their employees to work remotely, either from home or while they are "on the road." In either case, a VPN represents a trusted connection to the internal network. The test team will attempt to gain access to the VPN by either compromising the remote endpoint or gaining access to the VPN tunnel so that they have a "blessed" connection to the internal company network.

In addition to testing the applicable items in the blocks on the previous diagram, the penetration test team must also be familiar with and able to test for compliance with the regulatory requirements to which the tested organization is subject. Each standard has specific areas that must be tested, the process and procedures of which may not be part of a standard penetration test.

I'm sure that as you read the previous paragraphs, there was a nagging thought in the back of your mind: What are the risks involved? Let's talk about the risks.

9. PENETRATION TESTING RISKS

The difference between a real attack and a penetration test is the penetration tester's intent, authority to conduct the test, and lack of malice. Because penetration testers may use the same tools and procedures as a real attacker, it should be obvious that penetration testing can have serious repercussions if it's not performed correctly.

Even if your target company ceased all operations for the time the penetration test was being conducted, there is still a danger of data loss, corruption, or system crashes that might require a reinstall from "bare metal." Few, if any, companies can afford to stop functioning while a penetration test is being performed. Therefore it is incumbent on both the target organization and the penetration test team to do everything in their power to prevent an interruption of normal business processes during penetration testing operations.

Target companies should be urged to back up all their critical data before testing begins. They should always have IT personnel present to immediately begin restoration in the unfortunate event that a system crashes or otherwise becomes unavailable. The test team must be prepared to lend all possible assistance to the target company in helping to restore any system that is affected by penetration testing activities.

10. LIABILITY ISSUES

Although we just discussed some of the risks involved with conducting a penetration test, the issue of liability deserves its own special section. A botched penetration test can mean serious liability for the penetration test company that conducted the testing. The penetration test company should ensure that the documentation for the penetration test includes a liability waiver.

The waiver must be signed by an authorized representative of the target company and state that the penetration testing firm cannot be held responsible for the consequences of items such as:

- Damage to systems
- Unintentional denial-of-service conditions
- Data corruption
- System crashes or unavailability
- Loss of business income

11. LEGAL CONSEQUENCES

The legal consequences of a penetration test gone wrong can be devastating to both the target company and the penetration testers performing the test. The company may become the target of lawsuits by customers. The penetration testers may become the target of lawsuits by the target company. The only winners in this situation are the lawyers. It is imperative that proper written permission is obtained from the target company before *any* testing is conducted.

Legal remedies are normally contained in a penetration testing contract that is drawn up in addition to the testing control documentation. Both the penetration test company and the target company should seek legal counsel to review the agreement and to protect their interests. The authorization to perform testing must come from a senior member of the test company, and that senior member must be someone who has the authority to authorize such testing, not just the network administrator or LAN manager.

Authorized representatives of both the penetration test company and the target company must sign the penetration testing contract to indicate that they agree with its contents and the contents of all documentation that may be included or included by reference, such as the Rules of Engagement, the test plan, and other test control documentation.

12. "GET OUT OF JAIL FREE" CARD

We just talked about how the target company and the penetration test company protect themselves. What about that individual team member crawling around in the dumpster at 2:00 A.M., or the unfortunate team member who's managed to get into the company president's office and log onto his or her computer? What protection do those individuals have when that 600-pound gorilla of a security guard clamps his hand on their shoulder and asks what they're doing?

A "Get Out of Jail Free" card might just work wonders in these and other cases. Though not really a card, it's usually requested by the penetration test team as "extra insurance" during testing. It is presented if they're detained or apprehended while in the performance of their duties, as proof that their actions are sanctioned by the officers of the company. The card may actually be a letter on the tested company's letterhead and signed by the senior officer authorizing the test. It states the specific tasks that can be performed under the protection of the letter and specifically names the bearer.

It contains language that the bearer is conducting activities and testing under the auspices of a contract and that no violation of policy or crime is or has been committed. It includes a 24-hour contact number to verify the validity of the letter. As you can imagine, these "Get Out of Jail Free" cards are *very* sensitive and are usually distributed to team members immediately before testing begins, collected, and returned to the target company immediately after the end of any testing requiring their use.

There is a tremendous amount of work involved in conducting a thorough and comprehensive penetration test. What we've just discussed is but a 40,000-foot flyover of what actually happens during the process. But we're not done yet! The one area that we haven't discussed is the personnel performing these tests.

13. PENETRATION TESTING CONSULTANTS

The quality of the penetration test performed for a client is directly dependent on the quality of the consultants performing the work, singularly and in the aggregate. There are hundreds if not thousands of self-proclaimed "security services providers" out there, both companies and individuals. If I'm in need of a penetration test, how can I possibly know whether the firm or individual I'm going to select is really and truly qualified to test my network comprehensively, accurately, and safely? What if I end up hiring a consultancy that employs hackers? What if the consultant(s) aren't hackers, but they just don't know what they're doing?

In these, the last pages of this chapter, I want to talk about the people who perform penetration testing services. First, you get another dose of my personal opinion. Then we'll talk about security services providers, those who provide penetration testing services. We'll talk about some of the questions that you might want to ask about their operations and their employees. Here's a hint for you: If the company is evasive in answering the questions or outright refuses to answer them—run!

What determines whether or not a penetration tester is "experienced"? There are few benchmarks to test the knowledge of a penetration tester. You can't ask her for a score: "Yes, I've performed 27 penetration tests, been successful in compromising 23 of those networks, and the overall degree of difficulty of each one of those tests was 7 on a scale of 1 to 10."

There really isn't a Better Business Bureau for penetration testers. You can't go to a Web site and see that XSecurity has had three complaints filed against them for crashing networks they've been testing or that "John Smith" has tested nine networks that were hacked within the following 24 hours. (Whoa! What an idea . . . ! Nah, wouldn't work.) Few companies would want to admit that they chose the wrong person or company to test their networks, and that kind of information would surely be used by attackers in the "intelligence-gathering phase" as a source of information for future attacks on any company that chose to report.

Well, if we can't do that, what can we do?

We pretty much have to rely on "word of mouth" that such-and-such a company does a good job. We have to pretty much rely on the fact that the tester has been certified to a basic standard of knowledge by a reputable certification body. We pretty much have to rely on the skill set of the individual penetration tester and that "the whole is more than the sum of its parts" thing called synergy, which is created when a group of penetration testers works together as a team.

I'm not going to insult you by telling you how to go ask for recommendations. I will tell you that there are security certification providers who are better than others and who hold their candidates to a higher standard of knowledge and professionalism than others. Since it's hard to measure the "synergy" angle, let's take a closer look at what skill sets should be present on the penetration team that you hire.

14. REQUIRED SKILL SETS

Your penetration test "dream team" should be well versed in areas such as these:

- Networking concepts
- Hardware devices such as routers, firewalls, and IDS/IPS
- Hacking techniques (ethical hacking, of course!)
- Databases

- Open-source technologies
- Operating systems
- Wireless protocols
- Applications
- Protocols
- Many others

That's a rather long list to demonstrate a simple concept: Your penetration team should be able to show proof that they have knowledge about all the hardware, software, services, and protocols in use within your network.

Okay. They have technical skills. Is that enough?

15. ACCOMPLISHMENTS

Are the members of the test team "bookworms" or have they had practical experience in their areas of expertise? Have they contributed to the security community? The list that follows should give you some indication of questions you can ask to determine the "experiences" of your test team:

- Have they conducted research and development in the security arena?
- Have they published research papers or articles in technical journals?
- Have they presented at seminars, either locally or internationally?
- What certifications do they hold? Where are those certifications from?
- Do they maintain membership/affiliation/ accreditation in organizations such as the EC-Council, ISC2, ISACA, and others?
- Have they written or contributed to security-related books and articles?

How about some simple questions to ask of the company that will perform your test?

16. HIRING A PENETRATION TESTER

Here are some of the questions you might consider asking prospective security service providers or things to think about when hiring a test team:

- Is providing security services the primary mission of the security service provider, or is this just an "additional revenue source" for another company?
- Does the company offer a comprehensive suite of services tailored to your specific requirements, or do they just offer service packages?
- Does the supplier have a methodology? Does their methodology follow a recognized authority in security such as OSSTMM, OWASP, or LPT?

- Does the supplier hire former hackers? Do they perform background checks on their employees?
- Can they distinguish (and articulate) between infrastructure and application testing?
- How many consultants does the supplier have who perform penetration testing? How long have those consultants been practicing?
- What will the final report look like? Does it meet your needs? Is the supplier willing to modify the format to suit your needs (within reason)?
- Is the report just a list of what's wrong, or does it contain mitigation strategies that will be tailored to your particular situation?
- Is the supplier a recognized contributor to the security community?
- Do they have references available to attest to the quality of work already performed?

That ought to get a company started down the road to hiring a good penetration test team. Now let's talk about why a company should hire you, either as an individual or as a member of a penetration testing team.

17. WHY SHOULD A COMPANY HIRE YOU?

When a prospective client needs a penetration test, they may publish a request for proposal (RFP) or just make an announcement that they are accepting solicitations for security services. When all the bids come in, they will only consider the most qualified candidates. How to you make sure that your or your company's bid doesn't end up in the "circular file?"

Qualifications

Highlight your or your company's qualifications to perform the desired services. Don't rely on "alphabet soup" after your name or your team's names to highlight qualifications. Take the time to explain the meaning of CISSP, LPT, or MCSE.

Work Experience

The company will provide some information about itself. Align your response by highlighting work (without naming specific clients!) in the same or related fields and of related size.

Cutting-Edge Technical Skills

It doesn't bode well when you list one of your primary skills as "MCSE in Windows NT 3.51 and NT 4.0."

Maintain your technical proficiency and showcase your most recent and most highly regarded certification accomplishments, such as CCNA, CEH, CHFI, CCNP, MCSE, LPT, CISA, and CISM.

Communication Skills

Whether your communicate with the prospective client through written or verbal methods, made sure you are well written or well spoken. Spell-check your written documents, and then look them over again. There are some errors that spell checkers just won't find. "Dude, I'm gonna hack yer network!" isn't going to cut it in a second-round presentation.

Attitude

Let's face it: Most of us in the security arena have a bit of an ego and sometimes come off as a bit arrogant. Though that may hold some sway with your peers, it won't help your case with a prospective client. Polite and professional at all times is the rule.

Team Skills

There is no synergy if there is no team. You must be a good team player who can deal with subordinates, superiors, and clients professionally, even in the most critical moments of an engagement.

Okay. You've done all this. What else do you need to know to get hired? What about the concerns of the company that will hire you?

Company Concerns

You can have a sterling record and the best qualifications around and still not get hired. Here are some of the "influencing factors" companies may consider when looking to hire a penetration testing team:

- Companies usually want to work in collaboration with reputable and well-established firms such as Foundstone, ISS, EC-Council, and others.
- Companies may want to verify the tools that will be run during a test and the equipment on which the tools run.
- Companies will want references for the individuals on the team as well as recommendations about the company itself.
- Companies demand security-related certifications such as CISSP, CEH, and TICSA to confirm the authenticity of the testing company.

- Companies usually have an aversion to hiring those who are known or suspected hackers.
- Companies may require security clearances.
- Companies may inquire about how and where their data will be stored while in the testing company's possession.

  Okay, you get the idea, right?

18. ALL'S WELL THAT ENDS WELL

Anybody got an aspirin? I'm sure you probably need one after reading all the information I've tried to throw at you in this chapter. I've only barely scratched the surface of what a penetration test is, what it's meant to accomplish, how it's done, and how you report the findings to the client, but I'm out of space to tell you more.

Let me take these last couple of inches on the page to summarize. If you've got a network, the question is not "if" you'll be attacked, but "when." If you're going to make your network as safe as possible, you need to find the weaknesses and then test them to see which ones are really, truly the things that need to be fixed "yesterday." If you only conduct a penetration test once a year, a real hacker has 364 "unbirthdays" in which to attack and compromise your network. Don't give them the opportunity. Get someone on your staff certified as an ethical hacker and a Licensed Penetration Tester so that they can perform ethical hacks and penetrations on a regular basis to help protect your network.

## Chapter 23

What Is Vulnerability Assessment?

Almantas Kakareka

Terremark Worldwide, Inc.

In computer security, the term *vulnerability* is applied to a weakness in a system that allows an attacker to violate the integrity of that system. Vulnerabilities may result from weak passwords, software bugs, a computer virus or other malware (malicious software), a script code injection, or an SQL injection, just to name a few.

A security risk is classified as vulnerability if it is recognized as a possible means of attack. A security risk with one or more known instances of a working or fully implemented attack is classified as an *exploit*. Constructs in programming languages that are difficult to use properly can be large sources of vulnerabilities.

Vulnerabilities always existed, but when the Internet was in its early stage they were not as often used and exploited. The media did not report news of hackers who were getting put in jail for hacking into servers and stealing vital information.

Vulnerability assessment may be performed on many objects, not only computer systems/networks. For example, a physical building can be assessed so it will be clear what parts of the building have what kind of flaw. If the attacker can bypass the security guard at the front door and get into the building via a back door, it is definitely a vulnerability. Actually, going through the back door and using that vulnerability is called an *exploit*. The physical security is one of the most important aspects to be taken into account. If the attackers have physical access to the server, the server is not yours anymore! Just stating, "Your system or network is vulnerable" doesn't provide any useful information. Vulnerability assessment without a comprehensive report is pretty much useless. A vulnerability assessment report should include:

- Identification of vulnerabilities
- Quantity of vulnerabilities

It is enough to find one critical vulnerability, which means the whole network is at risk, as shown in Figure 23.1.

Vulnerabilities should be sorted by severity and then by servers/services. Critical vulnerabilities should be at the top of the report and should be listed in descending order, that is, critical, then high, medium, and low.[1]

1. REPORTING

Reporting capability is of growing importance to administrators in a documentation-oriented business climate where you must not only be able to do your job, you must also provide written proof of how you've done it. In fact, respondents to Sunbelt's survey[2] indicate that flexible and prioritizing reporting is their number-one favorite feature.

A scan might return hundreds or thousands of results, but the data is useless unless it is organized in a way that can be understood. That means that ideally you will be able to sort and cross-reference the data, export it to other programs and formats (such as CSV, HTML, XML, MHT, MDB, Excel, Word, and/or Lotus), view it in different ways, and easily compare it to the results of earlier scans.

Comprehensive, flexible, and customizable reporting is used within your department to provide a guideline of technical steps you need to take, but that's not all. Good reports also give you the ammunition you need to justify to management the costs of implementing security measures.

2. THE "IT WON'T HAPPEN TO US" FACTOR

Practical matters aside, CEOs, CIOs, and administrators are all human beings and thus subject to normal human tendencies—including the tendency to assume that bad things happen to "other people," not to us. Organizational decision makers assume that their companies aren't likely targets for hackers ("Why would an attacker want

---

1 http://en.wikipedia.org/wiki/Vulnerability_assessment.
2 www.sunbeltsoftware.com/documents/snsi_whitepaper.pdf.

FIGURE 23.1 One critical vulnerability affects the entire network.

to break into the network of Widgets, Inc., when they could go after the Department of Defense or Microsoft or someone else who's much more interesting?").[2]

3. WHY VULNERABILITY ASSESSMENT?

Organizations have a tremendous opportunity to use information technologies to increase their productivity. Securing information and communications systems will be a necessary factor in taking advantage of all this increased connectivity, speed, and information. However, no security measure will guarantee a risk-free environment in which to operate. In fact, many organizations need to provide easier user access to portions of their information systems, thereby increasing potential exposure. Administrative error, for example, is a primary cause of vulnerabilities that can be exploited by a novice hacker, whether an outsider or insider in the organization. Routine use of vulnerability assessment tools along with immediate response to identified problems will alleviate this risk. It follows, therefore, that routine vulnerability assessment should be a standard element of every organization's security policy. Vulnerability assessment is used to find unknown problems in the systems. The main purpose of vulnerability assessment is to find out what systems have flaws and take action to mitigate the risk. Some industry standards such as DSS PCI require organizations to perform vulnerability assessments on their networks. The sidebar "DSS PCI Compliance" gives a brief look.

DSS PCI Compliance

PCI DSS stands for Payment Card Industry Data Security Standard. This standard was developed by leading credit-card companies to help merchants be secure and follow common security criteria to protect sensitive customers' credit-card data. Before that every credit card company had a similar standard to protect customer data on the merchant side. Any company that does transactions via credit cards needs to be PCI compliant. One of the requirements to be PCI compliant is to regularly test security systems and processes. This can be achieved via vulnerability assessment. Small companies that don't process a lot of transactions are allowed to do self-assessment via questionnaire. Big companies that process a lot of transactions are required to be audited by third parties.[3]

---

3 www.pcisecuritystandards.org.

4. PENETRATION TESTING VERSUS VULNERABILITY ASSESSMENT

There seems to be a certain amount of confusion within the security industry about the difference between penetration testing and vulnerability assessment. They are often classified as the same thing but in fact they are not. Penetration testing sounds a lot more exciting, but most people actually want a vulnerability assessment and not a penetration test, so many projects are labeled as penetration tests when in fact they are 100% vulnerability assessments.

A penetration test mainly consists of a vulnerability assessment, but it goes one step further. A penetration test is a method for evaluating the security of a computer system or network by simulating an attack by a malicious hacker. The process involves an active analysis of the system for any weaknesses, technical flaws, or vulnerabilities. This analysis is carried out from the position of a potential attacker and will involve active exploitation of security vulnerabilities. Any security issues that are found will be presented to the system owner, together with an assessment of their impact and often with a proposal for mitigation or a technical solution.

A vulnerability assessment is what most companies generally do, since the systems they are testing are live production systems and can't afford to be disrupted by active exploits that might crash the system. Vulnerability assessment is the process of identifying and quantifying vulnerabilities in a system. The system being studied could be a physical facility such as a nuclear power plant, a computer system, or a larger system (for example, the communications infrastructure or water infrastructure of a region). Vulnerability assessment has many things in common with risk assessment. Assessments are typically performed according to the following steps:

1. Cataloging assets and capabilities (resources) in a system
2. Assigning quantifiable value and importance to the resources
3. Identifying the vulnerabilities or potential threats to each resource
4. Mitigating or eliminating the most serious vulnerabilities for the most valuable resources

This is generally what a security company is contracted to do, from a technical perspective—not to actually penetrate the systems but to assess and document the possible vulnerabilities and to recommend mitigation

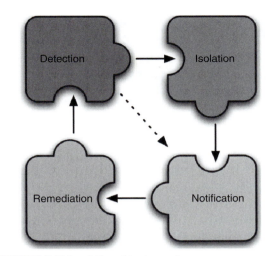

FIGURE 23.2 Vulnerability mitigation cycle.

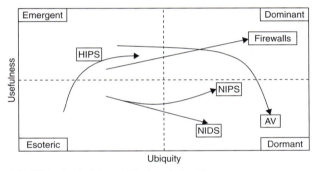

FIGURE 23.3 Usefulness/ubiquity relationship.

measures and improvements. Vulnerability detection, mitigation, notification, and remediation are linked, as shown in Figure 23.2.[4]

5. VULNERABILITY ASSESSMENT GOAL

The theoretical goal of network scanning is elevated security on all systems or establishing a networkwide minimal operation standard. Figure 23.3 shows how usefulness is related to ubiquity.

- HIPS: Host-Based Intrusion Prevention System
- NIDS: Network-Based Intrusion Detection System
- AV: Antivirus
- NIPS: Network-Based Intrusion Prevention System

6. MAPPING THE NETWORK

Before we start scanning the network we have to find out what machines are alive on it. Most of the scanners

have a built-in network mapping tool, usually the Nmap network mapping tool running behind the scenes. The Nmap Security Scanner is a free and open-source utility used by millions of people for network discovery, administration, inventory, and security auditing. Nmap uses raw IP packets in novel ways to determine what hosts are available on a network, what services (application name and version) those hosts are offering, what operating systems they are running, what type of packet filters or firewalls are in use, and more. Nmap was named "Information Security Product of the Year" by *Linux Journal* and *Info World*. It was also used by hackers in the movies *Matrix Reloaded, Die Hard 4*, and *Bourne Ultimatum*. Nmap runs on all major computer operating systems, plus the Amiga. Nmap has a traditional command-line interface, as shown in Figure 23.4.

Zenmap is the official Nmap Security Scanner GUI (see Figure 23.5). It is a multiplatform (Linux, Windows, Mac OS X, BSD, etc.), free and open-source application that aims to make Nmap easy for beginners to use while providing advanced features for experienced Nmap users. Frequently used scans can be saved as profiles to make them easy to run repeatedly. A command creator allows interactive creation of Nmap command lines. Scan results can be saved and viewed later. Saved scan results can be compared with one another to see how they differ. The results of recent scans are stored in a searchable database.

Gordon Lyon (better known by his nickname, Fyodor) released Nmap in 1997 and continues to coordinate its development. He also maintains the Insecure. Org, Nmap.Org, SecLists.Org, and SecTools.Org security resource sites and has written seminal papers on OS detection and stealth port scanning. He is a founding member of the Honeynet project and coauthored the books *Know Your Enemy: Honeynets* and *Stealing the Network: How to Own a Continent*. Gordon is President of Computer Professionals for Social Responsibility (CPSR), which has promoted free speech, security, and privacy since 1981.[5,6]

Some systems might be disconnected from the network. Obviously, if the system is not connected to any network at all it will have a lower priority for scanning. However, it shouldn't be left in the dark and not be scanned at all, because there might be other nonnetwork related flaws, for example, a Firewire exploit that can be used to unlock the Windows XP SP2 system. Exploits work like this: An attacker approaches a locked Windows XP

4 www.darknet.org.uk/2006/04/penetration-testing-vs-vulnerability-assessment/.

5 http://en.wikipedia.org/wiki/Gordon_Lyon.
6 www.nmap.org.

```
# nmap -sVC -O -T4 scanme.nmap.org

Starting Nmap ( http://nmap.org )
Interesting ports on scanme.nmap.org (64.13.134.52):
Not shown: 1710 filtered ports
PORT      STATE   SERVICE VERSION
22/tcp    open    ssh       OpenSSH 4.3 (protocol 2.0)
53/tcp    open    domain
70/tcp    closed  gopher
80/tcp    open    http      Apache httpd 2.2.2 ((Fedora))
|_ HTML title: Go ahead and ScanMe!
113/tcp   closed  auth
Device type: general purpose
Running: Linux 2.6.X
OS details: Linux 2.6.20-1 (Fedora Core 5)
Uptime: 5.378 days
Nmap done: 1 IP address (1 host up) scanned in 51.818 s
```

FIGURE 23.4 Nmap command-line interface.

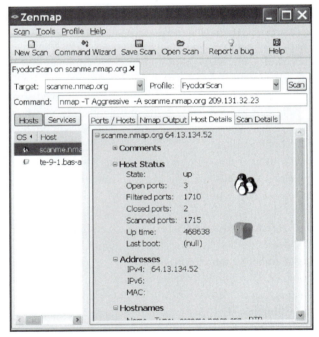

FIGURE 23.5 Zenmap graphical user interface.

SP2 station, plugs a Firewire cable into it, and uses special commands to unlock the locked machine. This technique is possible because Firewire has direct access to RAM. The system will accept any password and unlock the computer.[7,8]

7 http://en.wikipedia.org/wiki/FireWire.
8 http://storm.net.nz/projects/16.

7. SELECTING THE RIGHT SCANNERS

Scanners alone don't solve the problem; using scanners well helps solve *part* of the problem. Start with one scanner but consider more than one. It is a good practice to use more than one scanner. This way you can compare results from a couple of them. Some scanners are more focused on particular services. A typical scanner architecture is shown in Figure 23.6.

For example, Nessus is an outstanding general-purpose scanner, but Web application-oriented scanners such as HP Web Inspect or Hailstorm will do a much better job of scanning a Web server. In an ideal situation, scanners would not be needed because everyone would maintain patches and tested hosts, routers, gateways, workstations, and servers. However, the real world is different; we are humans and we tend to forget to install updates, patch systems, and/or configure systems properly. Malicious code will always find a way into your network! If a system is connected to the network, that means there is a possibility that this system will be infected at some time in the future. The chances might be higher or lower depending on the system's maintenance level. The system will never be secure 100%. There is no such thing as 100% security; if well maintained, it might be 99.9999999999% secure, but never 100%. There is a joke that says, if you want to make a computer secure, you have to disconnect it from the network and power outlet and then put it into a safe and lock it. This system will be *almost* 100%

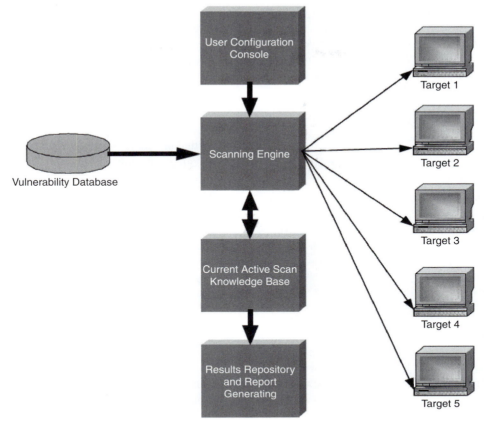

FIGURE 23.6 Typical scanner architecture.

secure (although not useful), because social engineering cons may call your employees and ask them to remove that system from the safe and plug it back into the network.[9,10,11]

8. CENTRAL SCANS VERSUS LOCAL SCANS

The question arises: Should we scan locally or centrally? Should we scan the whole network at once, or should we scan the network based on subdomains and virtual LANs? Table 23.1 shows pros and cons of each method.

With localized scanning with central scanning verification, central scanning becomes a verification audit. The question again arises, should we scan locally or centrally? The answer is both. Central scans give overall visibility

TABLE 23.1 Pros and Cons of Central Scans and Local Scans

	Centrally Controlled and Accessed Scanning	Decentralized Scanning
Pros	Easy to maintain	Scan managers can scan at will
Cons	Slow; most scans must be queued	Patching of the scanner is often overlooked

into the network. Local scans may have higher visibility into the local network. Centrally driven scans serve as the baseline. Locally driven scans are key to vulnerability reduction. Scanning tools should support both methodologies. Scan managers should be empowered to police their own area and enforce policy. So what will hackers target? Script kiddies will target any easily exploitable system; dedicated hackers will target some particular network/organization (see sidebar, "Who Is the Target?").

9 www.scmagazineus.com/HP-WebInspect-77/Review/2365/.

10 www.cenzic.com/products_services/products_overview.php.

11 http://en.wikipedia.org/wiki/Social_engineering_(computer_security).

9. DEFENSE IN DEPTH STRATEGY

Defense in depth is an information assurance (IA) strategy in which multiple layers of defense are placed throughout an IT system. Defense in depth addresses security vulnerabilities in personnel, technology, and operations for the duration of the system's life cycle. The idea behind this approach is to defend a system against any particular attack using several varying methods. It is a layering tactic, conceived by the National Security Agency (NSA) as a comprehensive approach to information and electronic security. Defense in depth was originally a military strategy that seeks to delay, rather than prevent, the advance of an attacker by yielding space in order to buy time. The placement of protection mechanisms, procedures, and policies is intended to increase the dependability of an IT system where multiple layers of defense prevent espionage and direct attacks against critical systems. In terms of computer network defense, defense-in-depth measures should not only prevent security breaches, they should give an organization time to detect and respond to an attack, thereby reducing and mitigating the impact of a breach. Using more than one of the following layers constitutes defense in depth:

- Physical security (e.g., deadbolt locks)
- Authentication and password security

- Antivirus software (host based and network based)
- Firewalls (hardware or software)
- Demilitarized zones (DMZs)
- Intrusion detection systems (IDSs)
- Packet filters (deep packet inspection appliances and stateful firewalls)
- Routers and switches
- Proxy servers
- Virtual private networks (VPNs)
- Logging and auditing
- Biometrics
- Timed access control
- Proprietary software/hardware not available to the public[12]

10. VULNERABILITY ASSESSMENT TOOLS

There are many vulnerability assessment tools. The top 10 tools according to www.sectools.org are listed here. Each tool is described by one or more attributes:

- Generally costs money; a free limited/demo/trial version may be available
- Works natively on Linux
- Works natively on OpenBSD, FreeBSD, Solaris, and/or other Unix-like systems
- Works natively on Apple Mac OS X
- Works natively on Microsoft Windows
- Features a command-line interface
- Offers a GUI (point-and-click) interface
- Source code available for inspection

Nessus

Nessus is a premier vulnerability assessment tool. There is a 2.x version that is open source and a 3.x version that is closed source. Unix-like implementations have CLI and Windows implementations have GUI only. Nessus was a popular free and open-source vulnerability scanner until it closed the source code in 2005 and removed the free "registered feed" version in 2008. A limited "home feed" is still available, though it is only licensed for home network use. Some people avoid paying by violating the "home feed" license or by avoiding feeds entirely and using just the plug-ins included with each release. But for most users, the cost has increased from free to $1200/year. Despite this, Nessus is still the best Unix vulnerability scanner available and among the best

---

12 www.nsa.gov/snac/support/defenseindepth.pdf.

to run on Windows. Nessus is constantly updated, with more than 20,000 plug-ins. Key features include remote and local (authenticated) security checks, a client/server architecture with a GTK graphical interface, and an embedded scripting language for writing your own plug-ins or understanding the existing ones.

GFI LANguard

A commercial network security scanner for Windows, GFI LANguard scans IP networks to detect what machines are running. Then it tries to discern the host OS and what applications are running. It also tries to collect Windows machines' service pack level, missing security patches, wireless access points, USB devices, open shares, open ports, services/applications active on the computer, key registry entries, weak passwords, users and groups, and more. Scan results are saved to an HTML report, which can be customized and queried. It also includes a patch manager that detects and installs missing patches. A free trial version is available, though it only works for up to 30 days.

Retina

Commercial vulnerability assessment scanner by eEye. Like Nessus, Retina's function is to scan all the hosts on a network and report on any vulnerabilities found. It was written by eEye, well known for security research.

Core Impact

An automated, comprehensive penetration testing product, Core Impact isn't cheap (be prepared to spend tens of thousands of dollars), but it is widely considered to be the most powerful exploitation tool available. It sports a large, regularly updated database of professional exploits and can do neat tricks, such as exploiting one machine and then establishing an encrypted tunnel through that machine to reach and exploit other boxes. If you can't afford Impact, take a look at the cheaper Canvas or the excellent and free Metasploit Framework. Your best bet is to use all three.

ISS Internet Scanner

Application-level vulnerability assessment Internet Scanner started off in 1992 as a tiny open-source scanner by Christopher Klaus. Now he has grown ISS into a billion-dollar company with myriad security products.

X-Scan

A general scanner for scanning network vulnerabilities, X-Scan is a multithreaded, plug-in-supported vulnerability scanner. X-Scan includes many features, including full NASL support, detecting service types, remote OS type/version detection, weak user/password pairs, and more. You may be able to find newer versions available at the X-Scan site if you can deal with most of the page being written in Chinese.

SARA

Security Auditor's Research Assistant SARA is a vulnerability assessment tool that was derived from the infamous SATAN scanner. Updates are released twice a month and the company tries to leverage other software created by the open-source community (such as Nmap and Samba).

QualysGuard

A Web-based vulnerability scanner delivered as a service over the Web, QualysGuard eliminates the burden of deploying, maintaining, and updating vulnerability management software or implementing ad hoc security applications. Clients securely access QualysGuard through an easy-to-use Web interface. QualysGuard features 5000+ unique vulnerability checks, an inference-based scanning engine, and automated daily updates to the QualysGuard vulnerability knowledge base.

SAINT

Security Administrator's Integrated Network Tool (SAINT) is another commercial vulnerability assessment tool (like Nessus, ISS Internet Scanner, or Retina). It runs on Unix and used to be free and open source but is now a commercial product.

MBSA

Microsoft Baseline Security Analyzer (MBSA) is an easy-to-use tool designed for the IT professional that helps small and medium-sized businesses determine their security state in accordance with Microsoft security recommendations, and offers specific remediation guidance. Built on the Windows Update Agent and Microsoft Update infrastructure, MBSA ensures consistency with other Microsoft management products, including Microsoft Update (MU), Windows Server Update Services (WSUS), Systems

Management Server (SMS), and Microsoft Operations Manager (MOM). Apparently MBSA, on average, scans over three million computers each week.[13]

11. SCANNER PERFORMANCE

A vulnerability scanner can use a lot of network bandwidth, so you want the scanning process to complete as quickly as possible. Of course, the more vulnerabilities in the database and the more comprehensive the scan, the longer it will take, so this can be a tradeoff. One way to increase performance is through the use of multiple scanners on the enterprise network, which can report back to one system that aggregates the results.[12]

12. SCAN VERIFICATION

The best practice is to use few scanners during your vulnerability assessment, then use more than one scanning tool to find more vulnerabilities. Scan your networks with different scanners from different vendors and compare the results. Also consider penetration testing, that is, hire white/gray-hat hackers to hack your own systems.[14,15]

13. SCANNING CORNERSTONES

All orphaned systems should be treated as hostile. Something in your organization that is not maintained or touched poses the largest threat. For example, say that you have a Web server and you inspect every byte of DHTML and make sure it has no flaws, but you totally forget to maintain the SMTP service with open relay that it is also running. Attackers might not be able to deface or harm your Web page, but they will be using the SMTP server to send out spam emails via your server. As a result, your company's IP ranges will be put into spammer lists such as spamhaus and spamcop.[16,17]

14. NETWORK SCANNING COUNTERMEASURES

A company wants to scan its own networks, but at the same time the company should take countermeasures to protect itself from being scanned by hackers. Here is a checklist of countermeasures to use when you're considering technical modifications to networks and filtering devices to reduce the effectiveness of network scanning and probing undertaken by attackers:

- Filter inbound Internet Control Message Protocol (ICMP) message types at border routers and firewalls. This forces attackers to use full-blown TCP port scans against all your IP addresses to map your network correctly.
- Filter all outbound ICMP type 3 unreachable messages at border routers and firewalls to prevent UDP port scanning and firewalking from being effective.
- Consider configuring Internet firewalls so that they can identify port scans and throttle the connections accordingly. You can configure commercial firewall appliances (such as those from Check Point, NetScreen, and WatchGuard) to prevent fast port scans and SYN floods being launched against your networks. On the open-source side, many tools such as port sentry can identify port scans and drop all packets from the source IP address for a given period of time.
- Assess the way that your network firewall and IDS devices handle fragmented IP packets by using fragtest and fragroute when performing scanning and probing exercises. Some devices crash or fail under conditions in which high volumes of fragmented packets are being processed.
- Ensure that your routing and filtering mechanisms (both firewalls and routers) can't be bypassed using specific source ports or source-routing techniques.
- If you house publicly accessible FTP services, ensure that your firewalls aren't vulnerable to stateful circumvention attacks relating to malformed PORT and PASV commands.
- If a commercial firewall is in use, ensure the following:
  - The latest service pack is installed.
  - Antispoofing rules have been correctly defined so that the device doesn't accept packets with private spoofed source addresses on its external interfaces.
  - Fastmode services aren't used in Check Point Firewall-1 environments.
- Investigate using inbound proxy servers in your environment if you require a high level of security. A proxy server will not forward fragmented or malformed packets, so it isn't possible to launch FIN scanning or other stealth methods.
- Be aware of your own network configuration and its publicly accessible ports by launching TCP and UDP

13 www.sectools.org.
14 http://en.wikipedia.org/wiki/White_hat.
15 http://en.wikipedia.org/wiki/Grey_hat.
16 www.spamhaus.org
17 www.spamcop.net.

port scans along with ICMP probes against your own IP address space. It is surprising how many large companies still don't properly undertake even simple port-scanning exercises.[18]

15. VULNERABILITY DISCLOSURE DATE

The time of disclosure of vulnerability is defined differently in the security community and industry. It is most commonly referred to as "a kind of public disclosure of security information by a certain party." Usually vulnerability information is discussed on a mailing list or published on a security Web site and results in a security advisory afterward.

The *time of disclosure* is the first date that security vulnerability is described on a channel where the disclosed information on the vulnerability has to fulfill the following requirements:

- The information is freely available to the public.
- The vulnerability information is published by a trusted and independent channel/source.
- The vulnerability has undergone analysis by experts such that risk rating information is included upon disclosure.

The method of disclosing vulnerabilities is a topic of debate in the computer security community. Some advocate immediate full disclosure of information about vulnerabilities once they are discovered. Others argue for limiting disclosure to the users placed at greatest risk and only releasing full details after a delay, if ever. Such delays may allow those notified to fix the problem by developing and applying patches, but they can also increase the risk to those not privy to full details. This debate has a long history in security; see full disclosure and security through obscurity. More recently a new form of commercial vulnerability disclosure has taken shape, as some commercial security companies offer money for exclusive disclosures of zero-day vulnerabilities. Those offers provide a legitimate market for the purchase and sale of vulnerability information from the security community.

From the security perspective, a free and public disclosure is successful only if the affected parties get the relevant information prior to potential hackers; if they did not, the hackers could take immediate advantage of the revealed exploit. With security through obscurity, the same rule applies but this time rests on the hackers finding the vulnerability themselves, as opposed to being given the

information from another source. The disadvantage here is that fewer people have full knowledge of the vulnerability and can aid in finding similar or related scenarios.

It should be unbiased to enable a fair dissemination of security-critical information. Most often a channel is considered trusted when it is a widely accepted source of security information in the industry (such as CERT, SecurityFocus, Secunia, and FrSIRT). Analysis and risk rating ensure the quality of the disclosed information. The analysis must include enough details to allow a concerned user of the software to assess his individual risk or take immediate action to protect his assets.

Find Security Holes Before They Become Problems

Vulnerabilities can be classified into two major categories:

- Those related to errors made by programmers in writing the code for the software
- Those related to misconfigurations of the software's settings that leave systems less secure than they could be (improperly secured accounts, running of unneeded services, etc.)

Vulnerability scanners can identify both types. Vulnerability assessment tools have been around for many years. They've been used by network administrators and misused by hackers to discover exploitable vulnerabilities in systems and networks of all kinds. One of the early well-known Unix scanners, System Administrator Tool for Analyzing Networks (SATAN), later morphed into SAINT (Security Administrator's Integrated Network Tool). These names illustrate the disparate dual nature of the purposes to which such tools can be put.

In the hands of a would-be intruder, vulnerability scanners become a means of finding victims and determining those victims' weak points, like an undercover intelligence operative who infiltrates the opposition's supposedly secure location and gathers information that can be used to launch a full-scale attack. However, in the hands of those who are charged with protecting their networks, these scanners are a vital proactive defense mechanism that allows you to see your systems through the eyes of the enemy and take steps to lock the doors, board up the windows, and plug up seldom used passageways through which the "bad guys" could enter, before they get a chance.

In fact, the first scanners were designed as hacking tools, but this is a case in which the bad guys' weapons have been appropriated and used to defend against them. By "fighting fire with fire," administrators gain a much-needed advantage. For the first time, they are able to battle

---

18 www.trustmatta.com/downloads/pdf/Matta_IP_Network_Scanning.pdf.

intruders proactively.[12] Once the vulnerabilities are found, we have to remove them (see sidebar, "Identifying and Removing Vulnerabilities").

> ### Identifying and Removing Vulnerabilities
>
> Many software tools can aid in the discovery (and sometimes removal) of vulnerabilities in a computer system. Though these tools can provide an auditor with a good overview of possible vulnerabilities present, they cannot replace human judgment. Relying solely on scanners will yield false positives and a limited-scope view of the problems present in the system.
>
> Vulnerabilities have been found in every major operating system including Windows, Mac OS, various forms of Unix and Linux, OpenVMS, and others. The only way to reduce the chance of a vulnerability being used against a system is through constant vigilance, including careful system maintenance (e.g., applying software patches), best practices in deployment (e.g., the use of firewalls and access controls), and auditing during development and throughout the deployment life cycle.

16. PROACTIVE SECURITY VERSUS REACTIVE SECURITY

There are two basic methods of dealing with security breaches:

- The *reactive method* is passive; when a breach occurs, you respond to it, doing damage control at the same time you track down how the intruder or attacker got in and cut off that means of access so it won't happen again.
- The *proactive method* is active; instead of waiting for the hackers to show you where you're vulnerable, you put on your own hacker hat in relation to your own network and set out to find the vulnerabilities yourself, before anyone else discovers and exploits them.

The best security strategy employs both reactive and proactive mechanisms. Intrusion detection systems (IDSs), for example, are reactive in that they detect suspicious network activity so that you can respond to it appropriately.

Vulnerability assessment scanning is a proactive tool that gives you the power to anticipate vulnerabilities and keep out attackers instead of spending much more time and money responding to attack after attack. The goal of proactive security is to prevent attacks before they happen, thus decreasing the load on reactive mechanisms. Being proactive is more cost effective and usually easier; the difference can be illustrated by contrasting the time and cost required to clean up after vandals break into your home or office with the effort and money required to simply install better locks that will keep them out.

Despite the initial outlay for vulnerability assessment scanners and the time spent administering them, potential return on investment is very high in the form of time and money saved when attacks are prevented.[12]

17. VULNERABILITY CAUSES

The following are vulnerability causes:

- Password management flaws
- Fundamental operating system design flaws
- Software bugs
- Unchecked user input

Password Management Flaws

The computer user uses weak passwords that could be discovered by brute force. The computer user stores the password on the computer where a program can access it. Users reuse passwords between many programs and Web sites.

Fundamental Operating System Design Flaws

The operating system designer chooses to enforce suboptimal policies on user/program management. For example, operating systems with policies such as *default permit* grant every program and every user full access to the entire computer. This operating system flaw allows viruses and malware to execute commands on behalf of the administrator.

Software Bugs

The programmer leaves an exploitable bug in a software program. The software bug may allow an attacker to misuse an application through (for example) bypassing access control checks or executing commands on the system hosting the application. Also the programmer's failure to check the size of data buffers, which can then be overflowed, can cause corruption of the stack or heap areas of memory (including causing the computer to execute code provided by the attacker).

Unchecked User Input

The program assumes that all user input is safe. Programs that do not check user input can allow unintended direct

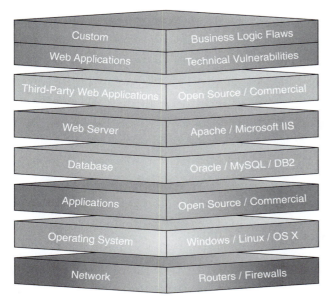

FIGURE 23.7 Vulnerabilities with the biggest impact.

execution of commands or SQL statements (known as Buffer overflows, SQL injection, or other nonvalidated inputs). The biggest impact on the organization would be if vulnerabilities are found in core devices on the network (routers, firewalls, etc.), as shown in Figure 23.7.[19]

18. DIY VULNERABILITY ASSESSMENT

If you perform credit-card transactions online, you're most likely PCI compliant or working on getting there. In either case, it is much better to resolve compliancy issues on an ongoing basis rather than stare at a truckload of problems as the auditor walks into your office. Though writing and reviewing policies and procedures is a big part of reaching your goal, being aware of the vulnerabilities in your environment and understanding how to remediate them are just as important. For most small businesses, vulnerability assessments sound like a lot of work and time that you just don't have. What if you could have a complete understanding of all vulnerabilities in your network and a fairly basic resolution

for each, outlined in a single report within a couple of hours? Sound good? What if I also told you the tool that can make this happen is currently free and doesn't require an IT genius to run it? Sounding better?

It isn't very pretty and it's not always right, but it can give you some valuable insight into your environment. Tenable's Nessus vulnerability scanner is one of the most widely used tools in professional vulnerability assessments today. In its default configuration, all you need to do is provide the tool with a range of IP addresses and click Go. It will then compare its database of known vulnerabilities against the responses it receives from your network devices, gathering as much information as possible without killing your network or servers, usually. It does have some very dangerous plug-ins that are disabled by default, and you can throttle down the amount of bandwidth it uses to keep the network noise levels to a minimum. The best part about Nessus is that it's, very well documented, and used by over 75,000 organizations worldwide, so you know you're dealing with trustworthy product. I urge you to take a look Tenable's enterprise offerings as well. You might just be surprised at how easy it is to perform a basic do-it-yourself vulnerability assessment! Related links:

- Tenable's Nessus: www.nessus.org
- Tenable Network Security: www.tenablesecurity.com

19. CONCLUSION

Network- and host-based vulnerability assessment tools are extremely useful in determining what vulnerabilities might exist on a particular network. However, these tools are not useful if the vulnerability knowledge base is not kept current. Also, these tools can only take a snapshot of the systems at a particular point in time. Systems administrators will continually update code on the target systems and will continuously add/delete services and configure the system. All found vulnerabilities should be promptly patched (especially critical ones).

---

19 www.webappsec.org.

Part III

Encryption Technology

## Chapter 24

Data Encryption

Dr. Bhushan Kapoor
California State University

Dr. Pramod Pandya
California State University

This chapter is about security and the role played by cryptographic technology in data security. Securing data while it is in storage or in transition from an unauthorized access is a critical function of information technology. All forms of ecommerce activities such as online credit card processing, purchasing stocks, and banking data processing would, if compromised, lead to businesses losing billions of dollars in revenues, as well as customer confidence lost in ecommerce.

The Internet evolved over the years as a means for users to access information and exchange emails. Later, once the bandwidth became available, businesses exploited the Internet's popularity to reach customers online. In the past few years it has been reported that organizations that store and maintain customers' private and confidential records were compromised on many occasions by hackers breaking into the data networks and stealing the records from storage media. More recently we have come across headline-grabbing security breaches regarding laptops with sensitive data being lost or stolen, and most recently the Feds have encrypted around 1 million laptops with encryption software loaded to secure data such as names and Social Security numbers.

Data security is not limited to wired networks but is equally critical for wireless communications such as in Wi-Fi and cellular. A very recent case was highlighted when the Indian government requested to Research In Motion (RIM) to share the encryption algorithm used in the BlackBerry cellular device. Of course, RIM refused to share the encryption algorithm. This should demonstrate that encryption is an important technology in all forms of communication. It is hard to accept that secured systems could ever remain secured, since they are designed by us and therefore must be breakable by one of us, given enough time. Every human-engineered system must have a flaw, and it is only a matter of time before someone finds it, thus demanding new innovations by exploring applications from algebraic structures such as groups and rings, elliptic curves, and quantum physics.

Over the past 20 years we have seen classical cryptography evolve to quantum cryptography, a branch of quantum information theory. Quantum cryptography is based on the framework of quantum physics, and it is meant to solve the problem of key distribution, which is an essential component of cryptography that enables us to secure data. The key allows the data to be coded so that to decode it, one would need to know the key that was used to code it. This coding of the given data using a key is known as *encryption*, and decoding of the encrypted data, the reverse step-by-step process, is known as *decryption*. At this stage we point out that the encryption algorithm comes in two flavors: symmetric and asymmetric, of which we will get into the details later on. Securing data requires a three-pronged approach: detection, prevention, and response. Data normally resides on storage media that are accessible over a network. This network is designed with a perimeter around it, such that a single access point provides a route for inbound and outbound traffic through a router supplemented with a firewall.

Data encryption prevents data from being exposed to unauthorized access and makes it unusable. Detection enables us to monitor the activities of network users and provides a means to differentiate levels of activities and offers a possible clue to network violations. Response is equally important, since a network violation must not be allowed to be repeated. Thus the three-pronged approach is evolutionary, and therefore systems analysis and design principles must be taken into account when we design a secured data network.

1. NEED FOR CRYPTOGRAPHY

Data communication normally takes place over an unsecured channel, as is the case when the Internet provides the pathways for the flow of data. In such a case the cryptographic protocols would enable secured communications by addressing the following.

Authentication

Alice sends a message to Bob. How can Bob verify that the message originated from Alice and not from Eve pretending to be Alice? Authentication is critical if Bob is to believe the message—for example, if the bank is trying to verify your Social Security or account number.

Confidentiality

Alice sends a message to Bob. How can Bob be sure that the message was not read by Eve? For example, personal communications need to be maintained as confidential.

Integrity

Alice sends a message to Bob. How does Bob verify that Eve did not intercept the message and change its contents?

Nonrepudiation

Alice could send a message to Bob and later deny that she ever sent a message to Bob. In such a case, how could Bob ever determine who actually sent him the message?

2. MATHEMATICAL PRELUDE TO CRYPTOGRAPHY

We will continue to describe Alice and Bob as two parties exchanging messages and Eve as the eavesdropper. Alice sends either a character string or a binary string that constitutes her message to Bob. In mathematical terms we have the *domain* of the message. The message in question needs to be secured from the eavesdropper Eve—hence it needs to be encrypted.

Mapping or Function

The encryption of the message can be defined as *mapping* the message from the domain to its range such that the inverse mapping should recover the original message.

This mapping is a mathematical construct known as the *function*.

So we have a domain, and the range of the function is defined such that the elements of the domain will always map to the range of the function, never outside it. If f represents the function, and the message $m \in$ the domain, then:

$$f(m) = M \in \text{the range}$$

This function can represent, for example, swapping (shifting by k places) the characters positions in the message as defined by the function:

$$f(m, k) = M \in \text{the range}$$

The inverse of this function f must recover the original message, in which case the function is invertible and one-to-one defined. If we were to apply two functions such as f followed by g, the composite function $(g \circ f)$ must be defined and furthermore invertible and one-to-one to recover the original message:

$$(g \circ f)(m) = g(f(m))$$

We will later see that this function is an algorithm that tells the user in a finite number of ways to disguise (encrypt) the given message. The inverse function, if it does exist, would enable us to recover the original message, which is known as the decryption.

Probability

Information security is the goal of the secured data encryption; hence if the encrypted data is truly randomly distributed in the message space (range), to the hacker the encrypted message is equally likely to be in any one of the states (encrypted). This would amount to maximum entropy, so one could reasonably ask as to the likelihood of a hacker breaking the encrypted message, that is, what is the probability of an insecure event taking place? This is conceptually similar to a system being in statistical equilibrium, when it could be equally likely to be in any one of the states. This could lay the foundations of cryptanalysis in terms of how secure the encryption algorithm is, and can it be broken in polynomial time?

Complexity

Computational complexity deals with problems that could be solved in polynomial time, for a given input.

If a given encryption algorithm is known to be difficult to solve and may have a number of solutions, the hacker would have a surmountable task to solve it. Therefore, secured encryption can be examined within the scope of computational complexity to determine whether a solution exists in polynomial time. There is a class of problems that have solutions in polynomial time for a given input, designated as *P*. By contrast, *NP* is the set of all problems that have solutions in polynomial time but the correctness of the problem cannot be ascertained. Therefore, *NP* is a larger set containing the set *P*. This is useful, for it leads us to *NP*-completeness, which reduces the solvability of problems in class *P* to class *NP*.

Consider a simple example—a set $S = \{4, 7, 12, 1, 10\}$ of five numbers. We want any three numbers to add to 23. Each of the numbers is either selected once only or not selected. The target is 23. Is there an algorithm for the target 23? If there is one, do we have more than one solution? Let's explore whether we can add three numbers to reach a target of 25. Is there a solution for a target of 25? Does a solution exist, and can we investigate in polynomial time? We could extend this concept of computational complexity to crack encryption algorithm that is public, but the key used to encrypt and decrypt the message is kept private. So, in essence the cryptoanalysis deals with discovering the key.

3. CLASSICAL CRYPTOGRAPHY

The conceptual foundation of cryptography was laid out around 3000 years ago in India and China. The earlier work in cryptology was centered on messages that were expressed using alphanumeric symbols; hence encryption involved simple algorithms such as shifting characters within the string of the message in a defined manner, which is now known as shift cipher. We will also introduce the necessary mathematics of cryptography: integer and modular arithmetic, linear congruence, Euclidean and Extended Euclidean algorithms, Fermat's theorem, and elliptic curves. We will specify useful notations in context.

Take the set of integers:

$$Z = \{............, -3, -2, -1, 0, 1, 2, 3, ...\}$$

For any integers *a* and *n*, we say that *n* divides *a* if the remainder is zero after the division, or else we write:

$$a = q \bullet n + r \quad q: \text{quotient, } r: \text{remainder}$$

The Euclidean Algorithm

Given two positive integers, *a* and *b*, find the greatest common divisors of *a* and *b*. Let *d* be the greatest common divisors (*gcd*) of *a* and *b*, then,

$$d = \gcd(a,b)$$

Use the following example:

$$\gcd(36,10) = \gcd(10,6) = \gcd(6,4) = \gcd(4,2)$$
$$= \gcd(2,0) = 2$$

Hence:

$$\gcd(36, 10) = 2$$

The Extended Euclidean Algorithm

Let *a* and *b* be two positive integers, then

$$d = \gcd(a, b) = ax + by$$

Use the following example:

$$\gcd(540, 168) = \gcd(168, 36) = \gcd(36, 24)$$
$$= \gcd(24, 12) = \gcd(12,0) = 12$$

$540 = 3(168) + 36$	$36 = 540 - 3(168)$
$168 = 4(36) + 24$	$24 = 168 - 4(36)$
$36 = 1(24) + 12$	$12 = 36 - 1(24)$

$$12 = 540 - 3(168) - 168 + 4(36)$$
$$= 540 - 4(168) + 4(36)$$
$$= 540 - 4(168) + 4(540) - 12(168)$$
$$= 5(540) - 16(168)$$

Therefore:

$$x = 5 \text{ and } y = -16$$

Hence:

$$12 = (5)540 - (16)168$$

Modular Arithmetic

For a given integer *a*, positive integer *m*, and the remainder *r*,

$$r = a \pmod{m}$$

Consider examples:

$$2 = 27 \bmod 5$$
$$10 = -18 \bmod 14$$

{divide − 18 by 14 leaves − 4 as a remainder, then add 14 to − 4 so that $(-4 + 14) = 10$ so the remainder is nonnegative}

A set of *residues* is a set consisting of remainders obtained by dividing positive integers by a chosen positive number m (modulus).

$$Z_m = a \ (\text{mod } m) = \{0, 1, 2, 3, \ldots, m - 1\}$$

Take $m = 7$, then

$$Z_7 = \{0, 1, 2, 3, 4, 5, 6\}$$

Congruence

In arithmetic we normally use the relational operator, equal (=), to express that the pair of numbers are equal to each other, which is a binary operation. In cryptography we use *congruence* to express that the residue is the same for a set of integers divided by a positive integer. This essentially groups the positive integers into equivalence classes. Let's look at some examples:

$$2 \equiv 2 \ \text{mod } 10; 2 \equiv 12 \ \text{mod } 10; 2 \equiv 22 \ \text{mod } 10$$

Hence we say that the set {2, 12, 22} are congruent mod 10.

Residue Class

A residue class is a set of integers congruent mod m, where m is a positive integer.

Take m = 7:

$$[0] = \{\ldots\ldots, -21, -14, -7, 0, 7, 14, 21, \ldots\ldots\}$$
$$[1] = \{\ldots\ldots, -20, -13, -6, 1, 8, 15, 22, \ldots\ldots\}$$
$$[2] = \{\ldots\ldots, -19, -12, -5, 2, 9, 16, 23, \ldots\ldots\}$$
$$[3] = \{\ldots\ldots, -18, -11, -4, 3, 10, 17, 24, \ldots\ldots\}$$
$$[4] = \{\ldots\ldots, -17, -10, -3, 4, 11, 18, 25, \ldots\ldots\}$$
$$[5] = \{\ldots\ldots, -16, -9, -2, 5, 12, 19, 26, \ldots\ldots\}$$
$$[6] = \{\ldots\ldots, -15, -8, -1, 6, 13, 20, 27, \ldots\ldots\}$$

Some more useful operations defined in $\mathbf{Z}_m$:

$$(a + b) \ \text{mod } m = \{(a \ \text{mod } m) + (b \ \text{mod } m)\} \ \text{mod } m$$
$$(a - b) \ \text{mod } m = \{(a \ \text{mod } m) - (b \ \text{mod } m)\} \ \text{mod } m$$
$$(a * b) \ \text{mod } m = \{(a \ \text{mod } m) * (b \ \text{mod } m)\} \ \text{mod } m$$

$$\mathbf{10}^n \ (\text{mod } x) = \langle \mathbf{10 \ mod \ } x \rangle^n \ \text{mod } m$$

Inverses

In everyday arithmetic, it is quite simple to find the inverse of a given integer if the binary operation is either additive or multiplicative, but such is not the case with modular arithmetic.

We will begin with the additive inverse of two numbers $a, b \in Z_m$

$$(a + b) \equiv 0 \ (\text{mod } m)$$

That is, the additive inverse of a is $b = (m - a)$.
Given

$$a = 4, \text{ and } m = 10$$

then:

$$b = m - a = 10 - 4 = 6$$

Verify:

$$4 + 6 \equiv 0 \ (\text{mod } 10)$$

Similarly, the multiplicative inverse of two integers $a, b \in Z_m$ if

$$a * b \equiv 1 \ (\text{mod } m)$$

a has a multiplicative inverse $b \in Z_m$ if and only if

$$\gcd(m, a) = 1$$

in which case (m, a) are relative prime.

We remind the reader that a prime number is any number greater than 1 that is divisible (with a remainder 0) only by itself and 1. For example, {2, 3, 5, 7, 11, 13, ... } are prime numbers, and we quote the following theorem for the reader.

Fundamental Theorem of Arithmetic

Each positive number is either a prime number or a composite number, in which case it can be expressed as a product of prime numbers.

Let's consider a set of integers mod 10 to find the multiplicative inverse of the numbers in the set:

$$Z_{10} = \{0, 1, 2, 3, 4, 5, 6, 7, 8, 9\}$$
$$(1 * 1) \ \text{mod } 10 = 1$$
$$(3 * 7) \ \text{mod } 10 = 1$$
$$(9 * 9) \ \text{mod } 10 = 1$$

then there are only three pairs (1,1); (3,7); and (9,9):

$$Z_{10*} = \{1, 3, 7, 9\}$$

The numbers {0, 2, 4, 5, 6, 8} have no multiplicative inverse.

Consider a set:

$$Z_6 = \{0, 1, 2, 3, 4, 5\}$$

Then,

$$Z_{6*} = \{1, 5\}$$

You will note that Z_{n*} is a subset of Z_n with unique multiplicative inverse.

Each member of Z_n has a unique additive inverse, whereas each member of Z_{n*} has a unique multiplicative inverse.

Congruence Relation Defined

The a is congruent to b (mod m) if m divides $(a - b)$, that is, the remainder is zero.

$$a \equiv b \bmod m$$

Examples: $87 \equiv 27 \bmod 4$, $67 \equiv 1 \bmod 6$.

Next we quote three theorems:

Theorem 1: Suppose that a $\equiv$ c mod m and b $\equiv$ = d mod m, then

$$a + b \equiv c + d \ (\bmod\ m)$$
$$a * b \equiv c * d \ (\bmod\ m)$$

Theorem 2: Suppose a*b $\equiv$ a*c (mod m)

and gcd(a, m) = 1
then b $\equiv$ c (mod m)

Theorem 3: Suppose a*b $\equiv$ a*c (mod m)

and d = gcd(a, m)
then b $\equiv$ c (mod m/d)

Example to illustrate the use of the theorems just stated:

$$6 \equiv 36 \ (\bmod\ 10)$$

then

$$3 \times 2 \equiv 3 \times 12 \ (\bmod\ 10)$$

since

$$\gcd(3,10) = 1$$

therefore,

$$2 \equiv 12 \ (\bmod\ 10)$$

also

$$2 = \gcd(6,10)$$

therefore,

$$1 \equiv 6 \ (\bmod\ 5)$$

Given,

$$14x \equiv 12 \ (\bmod\ 18)$$

find x.

Since

$$\gcd(14, 18) = 2$$

therefore,

$$7x \equiv 6 \ (\bmod\ 9)$$

you will observe that,

$$\gcd(7, 9) = 1$$

therefore,

$$x \equiv 6(7^{-1}) \bmod 9$$

and the multiplicative inverse of 7^{-1} is 4, therefore,

$$x \equiv (6 * 4) \ (\bmod\ 9) = 6$$

Substitution Cipher

Shift ciphers, also known as *additive ciphers*, are an example of a monoalphabetic character cipher in which each character is mapped to another character, and a repeated character maps to the same character irrespective of its position in the string. We give a simple example of an additive cipher, where the key is 3, and the algorithm is "add." We restrict the mapping to $\{0, 1, \ldots, 7\}$ (see Table 24.1)—that is, we use mod 8. This is an example of finite domain and the range for mapping, so the inverse of the function can be determined easily from the ciphertext.

Observations:

- The domain of the function is x = {0,1,2,3,4,5,6,7}.
- The range of the function is y = {0,1,2,3,4,5,6,7}.
- The function is 1 to 1.
- The function is invertible.
- The inverse function is x = (y − 3) mod 8.

TABLE 24.1 Table of values for $y = (x + 3)$ mod 8, given values of $x = \{0,1, \ldots 7\}$

x	0	1	2	3	4	5	6	7
y	3	4	5	6	7	0	1	2

The affine cipher has two operations, addition and multiplication, with two keys. Once again the arithmetic is mod *m*, where *m* is a chosen positive integer.

$$y = (kx + b) \bmod m$$

where *k* and *b* are chosen from integers $\{0, 1, 2, 3, \ldots\ldots, (m - 1)\}$, and *x* is the symbol to be encrypted.

The decryption is given as:

$$x = [(y - b) * k^{-1}] \bmod m$$

where

$$k^{-1}$$

is the multiplicative inverse of k in Z_{n^*}

$(-b)$ is the additive inverse in Z_n

Consider,

$$y = (5 * x + 3) \bmod 8$$

Then,

$$x = (y - 3)5 \bmod 8$$

In this case, the multiplicative inverse of 5 happens to be 5.

Monoalphabetic substitution ciphers are easily broken, since the key size is small (see Table 24.2).

$$Z_8 = \{0, 1, 2, 3, 4, 5, 6, 7\}$$
$$Z_{8*} = \{1, 3, 5\}$$

Transposition Cipher

A transposition cipher changes the location of the character by a given set of rules known as *permutation*. A cyclic group defines the permutation with a single key to encrypt, and the same key is used to decrypt the ciphered message. Table 24.3 provides an illustration.

TABLE 24.2 Monoalphabetic Substitution Cipher

x	0	1	2	3	4	5	6	7
y	3	0	5	2	7	4	1	6

TABLE 24.3 Transposition Cipher

1	2	3	4	5
3	1	4	5	2

4. MODERN SYMMETRIC CIPHERS

Computers internally represent printable data in binary format as strings of zeros and ones. Therefore any data is represented as a large block of zeros and ones. The processing speed of a computer is used to encrypt the block of zeros and ones. Securing all the data in one go would not be practical, nor would it secure the data; hence the scheme to treat data in chunks of blocks, leading to the concept of block ciphers.

The most common value of a block is 64, 128, 256, or 512 bits. You will observe that these values are powers of 2, since computers process data in binary representation using modular arithmetic with modulus 2. We need an algorithm and a key to encrypt the blocks of binary data such that the ciphered data is confusing and diffusing to the hacker. The algorithm is made public, whereas the key is kept secret from unauthorized users so that hackers could establish the robustness of the cipher by attempting to break the encrypted message. The logic of the block cipher is as follows:

- Each bit of ciphertext should depend on all bits of the key and all bits of the plaintext.
- There should be no evidence of statistical relationship between the plaintext and the ciphertext.

In essence, this is the goal of an encryption algorithm: Confuse the message so that there is no apparent relationship between the ciphertext and the plaintext. This is achieved by the substitution rule (S-boxes) and the key.

If changing one bit in the plaintext has a minimal effect on the encrypted text, it might be possible for the hacker to work backward from the encrypted text to the plaintext by changing the bits. Therefore a minimal change in the plaintext should lead to a maximum change in the ciphertext, resulting in spreading, which is known as *diffusion*. Permutation or P-boxes implement the diffusion.

The symmetric cipher consists of an algorithm and a key. The algorithm is made public, whereas the key is kept secret and is known only to the parties that are exchanging messages. Of course, this does create a huge problem, since every pair that is going to exchange messages will need a secret key, growing indefinitely in number as the number of pairs increases. We also would need a mechanism by which to manage the secret keys. We will address these issues later on.

The symmetric algorithm would consist of finite rounds of S-boxes and P-boxes. Once the plaintext is encrypted using the algorithm and the key, it would need to be decrypted using the same algorithm and key.

The decryption algorithm and the key would need to work backward in some sense to revert the encrypted message to its original message.

So you begin to see that the algorithm must consist of a finite number of combinations of S-boxes and P-boxes; encryption is mapping from message space (domain) to another message space (range), that is, mapping should be a closed operation, a "necessary" condition on the encryption algorithm. This implies that message strings get mapped to message strings, and of course these message strings belong to a set of messages. We are not concerned with the semantics of the message; we leave this to the message sender and receiver. The S-boxes and P-boxes would define a set of operations on the messages or bits that represent the string of messages. Therefore we require that this set of operations should also be able to undo the encryption, that is, mapping must be invertible in the mathematical sense. Hence the set of operations must have definite relationships among them, resulting in some structural and logical connection. In mathematics an example of this is an algebraic structure such as group, ring, and field, which we explore in the next section.

S-Box

The reader should note that an S-box can have a 3-bit input binary string, and its output may be a 2-bit. The S-box may use a key or be keyless. Let $S(x)$ be the linear function computed by the following function [1]:

$$S(x_1\ x_2\ x_3) = [(1 + x_1 + x_2 + x_3 + x_1 \cdot x_2)\,\mathrm{mod}\,2]$$
$$[(1 + x_3 + x_1 \cdot x_3 + x_1 \cdot x_2)\,\mathrm{mod}\,2]$$

Such a function is referred to as an *S-box*. For a given 4-bit block of plaintext $x_1x_2x_3x_4$ and the 3-bit key, $k_1k_2k_3$, let

$$E(x_1x_2x_3x_4, k_1k_2k_3) = x_1x_2(x_3x_4 \oplus$$
$$S(x_2x_1x_2 \oplus k_1k_2k_3))$$

where $\oplus$ represents exclusive OR

Given ciphertext, $y_1y_2y_3y_4$ computed with E and the key, $k_1k_2k_3$, compute

$$D(y_1y_2y_3y_4, k_1k_2k_3 = (y_1y_2 \oplus S(y_4y_3y_4 \oplus k_1k_2k_3))y_3y_4$$

S-boxes are classified as linear if the number of output bits is the same as the number of input bits, and they're nonlinear if the number of output bits is different from the number of input bits. Furthermore, S-boxes can be invertible or noninvertible.

P-Boxes

A *P-box* (permutation box) will permute the bits per specification. There are three different types of P-boxes, as shown in Tables 24.4, 24.5, and 24.6.

In the compression P-box, inputs 2 and 4 are blocked.

The expansion P-box maps elements 1, 2, and 3 only.

Let's consider a permutation group with the mapping defined, as shown in Table 24.7.

TABLE 24.4 Straight P-box

1	2	3	4	5
4	1	5	3	2

TABLE 24.5 Compression P-box

1	2	3	4	5
1		2		3

TABLE 24.6 Expansion P-box

1	3	3	1	2
1	2	3	4	5

TABLE 24.7 The permutation group

	1	2	3	4	5	6	7	8
a	2	6	3	1	4	8	5	7
	1	1	1	1	0	0	1	0
	1	0	1	1	1	0	0	1
a^2	6	8	3	2	1	7	4	5
	0	0	1	1	1	1	1	0
a^3	8	7	3	6	2	5	1	4
	0	1	1	0	1	0	1	1
a^4	7	5	3	8	6	4	2	1
	1	0	1	0	0	1	1	1
a^5	5	4	3	7	8	1	6	2
	0	1	1	1	0	1	0	1
a^6	4	1	3	5	7	2	8	6
	1	1	1	0	1	1	0	0
$a^7 = e$	1	2	3	4	5	6	7	8
	1	1	1	1	0	0	1	0

This group is a cyclic group with elements:

$$G = (e, a, a^2, a^3, a^4, a^5, a^6)$$

The identity mapping is given by $a^7 = e$. The inverse element is a^{-1}.

Table 24.7 shows a permutation of an 8-bit string (11110010).

Product Ciphers

Modern block ciphers are divided into two categories. The first category of the cipher uses both invertible and noninvertible components. A Feistel cipher belongs to the first category, and DES is a good example of a Feistel cipher. This cipher uses the combination of S-boxes and P-boxes with compression and expansion (noninvertible).

The second category of cipher only uses invertible components, and Advanced Encryption Standard (AES) is an example of a non-Feistel cipher. AES uses S-boxes with an equal number of inputs and outputs and a straight P-box that is invertible.

Alternation of substitutions and transpositions of appropriate forms when applied to a block of plaintext can have the effect of obscuring statistical relationships between the plaintext and the ciphertext and between the key and the ciphertext (diffusion and confusion).

5. ALGEBRAIC STRUCTURE

Modern encryption algorithms such as DES, AES, RSA, and ElGamal, to name a few, are based on algebraic structures such as group theory and field theory as well as number theory. We will begin with a set S, with a finite number of elements and a binary operation (∗) defined between any two elements of the set:

$$* : S \times S \to S$$

that is, if a and $b \in S$, then $a * b \in S$. This is important because it implies that the set is closed under the binary operation. We have seen that the message space is finite, and we want to make sure that any algebraic operation on the message space satisfies the closure property. Hence, we want to treat the message space as a finite set of elements. We remind the reader that messages that get encrypted must be finally decrypted by the received party, so the encryption algorithm must run in polynomial time; furthermore, the algorithm must have the property that it be reversible, to recover the original message.

The goal of encryption is to confuse and diffuse the hacker to make it almost impossible for the hacker to break the encrypted message. Therefore, encryption must consist of finite number substitutions and transpositions. The algebraic structure *classical group* facilitates the coding of encryption algorithms.

Next we give some relevant definitions and examples before we proceed to introduce the essential concept of a Galois field, which is central to formulation of a Rijndael algorithm used in the Advanced Encryption Standard.

Definition Group

A definition group $(G, \bullet)$ is a finite set G together with an operation • satisfying the following conditions [2]:

- Closure: $\forall\ a, b \in G$, then $(a \bullet b) \in G$
- Associativity: $\forall\ a, b, c \in G$, then $a \bullet (b \bullet c) = (a \bullet b) \bullet c$
- Existence of identity: $\exists$ a unique element $e \in G$ such that $\forall\ a \in G$: $a \bullet e = e \bullet a$
- $\forall\ a \in G$: $\exists\ a^{-1} \in G$: $a^{-1}\ a = a^{-1} \bullet a = e$

Definitions of Finite and Infinite Groups (Order of a Group)

A group G is said to be finite if the number of elements in the set G is finite; otherwise the group is infinite.

Definition Abelian Group

A group G is abelian if for all $a, b \in G$, $a \bullet b = b \bullet a$

The reader should note that in a group, the elements in the set do not have to be numbers or objects; they can be mappings, functions, or rules.

Examples of a Group

The set of integers Z is a group under addition (+), that is, $(Z, +)$ is a group with identity $e = 0$, and inverse of an element a is $(-a)$. This is an additive abelian group, but infinite.

Nonzero elements of Q (rationals), R (reals), and C (complex) form a group under multiplication, with the identity element $e = 1$, and a^{-1} being the multiplicative inverse.

For any $n \geq 1$, the set of integers modulo n forms a finite additive group of n elements.

$G = \ <Z_n, +>$ is an abelian group.

The set of Z_{n*} with multiplication operator , $G = \ <Z_{n*}, x>$ is also an abelian group.

The set Z_{n*}, is a subset of Z_n and includes only integers in Z_n that have a unique multiplicative inverse.

$$Z_{13} = \{0,1,2,3,4,5,6,7,8,9,10,11,12\}$$
$$Z_{13*} = \{1,2,3,4,5,6,7,8,9,10,11,12\}$$

Definition: Subgroup

A subgroup of a group G is a non empty subset H of G, which itself is a group under the same operations as that of G. We denote that H is a subgroup of G as $H \subseteq G$, and $H \subset G$ is a proper subgroup of G if the set $H \neq G$ [2]:

Examples of subgroups:

Under addition, $Z \subseteq Q \subseteq R \subseteq C$.

$H = <Z_{10}, + >$ is a proper subgroup of $G = < Z_{12}, + >$

Definition: Cyclic Group

A group G is said to be cyclic if there exists an element $a \in G$ such that for any $b \in G$, and $i \geq 0$, $b = a^i$. Element a is called a generator of G.

The group $G = < Z_{10*}, x >$ is a cyclic group with generators $g = 3$ and $g = 7$.

$$Z_{10*} = \{1,3,7,9\}$$

The group $G = < Z_6, + >$ is a cyclic group with generators $g = 1$ and $g = 5$.

$$Z_6 = \{0, 1, 2, 3, 4, 5\}$$

Rings

Let R be a non-empty set with two binary operations addition $(+)$ and multiplication $(*)$. Then R is called a *ring* if the following axioms are met:

- Under addition, R is an abelian group with zero as the additive identity.
- Under multiplication, R satisfies the closure, the associativity, and the identity axiom; 1 is the multiplicative identity, and that $1 \neq 0$.
- For every a and b that belongs to R, $a \bullet b = b \bullet a$.
- For every a, b, and c that belongs to R, then $a \bullet (b + c) = a \bullet b + a \bullet c$.

Examples

Z, Q, R, and C are all rings under addition and multiplication. For any $n > 0$, Z_n is a ring under addition and

multiplication modulo n with 0 as identity under addition, 1 under multiplication.

Definition: Field

If the nonzero elements of a ring form a group under multiplication, the ring is called a *field*.

Examples

Q, R, and C are all fields under addition and multiplication, with 0 and 1 as identity under addition and multiplication.

Note: Z under integer addition and multiplication is not a field because any nonzero element does not have a multiplicative inverse in Z.

Finite Fields GF(2ⁿ)

Construction of finite fields and computations in finite fields are based on polynomial computations. Finite fields play a significant role in cryptography and cryptographic protocols such as the Diffie and Hellman key exchange protocol, ElGamal cryptosystems, and AES.

For a prime number p, the quotient Z/p (or F_p) is a finite field with p number of elements. For any positive integer q, $GF(q) = F_q$. We define A to be algebraic structure such as a ring, group, or field.

Definition: A polynomial over A is an expression of the form

$$f(x) = \sum_{i=0}^{n} a_i x^n$$

where n is a nonnegative integer, the coefficient $a_i \in A$, $0 \leq i \leq n$, and $x \notin A$ [2].

Definition: A polynomial $f \in A[x]$ is said to be irreducible in $A[x]$ if f has a positive degree and $f = gh$ for some g, $h \in A[x]$ implies that either g or h is a constant polynomial [2].

The reader should be aware that a given polynomial can be reducible over one structure but irreducible over another.

Definition: Let f, g, q, and $r \in A[x]$ with $g \neq 0$. Then we say that r is a *remainder* of f divided by g:

$$r \equiv f(\bmod g)$$

The set of remainders of all the polynomials in $A[x](\bmod g)$ denoted as $A[x]_g$.

Theorem: Let F be a field and f be a nonzero polynomial in $F[x]$. Then $F[x]_f$ is a ring and is a field if f is irreducible over F.

Theorem: Let F be a field of p elements, and f be an irreducible polynomial over F. Then the number of elements in the field $F[x]_f$ is p^n [2].

For every prime p and every positive integer n there exists a finite field of p^n number of elements.

For any prime number p, Z_p is a finite field under addition and multiplication modulo p with 0 and 1 as the identity under addition and multiplication.

Z_p is an additive ring and the nonzero elements of Z_p, denoted by Z_{p*}, forms a multiplicative group.

Galois field, $GF(p^n)$ is a finite field with number of elements p^n, where p is a prime number and n is a positive integer.

Example: Integer representation of a finite field (Rijndael) element.

Polynomial $f(x) = x^8 + x^4 + x^3 + x + 1$ is irreducible over F_2.

The set of all polynomials(mod f) over F_2 forms a field of 2^8 elements; they are all polynomials over F_2 of degree less than 8. So any element in the field $F_2[x]_f$

$$b_7 x^7 + b_6 x^6 + b_5 x^5 + b_4 x^4 + b_3 x^3 + b_2 x^2 + b_1 x^1 + b_0$$

where $b_7, b_6, b_5, b_4, b_3, b_2, b_1, b_0 \in F_2$ thus any element in this field can represent an 8-bit binary number.

We often use F_{2^8} field with 256 elements because there exists an isomorphism between Rijndael and F_{2^8}.

Data inside a computer is organized in bytes (8 bits) and is processed using Boolean logic, that is, bits are manipulated using binary operations addition and multiplication. These binary operations are implemented using the logical operator XOR, or in the language of finite fields, $GF(2)$. Since the extended ASCII defines 8 bits per byte, an 8-bit byte has a natural representation using a polynomial of degree 8. Polynomial addition would be mod 2, and multiplication would be mod polynomial degree 8. Of course this polynomial degree 8 would have to be irreducible. Hence the Galois field $GF(2^8)$ would be the most natural tool to implement the encryption algorithm. Furthermore, this would provide a close algebraic formulation.

Consider polynomials over $GF(2)$ with $p = 2$ and $n = 1$.

$$1, x, x + 1, x^2 + x + 1, x^2 + 1, x^3 + 1$$

For polynomials with negative coefficients, -1 is the same as $+1$ in $GF(2)$. Obviously, the number of such polynomials is infinite. Algebraic operations of addition and multiplication in which the coefficients are added and multiplied according to the rules that apply to $GF(2)$ are sets of polynomials that form a ring.

Modular Polynomial Arithmetic Over $GF(2)$

The Galois field $GF(2^3)$: Construct this field with eight elements that can be represented by polynomials of the form

$$ax^2 + bx + c \text{ where } a, b, c \in GF(2) = \{0, 1\}$$

Two choices for a, b, c give $2 \times 2 \times 2 = 8$ polynomials of the form

$$ax^2 + bx + c \in GF_2[x]$$

What is our choice of the irreducible polynomials for this field?

$$(x^3 + x^2 + x + 1), (x^3 + x^2 + 1), (x^3 + x^2 + x),$$
$$(x^3 + x + 1), (x^3 + x^2)$$

These two polynomials have no factors: $(x^3 + x^2 + 1)$, $(x^3 + x + 1)$

So we choose polynomial $(x^3 + x + 1)$. Hence all polynomial arithmetic multiplication and division is carried out with respect to $(x^3 + x + 1)$.

The eight polynomials that belong to $GF(2^3)$:

$$\{0, 1, x, x^2, 1 + x, 1 + x^2, x + x^2, 1 + x + x^2\}$$

You will observe that $GF(8) = \{0,1,2,3,4,5,6,7\}$ is not a field, since every element (excluding zero) does not have a multiplicative inverse such as $\{2, 4, 6\}$ (mod 8) [2].

Using a Generator to Represent the Elements of $GF(2^n)$

It is particularly convenient to represent the elements of a Galois field with the help of a generator element. If α is a generator element, then every element of $GF(2^n)$, except for the 0 element, can be written as some power of α. A generator is obtained from the irreducible polynomial that was used to construct the finite field. If $f(\alpha)$ is the irreducible polynomial used, then α is that element that satisfies the equation $f(\alpha) = 0$. You do not actually solve this equation for its roots, since an irreducible polynomial cannot have actual roots in the field $GF(2)$.

Consider the case of $GF(2^3)$, defined with the irreducible polynomial $x^3 + x + 1$. The generator α is that element that satisfies $\alpha^3 + \alpha + 1 = 0$. Suppose α is a root in $GF(2^3)$ of the polynomial $p(x) = 1 + x + x^3$, that is, $p(\alpha) = 0$, then

$$\alpha^3 = -\alpha - 1 \ (\text{mod } 2) = \alpha + 1$$
$$\alpha^4 = \alpha(\alpha + 1) = \alpha^2 + \alpha$$
$$\alpha^5 = \alpha^4 . \alpha = (\alpha^2 + \alpha)\alpha = \alpha^3 + \alpha^2 = (\alpha^2 + \alpha + 1)$$
$$\alpha^6 = \alpha^5 . \alpha = \alpha.(\alpha^2 + \alpha + 1) = (\alpha^2 + 1)$$
$$\alpha^7 = (\alpha^2 + 1).\alpha = (2\alpha + 1) = 1$$

All powers of α generate nonzero elements of GF_8. The polynomials of $GF(2^3)$ represent bit strings, as shown in Table 24.8.

We now consider all polynomials defined over $GF(2)$, modulo the irreducible polynomial $x^3 + x + 1$. When an algebraic operation (polynomial multiplication) results in a polynomial whose degree equals or exceeds that of the irreducible polynomial, we will take for our result the remainder modulo the irreducible polynomial. For example,

$$(x^2 + x + 1) * (x^2 + 1) \ \text{mod} \ (x^3 + x + 1)$$
$$= (x^4 + x^3 + x^2) + (x^2 + x + 1) \ \text{mod} \ (x^3 + x + 1)$$
$$= (x^4 + x^3 + x + 1) \ \text{mod} \ (x^3 + x + 1)$$
$$= -x^2 + x$$
$$= x^2 + x$$

Recall that $1 + 1 = 0$ in $GF(2)$. With multiplications modulo $(x^3 + x + 1)$, we have only the following eight polynomials in the set of polynomials over $GF(2)$:

$$\{0, 1, x, x + 1, x^2, x^2 + 1, x^2 + x, x^2 + x + 1\}$$

We refer to this set as $GF(2^3)$, where the power of 2 is the degree of the modulus polynomial. The eight elements of Z_8 are to be integers modulo 8. Similarly,

TABLE 24.8 The polynomials of $GF(2^3)$

Polynomial	Bit String
0	000
1	001
x	010
x + 1	011
x^2	100
$x^2 + 1$	101
$x^2 + x$	110
$x^2 + x + 1$	111

$GF(2^3)$ maps all the polynomials over $GF(2)$ to the eight polynomials shown. But you will note the crucial difference between $GF(2^3)$ and 2^3: $GF(2^3)$ is a field, whereas Z_8 is *not* [2].

$GF(2^3)$ Is a Finite Field

We know that $GF(2^3)$ is an abelian group because the operation of polynomial addition satisfies all the requirements of a group operator and because polynomial addition is commutative. $GF(2^3)$ is also a commutative ring because polynomial multiplication is a distributive over polynomial addition. $GF(2^3)$ is a finite field because it is a finite set and because it contains a unique multiplicative inverse for every nonzero element.

$GF(2^n)$ is a finite field for every n. To find all the polynomials in $GF(2^n)$, we need an irreducible polynomial of degree n. AES arithmetic is based on $GF(2^8)$. It uses the following irreducible polynomial:

$$f(x) = x^8 + x^4 + x^3 + x + 1$$

The finite field $GF(2^8)$ used by AES obviously contains 256 distinct polynomials over $GF(2)$. In general, $GF(p^n)$ is a finite field for any prime p. The elements of $GF(p^n)$ are polynomials over $GF(p)$ (which is the same as the set of residues Z_p).

Next we show how the multiplicative inverse of a polynomial is calculated using the Extended Euclidean algorithm:

Multiplicative inverse of $(x^2 + x + 1)$
in $F_2[x]/(x^4 + x + 1)$ is $(x^2 + x)$

$$(x^2 + x)(x^2 + x + 1) = 1 \ \text{mod}(x^4 + x + 1)$$

Multiplicative inverse of $(x^6 + x + 1)$
in $F_2[x]/(x^8 + x^4 + x^3 + x + 1)$
is $(x^6 + x^5 + x^2 + x + 1)$

$$(x^6 + x + 1)(x^6 + x^5 + x^2 + x + 1) = 1$$
$$\text{mod} \ (x^8 + x^4 + x^3 + x + 1)[2,3]$$

6. THE INTERNAL FUNCTIONS OF RIJNDAEL IN AES IMPLEMENTATION

Rijndael is a block cipher. The messages are broken into blocks of a predetermined length, and each block is encrypted independently of the others. Rijndael operates on blocks that are 128-bits in length. There are actually three variants of the Rijndael cipher, each of which uses a different key length. The permissible key lengths are 128, 192, and 256 bits. The details of Rijndael may be found in Bennett and Gilles (1984), but we give an overview here [2, 3].

Mathematical Preliminaries

Within a block, the fundamental unit operated on is a byte, that is, 8 bits. Bytes can be interpreted in two different ways. A byte is given in terms of its bits as $b_7 b_6 b_5 b_4 b_3 b_2 b_1 b_0$. We may think of each bit as an element in GF(2), the finite field of two elements (mod 2). First, we may think of a byte as a vector, $b_7 b_6 b_5 b_4 b_3 b_2 b_1 b_0$ in GF(2^8). Second, we may think of a byte as an element of GF(2^8), in the following way: Consider the polynomial ring GF(2)[X]. We may mod out by any polynomial to produce a factor ring. If this polynomial is irreducible and of degree n, the resulting factor ring is isomorphic to GF(2^n). In Rijndael, we mod out by the irreducible polynomial $X8 + X4 + X3 + X + 1$ and so obtain a representation for GF(2^8). The Rijndael algorithm deals with five units of data in the encryption scheme:

- Bit: A binary digit with a value of 0 or 1
- Byte: A group of 8 bits
- Word: A group of 32 bits
- Block: A block in AES is defined to be 128, 192 or 256 bits
- State: The data block is known as a *state*, and it is made up of a 4 × 4 matrix of 16 bytes (128 bits)

State

For our discussion purposes, we will consider a data block of 128 bits with a *ky* size of 128 bits. The state is 128 bits long. We think of the state as divided into 16 bytes, a_{ij} where $0 \le i, j \le 3$. We think of these 16 bytes as an array, or matrix, with 4 rows and 4 columns, such that a_{00} is the first byte, b_0 and so on (see Figure 24.1).

AES uses several rounds (10, 12, or 14) of transformations, beginning with a 128-bit block. A round is made up of four parts: S-box, permutation, mixing, and subkey addition. We discuss each part here [2, 3].

The S-Box (SubByte)

S-boxes, or substitution boxes, are common in block ciphers. These are 1-to-1 and onto functions, and therefore an inverse exists. Furthermore, these maps are

$$\begin{bmatrix} a_{00} = b_0 & a_{01} = b_4 & a_{02} = b_8 & a_{03} = b_{12} \\ a_{10} = b_1 & a_{11} = b_5 & a_{12} = b_9 & a_{13} = b_{13} \\ a_{20} = b_2 & a_{21} = b_6 & a_{22} = b_{10} & a_{23} = b_{14} \\ a_{30} = b_3 & a_{31} = b_7 & a_{32} = b_{11} & a_{33} = b_{15} \end{bmatrix}$$

FIGURE 24.1 State.

nonlinear to make them immune to linear and differential cryptoanalysis. The S-box is the same in every round, and it acts independently on each byte. Each byte belongs to GF(2^8) domain with 256 elements. For a given byte we compute the inverse of that byte in the GF(2^8) field. This sends a byte x to x^{-1} if x is nonzero and sends it to 0 if it is zero. This defines a nonlinear transformation, as shown in Table 24.9.

Next we apply an affine (over GF(2)) transformation. Think of the byte x as a vector in GF(2^8). Consider the invertible matrix A, as shown in Figure 24.2.

The structure of matrix A is relatively simple, successively shifting the prior row by 1. If we define the vector $v \in$ GF(2^8) to be (1, 1, 0, 0, 0, 1, 1, 0), then the second half of the S-box sends byte x to byte y through the affine transformation defined as:

$$y = A \cdot x^{-1} \oplus 1$$

Since the matrix A has an inverse, it is possible to recover x using the following procedure known as the InvSubByte:

$$x = [A^{-1}(y \oplus b)]^{-1}$$

We will demonstrate the action of an S-box by choosing an uppercase letter *S*, for which the hexadecimal representation is 53_{16} and binary representation is shown in Tables 24.10 and 24.11.

The letter S has a polynomial representation:

$$(x^6 + x^4 + x + 1)$$

The multiplicative inverse of $(x^6 + x^4 + x + 1)$ is $(x^7 + x^6 + x^3 + x)$, which is derived using the Extended Euclidean algorithm.

Next we multiply the multiplicative inverse x^{-1} with an invertible matrix A (see Figure 24.3) and add a column vector (b) and get the resulting column vector y (see Table 24.12). This corresponds to SubByte transformation and it is nonlinear [2].

$$y = A * x^{-1} + b$$

The column vector y represents a character ED_{16} in hexadecimal representation.

TABLE 24.9 SubByte Transformation

	0	1	2	3	4	5	6	7	8	9	A	B	C	D	E	F
0	63	7C	77	7B	F2	6B	6F	C5	30	01	67	2B	FE	D7	AB	76
1	CA	82	C9	7D	FA	59	47	F0	AD	D4	A2	AF	9C	A4	72	C0
2	B7	FD	93	26	36	3F	F7	CC	34	A5	E5	F1	71	D8	31	15
3	04	C7	23	C3	18	96	05	9A	07	12	80	E2	EB	27	B2	75
4	09	83	2C	1A	1B	6E	5A	A0	52	3B	D6	B3	29	E3	2F	84
5	53	D1	00	ED	20	FC	B1	5B	6A	CB	BE	39	4A	4C	58	CF
6	D0	EF	AA	FB	43	4D	33	85	45	F9	02	7F	50	3C	9F	A8
7	51	A3	40	8F	92	9D	38	F5	BC	B6	DA	21	10	FF	F3	D2
8	CD	0C	13	EC	5F	97	44	17	C4	A7	7E	3D	64	5D	19	73
9	60	81	4F	DC	22	2A	90	88	46	EE	B8	14	DE	5E	0B	DB
A	E0	32	3A	0A	49	06	24	5C	C2	D3	AC	62	91	95	E4	79
B	E7	CB	37	6D	8D	D5	4E	A9	6C	56	F4	EA	65	7A	AE	08
C	BA	78	25	2E	1C	A6	B4	C6	E8	DD	74	1F	4B	BD	8B	8A
D	70	3E	B5	66	48	03	F6	0E	61	35	57	B9	86	C1	1D	9E
E	E1	F8	98	11	69	D9	8E	94	9B	1E	87	E9	CE	55	28	DF
F	8C	A1	89	0D	BF	E6	42	68	41	99	2D	0F	B0	54	BB	16

$$A = \begin{bmatrix} 10001111 \\ 11000111 \\ 11110001 \\ 11110001 \\ 01111100 \\ 00111110 \\ 00011111 \end{bmatrix} \qquad b = \begin{pmatrix} 1 \\ 1 \\ 0 \\ 0 \\ 0 \\ 1 \\ 1 \\ 0 \end{pmatrix}$$

FIGURE 24.2 The invertible matrix.

TABLE 24.10 Hexadecimal and binary representation

a_7	a_6	a_5	a_4	a_3	a_2	a_1	a_0
0	1	0	1	0	0	1	1

The reader should note that this transformation using the GF(2^8) field is a pretty tedious computation, so instead we use an AES S-box lookup table (a 17×17 matrix expressed in hexadecimal) to replace the character with **a** replacement character. This corresponds to the SubByte transformation, and corresponding to the SubByte table there is an InvSubByte table that is the inverse of the SubByte table. The InvSubByte can be found in the references or is readily available on the Internet.

We will work with the following string: QUANTUMCRYPTOGOD, which is 16 bytes long, to illustrate AES (see Table 24.13). The state represents our string as a 4×4 matrix in the given arrangement using a hexadecimal representation of each byte (see Figure 24.4).

We apply SubByte transformation (see Figure 24.5) using the lookup table, which replaces each byte as defined in Table 24.13

The next two rounds of ShiftRows and Mixing in the encryption lead to a diffusion process. The ShiftRow is a permutation.

ShiftRows

In the first step, we take the state and apply the following logic. The first row is kept as is. The second row is shifted left by one byte. The third row is shifted left by two bytes, and the last row is shifted left by three bytes. The resulting state is shown in Figure 24.6.

InvShiftRows in decryption shift bytes toward the right, similar to ShiftRows.

Mixing

The second step, the MixColumns transformation, mixes the columns. We interpret the bytes of each column as

TABLE 24.11 Hexadecimal and binary representation

a_7	a_6	a_5	a_4	a_3	a_2	a_1	a_0
1	1	0	0	1	0	1	0

$$\begin{bmatrix} 10001111 \\ 11000111 \\ 11100011 \\ 11110001 \\ 11111000 \\ 01111100 \\ 00111110 \\ 00011111 \end{bmatrix} \begin{pmatrix} 0 \\ 1 \\ 0 \\ 1 \\ 0 \\ 0 \\ 1 \\ 1 \end{pmatrix} + \begin{pmatrix} 1 \\ 1 \\ 0 \\ 0 \\ 0 \\ 1 \\ 1 \\ 0 \end{pmatrix} \textbf{(mod 2)} = \begin{pmatrix} 1 \\ 0 \\ 1 \\ 1 \\ 0 \\ 1 \\ 1 \\ 1 \end{pmatrix}$$

FIGURE 24.3 Multiplying the multiplicative inverse with an invertible matrix.

TABLE 24.12 Vector y

y_7	y_6	y_5	y_4	y_3	y_2	y_1	y_0
1	1	1	0	1	1	0	1

the coefficients of a polynomial in $GF(2^8)[x]/(x^4 + 1)$. Then we multiply each column by the polynomial '03' x^3 + '02' x^2 + '01'x + '02'. Multiplication of the bytes is done in $GF(2^8)$ with mod ($x^4 + 1$).

The mixing transformation remaps the four bytes to a new four bytes by changing the contents of the individual bytes (see Figure 24.7). The MixColumns transformation is applied to each column of the state, hence each column is multiplied by a constant matrix to obtain a new state, S'_{0i}.

$$S'_{0i} = 2 \circ S_{0i} \oplus 3 \circ S_{1i} \oplus S_{2i} \oplus S_{3i}$$
$$S'_{00} = 2 \circ S_{00} \oplus 3 \circ S_{10} \oplus S_{20} \oplus S_{30}$$
$$S_{20} \oplus S_{30} = 53 \oplus 1B$$
$$= (01010011) \oplus (00011011)$$
$$= (01001000)$$
$$2 \circ S_{00} = (00000010) \circ (D1)$$
$$= (x) \circ (11010001)$$
$$= (x)(x^7 + x^6 + x^4 + 1)$$
$$= (x^8 + x^7 + x^5 + x) \bmod (x^8 + x^4 + x^3 + x + 1)$$
$$= (x^7 + x^5 + x^4 + x^3 + 1)$$
$$= (10111001)$$

$$3 \circ S_{10} = (00000011)(FC)$$
$$= (00000011)(11111100)$$
$$= \{ (x + 1)(x^7 + x^6 + x^5 + x^4 + x^3 + x^2) \}$$
$$\bmod (x^8 + x^4 + x^3 + x + 1)$$
$$= (00011111)$$
$$S'_{00} = (10111001) \oplus (00011111) \oplus (01001000)$$
$$= (1110\ 1110) = 0xEE$$

Subkey Addition

From the original key, we produce a succession of 128-bit keys by means of a key schedule. Let's recap that a word is a group of 32 bits. A 128-bit key is labeled as shown in Table 24.14.

word $W_0 = (k_0\ k_1\ k_2\ k_3)$ word $W_1 = (k_4\ k_5\ k_6\ k_7)$
word $W_2 = (k_8\ k_9\ k_{10}\ k_{11})$ word $W_3 = (k_{12}\ k_{13}\ k_{14}\ k_{15})$

which is then written as a 4 × 4 matrix (see Figure 24.8), where W_0 is the first column, W_1 is the second column, W_2 is the third column, and W_3 is the fourth column.

AES uses a process called *key expansion* that creates (10 + 1) round keys from the given cipher key. We start with four words and end with 44 words—four word per round key. Thus

$$(W_0, \ldots \ldots \ldots \ldots, W_{42},\ W_{43})$$

The algorithm to generate 10 round keys is as follows: The initial cipher key consists of words: $W_0\ W_1\ W_2\ W_3$
The other 10 round keys are made using the following logic:
If (j mod 4) $\neq$ 0

$$W_j = W_{j-1} \oplus W_{j-4}$$

else

$$W_j = Z \oplus W_{j-4}$$

where $Z = SubWord(RotWord(W_{j-1}) \oplus RCon_{j/4}$.

RotWord (rotate word) takes a word as an array of four bytes and shifts each byte to the left with wrapping. SubWord (substitute word) uses the SubByte lookup table to substitute the byte in the word [2, 3]. RCon (round constants) is a four-byte value in which the rightmost three bytes are set to zero [2, 3].

Let's work through an example, as shown in Figure 24.9.

TABLE 24.13 Illustrating AES

b_0	b_1	b_2	b_3	b_4	b_5	b_6	b_7	b_8	b_9	b_{10}	b_{11}	b_{12}	b_{13}	b_{14}	b_{15}
Q	U	A	N	T	U	M	C	R	Y	P	T	O	G	O	D
51	55	41	4E	54	55	4D	43	52	59	50	54	4F	47	4F	44

$$\text{State} = \begin{bmatrix} 5154524F \\ 55555947 \\ 414D504F \\ 4E435444 \end{bmatrix}$$

FIGURE 24.4 The state represents a string as a 4×4 matrix in the given arrangement using hexadecimal representation of each byte.

$$\text{State} = \begin{bmatrix} D1200084 \\ FCFCCBA0 \\ 83E35384 \\ 2F1A201B \end{bmatrix}$$

FIGURE 24.5 Applying the SubByte transformation.

$$\text{State} = \begin{bmatrix} D1200084 \\ FCCBA0FC \\ 538483E3 \\ 1B2F1A20 \end{bmatrix}$$

FIGURE 24.6 ShiftRows.

$$\begin{bmatrix} S'_{0i} \\ S'_{1i} \\ S'_{2i} \\ S'_{3i} \end{bmatrix} = \begin{bmatrix} 2311 \\ 1231 \\ 1123 \\ 3112 \end{bmatrix} \begin{bmatrix} S_{0i} \\ S_{1i} \\ S_{2i} \\ S_{3i} \end{bmatrix}$$

FIGURE 24.7 Mixing transformation.

Key: 2B 7E 15 16 28 AE D2 A6 AB F7 15 88 09 CF 4F 3C

W_0 = 2B 7E 15 16 W_1 = 28 AE D2 A6 W_2 = AB F7 15 88 W_3 = 09 CF 4F 3C

Compute W_4:

$$W_4 = Z \oplus W_0$$
$$\text{RotWord}(W_3) = \text{RotWord}(09\ CF\ 4F\ 3C)$$
$$= (CF\ 4F\ 3C\ 09)$$
$$\text{SubWord}(CF\ 4F\ 3C\ 09) = (8A\ 84\ EB\ 01)$$
$$Z = (8A\ 84\ EB\ 01) \oplus (01\ 00\ 00\ 00)_{16} = 8B\ 84\ EB\ 01$$

Hence,

$$W_4 = (8B\ 84\ EB\ 01) \oplus (2B\ 7E\ 15\ 16) = A0\ FA\ FE\ 17$$

(but proceeding to a final key XOR in that round). The resulting state is the ciphertext. We use the following labels to describe the encryption procedure (see Table 24.15):

Key 1 : K1 : $W_0\ W_1\ W_2\ W_3$
Key 2 : K2 : $W_4\ W_5\ W_6\ W_7$
Key 11: K11 : $W_{40}\ W_{41}\ W_{42}\ W_{43}$
The Initial State (IS) is the plaintext
The Output State (OS1)
SubByte (SB), ShiftRows (SR), MixColumns (MC)
Round
Pre-round PlainText $\oplus$ K1 = = = = ➡ OS1
Next we cycle through the decryption procedure:

InvSubByte (ISB), InvShiftRows (ISR), InvMixColumns (IMC)

Putting It Together

Put the input into the state: XOR is the state with the 0-th round key. We start with this because any actions before the first (or after the last) use of the key are pointless, since they are publicly known and so can be undone by an attacker. Then apply 10 of the preceding rounds, skipping the column mixing on the last round

Round

AES is a non-Feistel cipher, hence each set of transformations such as SubByte, ShiftRows, and MixColumns are invertible so that the decryption must consist of steps to recover the plaintext. You will observe that the round keys are used in the reverse order (see Table 24.16).

TABLE 24.14 Subkey Addition

k_0	k_1	k_2	k_3	k_4	k_5	k_6	k_7	k_8	k_9	k_{10}	k_{11}	k_{12}	k_{13}	k_{14}	k_{15}

$$\begin{bmatrix} k_{00}k_{01}k_{02}k_{03} \\ k_{10}k_{11}k_{12}k_{13} \\ k_{20}k_{21}k_{22}k_{23} \\ k_{30}k_{31}k_{32}k_{33} \end{bmatrix}$$

FIGURE 24.8 A 4×4 matrix.

$$\begin{bmatrix} 2B28AB09 \\ 7EAEF7CF \\ 15D2154F \\ 16A6883C \end{bmatrix}$$

FIGURE 24.9 RotWord and SubWord.

7. USE OF MODERN BLOCK CIPHERS

DES and AES are designed to encrypt and decrypt data blocks of fixed size. Most practical examples have data blocks of fewer than 64 bits or greater than 128 bits, and to address this issue currently, five different modes of operation have been set up. These five modes of operation are known as Electronic Code Book (ECB), Cipher-Block Chaining (CBC), Output Feedback (OFB), Cipher Feedback (CFB), and Counter (CTR) modes.

The Electronic Code Book (ECB)

In this mode, the message is split into blocks, and the blocks are sequentially encrypted. This mode is vulnerable to attack using the frequency analysis, the same sort used in simple substitution. Identical blocks would get encrypted to the same blocks, thus exposing the key [1].

Cipher-Block Chaining (CBC)

A logical operation is performed on the first block with what is known as an *initial vector* using the secret key so as to randomize the first block. The output of this step is logically combined with the second block and the key to generate encrypted text, which is then used with the third block and so on [1].

8. PUBLIC-KEY CRYPTOGRAPHY

In this section we cover what is known as *asymmetric encryption,* which uses a pair of keys rather than one

key, as used in symmetric encryption. This single-key encryption between the two parties requires that each party has its secret key, so that as the number of parties increases so does the number of keys. In addition, the distribution of the secret key becomes unmanageable as the number of keys increases. Of course, a longtime use of the same secret key between any pair would make it more vulnerable to cryptanalysis attack. So, to deal with these inextricable problems, a key distribution facility was born. Symmetric encryption is considered more practical in dealing with vast amounts of data consisting of strings of zeros and ones. Yet another scheme was invented to secure data while in transition, using tools from a branch of mathematics known as number theory. To begin, let's review the necessary number theory concepts [2, 3].

Review: Number Theory

Asymmetric-key encryption uses prime numbers, which are a subset of positive integers. Positive integers are all odd and even numbers, including the number 1, such that some of the numbers are composite, that is, products of numbers therein. This critical fact plays a significant role in generating keys. Next we will go through some statements of fact for the sake of completeness.

Coprimes

Two positive integers are said to be coprime or relatively prime if $\gcd(a,b) = 1$.

Cardinality of Primes

The number of primes is infinite. Given a number n, how many prime numbers are smaller than or equal to n? The answer to this question was discovered by Gauss and Lagrange as:

$$\{n/\ln(n) < \prod(n) < \{n/\ln(n) - 1.08366\}$$

where $\prod(n)$ is the number of primes smaller than or equal to n.

Check whether a given number 107 is a prime number. We take the square root of 107 to the nearest

TABLE 24.15 The Encryption Procedure

1.	OS1 →	SB →	SR →	MC ⊕	K2 →	OS2
2.	OS2 →	SB →	SR →	MC ⊕	K3 →	OS3
3.	OS3 →	SB →	SR →	MC ⊕	K4 →	OS4
4.	OS4 →	SB →	SR →	MC ⊕	K5 →	OS5
5.	OS5 →	SB →	SR →	MC ⊕	K6 →	OS6
6.	OS6 →	SB →	SR →	MC ⊕	K7 →	OS7
7.	OS7 →	SB →	SR →	MC ⊕	K8 →	OS8
8.	OS8 →	SB →	SR →	MC ⊕	K9 →	OS9
9.	OS9 →	SB →	SR →	MC ⊕	K10 →	OS10
10.	OS10 →	SB →	SR →	⊕	K11 →	Cipher Text (C)

TABLE 24.16 Round

						OS10
	C ⊕	K11 →				
1	OS10 →	ISR →	ISB ⊕	K10 →	IMC →	OS9
2	OS9 →	ISR →	ISB ⊕	K9 →	IMC →	OS8
10	S1 →		ISR →	ISB ⊕	K1 →	PlainText

whole number, which is 10. Then count the number of primes less than 10, which are 2, 3, 5, 7. Next we check whether any one of these numbers will divide 107. In our example none of these numbers can divide 107, so 107 is a prime number.

Euler's Phi-Function $\phi(n)$: Euler's totient function finds the number of integers that are both smaller than n and coprime to n.

- $\phi(1) = 0$
- $\phi(p) = p - 1$ if p is a prime
- $\phi(m \times n) = \phi(n) \times \phi(m)$ if m and n are coprime
- $\phi(p^e) = p^e - p^{e-1}$ if p is a prime

Examples:

$$\phi(2) = 1; \phi(3) = 2; \phi(4) = 2; \phi(5) = 4; \phi(6) = 2;$$
$$\phi(7) = 6; \phi(8) = 4$$

Factoring

The fundamental theorem of arithmetic states that every positive integer can be written as a product of prime numbers. There are a number of algorithms to factor large composite numbers.

Fermat's Little Theorem

In the 1970s, the creators of digital signatures and public-key cryptography realized that the framework for their research was already laid out in the body of work by Fermat and Euler. Generation of a key in public-key cryptography involves exponentiation modulo of a given modulus.

$$a \equiv b \pmod{m} \text{ then } a^e \equiv b^e \pmod{m} \text{ for}$$
$$\text{any positive integer e}$$
$$a^{e+d} \equiv a^e \cdot a^d \pmod{m}$$
$$(ab)^e \equiv a^e \cdot b^e \pmod{m}$$
$$(a^d)^e \equiv a^{de} \pmod{m}$$

Examples:

$$2^{13} \pmod{33} \equiv 2^{8+4+1} \equiv 25.16.2 \equiv 25.32 \equiv 8 \pmod{33}$$
$$6^{43} \pmod{13}$$
$$2^2 \equiv 4 \quad 3^2 \equiv 9$$
$$2^4 \equiv 4^2 \equiv 16 \equiv 3 \quad 33^4 \equiv 3$$
$$2^8 \equiv 3^2 \equiv 9 \quad 3^8 \equiv 9$$
$$2^{16} \equiv 9^2 \equiv 81 \equiv 3 \quad 33^{16} \equiv 3$$
$$2^{32} \equiv 3^2 \equiv 9 \pmod{13} \quad 3^{32} \equiv 9 \pmod{13}$$

Theorem. Let *p* be a prime number.

1. If a is coprime to p, then $a^{p-1} \equiv 1$ (mod p)
2. $a^p \equiv a$ (mod p) for any integer a

Examples:

$$43^{58} \equiv 1 \text{ (mod 59)}$$
$$86^{97} \equiv 86 \text{ (mod 97)}$$

Theorem: Let p and q be distinct primes.

1. If a is coprime to pq, then

$$a^{k(p-1)(q-1)} \equiv 1 (\text{mod pq}), k \text{ is any integer}$$

2. For any integer a,

$$a^{k(p-1)(q-1)+1} \equiv a (\text{mod pq}), k \text{ is any positive integer}$$

Example:

$$62^{60} \equiv 62^{(7-1)-(11-1)} \equiv 1 \text{ (mod 77)}$$

Discrete Logarithm

Here we will deal with multiplicative group $G = <Z_{n*},\ x>$. The order of a finite group is the number of elements in the group G. Let's take an example of a group,

$$G = <Z_{21*},\ x>$$
$$\phi(21) = \phi(3) \times \phi(7) = 2 \times 6 = 12$$

that is, 12 elements in the group, and each is coprime to 21.

$$\{1, 2, 4, 5, 8, 9, 10, 11, 13, 16, 17, 19, 20\}$$

The order of an element, ord(a) is the smallest integer i such that

$$a^i \equiv e \text{ (mod n)}$$

where e = 1.

Find the order of all elements in $G = <Z_{10*}, x>$

$$\phi(10) = \phi(2) \times \phi(5) = 1 \times 4 = 4$$
$$\{1, 3, 7, 9\}$$

Lagrange's theorem states that the order of an element divides the order of the group. In our example {1, 2, 4} each of them divide 4, therefore we need to check only these powers to find the order of the element.

$$1^1 \equiv 1 \text{ (mod 10)} \rightarrow \text{ord}(1) = 1$$
$$3^1 \equiv 3 \text{ (mod 10)}; 3^2 \equiv 9 \text{ (mod 10)}; 3^4 \equiv 1 \text{ (mod 10)}$$
$$\rightarrow \text{ord}(3) = 4$$
$$7^1 \equiv 7 \text{ (mod 10)}; 7^2 \equiv 9 \text{ (mod 10)}; 7^4 \equiv 1 \text{ (mod 10)}$$
$$\rightarrow \text{ord}(7) = 4$$
$$9^1 \equiv 9 \text{ (mod 10)}; 9^2 \equiv 1 \text{ (mod 10)} \rightarrow \text{ord}(9) = 2$$

If $a \in G = <Z_{n*},\ x>$, then $a^{\phi(n)} = 1$ mod n

Euler's theorem shows that the relationship $a^i \equiv 1$ (mod n) holds whenever the order (i) of an element equals $\phi(n)$.

Primitive Roots

In the multiplicative group, if $G = <Z_{n*},\ x>$ when the order of an element is the same as $\phi(n)$, then that element is called the primitive root of the group. This property of primitive root is used in ElGamal cryptosystem.

$G = <Z_{8*},\ x>$ has no primitive roots. The order of this group is $\phi(8) = 4$.

$$Z_{8*} = \{1, 3, 5, 7\}$$

1, 2, 4 each divide the order of the group, which is 4.

$$1^1 \equiv 1 \text{ (mod 8)} \quad \rightarrow \text{ord}(1) = 1$$
$$3^1 \equiv 3 \text{ (mod 8)}; 3^2 \equiv 1 \text{ (mod 8)} \quad \rightarrow \text{ord}(3) = 2$$
$$5^1 \equiv 5 \text{ (mod 8)}; 5^2 \equiv 1 \text{ (mod 8)} \quad \rightarrow \text{ord}(5) = 2$$
$$7^1 \equiv 7 \text{ (mod 8)}; 7^2 \equiv 1 \text{ (mod 8)} \quad \rightarrow \text{ord}(7) = 2$$

In this example none of the elements has an order of 4, hence this group has no primitive roots. We will rearrange our data as shown in Table 24.17 [2, 3].

Let's take another example: $G = <Z_{7*},\ x>$, then $\phi(7) = 6$, hence the order of the group is 6 with these members {1, 2, 3, 4, 5, 6}, which are all coprime to 7. We note that the order of each of these elements {1, 2, 3, 4, 5, 6} is the smallest integer i such that $a^i \equiv 1$ (mod 7). We note that the order of an element divides the order of the group. Thus the only numbers that divide 6 are {1, 2, 3, 6}:

A). $1^1 \equiv 1$ (mod 7); $1^2 \equiv 1$ (mod 7); 1^3
$\equiv 1$ (mod 7); $1^4 \equiv 1$ (mod 7);
$1^5 \equiv 1$ (mod 7); $1^6 \equiv 1$ (mod 7); ➔ ord(1) = 1

B). $2^1 \equiv 2$ (mod 7); $2^2 \equiv 4$ (mod 7); 2^3
$\equiv 1$ (mod 7); $2^4 \equiv 2$ (mod 7)
$2^5 \equiv 4$ (mod 7); $2^6 \equiv 1$ (mod 7) ➔ ord(2) = 3

TABLE 24.17 No Primitive Group

	i = 1	i = 2	i = 3	i = 4	i = 5	i = 6	i = 7
a = 1	x:1	x:1	x:1	x:1	x:1	x:1	x:1
a = 3	x:3	x:1	x:3	x:1	x:3	x:1	x:3
a = 5	x:5	x:1	x:5	x:1	x:5	x:1	x:5
a = 7	x:7	x:1	x:7	x:1	x:7	x:1	x:7

C). $3^1 \equiv 3\ (mod\ 7);\ 3^2 \equiv 2\ (mod\ 7);\ 3^3$

$\equiv 6\ (mod\ 7);\ 3^4 \equiv 4\ (mod\ 7);$

$3^5 \equiv 5\ (mod\ 7);\ 3^6 \equiv 1\ (mod\ 7);\ \rightarrow ord(3) = 6$

D). $4^1 \equiv 4\ (mod\ 7);\ 4^2 \equiv 2\ (mod\ 7);\ 4^3$

$\equiv 1\ (mod\ 7);\ 4^4 \equiv 4\ (mod\ 7);$

$4^5 \equiv 2\ (mod\ 7);\ 4^6 \equiv 1\ (mod\ 7) \rightarrow ord(4) = 3$

E). $5^1 \equiv 5\ (mod\ 7);\ 5^2 \equiv 4\ (mod\ 7);\ 5^3$

$\equiv 6\ (mod\ 7);\ 5^4 \equiv 2\ (mod\ 7);$

$5^5 \equiv 3\ (mod\ 7);\ 5^6 \equiv 1\ (mod\ 7;\ \rightarrow ord(5) = 6$

F). $6^1 \equiv 6\ (mod\ 7);\ 6^2 \equiv 1\ (mod\ 7)\ ;\ 6^3$

$\equiv 6\ (mod\ 7)\ ;\ 6^4 \equiv 1\ (mod\ 7)$

$6^5 \equiv 6\ (mod\ 7);\ 6^6 \equiv 1\ (mod\ 7) \rightarrow ord(6) = 2$

Since the order of the elements {3, 5} is 6, which is the order of the group, therefore the primitive roots of the group are {3, 5}. In here the smallest integer i = 6, $\phi(7) = 6$.

Solve for x in each of the following:

$$5^x \equiv 6\ (mod\ 7)$$

We can rewrite the above as:

$$x = \log_5 6\ (mod\ 7)$$

Using the third term in E). we see that x must be equal to 3.

The group $G = <Z_{n*},\ x>$ has primitive roots only if n is 2, 4, p^t, or $2p^t$, where p is an odd prime not including 2, and t is an integer.

If the group $G = <Z_{n*},\ x>$ has any primitive roots, the number of primitive roots is $\phi(\phi(n))$.

Group $G = <Z_{n*},\ x>$ has primitive roots, then it is cyclic, and each of its primitive roots is a generator of the whole group.

Group $G = <Z_{10*},\ x>$ has two primitive roots because $\phi(10) = 4$, and $\phi(\phi(10)) = 2$. These two primitive roots are {3, 7}.

$3^1\ mod\ 10 = 3\ 3^2\ mod\ 10 = 9\ 3^3\ mod\ 10 = 7\ 3^4$
$mod\ 10 = 1$

$7^1\ mod\ 10 = 7\ 7^2\ mod\ 10 = 9\ 7^3\ mod\ 10 = 3\ 7^4$
$mod\ 10 = 1$

Group $G = <Z_{p*},\ x>$ is always cyclic.

The group $G = <Z_{p*},\ x>$ has the following properties:

- Its elements are from 1 to $(p - 1)$ inclusive.
- It always has primitive roots.
- It is cyclic, and its elements can be generated using g where x is an integer from 1 to $\phi(n) = p - 1$.
- The primitive roots can be used as the base of a discrete logarithm.

Now that we have reviewed the necessary mathematical preliminaries, we will focus on the subject matter of asymmetric cryptography, which uses a public and a private key to encrypt and decrypt the plaintext. If Alice wants to send plaintext to Bob, she uses Bob's public key, which is advertised by Bob, to encrypt the plaintext and then send it to Bob via an unsecured channel. Bob decrypts the data using his private key, which is known to him only. Of course this would appear to be an ideal replacement for the asymmetric-key cipher, but it is much slower, since it has to encrypt each byte; hence it is useful in message authentication and communicating the secret key (see sidebar, "The RSA Cryptosystem").

The RSA Cryptosystem

Key generation algorithm:

1. Select two prime numbers p and q such that $p \neq q$.
2. Construct m = p x q.
3. Set up a commutative ring $R = <Z_\phi,\ +,\ x>$ which is public since m is made public.
4. Set up a multiplicative group $G = <Zr_{(m)}^*,\ x>$ which is used to generate public and private keys. This group is hidden from the public since $\phi(m)$ is kept hidden.

$$\phi(m) = (p - 1)(q - 1)$$

5. Choose an integer e such that, $1 < e < \phi(m)$ and e is coprime to $\phi(m)$.

6. Compute the secret exponent d such that, $1 < d < \phi(m)$ and that $ed \equiv 1\ (mod\ \phi(m))$.
7. The public key is "e" and the private key is "d." The value of p, q, and $\phi(m)$ are kept private.

Encryption:

1. Alice obtains Bob's public key (m, e).
2. The plaintext x is treated as a number to lie in the range $1 < x < m - 1$.
3. The ciphertext corresponding to x is $y = x^e\ (mod\ m)$.
4. Send the ciphertext y to Bob.

Decryption:

1. Bob uses his private key (m, d).
2. Compute the $x = y^d \pmod{m}$.

Why RSA works:

$$y^d \equiv (x^e \bmod m)^d$$
$$(x^{ed}) \bmod m$$
$$d \cdot e = 1 + km = 1 + k(p - 1)(q - 1)$$
$$y^d \equiv x^{ed} \equiv x^{1+k(p-1)(q-1)} \equiv x \pmod{m}$$

Example:

1. Choose p = 7 and q = 11, then m = p x q = 7 × 11 = 77

   $R = <Z_{77}, +, x>$ and $\phi(77) = \phi(7)\,\phi(11) = 6 \times 10 = 60$

2. The corresponding multiplicative group $G = <Z_{60}^{*}, x>$.
3. Choose e = 13 and d = 37 from Z_{60}^{*} such that $e \times d \equiv 1 \pmod{60}$.

   Plaintext = 5 $y = x^e \pmod{m} = 5^{13} \pmod{77} = 26$
   $x = y^d \pmod{m} = 26^{37} \pmod{77} = 5$

Note: 384-bit primes or larger are deemed sufficient to use RSA securely. The prime number $e = 2^{16} + 1$ is often used in modern RSA implementations [2, 3].

9. CRYPTANALYSIS OF RSA

RSA algorithm relies that *p* and *q*, the distinct prime numbers, are kept secret, even though $m = p \times q$ is made public. So if *n* is an extremely large number, the problem reduces to find the factors that make up the number *n*, which is known as the *factorization attack*.

Factorization Attack

If the middleman, Eve, can factor *n* correctly, then she correctly guesses *p*, *q*, and $\phi(m)$. Reminding ourselves that the public key *e* is public, then Eve has to compute the multiplicative inverse of e:

$$d \equiv e^{-1} \pmod{m}$$

So if the modulus m is chosen to be 1024 bits long, it would take considerable time to break the RSA system unless an efficient factorization algorithm could be found [2, 3] (see sidebars "Chosen-Ciphertext Attack" and "The eth Roots Problem").

Chosen-Ciphertext Attack

Z_n is a set of all positive integers from 0 to (n − 1). Z_n^{*} is a set all integers such that gcd(n,a) = 1, where $a \in Z_n^{*}$

$$Z_n^{*} \subset Z_n$$

$\Phi(n)$ calculates the number of elements in Z_n^{*} that are smaller than n and coprime to n.

$$\Phi(21) = \Phi(3) \times \Phi(7) = 2 \times 6 = 12$$

Therefore, the number of integers in $\in Z_{21}^{*}$ is 12.

$$Z_{21}^{*} = \{1, 2, 4, 5, 8, 10, 11, 13, 16, 17, 19, 20\}$$

Each of which is coprime to 21.

$$Z_{14}^{*} = \{1, 3, 5, 9, 11, 13\}$$

Each of which is coprime to 14.

$\Phi(14) = \Phi(2) \times \Phi(7) = 1 \times 6 = 6$ number of integers in Z_{14}^{*}

Example: Choose p = 3 and q = 7, then m = 3 × 7 = 21. Encryption and decryption take place in the ring, $R = <Z_{21}, +, x>$

$$\Phi(21) = \Phi(2)\,\Phi(6) = 12$$

Key-Generation Group , $G = <Z_{12}^{*}, x>$

$$\Phi(12) = \Phi(4)\,\Phi(3) = 2 \times 2 = 4 \text{ numbers in } Z_{12}^{*}$$
$$Z_{12}^{*} = \{1, 5, 7, 11\}$$

Alice encrypts the message P using the public key e of Bob and sends the encrypted message C to Bob.

$$C = P^e \bmod m$$

Eve, the middleman, intercepts the message and manipulates the message before forwarding to Bob.

1. Eve chooses a random integer $X \in Z_m^{*}$ (since m is public).
2. Eve calculates $Y = C \times X^e \pmod{m}$.
3. Bob receives Y from Eve, and he decrypts Y using his private key d.
4. $Z = Y^d \pmod{m}$.
5. Eve can easily discover the plaintext P as follows:

$$Z = Y^d \pmod{m} = [C \times X^e]^d \pmod{m}$$
$$= [C^d \times X^{ed}] \pmod{m} = [C^d \times X] \pmod{m}$$

Hence $Z = [P \times X] \pmod{m}$.

Using the Extended Euclidean algorithm, Eve can then compute the multiplicative inverse of X, and thus obtain P:

$$P = Z \times X^{-1} \pmod{m} \text{ [2, 3]}$$

> **The eth Roots Problem**
>
> Given:
>
> A composite number n, product of two prime numbers p and q
>
> An integer e $\geq$ 3
>
> gcd (e, Φ(n)) =1
>
> An integer c $\in Z_{12}^{*}$
>
> Find an integer m such that m^e $\equiv$ c mod n [2, 3].

Discrete Logarithm Problem

Discrete logarithms are perhaps simplest to understand in the group Z_{p*}, where p is the prime number. Let g be the generator of Z_{p*}, then the discrete logarithm problem reduces to computing a, given (g, p, g^a mod p) for a randomly chosen a $< (p - 1)$.

If we want to find the kth power of one of the numbers in this group, we can do so by finding its kth power as an integer and then finding the remainder after division by p. This process is called *discrete exponentiation*. For example, consider Z_{23*}. To compute 3^4 in this group, we first compute 3^4 = 81, then we divide 81 by 23, obtaining a remainder of 12. Thus 3^4 = 12 in the group Z_{23*}

A *discrete logarithm* is just the inverse operation. For example, take the equation 3^k $\equiv$ 12 (mod 23) for *k*. As shown above k = 4 is a solution, but it is not the only solution. Since 3^{22} $\equiv$ 1 (mod 23), it also follows that if *n* is an integer, then 3$^{4+22 \, n}$ $\equiv$ 12 $\times$ 1^n $\equiv$ 12 (mod 23). Hence the equation has infinitely many solutions of the form 4 + 22*n*. Moreover, since 22 is the smallest positive integer *m* satisfying 3^m $\equiv$ 1 (mod 23), that is, 22 is the order of 3 in Z_{23*} these are all solutions. Equivalently, the solution can be expressed as *k* $\equiv$ 4 (mod 22) [2, 3].

10. DIFFIE-HELLMAN ALGORITHM

The purpose of this protocol is to allow two parties to set up a shared secret key over an insecure communication channel so that they may exchange messages. Alice and Bob agree on a finite cyclic group G and a generating element g in G. We will write the group G multiplicatively [2, 3].

1. Alice picks a prime number p, with the base g, exponent a to generate a public key A
2. A = g^a mod p
3. (g, p, A) are made public, and a is kept private.
4. Bob picks a prime number p, base b, and an exponent b to generate a public key B.

5. B = g^b mod p
6. (g, p, B) are made public, and b is kept private,
7. Bob using A generates the shared secret key S.
8. S = A^b mod p
9. Alice using B generates the shared secret key S.
10. S = B^a mod p

Thus the shared secret key S is established between Bob and Alice.

Example:

Alice: p = 53, g =18, a =10
    A = 18^{10} mod 53 = 24
Bob: p = 53, g =18, b = 11
    B = 18^{11} mod 53 = 48
    S = 24^{11} mod 53 = 48^{10} mod 53 = 15

Diffie-Hellman Problem

The middleman Eve would know (g, p, A, B) since these are public. So for Eve to discover the secret key S, she would have to tackle the following two congruences:

$$g^a \equiv A \bmod p \text{ and } g^b \equiv B \bmod p$$

If Eve had some way of solving the discrete logarithm problem (DLP) in a time-efficient manner, she could discover the shared secret key S; no probabilistic polynomial-time algorithm exists that solves this problem. The set of values:

$$(g^a \bmod p, g^b \bmod p, g^a b \bmod p)$$

is called the *Diffie-Hellman problem*.

If the DLP problem can be efficiently solved, then so can the Diffie-Hellman problem.

11. ELLIPTIC CURVE CRYPTOSYSTEMS

For simplicity, we shall restrict our attention to elliptic curves over Zp, where *p* is a prime greater than 3. We mention, however, that elliptic curves can more generally be defined over any finite field [4]. An *elliptic curve E* over Z_p is defined by an equation of the form

$$y^2 = x^3 + ax + b \tag{24.1}$$

where *a*, *b* $\in Z_p$, and 4a^3 + 27b^2 $\neq$ 0 (mod *p*), together with a special point *O* called the *point at infinity*. The set $E(Z_p)$ consists of all points (*x*, *y*), *x* $\in Z_p$, *y* $\in Z_p$, which satisfy the defining equation (1), together with *O*.

TABLE 24.18 Elliptic Curve Cryptosystems

(0, 1)	(6, 4)	(12, 19)
(0, 22)	(6, 19)	(13, 7)
(1, 7)	(7, 11)	(13, 16)
(1, 16)	(7, 12)	(17, 3)
(3, 10)	(9, 7)	(17, 20)
(3, 13)	(9, 16)	(18, 3)
(4, 0)	(11, 3)	(18, 20)
(5, 4)	(11, 20)	(19, 5)
(5, 19)	(12, 4)	(19, 18)

We will digress to modular division: 4/3 mod 11. We are looking for a number, say t, such that $3 * t \bmod 11 = 4$. We need to multiply the left and right sides by 3^{-1}

$$3^{-1} * 3 * t \bmod 11 = 3^{-1} * 4$$
$$t \bmod 11 = 3^{-1} * 4$$

Next we use the Extended Euclidean algorithm and get (inverse) 3^{-1} is 4 ($3 * 4 = 12 \bmod 11 = 1$).

$$4 * 4 \bmod 11 = 5$$

Hence,

$$4/3 \bmod 11 = 5$$

An Example

Let $p = 23$ and consider the elliptic curve $E: y^2 = x^3 + x + 1$, defined over Z_{23}. (In the notation of Equation 24.1, we have $a = 1$ and $b = 1$.) Note that $4a^3 + 27b^2 = 4 + 4 = 8 \neq 0$, so E is indeed an elliptic curve. The points in $E(Z_{23})$ are O and the following are shown in Table 24.18.

Addition Formula

There is a rule for adding two points on an elliptic curve $E(Zp)$ to give a third elliptic curve point. Together with this addition operation, the set of points $E(Zp)$ forms a group with O serving as its identity. It is this group that is used in the construction of elliptic curve cryptosystems. The addition rule, which can be explained geometrically, is presented here as a sequence of algebraic formula [4].

1. $P + O = O + P = P$ for all $P \in E(Z_p)$
2. If $P = (x, y) \in E(Zp)$ then $(x, y) + (x, -y) = O$ (The point $(x, -y)$ is denoted by $-P$, and is called the *negative* of P; observe that $-P$ is indeed a point on the curve.)
3. Let $P = (x1, y1) \in E(Zp)$ and $Q = (x2, y2) \in E(Zp)$, where $P \neq -Q$. Then $P + Q = (x3, y3)$,

where:

$$x_3 = (\lambda^2 - x_1 - x_2) \bmod p$$
$$y_3 = (\lambda(x_1 - x_3) - y_1) \bmod p$$
$$\lambda = \frac{y_2 - y_1}{x_2 - x_1} \bmod p \text{ if } P \neq Q \text{ or}$$
$$\lambda = \frac{3x_1^2 + a}{2y_1} \bmod p \text{ if } P = Q$$

Example of Elliptic Curve Addition

Consider the elliptic curve defined in the previous example. (Also see sidebar, "EC Diffie-Hellman Algorithm.") [4].

1. Let $P = (3, 10)$ and $Q = (9, 7)$. Then $P + Q = (x3, y3)$ is computed as follows:

$$\lambda = \frac{7 - 10}{9 - 3} = \frac{-3}{6} = \frac{-1}{2} = 11 \in Z_{23}$$
$$x_3 = 11^2 - 3 - 9 = 6 - 3 - 9 = -6 \equiv 17 \,(\bmod\, 23), \text{ and}$$
$$y_3 = 11(3 - (-6)) - 10 = 11(9) - 10 = 89 \equiv 20 \,(\bmod\, 23).$$

Hence $P + Q = (17, 20)$.

2. Let $P = (3, 10)$. Then $2P = P + P = (x3, y3)$ is computed as follows:

$$\lambda = \frac{3(3^2) + 1}{20} = \frac{5}{20} = \frac{1}{4} = 6 \in Z_{23}$$
$$x_3 = 6^2 - 6 = 30 \equiv 7 \,(\bmod\, 23), \text{ and}$$
$$y_3 = 6\,(3 - 7) - 10 = -24 - 10 = -11 \in 12 \,(\bmod\, 23).$$

Hence $2P = (7, 12)$.

Consider the following elliptic curve with Z_p^*

$$y^2 \bmod p = (x^3 + ax + b) \bmod p$$

Set $p = 11$ and $a = 1$ and $b = 2$. Take a point P (4, 2) and multiply it by 3; the resulting point will be on the curve with (4, 9).

EC Diffie-Hellman Algorithm

1. Alice has her elliptic curve, and she chooses a secret random number d and computes a number on the curve $Q_A = d_A*P$ [4].
   Alice's public key: (p, a, b, Q_A)
   Alice's private key: d_A

2. Bob has his elliptic curve, and he chooses a secret random number d and computes a number on the curve $Q_B = d_B * P$:
   Bob's public key: (p, a, b, Q_B)
   Bob's private key: d_B

   3. Alice computes the shared secret key as

   $$S = d_A * Q_B$$

4. Similarly, Bob computes the shared secret key as

   $$S = d_B * Q_A$$

5. The shared secret key computed by Alice and Bob are the same for:

   $$S = d_B * Q_A = d_B * d_A * P$$

EC Security

Suppose Eve the middleman captures (p, a, b, Q_A, Q_B). Can Eve figure out the shared secret key without knowing either (d_B, d_A)? Eve could use

$$Q_A = P * d_A$$

to compute the unknown d_A, which is known as the Elliptic Curve Discrete Logarithm problem [4].

12. MESSAGE INTEGRITY AND AUTHENTICATION

We live in the Internet age, and a fair number of commercial transactions take place on the Internet. It has often been reported that transactions on the Internet between two parties have been hijacked by a third party, hence data integrity and authentication are critical if ecommerce is to survive and grow.

This section deals with message integrity and authentication. So far we have discussed and shown how to keep a message confidential. But on many occasions we need to make sure that the content of a message has not been changed by a third party, and we need some way of ascertaining whether the message has been tampered with. Since the message is transmitted electronically as a string of ones and zeros, we need a mechanism to make

sure that the count of the number of ones and zeros does not become altered, and furthermore, that zeros and ones are not changed in their position within the string.

We create a pair and label it as message and its corresponding message digest. A given block of messages is run through an algorithm hash function, which has its input the message and the output is the compressed message, the message digest, which is a fixed-size block but smaller in length. The receiver, say, Bob, can verify the integrity of the message by running the message through the hash function (the same hash function as used by Alice) and comparing the message digest with the message digest that was sent along with the message by, say, Alice. If the two message digests agree on their block size, the integrity of the message was maintained in the transmission.

Cryptographic Hash Functions

A cryptographic hash function must satisfy three criteria:

- Preimage resistance
- Second preimage resistance (weak collision resistance)
- Strong collision resistance

Preimage Resistance

Given a message m and the hash function hash, if the hash value $h = hash(m)$ is given, it should be hard to find any m such that $h = hash(m)$.

Second Preimage Resistance (Weak Collision Resistance)

Given input m_1, it should be hard to find another message m_2 such that $hash(m_1) = hash(m_2)$ and that $m_1 \neq m_2$

Strong Collision Resistance

It ought to be hard to find two messages $m_1 \neq m_2$ such that $hash(m_1) = hash(m_2)$. A hash function takes a fixed size input n-bit string and produces a fixed size output m-bit string such that m less than n in length. The original hash function was defined by Merkle-Damgard, which is an iterated hash function. This hash function first breaks up the original message into fixed-size blocks of size n. Next an initial vector H_0 (digest) is set up and combined with the message block M_1 to produce message digest H_1, which is then combined with M_2 to produce message digest H_1, and so on until the last message block produces the final message digest.

$$H_i = f(H_{i-1}, M_i) \quad i \geq 1$$

Message digest MD2, MD4, and MD5 were designed by Ron Rivest. MD5 as input block size of 512 bits and produces a message digest of 128 bits[1].

Secure Hash Algorithm (SHA) was developed by the National Institute of Standards and Technology (NIST). SHA-1, SHA-224, SHA-256, SHA-384, and SHA-512 are examples of the secure hash algorithm. SHA-512 produces a message digest of 512 bits.

Message Authentication

Alice sends a message to Bob. How can Bob be sure that the message originated from Alice and not someone else pretending to be Alice? If you are engaged in a transaction on the Internet using a Web client, you need to make sure that you are not engaged with a dummy Web site or else you could submit your sensitive information to an unauthorized party. Alice in this case needs to demonstrate that she is communicating and not an imposter.

Alice creates a message digest using the message (M), then using the shared secret key (known to Bob only) she combines the key with a message digest and creates a message authentication code (MAC). She then sends the MAC and the message (M) to Bob over an insecure channel. Bob uses the message (M) to create a hash value and then recreates a MAC using the secret shared key and the hash value. Next he compares the received MAC from Alice with his MAC. If the two match, Bob is assured that Alice was indeed the originator of the message [1].

Digital Signature

Message authentication is implemented using the sender's private key and verified by the receiver using the sender's public key. Hence if Alice uses her private key, Bob can verify that the message was sent by Alice, since Bob would have to use Alice's public key to verify. Alice's public key cannot verify the signature signed by Eve's private key [1].

Message Integrity Uses a Hash Function in Signing the Message

Nonrepudiation is implemented using a third party that can be trusted by parties that want to exchange messages with one another. For example, Alice creates a signature from her message and sends the message, her identity,

Bob's identity, and the signature to the third party, who then verifies the message using Alice's public key that the message came from Alice. Next the third party saves a copy of the message with the sender's and the recipient's identity and the time stamp of the message.

The third party then creates another signature using its private key from the message that Alice left behind. The third party then sends the message, the new signature, and Alice's and Bob's identity to Bob, who then uses the third party's public key to ascertain that the message came from the third party [1].

RSA Digital Signature Scheme

Alice and Bob are the two parties that are going to exchange the messages. So, we begin with Alice, who will generate her public and private key using two distinct prime numbers—say, p and q. Next she calculates n = p x q. Using $\Phi(n) = (p - 1)(q - 1)$, picks e and computes d such that e x d = 1 mod ($\Phi(n)$). Alice declares (e, n) public, keeping her private key d secret.

Signing: Alice takes the message and computes the signature as:

$$S = M^d \ (mod \ n)$$

She then sends the message M and the signature S to Bob.

Bob receives the message M and the signature S, and then, using Alice's public key e and the signature S, recreates the message $M' = S^e \ (mod \ n)$. Next Bob compares M' with M, and if the two values are congruent, Bob accepts the message [1].

RSA Digital Signature and the Message Digest

Alice and Bob agree on a hash function. Alice applies the hash function to the message M and generates the message digest, D = hash(M). She then signs the message digest using her private key,

$$S = D^d \ (mod \ n)$$

Alice sends the signature S and the message M to Bob. He then uses Alice's public key, and the signature S recreates the message digest $D' = S^e \ (mod \ n)$ as well as computes the message digest D= hash(M) from the received message M. Bob then compares D with D', and if they are congruent modulo n, he accepts the message [1].

13. SUMMARY

In this chapter we have attempted to cover cryptography from its very simple structure such as substitution ciphers to the complex AES and elliptic curve cryptosystems. There is a subject known as *cryptoanalysis* that attempts to crack the encryption to expose the key, partially or fully. We briefly discussed this in the section on the discrete logarithm problem. Over the past 10 years, we have seen the application of quantum theory to encryption in what is termed *quantum cryptology*, which is used to transmit the secret key securely over a public channel. The reader will observe that we did not cover the Public Key Infrastructure (PKI) due to lack of space in the chapter.

REFERENCES

[1] Thomas H. Barr, *Invitation to Cryptology*, Prentice Hall, 2002.

[2] Wenbo Mao, *Modern Cryptography, Theory & Practice*, Prentice Hall, New York, 2004.

[3] Behrouz A. Forouzan, *Cryptography and Network Security*, McGraw-Hill, 2008.

[4] A. Jurisic, A. J. Menezes, *Elliptic Curves and Cryptograph*, Dr. Dobb's Journals, April 01, 1997, http://www.ddj.com/architect/184410167.

## Chapter 25

Satellite Encryption

Daniel S. Soper
California State University

For virtually all of human history, the communication of information was relegated to the surface of the Earth. Whether written or spoken, transmitted by land, sea, or air, all messages had one thing in common: They were, like those who created them, inescapably bound to the terrestrial surface.

In February 1945, however, the landscape of human communication was forever altered when an article by the famous science fiction writer Arthur C. Clarke proposed the extraordinary possibility that artificial satellites placed into orbit above the Earth could be used to facilitate mass communication on a global scale. A year later, a Project RAND report concluded that "A satellite vehicle with appropriate instrumentation [could] be expected to be one of the most potent scientific tools of the 20th century," and that "The achievement of a satellite craft would produce repercussions comparable to the explosion of the atomic bomb." It was only 12 short years after Clarke's historic prediction that mankind's first artificial satellite, *Sputnik 1*, was transmitting information from orbit back to Earth.

In the decades that followed, satellite technology evolved rapidly from its humble beginnings to become an essential tool for such diverse activities as astronomy, communications, scientific research, defense, navigation, and the monitoring of global weather patterns. In the 21st century, satellites are helping to fuel globalization, and societies are relying heavily on the power of satellite technology to enable the modern lifestyle. It is for these reasons that satellite communications must be protected. Before examining satellite encryption in detail, however, a brief review of satellite communication in general may be useful.

For communications purposes, modern satellites can be classified into two categories: those that communicate exclusively with the surface of the Earth (which will be referred to here as "Type 1" satellites) and those that communicate not only with the surface of the Earth but also with other satellites or spacecraft (referred to here as "Type 2" satellites). The distinction between these two types of satellite communications is depicted in Figure 25.1.

As shown in the figure, there are several varieties of communication links that a satellite may support, and the classification of a particular satellite as Type 1 or Type 2 allows us to gain an understanding of its basic communications capabilities as well as insight into the sort of communications links that might need protecting. In the case of Type 1 satellites, the spacecraft may support uplink capabilities, downlink capabilities, or both. An *uplink channel* is a communications channel through which information is transmitted from the surface of the Earth to an orbiting satellite or other spacecraft. By contrast, a *downlink channel* is a communications channel through which information is transmitted from an orbiting satellite or other spacecraft to the terrestrial surface. While Type 2 satellites may possess the uplink and downlink capabilities of a Type 1 satellite, they are also capable of establishing links with spacecraft or other Type 2 satellites for purposes of extraplanetary communication. Type 2 satellites that can act as intermediaries between other spacecraft and the ground may be classified as relay satellites. Note that whether a particular link is used for sending or receiving information depends on the perspective of the viewer—from the ground, for example, an uplink channel is used to send information, but from the perspective of the satellite, the uplink channel is used to receive information.

1. THE NEED FOR SATELLITE ENCRYPTION

Depending on the type of satellite communications link that needs to be established, substantially different technologies, frequencies, and data encryption techniques might be required. The reasons for this lie as much in

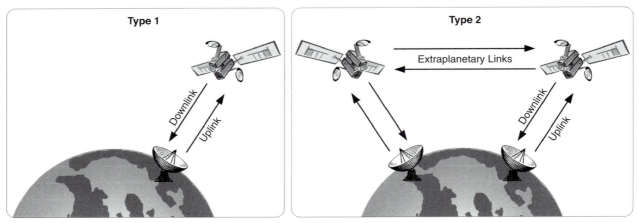

FIGURE 25.1 Comparison of Type 1 and Type 2 satellite communication capabilities.

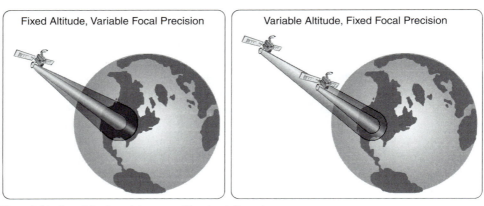

FIGURE 25.2 Effect of altitude and focal precision on satellite signal dispersion.

the realm of human behavior as they do in the realm of physics. Broadly speaking, it is not unreasonable to conclude that satellite encryption would be entirely unnecessary if every human being were perfectly trustworthy. That is to say, barring a desire to protect our messages from the possibility of extraterrestrial interception, there would be no need to encrypt satellite communications if only those individuals entitled to send or receive a particular satellite transmission actually attempted to do so. In reality, however, human beings, organizations, and governments commonly possess competing or contradictory agendas, thus implying the need to protect the confidentiality, integrity, and availability of information transmitted via satellite.

With human behavioral considerations in mind, the need for satellite encryption can be evaluated from a physical perspective. Consider, for example, a Type 1 communications satellite that has been placed into orbit above the Equator. Transmissions from the satellite to the terrestrial surface (i.e., the downlink channel) would

commonly be made by way of a parabolic antenna. Although such an antenna facilitates focusing the signal, the signal nevertheless disperses in a conical fashion as it departs the spacecraft and approaches the surface of the planet. The result is that the signal may be made available over a wider geographic area than would be optimally desirable for security purposes. As with terrestrial radio, in the absence of encryption anyone within range of the signal who possesses the requisite equipment could receive the message. In this particular example, the geographic area over which the signal would be dispersed would depend on both the focal precision of the parabolic antenna and the altitude of the satellite above the Earth. These concepts are illustrated in Figure 25.2.

Because the sender of a satellite message may have little or no control over to whom the transmission is made available, protecting the message requires that its contents be encrypted. For similar reasons, extraplanetary transmissions sent between Type 2 satellites must also be protected; with thousands of satellites orbiting the planet, the chances of an intersatellite communication being intercepted are quite good!

Aside from these considerations, the sensitivity of the information being transmitted must also be taken into account. Various entities possess different motivations for wanting to ensure the security of messages transmitted via satellite. An individual, for example, might want her private telephone calls or bank transaction details to be protected. Likewise, an organization may want to prevent its proprietary data from falling into the hands of its competition, and a government may want to protect its military communications and national security secrets from being intercepted or compromised by an enemy. As with terrestrial communications, the sensitivity of the data being transmitted via satellite must dictate the extent to which those data are protected. If the emerging global information society is to fully capitalize on the benefits of satellite-based communication, its citizens, organizations, and governments must be assured that their sensitive data are not being exposed to unacceptable risk. In light of these considerations, satellite encryption can be expected to play a key role in the future advancement of mankind.

2. SATELLITE ENCRYPTION POLICY

Given the rapid adoption of satellite communications, and the potential security implications associated therewith, many governments and multinational coalitions are increasingly establishing policy instruments with a view toward controlling and regulating the availability and use of satellite encryption in both the public and private sectors. Such policy instruments have wide-reaching economic, political, and cultural implications that commonly extend beyond national boundaries.

One might, for example, consider the export controls placed on satellite encryption technology by the U.S. government, which many consider the most stringent in the world. Broadly, these export controls were established in support of two primary objectives. First, the maintenance of a restrictive export policy allows the government to review and assess the merits of any newly developed satellite encryption technologies that have been proposed for export. If the export of those technologies is ultimately approved, the government will possess a detailed understanding of how the technologies operate, potentially allowing for their encryption schemes to be defeated if deemed necessary. Second, such controls allow the government to prevent satellite encryption technologies of particularly high merit from leaving the

country, especially if the utilization of those technologies by foreign entities would interfere with U.S. intelligence-gathering activities. Although these stringent controls may appear to be a legacy of the xenophobic policies of the Cold War, they are nevertheless still seen as prudent measures in a world where information and communication technologies can be readily leveraged to advance extreme agendas. Unfortunately, such controls have potentially negative economic implications insofar as U.S. firms may be barred from competing in the increasingly lucrative global market for satellite communication technologies.

The establishment and maintenance of satellite encryption policy also needs to be considered in the context of satellite systems of global import. Consider, for example, the NAVSTAR global positioning system (GPS), whose constellation of satellites enables anyone with a GPS receiver to accurately determine their current location, time, velocity, and direction of travel anywhere on or near the surface of the Earth. In recent years, GPS capabilities have been incorporated into the navigational systems of automobiles, oceangoing vessels, trains, commercial aircraft, military vehicles, and many other forms of transit all over the world. Despite their worldwide use, the NAVSTAR GPS satellites are currently operated by the 50th Space Wing of the U.S. Air Force, implying that satellite encryption policy decisions related to the GPS are controlled by the U.S. Department of Defense. One of the options available to the U.S. government through this arrangement is the ability to selectively or entirely block the transmission of civilian GPS signals while retaining access to GPS signals for military purposes. Additionally, the U.S. government reserves the right to introduce errors into civilian GPS signals, thus making them less accurate. As the U.S. government exercises exclusive control over the GPS system, users all over the world are forced to place a great deal of trust in the goodwill of its operators and in the integrity of the encryption scheme for the NAVSTAR uplink channel. Given the widespread use of GPS navigation, a global catastrophe could ensue if the encryption scheme used to control the NAVSTAR GPS satellites were to be compromised. Because the GPS system is controlled by the U.S. military, the resiliency and security of this encryption scheme cannot be independently evaluated.

In the reality of a rapidly globalizing and interconnected world, the effectiveness of national satellite encryption policy efforts may not be sustainable in the long run. Satellite encryption policies face the same legal difficulties as so many other intrinsically international issues; outside of international agreements, the ability of a specific country to enforce its laws extends only so far as its geographic

Type of Satellite Communications Link		
	Uplink	**Downlink**	**Extraplanetary Link**
High-Value	Category 01	Category 03	Category 05
Low-Value	Category 02	Category 04	Category 06

(Data Value)

FIGURE 25.3 Satellite communications categories as a function of data value and type of link.

boundaries. This problem is particularly relevant in the context of satellite communications because the satellites themselves orbit the Earth and hence do not lie within the geographic boundaries of any nation. Considered in conjunction with governments' growing need to share intelligence resources and information with their allies, future efforts targeted toward satellite encryption policy making may increasingly fall under the auspices of international organizations and multinational coalitions.

3. IMPLEMENTING SATELLITE ENCRYPTION

It was noted earlier in this chapter that information can be transmitted to or from satellites using three general types of communication links: surface-to-satellite links (uplinks), satellite-to-surface links (downlinks), and inter-satellite or interspacecraft links (extraplanetary links). Technological considerations notwithstanding, the specific encryption mechanism used to secure a transmission depends not only on which of these three types of links is being utilized but also on the nature and purpose of the message being transmitted. For purposes of simplicity, the value of transmitted information can be classified along two dimensions: high value and low value. The decision as to what constitutes high-value and low-value information largely depends on the perspective of the beholder; after all, one man's trash is another man's treasure. Nevertheless, establishing this broad distinction allows satellite encryption to be considered in the context of the conceptual model shown in Figure 25.3.

As shown in the figure, any satellite-based communication can be classified into one of six possible categories. In the subsections that follow, each of these categories will be addressed by considering the encryption of both high-value and low-value data in the context of the three types of satellite communication links. Before we consider the specific facets of encryption pertaining to satellite uplink, extraplanetary, and downlink transmissions, however, an examination of several of the more general issues associated with satellite encryption may be prudent.

General Satellite Encryption Issues

One of the problems common to all forms of satellite encryption relates to signal degradation. Satellite signals are typically sent over long distances using comparatively low-power transmissions and must frequently contend with many forms of interference, including terrestrial weather, solar and cosmic radiation, and many other forms of electromagnetic noise. Such disturbances may result in the introduction of gaps or errors into a satellite transmission. Depending on the encryption algorithm chosen, this situation can be particularly problematic for encrypted satellite transmissions because the entire encrypted message may be irretrievable if even a single bit of data is out of place. To resolve this problem, a checksum or cryptographic hash function may be applied to the encrypted message to allow errors to be identified and reconciled on receipt. This approach comes at a cost, however: Appending checksums or error-correcting code to an encrypted message increases the length of the message and by extension increases the time required for the message to be transmitted and lowers the satellite's overall communications capacity due to the extra burden placed on its limited resources.

Another common problem associated with satellite encryption relates to establishing the identity of the sender of a message. A satellite, for example, needs to know that the control signals it is receiving from the ground originate from an authorized source. Similarly, an intelligence agency receiving a satellite transmission from one of its operatives needs to establish that the transmission is authentic. To establish the identity of the sender, the message needs to be encrypted in such a way that from the recipient's perspective, only a legitimate sender could have encoded the message. The sender, of course, also wants to ensure that the message is protected while in transit and thus desires that only an authorized recipient would be able to decode the message on receipt. Both parties to the communication must therefore agree on an encryption algorithm that serves to identify the authenticity of the sender while affording a sufficient level of protection to the message while it is in transit. Although

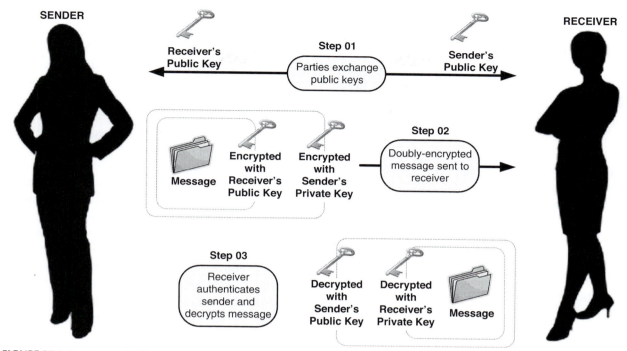

FIGURE 25.4 Ensuring sender identity and message security with asynchronously-keyed encryption.

keyless encryption algorithms may satisfy these two criteria, such algorithms are usually avoided in satellite communications, since the satellite may become useless if the keyless encryption algorithm is broken. Instead, keyed encryption algorithms are typically used to protect information transmitted via satellite. Using keyed encryption algorithms can be problematic, however.

To gain insight into the problems associated with keyed encryption, one might first consider the case of a symmetrically keyed encryption algorithm, wherein the same key is used to both encode and decode a message. If party A wants to communicate with party B via satellite using this method, then both A and B must agree on a secret key. As long as the key remains secret, it also serves to authenticate both parties. If party A also wants to communicate with party C, however, A and C must agree on their own unique secret key; otherwise party B could masquerade as A or C, or vice versa. A keyed encryption approach to satellite communication thus requires that each party establish a unique secret key with every other party with whom they would like to communicate. To further compound this problem, each party must obtain all its secret keys in advance because possession of an appropriate key is a necessary prerequisite to establishing a secure communications channel with another party.

To resolve these issues, an asymmetrically keyed encryption algorithm may be adopted wherein the key used to encrypt a message is different from the key used to decrypt the message. Such an approach requires each party to maintain only two keys, one of which is kept private and the other of which is made publicly available. If party A wants to send party B a secure transmission, A first asks B for her public key, which can be transmitted over an unsecured connection. Party A then encodes a secret message using B's public key. The message is secure because only B's private key can decode the message. To authenticate herself to B, party A needs only to reencode the entire message using her own private key before transmitting the message to B. On receiving the message, B can establish whether it was sent by A, because only A's private key could have encoded a message that can be decoded with A's public key. This process is depicted in Figure 25.4.

Unfortunately, even this approach to satellite encryption is not entirely foolproof. To understand why, consider how a malicious party M might interject himself between A and B to intercept the secure communication. To initiate the secure transmission, A must request B's public key over an unsecured channel. If this request is intercepted by M, M can supply A with his own (that is, M's) public key. A will then encrypt the message with M's public key, after which she will reencrypt the result of the first encryption operation with her own private key. A will then transmit the encrypted message to B, which will once again be intercepted by M. Using A's public key in conjunction with his own private key, M will be able to decrypt and read the message.

A will not know that the message has been intercepted, and B will not know that a message was even sent. Note that intercepting a secure communication is particularly easy for M if he owns or controls the satellite through which the message is being routed. In addition to the risk of interception, asynchronously keyed encryption algorithms are typically at least 10,000 times slower than synchronously keyed encryption algorithms—a situation that may place an enormously large burden on a satellite's limited computational resources. Until a means is developed of dynamically and securely distributing synchronous keys, satellite-based encryption will always require tradeoffs among security, computational complexity, and ease of implementation.

Uplink Encryption

Protecting a transmission that is being sent to a satellite from at or near the surface of the Earth requires much more than just cryptographic techniques—to wit, encrypting the message itself is a necessary but insufficient condition for protecting the transmission. The reason for this is that the actual transmission of the encrypted message to the satellite is but the final step in a long chain of custody that begins when the message is created and ends when the message is successfully received by the satellite. Along the way, the message may pass through many people, systems, or networks, the control of which may or may not reside entirely in the hands of the sender. If one assumes that the confidentiality and integrity of the message have not been compromised as the message has passed through all these intermediaries, then but two primary security concerns remain: the directional accuracy of the transmitting antenna and the method used to encrypt the message. In the case of the former, the transmitting antenna must be sufficiently well focused to allow the signal to be received by—and ideally *only* by—the target satellite. With thousands of satellites in orbit, a strong potential exists for a poorly focused transmission to be intercepted by another satellite, in which case the only remaining line of defense for a message is the strength of the encryption algorithm with which it was encoded. For this reason, a prudent sender should always assume that her message could be intercepted while in transit to the satellite and should implement message encryption accordingly.

When deciding on which encryption method to use, the sender must simultaneously consider the value of the data being transmitted, the purpose of the transmission, and the technological and computational limitations of the target satellite. A satellite's computational and technological capabilities are a function of its design specifications, its current workload, and any degradation that has occurred since the satellite was placed into orbit. These properties of the satellite can therefore be considered constraints; any encrypted uplink communications must work within the boundaries of these limitations. That having been said, the purpose of the transmission also features prominently in the choice of which encryption method to use. Here we must distinguish between two types of transmissions: commands, which instruct the satellite to perform one or more specific tasks, and transmissions in transit, which are intended to be retransmitted to the surface or to another satellite or spacecraft. Not only are command instructions of high value, they are also not typically burdened with the same low-latency requirements of transmissions in transit. Command instructions should therefore always be highly encrypted because control of the satellite could be lost if they were to be intercepted and compromised.

What remains, then, are transmissions in transit, which may be of either high value or low value. One of the basic tenants of cryptography states that the value of the data should dictate the extent to which the data are protected. As such, minimal encryption may be acceptable for low-value transmissions in transit. For such transmissions, adding an unnecessarily complex layer of encryption may increase the computational burden on the satellite, which in turn may delay message delivery and limit the satellite's ability to perform other tasks simultaneously. High-value transmissions in transit should be protected with a robust encryption scheme that reflects the value of the data being transmitted. The extent to which a highly encrypted transmission in transit will negatively impact a satellite's available resources depends on whether or not the message needs to be processed before being retransmitted. If the message is simply being relayed through the satellite without any additional processing, the burden on the satellite's resources may be comparatively small. If, however, a highly encrypted message needs to be processed by the satellite prior to retransmission (e.g., if the message needs to be decrypted, processed, and then re-encrypted), the burden on the satellite's resources may be substantial. Processing high-value, highly encrypted transmissions in transit may therefore vastly reduce a satellite's throughput capabilities when considered in conjunction with its technological and computational limitations.

Extraplanetary Link Encryption

Before a signal is sent to the terrestrial surface, it may need to be transmitted across an extraplanetary link.

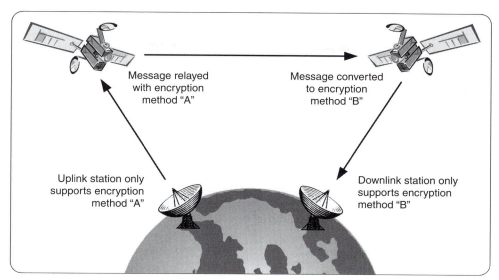

FIGURE 25.5 In-transit translation of message encryption in satellite communication.

Telemetry from a remote spacecraft orbiting Mars, for example, may need to be relayed to scientists by way of an Earth-orbiting satellite. Alternatively, a television signal originating in China may need to be relayed around the Earth by several intermediary satellites in order to reach its final destination in the United States. In such circumstances, several unique encryption-related issues may arise, each of which is associated with the routing of an extraplanetary transmission through one or more satellite nodes. Perhaps the most obvious of these issues is the scenario that arises when the signal transmitted from the source satellite or spacecraft is not compatible with the receiving capabilities of the target. For example, the very low-power signals transmitted from a remote exploratory spacecraft may not be detectable by a particular listening station on the planet's surface, or the data rate or signal modulation with which an extraplanetary transmission is sent may not be supported by the final recipient. In this scenario, the intermediary satellite through which the signal is being routed must act as an interpreter or translator of sorts, a situation illustrated in Figure 25.5.

From an encryption perspective, the situation we've illustrated implies that the intermediary satellite may need to decrypt the extraplanetary message and re-encrypt it using a different encryption scheme prior to retransmission. A similar issue may arise for legal or political reasons. Consider, for example, a message that is being transmitted from one country to another by way of several intermediary satellites. The first country may have no standing policies regarding the encryption of messages sent via satellite, whereas the second country may have policies that strictly regulate the encryption

standards of messages received via satellite. In this case, one or more of the orbiting satellites may need to alter the encryption of a message in transit to satisfy the legal and regulatory guidelines of both countries.

Downlink Encryption

Several issues impact the information where it is protected as it is transmitted from orbiting satellites to the surface of the Earth. As with uplink encryption, the technological and computational capabilities of the spacecraft may constrain the extent to which a particular message can be protected. If, for example, an older communications satellite does not possess the requisite hardware or software capabilities to support a newly developed downlink encryption scheme, that scheme simply cannot be used with the satellite. Similarly, if the utilization of a particular encryption scheme would reduce the efficiency or message-handling capacity of a satellite to a level that is deemed unacceptable, the satellite's operators may choose to prioritize capacity over downlink security. The precision with which a satellite is able to focus a downlink transmission may also impact the choice of encryption scheme; as noted earlier in this chapter, a widely dispersed downlink signal can be more readily intercepted than can a signal transmitted with a narrow focus. Though each of these computational and technological limitations must be considered when selecting a downlink encryption scheme, they are by no means the only factors requiring consideration.

Unlike uplink signals, which can only originate from the surface of the planet, messages to be transmitted over a downlink channel can come from one of three sources: the terrestrial surface, another spacecraft, or the satellite itself. The source of the message to be broadcast to the planet's surface plays a critical role in determining the method of protection for that message. Consider, for example, a message that originates from the planet's surface or from another spacecraft. In this case, one of two possible scenarios may exist. First, the satellite transmitting the message to Earth may be serving only as a simple signal router or amplifying transmitter; that is to say, the message is already encrypted on receipt, and the satellite is simply relaying the previously encrypted message to the surface. In this case, the satellite transmitting the downlink signal has very little to do with the encryption of the message, and only the integrity of the message and the retransmission capabilities of the satellite at the time the message is received need be considered. In the second scenario, a satellite may need to filter a message or alter its encryption method prior to downlink transmission. For example, a satellite may receive signals that have been optimized for extraplanetary communication from a robotic exploration spacecraft in the far reaches of the solar system. Prior to retransmission, the satellite may need to decrypt the data, process it, and then reencrypt the data using a different encryption scheme more suited to a downlink transmission. In this case, the technological capabilities of the satellite, the timeliness with which the data need to be delivered, and the value of the data themselves dictate the means through which those data are protected prior to downlink transmission.

Finally, one might consider the scenario in which the data being transmitted to the terrestrial surface originate from the satellite itself rather than from the surface or from another spacecraft. Such data can be classified as either telemetry relating to the status of the satellite or as information that the satellite has acquired or produced while performing an assigned task. In the case of the former, telemetry relating to the status of the satellite should always be highly protected, since it may reveal details about the satellite's capabilities, inner workings, or control systems if it were to be intercepted and compromised. In the case of the latter, however, the value of the data that the satellite has acquired or produced should dictate the extent to which those data are protected. Critical military intelligence, for example, should be subjected to a much higher standard of encryption than data that are comparatively less valuable. In the end, a satellite operator must weigh many factors when deciding on the extent to which a particular downlink transmission should be protected. It is tempting to conclude that the maximum level of encryption should be applied to every downlink transmission. Doing so, however, would unnecessarily burden satellites' limited resources and would vastly reduce the communications capacity of the global satellite network. Instead, a harmonious balance needs to be sought between a satellite's technological and computational capabilities, and the source, volume, and value of the data that it is asked to handle. Only by achieving such a balance can the maximum utility of a satellite be realized.

4. THE FUTURE OF SATELLITE ENCRYPTION

Despite the many challenges faced by satellite encryption, the potential advantages afforded by satellites to mankind are so tantalizing and alluring that the utilization of satellite-based communication can only be expected to grow for the foreseeable future. As globalization continues its indefatigable march across the terrestrial surface, access to secure high-speed communications will be needed from even the most remote and sparsely populated corners of the globe. Satellites by their very nature are well positioned to meet this demand and will therefore play a pivotal role in interconnecting humanity and enabling the forthcoming global information society. Furthermore, recent developments in the area of quantum cryptography promise to further improve the security of satellite-based encryption. This rapidly advancing technology allows the quantum state of photons to be manipulated in such a way that the photons themselves can carry a synchronous cryptographic key. The parties involved in a secure communication can be certain that the cryptographic key has not been intercepted, because eavesdropping on the key would introduce detectable quantum anomalies into the photonic transmission. By using a constellation of satellites in low Earth orbit, synchronous cryptographic keys could be securely distributed via photons to parties that want to communicate, thus resolving the key exchange problem. The parties could then establish secure communications using more traditional satellite channels. The further development and adoption of technologies such as quantum cryptography ensures that satellite-based communication has a bright—and secure—future.

There are, of course, risks to relying heavily on satellite-based communication. Specifically, if the ability to access critical satellite systems fails due to interference or damage to the satellite, disastrous consequences may ensue. What might happen, for example, if interference from a solar flare were to disrupt the constellation of global positioning satellites? What might happen if a micrometeoroid storm were to damage all the weather satellites monitoring the progress of a major hurricane? What might happen to a nation's ability to make war if antisatellite weapons were deployed to destroy its military communications and intelligence-gathering satellites? Questions such as these highlight the risks of relying too heavily on artificial satellites. Nevertheless, as the costs associated with building, launching, and operating satellites continue to decline, the utilization of satellite technology will, for the foreseeable future, become an increasingly common part of the human experience.

## Chapter 26

Public Key Infrastructure

Terence Spies
Voltage Security, Inc.

The ability to create, manipulate, and share digital documents has created a host of new applications (email, word processing, ecommerce Web sites), but it also created a new set of problems—namely how to protect the privacy and integrity of digital documents when they're stored and transmitted. The invention of public key cryptography in the 1970s[1]—most important, the ability to encrypt data without a shared key and the ability to "sign" data, ensuring its origin and integrity—pointed the way to a solution to those problems. Though these operations are quite conceptually simple, they both rely on the ability to bind a public key (which is typically a large mathematical object) reliably with an identity sensible to the application using the operation (for example, a globally unique name, a legal identifier, or an email address). Public Key Infrastructure (PKI) is the umbrella term used to refer to the protocols and machinery used to perform this binding.

This chapter explains the cryptographic background that forms the foundation of PKI systems, the mechanics of the X.509 PKI system (as elaborated by the Internet Engineering Task Force, or IETF), the practical issues surrounding the implementation of PKI systems, a number of alternative PKI standards, and alternative cryptographic strategies for solving the problem of secure public key distribution. PKI systems are complex objects that have proven difficult to implement properly.[2] This chapter aims to survey the basic architecture of PKI systems and some of the mechanisms used to implement them. It does not aim to be a comprehensive guide to all PKI standards or to contain sufficient technical detail to allow implementation of a PKI system. These systems are continually evolving, and the reader interested in building or operating a PKI is advised to consult the current work of standards bodies referenced in this chapter.

1. CRYPTOGRAPHIC BACKGROUND

To understand how PKI systems function, it is necessary to grasp the basics of public key cryptography. PKI systems enable the use of public key cryptography, and they also use public key cryptography as the basis for their operation. There are thousands of varieties of cryptographic algorithms, but we can understand PKI operations by looking at only two: signatures and encryption.

Digital Signatures

The most important cryptographic operation in PKI systems is the digital signature. If two parties are exchanging some digital document, it may be important to protect that data so that the recipient knows that the document has not been altered since it was sent and that any document received was indeed created by the sender. Digital signatures provide these guarantees by creating a data item, typically attached to the document in question that is uniquely tied to the data and the sender. The recipient then has some verification operation that confirms that the signature data matches the sender and the document.

Figure 26.1 illustrates the basic security problem that motivates signatures. An attacker controlling communications between the sender and receiver can insert a bogus document, fooling the receiver.

The aim of the digital signature is to block this attack by attaching a signature that can only be created by the sender, as shown in Figure 26.2.

Cryptographic algorithms can be used to construct secure digital signatures. These techniques (for example, the RSA or DSA algorithms) all have the same three basic operations, as shown in Table 26.1.

1 W. Diffie and M. E. Hellman, "New directions in cryptography," *IEEE Trans. Inform. Theory*, IT-22, 6, 1976, pp. 644–654.
2 P. Gutmann, "Plug-and-Play PKI: A PKI Your Mother Can Use," in *Proc. 12th Usenix Security Symp.*, Usenix Assoc., 2003, pp. 45–58.

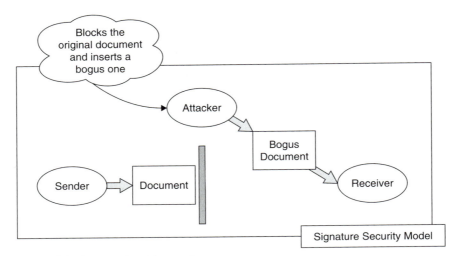

FIGURE 26.1 Block diagram of altering an unsigned document.

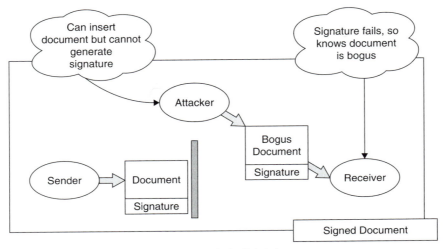

FIGURE 26.2 Block diagram showing prevention of an alteration attack via digital signature.

TABLE 26.1 The Three Fundamental Digital Signature Operations	
Key Generation	Using some random source, the sender creates a public and private key, called Kpublic and Kprivate. Using Kpublic, it is cryptographically difficult to derive Kprivate. The sender then distributes Kpublic, and keeps Kprivate hidden.
Signing	Using a document and Kprivate, the sender generates the signature data.
Verification	Using the document, the signature, and Kpublic, the receiver (or any other entity with these elements) can test that the signature matches the document, and could only be produced with the Kprivate matching Kpublic.

Public Key Encryption

Variants of the three operations used to construct digital signatures can also be used to encrypt data. Encryption uses a public key to scramble data in such a way that only the holder of the corresponding private key can unscramble it (see Figure 26.3).

Public key encryption is accomplished with variants of the same three operations used to sign data, as shown in Table 26.2.

The security of signature and encryption operations depends on two factors: first, the ability to keep the private key private and, second, the ability to reliably tie a public key to a sender. If a private key is known to an

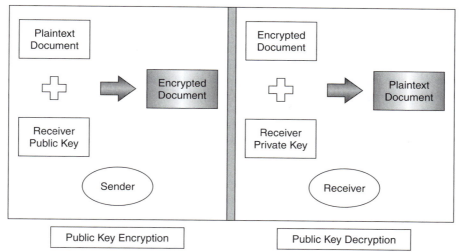

FIGURE 26.3 The public key encryption and decryption process.

TABLE 26.2 The three fundamental public key encryption operations

Key Generation	Using some random source, the sender creates a public and private key, called Kpublic and Kprivate. Using Kpublic, it is cryptographically difficult to derive Kprivate. The sender then distributes Kpublic, and keeps Kprivate hidden.
Encryption	Using a document and Kpublic, the sender encrypts the document.
Decryption	The receiver uses Kprivate to decrypt the document.

attacker, they can then perform the signing operation on arbitrary bogus documents and can also decrypt any document encrypted with the matching public key. The same attacks can be performed if an attacker can convince a sender or receiver to use a bogus public key.

PKI systems are built to securely distribute public keys, thereby preventing attackers from inserting bogus public keys. They do not directly address the security of private keys, which are typically defended by measures at a particular endpoint, such as keeping the private key on a smartcard, encrypting private key data using operating system facilities, or other similar mechanisms. The remainder of this section details the design, implementation, and operation of public key distribution systems.

2. OVERVIEW OF PKI

PKI systems solve the problem of associating meaningful names with essentially meaningless cryptographic

keys. For example, when encrypting an email, a user will typically specify a set of recipients that should be able to decrypt that mail. The user will want to specify these as some kind of name (email address or a name from a directory), not as a set of public keys. In the same way, when signed data is received and verified, the user will want to know what user signed the data, not what public key correctly verified the signature. The design goal of PKI systems is to securely and efficiently connect user identities to the public keys used to encrypt and verify data.

The original Diffie-Hellman paper[3] that outlined public key cryptography proposed that this binding would be done through storing public keys in a trusted directory. Whenever a user wanted to encrypt data to another user, they would consult the "public file" and request the public key corresponding to some user. The same operation would yield the public key needed to verify the signature on signed data. The disadvantage of this approach is that the directory must be online and available for every new encryption and verification operation. (Though this older approach was never widely implemented, variants of this approach are now reappearing in newer PKI designs. For more information, see the section on alternative PKI architectures.)

PKI systems solve this online problem and accomplish identity binding by distributing "digital certificates," chunks of data that contain an identity and a key, all authenticated by digital signature, and providing a mechanism to validate these certificates. Certificates,

---

3 W. Diffie and M. E. Hellman, "New directions in cryptography," *IEEE Trans. Inform. Theory*, IT-22, 6, 1976, pp. 644–654.

invented by Kohnfelder in 1978,[4] are essentially a digitally signed message from some authority stating "Entity X is associated with public key Y." Communicating parties can then rely on this statement (to the extent that they trust the authority signing the certificate) to use the public key Y to validate a signature from X or to send an encrypted message to X. Since time may pass between when the signed certificate is produced and when someone uses that certificate, it may be useful to have a validation mechanism to check that the authority still stands by the certificate. We will describe PKI systems in terms of producing and validating certificates.

There are multiple standards that describe the way certificates are formatted. The X.509 standard, promulgated by the ITU,[5] is the most widely used and is the certificate format used in the TLS/SSL protocols for secure Internet connections and the S/MIME standards for secured email. The X.509 certificate format also implies a particular model of how certification works. Other standards have attempted to define alternate models of operation and associated certificate models. Among the other standards that describe certificates are Pretty Good Privacy (PGP) and the Simple Public Key Infrastructure (SPKI). In this section, we'll describe the X.509 PKI model, then describe how these other standards attempt to remediate problems with X.509.

3. THE X.509 MODEL

The X.509 model is the most prevalent standard for certificate-based PKIs, though the standard has evolved such that PKI-using applications on the Internet are mostly based on the set of IETF standards that have evolved and extended the ideas in X.509. X.509-style certificates are the basis for SSL, TLS, many VPNs, the U.S. federal government PKI, and many other widely deployed systems.

The History of X.509

A quick historical preface here is useful to explain some of the properties of X.509. X.509 is part of the X.500 directory standard owned by the International Telecommunications Union Telecommunications Standardization Sector (ITU-T). X.500 specifies a hierarchical directory useful for the X.400 set of messaging standards. As such, it includes a naming system (called *distinguished naming*) that describes entities by their position in some hierarchy. A sample X.500/X.400 name might look like this:

> CN = Joe Davis, OU = Human Resources,
> O = WidgetCo, C = US

This name describes a person with a common name (CN) of Joe Davis who works in an organizational unit (OU) called Human Resources, in an organization called WidgetCo in the United States. These name components were intended to be run by their own directory components (so, for example, there would be Country directories that would point to Organizational directories, etc.), and this hierarchical description was ultimately reflected in the design of the X.509 system. Many of the changes made by IETF and other bodies that have evolved the X509 standard were made to reconcile this hierarchical naming system with the more distributed nature of the Internet.

The X.509 Certificate Model

The X.509 model specifies a system of certifying authorities (CAs) that issue certificates for end entities (users, Web sites, or other entities that hold private keys). A CA-issued certificate will contain (among other data) the name of the end entity, the name of the CA, the end entity's public key, a validity period, and a certificate serial number. All this information is signed with the CA's private key. (Additional details on the information in a certificate and how it is encoded appear in the section on the X.509 Certificate Format.) To validate a certificate, a relying party uses the CA's public key to verify the signature on the certificate, checks that the time falls within the validity period, and may also perform some other online checks.

This process leaves out one important detail: Where did the CA's public key come from? The answer is that another certificate is typically used to certify the public key of the CA. This "chaining" action of validating a certificate by using the public key from another certificate can be performed any number of times, allowing for arbitrarily deep hierarchies of CAs. Of course, this must terminate at some point, typically at a self-signed certificate that is trusted by the relying party. Trusted self-signed certificates are typically referred to as "root" certificates. Once the relying party has verified the chain of signatures from the end-entity certificate to a trusted root certificate, it can conclude that the end-entity certificate is properly signed and then move onto whatever other

---

4 Kohnfelder, L., "Towards a practical public-key cryptosystem," Bachelor's thesis, Department of Computer Science, Massachusetts Institute of Technology (June 1978).

5 ITU-T Recommendation X.509 (1997 E): Information Technology – Open Systems Interconnection – The Directory: Authentication Framework, June 1997.

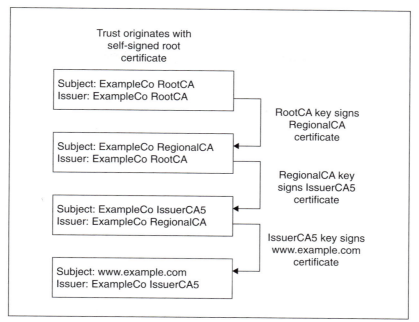

Trust originates with
self-signed root
certificate

Subject: ExampleCo RootCA
Issuer: ExampleCo RootCA

RootCA key signs
RegionalCA
certificate

Subject: ExampleCo RegionalCA
Issuer: ExampleCo RootCA

RegionalCA key
signs IssuerCA5
certificate

Subject: ExampleCo IssuerCA5
Issuer: ExampleCo RegionalCA

IssuerCA5 key signs
www.example.com
certificate

Subject: www.example.com
Issuer: ExampleCo IssuerCA5

FIGURE 26.4 An example X.509 certificate chain.

validation steps (proper key usage fields, validity dates in some time window, etc.) are required to fully trust the certificate. Figure 26.4 shows the structure of a typical certificate chain.

One other element is required for this system to function securely: CAs must be able to "undo" a certification action. Though a certificate binds an identity to a key, there are many events that may cause that binding to become invalid. For example, a CA operated by a bank may issue a certificate to a newly hired employee that gives that user the ability to sign messages as an employee of the bank. If that person leaves the bank before the certificate expires, the bank needs some way of undoing that certification. The physical compromise of a private key is another circumstance that may require invalidating a certificate. This is accomplished by a validation protocol, where (in the abstract) a user examining a certificate can ask the CA if a certificate is still valid. In practice, revocation protocols are used that simulate this action without actually contacting the CA.

Root certificates are critical to the process of validating public keys through certificates. They must be inherently trusted by the application, since no other certificate signs these certificates. This is most commonly done by installing the certificates as part of the application that will use the certificates under a set of root certificates. For example, Internet Explorer uses X.509 certificates to validate keys used to make Secure Socket Layer (SSL) connections. Internet Explorer has installed a large set of root certificates that can be examined by opening the

Internet Options menu item and selecting **Certificates** in the Content tab of the Options dialog box. A list like the one shown in Figure 26.5 will appear.

This dialog box can also be used to inspect these root certificates. The Microsoft Root certificate details look like the ones shown in Figure 26.6.

The meaning of these fields is explored in subsequent parts of this chapter.

4. X.509 IMPLEMENTATION ARCHITECTURES

In theory, the Certification Authority is the entity that creates and validates certificates, but in practice, it may be desirable or necessary to delegate the actions of user authentication and certificate validation to other servers. The security of the CA's signing key is crucial to the security of a PKI system. If we limit the functions of the server that holds that key, it should be subject to less risk of disclosure or illegitimate use. The X.509 architecture defines a delegated server role, the Registration Authority (RA), which allows delegation of authentication. Subsequent extensions to the core X.509 architecture have created a second delegated role, the Validation Authority (VA), which answers queries about the validity of a certificate after creation.

A Registration Authority is typically used to distribute the authentication function needed to issue a certificate without needing to distribute the CA key. The RA's

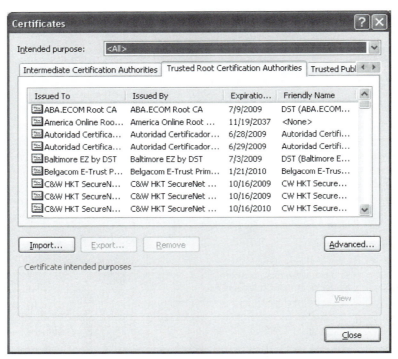

FIGURE 26.5 The Microsoft Internet Explorer trusted root certificates.

FIGURE 26.6 A view of the fields in an X.509 certificate using Microsoft Internet Explorer.

function is to perform the authentication needed to issue a certificate, then send a signed statement containing the fact that it performed the authentication, the identity to be certified, and the key to be certified. The CA validates the RA's message and issues a certificate in response.

For example, a large multinational corporation wants to deploy a PKI system using a centralized CA. It wants to issue certificates on the basis of in-person authentication, so it needs some way to distribute authentication to multiple locations in different countries. Copying and distributing the CA signing key creates a number of risks, not only due to the fact that the CA key will be present on multiple servers but also due to the complexities of creating and managing these copies. Sub-CAs could be created for each location, but this requires careful attention to controlling the identities allowed to be certified by each Sub-CA (otherwise, an attacker compromising one Sub-CA could issue a certificate for any identity he liked). One possible way to solve this problem is to create RAs at each location and have the CA check that the RA is authorized to authenticate a particular employee when a certificate is requested. If an attacker subverts a given RA signing key, he can request certificates for employees in the purview of that RA, but it is straightforward, once discovered, to deauthorize the RA, solve the security problem, and create a new RA key.

Validation Authorities are given the ability to revoke certificates (the specific methods used to effect revocation are detailed in the "X.509 Revocation Protocols" section) and offload that function from the CA.

Through judicious use of RAs and VAs, it is possible to construct certification architectures whereby the critical CA server is only accessible to a very small number of other servers, and network security controls can be used to reduce or eliminate threats from outside network entities.

5. X.509 CERTIFICATE VALIDATION

X.509 certificate validation is a complex process and can be done to several levels of confidence. This section outlines a typical set of steps involved in validating a certificate, but it is not an exhaustive catalog of the possible methods that can be used. Various applications will often require different validation techniques, depending on the application's security policy. It is rare for an application to implement certificate validation, since there are several APIs and libraries available to perform this task. Microsoft CryptoAPI, OpenSSL, and the Java JCE all provide certificate validation interfaces. The Server-based Certificate Validity Protocol (SCVP) can also be used to validate a certificate. However, all these interfaces offer a variety of options, and understanding the validation process is essential to properly using these interfaces.

A complete specification of the certificate validation process would require hundreds of pages, so here we supply just a sketch of what happens during certificate validation. It is not a complete description and is purposely simplified. The certificate validation process typically proceeds in three steps and typically takes three inputs. The first is the certificate to be validated, the second is any intermediate certificates acquired by the applications, and the third is a store containing the root and intermediate certificates trusted by the application. The following steps are a simplified outline of how certificates are typically validated. In practice, the introduction of bridge CAs and other nonhierarchical certification models have led to more complex validation procedures. IETF RFC 3280[6] presents a complete specification for certificate validation, and RFC 4158[7] presents a specification for constructing a certification path in environments where nonhierarchical certification structures are used.

Validation Step 1: Construct the Chain and Validate Signatures

The contents of the target certificate cannot be trusted until the signature on the certificate is validated, so the first step is to check the signature. To do so, the certificate for the authority that signed the target certificate must be located. This is done by searching the intermediate certificates and certificate store for a certificate with a *subject* field that matches the *issuer* field of the target certificate. If multiple certificates match, the validator can search the matching certificates for a Subject Key Identifier extension that matches the Issuer Key Identifier extension in the candidate certificates. If multiple certificates still match, the most recently issued candidate certificate can be used. (Note that, because of potentially revoked intermediate certificates, multiple chains may need to be constructed and examined through Steps 2 and 3 to find the actual valid chain.) Once the proper authority certificate is found, the validator checks the signature on the target certificate using the public key in the authority certificate. If the signature check fails, the validation process can be stopped, and the target certificate deemed invalid.

If the signature matches and the authority certificate is a trusted certificate, the constructed chain is then subjected to Steps 2–4. If not, the authority certificate is treated as a target certificate, and Step 1 is called recursively until it returns a chain to a trusted certificate or fails.

Constructing the complete certificate path requires that the validator is in possession of all the certificates in that path. This requires that the validator keep a database of intermediate certificates or that the protocol using the certificate supply the needed intermediates. The Server Certificate Validation Protocol (SCVP) provides a mechanism to request a certificate chain from a server, which can eliminate these requirements. The SCVP protocol is described in more detail in a subsequent section.

Validation Step 2: Check Validity Dates, Policy and Key Usage

Once a chain has been constructed, various fields in the certificate are checked to ensure that the certificate was issued correctly and that it is currently valid. The following checks should be run on the candidate chain:

The certificate chain times are correct. Each certificate in the chain contains a validity period with a not-before and not-after time. For applications outside validating the signature on a document, the current time must fall after the not-before time and before the not-after time. Some applications may require *time nesting*, meaning that the validity period for a certificate must fall entirely within the validity period of the issuer's certificate. It is up to the policy of the application whether it treats out-of-date certificates as invalid or treats them as warning cases that

6 R. Housely, W. Ford, W. Polk, and D. Solo, "Internet X.509 public key infrastructure certificate and certificate revocation list profile," IETF RFC 3280, April 2002.
7 M. Cooper, Y. Dzambasow, P. Hesse, S. Joseph, and R. Nicholas, "Internet X.509 public key infrastructure: certification path building," IETF RFC 4158, September 2005.

can be overridden by the user. Applications may also treat certificates that are not yet valid differently than certificates that have expired.

Applications that are validating the certificate on a stored document may have to treat validity time as the time that the document was signed as opposed to the time that the signature was checked. There are three cases of interest. The first, and easiest, is where the document signature is checked and the certificate chain validating the public key contains certificates that are currently within their validity time interval. In this case, the validity times are all good, and verification can proceed. The second case is where the certificate chain validating the public key is currently invalid because one or more certificates are out of date and the document is believed to be signed at a time when the chain was out of date. In this case, the validity times are all invalid, and the user should be at least warned.

The ambiguous case arises when the certificate chain is currently out of date, but the chain is believed to have been valid with respect to the time when the document was signed. Depending on its policy, the application can treat this case in several different ways. It can assume that the certificate validity times are strict, and fail to validate the document. Alternatively, it can assume that the certificates were good at the time of signing, and validate the document. The application can also take steps to ensure that this case does not occur by using a time-stamping mechanism in conjunction with signing the document or provide some mechanism for resigning documents before certificate chains expire.

Once the certificate chain has been constructed, the verifier must also verify that various X.509 extension fields are valid. Some common extensions that are relevant to the validity of a certificate path are:

- **BasicConstraints.** This extension is required for CAs and limits the depth of the certificate chain below a specific CA certificate.
- **NameConstraints.** This extension limits the namespace of identities certified underneath the given CA certificate. This extension can be used to limit a specific CA to issuing certificates for a given domain or X.400 namespace.
- **KeyUsage** and **ExtendedKeyUsage.** These extensions limit the purposes for which a certified key can be used. CA certificates must have *KeyUsage* set to allow certificate signing. Various values of *ExtendedKeyUsage* may be required for some certification tasks.

Validation Step 3: Consult Revocation Authorities

Once the verifier has concluded that it has a suitably signed certificate chain with valid dates and proper key-Usage extensions, it may want to consult the revocation authorities named in each certificate to check that the certificates are currently valid. Certificates may contain extensions that point to Certificate Revocation List (CRL) storage locations or to Online Certificate Status Protocol (OCSP) responders. These methods allow the verifier to check that a CA has not revoked the certificate in question.

The next section discusses these methods in more detail. Note that each certificate in the chain may need to be checked for revocation status. The following section on certificate revocation details the mechanisms used to revoke certificates.

6. X.509 CERTIFICATE REVOCATION

Since certificates are typically valid for a significant period of time, it is possible that during the validity period of the certificate, a key may be lost or stolen, an identity may change, or some other event may occur that causes a certificate's identity binding to become invalid or suspect. To deal with these events, it must be possible for a CA to revoke a certificate, typically by some kind of notification that can be consulted by applications examining the validity of a certificate. Two mechanisms are used to perform this task: Certificate Revocation Lists (CRLs) and the Online Certificate Status Protocol (OCSP).

The original X.509 architecture implemented revocation via a CRL, a periodically issued document containing a list of certificate serial numbers that are revoked by that CA. X.509 has defined two basic CRL formats, V1 and V2. When CA certificates are revoked by a higher-level CA, the serial number of the CA certificate is placed on an Authority Revocation List (ARL), which is formatted identically to a CRL. CRLs and ARLs, as defined in X.509 and IETF RFC 3280, are ASN.1 encoded objects that contain the information shown in Table 26.3.

This header is followed by a sequence of revoked certificate records. Each record contains the information shown in Table 26.4.

The list of revoked certificates is optionally followed by a set of CRL extensions that supply additional information about the CRL and how it should be processed. To process a CRL, the verifying party checks that the

TABLE 26.3 Data fields in an X.509 CRL

Version	Specifies the format of the CRL. Current version is 2
SignatureAlgorithm	Specifies the algorithm used to sign the CRL
Issuer	Name of the CA issuing the CRL
thisUpdate	Time from when this CRL is valid
nextUpdate	Time when the next CRL will be issued

TABLE 26.4 Format of a revocation record in an X.509 CRL

Serial Number	Serial number of a revoked certificate
Revocation Date	Date the revocation is effective
CRL Extensions	[Optional] specifies why the certificate is revoked

CRL has been signed with the key of the named issuer and that the current date is between the *thisUpdate* time and the *nextUpdate* time. This time check is crucial because if it is not performed, an attacker could use a revoked certificate by supplying an old CRL where the certificate had not yet appeared. Note that expired certificates are typically removed from the CRL, which prevents the CRL from growing unboundedly over time.

Note that CRLs can only revoke certificates on time boundaries determined by the *nextUpdate* time. If a CA publishes a CRL every Monday, for example, a certificate that is compromised on a Wednesday will continue to validate until its serial number is published in the CRL on the following Monday. Clients validating certificates may have downloaded the CA's CRL on Monday and are free to cache the CRL until the *nextUpdate* time occurs. This caching is important because it means that the CRL is only downloaded once per client per publication period rather than for every certificate validation. However, it has the unavoidable consequence of having a potential time lag between a certificate becoming invalid and its appearance on a CRL. The online certificate validation protocols detailed in the next section attempt to solve this problem.

The costs of maintaining and transmitting CRLs to verifying parties has been repeatedly identified as an important component of the cost of running a PKI system,[8,9] and several alternative revocation schemes have been proposed to lower this cost. The cost of CRL distribution was also a factor in the emergence of online certificate status-checking protocols such as OCSP and SCVP.

Delta CRLs

In large systems that issue many certificates, CRLs can potentially become quite lengthy. One approach to reducing the network overhead associated with sending the complete CRL to every verifier is to issue a Delta CRL along with a Base CRL. The Base CRL contains the complete set of revoked certificates up to some point in time, and the accompanying Delta CRL contains only the additional certificates added over some time period. Clients that are capable of processing the Delta CRL can then download the Base CRL less frequently and download the smaller Delta CRL to get recently revoked certificates. Delta CRLs are formatted identically to CRLs but have a critical extension added in the CRL that denotes that they are a Delta, not a Base, CRL. IETF RFC 3280[10] details the way Delta CRLs are formatted and the set of certificate extensions that indicate that a CA issues Delta CRLs.

Online Certificate Status Protocol

The Online Certificate Status Protocol (OCSP) was designed with the goal of reducing the costs of CRL transmission and eliminating the time lag between certificate invalidity and certificate revocation inherent in CRL-based designs. The idea behind OCSP is straightforward. A CA certificate contains a reference to an OCSP server. A client validating a certificate transmits the certificate serial number, a hash of the issuer name, and a hash of the subject name, to that OCSP server. The OCSP server checks the certificate status and returns an indication as to the current status of the certificate. This removes the need to download the entire list of revoked certificates and allows for essentially instantaneous revocation of invalid certificates. It has the design tradeoff of requiring that clients validating certificates have network connectivity to the required OCSP server.

8 Shimshon Berkovits, Santosh Chokhani, Judith A. Furlong, Jisoo A. Geiter, and Jonathan C. Guild, *Public Key Infrastructure Study: Final Report*, produced by the MITRE Corporation for NIST, April 1994.

9 S. Micali, "Efficient certificate revocation," technical report TM-542b, MIT Laboratory for Computer Science, March 22, 1996. http://citeseer.ist.psu.edu/micali96efficient.html.

10 R. Housely, W. Ford, W. Polk, and D. Solo, "Internet X.509 public key infrastructure certificate and certificate revocation list profile," IETF RFC 3280, April 2002.

OCSP responses contain the basic information as to the status of the certificate, in the set of "good," "revoked," or "unknown." They also contain a *thisUpdate* time, similarly to a CRL, and are signed. Responses can also contain a *nextUpdate* time, which indicates how long the client can consider the OCSP response definitive. The reason the certificate was revoked can also be returned in the response. OCSP is defined in IETF RFC 2560.[11]

7. SERVER-BASED CERTIFICATE VALIDITY PROTOCOL

The X.509 certificate path construction and validation process requires a nontrivial amount of code, the ability to fetch and cache CRLs, and, in the case of mesh and bridge CAs, the ability to interpret CA policies. The Server-based Certificate Validity Protocol[12] was designed to reduce the cost of using X.509 certificates by allowing applications to delegate the task of certificate validation to an external server. SCVP offers two levels of functionality: Delegated Path Discovery (DPD), which attempts to locate and construct a complete certificate chain for a given certificate, and Delegated Path Validation (DPV), which performs a complete path validation, including revocation checking, on a certificate chain. The main reason for this division of functionality is that a client can use an untrusted SCVP server for DPD operations, since it will validate the resulting path itself. Only trusted SCVP servers can be used for DPV, since the client must trust the server's assessment of a certificate's validity.

SCVP also allows certificate checking according to some defined certification policy. It can be used to centralize policy management for an organization that wants all clients to follow some set of rules with respect to what sets of CAs or certification policies are trusted and so on. To use SCVP, the client sends a query to an SCVP server that contains the following parameters:

- **QueriedCerts**. This is the set of certificates for which the client wants the server to construct (and optionally validate) paths.
- **Checks**. The *Checks* parameter specifies what the client wants the server to do. This parameter can be used to specify that the server should build a path, should build a path and validate it without checking

revocation, or should build and fully validate the path.

- **WantBack**. The *WantBack* parameter specifies what the server should return from the request. This can range from the public key from the validated certificate path (in which case the client is fully delegating certificate validation to the server) to all certificate chains that the server can locate.
- **ValidationPolicy**. The *ValidationPolicy* parameter instructs the server how to validate the resultant certification chain. This parameter can be as simple as "Use the default RFC 3280 validation algorithm" or can specify a wide range of conditions that must be satisfied. Some of the conditions that can be specified with this parameter are:
  - **KeyUsage and Extended Key Usage**. The client can specify a set of *KeyUsage* or *ExtendedKeyUsage* fields that must be present in the end-entity certificate. This allows the client to only accept, for example, certificates that are allowed to perform digital signatures.
  - **UserPolicySet**. The client can specify a set of certification policy OIDs that must be present in the CAs used to construct the chain. CAs can assert that they follow some formally defined policy when issuing certificates, and this parameter allows the client to only accept certificates issued under some set of these policies. For example, if a client wanted to only accept certificates acceptable under the Medium Assurance Federal Bridge CA policies, it could assert that policy identifier in this parameter. For more information on policy identifiers, see the section on X.509 extensions.
  - **InhibitPolicyMapping**. When issuing bridge or cross-certificates, a CA can assert that a certificate policy identifier in one domain is equivalent to some other policy identifier within its domain. Using this parameter, the client can state that it does not want to allow these policy equivalences to be used in validating certificates against values in the *UserPolicySet* parameter.
  - **TrustAnchors**. The client can use this parameter to specify some set of certificates that must be at the top of any acceptable certificate chain. By using this parameter a client could, for example, say that only VeriSign Class 3 certificates were acceptable in this context.
  - **ResponseFlags**. This specifies various options as to how the server should respond (if it needs to sign or otherwise protect the response) and if a cached response is acceptable to the client.

---

11 M. Myers, R. Ankeny, A. Malpani, S. Galperin, and C. Adams, "X.509 Internet public key infrastructure: Online Certificate Status Protocol – OCSP," IETF RFC 2560, June 1999.

12 T. Freeman, R. Housely, A. Malpani, D. Cooper, and W. Polk, "Server-Based Certificate Validation Protocol (SCVP)," IETF RFC 5055, December 2007.

– *ValidationTime*. The client may want a validation performed as though it was a specific time so that it can find out whether a certificate was valid at some point in the past. Note that SCVP does not allow for "speculative" validation in terms of asking whether a certificate will be valid in the future. This parameter allows the client to specify the validation time to be used by the server.

– *IntermediateCerts*. The client can use this parameter to give additional certificates that can potentially be used to construct the certificate chain. The server is not obligated to use these certificates. This parameter is used where the client may have received a set of intermediate certificates from a communicating party and is not certain that the SCVP server has possession of these certificates.

– *RevInfos*. Like the *IntermediateCerts* parameter, the *RevInfos* parameter supplies extra information that may be needed to construct or validate the path. Instead of certificates, the *RevInfos* parameter supplies revocation information such as OCSP responses, CRLs, or Delta CRLs.

8. X.509 BRIDGE CERTIFICATION SYSTEMS

In practice, large-scale PKI systems proved to be more complex than could be easily handled under the X.509 hierarchical model. For example, Polk and Hastings[13] identified a number of policy complexities that presented difficulties when attempting to build a PKI system for the U.S. federal government. In this case, certainly one of the largest PKI projects ever undertaken, they found that the traditional model of a hierarchical certification system was simply unworkable. They state:

> *The initial designs for a federal PKI were hierarchical in nature because of government's inherent hierarchical organizational structure. However, these initial PKI plans ran into several obstacles. There was no clear organization within the government that could be identified and agreed upon to run a governmental "root" CA. While the search for an appropriate organization dragged on, federal agencies began to deploy autonomous PKIs to enable their electronic processes. The search for a "root" CA for a hierarchical federal PKI was abandoned, due to the difficulties of imposing a hierarchy after the fact.*

Their proposed solution to this problem was to use a "mesh CA" system to establish a Federal Bridge Certification Authority. This Bridge architecture has since been adopted in large PKI systems in Europe and the financial services community in the United States. The details of the European Bridge CA can be found at www.bridge-ca.org. This part of the chapter details the technical design of bridge CAs and the various X.509 certificate features that enable bridges.

Mesh PKIs and Bridge CAs

Bridge CA architectures are implemented using a non-hierarchical certification structure called a *Mesh PKI*. The classic X.509 architecture joins together multiple PKI systems by subordinating them under a higher-level CA. All certificates chain up to this CA, and that CA essentially creates trust between the CAs below it. Mesh PKIs join together multiple PKI systems using a process called *cross-certification* that does not create this type of hierarchy. To cross-certify, the top-level CA in a given hierarchy creates a certificate for an external CA, called the *bridge CA*. This bridge CA then becomes, in a manner of speaking, a Sub-CA under the organization's CA. However, the bridge CA also creates a certificate for the organizational CA, so it can also be viewed as a top-level CA certifying that organizational CA.

The end result of this cross-certification process is that if two organizations, A and B, have joined the same bridge CA, they can both create certificate chains from their respective trusted CAs through the other organization's CA to the end-entity certificates that it has created. These chains will be longer than traditional hierarchical chains but will have the same basic verifiable properties. Figure 26.7 shows how two organizations might be connected through a bridge CA and what the resultant certificate chains look like.

In the case illustrated in the diagram, a user that trusts certificates issued by PKI A (that is, PKI A Root is a "trust anchor") can construct a chain to certificates issued by the PKI B Sub-CA, since it can verify Certificate 2 via its trust of the PKI A Root. Certificate 2 then chains to Certificate 3, which chains to Certificate 6. Certificate 6 is then a trusted issuer certificate for certificates issued by the PKI B Sub-CA.

Mesh architectures create two significant technical problems: path construction and policy evaluation. In a hierarchical PKI system, there is only one path from the root certificate to an end-entity certificate. Creating a certificate chain is as simple as taking the current certificate, locating the issuer in the subject field of another

---

13 W.T. Polk and N.E. Hastings, "Bridge certification authorities: connecting B2B public key infrastructures," white paper, U.S. National Institute of Standards and Technology, 2001, Available at http://csrc. nist.gov/groups/ST/crypto_apps_infra/documents/B2B-article.pdf.

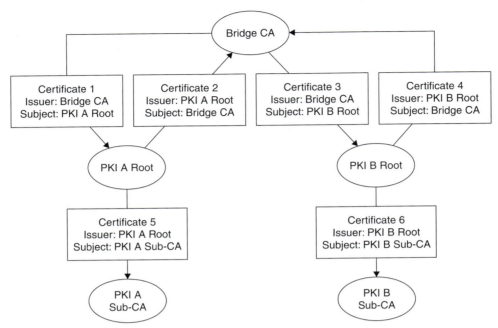

FIGURE 26.7 Showing the structure of two PKIs connected via a bridge CA.

certificate, and repeating until the root is reached (completing the chain) or no certificate can be found (failing to construct the chain). In a mesh system, there can now be cyclical loops in which this process can fail to terminate with a failure or success. This is not a difficult problem to solve, but it is more complex to deal with than the hierarchical case.

Policy evaluation becomes much more complex in the mesh case. In the hierarchical CA case, the top-level CA can establish policies that are followed by Sub-CAs, and these policies can be encoded into certificates in an unambiguous way. When multiple PKIs are joined by a bridge CA, these PKIs may have similar policies but can be expressed with different names. PKI A and PKI B may both certify "medium assurance" CAs that perform a certain level of authentication before issuing certificates, but they may have different identifiers for these policies. When joined by a bridge CA, clients may reasonably want to validate certificates issued by both CAs and understand the policies under which those certificates are issued. The *PolicyMapping* technique allows similar policies under different names from disjoint PKIs to be translated at the bridge CA.

Though none of these problems are insurmountable, they increase the complexity of certificate validation code and helped drive the invention of server-based validation protocols such as SCVP. These protocols delegate path discovery and validation to an external server rather than require that applications integrate this functionality.

Though this may lower application complexity, the main benefit of this strategy is that questions of acceptable policies and translation can be configured at one central verification server rather than distributed to every application doing certificate validation.

9. X.509 CERTIFICATE FORMAT

The X.509 standard (and the related IETF RFCs) specify a set of data fields that must be present in a properly formatted certificate, a set of optional extension data fields that can be used to supply additional certificate information, how these fields must be signed, and how the signature data is encoded. All these data fields (mandatory fields, optional fields, and the signature) are specified in Abstract Syntax Notation (aka ASN.1), a formal language that allows for exact definitions of the content of data fields and how those fields are arranged in a data structure. An associated specification, Determined Encoding Rules (DER), is used with specific certificate data and the ASN.1 certificate format to create the actual binary certificate data. The ASN.1 standard is authoritatively defined in ITU Recommendation X.693. (For an introduction to ASN.1 and DER, see Kaliski, November 1993.[14])

---

14 B.S. Kaliski, Jr., "A layman's guide to a subset of ASN.1, BER, and DER" An RSA Technical Note, Revised November 1, 1993, available at ftp.rsasecurity.com/pub/pkcs/ascii/layman.asc.

X.509 V1 and V2 Format

The first X.509 certificate standard was published in 1988 as part of the broader X.500 directory standard. X.509 was intended to provide public key-based access control to an X.500 directory and defined a certificate format for that use. This format, now referred to as X.509 v1, defined a static format containing an X.400 issuer name (the name of the CA), an X.400 subject name, a validity period, the key to be certified, and the signature of the CA. Though this basic format allowed for all the basic PKI operations, the format required that all names be in the X.400 form, and it did not allow for any other information to be added to the certificate. The X.509 v2 format added two more Unique ID fields but did not fix the primary deficiencies of the v1 format. As it became clear that name formats would have to be more flexible and certificates would have to accommodate a wider variety of information, work began on a new certificate format.

X.509 V3 Format

The X.509 certificate specification was revised in 1996 to add an optional extension field that allows encoding a set of optional additional data fields into the certificate (see Table 26.5). Though this change might seem minor, in fact it allowed certificates to carry a wide array of information useful for PKI implementation and for the certificate to contain multiple, non-X.400 identities. These extension fields allow key usage policies, CA policy information, revocation pointers, and other relevant information to live in the certificate. The v3 format is the most widely used X.509 variant and is the basis for the certificate profile in RFC 3280,[15] issued by the Internet Engineering Task Force.

X.509 Certificate Extensions

This section contains a partial catalog of common X.509 v3 extensions. There is no existing canonical directory of v3 extensions, so there are undoubtedly extensions in use outside this list.

The most common extensions are defined in RFC 3280,[16] which contains the IETF certificate profile used by S/MIME and many SSL/TLS implementations. These

TABLE 26.5 Data fields in an X.509 version 3 certificate

Version	The version of the standard used to format the certificate
Serial Number	A number, unique relative to the issuer, for this certificate
Signature Algorithm	The specific algorithm used to sign the certificate
Issuer	Name of the authority issuing the certificate
Validity	The time interval this certificate is valid for
Subject	The identity being certified
Subject Public Key	The key being bound to the subject
Issuer Unique ID	Obsolete field
Subject Unique ID	Obsolete field
Extensions	A list of additional certificate attributes
Signature	A digital signature by the issuer over the certificate data

extensions address a number of deficiencies in the base X.509 certificate specification, and, in many cases, are essential for constructing a practical PKI system. In particular, the Certificate Policy, Policy Mapping, and Policy Constraints extensions form the basis for the popular bridge CA architectures.

Authority Key Identifier

The Authority Key Identifier extension identifies which specific private key owned by the certificate issuer was used to sign the certificate. The use of this extension allows a single issuer to use multiple private keys and unambiguously identifies which key was used. This allows issuer keys to be refreshed without changing the issuer name and enables handling of events such as an issuer key being compromised or lost.

Subject Key Identifier

The Subject Key Identifier extension, like the Authority Key Identifier, indicates which subject key is contained in the certificate. This extension provides a way to quickly identify which certificates belong to a specific key owned by a subject. If the certificate is a CA certificate, the Subject Key Identifier can be used to construct chains by connecting a Subject Key Identifier with a matching Authority Key Identifier.

---

15 R. Housely, W. Ford, W. Polk, and D. Solo, "Internet X.509 public key infrastructure certificate and certificate revocation list profile," IETF RFC 3280, April 2002.

16 R. Housely, W. Ford, W. Polk, and D. Solo, "Internet X.509 public key infrastructure certificate and certificate revocation list profile," IETF RFC 3280, April 2002.

Key Usage

A CA might want to issue a certificate that limits the use of a public key. This could lead to an increase in overall system security by segregating encryption keys from signature keys and even segregating signature keys by utilization. For example, an entity may have a key used for signing documents and a key used for decryption of documents. The signing key may be protected by a smart card mechanism that requires a PIN per signing, whereas the encryption key is always available when the user is logged in. The use of this extension allows the CA to express that the encryption key cannot be used to generate signatures and notifies communicating users that they should not encrypt data with the signing public key.

The usage capabilities are defined in a bit field, which allows a single key to have any combination of the defined capabilities. The extension defines the following capabilities:

- *digitalSignature*. The key can be used to generate digital signatures.
- *nonRepudiation*. Signatures generated from this key can be tied back to the signer in such a way that the signer cannot deny generating the signature. This capability is used in electronic transaction scenarios in which it is important that signers cannot disavow a transaction.
- *keyEncipherment*. The key can be used to wrap a symmetric key that is then used to bulk-encrypt data. This is used in communications protocols and applications such as S/MIME in which an algorithm like AES is used to encrypt data, and the public key in the certificate is used to then encipher that AES key. In practice, almost all encryption applications are structured in this manner, since public keys are generally unsuitable for the encryption of bulk data.
- *dataEncipherment*. The key can be used to directly encrypt data. Because of algorithmic limitations of public encryption algorithms, the *keyEncipherment* technique is nearly always used instead of directly encrypting data.
- *keyAgreement*. The key can be used to create a communication key between two parties. This capability can be used in conjunction with the *encipherOnly* and *decipherOnly* capabilities.
- *keyCertSign*. The key can be used to sign another certificate. This is a crucial key usage capability because it essentially allows creation of subcertificates under this certificate, subject to *basicConstraints*. All CA certificates must have this usage bit set, and all end-entity certificates must *not* have it set.

- *cRLSign*. The key can be used to sign a CRL. CA certificates may have this bit set, or they may delegate CRL creation to a different key, in which case this bit will be cleared.
- *encipherOnly*. When the key is used for *keyAgreement*, the resultant key can only be used for encryption.
- *decipherOnly*. When the key is used for *keyAgreement*, the resultant key can only be used for decryption.

Subject Alternative Name

This extension allows the certificate to define non-X.400 formatted identities for the subject. It supports a variety of namespaces, including email addresses, DNS names for servers, Electronic Document Interchange (EDI) party names, Uniform Resource Identifiers (URIs), and IP addresses, among others.

Policy Extensions

Three important X.509 certificate extensions (Certificate Policy, Policy Mapping, and Policy Constraints) form a complete system for communicating CA policies for the way that certificates are issued and revoked and CA security is maintained. They are interesting in that they communicate information that is more relevant to business and policy decision-making than the other extensions that are used in the technical processes of certificate chain construction and validation. As an example, a variety of CAs run multiple Sub-CAs that issue certificates according to a variety of issuance policies, ranging from "Low Assurance" to "High Assurance." The CA will typically formally define in a policy document all of its operating policies, state them in a practice statement, define an ASN.1 Object Identifier (OID) that names this policy, and distribute it to parties that will validate those certificates.

The policy extensions allow a CA to attach a policy OID to its certificate, translate policy OIDs between PKIs, and limit the policies that can be used by Sub-CAs.

Certificate Policy

The Certificate Policy extension, if present in an issuer certificate, expresses the policies that are followed by the CA, both in terms of how identities are validated before certificate issuance as well as how certificates are revoked and the operational practices that are used to ensure integrity of the CA. These policies can be expressed in two ways: as an OID, which is a unique number that refers to one given policy, and as a human-readable Certificate Practice Statement (CPS). One Certificate Policy extension can contain both the computer-sensible OID and a printable CPS. One special OID has been set aside for *AnyPolicy*, which states that the CA may issue certificates under a free-form policy.

IETF RFC 2527[17] gives a complete description of what should be present in a CA policy document and CPS. More details on the 2527 guidelines are given in the "PKI Policy Description" section.

Policy Mapping

The Policy Mapping extension contains two policy OIDs, one for the issuer domain, the other for the subject domain. When this extension is present, a validating party can consider the two policies identical, which is to say that the subject OID, when present in the chain below the given certificate, can be considered to be the same as the policy named in the issuer OID. This extension is used to join together two PKI systems with functionally similar policies that have different policy reference OIDs.

Policy Constraints

The Policy Constraints extension enables a CA to disable policy mapping for CAs farther down the chain and to require explicit policies in all the CAs below a given CA.

10. PKI POLICY DESCRIPTION

In many application contexts, it is important to understand how and when certifying authorities will issue and revoke certificates. Especially when bridge architectures are used, an administrator may need to evaluate a certifying authority's policy to determine how and when to trust certificates issued under that authority. For example, the U.S. Federal Bridge CA maintains a detailed specification of its operating procedures and requirements for bridged CAs at the U.S. CIO office Web site (www.cio. gov/fpkipa/documents/FBCA_CP_RFC3647.pdf). Many other commercial CAs, such as VeriSign, maintain similar documents.

To make policy evaluation easier and more uniform, IETF RFC 2527[18] specifies a standard format for certifying authorities to communicate their policy for issuing and revoking certificates. This specification divides a policy specification document into the following sections:

- *Introduction.* This section describes the type of certificates that the CA issues, the applications in which those certificates can be used, and the OIDs used to identify CA policies. The Introduction also contains the contact information for the institution operating the CA.
- *General Provisions.* This section details the legal obligations of the CA, any warranties given as to the reliability of the bindings in the certificate, and details as to the legal operation of the CA, including fees and relationship to any relevant laws.
- *Identification and Authentication.* This section details how certificate requests are authenticated at the CA or RA and how events like name disputes or revocation requests are handled.
- *Operational Requirements.* This section details how the CA will react in case of key compromise, how it renews keys, how it publishes CRLs or other revocation information, how it is audited, and what records are kept during CA operation.
- *Physical, Procedural, and Personnel Security Controls.* This section details how the physical location of the CA is controlled and how employees are vetted.
- *Technical Security Controls.* This section explains how the CA key is generated and protected though its life cycle. CA key generation is typically done through an audited, recorded key generation ceremony to assure certificate users that the CA key was not copied or otherwise compromised during generation.
- *Certificate and CRL Profile.* The specific policy OIDs published in certificates generated by the CA are given in this section. The information in this section is sufficient to accomplish the technical evaluation of a certificate chain published by this CA.
- *Specification Administration.* The last section explains the procedures used to maintain and update the certificate policy statement itself.

These policy statements can be substantial documents. The Federal Bridge CA policy statement is 93 pages long; other certificate authorities have similarly exhaustive documents. The aim of these statements is to provide enough legal backing for certificates produced by these CAs so that they can be used to sign legally binding contracts and automate other legally relevant applications.

---

17 S. Chokhani and W. Ford, "Internet X.509 public key infrastructure: certificate policy and certification practices framework," IETF RFC 2527, March 1999.

18 S. Chokhani and W. Ford, "Internet X.509 public key infrastructure: certificate policy and certification practices framework," IETF RFC 2527, March 1999.

11. PKI STANDARDS ORGANIZATIONS

The PKIX Working Group was established in the fall of 1995 with the goal of developing Internet standards to support X.509-based PKIs. These specifications form the basis for numerous other IETF specifications that use certificates to secure various protocols, such as S/MIME (for secure email), TLS (for secured TCP connections), and IPsec (for securing Internet packets.)

IETF PKIX

The PKIX working group has produced a complete set of specifications for an X.509-based PKI system. These specifications span 36 RFCs, and at least eight more RFCs are being considered by the group. In addition to the basic core of X.509 certificate profiles and verification strategies, the PKIX drafts cover the format of certificate request messages, certificates for arbitrary attributes (rather than for public keys), and a host of other certificate techniques.

Other IETF groups have produced a group of specifications that detail the usage of certificates in various protocols and applications. In particular, the S/MIME group, which details a method for encrypting email messages, and the SSL/TLS group, which details TCP/IP connection security, use X.509 certificates.

SDSI/SPKI

The Simple Distributed Security Infrastructure (SDSI) group was chartered in 1996 to design a mechanism for distributing public keys that would correct some of the perceived complexities inherent in X.509. In particular, the SDSI group aimed at building a PKI architecture that would not rely on a hierarchical naming system but would instead work with local names that would not have to be enforced to be globally unique. The eventual SDSI design, produced by Ron Rivest and Butler Lampson,[19] has a number of unique features:

- *Public key-centric design.* The SDSI design uses the public key itself (or a hash of the key) as the primary indentifying name. SDSI signature objects can contain naming statements about the holder of a given key, but the names are not intended to be the "durable" name of a entity.
- *Free-form namespaces.* SDSI imposes no restrictions on what form names must take and imposes no

hierarchy that defines a canonical namespace. Instead, any signer may assert identity information about the holder of a key, but no entity is required to use (or believe) the identity bindings of any other particular signer. This allows each application to create a policy about who can create identities, how those identities are verified, and even what constitutes an identity.

- *Support for groups and roles.* The design of many security constructions (access control lists, for example) often include the ability to refer to groups or roles instead of the identity of individuals. This allows access control and encryption operations to protect data for groups, which may be more natural in some situations.

The Simple Public Key Infrastructure (SPKI) group was started at nearly the same time, with goals similar to the SDSI effort. In 1997, the two groups were merged and the SDSI/SPKI 2.0 specification was produced, incorporating ideas from both architectures.

IETF OpenPGP

The Pretty Good Privacy (PGP) public key system, created by Philip Zimmermann, is a widely deployed PKI system that allows for the signing and encryption of files and email. Unlike the X.509 PKI architecture, the PGP PKI system uses the notion of a "Web of Trust" to bind identities to keys. The Web of Trust (WoT)[20] replaces the X.509 idea of identity binding via an authoritative server, with identity binding via multiple semitrusted paths.

In a WoT system, the end user maintains a database of matching keys and identities, each of which are given two trust ratings. The first trust rating denotes how trusted the binding between the key and the identity is, and the second denotes how trusted a particular identity is to "introduce" new bindings. Users can create and sign a certificate as well as import certificates created by other users. Importing a new certificate is treated as an introduction. When a given identity and key in a database are signed by enough trusted identities, that binding is treated as trusted.

Because PGP identities are not bound by an authoritative server, there is also no authoritative server that can revoke a key. Instead, the PGP model states that the holder of a key can revoke that key by posting a signed revocation message to a public server. Any user seeing a properly

19 R. Rivest and B. Lampson, "SDSI-A simple distributed security infrastructure," Oct. 1996.

20 Alfarez Abdul-Rahman, "The PGP trust model," *EDI- Forum*, April 1997, available at www.cs.ucl.ac.uk/staff/F.AbdulRahman/docs/.

signed revocation message then removes that key from her database. Because revocation messages must be signed, only the holder of the key can produce them, so it is impossible to produce a false revocation without compromising the key. If an attacker does compromise the key, then production of a revocation message from that compromised key actually improves the security of the overall system because it warns other users not to trust that key.

12. PGP CERTIFICATE FORMATS

To support the unique features of the Web of Trust system, PGP invented a very flexible packetized message format that can encode encrypted messages, signed messages, key database entries, key revocation messages, and certificates. This packetized design, described in IETF RFC 2440, allows a PGP certificate to contain a variable number of names and signatures, as opposed to the single-certification model used in X.509.

A PGP certificate (known as a *transferrable public key*) contains three main sections of packetized data. The first section contains the main public key itself, potentially followed by some set of relevant revocation packets. The next section contains a set of User ID packets, which are identities to be bound to the main public key. Each User ID packet is optionally followed by a set of

Signature packets, each of which contains an identity and a signature of the User ID packet and the main public key. Each of these Signature packets essentially forms an identity binding. Because each PGP certificate can contain any number of these User ID/Signature elements, a single certificate can assert that a public key is bound to multiple identities (for example, multiple email addresses that correspond to a single user), certified by multiple signers. This multiple-signer approach enables the Web of Trust model. The last section of the certificate is optional and may contain multiple subkeys, which are single-function keys (for example, an encryption-only key) also owned by the holder of the main public key. Each of these subkeys must be signed by the main public key.

PGP Signature packets contain all the information needed to perform a certification, including time intervals for which the signature is valid. Figure 26.8 shows how the multiname, multisignature PGP format differs from the single-name with single-signature X.509 format.

13. PGP PKI IMPLEMENTATIONS

The PGP PKI system is implemented in commercial products sold by the PGP corporation, and several open-source projects, including GNU Privacy Guard (GnuPG) and OpenPGP. Thawte offers a Web of Trust service that connects people with "Web of Trust notaries" that can build trusted introductions. PGP Corporation operates a PGP Global Directory that contains PGP keys along with an email confirmation service to make key certification easier.

The OpenPGP group (www.openpgp.org) maintains the IETF specification (RFC 2440) for the PGP message and certificate format.

14. W3C

The World Wide Web Consortium (W3C) standards group has published a series of standards on encrypting and signing XML documents. These standards, XML Signature and XML Encryption, have a companion PKI specification called XKMS (XML Key Management Specification).

The XKMS specification describes a meta-PKI that can be used to register, locate, and validate keys that may be certified by an outside X.509 CA, a PGP referrer, a SPKI key signer, or the XKMS infrastructure itself. The specification contains two protocol specifications, X-KISS (XML Key Information Service Specification) and X-KRSS (XML Key Registration Service Specification). X-KISS is used to find and validate a public

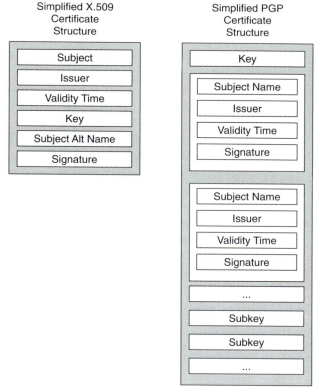

FIGURE 26.8 Comparing X.509 and PGP certificate structures.

key referenced in an XML document, and X-KRSS is used to register a public key so that it can be located by X-KISS requests.

15. ALTERNATIVE PKI ARCHITECTURES

PKI systems have proven remarkably effective tools for some protocols, most notably SSL, which has emerged as the dominant standard for encrypting Internet traffic. Deploying PKI systems for other types of applications or as a general key management system has not been as successful. The differentiating factor seems to be that PKI keys for machine end-entities (such as Web sites) do not encounter usability hurdles that emerge when issuing PKI keys for human end-entities. Peter Gutmann[21] has a number of overviews of PKI that present the fundamental difficulties of classic X.509 PKI architectures. Alma Whitten and Doug Tygar[22] published "Why Johnny Can't Encrypt," a study of various users attempting to encrypt email messages using certificates. This study showed substantial user failure rates due to the complexities of understanding certificate naming and validation practices. A subsequent study[23] showed similar results when using X.509 certificates with S/MIME encryption in Microsoft Outlook Express.

16. MODIFIED X.509 ARCHITECTURES

Some researchers have proposed modifications or redesigns of the X.509 architecture to make obtaining a certificate easier and to lower the cost of operating applications that depend on certificates. The goal of these systems is often to allow Internet-based services to use certificate-based signature and encryption services without requiring the user to consciously interact with certification services or even understand that certificates are being utilized.

Perlman and Kaufman's User-Centric PKI

Perlman and Kaufman proposed the User-Centric PKI,[24] which allows the user to act as his own CA, with authentication provided through individual registration with service providers. This method has several features that

Gutmann's Plug and Play PKI

Peter Gutmann's proposed "Plug and Play PKI"[25] provides for similar self-registration with a service provider and adds location protocols to establish ways to contact certifying services. The goal is to build a PKI that provides a reasonable level of security and that is essentially transparent to the end user.

Callas's Self-Assembling PKI

In 2003, Jon Callas[26] proposed a PKI system that would use existing standard PKI elements bound together by a "robot" server that would examine messages sent between users and attempt to find certificates that could be used to secure the message. In the absence of an available certificate, the robot would create a key on behalf of the user and send a message requesting authentication. This system has the benefit of speeding deployment of PKI systems for email authentication, but it loses many of the strict authentication attributes that drove the development of the X.509 and IETF PKI standards.

17. ALTERNATIVE KEY MANAGEMENT MODELS

PKI systems can be used for encryption as well as digital signatures, but these two applications have different operational characteristics. In particular, systems that use PKIs for encryption require that an encrypting party has the ability to locate certificates for its desired set of recipients. In digital signature applications, a signer only requires access to his own private key and certificate. The certificates required to verify the signature can be sent with the signed document, so there is no requirement for verifiers to locate arbitrary certificates. These difficulties have been identified as factors contributing to the difficulty of practical deployment of PKI-based encryption systems such as S/MIME.

In 1984, Adi Shamir[27] proposed an Identity-Based Encryption (IBE) system for email encryption. In the

21 P. Gutmann, "Plug-and-play PKI: A PKI your mother can use," in *Proc. 12th Usenix Security Symp.,* Usenix Assoc., 2003, pp. 45–58.
22 A. Whitten and J.D. Tygar, "Why Johnny can't encrypt: a usability evaluation of PGP 5.0," in *Proceedings of the 8th USENIX Security Symposium,* August 1999.
23 S. Garfinkel and R. Miller, "Johnny 2: A user test of key continuity management with S/MIME and outlook express," Symposium on Usable Privacy and Security, 2005.
24 R. Perlman and C. Kaufman, "User-centric PKI", 7th symposium on identity and trust on the internet.

25 P. Gutmann, "Plug-and-Play PKI: A PKI Your Mother Can Use," in *Proc. 12th Usenix Security Symp.,* Usenix Assoc., 2003, pp. 45–58.
26 J. Callas, "Improving Message Security With a Self-Assembling PKI," In *2nd Annual PKI Research Workshop Pre-Proceedings,* April 2003, http://citeseer.ist.psu.edu/callas03improving.html.
27 A. Shamir, "Identity-based Cryptosystems and Signature Schemes," *Advances in Cryptology – Crypto '84, Lecture Notes in Computer Science,* Vol. 196, Springer-Verlag, pp. 47–53, 1984.

identity-based model, any string can be mathematically transformed into a public key, typically using some public information from a server. A message can then be encrypted with this key. To decrypt, the message recipient contacts the server and requests a corresponding private key. The server is able to mathematically derive a private key, which is returned to the recipient. Shamir disclosed how to perform a signature operation in this model but did not give a solution for encryption.

This approach has significant advantages over the traditional PKI model of encryption. The most obvious is the ability to send an encrypted message without locating a certificate for a given recipient. There are other points of differentiation:

- *Key recovery.* In the traditional PKI model, if a recipient loses the private key corresponding to a certificate, all messages encrypted to that certificate's public key cannot be decrypted. In the IBE model, the server can recompute lost private keys. If messages must be recoverable for legal or other business reasons, PKI systems typically add mandatory secondary public keys to which senders must encrypt messages to.

- *Group support.* Since any string can be transformed to a public key, a group name can be supplied instead of an individual identity. In the traditional PKI model, groups are done by either expanding a group to a set of individuals at encrypt time or issuing group certificates. Group certificates pose serious difficulties with revocation, since individuals can only be removed from a group as often as revocation is updated.

In 2001, Boneh and Franklin gave the first fully described secure and efficient method for IBE.[28] This was followed by a number of variant techniques, including Hierarchical Identity-Based Encryption (HIBE) and Certificateless Encryption. HIBE allows multiple key servers to be used, each of which control part of the namespace used for encryption. Certificateless[29] encryption adds the ability to encrypt to an end user using an identity but in such a way that the key server cannot read messages. IBE systems have been commercialized and are the subject of standards under the IETF (RFC 5091) and IEEE (1363.3).

28 D. Boneh and M. Franklin, "Identity-based encryption from the Weil Pairing," *SIAM J. of Computing*, Vol. 32, No. 3, pp. 586–615, 2003.

29 S. S. Al-Riyami, K. Paterson, "Certificateless public key cryptography," In: C. S. Laih (ed.), *Advances in Cryptology – Asiacrypt 2003*, *Lecture Notes in Computer Science*, Vol. 2894, pp. 452–473, Springer-Verlag, 2003.

## Chapter 27

Instant-Messaging Security

Samuel J. J. Curry

RSA

Instant messaging (IM) has emerged as one of the most commonplace, prevalent technologies on the Internet. You would have to practically live under a rock (or at least not own a computer, personal digital assistant [PDA], or cell phone) to not have used it, much less to not know what it is. Luddites[1] notwithstanding, most people who use IM and even many people in information technology (IT) do not know how it works, why it is here, and what it means.

1. WHY SHOULD I CARE ABOUT INSTANT MESSAGING?

When considering IM, it is important to realize that it is first and foremost a technology; it is not a goal in and of itself. Like an ERP[2] system, an email system, a database or directory, or a provisioning system, IM must ultimately serve the business: It is a means to an end. The end should be measured in terms of *quantifiable* returns and should be put in context. Before engaging in an IM project, you should be clear about why you are doing it. The basic reasons you should consider IM are:

- Employee satisfaction
- Improving efficiency
- Performing transactions (some business transactions have been built, as you'll see later, to use IM infrastructures; those who do this are aware of it and those who have not seen it before are frequently horrified)
- Improving communications
- Improving response times and timelines

In many deployments, IM can be a valuable contributor to business infrastructure, but it shouldn't be adopted without due consideration of business value (that is, is this worth doing?), business risk (that is, what is at stake?), and the people, processes, and technologies that will make it valuable and secure. This chapter should help you make a plan, keep it current, and make sure that it makes a difference.

Business decisions revolve around the principle of acceptable risk for acceptable return, and as a result, your *security* decisions with respect to IM are effectively *business* decisions. To those of you reading this with a security hat on, you've probably seen the rapprochement of security and business in your place of work: IM is no exception to that. So let's look at IM, trends, the business around it, and then the security implications.

2. WHAT IS INSTANT MESSAGING?

IM is a technology in a continuum of advances (q.v) that have arisen for communicating and collaborating over the Internet. The most important characteristic of IM is that it has the appearance of being in "real time," and for all intents and purposes it is in real time.[3] Of course, some IM systems allow for synchronization with folks who

---

1 Luddites were a British social movement in the textile industry who protested against the technological changes of the Industrial Revolution in the 19th century (http://en.wikipedia.org/wiki/Luddites).

2 Enterprise resource planning is a category of software that ties together operations, finance, staffing, and accounting. Common examples include SAP and Oracle software.

3 The debate over what constitutes real time is a favorite in many technical circles and is materially important when dealing with events and their observation in systems in which volumes are high and distances and timing are significant. When dealing with human beings and the relatively simple instances of whom we interact with and our perceptions of communications, it is far simpler to call this "real time" than "near real time."

are offline and come online later through buffering and batching delivery.

IM technologies predate the Internet, with many early mainframe systems and bulletin board systems (BBS) having early chat-like functionality, where two or more people could have a continuous dialogue. In the post-mainframe world, when systems became more distributed and autonomous, chatting and early IM technologies came along, too. In the world of the Internet, two basic technologies have evolved: communications via a central server and communications directly between two peers. Many IM solutions involve a hybrid of these two basic technologies, maintaining a directory or registry of users that then enable a peer-to-peer (P2P) connection.

Some salient features that are relevant for the purposes of technology and will be important later in our approaches to securing instant messaging are as follows:

- *Simultaneity.* IM is a real time or "synchronous" form of communication—real-time opportunity and real-time risk.
- *Recording.* IM transactions are a form of written communication, which means that there are logs and sessions can be captured. This is directly analogous to email.
- *Nonrepudiation.* Instant messaging usually involves a dialogue and the appearance of nonrepudiation by virtue of an exchange, but there is no inherent nonrepudiation in most IM infrastructures. For example, talking to "Bobby" via IM does not in any way prove that it is registered to "Bobby" or is actually "Bobby" at the time you are talking to the other user.
- *Lack of confidentiality and integrity.* There is no guarantee that sessions are private or unaltered in most IM infrastructures without the implementation of effective encryption solutions.
- *Availability.* Most companies do not have guaranteed service-level agreements around availability and yet they depend on IM, either consciously or unknowingly.

Most users of an IM infrastructure also treat IM as an informal form of communication, not subject to the normal rules of behavior, formatting, and formality of other forms of business communication, such as letters, memoranda, and email.

3. THE EVOLUTION OF NETWORKING TECHNOLOGIES

Over time, technology changes and, usually, advances. Advancements in this context generally refer to being able to do more transactions with more people for more profit. Of course, generalizations of this sort tend to be true on the macroscopic level only as the tiny deltas in capabilities, offerings, and the vagaries of markets drive many small changes, some of which are detrimental. However, over the long term and at the macroscopic level, advances in technology enable us to do more things with more people more easily and in closer to real time.

There are more than a few laws that track the evolution of some distinct technology trends and the positive effects that are expected. A good example of this is Moore's Law, which has yet to be disproven and has proven true since the 1960s. Moore's Law,[4] put simply, postulates that the number of transistors that can be effectively integrated doubles roughly every two years, and the resultant computing power or efficiency increases along with that. Most of us in technology know Moore's Law, and it is arguable that we as a society depend on it for economic growth and stimulus: There is always more demand for more computing power (or has been to date and for the foreseeable future). A less known further example is Gilder's Law[5] (which has since been disproven) that asserts that a similar, related growth in available bandwidth occurs over time.

Perhaps the most important "law" with respect to networks and for instant messaging is Metcalfe's Law,[6] which states that the value of a telecommunications network increases exponentially with a linear increase in the number of users. (Actually, it states that it is proportional to the square of the users on the network.)

Let's also assume that over time the value of a network will increase; the people who use it will find new ways to get more value out of it. The number of connections or transactions will increase, and the value and importance of that network will go up. In a sense, it takes time once a network has increased in size for the complexity and number of transactions promised by Metcalfe's Law to be realized.

What does all this have to do with IM? Let's tie it together:

- Following from Moore's Law (and to a lesser extent Gilder), computers (and their networks) will get faster and therefore more valuable—and so connecting them in near real time (of which IM is an example of real-time communications) is a *natural occurrence* and will *increase value.*

---

4 http://en.wikipedia.org/wiki/Moore%27s_Law.
5 www.netlingo.com/lookup.cfm?term=Gilder's%20Law.
6 http://en.wikipedia.org/wiki/Metcalfe%27s_Law.

- Following from Metcalfe, over time networks will become increasingly valuable to users of those networks.

In other words, IM as a phenomenon is really a tool for increasing connections among systems and networks and for getting more value. For those of us in the business world, this is good news: Using IM, we should be able to realize more value from that large IT investment and should be able to do more business with more people more efficiently. That is the "carrot," but there is a stick, too: It is not all good news, because where there is value and opportunity, there is also threat and risk.

4. GAME THEORY AND INSTANT MESSAGING

Whenever gains or losses can be quantified for a given population, game theory[7] applies. Game theory is used in many fields to predict what is basically the *social* behavior or organisms in a system: people in economics and political science, animals in biology and ecology, and so on. When you can tell *how much* someone stands to gain or lose, you can build reasonably accurate predictive models for how they will behave; and this is in fact the foundation for many of our modern economic theories. The fact of the matter is that now that the Internet is used for business, we can apply game theory to human behavior with Internet technologies, too, and this includes IM.

On the positive side, if you are seeing more of your colleagues, employees, and friends adopt a technology, especially in a business context, you can be reasonably sure that there is some gain and loss equation that points to an increase in value behind the technology. Generally, people should not go out of their way to adopt technologies simply for the sake of adopting them on a wide scale (though actually, many people do just this and then suffer for it; technology adoption on a wide scale and over a long period of time generally means that something is showing a return on value). Unfortunately, in a business context, this may not translate into more business or more value for the business. Human beings not only do things for quantifiable, money-driven reasons; they also do things for moral and social reasons.

Let's explore the benefits of adopting IM technology within a company, and then we can explore the risks a little more deeply.

Your Workforce

Whether you work in an IT department or run a small company, your employees have things they need to do: process orders, work with peers, manage teams, talk to customers and to partners. IM is a tool they can and will use to do these things. Look at your workforce and their high-level roles: Do they need IM to do their jobs? IM is an entitlement within a company, not a right. The management of entitlements is a difficult undertaking, but it isn't without precedent. For older companies, you probably had to make a decision similar to the IM decision with respect to email or Internet access. The first response from a company is usually binary: Allow everyone or disallow everyone. This reactionary response is natural, and in many cases some roles are denied entitlements such as email or Internet access on a regular basis. Keep in mind that in some industries, employees make the difference between a successful, aggressively growing business and one that is effectively in a "maintenance mode" or, worse, is actively shrinking.

In the remainder of this chapter, we outline factors in your decision making, as follows with the first factor.

Factor #1

> *Factor #1:* Do your employees need IM? If so, which employees need IM and *what do they need it for?*

Examples of privileged IM entitlement include allowing developers, brokers, sales teams, executives, operations, and/or customer support to have access. *Warning:* If you provide IM for some parts of your company and not for others, you will be in a situation in which some employees have a privilege that others do not. This will have two, perhaps unintended, consequences:

- Employees without IM will seek to get it by abusing backdoors or processes to get this entitlement.
- Some employees will naturally be separated from other employees and may become the object of envy or of resentment. This could cause problems.

We have also touched on employee satisfaction, and it is important to understand the demographics of your workplace and its social norms. It is important to also consider physical location of employees and general demographic considerations with respect to IM because there could be cultural barriers, linguistic barriers, and, as we will see later, generational ones, too.

---

7 http://en.wikipedia.org/wiki/Game_Theory.

Factor #2

> *Factor #2:* Is IM important as a job satisfaction component?

Economists generally hold that employees work for financial, moral, and social reasons.[8] Financial reasons are the most obvious and, as we've seen, are the ones most easily quantified and therefore subject to game theory; companies have money, and they can use it to incent the behaviors they want. However, we as human beings also work on things for moral reasons, as is the case with people working in nonprofit organizations or in the open-source movement. These people work on things that matter to them for moral reasons.

However, the social incentives are perhaps the most important for job satisfaction. In speaking recently with the CIO of a large company that banned the use of external IM, the CIO was shocked that a large number of talented operations and development people refused lucrative offers on the grounds that IM was disallowed with people outside the company. This led to a discussion of the motivators for an important asset for this company: attracting and keeping the right talent. The lesson is that if you want to attract the best, you may have to allow them to use technologies such as IM.

After you have determined whether or not IM is needed for the job (Factor #1), interview employees on the uses of IM in a social context: with whom do they IM and for what purposes? Social incentives include a large number of social factors, including keeping in touch with parents, siblings, spouses, and friends but also with colleagues overseas, with mentors, and for team collaboration, especially over long distances.

Generational Gaps

An interesting phenomenon is observable in the generation now in schools and training for the future: They multitask frequently. Generational gaps and their attendant conflicts are nothing new; older generations are in power and are seen to bear larger burdens, and younger generations are often perceived in a negative light. Today IM may be at the forefront of yet another generational conflict.

If you've observed children recently, they do more all at once than adults have done in the past 20 years.

This is a generation that grows up in a home with multiple televisions, multiple computers, cell phones from a young age, PowerPoint in the classroom, text messaging, email,[9] and IM.

The typical older-generation values in a generational conflict that we must watch out for are assuming that the younger generation is inherently more lazy, is looking for unreasonable entitlement, wants instant gratification, or is lacking in intelligence and seasoning. If you catch yourself doing this, stop yourself and try to empathize with the younger folks. Likewise, the younger generation has its pitfalls and assumptions; but let's focus on the younger, emerging generation, because they will soon be entering the workforce. If you find yourself assuming that multitasking and responding to multiple concurrent stimuli is distracting and likely to produce a lack of efficiency, stop and run through a basic question: Is what's true for you immediately true for the people you are interacting with? This leads to Factors 3 and 4.

Factor #3

> *Factor #3:* Does IM improve or lessen efficiency?

With respect to IM, does IM (and the interruptions it creates) have to mean that someone is less efficient, or could they be more efficient because of it? As we've seen, it is possible that many younger employees can have multiple IM conversations and can potentially get a lot more done in less time compared to either sending out multiple emails or waiting for responses. In many respects, this question is similar to the questions that the BlackBerry raised when it was introduced to the workforce, and there are three ways that it can be answered:

- In some cases, jobs require isolation and focus, and a culture of IM can create conditions that are less effective.
- In some cases, it doesn't matter.
- In some cases, some employees may be much more effective when they receive maximum stimulus and input.

Factor #4

> *Factor #4:* Will this efficiency change over time, or is it in fact different for different demographics of my workforce?

---

8 http://en.wikipedia.org/wiki/Incentive. The actual incentive grouping that works on human beings is subject to debate, but it is limited to economic, moral, and social for the purposes of this chapter. This is a fascinating subject area well worth reading more about.

9 To my amusement, my goddaughter, who is 11, recently told me that "email was old fashioned" and she couldn't believe that I used it so heavily for work!

Consider generational differences and the evolution of your workforce. This may all be moot, or there may be a *de facto* acceptance of IM over time, much as there was with email and other, older technologies in companies. It is interesting to note that younger, newer companies never consider the important factors with respect to IM because *they culturally assume it is a right*. This assumption may form the basis of some real conflicts in the years to come. Imagine companies that shut off new technologies being sued over "cruel and unusual" work conditions because they are removing what employees assume to be a right. Of course, this conflict is small now, but it is important to have a process for dealing with new technologies within the corporation rather than being blindsided by them as they emerge or, worse, as a new generation of users find themselves cut off from stimuli and tools that they consider necessary for their job or for their quality of life.

In the end, the first four factors should help you define the following three items:

- Do you need IM as a company?
- Why do employees need it?
  - To do their jobs?
  - To improve efficiency?
  - To do more business?
  - To work with peers?
  - To improve employee satisfaction?
- Who needs it?

Without answers to these questions, which are all about the workforce as a whole, the role of IM will not be easily understood nor established within the company.

Transactions

Some companies have taken a bold step and use IM infrastructure for actual business processes. These are typically younger, fast-growing companies that are looking for more real-time transactions or processes. They typically accept a higher level of risk in general in exchange for greater potential returns. The unfortunate companies are the ones that have built product systems and processes on an IM infrastructure *unknowingly* and now have to deal with potentially unintended consequences of that infrastructure.

How does this happen? The infrastructures for IM on the Internet are large, ubiquitous, and fairly reliable, and it is natural that such infrastructures will get used. As we saw in the section on the evolution of Internet technologies, users will find ways to increase complexity and the value of networks over time, in essence fulfilling

Metcalfe's Law. This is why some companies find that a small team using IM (where a built in business process on an IM application has grown fast, with real-time response times for some processes) has now reached the point where sizeable business and transactions are conducted over IM.

Factor #5

> *Factor #5:* Does your company have a need or dependency on IM to do business?

If this is the case, you need to understand immediately which applications and infrastructures you rely on. You should begin a process for examining the infrastructure and mapping out the business processes:

- Where are the single points of failure?
- Where does liability lie?
- What is availability like?
- What is the impact of downtime on the business?
- What is the business risk?
- What are your disaster recovery and business continuity options?

The answers to these questions will lead to natural action plans and follow the basic rule of acceptable risk for acceptable return, unless you find you have a regulatory implication (in which case, build action plans immediately).

Factor #6

> *Factor #6:* Are you considering deploying a technology or process on an IM infrastructure?

If this is the case, you need to understand immediately which applications and infrastructures you will rely on. You should begin a process for understanding the infrastructure and quantifying and managing the business risk. Again, make sure, as with the workforce, that you in fact need the IM infrastructure in the first place.

5. THE NATURE OF THE THREAT

There are some clear threats, internal and external, and both inadvertent and malicious. These different threats call for the implementation of different countermeasures. Figure 27.1 shows a simple grid of the populations that a security professional will have to consider in the context of their security postures for IM.

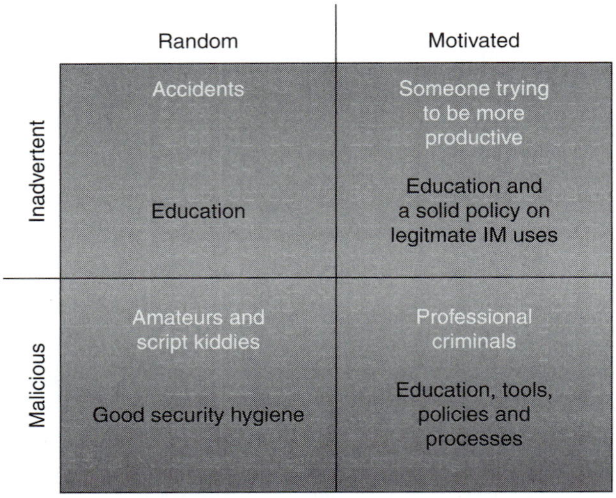

FIGURE 27.1 Populations that present a corporate risk and the correct responses to each.

Malicious Threat

We've looked at the good guys, who are basically looking within the company or are perhaps partners looking to use a powerful, real-time technology for positive reasons: more business with more people more efficiently. Now it is time to look at the bad guys: black hats.[10]

In the "old days," black hats were seen to be young kids in their parents' basements, or perhaps a disgruntled techie with an axe to grind. These were people who would invest a disproportionate amount of time in an activity, spending hundreds of hours to gain fame or notoriety or to enact revenge. This behavior led to the "worm of the week" and macro-viruses. They were, in effect, not a systematic threat but were rather background noise. We will calls these folks "amateurs" for reasons that will become clear.

There have also always been dedicated black hats, or "professionals," who plied their trade for gain or as mercenaries. These folks were at first in the minority and generally hid well among the amateurs. In fact, they had a vested interest in seeing the proliferation of "script kiddies" who could "hack" easily: This activity created background noise against which their actions would go unnoticed. Think of the flow of information and activity, of security incidents as a CSI scene where a smart criminal has visited barber shops, collected discarded hair from the floors, and then liberally spread them around the crime scene to throw off the DNA collection of forensic investigators. This is what the old-world professionals did and why they rejoiced at the "worms of the week" that

provided a constant background noise for them to hide their serious thefts.

Now we come to the modern age, and the professionals are in the majority. The amateurs have grown up and found that they can leave their parents' basements and go out and make money working for real organizations and companies, plying their skills to abuse the Internet and systems for real gain. This is what led to the proliferation of spyware; and because it is an *economic* activity, we can quantify losses and gains for this population and can begin to apply game theory to predicting their behaviors and *the technologies that they will abuse for gain.*

The bad guys are now a vested interest, as has been well documented[11] and analyzed; they are a sustained, real, commercial interest and present a clear and present risk to most IT infrastructures. Keep in mind the following general rules about these online criminals (spammers, spyware writers, virus writers, phishers, pharmers, and the like):

- It is not about ego or a particular trick; they are not above using or abusing any technology.
- They do what they do to make money. This is your money they are taking. They are a risk to you and to your company.
- They are sophisticated; they have supply and distribution agreements and partners, they have SLAs[12] and business relationships, and they even have quality labs and conferences.

In general, online criminals will seek to exploit IM if they can realize value in the target and if they can efficiently go after it. IM represents a technology against which it is easy for black hats to develop exploits, and even relatively small returns (such as a 1% click rate on SPIM, which stands for *spam instant messaging*) would have enormous potential value.

Factor #7

Factor #7: Does the value to the company of information and processes carried over IM represent something that is a valuable target (because it can either affect your business or realize a gain)? This should include the ability to blackmail employees and partners: Can someone learn things about key employees that they could use to threaten or abuse employees and partners?

The answer to this question will help put in perspective the potential for IM technology to be abused.

---

10 This term was a difficult one to choose. I opted not to go with *crackers* or *hackers* but rather with *black hats* because that is the most neutral term to refer to malicious computer exploiters.

11 www.rsa.com/blog/blog.aspx#Security-Blog.
12 Service-level agreement.

Factor #8

> *Factor #8:* If the IM technology were abused or compromised, what would be the risk to the business?

SPIM, worms, viruses, spyware, Trojans, rootkits, backdoors and other threats can spread over IM as readily as email, file shares, and other transmission vectors—in fact, it is arguable that it can spread more readily via IM. Will an incident over IM cause an unacceptable risk to the business? This should be answered in the same way as "Will an incident over email cause an unacceptable risk to the business?" For most organizations the answer should always be yes.

Vulnerabilities

Like any form of software (or hardware), IM applications and infrastructure are subject to vulnerabilities and weaknesses from poor configuration and implementation. Most of these applications do not have the same degree of rigor around maintenance, support, and patching as other enterprise software applications. As a result, it is important to have processes for penetration testing and security audits and to establish a relationship, if possible, with manufacturers and distributors for enterprise caliber support. In many cases, the total cost of ownership of an IM infrastructure and applications may rise considerably to make up for this lack. For this reason, using the freeware services may be a temptation, but the risks may quickly outweigh the savings.

Man-in-the-Middle Attacks

A man-in-the-middle attack is a class of attack in which a third party acts as a legitimate or even invisible broker. As shown in Figure 27.2, an attacker is posing to each user in an IM transaction as a legitimate part of the process while in fact recording or relaying information. This is a common attack philosophy, and without basic mutual authentication or encryption tools, it is inexpensive for black hats to carry out in a wide-scale manner.

As a security professional, it is possible to monitor IM protocols and the IP addresses with which they communicate, allowing IM to and from only certain recognized hubs. Even this is not perfect, because "X-in-the-middle" attacks in their most generic form can include everything from Trojans and keyloggers to line taps. It is also possible to monitor communications among peers, although effectively looking for man-in-the-middle attacks in this way is difficult.

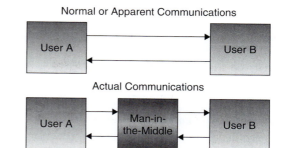

FIGURE 27.2 Normal versus man-in-the-middle communications.

Phishing and Social Engineering

Social engineering is the practice of fooling someone into giving up something they wouldn't otherwise surrender through the use of psychological tricks. Social engineers rely on the normal behavior of people presented with data or a social situation to respond in a predictable, human way. An attack of this sort will rely on presenting trusted logos and a context that seems normal but is in fact designed to create a vulnerability that the social engineer can exploit. This is relevant to IM because people can choose IM identities *similar to ones with whom the user normally communicates*. The simplest attack of all is to get an identity that is similar to a boss, sibling, friend, or spouse and then provide information to get information. Employees should be educated to always directly check with end users to ensure that they are in fact communicating with whom they believe they are communicating.

Knowledge Is the Commodity

It goes without saying that knowledge of business transactions is itself something that can be turned to profit. The contents of a formula, the nature of an experiment, the value and type of a financial transaction are all important to competitors and to speculators. Stock values rise and fall on rumors of activity, and material knowledge of what is happening can be directly translated into profit.

There are companies, organizations, and individuals that launder money and reap huge profits on the basis of insider information and intellectual property, and the bad guys are looking for exactly this information. Know what is being communicated and educate your employees about the open, real-time, and exposed nature of IM. Make sure that you have solid policies on what is acceptable to communicate over IM.

Factor #9

> *Factor #9:* What intellectual property, material information, corporate documents, and transaction data are at risk over IM?

Make sure that you know what people use IM for and, if you do not have the means to control it, consider denying access to IM or implementing content-filtering technologies. With false positives and technology failing to track context of communications, do not rely heavily on a technological answer; make sure you have educational options and that you document use of IM in your environment.

Data and Traffic Analysis

The mere presence of communications is enough, in some circumstances, to indicate material facts about a business or initiative. This is particularly well understood by national governments and interests with "signals intelligence." You do not have to know what someone is saying to have an edge. This has been seen throughout history, with the most obvious and numerous examples during World War II: If you know that someone is communicating, that is in effect intelligence.

Communicating with a lawyer, making a trade, and the synchronizing in real time of that information with public data may construe a material breach if it's intercepted. Wherever possible, artificial traffic levels and data content flags to the outside world should be used to disguise the nature and times of communication for transactions that indicate insider information or transactions that you otherwise wouldn't want the world to know about.

Factor #10

> *Factor #10:* What do transaction types and times tell people about your business? Is it acceptable for people to have access to this information?

Some of the most important events in history have occurred because of intelligence not of *what* was said but rather *how*, and most important *why*, a communication occurred.

Unintentional Threats

Perhaps the most insidious threat isn't the malicious one; it is the inadvertent one. Employees are generally seeking

to do more work more efficiently. This is what leads to them using their public, Web-based emails for working at home rather than only working in the office. Very often people who are working diligently do something to try to work faster, better, or in more places and they inadvertently cause a business risk. These are, in effect, human behaviors that put the company at risk, and the answer is both an educational one and one that can benefit from the use of certain tools.

Intellectual Property Leakage

Just as employees shouldn't leave laptops in cars or work on sensitive documents in public places such as an airport or coffee shop, they also should not use public IM for sensitive material. Intellectual property leakage of source code, insider information, trade secrets, and so on are major risks with IM when used incorrectly, although it should be noted that when deployed correctly, such transactions can be done safely over IM (when encrypted and appropriate, with the right mutual authentication).

Inappropriate Use

As with Web browsing and email, inappropriate use of IM can lead to risks and threats to a business. In particular, IM is an informal medium. People have their own lingo in IM, with acronyms[13] peculiar to the medium (e.g., B4N = bye for now, HAND = have a nice day, IRL = in real life, and so on). The very informal nature of the medium means that it is generally not conducted in a businesslike manner; it is more like our personal interactions and notes. When the social glue of an office becomes less business-oriented, it can lead to inappropriate advances, commentary, and exposure. Outlining inappropriate use of IM, as with any technology, should be part of the general HR policy of a company, and correct business use should be part of a regular regimen of business conduct training.

Factor #11

> *Factor #11:* What unintended exposure could the company face via IM? Which populations have this information and require special training, monitoring, or protection?

Make sure that your company has a strategy for categorization and management of sensitive information, in

---

13 A good source on these is found at AOL (www.aim.com/acronyms. adp).

particular personally identifiable information, trade secrets, and material insider information.

Regulatory Concerns

Last, but far from least, are the things that simply must be protected for legal reasons. In an age where customer information is a responsibility, not a privilege, where credit-card numbers and Social Security numbers are bartered and traded and insider trading can occur in real time (sometimes over IM), it is imperative that regulatory concerns be addressed in an IM policy. If you can't implement governance policies over IM technology, you might have to ban IM use until such time as you can govern it effectively—and you very well may have to take steps to actively root out and remove IM applications, with drastic consequences for those who break the company's IM policy. Examples of these are common in financial institutions, HR organizations, and healthcare organizations.

Factor #12

Factor #12: Do you have regulatory requirements that require a certain IM posture and policy?

No matter how attractive the technology, you may not be able to adopt IM if the regulatory concerns aren't addressed. If you absolutely need it, the project to adopt compliant IM will be driven higher in the priority queue; but the basic regulatory requirement and penalties could be prohibitive if this isn't done with utmost care and attention.

Remember also that some countries have explicit regulations about monitoring employees. In some jurisdictions in Europe and Asia in particular, it is *illegal to monitor employee behavior and actions*. This may seem alien to some in the United States, but multinationals and companies in other regions must conform to employee rights requirements.

6. COMMON IM APPLICATIONS

IM is a fact of life. Now it is time to decide which applications and infrastructures your company can and will be exposed to. You most likely will want to create a policy and to track various uses of IM and develop a posture and educational program about which ones are used in which contexts. You will want to review common IM applications in the consumer or home user domain because they

will find their ways into your environment and onto your assets. For example, many people install IM applications for personal use on laptops that they then take out of the company environment; they aren't using them at work, but those applications are on systems that have company intellectual property and material on them and they are used on insecure networks once they leave the building.

Consumer Instant Messaging

Numbers of subscribers are hard to come by in a consistent manner, although some analyst firms and public sites present disparate numbers. Wikipedia has a current view and commentary on relative sizes of IM networks[14] and concentrations that are worth examining and verifying in a more detailed fashion. The major IM programs are Windows Live Messenger/MSN, Skype, Jabber, AIM, Yahoo! Messenger, and eBuddy. There is also a good comparison of the technologies and infrastructure in use with various tools.[15] Others include a host of smaller applications such as ICQ and local ones, the most notable of which is QQ, which is primarily in China.

It is important to keep in mind who owns the infrastructures for private IM applications. In effect, the IM backbone passes information in the clear (unless an encryption program is used, and the owners of the infrastructure can see and collect data on who is communicating with whom, how, and what they are saying.

It could, for instance, with respect to quarterly earnings or an investigation or lawsuit, be materially important to know with whom the CFO is communicating and at what times. As a result, companies are well advised to educate employees on the risks of IM in general and the acceptable uses for certain applications. It may be acceptable to talk to your husband or wife on Yahoo! or QQ, but is it acceptable to talk to your lawyer that way?

Enterprise Instant Messaging

Some companies, such as IBM and Microsoft, offer IM solutions for internal use only. These are readily deployed and allow for good, real-time communications within the company. They of course do not address the issues of bridging communications with the outside world and the general public, but they are good for meeting some needs for improved productivity and efficiency

---

14 http://en.wikipedia.org/wiki/Instant_messaging.
15 http://en.wikipedia.org/wiki/Comparison_of_instant_messaging_clients.

that are clearly business related. The risk that these pose is in complacency—assuming that the IM application is exclusively used within the organization. Very often, they are used from public places or from private homes and even in some cases from employee-owned assets. As such, the ecosystem for remote access should be carefully considered.

Instant-Messaging Aggregators

There are some programs, such as Trillian,[16] for pulling together multiple IM applications. The danger here is similar to many applications that aggregate passwords or information: They should be legitimate companies, such as Cerulean Studios, with real privacy and security policies. Many illegitimate applications pose as IM aggregators, especially "free" ones, and are really in the business of establishing a spyware presence on PCs, especially corporate-owned PCs. To be clear, there are real, legitimate IM aggregators with real value, and you should look to do business with them, read their end-user license agreements (EULAs), and deploy and manage them correctly. There are also *illegitimate* companies and organizations that manufacture spyware but that pose as IM aggregators; these will come into your environment via well-meaning end users.

Most *illegitimate* applications should be caught with antispyware applications (note that some antivirus applications have antispyware capabilities; verify that this is the case with your vendor) that are resident on PCs, but there are some basic steps you should make sure that your security policies and procedures take into account:

- Make sure that you have antispyware software, that it is up to date and that it is active.
- Make sure that end users know the risks of these applications, especially on noncorporate systems (i.e., home or user-owned systems).
- Make sure that you survey communications into and out of the network for "phone home," especially encrypted communications and that you have a standard policy and procedure on what course of action to take should suspicious communications be discovered.

Backdoors: Instant Messaging Via Other Means (HTML)

Some IM applications have moved to HTML-based integrations with their network. The reason is obvious: This

is a way around the explicit IM protocols being blocked on corporate networks. Employees want to keep using their IM tools for personal or professional reasons, and they are finding workarounds. The obvious counter to this is HTML content filtering, especially at the gateways to networks. If your policy disallows IM, make sure the content-filtering blacklists are sensitive to IM IP addresses and communications. Many IM applications will actively scan for ports that are available on which they can piggyback communications, meaning that if you have any permissive rules for communications, the IM application will find it.

Mobile Dimension

Computing platforms and systems keep getting smaller and converging with their larger cousins; PDAs and phones are everywhere, and most major IM networks have an IM client for BlackBerry, cell phones, and the like. On corporate-owned assets with the latest generation of mobile technologies, it is fairly simple to lock down these applications to conform to the corporate IM policy. In some instances, however, it is more complex, especially in situations where PDAs are employee-owned or managed. In these cases, you actually have a larger potential problem and need a PDA and phone policy; the IM policy is secondary to that.

7. DEFENSIVE STRATEGIES

There are four basic postures that you can take within your company with respect to IM (actually this applies to all end-user applications more generally, although it needs to be rationalized for IM in particular):

- *Ban all IM.* This is the least permissive and most likely to fail over time. It is normally only advisable in cases of extremely high risk and in businesses that are very resistant to technology. This will be the hardest to enforce socially if not technically.
- *Allow internal IM.* This is the most common first step, but it demands a careful understanding and policies and procedures to enforce the ban on *external* or consumer IM.
- *Allow all IM.* Outright allowing all IM is not a common first policy, though some companies on due consideration may consider it.
- *Create a sophisticated IM policy.* This is the most difficult to do, but a sophisticated and granular IM policy, integrated with classic security measures, asset management, and a rigorous information policy,

---

16 Manufactured by Cerulean Studios: http://www.ceruleanstudios.com.

is the hallmark of a mature security organization. Incidentally, many of these exist already. It is not necessary to reinvent all of them if these sorts of policies have already been worked through and are a Web search away.

8. INSTANT-MESSAGING SECURITY MATURITY AND SOLUTIONS

Companies will likely go through an evolution of the security policy with respect to IM. Many (particularly older companies) begin with a ban and wind up over time settling on a sophisticated IM policy that takes into account asset policies, information policies, human behavior, risk, and corporate goals around employee satisfaction, efficiency, and productivity.

Asset Management

Many asset management solutions such as CA Unicenter, IBM Tivoli, and Microsoft SMS manage systems and the software they have. They are most effective for managing corporate-owned assets; make sure that employees have the right tools, correctly licensed and correctly provisioned. They also make sure that rogue, unlicensed software is minimized and can help enforce IM applications bans as in the case of a "ban of all IM" policy or a ban on external or consumer IM.

Built-In Security

Enterprise IM applications are generally the most readily adopted of solutions within a company or organization. Many of these IM platforms and "inside the firewall" IM applications provide some built-in security measures, such as the ability to auto-block inbound requests from unknown parties. Many of these features are good for hardening obvious deficiencies in the systems, but by themselves they do not typically do enough to protect the IM infrastructure.

Keep in mind also that "inside the firewall" is often misleading; people can readily sign on to these applications via virtual private network from outside the firewall or even from home computers, with a little work. Make sure the access policies and security features built into internal applications are understood and engaged correctly.

It is also generally good to ensure that strong authentication (multifactor authentication) is used in cases where people will be gaining remote access to the internal IM application. You want to make sure that the employee in question is in fact the employee and not a family member, friend, or someone who has broken into the employee's home or hotel room.

Content Filtering

A class of relatively new security products has arisen over the past few years specifically designed to do content filtering on IM. These are still not widely adopted and, when adopted, apply to only a limited set of users. Most companies that use these tools are those with strong regulatory requirements and then only to a limited set of users who expose the company most. The most common examples are insiders in financial firms or employees who can access customer data. Real-time leaks in a regulated or privileged environment are generally the most serious drivers here.

Classic Security

The perimeter is dead—long live the Internet. It is almost hackneyed these days to say that perimeter-centric security is dead; firewalls and IDSs aren't the solution. In many ways, modern security is about proving a negative—it can't be done. Human beings seeking to do better at their jobs, to communicate with friends and family, or to actively invade and bypass security will find new ways and new vectors around existing security controls. Having said that, it is important to realize that our job as security professionals is to first remove the inexpensive and easy ways to do get around security controls and then to efficiently *raise the security bar* for getting at what matters: the information. It is important to do a real, quantitative analysis of your cost threshold for the controls you are going to put in place and the amount by which it raises the bar and compare these to the risk and likelihood of loss.

In this regard, the traditional software for perimeter security *still serves a purpose;* in fact, many of these vendors are quite innovative at adding new features and new value over time. The classic products of proxies, corporate firewalls, virtual private networks, intrusion detection, and anti-malware continue to raise the bar for the most simple and inexpensive attack vectors and for stopping inadvertent leakage. This is true of adding layered protection to IM, and the classic security products should be leveraged to raise the security bar (that is, to lower basic business risk). They won't solve the problem, but it is important to use them in a layered approach to reducing business risk.

Compliance

Some industries have strict regulations that require that information be handled in certain ways. These industries have no choice but to comply or face punitive and legal damages and increased risk to their business. It is vital to consult with auditors and compliance departments regarding the implications of IM on corporate compliance.

Also, explicitly keep in mind employee rights legislation that may prohibit monitoring employees' IM communications. There are jurisdictions in which this kind of monitoring is illegal.

Data Loss Prevention

There is a new class of data loss prevention (DLP) product that can discover, classify, categorize, monitor, and enforce information-centric policies (at endpoint, network, datacenter, and "gateway" touchpoints) for a user population—either the whole company or a subset of the workforce population. There are tradeoffs to be made among applications of this type, in particular when it comes to false positives (wrongly identifying information as sensitive) and efficiency at particular times (filtering HR information during benefits enrollment periods or filtering financial-related information at the close of a quarter). This class of product can be massively powerful for enforcing the policy as a useful tool, but its efficiency and impact on *employee* efficiency need to be carefully applied. Further, the vital discovery, classification, and categorization features should be well understood, as should monitoring and enforcement applications.

Logging

Security information and event management (SIEM) systems are only as effective as what they instrument. In combination with content-filtering and DLP, this technology can be extremely effective. The best "real-world" analogy is perhaps insider trading. It is not impossible to commit insider trading, but it isn't as widespread as it could be because the Securities and Exchange Commission (and other regulatory bodies outside the United States) has effective logging and anomaly detection and reporting functions to catch transgressors. Logging in the form of SIEM on the right controls is both a good measure for active protection and a deterrent; just be sure to mention in your education processes that this is happening, to realize the deterrence benefit.

Archival

In conjunction with regulatory requirements, you may have either a process or audit requirement to keep logs for a certain period of time. Archival, storage, and retrieval systems are likely to form an important part of your post-event analysis and investigation and forensics policies and may actually be legally required for regulatory purposes.

9. PROCESSES

The lifeblood of any policy is the process and the people who enforce that policy. You will need a body of processes and owners that is documented and well maintained. Some of the processes you may need include, but aren't limited to, the following.

Instant-Messaging Activation and Provisioning

When someone is legitimately entitled to IM, how specifically do they get access to the application? How are they managed and supported? If you have IM, you will have issues and will have to keep the application and service current and functioning.

Application Review

Make sure that you know the state of the art in IM. Which applications have centralized structures, and what nations and private interests host these? Which applications are poorly written, contain weaknesses or, worse, have remote control vulnerabilities and are potentially spyware?

People

Make sure your IT staff and employees know the policies and why they matter. Business relevance is the best incentive for conformity. Work on adding IM to the corporate ethics, conduct, information, and general training policies.

Revise

Keep the policy up to date and relevant. Policies can easily fall into disuse or irrelevance, and given the nature of advances in Internet technologies, it is vital that you regularly revisit this policy on a quarterly or semiannual basis. Also ensure that your policy is enforceable; a policy that is not enforceable or is counterintuitive is useless.

Audit

Be sure to audit your environment. This is not auditing in the sense of a corporate audit, although that may also be a requirement, but do periodic examinations of network traffic for sessions and traffic that are out of policy. IM will leave proprietary protocol trails and even HTML trails in the network. Look in particular for rogue gateways and rogue proxies that have been set up by employees to work around the corporate policy.

10. CONCLUSION

Remember game theory with respect to your workforce and business; people will find ways to do more with the tools, networks, and systems at their disposal. They will find ways to use ungoverned technology, such as IM, to do more things with more people more efficiently. The siren call of real-time communications is too much to resist for a motivated IT department and a motivated workforce who want to do more with the tools that are readily available to them.

Let's review a few lists and what you must consider in formulating an IM security policy—and remember that this must always be *in service* to the business. In the following sidebar, "The 12 Factors," consider the factors and the posture in which these put you and your company.

The 12 Factors

Factor #1: Do your employees need IM? If so, which employees need IM and *what do they need it for?*

Factor #2: Is IM important as a job satisfaction component?

Factor #3: Does IM improve or lessen efficiency?

Factor #4: Will this efficiency change over time, or is it in fact different for different demographics of my workforce?

Factor #5: Does your company have a need or dependency on IM to do business?

Factor #6: Are you considering deploying a technology or process on an IM infrastructure?

Factor #7: Does the value to the company of information and processes carried over IM represent something that is a valuable target (because it can either affect your business or realize a gain)? This should include the ability to blackmail employees and partners; can someone learn things about key employees that they could use to threaten or abuse employees and partners?

Factor #8: If the IM technology were abused or compromised, what would be the risk to the business?

Factor #9: What intellectual property, material information, corporate documents, and transaction information is at risk over IM?

Factor #10: What do transaction types and times tell people about your business? Is it okay for people to have access to this information?

Factor #11: What unintended exposure could the company face via IM? Which populations have this information and require special training, monitoring, or protection?

Factor #12: Do you have regulatory requirements that require a certain IM posture and policy?

Now consider your responses to these factors in the context of your employees, your partners, your competitors, and the active threats your company will face. Next, consider the basic risks and returns and the infrastructure that you deploy:

- Where are the single points of failure?
- Where does liability lie?
- What is availability like?
- What is the impact of downtime on the business?
- What is the business risk?
- What are your disaster recovery and business continuity options?

Last, consider regulatory requirements and the basic business assets you must protect. You will most likely have to create or update your security policy to consider IM. This will mean having a posture on the following items, at a minimum:

- You must have formal, written policies for each of the following:
  - Intellectual property identification, monitoring, and protection
  - Sensitive information identification, monitoring, and protection
  - Entitlements by role for IM specifically
  - Legitimate, accepted uses for IM and specifically prohibited ones (if any)
  - Monitoring of IM traffic
  - Enforcement of IM policies
  - Logging of IM traffic
  - Archival of IM logs
  - Regulatory requirements and needs and the processes to satisfy them around IM
- Education
  - With respect to IM
  - With respect to regulations
  - With respect to intellectual property

Acme Inc.'s Answers to the 12 Factors

Factor #1: Do your employees need IM? If so, which employees need IM and *what do they need it for?*

Yes! All nonline working employees should have IM to allow for increased internal communications.

Factor #2: Is IM important as a job satisfaction component?

Yes!

Factor #3: Does IM improve or lessen efficiency?

IM should improve efficiency by allowing employees to get immediate answers/results and to be able to pull groups together quickly, compared to emails.

Factor #4: Will this efficiency change over time, or is it in fact different for different demographics of my workforce?

Efficiency should grow as adoption and comfort levels with IM technologies grow.

Factor #5: Does your company have a need for or dependency on IM to do business?

IM cannot be used for external business transactions or discussions.

Factor #6: Are you considering deploying a technology or process on an IM infrastructure?

Yes. We would need to implement an internal tool to perform IM services.

Factor #7: Does the value to the company of information and processes carried over IM represent something that is a valuable target (because it can either affect your business or realize a gain)? This should include the ability to blackmail employees and partners; can someone learn things about key employees that they could use to threaten or abuse employees and partners?

Yes. All IM communications must remain internal.

Factor #8: If the IM technology were abused or compromised, what would be the risk to the business?

Data loss: intellectual property.

Business plan loss: Sensitive information that we can't afford to let the competition see.

Customer data theft: Some Personally Identifiable Information (PII), but all customer-related information is treated as PII.

Factor #9: What intellectual property, material information, corporate documents, and transaction information is at risk over IM?

All internal data would be at risk.

Factor #10: What do transaction types and times tell people about your business? Is it okay for people to have access to this information?

Data will always remain on a need-to-know basis and the IM implementation must not result in the loss of data.

Factor #11: What unintended exposure could the company face via IM? Which populations have this information and require special training, monitoring, or protection?

Unintentional internal transfer of restricted data to internal staff without the required internal clearances.

Factor #12: Do you have regulatory requirements that require a certain IM posture and policy?

We are under PCI, HIPAA, ISO 27001, and SAS70 Type II guidelines.

- With respect to social engineering
- About enforcement, monitoring, and archival requirements (remember that these can have a deterrence benefit)
- Applications
  - Dealing with consumer IM and the applications employees will try to use
  - Internal, enterprise IM applications
  - Asset management
- Processes
  - Provisioning IM and accounts
  - Deprovisioning (via asset management processes) illegal IM clients
  - Revoking IM entitlements and accounts
- Do you have basic security hygiene configured correctly for an environment that includes IM?
  - Asset management software
  - Firewalls and proxies
  - Intrusion detection systems
  - Anti-malware
  - Virtual private networks and remote access
  - Strong authentication

- Advanced security
  - Monitoring and enforcement with DLP
  - Monitoring and SIEM

IM, like any other technology, can serve the business or be a risk to it. The best situation of all is where it is quantified like any other technology and helps promote the ability to attract talent and keep it while serving the business—driving more business with more people more efficiently and while minimizing risk for business return.

Example Answers to Key Factors

Let's take the example of Acme Inc., as shown in the sidebar, "Acme Inc.'s Answers to the 12 Factors." Acme is a publicly traded company that has international offices and groups that span geographies.

Giving answers to these simple questions mean that the scope of risk and the business relevance is known. These answers can now be used to formulate a security policy and begin the IT projects that are needed for enforcement and monitoring.

Part IV

Privacy and Access Management

## Chapter 28

NET Privacy

Marco Cremonini
University of Milan

Chiara Braghin
University of Milan

Claudio Agostino Ardagna
University of Milan

In recent years, large-scale computer networks have become an essential aspect of our daily computing environment. We often rely on a global information infrastructure for ebusiness activities such as home banking, ATM transactions, or shopping online. One of the main scientific and technological challenges in this setting has been to provide security to individuals who operate in possibly untrusted and unknown environments. However, beside threats directly related to computer intrusions, epidemic diffusion of malware, and outright frauds conducted online, a more subtle though increasing erosion of individuals' privacy has progressed and multiplied. Such an escalating violation of privacy has some direct harmful consequences—for example, identity theft has spread in recent years—and negative effects on the general perception of insecurity that many individuals now experience when dealing with online services.

Nevertheless, protecting personal privacy from the many parties—business, government, social, or even criminal—that examine the value of personal information is an old concern of modern society, now increased by the features of the digital infrastructure. In this chapter, we address these privacy issues in the digital society from different points of view, investigating:

- The various aspects of the notion of privacy and the debate that the intricate essence of privacy has stimulated
- The most common privacy threats and the possible economic aspects that may influence the way privacy is (and especially is not, in its current status) managed in most firms

- The efforts in the computer science community to face privacy threats, especially in the context of mobile and database systems
- The network-based technologies available to date to provide anonymity in user communications over a private network

1. PRIVACY IN THE DIGITAL SOCIETY

Privacy in today's digital society is one of the most debated and controversial topics. Many different opinions about what privacy actually is and how it could be preserved have been expressed, but still we can set no clear-cut border that cannot be trespassed if privacy is to be safeguarded.

The Origins, The Debate

As often happens when a debate heats up, the extremes speak louder and, about privacy, the extremes are those that advocate the ban of the disclosure of whatever personal information and those that say that all personal information is already out there, therefore privacy is dead. Supporters of the wide deployment and use of anonymizing technologies are perhaps the best representatives of one extreme. The chief executive officer of Sun Microsystems, Scott McNealy, with his "Get over it" comment, has gained large notoriety for championing the other extreme opinion.[1]

---

1 P. Sprenger, "Sun on privacy: 'get over it,'" *WIRED*, 1999, www.wired.com/politics/law/news/1999/01/17538.

However, these are just the extremes; in reality net privacy is a fluid concept that such radical positions cannot fully contain. It is a fact that even those supporting full anonymity recognize that there are several limitations to its adoption, either technical or functional. On the other side, even the most skeptical cannot avoid dealing with privacy issues, either because of laws and norms or because of common sense. Sun Microsystems, for example, is actually supporting privacy protection and is a member of the Online Privacy Alliance, an industry coalition that fosters the protection of individuals' privacy online.

Looking at the origins of the concept of privacy, Aristotle's distinction between the public sphere of politics and the private sphere of the family is often considered the root. Much later, the philosophical and anthropological debate around these two spheres of an individual's life evolved. John Stuart Mill, in his essay, *On Liberty*, introduced the distinction between the realm of governmental authority as opposed to the realm of self-regulation. Anthropologists such as Margaret Mead have demonstrated how the need for privacy is innate in different cultures that protect it through concealment or seclusion or by restricting access to secret ceremonies.

More pragmatically, back in 1898, the concept of privacy was expressed by U.S. Supreme Court Justice Brandeis, who defined privacy as "The right to be let alone."[2] This straightforward definition represented for decades the reference of any normative and operational privacy consideration and derivate issues and, before the advent of the digital society, a realistically enforceable ultimate goal. The Net has changed the landscape because the very concept of being let alone while interconnected becomes fuzzy and fluid.

In 1948, privacy gained the status of fundamental right of any individual, being explicitly mentioned in the United Nations Universal Declaration of Human Rights (Article 12): "No one shall be subjected to arbitrary interference with his privacy, family, home or correspondence, nor to attacks upon his honour and reputation. Everyone has the right to the protection of the law against such interference or attacks."[3] However, although privacy has been recognized as a fundamental right of each individual, the Universal Declaration of Human Rights does not explicitly define what privacy is, except for relating it to possible interference or attacks.

About the digital society, less rigorously but otherwise effectively in practical terms, in July 1993, *The New Yorker* published a brilliant cartoon by Peter Steiner that since then has been cited and reproduced dozen of times to refer to the supposed intrinsic level of privacy—here in the sense of anonymity or hiding personal traits—that can be achieved by carrying out social relations over the Internet. That famous cartoon shows one dog that types on a computer keyboard and says to the other one: "On the Internet, no one knows you're a dog."[4] The Internet, at least at the very beginning of its history, was not perceived as threatening to individuals' privacy; rather, it was seen as increasing it, sometimes too much, since it could easily let people disguise themselves in the course of personal relationships. Today that belief may look naïve with the rise of threats to individual privacy that have accompanied the diffusion of the digital society. Nevertheless, there is still truth in that cartoon because, whereas privacy is much weaker on the Net than in real space, concealing a person's identity and personal traits is technically even easier. Both aspects concur and should be considered.

Yet an unambiguous definition of the concept of privacy has still not been produced, nor has an assessment of its actual value and scope. It is clear, however, that with the term *privacy* we refer to a fundamental right and an innate feeling of every individual, not to a vague and mysterious entity. An attempt to give a precise definition at least to some terms that are strictly related to (and often used in place of) the notion of privacy can be found in[5,6], where the differences among *anonymity, unobservability,* and *unlinkability* are pointed out. In the digital society scenario, anonymity is defined as the state of not being identifiable, unobservability as the state of being indistinguishable, and unlinkability as the impossibility of correlating two or more actions/items/pieces of information. Privacy, however defined and valued, is a tangible state of life that must be attainable in both the physical and the digital society.

The reason that in the two realms—the physical and the digital—privacy behaves differently has been widely debated, too, and many of the critical factors that make

---

2 S. D. Warren, and L. D. Brandeis, "The right to privacy," *Harvard Law Review*, Vol. IV, No. 5, 1890.

3 United Nations, *Universal Declaration of Human Rights*, 1948, www.un.org/Overview/rights.html.

4 P. Steiner, "On the Internet, nobody knows you're a dog," Cartoonbank, *The New Yorker*, 1993, www.cartoonbank.com/item/22230.

5 A. Pfitzmann, and M. Waidner, "Networks without user observability – design options," *Proceedings of Workshop on the Theory and Application of Cryptographic Techniques on Advances in Cryptology (EuroCrypt'85)*, Vol. 219 LNCS Springer, Linz, Austria, pp. 245–253, 1986.

6 A. Pfitzmann, and M. Köhntopp, "Anonymity, unobservability, and pseudonymity—a proposal for terminology," in *Designing Privacy Enhancing Technologies*, Springer Berlin, pp. 1–9, 2001.

a difference in the two realms, the impact of technology and the Internet, have been spelled out clearly. However, given the threats and safeguards that technologies make possible, it often remains unclear what the goal of preserving net privacy should be—being that extreme positions are deemed unacceptable.

Lessig, in his book *Free Culture*,[7] provided an excellent explanation of the difference between privacy in the physical and in the digital world: "The highly inefficient architecture of real space means we all enjoy a fairly robust amount of privacy. That privacy is guaranteed to us by friction. Not by law [...] and in many places, not by norms [...] but instead, by the costs that friction imposes on anyone who would want to spy. [...] Enter the Internet, where the cost of tracking browsing in particular has become quite tiny. [...] The friction has disappeared, and hence any 'privacy' protected by the friction disappears, too."

Thus, privacy can be seen as the friction that reduces the spread of personal information, that makes it more difficult and economically inconvenient to gain access to it. The merit of this definition is to put privacy into a relative perspective, which excludes the extremes that advocate no friction at all or so much friction to stop the flow of information. It also reconciles privacy with security, being both aimed at setting an acceptable level of protection while allowing the development of the digital society and economy rather than focusing on an ideal state of perfect security and privacy.

Even in an historic perspective, the analogy with friction has sense. The natural path of evolution of a technology is first to push for its spreading and best efficiency. When the technology matures, other requirements come to the surface and gain importance with respect to mere efficiency and functionalities. Here, those frictions that have been eliminated because they are a waste of efficiency acquire new meaning and become the way to satisfy the new requirements, in terms of either safety or security, or even privacy. It is a sign that a technology has matured but not yet found a good balance between old and new requirements when nonfunctional aspects such as security or privacy become critical because they are not well managed and integrated.

Privacy Threats

Threats to individual privacy have become publicly appalling since July 2003, when the California Security Breach Notification Law[8] went into effect. This law was the first one to force state government agencies, companies, and nonprofit organizations that conduct business in California to notify California customers if personally identifiable information (PII) stored unencrypted in digital archives was, or is reasonably believed to have been, acquired by an unauthorized person.

The premise for this law was the rise of *identity theft*, which is the conventional expression that has been used to refer to the illicit impersonification carried out by fraudsters who use PII of other people to complete electronic transactions and purchases. The California Security Breach Notification Law lists, as PII: Social Security number, driver's license number, California Identification Card number, bank account number, credit- or debit-card number, security codes, access codes, or passwords that would permit access to an individual's financial account.[8] By requiring by law the immediate notification to the PII owners, the aim is to avoid direct consequences such as financial losses and derivate consequences such as the burden to restore an individual's own credit history. Starting on January 1, 2008, California's innovative data security breach notification law also applies to medical information and health insurance data.

Besides the benefits to consumers, this law has been the trigger for similar laws in the United States—today, the majority of U.S. states have one—and has permitted the flourishing of regular statistics about privacy breaches, once almost absent. Privacy threats and analyses are now widely debated, and research focused on privacy problems has become one of the most important. Figure 28.1 shows a chart produced by plotting data collected by Attrition.org Data Loss Archive and Database,[9] one of the most complete references for privacy breaches and data losses.

Looking at the data series, we see that some breaches are strikingly large. Etiolated.org maintains some statistics based on Attrition.org's database: In 2007, about 94 million records were hacked at TJX stores in the United States; confidential details of 25 million children have been lost by HM Revenue & Customs, U.K.; the Dai Nippon Printing Company in Tokyo lost more than 8 million records; data about 8.5 million people stored by a subsidiary of Fidelity National Information Services

---

7 L. Lessig, *Free Culture*, Penguin Group, 2003, www.free-culture.cc/.

8 California Security Breach Notification Law, Bill Number: SB 1386, February 2002, http://info.sen.ca.gov/pub/01-02/bill/sen/sb_1351-1400/sb_1386_bill_20020926_chaptered.html.

9 Attrition.org Data Loss Archive and Database (DLDOS), 2008, http://attrition.org/dataloss/.

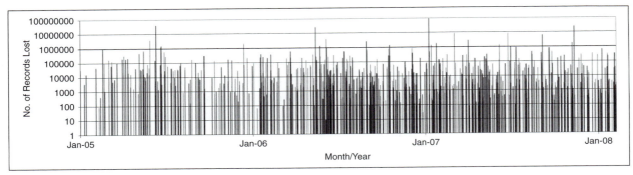

FIGURE 28.1 Privacy breaches from the Attrition.org Data Loss Archive and Database up to March 2008 (X-axis: Years 2000–2008; Y-axis (logarithmic): PII records lost).

were stolen and sold for illegal usage by a former employee. Similar paths were reported in previous years as well. In 2006, personal data of about 26.5 million U.S. military veterans was stolen from the residence of a Department of Veterans Affairs data analyst who improperly took the material home. In 2005, CardSystems Solutions—a credit card processing company managing accounts for Visa, MasterCard, and American Express—exposed 40 million debit- and credit-card accounts in a cyber break-in. In 2004, an employee of America Online Inc. stole 92 million email addresses and sold them to spammers. Still recently, in March 2008, Hannaford Bros. supermarket chain announced that, due to a security breach, about 4.2 million customer credit and debit card numbers were stolen.[10]

Whereas these incidents are the most notable, the phenomenon is distributed over the whole spectrum of breach sizes (see Figure 28.1). Hundreds of privacy breaches are reported in the order of a few thousand records lost and all categories of organizations are affected, from public agencies, universities, banks and financial institutions, manufacturing and retail companies, and so on.

The survey *Enterprise@Risk: 2007 Privacy & Data Protection*, conducted by Deloitte & Touche and Ponemon Institute,[11] provides another piece of data about the incidence of privacy breaches. Among the survey's respondents, over 85% reported at least one breach and about 63% reported multiple breaches requiring notification during the same time period. Breaches involving over 1000 records were reported by 33.9% of respondents; of those, almost 10% suffered data losses of more than 25,000 records. Astonishingly, about 21% of respondents

were not able to estimate the record loss. The picture that results is that of a pervasive management problem with regard to PII and its protection, which causes a continuous leakage of chunks of data and a few dramatic breakdowns when huge archives are lost or stolen.

It is interesting to analyze the root causes for such breaches and the type of information involved. One source of information is the *Educational Security Incidents (ESI) Year in Review–2007*,[12] by Adam Dodge. This survey lists all breaches that occurred worldwide during 2007 at colleges and universities around the world.

Concerning the causes of breaches, the results over a total of 139 incidents are:

- 38% are due to unauthorized disclosure
- 28% to theft (disks, laptops)
- 22% to penetration/hacking
- 9% to loss of data

Therefore, incidents to be accounted for by mismanagement by employees (unauthorized disclosure and loss) account for 47%, whereas criminal activity (penetration/hacking and theft) account for 40%.

With respect to the type of information exposed during these breaches, the result is that:

- PII have been exposed in 42% of incidents
- Social Security numbers in 34%
- Educational information in 11%
- Financial information in 7%
- Medical information in 5%
- Login accounts in 2%

Again, rather than direct economic consequences or illicit usage of computer facilities, such breaches represents threats to individual privacy.

---

10 Etiolated.org, "Shedding light on who's doing what with your private information," 2008, http://etiolated.org/.

11 Deloitte & Touche LLP and Ponemon Institute LLC, *Enterprise@ Risk: 2007 Privacy & Data Protection Survey*, 2007, www.deloitte. com/dtt/cda/doc/content/us_risk_s%26P_2007%20Privacy10Dec2007 final.pdf.

12 A. Dodge, *Educational Security Incidents (ESI) Year in Review 2007*, 2008. www.adamdodge.com/esi/yir_2006.

TABLE 28.1 Root causes of data breaches, 2006

	Private Sector (126 Incidents)	Public Sector (Inc. Military; 114 Incidents)	Higher Education (52 Incidents)	Medical Centers (30 Incidents)
Outside hackers	15%	13%	40%	3%
Insider malfeasance	10%	5%	2%	20%
Human/software incompetence	20%	44%	21%	20%
Theft (non-laptop)	15%	17%	17%	17%
Laptop theft	40%	21%	20%	40%

Source: *Privacy Rights Clearinghouse.*

Privacy Rights Clearinghouse is another organization that provides excellent data and statistics about privacy breaches. Among other things, it is particularly remarkable for its analysis of root causes for different sectors, namely the private sector, the public sector (military included), higher education, and medical centers.[13] Table 28.1 reports its findings for 2006.

Comparing these results with the previous statistics, the *Educational Security Incidents (ESI) Year in Review–2007*, breaches caused by hackers in universities look remarkably different. Privacy Rights ClearingHouse estimates as largely prevalent the external criminal activity (hackers and theft), which accounts for 77%, and internal problems, which account for 19%, whereas in the previous study the two classes were closer with a prevalence of internal problems.

Hasan and Yurcik[14] analyzed data about privacy breaches that occurred in 2005 and 2006 by fusing datasets maintained by Attrition.org and Privacy Rights ClearingHouse. The overall result partially clarifies the discrepancy that results from the previous two analyses. In particular, it emerges that considering the number of privacy breaches, education institutions are the most exposed, accounting for 35% of the total, followed by companies (25%) and state-level public agencies, medical centers, and banks (all close to 10%). However, by considering personal records lost by sector, companies lead the score with 35.5%, followed by federal agencies with 29.5%, medical centers with 16%, and banks with 11.6%. Educational institutions record a lost total of just 2.7% of the whole. Therefore, though universities are victimized by huge numbers of external attacks that cause a continuous leakage of PII, companies and federal agencies are those that have suffered or provoked ruinous losses of enormous archives of PII. For these sectors, the impact of external Internet attacks has been matched or even exceeded by internal fraud or misconduct.

The case of consumer data broker ChoicePoint, Inc., is perhaps the one that got the most publicity as an example of bad management practices that led to a huge privacy incident.[15] In 2006, the Federal Trade Commission charged that ChoicePoint violated the Fair Credit Reporting Act (FCRA) by furnishing consumer reports—credit histories—to subscribers who did not have a permissible purpose to obtain them and by failing to maintain reasonable procedures to verify both their identities and how they intended to use the information.[16]

The opinion that threats due to hacking have been overhyped with respect to others is one shared by many in the security community. In fact, it appears that root causes of privacy breaches, physical thefts (of laptops, disks, and portable memories) and bad management practices (sloppiness, incompetence, and scarce allocation of resources) need to be considered at least as serious as hacking. This is confirmed by the survey *Enterprise@Risk: 2007 Privacy & Data Protection*,[11] which concludes that most enterprise privacy programs are just in the early or middle stage of the maturity cycle. Requirements imposed by laws and regulations have the

13 Privacy Rights ClearingHouse, *Chronology of Data Breaches 2006: Analysis, 2007,* www.privacyrights.org/ar/DataBreaches2006-Analysis.htm.

14 R. Hasan, and W. Yurcik, "Beyond media hype: Empirical analysis of disclosed privacy breaches 2005–2006 and a dataset/database foundation for future work," *Proceedings of Workshop on the Economics of Securing the Information Infrastructure*, Washington, 2006.

15 S. D. Scalet, "The five most shocking things about the ChoicePoint data security breach," CSO online, 2005, www.csoonline.com/article/220340.

16 Federal Trade Commission (FTC), "ChoicePoint settles data security breach charges; to pay $10 million in civil penalties, $5 million for consumer redress, 2006," www.ftc.gov/opa/2006/01/choicepoint.shtm.

highest rates of implementation; operational processes, risk assessment, and training programs are less adopted. In addition, a minority of organizations seem able to implement measurable controls, a deficiency that makes privacy management intrinsically feeble. Training programs dedicated to privacy, security, and risk management look at the weakest spot. Respondents report that training on privacy and security is offered just annually (about 28%), just once (about 36.5%), or never (about 11%). Risk management is never the subject of training for almost 28% of respondents. With such figures, it is no surprise if internal negligence due to unfamiliarity with privacy problems or insufficient resources is such a relevant root cause for privacy breaches.

The ChoicePoint incident is paradigmatic of another important aspect that has been considered for analyzing privacy issues. The breach involved 163,000 records and it was carried out with the explicit intention of unauthorized parties to capture those records. However, actually, in just 800 cases (about 0.5%), that breach leads to identity theft, a severe offense suffered by ChoicePoint customers. Some analysts have questioned the actual value of privacy, which leads us to discuss an important strand of research about economic aspects of privacy.

2. THE ECONOMICS OF PRIVACY

The existence of strong economic factors that influence the way privacy is managed, breached, or even traded off has long been recognized.[17,18] However, it was with the expansion of the online economy, in the 1990s and 2000s, that privacy and economy become more and more entangled. Many studies have been produced to investigate, from different perspectives and approaches, the relation between the two. A comprehensive survey of works that analyzed the economic aspects of privacy can be found in[19].

Two issues among the many have gained most of the attention: assessing the value of privacy and examining to what extent privacy and business can coexist or are inevitably conflicting one with the other. For both issues the debate is still open and no ultimate conclusion has been reached yet.

The Value of Privacy

To ascertain the value of privacy on the one hand, people assign high value to their privacy when asked; on the other hand, privacy is more and more eroded and given away for small rewards. Several empirical studies have tested individuals' behavior when they are confronted with the decision to trade off privacy for some rewards or incentives and when confronted with the decision to pay for protecting their personal information. The approaches to these studies vary, from investigating the actual economic factors that determine people's choices to the psychological motivation and perception of risk or safety.

Syverson,[20] then Shostack and Syverson,[21] analyzed the apparently irrational behavior of people who claim to highly value privacy and then, in practice, are keen to release personal information for small rewards. The usual conclusion is that people are not actually able to assess the value of privacy or that they are either irrational or unaware of the risks they are taking. Though there is evidence that risks are often miscalculated or just unknown by most people, there are also some valid reasons that justify such paradoxical behavior. In particular, the analysis points to the cost of examining and understanding privacy policies and practices, which often make privacy a complex topic to manage. Another observation regards the cost of protecting privacy, which is often inaccurately allocated. Better reallocation would also provide government and business with incentives to increase rather than decrease protection of individual privacy.

One study that dates to 1999, by Culnan and Armstrong,[22] investigated how firms that demonstrate to adopt fair procedures and ethical behavior can mitigate consumer concerns about privacy. Their finding was that consumers who perceive that the collection of personal information is ruled by fair procedures are more willing to release their data for marketing use. This supported the hypothesis that most privacy concerns are motivated by an unclear or distrustful stance toward privacy protection that firms often exhibit.

17 J. Hirshleifer, "The private and social value of information and the reward to inventive activity," *American Economic Review*, Vol. 61, pp. 561–574, 1971.

18 R. A. Posner, "The economics of privacy," *American Economic Review*, Vol. 71, No. 2, pp. 405–409, 1981.

19 K. L. Hui, and I. P. L. Png, "Economics of privacy," in terrence hendershott (ed.), *Handbooks in Information Systems, Vol. 1*, Elsevier, pp. 471–497, 2006.

20 P. Syverson, "The paradoxical value of privacy," *Proceedings of the 2nd Annual Workshop on Economics and Information Security (WEIS 2003)*, 2003.

21 A. Shostack, and P. Syverson, "What price privacy? (and why identity theft is about neither identity nor theft)," In *Economics of Information Security*, Chapter 11, Kluwer Academic Publishers, 2004.

22 M. Culnan, and P. Armstrong, "Information privacy concerns, procedural fairness, and impersonal trust: an empirical evidence," *Organization Science*, Vol. 10, No. 1, pp. 104–1, 51999.

In 2007, Tsai et al.[23] published research that addresses much the same issue. The effect of privacy concerns on online purchasing decisions has been tested and the results are again that the role of incomplete information in privacy-relevant decisions is essential. Consumers are sensitive to the way privacy is managed and to what extent a merchant is trustful. However, in another study, Grosslack and Acquisti[24] found that individuals almost always choose to sell their personal information when offered small compensation rather than keep it confidential.

Hann, Lee, Hui, and Png have carried out a more analytic work in two studies about online information privacy. This strand of research[25] estimated how much privacy is worth for individuals and how economic incentives, such as monetary rewards and future convenience, could influence such values. Their main findings are that individuals do not esteem privacy as an absolute value; rather, information is available to trade off for economic benefits, and that improper access and secondary use of personal information are the most important classes of privacy violation. In the second work,[26] the authors considered firms that tried to mitigate privacy concerns by offering privacy policies regarding the handling and use of personal information and by offering benefits such as financial gains or convenience. These strategies have been analyzed in the context of the information processing theory of motivation, which considers how people form expectations and make decisions about what behavior to choose. Again, whether a firm may offer only partially complete privacy protection or some benefits, economic rewards and convenience have been found to be strong motivators for increasing individuals' willingness to disclose personal information.

Therefore, most works seems to converge to the same conclusion: Whether individuals react negatively when incomplete or distrustful information about privacy is presented, even a modest monetary reward is often sufficient for disclosing one's personal information.

Privacy and Business

The relationship between privacy and business has been examined from several angles by considering which incentives could be effective for integrating privacy with business processes and, instead, which disincentives make business motivations to prevail over privacy.

Froomkin[27] analyzed what he called "privacy-destroying technologies" developed by governments and businesses. Examples of such technologies are collections of transactional data, automated surveillance in public places, biometric technologies, and tracking mobile devices and positioning systems. To further aggravate the impact on privacy of each one of these technologies, their combination and integration result in a cumulative and reinforcing effect. On this premise, Froomkin introduces the role that legal responses may play to limit this apparently unavoidable "death of privacy."

Odlyzko[28,29,30,31] is a leading author that holds a pessimistic view of the future of privacy, calling "unsolvable" the problem of granting privacy because of price discrimination pressures on the market. His argument is based on the observation that the markets as a whole, especially Internet-based markets, have strong incentives to price discriminate, that is, to charge varying prices when there are no cost justifications for the differences. This practice, which has its roots long before the advent of the Internet and the modern economy—one of the most illustrative examples is 19th-century railroad pricing practices—provides relevant economic benefits to the vendors and, from a mere economic viewpoint, to the efficiency of the economy. In general, charging different prices to different segments of the customer base

23 J. Tsai, S. Egelman, L. Cranor, and A. Acquisti, "The effect of online privacy information on purchasing behavior: an experimental study," *Workshop on Economics and Information Security (WEIS 2007)*, 2007.

24 J. Grossklags, and A. Acquisti, "When 25 cents is too much: an experiment on willingness-to-sell and willingness-to-protect personal information," *Proceedings of Workshop on the Economics of Information Security (WEIS)*, Pittsburgh, 2007.

25 Il-H. Hann, K. L. Hui, T. S. Lee, and I. P. L. Png, "Online information privacy: measuring the cost-benefit trade-off," *Proceedings, 23rd International Conference on Information Systems*, Barcelona, Spain, 2002.

26 Il-H. Hann, K. L. Hui, T. S. Lee, and I. P. L. Png, "Analyzing online information privacy concerns: an information processing theory approach," *Journal of Management Information Systems*, Vol. 24, No. 2, pp. 13–42, 2007.

27 A. M. Froomkin, "The death of privacy?," 52 *Stanford Law Review*, pp. 1461–1469, 2000.

28 Odlyzko, A. M., "Privacy, economics, and price discrimination on the internet," *Proceedings of the Fifth International Conference on Electronic Commerce (ICEC2003)*, N. Sadeh (ed.), ACM, pp. 355–366, 2003.

29 A. M. Odlyzko, "The unsolvable privacy problem and its implications for security technologies," *Proceedings of the 8th Australasian Conference on Information Security and Privacy (ACISP 2003)*, R. Safavi-Naini and J. Seberry (eds.), Lecture Notes in Computer Science 2727, Springer, pp. 51–54, 2003.

30 A. M. Odlyzko, "The evolution of price discrimination in transportation and its implications for the Internet," *Review of Network Economics*, Vol. 3, No. 3, pp. 323–346, 2004.

31 A. M. Odlyzko, "Privacy and the clandestine evolution of ecommerce," *Proceedings of the Ninth International Conference on Electronic Commerce (ICEC2007)*, ACM, 2007.

permits vendors to complete transactions that would not take place otherwise. On the other hand, the public has often contrasted plain price discrimination practices since they perceive them as unfair. For this reason, many less evident price discrimination practices are in place today, among which bundling is one of the most recurrent. Privacy of actual and prospective customers is threatened by such economic pressures toward price discrimination because the more the customer base can be segmented—and thus known with greatest detail—the better efficiency is achieved for vendors. The Internet-based market has provided a new boost to such practices and to the acquisition of personal information and knowledge of customer habits.

Empirical studies seem to confirm such pessimistic views. A first review of the largest privately held companies listed in the Forbes Private 50[32] and a second study of firms listed in the Fortune 500[33] demonstrate a poor state of privacy policies adopted in such firms. In general, privately held companies are more likely to lack privacy policies than public companies and are more reluctant to publicly disclose their procedures relative to fair information practices. Even the larger set of the Fortune 500 firms exhibited a large majority of firms that are just mildly addressing privacy concerns.

More pragmatically, some analyses have pointed out that given the current privacy concerns, an explicitly fair management of customers' privacy may become a positive competitive factor.[34] Similarly, Hui et al.[35] have identified seven types of benefits that Internet businesses can provide to consumers in exchange for their personal information.

3. PRIVACY-ENHANCING TECHNOLOGIES

Technical improvements of Web and location technologies have fostered the development of online applications that use the private information of users (including physical position of individuals) to offer enhanced services. The increasing amount of available personal data and the decreasing cost of data storage and processing make it technically possible and economically justifiable to gather and analyze large amounts of data. Also, information technology gives organizations the power to manage and disclose users' personal information without restrictions. In this context, users are much more concerned about their privacy, and privacy has been recognized as one of the main reasons that prevent users from using the Internet for accessing online services. Today's global networked infrastructure requires the ability for parties to communicate in a secure environment while preserving their privacy. Support for digital identities and definition of privacy-enhanced protocols and techniques for their management and exchange then become fundamental requirements.

A number of useful privacy-enhancing technologies (PETs) have been developed for dealing with privacy issues, and previous works on privacy protection have focused on a wide variety of topics.[36,37,38,39,40,41] In this section, we discuss the privacy protection problem in three different contexts. We start by describing languages for the specification of access control policies and privacy preferences. We then describe the problem of data privacy protection, giving a brief description of some solutions. Finally, we analyze the problem of protecting privacy in mobile and pervasive environments.

Languages for Access Control and Privacy Preferences

Access control systems have been introduced for regulating and protecting access to resources and data owned

32 A. R. Peslak, "Privacy policies of the largest privately held companies: a review and analysis of the Forbes private 50," *Proceedings of the ACM SIGMIS CPR Conference on Computer Personnel Research*, Atlanta, 2005.

33 K. S. Schwaig, G. C. Kane, and V. C. Storey, "Compliance to the fair information practices: how are the fortune 500 handling online privacy disclosures?," *Inf. Manage.*, Vol. 43, No. 7, pp. 805–820, 2006.

34 M. Brown, and R. Muchira, "Investigating the relationship between internet privacy concerns and online purchase behavior," *Journal Electron. Commerce Res*, Vol. 5, No. 1, pp. 62–70, 2004.

35 K. L. Hui, B. C. Y. Tan, and C. Y. Goh, "Online information disclosure: Motivators and measurements," *ACM Transaction on Internet Technologies*, Vol. 6, No. 4, pp. 415–441, 2006.

36 C. A. Ardagna, E. Damiani, S. De Capitani di Vimercati, and P. Samarati, "Toward privacy-enhanced authorization policies and languages," *Proceedings of the 19th IFIP WG11.3 Working Conference on Data and Application Security*, Storrs, CT, pp. 16–27, 2005.

37 R. Chandramouli, "Privacy protection of enterprise information through inference analysis," *Proceedings of IEEE 6th International Workshop on Policies for Distributed Systems and Networks (POLICY 2005)*, Stockholm, Sweden, pp. 47–56, 2005.

38 L. F. Cranor, *Web Privacy with P3P*, O'Reilly & Associates, 2002.

39 G. Karjoth, and M. Schunter, "Privacy policy model for enterprises," *Proceedings of the 15th IEEE Computer Security Foundations Workshop*, Cape Breton, Nova Scotia, pp. 271–281, 2002.

40 B. Thuraisingham, "Privacy constraint processing in a privacy-enhanced database management system," *Data & Knowledge Engineering*, Vol. 55, No. 2, pp. 159–188, 2005.

41 M. Youssef, V. Atluri, and N. R. Adam, "Preserving mobile customer privacy: An access control system for moving objects and customer profiles," *Proceedings of the 6th International Conference on Mobile Data Management (MDM 2005)*, Ayia Napa, Cyprus, pp. 67–76, 2005.

by parties. However, the importance gained by privacy requirements has brought with it the definition of access control models that are enriched with the ability of supporting privacy requirements. These enhanced access control models encompass two aspects: to guarantee the desired level of privacy of information exchanged between different parties by controlling the access to services/resources, and to control all secondary uses of information disclosed for the purpose of access control enforcement.

In this context, many languages for access control policies and privacy preferences specification have been defined, among which eXtensible Access Control Markup Language (XACML),[42] Platform for Privacy Preferences Project (P3P),[38,43] and Enterprise Privacy Authorization Language (EPAL)[44,45] stand out.

The *eXtensible Access Control Markup Language (XACML),*[42] which is the result of a standardization effort by OASIS, proposes an XML-based language to express and interchange access control policies. It is not specifically designed for managing privacy, but it represents a relevant innovation in the field of access control policies and has been used as the basis for following privacy-aware authorization languages. Main features of XACML are: (1) policy combination, a method for combining policies on the same resource independently specified by different entities; (2) combining algorithms, different algorithms representing ways of combining multiple decisions into a single decision; (3) attribute-based restrictions, the definition of policies based on properties associated with subjects and resources rather than their identities; (4) multiple subjects, the definition of more than one subject relevant to a decision request; (5) policy distribution, policies can be defined by different parties and enforced at different enforcement points; (6) implementation independence, an abstraction layer that isolates the policy-writer from the implementation details; and (7) obligations,[46] a method for specifying the actions that must be fulfilled in conjunction with the policy enforcement.

Platform for Privacy Preferences Project (P3P)[38,43] is a World Wide Web Consortium (W3C) project aimed at protecting the privacy of users by addressing their need to assess that the privacy practices adopted by a server provider comply with users' privacy requirements. P3P provides an XML-based language and a mechanism for ensuring that users can be informed about privacy policies of the server before the release of personal information. Therefore, P3P allows Web sites to declare their privacy practices in a standard and machine-readable XML format known as P3P policy. A P3P policy contains the specification of the data it protects, the data recipients allowed to access the private data, consequences of data release, purposes of data collection, data retention policy, and dispute resolution mechanisms. Supporting privacy preferences and policies in Web-based transactions allows users to automatically understand and match server practices against their privacy preferences. Thus, users need not read the privacy policies at every site they interact with, but they are always aware of the server practices in data handling. In summary, the goal of P3P is twofold: It allows Web sites to state their data-collection practices in a standardized, machine-readable way, and it provides users with a solution to understand what data will be collected and how those data will be used.

The corresponding language that would allow users to specify their preferences as a set of preference rules is called a *P3P Preference Exchange Language* (APPEL).[47] APPEL can be used by users' agents to reach automated or semiautomated decisions regarding the acceptability of privacy policies from P3P-enabled Web sites. Unfortunately, interactions between P3P and APPEL[48] had shown that users can explicitly specify just what is unacceptable in a policy, whereas the APPEL syntax is cumbersome and error prone for users.

Finally, *Enterprise Privacy Authorization Language* (EPAL)[44,45] is another XML-based language for specifying and enforcing enterprise-based privacy policies. EPAL is specifically designed to enable organizations to translate their privacy policies into IT control statements and to enforce policies that may be declared and communicated according to P3P specifications.

In this scenario, the need for access control frameworks that integrate policy evaluation and privacy

42 eXtensible Access Control Markup Language (XACML) Version 2.0, February 2005, http://docs.oasis-open.org/xacml/2.0/access_control-xacml-2.0-core-spec-os.pdf.

43 World Wide Web Consortium (W3C), Platform for privacy preferences (P3P) project, 2002, www.w3.org/TR/P3P/.

44 P. Ashley, S. Hada, G. Karjoth, and M. Schunter, "E-P3P privacy policies and privacy authorization," *Proceedings of the ACM Workshop on Privacy in the Electronic Society (WPES 2002)*, Washington, pp. 103–109, 2002.

45 P. Ashley, S. Hada, G. Karjoth, C. Powers, and M. Schunter, "Enterprise privacy authorization language (epal 1.1)," 2003, www.zurich.ibm.com/security/enterprise-privacy/epal.

46 C. Bettini, S. Jajodia, X. S. Wang, and D. Wijesekera, "Provisions and obligations in policy management and security applications," *Proceedings of 28th Conference Very Large Data Bases (VLDB '02)*, Hong Kong, pp. 502–513, 2002.

47 World Wide Web Consortium (W3C). A P3P Preference Exchange Language 1.0 (APPEL1.0), 2002, www.w3.org/TR/P3P-preferences/.

48 R. Agrawal, J., Kiernan, R., Srikant, and Y. Xu, "An XPath based preference language for P3P," *Proceedings of the 12th International World Wide Web Conference*, Budapest, Hungary, pp. 629–639, 2003.

TABLE 28.2A Census Data

SSN	Name	Address	City	Date of Birth	ZIP	...
...	...	...	...	...	...	...
...	John Doe	...	New York	03/30/1938	10249	...
...	...	...	...	...	...	...

functionalities arose. A first attempt to provide a uniform framework for regulating information release over the Web has been presented by Bonatti and Samarati.[49] Later a solution that introduced a privacy-aware access control framework was defined by Ardagna et al.[50] This framework allows the integration, evaluation, and enforcement of policies regulating access to service/data and release of personal identifiable information, respectively, and provides a mechanism to define constraints on the secondary use of personal data for the protection of users' privacy. In particular, the following types of privacy policies have been specified:

- *Access control policies.* These govern access/release of data/services managed by the party (as in traditional access control).
- *Release policies.* These govern release of properties/credentials/personal identifiable information (PII) of the party and specify under which conditions they can be released.
- *Data handling policies.* These define how personal information will be (or should be) dealt with at the receiving parties.[51]

An important feature of this framework is to support requests for certified data, issued and signed by trusted authorities, and uncertified data, signed by the owner itself. It also allows defining conditions that can be satisfied by means of zero-knowledge proof[52,53] and based

on physical position of the users.[54] In the context of the Privacy and Identity Management for Europe (PRIME),[55] a European Union project for which the goal is the development of privacy-aware solutions and frameworks has been created.

Data Privacy Protection

The concept of anonymity was first introduced in the context of relational databases to avoid linking between published data and users' identity. Usually, to protect user anonymity, data holders encrypt or remove explicit identifiers such as name and Social Security number (SSN). However, data deidentification does not provide full anonymity. Released data can in fact be linked to other publicly available information to reidentify users and to infer data that should not be available to the recipients. For instance, a set of anonymized data could contain attributes that almost uniquely identify a user, such as, race, date of birth, and ZIP code. Table 28.2A and Table 28.2B show an example of where the anonymous medical data contained in a table are linked with the census data to reidentify users. It is easy to see that in Table 28.2a there is a unique tuple with a *male* born on *03/30/1938* and living in the area with ZIP code *10249*. As a consequence, if this combination of attributes is also unique in the census data in Table 28.2b, John Doe is identified, revealing that he suffers from obesity.

If in the past limited interconnectivity and limited computational power represented a form of protection against inference processes over large amounts of data, today, with the advent of the Internet, such an assumption no longer holds. Information technology in fact gives organizations the power to gather and manage vast amounts of personal information.

49 P. Bonatti, and P. Samarati, "A unified framework for regulating access and information release on the web," *Journal of Computer Security*, Vol. 10, No. 3, pp. 241–272, 2002.

50 C. A. Ardagna, M. Cremonini, S. De Capitani di Vimercati, and P. Samarati, "A privacy-aware access control system," *Journal of Computer Security*, 2008.

51 C. A. Ardagna, S. De Capitani di Vimercati, and P. Samarati, "Enhancing user privacy through data handling policies," *Proceedings of the 20th Annual IFIP WG 11.3 Working Conference on Data and Applications Security*, Sophia Antipolis, France, pp. 224–236, 2006.

52 J. Camenisch, and A. Lysyanskaya, "An efficient system for nontransferable anonymous credentials with optional anonymity revocation," *Proceedings of the International Conference on the Theory and Application of Cryptographic Techniques (EUROCRYPT 2001)*, Innsbruck, Austria, pp. 93–118, 2001.

53 J. Camenisch, and E. Van Herreweghen, "Design and implementation of the idemix anonymous credential system," *Proceedings of the 9th ACM Conference on Computer and Communications Security (CCS 2002)*, Washington, pp. 21–30, 2002.

54 C. A. Ardagna, M. Cremonini, E. Damiani, S. De Capitani di Vimercati, and P. Samarati, "Supporting location-based conditions in access control policies," *Proceedings of the ACM Symposium on Information, Computer and Communications Security (ASIACCS '06)*, Taipei, pp. 212–222, 2006.

55 Privacy and Identity Management for Europe (PRIME), 2004, www.prime-project.eu.org/.

TABLE 28.2B User reidentification

		Anonymous Medical Data				
SSN	Name	Date of Birth	Sex	ZIP	Marital Status	Disease
		09/11/1984	M	10249	Married	HIV
		09/01/1978	M	10242	Single	HIV
		01/06/1959	F	10242	Married	Obesity
		01/23/1954	M	10249	Single	Hypertension
		03/15/1953	F	10212	Divorced	Hypertension
		03/30/1938	**M**	**10249**	**Single**	**Obesity**
		09/18/1935	F	10212	Divorced	Obesity
		03/15/1933	F	10252	Divorced	HIV

To address the problem of protecting anonymity while releasing microdata, the concept of *k*-anonymity has been defined. *K*-anonymity means that the observed data cannot be related to fewer than *k* respondents.[56] Key to achieving *k*-anonymity is the identification of a *quasi-identifier*, which is the set of attributes in a dataset that can be linked with external information to reidentify the data owner. It follows that for each release of data, every combination of values of the quasi-identifier must be indistinctly matched to at least *k* tuples.

Two approaches to achieve *k*-anonymity have been adopted: *generalization* and *suppression*. These approaches share the important feature that the truthfulness of the information is preserved, that is, no false information is released.

In more detail, the *generalization* process generalizes some of the values stored in the table. For instance, considering the ZIP code attribute in Table 28.2B and supposing for simplicity that it represents a quasi-identifier, the ZIP code can be generalized by dropping, at each step of generalization, the least significant digit. As another example, the date of birth can be generalized by first removing the day, then the month, and eventually by generalizing the year.

On the contrary, the suppression process removes some tuples from the table. Again, considering Table 28.2B, the ZIP codes, and a *k*-anonymity requirement for *k* = 2, it is clear that all tuples already satisfy the *k* = 2 requirement except for the last one. In this case, to preserve the *k* = 2, the last tuple could be suppressed.

Research on *k*-anonymity has been particularly rich in recent years. Samarati[56] presented an algorithm based on generalization hierarchies and suppression that calculates the minimal generalization. The algorithm relies on a binary search on the domain generalization hierarchy to avoid an exhaustive visit of the whole generalization space. Bayardo and Agrawal[57] developed an optimal bottom-up algorithm that starts from a fully generalized table (with all tuples equal) and then specializes the dataset into a minimal *k*-anonymous table. LeFevre et al.[58] are the authors of *Incognito*, a framework for providing *k*-minimal generalization. Their algorithm is based on a bottom-up aggregation along dimensional hierarchies and *a priori* aggregate computation. The same authors[59] also introduced *Mondrian k*-anonymity, which models the tuples as points in *d*-dimensional spaces and applies a generalization process that consists of finding the minimal multidimensional partitioning that satisfy the *k* preference.

Although there are advantages of *k*-anonymity for protecting respondents' privacy, some weaknesses have been demonstrated. Machanavajjhala et al.[60] identified

56 P. Samarati, "Protecting respondents' identities in microdata release," *IEEE Transactions on Knowledge and Data Engineering*, Vol. 13, No. 6, pp. 1010–1027, 2001.

57 R. J. Bayardo, and R. Agrawal, "Data privacy through optimal k-anonymization," *Proceedings of the 21st International Conference on Data Engineering (ICDE'05)*, Tokyo, pp. 217–228, 2005.

58 K. LeFevre, D. J. DeWitt, and R. Ramakrishnan, "Incognito: Efficient full-domain k-anonymity," *Proceedings of the 24th ACM SIGMOD International Conference on Management of Data*, Baltimore, pp. 49–60, 2005.

59 K. LeFevre, D. J. DeWitt, and R. Ramakrishnan, "Mondrian multidimensional k-anonymity," *Proceedings of the 22nd International Conference on Data Engineering (ICDE'06)*, Atlanta, 2006.

60 A. Machanavajjhala, J. Gehrke, D. Kifer, and M. Venkitasubramaniam, "l-diversity: Privacy beyond k-anonymity," *Proceedings of the International Conference on Data Engineering (ICDE '06)*, Atlanta, 2006.

TABLE 28.3 An example of a 2-Anonymous table

Year of Birth	Sex	ZIP	Disease
1984	M	10249	HIV
1984	M	10249	Anorexia
1984	M	10249	HIV
1966	F	10212	Anorexia
1966	F	10212	Anorexia
...	...	...	...

two successful attacks to k-anonymous table: the *homogeneity attack* and the *background knowledge attack*. To explain the *homogeneity attack*, suppose that a k-anonymous table contains a single sensitive attribute. Suppose also that all tuples with a given quasi-identifier value have the same value for that sensitive attribute, too. As a consequence, if the attacker knows the quasi-identifier value of a respondent, the attacker is able to learn the value of the sensitive attribute associated with the respondent. For instance, consider the 2-anonymous table shown in Table 28.3 and assume that an attacker knows that Alice is born in *1966* and lives in the *10212* ZIP code. Since all tuples with quasi-identifier <1966,F,10212> suffer anorexia, the attacker can infer that Alice suffers anorexia. Focusing on the *background knowledge attack*, the attacker exploits some *a priori* knowledge to infer some personal information. For instance, suppose that an attacker knows that Bob has quasi-identifier <1984,M,10249> and that Bob is overweight. In this case, from Table 28.3, the attacker can infer that Bob suffers from HIV.

To neutralize these attacks, the concept of l-diversity has been introduced.[60] In particular, a cluster of tuples with the same quasi-identifier is said to be l-diverse if it contains at least l different values for the sensitive attribute (disease, in the example in Table 28.3). If a k-anonymous table is l-diverse, the homogeneity attack is ineffective, since each block of tuples has at least $l>=2$ distinct values for the sensitive attribute. Also, the background knowledge attack becomes more complex as l increases.

Although l-diversity protects data against attribute disclosure, it leaves space for more sophisticated attacks based on the distribution of values inside clusters of tuples with the same quasi-identifier.[61] To prevent this kind of attack, the *t-closeness* requirement has been defined. In particular,

a cluster of tuples with the same quasi-identifier is said to satisfy *t-closeness* if the distance between the probabilistic distribution of the sensitive attribute in the cluster and the one in the original table is lower than *t*. A table satisfies *t-closeness* if all its clusters satisfy *t-closeness*.

In the next section, where the problem of location privacy protection is analyzed, we also discuss how the location privacy protection problem has adapted the k-anonymity principle to a pervasive and distributed scenario, where users move on the field carrying a mobile device.

Privacy for Mobile Environments

The widespread diffusion of mobile devices and the accuracy and reliability achieved by positioning techniques make available a great amount of location information about users. Such information has been used for developing novel location-based services. However, if on one side such a pervasive environment provides many advantages and useful services to the users, on the other side privacy concerns arise, since users could be the target of fraudulent location-based attacks. The most pessimistic have even predicted that the unrestricted and unregulated availability of location technologies and information could lead to a "Big Brother" society dominated by total surveillance of individuals.

The concept of *location privacy* can be defined as the right of individuals to decide how, when, and for which purposes their location information could be released to other parties. The lack of location privacy protection could be exploited by adversaries to perform various attacks.[62]

- *Unsolicited advertising,* when the location of a user could be exploited, without her consent, to provide advertisements of products and services available nearby the user position
- *Physical attacks or harassment*, when the location of a user could allow criminals to carry out physical assaults on specific individuals
- *User profiling*, when the location of a user could be used to infer other sensitive information, such as state of health, personal habits, or professional duties, by correlating visited places or paths
- *Denial of service*, when the location of a user could motivate an access denial to services under some circumstances

61 N. Li, T. Li, and S. Venkatasubramanian, "t-closeness: Privacy beyond k-anonymity and l-diversity," *Proceedings of the 23nd International Conference on Data Engineering*, Istanbul, Turkey, pp. 106–115, 2007.

62 M. Duckham, and L. Kulik, "Location privacy and location-aware computing," *Dynamic & Mobile GIS: Investigating Change in Space and Time*, pp. 34–51, Taylor & Francis, 2006.

A further complicating factor is that location privacy can assume several meanings and introduce different requirements, depending on the scenario in which the users are moving and on the services the users are interacting with. The following categories of location privacy can then be identified:

- *Identity privacy* protects the identities of the users associated with or inferable from location information. To this purpose, protection techniques aim at minimizing the disclosure of data that can let an attacker infer a user identity. Identity privacy is suitable in application contexts that do not require the identification of the users for providing a service.
- *Position privacy* protects the position information of individual users by perturbing corresponding information and decreasing the accuracy of location information. Position privacy is suitable for environments where users' identities are required for a successful service provisioning. A technique that most solutions exploit, either explicitly or implicitly, consists of reducing the accuracy by scaling a location to a coarser granularity (from meters to hundreds of meters, from a city block to the whole town, and so on).
- *Path privacy* protects the privacy of information associated with individuals movements, such as the path followed while travelling or walking in an urban area. Several location-based services (personal navigation systems) could be exploited to subvert path privacy or to illicitly track users.

Since location privacy definition and requirements differ depending on the scenario, no single technique is able to address the requirements of all the location privacy categories. Therefore, in the past, the research community focusing on providing solutions for the protection of location privacy of users has defined techniques that can be divided into three main classes: *anonymity-based*, *obfuscation-based*, and *policy-based* techniques. These classes of techniques are partially overlapped in scope and could be potentially suitable to cover requirements coming from one or more of the categories of location privacy. It is easy to see that anonymity-based and obfuscation-based techniques can be considered dual categories. Anonymity-based techniques have been primarily defined to protect identity privacy and are not suitable for protecting position privacy, whereas obfuscation-based techniques are well suited for position protection and not appropriate for identity protection. Anonymity-based and obfuscation-based techniques could also be exploited for protecting path privacy. Policy-based techniques are in general suitable for

all the location privacy categories, although they are often difficult for end users to understand and manage.

Among the class of techniques just introduced, current research on location privacy has mainly focused on supporting anonymity and partial identities. Beresford and Stajano[63,64] proposed a method, called *mix zones*, which uses an anonymity service based on an infrastructure that delays and reorders messages from subscribers. Within a mix zone (i.e., an area where a user cannot be tracked), a user is anonymous in the sense that the identities of all users coexisting in the same zone are mixed and become indiscernible. Other works are based on the concept of k-anonymity. Bettini et al.[65] designed a framework able to evaluate the risk of sensitive location-based information dissemination. Their proposal puts forward the idea that the geo-localized history of the requests submitted by a user can be considered as a quasi-identifier that can be used to discover sensitive information about the user. Gruteser and Grunwald[66] developed a middleware architecture and an adaptive algorithm to adjust location information resolution, in spatial or temporal dimensions, to comply with users' anonymity requirements. To this purpose, the authors introduced the concepts of spatial cloaking. Spatial cloaking guarantees the k-anonymity by enlarging the area where a user is located to an area containing k indistinguishable users. Gedik and Liu[67] described another k-anonymity model aimed at protecting location privacy against various privacy threats. In their proposal, each user is able to define the minimum level of anonymity and the maximum acceptable temporal and spatial resolution for her location measurement. Mokbel et al.[68] designed a framework, named *Casper*, aimed at enhancing traditional location-based servers and query processors with anonymous services, which satisfies both k-anonymity and spatial

63 A. R. Beresford, and F. Stajano, "Location privacy in pervasive computing," *IEEE Pervasive Computing*, vol. 2, no. 1, pp. 46–55, 2003.
64 A. R. Beresford, and F. Stajano, "Mix zones: User privacy in location-aware services," *Proceedings of the 2nd IEEE Annual Conference on Pervasive Computing and Communications Workshops (PERCOMW04)*, Orlando, pp. 127–131, 2004.
65 C. Bettini, X. S. Wang, and S. Jajodia, "Protecting privacy against location-based personal identification," *Proceedings of the 2nd VLDB Workshop on Secure Data Management (SDM'05)*, Trondheim, Norway, pp. 185–199, 2005.
66 M. Gruteser, and D. Grunwald, "Anonymous usage of location-based services through spatial and temporal cloaking," *Proceedings of the 1st International Conference on Mobile Systems, Applications, and Services (MobiSys)*, San Francisco, pp. 31–42, 2003.
67 B. Gedik, and L. Liu, "Protecting location privacy with personalized k-anonymity: Architecture and algorithms," *IEEE Transactions on Mobile Computing*, vol. 7, no. 1, pp. 1–18, 2008.
68 M. F. Mokbel, C. Y. Chow, and W. G. Aref, "The new Casper: Query processing for location services without compromising privacy," *Proceedings of the 32nd International Conference on Very Large Data Bases (VLDB 2006)*, Seoul, South Korea, pp. 763–774, 2006.

user preferences in terms of the smallest location area that can be released. Ghinita et al.[69] proposed *PRIVE*, a decentralized architecture for preserving query anonymization, which is based on the definition of *k*-anonymous areas obtained exploiting the Hilbert space-filling curve. Finally, anonymity has been exploited to protect the path privacy of the users[70,71,72] Although interesting, these solutions are still at an early stage of development.

Alternatively, when the users' identity is required for location-based service provision, obfuscation-based techniques has been deployed. The first work providing an obfuscation-based technique for protecting location privacy was by Duckham and Kulik.[62] In particular, their framework provides a mechanism for balancing individual needs for high-quality information services and for location privacy. The idea is to degrade location information quality by adding *n* fake positions to the real user position. Ardagna et al.[73] defined different obfuscation-based techniques aimed at preserving location privacy by artificially perturbing location information. These techniques degrade the location information accuracy by (1) enlarging the radius of the measured location, (2) reducing the radius, and (3) shifting the center. In addition, a metric called *relevance* is used to evaluate the level of location privacy and balance it with the accuracy needed for the provision of reliable location-based services.

Finally, policy-based techniques are based on the notion of privacy policies and are suitable for all the categories of location privacy. In particular, privacy policies define restrictions that must be enforced when location of users is used by or released to external parties. The IETF Geopriv working group[74] addresses privacy and security issues related to the disclosure of location information over the Internet. The main goal is to define an environment supporting both location information and policy data.

4. NETWORK ANONYMITY

The wide diffusion of the Internet for many daily activities has enormously increased interest in security and privacy issues. In particular, in such a distributed environment, privacy should also imply anonymity: a person shopping online may not want her visits to be tracked, the sending of email should keep the identities of the sender and the recipient hidden from observers, and so on. That is, when surfing the Web, users want to keep secret not only the information they exchange but also the fact that they are exchanging information and with whom. Such a problem has to do with traffic analysis, and it requires ad hoc solutions. Traffic analysis is the process of intercepting and examining messages to deduce information from patterns in communication. It can be performed even when the messages are encrypted and cannot be decrypted. In general, the greater the number of messages observed or even intercepted and stored, the more can be inferred from the traffic. It cannot be solved just by encrypting the header of a packet or the payload: In the first case, the packet could still be tracked as it moves through the network; the second case is ineffective as well since it would still be possible to identify who is talking to whom.

In this section, we first describe the onion routing protocol,[75,76,77] one of the better-known approaches that is not application-oriented. Then we provide an overview of other techniques for assuring anonymity and privacy over networks. The key approaches we discuss are mix networks,[78,79] the Crowds system,[80] and the Freedom network.[81]

69 G. Ghinita, P. Kalnis, and S. Skiadopoulos, "PRIVE: Anonymous location-based queries in distributed mobile systems," *Proceedings of the International World Wide Web Conference (WWW 2007)*, Banff, Canada, pp. 371–380, 2007.

70 M. Gruteser, J. Bredin, and D. Grunwald, "Path privacy in location-aware computing," *Proceedings of the Second International Conference on Mobile Systems, Application and Services (MobiSys2004)*, Boston, 2004.

71 M. Gruteser, and X. Liu, "Protecting privacy in continuous location-tracking applications," *IEEE Security & Privacy Magazine*, Vol. 2, No. 2, pp. 28–34, 2004.

72 B. Ho, and M. Gruteser, "Protecting location privacy through path confusion," *Proceedings of IEEE/CreateNet International Conference on Security and Privacy for Emerging Areas in Communication Networks (SecureComm)*, Athens, Greece, pp. 194–205, 2005.

73 C.A. Ardagna, M. Cremonini, E. Damiani, S. De Capitani di Vimercati, and P. Samarati, "Location privacy protection through obfuscation-based techniques," *Proceedings of the 21st Annual IFIP WG 11.3 Working Conference on Data and Applications Security*, Redondo Beach, pp. 47–60, 2007.

74 Geographic Location/Privacy (geopriv), September 2006, www.ietf.org/html.charters/geopriv-charter.html.

75 D. Goldschlag, M. Reed, and P. Syverson, "Hiding routing information," In R. Anderson (ed.), *Information Hiding: First International Workshop*, Volume 1174 of Lecture Notes in Computer Science, Springer-Verlag, pp. 137–150, 1999.

76 D. Goldschlag, M. Reed, and P. Syverson, "Onion routing for anonymous and private internet connections," *Communication of the ACM*, Vol. 42, No. 2, pp. 39–41, 1999.

77 M. Reed, P. Syverson, and D. Goldschlag, "Anonymous connections and onion routing," *IEEE Journal on Selected Areas in Communications*, Vol. 16, No. 4, pp. 482–494, 1998.

78 D. Chaum, "Untraceable electronic mail, return address, and digital pseudonyms," *Communications of the ACM*, Vol. 24, No. 2, pp. 84–88, 1981.

79 O. Berthold, H. Federrath, and S. Kopsell, "Web MIXes: A system for anonymous and unobservable internet access," in H. Federrath (ed.), *Anonymity 2000*, Volume 2009 of Lecture Notes in Computer Science, Springer-Verlag, pp. 115–129, 2000.

80 M. Reiter, and A. Rubin, "Anonymous web transactions with crowds," *Communications of the ACM*, Vol. 42, No. 2, pp. 32–48, 1999.

81 P. Boucher, A. Shostack, and I. Goldberg, Freedom Systems 2.0 Architecture, 2000, www.freedom.net/info/whitepapers/Freedom_System_2_Architecture.pdf.

Onion Routing

Onion routing is intended to provide real-time bidirectional *anonymous connections* that are resistant to both eavesdropping and traffic analysis in a way that's transparent to applications. That is, if Alice and Bob communicate over a public network by means of onion routing, they are guaranteed that the content of the message remains confidential and no external observer or internal node is able to infer that they are communicating.

Onion routing works beneath the application layer, replacing socket connections with anonymous connections and without requiring any change to proxy-aware Internet services or applications. It was originally implemented on Sun Solaris 2.4 in 1997, including proxies for Web browsing (HTTP), remote logins (rlogin), email (SMTP), and file transfer (FTP). The *Tor*[82] generation 2 onion routing implementation runs on most common operating systems. It consists of a fixed infrastructure of onion routers, where each router has a longstanding socket connection to a set of neighboring ones. Only a few routers, called *onion router proxies*, know the whole infrastructure topology. In onion routing, instead of making socket connections directly to a responding machine, initiating applications make a socket connection to an onion routing proxy that builds an anonymous connection through several other onion routers to the destination. In this way, the onion routing network allows the connection between the initiator and responder to remain anonymous. Although the protocol is called onion routing, the routing that occurs during the anonymous connection is at the application layer of the protocol stack, not at the IP layer. However, the underlying IP network determines the route that data actually travels between individual onion routers. Given the onion router infrastructure, the onion routing protocol works in three phases:

- Anonymous connection *setup*
- *Communication* through the anonymous connection
- Anonymous connection *destruction*

During the first phase, the initiator application, instead of connecting directly with the destination machine, opens a socket connection with an onion routing proxy (which may reside in the same machine, in a remote machine, or in a firewall machine). The proxy first establishes a path to the destination in the onion router infrastructure, then

sends an *onion* to the first router of the path. The onion is a layered data structure in which each layer of the onion (public-key encrypted) is intended for a particular onion router and contains (1) the identity of the next onion router in the path to be followed by the anonymous connection; (2) the expiration time of the onion; and (3) a key seed to be used to generate the keys to encode the data sent through the anonymous connection in both directions. The onion is sent through the path established by the proxy: an onion router that receives an onion peels off its layer, identifies the next hop, records on a table the key seed, the expiration time and the identifiers of incoming and outgoing connections and the keys that are to be applied, pads the onion and sends it to the next onion router. Since the most internal layer contains the name of the destination machine, the last router of the path will act as the destination proxy and open a socket connection with the destination machine. Note that only the intended onion router is able to peel off the layer intended to it. In this way, each intermediate onion router knows (and can communicate with) only the previous and the next-hop router. Moreover, it is not capable of understanding the content of the following layers of the onion. The router, and any external observer, cannot know *a priori* the length of the path since the onion size is kept constant by the fact that each intermediate router is obliged to add padding to the onion corresponding to the fixed-size layer that it removed.

Figure 28.2 shows an onion for an anonymous connection following route *WXYZ*; the router infrastructure is as depicted in Figure 28.3, with *W* the onion router proxy.

Once the anonymous connection is established, data can be sent in both directions. The onion proxy receives data from the initiator application, breaks it into fixed-size packets, and adds a layer of encryption for each onion router in the path using the keys specified in the onion. As data packets travel through the anonymous connection, each intermediate onion router removes one layer of encryption. The last router in the path sends the plaintext to the destination through the socket connection that was opened during the setup phase. This encryption layering occurs in the reverse order when data is

82 R. Dingledine N. Mathewson and P. Syverson "Tor: The second-generation onion router," *Proceedings of the 13th USENIX Security Symposium*, San Diego, 2004.

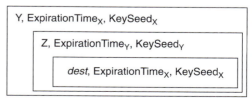

FIGURE 28.2 Onion message.

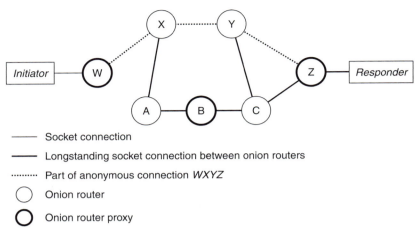

FIGURE 28.3 Onion routing network infrastructure.

sent backward from the destination machine to the initiator application. In this case, the initiator proxy, which knows both the keys and the path, will decrypt each layer and send the plaintext to the application using its socket connection with the application. As for the onion, data passed along the anonymous connection appears different to each intermediate router and external observer, so it cannot be tracked. Moreover, compromised onion routers cannot cooperate to correlate the data stream they see.

When the initiator application decides to close the socket connection with the proxy, the proxy sends a destroy message along the anonymous connection and each router removes the entry of the table relative to that connection.

There are several advantages in the onion routing protocol. First, the most trusted element of the onion routing infrastructure is the initiator proxy, which knows the network topology and decides the path used by the anonymous connection. If the proxy is moved in the initiator machine, the trusted part is under the full control of the initiator. Second, the total cryptographic overhead is the same as for link encryption but, whereas in link encryption one corrupted router is enough to disclose all the data, in onion routing routers cannot cooperate to correlate the little they know and disclose the information. Third, since an onion has an expiration time, replay attacks are not possible. Finally, if anonymity is also desired, then all identifying information must be additionally removed from the data stream before being sent over the anonymous connection. However, onion routing is not completely invulnerable to traffic analysis attacks: if a huge number of messages between routers is recorded and usage patterns analyzed, it would be possible to make a close guess about the routing, that is, also about the initiator and the responder. Moreover, the topology of the onion router infrastructure must be static and known *a priori* by

at least one onion router proxy, which make the protocol little adaptive to node/router failures.

Tor[82] generation 2 onion routing addresses some of the limitations highlighted earlier, providing a reasonable trade-off among anonymity, usability, and efficiency. In particular, it provides perfect forward secrecy and it does not require a proxy for each supported application protocol.

Anonymity Services

Some other approaches offer some possibilities for providing anonymity and privacy, but they are still vulnerable to some types of attacks. For instance, many of these approaches are designed for World Wide Web access only; being protocol-specific, these approaches may require further development to be used with other applications or Internet services, depending on the communication protocols used in those systems.

David Chaum[78,79] introduced the idea of *mix networks* in 1981 to enable unobservable communication between users of the Internet. Mixes are intermediate nodes that may reorder, delay, and pad incoming messages to complicate traffic analysis. A mix node stores a certain number of incoming messages that it receives and sends them to the next mix node in a random order. Thus, messages are modified and reordered in such a way that it is nearly impossible to correlate an incoming message with an outgoing message. Messages are sent through a series of mix nodes and encrypted with mix keys. If participants exclusively use mixes for sending messages to each other, their communication relations will be unobservable, even if the attacker records all network connections. Also, without additional information, the receiver does not have any clue about the identity of the message's sender. As in onion routing, each mix node knows only the previous and next node in a received message's route. Hence, unless the route only goes through a single node, compromising a mix node does not enable an attacker to violate either the sender nor the recipient privacy. Mix networks are not really efficient, since a mix needs to receive a large group of messages before forwarding them, thus delaying network traffic. However, onion routing has many analogies with this approach and an onion router can be seen as a real-time Chaum mix.

Reiter and Rubin[80] proposed an alternative to mixes, called *crowds*, a system to make only browsing anonymous, hiding from Web servers and other parties information about either the user or the information she retrieves. This is obtained by preventing a Web server from learning any information linked to the user, such as the IP address or domain name, the page that referred the user to its site, or the user's computing platform. The approach is based on the idea of "blending into a crowd," that is, hiding one's actions within the actions of many others. Before making any request, a user joins a crowd of other users. Then, when the user submits a request, it is forwarded to the final destination with probability *p* and to some other member of the crowd with probability *1-p*. When the request is eventually submitted, the end server cannot identify its true initiator. Even crowd members cannot identify the initiator of the request, since the initiator is indistinguishable from a member of the crowd that simply passed on a request from another.

Freedom network[81] is an overlay network that runs on top of the Internet, that is, on top of the application layer. The network is composed of a set of nodes called *anonymous Internet proxies*, which run on top of the existing infrastructure. As for onion routing and mix networks, the Freedom network is used to set up a communication channel between the initiator and the responder, but it uses different techniques to encrypt the messages sent along the channel.

5. CONCLUSION

In this chapter we discussed net privacy from different viewpoints, from historical to technological. The very nature of the concept of privacy requires such an enlarged perspective because it often appears indefinite, being constrained into the tradeoff between the undeniable need of protecting personal information and the evident utility, in many contexts, of the availability of the same information. The digital society and the global interconnected infrastructure eased accessing and spreading of personal information; therefore, developing technical means and defining norms and fair usage procedures for privacy protection are now more demanding than in the past.

Economic aspects have been introduced since they are likely to strongly influence the way privacy is actually managed and protected. In this area, research has provided useful insights about the incentive and disincentives toward better privacy.

We presented some of the more advanced solutions that research has developed to date, either for anonymizing stored data, hiding sensitive information in artificially inaccurate clusters, or introducing third parties and middleware in charge of managing online transactions and services in a privacy-aware fashion. Location privacy is a topic that has gained importance in recent years with the advent of mobile devices and that is worth a specific consideration.

Furthermore, the important issue of anonymity over the Net has been investigated. To let individuals surf the Web, access online services, and interact with remote parties in an anonymous way has been the goal of many efforts for years. Some important technologies and tools are available and are gaining popularity.

To conclude, whereas privacy over the Net and in the digital society does not look to be in good shape, the augmented sensibility of individuals to its erosion, the many scientific and technological efforts to introduce novel solutions, and a better knowledge of the problem with the help of fresh data contribute to stimulating the need for better protection and fairer use of personal information. For this reason, it is likely that Net privacy will remain an important topic in the years to come and more innovations toward better management of privacy issues will emerge.

## Chapter 29

Personal Privacy Policies[1]

Dr. George Yee
National Research Council of Canada, Ottawa

Larry Korba
National Research Council of Canada, Ottawa

The rapid growth of the Internet has been accompanied by a similar growth in the availability of Internet e-services (such as online booksellers and stockbrokers). This proliferation of e-services has in turn fueled the need to protect the personal privacy of e-service users or consumers. This chapter proposes the use of personal privacy policies to protect privacy. It is evident that the content must match the user's privacy preferences as well as privacy legislation. It is also evident that the construction of a personal privacy policy must be as easy as possible for the consumer. Further, the content and construction must not result in negative unexpected outcomes (an unexpected outcome that harms the user in some manner). The chapter begins with the derivation of policy content based on privacy legislation, followed by a description of how a personal privacy policy may be constructed semiautomatically. It then shows how to additionally specify policies so that negative unexpected outcomes can be avoided. Finally, it describes our Privacy Management Model that explains how to use personal privacy policies to protect privacy, including what is meant by a "match" of consumer and service provider policies and how nonmatches can be resolved through negotiation.

1. INTRODUCTION

The rapid growth of the Internet has been accompanied by a similar rapid growth in Internet based e-services targeting consumers. E-services are available for banking, shopping, stock investing, and healthcare, to name a few areas. However, each of these services requires a consumer's personal information in one form or another. This leads to concerns over privacy.

For e-services to be successful, privacy must be protected. In a recent U.S. study by MasterCard International, 60% of respondents were concerned with the privacy of transmitted data.[2] An effective and flexible way of protecting privacy is to manage it using privacy policies. In this approach, each provider of an e-service has a privacy policy specifying the private information required for that e-service. Similarly, each consumer of an e-service has a privacy policy specifying the private information she is willing to share for the e-service. Prior to the activation of an e-service, the consumer and provider of the e-service exchange privacy policies. The service is only activated if the policies are compatible (we define what "compatible" means in a moment). Where the personal privacy policy of an e-service consumer conflicts with the privacy policy of an e-service provider, we have advocated a negotiations approach to resolve the conflict.[3,4]

In our approach, the provider requires private information from the consumer for use in its e-service and so reduces the consumer's privacy by requesting such information. This reduction in consumer privacy is represented by the requirements for consumer private information in the provider's privacy policy. The consumer, on the other hand, would rather keep her private information to herself, so she tries to resist the provider's attempt to reduce her

1 NRC Paper number: NRC 50334

2 T. Greer, and M. Murtaza, "E-commerce security and privacy: Managerial vs. technical perspectives," Proceedings, *15th IRMA International Conference (IRMA 2004)*, New Orleans, May 2004.

3 G. Yee, and L. Korba, "Bilateral e-services negotiation under uncertainty," Proceedings, *The 2003 International Symposium on Applications and the Internet (SAINT 2003)*, Orlando, Jan 2003.

4 G. Yee, and L. Korba, "The negotiation of privacy policies in distance education," Proceedings, *14th IRMA International Conference*, Philadelphia, May 2003.

privacy. This means that the consumer would only be willing to have her privacy reduced by a certain amount, as represented by the privacy provisions in her privacy policy. There is a *match* between a provider's privacy policy and the corresponding consumer's policy where the amount of privacy reduction allowed by the consumer's policy is at least as great as the amount of privacy reduction required by the provider's policy (more details on policy matching follow). Otherwise, there is a *mismatch*. Where time is involved, a private item held for less time is considered less private. A privacy policy is considered *upgraded* if the new version represents more privacy than the prior version. Similarly, a privacy policy is considered *downgraded* if the new version represents less privacy than the prior version.

So far so good, but what should go into a personal privacy policy? How are these policies constructed? Moreover, what can be done to construct policies that do not lead to negative unexpected outcomes (an outcome that is harmful to the user in some manner)? Consumers need help in formulating personal privacy policies. The creation of such policies needs to be as easy as possible or consumers would simply avoid using them. Existing privacy specification languages such as P3P and APPE[5,6] that are XML-based are far too complicated for the average Internet user to understand. Understanding or changing a privacy policy expressed in these languages effectively requires knowing how to program. What is needed is an easy, semiautomated way of deriving a personal privacy policy.

In this chapter, we present two semiautomated approaches for obtaining personal privacy policies for consumers. We also show how these policies should be specified to avoid negative unexpected outcomes. Finally, we describe our Privacy Management Model that explains how personal privacy policies are used to protect consumer privacy, including how policies may be negotiated between e-service consumer and e-service provider.

The "Content of Personal Privacy Policies" section examines the content of personal privacy policies by identifying some attributes of private information collection. The "Semiautomated Derivation of Personal Privacy Policies" section shows how personal privacy policies can be semiautomatically generated. The "Specifying Well-Formed Personal Privacy Policies" section explains how to ensure that personal privacy policies do not lead to negative unexpected outcomes. "The Privacy Management Model" section presents our Privacy

Management Model, which explains how personal privacy policies can be used to protect consumer privacy, including how they may be negotiated between e-service consumer and e-service provider. The "Discussion and Related Work" section discusses our approaches and presents related work. The chapter ends with conclusions and a description of possible future work in these areas.

2. CONTENT OF PERSONAL PRIVACY POLICIES

In Canada, privacy legislation is enacted in the *Personal Information Protection and Electronic Documents Act* (PIPEDA)[7] and is based on the Canadian Standards Association's Model Code for the Protection of Personal Information,[8] recognized as a national standard in 1996. This code consists of ten Privacy Principles that for convenience, we label CSAPP.

Privacy Legislation and Directives

Data privacy in the European Union is governed by a very comprehensive set of regulations called the Data Protection Directive.[9] In the United States, privacy protection is achieved through a patchwork of legislation at the federal and state levels. Privacy legislation is largely sector-based.[10]

Requirements from Privacy Principles

In this section, we identify some attributes of private information collection or personally identifiable information (PII) collection using CSAPP as a guide. We then apply the attributes to the specification of privacy policy contents. Note that we use the terms *private information* and *PII* interchangeably. We use CSAPP because it is representative of privacy legislation in other countries (e.g., European Union, Australia) and has withstood the

---

5 W3C Platform, "The platform for privacy preferences," retrieved Sept. 2, 2002, from www.w3.org/P3P/.

6 W3C APPEL, "A P3P preference exchange language 1.0 (APPEL1.0)," W3C Working Draft 15, April 2002, retrieved Sept. 2, 2002, from: http://www.w3.org/TR/P3P-preferences/.

7 Canadian Standards Association, "Model code for the protection of personal information," retrieved Sept. 5, 2007, from www.csa.ca/standards/privacy/code/Default.asp?articleID = 5286&language = English.

8 Office of the Privacy Commissioner of Canada, "The personal information protection and electronic documents act," retrieved May 1, 2008, from www.privcom.gc.ca/legislation/02_06_01_e.asp.

9 European Union, "Directive 95/46/EC of the European Parliament and of the Council of 24 October 1995 on the protection of individuals with regard to the processing of personal data and on the free movement of such data," unofficial text retrieved Sept. 5, 2003, from http://aspe.hhs.gov/datacncl/eudirect.htm.

10 Banisar, D., "Privacy and data protection around the world," Proceedings, *21st International Conference on Privacy and Personal Data Protection*, September 13, 1999.

TABLE 29.1 CSAPP: The Ten Privacy Principles from the Canadian Standards Association

Principle	Description
1. Accountability	An organization is responsible for personal information under its control and shall designate an individual or individuals accountable for the organization's compliance with the privacy principles.
2. Identifying Purposes	The purposes for which personal information is collected shall be identified by the organization at or before the time the information is collected.
3. Consent	The knowledge and consent of the individual are required for the collection, use, or disclosure of personal information, except when inappropriate.
4. Limiting Collection	The collection of personal information shall be limited to that which is necessary for the purposes identified by the organization. Information shall be collected by fair and lawful means.
5. Limiting Use, Disclosure, and Retention	Personal information shall not be used or disclosed for purposes other than those for which it was collected, except with the consent of the individual or as required by the law. In addition, personal information shall be retained only as long as necessary for fulfillment of those purposes.
6. Accuracy	Personal information shall be as accurate, complete, and up to date as is necessary for the purposes for which it is to be used.
7. Safeguards	Security safeguards appropriate to the sensitivity of the information shall be used to protect personal information.
8. Openness	An organization shall make readily available to individuals specific information about its policies and practices relating to the management of personal information.
9. Individual Access	Upon request, an individual shall be informed of the existence, use and disclosure of his or her personal information and shall be given access to that information. An individual shall be able to challenge the accuracy and completeness of the information and have it amended as appropriate.
10. Challenging Compliance	An individual shall be able to address a challenge concerning compliance with the above principles to the designated individual or individuals accountable for the organization's compliance.

test of time, originating from 1996. In addition, CSAPP is representative of the Fair Information Practices, a set of standards balancing the information needs of the business with the privacy needs of the individual.[11] Table 29.1 shows CSAPP.

In Table 29.1, we interpret *organization* as "provider" and *individual* as "consumer." In the following, we use CSAPP.*n* to denote Principle *n* of CSAPP. Principle CSAPP.2 implies that there could be different providers requesting the information, thus implying a *collector* attribute. Principle CSAPP.4 implies that there is a *what* attribute, that is, what private information is being collected? Principles CSAPP.2, CSAPP.4, and CSAPP.5 state that there are *purposes* for which the private information is being collected. Principles CSAPP.3, CSAPP.5, and CSAPP.9 imply that the private information can be disclosed to other parties, giving a *disclose-to* attribute. Principle CSAPP.5 implies a *retention time* attribute for the retention of private information. Thus, from the CSAPP we derive five attributes of private information collection: *collector, what, purposes, retention time*, and *disclose-to*.

The Privacy Principles also prescribe certain operational requirements that must be satisfied between provider and consumer, such as identifying purpose and consent. Our service model and the exchange of privacy policies automatically satisfy some of these requirements, namely Principles CSAPP.2, CSAPP.3, and CSAPP.8. The satisfaction of the remaining operational requirements depends on compliance mechanisms (Principles CSAPP.1, CSAPP.4, CSAPP.5, CSAPP.6, CSAPP.9, and CSAPP.10) and security mechanisms (Principle CSAPP.7).

11 K. S. Schwaig, G. C. Kane, and V. C. Storey, "Privacy, fair information practices and the fortune 500: the virtual reality of compliance," *The DATA BASE for Advances in Information Systems*, 36(1), pp. 49–63, 2005.

Privacy Policy Specification

Based on these explorations, the contents of a privacy policy should, for each item of PII, identify (1) the *collector*—the person who wants to collect the information, (2) *what*—the nature of the information, (3) *purposes*—the purposes for which the information is being collected, (4) *retention time*—the amount of time for the provider to keep the information, and (5) *disclose-to*—the parties to whom the information will be disclosed. Figure 29.1 gives three examples of consumer personal privacy policies for use with an e-learning provider, an online bookseller, and an online medical help clinic. The *policy use* field indicates the type of online service for which the policy will be used. Since a privacy policy may change over time, we have a *valid* field to hold the time period during which the policy is valid. Figure 29.2 gives examples of provider privacy policies corresponding to the personal privacy policies of Figure 29.1.

A privacy policy thus consists of "header" information (*policy use*, *owner*, *valid*) together with one or more 5-tuples, or privacy rules:

$$< collector, what, purposes, retention\ time,$$
$$disclose\text{-}to >$$

where each 5-tuple or rule represents an item of private information and the conditions under which the information may be shared. For example, in Figure 29.1, the personal policy for e-learning has a header (top portion) plus two rules (bottom portion); the personal policy for a bookseller has only one rule.

3. SEMIAUTOMATED DERIVATION OF PERSONAL PRIVACY POLICIES

A semiautomated derivation of a personal privacy policy is the use of mechanisms (described in a moment) that may be semiautomated to obtain a set of privacy rules

Policy Use: E-learning Owner: Alice Consumer Valid: unlimited	Policy Use: Bookseller Owner: Alice Consumer Valid: June 2009	Policy Use: Medical Help Owner: Alice Consumer Valid: July 2009
Collector: any What: name, address, tel Purposes: identification Retention Time: unlimited Disclose-To: none Collector: any What: course marks Purposes: records Retention Time: 2 years Disclose-To: none	Collector: any What: name, address, tel Purposes: identification Retention Time: unlimited Disclose-To: none	Collector: any What: name, address, tel Purposes: contact Retention Time: unlimited Disclose-To: pharmacy Collector: Dr. A. Smith What: medical condition Purposes: treatment Retention Time: unlimited Disclose-To: pharmacy

FIGURE 29.1 Example of consumer personal privacy policies.

Policy Use: E-learning Owner: E-learning Unlimited Valid: unlimited	Policy Use: Bookseller Owner: All Books Online Valid: unlimited	Policy Use: Medical Help Owner: Medics Online Valid: unlimited
Collector: E-learning Unlimited What: name, address, tel Purposes: identification Retention Time: unlimited Disclose-To: none Collector: E-learning Unlimited What: course marks Purposes: records Retention Time: 1 years Disclose-To: none	Collector: All Books Online What: name, address, tel Purposes: identification Retention Time: unlimited Disclose-To: none Collector: All Books Online What: credit card Purposes: payment Retention Time: until paid Disclose-To: none	Collector: Medics Online What: name, address, tel Purposes: contact Retention Time: unlimited Disclose-To: pharmacy Collector: Medics Online What: medical condition Purposes: treatment Retention Time: 1 year Disclose-To: pharmacy

FIGURE 29.2 Example of corresponding provider privacy policies.

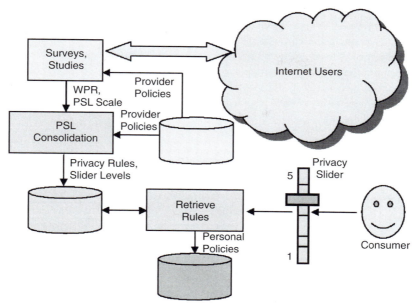

FIGURE 29.3 Derivation of personal privacy policies from surveys.

for a particular policy use. We present two approaches for such derivations. The first approach relies on third-party surveys (see sidebar, "Derivation Through Third Party Surveys") of user perceptions of data privacy (Figure 29.3). The second approach is based on retrieval from a community of peers.

Derivation Through Third-Party Surveys

(a) A policy provider makes use of third-party surveys performed on a regular basis, as well as those published in research literature, to obtain user privacy sensitivity levels (PSLs) or perceptions of the level of privacy for various combinations of <*what, purposes, retention time*> in provider policy rules. We call <*what, purposes, retention time*> WPR, for short. This gives a range of PSLs for different WPRs in different provider policies. Formally:

Let p_i represent a WPR from a provider policy, I represent the set of p_i over all provider policies, $f_{k,i}$ represent the privacy sensitivity function of person k to sharing p_i with a service provider. We restrict $f_{k,i}$ to an integer value in a standard interval $[M,N]$, that is, $M \leq f_{k,i} \leq N$ for integers M, N (e.g., $M = 1$, $N = 5$). Then the PSLs $s_{k,i}$ are obtained as

$$s_{k,i} = f_{k,i}(p_i) \; \forall \; k \in K, \; i \in I$$

where K is the set of consumers interested in the providers' services. This equation models a person making a choice of what PSL to assign a particular p_i.

(b) Corresponding to a service provider's privacy policy (which specifies the privacy rules required), a policy provider (or a software application used by the policy provider)

consolidates the PSLs from (a) such that the WPRs are selectable by a single value privacy level from a "privacy slider" for each service provider policy. There are different ways to do this consolidation. One way is to assign a WPR the median of its PSL range as its privacy level (illustrated in a moment). The outcome of this process is a set of consumer privacy rules (expressed using a policy language such as APPEL) ranked by privacy level for different providers, and with the *collector* and *disclose-to* fields as "any" and "none," respectively. (The consumer can change these fields later if desired.) Formally, using the notation introduced in (a):

Let P represent a provider's privacy policy. Then for each WPR $p_i \in P$, we have from (a) a set of PSLs: $S_i(P) = \{s_{k,i} \mid p_i \in P, \; \forall \; k \in K\}$. Our goal is to map $S_i(P)$ to a single privacy level from a privacy slider. Let g be such a mapping. Then this step performs the mapping $g(S_i(P)) = n$, where n is the privacy slider value. For example, the mapping g can be "take the median of" (illustrated below) or "take the average of." We have assumed that the range of slider values is the same as $[M,N]$ in (a). If this is not the case, g would need to incorporate normalization to the range of slider values.

(c) Consumers obtain online from the policy provider the privacy rules that make up whole policies. They do this by first specifying the provider for which a consumer privacy policy is required. The consumer is then prompted to enter the privacy level using the privacy slider for each WPR from the service provider's policy. The selected rules would then automatically populate the consumer's policy. The consumer then completes his privacy policy by adding the header information (i.e., *policy use, owner, valid*) and, if desired, add specific names to *collector* and *disclose-to* for all rules. This can be done through a human-computer interface that shelters the user from the complexity of the policy language. In this way, large populations of consumers may quickly obtain privacy policies for many service providers that reflect the privacy sensitivities of the communities surveyed.

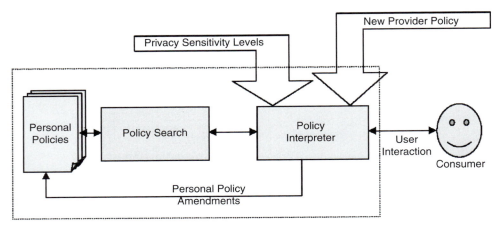

FIGURE 29.4 Adapting an existing personal privacy policy to a new provider.

Consumers may interactively adapt their existing privacy policies for new service provider policies based on the PSLs of the WPRs and the new provider policies, as illustrated in Figure 29.4. In Figure 29.4, the Policy Interpreter interactively allows the user to establish (using a privacy slider) the privacy levels of required rules based on the new provider policy and the PSLs from a policy provider. Policy Search then retrieves the user policy that most closely matches the user's privacy-established rules. This policy may then be further amended interactively via the Policy Interpreter to obtain the required personal privacy policy. This assumes the availability of an easy-to-understand interface for the user interaction as well as software to automatically take care of any needed conversions of rules back into the policy language (APPEL).

An Example

Suppose a consumer wants to generate a personal privacy policy for a company called E-learning Unlimited. For simplicity, suppose the privacy policy of E-learning Unlimited has only one WPR, namely *<course marks,*

records, 12 months >. The steps are implemented as follows:

1. The third-party survey generates the following results for the WPR (the lowest privacy sensitivity level is $M = 1$, the highest is $N = 5$).

WPR (p_i)	PSL ($s_{k,i}$)
< course marks, records, 6 months >	3
< course marks, records, 6 months >	4
< course marks, records, 6 months >	4
< course marks, records, 6 months >	5
< course marks, records, 12 months >	1
< course marks, records, 12 months >	1
< course marks, records, 12 months >	2
< course marks, records, 12 months >	3

Note that the higher the number of months the marks are retained, the lower the PSL (the lower the privacy perceived by the consumer). The different PSLs obtained constitute one part of the privacy sensitivity scale.

2. In this step, the policy provider consolidates the PSL in Step 1 using the median value from the corresponding PSL range. Thus for the four course-mark

retention times of 6 months, the lowest value is 3, the highest value is 5, and the median is 4. Therefore the rule <*any, course marks, records, 6 months, none* > is ranked with privacy level 4. Similarly, the rule <*any, course marks, records, 12 months, none* > is ranked with privacy level 2.

3. To obtain her privacy rules, the consumer specifies the service provider as E-learning Unlimited and a privacy slider value of 4 (for example) when prompted. She then obtains the rule:

<*any, course marks, records, 6 months, none* >

and proceeds to complete the policy by adding the header values and if desired, specific names for *collector* and *disclose-to*.

Retrieval from a Community of Peers

This approach assumes an existing community of peers already possessing specific use privacy policies with rules according to desired levels of privacy. A new consumer joining the community searches for personal privacy rules. The existing personal privacy policies may have been derived using the third-party surveys, as previously. Each privacy policy rule is stored along with its privacy level so that it may be selected according to this level and *purpose*. Where a rule has been adapted or modified by the owner, it is the owner's responsibility to ensure that the slider privacy value of the modified rule is consistent with the privacy sensitivity scale from surveys.

- All online users are peers and everyone has a privacy slider. The new consumer broadcasts a request for privacy rules to the community (see Figure 29.5a), specifying *purpose* and slider value. This is essentially a peer-to-peer search over all peers.
- The community responds by forwarding matching (in terms of *purpose* and slider value) rules to the consumer (see Figure 29.5b). This matching may also be fuzzy.
- The consumer compares the rules and selects them according to *what*, possibly popularity (those that are from the greater number of peers), and best fit in terms of privacy. After obtaining the rules, the consumer completes the privacy policies by

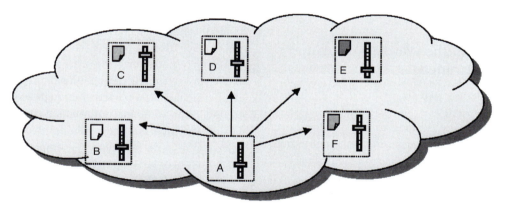

(a) New consumer "A" broadcasts request for privacy rules to the community

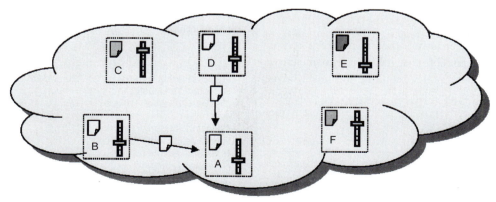

(b) Consumers B and D answer A's request

FIGURE 29.5 Retrieval of private policy rules from a community of peers.

completing the headers and possibly changing the *collector* and *disclose-to* as in the preceding derivation from surveys approach.

- The consumer adapts a privacy policy to the service provider's policy, as in the derivation by surveys approach (Figure 29.4), to try to fulfill provider requirements.

4. SPECIFYING WELL-FORMED PERSONAL PRIVACY POLICIES

This section explains how unexpected outcomes may arise from badly specified personal privacy policies. It then gives guidelines for specifying "well-formed" policies that avoid unexpected outcomes.

Unexpected Outcomes

We are interested in unexpected outcomes that result from the matching of consumer and provider policies. Unexpected outcomes result from (1) the way the matching policy was obtained, and (2) the content of the matching policy itself. We examine each of these sources in turn.

Outcomes From the Way the Matching Policy Was Obtained

The matching policy can be obtained through policy upgrades or downgrades. These policy changes can occur while the policy is being formulated for the first time or after a mismatch occurs, in an attempt to obtain a match (e.g., during policy negotiation[12,13]). Recall from the "Introduction" section that an upgraded policy reflects a higher level of privacy. On the other hand, a downgraded policy reflects a lower level of privacy.

Policy Upgrades

Given that a provider always tries to reduce a consumer's privacy, it is possible that the policy nonmatch was due to the provider's policy requiring too much privacy reduction. Suppose then that the match occurred after the provider upgraded its privacy policy to represent more

privacy, that is, require less privacy reduction. This could mean that the provider is requiring less information that is private. In this case, the provider or consumer may not realize the extra costs that may result from not having access to the private information item or items that were eliminated through upgrading. For example, leaving out the social security number may lead to more costly means of consumer identification for the provider. As another example, consider the provider and consumer policies of Figure 29.6. In this figure, suppose All Books Online upgraded its privacy policy by eliminating the credit-card requirement. This would lead to a match with Alice's privacy policy, but it could cost Alice longer waiting time to get her order, since she may be forced into an alternate and slower means of making payment (e.g., mailing a check) if payment is required prior to shipping.

Policy Downgrades

Since the consumer resists the provider's privacy reduction, it is possible that the policy nonmatch was due to the consumer's policy allowing too little privacy reduction. Suppose then that the match occurred after the consumer downgraded her privacy policy to represent less privacy, that is, to allow for more privacy reduction. This could mean that the consumer is willing to provide more information that is private. Then the provider or consumer may not realize the extra costs that result from having to safeguard the additional private information item or items that were added through downgrading. For example, the additional information might be a critical health condition that the consumer does not want anyone else to know, especially her employer, which could result in loss of her employment. The provider had better add sufficient (costly) safeguards to make sure that the

---

12 G. Yee, and L. Korba, "Bilateral e-services negotiation under uncertainty," Proceedings, *The 2003 International Symposium on Applications and the Internet (SAINT 2003)*, Orlando, Jan 2003.

13 G. Yee, and L. Korba, "The negotiation of privacy policies in distance education," Proceedings, *14th IRMA International Conference*, Philadelphia, May 2003.

Policy Use: Book Seller *Owner*: All Books Online *Valid*: unlimited	*Policy Use*: Book Seller *Owner*: Alice Consumer *Valid*: December 2009
Collector: All Books Online *What*: name, address, tel *Purposes*: identification *Retention Time*: unlimited *Disclose-To*: none *Collector*: All Books Online *What*: credit card *Purposes*: payment *Retention Time*: until payment complete *Disclose-To*: none	*Collector*: any *What*: name, address, tel *Purposes*: identification *Retention Time*: unlimited *Disclose-To*: none

FIGURE 29.6 Example online bookseller provider (left) and consumer privacy policies (right).

condition is kept confidential. The provider may not have fully realized the sensitivity of the extra information.

Outcomes from the Content of the Matching Policy

We give here some example unexpected outcomes due to the content of the matching policy. We examine the content of the header and privacy rules in turn, as follows.

Valid Field

If the *valid* field of the consumer's policy is not carefully specified, the provider may become confused upon expiry if there is not another consumer policy that becomes the new policy. In this state of confusion the provider could inadvertently disclose the consumer's private information to a party that the consumer does not want to receive the information.

Collector Field

Specification of who is to collect the consumer's private information needs to consider what happens if the collector is unavailable to receive the information. For example, consider the privacy policies of Figure 29.7. The policies are not compatible, since Alice will reveal her medical condition only to Dr. Smith, whereas the provider would like any doctor or nurse on staff to take the information. Suppose the provider upgrades its policy to satisfy Alice by allowing only Dr. Smith to receive information on Alice's condition. Then an unexpected outcome is that Alice cannot receive help from Nursing Online because Dr. Smith is not available (he might have been seriously injured in an accident), even though the policies would match and the service could theoretically proceed. There are various ways to solve this particular

situation (one way is simply to have an overriding condition that in an emergency, Alice *must* give her condition to any doctor or nurse on staff), but our point still holds: An improperly specified *collector* attribute can lead to unexpected serious consequences.

Retention Time

Care must also be taken to specify the appropriate retention time for a particular information item. The responsibility for setting an appropriate retention time lies with both the provider and the consumer. For example, consider once again the policies of Figure 29.7. Suppose Alice changes her privacy rule for medical condition from *Dr. A. Smith* to *any* and from *unlimited* to *2 years*. Then the policies match and the service can proceed. At the end of two years, the provider complies with the consumer's privacy policy and discards the information it has on Alice's medical condition. But suppose that after the two years, medical research discovers that Alice's condition is terminal unless treated with a certain new drug. Then Nursing Online cannot contact Alice to warn her, since it no longer knows that Alice has that condition. Poor Alice! Clearly, both the provider and the consumer are responsible for setting the appropriate retention time. One could conclude that in the case of a medical condition, the retention time should be *unlimited*. However, *unlimited* can also have its risks, such as retaining information beyond the point at which it no longer applies. For example, Alice could one day be cured of her condition. Then retention of Alice's condition could unjustly penalize Alice if it somehow leaked out when it is no longer true.

Disclose-To Field

If the *disclose-to* attribute of the consumer's privacy policy is not specified or improperly specified, providers can share the consumer's private information with other providers or consumers with resulting loss of privacy. Consider the following examples.

Suppose Alice has a critical health condition and she does not want her employer to know for fear of losing her job (the employer might dismiss her to save on sick leave or other benefits—this really happened![14]). Suppose that she is able to subscribe to Nursing Online as in the preceding examples. Then through the execution of the service, Nursing Online shares her condition with a pharmacy

Policy Use: Medical Help *Owner*: Nursing Online *Valid*: unlimited	*Policy Use*: Medical Help *Owner*: Alice Consumer *Valid*: December 2009
Collector: Nursing Online *What*: name, address, tel *Purposes*: contact *Retention Time*: unlimited *Disclose-To*: pharmacy	*Collector*: any *What*: name, address, tel *Purposes*: contact *Retention Time*: unlimited *Disclose-To*: pharmacy
Collector: Nursing Online *What*: medical condition *Purposes*: treatment *Retention Time*: 1 year *Disclose-To*: pharmacy	*Collector*: Dr. A. Smith *What*: medical condition *Purposes*: treatment *Retention Time*: unlimited *Disclose-To*: pharmacy

FIGURE 29.7 Example of medical help provider (left) and consumer privacy policies (right).

---

14 J. K. Kumekawa, "Health information privacy protection: crisis or common sense?", retrieved Sept. 7, 2003, from www.nursingworld.org/ojin/topic16/tpc16_2.htm.

to fill her prescription. Suppose the company that Alice works for is a pharmaceutical supplier and needs to know contact information of patients in the area where Alice lives so that the company can directly advertise to them about new drugs effective for Alice's condition. Suppose further that the pharmacy with which Nursing Online shared Alice's condition is a consumer of the pharmaceutical supplier and the pharmacy's privacy policy does not restrict the sharing of patient information that it receives secondhand. Then the pharmaceutical supplier, Alice's employer, can learn of her health condition from the pharmacy, and Alice could lose her job—an unexpected outcome with serious consequences. A possible solution to this situation is for Alice to specify *pharmacy, no further* for *disclose-to*. Then to comply with Alice's policy, Nursing Online, as a consumer of the pharmacy, in its privacy policy with the pharmacy would specify *none* for the *disclose-to* corresponding to Alice's condition, thus preventing Alice's employer from learning of her condition and so preserving her privacy.

As another example, suppose Alice, as a consumer, uses graphics services from company A and company B. Her privacy policy with these companies stipulates that the rates she pays them is private and not to be disclosed to any other party. Suppose she pays company A a higher rate than company B. Now suppose companies A and B are both consumers of company C, which provides data on rates paid for graphics services. To use company C's services, companies A and B must provide company C with deidentified information regarding rates they are paid. This does not violate the privacy policies of consumers of companies A and B, because the information is deidentified. However, company B now learns of the higher rate paid company A and seeks a higher rate from Alice. There does not appear to be any solution to this situation, since Alice has already specified *disclose-to* as *none*. This example shows that there can be unexpected outcomes that may not be preventable.

We have presented a number of unexpected outcomes arising from the way the policy match was obtained and how the content of the policy was specified. Our outcomes are all negative ones because they are the ones we need to be concerned about. There are also, of course, positive unexpected outcomes, but they are outside the scope of this chapter.

5. PREVENTING UNEXPECTED NEGATIVE OUTCOMES

The problem at hand is how to detect and prevent the unexpected outcomes that are negative or dangerous.

Since all unexpected outcomes derive from the personal privacy policy (at least in this work), it is necessary to ensure "well-formed" policies that can avoid unexpected negative outcomes. Further, if a non-well-formed policy matches the first time and leads to negative outcomes, it is too late to do anything about it. Based on the discussion of the preceding section, let's define our terms.

Definition 1

An *unexpected negative outcome* is an outcome of the use of privacy policies such that (1) the outcome is unexpected by both the provider and the consumer, and (2) the outcome leads to either the provider or the consumer or both experiencing some loss, which could be private information, money, time, convenience, job, and so on, even losses that are safety and health related.

Definition 2

A *well-formed (WF)* privacy policy (for either consumer or provider) is one that does not lead to unexpected negative outcomes. A *near well-formed (NWF)* privacy policy is one in which the attributes *valid, collector, retention time,* and *disclose-to* have each been considered against all *known* misspecifications that can lead to unexpected negative outcomes.

In Definition 2, the misspecifications can be accumulated as a result of experience (e.g., trial and error) or by scenario exploration (as earlier). We have already presented a number of them in the preceding section. An NWF privacy policy is the best that we can achieve at this time. Clearly, such a policy does not guarantee that unexpected negative outcomes will not occur; it just reduces the probability of an unexpected negative outcome.

Rules for Specifying Near Well-Formed Privacy Policies

Let's consider once more the content of a personal privacy policy by looking at the header and the privacy rules.

The header (Figure 29.1) consists of *policy use, owner,* and *valid. Policy use* and *owner* serve only to identify the policy and, assuming they are accurately specified, they are unlikely to lead to unexpected negative outcomes. That leaves *valid.* As discussed, *valid* must be specified so that it is never the case that the provider is in possession of the consumer's private information without a corresponding valid consumer policy (i.e., with the policy expired). Another way to look at this is that it must be true that the provider is no longer in possession of the consumer's information at the point of policy expiration. Hence we can construct a rule for specifying *valid*.

Rule for Specifying *Valid*

The time period specified for valid *must be at least as long as the longest retention time in the privacy policy.* This rule ensures that if the provider is in possession of the consumer's private information, there is always a corresponding consumer privacy policy that governs the information, which is what is needed to avoid the unexpected outcomes from an improperly specified *valid*.

Let's now consider the content of a privacy rule. The privacy rule consists of the attributes *collector*, *what*, *purposes*, *retention time*, and *disclose-to* (Figure 29.1). *What* and *purposes* serve only to identify the information and the purposes for which the information will be put to use. Assuming they are accurately specified, they are unlikely to lead to unexpected negative outcomes. That leaves *collector*, *retention-time*, and *disclose-to*, which we discussed. Based on this discussion, we can formulate specification rules for these attributes.

Rule for Specifying *Collector*

When specifying an individual for collector, *the consequences of the unavailability of the individual to receive the information must be considered. If the consequences do not lead to unexpected negative outcomes (as far as can be determined), proceed to specify the individual. Otherwise, or if there is doubt, specify the name of the provider (meaning anyone in the provider's organization).*

Rule for Specifying *Retention Time*

When specifying retention time, *the consequences of the expiration of the retention time (provider destroys corresponding information) must be considered. If the consequences do not lead to unexpected negative outcomes (as far as can be determined), proceed to specify the desired time. Otherwise, or if there is doubt, specify the length of time the service will be used.*

Rule for Specifying *Disclose-To*

When specifying disclose-to, *the consequences of successive propagation of your information starting with the first party mentioned in the* disclose-to *must be considered. If the consequences do not lead to unexpected negative outcomes (as far as can be determined), proceed with the specification of the* disclose-to *party or parties.*

Otherwise, or if there is doubt, specify none *or name of receiving party, no further.*

These rules address the problems discussed in the section "Outcomes from the Content of the Matching Policy" that lead to unexpected negative outcomes. Except for *valid*, in each case we require the consumer or provider to consider the consequences of the intended specification, and propose specification alternatives, where the consequences lead to unexpected negative outcomes or there is doubt. By definition, application of these rules to the specification of a privacy policy will result in a near well-formed policy. Undoubtedly, mathematical modeling of the processes at play together with state exploration tools can help to determine whether or not a particular specification will lead to unexpected negative outcomes. Such modeling and use of tools is part of future research.

Approach for Obtaining Near Well-Formed Privacy Policies

We propose that these rules for obtaining near well-formed policies be incorporated during initial policy specification. This is best achieved using an automatic or semiautomatic method for specifying privacy policies, such as the methods in the section "Semiautomated Derivation of Personal Privacy Policies." The rule for *valid* is easy to implement. Implementation of the remaining rules may employ a combination of artificial intelligence and human-computer interface techniques to assist the human specifier to reason out the consequences. Alternatively, the rules may be applied during manual policy specification in conjunction with a tool for determining possible consequences of a particular specification.

6. THE PRIVACY MANAGEMENT MODEL

In this part of the chapter, we explain how our Privacy Management Model works to protect a consumer's privacy through the use of personal privacy policies.

How Privacy Policies Are Used

An e-service provider has a privacy policy stating what PII it requires from a consumer and how the information will be used. A consumer has a privacy policy stating what PII the consumer is willing to share, with whom it may be shared, and under what circumstances it may be shared. An entity that is both a provider and a consumer has separate privacy policies for these two roles. A privacy policy is attached to a software agent, one that

FIGURE 29.8 Exchange of privacy policies (PP) between consumer agent (CA) and provider agent (PA).

acts for the consumer and another that acts for the provider. Prior to the activation of a particular service, the agent for the consumer and the agent for the provider undergo a privacy policy exchange, in which the policies are examined for compatibility (see Figure 29.8). The service is only activated if the policies are compatible, in which case we say that there is a "match" between the two policies.

The Matching of Privacy Policies

We define here the meaning of a match between a consumer personal privacy policy and a service provider privacy policy. Such matching is the comparison of corresponding rules that have the same *purposes* and similar *what*. Let *I* represent the set of rules in a consumer privacy policy and let *J* represent the set of rules in a service provider privacy policy. Let $p_{i,c}$, $i \in I$ and $p_{j,p}$, $j \in J$ represent corresponding WPRs of the consumer policy and the provider policy, respectively, that have the same *purposes* and similar *what*. We want to ascribe a function *pr* that returns a numerical level of privacy from the consumer's point of view when applied to $p_{i,c}$ and $p_{j,p}$. A high *pr* means a high degree of privacy; a low *pr* means a low degree of privacy—from the consumer's point of view. It is difficult to define *pr* universally because privacy is a subjective notion, and one consumer's view of degree of privacy may be different from another consumer's view. However, the privacy rules from the policy provider have corresponding privacy slider values and they are just what we need. We simply look up $p_{i,c}$ and $p_{j,p}$ in the policy provider database and assign the corresponding privacy slider values to them. This look-up and assignment can be done automatically.

Definition 3 (Matching Collector and Disclose-To)

The *collector* parameter from a consumer policy matches the *collector* parameter from a provider policy if and only if they are textually the same or the *collector* parameter from the consumer policy has the value *any*. The matching of *disclose-to* parameters is defined in the same way.

Definition 4 (Matching Rules)

There is a *match* between a rule in a consumer privacy policy and the corresponding (same *purposes* and similar *what*) rule in the provider policy if and only if:

$$pr(p_{i,c}) \leq pr(p_{j,p}), i \in I, j \in J$$

and the corresponding *collector* and *disclose-to* parameters match. If there is no corresponding rule in the provider policy, we say that the consumer rule corresponds to the *null* rule in the provider policy (called *consumer n-correspondence*), in which case the rules automatically match. If there is no corresponding rule in the consumer policy, we say that the provider rule corresponds to the *null* rule in the consumer policy (called *provider n-correspondence*), in which case the rules automatically mismatch.

In Definition 4, a match means that the level of privacy in the provider's rule is greater than the level of privacy in the consumer's rule (the provider is demanding less information than the consumer is willing to offer). Similarly, a consumer rule automatically matches a provider null rule because it means that the provider is not even asking for the information represented by the consumer's rule (ultimate rule privacy). A provider rule automatically mismatches a consumer null rule because it means the provider is asking for information the consumer is not willing to share, whatever the conditions (ultimate rule lack of privacy).

Definition 5 (Matching Privacy Policies)

A consumer privacy policy matches a service provider privacy policy if and only if all corresponding (same *purposes* and similar *what*) rules match and there are no cases of provider *n*-correspondence, although there may be cases of consumer *n*-correspondence.

Definition 6 (Upgrade and Downgrade of Rules and Policies)

A privacy rule or policy is considered *upgraded* if the new version represents more privacy than the prior version. A privacy rule or policy is considered *downgraded* if the new version represents less privacy than the prior version.

In comparing policies, it is not always necessary to carry out the comparison of each and every privacy rule as required by Definitions 4 and 5. We mention three shortcuts here.

Shortcut 1

Both policies are the same except one policy has fewer rules than the other policy. According to Definitions 4 and 5, there is a match if the policy with fewer rules belongs to the provider. There is a mismatch if this policy belongs to the consumer.

Shortcut 2

Both policies are the same except one policy has one or more rules with less retention time than the other policy. According to Definitions 4 and 5, there is a match if the policy with one or more rules with less retention time belongs to the provider. There is a mismatch if this policy belongs to the consumer.

Shortcut 3

Both policies are the same except one policy has one or more rules that clearly represent higher levels of privacy than the corresponding rules in the other policy. According to Definitions 4 and 5, there is a match if the policy with rules representing higher levels of privacy belongs to the provider. There is a mismatch if this policy belongs to the consumer.

Thus, in our example policies (Figures 29.1 and 29.2), there is a match for e-learning according to Shortcut 2, since the policy with lower retention time belongs to the provider. There is a mismatch for bookseller according to Shortcut 1, since the policy with fewer rules belongs to the consumer. There is a mismatch for medical help according to Shortcut 3, since the policy with the rule representing a higher level of privacy is the one specifying a particular collector (Dr. Smith), and this policy belongs to the consumer.

Personal Privacy Policy Negotiation

Where there is no match between a consumer's personal privacy policy and the privacy policy of the service provider, the consumer and provider may negotiate

TABLE 29.2 Example Negotiation Dialogue Showing Offers and Counteroffers

Provider	Employee
Okay for your exam results to be seen by your management?	Yes, but only David and Suzanne can see them.
Okay if only David and Bob see them?	No, only David and Suzanne can see them.
Can management from Divisions B and C also see your exam results?	Okay for management from Division C but not Division B.
How about letting Divisions C and D see your results?	That is acceptable.

with each other to try to achieve a match.[15,16] Consider the following negotiation to produce a privacy policy for an employee taking a course from an e-learning provider. Suppose the item for negotiation is the privacy of examination results. The employer would like to know how well the employee performed on a course in order to assign him appropriate tasks at work. Moreover, management (Bob, David and Suzanne) would like to share the results with management of other divisions, in case they could use the person's newly acquired skills. The negotiation dialogue can be expressed in terms of offers, counter-offers, and choices, as follows in Table 29.2 (read from left to right and down).

As shown in this example, negotiation is a process between two parties, wherein each party presents the other with offers and counter-offers until either an agreement is reached or no agreement is possible. Each party chooses to make a particular offer based on the value that the choice represents to that party. Each party chooses a particular offer because that offer represents the maximum value among the alternatives.

Each party in a negotiation shares a list of items to be negotiated. For each party and each item to be negotiated, there is a set of alternative positions with corresponding values. This set of alternatives is explored as new alternatives are considered at each step of the negotiation. Similarly, the values can change (or become apparent), based on these new alternatives and the other party's last offer.

---

15 G. Yee, and L. Korba, "Bilateral e-services negotiation under uncertainty," Proceedings, *The 2003 International Symposium on Applications and the Internet (SAINT 2003)*, Orlando, Jan 2003.

16 G. Yee, and L. Korba, "The negotiation of privacy policies in distance education," Proceedings, *14th IRMA International Conference*, Philadelphia, May 2003.

Let R be the set of items r_i to be negotiated, $R = \{r_1, r_2,...,r_n\}$. Let $A_{1,r,k}$ be the set of alternatives for party 1 and negotiation item r at step k, $k = 0,1,2,...,$ in the negotiation. $A_{1,r,0}$ is party 1's possible opening positions. Let $O_{1,r,k}$ be the alternative $a \in A_{1,r,k}$ that party 1 chooses to offer party 2 at step k. $O_{1,r,0}$ is party 1's chosen opening position. For example, for the first negotiation, the provider's opening position is *exam results can be seen by management*. Then for each alternative $a \in A_{1,r,k}$, $V_k(a)$ is the value function of alternative a for party 1 at step k, $k>0$, and

$$V_k(a) = f(I, O_{1,r,k-1}, O_{2,r,k-1}, \cdots)$$

where I is the common interest or purpose of the negotiation (e.g. negotiating privacy policy for "Psychology 101"), $O_{1,r,k-1}$ is the offer of party 1 at step $k \geq 1$, $O_{2,r,k-1}$ is the offer of party 2 at step $k \geq 1$, plus other factors which could include available alternatives, culture, sex, age, income level, and so on. These other factors are not required here, but their existence is without doubt since how an individual derives value can be very complex. Let $a_m \in A_{1,r,k}$ such that $V_k(a_m) = max \{V_k(a), a \in A_{1,r,k} \}$. Then at step k, $k > 0$ in the negotiation process, party 1 makes party 2 an offer $O_{1,r,k}$ where

$$O_{1,r,k} = a_m \quad if \quad V_k(a_m) > V_k(O_{2,r,k-1}), \qquad (1)$$

$$= O_{2,r,k-1} \quad if \quad V_k(a_m) \leq V_k(O_{2,r,k-1}). \qquad (2)$$

Equation 1 represents the case where party 1 makes a counter-offer to party 2's offer. Equation 2 represents the case where party 1 accepts party 2's offer and agreement is reached! A similar development can be done for party 2. Thus, there is a negotiation tree $\vec{r}$ corresponding to each item r to be negotiated, with two main branches extending from r at the root (see Figure 29.9). The two main branches correspond to the two negotiating parties. Each main branch has leaves representing the alternatives at each step. At each step, including the opening positions at step 0, each party's offer is visible to the other for comparison. As negotiation proceeds, each party does a traversal of its corresponding main branch. If the negotiation is successful, the traversals converge at the successful alternative (one of the parties adopts the other's offer as his own, Equation 2) and the negotiation tree is said to be complete. Each party may choose to terminate the negotiation if the party feels no progress is being made; the negotiation tree is then said to be *incomplete*.

In Figure 29.9, the influences arrows show that a particular alternative offered by the other party at step k will influence the alternatives of the first party at step $k + 1$. Figure 29.10 illustrates the negotiation tree using the above privacy of examination results negotiation.

Personal privacy policy negotiation may be used to avoid negative unexpected outcomes, even if the privacy policies involved are near well formed, since near well-formed policies may still not match. At a policies mismatch, the consumer or the provider upgrades or downgrades the individual policy to try to get a match. In so doing, each could inadvertently introduce new values into the policy or remove values from the policy that result in negative unexpected outcomes or loss of

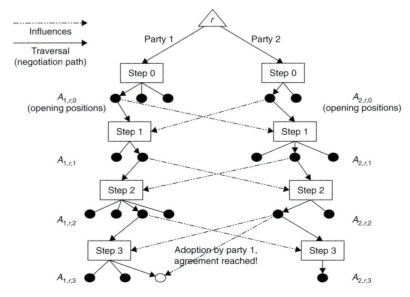

FIGURE 29.9 Negotiation tree $\vec{r}$ for a policy negotiation.

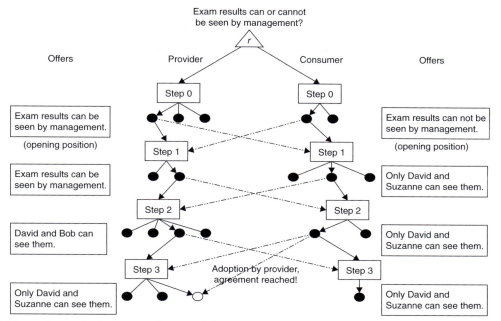

FIGURE 29.10 Negotiation tree for the first part of our negotiation.

TABLE 29.3 Preventing Unexpected Negative Outcomes: Nursing Online

Nursing Online (Provider)	Alice (Consumer)
Okay if a nurse on our staff is told your medical condition?	No, only Dr. Alexander Smith can be told my medical condition.
We cannot provide you with any nursing service unless we know your medical condition.	Okay, I'll see Dr. Smith instead.
You are putting yourself at risk. What if you need emergency medical help for your condition and Dr. Smith is not available?	You are right. Do you have any doctors on staff?
Yes, we always have doctors on call. Okay to allow them to know your medical condition?	That is acceptable. I will modify my privacy policy to share my medical condition with your doctors on call.

NWF-ness. We propose the use of privacy policy negotiation between consumer and provider agents to guide the policy upgrading or downgrading to avoid undoing the values already put in place for NWF-ness in the initial specification. Alternatively, negotiation may expose a needed application of the above rules for a policy to be near well formed. This is also a consequences exploration, but here both provider and consumer do the exploration while negotiating in real time.

For example, in the All Books Online example of the "Outcomes From How the Matching Policy Was Obtained" section, where Alice does not need to provide her credit card, negotiation between Alice and All Books Online could have identified the consequence that Alice would need to wait longer for her order and direct her to another, more viable alternative, such as agreeing to provide her credit card. Similarly, in the example (same

section) where the provider has to introduce more costly safeguards to protect the consumer's added highly sensitive information, negotiation could have uncovered the high sensitivity of the new information and possibly result in a different less costly alternative chosen (e.g., the new information may not be needed after all).

Table 29.3 illustrates how negotiation can detect and prevent the unexpected negative outcome of Alice having no access to medical service when it is needed (read from left to right and down). The result of this negotiation is that Nursing Online will be able to provide Alice with nursing service whenever Alice requires it, once she makes the change in her privacy policy reflecting the results of negotiation. If this negotiation had failed (Alice did not agree), Alice will at least be alerted to the possibility of a bad outcome, and may take other measures to avoid it. This example shows how negotiation

TABLE 29.4 Preventing Unexpected Negative Outcomes: All Books Online

All Books Online (Provider)	Alice (Consumer)
Okay if you provide your credit-card information?	No, I do not want to risk my credit-card number getting stolen.
If you do not provide your credit-card information, you will need to send us a certified check before we can ship your order. This will delay your order for up to three weeks.	I still don't want to risk my credit-card number getting stolen.
Your credit-card information will be encrypted during transmission and we keep your information in secure storage once we receive it. You need not worry.	Okay, I will modify my privacy policy to share my credit-card information.

may persuade the consumer to resolve a mismatch by applying the above rule for specifying *collector*.

Table 29.4 gives another example of negotiation at work using Alice's bookseller policy from Figure 29.1. This policy mismatched because Alice did not want to provide her credit-card information. At the end of the negotiation, Alice modifies her privacy policy and receives service from All Books Online.

Personal Privacy Policy Compliance

As we have seen, the above Privacy Principles require a provider to be accountable for complying with the Privacy Principles (CSAPP.1) and the privacy wishes of the consumer. In practice, a provider is required to appoint someone in its organization to be accountable for its compliance to Privacy Principles (CSAPP.1). This person is usually called the chief privacy officer (CPO). An important responsibility of the CPO is to put in place a procedure for receiving and responding to complaints or inquiries about the privacy policy and the practice of handling personal information. This procedure should be easily accessible and simple to use. The procedure should also refer to the dispute resolution process that the organization has adopted. Other responsibilities of the CPO include auditing the current privacy practices of the organization, formulating the organization's privacy policy, and implementing and maintaining this policy. *We propose that the CPO's duties be extended to include auditing the provider's compliance to the consumer's personal privacy policy.*

Further discussion of personal privacy policy compliance is beyond the scope of this chapter. We mention in passing that an alternative method of ensuring compliance is the use of a Privacy Policy Compliance System (PPCS) as presented in.[17]

---

17 G. Yee, and L. Korba, "Privacy policy compliance for web services," Proceedings, *2004 IEEE International Conference on Web Services (ICWS 2004)*, San Diego, July 2004.

7. DISCUSSION AND RELATED WORK

We have presented methods for the semiautomatic derivation of personal privacy policies. Given our Privacy Management Model, there needs to be a way for consumers to derive their personal privacy policies easily or consumers will simply not use the approach. The only "alternative" that we can see to semiautomated derivation is for the consumer to create his/her personal privacy policy manually. This can be done by a knowledgeable and technically inclined consumer, but would require a substantially larger effort (and correspondingly less likely to be used) than the semiautomated approaches. In addition to ease of use, our approaches ensure consistency of privacy rules by community consensus. This has the added benefit of facilitating provider compliance, since it is undoubtedly easier for a provider to comply to privacy rules that reflect the community consensus than rules that only reflect the feelings of a few.

We believe our approaches for the semiautomatic derivation of personal privacy policies are quite feasible, even taking account of the possible weaknesses described in this chapter. In the surveys approach, the consumer has merely to select the privacy level when prompted for the rules from the provider's policy. In fact, the user is already familiar with the use of a privacy slider to set the privacy level for Internet browsers (e.g., Microsoft Internet Explorer, under Internet Options). We have implemented the surveys approach in a prototype that we created for negotiating privacy policies. We plan to conduct experiments with this implementation, using volunteers to confirm the usability of the surveys approach. In the retrieval approach, the consumer is asked to do a little bit more—compare and select the rules received—but this should be no more complex than today's ecommerce transactions or the use of a word-processing program. Likewise, adapting a personal policy to a provider policy should be of the same level of complexity. Like anything else, the widespread use of these methods will take a little time to achieve, but people will come around to using them, just as they are using ecommerce; it is merely a matter of education and experience. Further, consumers are becoming more and more aware of their privacy rights as diverse jurisdictions enact privacy legislation to protect consumer privacy. In Canada, the Personal Information Protection and Electronic Documents Act has been in effect across all retail outlets since January 1, 2004, and consumers are reminded of their privacy rights every time they visit their optician, dentist, or other business requiring their private information.

We now discuss some possible weaknesses in our approaches. The surveys approach requires trust in the policy provider. Effectively, the policy provider becomes a trusted third party. Clearly, the notion of a trusted third party as a personal policy provider may be controversial to some. Any error made by the policy provider could affect PII for many hundreds or thousands of people. A certification process for the policy provider is probably required. For instance, in Canada, the offices for the provincial and federal privacy commissioners could be this certification body. They could also be policy providers themselves. Having privacy commissioners' offices take on the role of policy providers seems to be a natural fit, given their mandate as privacy watchdogs for the consumer. However, the process would have a cost. Costs could be recovered via micro-charges to the consumer, or the service provider for the policies provided. Aggregated information from the PII surveys could be sold to service providers who could use them to formulate privacy policies that are more acceptable to consumers.

There is a challenge in the retrieval approach regarding how to carry it out in a timely fashion. Efficient peer-to-peer search techniques will collect the rules in a timely manner, but the amount of information collected by the requester may be quite large. Furthermore, since the various rules collected will probably differ from one another, the requestor will have to compare them to determine which ones to select. Quick comparisons to reduce the amount of data collected could be done through a peer-to-peer rules search that employs a rules hash array containing hashed values for different portions of the rule.

In the section on policy compliance, a weakness of having the CPO be responsible for protecting consumer privacy is that the CPO belongs to the provider's organization. Will he be truly diligent about his task to protect the consumer's privacy? To get around this question, the CPO can use secure logs to answer any challenges doubting his organization's compliance. Secure logs automatically record all the organization's use of the consumer's

private information, both during and after the data collection. Cryptographic techniques[18] provide assurance that any modification of the secure log is detectable. In addition, database technology such as Oracle9i can tag the data with its privacy policy to evaluate the policy every time data is accessed.[19] The system can be set up so that any policy violation can trigger a warning to the CPO.

An objection could be raised that our approaches are not general, having been based on privacy policy content that was derived from Canadian privacy legislation. We have several answers for this objection. First, as we pointed out, Canadian privacy legislation is representative of privacy legislation in many countries. Therefore the content of privacy policies derived from Canadian privacy legislation is applicable in many countries. Second, as we also pointed out, Canadian privacy legislation is also representative of the Fair Information Practices standards, which have universal applicability. Third, all privacy policies regardless of their content will have to converge on the content that we presented, since such content is required by legislation. Finally, our approaches can be customized to any form of privacy policy, regardless of the content. We next discuss related work.

The use of privacy policies as a means of safeguarding privacy for ebusiness is relatively new. There is relatively little research on the use of personal privacy policies. For these reasons, we have not been able to find many authors who have written on the derivation of personal privacy policies. Dreyer and Olivier[20] worked on generating and analyzing privacy policies for computer systems, to regulate private information flows within the system, rather than generating personal privacy policies. Brodie et al.[21] describe a privacy management workbench for use by organizations. Within this workbench are tools to allow organizational users tasked with the responsibility to author organizational privacy policies. The tools allow these users to use natural language for policy creation and to visualize the results to ensure that they accomplished their intended goals. These authors

---

18 B. Schneier, and J. Kelsey, "Secure audit logs to support computer forensics," *ACM Transactions on Information and System Security*, 2(2), pp. 159-176, ACM, May 1999.

19 G. Yee, K. El-Khatib, L. Korba, A. Patrick, R. Song, and Y. Xu, "Privacy and trust in e-government," chapter in *Electronic Government Strategies and Implementation*, Idea Group Inc., 2004.

20 L. C. J. Dreyer, and M. S. Olivier, "A workbench for privacy policies," Proceedings, *The Twenty-Second Annual International Computer Software and Applications Conference (COMPSAC '98)*, pp. 350-355, August 19-21, 1998.

21 C. Brodie, C.-M. Karat, J. Karat, and J. Feng, "Usable security and privacy: a case study of developing privacy management tools," *Symposium On Usable Privacy and Security (SOUPS) 2005*, July 6-8, Pittsburgh, 2005.

do not address the creation of personal privacy policies. Irwin and Yu[22] present an approach for dynamically asking the user suitable questions to elicit the user's privacy preferences. They present a framework for determining which questions are suitable. However, there is no use of community consensus which means the resulting policies could be highly subjective. This means that providers would find it more difficult to use such policies to help them formulate provider privacy policies that would be acceptable to the majority of consumers.

Other work that uses privacy policies is primarily represented by the W3C Platform for Privacy Preferences.[23] This provides a Web site operator with a way of expressing the site's privacy policy using a P3P standard format and to have that policy automatically retrieved and interpreted by user agents (e.g., browser plug-in). The user can express rudimentary privacy preferences and have those preferences automatically checked against the web site's policy before proceeding. However, P3P cannot be used to fulfill the requirements of privacy legislation, has no compliance mechanism, and represents a "take it or leave it" view to privacy—if you don't like the privacy policy of the Web site, you leave it. There is no provision for negotiation. In addition, Jensen and Potts[24] evaluated the usability of 64 online privacy policies and the practice of posting them and determined that significant changes needed to be made to the practice in order to meet usability and regulatory requirements. Finally, Stufflebeam et al.[25] presented a case study in which they used P3P and Enterprise Privacy Authorization Language (EPAL) to formulate two healthcare Web site privacy policies and described the shortcomings they found with using these languages.

Negative outcomes arising from privacy policies may be regarded as a feature interaction problem, where policies "interact" and produce unexpected outcomes.[26] Traditionally, feature interactions have been considered mainly in the telephony or communication services domains.[27] More recent papers, however, have focused on other domains such as the Internet, multimedia systems, mobile systems,[28] and Internet personal appliances.[29] In this work, we have chosen not to frame negative outcomes from privacy policies as a feature interaction problem. In so doing, we have obtained new insights and results. Apart from feature interactions, other possible related work has to do with resolving conflicts in access control and mobile computing (e.g. [30,31]). However, it is believed that these methods and similar methods in other domains will not work for privacy due to the subjective nature of privacy, that is, personal involvement to consider each privacy rule is necessary.

Most negotiation research is on negotiation via autonomous software agents, focusing on methods or models for agent negotiation[32] and can incorporate techniques from other scientific areas such as game theory (e.g.[33]), fuzzy logic (e.g.[34]) and genetic algorithms (e.g.[35]). The research also extends to autonomous agent negotiation for specific application areas, such as ecommerce[36] and service-level agreements for the Internet.[37] Apart from

22 K. Irwin, and T. Yu, "Determining user privacy preferences by asking the right questions: an automated approach," Proceedings of the *2005 ACM Workshop on Privacy in the Electronic Society (WPES 2005)*, November 7, Alexandria, 2005.

23 W3C Platform, "The platform for privacy preferences," retrieved Sept. 2, 2002, from www.w3.org/P3P/.

24 Jensen, C., and Potts, C., "Privacy policies as decision-making tools: an evaluation of online privacy notices," Proceedings of the *2004 Conference on Human Factors in Computing Systems (CHI 2004)*, April 24-29, Vienna, 2004.

25 W. Stufflebeam, A. Anton, Q. He, and N. Jain, "Specifying privacy policies with P3P and EPAL: lessons learned," Proceedings of the *2004 ACM Workshop on Privacy in the Electronic Society (WPES 2004)*, October 28, Washington, D.C., 2004.

26 G. Yee, and L. Korba, "Feature interactions in policy driven privacy management", Proceedings, *Seventh International Workshop on Feature Interactions in Telecommunications and Software Systems*, Ottawa, Ontario, Canada, June 2003.

27 D. Keck, and P. Kuehn, "The feature and service interaction problem in telecommunications systems: a survey," in *IEEE Transactions on Software Engineering*, Vol. 24, No. 10, October 1998.

28 L. Blair, and J. Pang, "Feature interactions: life beyond traditional telephony," Distributed Multimedia Research Group, Computing Dept., Lancaster University, UK.

29 M. Kolberg, E. Magill, D. Marples, and S. Tsang, "Feature interactions in services for internet personal appliances," Proceedings, *IEEE International Conference on Communications (ICC 2002)*, Vol. 4, pp. 2613-2618, 2002.

30 T. Jaeger, R. Sailer, and X. Zhang, "Resolving constraint conflicts", *Proceedings of the Ninth ACM Symposium on Access Control Models and Technologies*, June 2004.

31 L. Capra, W. Emmerich, and C. Mascolo, "A micro-economic approach to conflict resolution in mobile computing," Proceedings of the *10th ACM SIGSOFT Symposium on Foundations of Software Engineering*, November 2002.

32 P. Huang, and K. Sycara, "A Computational model for online agent negotiation", Proceedings of the *35th Annual Hawaii International Conference on System Sciences*, 2002.

33 Y. Murakami, H. Sato, and A. Namatame, "Co-evolution in negotiation games," Proceedings, *Fourth International Conference on Computational Intelligence and Multimedia Applications*, 2001.

34 R. Lai, and M. Lin, "Agent negotiation as fuzzy constraint processing," Proceedings of the *2002 IEEE International Conference on Fuzzy Systems (FUZZ-IEEE'02)*, Vol. 2, 2002.

35 M. Tu, E. Wolff, and W. Lamersdorf, "Genetic algorithms for automated negotiations: a FSM-based application approach," Proceedings, *11th International Workshop on Database and Expert Systems Applications*, 2000.

36 M. Chung, and V. Honavar, "A Negotiation Model in Agent-mediated Electronic Commerce," Proceedings, *International Symposium on Multimedia Software Engineering*, 2000.

37 T. Nguyen, N. Boukhatem, Y. Doudane, and G. Pujolle, "COPS-SLS: A service level negotiation protocol for the internet," *IEEE Communications Magazine*, Vol. 40, Issue 5, May 2002.

negotiation by autonomous software agents, research has also been carried out on support tools for negotiation (e.g.[38]), which typically provide support in position communication, voting, documentation communication, and big picture negotiation visualization and navigation.

8. CONCLUSIONS AND FUTURE WORK

The protection of personal privacy is paramount if e-services are to be successful. A personal privacy policy approach to privacy protection seems best. However, for this approach to work, consumers must be able to derive their personal privacy policies easily. To describe semi-automated approaches to derive personal privacy policies, we first defined the content of a personal privacy policy using the Canadian Privacy Principles. We then presented two semiautomated approaches for obtaining the policies: one based on third-party surveys of consumer perceptions of privacy, the other based on retrieval from a peer community. Both approaches reflect the privacy sensitivities of the community, giving the consumer confidence that his/her privacy preferences are interpreted with the best information available. We then explained how personal privacy policies can lead to negative unexpected outcomes if not properly specified. We proposed specification rules that can be applied in conjunction with semi-automated policy derivation to result in near well-formed policies that can avoid the negative unexpected outcomes. We closed with our Privacy Management Model, which explains how privacy policies are used and the meaning of privacy policy matching. We described policy negotiation, not only for resolving policies that do not match, but also as an effective means for avoiding negative unexpected outcomes. Finally, we suggested how consumers could be assured that providers will comply with personal privacy policies.

We have based our work on our particular formulation of a privacy policy. An obvious question is whether our approaches apply to other formulations of privacy policies. We believe the answer is yes, for the following reasons: (1) privacy policy formulations (i.e., contents) cannot differ too much from one another since they must all conform to privacy legislation and our policy is a minimal policy that so conforms, and (2) if necessary, we can fit our approaches to any formulation by applying the same logic we used in this work.

Possible topics for future work include (1) looking at other methods for easily deriving personal privacy policies, (2) conducting experiments with volunteers, using the implementation of the surveys approach in our privacy policy negotiation prototype to confirm usability and resolve any scalability/performance issues, (3) investigating other possible unexpected outcomes from the interaction of privacy policies, (4) designing tools for outcomes exploration to identify the seriousness of each consequence, (5) exploring other methods for avoiding or mitigating negative unexpected outcomes from the interaction of privacy policies, and (6) investigating ways to facilitate personal privacy policy negotiation, such as improving trust, usability and response times.

---

38 D. Druckman, R. Harris, and B. Ramberg, "Artificial computer-assisted international negotiation: a tool for research and practice," Proceedings of the *35th Annual Hawaii International Conference on System Sciences*, 2002.

## Chapter 30

Virtual Private Networks

Jim Harmening
Computer Bits, Inc.

Joe Wright
Computer Bits, Inc.

With the incredible advance of the Internet, it has become more and more popular to set up virtual private networks (VPNs) within organizations. VPNs have been around for many years and have branched out into more and more varieties. (See Figure 30.1 for a high-level view of a VPN.) Once only the largest of organizations would utilize VPN technology to connect multiple networks over the Internet "public networks," but now VPNs are being used by many small businesses as a way to allow remote users access to their business networks from home or while traveling.

Consultants have changed their recommendations from dial-in systems and leased lines to VPNs for several reasons. Security concerns were once insurmountable, forcing the consultants to set up direct dial-in lines. Not that the public telephone system was much more secure, but it gave the feeling of security and with the right setup, dial-in systems approach secure settings. Sometimes they utilized automatic callback options and had their own encryption. Now, with advanced security, including random-number generator logins, a network administrator is far more likely to allow access to his network via a VPN. High-speed Internet access is now the rule instead of the exception. Costs have plummeted for the hardware and software to make the VPN connection as well. The proliferation of vendors, standardization of Internet Protocol (IP) networks, and ease of setup all played a role in the increasingly wide use and acceptance of VPN.

The key to this technology is the ability to route communications over a public network to allow access to office servers, printers, or data warehouses in an inexpensive manner. As high-speed Internet has grown and become prevalent throughout the world, VPNs over the public Internet have become common. Even inexpensive hotels are offering free Internet access to their customers. This is usually done through Wi-Fi connections, thus causing some concern for privacy, but the connections are out there. Moreover, the iPhone, Treo, and other multifunction Web-enabled phones are giving mobile users access to the Internet via their phones. Finally, one of the best ways to access the Internet is via a wireless USB or PCMCIA card from the major phone companies. These dedicated modem cards allow users to surf the Internet as long as they are in contact with the cell towers of their subscribing company.

One of the sources of our information on the overview of VPNs is James Yonan's talk at Linux Fest Northwest in 2004. You can read the entire presentation online at openvpn.net.

"Fundamentally, a VPN is a set of tools which allow networks at different locations to be securely connected, using a public network as the transport layer."[1] This quote from Yonan's talk states the basic premise incredibly well. Getting two computers to work together over the Internet is a difficult feat, but making two different computer networks be securely connected together via the public Internet is pure genius. By connecting different locations over the Internet, many companies cut out the cost of dedicated circuits from the phone companies. Some companies have saved thousands of dollars by getting rid of their Integrated Services Digital Network (ISDN) lines, too. Once thought of as the high-speed (128,000 bits per second, or 128kbs) Holy Grail, it is now utilized mainly by videoconferencing systems that require a direct sustained connection, but the two endpoints aren't usually known too much prior to the connection requirement. The ISDN lines are often referred

---

[1] www.openvpn.net/papers/BLUG-talk/2.html, copyright James Yonan 2003

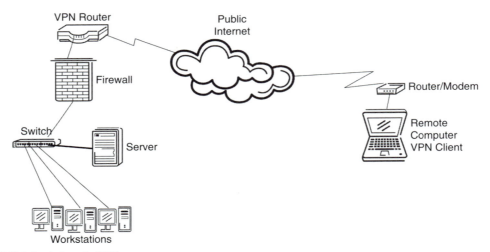

FIGURE 30.1 A high-level view of a VPN.

to as glorified fast dial-up connections. Some companies utilize multiple ISDN connections to get higher-quality voice or video.

Not all VPNs had security in the early days. Packets of information were transmitted as cleartext and could be easily seen. To keep the network systems secure, the information must be encrypted. Throughout the past 20 years, different encryption schemes have gained and lost favor. Some are too easy to break with the advanced speed of current computers; others require too much processing power at the router level, thus making their implementation expensive. This is one of those areas where an early technology seemed too expensive, but through time and technological advancements, the hardware processing power has caught up with requirements of the software. Encryption that seems secure in our current environments is often insecure as time passes. With supercomputers doing trillions of computations a second, we are required to make sure that the technology employed in our networks is up to the task. There are many different types of encryption, as we discuss later in the chapter.

Early in the VPN life-cycle, the goal for organizations was to connect different places or offices to remote computer systems. This was usually done with a dedicated piece of hardware at each site. This "point-to-point" setup allowed for a secure transmission between two sites, allowing users access to computer resources, data, and communications systems. Many of these sites were too expensive to access, so the advent of the point-to-point systems allowed access where none existed. Now multinational companies set up VPNs to access their manufacturing plants all over the world.

Accounting, order entry, and personnel databases were the big driving forces for disparate locations to be connected. Our desire to have more and more information

FIGURE 30.2 ATT logo; the company was often referred to as Ma Bell.

and faster and faster access to information has driven this trend. Now individuals at home are connecting their computers into the corporate network either through VPN connections or SSL-VPN Web connections. This proliferation is pushing vendors to make better security, especially in unsecure or minimally secure environments. Giving remote access to some, unfortunately, makes for a target to hackers and crackers.

1. HISTORY

Like many innovations in the network arena, the telephone companies first created VPNs. ATT, with it's familiar "Bell logo" (see Figure 30.2), was one of the leading providers of Centrex systems. The goal was to take advantage of different telephone enhancements for conferencing and dialing extensions within a company to connect to employees. Many people are familiar with the Centrex systems that the phone companies offered for many years.

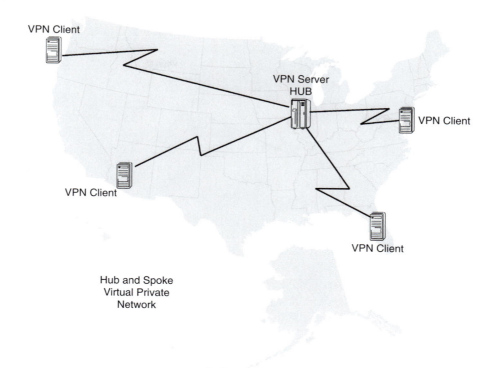

VPN Client

VPN Server
HUB

VPN Client

VPN Client

VPN Client

Hub and Spoke
Virtual Private
Network

FIGURE 30.3 The hub in the early days.

With Centrex the phone company did not require you to have a costly private branch exchange (PBX) switching system onsite. These PBXs were big, needed power, and cost a bundle of money. By eliminating the PBX and using the Centrex system, an organization could keep costs down yet have enhanced service and flexibility of the advanced phone services through the telephone company PBX.

The primary business of the phone companies was to provide voice service, but they also wanted to provide data services. Lines from the phone company from one company location to another (called *leased lines*) offered remote data access from one part of a company to another.

Many companies started utilizing different types of software to better utilize their leased lines. In the early days, the main equipment was located centrally, and all the offices connected to the "hub" (see Figure 30.3). This was a good system and many companies still prefer this network topography, but times are changing. Instead of having a hub-and-spoke design, some companies opted to daisy-chain their organization together, thus trying to limit the distance they would have to pay for their leased lines. So a company would have a leased line from New York to Washington, D.C., another from D.C. to Atlanta, and a third from Atlanta to Miami. This would cut costs over the typical hub-and-spoke system of having all the lines go through one central location (see Figure 30.4).

With the proliferation of the Internet and additional costs for Internet connections and leased-line connections, the companies pushed the software vendors to make cheap connections via the Internet. VPNs solved their problems and had a great return on investment (ROI). Within a year, the cost of the VPN equipment paid for itself through eliminating the leased lines. Though this technology has been around for years, some organizations still rely on leased lines due to a lack of high-speed Internet in remote areas.

In 1995, IPsec was one of the first attempts at bringing encryption to the VPN arena. One of the early downfalls of this technology was its complexity and requirement for fast processors on the routers to keep up with the high bandwidths. In 1995, according to ietf.org, "at least one hardware implementation can encrypt or decrypt at about 1 Gbps."[2] Yes, one installation that cost thousands of dollars.

Fortunately, Moore's Law has been at work, and today our processing speeds are high enough to get IPsec working on even small routers. Moore's Law is named after Intel cofounder Gordon Moore, who wrote in 1965: "the number of transistors on a chip will double about

---

2 http://tools.ietf.org/html/draft-ietf-ipsec-esp-des-cbc-03 "The ESP DES-CBC Transform"

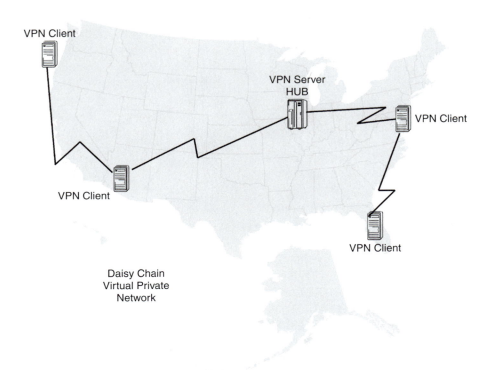

FIGURE 30.4 One central location for the hub-and-spoke system.

every two years."[3] This doubling of chip capacity allows for more and more computing to be done.

Another issue with early IPsec is that it is fairly inflexible, with differing IP addresses. Many home and home office computers utilize dynamic IP addresses. You may get a different IP address each time you turn on your computer and connect to the Internet. The IPsec connection will have to be reestablished and may cause a hiccup in your transmissions or the requirement that a password be reentered. This seems unreasonable to most users.

Another difficulty is the use of Network Address Translation (NAT) for some networks. Each computer on the network has the same IP address as far as the greater Internet is concerned. This is in part because of the shortage of legal IP addresses available in the IPv4 address space. As we move closer and closer to the IPv6 address space model, some of these issues will be moot, for a while. Soon, every device we own, including our refrigerators, radios, and heating systems, will have a static IP address. Maybe even our kitchen sinks will. Big Brother is coming, but won't it be cool to see what your refrigerator is up to?

In the late 1990s Linux began to take shape as a great test environment for networking. A technology called

tun, short for *tunnel*, allows data to be siphoned through the data stream to create virtual hardware. From the operating system perspective it looks like point-to-point network hardware, even though it is virtual hardware. Another technology, called *tap*, looks like Ethernet traffic but also uses virtual hardware to fool the operating system into thinking it is real hardware.

These technologies utilize a program running in the user area of the operating system software in order to look like a file. They can read and write IP packets directly to and from this virtual hardware, even though the systems are connected via the public Internet and could be on the other side of the world. Security is an issue with the tun/tap method. One way to build in security is to utilize the Secure Shell protocol (SSH) and transport the data via a User Datagram Protocol (UDP) or Transmission Control Protocol (TCP) packet sent over the network.

It is important to remember that IP is an unreliable protocol. There are collisions on all IP networks; high traffic times give high collisions and lost packets, but the protocol is good at resending the packets so that eventually all the data will get to its destination. On the other hand, TCP is a reliable protocol. So, like military and intelligence, we have the added problem of a reliable transportation protocol (TCP) using an unreliable transportation (IP) method.

---

3 www.intel.com/technology/mooreslaw/ Gordon Moore 1965.

So, how does it work if it is unreliable? Well, eventually all the packets get there; TCP makes sure of that, and they are put in order and delivered to the other side. Some may have to be retransmitted, but most won't and the system should work relatively quickly.

One way that we can gain some throughput and added security is by utilizing encapsulation protocols. Encapsulation allows you to stuff one kind of protocol inside another type of protocol. The idea is to encapsulate a TCP packet inside a UDP packet. This forces the application to worry about dropped packets and reliability instead of the TCP network layer, since UDP packets are not a reliable packet protocol. This really increases speed, especially during peak network usage times.

So, follow this logic: The IP packets are encrypted, then encapsulated and stored for transport via UDP over the Internet. On the receiving end the host system receives, decrypts, and authenticates the packets and then sends them to the tap or tun virtual adapter at the other end, thus giving a secure connection between the two sides, with the operating system not really knowing or caring about the encryption or transport methods. From the OS point of view, it is like a data file being transmitted; the OS doesn't have to know that the hardware is virtual. It is just as happy thinking that the virtual data file is real—and it processes it just like it processes a physical file locally stored on a hard drive.

OpenVPN is just one of many Open Source VPNs in use today. Google it and you will see a great example of a VPN system that employs IPsec.

IPsec is another way to ensure security on your VPN connection. IPsec took the approach that it needed to replace the IP stack and do it securely. IPsec looks to do its work in the background, without utilizing operating system CPU cycles. This is wonderful for its non-impact on servers, but it then relies heavily on the hardware.

A faster-growing encryption scheme involves Secure Socket Layer (SSL) VPN, as we talk about later in this chapter. This scheme gives the user access to resources like a VPN but through a Web browser. The end user only needs to install the browser plug-ins to get this VPN up and working, for remote access on the fly. One example of this SSL type of VPN is LogMeIn Rescue.[4] It sets up a remote control session within the SSL layer of the browser. It can also extend resources out to the remote user without initiating a remote-control session.

With all these schemes and more, we should take a look at who is in charge of helping to standardize

---

4 www.logmein.com

FIGURE 30.5 Logo for IETF

FIGURE 30.6 Logo for IEEE.

the hardware and software requirements of the VPN world.

2. WHO IS IN CHARGE?

For all this interconnectivity to actually work, there are several organizations that publish standards and work for cooperation among vendors in the sea of computer networking change. In addition to these public groups, there are also private companies that are working toward new protocols to improve speed and efficiency in the VPN arena.

The two biggest public groups are the Internet Engineering Task Force (www.ietf.org; see Figure 30.5) and the Institute of Electrical and Electronic Engineers (www.IEEE.org; see Figure 30.6). Each group has its own way of doing business and publishes its recommendations and standards.

As the IEEE Web site proclaims, the group's "core purpose is to foster technological innovation and excellence for the benefit of humanity." This is a wonderful and noble purpose. Sometimes they get it right and sometimes input and interference from vendors get in the way of moving technology forward—or worse yet, vendors go out and put up systems that come out before the specifications get published, leaving humanity with different standards. This has happened several times on the wireless networking standards group. Companies release their implementation of a standard prior to final agreement by the standards boards.

FIGURE 30.7 The ANSI logo.

The group's vision is stated thus: "IEEE will be essential to the global technical community and to technical professionals everywhere, and be universally recognized for the contributions of technology and of technical professionals in improving global conditions."[5]

The Internet Engineering Task Force (IETF) is a large, open international community of network designers, operators, vendors, and researchers concerned with the evolution of the Internet architecture and the smooth operation of the Internet. It is open to any interested individual. The IETF Mission Statement is documented in RFC 3935. According to the group's mission statement, "The goal of the IETF is to make the Internet work better."[6]

Finally, we can't get away from acronyms unless we include the United States Government. An organization called the American National Standards Institute (ANSI; www.ansi.org) is an 85-year-old organization with responsibilities that include writing voluntary standards for the marketplace to have somewhere to turn for standardizing efforts to improve efficiencies and interoperability (see Figure 30.7).

There are many standards for many physical things, such as the size of a light bulb socket or the size of an outlet on your wall. These groups help set standards for networking. Two international groups that are represented by ANSI are the International Organization for Standardization (ISO) and International Electrotechnical Commission (IEC).

These organizations have ongoing workgroups and projects that are tackling the various standards that will be in use in the future releases of the VPN standard. They also have the standards written for current interoperability. However, this does not require a vendor to follow the standards. Each vendor can and will implement parts and pieces of standards, but unless they meet all the requirements of a specification, they will not get to call their system compatible.

There are several IEEE projects relating to networking and the advancement of interconnectivity. If you are interested in networking, the 802 family of workgroups is your best bet. Check out www.ieee802.org.

3. VPN TYPES

As we talked about earlier, this encryption standard for VPN access is heavy on the hardware for processing the encryption and decrypting the packets. This protocol operates at the Layer 3 level of the Open Systems Interconnection (OSI) model. The OSI model dates to 1982 by the International Organization for Standardization.[7] IPsec is still used by many vendors for their VPN hardware.

IPsec

One of the weaknesses of VPNs we mentioned earlier is also a strength. Because the majority of the processing work is done by the interconnecting hardware, the application doesn't have to worry about knowing anything about IPsec at all.

There are two modes for IPsec. First, the transport mode secures the information all the way to each device trying to make the connection. The second mode is the transport mode, which is used for network-to-network communications. The latest standard for IPsec came out in 2005.

L2TP

Layer Tunneling Protocol was released in 1999; then to improve the reliability and security of Point-to-Point Tunneling Protocol (PPTP), L2TP was created. It really is a layer 5 protocol because it uses the session layer in the OSI model.

This was more cumbersome than PPTP and forced the users at each end to have authentication with one another. It also has weak security, thus most implementations of the L2TP protocol utilize IPsec to enhance security.

There is a 32-bit header for each packet that includes flags, versions, Tunnel ID, and Session IDs. There is also a space for the packet size.

Because this is a very weak protocol, some vendors combined it with IPsec to form L2TP/IPsec. In this implementation you take the strong, secure nature of IPsec as the secure channel, and the L2TP will act as the tunnel.

This protocol is a server/user setup. One part of the software acts as the server and waits for the user side of the software to make contact. Because this protocol can handle many users or clients at a time, some Asymmetric Digital Subscriber Line (ADSL) providers use this L2TP protocol and share the resources at the telephone central office. Their modem/routers utilize L2TP to phone home

---

5 www.ieee.org/web/aboutus/visionmission.html Copyright 2008 IEEE
6 www.ietf.org/rfc/rfc3935.txt Copyright The Internet Society 2004

7 http://en.wikipedia.org/wiki/Open_Systems_Interconnection

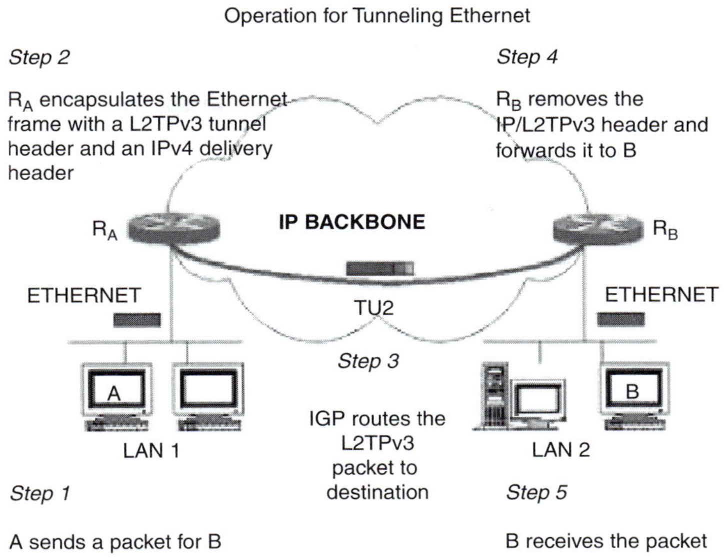

Operation for Tunneling Ethernet

Step 2

R_A encapsulates the Ethernet frame with a L2TPv3 tunnel header and an IPv4 delivery header

Step 4

R_B removes the IP/L2TPv3 header and forwards it to B

R_A **IP BACKBONE** R_B

ETHERNET   TU2   ETHERNET

A

Step 3

IGP routes the L2TPv3 packet to destination

B

LAN 1   LAN 2

Step 1   *Step 5*

A sends a packet for B   B receives the packet

FIGURE 30.8 The operation for tunneling Ethernet using the L2TPv3 protocol.

to the central office and share a higher capacity line out to the Internet.

For more information, see the IETF.org publication RFC 2661. You can delve deeper into the failover mode of L2TP or get far more detail on the standard.

L2TPv3

This is the draft advancement of the L2TP for large carrier-level information transmissions. In 2005, the draft protocol was released; it provides additional security features, improved encapsulation, and the ability to carry data links other than simply PPP over an IP network (e.g., Frame Relay, Ethernet, ATM). Figure 30.8 shows the operation for tunneling Ethernet using the L2TPv3 protocol and was taken from *Psuedo-wire Services and L2TPv3* from KPN/Quest.[8]

L2F

Cisco's Layer 2 Forwarding protocol is used for tunneling the link layer (layer 2 in the OSI model). This protocol allows for virtual dial-up that allows for the sharing of modems, ISDN routers, servers, and other hardware.

This protocol was popular in the mid- to late-1990s and was utilized by Shiva's products to share a bank

of modems to a network of personal computers. This was a fantastic cost savings for network administrators wanting to share a small number of modems and modem lines to a large user group. Instead of having 50 modems hooked up to individual PCs, you could have a bank of eight modems that could be used during the day to dial out and connect to external resources, becoming available at night for workers to dial back into the computer system for remote access to corporate data resources.

For those long-distance calls to remote computer systems, an employee could dial into the office network. For security and billing reasons, the office computer system would dial back to the home user. The home user would access a second modem line to dial out to a long distance computer system. This would eliminate all charges for the home user except for the initial call to get connected. RFC 2341 on IETF.org gives you the detailed standard.[9]

PPTP VPN

Point-to-Point Tunneling Protocol was created in the 1990s by Microsoft, Ascend, 3COM and a few other vendors to try and serve the user community. This VPN protocol allowed for easy implementation with Windows machines because it was included in Windows. It made for fairly secure transmissions, though not as secure as IPsec. Although Microsoft has a great deal of influence

8 www.ripe.net/ripe/meetings/ripe-42/presentations/ripe42-eof-pseudowires2/index.htmlKPN/Quest *Pseudo-wire Services and L2TPv3* presentation 5/14/2002

9 www.ietf.org/rfc/rfc2341.txt

in the computing arena, the IPsec and L2TP protocols are the standards-based protocols that most vendors use for VPNs.

Under PPTP, Microsoft has implemented MPPE—Microsoft Point-to-Point Encryption Protocol, which allows encryption keys of 40 to 128 bits. The latest updates were done in 2003 to strengthen the security of this protocol. A great excerpt from Microsoft Technet for Windows NT 4.0 Server explains the process of PPTP extremely well; check out http://technet.microsoft.com/en-us/library/cc768084.aspx for more information.

MPLS

MPLS is another system for large telephone companies or huge enterprises to get great response times for VPN with huge amounts of data. MPLS stands for MultiProtocol Label Switching. This protocol operates between layer 2 and layer 3 of the OSI model we have mentioned before. The Internet Engineering Task Force Web page with the specifications for the label switching architecture can be found at www.ietf.org/rfc/rfc3031.txt.

This protocol has big advantages over Asynchronous Transfer Mode (ATM) and Frame Relay. The overhead is lower and with the ability to have variable length data packets, audio and video will be transmitted much more efficiently. Another big advantage over ATM is the ATM requirement that the two endpoints have to handshake and make a connection before any data is ever transmitted.

The name MultiProtocol Label Switching came from the underlying way in which the endpoints find each other. The switches using this technology find their destination through the lookup of a label instead of the lookup of an IP address. Label Edge Routers are the beginning and ending points of an MPLS network. The big competitor for future network expansion is L2TPv3.

MPVPN™

Ragula Systems Development Company created Multi Path Virtual Private Network (MPVPN) to enhance the quality of service of VPNs. The basic concept is to allow multiple connections to the Internet at both endpoints and use the combination of connections to create a faster connection. So if you have a T1 line and a DS3 at your office, you can aggregate both lines through the MPVPN device to increase your response times. The data traffic will be load balanced and will increase your throughput.

FIGURE 30.9 SSH Communications Security logo.

SSH

This protocol lets network traffic run over a secured channel between devices. SSH uses public-key cryptography. Tatu Ylönen from Finland created the first version of SSH in 1995 to thwart password thieves at his university network. The company he created is called SSH Communications Security and can be reached at www.ssh.com (see Figure 30.9).

Utilizing public-key cryptography is a double-edged sword. If an inside user authenticates an attacker's public key, you have just let them into the system, where they can deploy man-in-the-middle hacks. Also, the intent for this security system was to keep out the bad guys at the gate. Once a person is authenticated, she is in and a regular user and can deploy software that would allow a remote VPN to be set up through the SSH protocol. Future versions of SSH may prevent these abuses.

SSL-VPN

Secure Socket Layer (SSL) VPN isn't really VPN at all. It's more of an interface that gives users the services that look like VPN through their Web browsers. There are many remote-control applications that take advantage of this layer in the Web browser to gain access to users' resources.

TLS

Transport Layer Security, the successor to SSL, is used to prevent eavesdropping on information being sent between computers. When using strong encryption algorithms, the security of your transmission is almost guaranteed.

Both SSL and TLS work very much the same way. First, the sessions at each endpoint contact each other for information about what encryption method is going to be employed. Second, the keys are exchanged. These could be RSA, Diffie-Hellman, ECDH, SRP, or PSK.

Finally, the messages are encrypted and authenticated, sometimes using Certificate of Authorities Public Key list. When you utilize SSL and TLS you may run into a situation where the server certificate does not match the information held in the Certificate of Authorities Public Key list. If this is the case, the user may override the error message or may choose not to trust the site and end the connection.

The whole public key/private key encryption is able to take place behind the scenes for a few reasons. During the beginning phase of the connection, the server and requesting computer generate a random number. Random numbers are combined and encrypted using the private keys. Only the owner of the public key can unencrypt the random number that is sent using their private key.

4. AUTHENTICATION METHODS

Currently, usernames and passwords are the most common authentication method employed in the VPN arena. We may transport the data through an SSL channel or via a secured and encrypted transport model, but when it comes to gaining access to the system resources, most often you will have to log into the VPN with a username and password.

As we talked about earlier, there are some edge-based systems that require a dongle, and a random number is generated on gaining access to the login screen. These tiered layers of security can be a great wall that will thwart a hacker's attempt to gain access to your network system in favor of going after easier networks.

Not all authentication methods are the same. We will talk about a few different types of protection schemes and point out weaknesses and strengths.

With each type of encryption we are concerned with its voracity along with concerns over the verification and authentication of the data being sent. Transmission speeds and overhead in encrypting and decrypting data are another consideration, but as mentioned earlier, Moore's Law has helped a great deal.

Hashing

Using a computer algorithm to mix up the characters in your encryption is fairly common. If you have a secret and want another person to know the answer, but you are fearful that it will be discovered, you can mix up the letters.

HMAC

HMAC (keyed Hash Message Authentication Code) is a type of encryption that uses an algorithm in conjunction with a key. The algorithm is only as strong as the complexity of the key and the size of the output. For HMAC either 128 or 160 bits are used.

This type of Message Authentication Code (MAC) can be defeated. One way is by using the birthday attack. To ensure that your data is not deciphered, choose a strong key; use upper- and lowercase letters, numbers, and special characters. Also use 160 bits when possible.

MD5

Message Digest 5 is one of the best file integrity checks available today. It is also used in some encryption schemes, though the voracity of its encryption strength is being challenged.

The method uses a 128-bit hash value. It is represented as a 32-digit hexadecimal number. A file can be "hashed" down to a single 32-digit hex number. The likelihood of two files with the same hash is 2^{128} but with the use of rainbow tables and collision theory, there have been a few successes in cracking this encryption.[10]

SHA-1

Secure Hash Algorithm was designed by the U.S. National Security Agency (NSA). There is also SHA-224, SHA-256, SHA-384, and SHA-512. The number of bits in SHA-1 is 160. The others have the number of bits following the SHA.

SHA-1 is purported to have been compromised, but the voracity of the reports has been challenged. In any case, the NSA has created the SHA-224 to SHA-512 specification to make it even more difficult to crack. At the Rump Session of CRYPTO 2006, Christian Rechberger and Christophe De Cannière claimed to have discovered a collision attack on SHA-1 that would allow an attacker to select at least parts of the message.[11]

The basic premise is the same as the MD5 hash: The data is encrypted utilizing a message digest. This method is the basis for several common applications including SSL, PGP, SSH, S/MIME, and IPsec.

NSA is working on the next-generation SHA-3 and is seeking vendors to compete in creating the next-generation

10 http://en.wikipedia.org/wiki/MD5#Vulnerability
11 http://en.wikipedia.org/wiki/SHA-1#Cryptanalysis_and_validation

hashing algorithms. Submissions were due October 31, 2008.

5. SYMMETRIC ENCRYPTION

Symmetric encryption requires that both the sender and receiver have the same key and each computes a common key that is subsequently used. Two of the most common symmetric encryption standards are known as DES (Data Encryption Standard) and AES (Advanced Encryption Standard). Once AES was released, DES was withdrawn as a standard and replaced with 3-DES, often referred to as Triple DES and TDES.

3-DES takes DES and repeats it two more times. So it is hashed with the 56-bit algorithm and password, and then done twice more. This prevents more brute-force attacks, assuming a strong key is used. Some VPN software is based on these symmetric keys, as we have discussed before.

Finally, a system of shared secrets allows encryption and decryption of data. This can either be done as a pre-shared password, which is known by both ends prior to communication, or some kind of key agreement protocol where the key is calculated from each end using a common identifier or public key.

6. ASYMMETRIC CRYPTOGRAPHY

The biggest example of asymmetric cryptography for VPNs is in the RSA protocol. Three professors at MIT, Ron Rivest, Adi Shamir, and Leonard Adelman (thus RSA), came up with the RSA encryption algorithm, which is an implementation of public/private key cryptography.

This is one of the coolest and most secure means of transmitting data. Not only is it used for transmission of data, but a person can also digitally sign a document with the use of RSA secure systems. Some states are creating systems for giving people their own digital signatures and holding the public keys in a server that can be accessed by all.

Although these systems have been around for a while, they are becoming more and more prevalent. For example, some states will allow accountants who sign up with them to transmit income tax forms electronically as long as they digitally sign the returns.

This algorithm uses two large random prime numbers. Prime number searching has been a pastime for many mathematical scientists. As the prime number gets larger and larger, its use for privacy and security systems is increased. Thus, many search for larger prime numbers.

Through the use of these numbers and a key, the data is secured from prying eyes.

When you are in a public system and don't have the luxury of knowing the keys in advance, there are ways to create a key that will work. This system is very interesting and is known as the *exponential key exchange* because it uses exponential numbers in the initial key exchange to come to an agreed-on cipher.

7. EDGE DEVICES

As with any system, having two locked doors is better than one. With the advent of many remote computing systems, a new type of external security has come into favor. For instance, the setting up an edge device, allows for a unique username and password, or better yet, a unique username and a random password that only the user and the computer system knows.

These edge systems often employ authentication schemes in conjunction with a key fob that displays a different random number every 30 to 60 seconds. The server knows what the random number should be based on the time and only authenticates the person into the edge of the network if the username and password match.

Once into the edge network, the user is prompted for a more traditional username and password to gain access to data, email, or applications under his username.

8. PASSWORDS

Your system and data are often only as good as the strength of your password. The weakest of passwords entails a single word or name. An attacker using common dictionary attacks will often break a weak password. For example, using the word *password* is usually broken very quickly.

Using multiple words or mixing spelling and upper- and lowercase will make your weak password a bit stronger. PassWOrd would be better. Adding numbers increases your passwords voracity. P2ssw9rd decreases your chance of getting hacked. Add in a few special characters and your password gets even more secure, as with P2#$w9rd.

But to get even stronger you need to use a password over 12 characters made up of upper- and lowercase letters, numbers, and special characters: P2#$w9rd.34HHlz. Stay away from acronyms.

Another way to keep your VPNs secure is to only allow access from fixed IP addresses. If the IP address isn't on the allowable list, you don't allow the computer in, no matter what. The unique address for each network card that is in the hardware is called the Media Access Control (MAC) address. This is another fixed ID that can be used to allow or disallow computers onto your VPN. The problem with this method is that both IP and MACs can be spoofed. So, if a person gets his hands on a valid MAC ID, he can get around this bit of security.

Some VPN systems will allow you to log in with a username and password, and then it will connect to a predefined IP address. So even if your passwords are stolen, unless the person knows the predefined IP address of the callback, they can't get into your system. This idea is a throwback to the dial-in networks that would allow a person to dial in, connect with their username and password, and then promptly disconnect and call the person's computer system back. It was an extra two minutes on the front end, but a great added level of security.

Finally, biometrics are playing a role in authentication systems. For example, instead of a password, your fingerprint is used. Some systems use voiceprint, hand geometry, retinal eye scan, or facial geometry. We can foresee the day when a DNA reader uses your DNA as your password.

9. HACKERS AND CRACKERS

Some good ways to prevent hackers and crackers from getting into your system is to enable the best security levels that your hardware has to offer. If you can utilize 256-bit encryption methods, then use them. If you can afford a random-number–generated edge security system, then use it.

Have your users change their VPN passwords frequently, especially if they are utilizing public Internet portals. Don't expect your local library to have the security that your own internal company has. If you access your VPN from an insecure public Internet hotspot, then make sure you change your VPN password.

Don't give out your VPN password for other people to use. This can cause you great difficulties if something sinister happens to the network and the connection is traced back to your username and password.

Another way to secure your network is to deactivate accounts that have not been used for 30 days. Yes, this can be a pain, but if a person is not regularly accessing the system, then maybe they don't need access in the first place.

Finally, remove stale VPN accounts from the system. One of the biggest problems with unauthorized VPN access is the employee who has retired but her account never got disabled. Maybe her logon and email were removed, but IT didn't remove her VPN account. Put in checks and balances on accounts.

## Chapter 31

Identity Theft

Markus Jacobsson*
Palo Alto Research Center

Alex Tsow*
The MITRE Corporation

Identity theft is commonly defined as unwanted appropriation of access credentials that allows creation and access of accounts and that allows the aggressor to pose as the victim. Phishing is a type of identity theft that is perpetrated on the Internet and that typically relies on social engineering to obtain the access credentials of the victim. Similar deceit techniques are becoming increasingly common in the context of crimeware. Crimeware, in turn, is often defined as economically motivated malware. Whereas computer science has a long-term tradition of studying and understanding security threats, the human component of the problem is traditionally ignored. In this chapter, we describe the importance of understanding the human factor of security and detail the findings from a study on deceit.

Social engineering can be thought of as an establishment of trust between an attacker and a victim, where the attacker's goal is to make the victim perform some action he would not have wanted to perform had he understood the consequences. Attackers leverage preexisting trust between victims and the chosen false identities to spur dubious actions (illegally transferring money, remailing stolen goods, installing malware on computers, and recommending fraudulent services to friends).

To understand deceit in this context, it is worth recalling that people are more likely to install software on their computer if they believe it is manufacturer-distributed patch rather than a third-party enhancement. Similarly, Internet users are more likely to visit a website when recommended by friends[1,2] and may agree to signing up to services that appear to be recommended by their friends. Moreover, when site-content hinges on accepting third-party browser extensions, friend recommendations prove highly effective in inducing the required installation.[3] When identity is used convincingly, these behaviors become social vectors for spreading crimeware and for causing users to opt in where they would not otherwise have.

Institutions and individuals project Internet identity through their Web sites and through email communication. How do attackers engineer contact with false identities? Clearly, email can be sent to anyone. Filters limit the quantity of unwanted messages, but spammers have successfully responded with increased volume and variation. Superficially, arranging contact with bogus Web sites appears to be a more difficult problem since legitimate content providers uncommonly link to spoofed Web hosts.

---

1 T. Jagatic, N. Johnson, M. Jakobsson, and F. Menczer, "Social phishing," *Communications of the ACM*, 2007, available at http://doi.acm.org/10.1145/1290958.1290968.

2 A. Genkina and L. J. Camp, "Phishing and countermeasures: understanding the increasing problem of electronic identity theft," chapter case study: *Net Trust*, John Wiley & Sons, 2007.

3 M. Gandhi, S. Stamm, M. Jakobsson, "verybigad.com: A study in socially transmitted malware," www.indiana.edu/~phishing/verybigad/.

Roughly 50% of Web requests (by volume) are not the result of site-to-site linking, based on results from over 100,000 Internet clients hosted by the Indiana University campuses, according to the Indiana University Advanced Network Management Lab.

The other half of Web visits follow from bookmarks, direct address bar manipulation, or linking from external sources (email, word-processor documents, and instant-messaging sessions). Social engineers influence these values through bogus links in email and by using domain names that are deceptive.

There are may studies of ways in which humans relate to deceit and treason, and there are many studies that focus on Internet security, but there is not an abundance of research on the combination of these two important fields. How do people relate to deceit on the Internet? This is an important question to ask—and to answer—for anybody who wants to improve Internet security.

This chapter focuses on identity manipulation tactics in email and Web pages. It describes the effects of features ranging from URL plausibility to trust endorsement graphics on a population of 398 subjects. The experiment presents these trust indicators in a variety of stimuli, since reactions vary according to context. In addition to testing specific features, the test gauges the potential of a tactic that spoofs third-party contractors rather than a brand itself. The results show that indeed graphic design can change authenticity evaluations and that its impact varies with context. We expected that authenticity-inspiring design changes would have the opposite effect when paired with an unreasonable request, but our data suggest that narrative strength, rather than underlying legitimacy, limits the impact of graphic design on trust and that these authenticity-inspiring design features improve trust in both legitimate and illegitimate media. Thus, it is not what is said that matters but how it is said: An eloquently stated unreasonable request is more convincing than a poorly phrased but quite reasonable request.

1. EXPERIMENTAL DESIGN

This experiment tests the ability to identify phishing, an Internet scam that spoofs emails and Web pages to trick victims into revealing sensitive information. Although cast in terms of phishing, the results generalize to identity spoofing for purposes beyond information theft. This experiment tests the effects of several media features—sometimes in multiple contexts—on an individual's evaluation of its phishing likelihood. This experiment

shows subjects six email screenshots followed by six Web page screenshots and asks them to rate their authenticity on a five-point scale: Certainly phishing, Probably phishing, No opinion, Probably not phishing, and Certainly not phishing (see Figure 31.1 for an example). The experiment was administered through SurveyMonkey.com,[4] an online Web survey service. Subjects were required to rate each screenshot before advancing to the next stimulus. The survey provided the following instructions to subjects:

- Phishing is a form of Internet fraud that spoofs emails and Web pages to trick people into disclosing sensitive information. When an email or Web page fraudulently represents itself, we classify it as phishing.
- This survey displays a sequence of email and Web site screenshots. Assume that your name is John Doe and that your email address is johndoe1972@gmail.com. Please rate each screenshot's authenticity using the five-point scale: Certainly phishing, Probably phishing, No opinion, Probably not phishing, Certainly not phishing.

This style of testing, termed *security first*, measures fraud-recognition skills rather than habits. Subjects are not trying to accomplish other work but are merely instructed to rate a series of legitimate and illegitimate stimuli. For this reason, security-first measurements place a plausible upper bound on fraud detection habits in normal computer usage. Even though security-first evaluations have shown high susceptibility to phishing,[5,6] role-playing experiments designed to measure fraud detection habits[7,8] demonstrate even more serious vulnerability.

Subjects were recruited from an undergraduate introductory noncomputer-science-major class on computer usage and literacy. Of a class size exceeding 600 students,

4 SurveyMonkey.com, "Surveymonkey.com-powerful tool for creating web surveys. online survey software made easy!" www.surveymonkey.com/, retrieved December 2006.

5 A. Genkina and L. J. Camp, "Phishing and countermeasures: understanding the increasing problem of electronic identity theft," chapter case study: *Net Trust*, John Wiley & Sons, 2007.

6 M. Jakobsson, A. Tsow, A. Shah, E. Blevis, and Y.-K. Lim, "What instills trust? A qualitative study of phishing," In submission, 2006.

7 J. S. Downs, M. B. Holbrook, and L. F. Cranor, "Decision strategies and susceptibility to phishing," In *SOUPS '06: Proceedings of the Second Symposium on Usable Privacy and Security*, pp. 79–90, New York, 2006, ACM Press.

8 M. Wu, R. C. Miller, and S. L. Garfinkel, "Do security toolbars actually prevent phishing attacks?" In *CHI '06: Proceedings of the SIGCHI Conference on Human Factors in Computing Systems*, pp 601–610, New York, 2006, ACM Press.

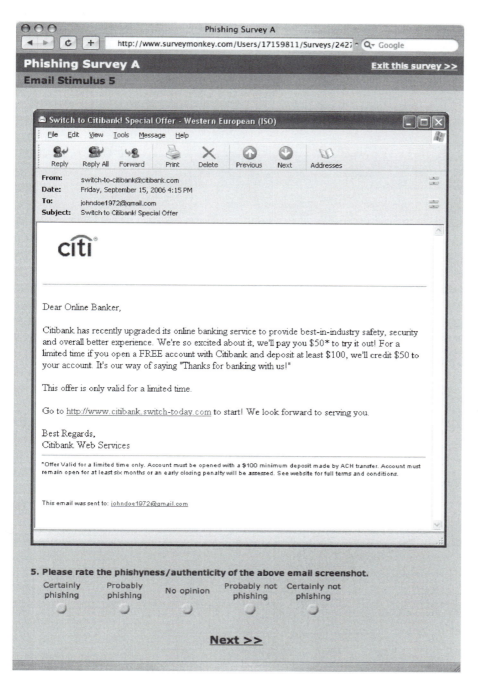

FIGURE 31.1 Subjects evaluate authenticity based on screenshots using a five-point scale. The survey required a judgment before proceeding to the next stimulus.

435 began this study. All but 12 subjects were between 17 and 22 years old; the gender split was 40.0% male to 57.9% female (2.0% did not respond to this question). Although the test population is not demographically representative of general computer users, their enrollment in the introductory course suggests that their computer skill level is generally representative. The class's only prerequisite is high-school algebra. Almost all students in this class had used computers before but had no particular expertise.

The experiment divided the population into two sets through random selection. The two sets completed different versions of the survey. For 10 of the stimuli, the two versions differ only by a target collection of test features. Our primary analysis compares the impact of the feature changes, by using the χ^9 to represent the difference

9 R. Dhamija, J. D. Tygar, and M. Hearst, "Why phishing works," In *CHI '06: Proceedings of the SIGCHI conference on Human Factors in computing systems*, pp. 581–590, New York, 2006, ACM Press.

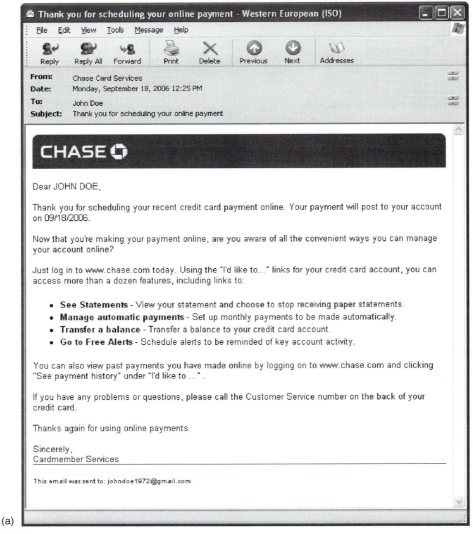

FIGURE 31.2 (a) Plain layout.

between response distributions. In two other question sets, subjects evaluate the authenticity of messages and Web pages under third-party administration (a potential vector for social engineering). We further designed the test to simulate a roughly equal number of authentic and phishing stimuli to avoid effective use of a trivial rating strategy: If there were significantly more phishing stimuli than authentic stimuli, subjects could employ an "always phishing" strategy that would correctly evaluate most of the stimuli without exercising due consideration.

Since the stimuli are only screenshots, their inauthentic features were designed to be evident on examination (rather than mouse-over or source analysis). For instance, incorrect domains are apparent in email hyperlinks; they are not disguised by an inconsistent *href* attribute. The domains we chose to simulate inauthentic URLs were not

in use at the time of testing, but some are owned by their respective companies, others are owned by unrelated companies, and the rest appear to be unregistered, according to the Whois database. Our use of these domains as representations of inauthentic URLs is still valid because none of these URLs exist with the content we present. We outline the stimuli, their relevant features, and what we hope to learn in Figures 31.2a and 31.2b.

Authentic Payment Notification: Plain versus Fancy Layout

These two email messages use actual payment notification text from Chase Bank (see sidebar, "A Strong Phishing Message"). The text personalizes its greeting and references a recent payment transaction; there are no hyperlinks. One

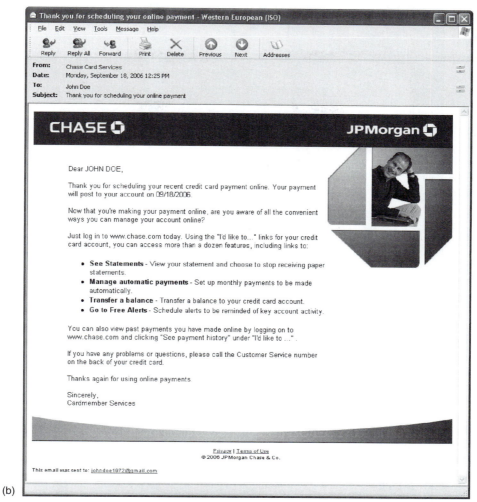

(b)

FIGURE 31.2 (*Continued*) (b) fancy layout.

A Strong Phishing Message

Dear John Doe,

JPMorgan Chase & Co. is proud to serve you as a former Bank One client.

Chase Online's patented ePIN technology is used both for eDebit transactions and for physical ATM access. While we will support the legacy 4 digit PIN for the remainder of the year, until December 31, 2006, we invite you to register for the ePIN program through our secure online server:

https://www.chase.ePIN-simplicity.com

If you have any questions about this or other Chase programs, do not hesitate to call our toll-free customer service number, 1-877-CHASEPC.

Sincerely,

Client Services

JPMorgan Chase & Co.

---

version uses the original layout (a one-color header containing the company logo followed by the message text); the other version uses an enhanced layout (a header that includes a continuous tone shiny logo and a photograph of a satisfied customer, a smooth gradient footer graphic that spans the page with a gentle concave arch, hyperlinks to Privacy and Terms of Use, and a copyright notice; these graphics were adapted from the Web page at www.bankone.com).

FIGURE 31.3 (a) Using a plain layout schema (b) using a fancy layout schema; and (c) using a plain and fancy layout schema.

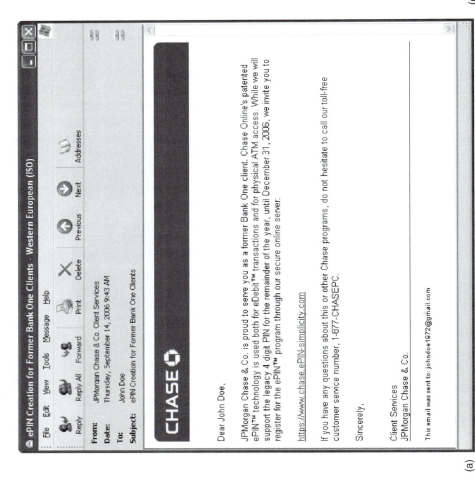

Strong Phishing Message: Plain Versus Fancy Layout

We constructed the phishing message text to sound as plausible as possible. Opening with a personalized greeting, the message explains that former Bank One customers will need to register for Chase's ePIN program—a replacement for ATM PINs that is also bundled with a new eDebit online service. It implicitly threatens service discontinuation by supporting "legacy 4 digit PINs for the rest of the calendar year." The bogus registration hyperlink uses the made-up URL https://www.chase.ePIN-simplicity.com. The message closes with a bogus phone number to call for assistance. The two versions of this message use the same plain and fancy layout schema described earlier, with one

exception: The fancy layout adds shiny letters proclaiming "Bank One is now Chase" (see Figure 31.3) between the header and message text.

Authentic Promotion: Effect of Small Footers

Figure 31.4 shows an authentic message from the AT&T Universal card that promotes the company's paperless billing system. It personalizes the greeting and includes the last four digits of the account number. There are multiple company logos, a blue outline around text, an Email Security Zone box, and a small-print footer filled with trademark, copyright, and contact notices as well as various

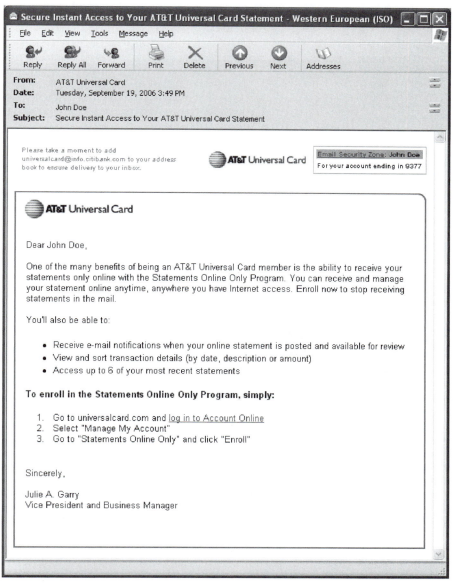

(a)

FIGURE 31.4 (a) An authentic message from the AT&T Universal card that promotes the company's paperless billing system.

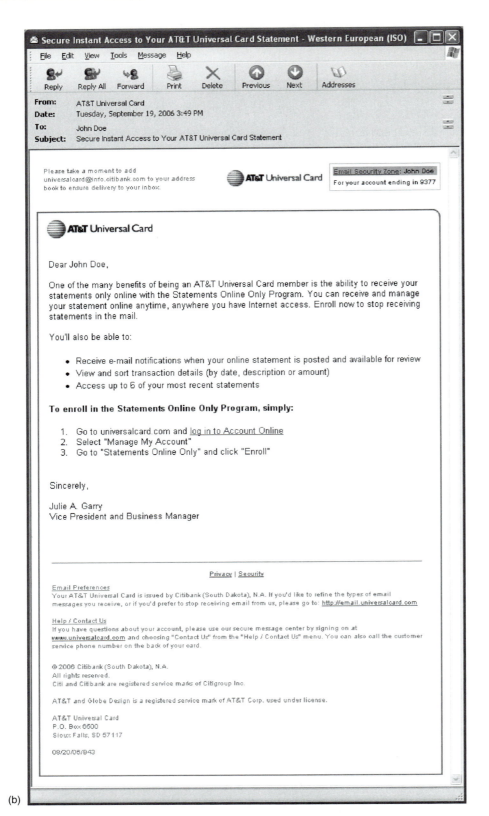

(b)

Please take a moment to add
universalcard@info.citibank.com to your address
(c) book to ensure delivery to your inbox.

(d) Email Security Zone: John Doe
For your account ending in 9377

To enroll in the Statements Online Only Program, simply:

(e)   1.   Go to universalcard.com and log in to Account Online

FIGURE 31.4 (*Continued*) (b) an authentic message from AT&T Universal card that personalizes the greeting and includes the last four digits of the account number; (c) header detail left side; (d) header detail right side; and (e) hyperlink detail.

> **Phishing Message**
>
> Dear Online Banker,
>
> Citibank has recently upgraded its online banking service to provide best-in-industry safety, security and overall better experience. We're so excited about it, we'll pay you $50* to try it out! For a limited time if you open a FREE account with Citibank and deposit at least $100, we'll credit $50 to your account. It's our way of saying "Thanks for banking with us!"
>
> This offer is only valid for a limited time. Go to http://www.citibank.switch-today.com to start! We look forward to serving you.
>
> Best Regards,
>
> Citibank Web Services
>
> *Offer valid for a limited time only. Account must be opened with $100 minimum deposit made by ACH transfer. Account must remain open for at least six months or an early closing penalty will be assessed. See website for full terms and conditions.

informational and administrative hyperlinks. The principal login hyperlink conceals its destination. The test pair consists of the original message and a modified version that excludes the small print footer.

Weak Phishing Message

The sidebar "Phishing Message" shows a phishing message promising $50 for opening an account with Citibank. There is a simple company logo in the header; a footer contains legal disclaimers about the offer. There is no personalization, and the lone hyperlink is a made-up domain (actually owned by an unrelated organization), www.citibank.switch-today.com. Figure 31.5 contains its screenshot. The two versions differ only by the presence of a center-aligned "VeriSign Secured" endorsement logo that follows the footer's legal disclaimers.

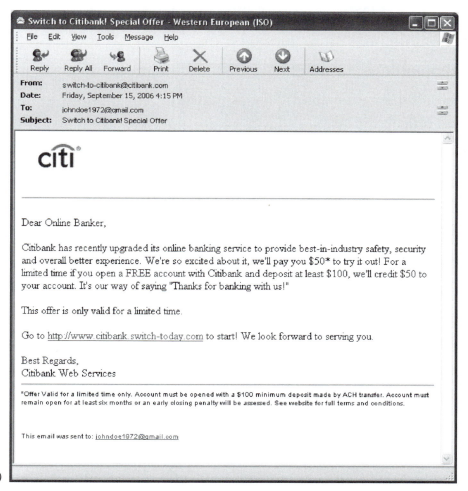

FIGURE 31.5 (a) Effect of endorsement logo.

(a)

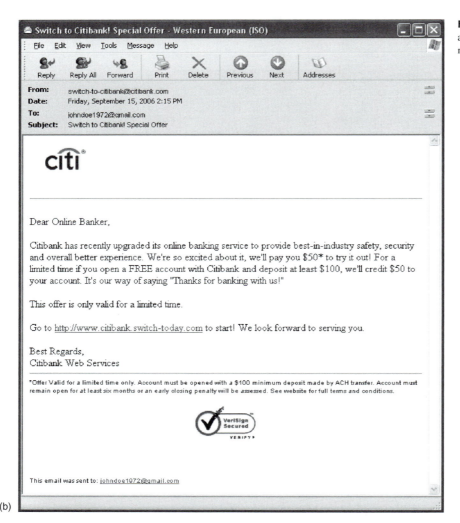

Authentic Message

The test determines the impact of a "VeriSign Secured" logo added to the footer of an authentic message, as shown in Figure 31.6. The notice begins with a personalized greeting and informs the client about changes in PayPal's logo insertion policy. The message body is considerably longer than all of the other messages except for the Netflix stimulus. The primary message contains no hyperlinks, but their small-print footer furnishes a hyperlink to unsubscribe from their newsletter. One interesting feature of the message is a boldfaced statement: "If you do not wish to have PayPal automatically inserted in your listings, you must update your preferences by 9/25." Though genuine, this message parallels the account shutdown threats brandished by many phishing messages. The header contains a monochrome company logo and a two-tone horizontal separation bar.

Login Page

We say that the URL is strongly aligned with the content of the page when these two "belong together." Imagine that one would look at some ten Web pages (without associated URLs), and then some ten randomly ordered URLs, each one belonging to one of the ten Web pages. The easier it is for a potential reader to correctly pair up Web pages and URLs, the stronger the alignment. If any Web page and associated URL is not correctly matched up, then the alignment is very weak.

Let's now turn to an example, as shown in Figure 31.7.

This browser's content window displays an exact copy of the AT&T Universal card login page. Like most Web login pages, it displays a high level of layout sophistication: photographs of happy clients, navigation bars, product pictures, a sidebar, promotional windows, and small-print legal disclaimers. It also displays a "VeriSign Secured" site

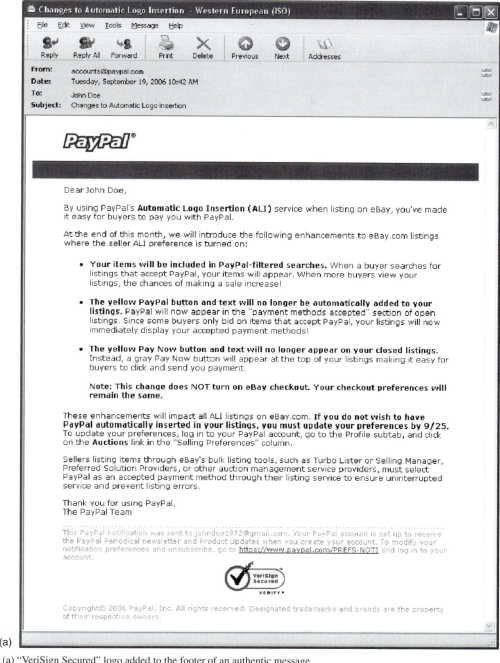

(a)

FIGURE 31.6 (a) "VeriSign Secured" logo added to the footer of an authentic message.

endorsement logo. The two versions of this stimulus differ by their address bar contents: version (a) uses https://www.accountonline.com/View?docId=Index&siteId=AC&langId=EN and consequently displays a browser frame padlock; version (b) uses the unencrypted URL http://www.attuniversalcard.com/ (owned by AT&T but not in use).

Login Page: Strong and Weak Content Alignment

This next set takes the alternative approach to aligning the address bar URL with content: change the content. Both pages (see Figure 31.8) use the unregistered URL www.citicardmembers.com/. Version (a) displays a

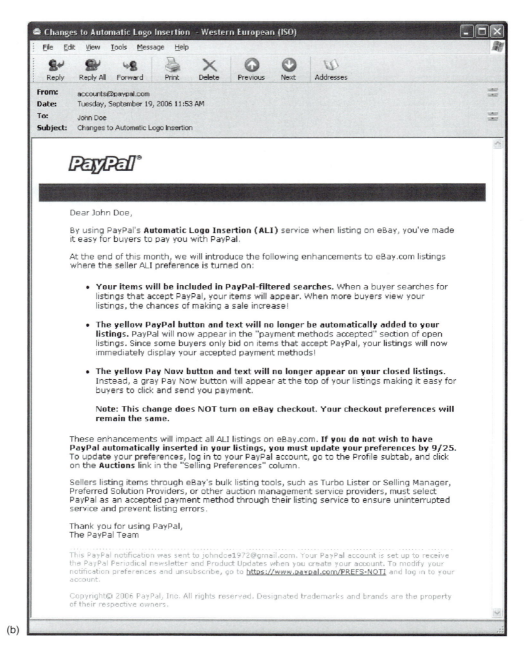

(b)

These enhancements will impact all ALI listings on eBay.com. **If you do not wish to have PayPal automatically inserted in your listings, you must update your preferences by 9/25.** To update your preferences, log in to your PayPal account, go to the Profile subtab, and click on the **Auctions** link in the "Selling Preferences" column.

(c)

This PayPal notification was sent to johndoe1972@gmail.com. Your PayPal account is set up to receive the PayPal Periodical newsletter and Product Updates when you create your account. To modify your notification preferences and unsubscribe, go to **https://www.paypal.com/PREFS-NOTI** and log in to your account.

Copyright© 2006 PayPal, Inc. All rights reserved. Designated trademarks and brands are the property of their respective owners.

(d)

FIGURE 31.6 (*Continued*) (b) authentic message—effect of endorsement logo; (c) shared body detail; (d) endorsement footer detail.

(a)

(b) Address 🔲 https://www.accountonline.com/View?docId=Index&siteId=AC&langId=EN

(c) Address 🔲 http://www.attuniversalcard.com/

FIGURE 31.7 (a) Strong and weak URL alignment; (b) weak alignment URL detail; (c) strong alignment URL detail.

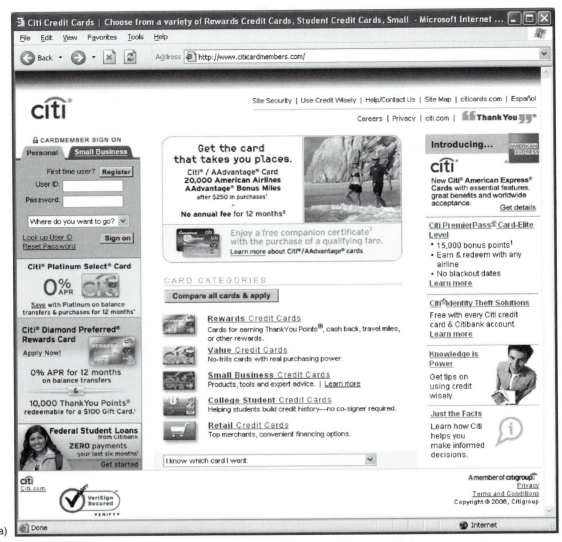

FIGURE 31.8 (a) A precise copy of the authentic Citi Credit Cards login page in its content window.

precise copy of the authentic Citi Credit Cards login page in its content window, whereas the version (b) content window displays modified logos and links (see Figure 31.9) for better alignment with the URL.

Figures 31.8a and 31.8b use a sophisticated layout with nearly all the same identifiable features of the AT&T Universal Card login: photographs of happy clients, navigation bars, product pictures, sidebars, promotional windows, and the "VeriSign Secured" logo.

Login Page: Authentic and Bogus (But Plausible) URLs

These two stimuli test the impact of changing a well-aligned authentic URL (see Figure 31.9), http://www.paypal.com/ebay, to a reasonably well-aligned bogus

URL, http://www.ebaygroup.com/paypal (domain owned by eBay but not in use). The main content window is the same for both: The eBay decorated version of the PayPal login page, which contains an eBay logo to the lower right of the primary PayPal logo. The page layout contains all the main features of the previous login pages but includes a more thorough set of third-party endorsement logos: "VeriSign Secured," "Reviewed by TRUST-e," and "Privacy: BBB OnLine." SSL is not used in either stimulus.

Login Page: Hard and Soft Emphasis on Security

Figure 31.10 tests whether it is possible to undermine confidence in an authentic login page with excessive

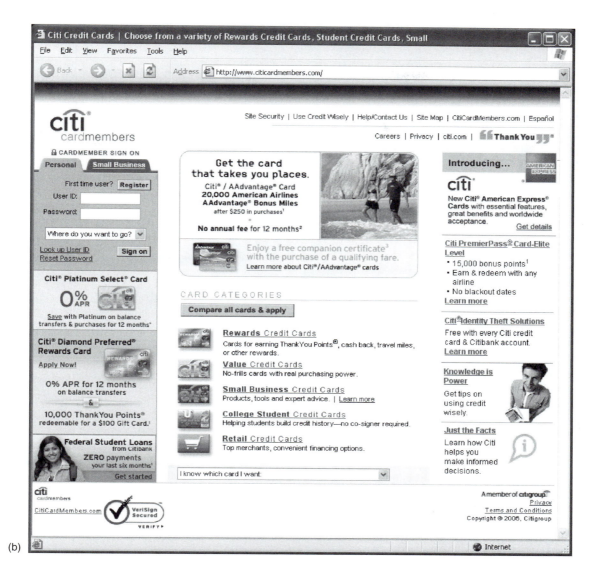

(b)

(e) citicards.com

(c) 🔒 CARDMEMBER SIGN ON   (f) CitiCardMembers.com

(g) Citi.com

cardmembers

(d) 🔒 CARDMEMBER SIGN ON   (h) CitiCardMembers.com

FIGURE 31.8 (*Continued*) (b) content window displays modified logos and links; (c) location of detail window; (d) original and modified detail window; (e) header menu of detail window; (f) Cardmember sign on detail window; (g) footer of detail window; and (h) Cardmembers of detail window.

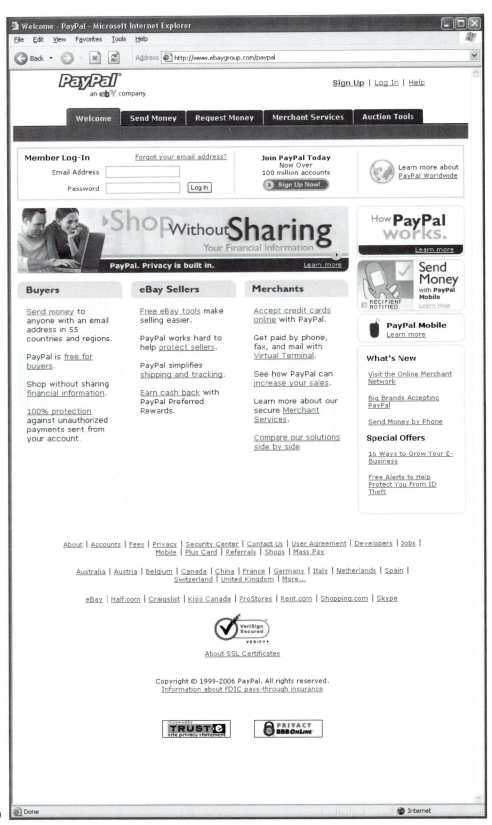

(a)

FIGURE 31.9 (a) A reasonably well-aligned bogus URL.

FIGURE 31.9 (*Continued*) (b) logo detail; (c) bogus URL detail; and (d) authentic URL detail.

concern about security and online fraud. These two stimuli represent an extreme but real-world case. Clients of the Indiana University Employees Federal Credit Union (IUCU) were targeted by a phishing attack in early August 2006. In response, the credit union altered its Web page to include a large banner, as shown in Figure 31.10f.

They further augmented the news section with a similar message: "Warning! Phishing Scam in progress (learn more)." Finally, a section named "Critical Fraud Alerts" contained the exact same warning as the one from the news section. The twin page eliminates all phishing warnings (including the banner) and changes the "Critical Fraud Alerts" section heading to read "Fraud Prevention Center." Generally, the language was changed to sound "in control" rather than alarmist.

Bad URL, with and without SSL and Endorsement Logo

Can an endorsement logo and SSL padlock overcome a bad domain name? This next set, as shown in Figure 31.11, tests these two features on a Wells Fargo phishing site based on the bogus domain www-wellsfargo.com. The login page is similar in layout to the others but does not feature photographs of people. The only continuous tone graphic is an image of a speeding horse-drawn carriage that evokes a Wild West money transfer service. One screenshot contains the original page content using an unencrypted connection; the other stimulus uses SSL and adds a center-aligned "VeriSign Secured" logo to the page's footer.

High-Profile Recall Notice

At the time of testing (10/02/2006–10/12/2006), the press had been alive with recent reports[10] of laptop battery recalls from both Dell and Apple. Sony, the source of the batteries, ultimately issued a direct recall for the same batteries, by adding several more brands on 10/23/2006.

As shown in Figure 31.12, this test set does not follow the controlled-pair format of the previous stimuli. One stimulus is a screenshot of the official Dell Battery Return Program Web page. The page layout is substantially simpler than all other Web stimuli. A four-color header logo adorns the top of the page. It presents the content as a letter to "Dell Customer," explaining the danger and how to determine eligibility for exchange. Notably, there is a single column of content, no photos, and no promotional content of any kind. They use the third-party domain dell-batteryprogram.com. Use of this domain for the official page makes the replacement service ripe for phishing.

We constructed a phishing email message using the header, footer, and textual content from this Web page. The phishing message omits the middle section on how to identify eligible batteries and instead requests that the recipient go to the bogus Web page at http://www.dellbatteryreplacements.com.

Low-Profile Class-Action Lawsuit

As shown in Figure 31.13, this last set of stimuli also follows the third-party email and Web page form of the previous set. Both stimuli are authentic, but they use altered dates to appear relevant at the time of testing. The email message is a lengthy notice that describes a class-action lawsuit against Netflix, a settlement to the lawsuit, and options for claiming benefits. There is no greeting, signature, color, or graphics. The only hyperlinks direct the user to the authentic third-party URL, http://www.netflixsettlement.com. The Web page has a similarly bare appearance but with much less text. It behaves as a hyperlink gateway for more information under the URL http://www.netflix.com/settlement/ (the result of redirection from http://www.netflixsettlement.com).

2. RESULTS AND ANALYSIS

Our experiment directly controls for the effect of several design features. There are some surprises in the direct

---

10 D. Darlin, "Dell will recall batteries in PCs," *New York Times*, 15 August 2006, http://select.nytimes.com/search/restricted/article?res=F10A1FF83C5A0C768DDDA10894DE404482.

(a)

⚠ Fraud Prevention Center

We're committed to your account security.

Protect yourself from fraud. Click here for effective fraud prevention strategies.

Concerned about fraud? IU Credit Union helps ensure online account safety—learn more

(c)

⚠ Critical Fraud Alerts

Your account security is very important to us.

Protect yourself from fraud. Click here for important security and blocked ATM/Visa Card updates.

(d)   Phishing Scam in Progress—learn more

FIGURE 31.10 (a) Soft emphasis on security; (b) hard emphasis on security; (c) soft security detail; (d) hard security detail; (d) hard security detail 1; (e) soft security detail 2; and (f) Web page warning.

(b)

Warning!
(e)   Phishing Scam in progress—learn more

(f)   ⚠**WARNING:** ALL IU CREDIT UNION MEMBERS PLEASE READ! ▨
Phishing Scam is in progress; click here for important information

FIGURE 31.10 (*Continued*)

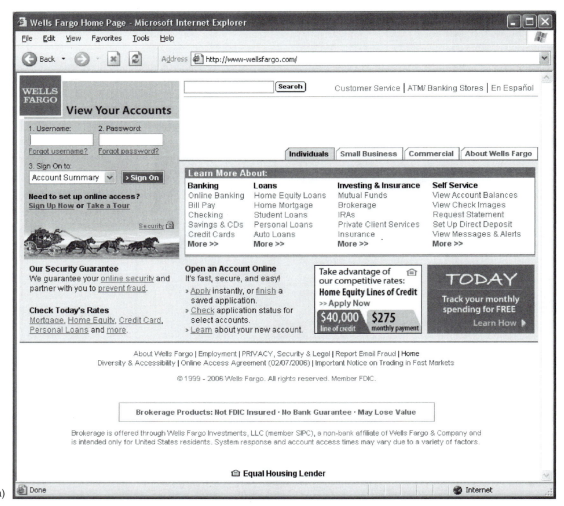

FIGURE 31.11 (a) Without SSL and endorsement logo.

results from these tests, including the stunning impact of a detailed small print footer on an otherwise well-conceived legitimate message; however, the experiment reveals an unexpected, but in retrospect obvious, lesson about email messages: The "story" of the message is critical. Messages with strong and succinct narrative components rated highly and their ratings appear to be less susceptible to changes in graphic design. On the other hand, authenticity perception changed significantly for messages that say little (such as a service promotion) under document feature variances. Two of the five sets of "twins" did not change significantly, according to the metric, when augmented with the very same features that produced significant changes in other messages. Subjects judged these messages principally on their narrative content.

The Chase phishing message uses the company's recent acquisition of Bank One as a pretext for imminent service change to ATM card authentication; the story further bundles this change with the addition of a new service, eDebit, and implicitly threatens discontinuation of service by claiming to "support the legacy 4 digit PIN for the remainder of the year." This consequence is much less direct than the standard "Your account will be suspended in 48 hours if ..." strategy used by many phishers. It works on a less urgent time scale and is pitched as a convenience to all clients rather than an anomaly specialized to a specific client. There was no significant difference in subject evaluation between the plainly formatted version of this message with the monochrome corporate header and the one with several customized continuous tone graphics.

Yet these same graphics, minus the shiny "Bank One is now Chase" banner, produced a significant change ($p = 0:018$) in evaluations of Chase's authentic payment notice. The payment notice thanks the receiver for a recent online payment, then goes on to inform the user

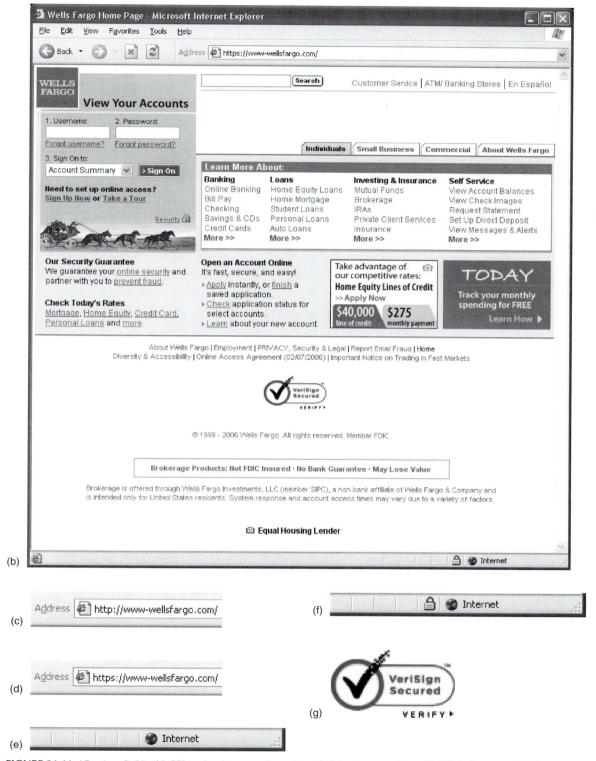

FIGURE 31.11 (*Continued*) (b) with SSL and endorsement logo; (c) no SSL/endorsement logo; (d) SSL/endorsement detail; (e) Internet no SSL/ endorsement status bar; (f) Internet SSL/endorsement status bar; and (g) VeriSign logo.

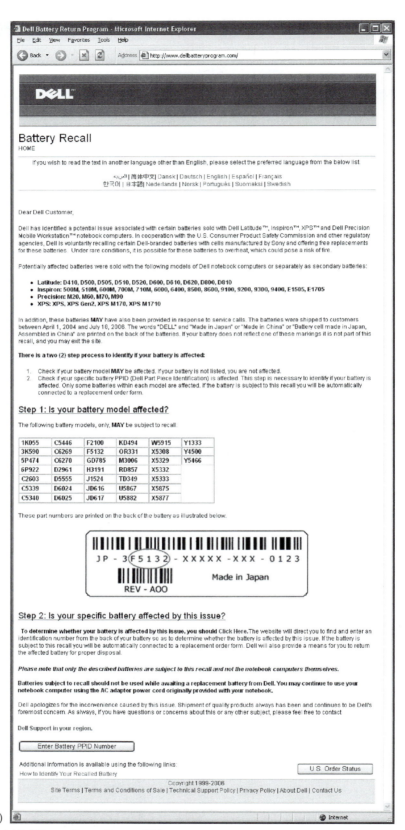

FIGURE 31.12 (a) The official Dell Battery Return Program Web page.

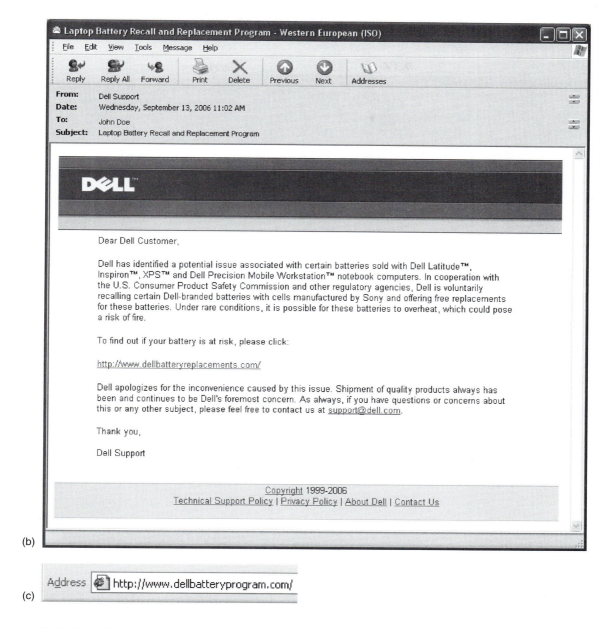

(b)

(c)

(d)

FIGURE 31.12 (*Continued*) (b) a letter to Dell customer; (c) genuine Web site URL detail; (d) bogus email body detail.

about features of their online account management interface. In terms of relevance, there is less potential impact on the user. Ignoring this message won't expose the client to any changes (good or bad). Assuming that the name and recent online interaction are correct, the message communicates little that would surprise the average client. So, in place of strong narrative components, the subject looks to formatting cues to further inform confidence. This message rated highly in its simple form and was pushed higher by the improved graphics. We attribute its initially high rating to its exclusion of hyperlinks, informative nature, and well-contextualized message.

Subject reactions to the presence of the "VeriSign Secured" logo differed dramatically between the two test messages. One message, a change of policy notice from PayPal, experienced no statistical difference in subject evaluations of its endorsed and unendorsed forms. The

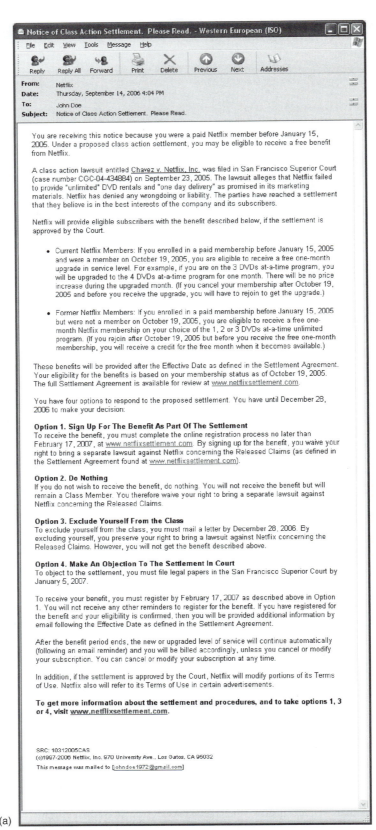

(a)

FIGURE 31.13 (a) Low-profile class-action suit.

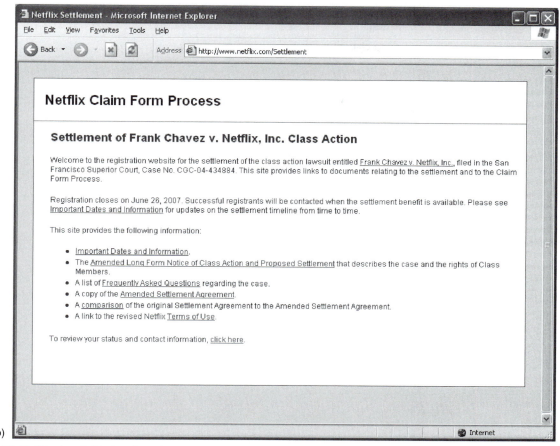

(b)

FIGURE 31.13 (*Continued*) (b) a lengthy notice that describes a class-action lawsuit against Netflix, a settlement to the lawsuit, and options for claiming benefits.

policy change notice shares several narrative features with the Chase phishing message: Both messages have a customized salutation, both inform users about an institution wide change (in this case, the particulars of their logo insertion policy), and both claim that inaction will result in a change of service. The PayPal message has no hyperlink in the message body but does contain a link in its small-font gray footer to manage user preferences; we think that this forecasts a potential phishing strategy.

The other message that tests the impact of the "VeriSign Secured" logo is a phishing message that exploits the Citibank brand. The experiment shows a statistically significant change in subject evaluations ($p = 0.047$) due to this single feature change. Of all the messages, this message makes the weakest connections to the receiver. It begins with a generic salutation. Worse, the first sentence promotes the goodness of their online service but fails to involve the receiver in any way. Not until the second sentence does the message's relevance become evident to the reader: They are offering "$50* to try it out!" These two messages had the lowest average ranking of all the email stimuli. Ignoring

this message has no impact on the user except for failing to miss out on an offer of dubious value. Ultimately, the stimulus fails to engage the reader, and so subjects base more of their evaluation on nonnarrative factors such as the endorsement logo and the bogus URL.

The Dell battery replacement program message presents a compelling story, but not directly. The incident received a high level of media coverage due to spectacular reports of exploding and burning laptop computers. The Dell message, which we manufactured, benefits from other sources spreading the story. Without this third-party validation, this message could have bordered on implausibility, but instead our subjects produced ratings that were statistically indistinguishable from the two most highly ranked email messages in the batch. This message contains a slightly nicer-than-average layout (multicolored header, footer graphic with links) but less personalization and a fraudulent (but semantically plausible) URL. The story was so powerful and present in the subjects' minds that they were willing to discount the suspicious link and generic greeting.

TABLE 31.1 The Other Third Party Attack

Stimulus Description	Mean	Diff.	χ^2	p
Chase card payment statement (legit)–plain layout	3.40	0.36	11.89	0.018
Chase card payment statement (legit)–fancy layout	3.76			
Chase phish-fancy layout	3.19	0.02	6.31	0.177
Chase phish-plain layout	3.18			
AT&T Universal Card statement without legal notices	3.05	0.62	30.18	0
AT&T Universal Card statement with legal notices	3.66			
PayPal policy change + VeriSign	3.19	0.11	5.75	0.219
PayPal policy change – no VeriSign	3.30			
Citibank phish – no VeriSign	2.40	0.29	9.62	0.047
Citibank phish + VeriSign	2.69			
AT&T Universal card login				
https://www.accountonline.com/View?docId=Index&siteId=AC&langId=EN	2.76	0.49	15.46	0.004
http://www.attuniversalcard.com	3.25			
Citbank (phish); URL=http://www.citicardmembers.com/	3.11	0.32	7.06	0.133
Copy of original site;	3.43			
Logos modified to better match domain				
PayPal Web site displaying eBay logo:				
URL=http://www.ebaygroup.com/paypal/	3.35	0.35	8.83	0.065
URL=http://www.paypal.com/ebay/	3.70			
Indiana University Credit Union homepage:				
Deemphasizes security language; no mention of "attacks"	3.69	0.32	11.45	0.022
Phishing attack banner + strong fraud warnings	3.37			
Wells Fargo phishing page:				
Reproduces original content;	3.17	0.31	10.83	0.029
URL=http://www-wellsfargo.com/				
Adds VeriSign endorsement; uses SSL;	3.48			
URL=https://www-wellsfargo.com/				
Netflix class-action settlement email (authentic)	2.72			
Netflix class-action settlement homepage (authentic)	2.55			
Dell battery replacement email (phishing)	3.61			
Dell battery replacement Web page (authentic)	3.54			

Note: The first section of the table reports on the differences between email messages; the next section reports on the Web pages; and the last section gives the average rating for the third-party attacks.

The other third-party attack (NetFlix) did not benefit from recent or high-profile media coverage (see Table 31.1). We may have further lowered its rating by altering the dates to appear relevant at the time of testing.

Subjects could have perceived the timeline as implausibly long (even for legal action) or may have been familiar with the case and known that the dates were incorrect. In addition to these changes, the original message is particularly poorly conceived. Though it has strong narrative elements that present lawsuit context, the elements of the settlement, and response options, the message is entirely too long. Message length and detail create an incentive for users to quickly evaluate according to nonnarrative features.

The most visually obvious features are the inclusion of blue hyperlinks—the only non-black-and-white symbols—that point to www.netflixsettlement.com. Though this is the legitimate domain, it should raise suspicion because it is an apparent "cousin domain" to the parent company's Web site. The lack of strong design features seals its poor evaluation. There is no company header—a feature present on every other stimulus—and no opening salutation or signature. The contact address appears to be an afterthought that does not even specify a division of the company, let alone an appropriate administrator.

The biggest surprise of the test appears in a pair of authentic AT&T Universal card messages. In many ways, this is the polar opposite of the Netflix settlements message: it has strong design elements and a short, weak narrative. The message promotes AT&T's Statements Online Only program without bundling it with a recent action (as Chase does with its payment notification). Ignoring this message will not produce any change in the receiver's service, nor does enrolling in the program provide any obvious benefit to the client; in fact, enrollment could result in unintended late payments due to imperfect spam interdiction of electronic billing notices. What the message lacks in narrative appeal it makes up for in design strength. It customizes the message to the receiver both in the opening salutation and in an "Email Security Zone" header box that displays client name and client account number suffix. The header also has a spam awareness message and company logo. A blue outline that complements the company logo encloses the rest of the content. The corporate logo appears a second time within the blue content box and the letter opens and closes with personalized salutations: "Dear John Doe," and "Sincerely, Julie A. Garry." The two versions of this message differ in the presence of a detailed small-print footer below the signature, which contains hyperlinks to privacy and security policies, as well as hyperlinks bearing the universalcard.com domain. The footer uses a small gray font and presents text for adjusting "Email Preferences" and a "Help/Contact Us" section containing the postal address and various trademark and copyright notices.

The one ambiguous feature of this email is a centrally located hyperlink, labeled "log in to Account Online." It does not indicate the URL in the text. Phishers frequently employ this sort of hyperlinking strategy to conceal the bogus server's URL. The footer may add confidence because its hyperlinks appear to reference URLs with legitimate and semantically aligned domain names; none of the hyperlinks outside the header indicate a target domain. Alternatively, the contact, copyright, and trademark notices themselves may improve confidence in the message. It is particularly interesting that even though the footer-less message displayed the last four digits of the credit-card number, customized the greeting, and employed generally strong design elements, except for the Netflix settlement, it was still ranked lower than any other legitimate message. This supports the experimental results in[11] that indicate indifference to customized greetings in certain contexts. Yet adding the footer boosts the evaluations to the point where it is statistically

indistinguishable from the other two most highly ranked messages—the Chase payment notification with fancy graphics and the Dell battery recall notice.

Web sites, particularly the login and information collection pages associated with phishing scams, do not present a story the way email messages do. For this reason, their credibility depends much more on document features and graphic design. Subjects assigned significantly different ratings to three of the five sets of twin stimuli. The results show that address bar alignment with page content, overwrought concerns about fraud, and third-party endorsements substantively change authenticity assessments.

The biggest rating difference among the Web page stimuli was measured between the two versions of the "AT&T Universal Card Sign-on" page. The official version, which uses the address URL https://www.accountonline.com/View?docId = Index&siteId = AC&langId = EN, has the lowest average rating of the ten Web stimuli in the paired testing. With an average rating of 2.76, it rated lower than a simulated phishing Web site based on the suspiciously formed domain www-wellsfargo.com (avg. rating: 3.17). Subjects who saw the unused domain http://www.attuniversalcard.com in the address bar of the AT&T card login page rated it significantly higher ($p = 0:004$) than the authentic page. The page content strongly aligns with the URL text http://www.attuniversalcard.com: the phrase "AT&T Universal" appears no less than seven times on the login page, whereas the phrase "AT&T Universal Card" appears four times in the content window. Interestingly, the official page uses HTTPS and displays an SSL padlock in the lower right-hand browser frame, whereas the attuniversalcard.com domain does not use SSL and consequently does not display the padlock on the browser frame. Subjects found the semantic alignment of the URL to be a much stronger indicator of authenticity than SSL utilization. In fairness, subjects could not examine the certificates, nor would they have been subject to the "Unable to verify the identity of host" pop-up window in the case of a self-signed certificate. Nevertheless, other user studies have found that in practice, subjects rarely consider these factors.[12,13]

---

11 M. Jakobsson and J. Ratkiewicz, "Designing ethical phishing experiments: a study of (rot13) ronl query features," In *WWW '06: Proceedings of the 15th International Conference on World Wide Web*, pp. 513–522, New York, 2006, ACM Press.

12 R. Dhamija, J. D. Tygar, and M. Hearst, "Why phishing works," In *CHI '06: Proceedings of the SIGCHI Conference on Human Factors in Computing Systems*, pp. 581–590, New York, 2006, ACM Press.

13 M. Wu, R. C. Miller, and S. L. Garfinkel, "Do security toolbars actually prevent phishing attacks?" In *CHI '06: Proceedings of the SIGCHI Conference on Human Factors in Computing Systems*, pp 601–610, New York, 2006, ACM Press.

Much to our surprise, the phishing simulation based on the URL www-wellsfargo.com rated significantly higher ($p = 0:00001$) than the official AT&T Universal card login page. Subjects valued semantic alignment between content and host domain more than domain well-formedness. Syntactically there is nothing wrong with the domain, but replacing the dot with a dash is clearly an attempt at deception. Adding SSL and a "VeriSign Secured" logo to the Wells-Fargo phishing page produced a significant improvement in authenticity ratings ($p = 0:029$). It's worth noting that the authentic login page (not in the test) does not display a VeriSign logo but does use SSL. In spite of subjects either failing to notice the dash-for-dot exchange or not thinking that it was suspicious, they did notice the presence of either SSL or the VeriSign logo. Note that the AT&T login page also used SSL and displayed a VeriSign endorsement, but neither of these features could overcome the mistrust of the accountonline.com domain.

The last statistically significant difference between twins in the Indiana University Credit Union homepage ($p = 0:022$) shows that too much concern about security can reduce customer confidence. Subjects responded positively to use of less fearful language and rated the softer, more constructive content significantly higher than the page that displayed stark warnings. Note that correct domain names and SSL were used on both stimuli. This is a case where a good-faith effort to educate clients about phishing undermines confidence in the Web site's authenticity. Login pages are no place for fear-provoking messages.

One way phishers align page content with URLs is by choosing an apt domain name; the other way is to change the page content. Though subjects gave a higher average rating to our modified Citibank cardmembers login page, the test showed that the two distributions were not significantly different ($p = 0:133$).

The last test pair was nearly significant ($p = 0:65$) but does not confirm that the two ratings come from different distributions. This pair compared the effects of a plausible parent company domain and subsidiary subdirectory, http://www.ebaygroup.com/paypal/, with the authentic URL that reverses their positions, http://www.paypal.com/ebay/. Although the ebaygroup.com domain is unbound, eBay has registered it. Nevertheless, this test shows a certain flexibility in user acceptance of domain alignment. No PayPal client has seen the PayPal page displayed under the http://www.ebaygroup.com/paypal/ address, yet their authenticity ratings are not significantly different. This result furthers our conviction that semantic alignment between content and URL is a principal factor in authenticity evaluations.

The last two Web stimuli sets are not twins; they are the Dell battery replacement page and the Netflix settlement page. Both pages are authentic, although the content of the Netflix page was altered to appear relevant at the time of testing. They received polar opposite ratings. The Dell battery page was statistically indistinguishable from the highest-rated page (the authentic PayPal site), and the Netflix page rated dead last—significantly lower than the second lowest rating ($p = 1:20 \ 10^{-7}$). As mentioned before, the Dell battery program stimuli benefit from a high visibility news story. It's noteworthy that the URL in the Web page (authentic) is different from the URL in the email (phishing), which subjects saw first. Subjects did not penalize the Web page for this inconsistency. Subjects may have had difficulty constructing a phishing scenario based on the informational nature of the page; there is no request for personal information.

Similarly, the Netflix settlement page does not make any overtures for personal information. Even more surprising is that the URL http://www.netflix.com/settlement/ aligns well with the content. Subjects may have dismissed the page based on mistrust of the email stimulus, which they viewed prior to (several screenshots before) the Web stimulus. The Netflix page is notable for its brevity and unsophisticated layout. It is the only page without graphics or logos of any kind. There are no apparent links back to the primary Netflix page. With the exception of the blue underlined hyperlinks and gray margins, the page is black and white. We take from this rating that utilizing minimalist design is a poor strategy for unsolicited communications, even for important and serious matters such as law.

3. IMPLICATIONS FOR CRIMEWARE

The experiment focused on design features and their effect on people's ability to distinguish authentic email and Web sites from malicious forgeries. Although presented in the context of phishing, we do not measure how often subjects disclose passwords or other sensitive data; rather, we identify design principles that convey authenticity. Just as phishing bait promises resolution upon revealing information, social crimeware bait may promise resolution contingent upon installing browser extensions or accepting self-signed Java applets. Presenting a convincing false identity to the victim is essential in both contexts. Toward this end, our results forecast the following social engineering tactics:

- Construct messages with weak narratives (bordering on innocuous) but use strong design elements (graphics, small-print footer, endorsement logos)

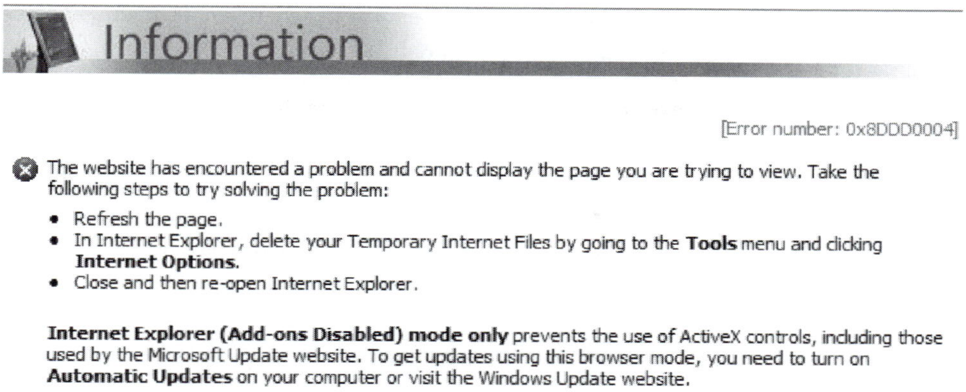

Information

[Error number: 0x8DDD0004]

⊗ The website has encountered a problem and cannot display the page you are trying to view. Take the following steps to try solving the problem:

- Refresh the page.
- In Internet Explorer, delete your Temporary Internet Files by going to the **Tools** menu and clicking **Internet Options**.
- Close and then re-open Internet Explorer.

Internet Explorer (Add-ons Disabled) mode only prevents the use of ActiveX controls, including those used by the Microsoft Update website. To get updates using this browser mode, you need to turn on **Automatic Updates** on your computer or visit the Windows Update website.

FIGURE 31.14 Suggested workarounds involving settings changes.

and identifying information to improve authenticity impressions.

- Use softer bait. Messages that do not encapsulate an imminent request for information, such as the Dell battery bait, rated highly in the test.
- Use plausibly unfamiliar administration pages; for example, the Dell Battery Return Program Web site provides a service that is not typically seen, such as a login page (so visitor expectations are less concrete).
- Leverage high-profile news to produce messages with credible and strong narratives. Personalization will be less important in these cases.
- Align domain names with page content. Although subjects were turned off by semantic mismatches between domain names and content, they were insensitive to malformed links (http://www-wellsfargo.com).

With respect to the final point, the "rock-phish" gang has proven that effective domain alignment can be achieved through deceptive subdomains,[14] the control of which is delegated to the domain owner rather than the registrar. The following URL, from a social engineering attack in the wild, illustrates this tactic:

www.paypal.com.cgi.bin.account.webscr.cmd.login. run.php.draciimasi.info/webscr.php?cmd=Login

The registered domain is draciimasi.info, but the owners have prepended it with a deep subdomain. Since subjects accepted the substitution of a dash for a dot in www-wellsfargo.com, they could easily accept a dot for a slash, as above. Moreover, the preponderance of subdirectory names such as cgi, bin, webscr, and the like further clouds the issue for the technically uninformed. This tactic may be particularly effective for download pages because they tend to be buried several directories deep; login pages, on the other hand, are frequently in the root of a domain.

Example: Vulnerability of Web-Based Update Mechanisms

Legitimate Web sites often make their services contingent upon changing settings, installing extensions, or accepting certificates. One important example is Microsoft's Windows Update Web site. It scans the client for installation detail through ActiveX extensions. When accessing the Web site through a professionally managed client at Indiana University, an update is not possible because the administrators have disabled the service. However, the Web site (see Figure 31.14) suggests workarounds involving settings changes.

None of these suggestions will enable remote update for this professionally managed computer, but subtle changes to the instructions could cause unsophisticated users to disengage important access controls. For example, the user could have been instructed to enter Add-ons Enabled mode. Subsequent installation of malicious add-ons will lead to a compromise. As long as the host's identity has been convincingly spoofed, users will be vulnerable to these kinds of attacks.

Example: The Unsubscribe Spam Attack

This attack leverages the first two tactics we discussed: weak narrative combined with strong design elements and softer bait. Some of the most highly rated email messages avoided hyperlinks in the main message text. The Chase account payment was completely devoid of hyperlinks and instead directed receivers to type www.chase.com into their address bar. Similarly, the PayPal message had no hyperlinks in its body, but it included a hyperlink in the footer to change preferences. The highly rated AT&T Universal card promotion also contains links in its small-print footer.

---

14 T. Moore and R. Clayton, "An empirical analysis of the current state of phishing attack and defense," The 2007 Workshop on the Economics of Information Security (WEIS 2007), 7–8 June 2007.

The attacker will send out promotional email that appears to come from the spoofed institution. The promotion would employ a weak narrative to shift user attention to a plethora of design features (graphical header, footer, small print, personalization, genuine but unlinked URLs in the body, and so on). The body will generate the perception of authenticity by referring the receivers to the phone number on back of her credit card or by requiring users to manually type in the promotional URL. Among the design features is a small-print footer with an unsubscribe hyperlink. This link will take users to a Web page that spreads crimeware simply by loading malicious JavaScript code, like a "drive-by pharming attack."

The bait message gets users to click on the link indirectly: annoyance with the volume of unsolicited messages. No suspicion is aroused through directions to change settings; the malware spreads on load.

The Strong Narrative Attack

The strong narrative attack engages the receiver with a plausible story, often bundling actions to well-known news stories. The Chase phishing message that promotes ePIN to incoming Bank One customers is such an example; it leverages in the news of the Bank One acquisition. The Dell battery program stimuli gain most of their credibility from the story's media coverage. The message maintains this credibility by deferring the request for personal information; standard attacks request an "account login" or "settings update" in the message body. This battery exchange program could have been turned into a "patch-now" attack by claiming that a firmware or operating system fix would prevent overheating.

Though scams that exploit strong narratives and current events are not new (many fraud cases capitalized on the September 11, 2001, and Hurricane Katrina tragedies[15,16]), our research suggests that they are less influenced by design features. This finding is supported by the persistence of the Nigerian code 419 advance fee scams.[17] One widespread form of this attack entices victims with a story of the death of a foreign dignitary and the need to move large amounts of money (allegedly to protect it from corrupt enemies); they offer the victim

a cut for moving the money. After drawing the victim into this illusion, the scammers request advance fees to enable the transfer of money. These messages break many design rules that promote trust: They use poor spelling and grammar, email messages are often plaintext, return addresses are essentially anonymous using free email accounts. Yet these scams still account for large amounts of Internet fraud, exceeding $3 billion in losses according to some estimates.[18]

4. CONCLUSION

This study tested the impact of several document features on user authenticity perceptions for both email messages and Web pages. The influence of these features was context dependent in email messages. We were surprised that this context was shaped more by a message's narrative strength, rather than its underlying authenticity. Third-party endorsements and glossy graphics proved to be effective authenticity stimulators when message content was short and unsurprising. The same document features failed to influence authenticity judgments in a significant way when applied to more involving messages. Most surprising was the huge increase in trust caused by a small-print footer in a message that already exhibited strong personalization with its greeting and presentation of a four-digit account number suffix.

The data suggest a link between narrative strength and susceptibility to trust-improving document features, but the experiment was not designed to test this hypothesis. Future work should characterize more precisely what kind of messages can benefit from these features and what kind of messages are resistant to their sway.

Since spoofed Web page content need not differ from the authentic pages, we focused three Web page tests on the effects of semantic alignment between address bar URLs and page content. The first showed a clear statistical preference for a simulated Web page whose domain name matched its content rather than the genuine page whose domain was only weakly aligned with the same content. The second test, which created better alignment with a bogus domain name by altering company logos, failed to register a statistically significant change in authenticity ratings. The third test compared an authentic page (and URL) with an authentic version of the same page content paired with a well-aligned but bogus URL; the results which favored the genuine URL were

---

15 Fraud Section, Criminal Division, U.S. Department of Justice. Special report on possible fraud schemes, www.usdoj.gov/criminal/fraud/WTCPent-SpecRpt.htm, 27 September 2001, retrieved December 2006.

16 B. Krebs, "Katrina phishing scams begin," WashingtonPost.com: Security Fix, 31 August 2005.

17 M. Zuckofi, "The perfect mark: How Massachusetts psychotherapist fell for a Nigerian e-mail scam," *The New Yorker*, 15 May 2006, www.newyorker.com/fact/content/articles/060515fa_fact.

18 Ultrascan Advanced Global Investigations, "Advance fee fraud in 37 nations," www.ultrascan.nl/html/aff_37_countries.html, 25 March 2006, retrieved December 2006.

just shy of statistical significance. In conclusion, we find that URL can change authenticity ratings.

This experiment also verified that it is possible to overuse well-intended notices about security and fraud. We observed a statistically significant negative effect of genuine, but heavy-handed, fraud warnings. Another test showed a statistically significant improvement in authenticity perception when using SSL and a third-party endorsement logo on a fraudulent Web page showing a suspiciously formed, but semantically well-aligned, domain name.

The experiment simulated two sequences (one email and one Web page) that appeared to be third parties charged with handling embarrassing incidents for their corporate clients. Though separated by many variables, one turned out to be among the most trusted stimuli in the test, whereas the other rank among the lowest. The poorly ranked one, though authentic, broke all the rules: poor publicity, long and rambling message, use of third-party domain names, and no graphics. The highly ranked one (whose bogus email message was concocted by the authors) benefited from a widely publicized recall message. The story overrode the message's poor personalization, illegitimate URL, and relatively simple layout.

These factors offer a glimpse into what kinds of social engineering tactics may be deployed in the future. We describe an unsubscribed attack which contains an innocuous message, many authenticity stimulating document features, and an unsubscribe link that leads to a noninteractively infectious Web site. Our tests with third-party administration suggest that organizations in the process of correcting an embarrassing incident are highly vulnerable to social engineering attacks. Finally, our findings suggest some common pitfalls for legitimate Internet communications to avoid: overuse of fraud warnings, utilization of poorly aligned domain names, failure to use HTTPS for rendering login pages, and long or rambling email messages.

## Chapter 32

VoIP Security

Dan Wing
Cisco Systems

Harsh Kupwade Patil
Southern Methodist University

The Internet has become an important medium for communication, and all kinds of media communications are carried on today's Internet. Telephony over the Internet has received a lot of attention in the last few years because it offers users advantages such as long distance toll bypass, interactive ecommerce, global online customer support, and much more.

1. INTRODUCTION

H.323 and *Session Initiation Protocol* (SIP) are the two standardized protocols for the realization of VoIP.[1,2] The multimedia conference protocol H.323 of the International Telecommunication Union (ITU) consists of multiple separate protocols such as the H.245 for control signaling and H.225 for call signaling. H.323 is difficult to implement because of its complexity and the bulkiness that it introduces into the client application.[3] In contrast, SIP is simpler than H.323 and also leaner on the client-side application. SIP uses the human-readable protocol (ASCII) instead of H.323's binary signal coding.

VoIP Basics

SIP is the *Internet Engineering Task Force* (IETF) standard for multimedia communications in an IP network. It is an application layer control protocol used for creating, modifying, and terminating sessions between one or more SIP *user agents*. It was primarily designed to support user location discovery, user availability, user capabilities, and session setup and management.

In SIP, the end devices are called *user agents* (UAs), and they send SIP requests and SIP responses to establish media sessions, send and receive media, and send other SIP messages (e.g., to send short text messages to each other or subscribe to an event notification service). A UA can be a SIP phone or SIP client software running on a PC or PDA.

Typically, a collection of SIP user agents belongs to an administrative domain, which forms a SIP network. Each administrative domain has a SIP proxy, which is the point of contact for UAs within the domain and for UAs or SIP proxies outside the domain. All SIP signaling messages within a domain are routed through the domain's own SIP proxy. SIP routing is performed using *Uniform Resource Identifiers* (URIs) for addressing user agents. Two types of SIP URIs are supported: the SIP URI and the TEL URI. A SIP URI begins with the keyword *sip* or *sips*, where *sips* indicates that the SIP signaling must be sent over a secure channel, such as TLS.[4] The SIP URI is similar to an email address and contains a user's identifier and the domain at which the user can be found. For example, it could contain a username such as *sip:alice@example.com*, a global E.164 telephone number[5] such as *sip:1 1-972-310-9882@example.com;user = phone*, or an extension such as *sip:1234@example.com*. The TEL URI only contains an E.164 telephone number and does not contain a domain name, for example, *tel: + 1.408.555.1234*.

A SIP proxy server is an entity that receives SIP requests, performs various database lookups, and then forwards ("proxies") the request to the next-hop proxy server. In this way,

1 ITU-T Recommendation H.323, Packet-Based Multimedia Communications System, www.itu.int/rec/T-REC-H.323-200606-I/en. 1998.

2 J. Rosenberg, H. Schulzrinne, G. Camarillo, J. Peterson, R. Sparks, M. Handley, and E. Schooler, "SIP: Session Initiation Protocol," IETF RFC 3261, June 2002.

3 H. Schulzrinne and J. Rosenberg, "A Comparison of SIP and H.323 for Internet telephony," in *Proceedings of NOSSDAV*, Cambridge, U.K., July 1998.

4 S. Fries and D. Ignjatic, "On the applicability of various MIKEY modes and extensions," IETF draft, March 31, 2008.

5 F. Audet, "The use of the SIPS URI scheme in the Session Initiation Protocol (SIP)," IETF draft, February 23, 2008.

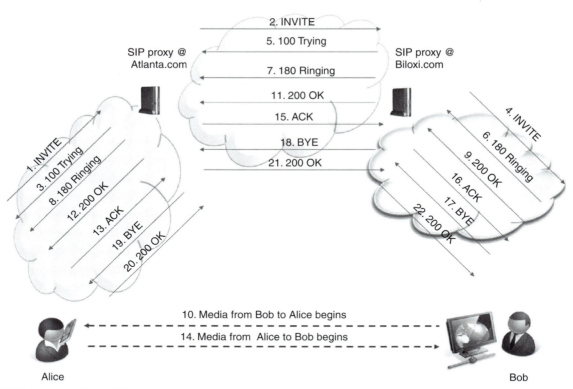

FIGURE 32.1 An example of a SIP session setup.

SIP messages are routed to their ultimate destination. Each proxy may perform some specialized function, such as external database lookups, authorization checks, and so on. Because the media does not flow through the SIP proxies—but rather only SIP signaling—SIP proxies are no longer needed after the call is established. In many SIP proxy designs, the proxies are stateless, which allows alternative intermediate proxies to resume processing for a failed (or overloaded) proxy. One type of SIP proxy called a *redirect server* receives a SIP request, performs a database query operation, and returns the lookup result to the requester (which is often another proxy). Another type of SIP proxy is a SIP *registrar server*, which receives and processes registration requests. Registration binds a SIP (or TEL) URI to the user's device, which is how SIP messages are routed to a user agent. Multiple UAs may register the same URI, which causes incoming SIP requests to be routed to all of those UAs, a process termed *forking*, which causes some interesting security concerns.

The typical SIP transactions can be broadly viewed by looking at the typical call flow mechanism in a SIP session setup, as shown in Figure 32.1. The term *SIP trapezoid* is often used to describe this message flow where the SIP signaling is sent to SIP proxies and the media is sent directly between the two UAs.

If Alice wants to initiate a session with Bob, she sends an initial SIP message (*INVITE*) to the local proxy

for her domain (Atlanta.com). Her *INVITE* has Bob's URI (bob@biloxi.com) as the Request-URI, which is used to route the message. Upon receiving the initial message from Alice, her domain's proxy sends a provisional *100 Trying* message to Alice, which indicates that the message was received without error from Alice. The Atlanta.com proxy looks at the *SIP Request-URI* in the message and decides to route the message to the Biloxi.com proxy. The Biloxi.com proxy receives the message and routes it to Bob. The Biloxi.com proxy delivers the *INVITE* message to Bob's SIP phone, to alert Bob of an incoming call. Bob's SIP phone initiates a provisional *180 Ringing* message back to Alice, which is routed all the way back to Alice; this causes Alice's phone to generate a ringback tone, audible to Alice. When Bob answers his phone a *200 OK* message is sent to his proxy, and Bob can start immediately sending media ("Hello?") to Alice. Meanwhile, Bob's 200 OK is routed from his proxy to Alice's proxy and finally to Alice's UA. Alice's UA responds with an *ACK* message to Bob and then Alice can begin sending media (audio and/or video) to Bob. Real-time media is almost exclusively sent using the Real-time Transport Protocol (RTP).[6]

6 H. Schulzrinne, R. Frederick, and V. Jacobson, "RTP: A transport protocol for real-time applications," IETF RFC 1889, Jan. 1996.

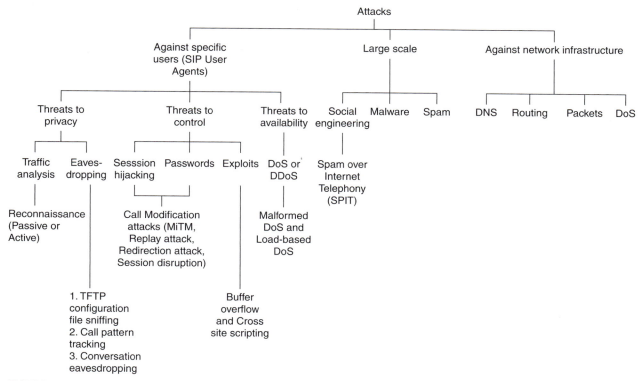

FIGURE 32.2 Taxonomy of threats.

At this point the proxies are no longer involved in the call and hence the media will typically flow directly between Alice and Bob. That is, the media takes a different path through the network than the signaling. Finally, when either Alice or Bob want to end the session, they send a *BYE* message to their proxy, which is routed to the other party and is acknowledged.

One of the challenging tasks faced by the industry today is secure deployment of VoIP. During the initial design of SIP the focus was more on providing new dynamic and powerful services along with simplicity rather than security. For this reason, a lot of effort is under way in the industry and among researchers to enhance SIP's security. The subsequent sections of this chapter deal with these issues.

2. OVERVIEW OF THREATS

Attacks can be broadly classified as attacks against specific users (SIP user agents), large scale (VoIP is part of the network) and against network infrastructure (SIP proxies or other network components and resources necessary for VoIP, such as routers, DNS servers, and bandwidth).[7]

This chapter does not cover attacks against infrastructure; the interested reader is referred to the literature.[8] The subsequent parts of this chapter deal with the attacks targeted toward the specific host and issues related to social engineering.

Taxonomy of Threats

The taxonomy of attacks is shown in Figure 32.2.

Reconnaissance of VoIP Networks

Reconnaissance refers to intelligent gathering or probing to assess the vulnerabilities of a network, to successfully launch a later attack; it includes *footprinting* the target (also known as *profiling* or *information gathering*).

The two forms of reconnaissance techniques are passive and active. Passive reconnaissance attacks include the collection of network information through indirect or direct methods but without probing the target; active reconnaissance attacks involve generating traffic with the intention of eliciting responses from the target. Passive reconnaissance techniques would involve searching for publicly

7 T. Chen and C. Davis, "An overview of electronic attacks," in *Information Security and Ethics: Concepts, Methodologies, Tools and Applications*, H. Nemati (ed.), Idea Group Publishing, to appear 2008.

8 A. Chakrabarti and G. Manimaran, "Internet infrastructure security: a taxonomy," IEEE Network, Vol. 16, pp. 13–21, Dec. 2002.

available SIP URIs in databases provided by VoIP service providers or on Web pages, looking for publicly accessible SIP proxies or SIP UAs. Examples include *dig* and *nslookup*. Although passive reconnaissance techniques can be effective, they are time intensive.

If an attacker can watch SIP signaling, the attacker can perform number harvesting. Here, an attacker passively monitors all incoming and outgoing calls to build a database of legitimate phone numbers or extensions within an organization. This type of database can be used in more advanced VoIP attacks such as signaling manipulation or Spam over Internet Telephony (SPIT) attacks.

Active reconnaissance uses technical tools to discover information on the hosts that are active on the target network. The drawback to active reconnaissance, however, is that it can be detected. The two most common active reconnaissance attacks are call walking attacks and port-scanning attacks.

Call walking is a type of reconnaissance probe in which a malicious user initiates sequential calls to a block of telephone numbers to identify what assets are available for further exploitation. This is a modern version of *wardialing*, common in the 1980s to find modems on the Public Switched Telephone Network (PSTN). Performed during nonbusiness hours, call walking can provide information useful for social engineering, such as voicemail announcements that disclose the called party's name.

SIP UAs and proxies listen on UDP/5060 and/or TCP/5060, so it can be effective to scan IP addresses looking for such listeners. Once the attacker has accumulated a list of active IP addresses, he can start to investigate each address further. The Nmap tool is a robust port scanner that is capable of performing a multitude of types of scans.[9]

Denial of Service

A denial-of-service (DoS) attack deprives a user or an organization of services or resources that are normally available. In SIP, DoS attacks can be classified as malformed request DoS and load-based DoS.

Malformed Request DoS

In this type of DoS attack, the attacker would craft a SIP request (or response) that exploits the vulnerability in a SIP proxy or SIP UA of the target, resulting in a partial or complete loss of function. For example, it has also been found that some user agents allow remote attackers

to cause a denial of service ("486 Busy" responses or device reboot) via a sequence of SIP INVITE transactions in which the Request-URI lacks a username.[10] Attackers have also shown that the IP implementations of some hard phones are vulnerable to IP fragmentation attacks [CAN-2002-0880] and DHCP-based DoS attacks [CAN-2002-0835], demonstrating that normal infrastructure protection (such as firewalls) is valuable for VoIP equipment. DoS attacks can also be initiated against other network services such as DHCP and DNS, which serve VoIP devices.

Load-Based DoS

In this case an attacker directs large volumes of traffic at a target (or set of targets) and attempts to exhaust resources such as the CPU processing time, network bandwidth, or memory. SIP proxies and session border controllers (SBCs) are primary targets for attackers because of their critical role of providing voice service and the complexity of the software running on them.

A common type of load-based attack is a flooding attack. In case of VoIP, we categorize flooding attacks into these types:

- Control packet floods
- Call data floods
- Distributed denial-of-service attack

Control Packet Floods

In this case the attacker will flood SIP proxies with SIP packets, such as INVITE messages, bogus responses, or the like. The attacker might purposefully craft authenticated messages that fail authentication, to cause the victim to validate the message. The attacker might spoof the IP address of a legitimate sender so that rate limiting the attack also causes rate limiting of the legitimate user as well.

Call Data Floods

The attacker will flood the target with RTP packets, with or without first establishing a legitimate RTP session, in an attempt to exhaust the target's bandwidth or processing power, leading to degradation of VoIP quality for other users on the same network or just for the victim.

Other common forms of load-based attacks that could affect the VoIP system are buffer overflow attacks, TCP SYN flood, UDP flood, fragmentation attacks, smurf attacks, and general overload attacks. Though VoIP

---

9 http://nmap.org/.

10 The common vulnerability and exposure list for SIP, http://cve. mitre.org/cgibin/cvekey.cgi?keyword=SIP.

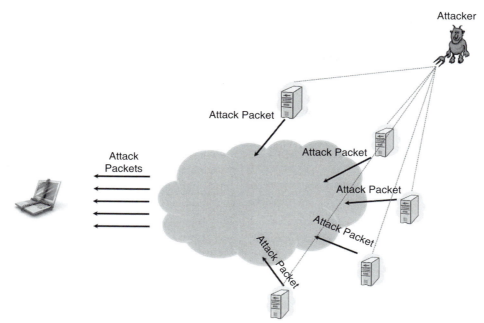

FIGURE 32.3 Distributed denial-of-service attack (DDoS).

equipment needs to protect itself from these attacks, these attacks are not specific to VoIP.

A SIP proxy can be overloaded with excessive legitimate traffic—the classic "Mother's Day" problem when the telephone system is most busy. Large-scale disasters (e.g., earthquakes) can also cause similar spikes, which are not attacks. Thus, even when not under attack, the system could be under high load. If the server or the end user is not fast enough to handle incoming loads, it will experience an outage or misbehave in such a way as to become ineffective at processing SIP messages. This type of attack is very difficult to detect because it would be difficult to sort the legitimate user from the illegitimate users who are performing the same type of attack.

Distributed Denial-of-Service Attack

Once an attacker has gained control of a large number of VoIP-capable hosts and formed a "zombies" network under the attacker's control, the attacker can launch interesting VoIP attacks, as illustrated in Figure 32.3.

Each zombie can send up to thousands of messages to a single location, thereby resulting in a barrage of packets, which incapacitates the victim's computer due to resource exhaustion.

Loss of Privacy

The four major eavesdropping attacks are:

- Trivial File Transfer Protocol (TFTP) configuration file sniffing

- Traffic analysis
- Conversation eavesdropping

TFTP Configuration File Sniffing

Most IP phones rely on a TFTP server to download their configuration file after powering on. The configuration file can sometimes contain passwords that can be used to directly connect back to the phone and administer it or used to access other services (such as the company directory). An attacker who is sniffing the file when the phone downloads this configuration file can glean through these passwords and potentially reconfigure and control the IP phone. To thwart this attack vector, vendors variously encrypt the configuration file or use HTTPS and authentication.

Traffic Analysis

Traffic analysis involves determining who is talking to whom, which can be done even when the actual conversation is encrypted and can even be done (to a lesser degree) between organizations. Such information can be beneficial to law enforcement and for criminals committing corporate espionage and stock fraud.

Conversation Eavesdropping

An important threat for VoIP users is eavesdropping on a conversation. In addition to the obvious problem of confidential information being exchanged between people, eavesdropping is also useful for credit-card fraud and identity theft. This is because some phone calls—especially to certain institutions—require users to enter credit-card numbers, PIN codes, or national identity numbers (e.g., Social Security numbers), which are sent as Dual-Tone Multi-frequency (DTMF) digits in RTP. An attacker can use tools like Wireshark, Cain & Abel, vomit (voice over misconfigured Internet telephones), VoIPong, and Oreka to capture RTP packets and extract the conversation or the DTMF digits.[11]

Man-in-the-Middle Attacks

The man-in-the-middle attack is a classic form of an attack where the attacker has managed to insert himself between the two hosts. It refers to an attacker who is able to read, and modify at will, messages between two parties without either party knowing that the link between them has been compromised. As such, the attacker has the ability to inspect or modify packets exchanged between two hosts or insert new packets or prevent packets from being sent to hosts. Any device that handles SIP messages as a normal course of its function could be a man in the middle: a compromised SIP proxy server or session border controller. If SIP messages are not authenticated, an attacker can also compromise a DNS server or use DNS poisoning techniques to cause SIP messages to be routed to a device under the attacker's control.

Replay Attacks

Replay attacks are often used to impersonate an authorized user. A replay attack is one in which an attacker captures a valid packet sent between the SIP UAs or proxies and resends it at a later time (perhaps a second later, perhaps days later). As an example with classic unauthenticated telnet, an attacker that captures a telnet username and password can replay that same username and password. In SIP, an attacker would capture and replay valid SIP requests. (Capturing and replaying SIP responses is usually not valuable, as SIP responses are discarded if their Call-Id does not match a currently outstanding request, which is one way SIP protects itself from replay attacks.)

If Real-time Transport Protocol (RTP) is used without authenticating Real-time Transport Control Protocol (RTCP) packets and without sampling synchronization source (SSRC), an attacker can inject RTCP packets into a multicast group, each with a different SSRC, and force the group size to grow exponentially. A variant on a replay attack is the cut-and-paste attack. In this scenario,

an attacker copies part of a captured packet with a generated packet. For example, a security credential can be copied from one request to another, resulting in a successful authorization without the attacker even discovering the user's password.

Impersonation

Impersonation is described as a user or host pretending to be another user or host, especially one that the intended victim trusts. In case of a phishing attack, the attacker continues the deception to make the victim disclose his banking information, employee credentials, and other sensitive information. In SIP, the From header is displayed to the called party, so authentication and authorization of the values used in the From header are important to prevent impersonation. Unfortunately, call forwarding in SIP (called *retargeting*) makes simple validation of the From header impossible. For example, imagine Bob has forwarded his phone to Carol and they are in different administrative domains (Bob is at work, Carol is his wife at home). Then Alice calls Bob. When Alice's INVITE is routed to Bob's proxy, her INVITE will be retargeted to Carol's UA by rewriting the Request-URI to point to Carol's URI. Alice's original INVITE is then routed to Carol's UA. When it arrives at Carol's UA, the INVITE needs to indicate that the call is from Alice. The difficulty is that if Carol's SIP proxy were to have performed simplistic validation of the From in the INVITE when it arrived from Bob's SIP proxy, Carol's SIP proxy would have rejected it—because it contained Alice's From. However, such retargeting is a legitimate function of SIP networks.

Redirection Attack

If compromised by an attacker or via a SIP man-in-the-middle attack, the intermediate SIP proxies responsible for SIP message routing can falsify any response. In this section we describe how the attacker could use this ability to launch a redirection attack. If an attacker can fabricate a reply to a SIP INVITE, the media session can be established with the attacker rather than the intended party. In SIP, a proxy or UA can respond to an INVITE request with a 301 Moved Permanently or 302 Moved Temporarily Response. The 302 Response will also include an Expires header line that communicates how long the redirection should last. The attacker can respond with a redirection response, effectively denying service to the called party and possibly tricking the caller into communicating with, or through, a rogue UA.

Session Disruption

Session disruption describes any attack that degrades or disrupts an existing signaling or media session. For

---

11 D. Endler and M. Collier, *Hacking VoIP Exposed: Voice over IP Security Secrets and Solutions,* McGraw-Hill, 2007.

example, in the case of a SIP scenario, if an attacker is able to send failure messages such as BYE and inject them into the signaling path, he can cause the sessions to fail when there is no legitimate reason why they should not continue. For this to be successful, the attacker has to include the Call-Id of an active call in the BYE message. Alternatively, if an attacker introduces bogus packets into the media stream, he can disrupt packet sequence, impede media processing, and disrupt a session. Delay attacks are those in which an attacker can capture and resend RTP SSRC packets out of sequence to a VoIP endpoint and force the endpoint to waste its processing cycles in resequencing packets and degrade call quality. An attacker could also disrupt a Voice over Wireless Local Area Network (WLAN) service by disrupting IEEE 802.11 WLAN service using radio spectrum jamming or a Wi-Fi Protected Access (WPA) Message Integrity Check (MIC) attack. A wireless access point will disassociate stations when it receives two invalid frames within 60 seconds, causing loss of network connectivity for 60 seconds. A one-minute loss of service is hardly tolerable in a voice application.

Exploits

Cross-Site Scripting (XSS) attacks are possible with VoIP systems because call logs contain header fields, and administrators (and other privileged users) view those call logs. In this attack, specially crafted From: (or other) fields are sent by an attacker in a normal SIP message (such as an INVITE). Then later, when someone such as the administrator looks at the call logs using a Web browser, the specially crafted From; causes a XSS attack against the administrator's Web browser, which can then do malicious things with the administrator's privileges. This can be a damaging attack if the administrator has already logged into other systems (HR databases, the SIP call controller, the firewall) and her Web browser has a valid cookie (or active session in another window) for those other systems.

Social Engineering

SPIT (Spam over Internet Telephony) is classified as a social threat because the callee can treat the call as unsolicited, and the term *unsolicited* is strictly bound to be a user-specific preference, which makes it hard for the system to identify this kind of transaction. SPIT can be telemarketing calls used for guiding callees to a service deployed to sell products. IM spam and presence spam could also be launched via SIP messages. IM spam is very similar to email spam; presence spam is defined as a set of unsolicited presence requests for the presence package. A subtle variation of SPIT called *Vishing* (VoIP phishing) is an attack that aims to collect personal data by redirecting users toward an interactive voice responder that could collect personal information such as the PIN for a credit card. From a signaling point of view, unsolicited communication is technically a correct transaction.

Unfortunately, many of the mechanisms that are effective for email spam are ineffective with VoIP, for many reasons. First, the email with its entire contents arrives at a server before it is seen by the user. Such a mail server can therefore apply many filtering strategies, such as Bayesian filters, URL filters, and so on. In contrast, in VoIP, human voices are transmitted rather than text. To recognize voices and to determine whether the message is spam or not is still a very difficult task for the end system. A recipient of a call only learns about the subject of the message when he is actually listening to it. Moreover, even if the content is stored on a voice mailbox, it is still difficult for today's speech recognition technologies to understand the context of the message enough to decide whether it is spam or not.

One mechanism to fight automated systems that deliver spam is to challenge such suspected incoming calls with a Turing test. These methods include:

- *Voice menu.* Before a call is put through, a computer asks the caller to press certain key combinations, for example "Press #55."
- *Challenge models.* Before a call is put through, a computer asks the caller to solve a simple equation and to type in the answer—for example, "Divide 10 by 2."
- *Alternative number.* Under the main number a computer announces an alternative number. This number may even be changed permanently by a call management server. All these methods can even be enforced by enriching the audio signal with noise or music. This prevents SPIT bots from using speech recognition.

Such Turing tests are attractive, since it is often hard for computers to decode audio questions. However, these puzzles cannot be made too difficult, because human beings must always be able to solve them.

One of the solutions to the SPIT problem is the whitelist. In a whitelist, a user explicitly states which persons are allowed to contact him. A similar technique is also used in Skype; where Alice wants to call Bob, she first has to add Bob to her contact list and send a contact request to Bob. Only when Bob has accepted this request can Alice make calls to Bob.

In general, whitelists have an introduction problem, since it is not possible to receive calls by someone who is not already on the whitelist. Blacklists are the opposite of whitelists but have limited effectiveness at blocking spam because new identities (which are not on the blacklist) can be easily created by anyone, including spammers.

Authentication mechanisms can be used to provide strong authentication, which is necessary for strong whitelists and reputation systems, which form the basis of SPIT prevention. Strong authentication is generally Public Key Infrastructure (PKI) dependent. Proactive publishing of incorrect information, namely SIP addresses, is a possible way to fill up spammers' databases with existing contacts. Consent-based communication is the other solution. Address obfuscation could be an alternative wherein spam bots are unable to identify the SIP URIs.

3. SECURITY IN VoIP

Much existing VoIP equipment is dedicated to VoIP, which allows placing such equipment on a separate network. This is typically accomplished with a separate VLAN. Depending on the vendor of the equipment, this can be automated using CDP (Cisco Discovery Protocol), LLDP (Link Layer Discovery Protocol), or 802.1x, all of which will place equipment into a separate "voice VLAN" to assist with this separation. This provides a reasonable level of protection, especially within an enterprise where employees lack much incentive to interfere with the telephone system.

Preventative Measures

However, the use of VLANs is not an ideal solution because it does not work well with softphones that are not dedicated to VoIP, because placing those softphones onto the "voice VLAN" destroys the security and management advantage of the separate network. A separate VLAN can also create a false sense of security that only benign voice devices are connected to the VLAN. However, even though 802.1x provides the best security, it is still possible for an attacker to gain access to the voice VLAN (with a suitable hub between the phone and the switch). Mechanisms that provide less security, such as CDP or LLDP, can be circumvented by software on an infected computer. Some vendors' Ethernet switches can be configured to require clients to request inline Ethernet power before allowing clients to join certain VLANs (such as the voice VLAN), which provides protection from such infected computers. But, as mentioned previously, such protection of the voice VLAN prevents deployment of softphones, which is a significant reason that most companies are interested in deploying VoIP.

Eavesdropping

To counter the threat of eavesdropping, the media can be encrypted. The method to encrypt RTP traffic is Secure RTP (RFC3711), which does not encrypt the IP, UDP, or RTP headers but does encrypt the RTP payload (the "voice" itself). SRTP's advantage of leaving the RTP headers unencrypted is that header compression protocols (e.g., cRTP,[12] ROHC,[13]) and protocol analyzers (e.g., looking for RTP packet loss and (S)RTCP reports) can still function with SRTP-encrypted media.

The drawback of SRTP is that approximately 13 incompatible mechanisms exist to establish the SRTP keys. These mechanisms are at various stages of deployment, industry acceptance, and standardization. Thus, at this point in time it is unlikely that two SRTP-capable systems from different vendors will have a compatible SRTP keying mechanism. A brief overview of some of the more popular keying mechanisms is provided here.

One of the popular SRTP keying mechanisms, Security Descriptions, requires a secure SIP signaling channel (SIP over TLS) and discloses the SRTP key to each SIP proxy along the call setup path. This means that a passive attacker, able to observe the unencrypted SIP signaling and the encrypted SRTP, would be able to eavesdrop on a call. S/MIME is SIP's end-to-end security mechanism, which Security Descriptions could use to its benefit, but S/MIME has not been well deployed and, due to specific features of SIP (primarily forking and retargeting), it is unlikely that S/MIME will see deployment in the foreseeable future.

Multimedia Internet Keying (MIKEY) has approximately eight incompatible modes defined; these allow establishing SRTP keys.[14] Almost all these MIKEY modes are more secure than Security Descriptions because they do not carry the SRTP key directly in the SIP message but rather encrypt it with the remote party's private key or perform a Diffie-Hellman exchange. Thus, for most of the MIKEY modes, the attacker would need to actively participate in the MIKEY exchange and obtain the encrypted SRTP to listen to the media.

Zimmermann Real-time Transport Protocol (ZRTP)[15] is another SRTP key exchange mechanism, which uses a

---

12 T. Koren, S. Casner, J. Geevarghese, B. Thompson, and P. Ruddy, "Enhanced compressed RTP (CRTP) for links with high delay," IETF RFC 3545, July 2003.

13 G. Pelletier and K. Sandlund, "Robust header compression version 2 (ROHCv2): Profiles for RTP, UDP, IP, ESP and UDP-Lite," IETF RFC 5225, April 2008.

14 S. Fries and D. Ignjatic, "On the applicability of various MIKEY modes and extensions," IETF draft, March 31, 2008.

15 P. Zimmermann, A. Johnston, and J. Callas, "ZRTP: Media path key agreement for secure RTP," IETF draft, July 9, 2007.

Diffie-Hellman exchange to establish the SRTP keys and detects an active attacker by having the users (or their computers) validate a short authentication string with each other. It affords useful security properties, including perfect forward secrecy and key continuity (which allows the users to verify authentication strings once, and never again), and the ability to work through session border controllers.

In 2006, the IETF decided to reduce the number of IETF standard key exchange mechanisms and chose DTLS-SRTP. DTLS-SRTP uses Datagram TLS (a mechanism to run TLS over a non-reliable protocol such as UDP) over the media path. To detect an active attacker, the TLS certificates exchanged over the media path must match the signed certificate fingerprints sent over the SIP signaling path. The certificate fingerprints are signed using SIP's identity mechanism.[16]

A drawback with SRTP is that it is imperative (for some keying mechanisms) or very helpful (with other keying mechanisms) for the SIP user agent to encrypt its SIP signaling traffic with its SIP proxy. The only standard for such encryption, today, is SIP-over-TLS which runs over TCP. To date, many vendors have avoided TCP on their SIP proxies because they have found SIP-over-TCP scales worse than SIP-over-UDP. It is anticipated that if this cannot be overcome we may see SIP-over-DTLS standardized. Another viable option, especially in some markets, is to use IPsec ESP to protect SIP.

Another drawback of SRTP is that diagnostic and troubleshooting equipment cannot listen to the media stream. This may seem obvious, but it can cause difficulties when technicians need to listen to and diagnose echo, gain, or other anomalies that cannot be diagnosed by examining SRTP headers (which are unencrypted) but can only be diagnosed by listening to the decrypted audio itself.

Identity

As described in the "Threats" section, it is important to have strong identity assurance. Today there are two mechanisms to provide for identity: P-Asserted-Identity,[17] which is used within a trust domain (e.g., within a company or between a service provider and its paying customers) and is simply a header inserted into a SIP request,

and SIP Identity,[18] which is used between trust domains (e.g., between two companies) and creates a signature over some of the SIP headers and over the SIP body.

SIP Identity is useful when two organizations connect via SIP proxies, as was originally envisioned as the SIP architecture for intermediaries between two organizations—often a SIP service provider. Many of these service providers operate session border controllers (SBCs) rather than SIP proxies, for a variety of reasons. One of the drawbacks of SIP Identity is that an SBC, by its nature, will rewrite the SIP body (specifically the m=/c=lines), which destroys the original signature. Thus, an SBC would need to rewrite the From header and sign the new message with the SBC's own private key. This effectively creates hop-by-hop trust; each SBC that needs to rewrite the message in this way is also able to manipulate the SIP headers and SIP body in other ways that could be malicious or could allow the SBC to eavesdrop on a call. Alternative cryptographic identity mechanisms are being pursued, but it is not yet known whether this weakness can be resolved.

Traffic Analysis

The most useful protection from traffic analysis is to encrypt your SIP traffic. This would require the attacker to gain access to your SIP proxy (or its call logs) to determine who you called.

Additionally, your (S)RTP traffic itself could also provide useful traffic analysis information. For example, someone may learn valuable information just by noticing where (S)RTP traffic is being sent (e.g., the company's in-house lawyers are calling an acquisition target several times a day). Forcing traffic to be concentrated to a device can help prevent this sort of traffic analysis. In some network topologies this can be achieved using a NAT, and in all cases it can be achieved with an SBC.

Reactive

An intrusion prevention system (IPS) is a useful way to react to VoIP attacks against signaling or media. An IPS with generic rules and with VoIP-specific rules can detect an attack and block or rate-limit traffic from the offender.

IPS

Because SIP is derived from, and related to, many well-deployed and well-understood protocols (HTTP), IDS/IPS vendors are able to create products to protect against

16 J. Peterson and C. Jennings, "Enhancements for authenticated identity management in the Session Initiation Protocol (SIP)," IETF RFC 4474, August 2006.
17 C. Jennings, J. Peterson and M. Watson, "Private extensions to the Session Initiation Protocol (SIP) for asserted identity within trusted networks," IETF RFC 3325, November 2002.
18 J. Peterson and C. Jennings, "Enhancements for authenticated identity management in the Session Initiation Protocol (SIP)," IETF RFC 4474, August 2006.

SIP quite readily. Often an IDS/IPS function can be built into a SIP proxy, SBC, or firewall, reducing the need for a separate IDS/IPS appliance. An IDS/IPS is marginally effective for detecting media attacks, primarily to notice an excessive amount of bandwidth is being consumed and to throttle it or alarm the event.

A drawback of IPS is that it can cause false positives and deny service to a legitimate endpoint, thus causing a DoS in an attempt to prevent a DoS. An attacker, knowledgeable of the rules or behavior of an IPS, may also be able to spoof the identity of a victim (the victim's source IP address or SIP identity) and trigger the IPS/IDS into reacting to the attack. Thus, it is important to deny attackers that avenue by using standard best practices for IP address spoofing[19] and employing strong SIP identity. Using a separate network (VLAN) for VoIP traffic can help reduce the chance of false positives, as the IDS/IPS rules can be more finely tuned for that one application running on the voice VLAN.

Rate Limiting

When suffering from too many SIP requests due to an attack, the first thing to consider doing is simple rate limiting. This is often naïvely performed by simply rate limiting the traffic to the SIP proxy and allowing excess traffic to be dropped. Though this does effectively reduce the transactions per second the SIP proxy needs to perform, it interferes with processing of existing calls to a significant degree. For example, a normal call is established with an INVITE, which is reliably acknowledged when the call is established. If the simplistic rate limiting were to drop the acknowledgment message, the INVITE would be retransmitted, incurring additional processing while the system is under high load. A separate problem with rate limiting is that both attackers and legitimate users are subject to the rate limiting; it is more useful to discriminate the rate limiting to the users causing the high rate. This can be done by distributing the simple rate limiting toward the users rather than doing the simple rate limiting near the server.

On the server, a more intelligent rate limiting is useful. These are usually proprietary rate-limiting schemes, but they attempt to process existing calls before processing new calls. For example, such a scheme would allow processing the acknowledgment message for a previously processed INVITE, as described above; process the BYE

associated with an active call, to free up resources; or process high-priority users' calls (the vice president's office is allowed to make calls, but the janitorial staff is blocked from making calls).

By pushing rate limiting toward users, effective use can be made of simple packet-based rate limiting. For example, even a very active call center phone does not need to send 100 Mb of SIP signaling traffic to its SIP proxy; even 1 Mb would be an excessive amount of traffic. By deploying simplistic, reasonable rate limiting very near the users, ideally at the Ethernet switch itself, bugs in the call processing application or malicious attacks by unauthorized software can be mitigated.

A similar situation occurs with the RTP media itself. Even high-definition video does not need to send or receive 100 Mb of traffic to another endpoint and can be rate-limited based on the applications running on the dedicated device. This sort of policing can be effective at the Ethernet switch itself, or in an IDS/IPS (watching for excessive bandwidth), a firewall, or SBC.

Challenging

A more sophisticated rate-limiting technique is to provide additional challenges to a high-volume user. This could be done when it is suspected that the user is sending spam or when the user has initiated too many calls in a certain time period. A simple mechanism is to complete the call with an interactive voice response system that requests the user to enter some digits ("Please enter 5, 1, 8 to complete your call"). Though this technique suffers from some problems (it does not work well for hearing-impaired users or if the caller does not understand the IVR's language), it is effective at reducing the calls per second from both internal and external callers.

4. FUTURE TRENDS

Certain SIP proxies have the ability to forward SIP requests to multiple user agents. These SIP requests can be sent in parallel, in series, or a combination of both series and parallel. Such proxies are called *forking proxies*.

Forking Problem in SIP

The forking proxy expects a response from all the user agents who received the request; the proxy forwards

---

19 P. Ferguson and D. Senie, "Network ingress filtering: Defeating denial of service attacks which employ IP source address spoofing," IETF 2827, May 2000.

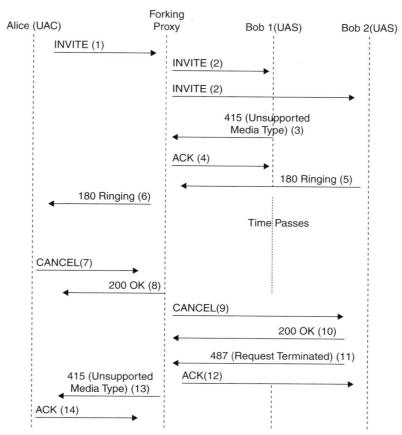

FIGURE 32.4 The heterogeneous error response forking problem.

only the "best" final response back to the caller. This behavior causes a situation known as the *heterogeneous error response forking problem* [HERFP], which is illustrated in Figure 32.4.[20]

Alice initiates an INVITE request that includes a body format that is understood by UAS2 but not UAS1. For example, the UAC might have used a MIME type of multipart/mixed with a session description and an optional image or sound. As UAC1 does not support this MIME format, it returns a 415 (Unsupported Media Type) response. Unfortunately the proxy has to wait until all the branches generate the final response and then pick the "best" response, depending on the criteria mentioned in RFC 3261. In many cases the proxy has to wait a long enough time that the human operating the UAC abandons the call. The proxy informs the UAS2 that the call has been canceled, which is acknowledged by UAS2. It then returns the 415 (Unsupported Media Type) back to

Alice, which could have been repaired by Alice by sending the appropriate session description.

Security in Peer-to-Peer SIP

Originally SIP was specified as a client/server protocol, but recent proposals suggest using SIP in a peer-to-peer setting.[21] One of the major reasons for using SIP in a peer-to-peer setting is its robustness, since there is no centralized control. As defined, "peer to peer (P2P) systems are distributed systems without any centralized control or hierarchical organization." This definition defines pure P2P systems. Even though many networks are considered P2P, they employ central authority or use supernodes. Early systems used flooding to route messages, which was found to be highly inefficient. To improve lookup time for a search request, structured overlay networks have been developed that provide load balancing and efficient routing of messages. They

20 H. Schulzrinne, D. Oran, and G. Camarillo, "The reason header field for the Session Initiation Protocol (SIP)," IETF RFC 3326, December 2002.

21 K. Singh and H. Schulzrinne, "Peer-to-peer Internet telephony using SIP," in *15th International Workshop on Network and Operating Systems Support for Digital Audio and Video,* June 2005.

use distributed hash tables (DHTs) to provide efficient lookup.[22] Examples of structured overlay networks are CAN, Chord, Pastry, and Tapestry.[23,24,25,26]

We focus on Chord Protocol because it is used as a prototype in most proposals for P2P-SIP. Chord has a ring-based topology in which each node stores at most $\log(N)$ entries in its finger table, which is like an application-level routing table, to point to other peers. Every node's IP address is mapped to an m bit chord identifier with a predefined hash function h. The same hash function h is also used to map any key of data onto a key ID that forms the distributed hash table. Every node maintains a finger table of $\log(N) = 6$ entries, pointing to the next-hop node location at distance 2^{i-1} (for i = 1,2...m) from this node identifier. Each node in the ring is responsible for storing the content of all key IDs that are equal to the identifier of the node's predecessor in the Chord ring. In a Chord ring each node n stores the IP address of m successor nodes plus its predecessor in the ring. The m successor entries in the routing table point to nodes at increasing distance from n. Routing is done by forwarding messages to the largest node-ID in the routing table that precedes the key-ID until the direct successor of a node has a longer ID than the key ID.

Singh and Schulzrinne envision a hierarchical architecture in which multiple P2P networks are represented by a DNS domain. A global DHT is used for interdomain routing of messages.

Join/Leave Attack

Security of structured overlay networks is based on the assumption that joining nodes are assigned node-IDs at random due to random assignment of IP addresses. This could lead to a join/leave attack in which the malicious attacker would want to control $O(\log N)$ nodes out of N nodes as

search is done on $O(\log N)$ nodes to find the desired key ID. With the adoption of IPv6, the join/leave attack can be more massive because the attacker will have more IP addresses. But even with IPv4, join/leave attacks are possible if the IP addresses are assigned dynamically. Node-ID assignment in Chord is inherently deterministic, thereby allowing the attacker to compute Node-IDs in advance where the attack could be launched by spoofing IP addresses. A probable solution would be to authenticate nodes before allowing them to join the overlay, which can involve authenticating the node before assigning the IP address.

Attacks on Overlay Routing

Any malicious node within the overlay can drop, alter, or wrongly forward a message it receives instead of routing it according to the overlay protocol. This can result in severe degradation of the overlay's availability. Therefore an adversary can perform one of the following:

- *Registration attacks.* One of the existing challenges to P2P-SIP registration is to provide confidentiality and message integrity to registration messages.
- *Man-in-the-middle attacks.* Let's consider the case where a node with ID 80 and a node with ID 109 conspire to form a man-in-the-middle attack, as shown in Figure 32.5. The honest node responsible for the key is node 180. Let's assume that a recursive approach is used for finding the desired key ID, wherein each routing node would send the request message to the appropriate node-ID until it reaches the node-ID responsible for the desired key-ID. The source node (node 30) will not have any control nor can it trace the request packet as it traverses through the Chord ring. Therefore node 32 will establish a dialog with node 119, and node 80 would impersonate node 32 and establish a dialog with node 108. This attack can be detected if an iterative routing mechanism is used wherein a source node checks whether the hash value is closer to the key-ID than the node-ID it received on the previous hop.[27] Therefore the source node (32) would get suspicious if node 80 redirected it directly to node 119, because it assumes that there exists a node with ID lower than Key ID 107.
- *Attacks on bootstrapping nodes.* Any node wanting to join the overlay needs to be bootstrapped with a static node or cached node or discover the bootstrap node

22 H. Balakrishnan, M. FransKaashoek, D. Karger, R. Morris, and I. Stoica, "Looking up data in P2P systems," *Communications of the ACM*, Vol. 46, No. 2, February 2003.

23 S. Ratnasamy, P. Francis, M. Handley, R. Karp, and S. Shenker, "A scalable content-addressable network," in *Proceedings of ACM SIGCOMM* 2001.

24 I. Stoica, R. Morris, D. Karger, M. F Kaashoek, and H. Balakrishnan, "Chord: A scalable peer-to-peer lookup service for internet applications," in *Proceedings of the 2001 Conference on Applications, Technologies, Architectures, and Protocols for Computer Communication*, pp. 149–160, 2001.

25 A. Rowstron and P. Druschel, "Pastry: Scalable, decentralized object location and routing for large-scale peer-to-peer systems," in *IFIP/ACM International Conference on Distributed Systems Platforms (Middleware)*, Heidelberg, Germany, pp. 329–350, 2001.

26 B. Y. Zhao, L. Huang, J. Stribling, S. C. Rhea, A. D. Joseph, and J. D. Kubiatowicz, "Tapestry: A resilient global-scale overlay for service deployment," *IEEE Journal on Selected Areas in Communications*, Vol. 22, No. 1, pp. 41–53, Jan. 2004.

27 M. Srivatsa and L. Liu, "Vulnerabilities and security threats in structured overlay networks: A quantitative analysis," in *Proceedings of 20th Annual Computer Science Application Conference*, Tucson, pp. 251–261, Dec. 6–10, 2004.

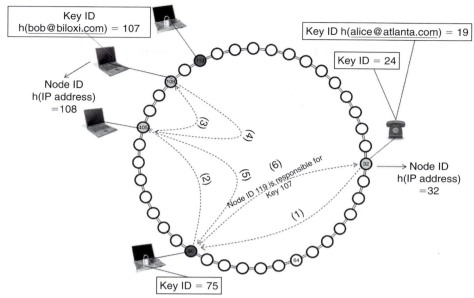

FIGURE 32.5 Man-in-the-middle attack.

through broadcast mechanisms (e.g., SIP-multicast). In any case, if an adversary gains access to the bootstrap node, the joining node can easily be attacked. Securing the bootstrap node is still an open question.

- *Duplicate identity attacks.* Preventing duplicate identities is one of the open problems whereby a hash of two IP addresses can lead to the same node-ID. The Singh and Schulzrinne approach reduces this problem somewhat by using a P2P network for each domain. Further, they suggest email-based authentication in which a joining node would receive a password via email and then use the password to authenticate itself to the network.

- *Free riding.* In a P2P system there is a risk of free riding in which nodes use services but fail to provide services to the network. Nodes use the overlay for registration and location service but drop other messages, which could eventually result in a reduction of the overlay's availability.

The other major challenges that are presumably even harder to solve for P2P-SIP are as follows:

- Prioritizing signaling for emergency calls in an overlay network and ascertaining the physical location of users in real time may be very difficult.

- With the high dynamic nature of P2P systems, there is no predefined path for signaling traffic, and therefore it is impossible to implement a surveillance system for law enforcement agencies with P2P-SIP.

End-to-End Identity with SBCs

As discussed earlier,[28] End-to-End Identity with SBCs provides identity for SIP requests by signing certain SIP headers and the SIP body (which typically contains the Session Description Protocol (SDP)). This identity is destroyed if the SIP request travels through an SBC, because the SBC has to rewrite the SDP as part of the SBC's function (to force media to travel through the SBC). Today, nearly all companies that provide SIP trunking (Internet telephony service providers, ITSPs) utilize SBCs. In order to work with[29] those SBCs, one would have to validate incoming requests (which is new), modify the SDP and create a new identity (which they are doing today), and sign the new identity (which is new). As of this writing, it appears unlikely that ITSPs will have any reason to perform these new functions.

A related problem is that, even if we had end-to-end identity, it is impossible to determine whether a certain identity can rightfully claim a certain E.164 phone number in the From: header. Unlike domain names, which can have their ownership validated (the way email address validation is performed on myriad Web sites today), there is no de facto or written standard to determine whether an identity can rightfully claim to "own" a certain E.164.

28 J. Peterson and C. Jennings, "Enhancements for authenticated identity management in the Session Initiation Protocol (SIP)," IETF RFC 4474, August 2006.

29 J. Peterson and C. Jennings, "Enhancements for authenticated identity management in the Session Initiation Protocol (SIP)," IETF RFC 4474, August 2006.

It is anticipated that as SIP trunking becomes more commonplace, SIP spam will grow with it, and the growth of SIP spam will create the necessary impetus for the industry to solve these interrelated problems. Solving the end-to-end identity problem and the problem of attesting E.164 ownership would allow domains to immediately create meaningful whitelists. Over time these whitelists could be shared among SIP networks, end users, and others, eventually creating a reputation system. But as long as spammers are able to impersonate legitimate users, even creating a whitelist is fraught with the risk of a spammer guessing the contents of that whitelist (e.g., your bank, family member, or employer).

5. CONCLUSION

With today's dedicated VoIP handsets, a separate voice VLAN provides a reasonable amount of security. Going forward, as nondedicated devices become more commonplace, more rigorous security mechanisms will gain importance. This will begin with encrypted signaling and encrypted media and will evolve to include spam protection and enhancements to SIP to provide cryptographic assurance of SIP call and message routing.

As VoIP continues to grow, VoIP security solutions will have to consider consumer, enterprise and policy concerns. Some VoIP applications, commonly installed on PCs may be against corporate security policies (e.g., Skype). One of the biggest challenges with enabling encryption is with maintaining a public key infrastructure and the complexities

involved in distributing public key certificates that would span to end users[30] and key synchronization between various devices belonging to the same end user agent.[31]

Using IPsec for VoIP tunneling across the Internet is another option; however, it is not without substantial overhead.[32] Therefore end-to-end mechanisms such as SRTP are specified for encrypting media and establishing session keys.

VoIP network designers should take extra care in designing intrusion detection systems that are able to identify never-before-seen activities and react according to the organization's policy. They should follow industry best practices for securing endpoint devices and servers. Current softphones and consumer-priced hardphones use the "haste-to-market" implementation approach and therefore become vulnerable to VoIP attacks. Therefore VoIP network administrators may evaluate VoIP endpoint technology, identify devices or software that will meet business needs and can be secured, and make these the corporate standards. With P2P-SIP, the lack of central authority makes authentication of users and nodes difficult. Providing central authority would dampen the spirit of P2P-SIP and would conflict the inherent features of distributed networks. A decentralized solution such as the reputation management system, where the trust values are assigned to nodes in the network based on prior behavior, would lead to a weak form of authentication because the credibility used to distribute trust values could vary in a decentralized system. Reputation management systems were more focused on file-sharing applications and have not yet been applied to P2P-SIP.

30 D. Berbecaru, A. Lioy, and M. Marian, "On the complexity of public key certificate validation," in *Proceedings of the 4th International Conference on Information Security, Lecture Notes in Computer Science*, Springer-Verlag, Vol. 2200, pp. 183–203, 2001.
31 C. Jennings and J. Fischl, "Certificate management service for the Session Initiation Protocol (SIP)," IETF draft April 5, 2008.
32 Z. Anwar, W. Yurcik, R. Johnson, M. Hafiz, and R. Campbell, "Multiple design patterns for voice over IP (VoIP) security," IPCCC 2006, pp. 485–492, April 10–12, 2006.

Part V

Storage Security

## Chapter 33

SAN Security

John McGowan
EMC Corporation

Jeffrey Bardin
Independent consultant

John McDonald
EMC Corporation

As with any IT subsystem, implementing the appropriate level of security for storage area networks (SANs) depends on many factors. The resources expended on protecting the SAN should reflect the value of the information stored on the SAN using a risk-based approach. A full assessment and classification of the data including threats, vulnerabilities, existing controls, and potential impact should the loss, disclosure, modification, interruption, and/or destruction of the data occur should be performed prior to configuration of the SAN. Anytime you consider security prior to actual build-out of a system or device, your expenditures are lower than attempting to bolt on the security after the fact. There are a number of inexpensive steps that can be taken to ensure that security is appropriate for the classification of data stored in the SAN.

As the use of SANs increases, the amount of data being stored increases exponentially, making the SAN a target for hackers, criminals, and disgruntled employees. To effectively protect a SAN, it is important to understand what actions increase security and what impact these actions have on the performance and usability of the environment. Ensuring a balance among protection capability, cost, performance, and operational considerations must be at the top of your list when applying controls to your SAN environment.

One thing to consider is that the most probable avenue of attack in a SAN is through the hosts connected to the SAN. There are potentially thousands of host, application, and operating system-specific security considerations that are beyond the scope of this chapter but should be followed as your systems and application administrators properly configure their owned devices.

Information security, that aspect of security that seeks to protect data confidentiality, data integrity, and access to the data, is an established commercial sector with a wide variety of vendors marketing mature products and technologies, such as VPNs, firewalls, antivirus, and content management. Recently there has been a subtle development in security. Organizations are expanding their security perspectives to secure not only end-user data access and the perimeter of the organization but also the data within the datacenter. Several factors drive these recent developments. The continuing expansion of the network and the continued shrinking of the perimeter expose datacenter resources and the storage infrastructure to new vulnerabilities. Data aggregation increases the impact of a security breach. IP-based storage networking potentially exposes storage resources to traditional network vulnerabilities. Recently the delineation between a back-end datacenter and front-end network perimeter is less clear. Storage resources are potentially becoming exposed to unauthorized users inside and outside the enterprise. In addition, as the plethora of compliance regulations continues to expand and become more complicated, IT managers are faced with addressing the threat of security breaches from both within and outside the organization. Complex international regulations require a greater focus on protecting not only the network but the data itself. This chapter describes best practices for enhancing and applying security of SANs.

1. ORGANIZATIONAL STRUCTURE

Every company has its own organizational structures and security requirements. These are typically driven by the type of business, types of regulations and statutes that focus corporate compliance, and the type of data stored in the SAN. All factors should be evaluated when developing a security policy that is appropriate for your environment. It is wise to incorporate existing security policies such as acceptable use policies (AUPs), data classification, and intellectual property policies along playbooks or standard operating procedures (SOPs) describing how the data is stored and managed.

As with best practice, implementation can lead to tradeoffs. Making a SAN more secure may result in additional management overhead or a reduction in ease-of-use capabilities or the introduction of ease-of-use capabilities that reduce the overall SAN security posture. The use of encryption could create an unacceptable performance hit if not applied properly. You may even find that SAN security best practices conflict with other IT policies. In some instances, functions required to implement a recommendation may not be available on a certain SAN. Other compensating controls need to be considered such as a process, policy, or triggered script that assists in implementing the control. Your implementation of security controls should be based on risk as defined in an assessment process during SAN deployment.

AAA

Authentication, authorization, and accounting (AAA) is a term for a framework for intelligently controlling access to computer resources, enforcing policies, auditing usage, and providing the information necessary to bill for services. These combined processes are important for effective network management and security.

Authentication provides a way of identifying a user, typically by having the user enter a valid username and password before granting access. The process of authentication is based on each user having a unique set of criteria for gaining access. The AAA server compares the user's credentials with credentials stored in a database. If the credentials match, the user is granted access to the resource.

Authorization is the process of enforcing policies: determining what types or qualities of activities, resources, or services a user is permitted. For example, after logging into a system, the user may try to issue commands. The authorization process determines whether the user has the authority to issue such commands. Once you have authenticated a user, she may be authorized for multiple types of access or activity.

The final process in the AAA framework is accounting, which measures the resources a user consumes during access. This can include the amount of system time or the amount of data a user has sent and/or received during a session. Accounting is accomplished by logging session statistics and usage information and is used for authorization control, billing, trend analysis, resource utilization, and capacity planning activities.

Authentication, authorization, and accounting services are often provided by a dedicated AAA server, a program that performs these functions. A common standard by which network access servers interface with the AAA server is the Remote Authentication Dial-In User Service (RADIUS).

Assessment and Design

The first step in developing adequate datacenter controls is to know what the controls need to address—for example, the vulnerabilities that can be exploited. Some threats may seem very difficult, and hence unlikely to be exploited, but it is an essential piece of the process to understand them so that you can demonstrate that they are either mitigated or that it is not commercially reasonable to fix the problem. This step is essential since it is not usually the vulnerabilities that you already know about that will be exploited. Once you have identified the gaps in the datacenter, you can communicate the vulnerabilities to your data by implementing a comprehensive SAN security program. The first step is to develop a storage security standard that outlines the architecture, workflow process, and technologies to leverage when deploying enterprisewide storage networks. Today SAN security solutions are available to meet some needs of every individual topology, incorporating a wide variety of vendor products and architectural needs. It is essential that corporations aggressively take on the challenge of integrating these new security features and technologies to interoperate with existing security technologies while complying with and redefining existing standards, policies, and processes.

The remainder of this section details the tasks within the planning and design phase. Included in this section are architecture planning and design details, considerations for design, best practices, and notes on data collection and documentation.

Review Topology and Architecture Options

Fabric security augments overall application security. It is not sufficient on its own; host and disk security are also required. You should consider each portion of the customer's SAN when determining the correct security configuration. Review the current security infrastructure and discuss present and future needs. Listed here are the most common discussion segments:

- *SAN management access.* Secure access to management services.
- *Fabric access.* Secure device access to fabric service.

- *Target access.* Secure access to targets and Logical Unit Numbers (LUNs).
- *SAN protocol.* Secure switch-to-switch communication protocols.
- *IP storage access.* Secure Fibre Channel over TCP/IP (FCIP) and Internet Small Computer System Interface (iSCSI) services.
- *Data integrity and secrecy.* Encryption of data both in transit and at rest.

Additional subjects to include in a networked storage strategy involve:

- Securing storage networking ports and devices
- Securing transmission and ISL interfaces
- Securing management tools and interfaces (Simple Network Management Protocol (SNMP), Telnet, IP interfaces)
- Securing storage resources and volumes

- Disabling SNMP management interfaces not used or needed
- Restricting use and access to Telnet and FTP for components

There are a several major areas of focus for securing storage networks. These include securing the fabric and its access, securing the data and where it is stored, securing the components, securing the transports, and securing the management tools and interfaces. This part of the chapter describes the following components:

- Protection rings (see sidebar, "Security and Protection")
- Restricting access to storage
- Access control lists (ACLs) and policies
- Port blocks and port prohibits
- Zoning and isolating resources

Security and Protection

Establish an overall security perimeter that is both physical and logical to restrict access to components and applications. Physical security includes placing equipment in locked cabinets and facilities that have access monitoring capabilities. Logical security involves securing those applications, servers, and other interfaces, including management consoles and maintenance ports, from unauthorized access. Also, consider who has access to backup and removable media and where the company stores them as part of an overall security perimeter and defense.

Secure your networks, including Local Area Networks (LANs), Metropolitan Area Networks (MANs), and Wide Area Networks (WANs), with various subnets and segments including Internet, intranet, and extranets with firewalls and DMZ access where applicable.

Secure your servers so that if someone attempts to access them using other applications, using public or private networks, or simply by walking up to a workstation or console, the servers are protected. Server protection is important; it is one of the most common points that an attacker will target. Make sure that the server has adequate protection on usernames, passwords, files, and application access permissions.

Control and monitor who has access to root and other supervisory modes of access, as well as who can install and configure software.

Protect your storage network interfaces including Fibre Channel, Ethernet for iSCSI, and NAS as well as management ports, interfaces, and tools. Tools including zoning, access control lists, binding, segmentation, authorizing, and authentication should be deployed within the storage network.

Protect your storage subsystems using zoning and LUN/volume mapping and masking. Your last line of defense should be the storage system itself, so make sure it is adequately protected.

Protect wide area interfaces when using Internet File Channel Protocol (iFCP), Fibre Channel over Internet Protocol (FCIP), Internet Small Computer System Interface (iSCSI), Synchronous Optical Networking/Synchrous Digital Hierarchy (SONET/SDH), Asynchrous Transfer Mode (ATM); and other means for moving data between locations. Set up VPNs to help guard data while it's in transit, along with compression and encryption. Maintain access control and audit trails of the management interface tools, and make sure that you change their passwords.

- File system permissions for Network-attached Storage (NAS) file access using Network File System (NFS), and Common Internet File System (CIFS)
- Operating system access control and management interfaces
- Control and monitor root and other supervisory access
- Physical and logical security and protection
- Virus protection and detection on management servers and PC

Restricting Access to Storage

Securing a storage network involves making sure that you protect the SAN itself as well as the storage. LUN mapping works by creating an access table on the storage device or host servers (persistent binding) that determines what servers, using World Wide Node Names (WWNN) or World Wide Port Names (WWPN), can access (read, read/write, etc.) a specific volume or LUN. Servers that do not have access to the specific LUN receive an I/O reject error or may not see the storage at all. Storage-based security is the last line of defense when it comes to controlling access to a storage resource LUN.

Device masking hides the existence of a storage device from all but a desired set of host connections. Because Fibre Channel fabrics support zoning based on individual devices (WWN Zoning) it is possible to perform device masking in the fabric (King, 2001).

2. ACCESS CONTROL LISTS (ACL) AND POLICIES

Authentication involves verifying the identity of people and devices that are attempting to gain authorization to storage network resources. Authentication involves use of a server such as a remote access dial-up server (RADIUS) commonly used in network environments to verify identity credentials. Access control lists implement authorization to determine who and what can have access to storage network resources. When looking at controlling access and isolating traffic within a single switch or director as well as in a single fabric of two or more switches all connected together, use the following techniques:

- Fabric, switch, and port binding with policies and ACLs
- Fabric and device zoning to control access
- Networking segmentation (traffic isolation)
- Port isolation (port blocks, prohibits, port isolation, and disablement)
- Partitioning and segmentation (logical domains, Virtual Storage Area Network (VSAN), Logical Storage Area Network (LSAN), virtual switches)

Data Integrity Field (DIF)

DIF provides a standard data-checking mechanism to monitor the integrity of data. DIF sends a block of information with integrity checks to an HBA. The HBA validates the data and sends the data block with its integrity check across the Fibre Channel fabric to the storage array. The storage array in turn validates the metadata and writes the data to Redundant Array of Independent Disks (RAID) memory. The array then sends the block of data to the disk, which validates the information before writing it to disk. DIF pinpoints where in the process of writing data to disk that the corruption occurred.

Diffie-Hellman: Challenge Handshake Authentication Protocol (DH-CHAP)

DH-CHAP is a forthcoming Internet Standard for the authentication of devices connecting to a Fibre Channel switch. DH-CHAP is a secure key-exchange authentication protocol that supports both switch-to-switch and host-to-switch authentication. DH-CHAP supports MD-5 and SHA-1 algorithm-based authentication.

Fibre-Channel Security Protocol (FC-SP)

FC-SP is a security framework that includes protocols to enhance Fibre Channel security in several areas, including authentication of Fibre Channel devices, cryptographically secure key exchange, and cryptographically secure communication between Fibre Channel devices. FC-SP is focused on protecting data in transit throughout the Fibre Channel network. FC-SP does not address the security of data which is stored on the Fibre Channel network.

Fibre-Channel Authentication Protocol (FCAP)

FCAP is an optional authentication mechanism employed between any two devices or entities on a Fibre Channel network using certificates or optional keys.

Fibre-Channel Password Authentication Protocol (FCPAP)

FCPAP is an optional password based authentication and key exchange protocol that is utilized in Fibre Channel networks. FCPAP is used to mutually authenticate Fibre Channel ports to each other.

Switch Link Authentication Protocol (SLAP)

SLAP is an authentication method for Fibre Channel switches that utilizes digital certificates to authenticate switch ports. SLAP was designed to prevent the unauthorized addition of switches into a Fibre Channel network.

Port Blocks and Port Prohibits

You can use zoning to isolate ports—for example, Fiber Connectivity (FICON) ports from open systems ports, and traffic. Other capabilities that exist on switches and directors that support Enterprise Systems Connection (ESCON) or FICON are port blocks and port prohibits. Port blocks and port prohibits are another approach independent of the upper-layer fabric and name server for protecting ESCON and FICON ports. Unlike fabric zoning that can span multiple switches and directors in a fabric, port blocks and prohibits are specific to an individual director.

Zoning and Isolating Resources

While a Fibre Channel-based storage network can theoretically have approximately 16 million addresses for servers, devices, and switches, the reality is a bit lower. Zones can be unique with devices isolated from each, or they can overlap with devices existing in different overlapping zones. You can accomplish port and fabric security using zoning combinations, including WWNN Soft zoning, WWPN Soft zoning as part of the T11 FC-SW-2 standard, along with hardware enforced port zoning.

3. PHYSICAL ACCESS

Physical access is arguably one of the most critical aspects of Fibre Channel SAN security. The Fibre Channel protocol is not designed to be routed (although SANs can be bridged), which means that what happens in the SAN should stay in the SAN. By implementing the rest of the best practices discussed in this chapter, strong physical access controls can almost ensure that any attempts to access the SAN from the outside will be thwarted, since an attacker would need to physically connect a fiber optic cable to a switch or array to gain access.

Physical controls should also include clear labeling for all cables and components. In performing a physical audit of the infrastructure, clear and accurate labeling will ensure that any changes are immediately detectable.

Controlling physical access to any storage medium is also critical. This applies not only to the disk drives in a SAN storage system but to any copies of the data, such as backup tapes. The best security management system can be easily defeated if an attacker can walk into a lightly controlled office area and walk out with backup tapes that were stored there.

4. CHANGE MANAGEMENT

A documented and enforced process should be in place for any actions that may change the configuration of any component connected to the SAN. Changes should be reviewed beforehand to ensure that they will not compromise security, and any unapproved changes uncovered during a regular audit (discussed shortly) should be thoroughly investigated.

5. PASSWORD POLICIES

Normal password-related best practices, such as regular changing of passwords and the use of hard-to-guess passwords, should be implemented for all components on the SAN. This includes the storage systems, switches and hubs, hosts, and so on.

The generally accepted best practice for the industry is that passwords should be changed every three to six months, and passwords should be a minimum of eight characters long and include at least one number or symbol. However, customers should follow the policies that have been established to address their particular business requirements.

6. DEFENSE IN DEPTH

No single method of protecting a SAN can be considered adequate in the light of constantly evolving threats. The best possible approach is to implement a policy of layers of protection for every aspect of the environment, which forces an attacker to defeat multiple mechanisms to achieve their goal, increasing the probability of an attack being detected and defeated. The LAN that interconnects the SAN component's management interfaces, which is the most likely avenue of attack, should be protected by multiple layers of security measures, such as firewalls, security monitoring tools, and so forth. The first phase of many attempts to attack the SAN will usually come through these LAN (Ethernet) management connections.

7. VENDOR SECURITY REVIEW

In considering new hardware and software that will be installed in or interact with the SAN, a security review should be performed with customer security personnel, customer technical/administrative personnel, and vendor technical personnel to gain a complete understanding of the security capabilities of the product and how they can be integrated into the existing security framework.

Failure to implement any of these basic security practices can increase the possibility that a SAN may come under attack and that any such an attack may succeed in impacting the ability of the SAN to perform its functions. For additional information on IT security best practices, refer to the SANS Institute's Resources Web site (www.sans.org/resources/) and to the SAN Security site (www.sansecurity.com).

8. DATA CLASSIFICATION

To develop and implement security policies and tools that effectively protect the data in a SAN at an appropriate level, it is important to understand the value of the data to the organization. Though implementing a one-size-fits-all approach to protecting all the data can simplify security management, such an approach may impose excessive costs for certain types of data while leaving other data underprotected. For example, encrypting data on the host can provide a significant level of protection; however, such encryption can impose significant overhead on the host processing, reducing performance for the entire environment.

A review of all data on the SAN should be performed and appropriate classifications assigned based on business requirements. These classifications should be assigned appropriate protection requirements.

9. SECURITY MANAGEMENT

When any new SAN component (such as a storage array, switch, or host) is installed, it usually contains at least one factory configured access method (such as a default username/password). It is imperative that any such access method be immediately reconfigured to conform to the security policies that have been set up for the rest of the environment. Strong passwords should be utilized (as discussed shortly) and, if possible, the account name should be changed.

Security Setup

More complex components, such as the hosts and storage systems, provide even more sophisticated security mechanisms, such as support for access domains, which allow them to be integrated into a broader security infrastructure. The mechanism should be configured according to established security policies immediately on installation.

Unused Capabilities

Most SAN hardware provides multiple methods of access and monitoring, such as a Web-based interface, a telnet command-line interface, and an SNMP interface. Many also provide some method for uploading new versions of firmware, such as FTP or Trivial File Transfer Protocol (TFTP). Any interface capabilities that will not be utilized on a regular basis should be explicitly disabled on every SAN device. Update interfaces such as FTP should only be enabled while an update is being performed and should be immediately disabled when done, to prevent them from being exploited during attacks.

On SAN switches any ports that will not be used in the configuration should also be explicitly disabled to prevent them from being utilized if an attacker does manage to gain physical access to the SAN.

10. AUDITING

Virtually every component in a SAN provides some form of capability to log changes when they occur. For example, some storage systems make a log entry when a new LUN is created; most Fibre Channel switches make log entries when zoning is changed. Regular audits should

be performed to ensure that the current configuration of the SAN and all its components agree with the currently documented configuration, including any changes made through the change management system.

Automated tools and scripts can be used to implement an effective auditing process. Most SAN components provide the capability to download a detailed text listing that shows the current configuration. By performing this task on a regular basis and comparing the results to established baseline configurations, changes can be quickly detected and, if necessary, investigated.

Updates

All patches and software/firmware updates to any SAN components should be reviewed in a timely manner to determine whether they may have an impact on security. If a particular update includes changes to address known security vulnerabilities, it should be applied as quickly as possible.

Monitoring

It is important to continuously monitor an infrastructure to detect and prevent attacks. For example, a brute-force password attack that generates an abnormally high amount of TCP/IP network traffic to a SAN switch can be easily detected and stopped using standard network monitoring tools before any impact occurs.

Monitoring can also detect changes to the SAN configuration that may indicate an attack is underway. For example, if an attacker attempts to "spoof" the world wide name (WWN) of another server to gain access to its storage, most switches will detect the existence of a duplicate WWN and generate error messages.

Security Maintenance

The security configuration of the SAN should be updated in a timely manner to reflect changes in the environment—for example, the removal of a previously authorized user or host from the infrastructure due to termination or transfer. SAN ports should be managed to ensure that any unused ports are explicitly disabled when not being used, such as when a previously connected server is removed from the SAN.

Configuration Information Protection

All attacks on a SAN start with obtaining information on the SAN's configuration, such as number and types of components, their configuration, and existing accounts. Without sufficient information it is virtually impossible to carry out a successful attack on a SAN environment. It is therefore critical that any information that provides details on how the IT infrastructure (including the SAN) is configured be carefully controlled. Some examples of information that can be used to plan an attack include:

- Network diagrams with TCP/IP addresses of SAN components
- SAN diagrams with component information
- Lists of usernames and users
- Inventory lists of components with firmware revisions

All such information should be labeled appropriately and its distribution restricted to only IT personnel with a confirmed need to know. When it is necessary to share this information with outside agencies (such as vendors when creating a Request for Proposal (RFP)). the information should be distributed utilizing positive controls, such as a password-protected view-only Adobe Acrobat PDF document.

11. MANAGEMENT ACCESS: SEPARATION OF FUNCTIONS

Management of functions supported by the SAN should be divided up among personnel to ensure that no single person has control over the entire SAN. For example, one individual should be responsible for managing the storage systems, one responsible for configuring the SAN hardware itself, and a different individual should be responsible for managing the hosts connected to the SAN. When a change needs to be made it should be requested utilizing the change management system (see previous discussion), reviewed by all personnel involved, and thoroughly documented.

Limit Tool Access

Many Fibre Channel Host Bus Adapter (HBA) vendors provide the capability to change the world wide name of an HBA. This is usually accomplished via either a host-based utility or a firmware utility that gets executed when the host is booted. In the case of a host-based utility, such utilities should be removed and the host should be regularly scanned to ensure that they have not been reinstalled. For management purposes the utilities should be copied to a CD-ROM and kept locked up until needed. For firmware-based utilities, many vendors provide the ability to disable the utility at boot time.

Note that in either case changing the WWN of an HBA usually requires that the host be rebooted. Monitoring of

the environment should detect any unscheduled reboots and report them immediately. Also, any switches that the host is connected to should detect the change in the WWN and report an entry in its internal log; monitoring of these logs should also be performed and a security report issued when such changes are detected.

Limit Connectivity

The management ports on most SAN components are arguably the weakest points in terms of security. Most utilize a standard TCP/IP connection and some form of Web-based or telnet protocol to access the management interface. In most environments these connections are utilized infrequently—usually only when making a change to the configuration or requesting access to a log for auditing purposes. To maximize security and defeat denial-of-service forms of attacks, the port on the Ethernet switch that these interfaces are connected to should be disabled when they are not being used. This minimizes the number of potential attack points within the SAN.

> Note: If a host requires network access to a storage system to perform its functions, disabling the port may not be possible.

Secure Management Interfaces

LAN connections to management interfaces should be secured utilizing some form of TCP/IP encryption such as Secure Sockets Layer (SSL) for Web-based interfaces or Secure Shell (SSH) for command-line interfaces. This can ensure that even in the event an attacker does manage to gain access to a management LAN, it will be difficult for them to gain any useful information, such as usernames and passwords.

12. HOST ACCESS: PARTITIONING

Partitioning defines methods to subdivide networks to restrict which components have access to other components. For Fibre Channel SANs this involves two distinct networks: the LAN to which the management interfaces of the components are connected and the SAN itself.

The network management interfaces for all SAN components should be connected to an isolated LAN (e.g., a VLAN). One or two management stations should be configured into the VLAN for management purposes. If a host requires LAN access to SAN components to function, a dedicated Network Interface Card (NIC) should be used in that host and included in the VLAN. For maximum security there should be no external routes into this management LAN.

The SAN itself should be partitioned using zoning. There are two forms of zoning: soft (or world wide name) zoning, which restricts access based on the world wide name (WWN), and hard zoning, which restricts access based on the location of the actual physical connection. Soft zoning is generally easier to implement and manage, since changes to zones are done entirely via the management interface and don't require swapping physical connections. However, should an attacker manage to gain control of a host connected to a SAN and fake the world wide name of another server (sometimes referred to as *WWN spoofing*), they could potentially gain access to a broader range of the storage on the SAN. Hard zoning requires slightly more effort when making changes, but it provides a much higher level of security, since an attacker would have to gain physical access to the SAN components to gain access outside the server they subverted. Note that for most current SAN switches, hard zoning is the default form of zoning.

A relatively new partitioning capability provided by some switch vendors is the concept of a virtual SAN, or VSAN. VSANs are similar to VLANs on an Ethernet network in that each VSAN appears to be a fully separate physical SAN with its own zoning, services, and management capabilities, even though multiple VSANs may reside on a single physical SAN switch. Strict segregation is maintained between VSANs, ensuring that no traffic can pass between them.

Finally, the storage systems themselves should be partitioned utilizing LUN masking, which controls which servers can access which LUNs on the storage system. Most modern SAN storage systems provide some form of LUN masking.

Combining VSANs and port zoning with LUN masking on the storage system provides a degree of defense in depth for the SAN, since an attacker would need to penetrate multiple separate levels of controls to gain access to the data.

S_ID Checking

When packets are transmitted through a SAN, they usually contain two fields that define where the packet originated: the source ID (S_ID) and the destination ID (D_ID). Under some configurations, such as soft zoning, the S_ID may not be validated, allowing an illegal host on the SAN to send packets to a storage server. Some switch vendors provide the capability to force S_ID checking under all

configurations; if this capability is available it should be enabled. Note that hard zoning (discussed earlier) will minimize the need for S_ID checking, since the available path for any SAN traffic will be strictly controlled.

Some high-end storage systems provide an even stricter method of defeating S_ID attacks, called *S_ID lockdown*. This SID feature provides additional security for data residing within the system. Since a WWN can potentially be spoofed to match the current WWN of another HBA, a host with a duplicate WWN can gain access to the data destined for the spoofed HBAs. S_ID lockdown prevents an unauthorized user from spoofing the WWN of an HBA. When the S_ID lockdown feature is enabled, the source ID (SID) of the switch port to which the protected HBA is connected is added to the Virtual Configuration Management Database (VCMDB) record. Once an association between the HBA's WWN, the SID, and the fiber adapter is created, the HBA is considered locked. When a SID is locked, no user with a spoofed WWN can log in. If a user with a spoofed WWN is already logged in, that user loses all access through that HBA.

13. DATA PROTECTION: REPLICAS

Many practices can be implemented that can significantly enhance the security of Fibre Channel SANs, but it is virtually impossible to guarantee that no attack will ever succeed. Though little can be done after data has been stolen, having in a SAN multiple replicas of the data that are updated regularly can help an organization recover from an attempted denial-of-service attack (see the section titled "Denial-of-Service Attacks" for more details). This includes not only having backups but maintaining regular disk-based replicas as well. For example, performing a point-in-time incremental update of a clone of a LUN every four hours provides a recovery point in the event the LUN gets corrupted or deleted by an attacker. It is critical that all replicas, whether they are disk or tape based, be protected at the same level as the original data.

Erasure

Any data that is stored in a Fibre Channel SAN is generally stored on some form of nonvolatile media (e.g., disk drive, tape, and so on). When that media reaches the end of its useful life, such as when upgrading to a new storage system, it is usually disposed of in the most efficient manner possible, usually with little consideration that the media may still contain sensitive data.

Any media that may have ever contained sensitive data should undergo a certified full data erasure procedure before leaving your infrastructure or be disposed of by a vendor that can provide assurance that the media will undergo such a procedure and will be under positive control until the procedure occurs. For extremely sensitive data, certified destruction of the media should be considered. The same level of consideration should be given to any media that may have contained sensitive data at one time, such as disks used to store replicas of data (e.g., snapshots or clones).

Potential Vulnerabilities and Threats

To effectively understand how secure a SAN is, it is important to understand what potential vulnerabilities exist and the types of attacks it could potentially face.

Physical Attacks

Physical attacks involve gaining some form of physical access to the SAN or the data stored on it. This may involve gaining access to the SAN switches to plug in an illegal host to be used for other attacks, stealing the disk drives themselves, or stealing backup tapes. It may also involve even more subtle methods, such as purchasing used disk media to search them for data that hasn't been erased or "dumpster diving" for old backup tapes that may have been disposed of in the trash. The following are physical attack countermeasures:

- Solid physical security practices, such as access control to the datacenter and locking racks for equipment, will defeat most physical attacks.
- Security monitoring of the environment will detect any changes to the SAN, such as a new host attempting to log in and fabric topology changes.
- Host-based encryption of critical data will ensure that the data on any stolen media cannot be accessed.
- Hard zoning and VSANs will limit the amount of access an attacker can obtain even if they do manage to gain access to an unused port.
- Explicitly disabling any unused (open) ports on a SAN switch will prevent them from being used in the event an attacker does gain access. The attacker will be forced to unplug an existing connection to gain access, which should become immediately apparent in any environment with even minimal monitoring.
- Regular audits can detect any changes in the physical infrastructure.
- Implementing data erasure procedures can prevent an attacker from gaining access to data after old media has been disposed of.

Management Control Attacks

Management control attacks involve an attacker attempting to gain control of the management interface to a SAN component. This involves accessing the LAN that the management interface is on and utilizing some form of username/password cracking technique or TCP/IP attack (e.g., buffer overflow) to gain control of the interface. This type of attack is usually the first phase in a more detailed attack or else an attempt to deny access to SAN resources. The following are management control attack countermeasures:

- Setting up the initial security utilizing strong security policies will increase the ability of the SAN to resist these types of attacks.
- Strong password policies will hinder these types of attacks by making it difficult for an attacker to guess the passwords.
- A formal change management system and regular auditing will allow any successful attacks to be detected.
- Partitioning these interfaces into a VLAN will minimize the number of potential avenues of attack.
- Defense-in-depth will force an attacker to penetrate many layers of security to gain access to the management interfaces, significantly decreasing the probability of success and increasing the probability of detection.
- Regular security maintenance will ensure that an attacker cannot gain access by using an old account.
- Active monitoring will detect significant changes in LAN traffic going to these interfaces.
- Limiting connectivity to management ports when not required can limit the available window for such an attack.
- Regular auditing will detect any changes to the management environment and ensure that the security configuration is up to date.
- Performing a vendor security review will ensure that the SAN components have been configured for the maximum level of security.

Host Attacks

Host attacks have the greatest potential risk of occurring, since attacking operating systems via a TCP/IP network is the most widely understood and implemented form of attack in the IT industry. These types of attacks usually involve exploiting some form of weakness in the operating system. Once an attacker has gained control of the host, they can then proceed to attack the SAN. The following are host attack countermeasures:

- A solid initial security setup will minimize the number of potential vulnerabilities on a host.
- Strong password policies will minimize the risk of an attacker gaining access to the host.
- A formal change management system and regular and active auditing and monitoring will detect the changes an attacker will have to make to a host to gain access to the SAN.
- Hard zoning on the SAN and LUN masking will limit the amount of data an attacker may be able to gain access to if they manage to subvert a host on the SAN.
- Defense in depth will reduce the probability of an attacker gaining access to a host in the first place.
- Timely security maintenance will ensure that an attacker cannot penetrate the host utilizing an unused account.
- Installing security updates in a timely manner will ensure that an attacker cannot exploit known vulnerabilities in the host's operating system.
- Regular auditing can detect changes in the host environment that may indicate an increased level of vulnerability.
- Classification of the data in the SAN can ensure that each host is protected at the level that is appropriate for the data it can access.

World Wide Name Spoofing

WWN spoofing involves an attacker assuming the identity of another host by changing the WWN of an HBA to gain access to that host's storage. This type of attack can occur in one of two ways: by subverting an existing host and changing its existing WWN or by installing a new host that the attacker controls on the SAN. Note that changing the WWN name of an HBA requires a host to be rebooted, which should be easily detectable with standard monitoring tools. The following are WWN spoofing countermeasures:

- Installing a new host requires physical access to the SAN, which can be defeated by the methods described in the section titled "Physical Attacks."
- Partitioning the SAN utilizing hard zoning tightly controls what resources an existing host can access, even if its WWN changes.
- Enabling port binding on the switch to uniquely identify a host by WWN and port ID on the fabric.
- Enable S_ID lockdown if the feature is available.

- Changing the WWN of an HBA in an existing host requires the attacker to first subvert the host, which is addressed in the section titled "Host Attacks."
- Utilizing host-based encryption can prevent an attacker from reading any data, even if they do manage to subvert the SAN, since the host performing the spoofing should not have access to the encryption keys used by the original host.
- Ensuring the tools necessary to change the WWN of an HBA are not installed on any host can prevent an attacker from spoofing a WWN.

Man-in-the-Middle Attacks[1]

Man-in-the-middle attacks involve an attacker gaining access to Fibre Channel packets as they are being exchanged between two valid components on the SAN and requires the attacker have a direct connection to the SAN. These types of attacks are roughly analogous to Ethernet sniffer attacks whereby packets are captured and analyzed. Implementing this type of attack requires some method that allows an attacker to gain access to packets being sent to other nodes on the SAN (referred to as *promiscuous mode* on Ethernet LANs), which is not generally supported in the Fibre Channel protocol. The following are man-in-the-middle attack countermeasures:

- Since this type of attack requires that an attacker be physically plugged into the SAN, they can be defeated by the methods described in the section titled "Physical Attacks."
- Disable any port-mirroring features on a SAN switch if they are not being used. This prevents an attacker from gaining access to SAN configuration data.
- By utilizing host-based encryption the data contained in any intercepted packets cannot be read by the attacker.

E-Port Replication Attack

In an e-port attack, an attacker plugs another switch or a specially configured host into the e-port on an existing switch in the SAN. When the switch sees a new valid peer connected on the e-port, it will send it a copy of all its configuration tables and information. This method is not necessarily an actual attack in and of itself but a method to gain information to be used to perpetuate other attacks. The following are e-port replication attack countermeasures:

- Since this type of attack requires that an attacker be physically plugged into the SAN, they can be

---

[1] An attack in which an attacker is able to read, insert, and modify messages between two parties without either party knowing that the link between them has been compromised.

defeated by the methods described in the section titled "Physical Attacks."

- Enable switch and Fabric binding on the switch to "lock down" the topology and connectivity of the fabric after initial configuration and after any legitimate changes are made.

Denial-of-Service Attacks

Denial-of-service (DoS) attacks are designed to deprive an organization of access to the SAN and the resources it contains. These types of attacks can take many forms, but they usually involve one of the following:

- Saturating a component with so much traffic that it cannot perform its primary function of delivering data to hosts
- Taking advantage of a known vulnerability and crashing a component in the SAN
- Gaining access to the management interface and deleting LUNs to deprive the owner of access to the data

A new type of attack that has surfaced recently also fits into this category. An attacker gains access to the data, usually through a host, encrypts the data, and then demands payment to decrypt the data (that is, extortion). The following are DoS attack countermeasures:

- Partitioning the LAN that the SAN component management interfaces are on can prevent an attacker from ever gaining access to those components to implement a DoS attack. This includes disabling those interfaces when they are not in use.
- Defense in depth will force an attacker to defeat several security layers to launch the DoS attack, reducing the probability of success and increasing the probability of detection before the attack can be launched.
- Deploying VSANs will prevent DoS traffic on one SAN from interfering with the others in the event of a successful attack.
- Maintaining up-to-date protected replicas of all data can allow easy recovery in the event a DoS attack results in data being deleted or encrypted.

Session Hijacking Attacks

A session hijacking attack involves an attacker intercepting packets between two components on a SAN and taking control of the session between them by inserting their own packets onto the SAN. This is basically a variant of the man-in-the-middle attack but involves taking control of an aspect of the SAN instead of just capturing data

packets. As with man-in-the-middle attacks, the attacker must gain physical access to the SAN to implement this approach. Session hijacking is probably more likely to occur on the LAN in an attempt to gain access to the management interface of a SAN component. The following is a session hijacking attack countermeasure: Since this type of attack requires that an attacker be physically plugged into the SAN, they can be defeated by the methods described in the section titled "Physical Attacks."

Table 33.1 summarizes the various best practices and the potential vulnerabilities they address.

15. ENCRYPTION IN STORAGE

Encryption is used to prevent disclosure of either stored or transmitted data by converting data to an unintelligible form called *ciphertext*. Decryption of the ciphertext converts the data back into its original form, called *plaintext*.

For environments that require even higher levels of security you can encrypt all transmissions (data and control) within the SAN utilizing a commercially available SAN encryption device. Also, for extremely sensitive data, host-based encryption should be considered. Most modern operating systems provide some form of encryption for their file systems. By utilizing these capabilities, all data is encrypted before it even leaves the host and is never exposed on the SAN in an unencrypted form.

The Process

Encryption simplifies the problem of securely sharing information by securely sharing a small key used to encrypt the information. In a two-party system, a process similar to these steps would be followed.[2]

1. Alice and Bob agree on an encryption algorithm to be used.
2. Alice and Bob agree on a key to be used for encryption/decryption.
3. Alice takes her plaintext message and encrypts it using the algorithm and key.
4. Alice sends the resulting ciphertext message to Bob.
5. Bob decrypts the ciphertext message with the same algorithm and key as the original encryption process.
6. Any change in the key or encryption algorithm has to be agreed on between Alice and Bob. The process of converting to a new key or algorithm requires decrypting the ciphertext using the original key and algorithm and reencrypting with the new key and algorithm. It is important that the key management system used

---

2 N. Ferguson, *Practical Cryptography*, Wiley Publishing, 2003.

TABLE 33.1 Best Practices and Potential Vulnerabilities

Best Practices	Threats							
	Physical	Mgmt. Control	Host	WWN Spoof	Man-in-the-Middle	E-Port Replication	DoS	Session Hijack
Physical access	X			X	X	X		X
Change management		X	X	X				
Password policies		X	X	X				
Defense in depth		X	X	X			X	
Vendor review		X						
Data classification			X					
Security setup	X	X	X	X				
Unused capabilities	X	X						
Auditing	X	X	X					
Updates			X	X				
Monitoring	X	X						
Security maintenance		X	X	X				
Configuration information protection	X	X	X	X	X	X	X	X
Separation of functions		X						
Tool access				X				
Limit connectivity		X						
Partitioning	X	X	X	X	X	X	X	
S_ID checking				X				
Encryption	X			X	X			
Replicas							X	
Erasure	X							

securely preserves the old key for as long as the data retention policy for that data prescribes. Premature destruction of the key will result in loss of data.

The secure exchange of data in a two-party system is typically accomplished using a public/private key mechanism. Protecting data at rest, however, is best handled with a symmetric (private) key because the data is accessed from fixed and/or known locations. Typically one host would use the same algorithm and key to encrypt the data when writing to disk/tape and to decrypt the data when reading from disk/tape. In the case of multipathing or situations in which multiple applications from different nodes will access the data, centralized key management is essential.

Throughout the remainder of the chapter, only symmetric-key encryption will be discussed and will be referred to simply as *encryption. Symmetric-key encryption*, as noted, refers to the process by which data is encrypted and decrypted with the same key. This method of encryption is more suited to the performance demands of data path operations. *Asymmetric-key encryption* refers to the process where encryption is performed with one key and decryption is performed with another key, often referred to as a *public/private key pair*. Asymmetric-key encryption is not well suited to encrypting bulk data at rest due to performance constraints and manageability.

Encryption Algorithms

The algorithm used can be any one of a variety of well-known cryptosystems described in the industry.

The U.S. Federal Information Processing Standards (FIPS) document the Advanced Encryption Standard (AES[3]) and specify it as the industry-standard algorithm in the United States. AES is the most common algorithm implemented in the current encryption methods described as follows. Triple-DES (Data Encryption Standard) is still a certified algorithm by the National Institute of Standards and Technology (NIST) and may be used but is not recommended.[4]

Encryption algorithms typically operate on block lengths of 64 to 128 bytes. To encrypt longer messages an encryption mode of operation may be used, such as:

- CBC–Cipher-block chaining
- CTR–Counter
- XTS–Tweakable narrow block
- GCM–Galois/counter mode

The CBC, CTR, and GCM modes of operation used for encryption require the use of an initialization vector (IV), or nonce. The IV is a seed block used to start and provide randomization to the encryption process. The same IV and key combination must not be used more than once. XTS is the only one of the four that does not require an IV but instead has a second key called the *tweak key*.

In the event the length of the message to be encrypted is not a multiple of the block size, it may be required to pad the final block.

Key Management

The protection potentially afforded by encryption is only as good as the management, generation, and protection of the keys used in the encryption process. Keys must be available and organized in such a fashion that they can be easily retrieved, but at the same time, access to keys must be tightly controlled and limited only to authorized users. This attention to key management must persist for the lifetime of the data, not just the lifetime of the system that generates or encrypts the data. Generation of keys should follow some simple guidelines:

- The key generated must be random, for example, as specified by FIPS 186-2.[5] There can be no predictability to the key used for encryption; pseudorandom number generators are not acceptable for key generation.

- Key length for AES can be 128, 192, or 256 bits.

Once the keys are generated, their protection is crucial to guaranteeing confidentiality. This requires the following:

- *Secure access to the key management solution.* The key management solution must provide a method to guarantee that unauthorized access to keys is restricted. This access restriction should also extend to the facility for generating and managing keys. This can be accomplished via a number of mechanisms including secure Web, smart cards, or split key arrangements. The key management solution must also protect against physical tampering as outlined in FIPS 140-2.[6]
- *Backup and recovery facilities for configuration and key information.* This information itself must be encrypted and stored to a secure backup medium (for example, a smart card). The keys used for encryption must never be visible in plaintext outside the key management solution and, under most circumstances, should not be visible at all. For additional security, the recovery of the configuration/keys should be performed by a group of security administrators. This eliminates the potential for misuse due to corruption of a single administrator and utilizes a group key recovery model where M of N (that is, 2 of 3, 3 of 5, and so on) or a quorum of administrators is needed to reconstruct an encrypted configuration.
- *The ability to apply high availability and business continuity practices and protocols* to key stores.
- *The ability to store keys and identify where they have been used for the lifetime of the data.* This covers data that is written to tape and that may be read up to 30 years later.
- *Integrity checking of keys.* This is particularly important if there are no integrity checks on the data.
- *Comprehensive logging and regular auditing* of how and when the keys are used.

Key management can be distributed or centralized. A common implementation of these requirements is a key management station that can reside either online with the encryption engine or out of band via TCP/IP. The key management station provides a centralized location where keys can be managed and stored securely and meet the

3 FIPS 197, http://csrc.nist.gov/publications/fips/fips197/fips-197.pdf.
4 FIPS 46-3, http://csrc.nist.gov/publications/fips/fips46-3/fips46-3.pdf.
5 http://csrc.nist.gov/publications/fips/fips186-2/fips186-2-change1.pdf.

6 http://csrc.nist.gov/cryptval/140-2.htm.

stringent standards of FIPS 140-2. At this point, there are very few certified, standalone key management systems.

Configuration Management

In configuring any of the methods for encrypting data described here, there are several common steps that need to be executed. The unit to be encrypted needs to be identified (for example, record, file, file system, volume, tape) and an associated key needs to be generated. This configuration information needs to be recorded, securely transmitted to the encryption engine, and securely stored for the lifetime of the encrypted data.

To ensure access to the encrypted data, the configuration must account for all paths available to the data and identify which applications, hosts, or appliances will access the data through those paths. Each needs access to the algorithm and key to be able to read/write uniformly from each path. In addition, replicas (for example, snaps, clones, and mirrors) need to be identified and associated with the original source data to ensure that they can also be correctly decoded when read.

16. APPLICATION OF ENCRYPTION

Encryption is only one tool that can be applied as part of a comprehensive information security strategy, and as such, should be applied selectively, only where it makes sense. Determining exactly where and how this takes place begins with an assessment of risks to the data, the suitability of encryption to address the risk, and then, if appropriate, the options for deployment of the technology.

Risk Assessment and Management

Risk assessment is a calculation that requires three key pieces of information: the number and nature of threats, the likelihood of a threat being realized in the form of an attack, and the impact to the business in the event the attack succeeds. Let's consider these in the context of a decision of whether it is appropriate to deploy encryption technology.

As administrators manage the flow of data from application to storage, they need to understand the nature of possible threats to the data and the likelihood of occurrence. These threats may take the form of:

- Unauthorized disclosure
- Destruction

- Denial of service
- Unauthorized access
- Unauthorized modification
- Masquerade[7]
- Replay[8]
- Man-in-the-middle attacks

These threats may occur at any point from where the information is generated to where it is stored. For each of these threats, an evaluation must be made as to the likelihood of attacks occurring and succeeding in light of existing protection measures. If any attack is determined to be likely, the value of the information subject to threat must be also considered. If the value to the business of the data being threatened is low, it ultimately may not warrant additional protection.

For those risks deemed to be significant, another calculation is required: are the tradeoffs of the proposed solution (in this case, encryption) worth making in context of the level of threat to the data. Considerations should include:

- Cost to deploy
- Level of threat
- Severity of vulnerability
- Consequences
- Detection time
- Response time
- Recovery time
- New risks introduced by encryption, such as premature loss of keys

In this case, by restricting access to the information via authentication and authorization, the administrator can identify who has rights to use the information as well as who has attempted to use the information. Access privileges can be granted at various points in the information flow: at the application, operating system, network, and storage platform layers. If these measures are deemed insufficient, encryption might provide another layer of defense.

Modeling Threats

To make this process more specific to the problem at hand, Figure 33.1 illustrates some of the risks to data

---

7 An attack in which a third party tries to mislead participants in a privileged conversation using forged information.
8 A form of network attack in which a valid transmission is maliciously or fraudulently repeated or delayed.

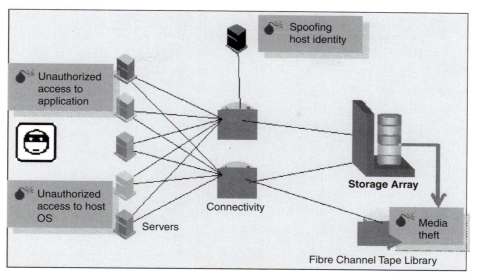

FIGURE 33.1 Threats to plaintext customer data.

in the enterprise. By understanding the attacks that can occur, administrators can determine where encryption may help to protect data and where it would not be applicable.

Figure 33.1 shows the following:

- Encrypting the information at the application level protects against unauthorized viewing of information at the operating system (user) and network levels, as well as protects against media theft. However, encryption at this level will not protect against unauthorized access at the application level (as the information is decrypted at that point) nor root access from the operating system unless strong application access controls are in place.
- Encrypting the information at the host or operating system level protects against unauthorized viewing of information at the network level as well as protects against media theft. Encryption at this level will not protect against unauthorized access at the application or operating system level as the information is decrypted at that point. Access control technology would be required to provide additional security at the operating system and application levels.
- Encrypting the information in the network protects against unauthorized viewing of information from the encryption device to the storage device in the network as well as protects against media theft. Encryption at this level will not protect against unauthorized access at the application or operating system level or in the network up to the encryption device as the information is decrypted at that point.

- Encrypting the information at the device level protects against media theft. Encryption at this level will not protect against unauthorized access at the application or operating system level or in the network as all data external to the device is unencrypted.

Use Cases for Protecting Data at Rest

The following are some specific use cases that warrant deployment of encryption of data at rest. The primary use case is protecting data that leaves administrators' direct control. Some examples of this situation include:

- Backup to tape
  - Tapes that are sent offsite
- Removal of disk for repair
  - Key-based data erasure for removed disk or array for return
  - Data sent to a disaster recovery or remote site
- Protection of data between and in disaster recovery sites
  - Consolidating data from many geographies to a single datacenter while still following each country's security laws
  - Using Type 1 encryption to share data between multiple secure sites
  - Data in harm's way (used for military applications such as planes, Humvees, embassies)
- Data extracts sent to service providers and partners
  - Outsourcing scenarios where sensitive data resides in vendor systems

A second use case is protecting data from unauthorized access in the datacenter when existing access controls are deemed to be insufficient. Some examples of this situation are:

- Shared/consolidated storage used by numerous groups
  - Sharing a single datacenter/array for multiple levels of security
  - Sharing a platform between an intranet and Internet for consolidation
- Protecting data from insider theft (employees, administrators, contractors, janitors)
- Protection of application/executables from alteration

In addition, data encryption is mandated or recommended by a number of regulations. Deploying encryption will enable or aid in compliance. Selected examples of these regulations include:

- *Sarbanes-Oxley Act.* U.S. regulation with respect to disclosure of financial and accounting information.
- *CA 1798 (formerly SB-1386).* California state legislation requiring public disclosure when unencrypted personal information is compromised.
- *HIPAA.* U.S. health-care regulation that recommends encryption for security of personal information.
- *Personal Information Protection Act.* Japanese regulation on information privacy.
- *Gramm-Leach-Bliley Act.* U.S. finance industry regulation requiring public disclosure of personal data breaches.
- *EU Data Protection Directive.* European Union directive on privacy and electronic communications.
- *National data privacy laws.* Becoming pervasive in many nations, including Spain, Switzerland, Australia, Canada, and Italy.

Use Considerations

There are additional factors to consider when using encryption:

- Data deduplication at the disk level may be affected. Any good encryption algorithm will generate different ciphertext for the same plaintext in different circumstances. As a result, algorithms for capacity reduction by analyzing the disk for duplicate blocks will not work on encrypted data.
- Encrypted data is not compressible. Lossless compression algorithms could potentially expand as often as they compress encrypted data if applied. This will impact any WAN connectivity needing to transmit encrypted traffic.

- There is overhead in converting current plaintext data to ciphertext. This is done as a data migration project, even when it is done in place. Host resources, impact to CPU utilization, and running applications must be considered.
- An additional benefit to encrypting data at any level described is the ability to provide data shredding with the destruction of the key. This is especially efficient when there are multiple, distributed copies of the data encrypted with the same key. For the data to be considered shredded, all management copies of the key need to be destroyed for all security administrators, smart cards, backups, key management stations, and so on. Key destruction must follow similar guidelines as to the data erasure outlined in NIST SP 800-88.

Deployment Options

As we have seen, the use cases discuss why encryption would be used and the threats being protected against determine where encryption should be deployed. The following sections discuss in further detail deployments at each layer of the infrastructure.

Application Level

Perhaps the greatest control over information can be exercised where it originates, from the application. The application has the best opportunity to classify the information and manage who can access it, during what times and for what purpose. If the administrator has concerns/risks over the information at all levels in the infrastructure, it makes sense to begin with security at the application level and work down. In this case application-based encryption should be an option. Adding encryption at the application level allows for granular, specific information to be secured as it leaves the application. For example, a database could encrypt specific rows/columns of sensitive information (for example, Social Security numbers or credit-card numbers) while leaving less sensitive information unencrypted. Attempts to snoop writes-to-disk or to read-data directly from disk without the application decrypting it would yield useless information.

Encryption at the application level provides security from access at the operating system level as well as from other applications on the server as shown in Figure 33.2. The application would still need to provide user authentication and authorization to guarantee that only those with a need to know can access the application and the data. If the application lacks these strong access controls, application-based encryption will provide no additional security benefit. End-user activities with data after it is converted to clear text are potentially the highest security risk for organizations.

There are some drawbacks to encrypting at the application level. First, encryption is done on a per-application basis. If multiple applications need encryption, each would have to handle the task separately, creating additional management complexities to ensure that all confidential data is protected. Second, application-level encryption solutions are typically software based. Encryption is a CPU-intensive process and will compete with normal operating resources on the server. In addition, the encryption keys will be stored in dynamic, nonvolatile memory on the server. If a hacker were to break into the server and find the keys, the information can be decrypted. Externalizing the encryption engine or key manager may address these issues at the expense of additional solution cost. An external key manager also enables clustered applications to share key information across nodes and geography (provided that each node can supply a secure channel from the server to the key manager.) If FIPS 140-2 compliance is a requirement for the encryption solution, an external appliance is typically used.

Application-based encryption also presents challenges in the area of rekeying. Any effort to rekey the data (to protect the integrity of the keys) will have to be done by the application. The application will need to read and decrypt the data using the old key and reencrypt and rewrite to disk using the new key. The application will also have to manage old and new key operations until all the previously encrypted information is reencrypted with the new key. This most likely will be done while the application is handling normal transactions, again presenting resource contention issues.

Another challenge occurs with the introduction of ediscovery solutions in the enterprise. Encryption at the application level will expose only encrypted information to other applications (including backup) and devices in the stack. Any attempt to perform analysis on the data will be useless as patterns and associations will be lost through the randomization process of encryption. To accomplish any analysis the ediscovery applications will need to be associated and linked to the application performing encryption to allow for a decryption of data at a level outside of the application, and a possible security risk could be introduced.

Application-based encryption (see Figure 33.2) must also account for variable record lengths. Encryption schemes must pad data up to their block size to generate valid signatures. Depending on the implementation, this may require some changes to application source code.

Application-based encryption doesn't take into account the impact on replicated data. Any locally replicated information at the storage layer, that is, a clone, does not have visibility into the application and the keys and the application does not have visibility into the replication process. Key management can become more complex. In addition, compression in the WAN is impossible for remote replication of the encrypted information causing WAN capacity issues.

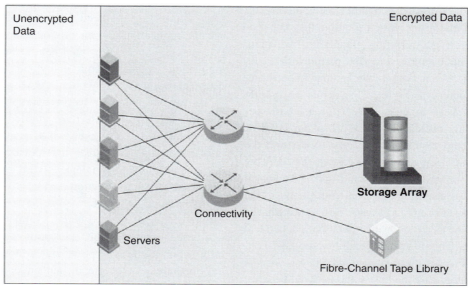

FIGURE 33.2 Coverage for application-based encryption.

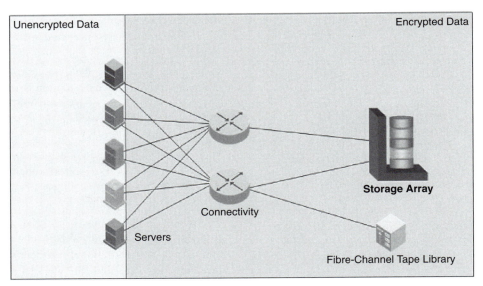

Unencrypted Data

Encrypted Data

Storage Array

Connectivity

Servers

Fibre-Channel Tape Library

FIGURE 33.3 Coverage for host-based encryption.

Host Level

Encrypting at the host level provides very similar benefits and tradeoffs to application-based encryption. At the host level, there are still opportunities to classify the data, but on a less granular basis; encryption can be performed at the file level for all applications running on the host (as shown in Figure 33.3). However, there are options for a host-based adapter or software to provide encryption of any data leaving the host as files, blocks, or objects. As with application-level implementations, the operating system must still provide user authentication and authorization to prevent against host-level attacks. If these strong access controls are absent, host-level encryption will provide no additional security benefit (aside from protection against loss or theft of media). If implemented correctly and integrated with the encryption solution, they can provide some process authorization granularity, managing which users should be allowed to view plaintext data.

At the host level, encryption can be done in software, using CPU resources to perform the actual encryption and storing the keys in memory, or offloaded to specialized hardware. Offload involves use of an HBA or an accelerator card resident in the host to perform the actual encryption of the data. In the case of the HBA the encryption can be performed in-band and is dedicated to the particular transport connection from the host, that is, Fibre Channel. For an accelerator card approach, the encryption is done as a look-aside operation independent of the transport. This provides flexibility for host connectivity but increases the memory and I/O bus load in the system. In either case the host software would control

the connection to the key manager and management of the keys.

There may be a need in the enterprise for the host-based encryption solution to support multiple operating systems, allowing for interoperability across systems or consistency in the management domain, something to consider when evaluating solutions. In addition, when encryption is implemented at the host level, there is the flexibility of being storage and array independent, allowing for support of legacy storage with no new hardware needed. Host-based encryption does present a challenge when coupled with storage-based functionality, that is, replication. If replication is employed underneath the host encryption level the host implementation must have the ability to track replicas and associate encryption keys, eliminating the need for users to manually manage the replication and encryption technology. As host encryption supplies encrypted data to the array, remote replication would transmit encrypted, uncompressible data. This would severely impact WAN performance.

As with application-based encryption, ediscovery solutions in the enterprise pose additional complexities. Encryption at the host level will expose only encrypted information to other hosts and devices in the stack, introducing the same challenges with analysis as those described in the prior section.

As encryption is performed at the host level, the data can be of variable record length. Similar to the application-based approach, the encryption solution can add information to the encryption payload to allow for a digital signature or cryptographic authentication. This would prevent a "man-in-the-middle" from substituting bad packets for the good encrypted packets from the host.

Network Level

If the threats in the enterprise are not at the server, operating system, or application level, but instead at the network or storage level, then a network-based appliance approach for encryption may work best. This approach is operating system independent and can be applied to file, block, tape, Fibre Channel, iSCSI, or NAS data. Encryption and key management are handled entirely in hardware and run at wire speed for the connection. The appliance presents an "unencrypted side" and "encrypted side" to the network. Encryption can be designated on a per block, file or tape basis and the keys maintained for the life of the data. Appliances available today are typically FIPS 140-2 level 3 validated.

There are two implementations for a network-based appliance design: store-and-forward or transparent. The store-and-forward design appears as storage to the server and a server to the storage, and supports iSCSI, Fibre Channel, SAN, NAS, and tape. An I/O operation comes to the appliance, is terminated, the data encrypted, and then forwarded to the destination storage device. This approach adds latency and as a result, some form of "cut-through" ideally needs to be offered to minimize the impact of the device for nonencrypted traffic. In addition, to appear as both server and storage, the store-and-forward appliance either needs to spoof the identities of the attached devices or rely on robust security practices to counteract the attempts to circumvent the appliance. While there may be a latency penalty for encrypting data through the appliance, the store-and-forward-based design has the benefit of allowing the attached storage devices to be rekeyed in the background. This is performed with no disruption to host operations as all I/O operations to the storage are handled independently of the host. There may still be some performance impact to the rekeying process, depending on the I/O load on the encryptor.

The transparent approach provides a flow-through model for the data being encrypted, supporting Fibre Channel SAN and tape. The appliance inspects SCSI headers as data flows through the appliance and encrypts only the data payloads that match preset source/destination criteria in the appliance configuration. The latency associated with this approach is minimal. The transparent design does, however, have a drawback when the encrypted data needs to be rekeyed. Unlike the store-and-forward design, the device is essentially transparent in the data flow, requiring the host to perform the reads and writes required in rekeying the encrypted data. This process can be done by a separate host agent and could be performed while normal operations are in process.

For block-based implementations, the size of the encrypted data cannot increase. This means no additional information can be added to the encrypted payload (for example, a digital signature). This is not true for file or tape-based encryption where the record information may be variable. As noted in the discussion on standards, the IEEE is working to provide standards for encrypting block data at rest, in IEEE P1619.

There may be a need in the enterprise for the encryption to support multiple operating systems, allowing for interoperability across systems or consistency in the management domain. In addition, when encryption is implemented at the network level, there is the flexibility of being storage- and array-independent, allowing for support of legacy storage—at the cost of adding new hardware. Hardware in this case is added in increments of ports, typically two at a time, adding to the power, package, and cooling issues currently facing enterprises today. In addition, adding appliances in these increments can add complications in managing additional devices in the enterprise. Network-level encryption does present a challenge when coupled with storage-based functionality such as replication. If replication is employed underneath encryption at the network level, the implementation must have the ability to track replicas and associate encryption keys, eliminating the need for users to manually manage the replication and encryption technology. As network-level encryption supplies encrypted data to the array, remote replication would transmit encrypted, uncompressible data. This would severely impact WAN performance.

There are also implementations moving to use data integrity features as part of the protocols. Encryption in the network level (see Figure 33.4) would encrypt both the data and the data integrity, resulting in mismatches at this level of checking performed at the arrays.

Network-level encryption doesn't take into account the impact on replicated data. Any locally replicated information at the storage layer, that is, a clone, does not have visibility into the network device management and the keys and the network device does not have visibility into the replication process. Key management can become more complex and more manual. In addition, compression in the WAN is impossible for remote replication of the encrypted information causing WAN capacity issues.

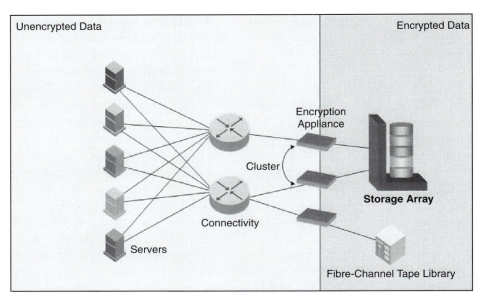

FIGURE 33.4 Coverage for network-based encryption.

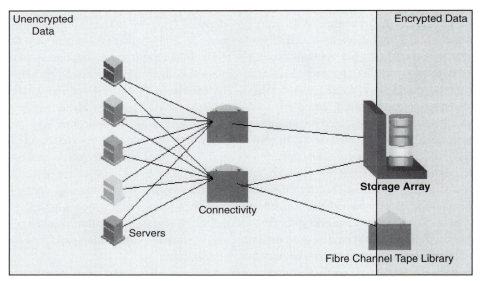

FIGURE 33.5 Coverage for device-based encryption.

Device Level

Encryption at the device level—array, disk, or tape—is a sufficient method of protecting sensitive data residing on storage media, which is a primary security risk many organizations are seeking to address. All data written to the device would be encrypted and stored as such and then decrypted when read from the device. Encryption at this level would be application and host independent and can be transport independent as well. When addressing media theft, the granularity for encryption, and keys, can be at the disk or tape level. As demonstrated in Figure 33.5, exposure for unencrypted data is increased as compared to the previous implementation examples.

Array-Level Encryption

There are a number of design points for encryption in the array, that is, at the disk or controller level. Design considerations for encryption include the interfaces to the array, software support, performance, FIPS validation, key management, and encryption object granularity to name a few. The intent is to have the encryption implementation transparent to the hosts attached while protecting the removable media. The connected hosts may not be knowledgeable of the encryption implementation but may be with respect to management and performance. All aspects of the design must be considered.

One possible approach is to implement the encryption in the disk drive, at the back end of the array. Some points to consider:

- As encryption is on a per-drive basis, the computes required are included in the drive enclosure, allowing for a scalable solution, adding encryption with every unit. The downside to this is cost to the functionality that is added with every unit. So while performance scales, so can cost.
- Customers might be unable to verify that encryption is enabled and functioning on the array, because data is always plaintext when it is external to the disk drive.
- Any approach to encryption at this level would also require interoperability of the encryption implementation across drive vendors to maintain flexibility and customer choice.
- Bulk drive encryption would not provide key granularity at the LUN/device level, which in many cases would eliminate the possibility of erasing specific confidential projects via key deletion.
- Last, as driven by the Trusted Computing Group, encryption at this level may follow a different path for validation, an alternative to FIPS 140 yet to be developed. Without a standard to evaluate it is impossible to understand the disk drive encryption validation proposal.

Another approach might be to implement encryption in the I/O controller connected to the disk drives. Some points to consider for this potential implementation are:

- Encryption is on the interface level and is required to support full wire speed versus interface speed in the drive approach.
- The cost model would be based on a single controller versus tens of drives connected to a single controller.
- The controller approach has the ability to perform encryption at the I/O level, allowing the granularity for key management to be at the LUN or disk level. This approach allows for future support of LUN-based erasure and logical data management.
- The controller approach is drive-independent, not relying on any specific vendor or interface, allowing for all standard tools and failure analysis to be performed.
- In supporting encryption at the controller level the crypto boundary can be well defined, allowing for FIPS 140-2 validation.

- Encryption and key control would be separate from the disk drive containing the encrypted data. This allows the customer to validate the encryption functionality is working and not be concerned with keys leaving with a removed disk drive.

An alternative to the encryption option for the protection against media theft is data erasure. It addresses the same primary use case: protection of disk media containing sensitive data and is available today, as erasure services (for removed drives) and software (for in-frame erasure). Erasure overwrites data multiple times, in accordance with the Department of Defense specification 5220.22-M, removing the data from the media. One consideration is that a minority of drives are not erasable for mechanical reasons.

Tape Encryption

As part of normal operations, data is frequently written from storage devices to tape for backup/data protection or third-party use. Data on tape cartridges becomes susceptible to theft or loss due to the size of the tape cartridge and quantity of the number of tapes to track during normal backup operations. To best protect the data on tape against unintended/unauthorized viewing, it can be encrypted. There are several approaches to encrypting tape as part of the backup operation:

- Reading encrypted data from application/disk and writing as encrypted data to tape
- Reading unencrypted data from application/disk and encrypting as part of the backup application
- Encrypting any/all data sent to tape via an encryption appliance in the network
- Encrypting any/all data written to the tape via an encrypting tape library or tape device

Tape encryption also presents key management challenges. Tapes may be stored for an extended period of time before an attempt is made to recover information. During the normal process of managing encrypted data, the application may have rekeyed the data on disk, updating all data on the disk to use a new key. This process would present the application with active data using one key and data on tape using an older key. The application must be therefore be able to manage keys for the lifetime of the data, regardless of where the data is stored. The following are tape encryption deployment options.

Application Level

Backup is typically another operation running on a host as a peer to the encrypting application. Any peer application or process will read data from the storage array as encrypted data. This allows the backup process to write already encrypted data to tape without having to perform the encryption itself. It will, however, prevent data compression during the backup process, as encrypted data is not compressible. Because typical compression ratios reduce data volumes anywhere from 2:1 to 4:1, this will impact performance of the backup process if a large amount of bulk data is encrypted.

Applications providing encryption can also provide access for authorized peer applications to read data in encrypted or unencrypted form. This would allow a backup application to read data in unencrypted form and allow for compression followed by encryption to be performed as part of the backup process.

Operating System/Host

Backup is another process on the host when using host-based encryption. The encryption process in the host operating system has the option of allowing the backup process to read data in encrypted or unencrypted form. If the authorization module determines that the backup process can read plaintext data, backup will receive decrypted data to be sent to tape. Encryption will also need to be performed by the backup application to allow for writing secure tapes. The backup process could take advantage of compression in this data flow. If the backup process is not allowed to view decrypted data, it will read encrypted data from disk and write it as such to tape. As in the application-based approach, compression may not be able to be utilized on this encrypted data, creating potential performance issues. In addition, the encryption engine for the host will have to maintain the keys for the lifetime of the data to ensure that decryption can take place in the event a restore from tape is needed.

In the Network

If an encryption appliance is placed in the network, backup can be handled in one of two ways. If backup is volume based, any data read from the storage array may already be encrypted. The backup application will read the encrypted data and write it directly to tape. In this scenario, there would be no benefit of compression in the data path. If the backup is file or incremental based, the backup process would read the data through the appliance, decrypting it in the process, and could then write the data to tape. To provide encryption, a tape encryption appliance would be positioned in front of the tape device, compressing and encrypting the data as it is written to tape. The tape encryption appliance would manage the keys for the lifetime of the tape.

At the Tape Library/Drive

Data can be encrypted at the tape drive level, independent of the backup process and application software. All encryption is performed at the device, or library, when data is written to the tape and decryption performed at the drive when data is read from the tape. The backup application deals with nothing but plaintext data. The tape drive or library can be the management interface to the key manager, requesting generation of keys for new tapes written and retrieval of keys for each tape read. Association of keys to tapes is managed at the key manager appliance. In some cases the key manager can be integrated to work cooperatively with a volume pool policy defined with backup application. Jobs directed to use tapes in a pool associated with this policy begin with a request by the drive or library for an encryption key only when the backup or restore job uses tapes in this volume pool.

17. CONCLUSION

Security is a complex and constantly evolving practice in the IT industry. Companies must recognize that threats to information infrastructures require vigilance on the part of IT managers and the vendors they rely on.

The management, integrity, and availability of your data should be your first priority. As this analysis has shown, basic security best practices can be implemented to greatly increase the security of your Fibre Channel SAN and the data it contains. The available avenues of attack are minimized by carefully controlling access to resources, both physically and logically.

While many storage vendors are making extensive investments in the security of their SAN products, they also recognize that it is impossible to predict every possible current and future combination of threats that might impact an IT environment. Ensure that your vendor constantly monitor changes and advances in security threats and technology, and updates its products with new features and functionality to address any issues that might impact the data on your SAN.

Encryption is a tool that can be used to protect the confidentiality of the information in the enterprise. To understand if and how an encryption solution should be deployed, administrators need to understand and assess the risks of unauthorized access and disclosure at each point of the information flow. They must also understand how deployment of encryption technology may add risk to other areas of the business, including complexity added to management, and risks to availability of encrypted data to authorized users. Data unavailability can come

TABLE 33.2 Summary of encryption approaches

	Encryption	Key Management	Backup	Issues	Risks Addressed
Application	Typically done in software but can be done in hardware.	Typically stored in memory or file. Coordination of keys across applications presents challenges to sharing information. Needs external appliance to meet FIPS 140-2 Level 3	Peer process to the application and will back up encrypted data. No compression. Lifetime key management challenges.	Encryption can be host system intensive and is a per-application process. If more than one application is used on a host, sharing of information can be an issue. Storing keys for lifetime of data can also be an issue for application upgrades. Can impact ediscovery.	Protects against operating system and network attacks as well as media theft.
Host	Typically done in software but can be done in hardware. Can be file or block based.	Typically stored in memory but can have external appliance.	Peer process will back up data and host will need to re-encrypt.	Encryption can be host system intensive. Storing keys for lifetime of data can also be an issue for OS upgrades (if external key management facility is not used). Can impact ediscovery.	Protects against network attacks as well as media theft.
Network	Typically done in hardware.	Managed for the lifetime of data in hardware.	Can perform block-based encryption to disk or tape or file-based encryption. Can also incorporate compression for tape backup or coordination for replication.	A single aggregation point in the network for encryption can be a performance bottleneck.	Protects against some network attacks as well as media theft.
Disk based	Typically done in hardware but can be done in software.	Can be done per disk or LUN. Key management can be resident-to-array or leveraged from external appliance.	Always presents unencrypted data external to disk.	Handles very focused use case. Largest exposure of encrypted data in an enterprise.	Protects against media theft.

from something as simple as key management, which is perhaps the most important factor to consider in implementing an encryption solution. Encryption should be considered as part of a total security solution, but not the only solution; administrators need to take advantage of protection options at all levels of the information flow and architecture. Two general issues that are present across encryption implementations are:

- The conversion of plaintext to ciphertext when encrypting data for the first time or ciphertext to ciphertext when encrypting with a new key. Both are done as a data migration project, even when it is done in place. Host resources, impact to CPU utilization, and running applications must be considered.

- The replication of encrypted data across the WAN. Encryption, if done correctly, produces random, uncompressible data that will impact the utilization of remote connectivity.

Table 33.2 summarizes the various deployment options.

REFERENCES

[1] J.C. Blaul, *Storage Security*, Wiley Publishing, Inc., 2003.
[2] H. Dwivedi, *Securing Storage: A Practical Guide to SAN and NAS Security*, Pearson Education, Inc., 2006.
[3] B. King, *LUN Masking in a SAN*, Aliso Viejo, California, October 8, 2001.
[4] J. McDonald, *Security Considerations for Fibre Channel Storage Area Networks*, Hopkinton, Massachusetts, June 5, 2005.
[5] C. McGowan, *Approaches for Encryption of Data-at-Rest in the Enterprise*, Hopkinton, Massachusetts, September 10, 2008.

## Chapter 34

Storage Area Networking Security Devices

Robert Rounsavall
Terremark Worldwide, Inc.

Storage area networking (SAN) devices have become a critical IT component of almost every business today. The upside and intended consequences of using a SAN are to consolidate corporate data as well as reduce cost, complexity, and risks. The tradeoff and downside to implementing SAN technology are that the risks of large-scale data loss are higher in terms of both cost and reputation. With the rapid adoption of virtualization, SANs now house more than just data; they house entire virtual servers and huge clusters of servers in "enterprise clouds."[1] In addition to all the technical, management, deployment, and protection challenges, a SAN comes with a full range of legal regulations such as PCI, HIPAA, SOX, GLBA, SB1386, and many others. Companies keep their informational "crown jewels" on their SANs but in most cases do not understand all the architecture issues and risks involved, which can cost an organization huge losses. This chapter covers all the issues and security concerns related to storage area network security.

1. WHAT IS A SAN?

The Storage Network Industry Association (SNIA)[2] defines a SAN as a data storage system consisting of various storage elements, storage devices, computer systems, and/or appliances, plus all the control software, all communicating in efficient harmony over a network. Put in simple terms, a SAN is a specialized, high-speed network attaching servers and storage devices and, for this reason, it is sometimes referred to as "the network behind the servers." A SAN allows "any-to-any" connections across the network, using interconnected elements such as routers, gateways, hubs, switches, and directors. It eliminates the traditional dedicated connection between a server and storage as well as the concept that the server effectively "owns and manages" the storage devices. It also eliminates any restriction to the amount of data that a server can access, currently limited by the number of storage devices attached to the individual server. Instead, a SAN introduces the flexibility of networking to enable one server or many heterogeneous servers to share a common storage utility, which may comprise many storage devices, including disk, tape, and optical storage. Additionally, the storage utility may be located far from the servers that use it.

The SAN can be viewed as an extension to the storage bus concept, which enables storage devices and servers to be interconnected using similar elements to those used in local area networks (LANs) and wide area networks (WANs). SANs can be interconnected with routers, hubs, switches, directors, and gateways. A SAN can also be shared between servers and/or dedicated to one server. It can be local or extended over geographical distances.

2. SAN DEPLOYMENT JUSTIFICATIONS

Perhaps a main reason SANs have emerged as the leading advanced storage option is because they can often alleviate many if not all the data storage "pain points" of IT managers.[3] For quite some time IT managers have been in a predicament in which some servers, such as database servers, run out of hard disk space rather quickly, whereas other servers, such as application servers, tend to not need a whole lot of disk space and usually have storage to spare. When a SAN is implemented, the storage can be spread throughout servers on an as-needed basis.

---

1 The Enterprise Cloud by Terremark, www.theenterprisecloud.com.
2 Storage Network Industry Association, www.snia.org/home.

3 SAN justifications: http://voicendata.ciol.com/content/enterprise_zone/105041303.asp.

The following are further justifications and benefits for implementing a storage area network:

- They allow for more manageable, scalable, and efficient deployment of mission-critical data.
- SAN designs can protect resource investments from unexpected turns in the economic environment and changes in market adoption of new technology.
- SANs help with the difficulty of managing large, disparate islands of storage from multiple physical and virtual locations.
- SANs reduce the complexity of maintaining scheduled backups for multiple systems and difficulty in preparing for unscheduled system outages.
- The inability to share storage resources and achieve efficient levels of subsystem utilization is avoided.
- SANs help address the issue of a shortage of qualified storage professionals to manage storage resources effectively.
- SANs help us understand how to implement the plethora of storage technology alternatives, including appropriate deployment of Fibre Channel as well as Internet small computer systems interface (iSCSI), Fibre Channel over IP (FCIP), and InfiniBand.
- SANs allow us to work with restricted budgets and increasing costs of deploying and maintaining them, despite decreasing prices for physical storage in terms of average street price per terabyte.

In addition to all these benefits, the true advantage of implementing a SAN is that it enables the management of huge quantities of email and other business-critical data such as that created by many enterprise applications, such as customer relationship management (CRM), enterprise resource planning (ERP), and others. The popularity of these enterprise applications, regulatory compliance, and other audit requirements have resulted in an explosion of information and data that have become the lifeblood of these organizations, greatly elevating the importance of a sound storage strategy. Selecting a unified architecture that integrates the appropriate technologies to meet user requirements across a range of applications is central to ensuring storage support for mission-critical applications. Then matching technologies to user demands allows for optimized storage architecture, providing the best use of capital and IT resources.

A large number of enterprises have already implemented production SANs, and many industry analysts have researched the actual benefits of these implementations. A Gartner[4] study of large enterprise data center

managers shows that 64% of those surveyed were either running or deploying a SAN. Another study by the Aberdeen Group cites that nearly 60% of organizations that have SANs installed have two or more separate SANs. The study also states that 80% of those surveyed felt that they had satisfactorily achieved their main goals for implementing a SAN. Across the board, all vendor case studies and all industry analyst investigations have found the following core benefits of SAN implementation compared to a direct attached storage (DAS) environment:

- Ease of management
- Increased subsystem utilization
- Reduction in backup expense
- Lower Total Cost of Ownership (TCO)

3. THE CRITICAL REASONS FOR SAN SECURITY

SAN security is important because there is more concentrated, centralized, high-value data at risk than in normal distributed servers with built-in, smaller-scale storage solutions. On a SAN you have data from multiple devices and multiple parts of the network shared on one platform. This typically fast-growing data can be consolidated and centralized from locations all over the world. SANs also store more than just data; with the increasing acceptance of server virtualization, multiple OS images and the data they create are being retrieved from and enabled by SANs.

Why Is SAN Security Important?

Some large-scale security losses have occurred by intercepting information incrementally over time, but the vast majority of breaches involve access or loss of data from the corporate SAN. (For deeper insight into the numbers, check out the Data Loss Web site. This website tracks incidents and is a clearinghouse of data loss each month.[5])

A wide range of adversaries can attack an organization simply to access its SAN, which is where all the company data rests. Common adversaries who will be looking to access the organization's main data store are:

- Financially motivated attackers and competitors
- Identity thieves
- Criminal gangs
- State-sponsored attackers
- Internal employees
- Curious business partners

---

4 Gartner, www.gartner.com.

5 Data Loss Database, http://datalossdb.org/.

If one or some of these perpetrators were to be successful in stealing or compromising the data in the SAN, and if news got around that your customer data had been compromised, it could directly impact your organization monetarily and cause significant losses in terms of:

- Reputation
- Time lost
- Forensics investigations
- Overtime for IT
- Business litigation
- Perhaps even a loss of competitive edge—for example, if the organization's proprietary manufacturing process is found in the wild

4. SAN ARCHITECTURE AND COMPONENTS

In its simplest form, a SAN is a number of servers attached to a storage array using a switch. Figure 34.1 is a diagram of all the components involved.

SAN Switches

Specialized switches called SAN switches are at the heart of a typical SAN. Switches provide capabilities to match the number of host SAN connections to the number of connections provided by the storage array. Switches also provide path redundancy in the event of a path failure from host server to switch or from storage

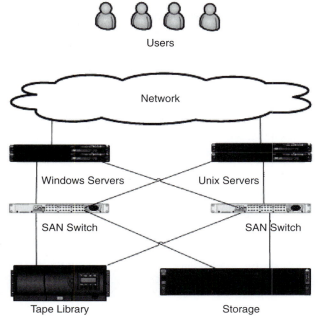

FIGURE 34.1 Simple SAN elements.

array to switch. SAN switches can connect both servers and storage devices and thus provide the connection points for the fabric of the SAN. For smaller SANs, the standard SAN switches are called *modular switches* and can typically support eight or 16 ports (though some 32-port modular switches are beginning to emerge). Sometimes modular switches are interconnected to create a fault-tolerant fabric. For larger SAN fabrics, director-class switches provide a larger port capacity (64 to 128 ports per switch) and built-in fault tolerance. The type of SAN switch, its design features, and its port capacity all contribute to its overall capacity, performance, and fault tolerance. The number of switches, types of switches, and manner in which the switches are interconnected define the topology of the fabric.

Network Attached Storage (NAS)

Network attached storage (NAS) is file-level data storage providing data access to many different network clients. The Business Continuity Planning (BCP) defined in this category address the security associated with file-level storage systems/ecosystems. They cover the Network File System (NFS), which is often used by Unix and Linux (and their derivatives') clients as well as SMB/CIFS, which is frequently used by Windows clients.

Fabric

When one or more SAN switches are connected, a *fabric* is created. The fabric is the actual network portion of the SAN. Special communications protocols such as Fibre Channel (FC), iSCSI, and Fibre Channel over Ethernet (FCoE) are used to communicate over the entire network. Multiple fabrics may be interconnected in a single SAN, and even for a simple SAN it is not unusual for it to be composed of two fabrics for redundancy.

HBA and Controllers

Host servers and storage systems are connected to the SAN fabric through ports in the fabric. A host connects to a fabric port through a Host Bus Adapter (HBA), and the storage devices connect to fabric ports through their controllers. Each server may host numerous applications that require dedicated storage for applications processing. Servers need not be homogeneous within the SAN environment.

Tape Library

A tape library is a storage device that is designed to hold, manage, label, and store data to tape. Its main benefit is related to cost/TB, but its slow random access relegates it to an archival device.

Protocols, Storage Formats and Communications

The following protocols and file systems are other important components of a SAN.

Block-Based IP Storage (IP)

Block-based IP storage is implemented using protocols such as iSCSI, Internet Fibre Channel Protocol (iFCP), and FCIP to transmit SCSI commands over IP networks.

Secure iSCSI

Internet SCSI or iSCSI, which is described in IETF RFC 3720, is a connection-oriented command/response protocol that runs over TCP and is used to access disk, tape, and other devices.

Secure FCIP

Fibre Channel over TCP/IP (FCIP), defined in IETF RFC 3821, is a pure Fibre Channel encapsulation protocol. It allows the interconnection of islands of Fibre Channel storage area networks through IP-based networks to form a unified storage area network.

Fibre Channel Storage (FCS)

Fibre Channel is a gigabit-speed network technology used for block-based storage and the Fibre Channel Protocol (FCP) is the interface protocol used to transmit SCSI on this network technology.

Secure FCP

Fibre Channel entities (host bus adapters or HBAs, switches, and storage) can contribute to the overall secure posture of a storage network by employing mechanisms such as filtering and authentication.

Secure Fibre Channel Storage Networks

A SAN is architected to attach remote computer storage devices (such as disk arrays, tape libraries, and optical jukeboxes) to servers in such a way that, to the operating system, the devices appear as though they're locally attached. These SANs are often based on a Fibre Channel fabric topology that utilizes the Fibre Channel Protocol (FCP).

SMB/CIFS

SMB/CIFS is a network protocol whose most common use is sharing files, especially in Microsoft operating system environments.

Network File System (NFS)

NFS is a client/server application, communicating with a remote procedure call (RPC)-based protocol. It enables file systems physically residing on one computer system or NAS device to be used by other computers in the network, appearing to users on the remote host as just another local disk.

Online Fixed Content

An online fixed content system usually contains at least some data subject to retention policies and a retention-managed storage system/ecosystem is commonly used for such data.

5. SAN GENERAL THREATS AND ISSUES

A SAN is a prime target of all attackers due to the goldmine of information that can be attained by accessing it. Here we discuss the general threats and issues related to SANs.

SAN Cost: A Deterrent to Attackers

Unlike many network components such as servers, routers, and switches, SANs are quite expensive, which does raise the bar for attackers a little bit. There are not huge numbers of people with SAN protocol expertise, and not too many people have a SAN in their home lab, unless they are a foreign government that has dedicated resources to researching and exploiting these types of vulnerabilities. Why would anyone go to the trouble when it would be much easier to compromise the machines of the people who manage the SANs or the servers that are themselves connected to the SAN?

The barrier to entry to directly attack the SAN is high; however, the ability to attack the management tools and administrators who access the SAN is not. Most are administered via Web interfaces, software applications, or command-line interfaces. An attacker simply has to gain root or administrator access on those machines to be able to attack the SAN.

Physical Level Threats, Issues, and Risk Mitigation

There can be many physical risks involved in using a SAN. It is important to take them all into consideration when planning and investing in a storage area network.

- Locate the SAN in a secure datacenter
- Ensure that proper access controls are in place

- Cabinets, servers, and tape libraries come with locks; use them
- Periodically audit the access control list
- Verify whether former employees can access the location where the SAN is located
- Perform physical penetration and social engineering tests on a regular basis

Physical Environment

The SAN must be located in an area with proper ventilation and cooling. Ensure that your datacenter has proper cooling and verify any service-level agreements with a third-party provider with regard to power and cooling.

Hardware Failure Considerations

Ensure that the SAN is designed and constructed in such a way that when a piece of hardware fails, it does not cause an outage. Schedule failover testing on a regular basis during maintenance windows so that it will be completed on time.

Secure Sensitive Data on Removable Media to Protect "Externalized Data"

Many of the data breaches that fill the newspapers and create significant embarrassments for organizations are easily preventable and involve loss of *externalized data* such as backup media. To follow are some ideas to avoid unauthorized disclosure while data is in transit:

- Offsite backup tapes of sensitive or regulated data should be encrypted as a general practice and must be encrypted when leaving the direct control of the organization; encryption keys must be stored separately from data.
- Use only secure and bonded shippers if not encrypted. (Remember that duty-of-care contractual provisions often contain a limitation of liability limited to the bond value. The risk transfer value is often less than the data value.)
- Secure sensitive data transferred between datacenters.
- Sensitive/regulated data transferred to and from remote datacenters must be encrypted in flight.
- Secure sensitive data in third-party datacenters.
- Sensitive/regulated data stored in third-party datacenters must be encrypted prior to arrival (both in-flight and at-rest).
- Secure your data being used by ediscovery tools.

Know Thy Network (or Storage Network)

It is not only a best practice but critical that the SAN is well documented. All assets must be known. All physical and logical interfaces must be known. Create detailed physical and logical diagrams of the SAN. Identify *all* interfaces on the SAN gear. Many times people overlook the network interfaces for the out-of-band management. Some vendors put a sticker with login and password physically on the server for the out-of-band management ports. Ensure that these are changed. Know what networks can access the SAN and from where. Verify all entry points and exit points for data, especially sensitive data such as financial information or PII. If an auditor asks, it should be simple to point to exactly where that data rests and where it goes on the network.

Use Best Practices for Disaster Recovery and Backup

Guidelines such as the NIST Special Publication 800-34[6] outline best practices for disaster recovery and backup. The seven steps for contingency planning are outlined below:

1. *Develop the contingency planning policy statement.* A formal department or agency policy provides the authority and guidance necessary to develop an effective contingency plan.
2. *Conduct the business impact analysis (BIA).* The BIA helps identify and prioritize critical IT systems and components. A template for developing the BIA is also provided to assist the user.
3. *Identify preventive controls.* Measures taken to reduce the effects of system disruptions can increase system availability and reduce contingency life-cycle costs.
4. *Develop recovery strategies.* Thorough recovery strategies ensure that the system may be recovered quickly and effectively following a disruption.
5. *Develop an IT contingency plan.* The contingency plan should contain detailed guidance and procedures for restoring a damaged system.
6. *Plan testing, training, and exercises.* Testing the plan identifies planning gaps, whereas training prepares recovery personnel for plan activation; both activities improve plan effectiveness and overall agency preparedness.
7. *Plan maintenance.* The plan should be a living document that is updated regularly to remain current with system enhancements.

---

6 NIST Special Publication 800-34, http://csrc.nist.gov/publications/nistpubs/800-34/sp800-34.pdf.

Logical Level Threats, Vulnerabilities, and Risk Mitigation

Aside from the physical risks and issues with SANs, there are also many logical threats. A threat is defined as any potential danger to information or systems. These are the same threats that exist in any network and they are also applicable to a storage network because Windows and Unix servers are used to access and manage the SAN. For this reason, it is important to take a defense-in-depth approach to securing the SAN.

Some of the threats that face a SAN are as follows:

- *Internal threats (malicious).* A malicious employee could access the sensitive data in a SAN via management interface or poorly secured servers.
- *Internal threats (nonmalicious).* Not following proper procedure such as using change management could bring down a SAN. A misconfiguration could bring down a SAN. Poor planning for growth could limit your SAN.
- *Outside threats.* An attacker could access your SAN data or management interface by compromising a management server, a workstation or laptop owned by an engineer, or other server that has access to the SAN.

The following parts of the chapter deal with protecting against these threats.

Begin with a Security Policy

Having a corporate information security policy is essential.[7] Companies should already have such policies, and they should be periodically reviewed and updated. If organizations process credit cards for payment and are subject to the Payment Card Industry (PCI)[8] standards, they are mandated to have a security policy. Federal agencies subject to certification and accreditation under guidelines such as DIACAP[9] must also have security policies.

Is storage covered in the corporate security policy? Some considerations for storage security policies include the following:

- Identification and classification of sensitive data such as PII, financial, trade secrets, and business-critical data

- Data retention, destruction, deduplication, and sanitization
- User access and authorization

Instrument the Network with Security Tools

Many of the network security instrumentation devices such as IDS/IPS have become a commodity, required for compliance and a minimum baseline for any IT network. The problem with many of those tools is that they are signature based and only provide alerts and packet captures on the offending packet alerts. Adding tools such as full packet capture and network anomaly detection systems can allow a corporation to see attacks that are not yet known. They can also find attacks that bypass the IDS/IPSs and help prove to customers and government regulators whether or not the valuable data was actually stolen from the network.

Intrusion Detection and Prevention Systems (IDS/IPS)

Intrusion detection and prevention systems can detect and block attacks on a network. Intrusion prevention systems are usually inline and can block attacks. A few warnings about IPS devices:

- Their number-one goal is to *not* bring down the network.
- Their number-two goal is to not block legitimate traffic.

Time after time attacks can slip by these systems. They will block the low-hanging fruit, but a sophisticated attacker can trivially bypass IDS/IPS devices. Commercial tools include TippingPoint, Sourcefire, ISS, and Fortinet. Open-source tools include Snort and Bro.

Network Traffic Pattern Behavior Analysis

Intrusion detection systems and vulnerability-scanning systems are only able to detect well-known vulnerabilities. A majority of enterprises have these systems as well as log aggregation systems but are unable to detect 0-day threats and other previously compromised machines. The answer to this problem is NetFlow data. NetFlow data shows all connections into and out of the network. There are commercial and open-source tools. Commercial tools are Arbor Networks and Mazu Networks. Open-source tools include nfdump and Argus.

Full Network Traffic Capture and Replay

Full packet capture tools allow security engineers to record and play back all the traffic on the network. This

---

7 Information Security Policy Made Easy, www.informationshield.com.
8 PCI Security Standards, https://www.pcisecuritystandards.org/.
9 DIACAP Certification and Accreditation standard, http://iase.disa.mil/ditscap/ditscap-to-diacap.html.

allows for validation of IDS/IPS alerts and validation of items that NetFlow or log data is showing. Commercial tools include Niksun, NetWitness, and NetScout. Open-source tools include Wireshark and tcpdump.

Secure Network and Management tools

It is important to secure the network and management tools. If physical separation is not possible, then at a very minimum logical separation must occur. For example:

- Separate the management network with a firewall.
- Ensure user space and management interfaces are on different subnets/VLANs.
- Use strong communication protocols such as SSH, SSL, and VPNs to connect to and communicate with the management interfaces.
- Avoid using out-of-band modems if possible. If absolutely necessary, use the callback feature on the modems.
- Have a local technician or datacenter operators connect the line only when remote dial-in access is needed, and then disconnect when done.
- Log all external maintenance access.

Restrict Remote Support

Best practice is to not allow remote support; however, most SANs have a "call home" feature that allows them to call back to the manufacturer for support. Managed network and security services are commonplace. If remote access for vendors is mandatory, take extreme care. Here are some things that can help make access to the SAN safe:

- Disable the remote "call home" feature in the SAN until needed.
- Do not open a port in the firewall and give direct external access to the SAN management station.
- If outsourcing management of a device, ensure that there is a VPN set up and verify that the data is transmitted encrypted.
- On mission-critical systems, do not allow external connections. Have internal engineers connect to the systems and use a tool such as WebEx or GoToAssist to allow the vendor to view while the trusted engineer controls the mouse and keyboard.

Attempt to Minimize User Error

It is not uncommon for a misconfiguration to cause a major outage. Not following proper procedure can cause major problems. Not all compromises are due to malicious behaviors; some may be due to mistakes made by trusted personnel.

Establish Proper Patch Management Procedures

Corporations today are struggling to keep up with all the vulnerabilities and patches for all the platforms they manage. With all the different technologies and operating systems it can be a daunting task. Mission-critical storage management gear and network gear cannot be patched on a whim whenever the administrator feels like it. There are Web sites dedicated to patch management software. Microsoft Windows Software Update Services (WSUS) is a free tool that only works with Windows. Other commercial tools can assist with cross-platform patch management deployment and automation:

- Schedule updates.
- Live within the change window.
- Establish a rollback procedure.
- Test patches in a lab if at all possible. Use virtual servers if possible, to save cost.
- Purchase identical lab gear if possible. Many vendors will sell "nonproduction" lab gear at more than 50% discount. This allows for test scenarios and patching in a nonproduction environment without rolling into production.
- After applying patches or firmware, validate to make sure that the equipment was actually correctly updated.

Use Configuration Management Tools

Many large organizations have invested large amounts of money in network and software configuration management tools to manage hundreds or thousands of devices around the network. These tools store network device and software configurations in a database format and allow for robust configuration management capabilities. An example is HP's Network Automation System,[10] which can do the following:

- Reduce costs by automating time-consuming manual compliance checks and configuration tasks.
- Pass audit and compliance requirements easily with proactive policy enforcement and out-of-the-box audit and compliance reports (IT Infrastructure Library (ITIL), Cardholder Information Security Program (CISP), HIPAA, SOX, GLBA, and others).
- Improve network security by recognizing and fixing security vulnerabilities before they affect the network, using an integrated security alert service.

---

10 HP Network Automation System, https://h10078.www1.hp.com/cda/hpms/display/main/hpms_content.jsp?zn=bto&cp=1-11-271-273_4000_100__.

- Increase network stability and uptime by preventing the inconsistencies and misconfigurations that are at the root of most problems.
- Use process-powered automation to deliver application integrations, which deliver full IT life-cycle workflow automation without scripting.
- Support SNMPv3 and IPv6, including dual-stack IPv4 and IPv6 support. HP Network Automation supports both of these technologies to provide flexibility in your protocol strategy and implementation.
- Use automated software image management to deploy wide-scale image updates quickly with audit and rollback capabilities.

Set Baseline Configurations

If a commercial tool is not available, there are still steps that can be taken. Use templates such as the ones provided by the Center for Internet Security or the National Security Agency. They offer security templates for multiple operating systems, software packages, and network devices. They are free of charge and can be modified to fit the needs of the organization. In addition:

- Create a base configuration for all production devices.
- Check with the vendor to see if they have baseline security guides. Many of them do internally and will provide them on request.
- Audit the baseline configurations.
- Script and automate as much as possible.

Center for Internet Security[11]

The Center for Internet Security (CIS) is a not-for-profit organization that helps enterprises reduce the risk of business and ecommerce disruptions resulting from inadequate technical security controls and provides enterprises with resources for measuring information security status and making rational security investment decisions.

National Security Agency[12]

NSA initiatives in enhancing software security cover both proprietary and open-source software, and we have successfully used both proprietary and open-source models in our research activities. NSA's work to enhance the security of software is motivated by one simple consideration:

---

11 Center for Internet Security, www.cisecurity.org.
12 National Security Agency security templates, www.nsa.gov/snac/index.cfm.

Use our resources as efficiently as possible to give NSA's customers the best possible security options in the most widely employed products. The objective of the NSA research program is to develop technologic advances that can be shared with the software development community through a variety of transfer mechanisms. The NSA does not favor or promote any specific software product or business model. Rather, it promotes enhanced security.

Vulnerability Scanning

PCI requirements include both internal and external vulnerability scanning. An area that is commonly overlooked when performing vulnerability scans is the proprietary devices and appliances that manage the SAN and network. Many of these have Web interfaces and run Web applications on board.

Vulnerability-scanning considerations:

- Use the Change Management/Change Control process to schedule the scans. Even trained security professionals who are good at not causing network problems sometimes cause network problems.
- Know exactly what will be scanned.
- Perform both internal and external vulnerability scans.
- Scan the Web application and appliances that manage the SAN and the network.
- Use more than one tool to scan.
- Document results and define metrics to know whether vulnerabilities are increasing or decreasing.
- Set up a scanning routine and scan regularly with updated tools.

System Hardening

System hardening is an important part of SAN security. Hardening includes all the SAN devices and any machines that connect to it as well as management tools. There are multiple organizations that provide hardening guides for free that can be used as a baseline and modified to fit the needs of the organization:

- Do not use shared accounts. If all engineers use the same account, there is no way to determine who logged in and when.
- Remove manufacturers' default passwords.
- If supported, use central authentication such as RADIUS.
- Use the principle of least privilege. Do not give all users on the device administrative credentials unless they absolutely need them. A user just working on storage does not need the ability to reconfigure the SAN switch.

Management Tools

It is common for management applications to have vulnerabilities that the vendor will refuse to fix or deny that they are vulnerabilities. They usually surface after a vulnerability scan or penetration test. When vulnerabilities are found, there are steps that can be taken to mitigate the risk:

- Contact the vendor regardless. The vendor needs to know that there are vulnerabilities and they should correct them.
- Verify if they have a hardening guide or any steps that can be taken to mitigate the risk.
- Physically or logically segregate the tools and apply strict ACLs or firewall rules.
- Place it behind an intrusion prevention device.
- Place behind a Web application firewall, if a Web application.
- Audit and log access very closely.
- Set up alerts for logins that occur outside normal hours.
- Use strong authentication if available.
- Review the logs.

Separate Areas of the SAN

In the world of security, a defense-in-depth strategy is often employed with an objective of aligning the security measures with the risks involved. This means that there must be security controls implemented at each layer that may create an exposure to the SAN system. Most organizations are motivated to protect sensitive (and business/mission-critical) data, which typically represents a small fraction of the total data. This narrow focus on the most important data can be leveraged as the starting point for data classification and a way to prioritize protection activities. The best way to be sure that there is a layered approach to security is to address each aspect of a SAN one by one and determine the best strategy to implement physical, logical, virtual, and access controls.

Physical

Segregating the production of some systems from other system classes is crucial to proper data classification and security. For example, if it is possible to physically segregate the quality assurance data from the research and development data, there is a smaller likelihood of data leakage between departments and therefore out to the rest of the world.

Logical

When a SAN is implemented, segregating storage traffic from normal server traffic is quite important because there is no need for the data to travel on the same switches as your end users browsing the Internet, for example. Logical

Unit Numbers (LUN) Masking, Fibre Channel Zoning, and IP VLANs can assist in separating data.

Virtual

One of the most prevalent uses recently for storage area networks is the storing of full-blown virtual machines that run from the SAN itself. With this newest of uses for SANs, the movement of virtual servers from one data store to another is something that is required in many scenarios and one that should be studied to identify potential risks.

Penetration Testing

Penetration testing like vulnerability scanning is becoming a regulatory requirement. Now people can go to jail for losing data and not complying with these regulations. Penetration-testing the SAN may be difficult due to the high cost of entry, as noted earlier. Most people don't have a SAN in their lab to practice pen testing.

Environments with custom applications and devices can be sensitive to heavy scans and attacks. Inexperienced people could inadvertently bring down critical systems. The security engineers who have experience working in these environments choose tools depending on the environment. They also tread lightly so that critical systems are not brought down. Boutique security firms might not have $100k to purchase a SAN so that their professional services personnel can do penetration tests on SANs. With the lack of skilled SAN technicians currently in the field, it is not likely that SAN engineers will be rapidly moving into the security arena. Depending on the size of the organization, there are things that can be done to facilitate successful penetration testing. An internal penetration testing team does the following:

- Have personnel cross-train and certify on the SAN platform in use.
- Provide the team access to the lab and establish a regular procedure to perform a pen test.
- Have a member of the SAN group as part of the pen-test team.
- Follow practices such as the OWASP guide for Web application testing and the OSSTMM for penetration-testing methodologies.

OWASP

The Open Web Application Security Project (OWASP; www.owasp.org) is a worldwide free and open community focused on improving the security of application software. Our mission is to make application security "visible" so that people and organizations can make informed decisions about application security risks.

OSSTMM

The Open Source Security Testing Methodology Manual (OSSTMM; www.isecom.org/osstmm/) is a peer-reviewed methodology for performing security tests and metrics. The OSSTMM test cases are divided into five channels (sections), which collectively test information and data controls, personnel security awareness levels, fraud and social engineering control levels, computer and telecommunications networks, wireless devices, mobile devices, physical security access controls, security processes, and physical locations such as buildings, perimeters, and military bases. The external penetration testing team does the following:

- Validates SAN testing experience through references and certification
- Avoids firms that do not have access to SAN storage gear
- Asks to see a sanitized report of a previous penetration test that included a SAN

Whether an internal or external penetration-testing group, it is a good idea to belong to one of the professional security associations in the area, such as the Information Systems Security Association (ISSA) or Information Systems Audit and Control Association (ISACA).

ISSA

ISSA (www.issa.org) is a not-for-profit, international organization of information security professionals and practitioners. It provides educational forums, publications, and peer interaction opportunities that enhance the knowledge, skill, and professional growth of its members.

ISACA

ISACA (www.isaca.org) got its start in 1967 when a small group of individuals with similar jobs—auditing controls in the computer systems that were becoming increasingly critical to the operations of their organizations—sat down to discuss the need for a centralized source of information and guidance in the field. In 1969 the group formalized, incorporating as the EDP Auditors Association. In 1976 the association formed an education foundation to undertake large-scale research efforts to expand the knowledge and value of the IT governance and control field.

Encryption

Encryption is the conversion of data into a form called *ciphertext* that cannot be easily understood by unauthorized

people. *Decryption* is the process of converting encrypted data back into its original form so that it can be understood.

Confidentiality

Confidentiality is the property whereby information is not disclosed to unauthorized parties. *Secrecy* is a term that is often used synonymously with confidentiality. Confidentiality is achieved using encryption to render the information unintelligible except by authorized entities.

The information may become intelligible again by using decryption. For encryption to provide confidentiality, the cryptographic algorithm and mode of operation must be designed and implemented so that an unauthorized party cannot determine the secret or private keys associated with the encryption or be able to derive the plaintext directly without deriving any keys.[13]

Data encryption can save a company time, money, and embarrassment. There are countless examples of lost and stolen media, especially hard drives and tape drives. A misplacement or theft can cause major headaches for an organization. Take, for example, the University of Miami[14]:

> A private off-site storage company used by the University of Miami has notified the University that a container carrying computer back-up tapes of patient information was stolen. The tapes were in a transport case that was stolen from a vehicle contracted by the storage company on March 17 in downtown Coral Gables, the company reported. Law enforcement is investigating the incident as one of a series of petty thefts in the area.
>
> Shortly after learning of the incident, the University determined it would be unlikely that a thief would be able to access the back-up tapes because of the complex and proprietary format in which they were written. Even so, the University engaged leading computer security experts at Terremark Worldwide[15] to independently ascertain the feasibility of accessing and extracting data from a similar set of back-up tapes.
>
> Anyone who has been a patient of a University of Miami physician or visited a UM facility since January 1, 1999, is likely included on the tapes. The data included names, addresses, Social Security numbers, or health information. The University will be notifying by mail the 47,000 patients whose data may have included credit card or other financial information regarding bill payment.

13 NIST Special Publication 800-57, Recommendation for Key Management Part 1, http://csrc.nist.gov/publications/nistpubs/800-57/SP800-57-Part1.pdf.
14 Data Loss Notification from the University of Miami, www6.miami.edu/dataincident/index.htm.
15 Terremark Worldwide, www.terremark.com

Even thought it was unlikely that the person who stole the tapes had access to the data or could read the data, the university still had to notify 47,000 people that their data may have been compromised. Had the tape drives been encrypted, they would not have been in the news at all and no one would have had to worry about personal data being compromised.

Deciding What to Encrypt

Deciding what type of data to encrypt and how best to do it can be a challenge. It depends on the type of data that is stored on the SAN. Encrypt backup tapes as well.

There are two main types of encryption to focus on: data in transit and data at rest. SNIA put out a white paper called *Encryption of Data At-Rest: Step-by-Step Checklist*, which outlines nine steps for encrypting data at rest:[16]

1. Understand confidentiality drivers.
2. Classify the data assets.
3. Inventory data assets.
4. Perform data flow analysis.
5. Determine the appropriate points of encryption.
6. Design encryption solution.
7. Begin data realignment.
8. Implement solution.
9. Activate encryption.

Many of the vendors implement encryption in different ways. NIST SP 800-57 contains best practices for key management and information about various cryptographic ciphers.

The following are the recommended minimum symmetric security levels, defined as bits of strength (not key size):

- 80 bits of security until 2010 (128-bit AES and 1024-bit RSA)
- 112 bits of security through 2030 (3DES, 128-AES and 2048-bit RSA)
- 128 bits of security beyond 2030 (128-AES and 3072-bit RSA)

Type of Encryption to Use

The type of encryption used should contain a strong algorithm and be publicly known. Algorithms such as ASE, RSA, SHA, and Twofish are known and tested. All the aforementioned encryption algorithms have been tested and proven to be strong if properly implemented. Organizations should be wary of vendors saying that they have their own "unknown" encryption algorithm. Many

times it is just data compression or a weak algorithm that the vendor wrote by itself. Though it sounds good in theory, the thousands of mathematicians employed by the NSA spend years and loads of computer power trying to break well-known encryption algorithms.

Proving That Data Is Encrypted

A well-architected encryption plan should be transparent to the end user of the data. The only way to know for sure that the data is encrypted is to verify the data. Data at rest can be verified using forensic tools such as dd for Unix or the free FTK[17] imager for Windows. Data in transit can be verified by network monitoring tools such as Wireshark.

Turn on event logging for any encryption hardware or software. Make sure it is logging when it turns on or off. Have a documented way to verify that the encryption was turned on while it had the sensitive data on the system (see Figure 34.2).

Encryption Challenges and Other Issues

No method of defense is perfect. Human error and computer vulnerabilities do pose encryption challenges (see Figure 34.3). A large financial firm had personal information on its network, including 34,000 credit cards with names and account numbers. The network administrator had left the decryption key on the server. After targeting the server for a year and a half, the attacker was able to get the decryption key and finally able to directly query the fully encrypted database and pull out 34,000 cards.

Logging

Logging is an important consideration when it comes to SAN security. There are all sorts of events that can be logged. When a security incident happens, having proper log information can mean the difference between solving the problem and not knowing whether your data was compromised. NIST has an excellent guide to Security Log Management. The SANS Institute has a guide on the top five most essential log reports.

There are multiple commercial vendors as well as open-source products for log management. Log management has evolved from standalone syslog servers to complex architectures for Security Event/Information Management. Acronyms used for these blend together as SEM, SIM, and SEIM. In addition to log data, they can take in data from IDSs, vulnerability assessment products, and many other security tools to centralize and speed up the analysis and

---

16 www.snia.org/forums/ssif/knowledge_center/white_papers.

17 Access Data Forensic Toolkit Imager, www.accessdata.com/downloads.html.

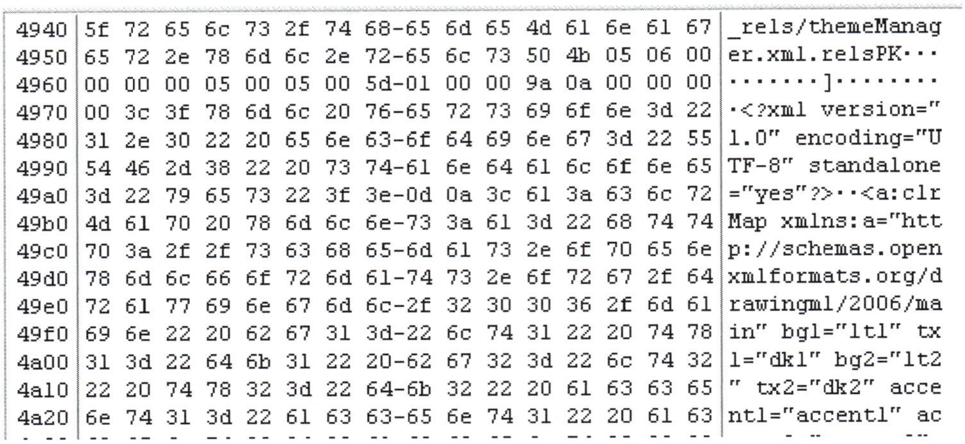

4940 5f 72 65 6c 73 2f 74 68-65 6d 65 4d 61 6e 61 67 _rels/themeManag
4950 65 72 2e 78 6d 6c 2e 72-65 6c 73 50 4b 05 06 00 er.xml.relsPK···
4960 00 00 00 05 00 05 00 5d-01 00 00 9a 0a 00 00 00 ·······]········
4970 00 3c 3f 78 6d 6c 20 76-65 72 73 69 6f 6e 3d 22 ·<?xml version="
4980 31 2e 30 22 20 65 6e 63-6f 64 69 6e 67 3d 22 55 1.0" encoding="U
4990 54 46 2d 38 22 20 73 74-61 6e 64 61 6c 6f 6e 65 TF-8" standalone
49a0 3d 22 79 65 73 22 3f 3e-0d 0a 3c 61 3a 63 6c 72 ="yes"?>··<a:clr
49b0 4d 61 70 20 78 6d 6c 6e-73 3a 61 3d 22 68 74 74 Map xmlns:a="htt
49c0 70 3a 2f 2f 73 63 68 65-6d 61 73 2e 6f 70 65 6e p://schemas.open
49d0 78 6d 6c 66 6f 72 6d 61-74 73 2e 6f 72 67 2f 64 xmlformats.org/d
49e0 72 61 77 69 6e 67 6d 6c-2f 32 30 30 36 2f 6d 61 rawingml/2006/ma
49f0 69 6e 22 20 62 67 31 3d-22 6c 74 31 22 20 74 78 in" bg1="lt1" tx
4a00 31 3d 22 64 6b 31 22 20-62 67 32 3d 22 6c 74 32 1="dk1" bg2="lt2
4a10 22 20 74 78 32 3d 22 64-6b 32 22 20 61 63 63 65 " tx2="dk2" acce
4a20 6e 74 31 3d 22 61 63 63-65 6e 74 31 22 20 61 63 nt1="accent1" ac

FIGURE 34.2 Notice the clear, legible text on the right.

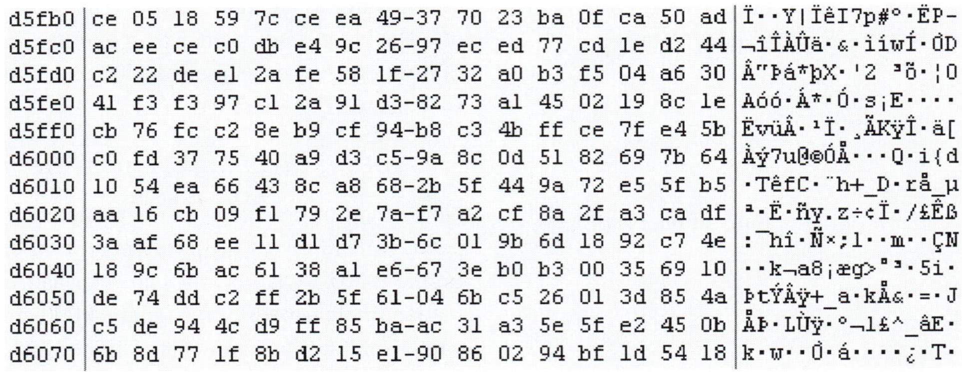

d5fb0 ce 05 18 59 7c ce ea 49-37 70 23 ba 0f ca 50 ad
d5fc0 ac ee ce c0 db e4 9c 26-97 ec ed 77 cd 1e d2 44
d5fd0 c2 22 de e1 2a fe 58 1f-27 32 a0 b3 f5 04 a6 30
d5fe0 41 f3 f3 97 c1 2a 91 d3-82 73 a1 45 02 19 8c 1e
d5ff0 cb 76 fc c2 8e b9 cf 94-b8 c3 4b ff ce 7f e4 5b
d6000 c0 fd 37 75 40 a9 d3 c5-9a 8c 0d 51 82 69 7b 64
d6010 10 54 ea 66 43 8c a8 68-2b 5f 44 9a 72 e5 5f b5
d6020 aa 16 cb 09 f1 79 2e 7a-f7 a2 cf 8a 2f a3 ca df
d6030 3a af 68 ee 11 d1 d7 3b-6c 01 9b 6d 18 92 c7 4e
d6040 18 9c 6b ac 61 38 a1 e6-67 3e b0 b3 00 35 69 10
d6050 de 74 dd c2 ff 2b 5f 61-04 6b c5 26 01 3d 85 4a
d6060 c5 de 94 4c d9 ff 85 ba-ac 31 a3 5e 5f e2 45 0b
d6070 6b 8d 77 1f 8b d2 15 e1-90 86 02 94 bf 1d 54 18

FIGURE 34.3 Notice Encrypted Data on the right-hand side.

processing of huge amounts of logs. More of a difference is being made between Security Event Management and audit logging. The former is geared toward looking at events of interest on which to take action; the latter is geared to compliance. In today's legal and compliance environment an auditor will ask an enterprise to immediately provide logs for a particular device for a time period such as the previous 90 days. With a solid log management infrastructure, this request becomes trivial and a powerful tool to help solve problems. NIST Special Publication 800-92[18] makes the following recommendations:

- Organizations should establish policies and procedures for log management.
- Organizations should prioritize log management appropriately throughout the organization.
- Organizations should create and maintain a log management infrastructure.
- Organizations should provide proper support for all staff with log management responsibilities.
- Organizations should establish standard log management operational processes.

Policies and Procedures

To establish and maintain successful log management activities, an organization should develop standard processes for performing log management. As part of the planning process, an organization should define its logging requirements and goals.

Prioritize Log Management

After an organization defines its requirements and goals for the log management process, it should then prioritize the requirements and goals based on the organization's perceived reduction of risk and the expected time and resources needed to perform log management functions.

Create and Maintain a Log Management Infrastructure

A log management infrastructure consists of the hardware, software, networks, and media used to generate, transmit, store, analyze, and dispose of log data. Log management

18 NIST SP 800-92 http://csrc.nist.gov/publications/nistpubs/800-92/SP800-92.pdf.

infrastructures typically perform several functions that support the analysis and security of log data.

Provide Support for Staff With Log Management Responsibilities

To ensure that log management for individual systems is performed effectively throughout the organization, the administrators of those systems should receive adequate support.

Establish a Log Management Operational Process

The major log management operational processes typically include configuring log sources, performing log analysis, initiating responses to identified events, and managing long-term storage.

What Events Should Be Logged for SANs?

For storage networks the same type of data should be collected as for other network devices, with focus on the storage management systems and any infrastructure that supports the SAN, such as the switches and servers. According to the SANS Institute, the top five most essential log reports[19] are as follows.

Attempts to Gain Access Through Existing Accounts

Failed authentication attempts can be an indication of a malicious user or process attempting to gain network access by performing password guessing. It can also be an indication that a local user account is attempting to gain a higher level of permissions to a system.

Failed File or Resource Access Attempts

Failed file or resource access attempts is a broad category that can impact many different job descriptions. In short, failed access attempts are an indication that someone is attempting to gain access to either a nonexistent resource or a resource to which they have not been granted the correct permissions.

Unauthorized Changes to Users, Groups and Services

The modification of user and group accounts, as well as system services, can be an indication that a system has become compromised. Clearly, modifications to all three will occur legitimately in an evolving network, but they warrant special attention because they can be a final indication that all other defenses have been breached and an intrusion has occurred.

Systems Most Vulnerable to Attack

As indicated in the original SANS Top 10 Critical Vulnerabilities list as well as the current Top 20, one of the most important steps you can take in securing your network is to stay up to date on patches. In an ideal world all systems would remain completely up to date on the latest patches; time management, legacy software, availability of resources, and so on can result in a less than ideal posture. A report that identifies the level of compliance of each network resource can be extremely helpful in setting priorities.

Suspicious or Unauthorized Network Traffic Patterns

Suspect traffic patterns can be described as unusual or unexpected traffic patterns on the local network. This not only includes traffic entering the local network but traffic leaving the network as well. This report option requires a certain level of familiarity with what is "normal" for the local network. With this in mind, administrators need to be knowledgeable of local traffic patterns to make the best use of these reports. With that said, there are some typical traffic patterns that can be considered to be highly suspect in nearly all environments.

6. CONCLUSION

The financial and IT resource benefits of consolidating information into a storage area network are compelling, and our dependence on this technology will continue to grow as our data storage needs grow exponentially. With this concentration and consolidation of critical information come security challenges and risks that must be recognized and appropriately addressed. In this chapter we covered these risks as well as the controls and processes that should be employed to protect the information stored on a SAN. Finally, we have emphasized why encryption of data at rest and in flight is a critical protection method that must be employed by the professional SAN administrator. Our intention is for you to understand all these risks to your SAN and to use the methods and controls described here to prevent you or your company from becoming a data loss statistic.

---

19 SANS Institute, www.sans.org/free_resources.php.

## Chapter 35

Risk Management

Sokratis K. Katsikas
University of Piraeus

Integrating security measures with the operational framework of an organization is neither a trivial nor an easy task. This explains to a large extent the low degree of security that information systems operating in contemporary businesses and organizations enjoy. Some of the most important difficulties that security professionals face when confronted with the task of introducing security measures in businesses and organizations are:

- The difficulty to justify the cost of the security measures
- The difficulty to establish communication between technical and administrative personnel
- The difficulty to assure active participation of users in the effort to secure the information system and to commit higher management to continuously supporting the effort
- The widely accepted erroneous perception of information systems security as a purely technical issue
- The difficulty to develop an integrated, efficient and effective information systems security plan
- The identification and assessment of the organizational impact that the implementation of a security plan entails

The difficulty in justifying the cost of the security measures, particularly those of a procedural and administrative nature, stems from the very nature of security itself. Indeed, the justification of the need for a security measure can only be proved "after the (unfortunate) event," whereas, at the same time, there is no way to prove that already implemented measures can adequately cope with a potential new threat. This cost does not only pertain to acquiring and installing mechanisms and tools for protection. It also includes the cost of human resources, the cost of educating and making users aware, and the cost for carrying out tasks and procedures relevant to security.

The difficulty in expressing the cost of the security measures in monetary terms is one of the fundamental factors that make the communication between technical and administrative personnel difficult. An immediate consequence of this is the difficulty in securing the continuous commitment of higher management to supporting the security enhancement effort. This becomes even more difficult when organizational and procedural security measures are proposed. Both management and users are concerned about the impact of these measures in their usual practice, particularly when the widely accepted concept that security is purely a technical issue is put into doubt.

Moreover, protecting an information system calls for an integrated, holistic study that will answer questions such as: Which elements of the information system do we want to protect? Which, among these, are the most important ones? What threats is the information system facing? What are its vulnerabilities? What security measures must be put in place? Answering these questions gives a good picture of the current state of the information system with regard to its security. As research[1] has shown, developing techniques and measures for security is not enough, since the most vulnerable point in any information system is the human user, operator, designer, or other human. Therefore, the development and operation of secure information systems must equally consider and take account of both technical and human factors. At the same time, the threats that an information system faces are characterized by variety, diversity, complexity, and continuous variation. As the technological and societal environment continuously evolves, threats change and evolve, too. Furthermore, both information systems and threats against them are dynamic; hence the need for continuous monitoring and managing of the information system security plan.

---

1 E. A. Kiountouzis and S. A. Kokolakis, "An analyst's view of information systems security", in *Information Systems Security: Facing the Information Society of the 21st Century,* Katsikas, S. K., and Gritzalis, D. (eds.), Chapman & Hall, 1996.

The most widely used methodology that aims at dealing with these issues is the information systems risk management methodology. This methodology adopts the concept of risk that originates in financial management, and substitutes the unachievable and immeasurable goal of fully securing the information system with the achievable and measurable goal of reducing the risk that the information system faces to within acceptable limits.

1. THE CONCEPT OF RISK

The concept of risk originated in the 17th century with the mathematics associated with gambling. At that time, risk referred to a combination of probability and magnitude of potential gains and losses. During the 18th century, risk, seen as a neutral concept, still considered both gains and losses and was employed in the marine insurance business. In the 19th century, risk emerged in the study of economics. The concept of risk, then, seen more negatively, caused entrepreneurs to call for special incentives to take the risk involved in investment. By the 20th century a total negative connotation was made when referring to outcomes of risk in engineering and science, with particular reference to the hazards posed by modern technological developments.[2,3]

Within the field of IT security, the risk R is calculated as the product of P, the probability of an exposure occurring a given number of times per year times C, the cost or loss attributed to such an exposure, that is, $R = P \times C$.[4]

The most recent standardized definition of risk comes from the ISO,[5] voted for on April 19, 2008, where the information security risk is defined as "the potential that a given threat will exploit vulnerabilities of an asset or group of assets and thereby cause harm to the organization."

To complete this definition, definitions of the terms *threat, vulnerability,* and *asset* are in order. These are as follows: A threat is "a potential cause of an incident, that may result in harm to system or organization." A vulnerability is "a weakness of an asset or group of assets that can be exploited by one or more threats." An asset is "anything that has value to the organization, its business operations and their continuity, including information resources

that support the organization's mission."[6] Additionally, harm results in impact, which, is "an adverse change to the level of business objectives achieved."[7] The relationships among these basic concepts are pictorially depicted in Figure 35.1.

2. EXPRESSING AND MEASURING RISK

As noted, risk "is measured in terms of a combination of the likelihood of an event and its consequence."[8] Because we are interested in events related to information security, we define an information security event as "an identified occurrence of a system, service or network state indicating a possible breach of information security policy or failure of safeguards, or a previously unknown situation that may be security relevant."[9] Additionally, an information security incident is "indicated by a single or a series of unwanted information security events that have a significant probability of compromising business operations and threatening information security."[10] These definitions actually invert the investment assessment model, where an investment is considered worth making when its cost is less than the product of the expected profit times the likelihood of the profit occurring. In our case, the risk R is defined as the product of the likelihood L of a security incident occurring times the impact I that will be incurred to the organization due to the incident, that is, $R = L \times I$.[11]

To measure risk, we adopt the fundamental principles and the scientific background of statistics and probability theory, particularly of the area known as Bayesian statistics, after the mathematician Thomas Bayes (1702–1761), who formalized the namesake theorem. Bayesian statistics is based on the view that the likelihood of an event happening in the future is measurable. This likelihood can be calculated if the factors affecting it are analyzed. For example, we are able to compute the probability

2 M. Gerber and R. von Solms, "Management of risk in the information age," *Computers & Security*, Vol. 24, pp. 16–30, 2005.

3 M. Douglas, "Risk as a forensic resource," *Daedalus*, Vol. 119, Issue 4, pp. 1–17, 1990.

4 R. Courtney, "Security risk assessment in electronic data processing," in the *AFIPS Conference Proceedings of the National Computer Conference 46*, AFIPS, Arlington, pp. 97–104, 1977.

5 ISO/IEC, "Information technology—Security techniques—information security risk management," ISO/IEC FDIS 27005:2008 (E).

6 British Standards Institute, "Information technology—Security techniques—Management of information and communications technology security—Part 1: Concepts and models for information and communications technology security management," BS ISO/IEC 13335-1:2004.

7 ISO/IEC, "Information technology—security techniques–information security risk management," ISO/IEC FDIS 27005:2008 (E).

8 ISO/IEC, "Information technology—security techniques–information security risk management," ISO/IEC FDIS 27005:2008 (E).

9 British Standards Institute, "Information technology—Security techniques—Information security incident management," BS ISO/IEC TR 18044:2004.

10 British Standards Institute, "Information technology—Security techniques—Information security incident management," BS ISO/IEC TR 18044:2004.

11 R. Baskerville, "Information systems security design methods: implications for information systems development," *ACM Computing Surveys*, Vol. 25, No. 4, pp. 375–414, 1993.

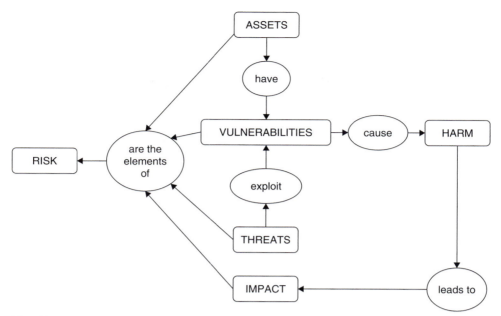

FIGURE 35.1 Risk and its related concepts.

of our data to be stolen as a function of the probability an intruder will attempt to intrude into our system and of the probability that he will succeed. In risk analysis terms, the former probability corresponds to the likelihood of the threat occurring and the latter corresponds to the likelihood of the vulnerability being successfully exploited. Thus, risk analysis assesses the likelihood that a security incident will happen by analyzing and assessing the factors that are related to its occurrence, that is, the threats and the vulnerabilities. Subsequently, it combines this likelihood with the impact resulting from the incident occurring to calculate the system risk. Risk analysis is a necessary prerequisite for subsequently treating risk. Risk treatment pertains to controlling the risk so that it remains within acceptable levels. Risk can be reduced by applying security measures; it can be transferred, perhaps by insuring; it can be avoided; or it can be accepted, in the sense that the organization accepts the likely impact of a security incident.

The likelihood of a security incident occurring is a function of the likelihood that a threat appears and of the likelihood that the threat can successfully exploit the relevant system vulnerabilities. The consequences of the occurrence of a security incident are a function of the likely impact that the incident will have to the organization as a result of the harm that the organization assets will sustain. Harm, in turn, is a function of the value of the assets to the organization. Thus, the risk R is a function of four elements: (a) V, the value of the assets; (b) T, the severity and likelihood of appearance of the threats;

(c) V, the nature and the extent of the vulnerabilities and the likelihood that a threat can successfully exploit them; and (d) I, the likely impact of the harm should the threat succeed, that is, $R = f(A, T, V, I)$.

If the impact is expressed in monetary terms, the likelihood being dimensionless, then risk can be also expressed in monetary terms. This approach has the advantage of making the risk directly comparable to the cost of acquiring and installing security measures. Since security is often one of several competing alternatives for capital investment, the existence of a cost/benefit analysis that would offer proof that security will produce benefits that equal or exceed its cost is of great interest to the management of the organization. Of even more interest to management is the analysis of the investment opportunity costs, that is, its comparison to other capital investment options.[12] However, expressing risk in monetary terms is not always possible or desirable, since harm to some kinds of assets (e.g., human life) cannot (and should not) be assessed in monetary terms. This is why risk is usually expressed in nonmonetary terms, on a simple dimensionless scale.

Assets in an organization are usually quite diverse. Because of this diversity, it is likely that some assets that have a known monetary value (e.g., hardware) can be valued in the local currency, whereas others of a more qualitative nature (e.g., data or information) may be assigned a

12 R. Baskerville, "Risk analysis as a source of professional knowledge," *Computers & Security*, Vol. 10, pp. 749–764, 1991.

numerical value based on the organization's perception of their value. This value is assessed in terms of the assets' importance to the organization or their potential value in different business opportunities. The legal and business requirements are also taken into account, as are the impacts to the asset itself and to the related business interests resulting from a loss of one or more of the information security attributes (confidentiality, integrity, availability). One way to express asset values is to use the business impacts that unwanted incidents, such as disclosure, modification, nonavailability, and/or destruction, would have to the asset and the related business interests that would be directly or indirectly damaged. An information security incident can impact more than one asset or only a part of an asset. Impact is related to the degree of success of the incident. Impact is considered as having either an immediate (operational) effect or a future (business) effect that includes financial and market consequences. Immediate (operational) impact is either direct or indirect.

Direct impact may result because of the financial replacement value of lost (part of) asset or the cost of acquisition, configuration and installation of the new asset or backup, or the cost of suspended operations due to the incident until the service provided by the asset(s) is restored. Indirect impact may result because financial resources needed to replace or repair an asset would have been used elsewhere (opportunity cost) or from the cost of interrupted operations or due to potential misuse of information obtained through a security breach or because of violation of statutory or regulatory obligations or of ethical codes of conduct.[13]

These considerations should be reflected in the asset values. This is why asset valuation (particularly of intangible assets) is usually done through impact assessment. Thus, impact valuation is not performed separately but is rather embedded within the asset valuation process.

The responsibility for identifying a suitable asset valuation scale lies with the organization. Usually, a three-value scale (low, medium, and high) or a five-value scale (negligible, low, medium, high, and very high) is used.[14]

Threats can be classified as deliberate or accidental. The likelihood of deliberate threats depends on the motivation, knowledge, capacity, and resources available to possible attackers and the attractiveness of assets to sophisticated attacks. On the other hand, the likelihood of accidental threats can be estimated using statistics and experience. The likelihood of these threats might also be related to the organization's proximity to sources of danger, such as major roads or rail routes, and factories dealing with dangerous material such as chemical materials or petroleum. Also the organization's geographical location will affect the possibility of extreme weather conditions. The likelihood of human errors (one of the most common accidental threats) and equipment malfunction should also be estimated.[15] As already noted, the responsibility for identifying a suitable threat valuation scale lies with the organization. What is important here is that the interpretation of the levels is consistent throughout the organization and clearly conveys the differences between the levels to those responsible for providing input to the threat valuation process. For example, if a three-value scale is used, the value *low* can be interpreted to mean that it is not likely that the threat will occur, there are no incidents, statistics, or motives that indicate that this is likely to happen. The value *medium* can be interpreted to mean that it is possible that the threat will occur, there have been incidents in the past or statistics or other information that indicate that this or similar threats have occurred sometime before, or there is an indication that there might be some reasons for an attacker to carry out such action. Finally, the value *high* can be interpreted to mean that the threat is expected to occur, there are incidents, statistics, or other information that indicate that the threat is likely to occur, or there might be strong reasons or motives for an attacker to carry out such action.[16]

Vulnerabilities can be related to the physical environment of the system, to the personnel, management, and administration procedures and security measures within the organization, to the business operations and service delivery or to the hardware, software, or communications equipment and facilities. Vulnerabilities are reduced by installed security measures. The nature and extent as well as the likelihood of a threat successfully exploiting the three former classes of vulnerabilities can be estimated based on information on past incidents, on new developments and trends, and on experience. The nature and extent as well as the likelihood of a threat successfully exploiting the latter class, often termed technical vulnerabilities, can be estimated using automated vulnerability-scanning tools, security testing and evaluation, penetration testing, or code review.[17]

---

13 ISO/IEC, "Information technology—security techniques–information security risk management," ISO/IEC FDIS 27005:2008 (E).
14 British Standards Institute, "ISMSs—Part 3: Guidelines for information security risk management," BS 7799-3:2006.

15 British Standards Institute, "ISMSs—Part 3: Guidelines for information security risk management," BS 7799-3:2006.
16 British Standards Institute, "ISMSs—Part 3: Guidelines for information security risk management," BS 7799-3:2006.
17 ISO/IEC, "Information technology—security techniques–information security risk management," ISO/IEC FDIS 27005:2008 (E).

TABLE 35.1 Risk management constituent processes

ISO/IEC FDIS 27005:2008 (E)	BS 7799-3:2006	SP 800-30
Context establishment	Organizational context	
Risk assessment	Risk assessment	Risk assessment
Risk treatment	Risk treatment and management decision making	Risk mitigation
Risk acceptance		
Risk communication	Ongoing risk management activities	
Risk monitoring and review		Evaluation and assessment

As in the case of threats, the responsibility for identifying a suitable vulnerability valuation scale lies with the organization. If a three-value scale is used, the value *low* can be interpreted to mean that the vulnerability is hard to exploit and the protection in place is good. The value *medium* can be interpreted to mean that the vulnerability might be exploited, but some protection is in place. The value *high* can be interpreted to mean that it is easy to exploit the vulnerability and there is little or no protection in place.[18]

3. THE RISK MANAGEMENT METHODOLOGY

The term *methodology* means an organized set of principles and rules that drives action in a particular field of knowledge. A *method* is a systematic and orderly procedure or process for attaining some objective. A *tool* is any instrument or apparatus that is necessary to the performance of some task. Thus, methodology is the study or description of methods.[19] A methodology is instantiated and materializes by a set of methods, techniques, and tools. A methodology does not describe specific methods; nevertheless, it does specify several processes that need to be followed. These processes constitute a generic framework. They may be broken down into subprocesses, they may be combined, or their sequence may change. However, every risk management exercise must carry out these processes in some form or another.

Risk management consists of six processes, namely context establishment, risk assessment, risk treatment, risk

acceptance, risk communication, and risk monitoring and review.[20] This is more or less in line with the approach where four processes are identified as the constituents of risk management, namely, putting information security risks in the organizational context, risk assessment, risk treatment, and management decision-making and ongoing risk management activities.[21] Alternatively, risk management is seen to comprise three processes, namely risk assessment, risk mitigation, and evaluation and assessment.[22] Table 35.1 depicts the relationships among these processes.[23,24]

Context Establishment

The context establishment process receives as input all relevant information about the organization. Establishing the context for information security risk management determines the purpose of the process. It involves setting the basic criteria to be used in the process, defining the scope and boundaries of the process, and establishing an appropriate organization operating the process. The output of context establishment process is the specification of these parameters.

The purpose may be to support an information security management system (ISMS); to comply with legal requirements and to provide evidence of due diligence;

18 British Standards Institute, "ISMSs—Part 3: Guidelines for information security risk management," BS 7799-3:2006.

19 R. Baskerville, "Risk analysis as a source of professional knowledge," *Computers & Security*, Vol. 10, pp. 749–764, 1991.

20 ISO/IEC, "Information technology—security techniques–information security risk management," ISO/IEC FDIS 27005:2008 (E).

21 British Standards Institute, "ISMSs—Part 3: Guidelines for information security risk management," BS 7799-3:2006.

22 G. Stoneburner, A. Goguen and A. Feringa, *Risk Management guide for information technology systems*, National Institute of Standards and Technology, Special Publication SP 800-30, 2002.

23 ISO/IEC, "Information technology—security techniques–information security risk management," ISO/IEC FDIS 27005:2008 (E).

24 British Standards Institute, "ISMSs—Part 3: Guidelines for information security risk management," BS 7799-3:2006.

to prepare for a business continuity plan; to prepare for an incident reporting plan; or to describe the information security requirements for a product, a service, or a mechanism. Combinations of these purposes are also possible.

The basic criteria include risk evaluation criteria, impact criteria, and risk acceptance criteria. When setting risk evaluation criteria the organization should consider the strategic value of the business information process; the criticality of the information assets involved; legal and regulatory requirements and contractual obligations; operational and business importance of the attributes of information security; and stakeholders expectations and perceptions, and negative consequences for goodwill and reputation. The impact criteria specify the degree of damage or costs to the organization caused by an information security event. Developing impact criteria involves considering the level of classification of the impacted information asset; breaches of information security; impaired operations; loss of business and financial value; disruption of plans and deadlines; damage of reputation; and breaches of legal, regulatory or contractual requirements. The risk acceptance criteria depend on the organization's policies, goals, objectives and the interest of its stakeholders. When developing risk acceptance criteria the organization should consider business criteria; legal and regulatory aspects; operations; technology; finance; and social and humanitarian factors.[25]

The scope of the process needs to be defined to ensure that all relevant assets are taken into account in the subsequent risk assessment. Any exclusion from the scope needs to be justified. Additionally, the boundaries need to be identified to address those risks that might arise through these boundaries. When defining the scope and boundaries, the organization needs to consider its strategic business objectives, strategies, and policies; its business processes; its functions and structure; applicable legal, regulatory, and contractual requirements; its information security policy; its overall approach to risk management; its information assets; its locations and their geographical characteristics; constraints that affect it; expectations of its stakeholders; its socio-cultural environment; and its information exchange with its environment. This involves studying the organization (i.e., its main purpose, its business; its mission; its values; its structure; its organizational chart; and its strategy). It also involves identifying its constraints. These may be of a political, cultural, or strategic nature; they may be territorial, organizational, structural, functional, personnel, budgetary, technical, or

environmental constraints; or they could be constraints arising from preexisting processes. Finally, it entails identifying legislation, regulations, and contracts.[26]

Setting up and maintaining the organization for information security risk management fulfills part of the requirement to determine and provide the resources needed to establish, implement, operate, monitor, review, maintain, and improve an ISMS.[27] The organization to be developed will bear responsibility for the development of the information security risk management process suitable for the organization; for the identification and analysis of the stakeholders; for the definition of roles and responsibilities of all parties, both external and internal to the organization; for the establishment of the required relationships between the organization and stakeholders, interfaces to the organization's high-level risk management functions, as well as interfaces to other relevant projects or activities; for the definition of decision escalation paths; and for the specification of records to be kept. Key roles in this organization are the senior management; the chief information officer (CIO); the system and information owners; the business and functional managers; the information systems security officers (ISSO); the IT security practitioners; and the security awareness trainers (security/subject matter professionals).[28] Additional roles that can be explicitly defined are those of the *risk assessor* and of the *security risk manager.*[29]

Risk Assessment

This process comprises two subprocesses, namely risk analysis and risk evaluation. Risk analysis, in turn, comprises risk identification and risk estimation. The process receives as input the output of the context establishment process. It identifies, quantifies or qualitatively describes risks and prioritizes them against the risk evaluation criteria established within the course of the context establishment process and according to objectives relevant to the organization. It is often conducted in more than one iteration, the first being a high-level assessment aiming at identifying potentially high risks that warrant further assessment, whereas the second and possibly

25 ISO/IEC, "Information technology—security techniques—information security risk management," ISO/IEC FDIS 27005:2008 (E).

26 ISO/IEC, "Information technology—security techniques—information security risk management," ISO/IEC FDIS 27005:2008 (E).
27 ISO/IEC, "Information security management—specification with guidance for use," ISO 27001.
28 G. Stoneburner, A. Goguen and A. Feringa, *Risk Management guide for information technology systems*, National Institute of Standards and Technology, Special Publication SP 800-30, 2002.
29 British Standards Institute, "ISMSs—Part 3: Guidelines for information security risk management," BS 7799-3:2006.

subsequent iterations entail further in-depth examination of potentially high risks revealed in the first iteration. The output of the process is a list of assessed risks prioritized according to risk evaluation criteria.[30]

Risk identification seeks to determine what could happen to cause a potential loss and to gain insight into how, where, and why the loss might happen. It involves a number of steps, namely identification of assets; identification of threats; identification of existing security measures; identification of vulnerabilities; and identification of consequences. Input to the subprocess is the scope and boundaries for the risk assessment to be conducted, an asset inventory, information on possible threats, documentation of existing security measures, possibly preexisting risk treatment implementation plans, and the list of business processes. The output of the subprocess is a list of assets to be risk-managed together with a list of business processes related to these assets; a list of threats on these assets; a list of existing and planned security measures, their implementation and usage status; a list of vulnerabilities related to assets, threats and already installed security measures; a list of vulnerabilities that do not relate to any identified threat; and a list of incident scenarios with their consequences, related to assets and business processes.[31]

Two kinds of assets can be distinguished, namely *primary assets*, which include business processes and activities and information, and *supporting assets*, which include hardware, software, network, personnel, site, and the organization's structure. Hardware assets comprise data-processing equipment (transportable and fixed), peripherals, and media. Software assets comprise the operating system; service, maintenance or administration software; and application software. Network assets comprise medium and supports, passive or active relays, and communication interfaces. Personnel assets comprise decision makers, users, operation/maintenance staff, and developers. The site assets comprise the location (and its external environment, premises, zone, essential services, communication and utilities characteristics) and the organization (and its authorities, structure, the project or system organization and its subcontractors, suppliers and manufacturers).[32]

Threats are classified according to their type and to their origin. Threat types are physical damage (e.g., fire, water, pollution); natural events (e.g., climatic phenomenon, seismic phenomenon, volcanic phenomenon); loss of

essential services (e.g., failure of air-conditioning, loss of power supply, failure of telecommunication equipment); disturbance due to radiation (electromagnetic radiation, thermal radiation, electromagnetic pulses); compromise of information (eavesdropping, theft of media or documents, retrieval of discarded or recycled media); technical failures (equipment failure, software malfunction, saturation of the information system); unauthorized actions (fraudulent copying of software, corruption of data, unauthorized use of equipment); and compromise of functions (error in use, abuse of rights, denial of actions).[33] Threats are classified according to origin into deliberate, accidental or environmental. A deliberate threat is an action aiming at information assets (e.g., remote spying, illegal processing of data); an accidental threat is an action that can accidentally damage information assets (equipment failure, software malfunction); and an environmental threat is any threat that is not based on human action (a natural event, loss of power supply). Note that a threat type may have multiple origins.

Vulnerabilities are classified according to the asset class they relate to. Therefore, vulnerabilities are classified as hardware (e.g., susceptibility to humidity, dust, soiling; unprotected storage); software (no or insufficient software testing, lack of audit trail); network (unprotected communication lines, insecure network architecture); personnel (inadequate recruitment processes, lack of security awareness); site (location in an area susceptible to flood, unstable power grid); and organization (lack of regular audits, lack of continuity plans).[34]

Risk estimation is done either quantitatively or qualitatively. Qualitative estimation uses a scale of qualifying attributes to describe the magnitude of potential consequences (e.g., low, medium or high) and the likelihood that these consequences will occur. Quantitative estimation uses a scale with numerical values for both consequences and likelihood. In practice, qualitative estimation is used first, to obtain a general indication of the level of risk and to reveal the major risks. It is then followed by a quantitative estimation on the major risks identified.

Risk estimation involves a number of steps, namely assessment of consequences (through valuation of assets); assessment of incident likelihood (through threat and vulnerability valuation); and assigning values to the likelihood and the consequences of a risk. We discussed valuation of assets, threats, and vulnerabilities in an earlier

30 ISO/IEC, "Information technology—security techniques—information security risk management," ISO/IEC FDIS 27005:2008 (E).
31 ISO/IEC, "Information technology—security techniques—information security risk management," ISO/IEC FDIS 27005:2008 (E).
32 ISO/IEC, "Information technology—security techniques—information security risk management," ISO/IEC FDIS 27005:2008 (E).
33 ISO/IEC, "Information technology—security techniques—information security risk management," ISO/IEC FDIS 27005:2008 (E).
34 ISO/IEC, "Information technology—security techniques—information security risk management," ISO/IEC FDIS 27005:2008 (E).

section. Input to the subprocess is the output of the risk identification subprocess. Its output is a list of risks with value levels assigned.

Having valuated assets, threats, and vulnerabilities, we should be able to calculate the resulting risk, if the function relating these to risk is known. Establishing an analytic function for this purpose is probably impossible and certainly ineffective. This is why, in practice, an empirical matrix is used for this purpose. Such a matrix, an example of which is shown in Table 35.2, links asset values and threat and vulnerability levels to the resulting risk. In this example, asset values are expressed on a 0–4 scale, whereas threat and vulnerability levels are expressed on a Low-Medium-High scale. The risk values are expressed on a scale of 1 to 8. When linking the asset values and the threats and vulnerabilities, consideration needs to be given to whether the threat/vulnerability combination could cause problems to confidentiality, integrity, and/or availability. Depending on the results of these considerations, the appropriate asset value(s) should be chosen, that is, the one that has been selected to express the impact of a loss of confidentiality, or the one that has been selected to express the loss of integrity, or the one chosen to express the loss of availability. Using this method can lead to multiple risks for each of the assets, depending on the particular threat/vulnerability combination considered.[35]

Finally, the risk evaluation process receives as input the output of the risk analysis process. It compares the levels of risk against the risk evaluation criteria and risk acceptance criteria that were established within the context establishment process. The process uses the understanding of risk obtained by the risk assessment process to make decisions about future actions. These decisions include whether an activity should be undertaken and setting priorities for risk treatment. The output of the process is a list of risks prioritized according to the risk evaluation criteria, in relation to the incident scenarios that lead to those risks.

Risk Treatment

When the risk is calculated, the risk assessment process finishes. However, our actual ultimate goal is treating the risk. The risk treatment process aims at selecting security measures to reduce, retain, avoid, or transfer the risks and at defining a risk treatment plan. The process receives as input the output of the risk assessment process and produces as output the risk treatment plan and the residual risks subject to the acceptance decision by the management of the organization.

The options available to treat risk are to reduce it, to accept it, to avoid it, or to transfer it. Combinations of these options are also possible. The factors that might influence the decision are the cost each time the incident related to the risk happens; how frequently it is expected to happen; the organization's attitude toward risk; the ease of implementation of the security measures required to treat the risk; the resources available; the current business/technology priorities; and organizational and management politics.[37]

For all those risks where the option to reduce the risk has been chosen, appropriate security measures should be

TABLE 35.2 Example Risk Calculation Matrix[36]

Asset Value	Level of Threat								
	Low			Medium			High		
	Level of Vulnerability								
	L	M	H	L	M	H	L	M	H
0	0	1	2	1	2	3	2	3	4
1	1	2	3	2	3	4	3	4	5
2	2	3	4	3	4	5	4	5	6
3	3	4	5	4	5	6	5	6	7
4	4	5	6	5	6	7	6	7	8

35 British Standards Institute, "ISMSs—Part 3: Guidelines for information security risk management," BS 7799-3:2006.

36 British Standards Institute, "ISMSs—Part 3: Guidelines for information security risk management," BS 7799-3:2006.
37 ISO/IEC, "Information technology—security techniques—information security risk management," ISO/IEC FDIS 27005:2008 (E).

implemented to reduce the risks to the level that has been identified as acceptable, or at least as much as is feasible toward that level. These questions then arise: How much can we reduce the risk? Is it possible to achieve zero risk?

Zero risk is possible when either the cost of an incident is zero or when the likelihood of the incident occurring is zero. The cost of an incident is zero when the value of the implicated asset is zero or when the impact to the organization is zero. Therefore, if one or more of these conditions are found to hold during the risk assessment process, it is meaningless to take security measures. On the other hand, the likelihood of an incident occurring being zero is not possible, because the threats faced by an open system operating in a dynamic, hence highly variable, environment, as contemporary information systems do, and the causes that generate them are extremely complex; human behavior, which is extremely difficult to predict and model, plays a very important role in securing information systems; and the resources that a business or organization has at its disposal are finite.

When faced with a nonzero risk, our interest focuses on reducing the risk to acceptable levels. Because risk is a nondecreasing function in all its constituents, security measures can reduce it by reducing these constituents. Since the asset value cannot be directly reduced,[38] it is possible to reduce risk by reducing the likelihood of the threat occurring or the likelihood of the vulnerability being successfully exploited or the impact should the threat succeed. Which of these ways (or a combination of them) an organization chooses to adopt to protect its assets is a business decision and depends on the business requirements, the environment, and the circumstances in which the organization needs to operate. There is no universal or common approach to the selection of security measures. A possibility is to assign numerical values to the efficiency of each security measure, on a scale that matches that in which risks are expressed, and select all security measures that are relevant to the particular risk and have an efficiency score of at least equal to the value of the risk. Several sources provide lists of potential security measures.[39,40]

Documenting the selected security measures is important in supporting certification and enables the organization to track the implementation of the selected security measures.

When considering reducing a risk, several constraints may appear. These may be related to the timeframe; to financial or technical issues; to the way the organization operates or to its culture; to the environment within which the organization operates; to the applicable legal framework or to ethics; to the ease of use of the appropriate security measures; to the availability and suitability of personnel; or to the difficulties of integrating new and existing security measures. Due to the existence of these constraints, it is likely that some risks will exist for which either the organization cannot install appropriate security measures or for which the cost of implementing appropriate measures outweighs the potential loss through the incident related to the risk occurring. In these cases, a decision may be made to accept the risk and live with the consequences if the incident related to the risk occurs. These decisions must be documented so that management is aware of its risk position and can knowingly accept the risk. The importance of this documentation has led risk acceptance to be identified as a separate process.[41] A special case where particular attention must be paid is when an incident related to a risk is deemed to be highly unlikely to occur but, if it occurred, the organization would not survive. If such a risk is deemed to be unacceptable but too costly to reduce, the organization could decide to transfer it.

Risk transfer is an option whereby it is difficult for the organization to reduce the risk to an acceptable level or the risk can be more economically transferred to a third party. Risks can be transferred using insurance. In this case, the question of what is a fair premium arises.[42] Another possibility is to use third parties or outsourcing partners to handle critical business assets or processes if they are suitably equipped for doing so. Combining both options is also possible; in this case, the fair premium may be determined.[43]

---

38 As we will see later, it is possible to indirectly reduce the value of an asset. For example, if sensitive personal data are stored and the cost of protecting them is high, it is possible to decide that such data are too costly to continue storing. This constitutes a form of risk avoidance. As another example, we may decide that the cost for protecting our equipment is too high and to resort to outsourcing. This is a form of risk transfer.

39 ISO/IEC, "Information security management—specification with guidance for use," ISO 27001.

40 British Standards Institute, "Information technology—Security techniques—Information security incident management," BS ISO/IEC 17799:2005.

41 ISO/IEC, "Information technology—security techniques—information security risk management," ISO/IEC FDIS 27005:2008 (E).

42 C. Lambrinoudakis, S. Gritzalis, P. Hatzopoulos, A. N. Yannacopoulos, and S. K. Katsikas, "A formal model for pricing information systems insurance contracts," Computer Standards and Interfaces, Vol. 27, pp. 521–532, 2005.

43 S. Gritzalis, A. N. Yannacopoulos, C. Lambrinoudakis, P. Hatzopoulos, S. K. Katsikas, "A probabilistic model for optimal insurance contracts against security risks and privacy violation in IT outsourcing environments," International Journal of Information Security, Vol. 6, pp. 197–211, 2007.

Risk avoidance describes any action where the business activities or ways to conduct business are changed to avoid any risk occurring. For example, risk avoidance can be achieved by not conducting certain business activities, by moving assets away from an area of risk, or by deciding not to process particularly sensitive information. Risk avoidance entails that the organization consciously accepts the impact likely to occur if an incident occurs. However, the organization chooses not to install the required security measures to reduce the risk. There are several cases where this option is exercised, particularly when the required measures contradict the culture and/or the policy of the organization.

After the risk treatment decision(s) have been taken, there will always be risks remaining. These are called *residual risks*. Residual risks can be difficult to assess, but at least an estimate should be made to ensure that sufficient protection is achieved. If the residual risk is unacceptable, the risk treatment process may be repeated.

Once the risk treatment decisions have been taken, the activities to implement these decisions need to be identified and planned. The risk treatment plan needs to identify limiting factors and dependencies, priorities, deadlines and milestones, resources, including any necessary approvals for their allocation, and the critical path of the implementation.

Risk Communication

Risk communication is a horizontal process that interacts bidirectionally with all other processes of risk management. Its purpose is to establish a common understanding of all aspects of risk among all the organization's stakeholders. Common understanding does not come automatically, since it is likely that perceptions of risk vary widely due to differences in assumptions, needs, concepts, and concerns. Establishing a common understanding is important, since it influences decisions to be taken and the ways in which such decisions are implemented. Risk communication must be made according to a well-defined plan that should include provisions for risk communication under both normal and emergency conditions.

Risk Monitoring and Review

Risk management is an ongoing, never-ending process that is assigned to an individual, a team, or an outsourced third party, depending on the organization's size and operational characteristics. Within this process, implemented security measures are regularly monitored and reviewed to ensure that they function correctly and effectively and that changes in the environment have not

rendered them ineffective. Because over time there is a tendency for the performance of any service or mechanism to deteriorate, monitoring is intended to detect this deterioration and initiate corrective action. Maintenance of security measures should be planned and performed on a regular, scheduled basis.

The results from an original security risk assessment exercise need to be regularly reviewed for change, since there are several factors that could change the originally assessed risks. Such factors may be the introduction of new business functions, a change in business objectives and/or processes, a review of the correctness and effectiveness of the implemented security measures, the appearance of new or changed threats and/or vulnerabilities, or changes external to the organization. After all these different changes have been taken into account, the risk should be recalculated and *necessary* changes to the risk treatment decisions and security measures identified and documented.

Regular internal audits should be scheduled and should be conducted by an independent party that does not need to be from outside the organization. Internal auditors should not be under the supervision or control of those responsible for the implementation or daily management of the ISMS. Additionally, audits by an external body are not only useful, they are essential for certification.

Finally, complete, accessible, and correct documentation and a controlled process to manage documents are necessary to support the ISMS, although the scope and detail will vary from organization to organization. Aligning these documentation details with the documentation requirements of other management systems, such as ISO 9001, is certainly possible and constitutes good practice. Figure 35.2 pictorially summarizes the different processes within the risk management methodology, as we discussed earlier.

Integrating Risk Management into the System Development Life Cycle

Risk management must be totally integrated into the system development life cycle. This cycle consists of five phases: initiation; development or acquisition; implementation; operation or maintenance; and disposal. Within the initiation phase, identified risks are used to support the development of the system requirements, including security requirements and a security concept of operations. In the development or acquisition phase, the risks identified can be used to support the security analyses of the system that may lead to architecture and design tradeoffs during system development. In the implementation phase, the risk management process supports the assessment of

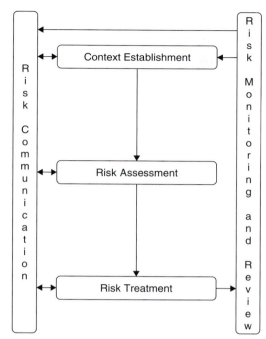

FIGURE 35.2 The risk management methodology.

the system implementation against its requirements and within its modeled operational environment. In the operation or maintenance phase, risk management activities are whenever major changes are made to a system in its operational environment. Finally, in the disposal phase, risk management activities are performed for system components that will be disposed of or replaced to ensure that the hardware and software are properly disposed of, that residual data is appropriately handled, and that system migration is conducted in a secure and systematic manner.[44]

Critique of Risk Management as a Methodology

Risk management as a scientific methodology has been criticized as being shallow. The main reason for this rather strong and probably unfair criticism is that risk management does not provide for feedback of the results of the selected security measures or of the risk treatment decisions. In most cases, even though the trend has already changed, information systems security is a low-priorityproject for management, until some security incident happens. Then, and only then, does management

44 G. Stoneburner, A. Goguen and A. Feringa, *Risk Management Guide for Information Technology Systems*, National Institute of Standards and Technology, Special Publication SP 800-30, 2002.

seriously engage in an effort to improve security measures. However, after a while, the problem stops being the center of interest, and what remains is a number of security measures, some specialized hardware and software, and an operationally more complex system. Unless an incident happens again, there is no way for management to know whether their efforts were really worthwhile. After all, in many cases the information system had operated for years in the past without problems, without the security improvements that the security professionals recommended.

The risk management methodology, as has already been stated, is based on the scientific foundations of statistical decision making. The Bayes Theorem, on which the theory is based, pertains to the statistical revision of *a priori* probabilities, providing *a posteriori* probabilities, and is applied when a decision is sought based on imperfect information. In risk management, the decision for quantifying an event may be a function of additional factors, other than the probability of the event itself occurring. For example, the probability for a riot to occur may be related to the stability of the political system. Thus, the calculation of this probability should involve quantified information relevant to the stability of the political system. The overall model accepts the possibility that any information (e.g., "The political system is stable") may be inaccurate. In comparison to this formal framework, risk management, as applied by the security professionals, is simplistic. Indeed, by avoiding the complexity that accompanies the formal probabilistic modeling of risks and uncertainty, risk management looks more like a process that attempts to guess rather than formally predict the future on the basis of statistical evidence.

Finally, the risk management methodology is highly subjective in assessing the value of assets, the likelihood of threats occurring, the likelihood of vulnerabilities being successfully exploited by threats, and the significance of the impact. This subjectivity is frequently obscured by the formality of the underlying mathematical-probabilistic models, the systematic way in which most risk analysis methods work, and the objectivity of the tools that support these methods.

If indeed the skepticism about the scientific soundness of the risk management methodology is justified, the question: Why, then, has risk management as a practice survived so long? becomes crucial. There are several answers to this question.

Risk management is a very important instrument in designing, implementing, and operating secure information systems, because it systematically classifies and drives the process of deciding how to treat risks. In doing so, it facilitates better understanding of the nature and the operation of the information system, thus constituting a means for documenting and analyzing the system. Therefore, it is necessary for supporting the efforts of the organization's management to design, implement, and operate secure information systems.

Traditionally, risk management has been seen by security professionals as a means to justify to management the cost of security measures. Nowadays, it does not only that, but it also fulfills legislative and/or regulatory provisions that exist in several countries, which demand information systems to be protected in a manner commensurate with the threats they face.

Risk management constitutes an efficient means of communication between technical and administrative personnel, as well as management, because it allows us to express the security problem in a language comprehensible by management, by viewing security as an investment that can be assessed in terms of cost/benefit analysis.[45] Additionally, it is quite flexible, so it can fit in several scientific frameworks and be applied either by itself or in combination with other methodologies. It is the most widely used methodology for designing and managing information systems security and has been successfully applied in many cases.

Finally, an answer frequently offered by security professionals is that there simply is no other efficient way to carry out the tasks that risk management does. Indeed, it has been proved in practice that by simply using methods of management science, law, and accounting, it is not possible to reach conclusions that can adequately justify risk treatment decisions.

Risk Management Methods

Many methods for risk management are available today. Most of them are supported by software tools. Selecting the most suitable method for a specific business environment and the needs of a specific organization is very important, albeit quite difficult, for a number of reasons[46]:

- There is a lack of a complete inventory of all available methods, with all their individual characteristics.
- There exists no commonly accepted set of evaluation criteria for risk management methods.

- Some methods only cover parts of the whole risk management process. For example, some methods only calculate the risk, without covering the risk treatment process. Some others focus on a small part of the whole process (e.g., disaster recovery planning). Some focus on auditing the security measures, and so on.
- Risk management methods differ widely in the analysis level that they use. Some use high-level descriptions of the information system under study; others call for detailed descriptions.
- Some methods are not freely available to the market, a fact that makes their evaluation very difficult, if at all possible.

The National Institute of Standards and Technology (NIST) compiled, in 1991, a comprehensive report on risk management methods and tools.[47] The European Commission, recognizing the need for a homogenized and software-supported risk management methodology for use by European businesses and organizations, assigned, in 1993, a similar project to a group of companies. Part of this project's results were the creation of an inventory and the evaluation of all available risk management methods at the time.[48] In 2006 the European Network and Information Security Agency (ENISA) recently repeated the endeavor. Even though preliminary results toward an inventory of risk management/risk assessment methods have been made available,[49] the process is still ongoing.[50] Some of the most widely used risk management methods[51] are briefly described in the sequel.

CRAMM (CCTA Risk Analysis and Management Methodology)[52] is a method developed by the British government organization CCTA (Central Communication and Telecommunication Agency), now renamed the Office of Government Commerce (OGC). CRAMM was first

45 R. Baskerville, "Information systems security design methods: implications for information systems development," *ACM Computing Surveys*, Vol. 25, No. 4, pp. 375–414, 1993.

46 R. Moses, "A European standard for risk analysis", in *Proceedings, 10th World Conference on Computer Security, Audit and Control*, Elsevier Advanced Technology, pp. 527–541, 1993.

47 NIST, *Description of automated risk management packages that NIST/NCSC risk management research laboratory have examined*, March 1991, available at http://w2.eff.org/Privacy/Newin/New_nist/risktool.txt, accessed April 28, 2008.

48 INFOSEC 1992, Project S2014—Risk Analysis, *Risk Analysis Methods Database*, January 1993.

49 ENISA Technical department (Section Risk Management), *Risk Management: Implementation principles and Inventories for Risk Management/Risk Assessment methods and tools*, available at www.enisa.europa.eu/rmra/files/D1_Inventory_of_Methods_Risk_Management_Final.pdf, June 2006, accessed April 28, 2008.

50 www.enisa.europa.eu/rmra/rm_home_01.html, accessed April 28, 2008.

51 ENISA Technical department (Section Risk Management), *Risk Management: Implementation principles and Inventories for Risk Management/Risk Assessment methods and tools*, available at www.enisa.europa.eu/rmra/files/D1_Inventory_of_Methods_Risk_Management_Final.pdf, June 2006, accessed April 28, 2008.

52 www.cramm.com, accessed April 28, 2008.

released in 1985. At present CRAMM is the U.K. government's preferred risk analysis method, but CRAMM is also used in many countries outside the U.K. CRAMM is especially appropriate for large organizations, such as government bodies and industry. CRAMM provides a staged and disciplined approach embracing both technical and nontechnical aspects of security. To assess these components, CRAMM is divided into three stages: asset identification and valuation; threat and vulnerability assessment; and countermeasure selection and recommendation. CRAMM enables the reviewer to identify the physical, software, data, and location assets that make up the information system. Each of these assets can be valued. Physical assets are valued in terms of their replacement cost. Data and software assets are valued in terms of the impact that would result if the information were to be unavailable, destroyed, disclosed, or modified. CRAMM covers the full range of deliberate and accidental threats that may affect information systems. This stage concludes by calculating the level of risk. CRAMM contains a very large countermeasure library consisting of over 3000 detailed countermeasures organized into over 70 logical groupings. The CRAMM software, developed by Insight Consulting,[53] uses the measures of risks determined during the previous stage and compares them against the security level (a threshold level associated with each countermeasure) to identify whether the risks are sufficiently great to justify the installation of a particular countermeasure. CRAMM provides a series of help facilities, including backtracking, what-if scenarios, prioritization functions, and reporting tools, to assist with the implementation of countermeasures and the active management of the identified risks. CRAMM is ISO/IEC 17799, Gramm-Leach-Bliley Act (GLBA), and Health Insurance Portability and Accountability Act (HIPAA) compliant.

The methodological approach offered by EBIOS (Expression des Besoins et Identification des Objectifs de Sécurité)[54] provides a global and consistent view of information systems security. It was first released in 1995. The method takes into account all technical entities and nontechnical entities. It allows all personnel using the information system to be involved in security issues and offers a dynamic approach that encourages interaction among the organization's various jobs and functions by examining the complete life cycle of the system. Promoted by the DCSSI (Direction Centrale de la Sécurité des Systèmes d' Information) of the French government and recognized by

the French administrations, EBIOS is also a reference in the private sector and abroad. It is compliant with major IT security standards. The EBIOS approach consists of five phases. Phase 1 deals with context analysis in terms of global business process dependency on the information system. Security needs analysis and threat analysis are conducted in Phases 2 and 3. Phases 4 and 5 yield an objective diagnostic on risks. The necessary and sufficient security objectives (and further security requirements) are then stated, proof of coverage is furnished, and residual risks made explicit. Local standard bases (e.g., German IT Grundschutz) are easily added on to its internal knowledge bases and catalogues of best practices. EBIOS is supported by a software tool developed by Central Information Systems Security Division (France). The tool helps the user to produce all risk analysis and management steps according to the EBIOS method and allows all the study results to be recorded and the required summary documents to be produced. EBIOS is compliant with ISO/IEC 27001, ISO/IEC 13335 (GMITS), ISO/IEC 15408 (Common Criteria), ISO/IEC 17799, and ISO/IEC 21827.

The Information Security Forum's (ISF) Standard of Good Practice[55] provides a set of high-level principles and objectives for information security together with associated statements of good practice. The Standard of Good Practice is split into five distinct aspects, each of which covers a particular type of environment. These are security management; critical business applications; computer installations; networks; and systems development. FIRM (Fundamental Information Risk Management) is a detailed method for monitoring and controlling information risk at the enterprise level. It has been developed as a practical approach to monitoring the effectiveness of information security. As such, it enables information risk to be managed systematically across enterprises of all sizes. It includes comprehensive implementation guidelines, which explain how to gain support for the approach and get it up and running. The Information Risk Scorecard is an integral part of FIRM. The Scorecard is a form used to collect a range of important details about a particular information resource such as the name of the owner, criticality, level of threat, business impact, and vulnerability. The ISF's Information Security Status Survey is a comprehensive risk management tool that evaluates a wide range of security measures used by organizations to control the business risks associated with their IT-based information systems. SARA (Simple

53 www.insight.co.uk/, accessed April 28, 2008.
54 www.ssi.gouv.fr/en/confidence/ebiospresentation.html, accessed April 28, 2008.

55 Information Security Forum, *The standard of good practice for information security*, 2007 (available at https://www.isfsecuritystandard.com/SOGP07/index.htm, accessed April 28, 2008).

to Apply Risk Analysis) is a detailed method for analyzing information risk in critical information systems.
SPRINT (Simplified Process for Risk Identification) is
a relatively quick and easy-to-use method for assessing
business impact and for analyzing information risk in
important but not critical information systems. The full
SPRINT method is intended for application to important, but not critical, systems. It complements the SARA
method, which is better suited to analyzing the risks associated with critical business systems. SPRINT first helps
decide the level of risk associated with a system. After
the risks are fully understood, SPRINT helps determine
how to proceed and, if the SPRINT process continues,
culminates in the production of an agreed plan of action
for keeping risks within acceptable limits. SPRINT can
help identify the vulnerabilities of existing systems and
the safeguards needed to protect against them; and define
the security requirements for systems under development
and the security measures needed to satisfy them. The
method is compliant to ISO/IEC 17799.

IT-Grundschutz[56] provides a method for an organization to establish an ISMS. It was first released in 1994. It
comprises both generic IT security recommendations for
establishing an applicable IT security process and detailed
technical recommendations to achieve the necessary IT
security level for a specific domain. The IT security process suggested by IT-Grundschutz consists of the following
steps: initialization of the process; definition of IT security goals and business environment; establishment of an
organizational structure for IT security; provision of necessary resources; creation of the IT security concept; IT
structure analysis; assessment of protection requirements;
modeling; IT security check; supplementary security
analysis; implementation planning and fulfillment; maintenance, monitoring, and improvement of the process; and
IT-Grundschutz Certification (optional). The key approach
in IT-Grundschutz is to provide a framework for IT security management, offering information for commonly
used IT components (modules). IT-Grundschutz modules
include lists of relevant threats and required countermeasures in a relatively technical level. These elements can be
expanded, complemented, or adapted to the needs of an
organization. IT-Grundschutz is supported by a software
tool named *Gstool* that has been developed by the Federal
Office for Information Security (BSI). The method is
compliant with ISO/IEC 17799 and ISO/IEC 27001.

MEHARI (Méthode Harmonisée d'Analyse de Ris-
ques Informatiques)[57] is a method designed by security

experts of the CLUSIF (Club de la Sécurité Informatique
Français) that replaced the earlier CLUSIF-sponsored
MARION and MELISA methods. It was first released
in 1996. It proposes an approach for defining risk reduction measures suited to the organization objectives.
MEHARI provides a risk assessment model and modular components and processes. It enhances the ability
to discover vulnerabilities through audit and to analyze
risk situations. MEHARI includes formulas facilitating threat identification and threat characterization and
optimal selection of corrective actions. MEHARI allows
for providing accurate indications for building security
plans, based on a complete list of vulnerability control
points and an accurate monitoring process in a continual
improvement cycle. It is compliant with ISO/IEC 17799
and ISO/IEC 13335.

The OCTAVE (Operationally Critical Threat, Asset,
and Vulnerability Evaluation)[58] method, developed by
the Software Engineering Institute of Carnegie-Mellon
University, defines a risk-based strategic assessment and
planning technique for security. It was first released in
1999. OCTAVE is self-directed in the sense that a small
team of people from the operational (or business) units
and the IT department work together to address the
security needs of the organization. The team draws on
the knowledge of many employees to define the current state of security, identify risks to critical assets, and
set a security strategy. OCTAVE is different from typical technology-focused assessments in that it focuses on
organizational risk and strategic, practice-related issues,
balancing operational risk, security practices, and technology. The OCTAVE method is driven by operational
risk and security practices. Technology is examined only
in relation to security practices. OCTAVE-S is a variation of the method tailored to the limited means and
unique constraints typically found in small organizations
(less than 100 people). OCTAVE Allegro is tailored
for organizations focused on information assets and a
streamlined approach. The Octave Automated Tool has
been implemented by Advanced Technology Institute
(ATI) to help users with the implementation of the
OCTAVE method.

Callio Secura 17799[59] is a product from Callio
Technologies. It was first released in 2001. It is a multiuser Web application with database support that lets the
user implement and certify an ISMS and guides the user
through each of the steps leading to ISO 27001 / 17799
compliance and BS 7799-2 certification. Moreover, it

56 www.bsi.de/english/gshb/index.htm, accessed April 28, 2008.
57 https://www.clusif.asso.fr/en/production/mehari/, accessed April 28, 2008.

58 www.cert.org/octave/, accessed April 28, 2008.
59 www.callio.com/secura.php, accessed April 28, 2008.

provides document management functionality as well as customization of the tool's databases. It also allows carrying out audits for other standards, such as COBIT, HIPAA, and Sarbanes-Oxley, by importing the user's own questionnaires. Callio Secura is compliant with ISO/IEC 17799 and ISO/IEC 27001.

COBRA[60] is a standalone application for risk management from C&A Systems Security. It is a questionnaire-based Windows PC tool, using expert system principles and a set of extensive knowledge bases. It has also embraced the functionality to optionally deliver other security services, such as checking compliance with the ISO 17799 security standard or with an organization's own security policies. It can be used for identification of threats and vulnerabilities; it measures the degree of actual risk for each area or aspect of a system and directly links this to the potential business impact. It offers detailed solutions and recommendations to reduce the risks and provides business as well as technical reports. It is compliant with ISO/IEC 17799.

Allion's product CounterMeasures[61] performs risk management based on the US-NIST 800 series and OMB Circular A-130 USA standards. The user standardizes the evaluation criteria and, using a "tailor-made" assessment checklist, the software provides objective evaluation criteria for determining security posture and/or compliance. CounterMeasures is available in both networked and desktop configurations. It is compliant with the NIST 800 series and OMB Circular A-130 USA standards.

Proteus[62] is a product suite from InfoGov. It was first released in 1999. Through its components the user can perform gap analysis against standards such as ISO 17799 or create and manage an ISMS according to ISO 27001 (BS 7799-2). Proteus Enterprise is a fully integrated Web-based Information Risk Management, Compliance and Security solution that is fully scalable. Using Proteus Enterprise, companies can perform any number of online compliance audits against any standard and compare between them. They can then assess how deficient compliance security measures affect the company both financially and operationally by mapping them onto its critical business processes. Proteus then identifies risks and mitigates those risks by formulating a work plan, maintains a current and demonstrable compliance status to the regulators and senior management alike. The system works with the company's existing infrastructure and uses RiskView to bridge the gap between the technical/

regulatory community and senior management. Proteus is a comprehensive system that includes online compliance and gap analysis, business impact, risk assessment, business continuity, incident management, asset management, organization roles, policy repository, and action plans. Its compliance engine supports any standard (international, industry, and corporate specific) and is supplied with a choice of comprehensive template questionnaires. The system is fully scalable and can size from a single user up to the largest of multinational organizations. The product maintains a full audit trail. It can perform online audits for both internal departments and external suppliers. It is compliant with ISO/IEC 17799 and ISO/IEC 27001.

RA2 art of risk[63] is the new risk assessment tool from AEXIS, the originators of the RA Software Tool. It was first released in 2000. It is designed to help businesses to develop an ISMS in compliance with ISO/IEC 27001:2005 (previously BS 7799 Part 2:2002), and the code of practice ISO/IEC 27002. It covers a number of security processes that direct businesses toward designing and implementing an ISMS. RA2 art of risk can be customized to meet the requirements of the organization. This includes the assessment of assets, threats, and vulnerabilities applicable to the organization, and the possibilities to include security measures additional to the ones in ISO/IEC 27002 in the assessment. It also includes a set of editable questions that can be used to assess the compliance with ISO/IEC 27002. RA2 Information Collection Device, a component that is distributed along with the tool, can be installed anywhere in the organization as needed to collect and feed back information into the risk assessment process. It is compliant with ISO/IEC 17799 and ISO/IEC 27001.

RiskWatch for Information Systems & ISO 17799[64] is the RiskWatch company's solution for information system risk management. Other relevant products in the same suite are RiskWatch for Financial Institutions, RiskWatch for HIPAA Security, RiskWatch for Physical & Homeland Security, RiskWatch for University and School Security, and RiskWatch for NERC (North American Electric Reliability Corporation) and C-TPAT-Supply Chain. The RiskWatch for Information Systems & ISO 17799 tool conducts automated risk analysis and vulnerability assessments of information systems. All RiskWatch software is fully customizable by the user. It can be tailored to reflect any corporate or government policy, including incorporation of unique standards, incident report data, penetration

60 www.riskworld.net/method.htm, accessed April 28, 2008.
61 www.countermeasures.com, accessed April 28, 2008.
62 www.infogov.co.uk/proteus/, accessed April 28, 2008.

63 www.aexis.de/RA2ToolPage.htm, accessed April 28, 2008.
64 www.riskwatch.com/index.php?option=com_content&task =view&id=22&Itemid=34, accessed April 28, 2008.

test data, observation, and country-specific threat data. Every product includes both information security as well as physical security. Project plans and a simple workflow make it easy to create accurate and supportable risk assessments. The tool includes security measures from the ISO 17799 and USNIST 800-26 standards, with which it is compliant.

The SBA (Security by Analysis) method[65] is a concept that's existed since the beginning of the 1980s. It is more of a way of looking at analysis and security work in computerized businesses than a fully developed method. It could be called the "human model" concerning risk and vulnerability analyses. The human model implies a very strong confidence in knowledge among staff and individuals within the analyzed business or organizations. It is based on the fact that it is those who are working with the everyday problems, regardless of position, who have got the greatest possibilities to pinpoint the most important problems and to suggest the solutions. SBA is supported by three software tools. Every tool has its own special method, but they are based on the same concept: gathering a group of people who represent the necessary breadth of knowledge. SBA Check is primarily a tool for anyone working with or responsible for information security issues. The role of analysis leader is central to the use of SBA Check. The analysis leader is in charge of ensuring that the analysis participants' knowledge of the operation is brought to bear during the analysis process in a way that is relevant, so that the description of the current situation and opportunities for improvement retain their consistent quality. SBA Scenario is a tool that helps evaluate business risks methodically through quantitative risk analysis. The tool also helps evaluate which actions are correct and financially motivated through risk management. SBA Project is an IT support tool and a method that helps identify conceivable problems in a project as well as providing suggestions for conceivable measures to deal with those problems. The analysis participants' views and knowledge are used as a basis for providing a good picture of the risk in the project.

4. RISK MANAGEMENT LAWS AND REGULATIONS

Many nations have adopted laws and regulations containing clauses that, directly or indirectly, pertain to aspects of information systems risk management. Similarly, a large number of international laws and regulations exist.

In the following, a brief description of such documents with an international scope, directly relevant to information systems risk management,[66] is given.

The "Regulation (EC) No 45/2001 of the European Parliament and of the Council of 18 December 2000 on the protection of individuals with regard to the processing of personal data by the Community institutions and bodies and on the free movement of such data"[67] requires that any personal data processing activity by Community institutions undergoes a prior risk analysis to determine the privacy implications of the activity and to determine the appropriate legal, technical, and organizational measures to protect such activities. It also stipulates that such activity is effectively protected by measures, which must be state of the art, keeping into account the sensitivity and privacy implications of the activity. When a third party is charged with the processing task, its activities are governed by suitable and enforced agreements. Furthermore, the regulation requires the European Union's (EU) institutions and bodies to take similar precautions with regard to their telecommunications infrastructure, and to properly inform the users of any specific risks of security breaches.[68]

The European Commission's Directive on Data Protection went into effect in October 1998 and prohibits the transfer of personal data to non-EU nations that do not meet the European "adequacy" standard for privacy protection. The United States takes a different approach to privacy from that taken by the EU; it uses a sectoral approach that relies on a mix of legislation, regulation, and self-regulation. The EU, however, relies on comprehensive legislation that, for example, requires creation of government data protection agencies, registration of data bases with those agencies, and in some instances prior approval before personal data processing may begin. The Safe Harbor Privacy Principles[69] aim at bridging this gap by providing that an EU-based entity self-certifies its compliance with them.

The "Commission Decision of 15 June 2001 on standard contractual clauses for the transfer of personal

---

65 www.thesbamethod.com, accessed April 28, 2008.

66 J. Dumortier and H. Graux, "Risk management/risk assessment in European regulation, international guidelines and codes of practice," ENISA, June 2007 (available at www.enisa.europa.eu/rmra/files/rmra_regulation.pdf).

67 http://europa.eu.int/smartapi/cgi/sga_doc?smartapi!celexapi!prod!CELEXnumdoc&lg=EN&numdoc=32001R0045&model=guichett, accessed April 29, 2008.

68 J. Dumortier and H. Graux, "Risk management/risk assessment in European regulation, international guidelines and codes of practice," ENISA, June 2007 (available at www.enisa.europa.eu/rmra/files/rmra_regulation.pdf).

69 www.export.gov/safeharbor/SH_Documents.asp, accessed April 29, 2008.

data to third countries, under Directive 95/46/EC" and the "Commission Decision of 27 December 2004 amending Decision 2001/497/EC as regards the introduction of an alternative set of standard contractual clauses for the transfer of personal data to third countries"[70] provide a set of voluntary model clauses that can be used to export personal data from a data controller who is subject to EU data protection rules to a data processor outside the EU who is not subject to these rules or to a similar set of adequate rules. Upon acceptance of the model clauses, the data controller must warrant that the appropriate legal, technical, and organizational measures to ensure the protection of the personal data are taken. Furthermore, the data processor must agree to permit auditing of its security practices to ensure compliance with applicable European data protection rules.[71]

The Health Insurance Portability and Accountability Act of 1996[72] is a U.S. law with regard to health insurance coverage, electronic health, and requirements for the security and privacy of health data. Title II of HIPAA, known as the Administrative Simplification (AS) provisions, requires the establishment of national standards for electronic health care transactions and national identifiers for providers, health-insurance plans, and employers. Per the requirements of Title II, the Department of Health and Human Services has promulgated five rules regarding Administrative Simplification: the Privacy Rule, the Transactions and Code Sets Rule, the Security Rule, the Unique Identifiers Rule, and the Enforcement Rule. The standards are meant to improve the efficiency and effectiveness of the U.S. health care system by encouraging the widespread use of electronic data interchange.

The "Directive 2002/58/EC of the European Parliament and of the Council of 12 July 2002 concerning the processing of personal data and the protection of privacy in the electronic communications sector (Directive on privacy and electronic communications)"[73] requires that any provider of publicly available electronic communications services takes the appropriate legal, technical and organizational measures to ensure the security of its services; informs his subscribers of any particular risks of security breaches; and takes the necessary measures to prevent such breaches, and indicates the likely costs of security breaches to the subscribers.[74]

The "Directive 2006/24/EC of the European Parliament and of the Council of 15 March 2006 on the retention of data generated or processed in connection with the provision of publicly available electronic communications services or of public communications networks and amending Directive 2002/58/EC"[75] requires the affected providers of publicly accessible electronic telecommunications networks to retain certain communications data to be specified in their national regulations, for a specific amount of time, under secured circumstances in compliance with applicable privacy regulations; to provide access to this data to competent national authorities; to ensure data quality and security through appropriate technical and organizational measures, shielding it from access by unauthorized individuals; to ensure its destruction when it is no longer required; and to ensure that stored data can be promptly delivered on request from the competent authorities.[76]

The "Regulation (EC) No 1907/2006 of the European Parliament and of the Council of 18 December 2006 concerning the Registration, Evaluation, Authorisation and Restriction of Chemicals (REACH), establishing a European Chemicals Agency, amending Directive 1999/45/EC and repealing Council Regulation (EEC) No 793/93 and Commission Regulation (EC) No 1488/94 as well as Council Directive 76/769/EEC and Commission Directives 91/155/EEC, 93/67/EEC, 93/105/EC and 2000/21/EC"[77] implants risk management obligations by imposing a reporting obligation on producers and importers of articles covered by the regulation, with regard to the qualities of certain chemical substances, which includes a risk assessment and obligation to examine how such risks can be managed. This information is to be registered in a central database. It also stipulates that a Committee for Risk Assessment within the European Chemicals Agency established by the Regulation is established and requires that the information provided is kept up to date with regard to potential risks to human health

70 http://ec.europa.eu/justice_home/fsj/privacy/modelcontracts/index_en.htm, accessed April 29, 2008.

71 J. Dumortier and H. Graux, "Risk management/risk assessment in European regulation, international guidelines and codes of practice," ENISA, June 2007 (available at www.enisa.europa.eu/rmra/files/rmra_regulation.pdf).

72 www.legalarchiver.org/hipaa.htm, accessed April 29, 2008.

73 http://europa.eu.int/smartapi/cgi/sga_doc?smartapi!celexapi!prod!CELEXnumdoc&lg=en&numdoc=32002L0058&model=guichett, accessed April 29, 2008.

74 J. Dumortier and H. Graux, "Risk management/risk assessment in European regulation, international guidelines and codes of practice," ENISA, June 2007 (available at www.enisa.europa.eu/rmra/files/rmra_regulation.pdf).

75 http://eurlex.europa.eu/LexUriServ/LexUriServ.do?uri=CELEX:32006L0024:EN:NOT, accessed April 29, 2008.

76 J. Dumortier and H. Graux, "Risk management/risk assessment in European regulation, international guidelines and codes of practice," ENISA, June 2007 (available at www.enisa.europa.eu/rmra/files/rmra_regulation.pdf).

77 http://eurlex.europa.eu/LexUriServ/LexUriServ.do?uri=OJ:L:2006:396:0001:0849:EN:PDF, accessed April 29, 2008.

or the environment, and that such risks are adequately managed.[78]

The "Council Framework Decision 2005/222/JHA of 24 February 2005 on attacks against information systems"[79] contains the conditions under which legal liability can be imposed on legal entities for conduct of certain natural persons of authority within the legal entity. Thus, the Framework decision requires that the conduct of such figures within an organization is adequately monitored, also because the decision states that a legal entity can be held liable for acts of omission in this regard. Additionally, the decision defines a series of criteria under which jurisdictional competence can be established. These include the competence of a jurisdiction when a criminal act is conducted against an information system within its borders.[80]

The "OECD Guidelines for the Security of Information Systems and Networks: Towards a Culture of Security" (25 July 2002)[81] aim to promote a culture of security; to raise awareness about the risk to information systems and networks (including the policies, practices, measures, and procedures available to address those risks and the need for their adoption and implementation); to foster greater confidence in information systems and networks and the way in which they are provided and used; to create a general frame of reference; to promote cooperation and information sharing; and to promote the consideration of security as an important objective. The guidelines state nine basic principles underpinning risk management and information security practices. No part of the text is legally binding, but noncompliance with any of the principles is indicative of a breach of risk management good practices that can potentially incur liability.[82]

The "Basel Committee on Banking Supervision—Risk Management Principles for Electronic Banking"[83] identifies 14 Risk Management Principles for Electronic Banking to help banking institutions expand their existing risk oversight policies and processes to cover their ebanking activities. The Risk Management Principles fall into three broad, and often overlapping, categories of issues that are grouped to provide clarity: board and management oversight; security controls; and legal and reputational risk management. The Risk Management Principles are not put forth as absolute requirements or even "best practice," nor do they attempt to set specific technical solutions or standards relating to ebanking. Consequently, the Risk Management Principles and sound practices are expected to be used as tools by national supervisors and to be implemented with adaptations to reflect specific national requirements and individual risk profiles where necessary.

The "Commission Recommendation 87/598/EEC of 8 December 1987, concerning a European code of conduct relating to electronic payments"[84] provides a number of general nonbinding recommendations, including an obligation to ensure that privacy is respected and that the system is transparent with regard to potential security or confidentiality risks, which must obviously be mitigated by all reasonable means.[85]

The "Public Company Accounting Reform and Investor Protection Act of 30 July 2002" (commonly referred to as *Sarbanes-Oxley* and often abbreviated to *SOX* or *Sarbox*),[86] even though indirectly relevant to risk management, is discussed here due to its importance. The Act is a U.S. federal law passed in response to a number of major corporate and accounting scandals including those affecting Enron, Tyco International, and WorldCom (now MCI). These scandals resulted in a decline of public trust in accounting and reporting practices. The legislation is wide ranging and establishes new or enhanced standards for all U.S. public company boards, management, and public accounting firms. Its provisions range from additional Corporate Board responsibilities to criminal penalties, and require the Securities and Exchange Commission (SEC) to implement rulings on requirements to comply with the new law. The first and most important part of the Act establishes a new quasi-public agency, the Public Company Accounting Oversight Board (www.pcaobus.org), which is charged with overseeing, regulating, inspecting, and disciplining accounting firms in their roles as auditors of public companies. The Act

78 J. Dumortier and H. Graux, "Risk management/risk assessment in European regulation, international guidelines and codes of practice," ENISA, June 2007 (available at www.enisa.europa.eu/rmra/files/rmra_regulation.pdf).

79 http://eurlex.europa.eu/LexUriServ/LexUriServ.do?uri = CELEX: 32005F0222:EN:NOT, accessed April 29, 2008.

80 J. Dumortier and H. Graux, "Risk management/risk assessment in European regulation, international guidelines and codes of practice," ENISA, June 2007 (available at www.enisa.europa.eu/rmra/files/rmra_regulation.pdf).

81 www.oecd.org/dataoecd/16/22/15582260.pdf, accessed April 29, 2008.

82 J. Dumortier and H. Graux, "Risk management/risk assessment in European regulation, international guidelines and codes of practice," ENISA, June 2007 (available at www.enisa.europa.eu/rmra/files/rmra_regulation.pdf).

83 www.bis.org/publ/bcbs98.pdf, accessed April 29, 2008.

84 http://eurlex.europa.eu/LexUriServ/LexUriServ.do?uri=CELEX:31987H0598:EN:HTML, accessed April 29, 2008.

85 J. Dumortier and H. Graux, "Risk management/risk assessment in European regulation, international guidelines and codes of practice," ENISA, June 2007 (available at www.enisa.europa.eu/rmra/files/rmra_regulation.pdf).

86 http://frwebgate.access.gpo.gov/cgi-bin/getdoc.cgi?dbname=107_cong_bills&docid=f:h3763enr.tst.pdf, accessed April 29, 2008.

also covers issues such as auditor independence, corporate governance and enhanced financial disclosure.

The "Office of the Comptroller of the Currency (OCC) – Electronic Banking Guidance"[87] is fairly high level and should be indicative of the subject matter to be analyzed and assessed by banking institutions, rather than serving as a yardstick to identify actual problems.[88]

The "Payment Card Industry (PCI) Security Standards Council—Data Security Standard (DSS)"[89] provides central guidance allowing financial service providers relying on payment cards to implement the necessary policies, procedures, and infrastructure to adequately safeguard their customer account data. PCI DSS has no formal binding legal power. Nevertheless, considering its origins and the key participants, it holds significant moral authority, and noncompliance with the PCI DSS by a payment card service provider may be indicative of inadequate risk management practices.[90]

The "Directive 2002/65/EC of the European Parliament and of the Council of 23 September 2002 concerning the distance marketing of consumer financial services and amending Council Directive 90/619/EEC and Directives 97/7/EC and 98/27/EC (the 'Financial Distance Marketing Directive')"[91] requires that, as a part of the minimum information to be provided to a consumer prior to concluding a distance financial services contract, the consumer must be clearly and comprehensibly informed of any specific risks related to the service concerned.[92]

5. RISK MANAGEMENT STANDARDS

Various national and international, de jure, and de facto standards exist that are related, directly or indirectly, to information systems risk management. In the following, we briefly describe the most important international standards that are directly related to risk management.

The "ISO/IEC 13335-1:2004—Information technology—Security techniques—Management of information and communications technology security—Part 1: Concepts and models for information and communications technology security management" standard[93] defines and describes the concepts associated with the management of IT security. It also identifies the relationships between the management of IT security and management of IT in general. Further, it presents several models, which can be used to explain IT security, and provides general guidance on the management of IT security. It is a commonly used code of practice and serves as a resource for the implementation of security management practices and as a yardstick for auditing such practices.[94]

The "BS 25999-1:2006—Business continuity management—Part 1: Code of Practice" standard[95] is a code of practice that takes the form of guidance and recommendations. It establishes the process, principles, and terminology of business continuity management (BCM), providing a basis for understanding, developing, and implementing business continuity within an organization and to provide confidence in business-to-business and business-to-customer dealings. In addition, it provides a comprehensive set of security measures based on BCM best practice and covers the whole BCM life cycle.[96]

The "ISO/IEC TR 15443-1:2005—Information technology—Security techniques—A framework for IT security assurance"[97] technical report introduces, relates, and categorizes security assurance methods to a generic life-cycle model in a manner enabling an increased level of confidence to be obtained in the security functionality of a deliverable. It allows security professionals to determine a suitable methodology for assessing a security service, product, or environmental factor (a deliverable). Following this technical report, it can be determined which level of security assurance a deliverable is intended

87 www.occ.treas.gov/netbank/ebguide.htm, accessed April 29, 2008.
88 J. Dumortier and H. Graux, "Risk management/risk assessment in European regulation, international guidelines and codes of practice," ENISA, June 2007 (available at www.enisa.europa.eu/rmra/files/rmra_regulation.pdf).
89 https://www.pcisecuritystandards.org/tech/download_the_pci_dss.htm, accessed April 29, 2008.
90 J. Dumortier and H. Graux, "Risk management/risk assessment in European regulation, international guidelines and codes of practice," ENISA, June 2007 (available at www.enisa.europa.eu/rmra/files/rmra_regulation.pdf).
91 http://eurlex.europa.eu/LexUriServ/LexUriServ.do?uri=CELEX:32002L0065:EN:NOT, accessed April 29, 2008.
92 J. Dumortier and H. Graux, "Risk management/risk assessment in European regulation, international guidelines and codes of practice," ENISA, June 2007 (available at www.enisa.europa.eu/rmra/files/rmra_regulation.pdf).

93 British Standards Institute, "Information technology—Security techniques—Management of information and communications technology security—Part 1: Concepts and models for information and communications technology security management," BS ISO/IEC 13335-1:2004.
94 J. Dumortier and H. Graux, "Risk management/risk assessment in European regulation, international guidelines and codes of practice," ENISA, June 2007 (available at www.enisa.europa.eu/rmra/files/rmra_regulation.pdf).
95 British Standards Institute, "Business continuity management—Code of practice," BS 25999-1:2006.
96 J. Dumortier and H. Graux, "Risk management/risk assessment in European regulation, international guidelines and codes of practice," ENISA, June 2007 (available at www.enisa.europa.eu/rmra/files/rmra_regulation.pdf).
97 ISO/IEC, "Information technology—security techniques—a framework for IT security assurance—overview and framework," ISO/IEC TR 15443-1:2005.

to meet and whether this threshold is actually met by the deliverable.

The "ISO/IEC 17799:2005— Information technology— Security techniques—Code of practice for information security management" standard[98] establishes guidelines and general principles for initiating, implementing, maintaining, and improving information security management in an organization. It provides general guidance on the commonly accepted goals of information security management. The standard contains best practices of security measures in many areas of information security management. These are intended to be implemented to meet the requirements identified by a risk assessment. The standard is intended as a common basis and practical guideline for developing organizational security standards and effective security management practices, and to help build confidence in interorganizational activities.

The "ISO/IEC 18028:2006—Information technology—Security techniques—IT network security" standard[99] extends the security management guidelines provided in ISO/IEC TR 13335 and ISO/IEC 17799 by detailing the specific operations and mechanisms needed to implement network security measures in a wider range of network environments, providing a bridge between general IT security management issues and network security technical implementations. The standard provides detailed guidance on the security aspects of the management, operation and use of IT networks, and their interconnections. It defines and describes the concepts associated with, and provides management guidance on, network security, including on how to identify and analyze the communications-related factors to be taken into account to establish network security requirements, with an introduction to the possible areas where security measures can be applied and the specific technical areas.

The "ISO/IEC 27001:2005—Information technology—Security techniques—Information security management systems—Requirements" standard[100] is designed to ensure the selection of adequate and proportionate security measures that protect information assets and give confidence to interested parties. The standard covers all types of organizations (e.g., commercial enterprises, government agencies, not-for-profit organizations) and specifies the requirements for establishing, implementing,

operating, monitoring, reviewing, maintaining, and improving a documented ISMS within the context of the organization's overall business risks. Further, it specifies requirements for the implementation of security measures customized to the needs of individual organizations or parts thereof. Its application in practice is often combined with related standards, such as BS 7799-3:2006 which provides additional guidance to support the requirements given in ISO/IEC 27001:2005.

The "BS 7799-3:2006—Information security management systems—Guidelines for information security risk management" standard[101] gives guidance to support the requirements given in BS ISO/IEC 27001:2005 regarding all aspects of an ISMS risk management cycle and is therefore typically applied in conjunction with this standard in risk assessment practices. This includes assessing and evaluating the risks, implementing security measures to treat the risks, monitoring and reviewing the risks, and maintaining and improving the system of risk treatment. The focus of this standard is effective information security through an ongoing program of risk management activities. This focus is targeted at information security in the context of an organization's business risks.

The "ISO/IEC TR 18044:2004—Information technology—Security techniques—Information security incident management" standard[102] provides advice and guidance on information security incident management for information security managers, and information system, service, and network managers. It is a high-level resource introducing basic concepts and considerations in the field of incident response. As such, it is mostly useful as a catalyst to awareness raising initiatives in this regard.

The "ISF Standard of Good Practice" standard[103] is a commonly quoted source of good practices and serves as a resource for the implementation of information security policies and as a yardstick for auditing such systems and/ or the surrounding practices.[104] The standard covers six distinct aspects of information security, each of which relates to a particular type of environment. The standard focuses on how information security supports an organization's key business processes.

---

98 British Standards Institute, "Information technology—Security techniques—Code of practice for information security management," BS ISO/IEC 17799:2005.

99 ISO/IEC, "Information technology—security techniques—IT network security—part 1: network security management," ISO/IEC TR 18028:2006.

100 ISO/IEC, "Information security management—specification with guidance for use," ISO 27001.

101 British Standards Institute, "ISMSs—Part 3: Guidelines for information security risk management," BS 7799-3:2006.

102 British Standards Institute, "Information technology—Security techniques—Information security incident management," BS ISO/IEC TR 18044:2004.

103 Information Security Forum, *The standard of good practice for information security*, 2007 (available at https://www.isfsecuritystandard.com/SOGP07/index.htm, accessed April 28, 2008).

104 J. Dumortier and H. Graux, "Risk management/risk assessment in European regulation, international guidelines and codes of practice," ENISA, June 2007 (available at www.enisa.europa.eu/rmra/files/rmra_regulation.pdf).

The "ISO/TR 13569:2005—Financial services—Information security guidelines" standard[105] provides guidelines on the development of an information security program for institutions in the financial services industry. It includes discussion of the policies, organization and the structural, legal and regulatory components of such a program. Considerations for the selection and implementation of security measures, and the elements required to manage information security risk within a modern financial services institution are discussed. Recommendations are given that are based on consideration of the institution's business environment, practices, and procedures. Included in this guidance is a discussion of legal and regulatory compliance issues, which should be considered in the design and implementation of the program.

The U.S. General Accounting Office "Information security risk assessment: practices of leading organizations" guide[106] is intended to help federal managers implement an ongoing information security risk assessment process by providing examples, or case studies, of practical risk assessment procedures that have been successfully adopted by four organizations known for their efforts to implement good risk assessment practices. More important, it identifies, based on the case studies, factors that are important to the success of any risk assessment program, regardless of the specific methodology employed.

The U.S. NIST SP 800-30 "Risk management guide for information technology systems"[107] developed by NIST in 2002, provides a common foundation for experienced and inexperienced, technical, and nontechnical personnel who support or use the risk management process for their IT systems. Its guidelines are for use by federal organizations which process sensitive information and are consistent with the requirements of OMB Circular A-130, Appendix III. The guidelines may also be used by nongovernmental organizations on a voluntary basis, even though they are not mandatory and binding standards.

Finally, the U.S. NIST SP 800-39 "Managing Risk from Information Systems: An Organizational Perspective" standard[108] provides guidelines for managing risk to organizational operations, organizational assets, individuals, other organizations, and the nation resulting from the operation and use of information systems. It provides a structured yet flexible approach for managing that portion of risk resulting from the incorporation of information systems into the mission and business processes of organizations.

6. SUMMARY

The information systems risk management methodology was developed with an eye to guiding the design and the management of security of an information system within the framework of an organization. It aims at analyzing and assessing the factors that affect risk, to subsequently treat the risk, and to continuously monitor and review the security plan. Central concepts of the methodology are those of the threat, the vulnerability, the asset, the impact, and the risk. The operational relationship of these concepts materializes when a threat exploits one or more vulnerabilities to harm assets, an event that will impact the organization. Once the risks are identified and assessed, they must be treated, that is, transferred, avoided, or accepted. Treating the risks is done on the basis of a carefully designed security plan, which must be continuously monitored, reviewed, and amended as necessary. Many methods implementing the whole or parts of the risk management methodology have been developed. Even though most of them follow closely the methodology as described in pertinent international standards, they differ considerably in both their underlying philosophy and in their specific steps. The risk management methodology has been and is being applied internationally with considerable success and enjoys universal acceptance. However, it does suffer several disadvantages that should be seriously considered in the process of applying it. Particular attention must be paid to the subjectivity of its estimates, which is often obscured by the formality of the underlying probabilistic models and by the systematic nature of most of the risk management methods. Subjectivity in applying the methodology is unavoidable and should be accepted and consciously managed. A number of international laws and regulations contain provisions for information system risk management, in addition to national provisions. The risk management methodology is standardized by international organizations.

105 ISO, *Financial services-Information security guidelines*, ISO/TR 13569:2005.

106 U.S. General Accounting Office, *Information security risk assessment: practices of leading organizations,* 1999.

107 G. Stoneburner, A. Goguen and A. Feringa, *Risk Management guide for information technology systems*, National Institute of Standards and Technology, Special Publication SP 800-30, 2002.

108 R. Ross, S. Katzke, A. Johnson, M. Swanson and G. Stoneburner, *Managing Risk from Information Systems: An Organizational Perspective,* US NIST SP 800-39, 2008 (available at http://csrc.nist.gov/publications/PubsDrafts.html#SP-800-39, accessed April 29, 2008).

Physical Security

## Chapter 36

Physical Security Essentials

William Stallings

Independent consultant

Platt[1] distinguishes three elements of information system (IS) security:

- *Logical security.* Protects computer-based data from software-based and communication-based threats.
- *Physical security.* Also called *infrastructure security.* Protects the information systems that house data and the people who use, operate, and maintain the systems. Physical security must also prevent any type of physical access or intrusion that can compromise logical security.
- *Premises security.* Also known as *corporate* or *facilities security.* Protects the people and property within an entire area, facility, or building(s) and is usually required by laws, regulations, and fiduciary obligations. Premises security provides perimeter security, access control, smoke and fire detection, fire suppression, some environmental protection, and usually surveillance systems, alarms, and guards.

This chapter is concerned with physical security and with some overlapping areas of premises security. We begin by looking at physical security threats and then consider physical security prevention measures.

1. OVERVIEW

For information systems, the role of physical security is to protect the physical assets that support the storage and processing of information. Physical security involves two complementary requirements. First, physical security must prevent damage to the physical infrastructure that sustains the information system. In broad terms, that infrastructure includes the following:

- *Information system hardware.* Including data processing and storage equipment,

transmission and networking facilities, and offline storage media. We can include in this category supporting documentation.
- *Physical facility.* The buildings and other structures housing the system and network components.
- *Supporting facilities.* These facilities underpin the operation of the information system. This category includes electrical power, communication services, and environmental controls (heat, humidity, etc.).
- *Personnel.* Humans involved in the control, maintenance, and use of the information systems.

Second, physical security must prevent misuse of the physical infrastructure that leads to the misuse or damage of the protected information. The misuse of the physical infrastructure can be accidental or malicious. It includes vandalism, theft of equipment, theft by copying, theft of services, and unauthorized entry.

Figure 36.1, based on Bosworth and Kabay[2], suggests the overall context in which physical security concerns arise. The central concern is the information assets of an organization. These information assets provide value to the organization that possesses them, as indicated by the upper four items in the figure. In turn, the physical infrastructure is essential to providing for the storage and processing of these assets. The lower four items in the figure are the concern of physical security. Not shown is the role of logical security, which consists of software- and protocol-based measures for ensuring data integrity, confidentiality, and so forth.

The role of physical security is affected by the operating location of the information system, which can be characterized as static, mobile, or portable. Our concern in this chapter is primarily with static systems, which are installed at fixed locations. A mobile system is installed in a vehicle, which serves the function of a structure for

---

1 F. Platt, "Physical threats to the information infrastructure," in S. Bosworth, and M. Kabay, (eds.), *Computer Security Handbook,* Wiley, 2002.

2 S. Bosworth and M. Kabay (eds.), *Computer Security Handbook,* Wiley, 2002.

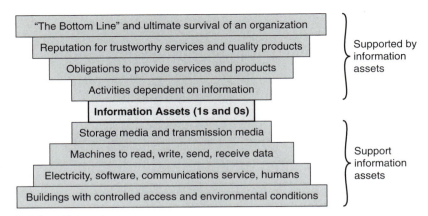

FIGURE 36.1 A context for information assets.

the system. Portable systems have no single installation point but may operate in a variety of locations, including buildings, vehicles, or in the open. The nature of the system's installation determines the nature and severity of the threats of various types, including fire, roof leaks, unauthorized access, and so forth.

2. PHYSICAL SECURITY THREATS

In this section, we first look at the types of physical situations and occurrences that can constitute a threat to information systems. There are a number of ways in which such threats can be categorized. It is important to understand the spectrum of threats to information systems so that responsible administrators can ensure that prevention measures are comprehensive. We organize the threats into the following categories:

- Environmental threats
- Technical threats
- Human-caused threats

We begin with a discussion of natural disasters, which are a prime, but not the only, source of environmental threats. Then we look specifically at environmental threats, followed by technical and human-caused threats.

Natural Disasters

Natural disasters are the source of a wide range of environmental threats to datacenters, other information processing facilities, and their personnel. It is possible to assess the risk of various types of natural disasters and take suitable precautions so that catastrophic loss from natural disaster is prevented.

Table 36.1 lists six categories of natural disasters, the typical warning time for each event, whether or not personnel evacuation is indicated or possible, and the typical

duration of each event. We comment briefly on the potential consequences of each type of disaster.

A tornado can generate winds that exceed hurricane strength in a narrow band along the tornado's path. There is substantial potential for structural damage, roof damage, and loss of outside equipment. There may be damage from wind and flying debris. Off site, a tornado may cause a temporary loss of local utility and communications. Offsite damage is typically followed by quick restoration of services.

A hurricane, depending on its strength, may also cause significant structural damage and damage to outside equipment. Off site, there is the potential for severe regionwide damage to public infrastructure, utilities, and communications. If onsite operation must continue, then emergency supplies for personnel as well as a backup generator are needed. Further, the responsible site manager may need to mobilize private post-storm security measures, such as armed guards.

A major earthquake has the potential for the greatest damage and occurs without warning. A facility near the epicenter may suffer catastrophic, even complete, destruction, with significant and long-lasting damage to datacenters and other IS facilities. Examples of inside damage include the toppling of unbraced computer hardware and site infrastructure equipment, including the collapse of raised floors. Personnel are at risk from broken glass and other flying debris. Off site, near the epicenter of a major earthquake, the damage equals and often exceeds that of a major hurricane. Structures that can withstand a hurricane, such as roads and bridges, may be damaged or destroyed, preventing the movement of fuel and other supplies.

An ice storm or blizzard can cause some disruption of or damage to IS facilities if outside equipment and the building are not designed to survive severe ice and snow accumulation. Off site, there may be widespread

TABLE 36.1 Characteristics of Natural Disasters

	Warning	Evacuation	Duration
Tornado	Advance warning of potential; not site specific	Remain at site	Brief but intense
Hurricane	Significant advance warning	May require evacuation	Hours to a few days
Earthquake	No warning	May be unable to evacuate	Brief duration; threat of continued aftershocks
Ice storm/ blizzard	Several days warning generally expected	May be unable to evacuate	May last several days
Lightning	Sensors may provide minutes of warning	May require evacuation	Brief but may recur
Flood	Several days warning generally expected	May be unable to evacuate	Site may be isolated for extended period

Source: ComputerSite Engineering, Inc.

disruption of utilities and communications and roads may be dangerous or impassable.

The consequences of lightning strikes can range from no impact to disaster. The effects depend on the proximity of the strike and the efficacy of grounding and surge protector measures in place. Off site, there can be disruption of electrical power and there is the potential for fires.

Flooding is a concern in areas that are subject to flooding and for facilities that are in severe flood areas at low elevation. Damage can be severe, with long-lasting effects and the need for a major cleanup operation.

Environmental Threats

This category encompasses conditions in the environment that can damage or interrupt the service of information systems and the data they house. Off site, there may be severe regionwide damage to the public infrastructure and, in the case of severe hurricanes, it may take days, weeks, or even years to recover from the event.

Inappropriate Temperature and Humidity

Computers and related equipment are designed to operate within a certain temperature range. Most computer systems should be kept between 10 and 32 degrees Celsius (50 and 90 degrees Fahrenheit). Outside this range, resources might continue to operate but produce undesirable results. If the ambient temperature around a computer gets too high, the computer cannot adequately cool itself, and internal components can be damaged. If the temperature gets too cold, the system can undergo thermal shock when it is turned on, causing circuit boards or integrated

TABLE 36.2 Temperature Thresholds for Damage to Computing Resources

Component or Medium	Sustained Ambient Temperature at which Damage May Begin
Flexible disks, magnetic tapes, etc.	38 °C (100 °F)
Optical media	49 °C (120 °F)
Hard disk media	66 °C (150 °F)
Computer equipment	79 °C (175 °F)
Thermoplastic insulation on wires carrying hazardous voltage	125 °C (257 °F)
Paper products	177 °C (350 °F)

Source: Data taken from National Fire Protection Association.

circuits to crack. Table 36.2 indicates the point at which permanent damage from excessive heat begins.

Another temperature-related concern is the internal temperature of equipment, which can be significantly higher than room temperature. Computer-related equipment comes with its own temperature dissipation and cooling mechanisms, but these may rely on, or be affected by, external conditions. Such conditions include excessive ambient temperature, interruption of supply of power or heating, ventilation, and air-conditioning (HVAC) services, and vent blockage.

High humidity also poses a threat to electrical and electronic equipment. Long-term exposure to high humidity can result in corrosion. Condensation can threaten magnetic and optical storage media. Condensation can also cause a short circuit, which in turn can damage circuit boards. High humidity can also cause a galvanic effect that results in electroplating, in which metal from one connector slowly migrates to the mating connector, bonding the two together.

Very low humidity can also be a concern. Under prolonged conditions of low humidity, some materials may change shape and performance may be affected. Static electricity also becomes a concern. A person or object that becomes statically charged can damage electronic equipment by an electric discharge. Static electricity discharges as low as 10 volts can damage particularly sensitive electronic circuits, and discharges in the hundreds of volts can create significant damage to a variety of electronic circuits. Discharges from humans can reach into the thousands of volts, so this is a nontrivial threat.

In general, relative humidity should be maintained between 40% and 60% to avoid the threats from both low and high humidity.

Fire and Smoke

Perhaps the most frightening physical threat is fire. It is a threat to human life and property. The threat is not only from the direct flame but also from heat, release of toxic fumes, water damage from fire suppression, and smoke damage. Further, fire can disrupt utilities, especially electricity.

The temperature due to fire increases with time, and in a typical building, fire effects follow the curve shown in Figure 36.2. The scale on the right side of the figure shows the temperature at which various items melt or are damaged and therefore indicates how long after the fire is started such damage occurs.

Smoke damage related to fires can also be extensive. Smoke is an abrasive. It collects on the heads of unsealed magnetic disks, optical disks, and tape drives. Electrical fires can produce an acrid smoke that may damage other equipment and may be poisonous or carcinogenic.

The most common fire threat is from fires that originate within a facility, and, as discussed subsequently, there are a number of preventive and mitigating measures that can be taken. A more uncontrollable threat is faced from wildfires, which are a plausible concern in the western United States, portions of Australia (where the term *bushfire* is used), and a number of other countries.

Water Damage

Water and other stored liquids in proximity to computer equipment pose an obvious threat. The primary danger is an electrical short, which can happen if water bridges between a circuit board trace carrying voltage and a trace carrying ground. Moving water, such as in plumbing, and weather-created water from rain, snow, and ice also pose threats. A pipe may burst from a fault in the line or from freezing. Sprinkler systems, despite their security function, are a major threat to computer equipment and paper and electronic storage media. The system may be set off by a faulty temperature sensor, or a burst pipe may cause water to enter the computer room. For a large computer installation, an effort should be made to avoid any sources of water from one or two floors above. An example of a hazard from this direction is an overflowing toilet.

Less common but more catastrophic is floodwater. Much of the damage comes from the suspended material in the water. Floodwater leaves a muddy residue that is extraordinarily difficult to clean up.

Chemical, Radiological, and Biological Hazards

Chemical, radiological, and biological hazards pose a growing threat, both from intentional attack and from accidental discharge. None of these hazardous agents should be present in an information system environment, but either accidental or intentional intrusion is possible. Nearby discharges (e.g., from an overturned truck carrying hazardous materials) can be introduced through the ventilation system or open windows and, in the case of radiation, through perimeter walls. In addition, discharges in the vicinity can disrupt work by causing evacuations to be ordered. Flooding can also introduce biological or chemical contaminants.

In general, the primary risk of these hazards is to personnel. Radiation and chemical agents can also cause damage to electronic equipment.

Dust

Dust is a prevalent concern that is often overlooked. Even fibers from fabric and paper are abrasive and mildly conductive, although generally equipment is resistant to such contaminants. Larger influxes of dust can result from a number of incidents, such as a controlled explosion of a nearby building and a windstorm carrying debris from a wildfire. A more likely source of influx comes from dust surges that originate within the building due to construction or maintenance work.

Equipment with moving parts, such as rotating storage media and computer fans, are the most vulnerable to

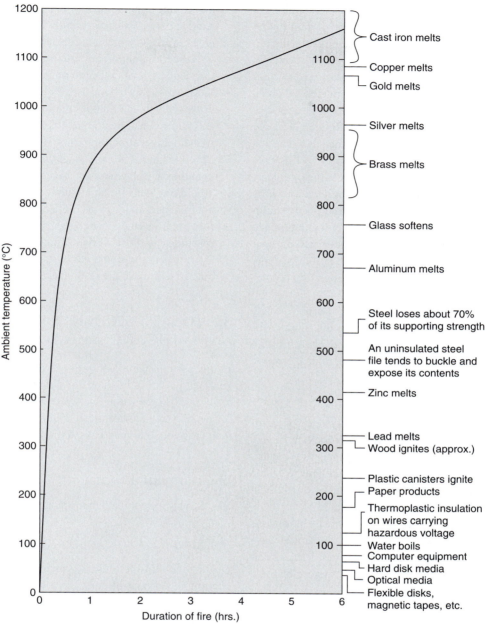

FIGURE 36.2 Fire effects.

damage from dust. Dust can also block ventilation and reduce radiational cooling.

Infestation

One of the less pleasant physical threats is infestation, which covers a broad range of living organisms, including mold, insects, and rodents. High-humidity conditions can lead to the growth of mold and mildew, which can be harmful to both personnel and equipment. Insects, particularly those that attack wood and paper, are also a common threat.

Technical Threats

This category encompasses threats related to electrical power and electromagnetic emission.

Electrical Power

Electrical power is essential to the operation of an information system. All the electrical and electronic devices in the system require power, and most require uninterrupted utility power.

Power utility problems can be broadly grouped into three categories: undervoltage, overvoltage, and noise.

An *undervoltage* occurs when the IS equipment receives less voltage than is required for normal operation. Undervoltage events range from temporary dips in the voltage supply to brownouts (prolonged undervoltage) and power outages. Most computers are designed to withstand prolonged voltage reductions of about 20% without shutting down and without operational error. Deeper dips or blackouts lasting more than a few milliseconds trigger a system shutdown. Generally, no damage is done, but service is interrupted.

Far more serious is an *overvoltage*. A surge of voltage can be caused by a utility company supply anomaly, by some internal (to the building) wiring fault, or by lightning. Damage is a function of intensity and duration and the effectiveness of any surge protectors between your equipment and the source of the surge. A sufficient surge can destroy silicon-based components, including processors and memories.

Power lines can also be a conduit for *noise*. In many cases, these spurious signals can endure through the filtering circuitry of the power supply and interfere with signals inside electronic devices, causing logical errors.

Electromagnetic Interference

Noise along a power supply line is only one source of electromagnetic interference (EMI). Motors, fans, heavy equipment, and even other computers generate electrical noise that can cause intermittent problems with the computer you are using. This noise can be transmitted through space as well as nearby power lines.

Another source of EMI is high-intensity emissions from nearby commercial radio stations and microwave relay antennas. Even low-intensity devices, such as cellular telephones, can interfere with sensitive electronic equipment.

Human-Caused Physical Threats

Human-caused threats are more difficult to deal with than the environmental and technical threats discussed so far. Human-caused threats are less predictable than other types of physical threats. Worse, human-caused threats are specifically designed to overcome prevention measures and/or seek the most vulnerable point of attack. We can group such threats into the following categories:

- *Unauthorized physical access*. Those who are not employees should not be in the building or building complex at all unless accompanied by an authorized individual. Not counting PCs and workstations, information system assets, such as servers,

mainframe computers, network equipment, and storage networks, are generally housed in restricted areas. Access to such areas is usually restricted to only a certain number of employees. Unauthorized physical access can lead to other threats, such as theft, vandalism, or misuse.

- *Theft*. This threat includes theft of equipment and theft of data by copying. Eavesdropping and wiretapping also fall into this category. Theft can be at the hands of an outsider who has gained unauthorized access or by an insider.
- *Vandalism*. This threat includes destruction of equipment and destruction of data.
- *Misuse*. This category includes improper use of resources by those who are authorized to use them, as well as use of resources by individuals not authorized to use the resources at all.

3. PHYSICAL SECURITY PREVENTION AND MITIGATION MEASURES

In this section, we look at a range of techniques for preventing, or in some cases simply deterring, physical attacks. We begin with a survey of some of the techniques for dealing with environmental and technical threats and then move on to human-caused threats.

Environmental Threats

We discuss these threats in the same order.

Inappropriate Temperature and Humidity

Dealing with this problem is primarily a matter of having environmental-control equipment of appropriate capacity and appropriate sensors to warn of thresholds being exceeded. Beyond that, the principal requirement is the maintenance of a power supply, discussed subsequently.

Fire and Smoke

Dealing with fire involves a combination of alarms, preventive measures, and fire mitigation. Martin provides the following list of necessary measures[3]:

- Choice of site to minimize likelihood of disaster. Few disastrous fires originate in a well-protected computer room or IS facility. The IS area should be

---

3 J. Martin, *Security, Accuracy, and Privacy in Computer Systems*, Prentice Hall, 1973.

chosen to minimize fire, water, and smoke hazards from adjoining areas. Common walls with other activities should have at least a one-hour fire-protection rating.

- Air conditioning and other ducts designed so as not to spread fire. There are standard guidelines and specifications for such designs.
- Positioning of equipment to minimize damage.
- Good housekeeping. Records and flammables must not be stored in the IS area. Tidy installation of IS equipment is crucial.
- Hand-operated fire extinguishers readily available, clearly marked, and regularly tested.
- Automatic fire extinguishers installed. Installation should be such that the extinguishers are unlikely to cause damage to equipment or danger to personnel.
- Fire detectors. The detectors sound alarms inside the IS room and with external authorities, and start automatic fire extinguishers after a delay to permit human intervention.
- Equipment power-off switch. This switch must be clearly marked and unobstructed. All personnel must be familiar with power-off procedures.
- Emergency procedures posted.
- Personnel safety. Safety must be considered in designing the building layout and emergency procedures.
- Important records stored in fireproof cabinets or vaults.
- Records needed for file reconstruction stored off the premises.
- Up-to-date duplicate of all programs stored off the premises.
- Contingency plan for use of equipment elsewhere should the computers be destroyed.
- Insurance company and local fire department should inspect the facility.

To deal with the threat of smoke, the responsible manager should install smoke detectors in every room that contains computer equipment as well as under raised floors and over suspended ceilings. Smoking should not be permitted in computer rooms.

For wildfires, the available countermeasures are limited. Fire-resistant building techniques are costly and difficult to justify.

Water Damage

Prevention and mitigation measures for water threats must encompass the range of such threats. For plumbing leaks, the cost of relocating threatening lines is generally difficult to justify. With knowledge of the exact layout of water supply lines, measures can be taken to locate equipment sensibly. The location of all shutoff valves should be clearly visible or at least clearly documented, and responsible personnel should know the procedures to follow in case of emergency.

To deal with both plumbing leaks and other sources of water, sensors are vital. Water sensors should be located on the floor of computer rooms as well as under raised floors and should cut off power automatically in the event of a flood.

Other Environmental Threats

For chemical, biological, and radiological threats, specific technical approaches are available, including infrastructure design, sensor design and placement, mitigation procedures, personnel training, and so forth. Standards and techniques in these areas continue to evolve.

As for dust hazards, the obvious prevention method is to limit dust through the use and proper filter maintenance and regular IS room maintenance.

For infestations, regular pest control procedures may be needed, starting with maintaining a clean environment.

Technical Threats

To deal with brief power interruptions, an uninterruptible power supply (UPS) should be employed for each piece of critical equipment. The UPS is a battery backup unit that can maintain power to processors, monitors, and other equipment for a period of minutes. UPS units can also function as surge protectors, power noise filters, and automatic shutdown devices when the battery runs low.

For longer blackouts or brownouts, critical equipment should be connected to an emergency power source, such as a generator. For reliable service, a range of issues need to be addressed by management, including product selection, generator placement, personnel training, testing and maintenance schedules, and so forth.

To deal with electromagnetic interference, a combination of filters and shielding can be used. The specific technical details will depend on the infrastructure design and the anticipated sources and nature of the interference.

Human-Caused Physical Threats

The general approach to human-caused physical threats is physical access control. Based on Michael,[4] we can

---

4 M. Michael, "Physical security measures," In H. Bidgoli, (ed.), *Handbook of Information Security*, Wiley, 2006.

suggest a spectrum of approaches that can be used to restrict access to equipment. These methods can be used in combination.

- Physical contact with a resource is restricted by restricting access to the building in which the resource is housed. This approach is intended to deny access to outsiders but does not address the issue of unauthorized insiders or employees.
- Physical contact with a resource is restricted by putting the resource in a locked cabinet, safe, or room.
- A machine may be accessed, but it is secured (perhaps permanently bolted) to an object that is difficult to move. This will deter theft but not vandalism, unauthorized access, or misuse.
- A security device controls the power switch.
- A movable resource is equipped with a tracking device so that a sensing portal can alert security personnel or trigger an automated barrier to prevent the object from being moved out of its proper security area.
- A portable object is equipped with a tracking device so that its current position can be monitored continually.

The first two of the preceding approaches isolate the equipment. Techniques that can be used for this type of access control include controlled areas patrolled or guarded by personnel, barriers that isolate each area, entry points in the barrier (doors), and locks or screening measures at each entry point.

Physical access control should address not just computers and other IS equipment but also locations of wiring used to connect systems, the electrical power service, the HVAC equipment and distribution system, telephone and communications lines, backup media, and documents.

In addition to physical and procedural barriers, an effective physical access control regime includes a variety of sensors and alarms to detect intruders and unauthorized access or movement of equipment. Surveillance systems are frequently an integral part of building security, and special-purpose surveillance systems for the IS area are generally also warranted. Such systems should provide real-time remote viewing as well as recording.

4. RECOVERY FROM PHYSICAL SECURITY BREACHES

The most essential element of recovery from physical security breaches is redundancy. Redundancy does not undo any breaches of confidentiality, such as the theft of data or documents, but it does provide for recovery from loss of data. Ideally, all the important data in the system should be available off site and updated as near to real time as is warranted based on a cost/benefit tradeoff. With broadband connections now almost universally available, batch encrypted backups over private networks or the Internet are warranted and can be carried out on whatever schedule is deemed appropriate by management. At the extreme, a *hotsite* can be created off site that is ready to take over operation instantly and has available to it a near-real-time copy of operational data.

Recovery from physical damage to the equipment or the site depends on the nature of the damage and, importantly, the nature of the residue. Water, smoke, and fire damage may leave behind hazardous materials that must be meticulously removed from the site before normal operations and the normal equipment suite can be reconstituted. In many cases, this requires bringing in disaster recovery specialists from outside the organization to do the cleanup.

5. THREAT ASSESSMENT, PLANNING, AND PLAN IMPLEMENTATION

We have surveyed a number of threats to physical security and a number of approaches to prevention, mitigation, and recovery. To implement a physical security program, an organization must conduct a threat assessment to determine the amount of resources to devote to physical security and the allocation of those resources against the various threats. This process also applies to logical security.

Threat Assessment

In this subsection, we follow Platt[5] in outlining a typical sequence of steps that an organization should take:

1. *Set up a steering committee.* The threat assessment should not be left only to a security officer or to IS management. All those who have a stake in the security of the IS assets, including all of the user communities, should be brought into the process.
2. *Obtain information and assistance.* Historical information concerning external threats, such as flood and fire is the best starting point. This information can often be obtained from

5 F. Platt, "Physical threats to the information infrastructure," in S. Bosworth, and M. Kabay, (eds.), *Computer Security Handbook*, Wiley, 2002.

government agencies and weather bureaus. In the United States, the Federal Emergency Management Agency (FEMA) can provide much useful information. FEMA has a number of publications available online that provide specific guidance in a wide variety of physical security areas (www.fema.gov/business/index.shtm). The committee should also seek expert advice from vendors, suppliers, neighboring businesses, service and maintenance personnel, consultants, and academics.

3. *Identify all possible threats.* List all possible threats, including those that are specific to IS operations as well as those that are more general, covering the building and the geographic area.

4. *Determine the likelihood of each threat.* This is clearly a difficult task. One approach is to use a scale of 1 (least likely) to 5 (most likely) so that threats can be grouped to suggest where attention should be directed. All the information from Step 2 can be applied to this task.

5. *Approximate the direct costs.* For each threat, the committee must estimate not only the threat's likelihood but also its severity in terms of consequences. Again a relative scale of 1 (low) to 5 (high) in terms of costs and losses is a reasonable approach. For both Steps 4 and 5, an attempt to use a finer-grained scale, or to assign specific probabilities and specific costs, is likely to produce the impression of greater precision and knowledge about future threats than is possible.

6. *Consider cascading costs.* Some threats can trigger consequential threats that add still more impact costs. For example, a fire can cause direct flame, heat, and smoke damage as well as disrupt utilities and result in water damage.

7. *Prioritize the threats.* The goal here is to determine the relative importance of the threats as a guide to focusing resources on prevention. A simple formula yields a prioritized list:

$$\text{Importance} = \text{Likelihood} \times [\text{Direct Cost} + \text{Secondary Cost}]$$

where the scale values (1 through 5) are used in the formula.

8. *Complete the threat assessment report.* The committee can now prepare a report that includes the prioritized list, with commentary on how the results were achieved. This report serves as the reference source for the planning process that follows.

Planning and Implementation

Once a threat assessment has been done, the steering committee, or another committee, can develop a plan for threat prevention, mitigation, and recovery. The following is a typical sequence of steps an organization could take:

1. *Assess internal and external resources.* These include resources for prevention as well as response. A reasonable approach is again to use a relative scale from 1 (strong ability to prevent and respond) to 5 (weak ability to prevent and respond). This scale can be combined with the threat priority score to focus resource planning.

2. *Identify challenges and prioritize activities.* Determine specific goals and milestones. Make a list of tasks to be performed, by whom and when. Determine how you will address the problem areas and resource shortfalls that were identified in the vulnerability analysis.

3. *Develop a plan.* The plan should include prevention measures and equipment needed and emergency response procedures. The plan should include support documents, such as emergency call lists, building and site maps, and resource lists.

4. *Implement the plan.* Implementation includes acquiring new equipment, assigning responsibilities, conducting training, monitoring plan implementation, and updating the plan regularly.

6. EXAMPLE: A CORPORATE PHYSICAL SECURITY POLICY

To give the reader a feel for how organizations deal with physical security, we provide a real-world example of a physical security policy. The company is a European Union (EU)-based engineering consulting firm that specializes in the provision of planning, design, and management services for infrastructure development worldwide. With interests in transportation, water, maritime, and property, the company is undertaking commissions in over 70 countries from a network of more than 70 offices.

Figure 36.3 is extracted from the company's security standards document. For our purposes, we have changed the name of the company to *Company* wherever it appears in the document. The company's physical security policy relies heavily on ISO 17799 (*Code of Practice for Information Security Management*).

5. Physical and Environmental Security

5.1. Secure Areas

5.1.1. **Physical Security Perimeter** – Company shall use security perimeters to protect all non-public areas, commensurate with the value of the assets therein. Business critical information processing facilities located in unattended buildings shall also be alarmed to a permanently manned remote alarm monitoring station.

5.1.2. **Physical Entry Controls** – Secure areas shall be segregated and protected by appropriate entry controls to ensure that only authorised personnel are allowed access. Similar controls are also required where the building is shared with, or accessed by, non-Company staff and organisations not acting on behalf of Company.

5.1.3. **Securing Offices, Rooms and Facilities** – Secure areas shall be created in order to protect office, rooms and facilities with special security requirements.

5.1.4. **Working in Secure Areas** – Additional controls and guidelines for working in secure areas shall be used to enhance the security provided by the physical control protecting the secure areas.

> *Employees of Company should be aware that additional controls and guidelines for working in secure areas to enhance the security provided by the physical control protecting the secure areas might be in force. For further clarification they should contact their Line Manager.*

5.1.5. **Isolated Access Points** – Isolated access points, additional to building main entrances (e.g. Delivery and Loading areas) shall be controlled and, if possible, isolated from secure areas to avoid unauthorised access.

5.1.6. **Sign Posting Of Computer Installations** – Business critical computer installations sited within a building must not be identified by the use of descriptive sign posts or other displays. Where such sign posts or other displays are used they must be worded in such a way so as not to highlight the business critical nature of the activity taking place within the building.

5.2. Equipment Security

5.2.1. **Equipment Sitting and Protection** – Equipment shall be sited or protected to reduce the risk from environmental threats and hazards, and opportunity for unauthorised access.

5.2.2. **Power Supply** – The equipment shall be protected from power failure and other electrical anomalies.

5.2.3. **Cabling Security** – Power and telecommunication cabling carrying data or supporting information services shall be protected from interception or damage commensurate with the business criticality of the operations they serve.

5.2.4. **Equipment Maintenance** – Equipment shall be maintained in accordance with manufacturer's instruction and/or documented procedures to ensure its continued availability and integrity.

5.2.5. **Security of Equipment off-premises** – Security procedures and controls shall be used to secure equipment used outside any Company's premises.

> *Employees are to note that there should be security procedures and controls to secure equipment used outside any Company premises. Advice on these procedures can be sought from the Group Security Manager.*

5.2.6. **Secure Disposal or Re-use of Equipment** – Information shall be erased from equipment prior to disposal or reuse.

> *For further guidance contact the Group Security Manager.*

5.2.7. **Security of the Access Network** – Company shall implement access control measures, determined by a risk assessment, to ensure that only authorised people have access to the Access Network (including: cabinets, cabling, nodes etc.).

5.2.8. **Security of PCs** – Every Company owned PC must have an owner who is responsible for its general management and control. Users of PCs are personally responsible for the physical and logical security of any PC they use. Users of Company PCs are personally responsible for the physical and logical security of any PC they use, as defined within the Staff Handbook.

5.2.9. **Removal of "Captured Data"** – Where any device (software or hardware based) has been introduced to the network that captures data for analytical purposes, all data must be wiped off of this device prior to removal from the Company Site. The removal of this data from site for analysis can only be approved by the MIS Technology Manager.

FIGURE 36.3 The Company's physical security policy.

5.3. General Controls

5.3.1. **Security Controls** – Security Settings are to be utilised and configurations must be controlled

No security settings or software on Company systems are to be changed without authorisation from MIS Support.

5.3.2. **Clear Screen Policy** – Company shall have and implement clear-screen policy in order to reduce the risks of unauthorised access, loss of, and damage to information.

This will be implemented when all Users of the Company system have Windows XP operating system.

When the User has the Windows XP system they are to carry out the following:

- *Select the Settings tab within the START area on the desktop screen.*
- *Select Control Panel.*
- *Select the icon called DISPLAY.*
- *Select the Screensaver Tab.*
- *Set a Screen saver.*
- *Set the time for 15 Mins.*
- *Tick the Password Protect box; remember this is the same password that you utilise to log on to the system.*

Staff are to lock their screens using the Ctrl-Alt-Del when they leave their desk.

5.3.3. **Clear Desk Policy** – Staff shall ensure that they operate a Clear Desk Policy.

Each member of staff is asked to take personal and active responsibility for maintaining a "clear desk" policy whereby files and papers are filed or otherwise cleared away before leaving the office at the end of each day.

5.3.4. **Removal of Property** – Equipment, information or software belonging to the organisation shall not be removed without authorisation.

Equipment, information or software belonging to Company shall not be removed without authorisation from the Project Manager or Line Manager and the MIS Support.

5.3.5. **People Identification** – All Company staff must have visible the appropriate identification whenever they are in Company premises.

5.3.6. **Visitors** – All Company premises will have a process for dealing with visitors. All Visitors must be sponsored and wear the appropriate identification whenever they are in Company premises.

5.3.7. **Legal Right of Entry** – Entry must be permitted to official bodies when entry is demanded on production of a court order or when the person has other legal rights. Advice must be sought from management or the Group Security Manager as a matter of urgency.

FIGURE 36.3 *Continued.*

7. INTEGRATION OF PHYSICAL AND LOGICAL SECURITY

Physical security involves numerous detection devices, such as sensors and alarms, and numerous prevention devices and measures, such as locks and physical barriers. It should be clear that there is much scope for automation and for the integration of various computerized and electronic devices. Clearly, physical security can be made more effective if there is a central destination for all alerts and alarms and if there is central control of all automated access control mechanisms, such as smart card entry sites.

From the point of view of both effectiveness and cost, there is increasing interest not only in integrating automated physical security functions but in integrating, to the extent possible, automated physical security and logical security functions. The most promising area is that of access control. Examples of ways to integrate physical and logical access control include the following:

- Use of a single ID card for physical and logical access. This can be a simple magnetic-strip card or a smart card.
- Single-step user/card enrollment and termination across all identity and access control databases.

- A central ID-management system instead of multiple disparate user directories and databases.
- Unified event monitoring and correlation.

As an example of the utility of this integration, suppose that an alert indicates that Bob has logged on to the company's wireless network (an event generated by the logical access control system) but did not enter the building (an event generated from the physical access control system). Combined, these two events suggest that someone is hijacking Bob's wireless account.

For the integration of physical and logical access control to be practical, a wide range of vendors must conform to standards that cover smart card protocols, authentication and access control formats and protocols, database entries, message formats, and so on. An important step in this direction is FIPS 201-1 (*Personal Identity Verification (PIV) of Federal Employees and Contractors*), issued in 2006. The standard defines a reliable, governmentwide PIV system for use in applications such as access to federally controlled facilities and information systems. The standard specifies a PIV system within which common identification credentials can be created and later used to verify a claimed identity. The standard also identifies federal governmentwide requirements for security levels that are dependent on risks to the facility or information being protected.

Figure 36.4 illustrates the major components of FIPS 201-1 compliant systems. The PIV front end defines the physical interface to a user who is requesting access to a facility, which could be either physical access to a protected physical area or logical access to an information system. The PIV front-end subsystem supports up to three-factor authentication; the number of factors used depends on the level of security required. The front end makes use of a smart card, known as a *PIV card*, which is a dual-interface contact and contactless card. The card holds a cardholder photograph, X.509 certificates, cryptographic keys, biometric data, and the cardholder unique identifier (CHUID). Certain cardholder information may be read-protected and require a personal identification number (PIN) for read access by the card reader. The biometric reader, in the current version of the standard, is a fingerprint reader.

The standard defines three assurance levels for verification of the card and the encoded data stored on the card, which in turn leads to verifying the authenticity of the person holding the credential. A level of *some confidence* corresponds to use of the card reader and PIN. A level of *high confidence* adds a biometric comparison of a fingerprint captured and encoded on the card during the card-issuing process and a fingerprint scanned at the physical access point. A *very high confidence* level requires that the process just described is completed at a control point attended by an official observer.

The other major component of the PIV system is the *PIV card issuance and management subsystem*. This subsystem includes the components responsible for identity proofing and registration, card and key issuance and management, and the various repositories and services (e.g., public key infrastructure [PKI] directory, certificate status servers) required as part of the verification infrastructure.

The PIV system interacts with an *access control subsystem*, which includes components responsible for determining a particular PIV cardholder's access to a physical or logical resource. FIPS 201-1 standardizes data formats and protocols for interaction between the PIV system and the access control system.

Unlike the typical card number/facility code encoded on most access control cards, the FIPS 201 CHUID takes authentication to a new level, through the use of an expiration date (a required CHUID data field) and an optional CHUID digital signature. A digital signature can be checked to ensure that the CHUID recorded on the card was digitally signed by a trusted source and that the CHUID data have not been altered since the card was signed. The CHUID expiration date can be checked to verify that the card has not expired. This is independent of whatever expiration date is associated with cardholder privileges. Reading and verifying the CHUID alone provides only some assurance of identity because it authenticates the card data, not the cardholder. The PIN and biometric factors provide identity verification of the individual.

Figure 36.5, adapted from Forristal,[6] illustrates the convergence of physical and logical access control using FIPS 201-1. The core of the system includes the PIV and access control system as well as a certificate authority for signing CHUIDs. The other elements of the figure provide examples of the use of the system core for integrating physical and logical access control.

If the integration of physical and logical access control extends beyond a unified front end to an integration of system elements, a number of benefits accrue, including the following[7]:

- Employees gain a single, unified access control authentication device; this cuts down on misplaced

6 J. Forristal, "Physical/logical convergence," *Network Computing*, November 23, 2006.

7 J. Forristal, "Physical/logical convergence," *Network Computing*, November 23, 2006.

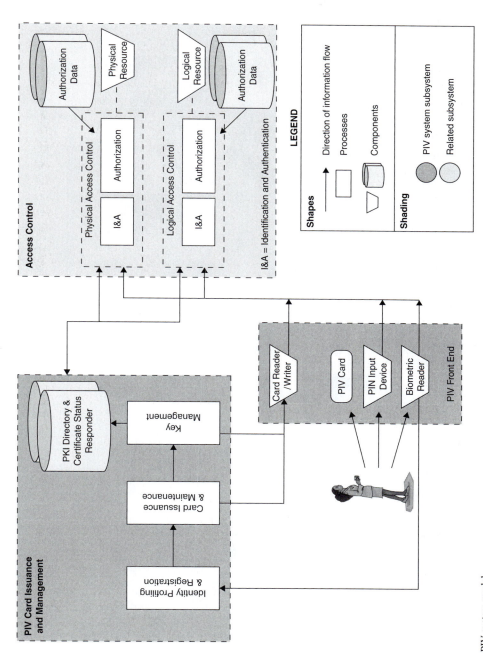

FIGURE 36.4 FIPS 201 PIV system model.

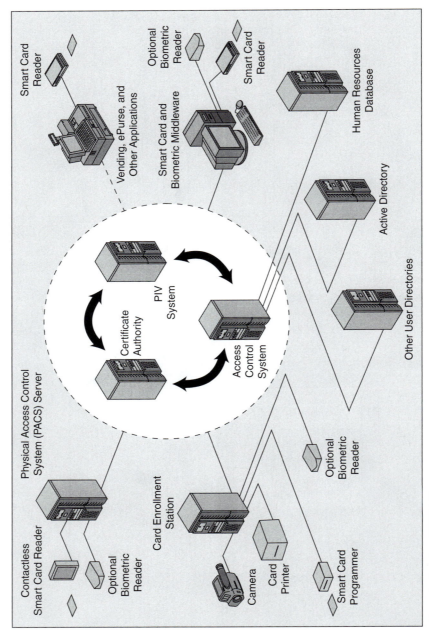

FIGURE 36.5 Convergence Example (based on [FORR06]).

tokens, reduces training and overhead, and allows seamless access.

- A single logical location for employee ID management reduces duplicate data entry operations and allows for immediate and real-time authorization revocation of all enterprise resources.
- Auditing and forensic groups have a central repository for access control investigations.
- Hardware unification can reduce the number of vendor purchase-and-support contracts.

- Certificate-based access control systems can leverage user ID certificates for other security applications, such as document esigning and data encryption.

REFERENCES

[1] H. Bidgoli (Ed.), *Handbook of Information Security*, Wiley, 2006.
[2] S. Bosworth, M. Kabay (Eds.), *Computer Security Handbook*, Wiley, 2002.

## Chapter 37

Biometrics

Luther Martin
Voltage Security

Biometrics is the analysis of biological observations and phenomena. People routinely use biometrics to recognize other people, commonly using the shape of a face or the sound of a voice to do so. Biometrics can also be used to create automated ways of recognizing a person based on her physiological or behavioral characteristics. Using biometrics as the basis of technologies that can be used to recognize people is not a new idea; there is evidence that fingerprints were used to sign official contracts in China as early as AD 700 and may have been used by ancient Babylonian scribes to sign cuneiform tablets as early as 2000 BC.[1] In both of these cases, a fingerprint was pressed in clay to form a distinctive mark that could characterize a particular person. It is likely that the sophistication of the techniques used to analyze biometric data has increased over the past 4000 years, but the principles have remained essentially the same.

Using biometrics in security applications is certainly appealing. Determining a person's identity through the presence of a physical object such as a key or access card has the problem that the physical token can be lost or stolen. Shared secrets such as passwords can be forgotten. Determining a person's identity using biometrics seems an attractive alternative. It allows an identity to be determined directly from characteristics of the person. It is generally impossible for people to lose or forget their biometric data, so many of the problems that other means of verifying an identity are essentially eliminated if biometrics can be used in this role.

Not all biometric data is suitable for use in security applications, however. To be useful, such biometric data should be as unique as possible (uniqueness), should occur in as many people as possible (universality), should stay relatively constant over time (permanence), and should be able to be measured easily (measurability) and without causing undue inconvenience or distress to a user (acceptability). Examples of technologies that seem to meet these criteria to varying degrees are those that recognize a person based on his DNA, geometry of his face, fingerprints, hand geometry, iris pattern, retina pattern, handwriting, or voice. Many others are also possible. Not all biometrics are equally suited for use in security applications. Table 37.1 compares the properties of selected biometric technologies, rating each property as high, medium, or low. This table shows that there is no "best" biometric for security applications. Though this is true, each biometric has a set of uses for which its particular properties make it more attractive than the alternatives.

Biometrics systems can be used as a means of authenticating a user. When they are used in this way, a user presents his biometric data along with his identity, and the biometric system decides whether or not the biometric data presented is correct for that identity. Biometrics used as a method of authentication can be very useful, but authentication systems based on biometrics also have very different properties from other authentication technologies, and these differences should be understood before biometrics are used as part of an information security system.

Systems based on biometrics can also be used as a means of identification. When they are used in this way, captured biometric data is compared to entries in a database, and the biometric system determines whether or not the biometric data presented matches any of these existing entries. When biometrics are used for identification, they have a property that many other identification systems do not have. In particular, biometrics do not always require the active participation of a subject. While a user always needs to enter her password when the password is used to authenticate her, it is possible to capture biometric data without the user's active involvement, perhaps even

---

[1] R. Heindl, *System und Praxis der Daktyloskopie und der sonstigen technischen Methoden der Kriminalpolizei*, De Gruyter, 1922.

TABLE 37.1 Overview of Selected Biometric Technologies

Biometric	Uniqueness	Universality	Permanence	Measurability	Acceptability
DNA	High	High	High	Low	Low
Face geometry	Low	High	Medium	High	High
Fingerprint	High	Medium	High	Medium	Medium
Hand geometry	Medium	Medium	Medium	High	Medium
Iris	High	High	High	Medium	Low
Retina	High	High	Medium	Low	Low
Signature dynamics	Low	Medium	Low	High	High
Voice	Low	Medium	Low	Medium	High

without her knowledge. This lets data be used in ways that other systems cannot. It is possible to automatically capture images of customers in a bank, for example, and to use the images to help identify people who are known to commit check fraud. Or it is possible to automatically capture images of airline passengers in an airport and use the images to help identify suspicious travelers.

The use of biometrics for identification also has the potential to pose serious privacy issues. The interests of governments and individual citizens are often at odds. Law enforcement agencies might want to be able to track the movements of certain people, and the automated use of biometrics for identification can certainly support this goal. On the other hand, it is unlikely that most people would approve of law enforcement having a database that contains detailed information about their travels. Similarly, tax authorities might want to track all business dealings to ensure that they collect all the revenue they are due, but it seems unlikely that most people would approve of government agencies having a database that tracks all merchants they have had dealings with, even if no purchases were made. Using some biometrics may also inherently provide access to much more information that is needed to just identify a person. DNA, for example, can used to identify people, but it can also be used to determine information about genetic conditions that are irrelevant to the identification process. But if a user needs to provide a DNA sample as a means of identification, the same DNA sample could be used to determine genetic information that the user might rather have kept private.

Designing biometric systems is actually a very difficult problem. This problem has been made to look easier than it actually is by the way that the technology has been portrayed in movies and on television. Biometric systems are typically depicted as being easy to use and

secure, whereas encryption that would actually take billions of years of supercomputer time to defeat is often depicted as being easily bypassed with minimal effort. This portrayal of biometric systems may have increased expectations well past what current technologies can actually deliver, and it is important to understand the limitations of existing biometric technologies and to have realistic expectations of the security that such systems can provide in the real world.

Designing biometric systems has been dubbed a "grand challenge" by researchers,[2] indicating that a significant level of research will be required before it will be possible for real systems to approach the performance that is expected of the technology, but one that also has the possibility for broad scientific and economic impact when technology finally reaches that level. So, although biometric systems are useful today, we should expect to see them become even more useful in the future and for the technology to eventually become fairly commonly used.

1. RELEVANT STANDARDS

The American National Standard (ANS) X9.84, "Biometric Information Management and Security for the Financial Services Industry," is one of the leading standards that provide an overview of biometrics and their use in information security systems. It is a good high-level discussion of biometric systems, and the description of the technology in this chapter roughly follows the framework defined by this standard. This standard is particularly

---

2 A. Jain, et al., "Biometrics: A grand challenge," *Proceedings of the 17th International Conference on Pattern Recognition*, Cambridge, UK, August 2004, pp. 935–942.

TABLE 37.2 Current ISO/IEC Standards for Biometric Systems

Standard	Title
ISO/IEC 19784-1: 2006	Information technology – Biometric Application Programming Interface – Part 1: BioAPI Specification
ISO/IEC 19784-2: 2007	Information technology – Biometric Application Programming Interface – Part 2: Biometric Archive Function Provider Interface
ISO/IEC 19785-1: 2006	Information technology – Common Biometric Exchange Formats Framework (CBEFF) – Part 1: Data Element Specification
ISO/IEC 19785-2: 2006	Information technology – Common Biometric Exchange Formats Framework (CBEFF) – Part 2: Procedures for the Operation of the Biometric Registration Authority
ISO/IEC 19794-1: 2006	Information technology – Biometric data interchange format – Part 1: Framework
ISO/IEC 19794-2: 2005	Information technology – Biometric data interchange format – Part 2: Finger minutiae data
ISO/IEC 19794-3: 2006	Information technology – Biometric data interchange format – Part 3: Finger pattern spectral data
ISO/IEC 19794-4: 2005	Information technology – Biometric data interchange format – Part 4: Finger image data
ISO/IEC 19794-5: 2005	Information technology – Biometric data interchange format – Part 5: Face image data
ISO/IEC 19794-6: 2005	Information technology – Biometric data interchange format – Part 6: Iris image data
ISO/IEC 19794-7: 2006	Information technology – Biometric data interchange format – Part 7: Signature/sign time series data
ISO/IEC 19794-8: 2006	Information technology – Biometric data interchange format – Part 8: Finger pattern skeletal data
ISO/IEC 19794-9: 2007	Information technology – Biometric data interchange format – Part 9: Vascular image data
ISO/IEC 19795-1: 2006	Information technology – Biometric performance testing and reporting – Part 1: Principles and framework
ISO/IEC 19795-2: 2007	Information technology – Biometric performance testing and reporting – Part 2: testing methodologies for technology and scenario evaluation
ISO/IEC 24709.1: 2007	BioAPI Conformance Testing – Part 1: Methods and Procedures
ISO/IEC 24709.2: 2007	BioAPI Conformance Testing – Part 2: Test Assertions for Biometric Service Providers

useful to system architects and others concerned with a high-level view of security systems. On the other hand, this standard does not provide many details of how to implement such systems.

There are also several international (ISO/IEC) standards that cover the details of biometric systems with more detail than ANS X9.84 does. These are listed in Table 37.2. These standards provide a good basis for implementing biometric systems and may be useful to both engineers and others who need to build a biometric system, and others who need the additional level of detail that ANS X9.84 does not provide. Many other ISO/IEC standards for biometric systems are currently under development that address other aspects of such systems, and in the next few years it is likely that the number of these standards that have been finalized will at least double from the number that are listed here. The JTC 1/SC 37 technical committee of the ISO is responsible for the development of these standards.

2. BIOMETRIC SYSTEM ARCHITECTURE

All biometric systems have a number of common subsystems. These are the following:

- A data capture subsystem
- A signal processing subsystem
- A matching subsystem
- A data storage subsystem
- A decision subsystem

An additional subsystem, the adaptation subsystem, may be present in some biometric systems but not others.

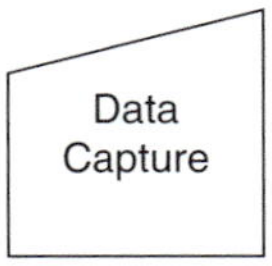

FIGURE 37.1 Symbol used to indicate a data capture subsystem.

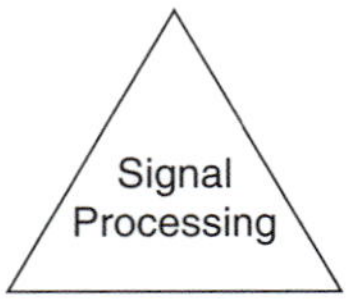

FIGURE 37.2 Symbol used to indicate a signal processing subsystem.

Data Capture

A data capture subsystem collects captured biometric data from a user. To do this, it performs a measurement of some sort and creates machine-readable data from it. This could be an image of a fingerprint, a signal from a microphone, or readings from a special pen that takes measurements while it is being used. In each case, the captured biometric data usually needs to be processed in some way before it can be used in a decision algorithm. It is extremely rare for a biometric system to make a decision using an image of a fingerprint, for example. Instead, features that make fingerprints different from other fingerprints are extracted from such an image in the signal processing subsystem, and these features are then used in the matching subsystem. The symbol that is used to indicate a data capture subsystem is shown in Figure 37.1.

The performance of a data capture subsystem is greatly affected by the characteristics of the sensor that it uses. A signal processing subsystem may work very well with one type of sensor, but much less well with another type. Even if identical sensors are used in each data capture subsystem, the calibration of the sensors may need to be consistent to ensure the collection of data that works well in other subsystems.

Environmental conditions can also significantly affect the operation of a data capture subsystem. Dirty sensors can result in images of fingerprints that are distorted or incomplete. Background noise can result in the collection of a data that makes it difficult for the signal processing subsystem to identify the features of a voice signal. Lighting can also affect any biometric data that is collected as an image so that an image collected against a gray background might not work as well as an image collected against a white background.

Because environmental conditions affect the quality and usefulness of captured biometric data, they also affect the performance of all the subsystems that rely on it. This means that it is essential to carry out all testing of biometric systems under conditions that duplicate the conditions under which the system will normally operate. Just because a biometric system performs well in a testing laboratory when operated by well-trained users does not mean that it will perform well in real-world conditions.

Because the data capture subsystem is typically the only one with which users directly interact, it is also the one that may require training of users to ensure that it provides useful data to the other subsystems.

Signal Processing

A signal processing subsystem takes the captured biometric data from a data capture subsystem and transforms the data into a form suitable for use in the matching subsystem. This transformed data is called a *reference*, or a *template* if it is stored in a data storage subsystem. A template is a type of reference, and it represents the average value that we expect to see for a particular user.

A signal processing subsystem may also analyze the quality of captured biometric data and reject data that is not of high enough quality. An image of a fingerprint that is not oriented correctly might be rejected, or a sample of speech that was collected with too much background noise might be rejected. The symbol that is used to indicate a signal processing subsystem is shown in Figure 37.2.

If the captured biometric data is not rejected, the signal processing subsystem then transforms the captured biometric data into a reference. In the case of fingerprints, for example, the signal processing subsystem may extract features such as the locations of branches and endpoints of the ridges that comprise a fingerprint. A biometric system that uses the speech of users to characterize them might convert the speech signal into frequency components using a Fourier transform and then look for patterns in the frequency components that uniquely characterize a particular speaker. A biometric that uses an image of a person's face might first look for large features such as the eyes, nose, and mouth and then look for distinctive features such as eyebrows or parts of the nose relative to the large ones, to uniquely identify a particular user. In any case, the output of the signal processing subsystem is the transformed data that comprises a reference. Although a reference contains information that has been extracted from captured biometric data, it may be possible to recover the

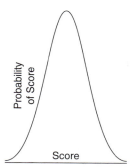

FIGURE 37.3 Distribution in comparison scores for a typical user.

captured biometric data, or a good approximation to it, from a template.[3]

Note that though several standards exist that define the format of biometric references for many technologies, these standards do not describe how references are obtained from captured biometric data. This means that there is still room for vendor innovation while remaining in compliance with existing standards.

Matching

A matching subsystem receives a reference from a signal processing subsystem and then compares the reference with a template from a data storage subsystem. The output of the matching subsystem is a numeric value called a *comparison score* that indicates how closely the two match.

Random variations occur in a data capture subsystem when it is used. This means that the reference created from the captured data is different each time, even for the same user. This makes the comparison score created for a particular user different each time they use the system, with random variations occurring around some average value. This concept is shown in Figure 37.3, in which the distribution of comparison scores that are calculated from repeated captures of biometric data from a single user are random. Such random data tend to be close to an average value every time that they are calculated from captured biometric data but not exactly the average value.

This is much like the case we get in other situations where observed data has a random component. Suppose that we flip a fair coin 100 times and count how many times the result "heads" appears. We expect to see this

FIGURE 37.4 Symbol used to indicate a matching subsystem.

FIGURE 37.5 Symbol used to indicate a data storage subsystem.

result an average of 50 times, but this average value actually occurs fairly rarely; exactly 50 out of 100 flips coming up heads happen less than 8% of the time. On the other hand, the number of heads will usually be not too far from the average value of 50, with the number being between 40 and 60 more than 95% of the time. Similarly, with biometrics, captured data will probably be close, but not identical, to an average value, and it will also not be too different from the average value.

The comparison score calculated by a matching subsystem is passed to a decision subsystem, where it is used to make a decision about the identity of the person who was the source of the biometric data. The symbol that is used to indicate a matching subsystem is shown in Figure 37.4.

Data Storage

A data storage subsystem stores templates that are used by the matching subsystem. The symbol that is used to indicate a data storage subsystem is shown in Figure 37.5.

A database is one obvious candidate for a place to store templates, but it is possible to store a template on a portable data storage device such as a chip card or a smart card. The relative strengths and weaknesses of different ways of doing this are discussed in the section on security considerations.

Decision

A decision subsystem takes a comparison score that is the output of a matching subsystem and returns a binary *yes* or *no* decision from it. This decision indicates whether or not the matching subsystem made a comparison which resulted in a match or not. The value *yes* is returned if the comparison was probably a match; the value *no* is returned is the comparison was probably not

3 M. Martinez-Diaz, et al., "Hill-climbing and brute-force attacks on biometric systems: A case study in match-on-card fingerprint verification," *Proceedings of the 40th IEEE International Carahan Conference on Security Technology*, Lexington, October 2006, pp. 151–159.

FIGURE 37.6 Symbol used to indicate a decision subsystem.

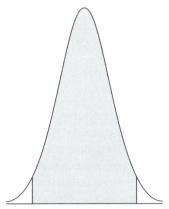

FIGURE 37.7 Comparison scores close to the average that result in a *yes* decision.

a match. The symbol that is used to indicate a decision subsystem is shown in Figure 37.6.

To make a *yes* or *no* decision, a decision subsystem compares a comparison score with a parameter called a *threshold*. The threshold value represents a measure of how good a comparison needs to be to be considered a match. If the comparison score is less than or equal to the threshold value then the decision subsystem returns the value *yes*. If the comparison score is greater than the threshold, it returns the value *no*. Comparison scores that will result in a *yes* or *no* response from a decision subsystem are shown in Figure 37.7. Comparison scores in the gray area of this illustration are close to the average value and result in a *yes*, whereas comparison scores that are outside the gray area are too far from the average value and result in a *no*. In Figure 37.7, the threshold value defines how far the gray area extends from the central average value. If the threshold is decreased, the size of the gray area will get narrower and decrease in size so that fewer comparison scores result in a *yes* answer. If the threshold is increased, the gray area will get wider and increase in size so that more comparison scores result in a *yes* answer.

Errors may occur in any decision subsystem. There are two general types of errors that can occur. In one case, a decision subsystem makes the incorrect decision of *no* instead of *yes*. In this case, a user is indeed who she claims to be, but large random errors occur in the

data capture subsystem and cause her to be incorrectly rejected. This type of error might result in the legitimate user Alice inaccurately failing to authenticate as herself.

This class of error is known as a *type-1* error by statisticians,[4] a term that would almost certainly be a contender for an award for the least meaningful terminology ever invented if such an award existed. It was once called *false rejection* by biometrics researchers and vendors, a term that has more recently been replaced by the term *false nonmatch*. One way in which the accuracy of biometric systems is now typically quantified is by their false nonmatch rate (FNMR), a value that estimates the probability of the biometric system making a type-1 error in its decision subsystem.

In the second case, a decision subsystem incorrectly returns a *yes* instead of a *no*. In this case, random errors occur that let a user be erroneously recognized as a different user. This might happen if the user Alice tries to authenticate as the user Bob, for example. This class of error is known as a *type-2* error by statisticians.[5] It was once called *false acceptance* by biometrics researchers and vendors, a term that has been more recently been replaced by the term *false match*. This leads to quantifying the accuracy of biometrics by their false match rate (FMR), a value that estimates the probability of the biometric system making a type-2 error.

For a particular biometric technology, it is impossible to simultaneously reduce both the FNMR and the FMR, although improving the technology does make it possible to do this. If the parameters used in a matching subsystem are changed so that the FNMR decreases, the FMR rate must increase; if the parameters used in a matching subsystem are changed so that the FMR decreases, the FNMR must increase. This relationship follows from the nature of the statistical tests that are performed by the decision subsystem and is not limited to just biometric systems. Any system that makes a decision based on statistical data will have the same property. The reason for this is shown in Figures 37.8 and 37.9.

Suppose that we have two users of a biometric system: Alice and Bob, whose comparison scores are distributed as shown in Figure 37.8. Note that the distributions of these values overlap so that in the area where they overlap, the comparison score could have come

4 J. Neyman and E. Pearson, "On the use and interpretation of certain test criteria for purposes of statistical inference: Part I," *Biometrika*, Vol. 20A, No. 1–2, pp. 175–240, July 1928.

5 S. King, H. Harrelson and G. Tran, "Testing iris and face recognition in a personnel identification application," 2002 Biometric Consortium Conference, February 2002.

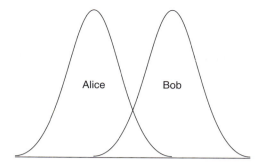

FIGURE 37.8 Overlap in possible comparison scores for Alice and Bob.

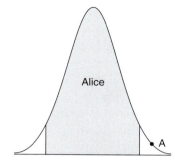

FIGURE 37.10 Type-1 error that causes a false nonmatch.

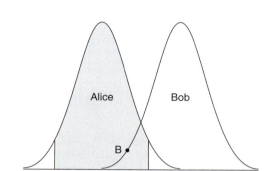

FIGURE 37.9 Type-2 error that causes a false match.

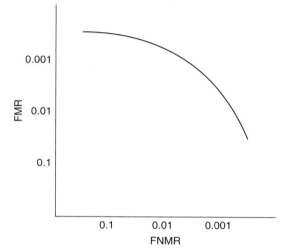

FIGURE 37.11 ROC for a hypothetical biometric system.

from either Alice or Bob, but we cannot tell which. If the average values that we expect for Alice and Bob are far enough apart, the chances of this happening may get extremely low, but even in such cases it is possible to have large enough errors creep into the data capture step to make even the rarest of errors possible.

Figure 37.9 shows how a false match can occur. Suppose that Bob uses our hypothetical biometric system but claims to be Alice when he does this, and the output of the matching subsystem is the point B that is shown in Figure 37.9. Because this point is close enough to the average that we expect from biometric data from Alice, the decision subsystem will erroneously decide that the biometric data that Bob presented is good enough to authenticate him as Alice. This is a false match, and it contributes to the FMR of the system.

Figure 37.10 shows how a false nonmatch can occur. Suppose that Alice uses our hypothetical biometric system and the output of the matching subsystem is the point A that is shown in Figure 37.10. Because this point is too far from the average that we expect when Alice uses the system, it is more likely to have come from someone else other than from Alice, and the decision subsystem will erroneously decide that the biometric data that Alice presented is probably not hers. This is a false nonmatch, and it contributes to the FNMR of the system.

Because the FNMR and FMR are related, the most meaningful way to represent the accuracy of a biometric system is probably by showing the relationship between the two error rates. The relationship between the two is known by the term *receiver operating characteristic*, or ROC, a term that originated in the study of the sensitivity of radio receivers as their operating parameters change. Figure 37.11 shows an ROC curve for a hypothetical biometric. Such an ROC curve assumes that the only way in which the error rates are changed is by changing the threshold value that is used in the decision subsystem. Note that this ROC curve indicates that when the FMR increases the FNMR decreases, and vice versa.

By adjusting the threshold that a decision subsystem uses it is possible to make the FMR very low while allowing the FNMR to get very high or to allow the FMR to get very high while making the FNMR very low. Between these two extreme cases lies the case where the FMR and the FNMR are the same. This point is sometimes the equal error rate (EER) or crossover error rate (CER) and is often used to simplify the discussions of error rates for biometric systems.

Though using a single value does indeed make it easier to compare the performance of different biometric systems, it can also be somewhat misleading. In high-security applications like those used by government or military organizations, keeping unauthorized users out may be much more important than the inconvenience caused by a high FNMR. In consumer applications, like ATMs, it may be more important to keep the FNMR low. This can help avoid the anger and accompanying support costs of dealing with customers who are incorrectly denied access to their accounts. In such situations, a low FNMR may be more important than the higher security that a higher FMR would provide. The error rates that are acceptable are strongly dependent on how the technology is being used, so be wary of trying to understand the performance of a biometric system by only considering the CER.

There is no theoretical way to accurately estimate the FMR and FNMR of biometric systems, so all estimates of these error rates need to be made from empirical data. Because testing can be expensive, the sample sizes used in such testing are often relatively small, so the results may not be representative of larger and more general populations. This is further complicated by the fact that some of the error rates that such testing attempts to estimate are fairly low. This means that human error from mislabeling data or other mistakes that occur during testing may make a bigger contribution to the measured error rates than the errors caused by a decision subsystem. It may be possible to create a biometric system that makes an error roughly only one time in 1 million operations, for example, but it is unrealistic to expect such high accuracy from the people who handle the data in an experiment that tries to estimate such an error rate. And because there are no standardized sample sizes and test conditions for estimating these error rates, there can be a wide range of reliability of error rate estimates. In one study,[5] a biometric system that performed well in a laboratory setting when used by trained users ended up correctly identifying enrolled users only 51% of the time when it was tested in a pilot project under real-world conditions, perhaps inviting an unenviable comparison with a system that recognizes a person by his ability to flip a coin and have it come up heads. Because of these effects, estimates of error rates should be viewed with a healthy amount of skepticism, particularly when extremely low rates are claimed.

Adaptation

Some biometric data changes over time. This may result in matches with a template becoming worse and worse over time, which will increase the FNMR of a biometric system.

FIGURE 37.12 Symbol used to indicate an adaptation subsystem.

One way to avoid the potential difficulties associated with having users eventually becoming unrecognizable is to update their template after a successful authentication. This process is called *adaptation*, and it is done by an optional part of a biometric system called an adaptation subsystem. If an adaptation subsystem is present, the symbol shown in Figure 37.12 is used to indicate it.

3. USING BIOMETRIC SYSTEMS

There are three main operations that a biometric system can perform. These are the following.

- *Enrollment.* During this operation, a biometric system creates a template that is used in later authentication and identification operations. This template, along with an associated identity, is stored in a data storage subsystem.
- *Authentication.* During this operation, a biometric system collects captured biometric data and a claimed identity and determines whether or not the captured biometric data matches the template stored for that identity. Although the term *authentication* is almost universally used in the information security industry for this operation, the term *verification* is often used by biometrics vendors and researchers to describe this.
- *Identification.* During this operation, a biometric system collects captured biometric data and attempts to find a match against any of the templates stored in a data storage subsystem.

Enrollment

Before a user can use a biometric system for either authentication or identification, a data storage subsystem needs to contain a template for the user. The process of initializing a biometric system with such a template is called *enrollment*, and it is the source of another error rate that can limit the usefulness of biometric systems. The interaction of the subsystems of a biometric system when enrolling a user is shown in Figure 37.13.

In the first step of enrollment, a user presents his biometric data to a data capture subsystem. The captured biometric data is then converted into a reference by a signal processing subsystem. This reference is then stored

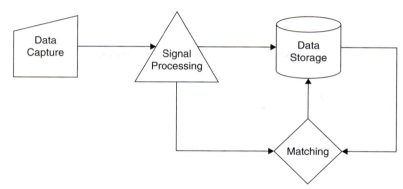

FIGURE 37.13 Enrollment in a biometric system.

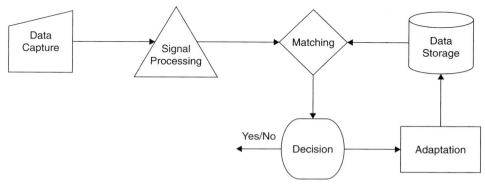

FIGURE 37.14 Authentication with a biometric system.

in a data storage subsystem, at which point it becomes a template. Such a template is typically calculated from several captures of biometric data to ensure that it reflects an accurate average value. An optional step includes using a matching subsystem to ensure that the user is not already enrolled.

The inherent nature of some captured biometric data as well as the randomness of captured biometric data can cause the enrollment process to fail. Some people have biometrics that are far enough outside the normal range of such data that they cause a signal processing subsystem to fail when it attempts to convert their captured data into a reference. The same types of random errors that contribute to the FMR and FNMR are also present in the enrollment process, and can be sometimes be enough to turn captured biometric data that would normally be within the range that the signal processing subsystem can handle into data that is outside this range. In some cases, it may even be impossible to collect some types of biometric data from some users, like the case where missing hands make it impossible to collect data on the geometry of the missing hands.

The probability of a user failing in the enrollment process is used to calculate the failure to enroll rate

(FER). Almost any biometric can fail sometimes, either temporarily or permanently. Dry air or sticky fingers can cause fingerprints to temporarily change. A cold can cause a voice to temporarily become hoarse. A broken arm can temporarily change the way a person writes his signature. Cataracts can permanently make retina patterns impossible to capture. Some skin diseases can even permanently change fingerprints.

A useful biometric system should have a low FER, but because all such systems have a nonzero value for this rate, it is likely that there will always be some users that cannot be enrolled in any particular biometric system, and a typical FER for a biometric system may be in the range of 1% to 5%. For this reason, biometric systems are often more useful as an additional means of authentication in multifactor authentication system instead of the single method used.

Authentication

After a user is enrolled in a biometric system, the system can be used to authenticate this user. The interaction of the subsystems of a biometric system when used to authenticate a user is shown in Figure 37.14.

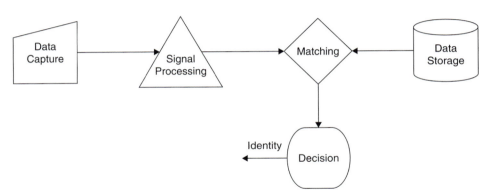

FIGURE 37.15 Identification with a biometric system.

To use a biometric system for authentication, a user first presents both a claimed identity and his biometric data to a data capture subsystem. The captured biometric data is then passed to a signal processing subsystem where features of the captured data are extracted and converted into a reference. A matching subsystem then compares this reference to a template from a data storage subsystem for the claimed identity and produces a comparison score. This comparison score is then passed to a decision subsystem, which produces a *yes* or *no* decision that reflects whether or not the biometric data agrees with the template stored for the claimed identity. The result of the authentication operation is the value returned by the decision subsystem.

A false match that occurs during authentication will allow one user to successfully authenticate as another user. So if Bob claims to be Alice and a false match occurs, he will be authenticated as Alice. A false nonmatch during authentication will incorrectly deny a user access. So if Bob attempts to authenticate as himself, he will be incorrectly denied assess if a false nonmatch occurs.

Because biometric data may change over time, an adaptation subsystem may update the stored template for a user after they have authenticated to the biometric system. If this is done, it will reduce the number or times that users will need to go through the enrollment process again when their biometric data changes enough to increase their FNMR rate to an unacceptable level.

Identification

A biometric system can be used to identify a user that has already enrolled in the system. The interaction of the subsystems of a biometric system when used for identification is shown in Figure 37.15.

To use a biometric system for identification, a user presents his biometric data to a data capture subsystem. The captured biometric data is then passed to a signal

processing subsystem where features of the captured data are extracted and converted into a reference. A matching subsystem then compares this reference to each of the templates stored in a data storage subsystem and produces a comparison score. Each of these comparison scores are passed to a decision subsystem, which produces a *yes* or *no* decision that reflects whether or not the reference is a good match for each template. If a *yes* decision is reached, then the identity associated with the template is returned for the identification operation. It is possible for this process to return more that one identity. This may or may not be useful, depending on the application. If a *yes* decision is not reached for any of the templates in a data storage subsystem, then a response that indicates that no match was found is returned for the identification operation.

A false match that occurs during identification will incorrectly identify a user as another enrolled user. So if Bob uses a biometric system for identification, he might be incorrectly identified as Alice if a false match occurs. Because there are typically many comparisons done when a biometric system is used for identification, the FMR can increase dramatically because there is an opportunity for a false match with every comparison. Suppose that for a single comparison we have an FMR of ε_1 and that ε_n represents the FMR for n comparisons. These two error rates are related by $\varepsilon_n = 1 - (1 - \varepsilon_1)^n$. If $n \cdot \varepsilon_1 \ll 1$, then we have that $\varepsilon_n \approx n \cdot \varepsilon_1$. This means that for a small FMR, the FMR is increased by a factor equal to the number of enrolled users when a system is used for identification instead of authentication. So an FMR of 10^{-6} when a system is used for authentication will be increased to approximately 10^{-3} if the identification is done by comparing to 1000 templates. A false nonmatch during identification will fail to identify an enrolled user as one who is enrolled in the system. So Bob might be incorrectly rejected, even though he is actually an enrolled user.

4. SECURITY CONSIDERATIONS

Biometric systems differ from most other authentication or identification technologies in several ways, and these differences should be understood by anyone considering using such systems as part of an information security architecture.

Biometric data is not secret, or at least it is not very secret. Fingerprints, for example, are not very secret because so-called latent fingerprints are left almost everywhere. On the other hand, reconstructing enough of a fingerprint from latent fingerprints to fool a biometric system is actually very difficult because latent fingerprints are typically of poor quality and incomplete. Because biometric data is not very secret, it may be useful to verify that captured biometric data is fresh instead of being replayed. There are technologies available that make it more difficult for an adversary to present fake biometric data to a biometric system for this very purpose. The technology exists to distinguish between a living finger and a manufactured copy, for example. Such technologies are not foolproof and can themselves be circumvented by clever attackers. This means that they just make it more difficult for an adversary to defeat a biometric system, but not impossible.

It is relatively easy to require users to frequently change their passwords and to enforce the expiration of cryptographic keys after their lifetime has passed, but many types of biometric data last for a long time, and it is essentially impossible to force users to change their biometric data. So when biometric data is compromised in some way, it is not possible to reissue new biometric data to the affected users. For that reason, it may be useful to both plan for alternate forms of authentication or identification in addition to a biometric system and to not rely on a single biometric system being useful for long periods of time.

Biometrics used for authentication may have much lower levels of security than other authentication technologies. This, plus the fact there is usually a non-zero FER for any biometric system, means that biometric systems may be more useful as an additional means of authentication than as a technology that can work alone.

Types of authentication technology can be divided into three general categories or "factors":

- Something that a user *knows*, such as a password or PIN
- Something that a user *has*, such as a key or access card
- Something that a user *is* or *does*, which is exactly the definition of a biometric

To be considered a *multifactor* authentication system, a system must use means from more than one of these categories to authenticate a user so that a system that uses two independent password-based systems for authentication does not qualify as a multifactor authentication system, whereas one that uses a password plus a biometric does. There is a commonly held perception that multifactor authentication is inherently more secure than authentication based on only a single factor, but this is not true. The concepts of *strong* authentication, in which an attacker has a small chance of bypassing the means of authentication, and multifactor authentication are totally independent. It is possible to have strong authentication based on only one factor. It is also possible to have weak authentication based on multiple authentication factors. So, including a biometric system as part of a multifactor authentication system should be done for reasons other than to simply use more than a single authentication factor. It may be more secure to use a password plus a PIN for authentication than to use a password plus a biometric, for example, even though both the password and PIN are the same type of authentication factor.

Error Rates

The usual understanding of biometric systems assumes that the FMR and FNMR of a biometric system are due to random errors that occur in a data capture subsystem. In particular, this assumes that the biometrics that are used in these systems are actually essentially unique. The existing market for celebrity lookalikes demonstrates that enough similarities exist in some physical features to justify the concern that similarities also exist in the more subtle characteristics that biometric systems use.

We assume, for example, that fingerprints are unique enough to identify a person without any ambiguity. This may indeed be true,[6] but there has been little careful research that demonstrates that this is actually the case. The largest empirical study of the uniqueness of fingerprints used only 50,000 fingerprints, a sample that could have come from as few as 5000 people, and has been criticized by experts for its careless use of statistics.[7] This is an area that deserves a closer look by researchers, but the expense of large-scale investigations probably means that they will probably never be carried out, leaving the uniqueness of biometrics an assumption that underlies the

6 S. Pankanti, S. Prabhakar and A. Jain, "On the individuality of fingerprints," *IEEE Transactions on Pattern Analysis and Machine Intelligence*, Vol. 24, No. 8, pp. 1010–1025, August 2002.
7 S. Cole, *Suspect Identities: A History of Fingerprinting and Criminal Identification*, Harvard University Press, 2002.

use of the technology for security applications. Note that other parts of information security also rely on assumptions that may never be proved. The security provided by all public-key cryptographic algorithms, for example, assumes that certain computational problems are intractable, but there are currently no proofs that this is actually the case.

The chances that the biometrics used in security systems will be found to be not unique enough for use in such systems is probably remote, but it certainly could happen. One easy way to prepare for this possibility is to use more than one biometric to characterize users. In such multi-modal systems, if one of the biometrics used is found to be weak, the others can still provide adequate strength. On the other hand, multi-modal systems have the additional drawback of being more expensive that a system that uses a single biometric.

Note that a given error rate can have many different sources. An error rate of 10% could be caused by an entire population having an error rate of 10%, or it could be caused by 90% of a population having an error rate of zero and 10% of the population having an error rate of 100%. The usability of the system is very different in each of these cases. In one case, all users are equally inconvenienced, but in the other case, some users are essentially unable to use the system at all. So understanding how errors are distributed can be important in understanding how biometric systems can be used. If a biometric system is used to control access to a sensitive facility, for example, it may not be very useful in this role if some of the people who need entry to the facility are unlucky enough to have a 100% FNMR. Studies have suggested that error rates are not uniformly distributed in some populations, but they are not quite as bad as the worst case. The nonuniform distribution of error rates that is observed in biometric systems is often called Doddington's Zoo and is named after the researcher who first noticed this phenomenon and the colorful names that he gave to the classes of users who made different contributions to the observed error rates.

Doddington's Zoo

Based on his experience testing biometric systems, George Doddington divided people into four categories: sheep, goats, lambs, and wolves.[8] Sheep are easily recognized by

a biometric system and comprise most of the population. Goats are particularly unsuccessful at being recognized. They have chronically high FNMRs, usually because their biometric is outside the range that a particular system recognizes. Goats can be particularly troublesome if a biometric system is used for access control, where it is critical that all users be reliably accepted. Lambs are exceptionally vulnerable to impersonation, so they contribute to the FMR. Wolves are exceptionally good false matchers and they also make a significant contribution to the FMR.

Doddington's goats can also cause another problem. Because their biometric pattern is outside the range that a particular biometric system expects, they may be unable to enroll in such a system and thus be major contributors to the FER of the system.

Note that users that may be sheep for one biometric may turn out to be goats for another, and so on. Because of this it is probably impossible to know in advance how error rates are distributed for a particular biometric system, it is almost always necessary to test such systems thoroughly before deploying them on a wide scale.

Birthday Attacks

Suppose that we have n users enrolled in a biometric system. This biometric system maps arbitrary inputs into $n + 1$ states that represent deciding on a match with one of the n users plus the additional "none of the above" user that represents the option of deciding on a match with none of the n enrolled users. From this point of view, this biometric system acts like a hash function so might try to use well-known facts about hash functions to understand the limits that this property puts on error rates. In particular, errors caused by the FMR of a biometric system look like a collision in this hash function, which happens when two different input values to a hash function result in the same output from the hash function. For this reason, we might think that the same "birthday attack" that can find collisions for a hash function can also increase the FMR of a biometric system. The reason for this is as follows.

For a hash function that maps inputs into m different message digests, the probability of finding at least one collision, a case where different inputs map to the same message digest, after calculating n message digests is approximately $1 - e^{-n^2/2m}$.[9] Considering birthdays as

8 G. Doddington, et al., "Sheep, goats, lambs and wolves: A statistical analysis of speaker performance in the NIST 1998 speaker recognition evaluation," *Proceedings of the Fifth International Conference on Spoken Language Processing*, Sydney, Australia, November–December, 1998, pp. 1351–1354.

9 D. Knuth, *The Art of Computer Programming, Volume 2: Sorting and Searching*, Addison-Wesley, 1973.

a hash function that maps people into one of 365 possible birthdays, this tells us that the probability of two or more people having the same birthday in a group of only 23 people is approximately $1 - e^{-23^2/2 \cdot 365} \approx 0.52$. This means that there is greater that a 50% chance of finding two people with the same birthday in a group of only 23 people, a result that is often counter to people's intuition. Using a biometric system is much like a hash function in that it maps biometric data into the templates in the data storage subsystem that it has a good match for, and collisions in this hash function cause a false match. Therefore, the FMR may increase as more users are added to the system, and if it does, we might expect the FMR rate to increase in the same way that the chances of a collision in a hash function do. This might cause false matches at a higher rate that we might expect, just like the chances of finding matching birthdays does.

In practice, however, this phenomenon is essentially not observed. This may be due to the nonuniform distribution in error rates of Doddingon's Zoo. If the threshold used in a decision subsystem is adjusted to create a particular FMR, it may be limited by the properties of Doddington's lambs. This may leave the sheep that comprise the majority of the user population with enough room to add additional users without getting too close to other sheep.

ANS X9.84 requires that the FMR for biometric systems provide at least the level of security provided by a four-digit PIN, which equates to an FMR of no greater than 10^{-4} and recommends that they provide an FMR of no more than 10^{-5}. In addition, this standard requires that the corresponding FNMR be no greater than 10^{-2} at the FMR selected for use. These error rates may be too ambitious for some existing technologies, but it is certainly possible to attain these error rates with some technologies.

On the other hand, these error rates compare very unfavorably with other authentication technologies. For example, an FMR of 10^{-4} is roughly the same as the probability of randomly guessing a four-digit PIN, a three-character password, or a 13-bit cryptographic key. And although few people would find three-character passwords or 13-bit cryptographic keys acceptable, they might have to accept an FMR of 10^{-4} from a biometric system because of the limitations of affordable current technologies. Table 37.3 summarizes how the security provided by various FMRs compares to both the security provided by all-numeric PINs and passwords that use only case-independent letters.

Comparing Technologies

There are many different biometrics that are used in currently available biometric systems. Each of these competing technologies tries to be better than the alternatives in some way, perhaps being easier to use, more accurate, or cheaper to operate. Because there are so many technologies available, however, it should come as no surprise that there is no single "best" technology for use in biometric systems. Almost any biometric system that is available is probably the best solution for some problem, and it is impossible to list all of the cases where each technology is the best without a very careful analysis of each authentication or identification problem. So any attempt to make a simple comparison between the competing technologies will be inherently inaccurate. Despite this, Table 37.4 attempts to make such a high-level comparison. In this table, the ease of use, accuracy and cost are rated as high, medium, or low.

Using DNA as a biometric provides an example of the difficulty involved in making such a rough classification.

TABLE 37.3 Comparison of Security Provided by Biometrics and Other Common Mechanisms

FMR	PIN Length	Password Length	Key Length
10^{-3}	3 digits	2 letters	10 bits
10^{-4}	4 digits	3 letters	13 bits
10^{-5}	5 digits	4 letters	17 bits
10^{-6}	6 digits	4 letters	20 bits
10^{-7}	7 digits	5 letters	23 bits
10^{-8}	8 digits	6 letters	27 bits

TABLE 37.4 Comparison of Selected Biometric Technologies

Biometric	Ease of use	Accuracy	Cost
DNA	Low	High	High
Face geometry	High	Medium	Medium
Fingerprint	High	High	Low
Hand geometry	Medium	Medium	Medium
Iris	High	High	High
Retina	Medium	High	High
Signature dynamics	Low	Medium	Medium
Voice	Medium	Low	Low
(Password)	(Medium)	(Low)	(Low)

The accuracy of DNA testing is limited by the fairly large number of identical twins that are present in the overall population, but in cases other than distinguishing identical twins it is very accurate. So if identical twins need to be distinguished, it may not be the best solution. By slightly abusing the usual understanding of what a biometric is, it is even possible to think of passwords as a biometric that is based purely on behavioral characteristics, along with the FMR, FNMR, and FER rates that come with their use, but they are certainly outside the commonly understood meaning of the term. Even if they are not covered by the usual definition of a biometric, passwords are fairly well understood, so they provide a point of reference for comparing against the relative strengths of biometrics that are commonly used in security systems. The accuracy of passwords here is meant to be that of passwords that users select for their own use instead of being randomly generated. Such passwords are typically much weaker than their length indicates because of the structure that people need to make passwords easy to remember. This means that the chances of guessing a typical eight-character case-insensitive password is actually much greater than the 26^{-8} that we would expect for strong passwords. Studies of the randomness in English words have estimated that there is approximately one bit of randomness per letter.[10] If we conservatively double this to estimate that there are approximately two bits of randomness per letter in a typical user-selected password, we get the estimate that an eight-character password probably provides only about 16 bits of randomness, which is close to the security provided by a biometric system with an FMR of 10^{-5}. This means that the security of passwords as used in practice is often probably comparable to that attainable by biometric systems, perhaps even less if weak passwords are used.

Storage of Templates

One obvious way to store the templates used in a biometric system is in a database. This can be a good solution, and the security provided by the database may be adequate to protect the templates that it stores. In other cases, it may be more useful for a user to carry his template with him on some sort of portable data storage device and to provide that template to a matching subsystem along with his biometric data. Portable, credit-card-sized data

storage devices are often used for this purpose. There are three general types of such cards that are used in this way, and each has a different set of security considerations that are relevant to it.

In one case, a memory card with unencrypted data storage can be used to store a template. This is the least expensive option, but also the least secure. Such a memory card can be read by anyone who finds it and can easily be duplicated, although it may be impossible for anyone other that the authorized user to use it. Nonbiometric data stored on such a card may also be compromised when a card is lost.

In principle, a nonauthorized user can use such a card to make a card that lets them authenticate as an authorized user. This can be done as follows. Suppose that Eve, a nonauthorized user, gets the memory card that stores the template for the authorized user Alice. Eve may be able to use Alice's card to make a card that is identical in every way to Alice's card but that has Eve's template in place of Alice's. Then when Eve uses this card to authenticate, she uses her biometric data, which then gets compared to her template on the card and gets her authenticated as the user Alice. Note that doing this relies on a fairly unsecured implementation.

A case that is more secure and also more expensive is a memory card in which data storage is encrypted. The contents of such a card can still be read by anyone who finds it and can easily be duplicated, but it is infeasible for an unauthorized user to decrypt and use the data on the card, which may also include any nonbiometric data on the card. Encrypting the data storage also makes it impractical for an unauthorized user to make a card that will let them authenticate as an authorized user. Though it may be possible to simply replace one template with another if the template is stored unencrypted on a memory card, carrying out the same attack on a memory card that stores data encrypted requires being able to create a valid encrypted template, which is just as difficult as defeating the encryption.

The most secure as well as the most expensive case is where a smart card with cryptographic capabilities is used to store a template. The data stored on such a smart card can only be read and decrypted by trusted applications, so that it is infeasible for anyone who finds a lost smart card to read data from it or to copy it. This makes it infeasible for unauthorized users to use a smart card to create a way to authenticate as an authorized user. It also protects any nonbiometric data that might be stored on the card.

---

10 C. Shannon, "Prediction and entropy of printed english," *Bell System Technical Journal*, Vol. 30, pp. 50–64, January 1951.

5. CONCLUSION

Using biometric systems as the basis for security technologies for authentication or identification is currently feasible. Each biometric has properties that may make it useful in some situations but not others, and security systems based on biometrics have the same property. This means that there is no single "best" biometric for such use and that each biometric technology has an application where it is superior to the alternatives.

There is still a great deal of research that needs to be done in the field, but existing technologies have progressed to the point that security systems based on biometrics are now a viable way to perform authentication or identification of users, although the properties of biometrics also make them more attractive as part of a multifactor authentication system instead of the single means that is used.

## Chapter 38

Homeland Security

Rahul Bhaskar Ph. D.
California State University

Bhushan Kapoor
California State University

The September 11, 2001, terrorist attacks, permanently changed the way the United States and the world's other most developed countries perceived the threat from terrorism. Massive amounts of resources were mobilized in a very short time to counter the perceived and actual threats from terrorists and terrorist organizations. In the United States, this refocus was pushed as a necessity for what was called *homeland security*. The homeland security threats were anticipated for the IT infrastructure as well. It was expected that not only the IT at the federal level was vulnerable to disruptions due to terrorism-related attacks but, due to the ubiquity of the availability of IT, any organization was vulnerable.

Soon after the terrorist attacks, the U.S. Congress passed various new laws and enhanced some existing ones that introduced sweeping changes to homeland security provisions and to the existing security organizations. The executive branch of the government also issued a series of Homeland Security Presidential Directives to maintain domestic security. These laws and directives are comprehensive and contain detailed provisions to make the U.S. secure from its vulnerabilities. Later in the chapter, we describe some principle provisions of these homeland security-related laws and presidential directives. Next, we discuss the organizational changes that were initiated to support homeland security in the United States. Then we highlight the 9-11 Commission that Congress charted to provide a full account of the circumstances surrounding the attacks and to develop recommendations for corrective measures that could be taken to prevent future acts of terrorism. We also detail the Intelligence Reform and Terrorism Prevention Act of 2004 and the Implementing the 9-11 Commission Recommendations Act of 2007. Finally, we summarize the chapter's discussion.

1. STATUTORY AUTHORITIES

Here we discuss the important homeland security-related laws passed in the aftermath of the terrorist attacks. These laws are listed in Figure 38.1.

The USA PATRIOT Act of 2001 (PL 107-56)

Just 45 days after the September 11 attacks, Congress passed the USA PATRIOT Act of 2001 (also known as

The USA PATRIOT Act of 2001
The Aviation and Transportation Security Act of 2001
Enhanced Border Security and Visa Entry Reform Act of 2002
Public Health Security, Bioterrorism Preparedness & Response Act of 2002
Homeland Security Act of 2002
E-Government Act of 2002

FIGURE 38.1 Laws passed in the aftermath of the 9/11 terrorist attacks.

TITLE I	Enhancing Domestic Security Against Terrorism
TITLE II	Enhanced Surveillance Procedures
TITLE III	International Money Laundering Abatement and Antiterrorist Financing Act of 2001
TITLE IV	Protecting the Border
TITLE V	Removing Obstacles to Investigate Terrorism
TITLE VI	Providing for Victims of Terrorism, Public Safety Officers, and their Families
TITLE VII	Increased Information Sharing for Critical Infrastructure Protection
TITLE VIII	Strengthening the Criminal Laws against Terrorism
TITLE IX	Improved Intelligence
TITLE X	Miscellaneous

FIGURE 38.2 USA PATRIOT Act titles.

the Uniting and Strengthening America by Providing Appropriate Tools Required to Intercept and Obstruct Terrorism Act of 2001). This Act, divided into 10 titles, expands law enforcement powers of the government and law enforcement authorities.[1] These titles are listed in Figure 38.2.

A summary of the titles is shown in the sidebar, "Summary of USA PATRIOT Act Titles."

Summary of USA PATRIOT Act Titles

Title I – Enhancing Domestic Security Against Terrorism

Increased funding for the technical support center at the Federal Bureau of Investigation, allowed military assistance to enforce prohibition in certain emergencies, and expanded National Electronic Crime Task Force Initiative.

Title II – Enhanced Surveillance Procedures

Authorized to intercept wire, oral, and electronic communications relating to terrorism, computer fraud and abuse offenses, to share criminal investigative information. It allowed seizure of voicemail messages pursuant to warrants and subpoenas for records of electronic communications. It provided delaying notice of the execution of a warrant, pen register and trap and trace authority under the Foreign Intelligence Surveillance Act, access to records and other items under FISA, interception of computer trespasser communications, and nationwide service of search warrants for electronic evidence.

Title III – International Money-laundering Abatement and Antiterrorist Financing Act of 2001

Special measures relating to the following three subtitles were created:

A. International Counter Money Laundering and Related Measures
B. Bank Secrecy Act Amendments and Related Improvements
C. Currency Crimes and Protection

Title IV – Protecting the Border

Special measures relating to the following three subtitles were created:

A. Protecting the Northern Border
B. Enhanced Immigration Provisions
C. Preservation of Immigration Benefits for Victims of Terrorism

Title V – Removing Obstacles to Investigating Terrorism

Attorney General and Secretary of State are authorized to pay rewards to combat terrorism. It allowed DNA identification of terrorists and other violent offenders, and allowed disclosure of information from National Center for Education Statistics (NCES) surveys.

Title VI – Providing for Victims of Terrorism, Public Safety Officers, and their Families

Special measures relating to the following subtitles were created:

A. Aid to Families of Public Safety Officers
B. Amendments to the Victims of Crime Act of 1984

Title VII – Increased Information Sharing for Critical Infrastructure Protection

Expansion of regional information sharing systems to facilitate federal, state, and local law enforcement response related to terrorist attacks.

---

1. "USA PATRIOT Act of 2001" U.S. Government Printing Office, http://frwebgate.access.gpo.gov/cgi-bin/getdoc.cgi?dbname=107_cong_public_laws&docid=f:publ056.107.pdf (downloaded 10/20/2008).

Title VIII – Strengthening the Criminal Laws against Terrorism

Strengthened laws against terrorist attacks and other acts of violence against mass transportation systems and crimes committed at U.S. facilities abroad.

Provided for the development and support of cyber security forensic capabilities and expanded the biological weapons statute.

Title IX – Improved Intelligence

Responsibilities of Director of Central Intelligence regarding foreign intelligence collected under the Foreign Intelligence Surveillance Act of 1978.

Inclusion of international terrorist activities within scope of foreign intelligence under National Security Act of 1947.

Disclosure to Director of Central Intelligence of foreign intelligence-related information with respect to criminal investigations.

Foreign terrorist asset tracking center.

Title X – Miscellaneous

Review of the Department of Justice.

A. Definition of electronic surveillance.
B. Venue in money-laundering cases.
C. Automated fingerprint identification system at overseas consular posts and points of entry to the United States.
D. Critical infrastructures protection.

Creation of an Undersecretary of Transportation for Security
Federalization of Airport Security Screeners
Assignment of Federal Security Managers
Airport Screening by Explosion Detection Devices
Allowing Pilots to Carry Firearms
Electronic Transmission of Passenger Manifests on International Flights

FIGURE 38.3 Key features of the Aviation and Transportation Security Act of 2001.

The Aviation and Transportation Security Act of 2001 (PL 107-71)

The series of September 11 attacks, perpetrated by 19 hijackers, killed 3000 people and brought commercial aviation to a standstill. It became obvious that enhanced laws and strong measures were needed to tighten aviation security. The Aviation and Transportation Security Act of 2001 transfers authority over civil aviation security from the Federal Aviation Administration (FAA) to the Transportation Security Administration (TSA).[2] With the passage of the Homeland Security Act of 2002, the TSA was later transferred to the Department of Homeland Security.

Key features of the act include the creation of an Undersecretary of Transportation for Security; federalization of airport security screeners; and the assignment of Federal Security Managers to each airport. Also included in the act are these provisions: airports provide for the screening of all checked baggage by explosive detection devices; allowing pilots to carry firearms; requiring the electronic transmission of passenger manifests on international flights prior to landing in the U.S.; requiring background checks, including national security checks, of persons who have access to secure areas at airports; and requiring that all federal security screeners be U.S. citizens.[3] These key features are highlighted in the Figure 38.3.

Enhanced Border Security and Visa Entry Reform Act of 2002 (PL 107-173)

This Act, divided into six titles, represents the most comprehensive immigration-related response to the terrorist threat.[4] The titles are listed in Figure 38.4.

A summary of these titles is shown in the sidebar, "Summary of the Border Security and Visa Entry Reform Act of 2002."

---

2 "Aviation and Transportation Security Act of 2001," National Transportation Library, http://ntl.bts.gov/faq/avtsa.html (downloaded 10/20/2008).

3 "Aviation and Transportation Security Act of 2001," National Transportation Library, http://ntl.bts.gov/faq/avtsa.html (downloaded 10/20/2008).

4 "Enhanced Border Security and Visa Entry Reform Act of 2002 (PL 107-173)," Center for Immigration Studies, www.cis.org/articles/2002/back502.html (downloaded 10/20/2008).

TITLE I	Funding
TITLE II	Interagency Information Sharing
TITLE III	Visa Issuance
TITLE IV	Inspection and Admission of Aliens
TITLE V	Removing the Obstacles to Investigate Terrorism
TITLE VI	Foreign Students and Exchange Visitors
TITLE VII	Miscellaneous

FIGURE 38.4 Border Security and Visa Entry Reform Act of 2002.

Summary of the Border Security and Visa Entry Reform Act of 2002

Title I – Funding

The Act provides for additional staff and training to increase security on both the northern and southern borders.

Title II – Interagency Information Sharing

The Act requires the President to develop and implement an interoperable electronic data system to provide current and immediate access to information contained in the databases of federal law enforcement agencies and the intelligence community that is relevant to visa issuance determinations and determinations of an alien's admissibility or deportability.

Title III – Visa Issuance

This requires consular officers issuing a visa to an alien to transmit an electronic version of the alien's visa file to the INS so that the file is available to immigration inspectors at U.S. ports of entry before the alien's arrival.

This Act requires the Attorney General and the Secretary of State to begin issuing machine-readable, tamper-resistant travel documents with biometric identifiers.

Title IV – Inspection and Admission of Aliens

It requires the President to submit to Congress a report discussing the feasibility of establishing a North American National Security Program to enhance the mutual security and safety of the U.S., Canada, and Mexico.

It also requires that all commercial flights and vessels coming to the U.S. from any place outside the country must provide to manifest information about each passenger, crew member, and other occupant prior to arrival in the U.S. In addition, each vessel or aircraft departing from the U.S. for any destination outside the U.S. must provide manifest information before departure.

Title VI – Foreign Students and Exchange Visitors

It requires the Attorney General, in consultation with the Secretary of State, to establish an electronic means to monitor and verify the various steps involved in the admittance to the U.S. of foreign students, such as: the issuance of documentation of acceptance of a foreign student by an educational institution or exchange visitor program.

Title VII – Miscellaneous

The Act requires the Comptroller General to conduct a study to determine the feasibility of requiring every nonimmigrant alien in the U.S. to provide the INS, on an annual basis, with a current address, and where applicable, the name and address of an employer.

It requires the Secretary of State and the INS Commissioner, in consultation with the Director of the Office of Homeland Security, to conduct a study on the procedures necessary for encouraging or requiring countries participating in the Visa Waiver Program to develop an intergovernmental network of interoperable electronic data systems.

Public Health Security, Bioterrorism Preparedness & Response Act of 2002 (PL 107-188)

The Act authorizes funding for a wide range of public health initiatives.[5] Title I of the Act addresses the national need to combat threats to public health, and to provide grants to state and local governments to help them prepare for public health emergencies, including emergencies resulting from acts of bioterrorism. The Act establishes opportunities for grants and cooperative agreements for states and local governments to conduct evaluations of public health emergency preparedness, and enhance public health infrastructure and the capacity to prepare for and respond to those emergencies. Other grants support efforts to combat antimicrobial resistance,

---

5 "Public Health Security, Bioterrorism Preparedness & Response Act of 2002," U.S. Government Printing Office, http://frwebgate. access.gpo.gov/cgi-bin/getdoc.cgi?dbname=107_cong_public_laws&docid=f:publ188.107 (downloaded 10/20/2008).

| Prevent Terrorist Attacks |
| Reduce the Vulnerability of the United States to Terrorism |
| Minimize the damage, and assist in recovery from terrorist attacks that do occur in the United States |

FIGURE 38.5 DHS mission.

improve public health laboratory capacity, and support collaborative efforts to detect, diagnose, and respond to acts of bioterrorism.

The Act also addresses other related public health security issues. Some of these provisions include:

- New controls on biological agents and toxins
- Additional safety and security measures affecting the nation's food and drug supply
- Additional safety and security measures affecting the nation's drinking water
- Measures affecting the Strategic National Stockpile and development of priority countermeasures to bioterrorism

Homeland Security Act of 2002 (PL 107-296)

This landmark Act establishes a new Executive Branch agency, the U.S. Department of Homeland Security (DHS), and consolidates the operations of 22 existing federal agencies.[6]

The primary mission of the DHS is given in Figure 38.5.

As a part of this act, a directorate of information analysis and infrastructure protection was set up. The primary role of this directorate is to[7]:

1. To access, receive, and analyze law enforcement information, intelligence information, and other information from agencies of the federal government, state and local government agencies (including law enforcement agencies), and private sector entities, and to integrate such information in order to:
   A. Identify and assess the nature and scope of terrorist threats to the homeland
   B. Detect and identify threats of terrorism against the United States
   C. Understand such threats in light of actual and potential vulnerabilities of the homeland
2. To carry out comprehensive assessments of the vulnerabilities of the key resources and critical

infrastructure of the United States, including the performance of risk assessments to determine the risks posed by particular types of terrorist attacks within the United States (including an assessment of the probability of success of such attacks and the feasibility and potential efficacy of various countermeasures to such attacks).

3. To integrate relevant information, analyses, and vulnerability assessments (whether such information, analyses, or assessments are provided or produced by the Department or others) in order to identify priorities for protective and support measures by the Department, other agencies of the federal government, state and local government agencies and authorities, the private sector, and other entities.

4. To ensure, pursuant to section 202, the timely and efficient access by the Department to all information necessary to discharge the responsibilities under this section, including obtaining such information from other agencies of the federal government.

5. To develop a comprehensive national plan for securing the key resources and critical infrastructure of the United States, including power production, generation, and distribution systems, information technology and telecommunications systems (including satellites), electronic financial and property record storage and transmission systems, emergency preparedness communications systems, and the physical and technological assets that support such systems.

6. To recommend measures necessary to protect the key resources and critical infrastructure of the United States in coordination with other agencies of the federal government and in cooperation with state and local government agencies and authorities, the private sector, and other entities.

7. To administer the Homeland Security Advisory System, including:
   A. Exercising primary responsibility for public advisories related to threats to homeland security.
   B. In coordination with other agencies of the federal government, providing specific warning

---

6 "Homeland Security Act of 2002," Homeland Security, www.dhs.gov/xabout/laws/law_regulation_rule_0011.shtm (downloaded 10/20/2008).
7 "Homeland Security Act of 2002," Homeland Security, www.dhs.gov/xabout/laws/law_regulation_rule_0011.shtm (downloaded 10/20/2008).

information, and advice about appropriate protective measures and countermeasures, to state and local government agencies and authorities, the private sector, other entities, and the public.

8. To review, analyze, and make recommendations for improvements in the policies and procedures governing the sharing of law enforcement information, intelligence information, intelligence-related information, and other information relating to homeland security within the federal government and between the federal government and state and local government agencies and authorities.

9. To disseminate, as appropriate, information analyzed by the Department within the Department, to other agencies of the federal government with responsibilities relating to homeland security, and to agencies of state and local governments and private sector entities with such responsibilities in order to assist in the deterrence, prevention, preemption of, or response to, terrorist attacks against the United States.

10. To consult with the Director of Central Intelligence and other appropriate intelligence, law enforcement, or other elements of the federal government to establish collection priorities and strategies for information, including law enforcement-related information, relating to threats of terrorism against the United States through such means as the representation of the Department in discussions regarding requirements and priorities in the collection of such information.

11. To consult with state and local governments and private sector entities to ensure appropriate exchanges of information, including law enforcement-related information, relating to threats of terrorism against the United States.

12. To ensure that:
    A. Any material received pursuant to this Act is protected from unauthorized disclosure and handled and used only for the performance of official duties.
    B. Any intelligence information under this Act is shared, retained, and disseminated consistent with the authority of the Director of Central Intelligence to protect intelligence sources and methods under the National Security Act of 1947 (50 U.S.C. 401 et seq.) and related procedures and, as appropriate, similar authorities of the Attorney General concerning sensitive law enforcement information.

13. To request additional information from other agencies of the federal government, state and local government agencies, and the private sector relating to threats of terrorism in the United States, or relating to other areas of responsibility assigned by the Secretary, including the entry into cooperative agreements through the Secretary to obtain such information.

14. To establish and utilize, in conjunction with the chief information officer of the Department, a secure communications and information technology infrastructure, including data mining and other advanced analytical tools, in order to access, receive, and analyze data and information in furtherance of the responsibilities under this section, and to disseminate information acquired and analyzed by the Department, as appropriate.

15. To ensure, in conjunction with the chief information officer of the Department, any information databases and analytical tools developed or utilized by the Department:
    A. Are compatible with one another and with relevant information databases of other agencies of the federal government.
    B. Treat information in such databases in a manner that complies with applicable federal law on privacy.

16. To coordinate training and other support to the elements and personnel of the Department, other agencies of the federal government, and state and local governments that provide information to the Department, or are consumers of information provided by the Department, in order to facilitate the identification and sharing of information revealed in their ordinary duties and the optimal utilization of information received from the Department.

17. To coordinate with elements of the intelligence community and with federal, state, and local law enforcement agencies, and the private sector, as appropriate.

18. To provide intelligence and information analysis and support to other elements of the Department.

19. To perform such other duties relating to such responsibilities as the Secretary may provide.

E-Government Act of 2002 (PL 107-347)

The E-Government Act of 2002 establishes a Federal Chief Information Officers Council to oversee government information and services, and creation of a new

Office of Electronic Government within the Office of Management and Budget.[8] The purposes of the Act are[9]:

- To provide effective leadership of federal government efforts to develop and promote electronic government services and processes by establishing an Administrator of a new Office of Electronic Government within the Office of Management and Budget.
- To promote use of the Internet and other information technologies to provide increased opportunities for citizen participation in government.
- To promote interagency collaboration in providing electronic government services, where this collaboration would improve the service to citizens by integrating related functions, and in the use of internal electronic government processes, where this collaboration would improve the efficiency and effectiveness of the processes.
- To improve the ability of the government to achieve agency missions and program performance goals.
- To promote the use of the Internet and emerging technologies within and across government agencies to provide citizen-centric government information and services.
- To reduce costs and burdens for businesses and other government entities.
- To promote better informed decision-making by policy makers.
- To promote access to high quality government information and services across multiple channels.
- To make the federal government more transparent and accountable.
- To transform agency operations by utilizing, where appropriate, best practices from public and private sector organizations.
- To provide enhanced access to government information and services in a manner consistent with laws regarding protection of personal privacy, national security, records retention, access for persons with disabilities, and other relevant laws.

Title III of the Act is known as the Federal Information Security Management Act of 2002. This act applies to the national security systems, that include any information systems used by an agency or a contractor of an agency involved in intelligence activities; cryptology activities related to the nation's security; command and control of military equipment that is an integral part of a weapon or weapons system or is critical to the direct fulfillment of military or intelligence missions. Nevertheless, this definition does not apply to a system that is used for routine administrative and business applications (including payroll, finance, logistics, and personnel management applications). The purposes of this Title are to:

- Provide a comprehensive framework for ensuring the effectiveness of information security controls over information resources that support federal operations and assets.
- Recognize the highly networked nature of the current federal computing environment and provide effective government-wide management and oversight of the related information security risks, including coordination of information security efforts throughout the civilian, national security, and law-enforcement communities.
- Provide for development and maintenance of minimum controls required to protect federal information and information systems.
- Provide a mechanism for improved oversight of federal agency information security programs.
- Acknowledge that commercially developed information security products offer advanced, dynamic, robust, and effective information security solutions, reflecting market solutions for the protection of critical information infrastructures important to the national defense and economic security of the nation that are designed, built, and operated by the private sector.
- Recognize that the selection of specific technical hardware and software information security solutions should be left to individual agencies from among commercially developed products.

2. HOMELAND SECURITY PRESIDENTIAL DIRECTIVES

Presidential directives are issued by the National Security Council and are signed or authorized by the President.[9] A series of Homeland Security Presidential

---

8 "E-Government Act of 2002," U.S. Government Printing Office, http://frwebgate.access.gpo.gov/cgi-bin/getdoc.cgi?dbname=107_cong_public_laws&docid=f:publ347.107.pdf (downloaded 10/20/2008).

9 "Presidential directives," Wikipedia, http://en.wikipedia.org, 2008 (downloaded 10/24/2008).

Directives (HSPDs) were issued by President George W. Bush on matters pertaining to Homeland Security[10]:

- HSPD 1: Organization and Operation of the Homeland Security Council. Ensures coordination of all homeland security-related activities among executive departments and agencies and promotes the effective development and implementation of all homeland security policies.
- HSPD 2: Combating Terrorism Through Immigration Policies. Provides for the creation of a task force which will work aggressively to prevent aliens who engage in or support terrorist activity from entering the United States and to detain, prosecute, or deport any such aliens who are within the United States.
- HSPD 3: Homeland Security Advisory System. Establishes a comprehensive and effective means to disseminate information regarding the risk of terrorist acts to federal, state, and local authorities and to the American people.
- HSPD 4: National Strategy to Combat Weapons of Mass Destruction. Applies new technologies, increased emphasis on intelligence collection and analysis, strengthens alliance relationships, and establishes new partnerships with former adversaries to counter this threat in all of its dimensions.
- HSPD 5: Management of Domestic Incidents. Enhances the ability of the United States to manage domestic incidents by establishing a single, comprehensive national incident management system.
- HSPD 6: Integration and Use of Screening Information. Provides for the establishment of the Terrorist Threat Integration Center.
- HSPD 7: Critical Infrastructure Identification, Prioritization, and Protection. Establishes a national policy for federal departments and agencies to identify and prioritize United States critical infrastructure and key resources and to protect them from terrorist attacks.
- HSPD 8: National Preparedness. Identifies steps for improved coordination in response to incidents. This directive describes the way federal departments and agencies will prepare for such a response, including prevention activities during the early stages of a terrorism incident. This directive is a companion to HSPD-5.

- HSPD 8 Annex 1: National Planning. Further enhances the preparedness of the United States by formally establishing a standard and comprehensive approach to national planning.
- HSPD 9: Defense of United States Agriculture and Food. Establishes a national policy to defend the agriculture and food system against terrorist attacks, major disasters, and other emergencies.
- HSPD 10: Biodefense for the 21st Century. Provides a comprehensive framework for our nation's Biodefense.
- HSPD 11: Comprehensive Terrorist-Related Screening Procedures. Implements a coordinated and comprehensive approach to terrorist-related screening that supports homeland security, at home and abroad. This directive builds upon HSPD 6.
- HSPD 12: Policy for a Common Identification Standard for Federal Employees and Contractors. Establishes a mandatory, government-wide standard for secure and reliable forms of identification issued by the federal government to its employees and contractors (including contractor employees).
- HSPD 13: Maritime Security Policy. Establishes policy guidelines to enhance national and homeland security by protecting U.S. maritime interests.
- HSPD 15: U.S. Strategy and Policy in the War on Terror.
- HSPD 16: Aviation Strategy. Details a strategic vision for aviation security while recognizing ongoing efforts, and directs the production of a National Strategy for Aviation Security and supporting plans.
- HSPD 17: Nuclear Materials Information Program.
- HSPD 18: Medical Countermeasures against Weapons of Mass Destruction. Establishes policy guidelines to draw upon the considerable potential of the scientific community in the public and private sectors to address medical countermeasure requirements relating to CBRN threats.
- HSPD 19: Combating Terrorist Use of Explosives in the United States. Establishes a national policy, and calls for the development of a national strategy and implementation plan, on the prevention and detection of, protection against, and response to terrorist use of explosives in the United States.
- HSPD 20: National Continuity Policy. Establishes a comprehensive national policy on the continuity of federal government structures and operations and a single National Continuity Coordinator responsible for coordinating the development and implementation of federal continuity policies.

---

10 "Homeland Security presidential directives," Homeland Security, https://www.drii.org/professional_prac/profprac_appendix.html#BUSINESS_CONTINUITY_PLANNING_INFORMATION, 2008 (downloaded 10/24/2008).

- HSPD 20 Annex A: Continuity Planning. Assigns executive departments and agencies to a category commensurate with their COOP/COG/ECG responsibilities during an emergency.
- HSPD 21: Public Health and Medical Preparedness. Establishes a national strategy that will enable a level of public health and medical preparedness sufficient to address a range of possible disasters.
- HSPD 23: National Cyber Security Initiative.
- HSPD 24: Biometrics for Identification and Screening to Enhance National Security. Establishes a framework to ensure that federal executive departments use mutually compatible methods and procedures regarding biometric information of individuals, while respecting their information privacy and other legal rights.

3. ORGANIZATIONAL ACTIONS

These laws and homeland security presidential directives called for deep and fundamental organizational changes to the executive branch of the government. The Homeland Security Act of 2002 established a new Executive Branch agency, the U.S. Department of Homeland Security (DHS), and consolidated the operations of 22 existing federal agencies.[11] This Department's overriding and urgent missions are (1) to lead the unified national effort to secure the country and preserve our freedoms, and (2) to prepare for and respond to all hazards and disasters. The citizens of the United States must have the utmost confidence that the Department can execute both of these missions.

Faced with the challenge of strengthening the components to function as a unified Department, DHS must coordinate centralized, integrated activities across components that are distinct in their missions and operations. Thus, sound and cohesive management is the key to department-wide and component-level strategic goals. We seek to harmonize our efforts as we work diligently to accomplish our mission each and every day.

The Department of Homeland Security is headed by the Secretary of Homeland Security. It has various departments, including management, science and technology, health affairs, intelligence and analysis, citizenship and immigration services, and national cyber security center.

Department of Homeland Security Subcomponents

There are various subcomponents of The Department of Homeland Security that are involved with Information Technology Security.[12] These include the following:

- The Office of Intelligence and Analysis is responsible for using information and intelligence from multiple sources to identify and assess current and future threats to the United States.
- The National Protection and Programs Directorate houses offices of the Cyber Security and Communications Department.
- The Directorate of Science and Technology is responsible for research and development of various technologies, including information technology.
- The Directorate for Management is responsible for department budgets and appropriations, expenditure of funds, accounting and finance, procurement, human resources, information technology systems, facilities and equipment, and the identification and tracking of performance measurements.
- The Office of Operations Coordination works to deter, detect, and prevent terrorist acts by coordinating the work of federal, state, territorial, tribal, local, and private-sector parties and by collecting and turning information from a variety of sources. It oversees the Homeland Security Operations Center (HSOC), which collects and fuses information from more than 35 federal, state, local, tribal, territorial, and private-sector agencies.

State and Federal Organizations

There are various organizations that support information sharing at the state and the federal levels. The Department of Homeland Security through the Office of Intelligence and Analysis provides personnel with operational and intelligence skills. The support to the state agencies is tailored to the unique needs of the locality and serves to:

- Help the classified and unclassified information flow
- Provide expertise
- Coordinate with local law enforcement and other agencies
- Provide local awareness and access

---

11 "Public Health Security, Bioterrorism Preparedness & Response Act of 2002," U.S. Government Printing Office, http://frwebgate. access.gpo.gov/cgi-bin/getdoc.cgi?dbname=107_cong_public_ laws&docid=f:publ188.107 (downloaded 10/20/2008).

12 "Public Health Security, Bioterrorism Preparedness & Response Act of 2002," U.S. Government Printing Office, http://frwebgate. access.gpo.gov/cgi-bin/getdoc.cgi?dbname=107_cong_public_ laws&docid=f:publ188.107 (downloaded 10/20/2008).

As of March 2008, there were 58 fusion centers around the country. The Department has provided more than $254 million from FY 2004–2007 to state and local governments to support the centers.

The Homeland Security Data Network (HSDN), which allows the federal government to move information and intelligence to the states at the Secret level, is deployed at 19 fusion centers. Through HSDN, fusion center staff can access the National Counterterrorism Center (NCTC), a classified portal of the most current terrorism-related information.

There are various organizations at the state levels that support the homeland security initiatives. These organizations vary in their size and budget from very large independently run departments to a department that is a part of a larger related department. As an example, California has the Office of Management Services that is responsible for any emergencies in the state of California. The Governor's Office of Homeland Security is responsible for the coordination among different departments to secure the state against potential terrorist threats. Very specific to IT security, the California Office of Information Security and Privacy Protection is functional.

The Governor's Office of Homeland Security

The Governor's Office of Homeland Security (OHS) acts as the Cabinet-level state office for the prevention of and preparation for a potential terrorist event.[13] OHS serves a diverse set of federal, state, local, private sector, and tribal entities by taking an "all-hazards" approach to reducing risk and increasing responder capabilities.

Because California is prone to floods, fires, and earthquakes in addition to the potential for an attack using manmade weapons of mass destruction, OHS is committed to contributing to a comprehensive, well-planned all-hazards strategy to prevent, prepare for, respond to, and recover from any possible emergency. OHS is responsible for several key state functions, including[14]:

- Analysis and dissemination of threat-related information
- Protection of California's critical infrastructure

- Management of the state's homeland security grants
- S/B training and exercising of first responders for terrorism events

California Office of Information Security and Privacy Protection

The California Office of Information Security and Privacy Protection (OISPP) unites consumer privacy protection with the oversight of government's responsible management of information. OISPP provides services to consumers, recommends practices to business, and provides policy direction, guidance, and compliance monitoring to state government.[15]

OISPP was established within the State and Consumer Services Agency by Chapter 183 of the Statutes of 2007 (Senate Bill 90), effective January 1, 2008. This legislation merged the Office of Privacy Protection, which opened in 2001 in the Department of Consumer Affairs with a mission of identifying consumer problems in the privacy area and encouraging the development of fair information practices, and the State Information Security Office, established within the Department of Finance with a mission of overseeing information security, risk management, and operational recovery planning within state government.[16]

Private Sector Organizations for Information Sharing

Intelligence sharing and analysis groups have been set up in many private infrastructure industries. As an example, National Electric Reliability Council has such a group, Electricity Sector Information Sharing and Analysis Center (ESISAC), which serves the electricity sector by facilitating communications between sector participants, federal governments, and other critical infrastructure organizations. It is the job of the ESISAC to promptly disseminate threat indications, analyses, and warnings, together with interpretations, to assist electricity sector participants take protective actions. Similarly, many other organizations in other infrastructure sectors are also members of an ISAC.

---

13 "The Governor's Office of Homeland Security (OHS)," www.homeland.ca.gov/ (downloaded 10/24/2008).

14 "The Governor's Office of Homeland Security (OHS)," www.homeland.ca.gov/ (downloaded 10/24/2008).

15 "California Office of Information Security and Privacy Protection," www.oispp.ca.gov/ (downloaded 10/20/2008).

16 "California Office of Information Security and Privacy Protection," www.oispp.ca.gov/ (downloaded 10/20/2008).

There are other organizations that share information among the member companies on issues related to incident response (see sidebar, "National Commission on Terrorist Attacks Upon the United States [The 9-11 Commission]"). These organizations include FIRST, the Forum of Incident Response and Security Teams,[17] which has as its members major corporations from all over the world. The FBI encourages organizations from the private sector to become members of InfraGard to encourage exchange of information among the members.[18]

National Commission on Terrorist Attacks Upon the United States (The 9-11 Commission)

Congress charted the National Commission on Terrorist Attacks Upon the United States (known as the 9-11 Commission) by Public Law 107-306, signed by the President on November 27, 2002, to provide a "full and complete accounting" of the attacks of September 11, 2001 and recommendations as to how to prevent such attacks in the future.[19] On July 22, 2004, the 9-11 Commission issued its final report, which included 41 wide-ranging recommendations to help prevent future terrorist attacks.[20] Many of these recommendations were put in place with the passage of the Intelligence Reform and Terrorism Prevention Act of 2004 (PL 108-458), which brought about significant reorganization of the intelligence community. Soon after the Democratic Party came into the majority in the House of Representatives, the 110th Congress passed another act, Implementing Recommendations of the 9-11 Commission Act of 2007 (PL 110-53). This section is subdivided into the following four subsections:

1. Creation of the National Commission on Terrorist Attacks Upon the United States (the 9-11 Commission)
2. Final Report of the National Commission on Terrorist Attacks Upon the United States (the 9-11 Commission Report)
3. Intelligence Reform and Terrorism Prevention Act of 2004 (PL 108-458)
4. Implementing Recommendations of the 9-11 Commission Act of 2007 (PL 110-53)

Creation of the National Commission on Terrorist Attacks Upon the United States (The 9-11 Commission)

Congress created the National Commission on Terrorist Attacks Upon the United States (known as the 9-11 Commission) to provide a "full and complete accounting" of the terrorist attacks and recommendations as to how to prevent such attacks in the future.[21] Specifically, the Commission was required to investigate "facts and circumstances relating to the terrorist attacks of September 11, 2001," including those relating to intelligence agencies; law-enforcement agencies; diplomacy; immigration, nonimmigrant visas, and border control; the flow of assets to terrorist organizations; commercial aviation; the role of congressional oversight and resource allocation; and other areas determined relevant by the Commission for its inquiry.

The Commission was composed of 10 members, of whom not more than five members of the Commission were from the same political party.

In response to the requirements under law, the Commission organized work teams to address each of the following eight topics[22]:

1. Al Qaeda and the organization of the 9-11 attack
2. Intelligence collection, analysis, and management (including oversight and resource allocation)
3. International counterterrorism policy, including states that harbor or harbored terrorists, or offer or offered terrorists safe havens
4. Terrorist financing
5. Border security and foreign visitors
6. Law enforcement and intelligence collection inside the United States
7. Commercial aviation and transportation security, including an Investigation into the circumstances of the four hijackings
8. The immediate response to the attacks at the national, state, and local levels, including issues of continuity of government.

---

17 "Forum of incident response and security teams," www.first.org/ downloaded 10/20/2008).

18 InfraGard, www.infragard.net/ (downloaded 10/20/2008).

19 "National Commission on Terrorist Attacks upon the United States Act of 2002," www.9-11commission.gov/about/107-306.pdf (downloaded 10/20/2008).

20 "The 9-11 Commission Report," National Commission on Terrorist Attacks upon the United States, http://govinfo.library.unt.edu/911/report/911Report.pdf (downloaded 10/20/2008).

21 "National Commission on Terrorist Attacks upon the United States Act of 2002," www.9-11commission.gov/about/107-306.pdf (downloaded 10/20/2008).

22 "National Commission on Terrorist Attacks upon the United States Act of 2002," www.9-11commission.gov/about/107-306.pdf (downloaded 10/20/2008).

Final Report of the National Commission on Terrorist Attacks Upon the United States (The 9-11 Commission Report)

The 9-11 Commission interviewed more than 1000 individuals in 10 countries and held at least 10 days of public hearings, receiving testimony from more than 110 federal, state, and local officials and experts from the private sector. The Commission issued three subpoenas to government agencies: the Federal Aviation Administration (FAA), the Department of Defense, and the City of New York. On July 22, 2004, the 9-11 Commission issued its final report, which included 41 wide-ranging recommendations to help prevent future terrorist attacks. This report covers both general and specific findings. Here is the summary of their general findings:

Since the plotters were flexible and resourceful, we cannot know whether any single step or series of steps would have defeated them. What we can say with confidence is that none of the measures adopted by the U.S. government from 1998 to 2001 disturbed or even delayed the progress of the al Qaeda plot. Across the government, there were failures of imagination, policy, capabilities, and management.[23]

Imagination

The most important failure was one of imagination. We do not believe leaders understood the gravity of the threat. The terrorist danger from Bin Laden and al Qaeda was not a major topic for policy debate among the public, the media, or in Congress. Indeed, it barely came up during the 2000 presidential campaign.

Al Qaeda's new brand of terrorism presented challenges to U.S. governmental institutions that they were not well-designed to meet. Though top officials all told us that they understood the danger, we believe there was uncertainty among them as to whether this was just a new and especially venomous version of the ordinary terrorist threat the United States had lived with for decades, or it was indeed radically new, posing a threat beyond any yet experienced.

As late as September 4, 2001, Richard Clarke, the White House staffer long responsible for counterterrorism policy coordination, asserted that the government had not yet made up its mind how to answer the question: "Is al Qaeda a big deal?"

A week later came the answer.

Terrorism was not the overriding national security concern for the U.S. government under either the Clinton or the pre-9/11 Bush administration.

The policy challenges were linked to this failure of imagination. Officials in both the Clinton and Bush administrations

regarded a full U.S. invasion of Afghanistan as practically inconceivable before 9/11.

Capabilities

Before 9/11, the United States tried to solve the al Qaeda problem with the capabilities it had used in the last stages of the Cold War and its immediate aftermath. These capabilities were insufficient. Little was done to expand or reform them.

The CIA had minimal capacity to conduct paramilitary operations with its own personnel, and it did not seek a large-scale expansion of these capabilities before 9/11. The CIA also needed to improve its capability to collect intelligence from human agents.

At no point before 9/11 was the Department of Defense fully engaged in the mission of countering al Qaeda, even though this was perhaps the most dangerous foreign enemy threatening the United States.

America's homeland defenders faced outward. North American Aerospace Defense Command (NORAD) itself was barely able to retain any alert bases at all. Its planning scenarios occasionally considered the danger of hijacked aircraft being guided to American targets, but only aircraft that were coming from overseas.

The most serious weaknesses in agency capabilities were in the domestic arena. The FBI did not have the capability to link the collective knowledge of agents in the field to national priorities. Other domestic agencies deferred to the FBI.

FAA capabilities were weak. Any serious examination of the possibility of a suicide hijacking could have suggested changes to fix glaring vulnerabilities—expanding no-fly lists, searching passengers identified by the Computer Assisted Passenger Prescreening System (CAPPS) screening system, deploying federal air marshals domestically, hardening cockpit doors, alerting air crews to a different kind of hijacking possibility than they had been trained to expect. Yet the FAA did not adjust either its own training or training with NORAD to take account of threats other than those experienced in the past.

Management

The missed opportunities to thwart the 9/11 plot were also symptoms of a broader inability to adapt the way government manages problems to the new challenges of the twenty-first century. Action officers should have been able to draw on all available knowledge about al Qaeda in the government. Management should have ensured that information was shared and duties were clearly assigned across agencies, and across the foreign-domestic divide.

There were also broader management issues with respect to how top leaders set priorities and allocated resources.

---

23 "The 9-11 Commission Report," National Commission on Terrorist Attacks upon the United States, http://govinfo.library.unt.edu/911/report/911Report.pdf (downloaded 10/20/2008).

For instance, on December 4, 1998, Director of Central Intelligence (DCI), Tenet issued a directive to several CIA officials and the Deputy Director of Central Intelligence (DDCI) for Community Management, stating: "We are at war. I want no resources or people spared in this effort, either inside CIA or the Community." The memorandum had little overall effect on mobilizing the CIA or the intelligence community. This episode indicates the limitations of the DCI's authority over the direction of the intelligence community, including agencies within the Department of Defense.

The U.S. government did not find a way of pooling intelligence and using it to guide the planning and assignment of responsibilities for joint operations involving entities as disparate as the CIA, the FBI, the State Department, the military, and the agencies involved in homeland security.

Intelligence Reform and Terrorism Prevention Act of 2004 (PL 108-458)

Many of the recommendations of the Final Report of the National Commission on Terrorist Attacks Upon the United States (The 9-11 Commission Report) were put into the Intelligence Reform and Terrorism Prevention Act of 2004. This Act, divided into 10 titles, brought about significant reorganization of intelligence community and critical infrastructures protection.[24]

Title I—Reform of the Intelligence Community

Special measures relating to the following subtitles were created:

A. Establishment of Director of National Intelligence
B. National Counterterrorism Center, National Counter Proliferation Center, and National Intelligence Centers
C. Joint Intelligence Community Council
D. Improvement of education for the intelligence community
E. Additional improvements of intelligence activities
F. Privacy and civil liberties
G. Conforming and other amendments
H. Transfer, termination, transition, and other provisions
I. Other matters

Title II—Federal Bureau of Investigation

Improvement of intelligence capabilities of the Federal Bureau of Investigation

Title III—Security Clearances

Special measures relating to the security clearances have been created.

Title IV—Transportation Security

Special measures relating to the following subtitles were created:

A. National strategy for transportation security

B. Aviation security
C. Air cargo security
D. Maritime security
E. General provisions

Title V—Border Protection, Immigration, and Visa Matters

Special measures relating to the following subtitles were created:

A. Advanced Technology Northern Border Security Pilot Program
B. Border and immigration enforcement
C. Visa requirements
D. Immigration reform
E. Treatment of aliens who commit acts of torture, extrajudicial killings, or other atrocities abroad

Title VI—Terrorism Prevention

Special measures relating to the following subtitles were created:

A. Individual terrorists as agents of foreign powers
B. Money laundering and terrorist financing
C. Money laundering abatement and financial antiterrorism technical corrections
D. Additional enforcement tools
E. Criminal history background checks
F. Grand jury information sharing
G. Providing material support to terrorism
H. Stop Terrorist and Military Hoaxes Act of 2004
I. Weapons of Mass Destruction Prohibition Improvement Act of 2004
J. Prevention of Terrorist Access to Destructive Weapons
K. Pretrial detention of terrorists

Title VII—Implementation of 9-11 Commission Recommendations

Special measures relating to the following subtitles were created:

A. Diplomacy, foreign aid, and the military in the war on terrorism
B. Terrorist travel and effective screening
C. National preparedness
D. Homeland security
E. Public safety spectrum
F. Presidential transition
G. Improving international standards and cooperation to fight terrorist financing
H. Emergency financial preparedness

24 "Intelligence Reform and Terrorism Prevention Act of 2004," U.S. Senate Select Committee on Intelligence http://intelligence.senate.gov/laws/pl108-458.pdf (downloaded 10/20/2008).

Title VIII—Other Matters

Special measures relating to the following subtitles were created:

A. Intelligence matters
B. Department of homeland security matters
C. Homeland security civil rights and civil liberties protection

Implementing Recommendations of the 9-11 Commission Act of 2007 (PL 110-53)

Soon after the Democratic Party came into the majority in the House of Representatives, the 110th Congress passed another act, "Implementing Recommendations of the 9-11 Commission Act of 2007 (PL 110-53, August 3, 2007)."[25] Approximately a year after the passing of this law, the Majority Staffs of the Committees on Homeland and Foreign Affairs put its attention on the extent to which the law was indeed implemented and issued a report on "Wasted Lessons of 9/11: How The Bush Administration Ignored the Law and Squandered Its Opportunities to Make Our Country Safer."[26]

This comprehensive Homeland Security legislation included provisions to strengthen the nation's security against terrorism by requiring screening of all cargo placed on passenger aircraft; securing mass transit, rail and bus systems; assuring the scanning of all U.S.-bound maritime cargo; distributing Homeland Security grants based on risk; creating a dedicated grant program to improve inter-operable radio communications; creating a coordinator for U.S. nonproliferation programs and improving international cooperation for interdiction of weapons of mass destruction; developing better mechanisms for modernizing education in Muslim communities and Muslim-majority countries, and creating a new forum for reform-minded members of those countries; formulating coherent strategies for key countries; establishing a common coalition approach on the treatment

of detainees; and putting resources into making democratic reform an international effort, rather than a unilaterally U.S. one. When President George W. Bush signed H.R. 1 into law on August 3, 2007 without any limiting statement, it seemed that the unfulfilled security recommendations of the 9-11 Commission would finally be implemented. To ensure that they were, over the past year the Majority staffs of the Committees on Homeland Security and Foreign Affairs have conducted extensive oversight to answer the question, *How is the Bush Administration doing on fulfilling the requirements of the "Implementing Recommendations of the 9-11 Commission Act of 2007 (P.L. 110-53)?* The Majority staffs of the two Committees prepared this report to summarize their findings. While the Majority staffs of the Committees found that the Bush Administration has taken some steps to carry out the provisions of the Act, this report focuses on the Administration's performance with respect to key statutory requirements in the following areas: (1) aviation security; (2) rail and public transportation security; (3) port security; (4) border security; (5) information sharing; (6) privacy and civil liberties; (7) emergency response; (8) biosurveillance; (9) private sector preparedness; and (10) national security. In each of the 25 individual assessments in this report, a status update is provided on the Bush Administration's performance on these key provisions. The status of the key provisions identified in the report, help explain why the report is entitled "Wasted Lessons of 9/11: How the Bush Administration Has Ignored the Law and Squandered Its Opportunities to Make Our Country Safer."[27]

Based on this report, it is clear that the Bush Administration did not deliver on myriad critical homeland and national security mandates set forth in the "Implementing the Recommendations of 9-11 Commission Act of 2007." Members of the Committees were alarmed that the Bush Administration did not make more progress on implementing these key provisions.

4. CONCLUSION

Within about a year after the terrorist attacks, Congress passed various new laws, such as The USA PATRIOT Act, Aviation and Transportation Security Act, Enhanced Border Security and Visa Entry Reform Act, Public Health Security, Bioterrorism Preparedness & Response Act, Homeland Security Act, and E-Government Act,

and introduced sweeping changes to homeland security provisions and to the existing security organizations. The executive branch of the government also issued a series of Homeland Security Presidential Directives (HSPDs) to maintain domestic security. These laws and directives are comprehensive and contain detailed provisions to make the United States secure. For example, HSPD 5 enhances the ability of the United States to manage domestic incidents by establishing a single, comprehensive national incident management system.

25 "Implementing Recommendations of the 9-11 Commission Act of 2007," The White House, www.whitehouse.gov/news/releases/2007/08/20070803-1.html (downloaded 10/24/2008).

26 "Wasted lessons of 9/11: How the bush administration ignored the law and squandered its opportunities to make our country safer," *The Gavel*, http://speaker.house.gov/blog/?p=1501 (downloaded 10/24/2008).

27 "Wasted lessons of 9/11: How the bush administration ignored the law and squandered its opportunities to make our country safer," *The Gavel*, http://speaker.house.gov/blog/?p=1501 (downloaded 10/24/2008)

These laws and homeland security presidential directives call for deep and fundamental organizational changes to the executive branch of the government. For example, the Homeland Security Act of 2002 established a new Executive Branch agency, the U.S. Department of Homeland Security (DHS), and consolidated the operations of 22 existing federal agencies. Intelligence-sharing and analysis groups have been set up in many private infrastructure industries as well. For example, the National Electric Reliability Council has such a group, the Electricity Sector Information Sharing and Analysis Center (ESISAC), which serves the electricity sector by facilitating communications between sector participants, federal governments, and other critical infrastructure organizations.

Congress charted the "National Commission on Terrorist Attacks Upon the United States (The 9-11 Commission)" on November 27, 2002, to provide a "full and complete accounting" of the attacks of September 11, 2001, and recommendations as to how to prevent such attacks in the future. On July 22, 2004, the 9-11 Commission issued its final report, which included 41 wide-ranging recommendations to help prevent future terrorist attacks. Many of these recommendations were put in place with the passage of the "Intelligence Reform and Terrorism Prevention Act" and "Implementing Recommendations of the 9-11 Commission Act of 2007."

About a year after the passing of this law, the Majority Staffs of the Committees on Homeland and Foreign Affairs drew its attention on the extent to which the law was indeed implemented and issued a report on "Wasted Lessons of 9/11: How the Bush Administration Ignored the Law and Squandered Its Opportunities to Make Our Country Safer." This report demonstrates that it is clear that the Bush Administration did not deliver on myriad critical homeland and national security mandates set forth in the "Implementing the 9-11 Commission Recommendations Act of 2007." Fulfilling the unfinished business of the 9-11 Commission will most certainly be a major focus of President Obama, as many of the statutory requirements are to be met in stages.

## Chapter 39

Information Warfare

Jan Eloff
University of Pretoria

Anna Granova
University of Pretoria

The times we live in are called the Information Age for very good reasons: Today information is probably worth much more than any other commodity. Globalization, the other important phenomenon of the times we live in, has taken the value of information to new heights. Citizens of one country now feel entitled to know exactly what is happening in other countries around the globe. To this end, the capabilities of the Internet have been put to use and people have become accustomed to receiving information about everyone and everything as soon as it becomes available.

October 20, 1969, marked the first message sent on the Internet,[1] and almost 40 years on we cannot imagine our lives without it. Internet banking, online gaming, and online shopping have become just as important to some as food and sleep. As the world has become more dependent on automated environments, interconnectivity, networks, and the Internet, instances of abuse and misuse of information technology infrastructures have increased proportionately.[2] Such abuse has, unfortunately, not been limited only to the abuse of business information systems and Web sites but over time has also penetrated the military domain of state security. Today this penetration of governmental IT infrastructures, including, among others, the military domain, is commonly referred to as *information warfare*. However, the concept of information warfare is not yet clearly defined and understood. Furthermore, information warfare is a multidisciplinary field requiring expertise from technical, legal, offensive, and defensive perspectives. Information security professionals are challenged to respond to information warfare issues in a professional and knowledgable way.

The purpose of this chapter is to define information warfare (IW), discuss its most common tactics, weapons, and tools, compare IW terrorism with conventional warfare, and address the issues of liability and the available legal remedies under international law. To have this discussion, a proper model and definition of IW first needs to be established.

1. INFORMATION WARFARE MODEL

The author proposes a model for IW by mapping important concepts regarding IW on a single diagrammatic representation (see Figure 39.1). This aids in simplifying a complex concept as well as providing a holistic view on the phenomenon. To this end, this chapter addresses the four axes of IW: technical, legal, offensive, and defensive, as depicted in Figure 39.1.

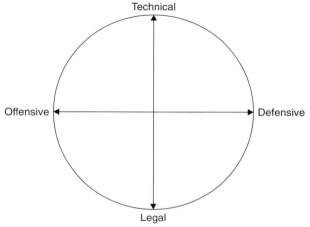

FIGURE 39.1 A perspective on IW.

---

1 *An Internet History* (2008), www.services.ex.ac.uk/cmit/modules/the_internet/webct/ch-history.html, accessed on 19 February 2008.

2 *Symantec Global Internet Security Threat Report Trends for July–December 07* (2008) Vol. 13, published April 2008 available at http://eval.symantec.com/mktginfo/enterprise/white_papers/b-whitepaper_internet_security_threat_report_xiii_04-2008.en-us.pdf, accessed on 21 April 2008.

The technical side of IW deals with technical exploits on one side and defensive measures on the other. As is apparent from Figure 39.1, these range from the most destructive offensive strategies, such as a distributed denial-of-service (DDoS) attack, to various workstation emergency response teams, such as US-CERT.

Considered from a legal perspective, IW can range from criminal prosecutions in international courts to use of force in retaliation. Therefore, the four axes of IW continuously interact and influence each other, as will become clearer from the discussion that follows.

2. INFORMATION WARFARE DEFINED

The manner in which war is being conducted has evolved enormously,[3] and IW has been accepted as a new direction in military operations.[4] A number of definitions are relevant for the purposes of this chapter. Some authors[5] maintain that IW covers "the full range of competitive information operations from destroying IT equipment to subtle perception management, and from industrial espionage to marketing." If one regards the more "military" definition of IW, one could say that IW is "a subset of information operations"—in other words "actions taken to adversely affect information and information systems while defending one's own information and information systems."[6]

The UN Secretary-General's report on *Development in the Field on Information and Telecommunications in the context of International Security* describes IW as "actions aimed at achieving information superiority by executing measures to exploit, corrupt, destroy, destabilise, or damage the enemy's information and its functions."[7] This definition is very similar to one of the more recent and accepted definitions found in literature that states that IW is "actions taken in support of objectives that influence decision-makers by affecting the information and/or information systems of others while protecting your own information and/or information systems."[8] If one, however, looks at IW in purely a military light, the following

technical definition seems to be the most appropriate: "The broad class of activities aimed at leveraging data, information and knowledge in support of military goals."[9]

In light of the preceding, it is clear that IW is all about information superiority because "the fundamental weapon and target of IW is information."[10] This being so, some authors[11] outline the basic strategies of IW as follows:

1. Deny access to information
2. Disrupt/destroy data
3. Steal data
4. Manipulate data to change its context or its perception

A slightly different perspective on the aims of IW is perhaps to see it as "an attack on information systems for military advantage using tactics of destruction, denial, exploitation or deception."[12]

With these definitions in mind, it is now appropriate to consider whether IW is a concept that has been created by enthusiasts such as individual hackers to impress the rest of the world's population or is, in fact, part of daily military operations.

3. IW: MYTH OR REALITY?

Groves once said: ". . . nowhere it is safe … no one knows of the scale of the threat, the silent deadly menace that stalks the network."[13] With the growing risk of terrorists and other hostile entities engaging in missions of sabotaging, either temporarily or permanently, important public infrastructures through cyber attacks, the number of articles[14] on the topic has grown significantly. To understand the gravity of IW and its consequences, the following real-life examples need to be considered. At the outset, however, it is important to mention that the reason there is so little regulation of computer-related activities with specific reference to IW both on national and international planes is that lawyers are very reluctant to venture into the unknown. The following examples, however, demonstrate that IW has consistently taken place since at

---

3 Schmitt, "Wired Warfare-Workstation Network Attack and *jus in bello*" 2002 *International Review of the Red Cross*, 365.

4 Rogers "Protecting America against Cyberterrorism" 2001 *United States Foreign Policy Agenda*, 15.

5 Hutchinson and Warren, *IW – Corporate Attack and Defence in a Digital World (2001) and XVIIII.*

6 Schmitt, "Wired Warfare-Workstation Network Attack and *jus in bello*" 2002 *International Review of the Red Cross* 365. See also the definition by Goldberg available on line at http://psycom.net/iwar.2.html.

7 UNG.A.Res A/56/164 dated 3 July 2001.

8 Thornton, R, *Asymmetric Warfare – Threat and Response in the 20-First Century* 2007.

9 Vacca, J. R., *Computer Forensics: Computer Crime Scene Investigation (2nd Edition)* Charles River Media, 2005.

10 Hutchinson and Warren, *IW – Corporate Attack and Defence in a Digital World (2001), p. xviiii.*

11 Hutchinson and Warren, *IW – Corporate Attack and Defence in a Digital World (2001) p. xviiii.*

12 Vacca, J. R., *Computer Forensics: Computer Crime Scene Investigation (2nd Edition)* Charles River Media, 2005.

13 Lloyd, I. J., *Information Technology Law* Oxford University Press 181 (5th Edition) 2008.

14 Groves, The War on Terrorism: Cyberterrorist be Ware, *Informational Management Journal*, Jan-Feb 2002.

least 1991. One of the first IW incidents was recorded in 1991 during the first Gulf War, where IW was used by the United States against Iraq.[15]

In 1998 an Israeli national hacked into the government workstations of the United States.[16] In 1999, a number of cyber attacks took place in Kosovo. During the attacks the Serbian and NATO Web sites were taken down with the aim of interfering with and indirectly influencing the public's perception and opinion of the conflict.[17]

These cyber attacks were executed for different reasons: Russians hacked U.S. and Canadian websites "in protest" against NATO deployment,[18] Chinese joined the online war because their embassy in Belgrade was bombed by NATO,[19] and U.S. nationals were paralyzing the White House[20] and NATO[21] Web sites "for fun." In 2000, classified information was distributed on the Internet,[22] and attacks were launched on NASA's laboratories,[23] the U.S. Postal Service, and the Canadian Defense Department.[24] As early as 2001, detected intrusions into the U.S. Defense Department's Web site numbered 23,662.[25] Furthermore, there were 1300 pending investigations into activities "ranging from criminal activity to national security intrusions."[26] Hackers also attempted to abuse the U.S. Federal Court's database[27] to compromise the peace process in the Middle East.[28]

In 2002, incidents of cyber terrorism in Morocco, Spain, Moldova, and Georgia[29] proved once again that a "hacker influenced by politics is a terrorist," illustrated by more than 140,000 attacks in less than 48 hours allegedly executed by the "G-Force" (Pakistan)[30]. During this period, a series of convictions on charges of conspiracy, the destruction of energy facilities,[31] the destruction of telecommunications facilities, and the disabling of air navigation facilities,[32] as well as cases of successful international luring and subsequent prosecutions, were recorded.[33]

In the second half of 2007, 499,811 new malicious code threats were detected, which represented a 571% increase from the same period in 2006.[34] With two thirds of more than 1 million identified viruses created in 2007,[35] the continued increase in malicious code threats has been linked to the sharp rise in the development of new Trojans and the apparent existence of institutions that employ "professionals" dedicated to creation of new threats.[36] In 2008 it has been reported in the media that "over the past year to 18 months, there has been 'a huge increase in focused attacks on our [United States] national infrastructure networks . . . . and they have been coming from outside the United States.'"[37]

It is common knowledge that over the past 10 years, the United States has tried to save both manpower and costs by establishing a system to remotely control and monitor the electric utilities, pipelines, railroads, and oil

15 Goodwin "Don't Techno for an Answer: The false promise of IW."

16 *Israeli citizen arrested in Israel for hacking United States and Israeli Government Workstations* (1998) http://www.usdoj.gov/criminal/cybercrime/ehudpr.hgm(accessed on 13 October 2002).

17 Hutchinson and Warren, *IW – Corporate Attack and Defence in a Digital World (2001)*.

18 Skoric (1999), http://amsterdam.nettime.org/Lists-Archives/nettime-l-9906/msg00152.html, (accessed on 03 October 2002).

19 Messmer (1999) http://www.cnn.com/TECH/computing/9905/12/cyberwar.idg/, (accessed on 03 October 2002).

20 *"Web Bandit" Hacker Sentenced to 15 Months Imprisonment, 3 Years of Supervised Release, for Hacking USIA, NATO, Web Sites* (1999), www.usdoj.gov/criminal/cybercrime/burns.htm (accessed on 13 October 2002).

21 *Access to NATO's Web Site Disrupted* (1999), www.cnn.com/WORLD/europe/9903/31/nato.hack/ (accessed on 03 October 2002).

22 Lusher (2000), www.balkanpeace.org/hed/archive/april00/hed30.shtml (accessed on 03 October 2002).

23 *Hacker Pleads Guilty in New York City to Hacking into Two NASA Jet Propulsion Lab Workstations Located in Pasadena, California* (2000), www.usdoj.gov/criminal/cybercrime/rolex.htm (accessed on 13 October 2002).

24 (2000) www.usdoj.gov/criminal/cybercrime/VAhacker2.htm (accessed on 13 October 2002).

25 www.coe.int/T/E/Legal_affairs/Legal_co-operation/Combating_economic_crime/Cybercrime/International_conference/ConfCY(2001)5E-1.pdf (accessed on 9 October 2002).

26 Rogers, *Protecting America against Cyberterrorism* U.S. Foreign Policy Agenda (2001).

27 (2001) "Hacker Into United States Courts' Information System Pleads Guilty," www.usdoj.gov/criminal/cybercrime/MamichPlea.htm (accessed on 13 October 2002).

28 (2001) "Computer Hacker Intentionally Damages Protected Computer" www.usdoj.gov/criminal/cybercrime/khanindict.htm (accessed on 13 October 2002).

29 *Hacker Influenced by Politics is Also a Terrorist* (2002), www.utro.ru/articles/2002/07/24/91321.shtml (accessed on 24 July 2002).

30 www.echocct.org/main.html (accessed on 20 September 2002).

31 *Hackers Hit Power Companies* (2002) www.cbsnews.com/stories/2002/07/08/tech/main514426.shtml (accessed on 20 September 2002).

32 U.S. v. Konopka (E.D.Wis.), www.usdoj.gov/criminal/cybercrime/konopkaIndict.htm (accessed on 13 October 2002).

33 U.S. v. Gorshkov (W.D.Wash), www.usdoj.gov/criminal/cybercrime/gorshkovSent.htm (accessed on 13 October 2002).

34 *Symantec Global Internet Security Threat Report Trends for July–December 07* (2008) Vol. 13, published April 2008 available at http://eval.symantec.com/mktginfo/enterprise/white_papers/b-whitepaper_internet_security_threat_report_xiii_04-2008.en-us.pdf accessed on 21 April 2008 at p.45.

35 *Symantec Global Internet Security Threat Report Trends for July–December 07* (2008) Vol. 13, published April 2008 available at http://eval.symantec.com/mktginfo/enterprise/white_papers/b-whitepaper_internet_security_threat_report_xiii_04-2008.en-us.pdf accessed on 21 April 2008 at p. 45.

36 *Symantec Global Internet Security Threat Report Trends for July–December 07* (2008) Vol. 13, published April 2008 available at http://eval.symantec.com/mktginfo/enterprise/white_papers/b-whitepaper_internet_security_threat_report_xiii_04-2008.en-us.pdf accessed on 21 April 2008 at p. 46.

37 Nakashima, E and Mufson, S, "Hackers have attacked foreign utilities, CIA Analysts says," 19 January 2008, available at www.washingtonpost.com/wp/dyn/conmttent/atricle/2008/01/18/AR2008011803277bf.html, accessed on 28 January 2008.

companies all across the United States.[38] The reality of the threat of IW has been officially confirmed by the U.S. Federal Energy Regulatory Commission, which approved eight cyber-security standards for electric utilities, which include "identity controls, training, security 'parameters' physical security of critical cyber equipment, incident reporting and recovery."[39] In January 2008, a CIA analyst warned the public that cyber attackers have hacked into the workstation systems of utility companies outside the United States and made demands, which led to at least one instance where, as a direct result, a power outage that affected multiple cities took place.[40]

To be able to appreciate the reality of the threat of IW, one only needs to look at the mild disruption of electricity in South Africa, which led to nervousness both within the South African local population as well as among international investors, who, as a direct result, withdrew more than US$500,000 from the South African economy. The blanket disruption of all essential services of a country may not only grind that country to a halt but could cause major population riots and further damage to an economy. The appropriate questions that then arise are, How can IW be brought about and how can one ward against it?

4. INFORMATION WARFARE: MAKING IW POSSIBLE

To conduct any form of warfare, one would require an arsenal of weapons. As far as IW is concerned, two general groups of strategies need to be considered: offensive strategies and defensive strategies. The nature of the beast that is IW is that constant research is essential and the most recent technological advances need to be employed to effectively employ and resist IW.

Offensive Strategies

The arsenal of IW includes weapons of psychological and technical nature. Both are significant and a combination

of the two can bring about astounding and highly disruptive results.

Psychological Weapons

Psychological weapons include social engineering techniques and psychological operations (*psyops*). Psyops include deceptive strategies. Deception has been part of warfare in general for hundreds of years.

Sun Tzu, in his fundamental work on warfare, says that "All warfare is based on deception."[41] Deception has been described as "a contrast and rational effort … to mislead an opponent."[42] In December 2005, it became known that the Pentagon was planning to launch a US$300 million operation to place pro-U.S. messages "in foreign media and on items such as T-shirts and bumper stickers without disclosing the U.S. government as the source."[43]

Trust is a central concept and a prerequisite for any psyops to succeed. The first known exploitation of trust in the cyber environment relates to Kevin Mitnick's exploitation of a network system.[44] The dissemination of workstation viruses as attachments to emails sent from people that you know and trust is another example of a psyops, such as the distribution of "I Love You" virus from a number of years ago.[45]

However, this does not represent an exhaustive list of psyops. Psyops can also target the general population by substituting the information on well-trusted news agencies' Web sites as well as public government sites with information favorable to the attackers. A good example is where the information on the Internet is misleading and does not reflect the actual situation on the ground.

The problem with psyops is that they cannot be used in isolation because once the enemy stops trusting the information it receives and disregards the bogus messages posted for its attention, psyops become useless, at least for some time. Therefore, technical measures of IW should also be employed to achieve the desired effect, such as DoS and botnet attacks. That way, the enemy might not only be deceived but the information the enemy holds can be destroyed, denied, or even exploited.

38 Nakashima, E and Mufson, S, "Hackers have attacked foreign utilities, CIA Analysts says," 19 January 2008, available at www.washingtonpost.com/wp/dyn/conmttent/atricle/2008/01/18/AR2008011803277bf.html, accessed on 28 January 2008.

39 Nakashima, E and Mufson, S, "Hackers have attacked foreign utilities, CIA Analysts says," 19 January 2008, available at www.washingtonpost.com/wp/dyn/conmttent/atricle/2008/01/18/AR2008011803277bf.html, accessed on 28 January 2008.

40 Nakashima, E and Mufson, S. (2008), "Hackers have attacked foreign utilities, CIA Analysts says," www.washingtonpost.com/wp/dyn/conmttent/atricle/2008/01/18/AR2008011803277bf.html, accessed on 28 January 2008.

41 Sun Tzu, *Art of War*.

42 Thornton, R., *Asymmetric Warfare – Threat and Response in the Twenty-First Century*, 2007.

43 www.infowar-monitor.net/modules.php?op=modload&name=News&sid=1302, accessed on 28 September 2006.

44 Vacca, J. R., *Computer Forensics: Computer Crime Scene Investigation (2nd Edition)* Charles River Media, 2005.

45 Vacca, J. R., *Computer Forensics: Computer Crime Scene Investigation (2nd Edition)* Charles River Media, 2005.

Technical Weapons

The technical weapons in IW can be subdivided into network, hardware, and software weapons. Network-based weapons relate to DoS attacks as well as the DDoS attacks. In plain language, it means that a specific workstation that contains required information cannot be accessed because of the intense volume of simultaneous requests sent from different workstations that have access to that workstation overload the system. It is unable to deal with the sheer volume of requests for access and so crashes.

Hardware-based weapons include putting defective parts into computer hardware, aiming to physically damage the whole unit. An example is the Exocets, French missiles that were reportedly sold to the Iraqis and contained backdoors to their workstation guidance systems,[46] which would ultimately render them harmless to French-allied troops.[47]

Software-based technical weapons are quite varied and have been recognized as important techniques of strategic IW.[48] Such malicious software includes Trojans, (distributed) DoS attacks, viruses, worms, and time bombs.

Trojans

Trojans have been defined as an advanced technique in hacking and pieces of code hidden in a benign/useful program—for example, a "green saver." Trojans require cooperation from the user, and in this sense this weapon overlaps the psyops. Trojans can also, however, be introduced by an executable script that is forcefully implanted into a user's workstation. Well-known scripts used for these purposes are, among others, JavaScript or Active Control. Trojans exploit the security deficiencies of the system to gain unauthorized access to sources such as an FBI database. Trojans represent a perfect accomplice for DoS or DDoS attacks.

It is therefore no surprise that five of the top 10 new malicious code families discovered in the latter half of 2007 were all Trojans. The Farfli Trojan77, for instance, took third place on the list of the new and most-spread malicious codes in that period. The distinct feature of this Trojan was not just its capability to download and install other threats onto the compromised workstation but the fact that the affected browsers were developed by Chinese programmers and were specifically aimed at Chinese users.[49] Since a Trojan creates an opportunity for a two-stage attack, it has become uniquely useful as a stepping stone for putting in place DoS and DDoS attacks in the IW context.

Denial-of-Service Attacks

Considering network attacks, it is important to remember that networks use a layered approach in moving data from one point to another. These layers are conceptual, and the model most commonly used is the ISO Open Systems Interconnect (OSI) model (Information Processing Systems, 1994). Lower layers are nearer the hardware and deal with transporting bytes across networks and applications; upper layers are concerned with presenting and adapting information for the user.

For attacks directed at lower levels in the OSI model, it is often the case that actual network components are targeted. For example, one crude but highly effective strike is the DoS attack.

DoS attacks constitute a serious threat to any network-dependant environment.[50] Both Windows and Unix platforms are susceptible to this type of attack.[51]

Although no data is usually destroyed[52] in a DoS assault, the service to legitimate users, networks, systems, or other resources is completely disrupted and/or denied.[53] A network is therefore rendered inaccessible due to the type or amount of traffic generated, which, in turn, "crashes servers, overwhelms the routers, or otherwise prevents the network's devices from functioning properly."[54] There are a number of ways a DoS attack can be carried out. A server's resources could, for

46 Lough, B. C., and Mungo, P. (1992), *Approaching Zero: Data Crime and the Workstation Underworld*, Faber and Faber, 186–187.
47 These back doors would allow the French military to send a radio signal to the on-board workstation. See also B. C. Lough, and P. Mungo, (1992), *Approaching Zero: Data Crime and the Workstation Underworld*, Faber and Faber, 187.
48 Lonsdale, D.J., *The Nature of War and Information Age: Clausewitzian Future*, Frank Cass, 2004.
49 *Symantec Global Internet Security Threat Report Trends for July–December 07* (2008), Vol. 13, p. 47–48, http://eval.symantec.com/mktginfo/enterprise/white_papers/b-whitepaper_internet_security_threat_report_xiii_04-2008.en-us.pdf, accessed on 21 April 2008.
50 McClure, S., Scambray, J., and Kurtz, G. (2003), *Hacking Exposed: Network Security Secrets & Solutions,* 4th ed., McGraw-Hill/Osborne.
51 McClure, S., Scambray, J., and Kurtz, G. (2003), *Hacking Exposed: Network Security Secrets & Solutions,* 4th ed., McGraw-Hill/Osborne.
52 Shinder, D. L. (2002), *Scene of the Cybercrime: Workstation Forensics Handbook*, Syngress Publishing.
53 McClure, S., Scambray, J., and Kurtz, G. (2003), *Hacking Exposed: Network Security Secrets & Solutions,* 4th ed., McGraw-Hill/Osborne. 504. See also Conklin, W. A., White, G. B., Cothren, C., Williams, D., and Davis, R. L. (2004), *Principles of Workstation Security: Security + and Beyond*, McGraw-Hill Technology Education.
54 Shinder, D. L. (2002), *Scene of the Cybercrime: Workstation Forensics Handbook,* Syngress Publishing.

example, be tied up or a particular workstation may need to be rebooted all the time.[55]

What makes this attack even more dangerous is that often there are no skill requirements on the part of the hacker because most, if not all, of the necessary tools are readily available on the Internet.[56] In other words, many DoS tools are classified as "point and click" and require "very little technical skill to run."[57] The fact that so-called "most-skilled hackers" frown[58] on the use of DoS attacks by amateurs does not detract from its malicious nature or destructive potential.

In recent years, profit-taking and invisibility dominated the underworld of the Internet. This is evidenced by the use of bots, programs covertly installed on an end user's machine to "allow an unauthorized user to remotely control the targeted system through a communication channel, such as IRC, peer-to-peer (P2P), or HTTP."[59] Once a substantial number of workstations are compromised, they can, in turn, be used in a DoS attack against a specific network.

The adoption of Supervisory Control and Data Acquisition (SCADA) network-connected systems for the U.S. infrastructure, such as power, water, and utilities,[60] has made a DoS attack a lethal weapon of choice. The susceptibility of the networking protocols, such as TCP/IP, to DoS attacks is easily explained. First, these protocols were designed to be used in a trusted environment.[61] Furthermore, the number of flaws on the network stack level in operating systems and network devices creates an environment in which attacks become irresistible and inevitable.[62]

Whether it is bandwidth consumption,[63] resource starvation,[64] programming flaws,[65] routing,[66] or a generic DoS[67] does not affect the damage capabilities of this attack.

An example of a DoS attack is a "fraggle" attack, which works as follows: Ping packets are sent to a subnet by the attacker, allegedly from the IP address of the targeted victim.[68] As a result, all workstations on the subnet flood the victim's machine with echo reply messages.[69] In 1999, this type of DoS was used by hackers while the Kosovo crisis was under way.[70] In particular, the pro-Serbian "hacktivists" on a continuous basis "fraggled" the U.S. and NATO Web sites with the purposes of overloading and bringing them down.[71]

DoS attacks are not only used to prevent access to a system. A SYN flooding attack, for example, is employed to temporarily interrupt the flow of normal service so that a trusted relationship between the compromised system and another system can be taken advantage of.[72]

To protect a network from a DoS attack, continuous improvement of a network's security is required. This entails daily updates of antivirus definitions, use of intrusion detection and intrusion prevention systems, and employment of ingress and egress filtering[73] on all network traffic, in combination with other behavior-blocking technologies. Most of the time, however, these techniques are outdated, and it may be that only certain types of DoS

---

55 Shinder, D. L. (2002), *Scene of the Cybercrime: Workstation Forensics Handbook,* Syngress Publishing, 317.

56 McClure, S., Scambray, J., and Kurtz, G. (2003), *Hacking Exposed: Network Security Secrets & Solutions,* 4th ed., McGraw-Hill/Osborne, 504. See also Shinder, D. L. (2002), *Scene of the Cybercrime: Workstation Forensics Handbook*, Syngress Publishing, 317.

57 McClure, S., Scambray, J., and Kurtz, G. (2003), *Hacking Exposed: Network Security Secrets & Solutions,* 4th ed., McGraw-Hill/Osborne, 504. See also Shinder, D. L. (2002), *Scene of the Cybercrime: Workstation Forensics Handbook*, Syngress Publishing, 317.

58 McClure, S., Scambray, J., and Kurtz, G. (2003), *Hacking Exposed: Network Security Secrets & Solutions,* 4th ed., McGraw-Hill/Osborne, 505.

59 *Symantec Global Internet Security Threat Report Trends for July–December 07* (2008), Vol. 13, p. 20, http://eval.symantec.com/mktginfo/enterprise/white_papers/b-whitepaper_internet_security_threat_report_xiii_04-2008.en-us.pdf, accessed on 21 April 2008.

60 McClure, S., Scambray, J., and Kurtz, G. (2003), *Hacking Exposed: Network Security Secrets & Solutions,* 4th ed., McGraw-Hill/Osborne, 505.

61 McClure, S., Scambray, J., and Kurtz, G. (2003), *Hacking Exposed: Network Security Secrets & Solutions,* 4th ed., McGraw-Hill/Osborne, 505.

62 McClure, S., Scambray, J., and Kurtz, G. (2003), *Hacking Exposed: Network Security Secrets & Solutions,* 4th ed., McGraw-Hill/Osborne, 505. See also Conklin, W. A., White, G. B., Cothren, C., Williams, D., and Davis, R. L. (2004), *Principles of Workstation Security: Security + and Beyond*, McGraw-Hill Technology Education, 396.

63 McClure, S., Scambray, J., and Kurtz, G. (2003), *Hacking Exposed: Network Security Secrets & Solutions,* 4th ed., McGraw-Hill/Osborne, 506.

64 McClure, S., Scambray, J., and Kurtz, G. (2003), *Hacking Exposed: Network Security Secrets & Solutions,* 4th ed., McGraw-Hill/Osborne, 506.

65 McClure, S., Scambray, J., and Kurtz, G. (2003), *Hacking Exposed: Network Security Secrets & Solutions,* 4th ed., McGraw-Hill/Osborne, 506.

66 McClure, S., Scambray, J., and Kurtz, G. (2003), *Hacking Exposed: Network Security Secrets & Solutions,* 4th ed., McGraw-Hill/Osborne, 507.

67 McClure, S., Scambray, J., and Kurtz, G. (2003), *Hacking Exposed: Network Security Secrets & Solutions,* 4th ed., McGraw-Hill/Osborne, 508–509.

68 Shinder, D. L. (2002), *Scene of the Cybercrime: Workstation Forensics Handbook*, Syngress Publishing, 320.

69 Shinder, D. L. (2002), *Scene of the Cybercrime: Workstation Forensics Handbook*, Syngress Publishing, 320.

70 Shinder, D. L. (2002), *Scene of the Cybercrime: Workstation Forensics Handbook*, Syngress Publishing, 320.

71 Shinder, D. L. (2002), *Scene of the Cybercrime: Workstation Forensics Handbook*, Syngress Publishing, 320.

72 Conklin, W. A., White, G. B., Cothren, C., Williams, D., and Davis, R. L. (2004), *Principles of Workstation Security: Security + and Beyond*, McGraw-Hill Technology Education, 396.

73 *Symantec Global Internet Security Threat Report Trends for July–December 07* (2008), Vol. 13, p. 23, http://eval.symantec.com/mktginfo/enterprise/white_papers/b-whitepaper_internet_security_threat_report_xiii_04-2008.en-us.pdf, accessed on 21 April 2008.

attacks are guarded against at any given time as a result of new attacks that enter the realm of the Internet on a daily basis.

The picture would, however, remain incomplete without mentioning that the U.S. law enforcement agencies are hot on the heels of the intruders. In 2007 their actions, through Operation Bot Roast II, led to an 11% decrease in botnet attacks and the indictment of eight people for crimes related to botnet activity.[74]

Distributed Denial-of-Service Attacks

The DDoS attack is another type of attack at the OSI level of the network. The first mass DDoS attack took place in February 2000.[75] Although the attack was reminiscent of a by then well-known DoS strategy, its ferocity justified placing it in a class of its own.[76] Seven major Web sites at the time,[77] including eBay, CNN, Amazon, and Yahoo!,[78] fell victim to the first DDoS. In recent years, DDoS assaults have become increasingly popular, largely due to the availability of exploits, which require little knowledge and/or skills to implement.[79]

Unlike a DoS attack, the source of a DDoS attack originates from a multitude[80] of workstations, possibly located all across the world.[81] Its aim, however, is identical: to bar legitimate parties from accessing and using a specific system or service.[82]

The use of intermediate workstations, sometimes referred to as *agents*[83] or *zombies*,[84] presupposes that in carrying out a DDoS assault, the perpetrator would go through a two-step process.[85] First, a number of workstations (which may number in the thousands)[86] are compromised to turn them into a weapon in the main action. To achieve this goal, the attacker must either gain unauthorized access to the system or induce an authorized user or users to install software that is instrumental for the purposes of the DDoS assault.[87]

Thereafter, the hacker launches the attack against a third system by sending appropriate instructions with data[88] on the specific target system to the compromised machines.[89] Thus the attack is carried out against a third system through remote control of other systems over the Internet.[90] Application, operating system, and protocol exploits could all be used to cause a system to overload and consequently create a DoS on an unprecedently large scale.[91] The end result would depend on the size of the attack network in question, keeping in mind that even ordinary Web traffic may be sufficient to speedily overwhelm even the largest of sites[92] and render them absolutely useless.[93]

Tribe FloodNet (also known as TFN), TFN2K, Trinoo, and Stacheldraht are all examples of DDoS tools. Some of them (the TFN2K) can be used against both Unix and Windows systems.[94]

74 *Symantec Global Internet Security Threat Report Trends for July–December 07* (2008), Vol. 13, p. 22, http://eval.symantec.com/mktginfo/enterprise/white_papers/b-whitepaper_internet_security_threat_report_xiii_04-2008.en-us.pdf, accessed on 21 April 2008.
75 McClure, S., Scambray, J., and Kurtz, G. (2003), *Hacking Exposed: Network Security Secrets & Solutions*, 4th ed., McGraw-Hill/Osborne, 518.
76 McClure, S., Scambray, J., and Kurtz, G. (2003), *Hacking Exposed: Network Security Secrets & Solutions*, 4th ed., McGraw-Hill/Osborne, 504.
77 McClure, S., Scambray, J., and Kurtz, G. (2003), *Hacking Exposed: Network Security Secrets & Solutions*, 4th ed., McGraw-Hill/Osborne, 518.
78 Harrison A (2000) "Cyber assaults hit Buy.com, eBay, CNN and Amazon," available online at www.workstationworld.com/news/2000/story/0,11280,43010,00.html and accessed on 16 May 2005. See also Conklin, W. A., White, G. B., Cothren, C., Williams, D., and Davis, R. L. (2004), *Principles of Workstation Security: Security + and Beyond*, McGraw-Hill Technology Education, 397.
79 McClure, S., Scambray, J., and Kurtz, G. (2003), *Hacking Exposed: Network Security Secrets & Solutions,* 4th ed., McGraw-Hill/Osborne, 525.
80 McClure, S., Scambray, J., and Kurtz, G. (2003), *Hacking Exposed: Network Security Secrets & Solutions,* 4th ed., McGraw-Hill/Osborne, 518. See also Conklin, W. A., White, G. B., Cothren, C., Williams, D., and Davis, R. L. (2004), *Principles of Workstation Security: Security + and Beyond*, McGraw-Hill Technology Education, 397.
81 Shinder DL (2002) *Scene of the Cybercrime: Workstation Forensics Handbook* (Syngress Publishing, Inc, Rockland) 317.
82 Conklin, W. A., White, G. B., Cothren, C., Williams, D., and Davis, R. L. (2004), *Principles of Workstation Security: Security + and Beyond*, McGraw-Hill Technology Education, 397.

83 Shinder, D. L. (2002), *Scene of the Cybercrime: Workstation Forensics Handbook*, Syngress Publishing, 317.
84 Conklin, W. A., White, G. B., Cothren, C., Williams, D., and Davis, R. L. (2004), *Principles of Workstation Security: Security + and Beyond*, McGraw-Hill Technology Education, 397.
85 Conklin, W. A., White, G. B., Cothren, C., Williams, D., and Davis, R. L. (2004), *Principles of Workstation Security: Security + and Beyond*, McGraw-Hill Technology Education, 397.
86 Shinder, D. L. (2002), *Scene of the Cybercrime: Workstation Forensics Handbook*, Syngress Publishing, 317.
87 Conklin, W. A., White, G. B., Cothren, C., Williams, D., and Davis, R. L. (2004), *Principles of Workstation Security: Security + and Beyond*, McGraw-Hill Technology Education, 397.
88 Conklin, W. A., White, G. B., Cothren, C., Williams, D., and Davis, R. L. (2004), *Principles of Workstation Security: Security + and Beyond*, McGraw-Hill Technology Education, 397.
89 Shinder, D. L. (2002), *Scene of the Cybercrime: Workstation Forensics Handbook*, Syngress Publishing, 317.
90 McClure, S., Scambray, J., and Kurtz, G. (2003), *Hacking Exposed: Network Security Secrets & Solutions*, 4th ed., McGraw-Hill/Osborne, 518.
91 Shinder, D. L. (2002), *Scene of the Cybercrime: Workstation Forensics Handbook*, Syngress Publishing, 317.
92 Conklin, W. A., White, G. B., Cothren, C., Williams, D., and Davis, R. L. (2004), *Principles of Workstation Security: Security + and Beyond*, McGraw-Hill Technology Education, 397.
93 McClure, S., Scambray, J., and Kurtz, G. (2003), *Hacking Exposed: Network Security Secrets & Solutions*, 4th ed., McGraw-Hill/Osborne, 525.
94 Shinder, D. L. (2002), *Scene of the Cybercrime: Workstation Forensics Handbook*, Syngress Publishing, 317.

What is interesting is that not only hackers have contemplated the use of DoS and DDoS attacks to further their aims. Information recently leaked from military sources indicates that warfare capabilities are currently officially classified to include DoS attacks as opposed to just conventional weapons of massive destruction.[95] The logical conclusion, therefore, is that a DDoS assault, as part of IW, represents a type of attack that is considered capable of bringing any country to a standstill.

In considering technical remedies for a DDoS, it should be kept in mind that DDoS attacks pose a dual threat[96] to both a primary or secondary victim network in that a network could be either the target or the vehicle of the DDoS assault. As is the case with DoS, the most effective precaution against a DDoS attack is ensuring that the latest patches and upgrades are installed on the system concerned.[97] Finally, the system administrator may also adjust "the timeout option for TCP connections"[98] as well as try to intercept or block the attack messages.[99]

Viruses

A virus is defined as "a program designed to spread itself by first infecting the executable files or the system areas of hard or floppy disks and then making copies of itself. Viruses usually operate without the knowledge or desire of the workstation user."[100]

Three types of viruses are prevalent: boot sector, program, and macro viruses. Boot-sector viruses attack the boot sector and render the whole system inoperable, whether temporarily or permanently. Program-type viruses come in executable format and load automatically and do not need to be launched, whether by the user or otherwise. Macro viruses are small applications embedded in a file, such as a Microsoft Word document, and automate "the performance of some task or sequence."[101]

In the last six months of 2007, 15% of the top 50 potential malicious code infections consisted of viruses, up from 10% in the previous six-month period and 5% in the last half of 2006.[102] Recently, however, viruses have been used as an introductory agent or "payload" for a worm, which causes more harm than the virus would cause by itself. In 2007, Symantec recorded a 5% increase in viruses but noted that the popularity of a virus as a technique could be solely attributed to its use as an introductory agent for worms that incorporate a "viral infection component."[103]

Worms

The difference between viruses and worms is that worms are automated programs that penetrate the network and each and every workstation that is on it, subject to any antivirus programs that may be installed on them. As with any workstation program, worms range from very simple to most sophisticated, making them some of the most security-destructive articles available on the Net. The classic examples of worms are Love-bug and CodeRed, which are well-known in the IT world.

It is no surprise that in 2007, half of the top 10 malicious code families were worms. The variation among their types speaks for itself: Two of the 10 were straightforward worms, two were worms with a backdoor component, and one had a virus component.[104]

The first and second most popular malicious code families in 2007 were the Invadesys worm.75 and the Niuniu76 worms. Their distinct features lie in the fact that they prepend their codes to Web pages that the user of the compromised workstation visits regularly, giving rise to a new and rapidly growing trend in malicious codes.[105] The popularity of the trend is largely attributed to the fact that the author usually redirects the victim's Internet Explorer to his own page and thus earns money from the sponsors who place links on his Web page.

95 McClure, S., Scambray, J., and Kurtz, G. (2003), *Hacking Exposed: Network Security Secrets & Solutions*, 4th ed., McGraw-Hill/Osborne, 525.

96 Shinder, D. L. (2002), *Scene of the Cybercrime: Workstation Forensics Handbook*, Syngress Publishing, 317.

97 Conklin, W. A., White, G. B., Cothren, C., Williams, D., and Davis, R. L. (2004), *Principles of Workstation Security: Security + and Beyond*, McGraw-Hill Technology Education, 397.

98 Conklin, W. A., White, G. B., Cothren, C., Williams, D., and Davis, R. L. (2004), *Principles of Workstation Security: Security + and Beyond*, McGraw-Hill Technology Education, 398.

99 Conklin, W. A., White, G. B., Cothren, C., Williams, D., and Davis, R. L. (2004), *Principles of Workstation Security: Security + and Beyond*, McGraw-Hill Technology Education, 398.

100 Young, S., and Aitel, D., *The Hackers Handbook: The strategy behind breaking into and defending networks*, p. 529.

101 Shinder, D. L. (2002), *Scene of the Cybercrime: Workstation Forensics Handbook*, Syngress Publishing, 337.

102 *Symantec Global Internet Security Threat Report Trends for July–December 07* (2008), Vol. 13, p. 50, http://eval.symantec.com/mktginfo/enterprise/white_papers/b-whitepaper_internet_security_threat_report_xiii_04-2008.en-us.pdf, accessed on 21 April 2008.

103 *Symantec Global Internet Security Threat Report Trends for July–December 07* (2008), Vol. 13, p. 50, http://eval.symantec.com/mktginfo/enterprise/white_papers/b-whitepaper_internet_security_threat_report_xiii_04-2008.en-us.pdf, accessed on 21 April 2008.

104 *Symantec Global Internet Security Threat Report Trends for July–December 07* (2008), Vol. 13, p. 47, http://eval.symantec.com/mktginfo/enterprise/white_papers/b-whitepaper_internet_security_threat_report_xiii_04-2008.en-us.pdf, accessed on 21 April 2008.

105 *Symantec Global Internet Security Threat Report Trends for July–December 07* (2008), Vol. 13, p. 47, http://eval.symantec.com/mktginfo/enterprise/white_papers/b-whitepaper_internet_security_threat_report_xiii_04-2008.en-us.pdf, accessed on 21 April 2008.

Time Bombs

Time bombs are another category of malicious software that may be employed for purposes of IW. Time bombs are intentionally installed by illegitimate users who fully understand the implications of their actions and deliberately seek the outcome thereof. In the commercial sense of the word, a time bomb may be installed for the purposes of bringing down the whole network infrastructure of a company that trades on a national level at various shopping centers, thereby causing great loss of sales and, ultimately, loss of profits.[106] In the conduct of IW, the implementation of malicious software that can crash a banking system, electricity source, and water supply at the same time may be very effective, together with the distribution of pamphlets that say that these types of failures are only the beginning of the offensive. The other examples of malicious software with nefarious purposes are those nonautomated hacking tools that are available for download from the Internet. Such tools include, for instance, a tool one could use to hack into one workstation on a system, such as an FBI database.

All of these types of malicious software, used in combination with psychological weapons, may prove very effective at attacking in a high-tech country such as the United States or the United Kingdom and rendering it defenseless. For these reasons the aforesaid countries have put in place stringent policies and institutions to deal with IW attacks of the present or future.

5. PREVENTATIVE STRATEGIES

As far as prevention is concerned, experts agree that "there is no silver bullet against IW attacks."[107] The U.S. Department of Defence in Information Operation Roadmap recommends that a special unit be created with a budget of US$15 million to improve the current psyops force structure that exists in the United States.[108] The roadmap specifically acknowledges that these remedies are necessary but require an advanced "21st-century technology" to attain "the long-range dissemination of psyops messages by new information venues such as solid satellites, the Internet, personal digital assistants and cell phones."[109]

For the most part, the attacks listed here are preventable and detectable. The problem facing a large target entity such as a sovereign nation is to coordinate its defense of many possible individual targets. Policies and procedures must be consistent and thoroughly followed. This is a mammoth task, given the heterogeneous nature of large computing systems.

Current solutions are of an organizational nature. Many developed countries have response teams such as the Computer Emergency Response Teams (CERT), but these deal only with technicalities of attacks. Higher-level involvement from government is required to act as a line of defense for IW. The U.S. Department of Homeland Security has forged a link with the private and public sector in the form of the US-CERT, with the blessing of a national strategy for cyber defense. In the U.K., a similar role is played by the National Infrastructure Security Co-ordination Centre.

South Africa, as an example country of the developing world, does not yet have a high-level commitment to digital defense; however, there are initiatives in the pipeline to address IW issues. A number of international efforts that aim at securing the Internet and preventing attacks such as the ones mentioned here have been implemented. One such initiative is the adoption of the European Convention of Cybercrime 2001, which deals with the commercial aspects of the Internet transactions. As far as the military aspects of IW are concerned, there have been calls from a number of countries, notably Russia, that the Internet be placed under control of the United Nations.[110]

As far as offensive weapons are concerned, the countermeasures that can be employed to prevent the attacks mostly consist of countermeasures that resemble the type of the original attack. For example, to avoid information by country B inflicting damage, country A may very well start with an offensive psyops itself, which may lead to the confusion of country B's government and the eventual cancellation of the original psyops it itself had planned.

Other technical measures usually involve information security services such as proactive creation of antiviruses, network security suits, and extensive use of encryption. The only problem with encryption, however, is that control over it is not centralized and it is therefore not possible for a government to govern and control the Internet from a global perspective in this manner.

106 Eloff, J., and Granova, A. (2003) (Computer Crime Case), *Computer Fraud and Security*, October 2003, p 14.
107 Lonsdale, D. J., *The Nature of War and Information Age: Clausewitzian Future* at 140.
108 U.S. Department of Defense *Information Operation Roadmap* dated 30 October 2003, p. 64.
109 U.S. Department of Defense *Information Operation Roadmap* dated 30 October 2003, p. 65.

110 (2003) *"Russia wants the UN to take control over the Internet,"* www.witrina.ru/witrina/internet/?file_body = 20031118oon.htm, accessed on 10 May 2005.

The Echelon system is well known as the system the U.S. implemented for purposes of monitoring the information flow on the Internet. It is well documented, and for purposes of this discussion it suffices to say that the Echelon system may not be the best system to use. Some estimate that a new Web site is created every four seconds, which makes the Internet almost impossible to monitor, especially if law enforcement is, as is true in some instances, 10 years behind the current transnational crime curve.[111]

In this light, it is clear that IW is a reality that exists as a direct result of the various psychological and technological advances of the human race. The question, however, remains: Is IW war or just an act of terrorism?

6. LEGAL ASPECTS OF IW

The fact that the Internet is, by definition, international implies that any criminal activity that occurs within its domain is almost always of an international nature.[112] The question that raises concern, however, is the degree of severity of the cyber attacks. This concern merits the following discussion.

Terrorism and Sovereignty

Today more than 110 different definitions of terrorism exist and are in use. There is consensus only on one part of the definition, and that is that the act of terrorism must "create a state of terror" in the minds of the people.[113]

The following definition of "workstation terrorism" as a variation of IW is quite suitable: "Computer terrorism is the act of destroying or of corrupting workstation systems with an aim of destabilizing a country or of applying pressure on a government,"[114] because the cyber attack's objective, *inter alia*, is to draw immediate attention by way of causing shock in the minds of a specific populace and thus diminishing that populace's faith in government.

Incidents such as hacking into energy plants, telecommunications facilities, and government Web sites cause a sense of instability in the minds of a nation's people, thereby applying pressure on the government of a particular country; therefore, these acts do qualify as terrorism and should be treated as such. Factual manifestations of war, that is, use of force and overpowering the enemy, ceased to be part of the classical definition of "war" after World War I,[115] and international writers began to pay more attention to the factual circumstances of each case to determine the status of an armed conflict. This is very significant for current purposes because it means that, depending on the scale and consequences of a cyber attack, the latter may be seen as a fully fledged war,[116] and the same restrictions—for example, prohibition of an attack on hospitals and churches—will apply.[117]

IW may seem to be a stranger to the concepts of public international law. This, however, is not the case, for there are many similarities between IW and the notions of terrorism and war as embodied in international criminal law.

The impact of the aforesaid discussion on sovereignty is enormous. Admittedly a cornerstone of the international law, the idea of sovereignty, was officially entrenched in 1945 in article 2(1) of the United Nations (UN) Charter.[118] This being so, any IW attack, whatever form or shape it may take, will no doubt undermine the affected state's political independence, because without order there is no governance.

Furthermore, the prohibition of use of force[119] places an obligation on a state to ensure that all disputes are solved at a negotiation table and not by way of crashing of the other state's Web sites or paralyzing its telecommunications facilities, thereby obtaining a favorable outcome of a dispute under duress. Finally, these rights of nonuse of force and sovereignty are of international character and therefore "international responsibility"[120] for all cyber attacks may undermine regional or even international security.

Liability Under International Law

There are two possible routes that one could pursue to bring IW wrongdoers to justice: using the concept of "state responsibility," whereby the establishment

---

111 Webster, W. H. (1998), *Cyber crime, Cyber terrorism, Cyber warfare: Averting an Electronic Waterloo*, CSIS Press: p. xiv.
112 Corell (2002), www.un.org/law/counsel/english/remarks.pdf (accessed on 20 September 2002).
113 J. Dugard, International Law: A South African Perspective 149 (2nd ed. 2000).
114 Galley (1996), http://homer.span.ch/~spaw1165/infosec/sts_en/ (accessed on 20 September 2002).

115 P. Macalister-Smith, Encyclopaedia of Public International Law 1135 (2000).
116 Barkham, *Informational Warfare and International Law*, 34 Journal of International Law and Politics, Fall 2001, at 65.
117 P. Macalister-Smith, Encyclopaedia of Public International Law 1400 (2000).
118 www.unhchr.ch/pdf/UNcharter.pdf (accessed on 13 October 2002).
119 www.unhchr.ch/pdf/UNcharter.pdf (accessed on 13 October 2002).
120 *Spanish Zone of Morocco* claims 2 RIAA, 615 (1923) at 641.

of a material link between the state and the individual executing the attack is imperative, or acting directly against the person, who might incur individual criminal responsibility.

State Responsibility

Originally, states were the only possible actors on the international plane and therefore a substantial amount of jurisprudence has developed concerning state responsibility. There are two important aspects of state responsibility that are important for our purposes: presence of a right on the part of the state claiming to have suffered from the cyber attack and imputation of the acts of individuals to a state.

Usually one would doubt that such acts as cyber attacks, which are so closely connected to an individual, could be attributable to a state, for no state is liable for acts of individuals unless the latter acts on its behalf.[121] The situation, however, would depend on the concrete facts of each case, as even an *ex post facto* approval of students' conduct by the head of the government[122] may give rise to state responsibility. Thus, this norm of international law has not become obsolete in the technology age and can still serve states and their protection on the international level.

Individual Liability

With the advent of a human rights culture after the Second World War, there is no doubt that individuals have become participants in international law.[123] There are, however, two qualifications to the statement: First, such participation was considered indirect in that nationals of a state are only involved in international law if they act on the particular state's behalf. Second, individuals were regarded only as beneficiaries of the protection offered by the international law, specifically through international human rights instruments.[124]

Individual criminal responsibility, however, has been a much more debated issue, for introduction of such a concept would make natural persons equal players in international law. This, however, has been done in cases of Nuremberg, the former Yugoslavia, and the Rwanda

tribunals, and therefore,[125] cyber attacks committed during the time of war, such as attacks on NATO web sites in the Kosovo war, should not be difficult to accommodate.

The difficulty is encountered with justification of use of the same terms and application of similar concepts to acts of IW, where the latter occurs independently from a conventional war. Conventionally, IW as an act of war sounds wrong, and to consider it as such requires a conventional classification. The definition of "international crimes" serves as a useful tool that saves the situation: being part of *jus cogens*,[126] crimes described by terms such as "aggression," "torture," and "against humanity" provide us with ample space to fit all the possible variations of IW without disturbing the very foundation of international law. Thus, once again there is support for the notions of individual criminal responsibility for cyber crimes in general public international law, which stand as an alternative to state responsibility.

In conclusion, it is important to note that international criminal law offers two options to an agreed state, and it is up to the latter to decide which way to go. The fact that there are no clear pronouncements on the subject by an international forum does not give a blank amnesty to actors on an international plane to abuse the apparent *lacuna*, ignore the general principles, and employ unlawful measures in retaliation.

Remedies Under International Law

In every discussion, the most interesting part is the one that answers the question: What are we going to do about it? In our case there are two main solutions or steps that a state can take in terms of international criminal law in the face of IW: employ self-defense or seek justice by bringing the responsible individual before an international forum.

Self-Defense

States may only engage in self-defense in cases of an armed attempt[127] which in itself has become a hotly debated issue. This is due to recognition of obligation of nonuse of force in terms of Art.2(4) of the UN Charter as being not only customary international law but also *jus cogens*.[128]

---

121 M.N. Shaw, International Law 414 (2nd ed. 1986).
122 For example, in *Tehran Hostages Case (v.) I.C.J. Reports*, 1980 at 3, 34–35.
123 J. Dugard, International Law: a South African Perspective (2nd ed. 2000), p. 1.
124 J. Dugard, International Law: a South African Perspective 1 (2nd ed. 2000), p. 234.

125 M.C. Bassiouni, International Criminal Law (2nd ed. 1999), p. 26.
126 M.C. Bassiouni, International Criminal Law (2nd ed. 1999), p. 98.
127 U.N. Charter art. 51.
128 M.Dixon, Cases and Materials on International Law 570 (3rd ed., 2000).

Armed attack, however, can be explained away by reference to the time when the UN Charter was written, therefore accepting that other attacks may require the exercise of the right to self-defense.[129] What cannot be discarded is the requirement that this inherent right may be exercised only if it aims at extinguishing the armed attack to avoid the conclusion of it constituting a unilateral use of force.[130] Finally, a state may invoke "collective self-defense" in the cases of IW. Though possible, this type of self-defense requires, first, an unequivocal statement by a third state that it has been a victim of the attack, and second, such a state must make a request for action on its behalf.[131]

Therefore, invoking self-defense in cases of IW today, though possible,[132] might not be a plausible option, because it requires solid proof of an attack, obtained promptly and before the conclusion of such an attack,[133] which at this stage of technological advancement is quite difficult. The requirement that the attack should not be completed by the time the victim state retaliates hinges on the fact that once damage is done and the attack is finished, states are encouraged to turn to international courts and through legal debate resolve their grievances without causing more loss of life and damage to infrastructure.

International Criminal Court

The International Criminal Court (ICC) established by the Rome Statute of 1998 is not explicitly vested with a jurisdiction to try an individual who committed an act of terrorism. Therefore, in a narrow sense, cyber terrorism would also fall outside the competence of the ICC.

In the wide sense, however, terrorism, including cyber terrorism, could be and is seen by some authors as torture.[134] That being so, since torture is a crime against humanity, the ICC will, in fact, have a jurisdiction over cyber attacks, too.[135]

Cyber terrorism could also be seen as crime against peace, should it take a form of fully fledged "war on the Internet," for an "aggressive war" has been proclaimed an international crime on a number of occasions.[136] Though not clearly pronounced on by the Nuremberg Trials,[137] the term "crime of aggression" is contained in the ICC Statute and therefore falls under its jurisdiction.[138]

Cyber crimes can also fall under crimes against nations, since in terms of customary international law states are obliged to punish individuals committing crimes against third states.[139] Furthermore, workstation-related attacks evolved into crimes that are universally recognized to be criminal and therefore against nations.[140] Therefore, thanks to the absence of *travaux préparatoires* of the Rome Statute, the ICC will be able to interpret provisions of the statute to the advantage of the international community, allow prosecutions of cyber terrorists, and ensure international peace and security.

Other Remedies

Probably the most effective method of dealing with IW is by way of treaties. At the time of this writing, there has been only one such convention on a truly international level, the European Convention on Cybercrime 2001.

The effectiveness of the Convention can be easily seen from the list of states that have joined and ratified it. By involving such technologically advanced countries as the United States, Japan, the United Kingdom, Canada, and Germany, the Convention can be said to have gained the status of instant customary international law,[141] as it adds *opinio juris* links to already existing practice of the states.

Furthermore, the Convention also urges the member states to adopt uniform national legislation to deal with the ever-growing problem of this century[142] as well as

129 P. Macalister-Smith, Encyclopaedia of Public International Law 362 (2000).

130 Military and Paramilitary Activities in and against Nicaragua (*Nic. v. U.S.A.*), www.icj-cij.org/icjwww/Icases/iNus/inus_ijudgment/inus_ijudgment_19860627.pdf (accessed on 11 October 2002).

131 M.Dixon, Cases and Materials on International Law 575 (3rd ed. 2000).

132 Barkham, *Informational Warfare and International Law*, Journal of International Law and Politics (2001), p. 80.

133 otherwise a reaction of a state would amount to reprisals, that are unlawful; see also *Nic. v. U.S.A.* case in this regard, www.icj-cij.org/icjwww/Icases/iNus/inus_ijudgment/inus_ijudgment_19860627.pdf (accessed on 11 October 2002).

134 J. Rehman, International Human Rights Law: A Practical Approach 464–465 (2002).

135 Rome Statute of the International Criminal Court of 1998 art.7, www.un.org/law/icc/statute/english/rome_statute(e).pdf (accessed on 13 October 2002).

136 League of Nations Draft Treaty of Mutual Assistance of 1923, www.mazal.org/archive/imt/03/IMT03-T096.htm (accessed on 13 October 2002); Geneva Protocol for the Pacific Settlement of International Disputes 1924, www.worldcourts.com/pcij/eng/laws/law07.htm (accessed on 13 October 2002).

137 P. Macalister-Smith, Encyclopaedia of Public International Law 873–874 (1992).

138 Art.5(1)(d) of the Rome Statute of the International Criminal Court 1998, www.un.org/law/icc/statute/english/rome_statute(e).pdf (accessed on 13 October 2002).

139 P. Macalister-Smith, Encyclopaedia of Public International Law 876 (1992).

140 P. Macalister-Smith, Encyclopaedia of Public International Law 876 (1992).

141 http://conventions.coe.int/Treaty/en/Treaties/Html/185.htm (accessed on 9 October 2002).

142 European Convention on Cybercrime of 2001 art. 23, http://conventions.coe.int/Treaty/en/Treaties/Html/185.htm (accessed on 9 October 2002).

provide a platform for solution of disputes on the international level.[143] Finally, taking the very nature of IW into consideration, "hard" international law may be the solution to possible large-scale threats in future.

The fact that remedies bring legitimacy of a rule cannot be overemphasized, for it is the remedies available to parties at the time of a conflict that play a decisive role in the escalation of the conflict to possible loss of life. By discussing the most pertinent remedies under international criminal law, the authors have shown that its old principles are still workable solutions, even for such a new development as the Internet.

Developing Countries Response

The attractiveness of looking into developing countries' response to an IW attack lies in the fact that usually these are the countries that appeal to transnational criminals due to lack of any criminal sanctions for crimes they want to commit. For purposes of this chapter, the South African legal system will be used to answer the question of how a developing country would respond to such an instance of IW.

In a 1989 "end conscription" case, South African courts defined war as a "hostile contest between nations, states or different groups within a state, carried out by force of arms against the foreign power or against an armed and organised group within the state."[144] In the 1996 *Azapo* case, the Constitutional Court, the highest court of the land, held that it had to consider international law when dealing with matters like these.[145] In the 2005 *Basson* case, the Constitutional Court further held that South African courts have jurisdiction to hear cases involving international crimes, such as war crimes and crimes against humanity.[146]

A number of legislative provisions in South Africa prohibit South African citizens from engaging, directly or indirectly, in IW activities. These Acts include the Internal Security Intimidation Act 13 of 1991 and the Regulation of Foreign Military Assistance Act 15 of 1998. The main question here is whether the South African courts would have jurisdiction to hear matters

in connection therewith. A number of factors will play a role. First, if the incident takes place within the air, water, or *terra firma* space of South Africa, the court would have jurisdiction over the matter.[147]

The implementation of the Rome Statute Act will further assist the South African courts to deal with the matter because it confers jurisdiction over the citizens who commit international crimes. It is well known that interference with the navigation of a civil aircraft, for example, is contrary to international law and is clearly prohibited in terms of the Montreal Convention.[148]

A further reason for jurisdiction is found in the 2004 Witwatersrand Local Division High Court decision of *Tsichlas v Touch Line Media*,[149] where Acting Judge Kuny held that publication on a Web site takes place where it is accessed. In our case, should the sites in question be accessed in South Africa, the South African courts would have jurisdiction to hear the matter, provided that the courts can effectively enforce its judgment against the members of the group.

Finally, in terms of the new Electronic Communications and Transactions (ECT) Act,[150] any act or preparation taken toward the offense taking place in South Africa would confer jurisdiction over such a crime, including interference with the Internet. This means that South African courts can be approached if preparation for the crime takes place in South Africa. Needless to say, imprisonment of up to five years would be a competent sentence for each and every participant of IW, including coconspirators.[151]

7. HOLISTIC VIEW OF INFORMATION WARFARE

This chapter has addressed the four axes of the IW model[152] presented at the beginning of this discussion: technical, legal, offensive, and defensive. Furthermore, the specific subgroups of the axes have also been discussed. For the complete picture of IW as relevant to the discussion at hand, however, Figure 39.2 places each subgroup into its own field.[153]

---

143 European Convention on Cybercrime of 2001 art. 45, http://conventions.coe.int/Treaty/en/Treaties/Html/185.htm (accessed on 9 October 2002).
144 Transcription *Campaign and Another v Minister of Defence and Another* 1989 (2) SA 180 (C).
145 *Azanian People's Organisation (AZAPO) v Truth and Reconciliation Commission* 1996 (4) SA 671 (CC).
146 *State v Basson* 2005, available at www.constitutionalcourt.org.za.

147 Supreme Court Act 59 of 1959 (South Africa).
148 Montreal Convention of 1971.
149 *Tsichlas v Touch Media* 2004 (2) SA 211 (W).
150 Electronic Communications and Transactions Act 25 of 2002.
151 Electronic Communication and Transaction Act 25 of 2002.
152 Supreme Court Act 59 of 1959 (South Africa).
153 Implementation of the Rome Statute of the International Criminal Court Act 27 of 2002 (South Africa).

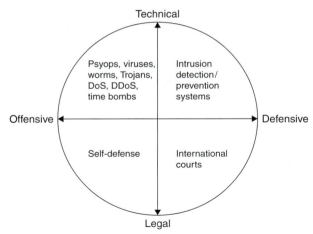

FIGURE 39.2 Holistic view of IW.

8. CONCLUSION

This discussion clearly demonstrated that IW is not only possible, it has already taken place and is growing internationally as a preferred way of warfare. It is clearly demonstrated that successful strategies, offensive or defensive, are dependent on taking a holistic view of the matter. Information security professionals should refrain from focusing only on the technical aspects of this area, since it is shown that legal frameworks, national as well as international, also have to be considered. The prevailing challenge for countries around the globe is to foster collaboration among lawyers, information security professionals, and technical IT professionals. They should continue striving to at least keep the registry of IW arsenal and remedies updated, which may, in turn, incite adversaries to provide us with more material for research.

Advanced Security

## Chapter 40

Security Through Diversity

Kevin Noble
Terremark Worldwide, Inc.

Security through diversity is a calculated and measured response to attacks against the mainstream and is usually used to survive and withstand uniform attacks. This response involves intentionally making things slightly different to completely different, forcing an attacker to alter a standard attack vector, tactics, and methodology. It can also be a matter of survival; having very different environments from everyone else might keep you operational. Intentionally going against the trend might be the right amount of diversity that puts your efforts ahead of the game or way behind it. Implementing diversity as a matter of doctrine can be scaled to having a completely different array of equipment for your production, test, and development or creating enough of a difference to protect information in the event of a disaster.

Where does one choose to deploy the diversity strategy? The most common diversity strategy is in use today by most large-scale businesses that choose to store data far enough away from the original site as to be unaffected by natural disasters and phenomena such as power outages. But is this enough? Natural disasters cover only one threat vector to sustainability and operational readiness.

This chapter covers some of the industry trends in adapting diversity in hardware, software, and application deployments. It also covers the risk of uniformity, conformity, and the ubiquitous impact of adapting standard organizational principals without the consideration of security.

1. UBIQUITY

Most modern attacks take advantage of the fact that the majority of personal computers on the Internet are quite nearly in the same state. That is, those home computers tend to be a few patches behind in many applications and with the operating system itself. Home users also tend not to patch software unless prompted by the self-updating software. Most home computers also tend to have an antivirus product installed with updated antivirus signatures. Working with this knowledge, an attacker will seek to automate an attack by taking advantage of the available common systems. This way, getting the most out of an attack seems reasonable.

Imagine for a moment that you're an attacker. You'd select the most frequently used operating systems with the most common software packages for your target list. The only thing that changes is the IP address itself. An economist might see the concept as a "probability density function," or what is simply referred to as "getting the most bang for the buck." It is certain that as a given computer system moves away from the densest pool of common systems, an attacker needs to work harder to accommodate the difference, which thus can reduce the likelihood of compromise.

When does diversity work against you? It might not be possible to quantify the advantage of selecting diversity over ubiquity other than the cost in procurement, training, and interoperability. It is quite possible that an investment in "bucking the system" and using uncommon systems and services won't just cause issues; it would drive your competitive advantage into oblivion. This is the single biggest reason to avoid security through diversity, and it will be pointed out repeatedly. Security through diversity starts early and is embraced as a matter of survival. Military and financial institutions abide by the diversity principals in investments and decision making. Though a threat is not always understood, the lessons learned during an attack tend to live on, forcing change and adaptation that require diversity as a fundamental principal of survival.

The introduction of complexity over engineering rarely leads to any sort of natural diversity. Engineering to requirements with anticipated tolerances might still be the best approach for any design. "All security involves trade-offs."[1] To that end diversity is not a security strategy in itself but is an aspect of defense in depth, part of a holistic approach to security and possibly an insurance policy against unenforceable odds.

2. EXAMPLE ATTACKS AGAINST UNIFORMITY

Ubiquitous systems are good, cheap, replaceable, and reliable—until mass failure occurs. It certainly pays to know that ubiquity and uniformity are the absolute right choices in the absence of threats. That is not the world we occupy, even if not acknowledged. What would it take to survive an attack that had the potential to effectively disrupt a business or even destroy it?

If you operate in a service industry that is Internet based, this question is perhaps what keeps you up at night—an attack against all your systems and services, from which you might not recover. Denial of Service (DoS) is a simple and straightforward attack that involves an attacker making enough requests to saturate your network or service to the point at which legitimate business and communications fails. The distributed denial-of-service (DDoS) attack is the same type of attack against a uniform presence in the Internet space but with many attacking hosts operating in unison against a site or service.

Businesses with real bricks-and-mortar locations in addition to selling goods and services over the Internet can survive a sustainable DDoS attack against the Internet-based business because the bricks-and-mortar transactions can carry the company's survival. Inversely, businesses with the ubiquitous use of credit cards that require the merchant authorization process can suffer when the point-of-sale system can't process credit cards. That business will simply and routinely have to turn away customers who can only pay by credit card. Yet a business with both a strong Internet and a solid bricks-and-mortar presence can survive an outage through diversity.

For years DDoS was used as a form of extortion. Internet-based gambling businesses were frequent targets of this type of attack and frequently made payouts to criminal attackers. It is common for Internet-based businesses to utilize DDoS mitigation services to absorb or offload the undesired traffic. The various means that an attacker can use in combination to conduct DDoS have escalated into a shifting asymmetrical warfare, with each side adapting to new techniques deployed by the other side.

Companies have failed to counter the straightforward attack and have gone out of business or ceased operations. A company called Blue Security Inc. that specialized in combating unsolicited email messages (spam) by automating a reply message to the senders had its subscribers attacked. Blue Security's antispam model failed in 2006 when spammers attacked its very customers, causing the company to shut down the service in the interest of protecting the customers.[2]

Successfully mitigating and combating an attack is achieved by either having enough resources to absorb the attack or offloading the attack at some point prior to reaching a site or service. The DDoS attack is partially successful where the target is uniformly presented and responsive and does not react fast enough to the attacks. A common means to protect against DDoS or Internet-based outages is to have a diverse business model that does not rely only on the Internet as a means to conduct business. Diverse business models may hold considerable cost and bring in differential revenue, but they ensure that one model may in fact support the other through sustained attacks, disasters, or even tough times. Employing the concept of security through diversity gives decision makers more immediate options.

Though the DDoS attack represents the most simplistic and basic attack against an Internet-based institution, it does require an attacker to use enough resources against a given target to achieve bottlenecking or saturation. This represents the immediate and intentional attack, with one or more attackers making a concentrated effort against a target.

3. ATTACKING UBIQUITY WITH ANTIVIRUS TOOLS

Attackers use obfuscation, encryption, and compression to install malicious code such as viruses, worms, and Trojans. These techniques are tactical responses to bypass common antivirus solutions deployed by just about everyone. The number of permutations possible on a single executable file while retaining functionality is on the order of tens of thousands, and these changes create just enough diversity in each iteration to achieve a successful infection. An attacker needs to mutate an executable only enough to bypass detection from

---

1 Bruce Schneier, *Beyond Fear,* Springer-Verlag, 2003.

2 "Blue Security, spam victim or just a really bad idea," *InfoWorld/Tech Watch* article, May 19, 2006.

signature-based antivirus tools, the most common antivirus solutions deployed.[3]

It is possible for anyone to test a given piece of malicious code against a litany of antivirus solutions. It is common practice for attackers and defenders both to submit code to sites such as www.virustotal.com for inspection and detection against 26 or more common antivirus solutions. Attackers use the information to verify whether a specific antivirus product will fail to detect code while defenders inspect suspected binaries.

At the root of the problem is the signature-based method used to inspect malicious code. Not all antivirus solutions use signature-based detection exclusively, but in essence, it is the fast, cheap, and, until recently, most effective method. If malware sample A looks like signature X, it is most likely X. A harder and less reliable way to detect malicious code is through a technique known as *heuristics*. Each antivirus will perform heuristics in a different manner, but it makes a guess or best-effort determination and will classify samples ranging from safe to highly suspect. Some antivirus solutions may declare a sample malicious, increasing the chances of finding a false positive.

Another factor in analysis is entropy, or how random the code looks upon inspection. Here again you can have false positives when following the trend to pack, distort, encrypt, and otherwise obfuscate malicious code. The measurement of entropy is a good key indicator that something has attempted to hide itself from inspection. Keep in mind that because commercial software uses these techniques as well, you have a chance of false positives.

At the 2008 annual DEFCON conference in Las Vegas, a new challenge was presented: Teams were provided with existing malicious code and modified the code without changing functionality, to bypass all the antivirus solutions. The team that could best defeat detection won. The contest was called "race to zero." The organizers hoped to raise awareness about the decreased reliability on signature-based antivirus engines. It is very important to say again that the code is essentially the same except that it can avoid detection (or immediate detection).

Given that it is possible and relatively easy for attackers to modify existing malicious code enough to bypass all signature-based solutions yet retain functionality, it can be considered a threat against any enterprise that has a ubiquitous antivirus solution deployment. Infections are possible and likely and increasing; the risk is not a doomed enterprise, but usually information disclosure could lead to other things.

Those who choose Apple's OS X over PC operating systems enjoy what might be coined in some circles as immunity or resistance in the arena of malicious code. An attacker would have to invest time and effort into attack strategies against the Apple platform over and above the efforts of attacking Windows, for example. Without getting caught up in market share percentages, Apple is not as attractive for attackers (at the time of this writing) from the operating system perspective.

One might think the application of diversity can be applied simply by hosting differential operating systems. This is true but rarely works if derived from a strict security perspective. It could be beneficial to switch entirely to a less attacked platform or host a differential operating system in a single environment. On the sliding scales of diversity and complexity, you might have immune hosts to one attack type against a given operating system. This also means that internal information technology and support teams would have to maintain support skills that can support each different platform hosted. Usually business decisions make better drivers for using and supporting diverse operating systems than a strategy of diversity alone. In my observations, routine support will be applied where individuals have stronger skills and abilities while other platforms are neglected.

4. THE THREAT OF WORMS

In 2003 and 2004, the fast-spreading worm's probability represented the bigger threat for the Internet community at large because patching was not as commonplace and interconnectivity was largely ignored compared to today. A number of self-replicating viruses propagating to new hosts autonomously are known as *worms*. A worm-infected host would seek to send the worm to other hosts, using methods that would allow for extremely aggressive and rapid spread. Infected hosts did not experience much in the way of damage or intentional data loss but simply were not able to communicate with other hosts on heavily infected networks. Essentially, the worms became an uncontrolled DDoS tool, causing outages and performance issues in networks in which the worm gained enough hosts to saturate the networks by seeking yet more hosts.

While responding to the outbreaks of both the Nachi and MSBlas worms in 2003 for a large business, there was enough statistical information about both worms from the various logs, host-based protection, and packet captures to reconstruct the infection process (see

---

3 G. Ollmann, "X-morphic exploitation," IBM Global Technology Services, May 2007.

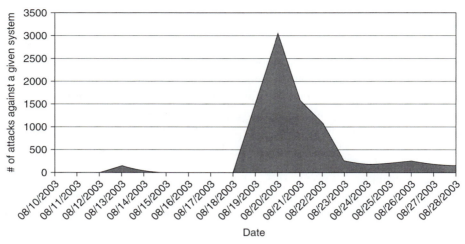

FIGURE 40.1 Tracking infected hosts as part of the Nachi outbreak.

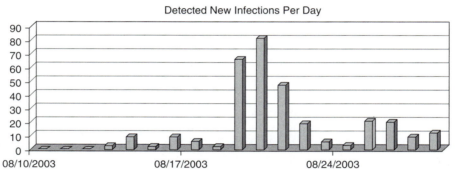

FIGURE 40.2 Nachi finding new hosts to infect.

Figure 40.1). The Nachi worm in particular appeared to have an optimized IP address-generating algorithm allowing nodes closer on the network to become infected faster. When you consider that the worm could only infect Windows-based systems against the total variety of hosts, you end up with a maximum threshold of targets. The network-accessible Windows hosts at the time of the worm attack were about 79.8% of the total network; other platforms and systems were based on Unix, printers, and routers. Certainly some of the hosts were patched against this particular vulnerability. Microsoft had released a patch prior to the outbreak. But at the time of the Nachi worm outbreak, patching was deployed at set intervals in excess of 60 days, and the particular vulnerability exploited by Nachi was not patched. The theoretical estimated number of systems that could succumb to infection was right at the total number of Windows systems on the network—just under 80%, as shown in Figure 40.2— meaning that the network was fairly uniform.[4]

Given this scenario, it would stand to reason that the infection would achieve 100% and only depend on each newly infected system coming up with the appropriate IP address to infect new hosts. Yet the data reveals that the total infection was only 36% of the total Windows systems and took 17 days to really become effective, as shown in Figure 40.3. It seemed that enough vulnerable Windows hosts had to be infected to seed the next wave of infected hosts.

The worm's pseudorandom IP address selection was a factor in the success of its spread; you had to have a vulnerable system online with a specific IP that was targeted at that time. Once enough seed systems became infected, even a poor pseudorandom IP generator would have been successful in allowing the worm to spread at speeds similar to a chemical chain reaction. Systems would become infected within seconds rather than minutes or hours of connecting to a network.

Other factors for a successful defense against the worm included a deployment of host-based firewalls that blocked port traffic. The Nachi worm traffic was mostly

4 K. Noble, "Profile of an intrusion." research paper, Aug. 2003.

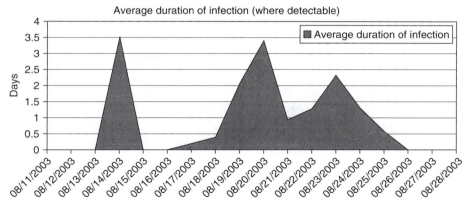

FIGURE 40.3 The Nachi worm requires continual infection to achieve network saturation.

from nonlocal untrusted networks making port filtering an easy block for the attack. Other factors that reduced the spread included the fact that a number of systems, such as mobile laptop computers, did not remain connected after business hours (users taking the laptops home, for example). Emergency patching and efforts to contain the spread by various groups was also a big factor in reducing the number of vulnerable systems. The Nachi worm itself also prevented infection to some systems by simply generating too much traffic, causing a DoS within the network. Network engineers immediately began blocking traffic as generated by the Nachi worm and blocking entire subnets altogether. The speed of the infection caused a dramatic increase in traffic on infected networks and induced a reaction by many network engineers looking for the root cause and attacking the problem by blocking specific traffic.

Additional resistance to infection from the Nachi worm in this case was achieved through unintended diversity in time, location, and events surrounding the vulnerable systems. Perhaps we can call this being lucky; vulnerable hosts were protected by not being connected or not needing to connect during the potential infection window. The last interesting thing about worms that achieved mass infection during 2003 is that those worms still generate traffic on the Internet today—perhaps an indication of a sustained infection, reinfection, or intentional attacks.

Though unintentional diversity and rapid response to the outbreak were success factors, an emerging response to automated attacks was intrusion detection systems (IDSs) being deployed in greater numbers. Though prevention is ideal, detection is the absolute first and necessary step in the process of defense. A natural transition to automating defense was the mass implementation of intrusion protection systems (IPSs), which detect and block based on predefined understandings of past attacks and in some cases block based on attack behavior.

Making a choice to be diverse as a means to improve security alone might not be beneficial. If you choose two different backup methodologies or split offices between two different operating systems just for the sake of security and not business as the driver, then cost in theory nearly doubles without gaining much. Ideally diversity is coupled with other concepts, such as security.

5. AUTOMATED NETWORK DEFENSE

Computer systems that transact information at great speed have similar properties to chemical reactions that, once started, are quite difficult or impossible to stop. Though an IPS will trade speed for security, it ultimately tries not to impede the traffic overall and has a default threshold for when to allow traffic unabated. This seems to be a default objective for IPSs—trying to keep out most of the bad things while allowing everything else to traverse without interference, reflecting customer demand.

If an IPS took time to inspect every anomaly to the point where overall traffic performance were degraded, it would be advantageous for an attacker to exploit the heavy inspection process to create a performance issue up to the point of denying service. This very consideration causes both the default policies on IPS and IPS customers to acquiesce and to allow a percentage of bad traffic as a trade for performance or connectivity in general.

At first you might be surprised at the position taken by IPS vendors and customers. Denying all anomalous and malicious traffic might be the sales pitch from IPS vendors, but the dichotomy of having a device designed for automated protection being used for automated DoS by an attacker against the very business it was suppose to protect would scare off anyone. IDS as an industry does nothing more than strike a balance between common attack prevention while allowing everything else—perhaps a worthy goal on some fronts.

6. DIVERSITY AND THE BROWSER

An evolutionary adaptation to security has driven attackers to exploit the Web browser. Because everyone has one, the Web browser represents the most promising avenue to information exploitation. Straightforward attacks involving simply spraying an attack across the Internet are not how one exploits browers. Attacks usually take advantage of vulnerabilities only after a browser retrieves code from a malicious Web site. The remote attack is not a sustainable attack. Most popular browsers that host the means for automatic patching allow the browsers to be secured against known vulnerabilities. Still, not everyone takes advantage of new browser releases that include patches for remote exploits and serious issues. Attacking the user behind the browser along with attacking the browser seems to be a winning combination yielding a higher percentage of compromised hosts for attackers.

Conceptually, could the browser be the weapon of choice that collapses an entire enterprise? It is possible but highly unlikely. The two most common browsers are Microsoft's Internet Explorer and Mozilla's Firefox, making them the most targeted. Most browsers are not monolithic; adding code to view pages and perform animation are common practices. Browser extensibility allows anyone to integrate software components. Serious vulnerabilities and poor implementation in some of these extensions has led to exploitable code but usually demands a visit from a vulnerable browser. Since many of us don't use the same software package added to our browsers, this sort of threat, though risky to any enterprise from the standpoint of information disclosure, does not represent the sort of survivability issues security diversity seeks to remedy.

The application of diversity to browsers could be remedied by the selection of an uncommon browser or by choosing extensibility options offered by vendors other than the most common ones. The tradeoff is gaining a host of compatibility issues for the ability to thwart browser-specific attacks.

Operating systems (OSs) are the Holy Grail of attacked platforms. All attacks in some form or fashion seek to gain authority within the OS or to dominate the OS altogether. Rootkits seek to hide the behavior of code and allow code (usually malicious) to operate with impunity on a given system. Even when the browser or other services are attacked, it would probably be more advantageous for the attacker to seek a way into the OS without detection.

The Windows OS, with the lion's share of systems, is the ubiquitous platform of choice for attackers. Microsoft has made considerable efforts in the past few years to combat the threats and has introduced technologies such as stack cookies, safe handler and chain validation, heap protection, data execution prevention (DEP), and address space layout randomization (ASLR). Each is designed to thwart or deter attacks and protect code execution from exploitation through any vulnerability.

Of each of these low-level defenses implemented in code today, ASLR seeks to increase security through diversity in the Vista OS. Theoretically, on a given system on which an attack is possible, it will not be possible again on another system or even the same system after a layout change that occurs after a reboot. Certainly altering the behavior between systems reduces risk.

The current implementation of ASLR on Vista requires complete randomized process address spacing to offer complete security from the next wave of attacks.[5] Certainly the balance of security falters and favors the attacker when promiscuous code meets any static state or even limited entropy of sorts.

7. SANDBOXING AND VIRTUALIZATION

The technique of *sandboxing* is sometimes used to contain code or fault isolation. Java, Flash, and other languages rely heavily on containing code as a security measure. Though sandboxing can be effective, it has the same issues as anything else that is ubiquitous—one flaw that can be exploited for a single sandbox can be exploited for all sandboxes.

Expanding the concept in a different way is the virtual hosting of many systems on a single system through the use of a *hypervisor*. Each instance of an OS connects to the physical host through the hypervisor, which acts as the hardware gateway and as a kernel of sorts. Frequently the concept of virtualization is coupled to security as the layer of abstraction and offers quite a bit of protection between environments in the absence of vulnerabilities.

The concept of virtualization has considerable long-term benefits by offering diversity within a single host but requires the same diligence as any physical system

---

5 M. Dowd and A. Sotirov, 2008 Black Hat paper, "Bypassing browser memory protections," http://taossa.com/archive/bh08sotirovdowd.pdf.

compounded by the number of virtual systems hosted. It is fair to say that each host that contains vulnerabilities may therefore put other hosts or the entire core of the hosting physical system at risk. The risk is no different than an entire room full of interconnected systems that have emergent properties. Frequently, security professionals and attackers alike use virtualization as a platform for testing code and the ability to suspend and record activity, similar to a VCR.

In many cases the push to virtualize systems and services is driven by sharing unused resources as a business decision. However, with increased frequency, security is considered a benefit of virtualization. This is true only in the context of virtual environments achieving isolation between guests or host and guest. This is a clear goal of all the hypervisors on the market, from the VMware product line to Windows Virtualization products.

For quite some time it was possible for security researchers to work with malicious samples in a virtualized state. This allowed researchers to essentially use the context of a computer running on a computer with features similar to a digital video recorder, where time (for the malicious sample) can be recorded and played back at a speed of their choosing. That was true until the advent of malicious code with the ability to test whether it was hosted in a virtualized environment or not. Recent research has shown that it is possible for malicious code to escape the context of the virtual world and attack the host system or at least glean information from it.

Two competing factors nullify using virtualized environments as a means of archiving simple security through diversity. It will continue to be possible to detect hosting in a virtual environment, and it is possible to find the means to exploit virtual environments, even if the difficulty increases. However, this just means that you can't rely on the hypervisor alone. Vulnerabilities are at the heart of all software, and the evolutionary state of attacking the virtualized environments and the hypervisor will continue to progress.

The decline of virtualized environments as a security tool was natural as so many in the security field became dependent on hypervisors. In response, the security field will essentially adapt new features and functions to offset vulnerabilities and detect attacks. Examples include improved forensics and hosting virtualized environments in ways to avoid detection.

In nature, colorful insects represent a warning to others of toxicity or poison if eaten. Similarly, some in the security field have taken to setting virtualization flags on real, physical machines simply to foil malicious code. The more hostile malicious code will shut itself down

and delete itself when it determines it is in a virtual host, thus preventing some infections.

8. DNS EXAMPLE OF DIVERSITY THROUGH SECURITY

It is fair to say that the Internet requires a means to resolve IP addresses to names and names back to IP addresses. The resolving capabilities are solved by Domain Name Services with a well-defined explanation on how any DNS is supposed to function being published and publicly available. In most cases you may choose to use a provider's implementation of DNS as a resolver or deploy your own to manage internal names and perform a lookup from other domains.

If prior to 2008 you had selected the less popular DJBDNS[6] over the more popular BIND, you would have been inoculated (for the most part[7]) against the DNS cache-poisoning attack made famous by Dan Kaminski. Depending on your understanding of the attack against what you are trying to protect, theoretically all information transacted over the Internet was at the complete mercy of an attacker. Nothing could be trusted. This is actually not the limit of the capabilities, but it is the most fundamental. The threat to survivability was real and caused many to consider secure DNS alternatives after the attack was made public.

Rapid and automated response is the most common defense technique. Making the decision to act late is still beneficial but risky because the number of attackers capable of performing the attack increases with time. Reaction is both a good procedural defense and offers immunity and lessons learned. As part of the reaction, you could assume that the DNS is not trusted and continue to operate with the idea that some information not be from the intended sources. You could also make a decision to disconnect from the Internet until the threat is mitigated to a satisfactory level. Neither would seem reasonable, but it is important to know what threat would constitute such a reaction.

9. RECOVERY FROM DISASTER IS SURVIVAL

Disaster recovery is often thought of as being able to recover from partial data loss or complete data loss by

---

6 D. J. Bernstein, http://cr.yp.to/djbdns.html.
7 Though DNS queries might be verified where DJBDNS was deployed, the upstream DNS server could still be vulnerable, making it important to know from where you get your DNS names.

restoring data from tape. With the considerably lower cost of dense media, it is now possible to continuously stream a copy of the data and recover at any point in time rather than the scheduled time associated with evening backup events. In many cases the backup procedure is tested frequently, whereas the recovery procedure is not.

Unfortunately, many assume that simply having backups means that recovery is inevitable or a foregone conclusion. For others, the risk associated with recovery has led to many organizations never testing the backups for fear of disruption or failure. Perhaps in the interest of diversity from the norm it is beneficial to frequently and procedurally test restore operations. Though security diversity is a survival technique, recovery is the paramount survival tool in everyone's arsenal.

10. CONCLUSION

Disaster recovery seems the ideal area in which to institute a separate and diverse architecture from that of a production environment. Segregation between environments offers a tangible boundary that accounts for attacks, unintended consequences, and disasters, but it is only part of a solution. As Dan Greer indicated in his essay on the evolution of security,[8] we already have an evolutionary approach to systems by centralizing enterprises into safe, climate-controlled environments. We protect systems with IDS all while making copies of critical data and systems, just in case. Making changes to systems as we acquire them is rarely undertaken to the level necessary to ensure survival; most systems have very few changes from the "out-of-box" state or factory default because we fear that the changes will make the system unstable or ineffective.

The best ways to make the leap to complete diversity will inevitably be performed on as many fronts as possible and at the lowest levels—differential hardware, platforms, and interfaces. At the higher levels, consideration

for a process to apply hygiene to each protocol and every piece of data, to change states from the original format into anything other than the original, to ensure that any native attack code becomes inoculated. Adaptation and rapid response might just be enough diversity for survival.

In selecting diversity and all the investment and issues that go along with it, an instant beneficial byproduct is a rich set of choices in many areas, not just security. Decision makers have options not available to monocultural networks and systems. For example, if you have deployed in production at least two different manufacturers, routers or firewalls, you will have people trained specifically for each or both. Instead of a competitive nature of driving out competition, you have the ability to match the appropriate models to various parts of a given network and not depend on the product catalog of a single vendor. In the immediate situation of threats to an entire product line, a diverse decision process such as exchanging routers is available. Someone with a single affected vendor has a limited choice bracket of solutions. Additionally, anyone trained or certified in more than one company's equipment portfolio can more easily adapt to any additional needs increasing choices and options.

Of all the security diversity solutions available, perhaps having a skilled and adaptable workforce trained in all the fundamental aspects of computer security offers the best solution. The simplistic statement of "the best defense is a good offense" means that security professionals should be able to defend from attacks, understand attacks, and be prepared to perform the forensic analysis and reverse-engineering needed to understand attacks.

Having both an archive of skills and knowledge along with just-in-time knowledge is the true application of diversity in a security situation. Execution of a diverse skill set during a given threat to survival makes all the difference in the world.

---

8 D. Greer, "The evolution of security," *ACM Queue*, April 2007

## Chapter 41

Reputation Management

Dr. Jean-Marc Seigneur
University of Geneva

Reputation management is a rather new field in the realm of computer security, mainly due to the fact that computers and software are more and more involved in open networks. In these open networks, any encountered users may become part of the user base and associated interactions, even if there is no *a priori* information about those new users. The greater openness of these networks implies greater uncertainty regarding the outcomes of these interactions. Traditional security mechanisms, for example, access control lists, working under the assumption that there is *a priori* information about who is allowed to do what, fail in these open situations.

Reputation management has been used for ages in the real world to mitigate the risk of negative interaction outcomes among an open number of potentially highly profitable interaction opportunities. Reputation management is now being applied to the open computing world of online interactions and transactions. After the introduction, this chapter discusses the general understanding of the notion of reputation. Next, we explain where this concept of reputation fits into computer security. Then we present the state of the art of robust computational reputation. In addition, we give an overview of the current market for online reputation services. The conclusion underlines the need to standardize online reputation for increased adoption and robustness.

During the past three decades, the computing environment has changed from centralized stationary computers to distributed and mobile computing. This evolution has profound implications for the security models, policies, and mechanisms needed to protect users' information and resources in an increasingly globally interconnected, open computing infrastructure. In centralized stationary computer systems, security is typically based on the authenticated identity of other parties. Strong authentication mechanisms, such as Public Key Infrastructures

(PKIs),[1,2] have allowed this model to be extended to distributed systems within a single administrative domain or within a few closely collaborating domains. However, small mobile devices are increasingly being equipped with wireless network capabilities that allow ubiquitous access to corporate resources and allow users with similar devices to collaborate while on the move. Traditional, identity-based security mechanisms cannot authorize an operation without authenticating the claiming entity. This means that no interaction can take place unless both parties are known to each others' authentication framework. Spontaneous interactions would therefore require that a single or a few trusted Certificate Authorities (CAs) emerge, which, based on the inability of a PKI to emerge over the past decade, seems highly unlikely for the foreseeable future. In the current environment, a user who wants to partake in spontaneous collaboration with another party has the choice between enabling security and thereby disabling spontaneous collaboration or disabling security and thereby enabling spontaneous collaboration.

The state of the art is clearly unsatisfactory; instead, mobile users and devices need the ability to autonomously authenticate and authorize other parties that they encounter on their way, without relying on a common authentication infrastructure. The user's mobility implies that resources left in the home environment must be accessed via interconnected third parties. When the user moves to a foreign place for the first time, it is highly probable that the third parties of this place are *a priori* unknown strangers. However, it is still necessary for a user to interact with

---

1 C. Ellison, and B. Schneier, "Ten risks of PKI: What you're not being told about Public Key Infrastructure", *Computer Security Journal*, Winter (2000).
2 R. Housley, and T. Polk, *Planning for PKI: Best Practices Guide for Deploying Public Key Infrastructure*, Wiley (2001).

these strangers to, for example, access her remote home environment. It is a reality that users can move to potentially harmful places; for example, by lack of information or due to uncertainty, there is a probability that previously unknown computing third parties used to provide mobile computing in foreign places are malicious. The assumption of a known and closed computing environment held for fixed, centralized, and distributed computers until the advent of the Internet and more recently mobile computing. Legacy security models and mechanisms rely on the assumption of closed computing environments, where it is possible to identify and fortify a security perimeter that protects against potentially malicious entities. However, in these models, there is no room for "anytime, anywhere" mobility. Moreover, it is supposed that inside the security perimeter there is a common security infrastructure, a common security policy, or a common jurisdiction in which the notion of identity is globally meaningful. It does not work in the absence of this assumption.

A fundamental requirement for Internet and mobile computing environments is to allow for potential interaction and collaboration with unknown entities. Due to the potentially large number of previously unknown entities and for simple economic reasons, it makes no sense to assume the presence of a human administrator who configures and maintains the security framework for all users in the Internet, for example, in an online auction situation or even in proximity, as when a user moves within a city from home to workplace. This means that either the individuals or their computing devices must decide about each of these potential interactions themselves. This applies to security decisions, too, such as those concerning the enrollment of a large number of unknown entities. There is an inherent element of risk whenever a computing entity ventures into collaboration with a previously unknown party. One way to manage that risk is to develop models, policies, and mechanisms that allow the local entity to assess the risk of the proposed collaboration and to explicitly reason about the trustworthiness of the other party, to determine whether the other party is trustworthy enough to mitigate the risk of collaboration. Formation of trust may be based on previous experience, recommendations from reachable peers, or the perceived reputation of the other party. Reputation, for example, could be obtained through a reputation system such as the one used on eBay.[3] This chapter focuses on this new approach to computer security—namely, reputation management.

1. THE HUMAN NOTION OF REPUTATION

Reputation is an old human notion; the Romans called it *reputatio*, as in "*reputatio est vulgaris opinio ubi non est veritas.*"[4] Reputation may be considered a social control mechanism,[5] where it is better to tell the truth than to have the reputation of being a liar. That social control mechanism may have been challenged in the past by the fact that people could change their physical locale to clear their reputation. However, as we move toward an information society world, changing locales should have less and less impact in this regard because reputation information is no longer bound to a specific location, which is also good news for reputable people who have to move to other regions for other reasons such as job relocation. For example, someone might want to know the reputation of a person he does not know, especially when this person is being considered to carry out a risky task among a set of potential new collaborators. Another case may be that the reputation of a person is simply gossiped about. The reputation information may be based on real, biased, or faked "facts," perhaps faked by a malicious recommender who wants to harm the target person or positively biased by a recommender who is a close friend of the person to be recommended. The above Latin quote translates to "reputation is a vulgar opinion where there is no truth."[6] The target of the reputation may also be an organization, a product, a brand, or a location. The source of the reputation information may not be very clear; it could come from gossip or rumors, the source of which is not exactly known, or it may come from a known group of people. When the source is known, the term *recommendation* can be used. Reputation is different from recommendation, which is made by a known specific entity. Figure 41.1 gives an overview of the reputation primitives.

As La Rochefoucauld wrote[7] a long time ago, recommending is also a trusting behavior. It has not only an impact on the recommender's overall trustworthiness (meaning it goes beyond recommending trustworthiness)

---

3 P. Resnick, R. Zeckhauser, J. Swanson, and K. Lockwood, *The Value of Reputation on eBay: A Controlled Experiment*, Division of Research, Harvard Business School (2003).

---

4 M. Bouvier, "Maxims of law," *Law Dictionary* (1856).

5 K. Kuwabara, "Reputation: Signals or incentives?" In *The Annual Meeting of the American Sociological Association* (2003).

6 M. Bouvier, "Maxims of law," *Law Dictionary* (1856).

7 Original quotation in French: *La confiance ne nous laisse pas tant de liberté, ses règles sont plus étroites, elle demande plus de prudence et de retenue, et nous ne sommes pas toujours libres d'en disposer: il ne s'agit pas de nous uniquement, et nos intérêts sont mêlés d'ordinaire avec les intérêts des autres. Elle a besoin d'une grande justesse pour ne livrer pas nos amis en nous livrant nous-mêmes, et pour ne faire pas des présents de leur bien dans la vue d'augmenter le prix de ce que nous donnons.*

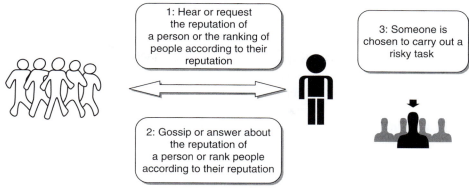

FIGURE 41.1 Overview of the reputation primitives.

but also on the overall level of trust in the network of the involved parties. La Rochefoucauld highlighted that when one recommends another, they should be aware that the outcome of their recommendation will reflect on their own trustworthiness and reputation, since they are partly responsible for this outcome. Benjamin Franklin noted that each time he made a recommendation, his recommending trustworthiness was impacted: "In consequence of my crediting such recommendations, my own are out of credit."[8] However, his letter underlines that still he had to make recommendations about not very well-known parties because they made the request and not making recommendations could have upset them. This is in line with Covey's "Emotional Bank Account,"[9,10] where any interaction modifies the amount of trust between the interacting parties and can be seen as favor or disfavor—a deposit or withdrawal. As Romano underlined in her thesis, there are many definitions of trust in a wide range of domains,[11] for example, psychology, economics, or sociology. In this chapter, we use Romano's definition of trust, which is supposed to integrate many aspects of previous work on trust research:

> *Trust is a subjective assessment of another's influence in terms of the extent of one's perceptions about the quality and significance of another's impact over one's outcomes in a given situation, such that one's expectation of, openness to, and inclination toward such influence provide a sense of control over the potential outcomes of the situation.[12]*

8 B. Franklin, *The Life and Letters of Benjamin Franklin.*, G. M. Hale & Co., 1940.

9 S. R. Covey, *The seven habits of highly effective people* (1989).

10 J. Seigneur, J. Abendroth, and C. D. Jensen, "Bank accounting and ubiquitous brokering of trustos" (2002) *7th Cabernet Radicals Workshop.*

11 D. M. Romano, *The Nature of Trust: Conceptual and Operational Clarification* (2003).

12 D. M. Romano, *The Nature of Trust: Conceptual and Operational Clarification* (2003).

In social research, there are three main types of trust: interpersonal trust, based on the outcomes of past interactions with the trustee; dispositional trust, provided by the trustor's general disposition toward trust, independent of the trustee; and system trust, provided by external means such as insurance or laws.[13] Depending on the situation, a high level of trust in one of these types can become sufficient for the trustor to make the decision to trust. When there is insurance against a negative outcome or when the legal system acts as a credible deterrent against undesirable behavior, it means that the level of system trust is high and the level of risk is negligible; therefore the levels of interpersonal and dispositional trust are less important. It is usually assumed that by knowing the link to the real-world identity, there is insurance against harm that may be done by this entity. In essence, this is security based on authenticated identity and legal recourse. In this case, the level of system trust seems to be high, but one may argue that in practice the legal system does not provide a credible deterrent against undesirable behavior, that is, it makes no sense to sue someone for a single spam email, since the effort expended to gain redress outweighs the benefit.

The information on the outcomes of past interactions with the trustee that are used for trust can come from different sources. First, the information on the outcomes may be based on direct observations—when the trustor has directly interacted with the requesting trustee and personally experienced the observation. Another type of observation is when a third party himself observes an interaction between two parties and infers the type of outcome. Another source of information may be specific recommenders who report to the trustor the outcomes of

13 D. H. McKnight, and N. L. Chervany, "What is trust? A conceptual analysis and an interdisciplinary model," In *The Americas conference on information systems* (2000).

interactions that have not been directly observed by the trustor but by themselves or other recommenders. In this case, care must be taken not to count twice or many more times the same outcomes reported by different recommenders.

Finally, reputation is another source of trust information but more difficult to analyze because generally it is not exactly known who the recommenders are, and the chance to count many times the same outcomes of interactions is higher. As said in the introduction, reputation may be biased by faked evidence or other controversial influencing means. Reputation evidence is the riskiest type of evidence to process. When the evidence recommender is known, it is possible to take into account the recommender trustworthiness. Since some recommenders are more or less likely to produce good recommendations, even malicious ones, the notion of recommending trustworthiness mitigates the risk of bad or malicious recommendations. Intuitively, recommendations must only be accepted from senders that the local entity trusts to make judgments close to those that it would have made about others. We call the trust in a given situation the *trust context*. For example, recommending trustworthiness happens in the context of trusting the recommendation of a recommender. Intuitively, recommendations must only be accepted from senders the local entity trusts to make judgments close to those that it would have made about others. For our discussion in the remainder of this chapter, we define reputation as follows:

> *Reputation is the subjective aggregated value, as perceived by the requester, of the assessments by other people, who are not exactly identified, of some quality, character, characteristic or ability of a specific entity with whom the requester has never interacted with previously.*

To be able to perceive the reputation of an entity is only one aspect of reputation management. The other aspects of reputation management for an entity consist of the following:

- Monitoring the entity reputation as broadly as possible in a proactive way
- Analyzing the sources spreading the entity reputation
- Influencing the number and content of these sources to spread an improved reputation

Therefore, reputation management involves some marketing and public relations actions. Reputation management may be applied to different types of entities: personal reputation management, which is also called "personal branding,"[14] or business reputation management. It is now common for businesses to employ full-time staff to influence the company's reputation via the traditional media channels. Politicians and stars also make use of public relations services. For individuals, in the past few years media have become available to easily retrieve information, but as more and more people use the Web and leave digital traces, it now becomes possible to find information about any Web user via Google. For example, in a recent survey of 100 executive recruiters,[15] 77% of these executive recruiters declared that they use search engines to learn more about candidates.

2. REPUTATION APPLIED TO THE COMPUTING WORLD

Trust engines, based on computational models of the human notion of trust, have been proposed to make security decisions on behalf of their owners. For example, the EU-funded SECURE project[16] has built a generic and reusable trust engine that each computing entity would run. These trust engines allow the entities to compute levels of trust based on sources of trust evidence, that is, knowledge about the interacting entities: local observations of interaction outcomes or recommendations. Based on the computed trust value and given a trust policy, the trust engine can decide to grant or deny access to a requesting entity. Then, if access is given to an entity, the actions of the granted entity are monitored and the outcomes, positive or negative, are used to refine the trust value. The computed trust value represents the interpersonal trust part and is generally defined as follows:

- A trust value is an unenforceable estimate of the entity's future behavior in a given context based on past evidence.
- A trust metric consists of the different computations and communications carried out by the trustor (and her network) to compute a trust value in the trustee.

Figure 41.2 depicts the high-level view of a computational trust engine called when:

- A requested entity has to decide what action should be taken due to a request made by another entity, the requesting entity
- The decision has been decided by the requested entity

---

14 T. Peters, "The brand called you," *Fast Company* (1997).

15 Execunet, www.execunet.com.
16 J. M. Seigneur, *Trust, Security and Privacy in Global Computing* (2005).

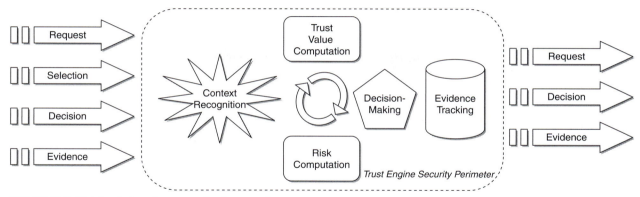

FIGURE 41.2 High-level view of a computational trust engine.

- Evidence about the actions and the outcomes is reported
- The trustor has to select a trustee among several potential trustees

A number of subcomponents are used for the preceding cases:

- A component that is able to recognize the context, especially to recognize the involved entities. Depending on the confidence level in recognition of the involved entities, for example, the face has only been recognized with 82% of confidence, which may impact the overall trust decision. Context information may also consist of the time, the location, and the activity of the user.[17]
- Another component that can dynamically compute the trust value, that is, the trustworthiness of the requesting entity based on pieces of evidence (for example, direct observations, recommendations or reputation).
- A risk module that can dynamically evaluate the risk involved in the interaction based on the recognized context. Risk evidence is also needed.

The chosen decision should maintain the appropriate cost/benefit ratio. In the background, another component is in charge of gathering and tracking evidence: recommendations and comparisons between expected outcomes of the chosen actions and real outcomes. This evidence is used to update risk and trust information. Thus, trust and risk follow a managed life cycle.

Depending on dispositional trust and system trust, the weight of the trust value in the final decision may be small. The level of dispositional trust may be set due to two main facts. First, the user manually sets a general level of trust, which is used in the application to get the level of trust in entities, independently of the entities. Second, the current balance of gains and losses is very positive and the risk policy allows any new interactions as long as the balance is kept positive. Marsh uses the term *basic trust*[18] for dispositional trust; it may also be called self-trust.

Generally, as introduced by Rahman and Hailes,[19] there are two main contexts for the trust values: *direct*, which is about the properties of the trustee, and *recommend*, which is the equivalent of recommending trustworthiness. In their case, recommending trustworthiness is based on consistency on the "semantic distance" between the real outcomes and the recommendations that have been made. The default metric for consistency is the standard deviation based on the frequency of specific semantic distance values: the higher the consistency, the smaller the standard deviation and the higher the trust value in recommending trustworthiness.

As said previously, another source for trust in human networks consists of real-world recourse mechanisms such as insurance or legal actions. Traditionally, it is assumed that if the actions made by a computing entity are bound to a real-world identity, the owner of the faulty computing entity can be brought to court and reparations are possible. In an open environment with no unique authority, the feasibility of this approach is questionable. An example where prosecution is ineffective occurs when email spammers do not mind moving operations abroad where antispam laws are less developed, to escape any risk of prosecution. It is a fact that worldwide there are multiple jurisdictions. Therefore, security based on authenticated identity may be superfluous. Furthermore,

17 A. K. Dey, "Understanding and using context", *Personal and Ubiquitous Computing Journal* (2001).

18 S. Marsh, *Formalizing Trust as a Computational Concept* (1994).
19 A. Rahman, and S. Hailes, *Using Recommendations for Managing Trust in Distributed Systems* (1997).

there is the question of which authority is in charge of certifying the binding with the real-world identity, since there are no unique global authorities. "Who, after all, can authenticate U.S. citizens abroad? The UN? Or thousands of pair wise national cross-certifications?"[20]

More important, is authentication of the real-world identity necessary to be able to use the human notion of trust? Indeed, a critical element for the use of trust is to retrieve trust evidence on the interacting entities, but trust evidence does not necessarily consist of information about the real-world identity of the owner; it may simply be the count of positive interactions with a pseudonym, as defended in[21]. As long as the interacting computing entities can be recognized, direct observations and recommendations can be exchanged to build trust, interaction after interaction. This level of trust can be used for trusting decisions. Thus, trust engines can provide dynamic protection without the assumption that real-world recourse mechanisms, such as legal recourse, are available in case of harm.

The terms *trust/trusted/trustworthy*, which appear in the traditional computer science literature, are not grounded on social science and often correspond to an implicit element of trust. For example, we have already mentioned the use of trusted third parties, called CAs, which are common in PKIs. Another example is *trusted computing*,[22] the goal of which is to create enhanced hardware by using cost-effective security hardware (more or less comparable to a smart-card chip) that acts as the "root of trust." *They are trusted* means that they are assumed to make use of some (strong) security protection mechanisms. Therefore they can/must implicitly be blindly trusted and cannot fail. This cannot address security when it is not known who or whether or not to blindly trust. The term *trust management* has been introduced in computer security by Blaze et al.,[23] but others have argued that their model still relies on an implicit notion of trust because it only describes "a way of exploiting established trust relationships for distributed security policy management without determining how these relationships are formed."[24] There is a need for trust formation mechanisms from scratch between two strangers. Trust engines build trust explicitly based on evidence either personal, reported by known recommenders or through reputation mechanisms.

As said previously, reputation is different than a recommendation made by a known specific entity. However, in the digital world, it is still less easy to exactly certify the identity of the recommender and in many cases the recommender can only be recognized to some extent. The entity recognition occurs with the help of a context recognition module, and the level of confidence in recognition may be taken into account in the final trust computation—for example, as done in advanced computational trust engines.[25] In the remainder of this chapter, for simplicity's sake (since this chapter focuses on reputation rather than trust), we assume that each entity can be recognized with a perfect confidence level in recognition. Thus, we obtain the two layers depicted in Figure 41.3: the identity management layer and the reputation management layer. In these layers, although we mention the world *identity*, we do not mean that the real-world identity behind each entity is supposed to be certified; we assume that it is sufficient to recognize the entity at a perfect level of confidence in recognition—for example, if a recommendation is received from an eBay account, it is sure that it comes from this account and that it is not spoofed. There are different round-edged rectangles at the top of the reputation layer that represent a few of the different reputation services detailed later in the chapter. There are also a number of round-edged rectangles below the identity layer that represent the various types of authentication schemes that can be used to recognize an entity. Although password-based or OpenID[26]-based[27] authentication may be less secure than multimodal authentication combining biometrics, smart cards, and crypto-certificates,[28] since we assume that the level of confidence in recognition is perfect, as stated previously, the different identity management technologies are abstracted to a unique identity management layer for the remainder of the chapter.

As presented previously, reputation management goes beyond mere reputation assessment and encompasses monitoring, analysis, and influence of reputation sources. It is the reason that we introduce the following categories, depicted in Figure 41.4, for online reputation services:

- *Reputation calculation*. Based on evidence gathered by the service, the service either computes a value

20 R. Khare, *What's in a Name? Trust* (1999).

21 J. M. Seigneur, *Trust, Security and Privacy in Global Computing* (2005).

22 Trusted Computing Group, https://www.trustedcomputinggroup.org.

23 M. Blaze, J. Feigenbaum, and J. Lacy, "Decentralized trust management," In *The 17th IEEE Symposium on Security and Privacy* (1996).

24 S. Terzis, W. Wagealla, C. English, A. McGettrick, and P. Nixon, *The SECURE Collaboration Model* (2004).

25 J. M. Seigneur, *Trust, Security and Privacy in Global Computing* (2005).

26 Refer to Chapter 17 of this book on identity management to learn more about OpenID.

27 OpenID, http://openid.net/.

28 J. M. Seigneur, *Trust, Security and Privacy in Global Computing* (2005).

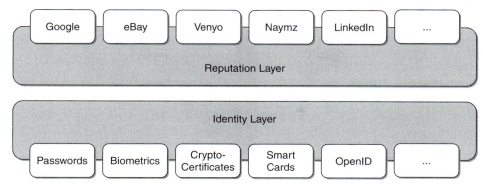

FIGURE 41.3 Identity management and reputation management layers.

Reputation Calculation

Monitoring, Analysis and Warnings

Influencing, Promotion and Rewards

Interaction Facilitation and Follow-up

Reputation Certification and Assurance

Fraud Protection, Mediation, Cleaning and Recovery

FIGURE 41.4 Online reputation management services categories.

representing the reputation of a specific entity or simply presents the reputation information without ranking.

- *Reputation monitoring, analysis, and warnings.* The service monitors Web-based media (Web sites, blogs, social networks, digitalized archived of paper-based press and trademarks) to detect any information impacting the entity reputation and warns the user in case of important changes.
- *Reputation influencing, promotion, and rewards.* The service takes actions to influence the perceived reputation of the entity. The service actively promotes the entity reputation, for example, by publishing Web pages carefully designed to reach a high rank in major search engines or paid online advertisements, such as, Google AdWords. Users reaching a higher reputation may gain other rewards than promotion, such as discounts. Based on the monitoring services analysis, the service may be able to list the most important reputation sources and allow the users to influence these sources. For example, in a 2006 blog bribe case, it was reported that free laptops preloaded with a new commercial operating system were shipped for free to the most

important bloggers in the field of consumer-oriented software, to improve the reputation of the new operating software.

- *Interaction facilitation and follow-up.* The service provides an environment to facilitate the interaction and its outcome between the trustor and the trustee. For example, eBay provides an online auction system to sellers and buyers as well as monitors the follow-up of the commercial transaction between the buyer and the seller.
- *Reputation certification and assurance.* That type of service is closer to the notion of system trust than the human notion of reputation because it relies on external means to avoid ending up in a harmful situation. For example, an insurance is paid as part of a commercial transaction. These services might need the certification of the link between the entity and its real-world identity in case of prosecutions. Our assumption does not hold for the services that require that kind of link, but that category of services had to be covered because a few services we surveyed make use of them.
- *Fraud protection, mediation, cleaning, and recovery.* These promotion services aim at improving the ranking of reputation information provided by the user rather than external information provided by third parties. However, even if external information is hidden behind more controlled information, it can still be found. It is the reason that some services try to force the owners of the external sites hosting damaging reputation information to delete the damaging information. Depending on where the server is located, this goal is more or less difficult to achieve. It may be as simple as filling an online form on the site hosting the defaming information to contact the technical support employee who will check to see whether the information is really problematic. In the case of a reluctant administrator,

lawyers or mediators specialized in online defamation laws have to be commissioned, which is more or less easy depending on the legislation in the country hosting the server. Generally, in countries with clear defamation laws, the administrators prefer deleting the information rather than going into a lengthy and costly legal process. Depending on the mediation and the degree of defamation, the host may have to add an apology in place of the defaming information, pay a fine, or more. Fraud protection is also needed against reputation calculation attacks. There are different types of attacks that can be carried out to flaw reputation calculation results.[29] The art of attack-resistant reputation computation is covered later in the chapter.

3. STATE OF THE ART OF ATTACK-RESISTANT REPUTATION COMPUTATION

In most commercial reputation services surveyed in this chapter, the reputation calculation does not take into account the attack resistance of its algorithm. This is a pity because there are many different types of attacks that can be carried out, especially at the identity level. In addition, most of these reputation algorithms correspond more to a trust metric algorithm rather than reputation as we have defined it earlier in the chapter, because they aggregate ratings submitted by recommenders or the rater itself rather than rely on evidence for which recommenders are unknown. Based on these ratings that we can consider as either direct observations or recommendations, the services compute a reputation score that we can consider a trust value, generally represented on a scale from 0% to 100% or from 0 to 5 stars. The exact reputation computation algorithm is not publicly disclosed by all services providers, and it is difficult to estimate the attack resistance of each of these algorithms without their full specification. However, it is clear that many of these algorithms do not provide a high level of attack-resistance for the following reasons:

- Besides eBay, where each transaction corresponds to a very clear trust context with quite well-authenticated users and a real transaction that is confirmed by real money transfers, most services occur in a decentralized environment and allow for the rating of unconfirmed transactions (without any real

evidence that the transaction really happened, and even worse, by anonymous users).

- Still, eBay experiences difficulties with its reputation calculation algorithm. In fact, eBay has recently changed its reputation calculation algorithm: the sellers on eBay are no longer allowed to leave unfavorable or neutral messages about buyers, to diminish the risk that buyers fear leaving negative feedback due to retaliatory negative feedback from sellers. Finally, accounts on eBay that are protected by passwords may be usurped. According to Twigg and Dimmock,[30] a trust metric is γ-resistant if more than γ nodes must be compromised for the attacker to successfully drive the trust value. For example, the Rahman and Hailes'[31] trust metric is not γ-resistant for $\gamma > 1$ (a successful attack needs only one victim).

In contrast to the centralized environment of eBay, in decentralized settings there are a number of specific attacks. First, real-world identities may form an alliance and use their recommendation to undermine the reputation of entities. On one hand, this may be seen as collusion. On the other hand, one may argue that real-world identities are free to vote as they wish. However, the impact is greater online. Even if more and more transactions and interactions are traced online, the majority of transactions and interactions that happen in the real world are not reported online. Due to the limited number of traced transactions and interactions, a few faked transactions and interactions can have a high impact on the computed reputation, which is not fair.

Second, we focus here on attacks based on vulnerabilities in the identity approach and subsequent use of these vulnerabilities. The vulnerabilities may have different origins, for example, technical weaknesses in the authentication mechanism. These attacks commonly rely on the possibility of identity multiplicity, meaning that a real-world identity uses many digital pseudonyms. A very well-known identity multiplicity attack in the field of computational trust is Douceur's Sybil attack.[32] Douceur argues that in large-scale networks where a centralized identity authority cannot be used to control the creation of pseudonyms, a powerful real-world entity may create as many digital pseudonyms as it likes and recommend one

29 J. M. Seigneur, *Trust, Security and Privacy in Global Computing* (2005).

30 A. Twigg, and N. Dimmock, "Attack-resistance of computational trust models" (2003) Proceedings of the Twelfth International Workshop on Enabling Technologies: Infrastructure for Collaborative Enterprises.

31 A. Rahman, and S. Hailes, *Using Recommendations for Managing Trust in Distributed Systems* (1997).

32 J. R. Douceur, "The sybil attack", *Proceedings of the 1st International Workshop on Peer-to-Peer Systems* (2002).

of these pseudonyms to fool the reputation calculation algorithm. This is especially important in scenarios where the possibility to use many pseudonyms is facilitated—for example, in scenarios where pseudonym creation is provided for better privacy protection.

In his Ph. D. thesis, Levien[33] says that a trust metric is attack resistant if the number of faked pseudonyms, owned by the same real-world identity and that can be introduced, is bounded. Levien argues that to mitigate the problem of Sybil-like attacks, it is required to compute "a trust value for all the nodes in the graph at once, rather than calculating independently the trust value independently for each node." Another approach proposed to protect against the Sybil attack is the use of mandatory "entry fees"[34] associated with the creation of each pseudonym. This approach raises some issues about its feasibility in a fully decentralized way and the choice of the minimal fee that guarantees protection. Also, "more generally, the optimal fee will often exclude some players yet still be insufficient to deter the wealthiest players from defecting."[35]

An alternative to entry fees may be the use of once-in-a-lifetime (1L[36]) pseudonyms, whereby an elected party per "arena" of application is responsible to certify only 1L to any real-world entity that possesses a key pair bound to this entity's real-world identity. The technique of blind signature[37] is used to keep the link between the real-world identity and its chosen pseudonym in the arena unknown to the elected party. However, there are still two unresolved questions about this approach: how the elected party is chosen and how much the users would agree to pay for this approach. More important, a Sybil attack is possible during the voting phase, so the concept of electing a trusted entity to stop Sybil attacks does not seem practical. However, relying on real money turns the trust mechanism into a type of system trust where the use of reputation becomes almost superfluous. In the real world, tax authorities are likely to require traceability of money transfers, which would completely break privacy. Thus, when using pseudonyms, another means must be present to prevent users from taking advantage of the fact that they can create as many pseudonyms as they want.

Trust transfer[38] has been introduced to encourage self-recommendations without attacks based on the creation and use of a large number of pseudonyms owned by the same real-world identity. In a system where there are pseudonyms that can potentially belong to the same real-world entity, a transitive trust process is open to abuse. Even if there is a high recommendation discounting factor due to recommending trustworthiness, the real-world entity can diminish the impact of this discounting factor by sending a huge number of recommendations from his army of pseudonyms in a Sybil attack. When someone recommends another person, she has influence over the potential outcome of interaction between this person and the trustor. The inclination of the trustor with regard to this influence "provides a goal-oriented sense of control to attain desirable outcomes."[39] So, the trustor should also be able to increase or decrease the influence of the recommenders according to his goals.

Moreover, according to Romano, trust is not multiple constructs that vary in meaning across contexts but a single construct that varies in level across contexts. The overall trustworthiness depends on the complete set of different domains of trustworthiness. This overall trustworthiness must be put in context: It is not sufficient to strictly limit the domain of trustworthiness to the current trust context and the trustee; if recommenders are involved, the decision and the outcome should impact their overall trustworthiness according to the influence they had. Kinateder et al.[40] also take the position that there is a dependence between different trust contexts. For example, a chef known to have both won cooking awards and murdered people may not be a trustworthy chef after all. Trust transfer introduces the possibility of a dependence between trustworthiness and recommending trustworthiness. Trust transfer relies on the following assumptions:

- The trust value is based on direct observations or recommendations of the count of event outcomes from recognized entities (for example, the outcome of an eBay auction transaction with a specific seller from a specific buyer recognized by their eBay account pseudos).
- A pseudonym can be neither compromised nor spoofed; an attacker can neither take control of a

33 R. Levien, *Attack Resistant Trust Metrics* (2004).
34 E. Friedman, and P. Resnick, *The Social Cost of Cheap Pseudonyms* (2001): pp. 173–199.
35 E. Friedman, and P. Resnick, *The Social Cost of Cheap Pseudonyms* (2001): pp. 173–199.
36 E. Friedman, and P. Resnick, *The Social Cost of Cheap Pseudonyms* (2001): pp. 173–199.
37 D. Chaum, "Achieving Electronic Privacy", *Scientific American* (1992): pp. 96–100.

38 J. M. Seigneur, *Trust, Security and Privacy in Global Computing* (2005).
39 D. M. Romano, *The Nature of Trust: Conceptual and Operational Clarification* (2003).
40 M. Kinateder, and K. Rothermel, "Architecture and Algorithms for a Distributed Reputation System", *Proceedings of the First Conference on Trust Management* (2003).

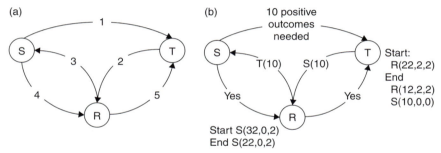

FIGURE 41.5 (a) Trust transfer process; (b) trust transfer process example.

pseudonym nor send spoofed recommendations; however, everyone is free to introduce as many pseudonyms as they wish.

- All messages are assumed to be signed and timestamped.

Trust transfer implies that recommendations cause trust on the trustor (T) side to be transferred from the recommender (R) to the subject (S) of the recommendation. A second effect is that the trust on the recommender side for the subject is reduced by the amount of transferred trustworthiness. If it is a self-recommendation, that is, recommendations from pseudonyms belonging to the same real-world identity, then the second effect is moot, since it does not make sense for a real-world entity to reduce trust in his own pseudonyms. Even if there are different trust contexts (such as trustworthiness in delivering on time or recommending trustworthiness), each trust context has its impact on the single construct trust value: they cannot be taken separately for the calculation of the single construct trust value. A transfer of trust is carried out if the exchange of communications depicted is successful. A local entity's Recommender Search Policy (RSP) dictates which contacts can be used as potential recommenders. Its Recommendation Policy (RP) decides which of its contacts it is willing to recommend to other entities and how much trust it is willing to transfer to an entity. Trust transfer (in its simplest form) can be decomposed into five steps:

1. The subject requests an action, requiring a total amount of trustworthiness TA in the subject, in order for the request to be accepted by the trustor; the actual value of TA is contingent upon the risk acceptable to the user, as well as dispositional trust and the context of the request; so the risk module of the trust engine plays a role in the calculation of TA.

2. The trustor queries its contacts, which pass the RSP, in order to find recommenders willing to transfer some of their positive event outcomes count to the subject. Recall that trustworthiness is based on event outcomes count in trust transfer.

3. If the contact has directly interacted with the subject and the contact's RP allows it to permit the trustor to transfer an amount $(A \leq TA)$ of the recommender's trustworthiness to the subject, the contact agrees to recommend the subject. It queries the subject whether it agrees to lose A of trustworthiness on the recommender side.

4. The subject returns a signed statement, indicating whether it agrees or not.

5. The recommender sends back a signed recommendation to the trustor, indicating the trust value it is prepared to transfer to the subject. This message includes the signed agreement of the subject.

Both the RSP and RP can be as simple or complex as the application environment demands. The trust transfer process is illustrated in Figures 41.5, where the subject requests an action that requires 10 positive outcomes. We represent the trust value as a tree of (s,i,c)-triples, corresponding to a mathematical event structure[41]: an event outcome count is represented as a (s,i,c)-triple, where s is the number of events that supports the outcome, i is the number of events that have no information or are inconclusive about the outcome, and c is the number of events that contradict the expected outcome. This format takes into account the element of uncertainty via i.

> *Note:* In Figure 41.5a, the circles represent the different involved entities: S corresponds to the sender, which is the subject of the recommendation and the requester; T is the trustor, which is also the target; and R is the recommender. The directed black arrows indicate a message sent from one entity to another. The arrows are chronologically ordered by their number.
>
> In Figure 41.5b, an entity E associated with a SECURE triple *(s-i-c)* is indicated by $E(s-i-c)$.

41 M. Nielsen, G. Plotkin, and G. Winskel, "Petri nets, event structures and domains," *Theoritical Computer Science* (1981): pp. 85–108.

The *RSP* of the trustor is to query a contact to propose to transfer trust if the *balance (s-i-c)* is strictly greater than *2TA*. This is because it is sensible to require that the recommender remains more trustworthy than the subject after the recommendation. The contact, having a balance passing the *RSP (s-i-c = 32-0-2 = 30)*, is asked by the trustor whether she wants to recommend 10 good outcomes. The contact's *RP* is to agree to the transfer if the subject has a trust value greater than *TA*. The balance of the subject on the recommender's side is greater than *10 (s-i-c = 22-2-2 = 18)*. The subject is asked by the recommender whether she agrees 10 good outcomes to be transferred. Trustor *T* reduces its trust in recommender *R* by 10 and increases its trust in subject *S* by *10*. Finally, the recommender reduces her trust in the subject by *10*.

The recommender could make requests to a number of recommenders until the total amount of trust value is reached (the search requests to find the recommenders are not represented in the figures). For instance, in the previous example, two different recommenders could be contacted, with one recommending three good outcomes and the other one seven.

A recommender chain in trust transfer is not explicitly known to the trustor. The trustor only needs to know his contacts who agree to transfer some of their trustworthiness. This is useful from a privacy point of view since the full chain of recommenders is not disclosed. This is in contrast to other recommender chains such as a public key web of trust.[42] Because we assume that the entities cannot be compromised, we leave the issue surrounding the independence of recommender chains in order to increase the attack resistance of the trust metric for future work. The reason for searching more than one path is that it decreases the chance of a faulty path (either due to malicious intermediaries or unreliable ones). If the full list of recommenders must be detailed to be able to check the independence of recommender chains, the privacy protection is lost. This can be an application-specific design decision.

Thanks to trust transfer, although a real-world identity has many pseudonyms, the Sybil attack cannot happen because the number of direct observations (and hence, total amount of trust) remains the same on the trustor side. One may argue that it is unfair for the recommender to lose the same amount of trustworthiness as specified in his/her recommendation, moreover if the outcome is ultimately good. It is envisaged that a more complex sequence of messages can be put in place in order to revise the decrease of trustworthiness after a successful outcome. This has been left for future work, because it can lead to vulnerabilities (for example, based on Sybil attacks with careful cost/benefit analysis). The current trust transfer approach is still limited to scenarios where there are many interactions between the recommenders and where the overall trustworthiness in the network (that is, the global number of good outcomes) is large enough that there is no major impact to entities when they agree to transfer some of their trust (such as in the email application domain[43]). Ultimately, without sacrificing the flexibility and privacy enhancing potential of limitless pseudonym creation, Sybil attacks are guaranteed to be avoided.

4. OVERVIEW OF CURRENT ONLINE REPUTATION SERVICE

As explained previously, most of the current online reputation services surveyed in this part of the chapter do not really compute reputation as we defined it earlier in the chapter. Their reputation algorithms correspond more to a trust metric because they aggregate direct observations and recommendations of different users rather than base their assessment on evidence from a group of an unknown number of unknown users. However, one may consider that these services present reputations to their users if we assume that their users do not take the time to understand how it was computed and who made the recommendations.

The remainder of this part of the chapter starts by surveying the current online reputation services and finishes with a recapitulating table. If not mentioned otherwise, the reputation services do not require the users to pay a fee.

eBay

Founded in 1995, eBay has been a very successful online auction marketplace where buyers can search for products offered by sellers and buy them either directly or after an auction. After each transaction, the buyers can rate the transaction with the seller as positive, negative, or neutral. Since May 2008, sellers have only the choice to rate the buyer experience as positive, nothing else. Short comments of a maximum of 80 characters can be left with the rating. User reputation is based on the number of positive and negative ratings that are aggregated in the Feedback Score as well as the comments. Buyers or sellers can affect each other's Feedback Scores by only one point per week. Each positive rating counts for 1

---

42 P. R. Zimmermann, *The Official PGP User's Guide* (1995).

43 J. M. Seigneur, *Trust, Security and Privacy in Global Computing* (2005).

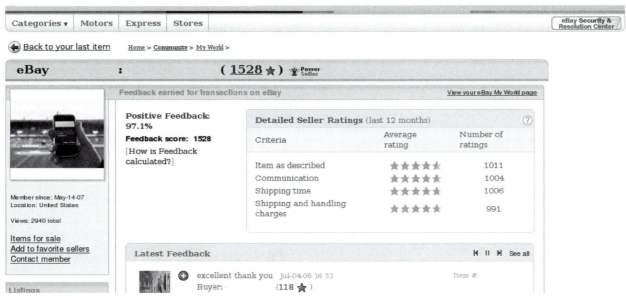

FIGURE 41.6 eBay's visual reputation representation.

point and each negative counts for -1 point. The balance of points is calculated at the end of the week and the Feedback Score is increased by 1 if the balance is positive or decreased by 1 if the balance is negative. Buyers can also leave anonymous Detailed Seller Ratings. composed of various criteria such as "Item as described," "Communication," and "Shipping Time," displayed as a number of stars from 0 to 5. Different image icons are also displayed to quickly estimate the reputation of the user—for example, a star whose color depends on the Feedback Score, as depicted in Figure 41.6. After 90 days, detailed item information is removed.

From a privacy point of view, on one hand it is possible to use a pseudonym; on the other hand, a pretty exhaustive list of what has been bought is available, which is quite a privacy concern. There are various auction Insertion and Final Value fees depending on the item type. eBay addresses the reputation service categories as follows:

- *Reputation calculation.* As detailed, reputation is computed based on transactions that are quite well tracked, which is important to avoid faked evidence. However, eBay's reputation calculation still has some problems. For example, as explained, the algorithm had to be changed recently; the value of the transaction is not taken into account at time of Feedback Score update (a good transaction of 10 Euros should count less than a good transaction of 10 kEuros); it is limited to the ecommerce application domain.

- *Monitoring, analysis, and warnings.* eBay does not monitor the reputation of its users outside of its service.

- *Influencing, promotion, and rewards.* eBay rewards its users through their public Feedback Scores and their associated icon images. However, eBay does not promote the user reputation outside its system and does not facilitate this promotion due to a strict access to its full evidence pool, although some Feedback Score data can be accessed through eBay software developer Application Programming Interface (API).

- *Interaction facilitation and follow-up.* eBay provides a comprehensive Web-based site to facilitate online auctions between buyers and sellers, including a dedicated messaging service and advanced tools to manage the auction. The follow-up based on the Feedback Score is pretty detailed.

- *Reputation certification and assurance.* eBay does not certify a user reputation per se but, given its leading position, eBay Feedback Score can be considered, to some extent, as some certified reputation evidence.

- *Fraud protection, mediation, cleaning, and recovery.* eBay facilitates communication between the buyer and the seller as well as a dispute console with eBay customer support employees. A rating and comment cannot be deleted since the Mutual Feedback Withdrawal has been removed. In extreme cases, if the buyer had paid through PayPal, which is now

Create Opinity Profile
This is your online self-portrait. Using your profile, you can lower barriers, gain instant respect, become better known.

Buy with confidence, sell with ease
Trying to sell something online? You can show people your history as a seller, no matter where it comes from.

Make better choices, get better dates
If you're using an online dating service, you can present yourself as you want to be seen, and you can ask others to show you more about themselves.

Blog your profile and profile your blog
Increase your blog readership. Put your Opinity signature on your blog so that people can find out more about you.

▸**Sign-Up Now**

Now supporting OpenID and Windows Cardspace

Opinity Profile Exchange

Share your information with others and gain trust. Securely and selectively.

Need to buy or sell something? Use Opinity Profile Exchange to gain trust.
Classifieds

Share your information with the one you want, no one else. Securely and selectively.
Dating

Put a button on your blog so that people can request your profile.
Blogs

FIGURE 41.7 Opinity OpenID support.

part of eBay, the item might be refunded after some time if the item is covered and depending on the item price. Finally, eBay works with a number of escrow services that act as third parties and that do not deliver the product until the payment is made. Again, if such third-party services are used, the use of reputation is less useful because these third-party services decrease a lot the risk of a negative outcome. eBay does not offer to clean a reputation outside its own Web site.

Opinity

Founded in 2004, Opinity[44] has been one of the first commercial efforts to build a decentralized online reputation for users in all contexts beyond eBay's limited ecommerce context (see Figure 41.7). However, at time of writing (March 2009), Opinity has been inactive for quite a while. After creating an account, the users had the possibility to specify their login and passwords of other Web sites, especially eBay, to retrieve and consolidate all

evidence in the user's Opinity account. Of course, asking users to provide their passwords was risky and seems not a good security practice. Another, safer option was for the users to put hidden text in the HTML pages of their external services, such as eBay. Opinity was quite advanced at the identity layer, since it supported OpenID and Microsoft Cardspace. In addition, Opinity could retrieve professional or education background and verify it to some extent using public listings or for a fee. Opinity users could rate other users in different contexts, such as plumbing or humor. Opinity addressed the different reputation service categories as follows:

- *Reputation calculation.* The reputation was calculated based on all the evidence sources and could be accessed by other Opinity partner sites. The reputation could be focused to a specific context called a *reputation category*.
- *Monitoring, analysis, and warnings.* Opinity did not really cover this category of services; most evidence was pointed out by the users as they added the external accounts that they owned.
- *Influencing, promotion, and rewards.* Opinity had a base Opinity Reputation Score, and it was possible to

---

44 Opinity, www.opinity.com.

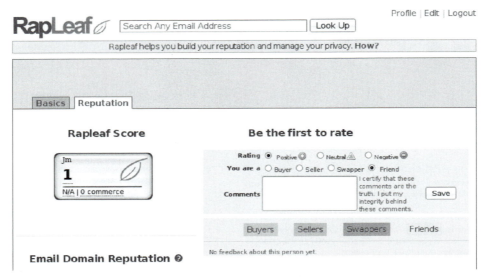

FIGURE 41.8 Rapleaf rating interface.

include a Web badge representation of that reputation on external Web sites.

- *Interaction facilitation and follow-up.* Opinity did not really cover this category of services besides the fact that users could mutually decide to disclose more details of their profiles via the Exchange Profile feature.

- *Reputation certification and assurance.* Opinity certified educational, personal, or professional information to some extent via public listings or for a fee to check the information provided by the users.

- *Fraud protection, mediation, cleaning, and recovery.* One of Opinity's relevant features in this category is its reputation algorithm. However, it is not known how strongly this algorithm was resistant to attacks, for example, against a user who creates many Opinity accounts and uses them to give high ratings to a main account. Another relevant feature was that users could appeal bad reviews via a formal dispute process. Opinity did not offer to clean the reputation outside its own Web site.

Rapleaf

Founded in 2006, Rapleaf[45] builds reputations around email addresses. Any Rapleaf user is able to rate any other email address, which may be open to defamation or other privacy issues because the users behind the email addresses may not have given their consent. If the email address to be rated has never been rated before, Rapleaf informs the potential rater that it has started crawling the

Web to search for information about that email address and that once the crawling is finished, it will invite the rater to add a rating. As depicted in Figure 41.8, different contexts are possible: Buyers, Sellers, Swappers, and Friends. Once a rating is entered, it cannot be removed. However, new comments are possible and users can rate an email address several times.

Online social networks are also crawled, and any external profile linked to the search email address are added to the Rapleaf profile. The email address owners may also add the other email addresses that they own to their profile to provide a unified view of their reputation. Rapleaf's investors are also involved in two other related services: Upscoop.com, which allows users to import their list of social network friends after disclosing their online social networks passwords (a risky practice, as already mentioned) and see in which other social networks their friends are subscribed (at time of writing Upscoop already has information about over 400 million profiles), and TrustFuse.com, a business that retrieves profile information for marketing businesses that submit their lists of email addresses to TrustFuse. Officially, Rapleaf will not sell its base of email addresses. However, according to its August 2007 policy, "information captured via Rapleaf may be used to assist TrustFuse services. Additionally, information collected by TrustFuse during the course of its business may also be displayed on Rapleaf for given profiles searched by email address," which is quite worrisome from a privacy point of view. Rapleaf has addressed the different reputation service categories as follows:

- *Reputation calculation.* The Rapleaf Score takes into account ratings evidence in all contexts as well

---

45 Rapleaf, www.rapleaf.com.

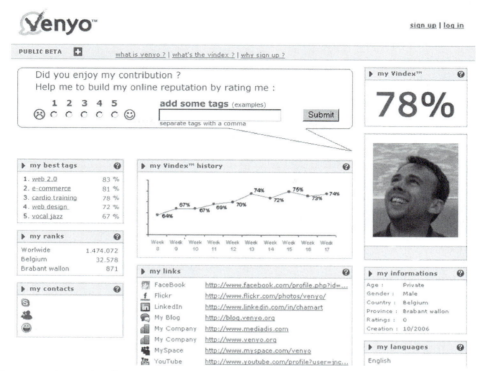

FIGURE 41.9 Venyo reputation user interface.

as how the users have rated others and their social network connections. Unfortunately, the algorithm is not public and thus its attack resistance is unknown. In contrast to eBay, the commercial transactions reported in Rapleaf are not substantiated by other facts than the rater rating information. Thus, the chance of faked transactions is higher. Apparently, a user may rate an email address several times. However, a user rating counts only once in the overall reputation of the target email address.

- *Monitoring, analysis, and warnings.* Rapleaf warns the target email address when a new rating is added.

- *Influencing, promotion, and rewards.* The Rapleaf Score can be embedded in a Web badge and displayed on external Web pages.

- *Interaction facilitation and follow-up.* At least it is possible for the target email address to be warned of a rating and to rate the rater back.

- *Reputation certification and assurance.* There is no real feature in this category.

- *Fraud protection, mediation, cleaning, and recovery.* There is a form that allows the owner of a particular email address to remove that email address from Rapleaf. For more important issues, such as defamation, a support email address is provided. Rapleaf does not offer to clean the reputation outside its own Web site.

Venyo

Founded in 2006, Venyo[46] provides a worldwide people reputation index, called the Vindex, based on either direct ratings through the user profile on Venyo Web site or indirect ratings through contributions or profiles on partner Web sites (see Figure 41.9). Venyo is privacy friendly because it does not ask users for their external passwords and it does not crawl the Web to present a user reputation without a user's initial consent. Venyo has addressed the different reputation service categories as follows:

- *Reputation calculation.* Venyo's reputation algorithm is not public and therefore its attack resistance is unknown. At time of rating, the rater specifies a value between 1 and 5 as well as keywords corresponding to the tags contextualizing the rating. The rating is also contextualized according to where the rating has been done. For example, if the rating is done from a GaultMillau restaurant blog article, the tag "restaurant recommendation" is automatically added to the list of tags.

- *Monitoring, analysis, and warnings.* Venyo provides a reputation history chart, as depicted, to help users

46 Venyo, www.venyo.org.

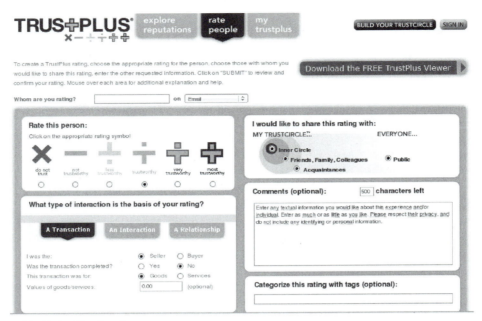

FIGURE 41.10 TrustPlus Rating User Interface.

monitor the evolution of their reputation on Venyo's and partner's Web sites. Venyo does not monitor external Web pages or information.

- *Influencing, promotion, and rewards.* The Vindex allows users to search for the most reputable users in different domains specified by tags and it can be tailored to specific locations. In addition, the Venyo Web badge can be embedded in external Web sites. There is also a Facebook plug-in to port Venyo reputation into a Facebook profile.

- *Interaction facilitation and follow-up.* The Vindex facilitates finding the most reputable user for the request context.

- *Reputation certification and assurance.* There is no Venyo feature in this category yet.

- *Fraud protection, mediation, cleaning, and recovery.* As mentioned, Venyo's reputation algorithm attack resistance cannot be assessed because Venyo's algorithm is not public. The cleaning feature is less relevant because the users do not know who has rated them. An account may be closed if the user requests it. As noted, Venyo is more privacy friendly than other services that request passwords or display reputation without their consent.

TrustPlus + XING + ZoomInfo + SageFire

Founded in 1999, ZoomInfo is more a people (and company) search directory than a reputation service. However, ZoomInfo, with its 42 million-plus users, 3.8 million

companies, and partnership with Xing.com (a business social network similar to LinkedIn.com), has recently formed an alliance with Trustplus,[47] an online reputation service founded in 2006. The main initial feature of TrustPlus is a Web browser plug-in that allows users to see the TrustPlus reputation of an online profile appearing on Web pages on different sites, such as, craiglist. org. At the identity layer, TrustPlus asks users to type their external accounts passwords, for example, eBay's or Facebook's, to validate that they own these external accounts as well as to create their list of contacts. This list of contacts can be used to specify who among the contacts can see the detail of which transactions or ratings.

As depicted in Figure 41.10, the TrustPlus rating user interface is pretty complex. There are different contexts: a commercial transaction, a relationship, and an interaction, for example, a chat or a date.

The TrustPlus score is also pretty complex, as depicted in Figure 41.11. Thanks to its partnership with SageFire, which is a trusted eBay Certified Solution Provider that has access to historical archives of eBay reputation data, TrustPlus is able to display and use eBay's reputation evidence when users agree to link their TrustPlus accounts with their eBay accounts. TrustPlus has addressed the different reputation service categories as follows:

- *Reputation calculation.* The TrustPlus reputation algorithm combines the different sources of reputation

---

47 Trustplus, www.trustplus.com.

FIGURE 41.11 The TrustPlus score.

evidence reported to TrustPlus by its users and partner sites. However, the TrustPlus reputation algorithm is not public and thus again it is difficult to assess its attack resistance. At time of rating a commercial transaction, it is possible to specify the amount involved in the transaction, which is interesting from a computational trust point of view. Unfortunately, the risk that this transaction is faked is higher than in eBay because there are no other real facts that corroborate the information given by the rating user.

- *Monitoring, analysis, and warnings.* TrustPlus warns the user when a new rating has been entered or a new request for rating has been added. However, there is no broader monitoring of the global reputation of the user.

- *Influencing, promotion, and rewards.* TrustPlus provides different tools to propagate the user reputation: a Web badge that may include the eBay reputation, visibility once the TrustPlus Web browser plug-in viewer has been installed, and link with the ZoomInfo directory.

- *Interaction facilitation and follow-up.* TrustPlus provides an internal messaging service that increases the tracking quality of the interactions between the rated users and the raters.

- *Reputation certification and assurance.* No reputation certification is done by TrustPlus per se, but the certification is a bit more formal when the users have chosen the option to link their eBay reputation evidence.

- *Fraud protection, mediation, cleaning, and recovery.* As noted, the attack resistance of the TrustPlus reputation algorithm is unknown. In case of defamation or rating disputes, a Dispute Rating button is available in the Explore Reputation part of the TrustPlus site. When a dispute is initiated, the users have to provide substantiating evidence to the TrustPlus support employees via email. TrustPlus does not offer to clean the reputation outside its own Web site.

Naymz + Trufina

Founded in 2006, Naymz[48] has formed an alliance with Trufina.com, which is in charge of certifying identity and background user information. Premium features cost $9.95 per month at time of writing. The users are asked for their passwords on external sites such as LinkedIn to invite their list of contacts on these external sites, which is a bad security practice, as we've mentioned several times. Unfortunately, it seems that Naymz has been too aggressive concerning its emails policy and a number of users have complained about receiving unsolicited emails from Naymz—for example, "I have been spammed several times over the past several weeks by a service called Naymz."[49]

48 Naymz, www.naymz.com.
49 www.igotspam.com/50226711/naymz_sending_spamas_you.php, accessed 16 July 2008.

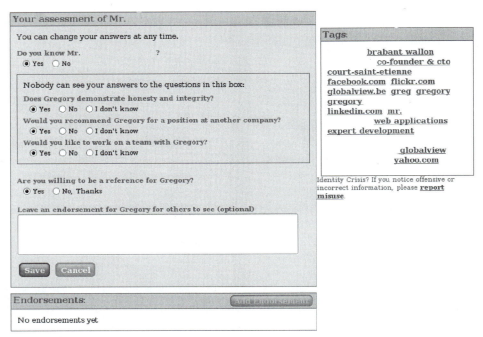

FIGURE 41.12 Reputation calculation on Naymz.

Naymz has addressed the different reputation service categories as follows:

- *Reputation calculation.* Naymz RepScore combines a surprising set of information—not only the ratings given by other users but also points for the user profile completeness and identity verifications from Trufina. Each rating is qualitative and focused on the professional contexts of the target user ("Would you like to work on a team with the user?"), as depicted in Figure 41.12. The answers can be changed at any time. Only users who are part of the target user list of contacts are allowed to rate the user. There is no specific transaction-based rating, for example, for an ecommerce transaction.

- *Monitoring, analysis, and warnings.* Naymz has many monitoring features for both inside and outside Naymz reputation evidence. There is a free list of Web sources (Web sites, forum, blogs) that mention the user's name. A premium monitoring tool allows the user to see on a worldwide map who has accessed the user Naymz profile, including the visitor's IP address. It is possible to subscribe to other profiles, recent Web activities if they are part of the user's confirmed contacts.

- *Influencing, promotion, and rewards.* In addition to the RepScore and Web badges, the users can get

ranking in Web search engines for a fee or for free if they maintain a RepScore higher than 9. The users can also get other features for free if they maintain a certain level of RepScore—for example, free detailed monitoring above 10. For a fee of $1995 at this writing, they also propose to shoot and produce high-quality, professional videos, to improve the user "personal brand."

- *Interaction facilitation and follow-up.* It is possible to search for users based on keywords but the search options and index are not advanced at this writing.

- *Reputation certification and assurance.* As said above, Trufina is in charge of certifying identity and background user information.

- *Fraud protection, mediation, cleaning, and recovery.* There are links to report offensive or defaming information to the support employees. The attack resistance of the RepScore cannot be assessed because the algorithm detail is not public. They have also launched a new service called Naymz Reputation Repair whereby a user can indicate the location of external Web pages that contain embarrassing information as well as some information regarding the issues, and after analysis Naymz may offer to take action to remove the embarrassing information for a fee.

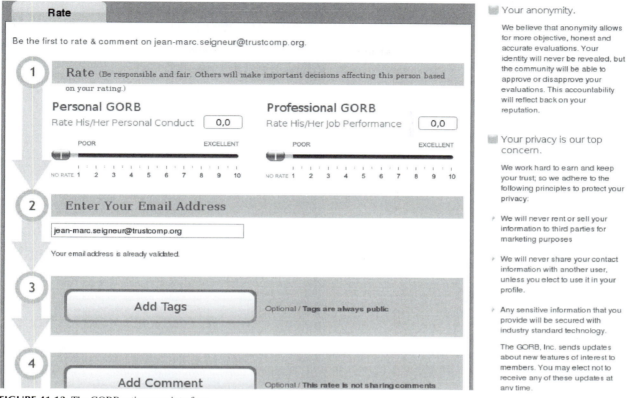

FIGURE 41.13 The GORB rating user interface.

The GORB

Founded in 2006, The GORB[50] allows anybody to rate any email address anonymously. Users can create an account to be allowed to display their GORB score with a Web badge and be notified of their and others' reputation evolution. The GORB is very strict regarding their rule of anonymity: Users are not allowed to know who has rated them (see Figure 41.13). The GORB has addressed the different reputation service categories as follows:

- *Reputation calculation.* The GORB argues that, although they only use anonymous ratings, their reputation algorithm is attack resistant, but it is impossible to assess because it is not public. Apparently, they allow a user to rate an email address several times, but they warn that multiple ratings may decrease the GORB score of the rater. The rating has two contexts on a 0 to 10 scale, as depicted in personal and professional. Keywords

called tags can be added to the rating as well as a textual comment.

- *Monitoring, analysis, and warnings.* The users can be notified by email when their reputation evolves or when the reputation of user-defined email addresses evolve. However, it does not monitor evidence outside The GORB.

- *Influencing, promotion, and rewards.* A Web browser plug-in can be installed to visualize the reputation of email addresses appearing on Web pages in the Web browser. There is a ranking of the users based on the GORB score.

- *Interaction facilitation and follow-up.* There is no follow-up because the ratings are anonymous.

- *Reputation certification and assurance.* There is no feature in this category.

- *Fraud protection, mediation, cleaning, and recovery.* The GORB does not allow users to remove their email address from their list of emails. The GORB asks for user passwords to import email addresses from the list of contacts of other Web sites. Thus, one may argue that The GORB, even if the ratings are anonymous, is not very privacy friendly.

---

50 The GORB, www.thegorb.com.

TABLE 41.1 Table Summarization

	eBay	Opinity	Rapleaf	TrustPlus	Venyo	The GORB	Naymz	Reputation Defender
Founding Year	1995	2004	2006	2006	2006	2006	2006	2006
Fee	%		N	P	N	N	P	Y
Reputation Calculation	**	*	*	*	*	*	*	
Monitoring, Analysis and Warnings			*	*	*	*	**	**
Influencing, Promotion and Rewards	**	*	*	**	**	**	***	**
Interaction Facilitation and Follow-up	***	*	*	*	**			
Reputation Certification and Assurance	*	**					*	
Fraud Protection, Mediation, Cleaning and Recovery	**	*	*	*	**		**	***

%: transaction percentage fee, P: premium services fee, N: No fee, Y: paid service

ReputationDefender

Founded in 2006, ReputationDefender[51] has the following products at this writing:

- MyReputation and MyPrivacy, which crawl the Web to find reputation information about users for $9.95 a month and allow them to ask for the deletion of embarrassing information for $39.95 per item.
- MyChild, which does the same but for $9.95 a month and per child.
- MyEdge, starting from $99 to $499, allows the user with the help of automated and professional copywriters to improve her online presence—for example, in search engines such as Google and with third-person biographies written by professional copywriters.

ReputationDefender has addressed the different reputation service categories as follows:

- *Reputation calculation.* There is no feature in this category.
- *Monitoring, analysis, and warnings.* As noted, the whole Web is crawled and synthetic online reports are provided.
- *Influencing, promotion, and rewards.* The user reputation may be improved based on expert advice and better positioned in Web search engines.

- *Interaction facilitation and follow-up.* There is no feature in this category.
- *Reputation certification and assurance.* There is no feature in this category.
- *Fraud protection, mediation, cleaning, and recovery.* There is no reputation algorithm. Cleaning may involve automated software or real people specialized in legal reputation issues.

Summarizing Table

Table 41.1 summarizes how well each current online reputation service surveyed in this chapter addresses each reputation service category.

5. CONCLUSION

Online reputation management is an emerging complementary field of computer security whose traditional security mechanisms are challenged by the openness of the World Wide Web, where there is no *a priori* information of who is allowed to do what. Technical issues remain to be overcome: the attack resistance of the reputation algorithm is not mature yet; it is difficult to represent in a consistent way reputation built from different contexts (ecommerce, friendship). Sustainable business models are still to be found: Opinity seems to have gone out of business; Rapleaf had to move from a reputation service to a privacy-risky business of email address profiling;

---

51 ReputationDefender, www.reputationdefender.com.

TrustPlus had to form an alliance with ZoomInfo, XING, and SageFire; Naymz decreased its own reputation by spamming its base of users in hope of increasing its traffic.

It seems that both current technical and commercial issues may be improved by a standardization effort of online reputation management. The attack resistance of reputation algorithms cannot be certified to the degree it deserves if the reputation algorithms remain private. It has been proven in other security domains that security through obscurity gives lower results—for example, concerning cryptographic algorithms that are now open to review by the whole security research community. Open reputation algorithms will also improve the credibility of the reputation results because it will be possible to clearly explain to users how the reputation has been calculated. Standardizing the representation of reputation will also diminish confusion in the eyes of the users. The clearer understanding of which reputation evidence is taken into account in reputation calculation will improve the situation regarding privacy and will open the door to stronger regulation on the way in which reputation information flows.

## Chapter 42

Content Filtering

Peter Nicoletti

Secure Information Systems

Content filtering is a powerful tool that, properly deployed, can offer parents, companies, and local, state, and federal governments protection from Internet-based content. It is disparaged as Orwellian and simultaneously embraced as a short-term positive ROI project, depending on who you are and how it affects your online behavior. In this chapter we examine the many benefits and justifications of Web-based content filtering, such as legal liability risk reduction, productivity gains, and bandwidth usage. We'll explore the downside and unintended consequences and risks that improperly deployed or misconfigured systems create. We'll also look into methods to subvert and bypass these systems and the reasons behind them.

It is important for people who are considering content filtering to be aware of all the legal implications, and we'll also review these. Content filtering is straightforward to deploy, and license costs are so reasonable they can offer extremely fast return on investment while providing a very effective risk reduction strategy. We'll make sure that your project turns out successfully, since we'll look at all the angles: Executives will be happy with the project results and employees won't key your car in the parking lot!

1. THE PROBLEM WITH CONTENT FILTERING

Access to information and supplications on the World Wide Web (WWW) has become a critical and integral part of modern personal and business life as well as a national pastime for billions of users. With millions of applications and worldwide access to information, email, video, music, instant messaging (IM), Voice over IP (VoIP), and more, the way we conduct business, communicate, shop, and entertain is evolving rapidly. With all the advancements of increased communications and productivity comes a bad side with a tangle of security risks. Productivity, accessibility, and conveniences of the World Wide Web have also brought us spam, viruses, worms, Trojans, keystroke

loggers, relentless joke forwarding, identity theft, Internet scams, and the dreaded chain letter. These are among the increasing risks associated with simple WWW access that was once taken for granted only a few years ago.

Surfing the Web is the most common of all Internet applications. It offers global access to all types of information, banking, buying and selling goods and services from the comfort of our computer, and online bill paying, and it's so entertaining in many different ways. For business, access to Web apps is mission critical, and other sites are productivity tools. Accessing the Internet from the office is constantly presenting new challenges to manage. Some of the negative impacts of doing the wrong thing and going to the "wrong places" include:

- Lost productivity due to nonbusiness-related Internet use
- Higher costs as additional bandwidth is purchased to support legitimate and illegitimate business applications
- Network congestion; valuable bandwidth is being used for nonbusiness purposes, and legitimate business applications suffer
- Loss or exposure of confidential information through chat sites, nonapproved email systems, IM, peer-to-peer file sharing, etc.
- Infection and destruction of corporate information and computing resources due to increased exposure to Web-based threats (viruses, worms, Trojans, spyware, etc.) as employees surf nonbusiness-related Web sites.
- Legal liability when employees access/download inappropriate and offensive material (pornography, racism, etc.)
- Copyright infringement caused by employees downloading and/or distributing copyrighted material such as music, movies, etc.
- Negative publicity due to exposure of critical company information, legal action, and the like

Casual nonbusiness-related Web surfing has caused many businesses countless hours of legal litigation as hostile work environments have been created by employees who view and download and show off or share offensive content. RIAA takedown notices and copyright infringement threats, fines, and lawsuits are increasing as employees use file-sharing programs to download, serve up, and share their favorite music and movie files. Government regulations and legal requirements are getting teeth with fines and consequences as company executives are accountable for their employees' actions. Corporate executives and IT professionals alike are now becoming more concerned about what their employees are viewing and downloading from the Internet.

Government regulations on Internet access and information security are being enforced by many countries and individual states: the Children's Internet Protection Act (CIPA) for schools and libraries, Japan's Internet Association's SafetyOnline2 to promote Internet filtering, HIPAA, Sarbanes-Oxley, Gramm-Leach-Bliley, and "duty of care" legal obligation legislation. Many independent reports and government agencies (such as the FBI) are now reporting that employees are the single highest risk and are the most common cause of network abuse, data loss, and legal action. Because employers can be ultimately held responsible for their employees' actions, many businesses are now working aggressively with their Human Resources departments to define acceptable Internet usage. Reports of Internet abuse include:

- Global consulting firm IDC reports that 30–40% of Internet access is being used for nonbusiness purposes.
- The American Management Association reports that 27% of Fortune 500 companies have been involved in sexual harassment lawsuits over their employees' inappropriate use of email and Internet.
- The Center of Internet Studies have reported that more than 60% of companies have disciplined employees over Internet and email use, with more than 30% terminating employees.

Numerous stories of employee dismissal, sexual harassment, and discipline with regard to Internet use can be found on the Internet[1]:

---

1 Stories of workers being dismissed for porn surfing: "IT manager fired for lunchtime Web surfing," www.theregister.co.uk/1999/06/16/it_manager_fired_for_lunchtime; "Xerox fires 40 in porn site clampdown," www.theregister.co.uk/2000/07/15/xerox_fires_40_in_porn; "41 District workers have been fired/suspended for visiting pornographic Web sites," www.wtopnews.com/?sid=1331641&nid=25.

- The Recording Industry Association of America (RIAA) and the Motion Picture Association of America (MPAA) have relentlessly pursued legal action against schools, corporations, and individuals (even printers!) over the illegal downloading of music and movies from the Internet. The RIAA recently won a case against an Arizona company for $1 million.
- An oil and gas company recently paid $2.2 million to settle a lawsuit for tolerating a hostile work environment created by the downloading and sharing of Internet pornography.

To address these issues, companies are creating or updating their computer usage polices to include Web, email, surfing, and general Internet usage security, to protect themselves from legal action and financial losses. To become compliant with many of these new policies, corporations need to start monitoring and controlling Web access. Web content filtering is gaining popularity, and the industry providing the tools and technology in this area has been growing rapidly; IDC predicted a compound annual growth rate of 27% year over year until 2007.

2. USER CATEGORIES, MOTIVATIONS, AND JUSTIFICATIONS

Let's look at the entities that should consider content filtering:

- Schools
- Commercial businesses
- Libraries
- Local, state, and federal government
- Parents

Each of these faces different risks, but they are all trying to solve one or more of the following challenges:

- Maintain compliance
- Protect company and client sensitive data
- Maximize employee productivity
- Avoid costly legal liabilities due to sexual harassment and hostile work environment lawsuits
- Preserve and claw back network bandwidth
- Enforce company acceptable use policies (also known as Internet access policies)
- Control access to customer records and private data
- Monitor communications going into and out of a company
- Protect children

Let's look at the specific risks driving these entities to review their motivation to filter content.

Schools

When "Little Johnny" shows the latest starlet's sex tape to his buddies in high school media class, he is not following a school board-approved agenda. His parents could argue that the school computers "allowed" the access simply by being a click away from pornographic content. All school computer use policies have been updated to forbid visits to offensive sites, most with serious consequences. About 95% of schools have deployed a content-filtering solution.

Commercial Business

Do you have abundant bandwidth? Are your employees productive? Then your content-filtering project may be as simple as blocking porn and logging all other behavior. Content filtering projects have to be well thought out and deployed as an enforcement of an appropriate IT security policy. Put in content filtering over the weekend and surprise your employees with a "This page is blocked" message when they check their fantasy sports team results and you'll have a mutiny around the water cooler!

Financial Organizations

Financial organizations traffic in sensitive data and have specific risks. Protecting credit card numbers, Social Security numbers, and other critical PII means they have no room for error. Employees can inadvertently or intentionally disclose sensitive information through Web-based email. This increases risk and puts organizations in financial and legal jeopardy.

Healthcare Organizations

In today's fast-paced technological world, healthcare organizations must keep their costs and risks down. When employees inadvertently disclose sensitive information through bad online behavior, they put health organizations in financial and legal jeopardy. With the Health Insurance Portability and Accountability Act (HIPAA) pushing to protect sensitive client data, healthcare organizations cannot afford to have less than the best in Internet security solutions.

Internet Service Providers

ISPs have three motivations in regard to content filtering. The first is bandwidth. If the ISP can throttle, constrain,

or limit the streaming Web content, the ISP may be able to lower costs. Second, ISPs have to comply and produce logs in response to lawful requests. Finally, ISPs must assist the government with the USA PATRIOT Act and CIPA and must have technology in place to monitor.

U.S. Government

In the United States, the military is attempting to reduce the number of Internet connection points from thousands to hundreds, to reduce the risks we've described. National secrets, military plans, and information about soldiers and citizens cannot be exposed to our enemies by inadvertent surfing to the wrong places and downloading Trojans, keystroke loggers, or zombie code.

Other Governments

Other countries only allow their government employees access to whitelisted sites, to control access to news and other sites that censors determine to be inappropriate. In Russia the ruling party routinely shuts off access to political rivals' Web sites. China has deployed and maintains a new and virtual "Great Firewall of China" (also know as the Golden Shield Project). Ministry of Public Security Authorities determine sites that they believe represent an ideological threat to the Chinese Communist Party and then prevent their citizenry surfing, blogging, and emailing to blocked sites with sophisticated content-filtering methods, including IP address blocking and even DNS cache poisoning. Russia, Tibet, North Korea, Australia, China, Iran, Cuba, Thailand, Saudi Arabia, and many other repressive governments use similar technology. The ironic part of these massive content-filtering efforts is that many U.S.-based technology companies have been involved in their construction, sometimes as a contingency for doing business in China or other censoring countries.[2]

Libraries

The use of Internet filters or content-control software varies widely in public libraries in the United States, since Internet use policies are established by local library boards. Many libraries adopted Internet filters after Congress conditioned the receipt of universal service discounts on the use of Internet filters through the Children's Internet

---

2 U.S. companies' involvement in the "Golden Shield" Chinese content-filtering project, www.forbes.com/forbes/2006/0227/090.html, www.businessweek.com/magazine/content/06_08/b3972061.htm.

Protection Act (CIPA). Other libraries do not install content control software, believing that acceptable use policies and educational efforts address the issue of children accessing age-inappropriate content while preserving adult users' right to freely access information. Some libraries use Internet filters on computers used by children only. Some libraries that employ content-control software allow the software to be deactivated on a case-by-case basis on application to a librarian; libraries that are subject to CIPA are required to have a policy that allows adults to request that the filter be disabled without having to explain the reason for their request. Libraries have other legal challenges as well. In 1998, a U.S. federal district court in Virginia ruled that the imposition of mandatory filtering in a public library violates the First Amendment of the U.S. Bill of Rights.[3] About 50% of libraries have deployed content-filtering solutions.

Parents

Responsible parents don't leave their adult magazines on the coffee table, their XXX DVDs in the player ready to play, or their porn channels available and not PIN protected on cable or satellite. If you allow minor children unfettered access to the Internet, you will have an incident. Good practices include teaching your kids about what is on the Internet, what to do if they inadvertently click on a link or a pop up, make sure they have their own personal login (not as an admin!) and profile on shared computers, and review browser logs ("Trust but Verify!"). Younger children can be allowed to surf with their parents' assistance and direct supervision in a common area. PC-based software apps will give parents control, blocking, logging, and piece of mind. About 30% of parents with teenage children have deployed a content-filtering solution.

3. CONTENT BLOCKING METHODS

There are many ways to block content. Most commercial products use a number of these techniques together to optimize their capability.

Banned Word Lists

This method allows the creation of a blacklist dictionary that contains words or phrases. URLs and Web content are compared against the blacklist to block unauthorized Web sites. In the beginning this technology was largely a manual process, with vendors providing blacklists as starting points, requiring customers to manually update/tune the lists by adding or excluding keywords. This method has improved over the years and vendor lists have grown to include millions of keywords and phrases. Updates are usually performed manually, and filtering accuracy may be impacted with specific categories. For example, medical research sites are often blocked because they are mistaken for offensive material.[4]

URL Block

The URL block method is a blacklist containing known bad or unauthorized Web site URLs. Entire URLs can be added to the blacklist and exemptions can usually be made to allow portions of the Web site through. Many vendors provide URL blacklists with their products to simplify the technology, giving the user the ability to add new sites and perform URL pattern matching. With both banned word lists and URL block lists, a customer must perform manual updates of the vendors' blacklists. Depending on the frequency of the updates, the blacklists may fall out of compliance with the corporate policy between updates.

Category Block

Category blocking is the latest Web content-filtering technology that greatly simplifies the management process of Web inspection and content filtering. Category blocking utilizes external services that help keep suspect Web sites up to date, relying on Web category servers that contain the latest URL ratings to perform Web filtering. With category blocking devices, there are no manual lists to install or maintain. Web traffic is inspected against rating databases installed on the category servers, and the results (good or bad sites) are cached to increase performance. The advantage is up-to-date Web URL and category information at all times, eliminating the need to manually manage and update local blacklists. This method ensures accuracy and real-time compliance with the company's Internet use policy in terms of:

● Wildcard pattern matching
● Multilanguage pattern matching

---

3 "Library content filtering is unconstitutional," Mainstream Loudon v. Board of Trustees of the Loudon County Library, 24 F. Supp. 2d 552 (E.D. Va. 1998).

4 Benjamin Edelman, "Empirical analysis of Google SafeSearch" http://cyber.law.harvard.edu/archived_content/people/edelman/google-safesearch/.

- URL block lists
- Web pattern lists
- URL exemption lists
- Web application block (Java Applet, Cookie, ActiveX)
- Category block

Bayesian Filters

Particular words and phrases have probabilities of occurring on Web sites. For example, most Web surfers users will frequently encounter the "word" XXX on a porn Web site but seldom see it on other Web pages. The filter doesn't know these probabilities in advance and must first be trained so it can build them up. To train the filter, the user or an external "grader" must manually indicate whether a new Web site is a XXX porn site or not. For all words on each page, the filter will adjust the probabilities that each word will appear in porn Web pages versus legitimate Web sites in its database. For instance, Bayesian content filters will typically have learned a very high probability as porn content for the words *big breasts* and *Paris Hilton sex tape* but a very low probability for words seen only on legitimate Web sites, such as the names of companies and commercial products.

Safe Search Integration to Search Engines with Content Labeling

Content labeling is considered another form of content-control software. The Internet Content Rating Association (ICRA), now part of the Family Online Safety Institute, developed a content rating system to self-regulate online content providers. Using an online questionnaire, a Webmaster describes the nature of his Web content. A small file is generated that contains a condensed, computer-readable digest of this description that can then be used by content-filtering software to block or allow that site.

ICRA labels are deployed in a couple of formats. These include the World Wide Web Consortium's Resource Description Framework (RDF) as well as Platform for Internet Content Selection (PICS) labels used by Microsoft's Internet Explorer Content Advisor.

ICRA labels are an example of self-policing and self-labeling. Similarly, in 2006 the Association of Sites Advocating Child Protection (ASACP) initiated the Restricted to Adults (RTA) self-labeling initiative. The RTA label, unlike ICRA labels, does not require a Webmaster to fill out a questionnaire or sign up to use. Like ICRA, the RTA label is free. Both labels are recognized by a wide variety of content-control software.

Content-Based Image Filtering (CBIF)

The latest in content-filtering technology is CBIF. All the text-based content-filtering methods use knowledge of a site and text matching to impose blocks. This technique makes it impossible to filter visual and audio media. Content-based image filtering may resolve this issue, as shown in Figure 42.1. The method consists of examining the image itself for flesh tone patterns, detecting objectionable material and then blocking the offending site.

Step 1: Skin Tone Filter

First the images are filtered for skin tones. The color of human skin is created by a combination of blood (red) and melanin (yellow, brown). These combinations restrict the range of hues that skin can possess (except for people from the planet Rigel 7). In addition, skin has very little texture. These facts allow us to ignore regions with high-amplitude variations and design a skin tone filter to separate images before they are analyzed.

> *Tip*: Determine if the image contains large areas of skin color pixels.

Step 2: Analyze

Since we have already filtered the images for skin tones, any images that have very little skin tones will be accepted into the repository. The remaining images are then automatically segmented and their visual signatures are computed.

> *Tip*: Automatically segment and compute a visual signature for the image.

Step 3: Compare

The visual signatures of the potentially objectionable images are then compared to a predetermined reference data set. If the new image matches any of the images in the reference set with over 70% similarity, the image is rejected. If the similarity falls in the range of 40–70%, that image is set aside for manual intervention. An operator can look at these images and decide to accept or reject them. Images that fall below 40% are accepted and added to the repository. These threshold values are arbitrary and are completely adjustable.[5]

---

5 Envision Search Technologies (permission to use pending), www.evisionglobal.com/index.html.

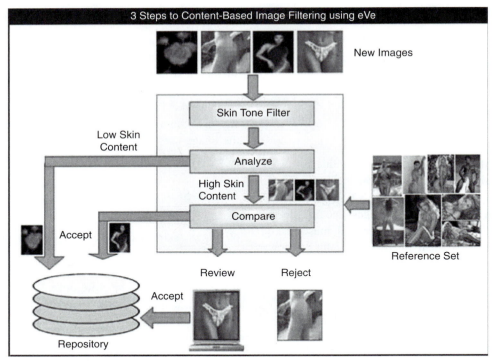

FIGURE 42.1 The process of content-based image filtering consists of three specific steps.

> *Tip*: Match the new image against a reference set of objectionable images and object regions.

4. TECHNOLOGY AND TECHNIQUES FOR CONTENT-FILTERING CONTROL

There are several different technologies that help facilitate Web monitoring, logging, and filtering of HTTP, FTP sites, and other Web-related traffic. The methods available for monitoring and controlling Internet access range from manual and educational methods to fully automated systems designed to scan, inspect, rate, and control Web activity.

Many solutions are software based and run on Intel-based servers that are attached to the network through a "mirrored" network port. Other solutions are dedicated appliances that are installed inline with the network, allowing it to see all the Internet traffic and allowing it to take fast, responsive action against unauthorized and malicious content. Common Web access control mechanisms include:

- Establishing a well-written usage policy
- Communicating the usage policy to every person in the organization
- Educating everyone on proper Internet, email, and computer conduct

- Installing monitoring tools that record and report on Internet usage
- Implementing policy-based tools that capture, rate, and block URLs
- Taking appropriate action when complaints are registered, policies violated, etc.

Now let's look at each enforcement point and the methods used for content filtering (see Figure 42.2).

This may be one of the most cost-effective and expeditious methods: Teach your employees about the risks and train them on WWW surfing policies. Then trust them, or not. Then select and use one of the solutions discussed next, to augment this important first step.

Internet Gateway-Based Products/Unified Threat Appliances

The fastest-growing area during the past several years has been the unified threat appliance market, as shown in Figure 42.3. These hardware platforms combine multiple security technologies working in concert to minimize threats.

Fortinet

Fortinet's unique approach to protecting networks against the latest vulnerabilities involves several key security components. By combining seven key security

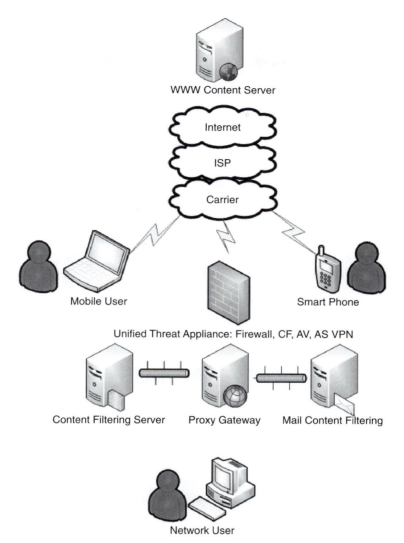

FIGURE 42.2 Deploy a policy for Internet use.

functions into one Aviation Security Identification Card (ASIC) accelerated security hardware and software platform, Fortinet has developed the world's first Dynamic Threat Prevention System. By sharing information between each component and relying on powerful firewall and IPS capabilities, threats are identified quickly and proactively blocked at the network level before they reach the endpoints to cause damage. Customers can create custom protection policies by turning on any of the seven security functions—Stateful Firewall, IPSec and SSL VPN, Antivirus, IDS & IPS, Web Content Filtering, Anti-Spam, and Bandwidth Shaping—in any combination and applying them to the interfaces on the FortiGate multifunction security platforms. Fortinet's Web Content Filtering technology allows customers to take a wide variety of actions to inspect, rate, and control Web traffic.

Included with each FortiGate security platform is the ability to control Web traffic via:

- Banned word lists
- Wildcard pattern matching
- Multilanguage pattern matching
- URL block lists
- Web pattern lists
- URL exemption lists
- Web application block (Java Applet, Cookie, ActiveX)
- Category block (via FortiGuard Service)

Customers can mix and match any of the Web content-filtering methods to achieve the correct balance for enforcement or select Fortinet's Automated Category Blocking option or FortiGuard Web Filtering Solution,

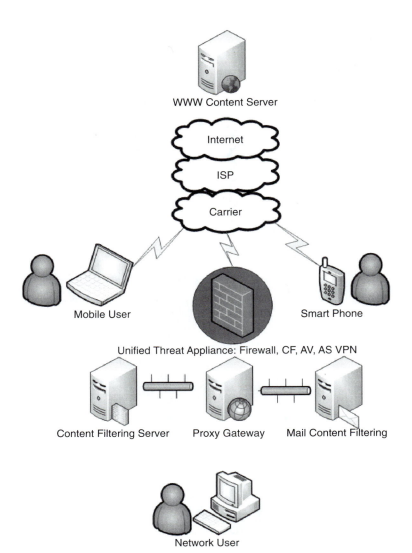

FIGURE 42.3 The unified threat appliance market.

by combining Fortinet's Web Content Filtering system with its Antivirus, IDS & IPS, and Anti-Spam functions. Increasingly, companies are looking to consolidate their security services into one multifunction appliance for license, management, and complexity justifications.[6]

Websense and Blue Coat

Websense is probably the most deployed system in commercial enterprises. Known for great flexibility in deployment and the perhaps the most granular category list, this product requires a third-party firewall to provide for a complete solution. Blue Coat, on the other hand, is a well-regarded leader in the secure Web gateway space.

Surf Control

Surf Control is a company purchased by Websense in 2008 and currently has an unclear product direction. Always well regarded, it has a large installed base and market percentage. Others include Secure Computing, Aladdin Knowledge Systems, Finjan, Marshal, FaceTime Communications, Webroot Software, Clearswift, CP Secure, IronPort Systems, ISS/IBM Proventia, Trend Micro, McAfee, MessageLabs, Barracuda Networks, ContentKeeper Technologies, Computer Associates, Cymphonix, Pearl Software, and St. Bernard.

PC Based

PC software such as Norton Internet Security includes parental controls. Operating Systems such as Mac OS X v10.4 offer parental controls for several applications.

---

6 Fortinet Multi-Threat Security Solution (permission to use pending), www.fortinet.com/doc/whitepaper/Webfilter_applicationNote.pdf.

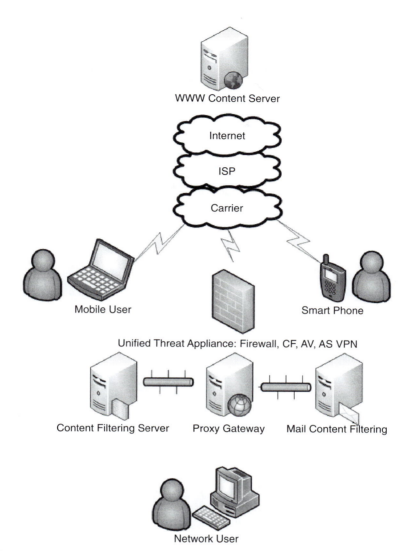

FIGURE 42.4 Content-filtering deployments.

Microsoft's Windows Vista operating system also includes content-control software. Other PC-based content-filtering software products are CyberPatrol, Cybersitter, EnoLogic NetFilter, iProtectYou Pro Web Filter, Net Nanny, Norton Internet Security, Safe Eyes Platinum, SentryPC, Bess, Crayon Crawler, Cyber Snoop, Covenant Eyes, K9 Web Protection, Naomi, Scieno Sitter, Sentry Parental Controls, Websense, Windows Live Family Safety, Windows Vista Parental Control, WinGate, X3Watch, and PlanetView. On the other hand, Mac software is available from Covenant Eyes, DansGuardian, Intego, and Mac OS X Leopard Parental Controls.

Remote corporate PCs and now the ever-increasing sophistication and capabilities of smart phones make them challenges for content-filtering deployments (see Figure 42.4). Usually a content-monitoring and control client is installed on a mobile PC or all surfing is only allowed after establishing a VPN connection back to HQ, and then HTTP requests can be served up and monitored.

ISP-Based Solutions

Many ISPs offer parental control browser-based options, among them Charter Communications, EarthLink, Yahoo!, and AOL (see Figure 42.5). Cleanfeed is offered by British Telecom in the U.K. and is an ISP administered content-filtering system that targets child sexual abuse content using offensive image lists from the Internet Watch Foundation.

Internet Cloud-Based Solutions

In 2008 the Google search engine adapted a software program to faster track child pornography accessible

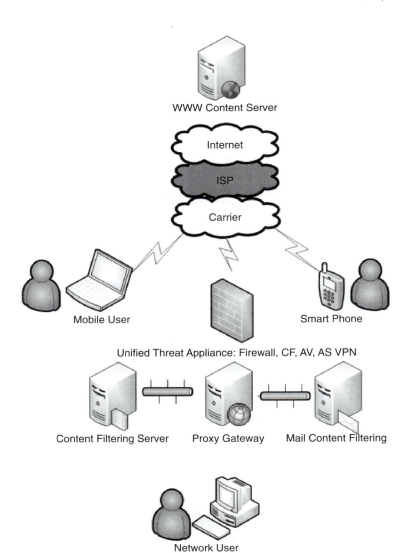

FIGURE 42.5 ISP-based solutions.

through its site. The software is based on a pattern rec-ognition engine.[7] Content distribution networks that are attached to the Internet, such as Akamai, Limelight, Panther Express, EdgeCast, CDNetworks, Level 3, and Internap, manage the content in their networks and will not distribute offensive images (see Figure 42.6). Many would also find it unacceptable that an ISP, whether by law or by the ISP's own choice, should deploy such software without allowing users to disable the filtering for their own connections. In addition, some argue that using content-control software may violate Sections 13 and 17 of the Convention on the Rights of the Child.[8]

7 Google Block Child Porn Content in Searches, http://en.wikipedia. org/wiki/Child_pornography#cite_note-44#cite_note-44.
8 Convention on the Rights of the Child, www.unhchr.ch/html/menu3/ b/k2crc.htm.

Proxy Gateway-Based Content Control

Companies that look to implement content-control solu-tions (see Figure 42.7) are also implementing security appliances at specialized network gateways, such as those from proprietary vendors like St. Bernard Software, Bloxx, CensorNet, Kerio, Untangle, and Winroute Firewall and content-filtering Web proxies like SafeSquid. Gateway-based content control solutions may be more difficult to bypass than desktop software solutions since they are less easily removed or disabled by the local user.

5. CATEGORIES

By various counts there were approximately 150 million Web sites in 2008. Most content-filtering companies have rated between 14 and 50 million Web sites. Facebook and

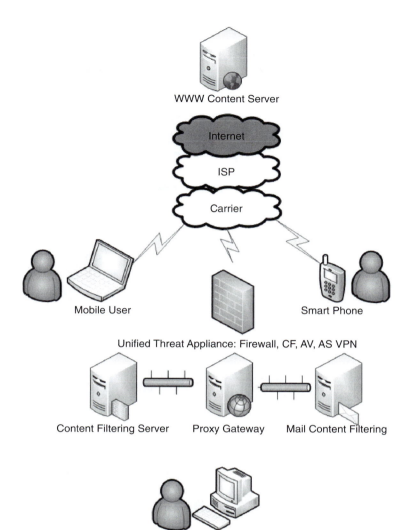

FIGURE 42.6 Internet cloud-based solutions.

other social networking sites are counted in the aggregate count but are generally not rated by content-filtering companies.

These rankings are rated by content-filtering companies into between 10 and 90 various categories. Typical subjects of content-control software include:

- Illegal content with reference to the legal domain being served by that company.
- Promote, enable, or discuss system cracking, software piracy, criminal skills, or other potentially illegal acts.
- Sexually explicit content, such as pornography, erotica, nudity, and nonerotic discussions of sexual topics such as sexuality or sex. Promote, enable, or discuss promiscuity, lesbian, gay, bisexual, transsexual, sexual activity outside of marriage, or other lifestyles seen to be immoral or alternative.

- Contain violence or other forms of graphic or "extreme" content.
- Promote, enable, or discuss bigotry or hate speech.
- Promote, enable, or discuss gambling, recreational drug use, alcohol, or other activities frequently considered to be vice.
- Are unlikely to be related to a student's studies, an employee's job function, or other tasks for which the computer in question may be intended, especially if they are likely to involve heavy bandwidth consumption.
- Are contrary to the interests of the authority in question, such as Web sites promoting organized labor or criticizing a particular company or industry.
- Promote or discuss politics, religion, health or other topics.
- Prevent people who are hypochondriacs from viewing Web sites related to health concerns.

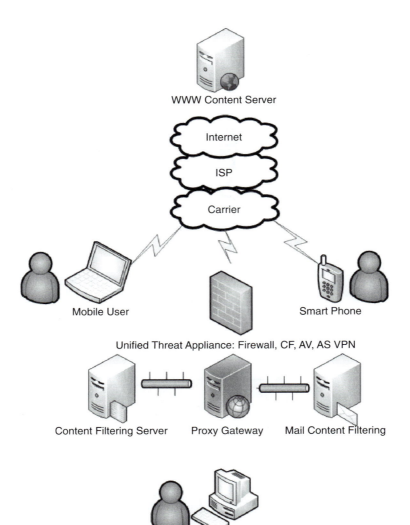

FIGURE 42.7 Proxy gateway-based content control.

- Include social networking opportunities that might expose children to predators.
- Potentially liable: drug abuse, folklore, hacking, illegal or unethical, marijuana, occult, phishing, plagiarism, proxy avoidance, racism and hate, violence, Web translation.
- Controversial: abortion, adult materials, advocacy groups/organizations, alcohol, extremist groups, gambling, lingerie and swimwear, nudity, pornography, sex education, sport hunting and war games, tasteless, tobacco, weapons.
- Potentially nonproductive: Advertising, brokerage and trading, digital postcards, freeware, downloads, games, instant messaging, newsgroups and message boards, Web chat, Web-based email.
- Potentially bandwidth consuming: Internet radio and TV, Internet telephony, multimedia

- download, peer-to-peer file sharing, personal storage.
- Potential security risks: Malware, spyware.
- General interest: Arts and entertainment, child education, culture, education, finance and banking, general organizations, health and wellness, homosexuality, job search, medicine, news and media, personal relationships, personal vehicles, personal Web sites, political organizations, real estate, reference, religion, restaurants and dining, search engines, shopping and auction, society and lifestyles, sports, travel.
- Business oriented: Armed forces, business, government and legal organizations, information technology, information/computer security.
- Others: Content servers, dynamic content, miscellaneous, secure Web sites, Web hosting.

6. LEGAL ISSUES

There are many legal issues to consider in content filtering. And once you think you have a handle on your particular organizational requirements and have ensured that they are legal, a court will make a ruling that changes the game. A number of Internet technology issues and related challenges have not yet been fully addressed by legislatures or courts and are subject to a wide range of interpretation. For example, virtual child pornography, pornographic images and text delivered by SMS messages, sexual age-play in virtual game worlds, the soft porn Manga genre of Lolicon and Rorikon are all challenges to current laws and issues that will need to be addressed as our society comes to grips with the Internet and what is "out there." The following discussion centers on the most relevant laws in the content-filtering space.

Federal Law: ECPA

The Electronic Communications Privacy Act (ECPA)[9] allows companies to monitor employees' communications when one of three provisions are met: one of the parties has given consent, there is a legitimate business reason, or the company needs to protect itself.

If your company has no content access policy in place, an employee could argue that he or she had a reasonable expectation of privacy. However, if the company has implemented a written policy whereby employees are informed about the possibility of Web site monitoring and warned that they should not have an expectation of privacy, the company is protected from this type of privacy claim.

CIPA: The Children's Internet Protection Act

CIPA provisions have both the "carrot and the stick." The U.S. government will pay you for equipment to access the Internet, but you have to play by its rules to get the money! Having been rebuffed by the courts in its previous efforts to protect children by regulating speech on the Internet, Congress took a new approach with the Children's Internet Protection Act (CIPA). See, for example *Reno v. ACLU*, 521 U.S. 844 (1997) (overturning the Communications Decency Act of 1996 on First Amendment grounds). With CIPA, Congress sought to condition federal funding for schools and libraries on the installation of filtering software on Internet-ready computers to block objectionable content.

CIPA is a federal law enacted by Congress in December 2000 to address concerns about access to offensive content over the Internet on school and library computers. CIPA imposes certain types of requirements on any school or library that receives funding for Internet access or internal connections from the E-rate program, which makes certain communications technology more affordable for eligible schools and libraries. In early 2001, the FCC issued rules implementing CIPA. CIPA made amendments to three federal funding programs: (1) the Elementary and Secondary Education Act of 1965, which provides aid to elementary and secondary schools; (2) the Library Services Technology Act, which provides grants to states for support of libraries; and (3) the E-Rate Program, under the Communications Act of 1934, which provides Internet and telecommunications subsidies to schools and libraries. The following are what CIPA requires[10]:

- Schools and libraries subject to CIPA may not receive the discounts offered by the E-Rate Program unless they certify that they have an Internet safety policy and technology protection measures in place. An Internet safety policy must include technology protection measures to block or filter Internet access to pictures that (a) are obscene, (b) are child pornography, or (c) are harmful to minors (for computers that are accessed by minors).
- Schools subject to CIPA are required to adopt and enforce a policy to monitor online activities of minors.
- Schools and libraries subject to CIPA are required to adopt and implement a policy addressing: (a) access by minors to inappropriate matter on the Internet; (b) the safety and security of minors when using electronic mail, chat rooms, and other forms of direct electronic communications; (c) unauthorized access, including so-called "hacking," and other unlawful activities by minors online; (d) unauthorized disclosure, use, and dissemination of personal information regarding minors; and (e) restricting minors' access to materials harmful to them.

Schools and libraries are required to certify that they have their safety policies and technology in place before receiving E-Rate funding, as follows:

- CIPA does not affect E-Rate funding for schools and libraries receiving discounts only for telecommunications, such as telephone service.

---

9 U.S. Code: Wire and Electronic Communications Interception and Interception of Oral Communications, www.law.cornell.edu/uscode/18/usc_sup_01_18_10_I_20_119.html.

10 What CIPA Requires, www.fcc.gov/cgb/consumerfacts/cipa.html.

- An authorized person may disable the blocking or filtering measure during any use by an adult to enable access for bona fide research or other lawful purposes.
- CIPA does not require the tracking of Internet use by minors or adults.

"Harmful to minors" is defined under the Act as:

> *any picture, image, graphic image file, or other visual depiction that (i) taken as a whole and with respect to minors, appeals to a prurient interest in nudity, sex, or excretion; (ii) depicts, describes, or represents, in a patently offensive way with respect to what is suitable for minors, an actual or simulated sexual act or sexual contact, actual or simulated normal or perverted sexual acts, or a lewd exhibition of the genitals; and (iii) taken as a whole, lacks serious literary, artistic, political, or scientific value as to minors.*

Court Rulings: CIPA From Internet Law Treatise

On June 23, 2003, the U.S. Supreme Court reversed a District Court's holding in *United States v. American Library Ass'n*, 539 U.S. 194 (2003).[11] It held that the use of Internet filtering software does not violate library patrons' First Amendment rights. Therefore, CIPA is constitutional and a valid exercise of Congress's spending power.

The Court held, in a plurality opinion, that libraries' filtering of Internet material should be subject to a rational basis review, not strict scrutiny. It explained that, because collective decisions regarding printed material have generally only been subject to a rational basis review, decisions regarding which Web sites to block should likewise be subject to the same test. It reasoned that libraries are no less entitled to make content-based judgments about their collections when they collect material from the Internet than when they collect material from any other source.

Further, it reasoned that heightened judicial scrutiny is also inappropriate because "Internet access in public libraries is neither a 'traditional' nor a 'designated' public forum" (*Id.* at 2304). Therefore, although filtering software may overblock constitutionally-protected speech and a less restrictive alternative may exist, because the government is not required to use the least restrictive means under a rational basis review, CIPA is nonetheless constitutional.

Moreover, the Court held that Congress did not exceed its spending power by enacting CIPA because, when the government uses public funds to establish a program, it is entitled to define its limits. By denying federal funding, the government is not penalizing libraries that refuse to filter the Internet, or denying their rights to provide their patrons with unfiltered Internet access. Rather, it "simply reflects Congress' decision not to subsidize their doing so" (*Id.* at 2308).[12]

The Trump Card of Content Filtering: The "National Security Letter"

The FBI, CIA, or DoD can issue an administrative subpoena to ISPs for Web site access logs, records, and connection logs for various individuals. Along with a gag order, this letter comes with no judicial oversight and does not require probable cause. In 2001, Section 505 of the PATRIOT Act powers were expanded for the use of the NSL. There are many contentious issues with these laws, and the Electronic Frontier Foundation and the American Civil Liberties Union (ACLU) are battling our government to prevent their expansion and open interpretation.[13]

ISP Content Filtering Might Be a "Five-Year Felony"

There are issues looming for ISPs that monitor their networks for copyright infringement or bandwidth hogs, since they may be committing felonies by breaking federal wiretapping laws. University of Colorado law professor Paul Ohm, a former federal computer crimes prosecutor, argues that ISPs such as Comcast, AT&T, and Charter Communications that are or are contemplating ways to throttle bandwidth, police for copyright violations, and serve targeted ads by examining their customers' Internet packets are putting themselves in criminal and civil jeopardy.[14]

State of Texas: An Example of an Enhanced Content-Filtering Law

Texas state law requires all Texas ISPs to link to blocking and filtering software sites. In 1997, during the 75th Regular Session of the Texas Legislature, House Bill 1300 was passed. HB 1300 requires ISPs to make a link

---

11 CIPA and E-Rate Ruling, www.cdt.org/speech/cipa/030623 decision.pdf.

12 IETF Fights CIPA, http://ilt.eff.org/index.php/Speech:_CIPA.

13 ACLU Sues Over Internet Privacy, Challenges ISPs Being Forced to Secretly Turn Over Customer Data, www.cbsnews.com/stories/2004/04/29/terror/main614638.shtml.

14 Forer Prosecutor: ISP Content Filtering Might be a 'Five Year Felony,' http://blog.wired.com/27bstroke6/2008/05/isp-content-f-1.html.

available on their first Web page that leads to Internet "censorware" software, also known as "automatic" blocking and screening software. The two most important portions of the law are shown here:

Sec. 35.102. SOFTWARE OR SERVICES THAT RESTRICT ACCESS TO CERTAIN MATERIAL ON INTERNET.

(a) A person who provides an interactive computer service to another person for a fee shall provide free of charge to each subscriber of the service in this state a link leading to fully functional shareware, freeware, or demonstration versions of software or to a service that, for at least one operating system, enables the subscriber to automatically block or screen material on the Internet.

(b) A provider is considered to be in compliance with this section if the provider places, on the provider's first page of world wide Web text information accessible to a subscriber, a link leading to the software or a service described by Subsection (a). The identity of the link or other on-screen depiction of the link must appear set out from surrounding written or graphical material so as to be conspicuous.

Sec. 35.103. CIVIL PENALTY.

(a) A person is liable to the state for a civil penalty of $2,000 for each day on which the person provides an interactive computer service for a fee but fails to provide a link to software or a service as required by Section 35.102. The aggregate civil penalty may not exceed $60,000.[15]

(b) The attorney general may institute a suit to recover the civil penalty. Before filing suit, the attorney general shall give the person notice of the person's noncompliance and liability for a civil penalty. If the person complies with the requirements of Section 35.102 not later than the 30th day after the date of the notice, the violation is considered cured and the person is not liable for the civil penalty.

The following are international laws involving content filtering:

- UK: Data Protection Act
- EU: Safer Internet Action Plan
- Many other countries have also enacted legislation

Additionally, the United Kingdom and some other European countries have data retention policies. Under these policies ISPs and carriers are obliged to retain a record of all their clients' Web browsing. The data retention period varies from six months to three years. In the U.K. this retained data is available to a very wide range of public bodies, including the police and security services. Anyone who operates a proxy service of any kind in one

of these countries needs to be aware that a record is kept of all Web browsing through their computers. On March 15, 2006, the European Union adopted Directive 2006/24/EC, which requires all member states to introduce statutory data retention. The United States does not have a statutory data retention specifically targeting information in this area, though such provisions are under consideration.

7. ISSUES AND PROBLEMS WITH CONTENT FILTERING

By far the biggest challenge to content-filtering deployments comes from those users who intend to bypass and gain access to their intended Web content. For content-filtering technologies to work well, developers have to understand all the methods that users will devise and employ to circumvent the content-filtering systems, inadvertently or otherwise.

Bypass and Circumvention

Some controls may be bypassed successfully using alternative protocols such as FTP, telnet, or HTTPS, by conducting searches in a different language, or by using a proxy server or a circumventor such as Psiphon or UltraSurf. Cached Web pages returned by Google or other searches may bypass some controls as well. Web syndication services may provide alternate paths to access content.

The primary circumvention method surfers use is proxies. There are basically five types of proxies:

- Client-based proxies
- Open proxies
- HTTP Web-based proxies
- Secure public and private Web-based proxies
- Secure anonymous Web-based proxies

Client-Based Proxies

These are programs that users download and run on their computers. Many of these programs are run as "portable applications," which means they don't require any installation or elevated privileges, so they can be run from a USB thumb drive by a user with limited privileges. The three most widely used include TorPark, which uses Firefox and the XeroBank network, Google Web Accelerator, and McAfee's Anonymizer.

These programs create a local proxy server using a nonstandard port. Then they configure the browser to use the local proxy by changing its proxy server settings to the form localhost:port = 127.0.0.1:9777, for example.

---

15 Texas ISP Laws can be found here: www.tlc.state.tx.us/legal/b&ccode/b&c_title10/80C258(3).HTML.

Web content requests are then tunneled through the proxy program to an appropriate proxy server using a custom protocol, which is typically encrypted. The content-filtering gateway doesn't see the browser-to-local proxy traffic, because it flies under its content inspection radar. All the gateway may see is the custom protocol that encapsulates the user's Web request.

The network of proxy servers is either static, as is the case with commercial programs such as McAfee's Anonymizer and Google Web Accelerator, or it's private and dynamic, as is the case with Psiphon and XeroBank. In both cases, the proxy server network is typically built by individuals who volunteer their home computers for use by installing the corresponding proxy server software.

Currently the UltraSurf proxy client is the most advanced tool available to circumvent gateway security Web content filters. UltraSurf was developed by an organization called UltraReach,[16] which was founded by a group of Chinese political dissidents. UltraReach developers continue to actively maintain and update UltraSurf. They designed UltraSurf specifically to allow Chinese citizens to circumvent the Chinese government's efforts to restrict Internet use in China. The UltraSurf application is a very sophisticated piece of software. It uses a distributed network of proxy servers, installed and maintained by volunteers around the world, much like a peer-to-peer network. It uses multiple schemes to locate the proxy servers in its network, spanning different protocols. It uses port and protocol tunneling to trick security devices into ignoring it or mishandling it. It also uses encryption and misdirection to thwart efforts to investigate how it works.

Ultrasurf is free and requires no registration, which makes it widely distributable. It requires no installation and can be run by a user who doesn't have administrative permissions to his computer, which makes it very portable. It can easily be carried around on a USB thumb drive and run from there.

Another formidable bypass application is Psiphon.[17] This is a distributed "personal trust" style Web proxy designed to help Internet users affected by Internet censorship securely bypass content-filtering systems typically set up by governments. Psiphon was developed by the Citizen Lab at the University of Toronto, building on previous generations of Web proxy software systems. Psiphon's recommended use is among private, trusted relationships that span censored and uncensored locations (such as those that exist among friends and family members, for example) rather than as an open public proxy. Traffic between clients

and servers in the Psiphon system is encrypted using the HTTPS protocol.

According to Nart Villeneuve, director of technical research at the Citizen Lab, "The idea is to get them to install this on their computer, and then deliver the location of that circumventor, to people in filtered countries by the means they know to be the most secure. What we're trying to build is a network of trust among people who know each other, rather than a large tech network that people can just tap into."[18]

Psiphon takes a different approach to censorship circumvention than other tools used for such purposes, such as The Onion Router, aka Tor. Psiphon requires no download on the client side and thus offers ease of use for the end user. But unlike Tor, Psiphon is not an anonymizer; the server logs all the client's surfing history. Psiphon differs from previous approaches in that the users themselves have access to server software. The developers of Psiphon have provided the user with a Microsoft Windows platform executable for the Psiphon server. If the server software attains a high level of use, this would result in a greater number of servers being online. A great number of servers online would make the task of attacking the overall user base more difficult for those hostile to use of the Psiphon proxy than attacking a few centralized servers, because each individual Web proxy would have to be disabled one by one.

There are inherent security risks in approaches such as Psiphon, specifically those presented by logging by the services themselves. The real-world risk of log keeping was illustrated by the turnover of the emails of Li Zhi to the Chinese government by Yahoo. Li was subsequently arrested, convicted, and sent to jail for eight years.[19] Some have raised concerns that the IP addresses and the Psiphon software download logs of Psiphon users could fall into the wrong hands if the Citizen Lab computers were to get hacked or otherwise compromised.

These tools are a double-edged sword: They are incredibly powerful tools for allowing political dissidents around the world to evade oppression, but they also provide end users on private, filtered networks with a way to access the Internet that violates acceptable use policies and introduces liability to an organization. The best way to block these types of circumventing technologies is by using packet inspection and blocking based on signatures of this application setting up or in process.

---

16 UltraReach Information can be found at www.ultrareach.com/.
17 Psiphon: http://psiphon.civisec.org/.

18 Psiphon Web Proxy Information can be found here: http://en.wikipedia.org/wiki/Psiphon#cite_note-2#cite_note-2.
19 Yahoo may have helped jail another Chinese user, www.infoworld.com/article/06/02/09/75208_HNyahoohelpedjail_1.html.

Open Proxies

Open proxies are accessed by changing the configuration of your browser. Your browser can be modified to send all traffic to a proxy at a specific IP and port. Usually the IT department builds an OS image that makes this configuration as a way of facilitating corporate installed Web filtering. To check it out on Internet Explorer, go to Tools | Internet Options | Connections | LAN Settings. This is where the IT department, school, or library normally locks you into using their proxy, or if you have administrative privileges you can configure your browser to use an open proxy.

When your PC is configured to use an open proxy, the browser simply sends all its Web content requests to the proxy, as opposed to resolving the URL to an IP and sending the request directly to the destination Web site. The open proxy then does the DNS name resolution, connects to the destination Web site, and returns that content to the browser.

Blocking this behavior is rather straightforward. When the end user attempts to access a blocked site through an open proxy, the name of the site is encoded right there in the request, and the content filter works just as it would if the browser wasn't configured to use an open proxy.

HTTP Web-Based Proxies (Public and Private)

These are Web sites that are purpose-built to proxy Web traffic. To use them, the user goes to the Web page of the proxy Web site, then types the desired URL into a text box on the HTML page that site serves. The browser makes requests to the proxy site, and the proxy site returns the content of a different site, the one the user actually wants to see. The content inspection gateway only sees traffic to the proxy site.

PHProxy and CGIProxy are the most well-known development efforts used for this purpose. Peacefire's Circumventor is an example of an application using these tools kits. The HTML code request and response from the proxy is specifically engineered to evade filtering. The more difficult it is to reverse engineer the URL of the proxied site from the HTTP traffic that's flowing between the browser and the proxy, the more successful this method of circumvention is.

The biggest benefit for these types of proxies for the circumventer is that they are simple to install on your home or office computer. A nontechnical user can do it in a matter of minutes. Once it is installed, the user has a Web-based proxy running on his home computer, which is presumably not filtered. He can then access his home computer from a filtered network (like an office or school network)

using just a browser, and circumvent your carefully crafted Web filtering policy.

Secure Public Web-Based Proxies

These proxies are basically the same as the HTTP Web-based proxies except that they use the SSL encrypted HTTPS protocol. There are two types of HTTPS proxies: public and anonymous. Public HTTPS proxies are built by organizations such as Proxy.org and Peacefire and are publicized via mailing lists and word of mouth. They intentionally look like completely legitimate sites, with properly constructed certificates that have been issued by trusted certificate authorities like VeriSign. These sites are blocked by IP addresses, since the content-filtering device cannot decrypt and look inside HTTPS packets.

The other type of secure anonymous Web-based proxies is more difficult to locate and block and makes the game much more interesting. In this case, the user takes that same proxy software package used by the public proxy sites and installs it on his home computer. The package generates a certificate and listens on HTTPS. Now the user has a secure Web-based proxy running on her home computer. Since these sites are anonymous and because in the sense that nobody links to them they can't be found by classic site discovery techniques like spidering links on known sites, building an IP list and blocking them is problematic and must be done with certificate examination and other heuristic techniques.

These proxy types combine the problems we've described; since they are encrypted using HTTPS there is one more huge risk to using these proxy portals. There are nefarious individuals on the Internet who build open proxies and publicize them through mailing lists and other sites. Often they are built with criminal intent, as a way to steal user credentials. The open proxy can see and capture and log everything you are sending and receiving, even HTTPS. Use caution if you dare to explore here.

Process Killing

Some of the more poorly designed PC installed content-filtering application programs and agents can be shut down by killing their processes: for example, in Microsoft Windows through the Windows Task Manager or in Mac OS using Activity Monitor.

Remote PC Control Applications

Windows RPC, VNC, Citrix GoToMyPc, BeAnywhere, WallCooler, I'm InTouch, eBLVD, BeamYourScreen,

PCMobilizr, and Cisco's WebEx are examples. Some of these applications are business critical and will not be blocked by corporately deployed content-filtering systems, and their intentional misuse is a serious risk.

Overblocking and Underblocking

Overblocking is the issue that occurs when the content-filtering technology blocks legitimate Web sites because of a tuning, filter update missing, or other technology limitation. Underblocking occurs when a content filter is deployed and does not block a Web site in a targeted category; the user will see the content and a policy violation will occur.

Blacklist and Whitelist Determination

There are countless conversations going on between HR and IT departments every day trying to appropriately tune the content filter's blacklist. Some strict companies, schools, and parents allow surfing only to sites that are on a whitelist.

Casual Surfing Mistake

A friend sends a link in email, a popup window offers up something interesting, or you mistype a Web site address and get a typo-squatter porn site. All these ways will land you on a Web site that is not approved by your content-filtering system. You better have a way to deal with this reality.

Getting the List Updated

Most content-filtering companies send out very frequent updates. These must be accessed, downloaded, and incorporated. There has to be an automatic function for this or your IT administration will avoid this task and your lists will become quickly outdated.

Time-of-Day Policy Changing

Benevolent companies sometimes allow for surfing before or after business hours. Setting this up and managing the policy enforcement is an HR and IT challenge.

Override Authorization Methods

Many content filters have an option that allows authorized people to bypass the content filter. This is especially useful in environments where the computer is being supervised and the content filter is aggressively blocking Web sites that need to be accessed. Usually the company owners and executives claim this privilege.

Hide Content in "Noise" or Use Steganography

The most devious and technical approaches to get information past filters is to hide this information in pictures or video or within normal communication noise.

Nonrepudiation: Smart Cards, ID Cards for Access

One of the strongest content access methods is to know, really know, who is browsing. If you don't have anonymity and you know that censors are controlling the content, the risks should be lower.

Warn and Allow Methods

This is a method of allowing the user to go to the desired site, but after a warning that the site may not meet HR or IT policy. Usually this type of warning is enough to make the surfer stop in her tracks.

Integration with Spam Filtering tools

Most new content-filtering technology has a related component that inspects mail and coordinates policy with the content-filtering gateway.

Detect Spyware and Malware in the HTTP Payload

Most new content-filtering technology goes beyond just blocking offensive content. The same technology is looking for and blocking malware and spyware in HTTP data. Don't select an enterprise product without this feature.

Integration with Directory Servers

The easiest way to manages content filtering that requires granular user-lever control is to set up groups within directory servers. For example, Trusted User Groups, Executive User Groups, Owner User Group, and Restricted User Group will have different browsing behavior allowed or disallowed.

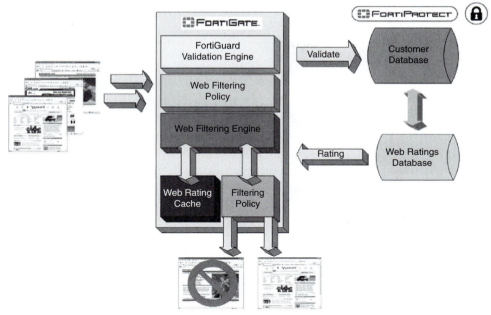

FIGURE 42.8 Cache Rating and Filtering Policy Engine.[20]

Language Support

The content-filtering gateway must have support for multiple languages or the surfer will just find Spanish porn sites, for example. Typically a global ratings database will support multiple languages.

Financial Considerations Are Important

Don't forget that a content filter project includes some of these items when calculating total cost of ownership for ROI payback:

- Licensing costs: Per user or per gateway.
- Servers: How many do you need to buy; how about high availability?
- Appliances: How many do you need to buy, how about high availability?
- Installation: Can you do it yourself or do you need a consultant or the manufacturer to help?
- Maintenance: Support and updates are necessary to keep your solution current.
- Ongoing administration from your IT staff.
- Patching, scanning, remediation by your IT staff.
- Some content filters need add-on server and license costs, for example:
  - ISA Server
  - MS Server
  - Logging Server
  - Analyzer Server
  - AV Server
  - Firewall
- Some content-filtering systems require integration costs with third-party enforcement points such as a firewall.

Scalability and Usability

Critical design issues must be addressed. So, how are out-of-cache queries handled (see Figure 42.8).

We'll use the Fortinet Unified Threat Appliance as an example. When a match is not found in the FortiGuard cache, a request is sent to the Fortinet Distribution Network (FDN) in parallel with the request sent to the Web server to retrieve the Web pages. The time to query the FDN for URL rating is often negligible and far less than the time to retrieve the Webpage because:

- FDN servers are strategically deployed close to the major backbones and the roundtrip time from a FortiGate unit to the FDN and back is usually less than the roundtrip time from the FortiGate unit to the Web site and back.
- The latency of responding to a query is less than 1ms, even when an FDN server is operating at its maximum capacity. This compares to generally hundreds of milliseconds to even several seconds to retrieve a Web page because of normal network and Web server latency.

20 Image Courtesy of Fortinet For a complete review of their wide range of Fortinet UTM Appliance, see www.fortinet.com.

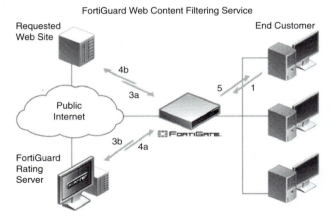

FortiGuard Web Content Filtering Service

FIGURE 42.9 FortiGuard URL query packet.***

- The average payload of a FortiGuard URL query packet is less than 256 bytes, and one round trip is enough to retrieve the rating. The average size of a Web page is 10 Kbytes and usually requires a minimum of three round trips. See the following procedural steps with regard to the FortiGuard URL query packet, as shown in Figure 42.9:

  1. User requests a URL.
  2. If the rating for the URL is already cached in the FortiGate unit, it is immediately compared with the policy for the user. If the site is allowed, the page is requested (3a) and the response is retrieved (4b).
  3. If the URL rating is not in the FortiGate cache, the page is requested (3a) and a rating request is made simultaneously to the FortiGuard Rating Server (3b).
  4. When the rating response is received by the FortiGate unit (4a), it is compared with the requestor's policy (2). The response from the Web site (4b) is queued by the FortiGate unit if necessary until the rating is received.
  5. If the policy is to allow the page, the Web site response (4b) is passed to the requestor (5). Otherwise, a user-definable "blocked" message is sent to the requestor and the event is logged in the content-filtering log.

Performance Issues

Testing and measuring Web content-filtering performance is a challenge because constantly changing network conditions have the greatest effect on performance. Every millisecond of delay for content inspection is multiplied by the entire user base. Poorly designed or constrained systems will affect Web access business efficiency.

Reporting Is a Critical Requirement

It's one thing to block Web content, but for businesses, schools, and parents it is critical to see results and issues that reports will illustrate. Real-time visibility to Internet usage, historical trending of Web traffic, and detailed forensic reporting help gauge user intent, help in enforcing Internet use policies, and enable retention of archived records to satisfy legal requirements and aid in regulatory compliance.

Typically Web filtering reports are generated and organized according to category and groups and users. There are per-group statistics in addition to the per-category statistics. Many reports should be supported including:

- *Management reports*. The most frequently used reports by customers or those of most interest to management. These include category, destination, disposition, group, risk, and user.
- *Summary reports*. Overview of usage with daily and grand totals. Summary Reports are used to view Internet usage trends.
- *User detail reports*. The most complete picture of Internet usage. Detail into one user's online activities.

Additionally this information is logged for reporting purposes:

- Source IP
- Destination IP
- URL
- Policy Action (allow, block, monitor)
- Content Category

Bandwidth Usage

Content-filtering systems should have the ability to display current protocol usage and report on patterns. Bandwidth savings give the most rapid ROI and need to be measurable. Figure 42.10 shows a bandwidth monitoring report from Fortinet.

Precision Percentage and Recall

The accuracy and efficacy of content-filtering systems are measured by precision and recall. Precision is the percentage of the number of relevant Web sites retrieved compared to the total number of irrelevant and relevant Web sites retrieved. Recall is the percentage of the number of relevant records retrieved compared to the total number of relevant records in the database. There is an inverse relationship between these two metrics that cannot be

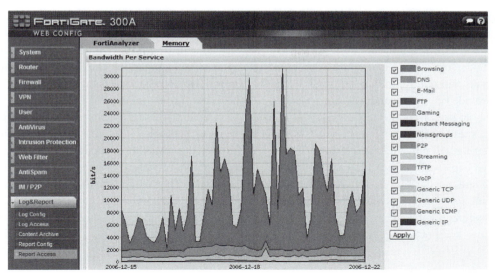

FIGURE 42.10 Shows that surfing consumes the majority of the bandwidth of an Internet connection.

avoided: Maximizing one minimizes the other, and vice versa. Precision and recall must be considered together. A single metric of adding the precision and recall together is a good overall indication of the accuracy and efficacy.

The categorization of Web sites is an information retrieval process whereby each URL or Web page can be considered a record. A correctly categorized URL is a relevant record retrieved, whereas an incorrectly categorized URL is an irrelevant record retrieved. The objective of Web filtering is to block Web pages that are designated to be blocked and allow Web pages that are permitted. Web filtering precision is a measure of underblocking, or letting pages through that should be blocked. Higher precision leads to lower underblocking.

Web filtering recall is a measure of overblocking. Overblocking results from false positives and means blocking pages that should not be blocked. High recall leads to fewer false positives and lower overblocking. A perfect Web filtering system would have 100% precision and 100% recall, or a score of 200% overall.

A customer's Internet access policies dictate the Web sites to block, and typically all Web sites that are potentially liable, objectionable, or controversial are blocked.

9. RELATED PRODUCTS

Instant messaging, IRC, FTP, telnet, and especially email are all forms of communication that can be inspected with content-filtering technology. Also, more and more companies are integrating DLP technologies to reduce the risk of confidential, HIPPA, PCI, and PII information from leaking out over Internet connections. DLP inspection and blocking enforce data leakage and encryption policies.

Expect to see this functionality become standard as content-filtering products mature.

On the other hand, Internet accountability software is a type of computer software that provides detailed reports that account for user behavior, surfing history, chat sessions, and actions on the Internet. Internet accountability software is used for various reasons, court-mandated sanctions, company policy obligations, and as a recovery step in porn addiction. Versions of accountability software monitor Internet use on a personal computer,or Internet use by a specific user on a computer. These software applications then generate reports of Internet use, monitored by a third party, that account for and manage an individual's Internet browsing.

The first vendor to offer Internet accountability software was Covenant Eyes. Available in March 2000, Covenant Eyes accountability software was developed to provide Internet users with a means of reporting their online activity to one or more "accountability partners." The term "accountability partner" is a well-known concept in addiction-recovery circles and 12-step programs, such as Alcoholics Anonymous and Sexaholics Anonymous. Accountability partners have access to a user's Internet browsing record, which eliminates the anonymity of Internet use, thus providing incentive to not view Internet pornography or other explicit sexual images online. Today there are several accountability software providers: Covenant Eyes, Promise Keepers, K9 Web Protection, and X3watch.

10. CONCLUSION

Content filtering is a fast-paced battle of new technologies and the relentless trumping of these systems by subversion and evasion. Altruistic development efforts by passionate programmers on a mission to support citizens in countries that block access to content will win, then lose, and then win again in a never-ending cycle. Other challenges include employees and kids who don't understand all the risks and don't think the abuse of a school- or company-provided computer and network is a big deal. Add new technologies, Web 2.0 applications, YouTube, and streaming sites, and the challenges and arguments for content filtering will not end anytime soon.

As we have explored, content filtering and its three objectives—accuracy, scalability, and maintainability—are at odds with each other. Accurate blocking makes it hard to scale and maintain, and easily scalable and maintainable systems are not as accurate. Companies that make content-filtering technology are attempting to make these challenges easier to manage and maintain.

Content filtering is controversial, and the law is frequently changing in the U.S. and internationally. IT policies try to cope and are being updated every year to deal with new legal issues.

Content filtering is morphing and aggregating with other technologies to address multifaceted threats. In the future, the standalone content filter/proxy will be just one important part of your security protection posture.

Finally, in the high-stakes chess game of content filtering, the censors and policy enforcers are always perpetually destined to have the worst move in chess: the second to last one.

## Chapter 43

Data Loss Protection

Ken Perkins

Blazent Incorporated

IT professionals are tasked with the some of the most complex and daunting tasks in any organization. Some of the roles and responsibilities are paramount to the company's livelihood and profitability and maybe even the ultimate survival of the organization. Some of the most challenging issues facing IT professionals today are securing communications and complying with the vast number of data privacy regulations. Secure communications must protect the organization against spam, viruses, and worms; securing outbound traffic; guaranteeing the availability and continuity of the core business systems (such as corporate email, Internet connectivity, and phone systems), all while facing an increasing workload with the same workforce. In addition, many organizations face challenges in meeting compliance goals, contingency plans for disasters, detecting and/or preventing data misappropriation, and dealing with hacking, both internally and externally.

Almost every week, IT professionals can open the newspaper or browse online news sites and read stories that would keep most people up at night (see sidebar, "Stealing Trade Secrets From E. I. du Pont de Nemours and Company"). The dollar amounts lost are staggering and growing each year (see sidebar, "Stored Secure Information Intrusions"). Pressures of compliance regulations, brand protection, and corporate intellectual property are all driving organizations to evaluate and/or adopt data loss protection (DLP) solutions.

Stealing Trade Secrets from E. I. du Pont de Nemours and Company

WILMINGTON, DE—Colm F. Connolly, United States Attorney for the District of Delaware; William D. Chase, Special Agent in Charge of the Baltimore Federal Bureau of Investigation (FBI) Field Office; and Darryl W. Jackson, Assistant Secretary of Commerce for Export Enforcement, announced today the unsealing of a one-count Criminal Information charging Gary Min, a.k.a. Yonggang Min, with stealing trade secrets from E. I. du Pont de Nemours and Company ("DuPont"). Min pleaded guilty to the charge on November 13, 2006. The offense carries a maximum prison sentence of 10 years, a fine of up to $250,000, and restitution.

Pursuant to the terms of the plea agreement, Min admitted that he misappropriated DuPont's proprietary trade secrets without the company's consent and agreed to cooperate with the government.

According to facts recited by the government and acknowledged by Min at Min's guilty plea hearing, Min began working for DuPont as a research chemist in November 1995. Throughout his tenure at DuPont, Min's research focused generally on polyimides, a category of heat and chemical resistant polymers, and more specifically on high-performance films. Beginning in July 2005, Min began discussions with Victrex PLC about possible employment opportunities in Asia. Victrex manufactures PEEK,™ a polymer compound that is a functional competitor with two DuPont products, Vespel® and Kapton®. On October 18, 2005, Min signed an employment agreement with Victrex, with his employment set to begin in January 2006. Min did not tell DuPont that he had accepted a job with Victrex, however, until December 12, 2005.

Between August 2005 and December 12, 2005, Min accessed an unusually high volume of abstracts and full-text .pdf documents off of DuPont's Electronic Data Library ("EDL"). The EDL server, which is located at DuPont's experimental station in Wilmington, is one of DuPont's primary databases for storing confidential and proprietary information. Min downloaded approximately 22,000 abstracts from the EDL and

---

accessed approximately 16,706 documents—fifteen times the number of abstracts and reports accessed by the next highest user of the EDL for that period. The vast majority of Min's EDL searches were unrelated to his research responsibilities and his work on high-performance films. Rather, Min's EDL searches covered most of DuPont's major technologies and product lines, as well as new and emerging technologies in the research and development stage. The fair market value of the technology accessed by Min exceeded $400 million.

After Min gave DuPont notice that he was resigning to take a position at Victrex, DuPont uncovered Min's unusually-high EDL usage. DuPont immediately contacted the FBI in Wilmington, which launched a joint investigation with the United States Attorney's Office and the United States Department of Commerce. Min began working at Victrex on January 1, 2006. On or about February 2, 2006, Min uploaded approximately 180 DuPont documents—including documents containing confidential, trade secret information—to his Victrex-assigned laptop computer. On February 3, 2006, DuPont officials told Victrex officials in London about Min's EDL activities and explained that Min had accessed confidential and proprietary action. Victrex officials seized Min's laptop computer from him on February 8, 2006, and subsequently turned it over to the FBI."[1]

Stored Secure Information Intrusions

Retailer TJX suffered an unauthorized intrusion or intrusions into portions of its computer system that process and store information related to credit and debit card, check and unreceipted merchandise return transactions (the intrusion or intrusions, collectively, the "Computer Intrusion"), which was discovered during the fourth quarter of fiscal 2007. The theft of customer data primarily related to portions of the transactions at its stores (other than Bob's Stores) during the periods 2003 through June 2004 and mid-May 2006 through mid-December 2006.

During the first six months of fiscal 2007 TJX incurred pretax costs of $38 million for costs related to the Computer Intrusion. In addition, in the second quarter ended July 28, 2007, TJX established a pretax reserve for its estimated exposure to potential losses related to the Computer Intrusion and recorded a pretax charge of $178 million. As of January 26, 2008, TJX reduced the reserve by $19 million, primarily due to insurance proceeds with respect to the Computer Intrusion, which had not previously been reflected in the reserve, as well as a reduction in estimated legal and other fees as the Company has continued to resolve outstanding disputes, litigation, and investigations. This reserve reflects the Company's current estimation of probable losses in accordance with generally accepted accounting principles with respect to the Computer Intrusion and includes a current estimation of total potential cash liabilities from pending litigation, proceedings, investigations and other claims, as well as legal and other costs and expenses, arising from the Computer Intrusion. This reduction in the reserve results in a credit to the Provision for Computer Intrusion related costs of $19 million in the fiscal 2007 fourth quarter and a pretax charge of $197 million for the fiscal year ended January 26, 2008.

The Provision for Computer Intrusion related costs increased fiscal 2008 fourth quarter net income by $11 million, or $0.02 per share, and reduced net income from continuing operations for the full fiscal 2008 year by $119 million, or $0.25 per share.[2]

Note: In the June 2007 General Accounting Office article, "GAO-07-737 Personal Information: Data Breaches Are Frequent, But Evidence of Resulting Identity Theft Is Limited; However, the Full Extent Is Unknown," 31 companies that responded to a 2006 survey said they incurred an average of $1.4 million per data breach.[3]

The list of concerning stories of companies and organizations affected by data breaches grows every year. The penalties are not limited to financial losses but sometimes hurt people personally through invasion of privacy. The organizations harmed are not limited to Wall Street and have implications of influencing the national security of countries worldwide. The pressures across entire organizations are growing to keep data in its place and keep it a secure manner. It is no wonder that DLP solutions are included in most IT organizations' initiatives for the next few years.

So, with this in mind, this chapter could be considered an introduction and a primer to the concepts of DLP. The terms, acronyms, and concepts discussed here will give the reader a baseline understanding of how to investigate and evaluate DLP applications in the market today. However, this chapter should not be considered the authoritative single source of information on the topic.

---

1 "Guilty plea in trade secrets case," Department of Justice Press Release, February 15, 2007.

2 "SEC EDGAR filing information form 8-K," TJX Companies, Inc., February 20, 2008.

3 "GAO-07-737 personal information: Data breaches are frequent, but evidence of resulting identity theft is limited; however, the full extent is unknown," General Accounting Office, June 2007.

1. PRECURSORS OF DLP

Even before the Internet and all the wonderful benefits it brings to the world, organizations' data were exposed to the outside world. Modems, telex, and fax machines were some of the first enablers of electronic communications. Electronic methods of communications, by default, increase the speed and ease of communication, but they also create inherent security risks. Once IT organizations noticed they were at risk, they immediately started focusing on creating impenetrable moats to surround the "IT castle." As communication protocols standardized and with the mainstream adoption of the Internet, Transmission Control Protocol/Internet Protocol (TCP/IP) became the generally accepted default language of the Internet. This phenomenon brought to light external-facing security technologies and consequently their quick adoption. Some common technologies that protect TCP/IP networks from external threats are:

- *Firewalls.* Inspect network traffic passing through it, and denies or permits passage based on a set of rules.
- *Intrusion detection systems (IDSs).* Sensors log potential suspicious activity and allow for the remediation of the issue.
- *Intrusion prevention systems (IPSs).* React to suspicious activity by automatically performing a reset to the connection or by adjusting the firewall to block network traffic from the suspected malicious source.
- *Antivirus protection.* Attempts to identify, neutralize, or eliminate malicious software.
- *Antispam technology.* Attempts to let in "good" emails and keep out "bad" emails.

The common thread in these technologies: Keep the "bad guys" out while letting normal, efficient business processes occur. These technologies initially offered some very high-level, nongranular features such as blocking a TCP/IP port, allowing communications to and from a certain range of IP addresses, identifying keywords (without context or much flexibility), signatures of viruses, and blocking spam that used common techniques used by spammers.

Once IT organizations had a good handle on external-facing services, the next logical thought comes to mind: What happens if the "bad guy," undertrained or undereducated users, already have access to the information contained in an organization? In some circles of IT, this animal is simply known as an employee. Employees, by their default, "inside" nature, have permission to access the company's most sensitive information to accomplish their jobs. Even though the behavior of nonmalicious employees might cause as much damage as an intentional act, the disgruntled employee or insider is a unique threat that needs to be addressed.

The disgruntled insider, working from within an organization, is a principal source of computer crimes. Insiders may not need a great deal of knowledge about computer hacking because their knowledge of a victim's system often allows them to gain unrestricted access to cause damage to the system or to steal system data. With the advent of technology outsourcing, even non-employees have the rights to view/create/delete some of the most sensitive data assets within an organization. The insider threat could also include contractor personnel and even vendors working onsite. To make matters worse, the ease of finding information to help with hacking systems is no harder than typing a search string into popular search engines. The following is an example of how easy it is for non-"black hats" to perform complicated hacks without much technical knowledge:

1. Open a browser that is connected to the Internet.
2. Go to any popular Internet search engine site.
3. Search for the string "cracking WEP How to."

> *Note:* Observe the number of articles, most with step-by-step instructions, on how to find the Wired Equivalent Privacy (WEP) encryption key to "hijack" a Wi-Fi access point.

So, what happens if an inside worker puts the organization at risk through his activity on the network or corporate assets? The next wave of technologies that IT organizations started to address dealt with the "inside man" issue. Some examples of these types of technologies include:

- *Web filtering.* Can allow/deny content to a user, especially when it is used to restrict material delivered over the Web.
- *Proxy servers.* Services the requests of its clients by forwarding requests to other servers and may block entire functionality such as Internet messaging/chat, Web email, and peer-to-peer file sharing programs.
- *Audit systems (both manual and automated).* Technology that records every packet of data that enters/leave the organization's network. Can be thought of as a network "VCR." Automated appliances feature post-event investigative reports. Manual systems might just use open-source packet-capture technologies writing to a disk for a record of network events.

- *Computer forensic systems.* Is a branch of forensic science pertaining to legal evidence found in computers and digital storage media. Computer forensics adheres to standards of evidence admissible in a court of law. Computer forensics experts investigate data storage devices (such as hard drives, USB drives, CD-ROMs, floppy disks, tape drives, etc.), identifying, preserving, and then analyzing sources of documentary or other digital evidence.
- *Data stores* for email governance.
- *IM- and chat-monitoring services.* The adoption of IM across corporate networks outside the control of IT organizations creates risks and liabilities for companies who do not effectively manage and support IM use. Companies implement specialized IM archiving and security products and services to mitigate these risks and provide safe, secure, productive instant-messaging capabilities to their employees.
- *Document management systems.* A computer system (or set of computer programs) used to track and store electronic documents and/or images of paper documents.

Each of these technologies are necessary security measures implemented in [or "by"] IT organizations to address point or niche areas of vulnerabilities in corporate networks and computer assets.

Even before DLP became a concept, IT organizations have been practicing the tenets of DLP for years. Firewalls at the edge of corporate networks can block access to IP addresses, subnets, and Internet sites. One could say this is the first attempt to keep data where it should reside, within

the organization. DLP should be looked at nothing more than the natural progression of the IT security life cycle.

2. WHAT IS DLP?

Data loss protection is a term that has percolated up from the alphabet soup of computer security concepts in the past few years. Known in the past as information leak detection and prevention (ILDP), used by IDC; information protection and control (IPC); information leak prevention (ILP), coined by Forrester; content monitoring and filtering (CMF), suggested by Gartner; or extrusion prevention system (EPS), the opposite of intrusion prevention system (IPS), the acronym DLP seems to have won out. No matter what acronym of the day is used, *DLP is an automated system to identify anything that leaves the organization that could harm the organization.*

DLP applications try to move away from the point or niche application and give a more holistic approach to coverage, remediation and reporting of data issues. One way of evaluating an organization's level of risk is to look around in an unbiased fashion. The most benign communication technologies could be used against the organization and cause harm.

Before embarking on a DLP project, understanding some example types of harm and/or the corresponding regulations can help with the evaluation. The following sidebar, "Current Data Privacy Legislation and Standards," addresses only a fraction of current data privacy legislation and standards but should give the reader a good understanding of the complexities involved in protecting data.

Current Data Privacy Legislation and Standards

Examples of Harm

Scenario

An administrative assistant confirms a hotel reservation for an upcoming conference by emailing a spreadsheet with employee's credit card numbers with expiration dates; sometimes if they want to make it really easy for the "bad guys," an admin will include the credit card's "secret" PIN, also known as card verification number (CVN).

Problem

Possible violation of GLBA and puts the organization's employees at risk for identity theft and credit card fraud.

Legislation

Gramm-Leach-Bliley Act

GLBA compliance is mandatory; whether a financial institution discloses nonpublic information or not, there must

be a policy in place to protect the information from foreseeable threats in security and data integrity.

Major components put into place to govern the collection, disclosure, and protection of consumers' nonpublic personal information; or personally identifiable information:

- Financial Privacy Rule
- Safeguards Rule
- Pretexting Protection

Financial Privacy Rule

(Subtitle A: Disclosure of Nonpublic Personal Information, codified at 15 U.S.C. § 6801–6809)

The Financial Privacy Rule requires financial institutions to provide each consumer with a privacy notice at the time the consumer relationship is established and annually thereafter. The privacy notice must explain the information collected about the consumer, where that information is shared, how that information is used, and how that information is protected. The notice must also identify the consumer's right to opt out of the information being shared with unaffiliated parties per the Fair Credit Reporting Act. Should the privacy policy change at any point in time, the consumer must be notified again for acceptance. Each time the privacy notice is reestablished, the consumer has the right to opt-out again. The unaffiliated parties receiving the nonpublic information are held to the acceptance terms of the consumer under the original relationship agreement. In summary, the financial privacy rule provides for a privacy policy agreement between the company and the consumer pertaining to the protection of the consumer's personal nonpublic information.

Safeguards Rule

(Subtitle A: Disclosure of Nonpublic Personal Information, codified at 15 U.S.C. § 6801–6809)

The Safeguards Rule requires financial institutions to develop a written information security plan that describes how the company is prepared for and plans to continue to protect clients' nonpublic personal information. (The Safeguards Rule also applies to information of those no longer consumers of the financial institution.) This plan must include:

- Denoting at least one employee to manage the safeguards
- Constructing a thorough risk management on each department handling the nonpublic information
- Developing, monitoring, and testing a program to secure the information
- Changing the safeguards as needed with the changes in how information is collected, stored, and used

This rule is intended to do what most businesses should already be doing: *protect their clients*. The Safeguards Rule forces financial institutions to take a closer look at how they manage private data and to do a risk analysis on their current processes. No process is perfect, so this has meant that every financial institution has had to make some effort to comply with the GLBA.

Pretexting Protection

(Subtitle B: Fraudulent Access to Financial Information, codified at 15 U.S.C. § 6821–6827)

Pretexting (sometimes referred to as *social engineering*) occurs when someone tries to gain access to personal nonpublic information without proper authority to do so. This may entail requesting private information while impersonating the account holder, by phone, by mail, by email, or even by phishing (i.e., using a phony Web site or email to collect data). The GLBA encourages the organizations covered by the GLBA to implement safeguards against pretexting.

For example, a well-written plan to meet GLBA's Safeguards Rule ("develop, monitor, and test a program to secure the information") ought to include a section on training employees to recognize and deflect inquiries made under pretext. In the United States, pretexting by individuals is punishable as a common law crime of False Pretenses.

Scenario

An HR employee, whose main job function is to process claims, forwards via email an employee's Explanation of Benefits that contains a variety of Protected Health Information. The email is sent in the clear, unencrypted, to the organization's healthcare provider.

Problem

Could violate the Health Insurance Portability and Accountability Act (HIPAA), depending on the type of organization.

Legislation

The Privacy Rule

The Privacy Rule took effect on April 14, 2003, with a one-year extension for certain "small plans." It establishes regulations for the use and disclosure of Protected Health Information (PHI). PHI is any information about health status, provision of health care, or payment for health care that can be linked to an individual. This is interpreted rather broadly and includes any part of a patient's medical record or payment history.

Covered entities must disclose PHI to the individual within 30 days upon request. They also must disclose PHI when required to do so by law, such as reporting suspected child abuse to state child welfare agencies.

A covered entity may disclose PHI to facilitate treatment, payment, or healthcare operations or if the covered entity has obtained authorization from the individual. However, when a covered entity discloses any PHI, it must make a reasonable effort to disclose only the minimum necessary information required to achieve its purpose.

The Privacy Rule gives individuals the right to request that a covered entity correct any inaccurate PHI. It also requires covered entities to take reasonable steps to ensure the confidentiality of communications with individuals. For example, an individual can ask to be called at his or her work number, instead of home or cell phone number.

The Privacy Rule requires covered entities to notify individuals of uses of their PHI. Covered entities must also keep track of disclosures of PHI and document privacy policies and procedures. They must appoint a Privacy Official and a contact person responsible for receiving complaints and train all members of their workforce in procedures regarding PHI.

An individual who believes that the Privacy Rule is not being upheld can file a complaint with the Department of Health and Human Services Office for Civil Rights (OCR).

Scenario

An employee opens an email whose subject is "25 Reasons Why Beer is Better than Women." The employee finds this joke amusing and forwards the email to other coworkers using the corporate email system.

Problem

Puts the organization in an exposed position for claims of sexual harassment and a hostile workplace environment.

Legislation

In the U.S., the Civil Rights Act of 1964 Title VII prohibits employment discrimination based on race, sex, color, national origin, or religion. The prohibition of sex discrimination covers both females and males. This discrimination occurs when the sex of the worker is made a condition of employment (i.e., all female waitpersons or male carpenters) or where this is a job requirement that does not mention sex but ends up barring many more persons of one sex than the other from the job (such as height and weight limits).

In 1998, Chevron settled, out of court, a lawsuit brought by several female employees after the "25 Reasons" email was widely circulated throughout the organization. Ultimately, Chevron settled out of court for $2.2 million.

Scenario

A retail store server electronically transmits daily point-of-sale (POS) transactions to the main corporate billing server. The POS system records the time, date, register number, employee number, part number, quantity, and if paid for by credit card, the card number. This transaction occurs nightly as part of a batch job and is transmitted over the store's Wi-Fi network.

Problem

PCI DSS stands for Payment Card Industry Data Security Standard. It was developed by the major credit card companies as a guideline to help organizations that process card payments prevent credit-card fraud, cracking, and various other security vulnerabilities and threats. A company processing, storing, or transmitting payment card data must be PCI DSS compliant or risk losing its ability to process credit card payments and being audited and/or fined. Merchants and payment card service providers must validate their compliance periodically. This validation gets conducted by auditors (that is persons who are the PCI DSS Qualified Security Assessors, or QSAs). Although individuals receive QSA status, reports on compliance can only be signed off by an individual QSA on behalf of a PCI council-approved consultancy. Smaller companies, processing *fewer* than about 80,000 transactions a year, are allowed to perform a self-assessment questionnaire. Penalties are often accessed and fines of $25,000 per month are possible for large merchants for noncompliance.

PCI DSS requires 12 requirements to be in compliance:

Requirement 1: Install and maintain a firewall configuration to protect cardholder data

Firewalls are computer devices that control computer traffic allowed into and out of a company's network, as well as traffic into more sensitive areas within a company's internal network. A firewall examines all network traffic and blocks those transmissions that do not meet the specified security criteria.

Requirement 2: Do not use vendor-supplied defaults for system passwords and other security parameters

Hackers (external and internal to a company) often use vendor default passwords and other vendor default settings to compromise systems. These passwords and settings are well known in hacker communities and easily determined via public information.

Requirement 3: Protect stored cardholder data

Encryption is a critical component of cardholder data protection. If an intruder circumvents other network security controls and gains access to encrypted data, without the proper cryptographic keys, the data is unreadable and unusable to that person. Other effective methods of protecting stored data should be considered as potential risk mitigation opportunities. For example, methods for minimizing risk include not storing cardholder data unless absolutely necessary, truncating cardholder data if full PAN is not needed and not sending PAN in unencrypted emails.

Requirement 4: Encrypt transmission of cardholder data across open, public networks

Sensitive information must be encrypted during transmission over networks that are easy and common for a hacker to intercept, modify, and divert data while in transit.

Requirement 5: Use and regularly update anti-virus software or programs

Many vulnerabilities and malicious viruses enter the network via employees' email activities. Antivirus software must be used on all systems commonly affected by viruses to protect systems from malicious software.

Requirement 6: Develop and maintain secure systems and applications

Unscrupulous individuals use security vulnerabilities to gain privileged access to systems. Many of these vulnerabilities are fixed by vendor-provided security patches. All systems must have the most recently released, appropriate software patches to protect against exploitation by employees, external hackers, and viruses. *Note:* Appropriate software patches are those patches that have been evaluated and tested sufficiently to determine that the patches do not conflict with existing security configurations. For in-house developed applications, numerous vulnerabilities can be avoided by using standard system development processes and secure coding techniques.

Requirement 7: Restrict access to cardholder data by business need-to-know

This requirement ensures critical data can only be accessed by authorized personnel.

Requirement 8: Assign a unique ID to each person with computer access

Assigning a unique identification (ID) to each person with access ensures that actions taken on critical data and systems are performed by, and can be traced to, known and authorized users.

Requirement 9: Restrict physical access to cardholder data

Any physical access to data or systems that house cardholder data provides the opportunity for individuals to access devices or data and to remove systems or hardcopies, and should be appropriately restricted.

Requirement 10: Track and monitor all access to network resources and cardholder data

Logging mechanisms and the ability to track user activities are critical. The presence of logs in all environments allows thorough tracking and analysis if something does go wrong. Determining the cause of a compromise is very difficult without system activity logs.

Requirement 11: Regularly test security systems and processes

Vulnerabilities are being discovered continually by hackers and researchers, and being introduced by new software. Systems, processes, and custom software should be tested frequently to ensure security is maintained over time and with any changes in software.

Requirement 12: Maintain a policy that addresses information security for employees and contractors

A strong security policy sets the security tone for the whole company and informs employees what is expected of them. All employees should be aware of the sensitivity of data and their responsibilities for protecting it.[4]

Organizations are facing pressures to become Sarbanes-Oxley compliant.

SOX Section 404: Assessment of internal control

The most contentious aspect of SOX is Section 404, which requires management and the external auditor to report on the adequacy of the company's internal control over financial reporting (ICFR). This is the most costly aspect of the legislation for companies to implement, as documenting and testing important financial manual and automated controls requires enormous effort.

Under Section 404 of the Act, management is required to produce an "internal control report" as part of each annual Exchange Act report. The report must affirm "the responsibility of management for establishing and maintaining an adequate internal control structure and procedures for financial reporting." The report must also "contain an assessment, as of the end of the most recent fiscal year of the Company, of the effectiveness of the internal control structure and procedures of the issuer for financial reporting." To do this, managers are generally adopting an internal control framework such as that described in Committee of Sponsoring Organization of the Treadway Commission (COSO).

Both management and the external auditor are responsible for performing their assessment in the context of a top-down risk assessment, which requires management to base both the scope of its assessment and evidence gathered on risk. Both the Public Company Accounting Oversight Board (PCAOB) and SEC recently issued guidance on this topic to help alleviate the significant costs of compliance and better focus the assessment on the most critical risk areas.

The recently released Auditing Standard No. 5 of the PCAOB, which superseded Auditing Standard No 2. has the following key requirements for the external auditor:

- Assess both the design and operating effectiveness of selected internal controls related to significant accounts and relevant assertions, in the context of material misstatement risks
- Understand the flow of transactions, including IT aspects, sufficiently to identify points at which a misstatement could arise
- Evaluate company-level (entity-level) controls, which correspond to the components of the COSO framework
- Perform a fraud risk assessment
- Evaluate controls designed to prevent or detect fraud, including management override of controls
- Evaluate controls over the period-end financial reporting process;
- Scale the assessment based on the size and complexity of the company
- Rely on management's work based on factors such as competency, objectivity, and risk
- Evaluate controls over the safeguarding of assets
- Conclude on the adequacy of internal control over financial reporting

The recently released SEC guidance is generally consistent with the PCAOB's guidance above, only intended for management.

---

4 "Portions of this production are provided courtesy of PCI Security Standards Council, LLC ("PCI SSC") and/or its licensors. © 2007 PCI Security Standards Council, LLC. All rights reserved. Neither PCI SSC nor its licensors endorses this product, its provider or the methods, procedures, statements, views, opinions or advice contained herein. All references to documents, materials or portions thereof provided by PCI SSC (the "PCI Materials") should be read as qualified by the actual PCI Materials. For questions regarding the PCI Materials, please contact PCI SSC through its Web site at https://www.pcisecuritystandards.org."

After the release of this guidance, the SEC required smaller public companies to comply with SOX Section 404, companies with year ends after December 15, 2007. Smaller public companies performing their first management assessment under Sarbanes-Oxley Section 404 may find their first year of compliance after December 15, 2007 particularly challenging. To help unravel the maze of uncertainty, Lord & Benoit, a SOX compliance company, issued "10 Threats to Compliance for Smaller Companies" (www.section404.org/pdf/sox_404_10_threats_to_compliance_for_smaller_public_companies.pdf), which gathered historical evidence of material weaknesses from companies with revenues under $100 million. The research was compiled aggregating the results of 148 first-time companies with material weaknesses and revenues under $100 million. The following were the 10 leading material weaknesses in Lord & Benoit's study: accounting and disclosure controls, treasury, competency and training of accounting personnel, control environment, design of controls/lack of effective compensating controls, revenue recognition, financial closing process, inadequate account reconciliations, information technology and consolidations, mergers, intercompany accounts.[5]

Scenario

A guidance counselor at a high school gets a request from a student's prospective college. The college asked for the student's transcripts. The guidance counselor sends the transcript over the schools email system unencrypted.

Problem

FERPA privacy concerns, depending on the age of the student.

Legislation

The Family Educational Rights and Privacy Act (FERPA) (20 U.S.C. § 1232g; 34 CFR Part 99) is a federal law that protects the privacy of student education records. The law applies to all schools that receive funds under an applicable program of the U.S. Department of Education.

FERPA gives parents certain rights with respect to their children's education records. These rights transfer to the student when he or she reaches the age of 18 or attends a school beyond the high school level. Students to whom the rights have transferred are "eligible students."

Parents or eligible students have the right to inspect and review the student's education records maintained by the school. Schools are not required to provide copies of records unless, for reasons such as great distance, it is impossible for parents or eligible students to review the records. Schools may charge a fee for copies.

Parents or eligible students have the right to request that a school correct records that they believe to be inaccurate or misleading. If the school decides not to amend the record, the parent or eligible student then has the right to a formal hearing. After the hearing, if the school still decides not to amend the record, the parent or eligible student has the right to place a statement with the record setting forth his or her view about the contested information.

Generally, schools must have written permission from the parent or eligible student in order to release any information from a student's education record. However, FERPA allows schools to disclose those records, without consent, to the following parties or under the following conditions (34 CFR § 99.31):

- School officials with legitimate educational interest
- Other schools to which a student is transferring
- Specified officials for audit or evaluation purposes
- Appropriate parties in connection with financial aid to a student
- Organizations conducting certain studies for or on behalf of the school
- Accrediting organizations
- To comply with a judicial order or lawfully issued subpoena
- Appropriate officials in cases of health and safety emergencies
- State and local authorities, within a juvenile justice system, pursuant to specific State law

Schools may disclose, without consent, "directory" information such as a student's name, address, telephone number, date and place of birth, honors and awards, and dates of attendance. However, schools must tell parents and eligible students about directory information and allow parents and eligible students a reasonable amount of time to request that the school not disclose directory information about them. Schools must notify parents and eligible students annually of their rights under FERPA. The actual means of notification (special letter, inclusion in a PTA bulletin, student handbook, or newspaper article) is left to the discretion of each school.

Scenario

Employee job hunting, posting resumes and trying to find another job while working. See Figure 43.1 for an example of a DLP system capturing the full content of a user going through the resignation process.

Problem

Loss of productivity for that employee.
Warning sign for a possible disgruntled employee.

---

5 Wikipedia contributors, "Sarbanes-Oxley Act," Wikipedia, Wednesday, 2008-05-14 14:31 UTC, http://en.wikipedia.org/wiki/Sarbannes_Oxley_Act.

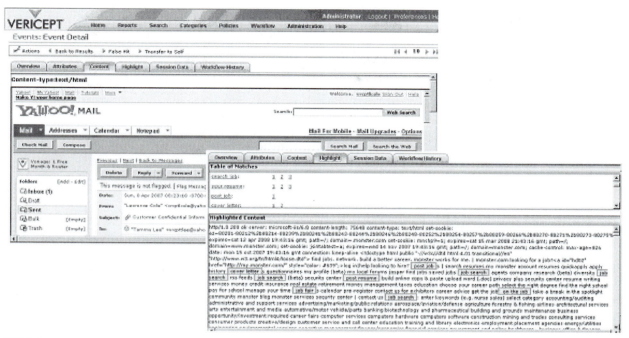

FIGURE 43.1 Webmail event: Content rendering of a resignation event.[6]

3. WHERE TO BEGIN?

A reasonable place to begin talking about DLP is with the department of the organization that handles corporate policy and/or governance (see sidebar, "An Example of an Acceptable Use Policy"). Monitoring employees is at best an interesting proposition. Corporate culture can drive whether monitoring of any kind is even allowed. A good litmus test would be the types of notice that appear in the employee handbook.

An Example of an Acceptable Use Policy

Use of Email and Computer Systems

All information created, accessed or stored using company applications, systems, or resources, including email, is the property of the company. Users do not have a right to privacy regarding any activity conducted using the company's system. The company can review, read, access, or otherwise monitor email and all activities on the company system or any other system accessed by use of the company system. In addition, the Company could be required to allow others to read email or other documents on the company's system in the context of a lawsuit or other legal action.

All users must abide by the rules of network etiquette, which include being polite and using the network and the Internet in a safe and legal manner. The company or authorized company officials will make a good faith judgment as to which materials, files, information, software, communications, and other content and activity are permitted and prohibited based on the following guidelines and under the particular circumstances.

Among the uses that are considered unacceptable and constitute a violation of this policy are the following:

- Using, transmitting, receiving, or seeking inappropriate, offensive, swearing, vulgar, profane, suggestive, obscene, abusive, harassing, belligerent, threatening, defamatory (harming another's reputation by lies), or misleading language or materials; revealing personal information such as another's home address, home telephone number, or Social Security number; making ethnic, sexual-preference, age or gender-related slurs or jokes.

- Users may never harass, intimidate, threaten others, or engage in other illegal activity (including pornography, terrorism, espionage, theft, or drugs) by email or other posting. All such instances should be reported to management for appropriate action. In addition to violating this policy, such behavior may also violate other company policies or civil or criminal laws.

---

6 Figures 43.1, 43.2 (a-c), and 43.3 (a-b), inclusive of the Vericept trademark and logo, are provided by Vericept Corporation solely for use as screenshots herein and may not be reproduced or used in any other way without the prior written permission of Vericept Corporation. All rights reserved.

- Among the uses that are considered unacceptable and constitute a violation of this policy are downloading or transmitting copyrighted materials without permission from the owner of the copyright on those materials. Even if materials on the network or the Internet are not marked with the copyright symbol, you should assume that they are protected under copyright laws unless there is explicit permission from the copyright holder on the materials to use them.
- Users must not use email or other communications methods, including but not limited to news group posting, blogs, forums, instant messaging, and chat servers, to send company proprietary or confidential information to any unauthorized party. Such information may be disclosed to authorized persons in encrypted files if sent over publicly accessible media such as the Internet or other broadcast media such as wireless communication. Such information may be sent in unencrypted files only within the company system. Users are responsible for properly labeling such information.

Certain specific policies extend the Company's acceptable use policy by placing further restrictions on that activity. Examples include, but are not limited to: software usage, network usage, shell policy, remote access policy, wireless policy, and the mobile email access policy. These and any additional policies are available from the IT Web site on the intranet.

Your use of the network and the Internet is a privilege, not a right. If you violate this policy, at a minimum you will be subject to having your access to the network and the Internet terminated. You breach this policy not only by affirmatively violating the above provisions but also by failing to report any violations of this policy by other users which come to your attention. Further, you violate this policy if you permit another to use your account or password to access the network or the Internet, including but not limited to someone whose access has been denied or terminated. Sharing your account with anyone is a violation of this policy. It is your responsibility to keep your account secure by choosing a sufficiently complex password and changing it on a regular basis.

Another good indicator that the organization would be a good fit for a DLP application is the sign-on screen that appears before or after a computer user logs on to her workstation (see sidebar, "Accessing a Company's Information System").

Accessing a Company's Information System

You are accessing a Company's information system (IS) that is provided for Company-authorized use only. By using this IS, you consent to the following conditions:

- The Company routinely monitors communications occurring on this IS, and any device attached to this IS, for purposes including, but not limited to, penetration testing, monitoring, network defense, quality control, and employee misconduct, law enforcement, and counterintelligence investigations.
- At any time the Company may inspect and/or seize data stored on this IS and any device attached to this IS.
- Communications occurring on or data stored on this IS, or any device attached to this IS, are not private. They are subject to routine monitoring and search.
- Any communications occurring on or data stored on this IS, or any device attached to this IS, may be disclosed or used for any Company-authorized purpose.
- Security protections may be utilized on this IS to protect certain interests that are important to the Company. For example, password, access cards, encryption or biometric access controls provide security for the benefit of the Company. These protections are not provided for your benefit or privacy and may be modified or eliminated at the Company's discretion.

Some organizations are more apt to take advantage of the laws and rights that companies have to defend themselves. Simply asking around and performing informal interviews with Human Resources, Security, and Legal can save days and weeks of time down the line.

In summary, implementing a DLP application without the proper Human Resources, Security, and Legal policies could be a waste of time because IT professionals *will* catch employees violating security standard. The events in a DLP system must be actionable and have "teeth" for changes to take place.

4. DATA IS LIKE WATER

As most anyone who has had a water leak in dwelling knows, water will find a way out of where it is supposed to go. Pipes are meant to direct the proper flow of water both in and out. If a leak happens, the occupant will eventually find a damp spot, a watermark, or a real drip. It might take minutes or days to notice the leak and might take just as long to find the source of the leak.

Much like the water analogy, employees are given data "pipes" to do their jobs with enabling technology provided by the IT organization. Instead of water flowing through, data can ingress/egress the organization in multiple methods.

Corporate email is a powerful efficient time saving tool that speeds communication. A user can attach a 10 megabyte file, personal pictures, a recipe for chili and next quarter's marketing plan or an acquisition target. Chat and

IM is the quickest growing form of electronic communication and a great enabler of efficient workflow. Files can be sent as well over these protocols or "pipes." Web mail is usually the "weapon of choice" by users who like to conduct personal business at work. Web mail allows users to attach files of any type.

Thus, the IT network "plumbing" needs to be monitored, maintained, and evaluated on an ongoing basis. The U.S. government has published a complete and well-rounded standard that organizations can use as a good first step to compare where they are strong and where they can use improvement.

The U.S. Government Federal Information Security Management Act of 2002 (FISMA) offers reasonable guidelines that most organizations could benefit by adopting. Even though FISMA is mandated for government agencies and contractors, it can be applied to the corporate world as well.

FISMA sets forth a comprehensive framework for ensuring the effectiveness of security controls over information resources that support federal operations and assets. FISMA's framework creates a cycle of risk management activities necessary for an effective security program, and these activities are similar to the principles noted in our study of the risk management activities of leading private sector organizations—assessing risk, establishing a central management focal point, implementing appropriate policies and procedures, promoting awareness, and monitoring and evaluating policy and control effectiveness. More specifically, FISMA requires the head of each agency to provide information security protections commensurate with the risk and magnitude of harm resulting from the unauthorized access, use, disclosure, disruption, modification, or destruction of information and information systems used or operated by the agency or on behalf of the agency. In this regard, FISMA requires that agencies implement information security programs that, among other things, include:

- Periodic assessments of the risk
- Risk-based policies and procedures
- Subordinate plans for providing adequate information security for networks, facilities, and systems or groups of information systems, as appropriate
- Security awareness training for agency personnel, including contractors and other users of information systems that support the operations and assets of the agency
- Periodic testing and evaluation of the effectiveness of information security policies, procedures, and practices, performed with a frequency depending on risk, but no less than annually

- A process for planning, implementing, evaluating, and documenting remedial action to address any deficiencies
- Procedures for detecting, reporting, and responding to security incidents
- Plans and procedures to ensure continuity of operations

In addition, agencies must develop and maintain an inventory of major information systems that is updated at least annually and report annually to the Director of OMB and several Congressional Committees on the adequacy and effectiveness of their information security policies, procedures, and practices and compliance with the requirements of the act. An internal risk assessment of what types of "communication," both manual and electronic, that are allowed within the organization can give the DLP evaluator a baseline of the type of transmission that are probably taking place.

Some types of communications that should be evaluated are not always obvious but could be just as damaging as electronic methods. The following list encompasses some of those obvious and not so obvious methods:

- Pencil and paper
- Photocopier
- Fax
- Voicemail
- Digital camera
- Jump drive
- MP3/iPod
- DVD/CD-ROM/3½ in. floppy
- Magnetic tape
- SATA drives
- IM/chat
- FTP/FTPS
- SMTP/POP3/IMAP
- HTTP post/response
- HTTPS
- Telnet
- SCP
- P2P
- Rogue ports
- GoToMyPC
- Web conferencing systems

5. YOU DON'T KNOW WHAT YOU DON'T KNOW

Embarking on a DLP evaluation or implementation can be a straightforward exercise. The IT professional usually has a mandate in mind and a few problems that the

DLP application will address. Invariably, many other issues will arise as DLP applications do a very good job at finding most potential security and privacy issues.

> *Reports that say that something hasn't happened are always interesting to me, because as we know, there are 'known knowns'; there are things we know we know. We also know there are 'known unknowns'; that is to say we know there are some things we do not know. But there are also 'unknown unknowns'—the ones we don't know we don't know.*
>
> —Donald Rumsfeld, U.S. Department of Defense, February 12, 2002

Once the corporate culture has established that DLP is worth investigating or worth implementing, the next logical step would be performing a risk/exposure assessment. Several DLP vendors offer free pilots or proof of concepts and should be leveraged to jumpstart the data risk assessment for a very low monetary cost.

A risk/exposure assessment usually involves placing a server on the edge of the corporate network and sampling/recording the network traffic that is egressing the organization. In addition, the assessment might involve look for high-risk files at rest and the activity of what is happening on the workstation environment. Most if not all DLP applications have predefined risk categories that cover a wide range of risk profiles. Some examples are:

- Regulations: GLBA, HIPAA, PCI-DSS, SOX, FERPA, PHI
- Acceptable use: Violence, gangs, profanity, adult themes, weapons, harassment, racism, pornography
- Productivity: Streaming media, resignation, shopping, Webmail
- Insider hacker activity: Root activity, nmap, stack, smashing code, keyloggers

Deciding what risk categories are most important to your organization can streamline the DLP evaluation. If data categories are turned on but not likely to impact what is truly important to the organization, the test/pilot result will contain a lot of "noise." Focus on the "low-hanging fruit." For example, if the organization's life blood is customer data, focus on the categories that address those types of leaks.

Precision versus Recall

Before the precision versus recall discussion can take place, definitions are necessary:

- *False positive.* A false positive occurs when the DLP application-monitoring or DLP application-blocking

techniques wrongly classify a legitimate transmission or event as "uninteresting" and, as a result, the event must be remediated anyway. Remediating an event is a time-consuming process which could involve one to many administrators dispositioning the event. A high number of false positives is normal during an initial implementation, but the number should fall after the DLP application is tuned.

- *False negative.* A false negative occurs when a transmission is not detected as interesting. The problem with false negatives is usually the DLP administrator does not know these transmissions are happening in the first place. An analogy would be a bank employee who embezzles thousands of dollars and the bank does not notice the theft until it is too late.
- *True positive.* Condition present and the DLP application records the event for remediation.
- *True negative.* Condition not present and the DLP application does not record it.

DLP application testing and tuning can involve a trade-off:

- The acceptable level of false positives (in which a nonmatch is declared to be a match).
- The acceptable level of false negatives (in which an actual match is not detected).

An evaluator can think of this process as a slider bar concept, with false negatives on the left side and false positives on the right. A properly tuned DLP application minimizes false positives and diminishes the chances of false negatives.

This iterative process of tuning is called *thresholding*. Creating the proper threshold eventually leads to the minimization of acceptable amounts of false positives with no or minimal false negatives.

An easy way to achieve thresholding is to make the test more restrictive or more sensitive. The more restrictive the test is, the higher the risk of rejecting true positives; and, the less sensitive the test is, the higher the risk of accepting false positives.

6. HOW DO DLP APPLICATIONS WORK?

The way that most DLP applications capture interesting events is through different kinds of analysis engines. Most support simple keyword matching. For example, any time you see the phrase "project phoenix" in a data transmission, the network event is stored for later review.

Keywords can be grouped and joined. Regular expression (RegEx) support is featured in most of today's DLP applications. Regular expressions provide a concise and flexible means for identifying strings of text of interest, such as particular characters, words, or patterns of characters. Regular expressions are written in a formal language that can be interpreted by a regular expression processor, a program that either serves as a parser generator or examines text and identifies parts that match the provided specification. A real-world example would be the expression:

$$(r|b)?ed$$

Any transmission that contained the word *red*, *bed*, or even *ed* would be captured for later investigation. Regular expressions can also do pattern matching on credit card number and U.S. Social Security numbers:

$$\wedge d\{3\} - ?\backslash d\{2\} - ?\backslash d\{4\}$$

which can be read: Any three numbers followed by an optional dash followed by any two numbers followed by an optional dash and then followed by any four numbers. Regular expressions offer a certain level of efficiencies but cannot address all DLP concerns. Weighting of either keyword(s) and/or RegEx's can help. A real-world example might be the word *red* is worth three points and the SSN is worth five points, but for an event to hit the transmission, it must contain 22 points. In this example, four SSNs and the word *red* would trigger an event (4 times 5 plus 3 equals 23, which would trigger the event score rule). Scoring can help address the thresholding issue. To address some of the limitation of simple keyword and RegEx's, DLP applications can also look for data "signatures" or hashes of data. Hashing creates a mathematical representation of the sensitive data and looks for that signature. Sensitive data or representative types of data can be bulk loaded from databases and example files.

7. EAT YOUR VEGETABLES

DLP is like the layers of an onion. Once the first layer of protection is implemented, the next layer should/could be addressed. There are many different forms of DLP applications, depending on the velocity and location of the sensitive data.

Data in Motion

Data in motion is an easy place to start implementing a DLP application because most can function in "passive" mode, meaning it looks at only a copy of the actual data egressing/ingressing the network. One way to look at data-in-motion monitoring is like a very intelligent VCR. Instead of recording every packet of information that passes in and out of an organization, DLP applications only capture, flag, and record the transmissions that fall within the categories/policies that are turned on (see sidebar, "Case Study: DLP Applications"). There are two main types of data-in-motion analysis:

- *Passive monitoring*. Using a Switched Port Analyzer (SPAN) on a router, port mirror on a switch or a network tap(s) that feeds the outbound network traffic to the DLP application for analysis.
- Active (inline) enforcement. Using an active egress port or through a proxy server, some DLP applications can stop the transmission from happening. The port itself can be reset or the proxy server can show a failure of transmission. The event that keyed off the reset or failure is still recorded.

Case Study: DLP Applications

Background

A Fortune 500 Company has tens of thousands of employees with access to the Internet through an authenticated method. The Company has recently retired a version of laptops with the associated docking station, monitors and mice. New laptops were purchased and given to the employees. The old assets were retired to a storage closet. One manager noticed some docking stations had gone missing. That in and of itself was not concerning as this company had a liberal policy of donating old computer assets to charity. After looking in the company's Asset Management System and talking to the organization's charity manager, the manager found this was not the case. An investigation was launched both electronically and through traditional investigative means.

Action

The organization had a DLP application in use with data-in-motion implemented. This particular DLP application had a strong acceptable use set of categories/policies. One of them was "Shopping," which covered both traditional shopping outlets but also popular online auction sites. The DLP investigator selected the report that returns all transmissions that violated the "Shopping" category and contained the keyword of the model number of the docking station. Within seconds, a user from within their network was found auctioning the exact same model docking stations as the ones the company had just retired.

Result

The Fortune 500 Company was able to remediate a situation quickly that not only stopped the loss of physical assets, but get rid of an employee that was stealing while at work. The real value of this exercise could have been, if an employee is "ok" with stealing assets to make a few extra dollars on the company's dime, one might ask, What else might an employee that thinks it is ok to steal do?

Data at Rest

Static computer files on drives, removable media or even tape can grow to the millions in large multinational organizations. Unless tight controls are implemented, data can spawn out of control. Even though email transmissions account for more than 80% of DLP violations, data-at-rest files that are resting where they are not supposed to be can be a major concern (see sidebar, "Case Study: Data-at-Rest Files").

Data-at-rest risk can occur in other places besides the personal computer's file system. One of the benefits of networked computer systems is the ability to share files. File shares can also pose a risk because the original owner of the file now has no idea what happened to the file after they share it.

The same can be said of many Web-based collaboration and document management platforms that are available in the market today. Collaboration tools can be used to host Web sites that can be used to access shared workspaces and documents, as well as specialized applications such as wikis, blogs, and many other forms of applications, from within a browser. Once again, the wonderful world of shared computing can also put an organization's data at risk.

DLP application can help with databases as well and half the battle is knowing where the organizations most sensitive data resides. The data-at-rest function of DLP applications can definitely help.

Data in Use

DLP applications can also help keep data where it is supposed to stay (see sidebar, "Case Study: Data-in-Use Files"). Agent-based technologies that run resident on the guest operating system can track, monitor,

---

Case Study: Data-at-Rest Files

Background

A Fortune 500 Company has multiple customer service centers located throughout the United States. Each customer server representative has a personal computer with a hard drive and Internet access. The representative's job entails taking inbound phone calls to help their customers with account management including auto-pay features. Auto-pay setup information could include taking a credit-card number and expiration date and/or setting up an electronic fund transfer payment which includes an ABA routing number and account number. This sensitive information is supposed to be entered directly into the corporate enterprise resource planning (ERP) system application. Invariably customer service representatives run into issues during this process (connectivity to the ERP system is interrupted, power goes down, computer needs to be rebooted, etc.) and sensitive data finds its way into unapproved places on the personal computer—a note text file, a word-processing document, an electronic spreadsheet, or in an email system.

Even though employees went through training for their job that included handling of sensitive data, the management suspected that data was finding a way out of the ERP system. Another issue that the management faced with a very high turnover ratio and that employee training was falling behind.

Action

A DLP data-at-rest pilot was performed and over one thousand files that contained credit-card numbers and other customer personal identifiable information were found.

Result

The Fortune 500 Company was able to cleanse the hard drives of files that contained sensitive data by using the legend the DLP application provided. More important, the systemic cause of the problem had to be readdressed with training and tightening down the security of the representative, personal computers.

block, report, quarantine or notify the usage of particular kinds of data files and/or the contents of the file itself. Policies can be centrally administered and "pushed" out of the organization's computer assets. Since the agent is resident on the computer, it can also create an inventory of every file on the hard drives, removable media and even music players. Since the agent knows of the

file systems down to the operating system level, it can allow or disallow certain types of removable media. For example, an organization might allow a USB storage device if and only if the device supports encryption. The agent will disallow any other types of USB devices such as music players, cameras, removable hard drives, and so on.

Case Study: Data-in-Use Files

Background

An electronics manufacturer has created a revolutionary new design for a cell phone and wants to keep the design and photographs of the prototype under wraps. They have had problems in the past with pictures ending up on blog sites, competitors "borrowing" design ideas, and even other countries creating similar products and launching an imitator within weeks of the initial product launch.

Action

Each document, whether a spreadsheet, document, diagram, or photograph, was secretly watermarked with a special secret code. At the same time, the main security

group created an organizational unit within their main LDAP application. This was the only group that had permission to access the watermarked files. At the same time, a DLP application agent was rolled out to the computer assets within the organization. If anyone "found" a marked file and tried to do something with it, unless they were in the privileged group, access was denied *and* an alert (see Figure 43.2c) went back to the main DLP reporting server.

Result

The electronics manufacturer was able to deliver its revolutionary product to market in a secure manner and on time.

Much like the different flavors of DLP that are available (data in motion, data at rest and data in use), conditions of the severity of action that DLP applications take on the event can vary. A good place to diagnose the problems organizations are currently facing would be to start with Monitoring (see sidebar, "Case Study in Monitoring"). Monitoring is only capturing the actual event that took place to review

at a later time. Most DLP applications offer real-time or near real-time monitoring of events that violated a policy. Monitoring coupled with escalation can help most organizations immediately. Escalation works well with monitoring as when an event happens, rules can be put into place on who should be notified and/or how the notification should take place. Email is the most common form of escalation.

Case Study in Monitoring

Background

A large data provider of financial account records dealt with millions of customer records. The customer records contained account numbers and other nonpublic, personal information (NPPI) and Social Security numbers. The data provider mandated the protection of this type of sensitive data was the top priority of the upcoming year.

Action

A DLP application was implemented. Social Security number, customer information, and NPPI categories were turned on. After one week, over 1000 data transmissions were captured

over various protocols (email, FTP, and Web traffic). After investigating the results, over 800 transmissions were found to have come from a pair of servers that was set up to transmit account information to partners.

Result

By simply changing the type of transmission to a secure, encrypted format, the data was secured with no interruption of normal business processes. Monitoring was the way to go in this case and made the organization more secure and minimized the number of processes that were impacted.

Another action that DLP application supports is notification. Notification can temporarily interrupt that transmission of an event and could require user interaction. See Figure 43.2a for an example of the kind of "bounce" email

a user could receive if she sends an email containing sensitive information. See Figure 43.2b for an example of the type of notification a user could see if he tries to open a sensitive data document. The DLP application could make

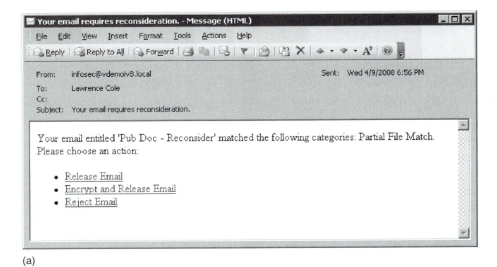

(a)

(b)

(c)

FIGURE 43.2 (a) Email with user notification on the fly; (b) PC user tries to access a protected document; and (c) policy prompts a justification alert.[6]

the user justify why access is needed, deny access, or simply log the attempt back to the main reporting console.

Notification can enhance the current user education program in place and serve as a gentle reminder. The onus of action lies solely on the end user and does not take resources from the already thinly stretched IT organization.

The next level of severity of implementing DLP could be quarantining and then outright blocking. Quarantining events places the transmission in "stasis" for review from a DLP administrator. The quarantine administrator can release, release with encryption, block, or send the event back to the offending user for remediation. Blocking is an action that stops the transmission in its entirety based upon the contents.

Both quarantining and blocking should be used sparingly and only after the organization feels comfortable

with the policies and procedures. The first time an executive tries to send a transmission and cannot because of the action set forth in the DLP application, the IT professional can potentially lose his job.

8. IT'S A FAMILY AFFAIR, NOT JUST IT SECURITY'S PROBLEM

The IT organization does and most likely maintains the corporate email system; almost everyone across all departments within an organization uses email. The same can be said for the DLP application. Even though IT will implement and maintain the DLP application, the events will most likely come from all different types of users across the entire organization. When concerning events are captured and there will be many captured

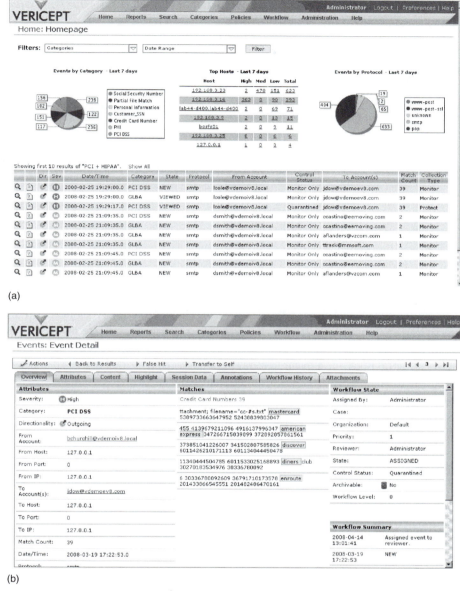

FIGURE 43.3 (a) Dashboard; (b) Email Event Overview.[6]

by the DLP application, most management will turn to IT to resolve the problem. The IT organization should not become the "police and judge." Each business unit should have published standards on how events should be handled and escalated.

Most DLP applications can segregate duties to allow non-IT personnel to review the disposition of the event captured. One way to address DLP would be to assign certain types of events to administrators in the appropriate department. If a racial email is captured, the most appropriate department might be a Human Resource employee. If a personal information transmission is captured, a compliance officer should be assigned. IT might be tasked if the nature of the event is hacking related.

Users can also have a level of privilege within the DLP application. Reviewers can be assigned to initial investigations of only certain types or all events. If necessary, an event can be escalated to a reviewer's superior. Users can have administrative or reports-only rights.

Each of these functions relates to the concept of workflow within the DLP application. Events need to be prioritized, escalated, reviewed, annotated, ignored and eventually closed. The workflow should be easy to use across the DLP community and reports should be easily assessable and created/tuned. See Figure 43.3a for an example of an Executive Dashboard that allows the user to quickly assess the state of risk and allows for a quick-click drill down for more granular information.

Figure 43.3b is the result of a click from the Executive Dashboard to the full content capture of the event.

9. VENDORS, VENDORS EVERYWHERE! WHO DO YOU BELIEVE?

At the end of the day the DLP market and applications are maturing at an incredible pace. Vendors are releasing new features and functions almost every calendar quarter. In the past, when monitoring seem sufficient to diagnose the central issue of data security, the marketplace was demanding more control, more granularity, easier user interfaces, and more actionable reports, as well as moving the DLP application off the main network egress point and parlaying the same functionality to the desktop/laptops, servers, and their respective end points to document storage repositories and databases.

In evaluating DLP applications, it is important to focus on the type of underlying engine that analyzes the data and then work up from that base. Next rate the ease of configuring the data categories and the ability to preload certain documents and document types. Look for a mature product with plenty of industry-specific references. Company stability and financial health should also come into play. Roadmaps of future offerings can give an idea of the features and functions coming in the next release. The relationship with the vendor is an important requirement to make sure that the purchase and subsequent implementation goes smoothly. The vendor should offer training that empowers the IT organization to be somewhat self-sustaining instead of having to go back to the vendor every time a configuration needs to be implemented. The vendor should offer best practices that other customers have used to help with quick adoption of policies. This allows for an effective system that will improve and lower the overall risk profile of the organization.

Analyst briefings about the DLP space can be found on the Internet for free and can provide an unbiased view from a third party of things that should be evaluated during the selection process.

10. CONCLUSION

DLP is an important tool that should at least be evaluated by organizations that are looking to protect their employees, customers, and stakeholders. An effectively implemented DLP application can augment current security safeguards. A well thought out strategy for a DLP application and implementation should be designed first before a purchase. All parts of the organization are likely to be impacted by DLP, and IT should not be the only organization to evaluate and create policies. A holistic approach will help foster a successful implementation that is supported by the DLP vendor and other departments, and ultimately the employees should improve the data risk profile of an organization. The main goal is to keep the brand name and reputation of the organization safe and to continue to operate with minimal data security interruptions. Many types of DLP approaches are available in the market today; picking the right vendor and product with the right features and functions can foster best practices, augment already implemented employee training and policies, and ultimately safeguard the most critical data assets of the organization.

Part VIII

Appendices

Configuring Authentication Service on Microsoft Windows Vista

John R. Vacca

This appendix describes the configuration of Windows Vista® authentication service features that are relevant to IT professionals. The authentication service features included with Windows Vista extend to a strong set of platform-based authentication features to help provide better security, manageability, and user experience. The features include the following:

- Backup and Restore of Stored Usernames and Passwords
- Credential Security Service Provider and SSO for Terminal Services Logon
- TLS/SSL Cryptographic Enhancements
- Kerberos Enhancements
- Smart Card Authentication Changes
- Previous Logon Information[1]

1. BACKUP AND RESTORE OF STORED USERNAMES AND PASSWORDS

In some environments, the stored usernames and passwords feature significantly affects user efficiency and productivity because it can store dozens of credentials for using network resources per user. Unfortunately, this same usefulness can lead to frustration if a user suddenly loses his or her stored usernames and passwords because of a hardware or software failure on the client computer she regularly uses.[1]

To resolve this potential source of user frustration (or to help organizations support this feature), Windows Vista includes a Backup and Restore Wizard that allows users to back up usernames and passwords they have requested

that Windows remember for them. This new functionality allows users to restore the usernames and passwords on any computer running Windows Vista. Restoring a backup file on a different computer allows users to effectively roam or move their saved usernames and passwords.[1]

> *Caution:* Restoring usernames and passwords from a backup file will replace any existing saved usernames and passwords the user has on the computer.

To access this feature, open **Control Panel**, double-click **User Accounts**, and then click **Manage your network passwords**. If you have previously saved any credentials, the **Back up** button is enabled.[1]

Automation and Scripting

For security reasons, this feature cannot be automated, nor can the backup process be initiated by an application that runs under standard user credentials. This feature requires Windows Vista.[1]

Security Considerations

The backup file is encrypted by using Advanced Encryption Standard (AES) and a password supplied by the user at the time the backup is performed. The password should be a strong password to avoid the possibility of the backup being compromised if the password is lost.[1]

2. CREDENTIAL SECURITY SERVICE PROVIDER AND SSO FOR TERMINAL SERVICES LOGON

Authentication protocols are implemented in Windows by security service providers. Windows Vista introduces

---

[1] "Windows Vista Authentication Features," Microsoft TechNet, © 2008 Microsoft Corporation; all rights reserved; Microsoft Corporation, One Microsoft Way, Redmond, WA 98052-6399, 2008.

a new authentication package called the Credential Security Service Provider, or CredSSP, that provides a single sign-on (SSO) user experience when starting new Terminal Services sessions. CredSSP enables applications to delegate users' credentials from the client computer (by using the client-side security service provider) to the target server (through the server-side security service provider) based on client policies. CredSSP policies are configured via Group Policy, and delegation of credentials is turned off by default.[1]

Like the Kerberos authentication protocol, CredSSP can delegate credentials from the client to the server, but it does so by using a completely different mechanism and with different usability and security characteristics. With CredSSP, when policy specifies that credentials should be delegated, users will be prompted for credentials (unlike Kerberos delegation) which means the user has some control over whether the delegation should occur and (more importantly) what credentials should be used. With Kerberos delegation, only the user's Active Directory® credentials can be delegated.[1]

Unlike the experience in Windows Server® 2003 Terminal Server, the credential prompt is on the client computer and not the server. Most importantly, the client credential prompt is on the secure desktop. Therefore, not even the Terminal Services client can see the credentials, which is an important Common Criteria requirement. Furthermore, the credentials obtained from the prompt will not be delegated until the server identity is authenticated (subject to policy configuration). Finally, the terminal server will not establish a session for the user (which consumes a significant amount of memory and CPU processing time on the server) before authenticating the client, which decreases the chances of successful denial-of-service attacks on the server.[1]

Requirements

This feature requires the Terminal Services client to run on Windows Vista or Windows Server 2008. It also requires that Terminal Services be hosted on a server that runs Windows Server 2008.[1]

Configuration

CredSSP policies, and by extension the SSO functionality they provide to Terminal Services, are configured via Group Policy. Use the Local Group Policy Editor to navigate to **Local Computer Policy | Computer Configuration | Administrative Templates | System |**

Credentials Delegation, and enable one or more of the policy options.[1]

Security Considerations

When credential delegation is enabled, the terminal server will receive the user credentials in plaintext form, which can introduce risk to the network environment if the servers are not well secured. An organization that wants to achieve this functionality should plan carefully for its deployment and ensure that an effective security program for the servers is in place beforehand.[1]

In addition, a few of the policy settings might increase or decrease the risk. For example, the **Allow Default Credentials with NTLM-only Server Authentication** and **Allow Fresh Credentials with NTLM-only Server Authentication** policy settings remove the restriction to require the Kerberos authentication protocol for authentication between the client and server. If a computer requires NTLM and either of these settings is selected, then NTLM will be used and will allow communication to occur successfully but at a higher security risk. The Kerberos protocol provides significant additional security in this scenario because it provides mutual authentication—that is, positive authentication of the server to the client. This functionality is important, because users should be protected from delegating their plaintext credentials to an attacker who might have taken control of a network session. Before enabling the NTLM-only policies, network administrators should first ensure that NTLM authentication is necessary in the scenario that they need to support.[1]

3. TLS/SSL CRYPTOGRAPHIC ENHANCEMENTS

Microsoft has added new TLS extensions that enable the support of both AES and new elliptic curve cryptography (ECC) cipher suites. In addition, custom cryptographic mechanisms can now be implemented and used with Schannel as custom cipher suites. Schannel is the Windows security package that implements TLS and SSL.[1]

AES Cipher Suites

The support for AES (which is not available in Microsoft Windows® 2000 Server or Windows Server 2003) is important, because AES has become a National Institute of Standards and Technology (NIST) standard. To ease the process of bulk encryption, cipher suites that support

AES have been added. The following list is the subset of TLS AES cipher suites defined in Request for Comments (RFC) 3268, Advanced Encryption Standard (AES) Ciphersuites for Transport Layer Security (TLS) (http://go.microsoft.com/fwlink/?LinkId=105879), that are available in Windows Vista:

- TLS_RSA_WITH_AES_128_CBC_SHA
- TLS_RSA_WITH_AES_256_CBC_SHA
- TLS_DHE_DSS_WITH_AES_128_CBC_SHA
- TLS_DHE_DSS_WITH_AES_256_CBC_SHA[1]

Requirements

To negotiate these new cipher suites, the client and server computers must be running either Windows Vista or Windows Server 2008.[1]

Configure AES

For information about the registry entries used to configure TLS/SSL ciphers in previous versions of Windows, see TLS/SSL Tools and Settings (http://go.microsoft.com/fwlink/?LinkId=105880). These settings are only available for cipher suites included with Windows operating systems earlier than Windows Vista and are not supported for AES. Cipher preferences are configured in Windows Vista by enabling the **SSL Cipher Suite Order** policy setting in **Administrative Templates | Network | SSL Configuration Settings.**[1]

> Tip: The Windows Vista-based computer must be restarted for any setting changes to take effect.

ECC Cipher Suites

ECC is a key-generation technique that is based on elliptic curve theory and is used to create more efficient and smaller cryptographic keys. ECC key generation differs from the traditional method that uses the product of very large prime numbers to create keys. Instead, ECC uses an elliptic curve equation to create keys. ECC keys are approximately six times smaller than the equivalent strength traditional keys, which significantly reduces the computations that are needed during the TLS handshake to establish a secure connection.[1]

In Windows Vista, the Schannel security service provider includes new cipher suites that support ECC cryptography. ECC cipher suites can now be negotiated as part of the standard TLS handshake. The subset of ECC cipher suites defined in RFC 4492, Elliptic

Curve Cryptography (ECC) Cipher Suites for Transport Layer Security (TLS) (http://go.microsoft.com/fwlink/?LinkId=105881), that are available in Windows Vista is shown in the following list:

- TLS_ECDHE_ECDSA_WITH_AES_128_CBC_SHA_P256
- TLS_ECDHE_ECDSA_WITH_AES_128_CBC_SHA_P384
- TLS_ECDHE_ECDSA_WITH_AES_128_CBC_SHA_P521
- TLS_ECDHE_ECDSA_WITH_AES_256_CBC_SHA_P256
- TLS_ECDHE_ECDSA_WITH_AES_256_CBC_SHA_P384
- TLS_ECDHE_ECDSA_WITH_AES_256_CBC_SHA_P521
- TLS_ECDHE_RSA_WITH_AES_128_CBC_SHA_P256
- TLS_ECDHE_RSA_WITH_AES_128_CBC_SHA_P384
- TLS_ECDHE_RSA_WITH_AES_128_CBC_SHA_P521
- TLS_ECDHE_RSA_WITH_AES_256_CBC_SHA_P256
- TLS_ECDHE_RSA_WITH_AES_256_CBC_SHA_P384
- TLS_ECDHE_RSA_WITH_AES_256_CBC_SHA_P521[1]

The ECC cipher suites use three NIST curves: P-256 (secp256r1), P-384 (secp384r1), and P-521 (secp521r1).[1]

Requirements

To use the ECDHE_ECDSA cipher suites, ECC certificates must be used. Rivest-Shamir-Adleman (RSA) certificates can be used to negotiate the ECDHE_RSA cipher suites. Additionally, the client and server computers must be running either Windows Vista or Windows Server 2008.[1]

Configure ECC Cipher Suites

Cipher preferences are configured in Windows Vista by using the **SSL Cipher Suite Order** policy setting in **Administrative Templates | Network | SSL Configuration Settings.**[1]

> Tip: The Windows Vista-based computer must be restarted for these settings to take effect.

TABLE A.1 Prioritized List of TLS and SSL Cipher Suites

Number	Cipher Suites
1.	TLS_RSA_WITH_AES_128_CBC_SHA
2.	TLS_RSA_WITH_AES_256_CBC_SHA
3.	TLS_RSA_WITH_RC4_128_SHA
4.	TLS_RSA_WITH_3DES_EDE_CBC_SHA
5.	TLS_ECDHE_ECDSA_WITH_AES_128_CBC_SHA_P256
6.	TLS_ECDHE_ECDSA_WITH_AES_128_CBC_SHA_P384
7.	TLS_ECDHE_ECDSA_WITH_AES_128_CBC_SHA_P521
8.	TLS_ECDHE_ECDSA_WITH_AES_256_CBC_SHA_P256
9.	TLS_ECDHE_ECDSA_WITH_AES_256_CBC_SHA_P384
10.	TLS_ECDHE_ECDSA_WITH_AES_256_CBC_SHA_P521
11.	TLS_ECDHE_RSA_WITH_AES_128_CBC_SHA_P256
12.	TLS_ECDHE_RSA_WITH_AES_128_CBC_SHA_P384
13.	TLS_ECDHE_RSA_WITH_AES_128_CBC_SHA_P521
14.	TLS_ECDHE_RSA_WITH_AES_256_CBC_SHA_P256
15.	TLS_ECDHE_RSA_WITH_AES_256_CBC_SHA_P384
16.	TLS_ECDHE_RSA_WITH_AES_256_CBC_SHA_P521
17.	TLS_DHE_DSS_WITH_AES_128_CBC_SHA
18.	TLS_DHE_DSS_WITH_AES_256_CBC_SHA
19.	TLS_DHE_DSS_WITH_3DES_EDE_CBC_SHA
20.	TLS_RSA_WITH_RC4_128_MD5
21.	SSL_CK_RC4_128_WITH_MD5
22.	SSL_CK_DES_192_EDE3_CBC_WITH_MD5
23.	TLS_RSA_WITH_NULL_MD5
24.	TLS_RSA_WITH_NULL_SHA

Schannel CNG Provider Model

Microsoft introduced a new implementation of the cryptographic libraries with Windows Vista that is referred to as Cryptography Next Generation, or CNG. CNG allows for an extensible provider model for cryptographic algorithms.[1]

Schannel, which is Microsoft's implementation of TLS/SSL for Windows Server 2008 and Windows Vista, uses CNG so that any underlying cryptographic mechanisms can be used. This allows organizations to create new cipher suites or reuse existing ones when used with Schannel. The new cipher suites included with Windows Server 2008 and Windows Vista are only available to applications running in user mode.[1]

Requirements

Because both the client and server computers must be able to negotiate the same TLS/SSL cipher, the Schannel CNG feature requires Windows Server 2008 and Windows Vista to use the same custom cipher configured for use on both the client and server computers. In addition, the custom cipher must be prioritized above other ciphers that could be negotiated.[1]

Configure Custom Cipher Suites

Cipher preferences, including preferences for custom cipher suites, are configured in Windows Vista by using the **SSL Cipher Suite Order** policy setting

TABLE A.2 Previous Cipher Suites

Number	Cipher Suites
1.	RSA_EXPORT_RC4_40_MD5
2.	RSA_EXPORT1024_RC4_56_SHA
3.	RSA_EXPORT1024_DES_CBC_SHA
4.	SSL_CK_RC4_128_EXPORT40_MD5
5.	SSL_CK_DES_64_CBC_WITH_MD5
6.	RSA_DES_CBC_SHA
7.	RSA_RC4_128_MD5
8.	RSA_RC4_128_SHA
9.	RSA_3DES_EDE_CBC_SHA
10.	RSA_NULL_MD5
11.	RSA_NULL_SHA
12.	DHE_DSS_EXPORT1024_DES_SHA
13.	DHE_DSS_DES_CBC_SHA
14.	DHE_DSS_3DES_EDE_CBC_SHA

in **Administrative Templates | Network | SSL Configuration Settings.**[1]

> *Tip:* The Windows Vista-based computer must be restarted for these settings to take effect.

Default Cipher Suite Preference

Windows Vista prioritizes the complete list of TLS and SSL cipher suites as shown in Table A.1.[1] The cipher suite negotiated will be the highest-listed cipher suite that is supported by both the client and the server computers.[1]

Previous Cipher Suites

The Microsoft Schannel provider supports the cipher suites listed in Table A.2.[1] However, the cipher suites are not enabled by default. To enable any of these cipher suites, use the **SSL Cipher Suite Order** policy setting in **Administrative Templates | Network | SSL Configuration Settings**.

> *Warning:* Enabling any of these SSL cipher suites is not recommended. Future versions of Windows might not support these cipher suites.

4. KERBEROS ENHANCEMENTS

Microsoft's implementation of the Kerberos authentication protocol is significantly improved in Windows Vista with the following features:

- AES support
- Improved security for Kerberos Key Distribution Centers (KDCs) located on branch office domain controllers[1]

AES

This Windows Vista security enhancement enables the use of AES encryption with the Kerberos authentication protocol. This enhancement includes the following changes from Windows XP:

- *AES support for the base Kerberos authentication protocol.* The base Kerberos protocol in Windows Vista supports AES for encryption of ticket-granting tickets (TGTs), service tickets, and session keys.
- *AES support for the Generic Security Service (GSS)-Kerberos mechanism. In* addition to enabling AES for the base protocol, GSS messages (which conduct client/server communications in Windows Vista) are protected with AES.[1]

Requirements

All Kerberos authentication requests involve three different parties: the client requesting a connection, the server that will provide the requested data, and the Kerberos KDC that provides the keys that are used to protect the various messages This discussion focuses on how AES can be used to protect these Kerberos authentication protocol messages and data structures that are exchanged among the three parties. Typically, when the parties are operating systems running Windows Vista or Windows Server 2008, the exchange will use AES. However, if one of the parties is an operating system running Windows 2000 Professional, Windows 2000 Server, Windows XP, or Windows Server 2003, the exchange will not use AES. The specific exchanges are:

- *TGT.* The TGT is created by the KDC and sent to the client if authentication to the KDC succeeds.
- *Service ticket.* A service ticket is the data created by the KDC, which is provided to the client and then sent by the client to the server to establish authentication of the client.

TABLE A.3 Usage of AES with Various Windows Operating Systems

Client	Server	KDC	Ticket/Message Encryption
Operating systems earlier than Windows Vista	Operating systems earlier than Windows Server 2008	Windows Server 2008	TGT might be encrypted with AES based on policy
Operating systems earlier than Windows Vista	Windows Server 2008	Windows Server 2008	Service ticket encrypted with AES
Windows Vista	Windows Server 2008	Windows Server 2008	All tickets and GSS encrypted with AES
Windows Vista	Windows Server 2008	Operating systems earlier than Windows Server 2008	GSS encrypted with AES
Windows Vista	Operating systems earlier than Windows Server 2008	Windows Server 2008	AS-REQ/REP and TGS-REQ/REP encrypted with AES
Operating systems earlier than Windows Vista	Windows Server 2008	Operating systems earlier than Windows Server 2008	No AES
Windows Vista	Operating systems earlier than Windows Server 2008	Operating systems earlier than Windows Server 2008	No AES
Operating systems earlier than Windows Vista	Operating systems earlier than Windows Server 2008	Operating systems earlier than Windows Server 2008	No AES

- *AS-REQ/REP.* The authentication service request/response (AS-REQ/REP) exchange is the Kerberos TGT request and reply messages sent to the KDC from the client. If the exchange is successful, the client is provided with a TGT.
- *TGS-REQ/REP.* The ticket-granting service request/response (TGS-REQ/REP) exchange is the Kerberos service ticket request and reply messages that are sent to the KDC from the client when it is instructed to obtain a service ticket for a server.
- *GSS.* The Generic Security Service application programming interface (GSS-API) and the Generic Security Service Negotiate Support Provider (GSS-SPNEGO) mechanisms negotiate a secure context for sending and receiving messages between the client and server by using key material derived from the previous ticket exchanges.[1]

Table A.3 shows whether AES is used in each exchange for different combinations of Windows operating systems.[1]

Read-Only Domain Controller and Kerberos Authentication

Windows Vista includes new Kerberos authentication protocol features to further protect a Windows Server 2008 domain controller that is physically located in a branch office. With the read-only domain controller

(RODC), the KDC issues TGTs to branch users only and forwards other requests to the hub domain controller.[1]

In the Windows implementation, the keys used to create TGTs are derived from the password of the **krbtgt** account. This account and its password are typically replicated to every domain controller in the domain. In the branch office scenario, the risk of theft or unauthorized access to the local domain controller (and therefore the security of the **krbtgt** account) is typically greater. To mitigate this risk, the RODC has a unique **krbtgt** account that does not have all of the capabilities of a standard **krbtgt** account on a standard domain controller. If the RODC is compromised, the scope of the breach in regards to the **krbtgt** account information is limited to that RODC, not the other KDCs.[1]

5. SMART CARD AUTHENTICATION CHANGES

Although Windows Server 2003 includes support for smart cards, the types of certificates that smart cards can contain are limited by strict requirements. Each certificate needs to be associated with a user principal name (UPN) and needs to contain the smart card logon object identifier (also known as OID) in the **Enhanced Key Usage** field. In addition, each certificate requires that signing be used in conjunction with encryption.[1]

To better support smart card deployments, Windows Vista enables support for a range of certificates.

Customers now have the ability to deploy smart cards with certificates that are not limited by the previous requirements. Specific certificate requirements that were changed are itemized in the following list:

- UPN is no longer required.
- For smart card logon, the **Enhanced Key Usage** (no need for smart card logon object identifier) and **Subject Alternative Name** (need not contain email ID) fields are not required. If an enhanced key usage is present, it must contain the Smart Card Logon enhanced key usage.
- You can enable any certificate to be visible for the smart card credential provider.
- Smart card logon certificates do not require a **Key Exchange** (AT_KEYEXCHANGE) field.
- **Certificate Revocation List (CRL)** is no longer a required field.[1]

Because the restrictions found in previous versions of Windows are still considered best practices for certificate deployment, the listed changes are not enabled by default except for multiple certificates support (some certificates are excluded). Administrators need to configure the registry keys on client computers to enable the functionality. Group Policy can be used to accomplish this configuration. In addition to these changes to the smart card requirements, the following functional changes have been made for smart card logon:

- When a smart card is inserted into a smart card reader, the logon process does not start automatically. Typically, users are now required to press Ctrl +Alt + Delete to start the logon process.
- All valid smart card logon certificates are enumerated and presented to users. The smart card must be inserted before users can enter a personal identification number (PIN).
- Keys are no longer restricted to being in the default container, and certificates in different smart cards can be chosen.
- Multiple Terminal Services sessions are supported in a single process. Because Windows Vista is closely integrated with Terminal Services to provide fast user switching, this functionality is an important improvement.[1]

Additional Changes to Common Smart Card Logon Scenarios

The following part of this appendix, describes the changes in Windows Vista for common smart card authentication and logon scenarios.[1]

Smart Card Logon of a Single User with One Certificate into Multiple Accounts

In Windows Vista, a single user certificate can be mapped to multiple accounts. For example, a user can log on to his or her user account or can log on as domain administrator.[1]

Smart Card Logon of Multiple Users into a Single Account

Windows Vista supports the ability for multiple users with unique smart card certificates to log on to a single account, such as an administrator's account.[1]

Smart Card Logon Across Forests

In some situations, such as logon across forests, there might not be enough information in the smart card certificate to reliably route the logon request. Windows Vista allows users to enter a "hint" in the form domain\ user username or a fully qualified UPN such as user@ DNSnameofdomain.com that allows reliable authentication routing. For the **Hint** field to appear during smart card logon, the *X509HintsNeeded* registry key must be set on the client computer.[1]

OCSP Support for PKINIT

The Public Key Cryptography for Initial Authentication in Kerberos (PKINIT) protocol is the smart card authentication mechanism for the Kerberos authentication protocol. Online Certificate Status Protocol (OCSP), defined in RFC 2560, X.509 Internet Public Key Infrastructure Online Certificate Status Protocol-OCSP (http://go.microsoft.com/fwlink/?LinkID=67082), enables applications to obtain timely information regarding the revocation status of a certificate.[1]

Because the Windows KDC is a high-volume transactional service, it benefits greatly by using OCSP instead of relying on CRLs. Windows Server 2008 KDCs will always attempt to use OCSP to verify certificate validity.[1]

Certificate Revocation Support

Table A.4 describes the registry key values you can use to disable CRL checking.[1]

> *Tip:* The settings must be enabled on both the client and KDC computers to disable CRL checking.

TABLE A.4 Registry Key Values to Disable CRL Checking

Key	Value
HKLM\SYSTEM\CCS\Services\Kdc\UseCachedCRLOnlyAndIgnore RevocationUnknownErrors	Type=DWORD Value=1
HKLM\SYSTEM\CCS\Control\LSA\Kerberos\Parameters\UseCachedCRL OnlyAndIgnoreRevocationUnknownErrors	Type=DWORD Value=1

Smart Card Root Certificate Requirements for Use When Joining a Domain

When using a smart card to join a domain, the smart card certificate must comply with one of the following conditions:

- The smart card certificate must contain a **Subject** field that contains the DNS domain name within the distinguished name. If it does not contain this field, resolution to the appropriate domain will fail, causing the domain join with smart card to fail.
- The smart card certificate must contain a UPN in which the domain part of the UPN must resolve to the actual domain. For example, the UPN username@engineering.corp.example.comwould work, but username@engineering.example.com would not work because the Kerberos client would not be able to find the appropriate domain.[1]

The solution for both of the listed conditions is to supply a hint (enabled via the **X509HintsNeeded** registry setting) in the credentials prompt when joining a domain. If the client computer is not joined to a domain, then the client will only be able to resolve the server domain by viewing the distinguished name on the certificate (as opposed to the UPN). For this scenario to work, the **Subject** field for the certificate must include "DC =" for domain name resolution. To deploy root certificates on smart cards for the currently joined domain, the following command can be used:[1]

certutil-scroots

Terminal Server Redirection

In terminal server scenarios, remote servers are used to run services. However, the smart card is local to the computers from which the connections are established. In smart card logon scenarios, the Smart Card service on the remote servers will appropriately redirect to the smart card readers that are connected to the remote computers from which users are trying to log on.[1]

Terminal Server Sign-On Experience

As a part of Common Criteria compliance requirements, the Terminal Services client must be able to be configured to use Stored User Names and Passwords to acquire and save users' passwords and smart card PINs. Common Criteria requires that applications must not have direct access to users' passwords or PINs.[1]

Specifically, the Common Criteria requirement is that passwords and PINs never leave the highly trusted Local Security Authority (LSA) unencrypted. When this requirement is applied to a distributed scenario, it should allow passwords and PINs to travel between one trusted LSA and another if they are encrypted during transit.[1]

In Windows Vista, smart card users will need to log on for every new Terminal Services session. However, users are not prompted for their PINs more than once to establish a Terminal Services session. For example, after a user double-clicks a Microsoft Word document icon that resides on a remote computer, the user will be prompted to enter his or her PIN. This PIN will be passed via a secure channel established by CredSSP. The PIN is routed to the Terminal Services client over the secure channel, where it is used to access the keys on the smart card. Users are not prompted again for their PINs unless a PIN is incorrect or if a smart card fails due to problems with the card or reader.[1]

Terminal Services and Smart Card Logon

This feature enables users to log on with smart cards by entering a PIN on the Terminal Services client, which securely relays this information to the server in a manner similar to authentication that uses a user name and password. Smart card logon with Terminal Server was first introduced in Windows XP. It is not available in any earlier versions of the Windows operating system. In Windows XP, users can use only one certificate from the default container to log on. To enable smart card logon to a terminal server, the KDC certificate must be present on the local Terminal Services client computer.[1]

Terminal Services and Smart Card Logon across Domains

With Windows Vista, it is now possible to use smart cards to log on across domains or from computers that were not joined to domains trusted by the users' account domains. Common scenarios where this functionality is required include:

- Using Routing and Remote Access to access an organization's network resources across the Internet.
- Using Terminal Services across domains that are not trusted or computers that are not joined to a domain.[1]

To enable this functionality, the root certificate for the user's account domain must be provisioned on the smart card. To provision the domain root certificate while using a computer that is a member of the domain, type the following at a command prompt:[1]

certutil-scroots update

In addition, for Terminal Services access across trusting domains, the KDC certificate of the domain of the Terminal Services computer needs to be present in the NTAuth store of the client computer. The following command can be used to provision this certificate onto the client computer:[1]

certutil-addstore-enterprise NTAUTH certfile

Replace certfile with the root certificate of the KDC certificate issuer.[1]

To log on to a terminal server by using a smart card from a client computer that is not a member of the domain, the smart card needs to be provisioned with the root certificate of the terminal server's domain controller. Furthermore, cross-domain terminal server logon will only work if the UPN attribute of the certificate is in the form username@domain_dns_name. If it is impossible or impractical to deploy certificates with the UPN attribute in this form, enabling domain hints with Group Policy is a potential solution.[1]

Terminal Services and Smart Card Logon Registry Settings

If smart card logon is the only form of logon that is supported, enable the following registry setting:[1]

HKEY_LOCAL_MACHINE\Software\Policies\
Microsoft|Windows\CredentialsDelega

AllowFreshCredentials

If the user also has a corresponding password-enabled account, enabling the following setting would also be useful:[1]

HKEY_LOCAL_MACHINE\Software\Policies\
Microsoft\Windows\CredentialDelegation

AllowFreshCredentialsWhenNTLMOnly

Delegation of default and saved credentials are not supported for Terminal Services with smart card logon. The following Group Policy settings are ignored:

- HKEY_LOCAL_MACHINE\Software\Policies\
  Microsoft\Windows\CredentialsDelegation
- AllowDefCredentials
- AllowDefCredentialsWhenNTLMOnly
- AllowSavedCredentials
- AllowSavedCredentialsWhenNTLMOnly[1]

6. PREVIOUS LOGON INFORMATION

This setting enables users to determine whether their accounts were used (or were attempted to be used) without their knowledge. When this policy is enabled and the Windows Vista–based computer is joined to a Windows Server 2008 functional-level domain, the following information is displayed after a successful interactive logon:

1. Date and time of the last successful logon by that user
2. Date and time of the last unsuccessful logon attempt with the same user name
3. The number of failed logon attempts since the last successful logon with the same username[1]

> *Note:* The source of this information is the Active Directory database or Security Accounts Manager (SAM) of the computer providing the information. For local accounts, this information is always up to date. However, in domain environments, domain controllers depend on replication, so the information might not be up to date.

> *Caution:* If this policy is enabled and the Windows Vista-based computer is not joined to a Windows Server 2008 functional-level domain, a warning message will appear stating that the information could not be retrieved and the user will not be able to log on. Do not enable this policy setting unless the Windows Vista–based computer is joined to a Windows Server 2008 functional-level domain.

Configuration

To enable this feature, use the Local Group Policy Editor to navigate to **Local Computer Policy | Computer Configuration | Administrative Templates | Windows Components | Windows Logon Options**, and enable **Display Information about previous logons during user logon**. Additional information is available on the **Explain Text** tab for this setting.[1]

Security Considerations

User training that accompanies the deployment of Windows Vista should include information about how to use this information and what to do if the information does not represent the user's actions.[1]

Security Management and Resiliency

John R. Vacca

The United States needs to strengthen the computer security management and resilience component of its homeland security strategy to mitigate the effect of successful terrorist attacks and other disasters. As a nation, the U.S. must be able to withstand a blow and then bounce back. That's resilience![1]

The U.S. can mitigate risk but cannot guarantee that another attack will not occur, nor can it prevent natural and accidental disasters. It requires this country to admit that some disasters cannot be avoided. It also requires the U.S. to acknowledge that, faced with disaster, most citizens, businesses, and other institutions will take action to rescue themselves and others.[1]

According to U.S. government analysts, 86% of the country's critical infrastructure is privately owned and operated. However, it isn't the job of the government to do the on-the-ground work of security management and resiliency.[1]

The private sector can provide the means and the execution. On the other hand, it should also be the champion and the facilitator of security management and resiliency chain; balancing the interests of stakeholders; setting broad objectives and strategies; and providing oversight.[1]

However, the creativity and ingenuity of the American people must also be taken into consideration, including the businesses they create. This also includes how government can prepare its citizens for a disaster or an emergency by giving them the necessary security management tools.[1]

The government's first goal is to provide timely and accurate security management information during a crisis. Government must also leverage technology to help inform citizens that danger is near. The Department of Homeland Security (DHS) has created the Ready Business program, which gives small-to-medium-size businesses guidance on which security management and resiliency tools and resources are available to them to ensure business continuity.[1]

The government's second goal is to provide order, so citizens can focus on disaster response, rather than protecting themselves from social chaos. While local and state forces can maintain order during a disaster; just in case they cannot, DHS is studying specialized law enforcement deployment teams (LEDTs). These teams from neighboring jurisdictions would assist local and state forces when they are taxed to the breaking point. LEDTs could help provide an organized system that would allow state and local law enforcement to assist each other to quickly resume normal police services, to an area hit by a terrorist attack or natural disaster (something Louisiana and New Orleans police did not have after Hurricane Katrina struck).[1]

Finally, the government can increase infrastructure security management and resilience after an attack or disaster. Nevertheless, this can be done through the dispersal of key functions across multiple service providers, flexible supply chains, and related systems.[1]

Business should build in such flexibility as well. Flexibility, is cheaper than redundancy, and it is also a smart business decision because it makes companies more competitive.[1]

A company that builds in the ability to respond to supply disruption is automatically building in the ability to respond to demand fluctuations and winning market share. For the past 16 years, AT&T has invested in mobile central offices: 500 trailers that hold everything

---

1 Matthew Harwood, "U.S. Must be More Resilient to Disasters and Terrorism, Experts Explain," Copyright © 2008, Security Management, Security Management, ASIS International, Inc. Worldwide Headquarters USA, 1625 Prince Street, Alexandria, Virginia 22314-2818, 2008.

the company needs to keep their network up and running. On 9/11, AT&T dispatched these trailers to New York because the terrorist attack had knocked out a company transport hub in the sixth subbasement of the World Trade Center's South Tower. Within 48 hours, the trailers were operational and accepting call traffic.[1]

Finally, the United States has been too focused on prevention to the detriment of security management and resilience. After 9/11, the Bush administration focused solely on preventing the next attack, as opposed to how best to recover should an incident occur. That, of course, is not the best approach.[1]

List of Top Security Implementation and Deployment Companies

Aaditya Corporation (www.aadityacorp.com/): Network Security Consultants offering specialization in network security policy definition.

Advent Information Management Ltd (www.advent-im.co.uk/): Knowledge-based consultancy offering information management advice, training and consultancy.

AMPEG Security Lighthouse (www.security-lighthouse.com/): Produce information security management software which provides a national and international perspective on your company's security status.

Atsec (www.atsec.com/01/index.php): Offers a range of services based on the Common Criteria standard, ISO 15408.

BindView Policy Compliance (www.symantec.com/business/solutions/index.jsp?ptid=tab2&ctid=tab2_2): Provides organizations with advanced tools to proactively build and measure security best practices across the enterprise.

CF6 Luxembourg S.A. (www.cf6.lu/): Security policies are the formalization of security needs in order to define security measures for implementation. CF6 Luxembourg proposes to help companies to develop and implement security policies.

Citicus ONE-security risk management (www.citicus.com/index.asp): Citicus provides tools for information risk management to ensure that compliance with security policy can be monitored and enhanced.

Computer Policy Guide (www.computerpolicy.com/): A commercial manual with sample policies. Topics include: Email; Internet Usage; Personal Computer Usage; Information Security; and Document Retention.

CoSoSys SRL (www.fortedownloads.com/CoSoSys-SRL-Surf-it-Easy/): Provides software to protect PC endpoints and networks.

Delta Risk LLC (www.delta-risk.net/): Provides information on a range of policy related services, including risk assessment, awareness and training.

DynamicPolicy – Efficient Policy Management (www.zequel.com/): DynamicPolicy is an Intranet application that enables companies to automatically create, manage and disseminate their corporate policies and procedures, particularly those related with Information Security.

FoolProof Software – Desktop Security for windows and MAC OS-education and libraries (www.foolproofsoftware.com/assets/cm.js): FoolProof Security provides complete protection for both Windows® and Macintosh® operating systems and desktops by preventing unwanted or malicious changes from being made to the system.

Information Management Technologies (www.imt.com.sa/files/index.asp): Saudi Arabia. BS7799 Audit; Forensic Services and Training; Data Recovery Laboratory; Managed Security Service Provider; Security Control Frameworks.

Information Security and IT Security Austria (www.eclipse-security.at/): Austrian Information Security and IT-Security Company offering Consulting Services, Information Security Awareness Training in German and English language, and M.M.O.S.S Software (Massive Multiuser Online Sensitiving Software).

Information Shield, Inc. (www.informationshield.com/): A global provider of prepackaged security policies and customizable implementation guidance.

IT Security Essentials Guide (www.ovitztaylor-gates.com/TheITSecurityEssentialsGuide.html): Management resources for enterprise projects, offering how-to workbooks, project plans and planning guides, tools, templates and checklists.

Layton Technology Inc. (www.laytontechnology.com/):
Offers a range of Windows based audit, monitoring
and access control software solutions.

Megaprime (www.megaprime.com.au/): Offers ISO/IEC
17799 compliant information security policy and
management systems, security architectures, secure
applications and networks.

Pirean Limited Homepage (www.pirean.com/):
Providing enterprise systems, risk management
and information security services, applications and
education with a focus on security management and
international standards (BS7799 / ISO17799).

Policy Manager – Cisco Systems (www.cisco.com/en/
US/products/sw/netmgtsw/ps996/ps5663/index.
html): Cisco Secure Policy Manager is a scalable,
powerful security policy management system for
Cisco firewalls and Virtual Private Network (VPN)
gateways. Assistance is also provided with the development and auditing of security policy.

Prolateral Consulting (www.prolateral.com/):
Consultancy for ISO17799 BS7799, Information
Security Management.

Prolify (www.prolify.com/): Prolify delivers Dynamic
Process Management (DPM) solutions for IT
Governance, enabling enterprises to achieve higher
levels of control, efficiency and compliance.

PSS Systems (www.pss-systems.com/): Document policy
management and enforcement for electronic documents. Enterprise software to protect, track and ensure
the destruction of highly mobile, distributed assets.

Ruskwig Security Portal (www.ruskwig.com/): Provides
security policies, an encryption package, security
policy templates, Internet and email usage policies.

Secoda Risk Management (www.secoda.com/):
RuleSafe from Secoda enables the people in your
organization to achieve real awareness of policies.
Expert content and compliance tracking help organizations implement security (BS7799), privacy and
regulatory requirements.

Security Policies & Baseline Standards: Effective
Implementation (www.security.kirion.net/
securitypolicy/): Discussion of topic with security
policies and baseline standards information.

- Singular Security (www.singularsecurity.com/):
A firm specializing in delivering security
configuration management services designed to
mitigate both computing and company-wide policy
compliance requirements.
- Spry Control LLC (www.sprycontrol.com/): Spry
Control provides Information Technology Audit
Services as a part of corporate oversight or external

audit that address information security, data privacy
and technology risks.
- VantagePoint Security (www.vantagepointsecurity.
com/): Professional services firm specializing in
security policy, assessments, risk mitigation, and
managed services.
- Vision training and consultancy: Dedicated to onsite
consultancy and training in the following elements:
BS7799 and ISO90012000.
- Xbasics, LLC: Offers information security and
FISMA-related software for government, industry
and consulting organizations.

LIST OF SAN IMPLEMENTATION AND DEPLOYMENT COMPANIES

There are many different SAN implementation and deployment companies that offer products and services, from very
large companies to smaller, lesser-known ones. A list of
some of the more well-known companies is offered here:

Bull: www.bull.com/index.php
Dell: www.dell.com
EMC: www.emc.com
Fujitsu: www.fujitsu.
com/global/services/computing/storage/system/
HP: welcome.hp.com/country/us/en/prodserv/storage.
html
Hitachi Data Systems: www.hds.
com/products/storage-networking/
IBM: www-03.ibm.com/systems/storage/
NetApp: www.netapp.com/us/
NEC: www.nec.co.jp/necstorage/global/index.shtml
3PAR: www.3par.com/index.html
Sun: www.sun.com/storagetek/networking.jsp
Xiotech: www.xiotech.com/

SAN SECURITY IMPLEMENTATION AND DEPLOYMENT COMPANIES:[1]

McData SANtegrity Security Suite Software (www.
mcdata.com/products/network/security/santegrity.
html): SANtegrity Security Suite enhances business
continuity by reducing the impact of human influences on your networked data. This robust suite of
software applications provides unsurpassed storage
area network (SAN) protection. SANtegrity lets

1 SAN Security www.sansecurity.com/san-security-vendors.shtml

you build secure storage networks by providing end-to-end security features for McD fabrics. Using SANtegrity software, you can apply layers of security to individual storage network ports, switches and entire fabrics through: Multi-level Access Control, Advanced Zoning Security, Secure Management zones, SANtegrity Features and Functions.

Brocade Secure Fabric OS (www.brocade.com/products/silkworm/silkworm_12000/fabric_os_datasheet.jsp): A Comprehensive SAN Security Solution. As a greater number of organizations implement larger Storage Area Networks (SANs), they are facing new challenges in regard to data and system security. Especially as organizations interconnect SANs over longer distances through existing networks, they have an even greater need to effectively manage their security and policy requirements. To help these organizations improve security, Brocade has developed Secure Fabric OS™, a comprehensive security solution for Brocade-based SAN fabrics that provides policy-based security protection for more predictable change management, assured configuration integrity, and reduced risk of downtime. Secure Fabric OS protects the network by using the strongest, enterprise-class security methods available, including digital certificates and digital signatures, multiple levels of password protection, strong password encryption, and Public Key Infrastructure (PKI)-based authentication, and 128-bit encryption of the switch's private key used for digital signatures.

Hifn 4300 HIPP III Storage Security Processor (www.hifn.com/products/4300.html): The Hifn™ HIPP III 4300 Storage Security Processor is the first security processor designed for the specific requirements of IP Storage applications. The 4300 offers a complete IPsec data path solution optimized for IP Storage based systems, combining inbound and outbound policy processing, SA lookup, SA context handling, and packet formatting – all within a single chip. Hifn's 4300 delivers industry-leading cryptographic functionality, supporting the DES/3DES-CBC, AES-CBC, AES-CTR, MD5, SHA-1 and AES-XCBC-MAC algorithms. Hifn also provides complete software support, including an optional onboard iSCSI-compliant IPsec software stack, offering an embedded HTML manager application.

HP StorageWorks Secure Fabric OS (javascript:var%20handle=window.open('h18006.www1.hp.com/products/storage/software/sansecurity/): HP Secure Fabric OS solutions include a comprehensive SAN infrastructure security software tool and value added services for 1 Gb and 2 Gb SAN Switches environments. With its flexible design, the Security feature enables organizations to customize SAN fabric security in order to meet specific policy requirements. In addition, Security Fabric OS works with security practices already deployed in many SAN environments such as Advanced Zoning. HP Services also provide a portfolio of services ranging from the broad SAN Design and Architecture that can provide a complete multisite security design, to a single site Security Installation & Startup service that shows you how to configure your Secure Fabric OS environment using the most used industry tested aspects of security. HP Secure Fabric OS is a complete solution for securing SAN infrastructures.

Decru Dataform Security Appliances (www.decru.com/): Decru DataFort™ is a reliable, multigigabit-speed encryption appliance that integrates transparently into NAS, SAN, DAS and tape backup environments. By locking down stored data with strong encryption, and routing all access through secure hardware, DataFort radically simplifies the security model for networked storage. DataFort appliances combine secure access controls, authentication, storage encryption, and secure logging to provide unprecedented protection for sensitive stored data. Because DataFort protects data at rest and in flight with strong encryption, even organizations that outsource IT management can be sure their data assets are secure. In short, DataFort offers a powerful and cost-effective solution to address a broad range of external, internal, and physical threats to sensitive data.

Kasten Chase Assurency (www.kastenchase.com/): Assurency™ SecureData provides comprehensive security for data storage, including SAN, NAS and DAS. Utilizing authentication, access control and strong industry-standard encryption, SecureData protects valuable information stored on online, near-line, and backup storage media. These safeguards extend to stored data both within the datacenter and at off-site data storage facilities. Assurency SecureData protects valuable data assets, such as email, financial and health care information, customer and personnel records and intellectual property. For government agencies, Assurency SecureData protects intelligence and national defense data, law enforcement information, and confidential citizen records. Helps build trusted brands that earn customer loyalty and retention.

List of Security Products

SECURITY SOFTWARE

Activeworx (www.crosstecsoftware.com/security/index. html): Activeworx provides organizations with comprehensive, real time expert security information analysis combined with strong correlation intelligence, flexible and robust reporting capabilities, and tight integration with our best of breed logging solution.

Ad-Aware 2008 Definition File (www.download. com/Ad-Aware-2008-Definition-File/3000-8022_4-10706164.html): Updates your Ad-Aware 2007 definition file to the latest release.

Ad-Aware 2008 (www.download.com/Ad-Aware-2008/3000-8022_4-10045910.html): Protects your personal home computer from malware attacks.

ArcSight (www.arcsight.com/product_overview.htm): The ArcSight SIEM Platform is an integrated set of products for collecting, analyzing, and managing enterprise event information. These products can be purchased and deployed separately or together, depending on organization size and needs.

Ashampoo FireWall (www.download.com/Ashampoo-FireWall/3000-10435_4-10575187.html): Sets up an effective firewall and prevents unauthorized online activity.

Avast Virus Cleaner Tool (www.download.com/Avast-Virus-Cleaner-Tool/3000-2239_4-10223809.html): Removes selected viruses and worms from your computer.

AVG Anti-Virus (www.download.com/AVG-Anti-Virus/3000-2239_4-10385707.html): Protects your computer from viruses and malicious programs.

AVG Internet Security (www.download.com/AVG-Internet-Security/3000-2239_4-10710160.html): Protects your PC from harmful Internet threats.

Avira AntiVir Personal-Free Antivirus (www.download. com/Avira-AntiVir-Personal-Free-Antivirus/3000-2239_4-10322935.html): Detects and eliminates viruses, get free protection for home users.

Avira Premium Security Suite (www.download. com/Avira-Premium-Security-Suite/3000-2239_4-10683930.html): Protects your workstation from viruses and online threats.

CCleaner (www.download.com/CCleaner/3000-2144_4-10315544.html): Cleans up junk files and invalid Registry entries.

Comodo Firewall Pro (www.download.com/Comodo-Firewall-Pro/3000-10435_4-10460704.html): Protects your PC from harmful threats.

ESET NOD32 Antivirus (www.download.com/ESET-NOD32-Antivirus/3000-2239_4-10185608.html): Protects your system against viruses.

Folder Lock (www.download.com/Folder-Lock/3000-2092_4-10063343.html): Password-protects, locks, hides or encrypts files, folders, drives and portable disks in seconds.

Hotspot Shield (www.download.com/Hotspot-Shield/3000-2092_4-10594721.html): Maintains your anonymity and protects your privacy when accessing free Wi-Fi hotspots.

Intelinet Spyware Remover (www.download.com/Intelinet-Spyware-Remover/3000-8022_4-10888927. html): Removes and blocks all types of spyware and PC errors on your computer.

Kaspersky Anti-Virus (www.download.com/Kaspersky-Anti-Virus/3000-2239_4-10259842.html): Monitors and detects viruses and protects your PC from viruses, malware, and Trojan attacks.

Kaspersky Anti-Virus Definition Complete Update (www.download.com/Kaspersky-Anti-Virus-Definition-Complete-Update/3000-2239_4-10059428.html): Updates your Kaspersky Anti-Virus with the latest overall set of virus definitions.

Kaspersky Internet Security (www.download. com/Kaspersky-Internet-Security/3000-2239_4-10012072.html): Detects and eliminates viruses and Trojan horses, even new and unknown ones.

KeyScrambler Personal (www.download.com/KeyScrambler-Personal/3000-2144_4-10571274.

html): Encrypts keystrokes to protect your username and password from keyloggers.

Malwarebytes' Anti-Malware (www.download. com/Malwarebytes-Anti-Malware/3000-8022_4-10804572.html): Detects and removes malware from your computer.

McAfee VirusScan Plus (www.download.com/ McAfee-VirusScan-Plus/3000-2239_4-10581368. html): Removes spyware or virus threats and prevents malicious applications from invading your PC.

Norton 360 (www.download.com/Norton-360/3000-2239_4-10651162.html): Surround yourself with protection from viruses, spyware, fraudulent Web sites, and phishing scams.

Norton AntiVirus 2009 (www.download.com/Norton-AntiVirus-2009/3000-2239_4-10592477.html): Protects yourself from all forms of online viruses.

Norton AntiVirus 2009 Definitions Update (www. download.com/Norton-AntiVirus-2009-Definitions-Update/3000-2239_4-10737487.html): Updates virus definitions for your Norton AntiVirus and Internet Security 2008 products.

Norton Internet Security (www.download.com/Norton-Internet-Security/3000-8022_4-10592551.html): Prevents viruses, spyware, and phishing attacks to enjoy secure Web connection.

Online Armor Personal Firewall (www.download.com/ Online-Armor-Personal-Firewall/3000-10435_4-10426782.html): Protects your system from parasites, viruses, and identity theft while surfing the Web.

ParentalControl Bar (www.download.com/ ParentalControl-Bar/3000-2162_4-10539075.html): Prevents your children from accessing adult-oriented Web sites.

Password Dragon (www.download.com/Password-Dragon/3000-2092_4-10844722.html): Manages your passwords and keeps them in a safe place.

PeerGuardian (www.download.com/PeerGuardian/3000-2144_4-10438288.html): Protect yourself on P2P networks by blocking IPs.

RSA Envision (www.rsa.com/node.aspx?id=3170): The RSA enVision platform provides the power to gather and use log data to understand your security, compliance, or operational status in real time or over any period of time.

Secunia Personal Software Inspector (www.download. com/Secunia-Personal-Software-Inspector/3000-2162_4-10717855.html): Scans your installed programs and categorizes them by their security-update status.

Spybot-Search & Destroy (www.download.com/Spybot-Search-amp-Destroy/3000-8022_4-10122137.html): Searches your hard disk and Registry for threats to your security and privacy.

SpywareBlaster (www.download.com/Spyware Blaster/3000-8022_4-10196637.html): Prevents spyware from being installed on your computer.

Spyware Doctor (www.download.com/Spyware-Doctor/3000-8022_4-10293212.html): Remove spyware, adware, Trojan horses, and key loggers with this popular and fast utility.

Syslog NG (www.balabit.com/network-security/syslog-ng/): The syslog-ng application is a flexible and highly scalable system logging application that is ideal for creating centralized and trusted logging solutions.

Trend Micro AntiVirus plus AntiSpyware (www. download.com/Trend-Micro-AntiVirus-plus-AntiSpyware/3000-2239_4-10440657.html): Detects and removes adware and spyware from your home computer.

Trend Micro HijackThis (www.download.com/Trend-Micro-HijackThis/3000-8022_4-10227353.html): Scans the Registry and hard drive for spyware.

ZoneAlarm Firewall (Windows 2000/XP): (www. download.com/ZoneAlarm-Firewall-Windows-2000-XP-/3000-10435_4-10039884.html): Protects your Internet connection from hackers and other security breaches.

ZoneAlarm Internet Security Suite (www.download. com/ZoneAlarm-Internet-Security-Suite/3000-8022_4-10291278.html): Equips your system to deal with Web-based security threats including hackers, viruses, and worms.

List of Security Standards

BITS Financial Services Roundtable (www.bits.org/ FISAP/index.php): Security assessment questionnaire and review process based on ISO/IEC 27002 (access requires free registration). Also information on the overlaps between ISO/IEC 27002, PCI-DSS 1.1 and COBIT.

Common Criteria (www.commoncriteriaportal.org/ thecc.html): Provides the Common Criteria for Information Technology Security Evaluation, also published as ISO/IEC 15408.

ISO 27001 Certificates (iso27001certificates.com/): List of organizations certified against ISO/IEC 27001 or equivalent national standards, maintained by the ISMS International User Group based on inputs from all the certification bodies.

ISO 27000 Directory (www.27000.org/): Information covering the ISO/IEC 27000 series of standards, including updates and consultants directory.

ISO 27001 Security (www.iso27001security.com/): Information about the ISO/IEC 27000-series information security standards and other related standards, with discussion forum and FAQ.

ISO 27000 Toolkit (www.17799-toolkit.com/): Package containing the ISO/IEC 27001 and 27002 standards plus supporting materials such as policies and a glossary.

ISO/IEC 27002 Explained (www.berr.gov.uk/whatwedo/ sectors/infosec/infosecadvice/legislationpolicy standards/securitystandards/isoiec27002/page33370. html): Information on ISO/IEC 27001 and 27002 from BERR, the UK government department for Business Enterprise and Regulatory Reform (formerly the DTI, the Department of Trade and Industry).

ISO/IEC 27001 Frequently Asked Questions (www. atsec. com/01/index.php?id=06-0101-01): FAQ covers the basics of ISO/IEC 27001, the ISO/IEC standard Specification for an Information Security Management System.

NIST Special Publication 800-53 (csrc.nist.gov/publications/nistpubs/800-53-Rev2/sp800-53-rev2-final. pdf): Recommended Security Controls for Federal Information Systems has a similar scope to ISO/IEC 27002 and cross-references the standard. [PDF]

Overview of Information Security Standards (www. infosec.gov.hk/english/technical/files/overview.pdf): Report by the Government of the Hong Kong Special Administrative Region outlines the ISO/IEC 27000-series standards plus related standards, regulations etc. including PCI-DSS, COBIT, ITIL/ISO 20000, FISMA, SOX and HIPAA. [PDF]

Praxiom Research Group Ltd. (praxiom.com/ #ISO%20IEC%2027001%20LIBRARY): Plain English descriptions of ISO/IEC 27001, 27002 and other standards, including a list of the controls.

The Security Practitioner (security.practitioner.com/introduction/): The ISO 27001 Perspective: An Introduction to Information Security is a guide to ISO/IEC 27001 and 27002 in the form of an HTML help file.

Veridion (www.veridion.net/): ISO/IEC 27001 and 27002 training courses including Lead Auditor and Lead Implementer, plus other information security, risk management and business continuity courses on BS 25999, CISSP, CISA, CISM, MEHARI and OCTAVE.

Appendix F

List of Miscellaneous Security Resources

The following is a list of miscellaneous security resources:

Conferences
Consumer Information
Directories
Help and Tutorials
Mailing Lists
News and Media
Organizations
Products and Tools
Research
Content Filtering Links
Other Logging Resources

CONFERENCES

Airscanner: Wireless Security Boot Camp (www.airscanner.com/wireless/): Wireless security training conference held in Dallas, Texas, USA.

AusCERT (conference.auscert.org.au/conf2009/): International conference focusing on IT security. Held near Brisbane, Australia.

DallasCon (www.dallascon.com/): Provides information and wireless security training with hands-on boot camps throughout the U.S. as well as annual conference in Dallas, Texax.

FIRST Conference (www.first.org/conference/): Annual international conference focused on handling computer security incidents. Location varies.

Infosecurity (www.infosec.co.uk/page.cfm/Link=18/t=m/trackLogID=2317009_A50169F58F): Global series of annual IT Security exhibitions.

International Computer Security Audit and Control Symposium (www.cosac.net/): This annual conference held in Ireland is for IT security professionals.

ITsecurityEvents (www.itsecurityevents.com/): Calendar listing IT security events worldwide.

Network and Distributed System Security Symposium (www.isoc.org/includes/javascript.js): Annual event aimed at fostering information exchange among research scientists and practitioners of network and distributed system security services. Held in San Diego, California

NISC (www.nisc.org.uk/): Information security conference in Scotland. Details of agenda, guest speakers and online booking form.

The Training Co. (www.thetrainingco.com/): Techno-Security conference organizers and computer security training providers. Conference details, including registration and pricing.

VP4S-06: Video Processing for Security (www.computer-vision.org/4security/): Conference focused on processing video data from security devices.

CONSUMER INFORMATION

AnonIC (www.anonic.org/): A free resource for those in need of Internet privacy. The aim of this site is to educate Internet users how to protect their privacy at little or no cost.

Business.gov: Information and Computer Security Guide (www.business.gov/guides/privacy/): Provides links to plain language government resources that help businesses secure their information systems, protecting mission-critical data.

Computer Security information for the rest of us. (www.secure-computing.info/): Computer Security information in plain language. Learn how to protect your computer from viruses, spyware and spam.

Consumer Guide to Internet Safety, Privacy and Security (nclnet.org/essentials/): Offers tips and advice for maintaining online privacy and security, and how to keep children safe online.

EFS File Encryption Tutorial (www.iopus.com/guides/efs.htm): Learn how to use the free Microsoft Encrypting File System (EFS) to protect your data and how to back up your private key to enable data recovery.

GRC Security Now (www.grc.com/securitynow.htm): Provides access to weekly podcasts and whitepapers on topics like Windows Vista, computer security, virus advisories, and other interesting hacking topics.

Home Network Security (www.cert.org/tech_tips/home_networks.html): Gives home users an overview of the security risks and countermeasures associated with Internet connectivity, especially in the context of "always-on" or broadband access services such as cable modems and DSL.

Internet Security Guide (www.internetsecurityguide.com/): Features articles on business and home user Internet security including SSL certificates and network vulnerability scanning.

Online Security Tips for Consumers of Financial Services (www.bits.org/ci_consumer.html): Advice for conducting secure online transactions.

Outlook Express Security Tutorial (www.iopus.com/guides/oe-backup.htm): Learn how to back up your Outlook Express (OE) email, investigate the Windows Registry and transfer your email account and rules settings to another PC.

An Overview of email and Internet Monitoring in the Workplace (www.fmew.com/archive/monitoring/): Compliance with the law that governs employer monitoring of employee Internet usage and personal email in the workplace.

Privacy Initiatives (www.ftc.gov/privacy/): Government Site that is run by the Federal Trade Commission. Information about how the government can help protect kids and the general public. It has lots of information about official policies.

Protect Your Privacy and email on the Internet (www.taci-roglu.com/p/): Guide to protecting privacy and personal information. Includes information on protecting passwords, email software, IP numbers, encryption, firewalls, anti-virus software, and related resources.

Spyware watch (www.spyware.co.uk/): Spyware information and tools.

Staysafe.org (staysafe.org/): Educational site intended to help consumers understand both the positive aspects of the Internet as well as how to manage a variety of safety and security issues that exist online.

Susi (www.besafeonline.org/English/safer_use_of_services_on_the_internet.htm): Information and advice to parents and teachers, about risks on the Internet and how to behave.

Wired Safety (www.wiredsafety.org/): Offers advice about things that can go wrong online, including con

artists, identity thieves, predators, stalkers, criminal hackers, fraud, cyber-romance gone wrong and privacy problems. Includes contact form.

DIRECTORIES

E-Evidence Information Center (www.e-evidence.info/): Directory of material relating to all aspects of digital forensics and electronic evidence.

Itzalist (www.itzalist.com/com/computer-security/index.html): Computer resources offering antivirus software, current virus news, antivirus patches, online protection, security software and other information about computer security.

The Laughing Bit (www.tlb.ch/): Collection of links to information on Windows NT and Checkpoint Firewall-1 security.

Safe World (soft.safeworld.info/): Directory of links to downloadable security software. Brief descriptions for each.

SecureRoot (www.secureroot.com/): Hacking and security related links. Also offers discussion forums.

HELP AND TUTORIALS

How to find security holes (www.canonical.org/%7Ekragen/security-holes.html): Short primer originally written for the Linux Security Audit project.

Ronald L. Rivest's Cryptography and Security (people.csail.mit.edu/rivest/crypto-security.html): Provides links to cryptography and security sites.

SANS Institute – The Internet Guide To Popular Resources On Computer Security (www.sans.org/410.php): Combination FAQ and library providing answers to common information requests about computer security.

MAILING LISTS

Alert Security Mailing List (www.w3.easynet.co.uk/unitel/services/alert.html): Monthly security tips and alert mailing list. Pay subscription service provides information, tips and developments to protect your Internet computer security

Computer Forensics Training Mailing List (www.infosecinstitute.com/courses/computer_forensics_training.html): Computer forensics and incident response mailing list

FreeBSD Resources (www.freebsd.org/doc/en_US.ISO8859-1/books/handbook/eresources.html):

Mailing lists pertaining to FreeBSD. freebsd-security and freebsd-security-notifications are sources of official FreeBSD specific notifications.

InfoSec News (www.infosecnews.org/): Privately-run medium traffic list that caters to distribution of information security news articles.

ISO17799 & ISO27001 News (www.molemag.net/): News, background and updates on these international security standards.

IWS INFOCON Mailing List (www.iwar.org.uk/general/mailinglist.htm): The INFOCON mailing list is devoted to the discussion of cyber threats and all aspects of information operations, including offensive and defensive information warfare, information assurance, psychological operations, electronic warfare.

Risks Digest (catless.ncl.ac.uk/Risks): Forum on risks to the public in computers and related systems.

SCADA Security List (www.infosecinstitute.com/courses/scada_security_training.html): Mailing list concerning DCS and SCADA Security.

SecuriTeam Mailing Lists (www.securiteam.com/mailinglist.html): Location of various security mailing lists pertaining to exploits, hacking tools, and others.

Security Clipper (www.securityclipper.com/alarm-systems.php): Mailing list aggregator offering a selection of security lists to monitor.

NEWS AND MEDIA

Security Focus (www.securityfocus.com/): News and editorials on security related topics, along with a database of security knowledge.

Computer Security News-Topix (www.topix.com/tech/computer-security): News on computer security continually updated from thousands of sources around the net.

Computer Security Now (www.computersecuritynow.com/): Computer security news and information now for the less security oriented members of the community.

Enterprise Security Today (www.enterprise-security-today.com/fullpage/fullpage.xhtml?dest = %2F): Computer security news for the I.T. Professional.

Hagai Bar-El-Information Security Consulting (www.hbarel.com/news.html): Links to recent information security news articles from a variety of sources.

Help Net Security (www.net-security.org/): Help Net Security is a security portal offering various information on security issues-news, vulnerabilities, press

releases, software, viruses and a popular weekly newsletter.

Investigative Research into Infrastructure Assurance Group (news.ists.dartmouth.edu/): News digests arranged by subject with links to full articles. Subjects include cybercrime, regulation, consumer issues and technology.

O'Reilly Security Center (oreilly.com/pub/topic/security): O'Reilly is a leader in technical and computer book documentation for Security.

SecureLab (www.securelab.com/): Computer and network security software, information, and news.

SecuriTeam (www.securiteam.com/): Group dedicated to bringing you the latest news and utilities in computer security. Latest exploits with a focus on both Windows and Unix.

Security Geeks (securitygeeks.shmoo.com/): Identity and information security news summaries with discussion and links to external sources.

SecurityTracker (securitytracker.com/): Information on the latest security vulnerabilities, free SecurityTracker Alerts, and customized vulnerability notification services.

Xatrix Security (www.xatrix.org/): Security news portal with articles, a search engine and books.

ORGANIZATIONS

Association for Automatic Identification and Mobility (www.aimglobal.org/): Global trade association for the Automatic Identification and Data Capture (AIDC) industry, representing manufacturers, consultants, system integrators, and users involved in technologies that include barcode, RFID, card technologies, biometrics, RFDC, and their associated industries.

Association for Information Security (www.iseca.org/): Non-profit organization aiming to increase public awareness and facilitate collaboration among information security professionals worldwide. Offers security documents repository, training, news and joining information. Headquarters in Sofia, Bulgaria.

First (www.first.org/): Forum of Incident Response and Security Teams.

Information Systems Audit and Control Association (www.isaca.org/): Worldwide association of IS professionals dedicated to the audit, control, and security of information systems. Offer CISA qualification and COBIT standards.

IntoIT (www.intosaiitaudit.org/): The journal of the INTOSAI EDP Audit Committee. Its main focuses are on information systems auditing, IT performance auditing, and IT support for auditing.

North Texas Chapter ISSA (issa-northtexas.org/): The Dallas and Fort Worth chapter of the Information Systems Security Association (ISSA).

RCMP Technical Security Branch (www.rcmp-grc. gc.ca/tsb/): Canadian organization dedicated to providing federal government clients with a full range of professional physical and information technology security services and police forces with high technology forensic services.

The Shmoo Group (www.shmoo.com/): Privacy, crypto, and security tools and resources with daily news updates.

Switch-CERT (www.switch.ch/cert/): Swiss CERT-Team from the Swiss research network (Switch).

PRODUCTS AND TOOLS

AlphaShield (www.alphashield.com/): Hardware product used with your DSL or cable modem which disconnects the "always on" connection when the Internet is not in use, and prevents unauthorized access to your computer.

Bangkok Systems & Software (www.bangkoksystem. com/): System and software security. Offices in Thailand and India.

Beijing Rising International Software Co.,Ltd (www. rising-global.com/): Chinese supplier of antivirus, firewall, content management and other network security software and products.

Beyond If Solutions (www.beyondifsolutions.com/): Supplier of encryption and biometric devices, mobile device management software and remote network access.

BootLocker Security Software (www.bootlocker.com/): BootLocker secures your computer by asking for a password on startup. Features include multiple user support, screensaver activation, system tray support, and logging.

Calyx Suite (www.calyxsuite.com/): Offer token or biometric based authentication, with associated firewall, encryption and single sign-on software. Technical documentation, reseller listings and trial downloads. Located in France.

CipherLinx (www.cipherlinx.com/): Secure remote control technology using Skipjack encryption.

ControlGuard (www.controlguard.com/): Provides access control solutions for portable devices and removable media storage. [May not work in all browsers.]

CT Holdings, Inc. (www.ct-holdings.com/): Develops, markets and supports security and administration software products for both computer networks and desktop personal computers. (Nasdaq: CITN).

Cyber-Defense (enclaveforensics.com/): Links to free software tools for security analysis, content monitoring and content filtering.

Data Circle (www.datacircle.com/app/homepage. asp): Products include Datapass, Dataware, and Dataguide.

Digital Pathways Services Ltd UK (www.digpath. co.uk/): Providing specialized security products for encryption, risk assessment, intrusion detection, VPNs, and intrusion detection.

Diversinet Corp. (www.dvnet.com/): Develops digital certificate products based on public-key infrastructures and technologies required for corporate networks, intranets and electronic commerce on the Internet for a variety of security authentication applications. (Nasdaq: DVNT).

DLA Security Systems, Inc. (www.dlaco.com/): Key control software, key records management software, master keying software.

DSH (www.dshi.com/): Commercial and GSA reseller for Arbor Networks, Entercept, Netforensics and Solsoft.

eLearning Corner (www.elearningcorner.com/): Flash based, scorm-compatible online computer security awareness courses to improve corporate IT security by modifying employee behaviors.

Enclave Data Solutions (enclavedatasolutions.com/): Reseller of MailMarshal, WebMarshal, Jatheon email archival, Akonix IM and other security products.

eye4you (www.eye4you.com.au/): Software to monitor and restrict PC usage, enforce acceptable use policies, teach classes and prevent students changing vital system files.

Faronics (www.faronics.com/): Develops and markets end-point non-restrictive, configuration management and whitelist based software security solutions.

Forensic Computers (www.forensic-computers.com/ index.php): Provides specialized computer systems, security and forensic hardware and software.

GFI Software Ltd (www.gfi.com/languard/): Offers network security software including intrusion detection, security scanner, anti virus for Exchange and anti virus for ISA server.

Global Protective Management.com (www.secureassess.com/): Providing Global Security Solutions. GPM has created a unique suite of PC-based security software applications called SecureAssess.

The SecureAssess product line takes full advantage of current mobile technologies to provide clients with tools to effectively address their security vulnerabilities.

GuardianEdge Technologies, Inc. (www.guardianedge. com/): Encryption for hard disks and removable storage, authentication, device control and smart phone protection, within a shared infrastructure giving consolidated administration.

Hotfix Reporter (www.maximized.com/freeware/ hotfixreporter/): Works with Microsoft Network Security Hotfix Checker (HfNetChk) to scan for security holes, and outputs Web pages complete with links to the Microsoft articles and security patches.

IPLocks Inc. (www.iplocks.com/): Database security, monitoring, auditing reporting for governance and compliance.

iSecurityShop (www.isecurityshop.com/): Offers hardware and software network security products including firewalls, cryptographic software, antivirus, and intrusion detection systems.

Juzt-Innovations Ltd. (www.juzt-innovations.ie/): PC data backup and recovery card, 3DES encryption utility and smart card access control system.

KAATAN Software (www.kaatansoftware.com/): Developer of security software including encryption of office documents and SQLserver database auditing.

Kilross Network Protection Ltd. (www.kilross.com/): Irish reseller of IT security products from eSoft, SecPoint, SafeNet and others.

Lexias Incorporated (www.lexias.com/): Provides next generation solutions in data security and high availability data storage.

Lexura Solutions Inc. (www.lexurasolutions.com/index. htm): Software for encryption, intruder alerting and cookie management.

Locum Software Services Limited (www.locumsoftware.co.uk/): Security solutions for Unisys MCP/AS systems.

Lumigent Technologies (www.lumigent.com/): Enterprise data auditing solutions that help organizations mitigate the inherent risks associated with data use and regulatory compliance.

Marshal (www.marshal.com/): Supplier of email and Web security software.

n-Crypt (www.n-crypt.co.uk/): Develops integrated security software products for the IT industry.

NetSAW: Take a look at your network (www.proquesys. com/). This is a new enterprise class network security product currently being developed by ProQueSys

that provides both security experts as well as hobbyists with an understanding of the communications on their computer networks.

Networking Technologies Inc. (www.nwtechusa.com/): Distributor of email security, antivirus, Web filtering and archival products.

New Media Security (www.newmediasecurity.com/): Provides solutions to protect data on mobile computers, laptops, PDAs, tablets and in emails and on CDs.

NoticeBored (www.noticebored.com/html/site_map. html): Information security awareness materials for staff, managers and IT professionals covering a fresh topic every month.

Noweco (www.noweco.com/smhe.htm): Proteus is a software tool designed to audit information security management systems according to ISO17799 standards.

Oakley Networks Inc. (www.oakleynetworks.com/): Security systems capable of monitoring 'leakage' of intellectual property through diverse routes such as Web, email, USB and printouts.

Pacom Systems (www.pacomsystems.com/): Provider of integrated and networked security solutions for single- and multisite organizations.

Paktronix Systems: Network Security (www.paktronix. com/): Design, supply, and implement secure networks. Provide secure border Firewall systems for connecting networks to the Internet or each other. Offer Network Address Translation (NAT), Virtual Private Networking (VPN), with IPSec, and custom port translation capabilities.

PC Lockdown (www.pclockdown.com.au/): Software that allows the remote lockdown of networked workstations. Product features, company information, FAQ and contact details.

Porcupine.org (www.porcupine.org/): Site providing several pieces of software for protecting computers against Internet intruders.

Powertech (www.powertech.com/powertech/index.asp): Security software for the IBM AS/400 and iSeries including intrusion detection, user access control, encryption and auditing.

Protocom Development Systems (www.actividentity. com/): Specializes in developing network security software for all needs with credential management, strong authentication, console security and password reset tools.

Sandstorm Enterprises (www.sandstorm.net/): Products include PhoneSweep, a commercial telephone line scanner and NetIntercept, a network analysis tool to reassemble TCP sessions and reconstruct files.

SecurDesk (www.cursorarts.com/ca_sd.html): Access control and verification, protection for sensitive files and folders, log usage, customizable desktop environment, administration, and limit use.

Secure Directory File Transfer System (www.owlcti. com/): An essential tool for organizations that demand the ultimate in security. This "special purpose firewall" will safeguard the privacy of your data residing on a private network, while at the same time, providing an inflow of information from the Internet or any other outside network.

Secure your PC (www.maths.usyd.edu.au/u/psz/securepc. html): A few notes on securing a Windows98 PC.

Security Awareness, Inc. (www.securityawareness. com/): Security awareness products for all types of organizations, including security brochures, custom screensavers, brochures and computer-based training.

Security Officers Management and Analysis Project (www.somap.org/): An Open Source collaborative project building an information security risk management method, manuals and toolset.

SecurityFriday Co. Ltd. (www.securityfriday.com/): Software to monitor access to Windows file servers, detect promiscuous mode network sniffers and quantify password strength.

SeQureIT (www.softcat.com/): Security solutions including WatchGuard firewalls, Check Point, Clearswift, Nokia and Netilla SSL VPN. Also provide managed and professional services.

Service Strategies Inc. (www.ssimail.com/): Email gateway and messaging, firewall, VPN and SSL software and appliances for AS/400 and PC networks.

Silanis Technology (www.silanis.com/index.html): Electronic and digital signature solution provider includes resources, white papers, product news and related information.

Simpliciti (simpliciti.biz/): Browser lockdown software to restrict Web browsing.

Smart PC Tools (www.smartpctools.com/en/index.html): Offers a range of PC software products, most of which relate to security.

Softcat plc (UK) (www.softcat.com/): Supplier of IT solutions, dealing with software, hardware and licensing.

Softek Limited (www.mailmarshal.co.uk/): Distributor of security software: anti-virus, anti-spam, firewall, VPN, Web filtering, USB device control etc.

Softnet Security (www.safeit.com/): Software to protect confidential communication and information. Product specifications, screenshots, demo downloads, and contact details.

Tech Assist, Inc. (www.toolsthatwork.com/): Applications for data recovery, network security, and computer investigation.

Tropical Software (www.tropsoft.com/): Security and Privacy products.

UpdateEXPERT (www.lyonware.co.uk/Update-Expert. htm): A hotfix and service pack security management utility that helps systems administrators keep their hotfixes and service packs up-to-date.

Visionsoft (www.visionsoft.com/): Range of security and software license auditing software for businesses, schools and personal users.

Wave Systems Corp. (www.wavesys.com/): Develops proprietary application specific integrated circuit which meters usage of data, graphics, software, and video and audio sequences which can be digitally transmitted and develops a software version of its application for use over the Internet. (Nasdaq: WAVX).

WhiteCanyon Security Software (www.whitecanyon. com/): Providing software products to securely clean, erase, and wipe electronic data from hard drives and removable media.

Wick Hill Group (www.wickhill.co.uk/): Value added distributor specializing in secure infrastructure solutions for ebusiness. Portfolio includes a range of security solutions, from firewalls to SSL VPN, as well as Web access and Web management products.

Winability Software Corporation (www.winability.com/ home/): Directory access control and inactivity timeout software for Windows systems.

xDefenders Inc. (www.xdefenders.com/): Security appliances combining spam, virus and Web content filtering with firewall and IDS systems, plus vulnerability assessment services.

ZEPKO (www.zepko.com/): SIM (Security Information Management) technology provider. Assessing business risks and technology vulnerabilities surrounding IT security products.

RESEARCH

Centre for Applied Cryptographic Research (www.cacr. math.uwaterloo.ca/): Cryptographic research organization at the University of Waterloo. Downloads of technical reports, upcoming conferences list and details of graduate courses available.

Cryptography Research, Inc (www.cryptography.com/): Research and system design in areas including tamper resistance, content protection, network security, and financial services. Service descriptions and white papers.

Dartmouth College Institute for Security Technology Studies (ISTS) (www.ists.dartmouth.edu/): Research group focusing on United States national cyber-security and technological counterterrorism. Administers the I3P consortium.

Penn State S2 Group (ist.psu.edu/s2/): General cyber security lab at the United States university. Includes current and past projects, software, publications, and events.

The SANS Institute (www.sans.org/): Offers computer security research, training and information.

SUNY Stony Brook Secure Systems Lab (seclab.cs.sunysb.edu/seclab1/): Group aimed at research and education in computer and network security. Projects, academic programs, and publications. Located in New York, United States.

CONTENT FILTERING LINKS

Content Filtering vs. Blocking (www.securitysoft.com/content_filtering.html): An interesting whitepaper from Security Software Systems discussing the pros and cons of content filtering and blocking.

GateFilter Plug-in (www.deerfield.com/products/gatefilter/): GateFilter Plug-in is a software Internet filter providing content filtering for WinGate. The plug-in uses technology based on Artificial Content Recognition (ACR), which analyzes the content of a Web site, determines if it is inappropriate, and blocks the site if necessary. Supports English, German, French, and Spanish

GFI Mail Essentials (www.gfi.com/mes/): Mail Essentials provides email content checking, antivirus software, and spam blocking for Microsoft Exchange and SMTP.

InterScan eManager (us.trendmicro.com/us/solutions/enterprise/security-solutions/web-security/index.html): Provides real-time content filtering, spam blocking, and reporting. Optional eManager plug-in integrates seamlessly with InterScan VirusWall to safeguard intellectual property and confidential information, block inappropriate email and attachments, and protect against viruses. eManager also enables Trend Micro Outbreak Prevention Services.

NetIQ (MailMarshal) (www.marshal.com/): NetIQ provides MailMarshal, imMarshal, and WebMarshal for content filtering coupled with antivirus protection (McAfee).

Postfix Add-on Software (www.postfix.org/addon.html): List and links of add-on software for Postfix, including content filtering and antivirus solutions.

Qmail-Content filtering (www.fehcom.de/qmail/filter.html): Scripts that provide content filtering for incoming email with Qmail.

SonicWALL's Content Filtering Subscription Service (www.sonicguard.com/ContentFilteringService.asp): Integrated with SonicWALL's line of Internet security appliances, the SonicWALL Content Filtering subscription enables organizations such as businesses, schools and libraries to maintain Internet access policies tailored to their specific needs.

SurfControl (www.websense.com/site/scwelcome/index.html): SurfControl is a London-based company providing email and Web filtering solutions. as well as Internet monitoring and policy management software. Recently purchased by Websense.

Tumbleweed (www.tumbleweed.com/): Tumbleweed provides secure messaging and email policy management solutions geared to the government, financial and healthcare industries.

WebSense (www.websense.com/content/home.aspx): Websense provides a wide range of solutions including Internet filters, monitoring software, content filtering, tracking, and policy management.

OTHER LOGGING RESOURCES

IETF Security Issues in Network Event Logging (www.ietf.org/html.charters/syslog-charter.html): USENIX Special Interest Group

Building a Logging Infrastructure (www.sage.org/pubs/12_logging/): Loganalysis.org is a volunteer not-for-profit organization devoted to furthering the state of the art in computer systems log analysis through dissemination of information and sharing of resources.

Warning: URLs may change or be deleted without notice.

Ensuring Built-in Frequency Hopping Spread Spectrum Wireless Network Security

The Sensors Directorate sponsored new technology developed by Robert Gold Comm Systems, Inc. (RGCS) under a Phase II Fast Track Small Business Innovation Research program. This technology provides powerful security protection for wireless computer networks, cell phones, and other radio communications. Benefits include highly secure communications with the overhead of encryption and selective addressability of receivers, individually or in groups.[1]

ACCOMPLISHMENT

Dr. Gold developed a built-in self-synchronizing and selective addressing algorithm based on times-of-arrival (TOA) measurements of a frequency-hopping radio system. These algorithms allow a monitor to synchronize to a frequency-hopping radio in a wireless network by making relatively brief observations of the TOAs on a single frequency. RGCS designed the algorithms for integration into spread-spectrum, frequency-hopping systems widely used for wireless communications such as wireless fidelity computer networks, cellular phones, and two-way radios used by the military, police, firefighters, ambulances, and commercial fleets.[1]

BACKGROUND

Although very convenient for users, wireless communication is extremely vulnerable to eavesdropping. For example, hackers frequently access wireless computer networks (laptop computers linking to the wireless network).[1]

Encrypting the data increases the security of these wireless networks, but encryption is complex, inconvenient, time consuming for users, and adds a significant amount of overhead information that reduces data throughput. In frequency-hopping (spread-spectrum) wireless networks now in wide use, users protect the data by sending it in brief spurts, with the transmitter and receiver skipping in a synchronized pattern among hundreds of frequencies. An intruder without knowledge of the synchronization pattern would just hear static.[1]

A major vulnerability of many spread-spectrum wireless networks involves compromising the network security by intercepting unprotected information. Originators must send the sync pattern information to authorized receivers, often unprotected.[1]

The Gold algorithms support code-division multiple access, frequency-hopping multiple access, and ultra-wide-band spread-spectrum communication systems. They are designed for incorporation into enhanced versions of existing products, most of which already include circuitry that manufacturers can adapt to implement the technology.[1]

ADDITIONAL INFORMATION

To receive more information about the preceding or other activities in the Air Force Research Laboratory, contact TECH CONNECT, AFRL/XPTC, (800) 203-6451, and you will be directed to the appropriate laboratory expert. (03-SN-21).[1]

---

1 "New technology provides powerful security protection for wireless communications," Air Force Research Laboratory AFRLAir AFRL, 1864 4th St., Bldg. 15, Room 225, WPAFB, OH 45433-7131, 2008.

Configuring Wireless Internet Security Remote Access

This Appendix describes how to configure and add wireless remote access points (APs) as RADIUS clients of the Microsoft 2003 and Vista Internet Authentication Service (IAS) servers.

ADDING THE ACCESS POINTS AS RADIUS CLIENTS TO IAS

You must add wireless remote APs as RADIUS clients to IAS before they are allowed to use RADIUS authentication and accounting services. The wireless remote APs at a given location will typically be configured to use an IAS server at the same location for their primary RADIUS server and another IAS server at the same or a different location as the secondary RADIUS server. The terms "primary" and "secondary" here do not refer to any hierarchical relationship, or difference in configuration, between the IAS servers themselves. The terms are relevant only to the wireless remote APs, each of which has a designated primary and secondary (or backup) RADIUS server. Before you configure your wireless remote APs, you must decide which IAS server will be the primary and which will be the secondary RADIUS server for each wireless remote AP[1].

The following procedures describe adding RADIUS clients to two IAS servers. During the first procedure, a RADIUS secret is generated for the wireless remote AP; this secret, or key, will be used by IAS and the AP to authenticate each other. The details of this client along with its secret are logged to a file. This file is used in the second procedure to import the client into the second IAS[1].

Tip: You must not use this first procedure to add the same client to two IAS servers. If you do this, the client entries on each server will have a different RADIUS secret configured and the wireless remote AP will not be able to authenticate to both servers.

ADDING ACCESS POINTS TO THE FIRST IAS SERVER

This part of the appendix describes the adding of wireless remote APs to the first IAS server. A script is supplied to automate the generation of a strong, random RADIUS secret (password) and add the client to IAS. The script also creates a file (defaults to Clients.txt) that logs the details of each wireless remote AP added. This file records the name, IP address, and RADIUS secret generated for each wireless remote AP. These will be required when configuring the second IAS server and wireless remote APs[1].

Tip: The RADIUS clients are added to IAS as "RADIUS Standard" clients. Although this is appropriate for most wireless remote APs, some APs may require that you configure vendor–specific attributes (VSA) on the IAS server. You can configure VSAs either by selecting a specific vendor device in the properties of the RADIUS clients in the Internet Authentication Service MMC or (if the device is not listed) by specifying the VSAs in the IAS remote access policy.

SCRIPTING THE ADDITION OF ACCESS POINTS TO IAS SERVER (ALTERNATIVE PROCEDURE)

If you do not want to add the wireless remote APs to the IAS server interactively using the previous procedure,

---

1 "Securing Wireless LANs with PEAP and Passwords, Chapter 5: Building the Wireless LAN Security Infrastructure," © 2008 Microsoft Corporation. All rights reserved. Microsoft Corporation, One Microsoft Way, Redmond, WA 98052-6399, 2007.

you can just generate the RADIUS client entries output files for each wireless remote AP without adding them to IAS. You can then import the RADIUS client entries into both the first IAS server and the second IAS server. Because you can script this whole operation, you may prefer to add your RADIUS clients this way if you have to add a large number of wireless remote APs[1].

> *Tip:* This procedure is an alternative method for adding RADIUS clients in a scripted rather than an interactive fashion.

CONFIGURING THE WIRELESS ACCESS POINTS

Having added RADIUS clients entries for the wireless remote APs to IAS, you now need to configure the wireless remote APs themselves. You must add the IP addresses of the IAS servers and the RADIUS client secrets that each AP will use to communicate securely with the IAS servers. Every wireless remote AP will be configured with a primary and secondary (or backup) IAS server. You should perform the procedures for the wireless remote APs at every site in your enterprise[1].

The procedure for configuring wireless remote APs varies depending on the make and model of the device. However, wireless remote AP vendors normally provide detailed instructions for configuring their devices. Depending on the vendor, these instructions may also be available online[1].

Prior to configuring the security settings for your wireless remote APs, you must configure the basic wireless network settings. These will include but are not limited to:

- IP Address and subnet mask of the wireless remote AP
- Default gateway
- Friendly name of the wireless remote AP
- Wireless Network Name (SSID)[1]

The preceding list will include a number of other parameters that affect the deployment of multiple wireless remote APs: settings that control the correct radio coverage across your site, for example, 802.11 Radio Channel, Transmission Rate, and Transmission Power, and so forth. Discussion of these parameters is outside the scope of this appendix. Use the vendor documentation as a reference when configuring these settings or consult a wireless network services supplier[1].

The guidance in this appendix assumes that you have set these items correctly and are able to connect to the wireless remote AP from a WLAN client using an unauthenticated connection. You should test this before configuring the authentication and security parameters listed later in this appendix[1].

ENABLING SECURE WLAN AUTHENTICATION ON ACCESS POINTS

You must configure each wireless remote AP with a primary and a secondary RADIUS server. The wireless remote AP will normally use the primary server for all authentication requests, and switch over to the secondary server if the primary server is unavailable. It is important that you plan the allocation of wireless remote APs and carefully decide which server should be made primary and which should be made secondary. To summarize:

In a site with two (or more) IAS servers, balance your wireless remote APs across the available servers so that approximately half of the wireless remote APs use server 1 as primary and server 2 as secondary, and the remaining use server 2 as primary and server 1 as secondary[1].

In sites where you have only one IAS server, this should always be the primary server. You should configure a remote server (in the site with most reliable connectivity to this site) as the secondary server[1].

In sites where there is no IAS server, balance the wireless remote APs between remote servers using the server with most resilient and lowest latency connectivity. Ideally, these servers should be at different sites unless you have resilient wide area network (WAN) connectivity[1].

Table H.1[1] lists the settings that you need to configure on your wireless remote APs. Although the names and descriptions of these settings may vary from one vendor to another, your wireless remote AP documentation helps you determine those that correspond to the items in Table H.1[1].

> *Tip:* The Key Refresh Time-out is set to 60 minutes for use with dynamic WEP. The Session Timeout value set in the IAS remote access policy is the same or shorter than this. Whichever of these has the lower setting will take precedence, so you only need to modify the setting in IAS. If you are using WPA, you should increase this setting in the AP to eight hours. Consult your vendor's documentation for more information.

Use the same RADIUS secrets procedure to add wireless remote APs to IAS. Although you may have

TABLE H.1 Wireless Access Point Configuration

Item	Setting
Authentication Parameters	
Authentication Mode	802.1X Authentication
Re-authentication	Enable
Rapid/Dynamic Re-keying	Enable
Key Refresh Time-out	60 minutes
Encryption Parameters (these settings usually relate to static WEP encryption)	(Encryption parameters may be disabled or be overridden when rapid re-keying is enabled)
Enable Encryption	Enable
Deny Unencrypted	Enable
RADIUS Authentication	
Enable RADIUS Authentication	Enable
Primary RADIUS Authentication Server	Primary IAS IP Address
Primary RADIUS Server Port	1812 (default)
Secondary RADIUS Authentication Server	Secondary IAS IP Address
Secondary RADIUS Server Port	1812 (default)
RADIUS Authentication Shared Secret	XXXXXX (replace with generated secret)
Retry Limit	5
Retry Timeout	5 seconds
RADIUS Accounting	
Enable RADIUS Accounting	Enable
Primary RADIUS Accounting Server	Primary IAS IP Address
Primary RADIUS Server Port	1813 (default)
Secondary RADIUS Accounting Server	Secondary IAS IP Address
Secondary RADIUS Server Port	1813 (default)
RADIUS Accounting Shared Secret	XXXXXX (replace with generated secret)
Retry Limit	5
Retry Timeout	5 seconds

not yet configured a secondary IAS server as a backup to the primary server, you can still add the server's IP address to the wireless remote AP now (to avoid having to reconfigure it later)[1].

Depending on the wireless remote AP hardware model, you may not have separate configurable entries for Authentication and Accounting RADIUS servers. If you have separate configurable entries, set them both to the same server unless you have a specific reason for doing otherwise. The RADIUS retry limit and timeout values given in Table H.1 are common defaults but these values are not mandatory[1].

Note: If you are currently using wireless remote APs with no security enabled or only static WEP, you need to plan your migration to an 802.1X–based WLAN.

ADDITIONAL SETTINGS TO SECURE WIRELESS ACCESS POINTS

In addition to enabling 802.1X parameters, you should also configure the wireless remote APs for highest security. Most wireless network hardware is supplied with

TABLE H.2 Wireless Access Point Security Configuration

Item	Recommended Setting	Notes
General		
Administrator Password	XXXXXX	Set to complex password.
Other Management Passwords	XXXXXX	Some devices use multiple management passwords to help protect access using different management protocols; ensure that all are changed from the defaults to secure values.
Management Protocols		
Serial Console	Enable	If no encrypted protocols are available, this is the most secure method of configuring wireless remote APs although this requires physical serial cable connections between the wireless remote APs and terminal and hence cannot be used remotely.
Telnet	Disable	All Telnet transmissions are in plaintext, so passwords and RADIUS client secrets will be visible on the network. If the Telnet traffic can be secured using Internet Protocol security (IPsec) or SSH, you can safely enable and use it.
HTTP	Disable	HTTP management is usually in plaintext and suffers from the same weaknesses as unencrypted telnet. HTTPS, if available, is recommended.
HTTPS (SSL or TLS)	Enable	Follow the vendor's instructions for configuring keys/certificates for this.
SNMP Communities		SNMP is the default protocol for network management. Use SNMP v3 with password protection for highest security. It is often the protocol used by GUI configuration tools and network management systems. However, you can disable it if you do not use it.
Community 1 Name	XXXXXX	The default is usually "public." Change this to a complex value.
Community 2 Name	Disabled	Any unnecessary community names should be disabled or set to complex values.

insecure management protocols enabled and administrator passwords set to well-known defaults, which poses a security risk. You should configure the settings listed in Table H.2[1]; however, this is not an exhaustive list. You should consult your vendor's documentation for authoritative guidance on this topic. When choosing passwords and community names for Simple Network Management Protocol (SNMP), use complex values that include upper and lowercase letters, numbers, and punctuation characters. Avoid choosing anything that can be guessed easily from information such as your domain name, company name, and site address[1].

You should not disable SSID (WLAN network name) broadcast since this can interfere with the ability of Windows XP to connect to the right network. Although disabling the SSID broadcast is often recommended as a security measure, it gives little practical security benefit if a secure 802.1X authentication method is being used. Even with SSID broadcast from the AP disabled, it is relatively easy for an attacker to determine the SSID by capturing client connection packets. If you are concerned about broadcasting the existence of your WLAN,

you can use a generic name for your SSID, which will not be attributable to your enterprise[1].

REPLICATING RADIUS CLIENT CONFIGURATION TO OTHER IAS SERVERS

Typically, the wireless remote APs in a given site are serviced by an IAS server at that site. For example, the site A IAS server services wireless remote APs in site A, while the site B server services wireless remote APs in site B and so on. However, other server settings such as the remote access policies will often be common to many IAS servers. For this reason the export and import of RADIUS client information is handled separately by the procedures described in this appendix. Although you will find relatively few scenarios where replicating RADIUS client information is relevant, it is useful in certain circumstances (for example, where you have two IAS servers on the same site acting as primary and secondary RADIUS servers for all wireless remote APs on that site)[1].

Frequently Asked Questions

Q. What is a firewall?

A. Firewall helps make your computer invisible to online attackers and blocks some malicious software such as viruses, worms, and Trojans. A firewall can also help prevent software on your computer from accessing the Internet to accept updates and modification without your permission[1].

Firewalls come in both software and hardware form, but hardware firewalls are intended for use *in addition* to a software firewall. It is important to have both a firewall and antivirus software turned on before you connect to the Internet[1].

Q. What is antivirus software?

A. Antivirus software helps protect your computer against *specific* viruses and related malicious software, such as worms and Trojans. Antivirus software must be kept up to date. Updates are generally available through a subscription from your antivirus vendor[1].

Q. Do you need both a firewall and antivirus software?

A. Yes. A firewall helps stop hackers and viruses before they reach your computer, while antivirus software helps get rid of known viruses if they manage to bypass the firewall or if they've already infected your computer. One way viruses get past a firewall is when you ignore its warning messages when you download software from the Internet or email[1].

Q. What is antispyware software?

A. Antispyware software helps detect and remove spyware from your computer. "Spyware" (also known as "adware") generally refers to software that is designed to monitor your activities on your computer[1].

Spyware can produce unwanted pop-up advertising, collect personal information about you, or change the configuration of your computer to the spyware designer's specifications. At its worst, spyware can enable criminals to disable your computer and steal your identity. Antispyware software is an important tool to help you keep your computer running properly and free from intrusion[1].

Note: Some "spyware" actually helps desirable software to run as it's intended, or enables some good software to be offered on a free-with-advertisements basis (such as many online email programs). Most antispyware software allows you to customize your settings so you can enable or disable programs.

Q. What is a spam filter?

A. Spam filters (sometimes broadly referred to as "email filters") evaluate incoming email messages to determine if they contain elements that are commonly associated with unwanted or dangerous bulk mailing. If the filter determines that an email message is suspicious, the message usually goes to a designated folder, and links and other code in it are disabled. Then you can evaluate the message more safely at your convenience[1].

Q: What is a phishing filter?

A: A phishing filter is usually a component of a Web browser or Internet toolbar. It evaluates Web sites for signs that they are connected with phishing scams.

Phishing scams use email and Web sites that look identical to those that belong to legitimate sources (such as financial or government institutions) but are actually hoaxes. If you click links in the email or enter your user name, password, and other data into these Web

---

1 "Security products and services FAQ," Microsoft TechNet, © 2008 Microsoft Corporation. All rights reserved. Microsoft Corporation, One Microsoft Way, Redmond, WA 98052-6399. 2008.

sites, it gives scammers information they can use to defraud you or to steal your identity[1].

Q: What are parental controls?

A: Parental controls can help you protect your children from inappropriate content, both on the Internet and in computer video games[1].

Q: Does my brand new computer come with these software security tools?

A: Maybe. When you buy a new computer, check your packing list to see if the manufacturer has included firewall, antivirus, or antispyware software in addition to the operating system[1].

Glossary

AAA: Administration, authorization, and authentication.

Access: A specific type of interaction between a subject and an object that results in the flow of information from one to the other. The capability and opportunity to gain knowledge of, or to alter information or materials including the ability and means to communicate with (i.e., input or receive output), or otherwise make use of any information, resource, or component in a computer system.

Access Control: The process of limiting access to the resources of a system to only authorized persons, programs, processes, or other systems. Synonymous with controlled access and limited access. Requires that access to information resources be controlled by or for the target system. In the context of network security, access control is the ability to limit and control the access to host systems and applications via communications links. To achieve this control, each entity trying to gain access must first be identified, or authenticated, so that access rights can be tailored to the individual.

Accreditation: The written formal management decision to approve and authorize an organization to operate a classified information system (IS) to process, store, transfer, or provide access to classified information.

AES: Advanced Encryption Standard.

Accreditation/Approval: The official management authorization for operation of an MIS. It provides a formal declaration by an Accrediting Authority that a computer system is approved to operate in a particular security mode using a prescribed set of safeguards. Accreditation is based on the certification process as well as other management considerations. An accreditation statement affixes security responsibility with the Accrediting Authority and shows that proper care has been taken for security.

Adequate Security: Security commensurate with the risk and magnitude of the harm resulting from the loss, misuse, or unauthorized access to or modification of information. This includes assuring that systems and applications used by the agency operate effectively and provide appropriate confidentiality, integrity, and availability, through the use of cost-effective management, personnel, operational and technical controls.

ADP: Automatic Data Processing. See also: Management Information System.

Application: A software organization of related functions, or series of interdependent or closely related programs, that when executed accomplish a specified objective or set of user requirements. See also: Major Application, Process.

Application Control: The ability for next generation content filter gateways to inspect the application and determine its intention and block accordingly.

Application Owner: The official who has the responsibility to ensure that the program or programs, which make up the application accomplish the specified objective or set of user requirements established for that application, including appropriate security safeguards. See also: Process Owner.

Attachment: The blocking of certain types of file (executable programs).

Audit: To conduct the independent review and examination of system records and activities.

Audit Capability: The ability to recognize, record, store, and analyze information related to security-relevant activities on a system in such a way that the resulting records can be used to determine which activities occurred and which user was responsible for them.

Audit Trail: A set of records that collectively provides documentary evidence of processing. It is used to aid in tracing from original transactions forward to related records and reports, and/or backwards from records and reports to their component source transactions.

Automated Information Systems (AIS): The infrastructure, organization, personnel, and components for the collection, processing, storage, transmission, display, dissemination, and disposition of information.

Automatic Data Processing (ADP): The assembly of computer hardware, firmware, and software used to categorize, sort, calculate, compute, summarize, store, retrieve, control, process, and/or protect data with a minimum of human intervention. ADP systems can include, but are not limited to, process control computers, embedded computer systems that perform general purpose computing functions, supercomputers, personal computers, intelligent terminals, offices automation systems (which includes standalone microprocessors, memory typewriters, and terminal connected to mainframes), firmware, and other implementations of MIS technologies as may be developed: they also include applications and operating system software. See also: Management Information System.

Authenticate/Authentication: The process to verify the identity of a user, device, or other entity in a computer system, often as a prerequisite to allowing access to resources in a system. Also, a process used to verify that the origin of transmitted data is correctly identified, with assurance that the identity is not false. To establish the validity of a claimed identity.

Authenticated User: A user who has accessed a MIS with a valid identifier and authentication combination.

Authenticator: A method of authenticating a classified information system (IS) in the form of knowledge or possession (for example, password, token card, key).

Authorization: The privileges and permissions granted to an individual by a designated official to access or use a program, process, information, or system. These privileges are based on the individual's approval and need-to-know.

Authorized Person: A person who has the need-to-know for sensitive information in the performance of official duties and who has been granted authorized access at the required level. The responsibility for determining whether a prospective recipient is an authorized person rests with the person who has, possession, knowledge, or control of the sensitive information involved, and not with the prospective recipient.

Availability: The property of being accessible and usable upon demand by an authorized entity. Security constraints must make MIS services available to authorized users and unavailable to unauthorized users.

Availability of Data: The state when data are in the place needed by the user, at the time the user needs them, and in the form needed by the user.

Backup: A copy of a program or data file for the purposes of protecting against loss if the original data becomes unavailable.

Backup and Restoration of Data: The regular copying of data to separate media and the recovery from a loss of information.

Backup Operation: A method of operations to complete essential tasks as identified by a risk analysis. These tasks would be employed following a disruption of the MIS and continue until the MIS is acceptably restored. See also: Contingency Plan, Disaster Recovery.

Bad Reputation Domains: Sites that appear on one or more security industry blacklists for repeated bad behavior, including hosting malware and phishing sites, generating spam, or hosting content linked to by spam email.

Botnet: Sites used by botnet herders for command and control of infected machines. Sites that known malware and spyware connects to for command and control by cyber criminals. These sites are differentiated from the Malcode category to enable reporting on potentially infected computers inside the network.

By URL: Filtering based on the URL. This is a suitable for blocking Web sites or sections of Web sites.

C2: A level of security safeguard criteria. See also: Controlled Access Protection, TCSEC.

Capstone: The U.S. Government's long-term project to develop a set of standards for publicly-available cryptography, as authorized by the Computer Security Act of 1987. The Capstone cryptographic system will consist of four major components and be contained on a single integrated circuit microchip that provides nonDoD data encryption for Sensitive But Unclassified information. It implements the Skipjack algorithm. See also: Clipper.

Certification: The comprehensive analysis of the technical and nontechnical features, and other safeguards, to establish the extent to which a particular MIS meets a set of specified security requirements. Certification is part of the accreditation process and carries with it an implicit mandate for accreditation. See also: Accreditation.

Channel: An information transfer path within a system or the mechanism by which the path is affected.

CHAP: Challenge Handshake Authentication Protocol developed by the IETF.

Child Pornography: Sites that promote, discuss or portray children in sexual acts and activity or the abuse of children. Pornographic sites that advertise or imply the depiction of underage models and that do not have a U.S.C. 2257 declaration on their main page. As of March 13, 2007, all sites categorized as child porn are actually saved into the URL Library in the Porn category and are automatically submitted to the Internet Watch Foundation for legal verification as child pornography (http://www.iwf.org.uk/). If the IWF agrees that a site and/or any of its hosted pages are child pornography, they add it those URLs to their master list. The master list is downloaded nightly and saved into the URL Library in the Child Porn category.

Cipher: An algorithm for encryption or decryption. A cipher replaces a piece of information (an element of plain text) with another object, with the intent to conceal meaning. Typically, the replacement rule is governed by a secret key. See also: Decryption, Encryption.

Ciphertext: Form of cryptography in which the *plain-text* is made unintelligible to anyone who intercepts it by a transformation of the information itself, based on some key.

CIO-Cyber Web Site: Provides training modules for Cyber Security subjects.

Classification: A systematic arrangement of information in groups or categories according to established criteria. In the interest of national security it is determined that the information requires a specific degree of protection against unauthorized disclosure together with a designation signifying that such a determination has been made.

Classified Distributive Information Network (CDIN): Any cable, wire, or other approved transmission media used for the clear text transmission of classified information in certain DOE access controlled environments. Excluded is any system used solely for the clear text transmission and reception of intrusion/fire alarm or control signaling.

Classified Information System (CIS): A discrete set of information resources organized for the collection, processing, maintenance, transmission, and dissemination of classified information, in accordance with defined procedures, whether automated or manual. Guidance Note: For the purposes of this document, an IS may be a standalone, single- or multiuser system or a network comprised of multiple systems and ancillary supporting communications devices, cabling, and equipment.

Classified Information Systems Security Plan (ISSP): The basic classified system protection document and evidence that the proposed system, or update to an existing system, meets the specified protection requirements. The Classified ISSP describes the classified IS, any interconnections, and the security protections and countermeasures. This plan is used throughout the certification, approval, and accreditation process and serves for the lifetime of the classified system as the formal record of the system and its environment as approved for operation. It also serves as the basis for inspections of the system.

Classified Information Systems Security Program: The Classified Information Systems Security Program provides for the protection of classified information on information systems at LANL.

Classified Information Systems Security Site Manager (ISSM): The manager responsible for the LANL Classified Information Systems Security Program.

Clear or Clearing (MIS Storage Media): The removal of sensitive data from MIS storage and other peripheral devices with storage capacity, at the end of a period of processing. It includes data removal in such a way that assures, proportional to data sensitivity, it may not be reconstructed using normal system capabilities, i.e., through the keyboard. See also: Object Reuse, Remanence.

Clipper: Clipper is an encryption chip developed and sponsored by the U.S. government as part of the Capstone project. Announced by the White House in April 1993, Clipper was designed to balance competing concerns of federal law-enforcement agencies and private citizens by using escrowed encryption keys. See also: Capstone, Skipjack.

Collaborator: A person not employed by the Laboratory who (1) is authorized to remotely access a LANL unclassified computer system located on the site or (2) uses a LANL system located off the site. Guidance note: A collaborator does not have an active Employee Information System record.

Commercial-off-the-Shelf (COTS): Products that are commercially available and can be utilized as generally marketed by the manufacturer.

Compromise: The disclosure of sensitive information to persons not authorized access or having a need-to-know.

Computer Fraud and Abuse Act of 1986: This law makes it a crime to knowingly gain access to a federal government computer without authorization and to affect its operation.

Computer Security: Technological and managerial procedures applied to MIS to ensure the availability, integrity, and confidentiality of information managed by the MIS. See also: Information Systems Security.

Computer Security Act of 1987: The law provides for improving the security and privacy of sensitive information in "federal computer systems"—"a computer system operated by a federal agency or other organization that processes information (using a computer system) on behalf of the federal government to accomplish a federal function."

Computer Security Incident: Any event or condition having actual or potentially adverse effects on an information system. See the Cyber Security Handbook.

Computing, Communications, and Networking (CCN) Division Web Sites: Describes network services and their use by system users.

Confidentiality: The condition when designated information collected for approved purposes is not disseminated beyond a community of authorized knowers. It is distinguished from secrecy, which results from the intentional concealment or withholding of information. [OTA-TCT-606] Confidentiality refers to: 1) how data will be maintained and used by the organization that collected it; 2) what further uses will be made of it; and 3) when individuals will be required to consent to such uses. It includes the protection of data from passive attacks and requires that the information (in an MIS or transmitted) be accessible only for reading by authorized parties. Access can include printing, displaying, and other forms of disclosure, including simply revealing the existence of an object.

Configuration Management (CM): The management of changes made to an MIS hardware, software, firmware, documentation, tests, test fixtures, test documentation, communications interfaces, operating procedures, installation structures, and all changes there to throughout the development and operational life-cycle of the MIS.

Contingency Plan: The documented organized process for implementing emergency response, backup operations, and post-disaster recovery, maintained for an MIS as part of its security program, to ensure the availability of critical assets (resources) and facilitate the continuity of operations in an emergency. See also: Disaster Recovery.

Contingency Planning: The process of preparing a documented organized approach for emergency response, backup operations, and post-disaster recovery that will ensure the availability of critical MIS resources and facilitate the continuity of MIS operations in an emergency. See also: Contingency Plan, Disaster Recovery.

Controlled Access Protection (C2): A category of safeguard criteria as defined in the Trusted Computer Security Evaluation Criteria (TCSEC). It includes identification and authentication, accountability,

auditing, object reuse, and specific access restrictions to data. This is the minimum level of control for SBU information.

Conventional Encryption: A form of cryptosystem in which encryption and decryption are performed using the same key. See also: Symmetric Encryption.

COTS: See: Commercial-off-the-Shelf.

COTS Software: Commercial-off the Shelf Software – software acquired by government contract through a commercial vendor. This software is a standard product, not developed by a vendor for a particular government project.

Countermeasures: See: Security Safeguards.

Cracker: See: Hacker.

Criminal Skills: Sites that promote crime or illegal activity such as credit card number generation, illegal surveillance and murder. Sites which commercially sell surveillance equipment will not be saved. Sample sites: www.illegalworld.com, www.password-crackers.com, and www.spy-cam-surveillance-equipment.com

Critical Assets: Those assets, which provide direct support to the organization's ability to sustain its mission. Assets are critical if their absence or unavailability would significantly degrade the ability of the organization to carry out its mission, and when the time that the organization can function without the asset is less than the time needed to replace the asset.

Critical Processing: Any applications, which are so important to an organization, that little or no loss of availability is acceptable; critical processing must be defined carefully during disaster and contingency planning. See also: Critical Assets.

Cryptanalysis: The branch of cryptology dealing with the breaking of a cipher to recover information, or forging encrypted information what will be accepted as authentic.

Cryptography: The branch of cryptology dealing with the design of algorithms for encryption and decryption, intended to ensure the secrecy and/or authenticity of messages.

Cryptology: The study of secure communications, which encompasses both cryptography and cryptanalysis.

Cyber Security Program: The program mandated to ensure that the confidentiality, integrity, and availability of electronic data, networks and computer systems are maintained to include protecting data, networks and computing systems from unauthorized access, alteration, modification, disclosure, destruction, transmission, denial of service, subversion of security measures, and improper use.

DAC: See: C2, Discretionary Access Control and TCSEC.

DASD (Direct Access Storage Device): A physical electromagnetic data storage unit used in larger computers. Usually these consist of cylindrical stacked multiunit assemblies, which have large capacity storage capabilities.

Data: A representation of facts, concepts, information, or instructions suitable for communication, interpretation, or processing. It is used as a plural noun meaning "facts or information" as in: *These data are described fully in the appendix*, or as a singular mass noun meaning "information" as in: *The data is entered into the computer*.

Data Custodian: The person who ensures that information is reviewed to determine if it is classified or sensitive unclassified. This person is responsible for generation, handling and protection, management, and destruction of the information. Guidance Note: An alternative name for the data custodian is classified information systems application owner.

DES: Digital Encryption Standard.

Data Encryption Standard (DES): Data Encryption Standard is an encryption block cipher defined and endorsed by the U.S. government in 1977 as an official standard (FIPS PUB 59). Developed by IBM®, it has been extensively studied for over 15 years and is the most well known and widely used cryptosystem in the world. See also: Capstone, Clipper, RSA, Skipjack.

Data Integrity: The state that exists when computerized data are the same as those that are in the source documents and have not been exposed to accidental or malicious alterations or destruction. It requires that the MIS assets and transmitted information be capable of modification only by authorized parties. Modification includes writing, changing, changing status, deleting, creating, and the delaying or replaying of transmitted messages. See also: Integrity, System Integrity.

Deciphering: The translation of encrypted text or data (called ciphertext) into original text or data (called plaintext). See also: Decryption.

Decryption: The translation of encrypted text or data (called ciphertext) into original text or data (called plaintext). See also: Deciphering.

Dedicated Security Mode: An operational method when each user with direct or indirect individual access to a computer system, its peripherals, and remote terminals or hosts has a valid personnel security authorization and a valid need-to-know for all information contained within the system.

Dedicated System: A system that is specifically and exclusively dedicated to and controlled for a specific mission, either for full time operation or a specified period of time. See also: Dedicated Security Mode.

Default: A value or setting that a device or program automatically selects if you do not specify a substitute.

Degaussing Media: Method to magnetically erase data from magnetic tape.

Denial of Service: The prevention of authorized access to resources or the delaying of time-critical operations. Refers to the inability of a MIS system or any essential part to perform its designated mission, either by loss of, or degradation of operational capability.

Department of Defense (DOD) Trusted Computer System Evaluation Criteria: The National Computer Security Center (NCSC) criteria intended for use in the design and evaluation of systems that will process and/or store sensitive (or classified) data. This document contains a uniform set of basic requirements and evaluation classes used for assessing the degrees of assurance in the effectiveness of hardware and software security controls built in the design and evaluation of MIS. See also: C2, Orange Book, TCSEC.

DES: See: Data Encryption Standard. See also: Capstone, Clipper, RSA, Skipjack.

Designated Accrediting Authority (DAA): A DOE official with the authority to formally grant approval for operating a classified information system; the person who determines the acceptability of the residual risk in a system that is prepared to process classified information and either accredits or denies operation of the system.

Designated Security Officer: The person responsible to the designated high level manager for ensuring that security is provided for and implemented throughout the life-cycle of an MIS from the beginning of the system concept development phase through its design, development, operations, maintenance, and disposal.

Dial-up: The service whereby a computer terminal can use the telephone to initiate and effect communication with a computer.

Digital Signature Standard: DSS is the Digital Signature Standard, which specifies a Digital Signature Algorithm (DSA), and is part of the U.S. government's Capstone project. It was selected by NIST and NSA to be the digital authentication standard of the U.S. government, but has not yet been officially adopted. See also: Capstone, Clipper, RSA, Skipjack.

Disaster Recovery Plan: The procedures to be followed should a disaster (fire, flood, etc.) occur. Disaster recovery plans may cover the computer center and other aspects of normal organizational functioning. See also: Contingency Plan.

Discretionary Access Control (DAC): A means of restricting access to objects based on the identity of subjects and/or groups to which they belong or on the possession of an authorization granting access to those objects. The controls are discretionary in the sense that a subject with a certain access permission is capable of passing that permission (perhaps indirectly) onto any other subject.

Discretionary access controls: Controls that limit access to information on a system on an individual basis.

Discretionary processing: Any computer work that can withstand interruption resulting from some disaster.

DSS: See: Capstone, Clipper, Digital Signature Standard, RSA, Skipjack.

Dubious/Unsavory: Sites of a questionable legal or ethical nature. Sites which promote or distribute products, information, or devices whose use may be deemed unethical or, in some cases, illegal: Warez, Unlicensed mp3 downloads, Radar detectors, and Street racing. Sample sites: www.thepayback.com and www.strangereports.com.

Emergency Response: A response to emergencies such as fire, flood, civil commotion, natural disasters, bomb threats, etc., in order to protect lives, limit the damage to property and the impact on MIS operations.

Enciphering: The conversion of plaintext or data into unintelligible form by means of a reversible translation that is based on a translation table or algorithm. See also: Encryption.

Encryption: The conversion of plaintext or data into unintelligible form by means of a reversible translation that is based on a translation table or algorithm. See also: Enciphering.

Entity: Something that exists as independent, distinct or self-contained. For programs, it may be anything that can be described using data, such as an employee, product, or invoice. Data associated with an entity are called attributes. A product's price, weight, quantities in stock, and description all constitute attributes. It is often used in describing distinct business organizations or government agencies.

Environment: The aggregate of external circumstance, conditions, and events that affect the development, operation, and maintenance of a system. Environment is often used with qualifiers such as computing environment, application environment, or threat environment, which limit the scope being considered.

Evaluation: Evaluation is the assessment for conformance with a preestablished metric, criteria, or standard.

Facsimile: A document that has been sent, or is about to be sent, via a fax machine.

Firewall: A collection of components or a system that is placed between two networks and possesses the following properties: 1) all traffic from inside to outside, and vice-versa, must pass through it; 2) only authorized traffic, as defined by the local security policy, is allowed to pass through it; 3) the system itself is immune to penetration.

Firmware: Equipment or devices within which computer programming instructions necessary to the performance of the device's discrete functions are electrically embedded in such a manner that they cannot be electrically altered during normal device operations.

Friendly Termination: The removal of an employee from the organization when there is no reason to believe that the termination is other than mutually acceptable.

Gateway: A machine or set of machines that provides relay services between two networks.

General Support System: An interconnected set of information resources under the same direct management control which shares common functionality. A system normally includes hardware, software, information, data, applications, communications, and people. A system can be, for example, a local area network (LAN) including smart terminals that support a branch office, an agency-wide backbone, a communications network, a departmental data processing center including its operating system and utilities, a tactical radio network, or a shared information processing service organization (IPSO).

Generic Remote Access: Web sites pertaining to the use of, or download of remote access clients.

Green Network: See Open Network.

Hack: Any software in which a significant portion of the code was originally another program. Many hacked programs simply have the copyright notice removed. Some hacks are done by programmers using code they have previously written that serves as a boilerplate for a set of operations needed in the program they are currently working on. In other cases it simply means a draft. Commonly misused to imply theft of software. See also: Hacker.

Hacker: Common nickname for an unauthorized person who breaks into or attempts to break into an MIS by circumventing software security safeguards. Also, commonly called a "cracker." See also: Hack, Intruder.

Hacking: Sites discussing and/or promoting unlawful or questionable tools or information revealing the ability to gain access to software or hardware/communications equipment and/or passwords: Password generation, Compiled binaries, Hacking tools and Software piracy (game cracking). Sample sites: www.happyhacker.org, and www.phreak.com.

Hardware: Refers to objects that you can actually touch, like disks, disk drives, display screens, keyboards, printers, boards, and chips.

Heuristic: Filtering based on heuristic scoring of the content based on multiple criteria.

Hostmaster Database: A relational database maintained by the Network Engineering Group (CCN-5) that contains information about every device connected to the Laboratory unclassified yellow and green networks.

HTML Anomalies: Legitimate companies keep their Web sites up to date and standards based to support the newest browser version support and features and are malicious code free. Malicious sites frequently have HTML code that is not compliant to standards.

Identification: The process that enables recognition of an entity by a system, generally by the use of unique machine-readable usernames.

Information Security: The protection of information systems against unauthorized access to or modification of information, whether in storage, processing or transit, and against the denial of service to authorized users or the provision of service to unauthorized users, including those measures necessary to detect, document, and counter such threats.

Information Security Officer (ISO): The person responsible to the designated high level manager for ensuring that security is provided for and implemented throughout the life-cycle of an MIS from the beginning of the system concept development phase through its design, development, operations, maintenance, and disposal.

Information System (IS): The entire infrastructure, organizations, personnel and components for the collection, processing, storage, transmission, display, dissemination and disposition of information.

Information Systems Security (INFOSEC): The protection of information assets from unauthorized access to or modification of information, whether in storage, processing, or transit, and against the denial of service to authorized users or the provision of service to unauthorized users, including those measures necessary to detect, document, and counter such threats. INFOSEC reflects the concept of the totality of MIS security. See also: Computer Security.

Information System Security Officer (ISSO): The worker responsible for ensuring that protection measures are installed and operational security is maintained

for one or more specific classified information systems and/or networks.

IKE: Internet Key Exchange.

Integrated Computing Network (ICN): LANL's primary institutional network.

Integrity: A subgoal of computer security which ensures that: 1) data is a proper representation of information; 2) data retains its original level of accuracy; 3) data remains in a sound, unimpaired, or perfect condition; 3) the MIS perform correct processing operations; and 4) the computerized data faithfully represent those in the source documents and have not been exposed to accidental or malicious alteration or destruction. See also: Data Integrity, System Integrity.

Interconnected System: An approach in which the network is treated as an interconnection of separately created, managed, and accredited MIS.

Internet: A global network connecting millions of computers. As of 1999, the Internet has more than 200 million users worldwide, and that number is growing rapidly.

Intranet: A network based on TCP/IP protocols (an Internet) belonging to an organization, usually a corporation, accessible only by the organization's members, employees, or others with authorization. An intranet's Web sites look and act just like any other Web sites, but the firewall surrounding an intranet fends off unauthorized access.

Intruder: An individual who gains, or attempts to gain, unauthorized access to a computer system or to gain unauthorized privileges on that system. See also: Hacker.

Intrusion Detection: Pertaining to techniques, which attempt to detect intrusion into a computer or network by observation of actions, security logs, or audit data. Detection of break-ins or attempts either manually or via software expert systems that operate on logs or other information available on the network.

Invalid Web Pages: Sites where a domain may be registered but no content is served or the server is offline.

Ipsec: Internet Protocol Security is a framework for a set of security protocols at the network or packet processing layer of network communications. IPsec is ubiquitous amongst firewall, VPNs, and routers.

ISO/AISO: The persons responsible to the Office Head or Facility Director for ensuring that security is provided for and implemented throughout the life-cycle of an IT from the beginning of the concept development plan through its design, development, operation, maintenance, and secure disposal.

Issue-Specific Policy: Policies developed to focus on areas of current relevance and concern to an office or facility. Both new technologies and the appearance of new threats often require the creation of issue-specific policies (email, Internet usage).

IT Security: Measures and controls that protect an IT against denial of and unauthorized (accidental or intentional) disclosure, modification, or destruction of ITs and data. IT security includes consideration of all hardware and/or software functions.

IT Security Policy: The set of laws, rules, and practices that regulate how an organization manages, protects, and distributes sensitive information.

IT Systems: An assembly of computer hardware, software and/or firmware configured to collect, create, communicate, compute, disseminate, process, store, and/or control data or information.

Kerberos: Kerberos is a secret-key network authentication system developed by MIT and uses DES for encryption and authentication. Unlike a public-key authentication system, it does not produce digital signatures. Kerberos was designed to authenticate requests for network resources rather than to authenticate authorship of documents. See also: DSS.

Key (digital): A set of code synonymous with key pairs as part of a public key infrastructure. The key pairs include 'private' and 'public' keys. Public keys are generally used for encrypting data and private keys are generally used for signing and decrypting data.

Key Distribution Center: A system that is authorized to transmit temporary session keys to principals (authorized users). Each session key is transmitted in encrypted form, using a master key that the key distribution shares with the target principal. See also: DSS, Encryption, Kerberos.

Label: The marking of an item of information that reflects its information security classification. An internal label is the marking of an item of information that reflects the classification of that item within the confines of the medium containing the information. An external label is a visible or readable marking on the outside of the medium or its cover that reflects the security classification information resident within that particular medium. See also: Confidentiality.

LAN (Local Area Network): An interconnected system of computers and peripherals. LAN users can share data stored on hard disks in the network and can share printers connected to the network.

Language: Content Filtering systems can be used to limit the results of an Internet search to those that are in your native language.

LANL Unclassified Network: The LANL unclassified network that consists of two internal networks: the unclassified protected network (Yellow Network) and the open network (Green Network).

LDAP: Short for Lightweight Directory Access Protocol, a set of protocols for accessing information directories. LDAP is based on the standards contained within the X.500 standard, but is significantly simpler. And unlike X.500, LDAP supports TCP/IP, which is necessary for any type of Internet access.

Least Privilege: The principle that requires each subject be granted the most restrictive set of privileges needed for the performance of authorized tasks. The application of this principle limits the damage that can result from accident, error, or unauthorized use.

Local Area Network: A short-haul data communications systems that connects IT devices in a building or group of buildings within a few square miles, including (but not limited to) workstations, front end processors, controllers, switches, and gateways.

Mail header: Filtering based solely on the analysis of e-mail headers. Antispam systems try to use this technique as well, but it is not very effective due to the ease of message header forgery.

Mailing List: Used to detect mailing list messages and file them in appropriate folders.

Major Application (MA): A computer application that requires special management attention because of its importance to an organization's mission; its high development, operating, and/or maintenance costs; or its significant role in the administration of an organization's programs, finances, property, or other resources.

Malicious Code/Virus: Sites that promote, demonstrate and/or carry malicious executable, virus or worm code that intentionally cause harm by modifying or destroying computer systems often without the user's knowledge.

Management Controls: Security methods that focus on the management of the computer security system and the management of risk for a system.

Management Information System (MIS): An MIS is an assembly of computer hardware, software, and/or firmware configured to collect, create, communicate, compute, disseminate, process, store, and/or control data or information. Examples include: information storage and retrieval systems, mainframe computers, minicomputers, personal computers and workstations, office automation systems, automated message processing systems (AMPSs), and those supercomputers and process control computers (e.g., embedded computer systems) that perform general purpose computing functions.

MIS Owner: The official who has the authority to decide on accepting the security safeguards prescribed for an MIS and is responsible for issuing an accreditation statement that records the decision to accept those safeguards. See also: Accreditation Approval (AA), Application Owner, Process Owner.

MIS Security: Measures or controls that safeguard or protect an MIS against unauthorized (accidental or intentional) disclosure, modification, destruction of the MIS and data, or denial of service. MIS security provides an acceptable level of risk for the MIS and the data contained in it. Considerations include: 1) all hardware and/or software functions, characteristics, and/or features; 2) operational procedures, accountability procedures, and access controls at all computer facilities in the MIS; 3) management constraints; 4) physical structures and devices; and 5) personnel and communications controls.

Microprocessor: A semiconductor central processing unit contained on a single integrated circuit chip.

Modem: An electronic device that allows a microcomputer or a computer terminal to be connected to another computer via a telephone line.

Multiuser Systems: Any system capable of supporting more than one user in a concurrent mode of operation.

National Computer Security Center (NCSC): The government agency part of the National Security Agency (NSA) and that produces technical reference materials relating to a wide variety of computer security areas. It is located at 9800 Savage Rd., Ft. George G. Meade, Maryland.

National Institute of Standards and Technology (NIST): The federal organization that develops and promotes measurement, standards, and technology to enhance productivity, facilitate trade, and improve the quality of life.

National Telecommunications and Information Systems Security Policy: Directs federal agencies, by July 15, 1992, to provide automated Controlled Access Protection (C2 level) for MIS, when all users do not have the same authorization to use the sensitive information.

Need-to-Know: Access to information based on clearly identified need to know the information to perform official job duties.

Network: A communications medium and all components attached to that medium whose responsibility is the transference of information. Such components may include MISs, packet switches, telecommunications controllers, key distribution centers, and technical control devices.

Network Security: Protection of networks and their services unauthorized modification, destruction, disclosure, and the provision of assurance that the network performs its critical functions correctly and there are no harmful side-effects.

NIST: National Institute of Standards and Technology in Gaithersburg, Maryland. NIST publishes a wide variety of materials on computer security, including FIPS publications.

Nonrepudiation: Method by which the sender is provided with proof of delivery and the recipient is assured of the sender's identity, so that neither can later deny having processed the data.

Nonvolatile Memory Units: Devices which continue to retain their contents when power to the unit is turned off (bobble memory, Read-Only Memory/ROM).

Object: A passive entity that contains or receives information. Access to an object potentially implies access to the information it contains. Examples of objects are records, blocks, pages, segments, files, directories, directory tree, and programs as well as bits, bytes, words, fields, processors, video displays, keyboards, clocks, printers, network nodes, etc.

Object Reuse: The reassignment to some subject of a medium (e.g., page frame, disk sector, or magnetic tape) that contained one or more objects. To be securely reassigned, no residual data from previously contained object(s) can be available to the new subject through standard system mechanisms.

Obscene/Tasteless: Sites that contain explicit graphical or text depictions of such things as mutilation, murder, bodily functions, horror, death, rude behavior, executions, violence, and obscenities etc. Sites which contain or deal with medical content *will not* be saved. Sample sites: www.celebritymorgue.com, www.rotten.com, and www.gruesome.com

Offline: Pertaining to the operation of a functional unit when not under direct control of a computer. See also: Online.

Online: Pertaining to the operation of a functional unit when under the direct control of a computer. See also: Offline.

Open Network: A network within the LANL Unclassified Network that supports LANL's public Internet presence and external collaborations. See LANL unclassified network.

Operating System: The most important program that runs on a computer. Every general-purpose computer must have an operating system to run other programs. Operating systems perform basic tasks, such as recognizing input from the keyboard, sending output to the display screen, keeping track of files and directories on the disk, and controlling peripheral devices such as disk drives and printers.

Operation Controls: Security methods that focus on mechanisms that primarily are implemented and executed by people (as opposed to systems).

Orange Book: Named because of the color of its cover, this is the DoD Trusted Computer System Evaluation Criteria, DoD 5200.28-STD. It provides the information needed to classify computer systems as security levels of A, B, C, or D, defining the degree of trust that may be placed in them. See also: C2, TCSEC.

Organizational Computer Security Representative (OCSR): A LANL person who has oversight responsibilities for one or more single-user, standalone classified or unclassified systems.

Overwrite Procedure: A process, which removes or destroys data recorded on a computer storage medium by writing patterns of data over, or on top of, the data stored on the medium.

Overwriting media: Method for clearing data from magnetic media. Overwriting uses a program to write (1s, 0s, or a combination) onto the media. Overwriting should not be confused with merely deleting the pointer to a file (which typically happens when a "delete" command is used).

Parity: The quality of being either odd or even. The fact that all numbers have parity is commonly used in data communication to ensure the validity of data. This is called parity checking.

PBX: Short for private branch exchange, a private telephone network used within an enterprise. Users of the PBX share a certain number of outside lines for making telephone calls external to the PBX.

Pass Code: A one-time-use "authenticator" that is generated by a token card after a user inputs his or her personal identification number (PIN) and that is subsequently used to authenticate a system user to an authentication server or workstation.

Password: A protected word, phrase, or string of symbols used to authenticate a user's identity to a system or network. Guidance note: One-time pass codes are valid only for a single authentication of a user to a system; reusable passwords are valid for repeated authentication of a user to a system.

Peripheral Device: Any external device attached to a computer. Examples of peripherals include printers, disk drives, display monitors, keyboards, and mice.

Personal Identification Number (PIN): A number known only to the owner of the token card and which, once entered, generates a one-time pass-code.

Personnel Security: The procedures established to ensure that all personnel who have access to any sensitive information have all required authorities or appropriate security authorizations.

Phishing: Deceptive information pharming sites that are used to acquire personal information for fraud or theft. Typically found in hoax e-mail, these sites falsely represent themselves as legitimate Web sites to trick recipients into divulging user account information, credit-card numbers, usernames, passwords, Social Security numbers, etc. Pharming, or crimeware misdirects users to fraudulent sites or proxy servers, typically through DNS hijacking or poisoning.

Phrases: Filtering based on detecting phrases in the content text and their proximity to other target phrases.

Physical Security: The application of physical barriers and control procedures as preventative measures or safeguards against threats to resources and information.

Pornography/Adult Content: Sites that portray sexual acts and activity.

Port: An interface on a computer to which you can connect a device.

Port Protection Device: A device that authorizes access to the port itself, often based on a separate authentication independent of the computer's own access control functions.

Privacy Act of 1974: A US law permitting citizens to examine and make corrections to records the government maintains. It requires that Federal agencies adhere to certain procedures in their record keeping and interagency information transfers. See also: System of Records.

Private Branch Exchange: Private Branch eXchange (PBX) is a telephone switch providing speech connections within an organization, while also allowing users access to both public switches and private network facilities outside the organization. The terms PABX, PBX, and PABX are used interchangeably.

Process: An organizational assignment of responsibilities for an associated collection of activities that takes one or more kinds of input to accomplish a specified objective that creates an output that is of value.

Process Owner: The official who defines the process parameters and its relationship to other Customs processes. The process owner has Accrediting Authority (AA) to decide on accepting the security safeguards prescribed for the MIS process and is responsible for issuing an accreditation statement that records the decision to accept those safeguards. See also: Application Owner.

Protected Distribution System (PDS): A type of protected conduit system used for the protection of certain levels of information. PDS is the highest level of protection and is used in public domain areas for SRD and lower.

Protected Transmission System: A cable, wire, conduit, or other carrier system used for the clear text transmission of classified information in certain DOE environments. Protected transmission systems comprise protected distribution systems (PDSs) and classified distributive information networks (CDINs). A wireline or fiber-optic telecommunications system that includes the acoustical, electrical, electromagnetic, and physical safeguards required to permit its use for the transmission of unencrypted classified information.

Public Law 100-235: Established minimal acceptable standards for the government in computer security and information privacy. See also: Computer Security Act of 1987.

RADIUS: Remote Authentication Dial-in User Service. A long-established de-facto standard whereby user profiles are maintained in a database that remote servers can share and authenticate dial-in users and authorize their request to access a system or service.

Rainbow Series: A series of documents published by the National Computer Security Center (NCSC) to discuss in detail the features of the DoD, Trusted Computer System Evaluation Criteria (TCSEC) and provide guidance for meeting each requirement. The name "rainbow" is a nickname because each document has a different color of cover. See also: NCSC.

Read: A fundamental operation that results only in the flow of information from an object to a subject.

Real Time: Occurring immediately. Real time can refer to events simulated by a computer at the same speed that they would occur in real life.

Recovery: The process of restoring an MIS facility and related assets, damaged files, or equipment so as to be useful again after a major emergency which resulted in significant curtailing of normal ADP operations. See also: Disaster Recovery.

Regular Expression: Filtering based on rules written as regular expressions.

Remanence: The residual information that remains on storage media after erasure. For discussion purposes, it is better to characterize magnetic remanence as the magnetic representation of residual information that remains on magnetic media after the media has been erased. The magnetic flux that remains in a magnetic circuit after an applied magnetomotive force has been removed. See also: Object Reuse.

Remote Access: Sites that provide information about or facilitate access to information, programs, online services or computer systems remotely. Sample sites: pcnow.webex.com, and www.remotelyanywhere.com.

Residual Risk: The risk of operating a classified information system that remains after the application of mitigating factors. Such mitigating factors include, but are not limited to minimizing initial risk by selecting a system known to have fewer vulnerabilities, reducing vulnerabilities by implementing countermeasures, reducing consequence by limiting the amounts and kinds of information on the system, and using classification and compartmentalization to lessen the threat by limiting the adversaries' knowledge of the system.

Risk: The probability that a particular threat will exploit a particular vulnerability of the system.

Risk Analysis: The process of identifying security risks, determining their magnitude, and identifying areas needing safeguards. An analysis of an organization's information resources, its existing controls, and its remaining organizational and MIS vulnerabilities. It combines the loss potential for each resource or combination of resources with an estimated rate of occurrence to establish a potential level of damage in dollars or other assets. See also: Risk Assessment, Risk Management.

Risk Assessment: Process of analyzing threats to and vulnerabilities of an MIS to determine the risks (potential for losses), and using the analysis as a basis for identifying appropriate and cost-effective measures. See also: Risk Analysis, Risk Management. Risk analysis is a part of risk management, which is used to minimize risk by specifying security measures commensurate with the relative values of the resources to be protected, the vulnerabilities of those resources, and the identified threats against them. The method should be applied iteratively during the system life-cycle. When applied during the implementation phase or to an operational system, it can verify the effectiveness of existing safeguards and identify areas in which additional measures are needed to achieve the desired level of security. There are numerous risk analysis methodologies and some automated tools available to support them.

Risk Management: The total process of identifying, measuring, controlling, and eliminating or minimizing uncertain events that may affect system resources. Risk management encompasses the entire system life-cycles and has a direct impact on system certification. It may include risk analysis, cost/benefit analysis, safeguard selection, security test and evaluation, safeguard implementation, and system review. See also: Risk Analysis, Risk Assessment.

Router: An interconnection device that is similar to a bridge but serves packets or frames containing certain protocols. Routers link LANs at the network layer.

ROM: Read Only Memory. See also: Nonvolatile Memory Units.

RSA: A public-key cryptosystem for both encryption and authentication based on exponentiation in modular arithmetic. The algorithm was invented in 1977 by Rivest, Shamir, and Adelman and is generally accepted as practical or secure for public-key encryption. See also: Capstone, Clipper, DES, RSA, Skipjack.

Rules of Behavior: Rules established and implemented concerning use of, security in, and acceptable level of risk for the system. Rules will clearly delineate responsibilities and expected behavior of all individuals with access to the system. Rules should cover such matters as work at home, dial-in access, connection to the Internet, use of copyrighted works, unofficial use of Federal Government equipment, the assignment and limitation of system privileges, and individual accountability.

Safeguards: Countermeasures, specifications, or controls, consisting of actions taken to decrease the organizations existing degree of vulnerability to a given threat probability, that the threat will occur.

Security Incident: An MIS security incident is any event and/or condition that has the potential to impact the security and/or accreditation of an MIS and may result from intentional or unintentional actions. See also: Security Violation.

Security Plan: Document that details the security controls established and planned for a particular system.

Security Policy: The set of laws, rules, directives, and practices that regulate how an organization manages, protects, and distributes controlled information.

Security Requirements: Types and levels of protection necessary for equipment, data, information, applications, and facilities to meet security policies.

Security Safeguards (Countermeasures): The protective measures and controls that are prescribed to meet the security requirements specified for a system. Those safeguards may include, but are not necessarily limited to: hardware and software security features; operating procedures; accountability procedures; access and distribution controls; management constraints; personnel security; and physical structures, areas, and devices. Also called safeguards or security controls.

Security Specifications: A detailed description of the security safeguards required to protect a system.

Security Violation: An event, which may result in disclosure of sensitive information to, unauthorized individuals, or that results in unauthorized modification or destruction of system data, loss of computer system processing capability, or loss or theft of any computer system resources. See also: Security Incident.

Sensitive Data: Any information, the loss, misuse, modification of, or unauthorized access to, could affect the national interest or the conduct of federal programs, or the privacy to which individuals are entitled under Section 552a of Title 5, U.S. Code, but has not been specifically authorized under criteria established by an Executive order or an act of Congress to be kept classified in the interest of national defense or foreign policy.

Sensitive Unclassified Information: Information for which disclosure, loss, misuse, alteration, or destruction could adversely affect national security or other federal government interests. Guidance Note: National security interests are those unclassified matters that relate to the national defense or to United States (US) foreign relations. Other government interests are those related to, but not limited to, a wide range of government or government-derived economic, human, financial, industrial, agricultural, technological, and law-enforcement information, and to the privacy or confidentiality of personal or commercial proprietary information provided to the U.S. government by its citizens. Examples are Unclassified Controlled Nuclear Information (UCNI), Official Use Only (OUO) information, Naval Nuclear Propulsion Information (NNPI), Export Controlled Information (ECI), In Confidence information, Privacy Act information (such as personal/medical information), proprietary information, for example, from a cooperative research and development agreement (CRADA), State Department Limited Official Use (LOU) information, and Department of Defense For Official Use Only (FOUO) information.

Sensitivity Level: Sensitivity level is the highest classification level and classification category of information to be processed on an information system.

Separation of Duties: The dissemination of tasks and associated privileges for a specific computing process among multiple users to prevent fraud and errors.

Server: The control computer on a local area network that controls software access to workstations, printers, and other parts of the network.

Site: Usually a single physical location, but it may be one or more MIS that are the responsibility of the DSO. The system may be a standalone MIS, a remote site linked to a network, or workstations interconnected via a local area network (LAN).

Skipjack: A classified NSA designed encryption algorithm contained in the Clipper Chip. It is substantially stronger than DES and intended to provide a federally mandated encryption process, which would enable law enforcement agencies to monitor and wiretap private communications. See also: Capstone, Clipper, DES, RSA, Skipjack.

Smart Card: A credit-card – sized device with embedded microelectronics circuitry for storing information about an individual. This is not a key or token, as used in the remote access authentication process.

SNMP: Simple Networking Management Protocol.

Software: Computer instructions or data. Anything that can be stored electronically is software.

Software Copyright: The right of the copyright owner to prohibit copying and/or issue permission for a customer to employ a particular computer program.

SPAM: To crash a program by overrunning a fixed-site buffer with excessively large input data. Also, to cause a person or newsgroup to be flooded with irrelevant or inappropriate messages.

Spyware: Sites that promote, offer or secretively install software to monitor user behavior, track personal information, record keystrokes, and/or change user computer configuration without the user's knowledge and consent malicious or advertising purposes. Includes sites with software that can connect to "phone home" for transferring user information.

Standard Security Procedures: Step-by-step security instructions tailored to users and operators of MIS that process sensitive information.

Standalone System: A single-user MIS not connected to any other systems.

Symmetric Encryption: See: Conventional Encryption.

System: An organized hierarchy of components (hardware, software, data, personnel, and communications, for example) having a specified purpose and performance requirements.

System Administrator: The individual responsible for the installation and maintenance of an information system, providing effective information system utilization, required security parameters, and implementation of established requirements.

System Availability: The state that exists when required automated informations can be performed within an acceptable time period even under adverse circumstances.

System Failure: An event or condition that results in a system failing to perform its required function.

System Integrity: The attribute of a system relating to the successful and correct operation of computing resources. See also: Integrity.

System of Records: A group of any records under the control of the Department from which information is retrieved by the name of an individual, or by some other identifying number, symbol, or other identifying particular assigned to an individual. See also: Privacy Act of 1974.

System Owner: The person, team, group, or division that has been assigned and accepted responsibility for Laboratory computer assets.

System Recovery: Actions necessary to restore a system's operational and computational capabilities, and its security support structure, after a system failure or penetration.

System User: An individual who can receive information from, input information to, or modify information on a LANL information system without an independent review. Guidance Note: This term is equivalent to computer information system user, or computer user, found in other Laboratory documentation. System users may be both LANL workers and collaborators. For desktop systems, a single individual may be a system user and system owner.

TCP/IP: Transmission Control Protocol/Internet Protocol. The Internet Protocol is based on this suite of protocols.

TCSEC: Trusted Computer System Evaluation Criteria (TCSEC). DoD 5200.28-STD, National Institute of Standards and Technology (NIST), Gaithersburg, Maryland, 1985. Establishes uniform security requirements, administrative controls, and technical measures to protect sensitive information processed by DoD computer systems. It provides a standard for security features in commercial products and gives a metric for evaluating the degree of trust that can be placed in computer systems for the securing of sensitive information. See also: C2, Orange Book.

Technical Controls: Security methods consisting of hardware and software controls used to provide automated protection to the system or applications. Technical controls operate within the technical system and applications.

Technical Security Policy: Specific protection conditions and/or protection philosophy that express the boundaries and responsibilities of the IT product in supporting the information protection policy control objectives and countering expected threats.

Telecommunications: Any transmission, emission, or reception of signals, writing, images, sound or other data by cable, telephone lines, radio, visual or any electromagnetic system.

Terrorist/Militant/Extremist: Sites that contain information regarding militias, anti-government groups, terrorism, anarchy, etc.: Anti-government/Anti-establishment and bomb-making/usage (Should also be saved in criminal skills). Sample sites: www.michiganmilitia.com, www.militiaofmontana.com, and www.ncmilitia.org

Test Condition: A statement defining a constraint that must be satisfied by the program under test.

Test Data: The set of specific objects and variables that must be used to demonstrate that a program produces a set of given outcomes. See also: Disaster Recovery, Test Program.

Test Plan: A document or a section of a document which describes the test conditions, data, and coverage of a particular test or group of tests. See also: Disaster Recovery, Test Condition, Test Data, Test Procedure (Script).

Test Procedure (Script): A set of steps necessary to carry out one or a group of tests. These include steps for test environment initialization, test execution, and result analysis. The test procedures are carried out by test operators.

Test Program: A program which implements the test conditions when initialized with the test data and which collects the results produced by the program being tested. See also: Disaster Recovery, Test Condition, Test Data, Test Procedure (Script).

The Computer Security Plans for General Support Systems (GSS) and Major Applications (MA): Plans that detail the specific protection requirements for major applications and general support systems.

The Cyber Security Handbook: A Web-site handbook that details the Cyber Security requirements required by system users, system administrators, and SRLMs who access electronic information.

Threat: An event, process, activity (act), substance, or quality of being perpetuated by one or more threat agents, which, when realized, has an adverse effect on organization assets, resulting in losses attributed to: direct loss, related direct loss, delays or denials, disclosure of sensitive information, modification of programs or databases and intangible (good will, reputation, etc.).

Threat Agent: Any person or thing, which acts, or has the power to act, to cause, carry, transmit, or support a threat. See also: Threat.

Token Card: A device used in conjunction with a unique PIN to generate a one-time pass code (for example, CRYPTOCard® or SecureID®).

Trapdoor: A secret undocumented entry point into a computer program, used to grant access without normal methods of access authentication. See also: Malicious Code.

Trojan Horse: A computer program with an apparently or actually useful function that contains additional (hidden) functions that surreptitiously exploit the legitimate authorizations of the invoking process to the detriment of security. See also: Malicious Code. Threat Agent.

Trusted Computer Base (TCB): The totality of protection mechanisms within a computer system, including hardware, firmware, and software, the combination of which is responsible for enforcing a security policy. A TCB consists of one or more components that together enforce a security policy over a product or system. See also: C2, Orange Book, TCSEC.

Trusted Computing System: A computer and operating system that employs sufficient hardware and software integrity measures to allow its use for simultaneously processing a range of sensitive information and can be verified to implement a given security policy.

Unclassified Cyber Security Program Plan: A plan that provides a single source of unclassified computer security program information, and specifies the minimum protections and controls and references the detailed source material that pertains to the program.

Unclassified Information Systems Security Site Manager: The manager responsible for the LANL Unclassified Information Systems Security Program.

Unclassified Protected Network: A network within the LANL unclassified network that is designed to protect the resident systems from unauthorized access and is separated from the Internet by a firewall that controls external access to the network. See also: LANL Unclassified Network.

Unfriendly Termination: The removal of an employee under involuntary or adverse conditions. This may include termination for cause, RIF, involuntary transfer, resignation for "personality conflicts," and situations with pending grievances.

UPS (Uninterruptible Power Supply): A system of electrical components to provide a buffer between utility power, or other power source, and a load that requires uninterrupted, precise power. This often includes a trickle-charge battery system which permits a continued supply of electrical power during brief interruption (blackouts, brownouts, surges, electrical noise, etc.) of normal power sources.

User: Any person who is granted access privileges to a given IT.

User Interface: The part of an application that the user works with. User interfaces can be text-driven, such as DOS, or graphical, such as Windows.

Verification: The process of comparing two levels of system specifications for proper correspondence.

Virus: Code imbedded within a program that causes a copy of itself to be inserted in one or more other programs. In addition to propagation, the virus usually performs some unwanted function. Note that a program need not perform malicious actions to be a virus; it need only infect other programs. See also: Malicious Code.

VSAN: Virtual SAN.

Vulnerability: A weakness, or finding that is non-compliant, non-adherent to a requirement, a specification or a standard, or unprotected area of an otherwise secure system, which leaves the system open to potential attack or other problem.

WAN (Wide Area Network): A network of LANs, which provides communication, services over a geographic area larger than served by a LAN.

WWW: See: World Wide Web.

World Wide Web: An association of independent information databases accessible via the Internet. Often called the Web, WWW, or W.

Worm: A computer program that can replicate itself and send copies from computer to computer across network connections. Upon arrival, the worm may be activated to replicate and propagate again. In addition to propagation, the worm usually performs some unwanted function. See also: Malicious Code.

Write: A fundamental operation that results only in the flow of information from a subject to an object.

Yellow Network: See LANL Unclassified Network.

Index